THE GOLDEN
ENCYCLOPEDIA
OF
MUSIC

THE GOLDEN

With a 24-Page Color Section on Instruments by

EMANUEL WINTERNITZ

Curator of Musical Instruments,
Metropolitan Museum of Art, New York

ENCYCLOPEDIA

OF

MUSIC

BY NORMAN LLOYD

GOLDEN PRESS NEW YORK

A DIVISION OF WESTERN PUBLISHING COMPANY, INC.

Racine, Wisconsin

Library of Congress Catalog Card Number: 68-17169

HOW TO USE THIS BOOK

The objective in THE GOLDEN ENCYCLOPEDIA OF MUSIC has been to provide explanation and understanding rather than a mere cataloguing of scattered facts. Longish articles have been preferred to short, dictionary-definition type entries—making it possible to discuss subjects within meaningful context rather than as isolated bits of information. Hence, not every subject will be found as a separate entry; instead, many topics are covered within larger articles.

We have used two standard devices to help the reader use the encyclopedia and to guide him to all the information within it: indexing and cross referencing.

THE INDEX

The reader will find the index an indispensable aid as he uses the encyclopedia and becomes familiar with its organization. The index should be used regularly, but particularly for the following two reasons: 1) If a topic sought is not found as a separate entry within the body of the encyclopedia, the reader should refer to the index; it will guide him to the material he seeks. 2) If the reader wishes to find supplementary material on a topic of special interest, he should, again, refer to the index. (This is because, in addition to the main entry on a subject, pertinent information often appears elsewhere in the encyclopedia, too.)

The index begins on page 703, and directions for using it are given there.

There is a separate index (on page 702) for the musical examples which appear throughout the book. The reader looking for examples of a particular composer's work should refer to this guide.

CROSS REFERENCES

Cross references appear in small capitals and direct the reader to main entry titles within the body of the encyclopedia. We have tried to keep cross references to a minimum, sending the reader only to articles bearing directly on the matter at hand. (More extensive cross referencing is provided by the index, and the reader who desires further information on a particular subject should refer to this invaluable tool.)

GLOSSARIES AND CHARTS

Information in specialized areas will be found by consulting:

Signs and Symbols Used in Music: page 670
Foreign Terms and Phrases Used in Music: page 671
Abbreviations Used in Music: page 673
Famous Names in Music: page 674

Acknowledgments and picture credits will be found on pages 699–702.

The Editors

FOREWORD

In view of the current availability of several detailed and authoritative dictionaries and encyclopedias of music and musicians, one's initial reaction to the appearance of the present volume might well be, "Do we really need it?" The answer—a distinctly affirmative "Yes"—is immediately apparent after even a superficial perusal of THE GOLDEN ENCYCLOPEDIA OF MUSIC. Norman Lloyd's many years as a teacher and administrator have endowed him with a unique ability to clarify the obscure, to separate sense from nonsense, and to penetrate to the very essence of a given musical subject. Together with his wife, Ruth (herself a renowned teacher and expert), Mr. Lloyd has fashioned a volume that will surely prove indispensable to the professional musician and the general listener alike.

It was given to this writer to read much of the manuscript almost as soon as it flowed from the Lloyd typewriter. The experience quickly took on the characteristics of an exciting, cliff-hanging adventure as I eagerly awaited the delivery of the next batch of completed material. Invariably it proved to be stimulating, informative, highly readable, and entertaining.

Curling up in front of the fire with an encyclopedia does not ordinarily rank very high on my list of life's exquisite pleasures. Yet I unhesitatingly suggest that THE GOLDEN ENCYCLOPEDIA OF MUSIC can be read like a novel from cover to cover; its cast of characters is extraordinary, and the skill of Norman and Ruth Lloyd in humanizing even the most pedantic and specialized of musical topics makes its publication a major event in the world of the Arts.

Martin Bookspan

INTRODUCTION

THE GOLDEN ENCYCLOPEDIA OF MUSIC is a personal guide to the enjoyment and understanding of all aspects of music. It was written to fill the need for a one-volume work that ranged, in scope, from fundamentals to broad questions of musical style, and that was of value to the layman as well as the professional. Such a book should not, I felt, merely catalogue numerous facts—it should place them in a meaningful context, enabling the reader to listen to or perform music with better understanding and greater appreciation and discrimination.

Obviously, a book that tries to give total yet scattered information answering such questions as "How did the French horn get its shape?" "What makes Brahms sound like Brahms?" and "Does a composer think first of a melody and then add the other notes?" had to be put into a form that had some kind of logic. Such a form is the encyclopedia, which organizes a variety of material alphabetically.

This, then, is an encyclopedia consisting of information about all fields of the art. The aim has not been, however, to produce a work that would take its place on the shelf along with Webster, Roget, and Bartlett as a reference book to be referred to only for specific bits of information. My hope is that this book will be consulted, browsed through, studied, played, and even argued about. I have tried to make it informative yet lively, scholarly yet interesting, so that it will be read as a series of continued stories about musical geniuses, musical history, musical instruments, and musical forms and styles.

Rather than try to mention briefly and dryly a vast number of composers, I have concentrated on approximately a hundred of the key figures in music. This has allowed me the luxury of going into detail about such musical giants as Bach and Mozart, and in many cases discussing and analyzing their works. Numerous other composers are mentioned throughout the text, and they are listed in the index—which is the basic key to the information given in the book. In addition, hundreds of composers are identified and discussed in the dictionary of *Famous Names in Music* beginning on page 674. On the contemporary scene, I have given emphasis to the contribution of American composers—from W. C. Handy to Leonard Bernstein—not out of a sense of chauvinism, but because, in general, the American composer is not sufficiently known even in his own country.

The more than 1,000 musical examples have been chosen from a wide variety of sources and from all fields of music: opera, symphony, song, chamber music. They are meant not only to illustrate the text but also to serve as hints to the reader who wants to explore compositions that are new to him. The pictorial illustrations have been chosen to give another dimension to the text—to show, for example, how a seventeenth-century ensemble looked as it performed or how early ballet dancers were costumed.

Some major works have been analyzed in detail—partly because the works are themselves landmarks in music, but even more to help the reader to better understand the creative process involved in musical composition. In such articles, and in others relating to music theory, I have tried to use language that is understandable to the layman.

By proper use of the comprehensive index, most musical questions can be answered. There are, in addition, tables of musical terms, abbreviations, and foreign words and phrases found in published scores; a glossary of musical signs and symbols; and a dictionary of famous names in music.

Many people have helped in the making of this book, including my teachers and colleagues over the years. I wish to express my thanks to Sarah Lawrence College, Juilliard School of Music, and Oberlin College for the use of their students' minds and their library facilities. Thanks are also due to the several editors who have helped shape the form and style of the book: Jean Le Corbeiller, Jerome Wyckoff, and Caroline Lynch Greenberg. Most of all I wish to pay tribute to my wife, who has been very much the co-author of this book. None of the above-mentioned persons are responsible for the errors of fact or the unorthodox interpretations that will undoubtedly be found. The author accepts the blame for errors and acknowledges certain heresies which he hopes will prove to be orthodoxies in the future.

Norman Lloyd

A: the tone that all instruments of the orchestra must match (see TUNING). In France and Italy it is called *la.* The A of the oboe is the first tone heard at an instrumental concert. In the United States, *A* is usually the tone made by 440 vibrations per second, but some orchestras—the Boston Symphony Orchestra, for example—tune to 444 and even higher. In Europe one hears a slightly lower A, usually 435 vibrations per second; one can hear it in Vienna by picking up the telephone and dialing 1507.

Every stringed instrument has an A string. On the violin, it is the third string; on the guitar, the second.

On the piano, A looks like this:

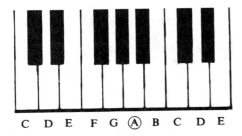

The A of the oboe, used in tuning, is the first one to the right of middle C.

The black key below A is called A-flat; the black key above A, A-sharp.

The most often used A's on the staff are:

The key signatures of the major and minor scales on A and A-flat are:

A Minor

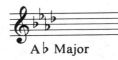
A Major   A♭ Major

Famous compositions written in the key of A major include Beethoven's Seventh Symphony, Mozart's Violin Concerto K. 219, Mendelssohn's "Italian" Symphony, and Liszt's Second Piano Concerto. Also in the key of A major are two well-known sonatas for violin and piano: one by César Franck and another by Brahms (Opus 100).

A-flat major, not used much before 1800, became more popular in the piano music of the early Romantic composers. It is the key of Beethoven's Piano Sonata Opus 110, Schumann's *Carnaval,* and many of the shorter works of Chopin.

A minor is the key of piano concertos by Schumann and Grieg, and of Mozart's Piano Sonata K. 310 and Rondo K. 511. Great chamber works in this key are Beethoven's Fifteenth Quartet (Opus 132), Brahm's Piano Trio (Opus 114), and Ravel's Piano Trio.

One modern work, Stravinsky's *Serenade en la,* is not actually in A major or in A minor, but is built around the tone A.

A CAPPELLA: an Italian phrase meaning "in the style of the chapel," used to designate a particularly pure style of choral music practiced in Italy during the Renaissance. It developed about the time of Josquin Des Prés, in the late fifteenth century, and reached its culmination a hundred years later in the music Palestrina wrote for the Sistine Chapel of the Vatican. No independent instrumental parts were written to accompany the voices; the choir thus sang unaccompanied or with instruments that exactly "doubled" some or all the vocal parts. By the seventeenth century, a cappella church music had lost ground to the cantata, in which the voices are accompanied by instruments playing independent parts.

In recent generations the expression *a cappella* has come to describe the performance of any music—religious or not—that is sung without accompaniment. Many schools in the United States have a cappella choirs, which are small groups made up of the best singers in the school.

ACCELERANDO: an Italian word that means "hastening." In music it means getting faster gradually, not suddenly. Composers use an accelerando passage to make a smooth transition from a slow section to a fast section. They also use it to suggest excitement or to promote it. Johann Strauss the Younger made the device the foundation of an entire piece, the "Acceleration Waltz," which he wrote in 1860. In scores the word is sometimes shortened to "accel."

ACCENT: the emphasis of one note over its companions. Composers accent a tone by making it longer (rhythmic accent) or higher (pitch accent) than the notes that come before it. The sixth tone of "The Star-Spangled Banner" is an accented tone because it is

Sistine Chapel, 1578 engraving

higher in pitch and longer in duration than the preceding five tones:

In most music written since 1600, there are accents at regular intervals, occurring on the first beat of the measure. This type of accent is called a measure accent. (See the article on METER.)

A composer can accent any note in his music by placing an accent mark (V or >) over or under the note. The use of the word *sforzando*—meaning "with force"—is another way to show that a note is to be accented. Sforzando is usually shortened to "sfz" or "sforz." See also SYNCOPATION.

ACCIDENTAL: a sharp (♯), double-sharp (×), flat (♭), double-flat (♭♭), or natural (♮) placed in front of a note to show that the note is to be raised, lowered, or restored to its former state. A sharp raises the pitch of a note one half step; a double-sharp raises it two half steps; a flat lowers it one half step; a double-flat lowers it two half steps; and a natural sign cancels all prior sharpings or flattings, including those in the key signature.

The accidental sign changes only the note that follows it and any repetition of that note on the same staff degree (line or space) within the measure. The sign has no effect on the note should the note appear in the next measure, unless the sign has been held over by a tie. The sign also has no effect on a note with the same letter name but a different line or space.

Here, the bottom note is F-sharp but the top one is F-natural:

The first accidental to be used was the flat, which was first applied to the note B. Since B was for a long time the only note to be flatted, the sign for B-flat, a rounded *b,* later came to be used whenever any note was to be flatted. The sharp was not used until about 1500. The natural, double-sharp, and double-flat came into music around the year 1700.

Before 1500, composers expected performers to raise or lower tones according to what their ears told them to do. This prac-

tice was called *musica ficta,* or "false music." Good musicians knew which tones to change without needing special symbols to tell them. They scorned accidentals as "signs for fools."

ACCOMPANIMENT: a musical composition, or part of a musical composition, that provides a background or support for something else—a melody, dance movement, or words. An accompaniment may just be rhythm, just chords, another melody, or a combination of these. It can be written for voices or for instruments.

The rhythmic accompaniment is probably the oldest form of accompaniment, and it may have been as simple as the hand-clapping that was used in primitive ritual dance, although drums and rattles appear early in man's history. Dancing and marching have always needed rhythmic support to keep groups of people moving together.

Chord accompaniments have been used mostly to accompany voices. Early operas—about 1600—were mostly melodies or recitative sung over a series of chords. These chords were not written out fully by the composer, but were indicated in a form of harmonic shorthand called figured bass. (Something like it is still used today in the form of chord names printed over the melody in sheet music. These indications, such as G7, are meant for guitarists. They tell the player which notes to play, but leave it up to him to distribute the notes over the six strings.) In the earliest operas, the chords called for by the figured bass were usually played on such instruments as the harpsichord, organ, lute, theorbo (a large lute), and

At right: *baritone Dietrich Fischer-Dieskau with the famous accompanyist Gerald Moore at the piano*

guitar, sometimes with the support of bowed instruments.

Soon composers began to add interest to their accompaniments by giving the accompanying instruments melodies of their own. A soloist would then be supported not only by instruments playing chords, but also perhaps by an oboe or flute weaving its own melodic line around his melody. This kind of melody is called an obbligato melody. A recent example of obbligato is the piccolo tune high above the melody in Sousa's "The Stars and Stripes Forever."

About 1800, composers began to make their accompaniments more dramatic. Schubert in his songs made the accompaniment sug-

gest the flow of a brook, the galloping of a horse, or the whirring of a spinning wheel. Ex. 1 gives the melody of "Gretchen at the Spinning Wheel," first with chords only, then with Schubert's accompaniment.

Throughout the nineteenth century, accompaniments became more and more intrinsic to the whole composition. In the hands of such composers as Schumann, Wagner, Wolf, and Mahler, accompaniments became at least equal partners with, not just supports for, the vocal or instrumental melodies.

Some patterns of accompaniment have come to be known by special names, such as those that are shown in Ex. 2.

Ex. 1—"Gretchen at the Spinning Wheel," Schubert

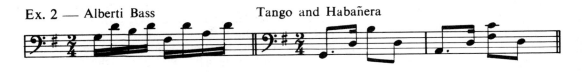

Stanley Darrow playing the Hohner accordion

Suzanne Farrell and Jacques d'Amboise in an adagio from George Balanchine's ballet Jewels

ACCORDION: a wind instrument that produces its sound in much the same way as two other instruments very different in size—the unassuming harmonica, or mouth organ, and the harmonium, an organlike piece of furniture dear to the Victorians. In all three instruments, air is forced through channels, each of which is partly blocked by a metal tongue called a reed. Each reed is fixed at one end only, so that the rush of air causes its free end to vibrate and produce a tone.

In the harmonica the air flow is produced by the player's breath, in the harmonium by bellows worked with pedals. In the accordion, sometimes known as the "squeezebox," the air is supplied by bellows that occupy the entire middle portion of the instrument. The bellows (in effect an airtight bag) are held between two end boards that carry keys or buttons. The end board played by the right hand is fixed, but the one worked by the left hand is free to move in and out, to enable the bellows to "breathe." To get a good tone, the player moves his left arm as smoothly as possible; otherwise his accordion will gasp and sputter.

The player's right hand plays the melody on a keyboard designed just like that of a piano, though usually only three octaves long. The fingers of his left hand work small buttons or studs (some accordions have as many as 120), each of which will sound a chord of three or four tones when it is pushed down. The player tells them apart partly by position and partly by the fact that some of them have a top that is scooped instead of rounded.

In its basic form the accordion was invented in Berlin in the 1820's by Friedrich Buschmann. Portable and easy to play, it soon became popular. The piano-style keyboard for the right hand was apparently invented as long ago as the 1850's, though it was hardly ever seen till after World War I. The fully chromatic series of chord studs for the left hand was added about 1910. Large concert accordions have studs that enable the player to change tone quality, and there is an expanded keyboard covering as many as four octaves.

The concertina, with its hexagonal endboards, is a small relative of the accordion. It was invented in 1829 by the English physicist Sir Charles Wheatstone.

ADAGIO: a tempo mark that tells the performer to play the music slowly and leisurely. (It comes from the Italian *ad agio,* "at ease," and like most tempo marks referred in its original use more to mood than to speed.) The metronome mark for an adagio tempo is about sixty beats per minute.

The slow movements of works by Haydn, Mozart, and Beethoven are often marked adagio and contain music that is deeply expressive and poetic. In adagio movements the music is often highly decorated, partly because the time distance from one beat to the next is long enough to allow many notes to be played. The second movements of Beethoven's Piano Sonata in G, Opus 31, Number 1, and Mozart's Piano Sonata in F, K. 332, are adagio melodies with much decoration.

Sometimes the composer gives the name "Adagio" to a complete composition. Two such works are Mozart's *Adagio in B Minor for Piano,* K. 540, and Samuel Barber's *Adagio for Strings.*

In ballet, the adagio is usually the duet, in which the ballerina, with the assistance and support of her partner (a man), displays extraordinary balance and control.

AIDA *(Aïda):* Giuseppe Verdi's most popular opera. *Aida* was composed under historic circumstances: the Suez Canal had finally been completed in 1869, and the Khedive, or viceroy, who ruled Egypt on behalf of Turkey commissioned Verdi to write an appropriately "national" opera to celebrate the occasion and, incidentally, to inaugurate the brand-new Cairo Opera House. The Egyptologist Mariette Bey (also remembered as the man who cleared the sand from the base of the Great Sphinx at Giza) produced a short plot based on historical accounts from the time of the Pharaohs; a French friend of Verdi's worked the draft into a full-length dramatic poem; and Verdi and a writer named Ghislanzoni together worked out the final Italian libretto. The opera was produced at the new opera house in Cairo on Christmas Eve, 1871.

The action takes place in ancient Egypt during a time of war with the Ethiopians. Aida, sung by a soprano, is a captive Ethiopian princess who is serving as a slave to the Pharaoh's daughter, Amneris (a mezzo-soprano). Radames (a tenor) is a young Egyptian army captain who falls in love with Aida. He pours out his love for her in one of the most famous of all operatic arias (Ex. 3). (An unusual feature of this aria is its placement early in the opera; composers usually save the "big aria" for a later act.) Princess Amneris is also in love with Radames. Finding that Aida is her rival, she threatens her with death.

Upon Radames' victorious return from an expedition against the Ethiopians, a triumphal procession passes across the stage to the tune of a rousing march (Ex. 4), in which the orchestra in the pit is joined by musicians on stage. Among the prisoners being led in the procession Aida discovers her father. She persuades Radames to contrive an escape for her father and herself. Radames tells Aida that he will lead them away by the secret road his army is to use on its next attack on Ethiopia. But the plot is discovered and Radames is imprisoned as a traitor. In spite of her jealousy Amneris tries to save the life of Radames, but he is condemned to be buried alive.

In the opera's final scene the stage is divided into two levels: above is the resplendent temple of Ptah; below, beneath the altar, is the dungeon that is to be Radames' grave. As the chanting priests lower the stone that is to seal the vault over him, Radames discovers that he is not alone: Aida has made her way to the tomb, prepared to share his fate. The two join in an impassioned farewell to life (Ex. 5), while above them priests and priestesses dance before the altar.

Verdi wrote some of his finest music for *Aida*. Although he did not use ancient Egyptian melodies (none being known), he did his best to give the priestesses, at the end of Act I, a melodic line that would sound properly archaic and oriental (Ex. 6). Though Verdi had no use for leitmotifs in any strict Wagnerian sense, he did give Aida a theme of her own (Ex. 7), heard from time to time as the story unfolds. It is the first theme heard in the overture.

A scene from Aida, *Act II, at the Metropolitan Opera House, with Birgit Nilsson in the title role*

Ex. 3 — "Celeste Aida"

Ex. 4 — Triumphal March

Ex. 5 — Final Duet

Ex. 6 — Song of the Egyptian Priestesses

Ex. 7 — Aida's Theme

Ex. 8 — Second Movement,
Sonata K. 332, Mozart

ALBERTI BASS: a style of accompaniment that was popular in the Classical period. Instead of writing simple chords for the left hand:

the composer takes the same notes and arranges them in a pattern that lies easily under the hand of the performer:

The Alberti bass was especially popular in music for the harpsichord and the early piano, whose tones fade away quickly; it is a way of keeping the tones sounding. It gets its name from the Italian composer Domenico Alberti (1710–c. 40). Although Alberti did not invent this form of "broken chords," his harpsichord sonatas show almost no other style of accompaniment. Mozart made great use of the Alberti bass in his piano sonatas in passages such as Ex. 8, above.

Although used primarily in keyboard music, it occasionally appears in second-violin and viola parts in ensemble music. It is a way of giving a feeling of motion to an accompaniment without letting the accompaniment become too important.

ALLA BREVE: duple measure, indicated by the time signature 2/2 or ¢ . (The Italian phrase means "in the short fashion.") The signature tells the performer that there are two main pulses per measure, the pulse note being the half note. Sometimes the phrase "alla breve" appears at the beginning of a new section of a work, usually after music in which the quarter note has been the pulse note. At this point the performer must mentally substitute ♩ for ♩ as the pulse note. Any tempo mark in alla breve time refers to the half note. Popularly, alla breve time is often called "cut" time (Ex. 9).

ALLEGRO: an Italian word meaning "cheerful." It has come to be used in music as a tempo mark calling for a fast rate of speed. The first movements of symphonies and sonatas are often marked "allegro."

Allegretto as a tempo means "fairly lively" but not so fast as allegro. The most famous allegretto is the second movement of Beethoven's Seventh Symphony.

Ex. 9 — Rondo from Sonata K. 533, Mozart

Positions and attitudes of the allemande

Ex. 10— Allemande in D Minor, Handel

ALLEMANDE: the most graceful and flowing court dance of the period around 1700. It came to the court of France from Germany (*allemande* is the French word for "German"). The man and the woman who were dance partners always kept both hands joined. The man turned the woman in various directions so that she circled and crossed under the arch made by their hands and arms. ("Allemande left" is the call for each man to turn the woman on his left with his left hand or arm.)

The music for the allemande was written in 2/2 or 4/4 time. Its speed was moderate, but the many rapid notes in the music suggested the flowing movement of the dance. Most of the keyboard suites of Bach and Handel open with an allemande in binary, or two-part, form. Many of them, such as Ex. 10 from Handel's Suite in D Minor, open with a characteristic "stutter" in which the first note appears twice, the first time lightly, just before the bar-line.

ALTO: the lower of the two natural ranges of women's voices. Since *alto* is an Italian word meaning "high," obviously the use of the word has undergone some changes.

In medieval music the tenor voice was expected to "hold" the melody; the voice immediately above it, being higher, was called *alto*. It was sung by men with high voices. Later this part came to be referred to as *contra alto* or contralto, and then simply alto. (A man singing in this range is today referred to as a countertenor.)

In four-part singing the alto has thus become the second voice from the top. Similarly, the second instrument from the top in woodwind families is now called alto. There are alto flutes, alto clarinets, alto recorders, alto saxophones. The mellophone often found in school bands is the circularly coiled alto of the saxhorn family.

The alto clef is a C clef with middle C on the third line:

Middle C

It is convenient for any musical part that ranges around middle C, and it is used for viola parts. (In France and Italy the viola itself is called alto.) In Ex. 11, from Bach's St. John Passion, the first two measures played by the violas are exactly the same pitches as those played by the violins.

Marian Anderson, famous American alto

Ex. 11 — St. John Passion, J.S. Bach

Violino I

Violino II

Viola

AMERICA: the favorite American hymn. The words were written in Andover, Massachusetts, in 1831 by a twenty-two-year-old Baptist minister from Boston, Samuel Francis Smith. Smith seems to have found the tune in a German collection lent him by the Boston hymn writer Lowell Mason. "I was looking over the books," he later wrote, "and fell in with the tune of 'God Save the King,' and at once took up my pen and wrote the piece in question. It was struck out at a sitting, without the slightest idea that it would ever attain the popularity it has since enjoyed." And so it was that "God save great George, our King . . ." ultimately became "My country, 'tis of thee. . . ." (For the origin of the tune that started it all—which seems to have reached its present form in the early years of the eighteenth century—see GOD SAVE THE QUEEN.)

"America" was first sung, by children, at a Fourth of July celebration in Boston in 1831 and was first published (by Lowell Mason) the following year. Its moving lines of tribute expressed in simple words what Americans felt for their new country, and it soon rivaled "Hail Columbia" and "The Star-Spangled Banner" in popularity. As things turned out, it was "The Star-Spangled Banner" that Congress chose in 1931 as the official national anthem of the United States, but "America" has remained the popular American national hymn.

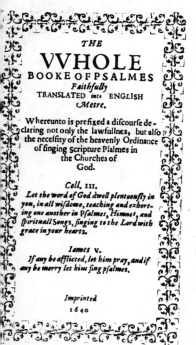

Title page of The Whole Booke of Psalms, *1640, commonly known as the* Bay Psalm Book

AMERICAN MUSIC: There was very little music in the early settlements in North America. To the Pilgrims, music and dancing were inventions of the devil. Musical instruments were banished altogether from early New England churches, the congregations' only musical outlet being the singing of psalms. (The *Bay Psalm Book* of 1640 was the first book printed in the English colonies in America.) In the towns drums, trumpets, and jew's harps were allowed. The drums and trumpets were good to sound the alarm in case of an Indian raid; why the jew's harp was tolerated has never been made clear.

As Germans and Swedes began to settle in Pennsylvania, they brought with them their love for music—and their musical instruments. In 1700 a Swedish church near Philadelphia installed the first pipe organ in the colonies. The Moravian settlements in and around Bethlehem, Pennsylvania, became centers of musical culture in the 1740's. It was the Moravians who put on the first American performances of Haydn's symphonies, as well as of his oratorios *The Creation* and *The Seasons*.

New York heard its first professional concert in 1736: a harpsichord recital by Carl Theodore Pachelbel, the son of a well-known German composer. A year before this the first opera in America was produced: in Charleston, South Carolina. Charleston, in 1762, was also the place of the founding of the first music society in the United States: the Saint Cecilia Society.

Many of the founding fathers of the United States took an active interest in music. Thomas Jefferson got up every morning at five to practice the violin. Benjamin Franklin not only wrote a string quartet but also invented a musical instrument, the glass harmonica. Francis Hopkinson (1737–91), a signer of the Declaration of Independence and a friend of George Washington, was one of America's first composers. He wrote many songs, of which the best known is "My Days Have Been So Wondrous Free."

The Revolutionary War was responsible for two rousing patriotic songs, "Yankee Doodle" and "Chester." "Yankee Doodle" was an English song that the Americans took for themselves after beating the British at Concord. "Chester" was a fighting hymn composed by William Billings (1746–1800), a Boston tanner and self-taught composer.

The words of three of America's national songs were written between 1798 and 1831. In 1798 Joseph Hopkinson, son of Francis, wrote the words of "Hail Columbia" to fit the tune of "The President's March." The War of 1812 was responsible for "The Star-Spangled Banner": its words were written by a young lawyer from Baltimore, Francis Scott Key, during the bombardment of Fort McHenry. The lyrics of "America" were written by Samuel Francis Smith for a Fourth of July celebration in Boston in 1831.

One of America's most important musicians in the mid-nineteenth century was Lowell Mason (1792–1872). Though he is best known for his hymns—"Nearer My God to Thee" and "From Greenland's Icy Mountains"—his life work was seeing that music had a place in the American public schools. It was Mason who laid the foundation for American musical education by training music teachers and organizing music festivals.

As the American pioneers moved westward, they heard the songs of the Indians. They heard these less as music than as war dances foreboding attacks. By the time the white man realized that the Indians had many beautiful songs, the Indians were on reservations and many of their songs were lost forever.

Some of the songs and dances of the pioneers came from Europe, often refurbished with new words. But many songs were new. No one knows the authors or composers of these folk songs, which grew as men worked and sang. There were songs about building the Erie Canal and the railroads, songs about the gold rush to California, songs about the nation's heroes, such as Washington and Lincoln, and songs about such legendary figures as John Henry and Paul Bunyan.

The most popular of all folk songs were those made by the black slaves. Many of these were work songs. Singing made it easier to pick cotton, load the steamboats, put down rails, and dig in the mines. The most beautiful slave songs were the spirituals, which were religious. But from Africa blacks had brought also a unique style of dancing. This loose-limbed shuffle and strutting cakewalk was accompanied by jangling banjos and clicking "bones."

These songs and dances became so popular that white men began to imitate them. A new kind of entertainment, the minstrel show, became America's favorite stage show. It was given by a group of white men with blackened faces. The performance was a series of songs, dances, jokes, and banjo solos, all in "Negro style" (minstrel shows were sometimes called banjo operas). This was the source of many of America's best-known songs—"Dixie," "Turkey in the Straw," "Old Dan Tucker," and "Big Sunflower," for example. And it was for minstrel shows that Stephen Foster wrote some of his most famous songs, among them "Old Folks at Home," "Oh, Susanna!" "My Old Kentucky Home," and "De Camptown Races."

The Civil War, which popularized "Dixie," also was responsible for "The Battle Hymn of the Republic," "The Bonnie Blue Flag," "Tramp, Tramp, Tramp, the Boys Are Marching," "Just Before the Battle, Mother," "Marching Through Georgia," and "The Battle Cry of Freedom."

After the Civil War the writing and publishing of popular music became big business. Song "pluggers" sang in saloons and restaurants, hoping their songs would catch on so that people would buy copies of the music. The period of the 1890's brought forth such dependable tear-jerkers as "A Little Lost Child," "The Letter Edged in Black," and "After the Ball Was Over." The Gay Nineties was the period also of such waltz songs as "East Side, West Side."

New kinds of popular music now came from blacks in the South. First was ragtime, an outgrowth of banjo sounds carried over to the piano. Then, from New Orleans,

Paul Revere frontispiece for Billings' The New England Psalm Singer, *1770*

Ben Franklin playing his glass harmonica

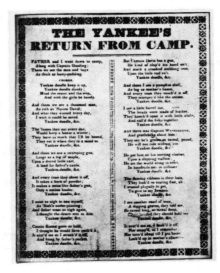

An early 19th-century broadside of "Yankee Doodle"

"Old Kentucky Home" by Eastman Johnson, 1859

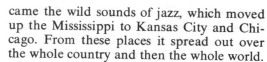

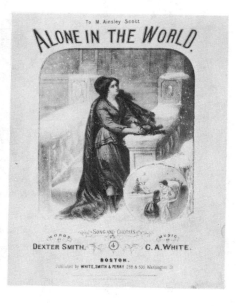

came the wild sounds of jazz, which moved up the Mississippi to Kansas City and Chicago. From these places it spread out over the whole country and then the whole world.

From the deeply moving songs of blacks came the written blues as we know them today. One of the first, and certainly the best-known, songs in this vein was "The St. Louis Blues," written by W. C. Handy in 1914. It is now as much a part of America as "Yankee Doodle."

As the country grew and developed, there came a demand for more music. European artists such as the celebrated singer Jenny Lind made the long ocean voyage. Opera companies, symphony orchestras, and music schools sprang up. There had been an opera house of sorts in New Orleans as early as 1808, but not until the Metropolitan Opera

Top left: *Louis Moreau Gottschalk*
Top right: *title page from a tearjerker of the late 19th century*
Middle left: *Jenny Lind, "The Swedish Nightingale," one of the first outstanding European artists to tour the United States (1852)*
Middle right: *Edward MacDowell in 1906 (photograph by E. Huntington Higgins)*
Bottom left: *Lincoln Center Plaza at night*
Bottom right: *Five American composers (top row: Barber and Copland; bottom row: Thomson, Menotti, and Schuman)*

Association was founded in New York, in 1883, was there an American opera company equal to any other in the world.

The oldest symphony orchestra in the United States, the New York Philharmonic, was founded in 1842. It was followed by the Boston Symphony (1881) and the Chicago Symphony (1891). The latter was organized by Theodore Thomas (1835–1905), who did much to set high standards of performance. It was Thomas who encouraged American composers to write for his orchestra and thus put them on equal footing with their European colleagues. Henceforth other cities began to organize their own orchestras: Cincinnati (1895), Los Angeles (1897), Philadelphia and Pittsburgh (1900), Minneapolis (1903), St. Louis (1907), San Francisco (1909), Detroit (1914), and Cleveland (1918). At last count American orchestras numbered more than 1,400.

The first conservatory of music in the United States was the Oberlin Conservatory (1865). Next were the New England and Cincinnati conservatories (both 1867) and the Peabody Institute of Baltimore (1868). In 1905 the Institute of Musical Art was founded in New York. Recently established conservatories of importance include the Eastman School of Music (1919), the Curtis Institute (1924), and the Juilliard School of Music (1926). Music departments were started in Harvard University and the University of Pennsylvania in 1875. Since then almost every large university and college throughout the country has added a music department to train composers, musicologists, teachers, and in some cases, performers.

American composers, with two exceptions, were not known outside the United States until after 1920. The exceptions were Louis Moreau Gottschalk (1829–69) and Edward MacDowell (1861–1908). Since 1920 the works of Ives, Copland, Harris, Hanson, Schuman, Barber, and many others have been played by orchestras in many parts of the world. Popular music—much of it from musical comedies written by such composers as Berlin, Kern, Gershwin, Rodgers, and Porter —is heard wherever there are radios, phonographs, and movies. Gershwin's songs, his *Rhapsody in Blue,* and his *Porgy and Bess* are universally popular. America's most recent musical export has been country and western music: a blend of jazz, folk, and rock styles.

The United States was slow in asserting its musical independence. In the past fifty years, however, it has produced composers and performers equal to any others in the world.

ANCIENT MUSIC:

What the music of ancient peoples was like is largely a matter of speculation and conjecture. Musical instruments have been found, and on surviving pottery, sculptures, and paintings there are representations of people playing these instruments. But most of what is known or surmised has come down to us through the centuries by way of story and legend. On the basis of the evidence we have, we know that music was as important in ancient times as it is today.

The presence of music in the life of ancient Egypt, the first great nation, is abundantly documented in many tomb paintings. Music was a part of the daily lives of the people as well as an adjunct to the festival and the ceremonial. The farmers sang as they planted the fields and reaped the harvest. Large orchestras of flutes and stringed instruments entertained at royal parties and festivals. The army marched to the sound of trumpet and drum. The Egyptian harp, seven feet tall, was played in the temples by priests who were also musicians. Dancing was done to the accompaniment of smaller stringed instruments. The great god Osiris was worshiped to the sound of blaring trumpets—instruments which, according to legend, he himself had invented.

The fierce neighbors of the Egyptians, the Assyrians, went into battle with their instruments strapped to their bodies. Their armies were welcomed home by large choruses and orchestras of hundreds of singers and players. For quieter music, the Assyrians used an instrument of many strings struck with small beaters, like a dulcimer.

In the Orient, the Chinese thousands of years ago had royal orchestras of drums, bells, gongs, and xylophones. For processionals they had also an instrument like the panpipes of Greece.

The Old Testament tells how the walls of Jericho were blown down by the sounding of the seven shofars, made from rams' horns. The shofar is the oldest musical instrument still in use. It is still sounded in the synagogue on high holy days.

The Jewish harp was the instrument of the home and the instrument of the poets. David, both as favorite to King Saul and as king himself, played the harp and composed and sang beautiful songs. These songs, the Psalms of the Bible, were chanted in the synagogue and later in the early Christian church. King Solomon, the son of David, had multitudes of singers, plus trumpeters and string players, in his orchestra. He started the first conservatory for the training of musicians.

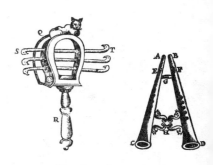

Ancient Egyptian sistrum (a percussion instrument) and Greek aulos (a woodwind)

Assyrian musicians, 7th century B.C.

Blowing a shofar

Musicians on an Egyptian tomb painting, XVIII dynasty (1567–1320 B.C.)

Above: *girl playing reed pipes, from a Grecian vase*
Left: *Ancient Chinese musicians, from a 3rd-century* A.D. *gravestone*

Ancient Roman bas-relief showing double reed pipes and a hand drum

In the ancient world, music rose to its greatest heights in Greece. Our word "music" comes from the Greek. The nine daughters of Zeus, the Muses, were in charge of the arts and sciences. Music had two Muses: one for sacred music, one for secular.

The invention of musical instruments was attributed by the Greeks to the gods. Legend has it that Pan, the goat-footed god of the woods and fields, invented the first "pipes" —the precursor of our woodwind instruments. Pursuing the beautiful nymph Syrinx, he was just about to embrace her when she changed herself into a bundle of reeds. Pan sighed as he held the reeds in his arms, and his breath through the reeds gave off a whistling sound. Pan then broke off the reeds, which were of different sizes, and bound them together. Learning to play melodies on this instrument, he named it the syrinx in honor of his lost love. This, according to the Greeks, was the first musical instrument.

Apollo is credited with making the first instrument with strings. By adding two animal horns to a tortoise shell and stretching several strings from one horn to the other, he made what was called the lyre—the plucked-string instrument with the soft voice. This was the instrument found in Greek homes and the one on which the young students in the family received their musical instruction. The study of music, along with poetry and athletics, formed the curriculum in early Greek schools.

The heroic stories sung by the Greek poets were accompanied by the sounds of the kithara, another stringed instrument. This was larger than the lyre and capable of being heard in the outdoor theaters where entertainment was provided for the citizens.

From their travels in Asia the Greeks brought back a wind instrument, the aulos, with a sound like that of our oboe. It became associated with the frenzied worship of Dionysius. Great strength was needed to play it, and the cheeks of the players had to be strapped tightly so that they would not burst.

The first scientific experiments with acoustics and the mathematical relationships of tones took place around 500 B.C. in the school of Pythagoras. The Greeks gave to the world also the idea of scales with different arrangements of whole steps and half steps. The scales were named after various tribes or cities of the ancient world: Ionian, Dorian, Lydian, and so on. The Greeks invented a system of musical notation so that their songs could be recorded and remembered. Unfortunately, few of the songs still exist, and there is considerable difference of opinion among scholars as to the real meaning of the notation.

Except for their invention of a kind of army trumpet which they called the tuba, the Romans did little for music except to carry it with them on their mighty conquests. Generally, their music was that of Greece, though they did bring the bagpipe into Europe from India. It became a great favorite with the Romans and probably was what Nero played while Rome burned.

When the early Christians began to compose hymns, they fell back on the only music they knew: that of Israel and Greece. From this developed the chants of the Roman Catholic and Greek Orthodox churches. And upon this foundation of ancient music was built, in turn, our own western European musical system.

Musical exercises by the philosopher Pythagoras of Samos

ANDANTE: a tempo mark that means "going" and indicates a moderate rate of speed —that of a strolling walk. (Andante does *not* mean "slowly.") It is the tempo mark of many songlike movements in the music of Mozart and Beethoven. This term is often combined with such other words as *cantabile* ("singing") and *con moto* ("with movement").

ANDANTINO: an Italian term meaning "little andante." Confusion has arisen because it has come to be used as a tempo mark in its own right. Then it can mean a tempo either slower or faster than andante. The performer can only try the composition at various speeds and use the tempo that seems best.

ANTHEM: originally, a choral composition sung in church. By extension the word has come to mean a hymn sung in glorification of one's country. In its original form the anthem appeared in the Church of England shortly before 1600. It was a counterpart to the Roman Catholic motet, having English rather than Latin words. Not a formal part of the service, it has survived in the form of an independent composition sometimes sung to organ accompaniment during the offertory. Some of the original Elizabethan and Jacobean anthems, notably the very beautiful short anthems of Orlando Gibbons, are still sung in Anglican churches today. Later composers made the anthem a freer and larger form, sometimes with verses sung by soloists. Purcell wrote some very fine ones in this freer vein, as did Handel after his arrival in England. The anthem is used in many Protestant churches, being most popular in English-speaking countries.

Orlando Gibbons

At right: *Martha Graham and May O'Donnell in* Appalachian Spring

APPALACHIAN SPRING: a modern-dance ballet by Martha Graham with music by Aaron Copland. It was first performed in Washington, D.C., in 1944. Originally, the music was written for a chamber orchestra of thirteen instruments; later Copland shortened the ballet score to make a concert version for full symphony orchestra.

This ballet is not so much a story as a mood piece. It takes place in the American past at a time when western Pennsylvania was a frontier settlement. Outside a newly built farmhouse a young couple are celebrating their coming marriage. Neighbors drop by and give them suggestions as to the joys and sorrows of life. At the end of the ballet the young couple are left "quiet and strong in their new house."

The score of *Appalachian Spring* has melodies (Ex. 12) that suggest pioneer songs and dances. Near the end Copland uses an old Shaker hymn, "The Gift to Be Simple," or "Simple Gifts" (Ex. 13).

Ex. 12

Allegro

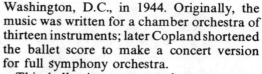

Ex. 13

Ex. 14— Sonata K. 309, Mozart

(a) Written

(b) Played

Ex. 15— Mazurka, Op. 17, No. 2, Chopin

Lento, ma non troppo

(App.)

(App.)

(App.)

APPOGGIATURA: a term that has two meanings in music theory. It is applied to a tone that is not a member of the chord of the moment and has "leaning" or "yearning" tendencies. In music of the Baroque and Classical periods it was always placed at a rhythmically strong point, such as the first beat of the measure, and was written as a small note (Ex. 14). Later the term was applied to any non-chordal tone that was approached by means of a leap and resolved by a step—upward or downward (Ex. 15).

ARIA: a melody sung by a soloist in an opera, oratorio, or cantata. It often follows a recitative, which is a kind of musical speech. An aria might be a love song (such as "Celeste Aida" from Verdi's *Aida*), a gay patter song ("Largo al factotum" from Rossini's *Barber of Seville*), a lament ("I Have Lost My Eurydice" from Gluck's *Orfeo*), a virtuoso piece for coloratura soprano ("The Bell Song" from Delibes' *Lakmé*), a religious statement ("He Shall Feed His Flock" from Handel's *Messiah*), or any other solo song in a dramatic work. The aria is the musical form in which the character in the opera, oratorio, or cantata expresses his innermost feelings.

An aria might be in any kind of musical form, but the majority of arias are written in the three-part form of the aria da capo. This musical form is made up of three sec-

tions, the first usually long and containing the important musical ideas of the aria, the second being in a different key and perhaps introducing new musical ideas, and the third being a repetition of the first section. The composer often does not write out the repetition; he writes "da capo" or "D.C." at the end of the second part. ("Da capo," meaning "from the head," is an instruction to go back to the beginning.) Alessandro Scarlatti (1659–1725) made the aria da capo the most significant feature of his operas, popularizing it so that for a hundred years it was the most-used musical form in opera.

Gabriella Tucci as Marguerite in Faust

In eighteenth-century operas the arias often interferred with the dramatic action. Everything stopped while the soloist stepped forward and sang his aria. About 1820 Carl Maria von Weber began to place the solo aria in a more meaningful context. Later composers, such as Mussorgsky, Wagner, and Verdi, made still further changes by using the aria as well as the other parts of the opera to make the scene a continuous flow of action and music, incorporating the aria only when the action demanded it. In Debussy's *Pelléas and Mélisande,* written about 1900, there are no arias—only a long succession of beautiful dialogues.

In early operas the accompaniment to the aria was quite simple, often being just a few supporting chords on the harpsichord. Later, accompaniments were written for a large orchestra and were as important as the vocal melody. The "Liebestod" at the end of Wagner's *Tristan and Isolde* is an aria in which the orchestra is equal in importance to the singer.

The title "Aria" is often given to a slow, songlike instrumental composition. Bach's "Goldberg" Variations, written for harpsichord solo, is entitled *Aria with Different Variations.*

ARMSTRONG, LOUIS (1900–1971): the king of jazz trumpet players. Born in New Orleans, the cradle of jazz, he learned to play the cornet while in the Waifs' Home. At eighteen he joined the famous jazz band of Kid Ory. After playing on Mississippi riverboats, he went to Chicago and became second trumpet to King Oliver. In 1924 Armstrong went to New York to join the big band of Fletcher Henderson, but he never cared much for playing in a big band and soon returned to Chicago, forming there his own small bands of five to seven pieces.

Armstrong discovered that his voice was as effective as his trumpet. A typical Armstrong record from 1929 on is a mixture of voice and trumpet with a few supporting instruments in the background. His style ranged from growling slow blues to hard-driving swing. Other instrumentalists copied his style, and his influence on the whole field of jazz was enormous.

Armstrong's trumpet technique was prodigious. He could play screaming high notes, seemingly forever, or subtle melodic variations on a tune. He once played 250 high C's in a row—and finished on a higher F. He taught composers and other trumpet players how agile the trumpet could be.

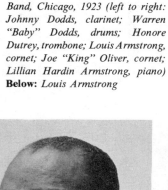

At right: *King Oliver's Creole Jazz Band, Chicago, 1923 (left to right: Johnny Dodds, clarinet; Warren "Baby" Dodds, drums; Honore Dutrey, trombone; Louis Armstrong, cornet; Joe "King" Oliver, cornet; Lillian Hardin Armstrong, piano)*
Below: *Louis Armstrong*

Some of his earliest records, made in the late 1920's, are jazz classics. These include his duets with blues singer Bessie Smith as well as his solos on "I Can't Give You Anything But Love, Baby," "Ain't Misbehavin'," and "Basin Street Blues." In later years, his gravelly voice delighted audiences with his fresh interpretations of "Hello, Dolly" and "Mack the Knife."

In 1936 he collected his memories of the early jazz years in the book *Swing That Music.* During the 1930's and again after World War II, Armstrong toured the world as a goodwill ambassador for the United States, playing, singing, and generating warmth and friendliness through his inimitable personal style.

ARPEGGIO: a chord whose notes are played one after another (as on a harp) rather than all together. The word arpeggio comes from the Italian *arpeggiare,* "to play on a harp."

Sometimes arpeggios are written out:

In other scores they are written as chords preceded by a wiggly line:

Arpeggios are often used as accompaniment patterns, as in Ex. 16, from Brahms's Fourth Symphony. They can be spread out over the whole range of the instrument—a traditional way of displaying the virtuosity of the performer, as in the first of Chopin's Études, Opus 10 (Ex. 17).

Arpeggios are best used on keyboard or stringed instruments. Rapid, long-legged

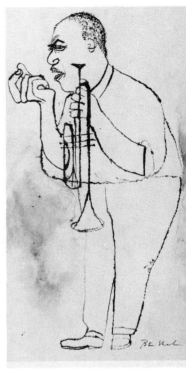

Louis Armstrong singing, by Ben Shahn

Ex. 16— Symphony No. 4, Brahms

Ex. 17— Étude No. 1, Chopin

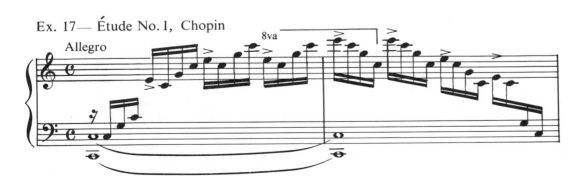

arpeggios are easy for the string player, who skips his bow from string to string (Ex. 36, page 316). They also are often found in woodwind passages and, less commonly, in the less playful brasses. Vocal arpeggios make good warmups for singers. Brilliant vocal arias often feature arpeggios to show off the dexterity of the singer, as in the operas of Bellini and Rossini.

In the time of Bach and Handel, arpeggios were not written out. The chord was shown as a block of notes with the word *arpeggione* written over it. The performer was expected to play the notes one after the other.

ARRANGEMENT: the provision of background or setting for melodies such as folk songs and popular music. "Arrangement" and "transcription" are two words with broadly overlapping meanings. Both are used to refer to the changing of a musical composition so that it can be performed by voices or instruments other than those for which it was originally written. Such musical adaptations are discussed under TRANSCRIPTION.

Folk songs do not have accompaniments until someone arranges them. Thus in folk music an arrangement can be an accompaniment that has been added to the melody. Such an arrangement might consist of a simple chordal background, suggesting a guitar, or an arranger might try to enhance the flavor of a song by making an elaborate or dramatic accompaniment.

In popular music, "arrangement" has a special meaning, since not all tunes are harmonized by the composer. When a popular tune is accepted for publication, the publisher usually turns it over to an editor for arranging. This is not the last arrangement the tune undergoes: before a dance band or singer uses the song, a new, special arrangement is written to bring out the individual style of the singer or band. Arrangers thus play an important role in giving much of the music we hear its characteristic flavor. Benny Goodman placed great value on Fletcher Henderson's arrangements, which were the foundation of much of the style of Goodman's band. Similarly, the orchestration of musical shows on Broadway is almost always turned over to professional arrangers. Robert Russell Bennett, the chief of these, has provided sparkling arrangements for Broadway musicals for over thirty years.

ATONALITY: the absence of tonality, or key center. Much contemporary music can be called atonal. The term is sometimes applied to twelve-tone music, although not all atonal music is built on the twelve-tone principle. "Atonal" is a non-descriptive word, and its meaning is purely negative. As listeners have become more sensitive to what they are hearing in contemporary music and more knowing about modern musical vocabulary, the word "atonal" is being used less often as a way to identify the musical idiom of a composition.

AUGMENTATION: the use of a theme, or musical idea, with the note values increased, usually to twice their value. In Ex. 18 the theme appears in its original form and in augmentation.

This compositional device is often found in contrapuntal works such as fugues and canons. It is also frequently used in the development section of symphonies.

AUGMENTED: a musical term meaning "made larger." The term applies to intervals and triads.

A major or perfect interval can be augmented by increasing its size by a half step:

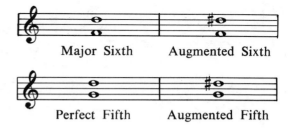

Major Sixth   Augmented Sixth

Perfect Fifth   Augmented Fifth

Ex. 18 — Fugue No. 2 from *The Well-tempered Clavier*, Book II, J. S. Bach

Except for the augmented fourth—the tritone—augmented intervals have no characteristic sound, since they sound like other intervals spelled enharmonically:

Augmented Fifth = Minor Sixth, in sound

An augmented triad is made by superimposing one major third on top of another major third:

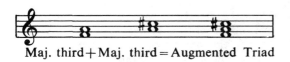

Maj. third + Maj. third = Augmented Triad

In diatonic music this triad occurs occasionally as the chord built on the third de-gree of the harmonic minor scale, as illustrated in this example:

In the whole-tone scale, all triads are augmented, as in the Prelude from Debussy's *Pour le Piano* (Ex. 19).

Augmented sixth chords, named for the augmented sixth interval from the bass note, are among the most important chromatic chords. They occur in three forms, called Italian, French, and German:

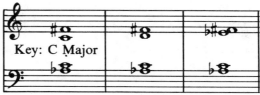

("Italian Sixth")   ("French Sixth")   ("German Sixth")

Ex. 19 — Prélude, *Pour le Piano*, Debussy
Assez animé et très rythmé

B: the white key to the right of the group of three black keys on the piano. In France and Italy it is called *si*. In Germany, B is called *H* and B-flat is called *B*. (German editions of Bach's B-minor Mass carry the title *Messe in H moll*—the *H* is pronounced *hah*). The first note to undergo chromatic change, around A.D. 1025, was B. The symbol for this lowering, or flatting, was the small round "b." The "natural" B was written as a square letter that looked like an "h." The black key below B is B-flat. Since there is no black key above B, B-sharp has the same pitch as C. The B's on the staff are shown here:

The key signatures for the scales on B and B-flat are:

B Major　B Minor　B♭ Major　B♭ Minor

Composers have avoided writing orchestral pieces in B major. Wind players have a hard time coping with five sharps, because of the nature of their instruments. But composers have occasionally turned to B major in compositions for the keyboard. Some of Chopin's mazurkas and the second passepied in Bach's keyboard *Overture in the French Manner* are written in B major.

B minor, on the other hand, has often been used in large-scale works, such as Bach's B-minor Mass, Schubert's Eighth Symphony (the "Unfinished"), and Tchaikovsky's Sixth Symphony (the "Pathétique"). Keyboard performers know B minor as the key of Liszt's only piano sonata, Chopin's Third Piano Sonata, Couperin's great Passacaglia of his eighth *Ordre,* one of Haydn's finest sonatas (Number 39, Peters edition), Mozart's Adagio K. 540, and the fourth bagatelle in the Opus 126 series of Beethoven.

The key of B-flat minor, used in Tchaikovsky's First Piano Concerto and Chopin's Second Piano Sonata (with the funeral march), has not been as popular with composers as B-flat major. Symphonies in B-flat major include Beethoven's Fourth and Schubert's Second and Fifth. Many concertos,

Portrait of young Bach by an unknown artist

including Mozart's K. 450, 456, and 595 as well as Beethoven's and Brahms's Second Piano Concertos, are in the key of B-flat major.

BACH, JOHANN SEBASTIAN (1685–1750): the outstanding member of the greatest musical family the world has ever known. Bach was the greatest peak in a mountain range of many peaks. Long before Johann Sebastian, musicians bearing the name Bach were known in Erfurt, Eisenach, Arnstadt, and other clusters of steep-roofed houses that dotted the wooded hills of Thuringia. Thuringia, whose capital was Weimar, was a ducal state about the size of Connecticut, just north of the larger state of Bavaria. During the sixteenth century it had been a stronghold of Luther's Reformation. Luther's parents were Thuringians, and young Luther himself had lived at both Erfurt and Eisenach in his student days. It is not surprising that Luther's fervent religious feeling is echoed in much of the music of Johann Sebastian Bach.

Bach was born in Eisenach on March 21, 1685, the fourth and last son of Ambrosius Bach, a violinist. The boy studied stringed instruments with his father until tragedy struck: both of Bach's parents died before he was ten. Bach was then cared for by his eldest brother, Johann Christoph, an organist at Ohrdruf, who gave the boy lessons on the harpsichord, clavichord, and organ. Johann Christoph was himself a pupil of one of the finest keyboard composers of the day, Johann Pachelbel. Pachelbel had studied with a pupil of the great Italian master Frescobaldi, and he played and composed in the southern style, which was much more relaxed in feeling than that of the northern German composers.

Bach was an outstanding student at the fine school in Ohrdruf. When there was an opening for a singer in the paid choir at St. Michael's Lutheran Church in Lüneberg, Bach's teacher, Herda, recommended him highly and he was hired. At the age of fifteen Bach became a professional musician. As a boy soprano he became familiar with the finest of choral music: the works of Lassus, Monteverdi, Schütz, and Carissimi. In Lüneberg, Bach also heard the music of Böhm, one of the great German organists, and in Hamburg he heard that of Jan Reinken. Reinken was the grand old man of the northern school of organists—his own teacher had been (around 1620) a pupil of Sweelinck, the founder of the tradition. So Bach, even though a very young man, had already come to know the southern tradition through his own brother Johann Christoph, and was now learning the northern one through Böhm and Reinken.

Bach's voice broke while he was at St. Michael's, but he was useful enough as an instrumentalist to be kept on. The choir's duties were lighter during the summer months, and during summers Bach explored various musical centers, among them the ducal court at Celle, some sixty miles south of Lüneberg. At Celle, Bach first came into contact with French music. The duke had a French wife, formal French gardens, and an orchestra of French instrumentalists with a French conductor. The elegance of the French music appealed to Bach, and throughout his life he turned spontaneously to the French ornamental melodies and French rhythms he first experienced at Celle.

In 1703, after a short sojourn in Weimar, where he played the violin in the orchestra of the younger brother of the Duke of Weimar, Bach became organist at the Lutheran Church of St. Boniface in Arnstadt. Back in the heart of "Bach country," he was happy to get acquainted with his brothers again. When one of them, Johann Jakob, was leaving to take up a new job as oboist at the Swedish court, Bach wrote one of his earliest surviving keyboard pieces. This was the *Capriccio on the Departure of His Beloved Brother,* a set of descriptive movements, which include a lament and a lively fugue based on the horn call of the stagecoach postilion.

In 1705 he requested and was granted a leave of absence for one month in order to travel to Lübeck, a city three hundred miles to the north. He set forth in October and traveled all or part of the way on foot. What drew Bach to Lübeck was the music at the Church of St. Mary, played and conducted by the Danish organist Dietrich Buxtehude.

Buxtehude, now nearing seventy, was the greatest organist of his generation. Hearing him improvise was undoubtedly a great treat for Bach, and he stayed on to hear the marvelous musical evenings that Buxtehude had planned for the six weeks before Christmas. These evenings featured not only the organ playing of Buxtehude, but also a cycle of cantatas for voices and instruments. For the first time, Bach had a vision of how to relate music to religious worship on a large scale. The Lübeck visit planted the seeds that would grow into the blossoming of Bach's finest organ works and his greatest achievements—his cantatas and oratorios.

Bach returned to Arnstadt three months late—a fact that did not endear him to his congregation. He began to experiment in his chorale accompaniments, using some of the techniques he had heard in Lübeck. The congregation became even more upset and objected to the "surprising variations and irrelevant ornaments" that made their chorales harder to sing. They took him to task for his poor relations with his choristers. They even made remarks about the fact that an "unknown young lady" was often found listening or singing in the church when Bach was practicing. The young lady was his distant cousin Maria Barbara Bach. Things got so bad that when there was a vacancy at St. Blasius' Church in Mühlhausen, Bach applied for the post.

In September 1707, Bach packed his furniture, his books, and his harpsichord into a hay wagon and left for Mühlhausen. Just at that time one of his uncles died, leaving him a sum of money. Bach composed a cantata for the funeral—a particularly fine

The house in Eisenach where Bach was born

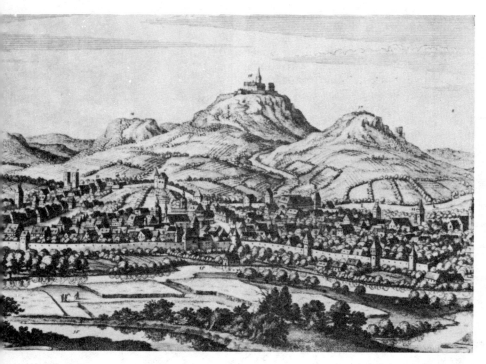

Eisenach around 1650 (engraving from Topographia, *by Merian)*

was built anywhere in central Germany, the man called to test it was Bach. The consultation brought him extra income, and he took genuine pleasure in inspecting a new instrument. He would first play a few chords with all the stops pulled out to see if the organ had "good lungs." Then he would play something that gave the various ranks of pipes a chance to be heard individually—a set of variations, for instance, in which a different registration could be used for each variation. One such set, which he began compiling at Lüneberg and later added to at Mühlhausen and Weimar, is the organ partita based on the chorale "Sei gegrusset, Jesu gutig" (Be Thou Blessed, Sweetest Jesus).

In his early works Bach was very much under the influence of Reinken and Buxtehude. The subjects of his fugues are long and sequential (Ex. 1), the music often rambling on as though not sure of its destination. But at Weimar, Bach learned the art of being concise. Here at the court he heard and played the music by the new Italian masters, Vivaldi, Corelli, and Albinoni. Bach took the string concertos by these men and arranged them for solo harpsichord. Sometimes he followed the original, note for note; at other times he added ornaments and even new inner voices. His own music became more tightly knit as he applied his own contrapuntal skills to the fast, athletic themes of the Italians. In his cantatas he brought together the religious intensity of the music of Buxtehude and the operatic forms and beautiful melodic writing of the Italians.

Bach took on new duties in Weimar as his family grew in size with the coming of children. He became concertmaster of the duke's orchestra, and the promotion entailed his writing new compositions every month for performance in the ducal chapel. But as happened so often in his life, he began looking around for a larger or different world of music from the one in which he was involved.

one: Number 106, *Gottes Zeit Ist allerbeste Zeit (God's Time Is the Best Time)*—and married Maria Barbara.

Bach found that a puritanical group within the Mühlhausen congregation were set against making music important in the church service. Accordingly, in the summer of 1708 Bach moved again—this time to Weimar, where he became a member of the orchestra of the reigning duke of Saxony-Weimar.

Although Bach was hired as an orchestral musician, his prowess as an organist soon secured for him a promotion to the post of Duke's Organist. During these years at Weimar, from 1708 to 1717, Bach wrote much of the organ music that is most familiar to us today—the Toccata and Fugue in D Minor, the Passacaglia and Fugue in C Minor, and other pieces in display style.

Bach had begun to achieve fame as an organist and as a tester of church organs. It almost seems that whenever a new organ

Ex. 1 — Fugue in A Minor for Organ

He heard of an opening as kapellmeister (conductor) at the ducal court of Cöthen, a hundred miles away. The post was given to him—but, alas, he had not asked permission of his employer, the Duke of Weimar. He was clapped into the duke's prison room for a month as punishment.

In December 1717, he was released and took up his duties at Cöthen. Cöthen was not a city known for its religious music, but this disadvantage was for Bach balanced by the musical enthusiasm of its young Prince Leopold. Leopold sang and played the violin, the viola da gamba, and various keyboard instruments. He kept a private orchestra of eighteen players, which Bach was hired to direct.

It was during the Cöthen period that Bach composed the bulk of his secular instrumental music—the sonatas for various instruments, the concertos, the four orchestral suites, and the "Brandenburg" Concertos. Many of Bach's most ambitious pieces for harpsichord solo date from this time: the Toccata in C Minor, the *Chromatic Fantasia and Fugue*. At this time, too, he began the composition of many keyboard works intended for his children and his pupils: the inventions and the *Orgelbüchlein (Little Organ Book)*, a set of short, imaginative organ preludes, each based on the melody of a standard Lutheran chorale. Since the words of the chorales are known, the *Little Organ Book* is helpful to listeners who want to unravel Bach's musical language—to see which rhythms and turns of phrase he seems to associate with certain ideas in the chorale texts. Of course, not every chorale prelude in the *Little Organ Book* is pictorial. Sometimes Bach is content to show how the melody could be treated contrapuntally—as a canon, as a thread around which to weave several other melodic lines.

Bach was always more than just an accomplished performer or composer. His logical mind was interested in organizing ideas into the proper form. As Bach's eldest son, Wilhelm Friedemann, became old enough to start his musical training, Bach began to write series of what today would be called teaching pieces. First came some twenty little preludes for keyboard, then the so-called "French" Suites and "English" Suites—pieces based on dance forms that show Bach in his most tuneful aspect. To teach Wilhelm Friedemann how to "play neatly" and "in a singing manner," as well as to give the boy a taste of contrapuntal composition, Bach wrote his cycles of two- and three-part inventions. The inventions move up the scale from C, one for each major and minor key except for those keys needing more than four sharps or flats in their key signatures.

It is in his *Das Wohltemperierte Clavier (The Well-tempered Clavier)*, Book I, that the inventiveness and logic of Bach's mind show most clearly. These twenty-four preludes and fugues, written as teaching pieces and to prove the value of tuning by means of a "tempered scale," are in a multiplicity of styles and textures. They are highly intellectual and at the same time expressive. In Bach, as in all the great composers, the intellect is always the servant of the emotions. Each prelude is based on a motive, usually an opening out of a simple triad, with or without decorations (Ex. 2a and b). The motive is then delightfully spun out over a harmonic plan, usually building to a climax of a dissonant diminished seventh chord and an ending wherein "all's well that ends well." Some of the preludes are in dance form; others are perpetual motions, arias, and even fugues.

The fugues follow no one set pattern, except that the voices enter one by one. Once they are all in, the music starts moving from key to key, the subject piles in on top of itself, new subjects are brought in, the old

Organ in Arnstadt museum, designed by Bach, on which many of his early works for organ were composed

Ex. 2a — Prelude No. 20 from *The Well-tempered Clavier*, Book I

Ex. 2b — Prelude No. 2 from *The Well-tempered Clavier*, Book I

A portion of the music manuscript for the B-minor Mass in Bach's own hand

subject is turned upside down or varied rhythmically. And always there is a sense of direction in the music, helped very much by Bach's treatment of the episodes—the connecting links or roads that lead from key to key. Where other composers used these links merely to get from key to key, Bach makes the episodes dramatic parts of the whole composition. They give a sense of suspense, which is relieved when the new key is reached and the fugue subject can be stated again. The whole form is a tightly knit one, helped by the new—for Bach—type of fugue subject. Where his earlier subjects tended to ramble (Ex. 1, page 30), he now constructs a fugue on as few as four notes, as here. Each subject seems whittled down to its smallest form.

Fugue No. 4 from *The Well-tempered Clavier,* Book I

His new style, combining all that Bach knew of German, French, and Italian music, resulted in a whole wealth of masterpieces for violin, with and without keyboard, and cello. The six sonatas for violin alone and the six suites for cello alone are still, almost 250 years later, towering landmarks in their respective fields. They are still the fiendishly difficult works by which the contemporary violinist or cellist proves himself to his audiences and his musical peers. Because these stringed instruments are less chordal than melodic, Bach spun for them long melodies in dance rhythms, rhapsodies, arias, and fugues. Although the use of two or three strings is possible, Bach preferred to make the audience imagine its own counterpoint at times. One melody might be heard (Ex. 3a), but the mind of the hearer must hear it as two voices (Ex. 3b).

Bach did not, of course, limit himself to music for just one or two instruments. His job and his far-ranging mind prompted otherwise. At Cöthen he wrote four orchestral suites for strings and wind instruments. When the Margrave of Brandenburg commissioned a set of concerti grossi, Bach wrote his six "Brandenburg" Concertos—virtuoso works that represent the high point of the concerto grosso form and style.

Suddenly, in the midst of success, Bach was hit by the saddest experience of his adult life. He had been on a long trip with Prince Leopold during the summer of 1720. When he came home, he discovered that his faithful wife had died. Bach was very much a family man, and Maria Barbara's death probably changed his whole feeling about life at Cöthen—and made him realize how far he had drifted from the service of the church. He began to look for another post, venturing as far as Hamburg. He did not get the Hamburg job (someone who could afford to contribute to the church treasury did), but he received the greatest of compliments from the ninety-seven-year-old Reinken, who was one of the judges. After Bach improvised for a half hour on the chorale "By the Waters of Babylon," Reinken said, "I thought this art was dead, but I see that in you it still lives."

Bach had his family of four children to think of. Toward the end of 1721 he married Anna Magdalena Wilcken, a twenty-year-old soprano who came from a musical family. It was for her that Bach wrote the charming little pieces in the *Anna Magdalena Notebook.*

Also in 1721 Prince Leopold decided to marry, and the young princess he chose turned out to be totally uninterested in music. She even resented the regard her music-mad prince showed to Bach. The atmosphere at Cöthen was indeed changing.

Meanwhile the appointment of a new cantor at the St. Thomas Church in Leipzig was being considered by the Leipzig City

Ex. 3a — Chaconne

Ex. 3b

Council. For this great Lutheran church the city fathers wanted the best musician they could get. They drew up two lists of possibilities; Bach was on neither. Finally the council decided that Bach should at least be *heard.* He went to Leipzig on the first Sunday in February 1723, and led the St. Thomas Choir in his cantata Number 22, *And Jesus Took the Twelve unto Him.* On Good Friday, Bach showed the Leipzig Council what he could do on a larger scale by conducting his St. John Passion. In April, securing his release from Prince Leopold, he wrote to the Leipzig Council pledging himself to undertake the duties they required but begging to be allowed to delegate the teaching of Latin to another instructor, whom he would compensate out of his own pocket. This the council agreed to, and on May 13 Bach was given the job.

He conducted his first service on May 30, 1723, not at St. Thomas' but at Leipzig's St. Nicholas, where the St. Thomas Choir also sang. On June 1 representatives of the City Council formally introduced him to the faculty and students of the St. Thomas School.

Bach was now thirty-eight and at the height of his powers. For the remaining quarter-century of his life these powers were to be dedicated to giving musical form to the public worship of his congregation. His main vehicle was the cantata, a form in which instruments and voices joined forces to illustrate a devotional text. And just as there is a whole world of personal experience in the Beethoven sonatas or in Mozart's operas, there is a whole world—emotional, musical, and devotional—in Bach's cantatas. Bach wrote over two hundred of these, most of them related to some passage of the Gospel appropriate to a given Sunday in the church calendar. For every Sunday (and also for holidays) he had to have a cantata ready for performance at St. Thomas and one for the associated church of St. Nicholas. Today a conductor who directs a program once a week isn't expected also to write the music for it, but Bach, although he sometimes performed works by other composers, usually provided the music himself. Especially in the first few years, in the 1720's, he composed a new cantata for almost every Sunday. Then, by the time he had built up a backlog of one or two cantatas for each Sunday in the church calendar, he could occasionally repeat these earlier ones and have more time to write new ones. For instance, in the single year 1725 there were thirty-two Sundays, birthdays, and holidays for which we know he wrote brand-new cantatas.

Johann Jacob Ihle's portrait of Bach at age thirty-five

Bach still occasionally wrote organ music, though not as much as before. Organ pieces from this period include a cheerful Prelude and Fugue in G Major and six trio sonatas. Bach's first biographer, a man named Forkel, reported that they were written for Wilhelm Friedemann, then in his teens. Other pieces from this period are the six partitas, the first one perhaps written for clavichord, the others all written for harpsichord. But the greatest achievement of these years is *The Passion According to St. Matthew,* one of Bach's most monumental works.

The occasion was Good Friday, April 15, 1729. It was the moment in the church devoted to the memory of Christ's supreme sacrifice. The service allowed room for one cantata before the pastor's sermon and one after, or for a long work in two parts, with the pastor's sermon set between them. Bach chose to write a two-part passion. In Part I, which lasts an hour and a half, Bach describes the persecution of Jesus, the last supper with the disciples, and the agony in the garden of Gethsemane. At this point Christian Weiss, the pastor of St. Thomas, delivered his sermon. Then followed Part II of the passion—Jesus brought before the high priest Caiaphas, Peter's denial and remorse, the Crucifixion, the descent from the Cross, and the burial.

Interior of St. Thomas Church, Leipzig

At right: *portrait of Bach in 1746 by Elias Gottlieb Hausman*

The entire service was of immense length, and Bach organized his part of it with great built-in variety and complexity. The story of the Passion was taken directly from the Gospel according to St. Matthew and told in recitative style by a tenor narrator; it was interspersed with quotations of the words of Jesus, sung by a bass, and with occasional outbursts from the crowd, shouted by the chorus. Bach's style here was conservative, in some ways going back to the passions of Heinrich Schütz. But between these narrative passages Bach inserted what amounted to a sermon of his own—lyrical and reflective recitatives and arias in late-Baroque oratorio style, with a great variety of instrumental and sometimes choral accompaniments. The text for these portions was written by a Leipzig post-office official who wrote verse under the pen name "Picander." Meanwhile Bach was not forgetting the congregation: he brought them into the unfolding drama by interspersing Lutheran chorales at various points in the passion. These chorales were sung by the choirs accompanied by the full orchestra, and the congregation, which had sung these chorales at hundreds of Sunday services, was able to join in. One chorale,

"O Sacred Head," now known as the "Passion Chorale," appears five times in the course of the oratorio. Bach used it as a way of achieving emotional as well as musical continuity. As the passion unfolds, it builds up a deeply stirring musical effect.

Bach's years at St. Thomas were not always easy ones. He himself was not an easy man to get along with. He demanded his rights and argued with his superiors if the occasion demanded it. He began to cast about to see if he could get a post near Leipzig that would add not just to his income but to his fame, thereby putting him in a better bargaining position with his superiors. When a new Elector of Saxony came to power in Dresden in 1733, Bach dedicated a Kyrie and Gloria to him, which he expanded two years later into the B-minor Mass. The elector was not immediately responsive but, a few years and several dedications later, did give Bach the title of Composer to the Court. The "honor" had no particular effect on Bach's situation at St. Thomas.

Bach's pupils were now going out into the world—at first his sons Wilhelm Friedemann and Carl Philipp Emanuel, and later some of the boys he had taught at St. Thomas. But he also, in effect, taught the community at large through the keyboard suites he published. In 1731 he issued the *Clavierübung* (literally, "Keyboard Exercise"), Part I, in which he grouped his partitas. Part II, which followed in 1735, included the *Overture in the French Manner* and the *Italian Concerto,* both for harpsichord. Part III (1739) gives organ preludes on chorales illustrating the central points of Lutheran belief, and Part IV (1742) contains the "Goldberg" Variations for harpsichord. Meanwhile Bach had been accumulating a great many keyboard preludes and fugues in various keys, and in 1744 he was able to bring out Book II of *The Well-tempered Clavier,* following the same key scheme as his first collection of 1722.

In 1740 Bach's most famous son, Carl Philipp Emanuel, was appointed harpsichordist to Frederick the Great at his court in Potsdam, near Berlin. Carl Philipp had since had a son of his own—Bach's first grandson—and in 1747 Bach decided to pay the growing young family a visit. Barely had he stepped down from the coach when he was summoned into the king's presence. Frederick was a good musician as kings go and made a point of canceling his regular afternoon concert to hear Bach improvise on the various harpsichords and Silbermann pianos he kept at the palace. At one point

Ex. 4

Ex. 5

the king took up his flute and gave Bach a theme (Ex. 4) on which to improvise. Bach enjoyed the theme, with its sparse opening and fashionable chromatic tailpiece, and improvised on it with the best skill he could muster on the moment. But back in Leipzig, after his return, he worked on it more carefully, and within three months he had had engraved an ambitious *Musikalisches Opfer (Musical Offering),* dedicated to the king. It included canons and ricercars on the king's "right royal theme" and a trio sonata in which the theme appeared in two of the movements, and in which the flute was given a prominent part.

Bach was sixty now. He had given up composing cantatas for St. Thomas, though he still taught at the school and led its choirs. But his imagination was still active, especially in the area of organ music and counterpoint. Ten years before, he had written some of his most searching music in his organ preludes and fugues in B minor and E minor. Now, in his last years, what he wanted to offer was his personal musical commentary on some of his favorite Lutheran chorales. This he did partly in the six organ preludes known as the "Schubler" Chorales —some of which were transcriptions of movements from his cantatas—and partly in the *Eighteen Chorales of Different Style,* which he did not live to complete. These chorale preludes allowed him to combine the chorale melodies that carried the faith of the Lutheran community as a whole with the personal musical symbolism conveying his personal meditations, weaving the two elements together with the counterpoint of which he was now the world's greatest master.

In 1749 he started work on *Die Kunst der Fuge (The Art of Fugue),* a collection of canons and fugues on a subject that is music reduced to its most elemental form (Ex. 5). Bach put all his skill into these pieces, which are testimonials to an art that would die with him. Meanwhile he suffered what appears to have been some sort of stroke, from which he lost the use of his eyes. In July 1750, he called his son-in-law Altnikol to

him and dictated his last chorale prelude, "Before Thy Throne, O God, I Stand," of which he managed to think out twenty-six measures. The piece was not finished. A few weeks later, on July 28, Bach was dead.

Bach had lived a long life, and the musical world of 1750 was very different from that of 1685. His son Carl Philipp Emanuel would be one of the early explorers, along with Haydn, of the sonata-allegro form, in which much of the music of the next hundred years would be cast. His son Johann Christian would be the model and guide of the young Mozart. Bach's own music would be studied with admiration by Beethoven, but generally would not be performed until "rediscovered" by Mendelssohn eighty years later. His scores would lie unused in attics and organ lofts, and not until 1850 would a *Bach Gesellschaft,* or Bach Society, be formed to rescue his scores; and by that time many of them would be lost.

Today, more than two centuries after his death, Bach's organ music is still the greatest that has been written; his sonatas and partitas for solo violin are still among the most exciting concert offerings. Today, more than ever, the inspiring heritage of his cantatas is being discovered. They continue to give testimony to the fact that music can be deeply personal and yet meaningful to the world at large—if the composer, like Bach, is willing to devote his entire life and talent to reaching out to mankind.

BACH'S SONS: Three of Johann Sebastian Bach's sons achieved greatness in the musical world—for the most part in a musical style quite different from that of their father. The eldest of the three, **Wilhelm Friedemann Bach** (1710–84), was the one whose musical upbringing was most carefully supervised by his father. At the age of nine he was given lessons at the clavichord, and the following year his father started a special notebook for him, filled with short piano pieces of graduated difficulty. Some of these compositions were later included in the first volume of

Wilhelm Friedemann Bach

Ex. 6 — Polonaise, Wilhelm Friedemann Bach
Allegro Moderato

The Well-tempered Clavier and the two- and three-part inventions. After some violin study Wilhelm Friedemann was graduated from the St. Thomas School in Leipzig; then he entered the city's university, where he studied law, philosophy, and mathematics.

Wilhelm Friedemann spent thirteen years in his first job, as organist at the School of St. Sophia in Dresden. While there he gave lessons and did a small amount of composing. But he was not happy in Dresden, being torn between the severe standards of his Lutheran father and the expectations of the Catholic, opera-oriented, worldly Saxon capital, which reflected the showy tastes of its new elector, Friedrich Augustus II. He was relieved to be able to move, in 1746, to the Church of Our Lady in Halle. After almost twenty years there he resigned, although he stayed on in Halle for a few years, teaching privately. In Halle he wrote some of his best-known compositions—twelve polonaises for clavichord. At the age of sixty he left to play in various German towns. His improvisations at the organ always created a fine impression on listeners in each town, but he was never invited to stay. His style in composition is a combination of his father's with the newer, lighter style of the Classical period (Ex. 6, above).

Carl Philipp Emanuel Bach (1714–88), four years younger than Wilhelm Friedemann, also benefited from the teachings of his father both privately and at the St. Thomas School. He too went to law school, first at the University of Leipzig, and later in the distant northern town of Frankfurt-on-the-Oder, east of Berlin. His keyboard playing caught the attention of Crown Prince Frederick, who hired him for his private orchestra. Frederick, an accomplished flute player, became king of Prussia in 1740, and when he gave his first solo performance as king, it was Carl Philipp Emanuel who accompanied him.

Carl Philipp Emanuel stayed with Frederick for the next twenty-eight years. Though much of this time was spent in the king's anterooms waiting for the signal that the king was ready for some music, much of it was also spent composing and performing concertos, symphonies, and all kinds of chamber music. Several collections of clavichord sonatas date from these years, as well as a great many harpsichord concertos and one very famous book, *Versuch über die wahre Art das Clavier zu spielen (Essay on the True Art of Playing Keyboard Instruments).* This is the most explicit and helpful testimony we have today on the way eighteenth-century music was actually performed. A translation of it by William J. Mitchell was published in New York in 1949, and it is now possible for anyone to take lessons (in effect) from one of the most sought-after teachers of the eighteenth century.

After more than a quarter-century as the King's Accompanist, Carl Philipp Emanuel became music director of the five main churches of the city of Hamburg. The vacancy he filled was created by the death of Georg Philipp Telemann, the most fashionable German composer of his generation and a godfather of Carl Philipp Emanuel. Bach held this job for the remainder of his life.

Carl Philipp Emanuel's position in Hamburg was much what his father's had been in Leipzig. His university training and his

C.P.E. Bach and Pastor Sturm, 1764

Ex. 7 — Fantasia No. 1, C. P. E. Bach

long years at the court of Frederick—intellectually the most advanced court in Europe —had prepared him well for the life of Germany's most cosmopolitan city. He turned out arias, cantatas, and passions for the church as the need arose, but possibly his most inspired "works" were his improvisations at the keyboard. We can get some idea of what his improvisations were like in the 1780's from the fantasias (Ex. 7) he included in the last three volumes of his clavichord sonatas "for connoisseurs and amateurs."

Carl Philipp Emanuel belongs to the generation that renewed music by contributing to the development of a new way of organizing musical composition—the sonata form. His earliest mature works (the "Württemburg" and "Prussian" Sonatas) date from the early 1740's, when his father was still alive

and composing. By the 1770's Mozart and Haydn were getting to know his symphonies, and Mozart personally conducted C. P. E.'s oratorio *Die Auferstehung und Himmelfahrt Jesu (The Resurrection and the Ascension of Jesus)*. His life spanned the end of the Baroque and the beginning of Classical times—but not in a smooth transition. Bits of Baroque, bits of Frederick the Great's favored *style galant,* and bits of Haydn-like Classicism all occur in C.P.E.'s work, sometimes side by side. One of the most "Romantic" pieces he ever wrote was his *Farewell to My Silbermann Clavichord,* which is filled with sequences of a yearning, chromatic quality (Ex. 8, below).

Johann Christian Bach (1735–82) was almost of a different generation from that of

Ex. 8 —"Abschied von meinem Silbermannischen Claviere," C. P. E. Bach

his two famous brothers. Born during the Leipzig years of his father's second marriage, to Anna Magdalena, Johann Christian was a pupil not of his father but of his elder half-brother Carl Philipp Emanuel in Berlin. When his apprenticeship to his brother was over, he managed somehow to get to Italy. What interested him most was opera, and to succeed in the opera world he set about systematically to Italianize himself, finding an Italian patron (Count Litta of Milan), becoming a Roman Catholic, and taking lessons with Italy's most renowned teacher of composition, Padre Martini of Bologna. In 1760 he became the organist of one of Italy's greatest churches, the Cathedral of Milan, and in the next two years he managed to get five of his operas performed in Naples. The taste for Italian opera had meanwhile taken root in England, and London's King's Theatre needed a competent composer of opera in the Italian style. In 1762 Johann Christian Bach set out for London, and there—as John Bach—he settled for the remainder of his life. His contract with the King's Theatre soon lapsed, but in 1763 he was appointed music master to the nineteen-year-old Queen Charlotte Sophia, and in 1764 he inaugurated one of the most famous concert series of all time, in partnership with a fellow immigrant, Karl Friedrich Abel. Abel was the last great viola da gamba virtuoso of the eighteenth century, and for many years he and J. C. Bach provided Londoners with concerts by subscription.

Almost more than for his own light and elegant compositions, J. C. Bach is remembered for his influence on the musical style of Mozart. Mozart came to London in 1764 (when he was eight years old) along with

Johann Christian Bach by Gainsborough

his sister "Nannerl." In the course of playing four-hand keyboard duets together, J. C. Bach and Mozart came to know each other. Bach was greatly impressed with the young Mozart's musicianship, and Mozart carried away from their meeting a warm feeling for the older man.

J. C. Bach died in 1782. In the twenty-seven years he had spent in London, he had written four-hand keyboard duets (a field in which he was a pioneer), quintets for woodwinds and strings, several sets of concertos, and a great number of short symphonies, of which more than forty were published in his lifetime. In addition he is remembered for the songs (notably "Cease Awhile") he provided for outdoor concerts held on summer evenings in London's Vauxhall Gardens. For an example of his music, see Ex. 9.

Ex. 9 — Sonata, Op. 17, No. 4, J. C. Bach

Allegro

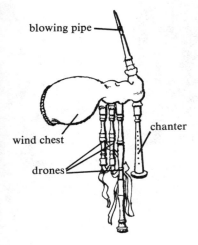

blowing pipe

wind chest

drones

chanter

BAGPIPE: a wind instrument that appears in many shapes and forms all over the world. It is basically an airtight bag with wooden pipes stuck into it. One pipe is held in the mouth and is used to blow air into the bag. The player's arm pumps air from the bag (which is held under the arm) to the other pipes, which make the sounds. At the end of each pipe is a tonguelike reed which vibrates as the air goes through it. One pipe, the chanter, has holes for the fingers to fit over; this is the pipe used to play a melody. Each of the other pipes, the drones, can sound only one note, and these provide the foundation for the melody.

Coming to Europe from India, the bagpipe became popular with the Romans who took it with them all over Europe. (From a remark by the Roman historian Suetonius, it appears that it was probably a bagpipe, not a fiddle, that Nero played while Rome burned.) In France the bagpipe became a favorite instrument for playing dance music. There it was called the musette, or cornemeuse.

In Scotland the bagpipe became the favorite national instrument. Each Scottish family or clan had its own piper and its own songs, which were handed down the generations by ear. The Highland bagpipe is one of the largest kinds, having a melodic range of a ninth.

The bagpipe is a solo instrument; it does not get along with anything but other bagpipes—partly because two of its tones are tuned sharp. Hence composers have tended to shy away from this instrument. But they

have imitated the sound of the bagpipe's drones on keyboard and wind instruments. Imitations can be heard in the middle part (titled "musette") of many gavottes. Echoes of bagpipe music can also be heard in other musical forms—the Siciliano, the pastorale, the loure.

Massed pipe bands, Edinburgh

Balalaika players in the Voronezh Student Ensemble of Folk Instruments

BALALAIKA: the favorite stringed instrument used in popular Russian music. Its body, made of wood, is shaped like a triangle. Of its three strings, two are tuned to the same pitch and one to a perfect fourth above:

The balalaika is strummed like a ukulele and can play chords or melodies.

Balalaikas are made in many sizes, from tiny sopranos held like mandolins to large basses that rest on the ground like string basses. The small balalaikas, which usually play the melody, are not able to hold long sustained tones—the player keeps the tone sounding by strumming rapidly.

Balalaikas are used only in Russia. There they are used mostly to accompany folk songs and dances, although there are large balalaika orchestras that play arrangements of light classical works.

BALLAD: originally, a song sung while dancing. The dance tunes often had several sets of words. Later "ballad" came to mean a song that tells a story. Many folk songs, such as "Barbara Allen," are old ballads that tell a story in many verses.

Composers of the nineteenth century tried to find musical forms or form names that would give their listeners a clue to the meanings of their compositions. Chopin, Brahms, and Liszt used the title "Ballade" for piano pieces that seemed to tell a story.

The ballad opera was a kind of musical show that combined speaking, dancing, and singing. The songs were folk songs or ballads, usually with a new set of words. The first ballad opera was *The Beggar's Opera,* produced in London in 1728. It was so successful that it led the way for the German Singspiel and English and American musical comedies.

BALLET MUSIC: originally, music specifically written to be danced to; but since Isadora Duncan and Michel Fokine in the early 1900's, any music used for theater dance. Music for dance usually has been characterized by a strong beat and by clear, definite cadences to indicate the endings of musical phrases. In the past fifty years, however, these limitations have disappeared and almost every style of music has been used by choreographers, from Beethoven to Webern and from Bach to electronic sounds.

Scores for ballet are usually the result of a collaboration between a composer and a

American balladeer: Woody Guthrie

choreographer. The choreographer devises a scenario for the composer, sometimes being as specific as to tell him how many measures of a certain kind of music he wants. On other occasions the choreographer prepares only a vague outline, leaving it to the composer to decide the lengths of sections. Contemporary dancers such as Martha Graham and José Limon have at times composed all the movement first, calling in the composer only after the dance is completed. In such a case the composer tailor-makes the music to fit the movement and mood of the dance. Just as choreographers have taken concert music and used it for dance purposes, many ballet scores have found their way into the concert hall without the dance. Some ballet scores, such as Stravinsky's *Le Sacre du printemps (The Rite of Spring)* and Copland's *Appalachian Spring,* are heard more often on orchestra programs than on ballet programs.

The earliest ballet music, beginning with that written by de Beaulieu and de Courville for the first ballet, *Le Ballet comique de la reine* (1581), used the social dance forms of the day—mostly slow processionals (Ex. 10). The founder of French opera, Lully, whose ballets and operas popularized the minuet and chaconne, continued the tradition of using stately dances. Wearing high-heeled shoes, elaborate costumes, and headdresses, the dancers could do little more than walk around in interesting patterns.

Rameau, Lully's successor in Paris, brought into his operas and ballets a wholly new approach to the writing of dance music. He introduced lively dances, such as the gavotte, bourrée, passepied, and gigue. But more important he introduced the idea of descriptive music into his ballets. Sometimes the music suggests motion, or even gestures, as in the swirling "Air for Zephire" (Ex. 11) in the spectacular ballet *Les Indes galantes* (1735). At other times his music suggests contrasts of mood, as in his air (Ex. 12) for "Sad Fools and Gay Fools" in *Platèe* (1749).

The great reformer of ballet, the dancer Jean-Georges Noverre (1727–1810), was responsible for a drastic change in dance music. Emphasizing pantomime and expressiveness in dancing, Noverre's theories led to such music as the dramatic Dance of the Furies and the serene Dance of the Blessed Spirits in Gluck's *Orfeo* (1762). A follower of Noverre's, Salvatore Vigano, commissioned Beethoven's *Creatures of Prometheus,* a not altogether successful ballet but one that drew much interesting music from its composer. (The theme of the finale of *Prometheus* was later used by Beethoven as the theme for a set of variations for piano and for the

Ex. 10 — Excerpt from *Le Ballet comique de la reine*

Ex. 11— "Air for Zephire" from *Les Indes galantes*, Rameau

Ex. 12 — "Sad Fools and Gay Fools" from *Platée*, Rameau

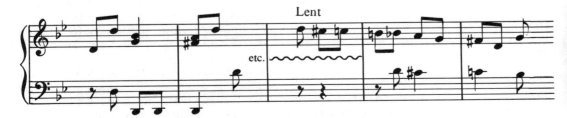

Jean-Georges Noverre

An early form of dance notation by Raoul Feuillet

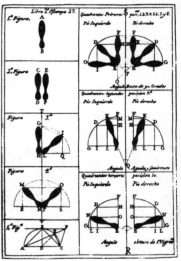

Marie Taglioni in La Sylphide

Above: *Michel Fokine*
Right: *Anna Pavlova*

Vaslav Nijinsky and Tamara Karsavina in Fokine's Spectre de la Rose

final movement of his great Third Symphony, the "Eroica.")

Until the French Revolution, most ballets were based on mythological subjects. One of the first to break from this tradition is also the oldest ballet still performed, *La Fille mal gardée* (1786). (The original production of this ballet used music by various composers. Later scores were written by Herold and Hertel.) With this break from tradition the ballet world was ready for the Romantic period.

The first truly Romantic ballet, involving the love between a supernatural being and a human, was *La Sylphide* (1832). The music for *La Sylphide* was by Jean Schneitzhöffer, a violinist in the Paris Opéra orchestra. It is typical theater music of the early nineteenth century, uncomplicated and with pantomime sections suggestive of later silent-movie music. (It is ironic that Schneitzhöffer, who wrote the music for this ballet that changed the whole trend of the art, is listed in almost no reference books.) If *La Sylphide* is not famous for its music, it is famous because of the costume worn by the ballerina Marie Taglioni—the snug bodice and the flaring white muslin skirt that became the typical costume for all Romantic ballets. This ballet is also a landmark because, in creating an ethereal character, Taglioni danced on the points of her slippers, creating the technique of toe dancing, or dancing on the points.

Paris had always been the home of the ballet. (This is why all ballet terms are in the French language.) It was where Lully's

and Rameau's spectacle ballets were performed, and where the most famous Romantic ballet, *Giselle* (music by Adolphe Adam), was given its première in 1841. For a while, during the middle 1800's, French ballet had a dull period, with no great composer writing dance music. Then Leo Delibes (1836–91) came along to prove that dance music did not have to be routine. *La Source* (1866), written in collaboration with Ludwig Minkus, official composer for the Bolshoi Theater in Moscow, was followed by *Coppélia* (1870) and *Sylvia* (1876). Delibes brought to ballet music a style of symphonic writing that was richly inventive and melodically sparkling.

The success of Delibes encouraged the greatest of all ballet composers, Peter Ilyitch Tchaikovsky, to try his hand. First came *Swan Lake* (1877), expanded from a little home entertainment piece to full evening length. There followed *The Sleeping Beauty* (1890) and *Nutcracker* (1892). Tchaikovsky's lilting waltzes, haunting melodies, and colorful instrumentation, along with the choreographic mastery of Marius Petipa, the creator of the Russian ballet style, made Moscow and St. Petersburg the dance centers of the world.

This ascendancy was short-lived. Sergei Diaghilev, greatest of opera and ballet impresarios, left Russia and moved his company of the finest Russian dancers to Paris. Here such legendary dancers and choreographers as Pavlova, Nijinsky, Karsavina, and Fokine danced to Rimsky-Korsakov's *Scheherazade* and Borodin's barbaric *Polovetzian Dances*. More important, Diaghilev commissioned such important contemporary composers as Debussy, Ravel, Prokofiev, Satie, and Stravinsky.

Stravinsky started by orchestrating a few of Chopin's works for Fokine's *Les Sylphides* (sometimes known as *Chopiniana*). From here he went on to *The Firebird* (1910), *Petrouchka* (1911), and the revolutionary *The Rite of Spring* (1913). This work, more than any other, ushered in the era of modern music. Its dissonant, primitive quality, its jagged rhythms which dominated the work, and its daring use of instruments in hitherto-unexplored registers made *The Rite of Spring* a work fiercely hated and fiercely defended. Like much ballet music of the past it was experimental, since composers for theater have always relied on effect and immediate impact rather than on detailed development of musical materials. Stravinsky's music, while difficult rhythmically, is always perfect for dance. More than any other composer he has had a feeling for movement, without which no composer can write effective ballet music.

After *The Rite of Spring,* Stravinsky started a ballet based on Russian peasant wedding ceremonies, *Les Noces (The Wedding).* In this work he experimented by using not an orchestra but, instead, four pianos, percussion, solo voices, and chorus. *Les Noces* was first produced in 1923, several years after *Pulcinella,* a light work based on the melodies and style of the composer Pergolesi.

Following *Les Noces* came a long line of ballets by Stravinsky, each one different from the others in musical style just as each ballet was different in subject matter. *Apollen musagète (Apollo, Master of the Muses,* 1928) was severely classical; *Le Baiser de la fée (The Fairy's Kiss,* 1928) used themes by Tchaikovsky; *Perséphone* (1934) was scored for reciter and chorus; and *Jeux de Cartes (Card Party,* 1937) and *Orpheus* (1948) were for conventional orchestra. Seemingly having tried all other styles, Stravinsky used in *Agon* (1957) the one technique he had previously avoided: the twelve-tone technique of Schoenberg and Webern.

After the death of Diaghilev in 1929, the Ballet Russe began to decline in importance. Fresh impetus came from the American modern dancers Martha Graham and Doris Humphrey. Their bold ideas of themes for dance and their revolutionary approach to movement, breaking away from formalized ballet figures, called for musical scores that were themselves completely contemporary. In the 1930's Graham and Humphrey commissioned Louis Horst, Wallingford Riegger, and Alex North to create a new kind of dance music: unsentimental and sparse. Because the dancers did not have money to hire a full orchestra, their music was written for small chamber orchestra, two pianos, or percussion ensemble. At times the choreographer combined words with music, as in Graham's *Letter to the World* (poems by Emily Dickinson, music by Hunter Johnson) and Humphrey's *Lament for Ignacio Sanchez Mejía,* composed for José Limon's company and using words by Garcia Lorca and music by Norman Lloyd.

By the present time almost every well-known contemporary composer has written music for dance. Among the most important scores are those by Prokofiev *(Romeo and Juliet),* Copland *(Billy the Kid, Rodeo, Appalachian Spring),* Bernstein *(Fancy Free),* Schuman *(Undertow, Judith, Night Journey),* Barber *(Cave of the Heart),* Dello Joio *(On Stage, There Is a Time, Diversion of Angels),* Persichetti *(King Lear),* and Morton Gould *(Fall River Legend* and *Interplay).*

Top left: *Maria Tallchief and Edward Bigelow in the original production of George Balanchine's ballet* Orpheus
Top right: *Sergei Diaghilev*
Middle left: *Martha Graham in her solo* Ekstasis
Middle right: *George Balanchine, choreographer of most of the later ballets by Stravinsky*
Bottom: Four Temperaments *(music by Hindemith; choreography by Balanchine)*

BAND: a group of wind-instrument and percussion players. Until the late 1600's any combination of instruments was called a band, even if the instruments were stringed. Today there are two kinds of band: the military or marching band, which plays at parades and football games; and the concert band, which plays at concerts. Both use the same instruments, but they play different music. The marching band plays mostly marches; the concert band plays as many kinds of music as a symphony orchestra and is sometimes known as the symphonic band.

Bands appeared hundreds of years ago in Europe. A group of trumpets and drums gave signals to an army, much like the bugle calls of today. Another kind of military band played tunes for the foot soldiers to march to. The instruments of this band were fifes, bagpipes, and drums; oboes and clarinets later took the place of the bagpipes. A third kind of group was the German town band: musicians who played trombones and *zinken,* wooden cornetts with finger holes like those of a recorder.

At first the job of the town band was to announce the hours from the town-hall tower. Later, bands were called upon to play chorales from the church tower in addition to accompanying the singing of the congregation in the church. The town band also played outdoor music for town ceremonies and festivals.

Band concerts became popular in Europe in the 1700's. A typical band of that time consisted of two oboes, two clarinets, two bassoons, and two horns. The program they played would be not too different from what a concert band might offer today: medleys of popular opera tunes, a few dances, and some original music written for band. Great composers such as Haydn, Mozart, and C. P. E. Bach wrote charming works for this small concert band. (In the second act of Mozart's *Don Giovanni* a band of wind instruments plays a concert of opera airs popular in the 1780's.)

In the late 1700's each European country began to take pride in its finest band. As instruments were added, the bands grew in size from eight or twelve to thirty-six players. Finally, in 1790, the band of the French National Guard reached the number of seventy players.

In the late eighteenth century Turkish bands, which featured percussion instruments, influenced the European bands (see JANISSARY MUSIC). Bass drums, snare drums, cymbals, and triangles were added to the usual kettledrums and military drums. The brilliant costumes of the Turks inspired the fancy uniforms and hats seen in parades today—as well as the strutting drum major and the baton twirlers.

The French Revolution led to the founding of many French bands, because Napoleon realized their value in inspiring his soldiers and also the crowds at patriotic celebrations. The seventy-piece band of the French National Guard used every known type of wind instrument. Its music was from the pens of the leading French composers of the time—Gossec, Cherubini, and Mehul. Its members started the National Conservatory of

Top: *Nuremberg town band (copy of mural on wall of the old town hall)*
Bottom: *Sousa and his band*

Music in Paris, one of the greatest of music schools.

The United States had bands during the Revolutionary War—mostly "pick-up" groups that did not stay together very long. The earliest American band still in existence is the United States Marine Corps Band, organized in 1798. The oldest permanent town band is the Allentown Band of Allentown, Pennsylvania, founded in 1828.

Patrick Gilmore, an Irish cornettist who came to Massachusetts in the 1850's, founded the first big concert band in the United States. Gilmore's first experience here was as leader of a band that served with a Massachusetts regiment during the Civil War; after the war he traveled about the country organizing monster-sized band festivals. His own band consisted of about eighty players, to which number he would add several other bands so that the total number of players ranged from five hundred to a thousand. Gilmore set the stage for the man who was to be the greatest popularizer of the band in the United States—the "March King," John Philip Sousa.

Sousa led the Marine Corps Band for twelve years; in 1892 he left this post to form his own concert group. Sousa's band traveled all over the United States and made several tours of Europe and one tour around the world. A combination of snappy marches, top-notch technique among the players, and military precision in marching made Sousa's band the best-known musical group of its time in the United States.

A band's basic musical repertoire is its marches. In addition, bands have always played transcriptions of operatic and symphonic music. For a long time there had not been much original music, other than marches, written for band. Beethoven wrote a Military March in D; Berlioz wrote a symphony for band and chorus; and Gounod, Wagner, Mendelssohn, and Rimsky-Korsakov wrote music for wind bands—mostly slight pieces. In the twentieth century, however, composers began to give bands more attention. The English composer Gustav Holst was first with his two Suites for Band, written about 1910. Soon almost every contemporary composer began to write original band music. Today's band repertoire includes works by Schoenberg, Milhaud, Schuman, Copland, Riegger, Cowell, and Gould.

Band music has reached a high peak in the United States—not only with Sousa's band but with the Goldman Band, which has given summer concerts in New York City since 1911 and pioneered in commissioning composers to write for band. Such big-city concert bands, as well as the bands of the large universities, have brought band performance up to the standard of the finest symphony orchestras.

BANJO: a stringed instrument that has played an important part in the musical history of the United States. Slaves brought from Africa to work the plantations of the New World carried with them one of their native instruments, the *banjar*. In the United States the slaves made their banjars by stretching a coon skin over a hollowed gourd, attaching a handle to the gourd, and running four strings along the length of the instrument. In time the instrument came to be known as the banjo and provided the favorite accompaniment to the plantation songs and dances.

The banjo gradually changed until it reached its present form, with five or six strings. The body of the instrument is a skin stretched tightly over a hoop of wood or metal. The common tunings of the five-string banjo are:

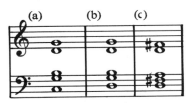

The banjo is played by strumming the strings with the right hand. Melodies can be played on the banjo, but chord accompaniments, beating out the pulse of the music, are more usual. A really accomplished player can give himself the harmonic background by playing fast arpeggios and still make the top notes come through as a melody—a technique also used by guitarists.

In the 1830's and -40's the banjo was played around the campfires of the westward-moving pioneers. Stephen Foster started his "Oh, Susanna!" with the words "Oh, I come from Alabama with my banjo on my knee." The banjo was also the characteristic instrument in the popular minstrel shows of the 1800's, often called banjo operas.

The syncopated melodies and chords played on the banjo led to the early jazz style called ragtime, and until 1930 the banjo remained a basic member of the rhythm section of dance bands. Then it was replaced by the smoother-sounding guitar. Today the banjo has once more become a popular instrument, thanks to a widespread interest in American folk music.

Folksinger Pete Seeger and his banjo

Samuel Barber

Eleanor Steber and Rosalind Elias in Vanessa

BARBER, SAMUEL (1910–): one of the most successful of American composers. He was born in West Chester, Pennsylvania. Barber's family was musical, and he started to compose when he was seven years old. At thirteen he became a student at Philadelphia's newly founded Curtis Institute. There he studied composition with Rosario Scalero, who developed his skill in counterpoint and his sensitivity to melody. For his graduation piece Barber composed a gay, bubbling overture based on Sheridan's *School for Scandal.* It achieved immediate success at its first public performance, which was by the Philadelphia Orchestra. Barber at twenty-two had achieved recognition for which many composers have waited a lifetime.

Thanks to two Pulitzer Traveling Scholarships and an American Prix de Rome, he spent the mid-1930's traveling in Europe. His First Symphony dates from these years (it was first performed in Rome), as does the piece by which he is still best known today, his *Adagio for Strings* (Ex. 13). It was Toscanini who launched the *Adagio* (originally written for string quartet), playing it on his South American tour with the NBC Symphony and broadcasting it over the radio. One of the most popular orchestral works ever written by an American, it has been recorded at least a dozen times.

Barber has written two symphonies, several concertos, chamber music, piano music, *Excursions* (1944), many songs (notably the "Hermit Songs" of 1953), *Essays for Orchestra* (1937 and 1942), the ballet music of *Cave of the Heart* (1946), written for Martha Graham, and two operas. His early music was simple and traditional in style. The long, flowing melodic line of his *Adagio for Strings* might have been written by a nineteenth-century composer. Barber's later works have in them all the variety of structure and content found in the music of his contemporaries. But his music even so has a consonance unusual in the music of today. He is not afraid to use the sounds of the Romantic period or to write a beautiful melody, and yet the context in which these sounds are heard is most certainly modern. Polytonality, the use of the twelve-tone technique, and the use of various Americana, including folk and jazz styles, are all to be found in Barber's works. Ex. 14 is the jazzy subject of the brilliant fugue finale from his *Sonata for Piano* (1949).

In 1958 Barber's opera *Vanessa,* with a libretto by Gian-Carlo Menotti, was given its first performance at the Metropolitan Opera House. It was so successful that it was soon given in several cities in Europe, becoming one of the first American operas to be so honored. It also brought him the Pulitzer Prize.

In 1962 he produced his most successful work thus far, his *Concerto for Piano and Orchestra.* His second opera, *Antony and Cleopatra,* was commissioned for the opening of the new Metropolitan Opera House at Lincoln Center in the fall of 1966.

Ex. 13 — Theme of *Adagio for Strings*

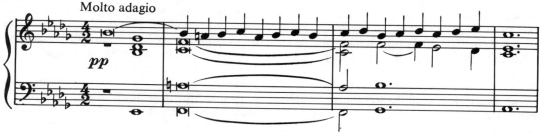

Ex. 14 — Fugue from *Sonata for Piano*

BARBER OF SEVILLE, THE (Il Barbiere di Siviglia):

BARBER OF SEVILLE, THE (*Il Barbiere di Siviglia*): one of the most popular comic operas ever to hold the stage. It was first produced in Rome in 1816, when its composer, Gioacchino Rossini, was not quite twenty-four years old. Rossini himself conducted the first performance, and he had a bad time of it—a guitar string snapped during a crucial serenade, a stray cat ambled across the stage, and the audience hooted and hissed. Nevertheless, by the third night it was a success. For his libretto Rossini used an adaptation of a comedy written a generation earlier by Beaumarchais, an adventurer and financial speculator who had been active in organizing supplies for the insurgent American colonies.

The heroine of the *Barber* is Rosina, a pretty young girl of Seville. Her old guardian, Don Bartolo, keeps her a prisoner in his house, hoping to marry her to get her money for himself. Count Almaviva, a rich young nobleman, sees Rosina and falls in love with her. He has serenades sung to her, but cannot get to see her and talk to her. Figaro, the local barber, druggist, doctor, and general schemer, tells the count that he can do anything—even find husbands for young girls. Figaro sings his praise of himself in the "Largo al factotum," a tongue-twisting, humorous bass aria sung at lightning speed (Ex. 15).

Rosina finds herself very much attracted to this mysterious stranger who serenades her. She sings (Ex. 16) of her growing love in "Una voce poco fa" (A voice, a little while ago. . . .).

Meanwhile the artful Figaro is working on schemes to bring Rosina and the count together. He smuggles letters in and out of the house. Getting the count inside by disguising him as a drunken soldier, he has him take the place of Basilio, Rosina's music teacher and a friend of Don Bartolo. While Figaro shaves Don Bartolo, the lovers plan an elopement at midnight.

Don Bartolo uses a letter written by the count to show Rosina that the count is not faithful to her. Jealous, she tells Don Bartolo of the plans for the elopement. He locks her in her room and sends his servant to call the police, and also sends Basilio to get a notary to draw up a wedding contract.

While Don Bartolo is away, Figaro and the count climb a ladder and come into Rosina's room through the window. She accuses the count of being unfaithful. The count convinces her that she is his only love, but when they get ready to leave they discover that the ladder has vanished.

When Basilio brings the notary in, he is amazed to find Figaro and the count with Rosina. The count threatens Basilio with a pistol and forces him to tell the notary to draw up a marriage contract for Rosina and the count. Then Don Bartolo arrives with the police, but it is too late. The count, however, tells Don Bartolo to keep Rosina's dowry; so everyone is happy, and the whole cast sings a joyful song as the opera comes to an end.

The overture is often played separately on concert programs. Although it goes well with the mood of *The Barber of Seville,* it has no musical connection with it, being in fact an overture Rossini had written three years before and used in two other operas.

Two scenes from The Barber of Seville. **Top:** *Dino Formichini, Robert Merrill, Giulletta Simionato, and Fernando Corena*
Bottom: *Maria Callas and Tito Gobbi*

Ex. 15

Lar - go al fac - to - tum del - la cit - tà, lar - go

Ex. 16

U - na vo - ce po - co fà qui nel cor mi ri - suo - no,

Ex. 17— "Venetian Boat Song" No. 1, Mendelssohn

Cantabile

Venetian scene from the 1913 Metropolitan Opera production of The Tales of Hoffmann

At right: a Baroque composer, Michel de la Barre, and the performers for his trio sonata

BARCAROLE *(barcarolo):* a boatman's song. (In Italy a boatman is a *barcarolo*.) The barcarole came from Venice, where the streets are canals and the taxis are gondolas. The gondoliers have long had a tradition of singing love songs as they row. Composers have imitated these songs by writing flowing melodies over an accompaniment that suggests the steady rhythm of the oars.

Barcaroles are usually in 6/8 time. The accompaniment pattern is based on these two rhythms:

(a)   (b)

The best-known barcaroles are by Chopin and Offenbach (the famous barcarole in Offenbach's *Tales of Hoffmann* first appeared in one of his earlier works, *The Rhine Nymphs*). Mendelssohn called his barcaroles (Ex. 17) "Venetian Boat Songs."

BAR-LINE: a straight line drawn through the musical staff. The space between one bar-line and the next is called a bar or—since it measures the distance from one measure accent to another—a measure. The beat just after the bar-line is the first count in the measure. It is often called the downbeat, because the conductor's baton comes down on the first beat of a measure. If a composition begins on any beat in a bar other than the first one, it is said to begin on an upbeat.

The meaning of the bar-line is often misunderstood. Students often practice music from the beginning of a bar to the end of a bar, although the greatest feeling of rhythmic drive occurs from the end of one measure to the beginning of the next. (Short note values are used by composers more often at the end of a measure than at the beginning. The rhythm of the short note values should be carried through to the next downbeat.) A bar-line should be felt not as a wall that stops the music, but as a short hurdle where the music jumps into the air with a great feeling of push.

The bar-line began to be used in musical notation in the sixteenth century. At that time it was used to show the end of a song phrase or to make a musical score easier to read. Most of the madrigals and motets of the late sixteenth century were written without bar-lines. Several hundred years later, bar-lines were added by editors.

The double bar is used at the end of a musical composition. It is also used at the end of a large section of a composition, particularly if there is to be a repeat of the section.

BAROQUE PERIOD: the musical period from just before 1600 until just after 1750. It is the period of these great composers: Monteverdi, Lully, Purcell, Corelli, Vivaldi, Rameau, Couperin, the Scarlattis, Handel, and Bach. It is the period that saw the beginning of opera, ballet, and oratorio. It is the period from which come most forms of instrumental music: sonata, concerto, concerto grosso, fugue, dance suite, toccata, passacaglia, chaconne, theme and variations, chorale prelude, and early symphony. It is the period that saw the development of the recitative and aria da capo as well as the opera overture.

The Baroque is the period during which harmonic theory and figured bass came into being. It is the period that saw the beginning of the orchestra—when composers first began to specify which instruments were to play what music. It is the period in which the major and minor scales replaced the old church modes in importance. It is the period when composers began to write Italian words, such as *forte* and *allegro,* to tell performers how to play their music. It is the period when composers and performers began to use the many kinds of musical decoration, such as the trill and the mordent. It is the period during which the violin family reached its highest development and the violin became the queen of instruments. It is the period that opened the road to all later music, up to the present day.

The Baroque period represented a revolt

Handel watching a rehearsal of one of his oratorios. The conductor is at a two-manual harpsichord, with the main body of the orchestra behind him and the choir in front. Solo vocalists are at his left. The principal instrumentalists (two violins, flute, cello) are at his right

against the kind of music that had been written in the fifteenth and sixteenth centuries: music mostly for voices; music that was based on the interweaving of melodic lines; music that used little dissonance; music that had a flowing, varied rhythm; music that did not try to portray emotions except of the simplest and noblest kinds.

The Baroque composers wanted their music to be extremely expressive—to deal with passionate emotions. The feelings were classified as various typical "affections": sorrow, pain, heroism, devotion, and so forth. It was the job of the composer to find the musical motive that would best give an audience the feeling of the "affection." This motive would be used throughout a composition and would serve to give it unity. The motive might be the all-important subject of a fugue. Or it might be an accompaniment pattern on top of which a composer might float a beautiful aria.

The Baroque age is often divided into three parts. The early Baroque saw the appearance of opera and of short instrumental pieces that were close to the forms of earlier music, such as the motet. The middle period saw the separation of the recitative from the aria, the beginning of a greater use of counterpoint, and the birth of the singing style called bel canto. The late Baroque is the period of the fugue and other large contrapuntal forms, the concerto style of writing, and chord progressions that are based on set patterns such as the "circle of fifths."

The Baroque period got its name from a term that was used to describe over-decorated church architecture. For a long time many people thought that Baroque was a poor descendant of the art of the Renaissance period. Now it is recognized for what it was—the beginning of almost all of the musical styles up to the present.

At right: "The Organ Grinder" (photograph by Krausz, Chicago, 1891)

BARREL ORGAN: a mechanical instrument that was a remote ancestor of the jukebox. The basic form was that of a revolving wooden barrel, operated by a crank or clockspring and equipped with protruding pins. As the barrel revolved, the pins tripped triggers which, in turn, opened organ pipes. Air pumped by the turning crank from bellows or chests of wind entered the pipes to make the sound. The music was pre-set into the barrel by the precise placement of the metal pins. Large barrels could hold as many as ten tunes. If more tunes were wanted, a new barrel could be put in place—much as one puts on a different record.

The pin-and-barrel principle goes back to the Middle Ages, when it was used for carillons. But the barrel organ proper was an eighteenth-century instrument known to Mozart, who wrote three large works for it. Big barrel organs were used to play popular dance tunes and operatic medleys. (Mozart was pleased when he went to Prague in 1787 and heard tunes from his *Marriage of Figaro* played on street-corner barrel organs.) In England the barrel organ was so popular that it put many church organists out of work during the eighteenth and nineteenth centuries.

A relative of the barrel organ, the modern hurdy-gurdy, or street organ, is the instrument associated with the begging monkey. This instrument is actually a form of mechanical piano with hammers activated by the pin-and-barrel device.

BARTÓK, BÉLA (1881–1945): an outstanding modern composer who wrote not only large orchestral works and string quartets, but also works for young musicians and students. He began to study music in his native Hungary at the age of six. At nine he was already composing short piano pieces. He studied at the Royal Academy in Budapest, to which he returned in 1907 as one of its youngest professors of piano.

Upon visiting a friend who lived in a far-off village, Bartók heard for the first time the kind of Hungarian music that was to influence his own music for the rest of his musical life. He and his fellow-composer Zoltán Kodály realized that what they had been hearing as Hungarian music in the city was really gypsy music and that there was a different world of Hungarian, or Magyar, folk music to be used and exploited. Bartók spent much time traveling through Hungary and Rumania listening to the music of the peasants, writing the tunes in his notebooks and, later, recording the original sounds of it. He went to North Africa and made recordings of Arabian music: altogether he gathered more than five thousand songs and dances.

From much of this folk material Bartók made delightful little piano pieces that preserve the warmth and the depth of the peasant songs. Some of the folk songs were in the old church modes, others in the pentatonic scales. Some used scales that were unknown to the musicians of his day. Because the Magyar melodies did not fit the Classical harmonies of Mozart and Beethoven, Bartók had to invent his own system of harmony, often basing it on dissonance.

Bartók experimented with his newly discovered harmonic ideas and used them as the foundation of various large compositions—his *Sonata for Piano,* six string quartets, three virtuoso piano concertos, three violin sonatas, and *Concerto for Orchestra.* He wrote for unusual combinations of instruments, as in his *Sonata for Two Pianos and Percussion; Music for String Instruments, Percussion and Celesta;* and *Contrasts* for violin, clarinet, and piano.

Bartók's works are tightly knit, growing out of small bits of musical material the way a plant grows from a seed. He would take a two-note motive and from it construct a whole composition. His driving rhythms, biting harmonies, and terse melodies were all woven together in a way unlike that of any other composer. But no matter how complex Bartók's music seems to be, it is basically crystal clear in its simplicity and beauty.

Bartók wrote one opera, *Bluebeard's Castle,*

and two large ballets. Success was late in coming to these, but his *Mikrokosmos,* a six-volume collection of short piano pieces, has become a basis for the study of the music of our time.

Bartók came to the United States in 1940. His royalties from publishers were cut off by the World War and Bartók suffered severe financial hardships. Honored and respected by musicians, he died practically unknown to the general public. Had he lived a little longer, he would have found his works among those most played in all modern music.

BASS: the lowest voice part in music. Each family of musical instruments includes at least one member that serves as its bass (pronounced "base"). The most usual bass instruments are the bassoon, bass clarinet, trombone, tuba, bass drum, and (string) double bass. The cello serves as bass in the string quartet.

Parts for bass instruments generally lie below middle C and are written in the bass CLEF, whose two dots enclose the line for F below middle C:

When music is written in several "parts" or "voices," the bass part is often the founda-

Top: *Bartók recording Hungarian folk songs in an Hungarian village*
Bottom: *Béla Bartók*

Basso Salvatore Baccaloni

tion on which the harmony is built. This special role is clearly seen in figured bass, a form of musical shorthand invented about the year 1600. Instead of writing all the notes of the chords that accompanied a melody, the composer merely wrote a bass part (the continuo) with numbers over the notes. The notes were played by a bass instrument, such as the bassoon or cello. The same part, with numbers, was given to the harpsichord player or organist, who filled in the notes of the chords as shown to him by the numbers. This was called "realizing" a figured bass (see HARMONY).

Most men speak or sing in the high bass voice that is called baritone. A true bass voice is rare, being marked not only by the ability to reach very low notes but also by deep *quality*. The bass voice has the range shown here:

In choral writing the part does not usually go as high or as low as in solo writing.

In opera the bass singer is rarely the romantic hero. Sometimes he is a regal personage, such as Boris in *Boris Godunov;* or a noble character, such as Hans Sachs in *Die Meistersinger;* or a lordly god, like Wotan in Wagner's *The Ring of the Nibelungs.* Sometimes he is a villain, like Mephistopheles in Gounod's *Faust,* but more often a comic character, like Leporello in Mozart's *Don Giovanni.* In Pergolesi's comic opera *La serva padrona* there are only two characters, one of them a bass.

The bass singer is often given long, low notes that bring out the grave quality of his voice. A singer with an exceptionally low voice is called a basso profundo. The part of the commander in *Don Giovanni* is written for such a voice.

The bass voice can be as agile as any other. The operas and oratorios of Handel, the songs of Purcell, and the cantatas of Bach are full of bass solos that have fast running passages as well as big leaps (Ex. 18).

BASS DRUM: the largest member of the drum family. In parades this two-headed drum looks almost as tall as the man who plays it. The bass drums used in some parades are so large that they are carried on small wagons. On the concert stage a drum about three feet in diameter is used, resting on a small wooden cradle. It is usually played with a short, heavy drumstick with a large felt knob at the end. In dance bands the bass drum is usually played by means of a pedal.

The bass drum cannot play fast notes: its head is so big that it takes a long time to start vibrating. It has no definite pitch, although the head can be tightened. In scores the bass drum's part is indicated by its French, Italian, or German name—*grosse caisse, cassa grande,* or *Grosse Trommel.* The part is usually written on the second space of the bass clef:

Sometimes it shares a staff with the snare drum or cymbals:

In a crowded score the bass drum's part is written on a single line:

The bass drum came into European music from Turkish Janissary bands, which had large percussion sections featuring drums, cymbals, triangles, and a jingling crescent. Gluck pioneered in the use of the bass drum in his operas written from 1764 on *(The Unforeseen Encounter),* and Haydn was the first to use this drum in a symphony. Haydn's "Military" Symphony (Number 100, 1794) contains an important part for the bass drum, to be played with two sticks (a practice still popular in high-school and military bands).

Jesse Kregal playing the bass drum

Ex. 18— Aria from Cantata No. 80: "A Mighty Fortress Is Our God," J. S. Bach

Al ———————————— les, Al ————————

———————— les, was von Gott ge - bo - ren, Al - les was von Gott ge - bo - ren.

Ex. 19— Second Movement, "Military" Symphony No. 100, Haydn

In his score Haydn showed by the direction of the note stem (Ex. 19) which hand was to play. Stems going up call for the left hand; stems going down, for the right.

Long after the Viennese craze for "Turkish" music had died down, the bass drum was kept on for its help in marking heavy accents. A roll on the bass drum, played with two timpani sticks, is a dramatic way of suggesting thunder or cannon. Composers often use the bass drum in funeral marches, and Berlioz used it all through the last two movements of his *Symphonie fantastique.*

BASSOON: the bass of the woodwind family. When taken apart to be carried, it looks like a bundle of sticks; hence the Italian and German names *fagotto* and *Fagott,* sometimes seen on the first page of a score. The bassoon's tube has a length of over eight feet but is doubled up into a U to allow the player to reach all the keys and levers. A strap around the bassoonist's neck helps him to support the instrument, leaving his hands free.

When it is played, the bassoon looks like a long, thin log with a bent straw sticking out from its side. This straw is actually a metal tube, one end of which carries the mouthpiece and the other end of which is attached to the shorter of the two wooden tubes that make up the body of the instrument.

The mouthpiece holds two reeds—a feature that gives the bassoon a characteristic biting tone color reminiscent of the other double-reed instruments, the oboe and the English horn. In spite of its penetrating quality, the tone of the bassoon is surprisingly soft for such a large instrument. Even more remarkable is the bassoon's range—from the B-flat below the staff to a few tones higher than the C above middle C:

This great range allows the bassoonist to play bass parts and tenor parts (which he reads in the bass and tenor clefs).

To many listeners the bassoon is hardly more than the clown of the orchestra. Bassoonists, who spend much of their playing time in orchestras holding long bass notes that no one ever notices, tend to take another view of the matter. Composers sometimes reinforce the clown image by giving the bassoon staccato melodies, as in Paul Dukas' *The Sorcerer's Apprentice* (Ex. 20). But in his Fifth Symphony, Tchaikovsky showed that the bassoon is perfectly capable of carrying a sweet melody (Ex. 21). And in his Sixth Symphony, the "Pathétique," we hear it express in a whisper the deepest of tragic feelings. The bassoon's highest register is

Kenneth Pasmanick playing the bassoon

Ex. 20 — *The Sorcerer's Apprentice*, Dukas

Ex. 21— Symphony No. 5, Tchaikovsky

Ex. 22— Symphony No. 97, Haydn

Vivace

George Longazo playing the contrabassoon

heard in the memorable opening of Stravinsky's *Rite of Spring,* where its plaintive tone sets the scene for the primitive dances that follow. Although one does not normally think of the bassoon as an especially nimble instrument, it can scamper up and down the scale at a rapid tempo if it has to, as in Haydn's Symphony Number 97, in C (Ex. 22).

The bassoon was invented around 1600. One of its earliest appearances in an orchestra is in one of Lully's operas (1674), where it is used along with two oboes to play the first trios. Many composers have found a role for the bassoon in woodwind quintets, and the American composer William Schuman has even written a quartet for four bassoons. But not many solos have been written for it apart from those in the half-dozen concertos for bassoon and orchestra by Vivaldi and the single concerto by Mozart, K. 191.

The contrabassoon (or double bassoon) is a rare instrument. It sounds an octave lower than the bassoon, its lowest tone being only a half tone above the lowest tone on the piano. To avoid an illegible piling up of ledger lines below the staff, its part is written an octave higher than it sounds. The contrabassoon can be heard at the beginning of Brahms' First Symphony, where its lowest C serves as a fundamental tone for the rest of the orchestra.

BATON: the thin, tapering stick, usually made of wood, that is used by the conductor to give silent signals to his ensemble. By his use of the baton a conductor keeps the group together, indicates entrances, and, by the size and quality of his beat, reminds the performers of dynamics and articulation.

Conductor Fritz Reiner, virtuoso of the baton

The baton as known today was first used about 1820, although violin bows and rolls of music paper had been tried several hundred years earlier. For a while its use met with opposition from orchestral players who had been accustomed to having the leader of the first violins or the harpsichordist give all signals. By the middle of the nineteenth century, however, the baton had won out, although some orchestral conductors and many choral conductors of today use their hands instead of a baton.

Each conductor chooses his own special design of baton, often having it made to order. Some like short batons, thin or stubby and barely a foot in length. Others prefer longer batons, particularly when conducting large forces as in opera or choral and orchestral works. In theaters, where the light in the orchestra pit is rather dim, some conductors use a baton with a small flashlight at its tip.

BATTLE HYMN OF THE REPUBLIC, THE: the marching song of the Northern troops during the Civil War. Its melody came originally from the South, having been composed there by William Steffe about 1856. It had been popular in black churches around Charleston, South Carolina, where it was sung to the words of

> *Say, brothers will you meet us—*
> *Say, brothers will you meet us—*
> *Say, brothers will you meet us—*
> *On Canaan's happy shore?*

in the verse. The chorus was the familiar "Glory, glory, hallelujah."

During the war the Northern soldiers sang the melody with new words: "John Brown's body lies a-mouldering in the grave. . . . But his soul goes marching on." Later the words were changed to "We'll hang Jeff Davis to a sour apple tree."

Julia Ward Howe, a Northern lady visiting the army camps outside Washington, heard the troops singing "John Brown's Body." She felt that there should be more inspiring words for the old hymn. In December 1861, she wrote the stirring verses of "The Battle Hymn of the Republic." This song became the Northern answer to "Dixie."

BEETHOVEN, LUDWIG VAN (1770–1827): master composer of symphonies, sonatas, concertos, and string quartets. Beethoven was born in Bonn, on the banks of the Rhine in Germany. His father was a poorly paid singer and instrumentalist in the court orchestra of the Elector of Cologne. Seeing that his son had musical talent, the father gave him lessons on the piano and the violin in the hope that Ludwig would be a prodigy who would make a fortune for the family. From the age of four Beethoven was made to practice many hours a day, and when he was eight he played his first recital.

At eleven Beethoven became a pupil of the court organist, Neefe. Neefe saw the genius that was in his pupil and became a kind of musical father to him, encouraging him to compose and even helping to get his early works published. He employed Beethoven as an assistant organist and as a violist in the court orchestra. The job did not mean much in money, but Beethoven did get to know the music of Bach and of the opera composers of the day.

Beethoven's mother died when he was seventeen; his father was a drunkard. Ludwig had to become head of the household, and for five years while he played in the orchestra he also took care of his father, two brothers, and a sister.

His piano playing and his compositions attracted the attention of several wealthy persons, who became his friends. They and the prince of the nearby city of Cologne encouraged Beethoven and offered to help him. In 1792 he was sent to Vienna, then the center of the musical world, to study and seek his fortune.

Beethoven had dreamed of studying with Mozart, but Mozart had died just the year before. Beethoven therefore asked Haydn to be his teacher, and was accepted. For a little more than a year Beethoven studied music theory with Haydn. The lessons were often stormy, for Beethoven always wanted to know the reason for any rule and Haydn, who broke the rules in his own music, was too busy to explain why a student should obey them. On the sly, Beethoven began to take his exercises to a teacher named Schenk for more intensive and pedantic corrections. Fortunately the lessons with Haydn stopped when Haydn left for a long trip to England, and Beethoven then studied with the noted theorist Albrechtsberger.

Beethoven began to make a career for himself as a pianist and composer. The people whose names appear and reappear in his dedications—Count Waldstein, Prince Lichnowsky, Count Rasoumovsky, Archduke Rudolf, and others—were all members of the nobility with great understanding of music who commissioned works to be written and provided for the performances. Beethoven was invited to their houses to play and improvise. He was a phenomenal improviser, and in fact many of his listeners were moved more by his improvisations than by his compositions.

After leaving Bonn, Beethoven never had a regular job as a musician. Most composers up to this time had worked for either church or court, but Beethoven was a new species of musician—the free-lance composer. Apart from the occasional piano lessons that he gave, he had two main sources of income: he sold his compositions to publishers and he wrote works for his friends among the nobility of Vienna. He had a scale of prices for his works, charging so much for a sonata, a little more for a string quartet, and the top price for a symphony. There were times

Beethoven's birthplace in Bonn

Miniature of Beethoven by Horneman, 1804

Beethoven's hearing aids, made by Johannes Maelzel, inventor of the metronome, in 1812–14

Beethoven in 1824

when he yearned to write a quartet, but if someone called for a sonata this was what he wrote.

At the end of his first ten years in Vienna, Beethoven was at the peak of his fame. He had written ten piano sonatas, six string quartets, two symphonies, two piano concertos, and his ballet *The Creatures of Prometheus*. He was in great demand as a pianist and conductor. His fame was spreading throughout Europe, and he might have become a traveling virtuoso pianist. Then a terrible misfortune overtook him: he began to lose his hearing. At first he was only slightly deaf; he could hear loud talking and loud music. Later, the whole world of sound became closed to him.

Most persons would have given up. Of what use is a musician who cannot hear? Beethoven had many moments of distress and misery, yet never lost faith in himself. In a letter to a friend he wrote, "I will struggle with fate; it shall never drag me down."

As his deafness increased, Beethoven began to close himself off more from the world of people. Conversation with him was difficult. A person had to write down everything he wanted to say to the composer. Beethoven, turning away from people, took walks in the woods to get close to nature, buried himself in great books, and poured his energies into composition.

Beethoven heard his music with what musicians call the "inner ear." Instead of limiting his expression, deafness seemed to free him to pursue new ideas. It was a time of violent changes—the period often referred to as *Sturm und Drang* (Storm and Stress) after the title of a German play of the 1770's. The American and French revolutions were declaring the importance of every man, not just the nobility. In the arts, stormy passions, simple directness, and warm tenderness began to take the place of aristocratic elegance and grace.

The spirit of freedom that was in the air inspired Beethoven to do many things that changed music. His early works were modeled on the sonatas, string quartets, and symphonies of Mozart and Haydn, but from the beginning his music was different from any other. Even when it was pure music—music without a story—it had a dramatic quality. It was full of violent contrasts, jumped from low to high registers, went from soft to loud explosively. His chord progressions were often unexpected or surprising, not like those of the classic pattern. His key changes did not follow the traditional modulations to closely related keys.

In his piano music Beethoven replaced the simple accompaniment pattern with hammering percussive chords. He used the sustaining pedal to get new sonorities. He used bold arpeggio figures.

With the orchestra of Haydn, Beethoven could not get the range of sound he needed. He added the piccolo and trombones in his Fifth Symphony, and the contrabassoon in the Ninth. He freed the double bass, cello, and timpani from their simple job of marking accents, and in his Ninth Symphony gave them important solo parts. The clarinet, a newcomer to the orchestra, was given a place equal to that of the oboe. Beethoven even used the whole orchestra for effects other than mere loudness. In the Ninth Symphony he had the whole orchestra play together softly, revealing for composers a new world of sound.

It was the musical form of the sonata that Beethoven changed more than anything else. Instead of writing four movements that had no themes in common, he connected the whole work by building the movements from themes that shared a central melodic kernel with one another, as in the Fifth Symphony, or quoting themes from previous movements, as in the finale of the Ninth Symphony. Thus he foreshadowed the cyclic form of later composers.

Beethoven was a master of proportion and of musical timing. He knew the dramatic force of a long build-up or transition section (see "EROICA"). He knew that a long development section needed to be balanced by a long coda. Realizing that the minuet form was out of date, he substituted for it dashing, abandoned scherzos. He saw that jolly finales were out of place after a series of deep, forceful movements; he replaced them with powerful, craggy fugues. The sonata form was no longer the same after it had been used by Beethoven.

Beethoven sometimes gave his compositions titles, such as *Sonate pathétique, Sinfonia eroica, Sinfonia pastorale*. The three-movement *Sonata for Piano*, Opus 81a, was subtitled *The Farewell, the Absence, and the Return*. These titles are Beethoven's own, and they have a different standing from those—such as "Moonlight," "Spring," or "Pastoral"—that were later attached to certain other sonatas, sometimes long after they were written. What Beethoven was getting at with his titles was something very characteristic of the Romantic age. What was music for? Was its purpose merely to decorate the idle daydreams of the upper classes or to make serious statements about mankind? One of Beethoven's convictions, in these years when the entire social order of Europe was being shaken by the French Revolution, was that man's birthright is to be free. It was in this spirit that he chose to set Schiller's "Ode to Joy" in the concluding movement of his Ninth Symphony. Its refrain, "All mankind are brothers," was Beethoven's own philosophy. To proclaim it, he added solo singers and a chorus to the symphony's orchestral forces. Only through the human voice, he felt, could he evoke the deepest feelings of mankind.

Beethoven did not always write sad or heroic music. He was fond of jokes; he loved to make puns—the worse they were, the more he liked them. All through his music there is the same love of fun. Sometimes it is a kind of practical joke on the audience—getting it off balance by putting accents in the wrong place. His scherzos are all wonderful musical jokes, some light-hearted and some gigantic. Only a master of musical timing could make his music bubble and bounce the way Beethoven does.

This composer's music is full of drama, yet he wrote but one opera, *Fidelio*. It contains some of his finest music but when it was first produced, in 1805, it was not a success. Beethoven had a great deal of trouble with *Fidelio*, writing and rewriting. Three overtures were put aside before he was satisfied. The first three of these are known as the Leonore Overtures, after the name of the heroine. The fourth, the Fidelio Overture, is the only one usually played before the opera today.

Many of Beethoven's overtures are really dramas in music. The Third Leonore Overture and the overtures to the plays *Egmont* and *Coriolanus* are early examples of the symphonic poem—music that seems to tell a story without the use of words.

Beethoven's life as a composer is often divided into three periods. The first is his youthful period, in which he was seeking himself. Very roughly, this corresponds to the first fifty opus numbers of his works as they were published—his first twenty-plus piano sonatas, the first nine of his violin sonatas, the string quartets of the Opus 18 group, the first three piano concertos, and the first two symphonies.

The opening shot of his second period is his Third Symphony, the "Eroica." This has been called by Paul Henry Lang "the greatest single step made by an individual composer in the history of the symphony and in the history of music in general." Thereafter Beethoven made greater and greater demands on performers and audiences. He was now widely criticized for his

Portrait of Beethoven by Ferdinand Waldmüller, 1823

lack of elegance and measure, for his wildness. Even his Fifth Symphony—today the most popular of all symphonies—was held up by music teachers as an example of how *not* to start a symphony. The compositions of this period include the items most associated with the name "Beethoven" in the concert world today—the piano sonatas, from the "Waldstein" Sonata, Opus 53, to the Sonata in E Minor, Opus 90; the last sonata for violin and piano, in G major, Opus 96; the piano trios of Opus 70, and the "Archduke," Opus 97; the "Rasoumovsky" string quartets, Opus 59, and the quartets of Opus 74 (the "Harp") and 95; many of the most familiar overtures—the Coriolanus, Leonore (Numbers 1, 2 and 3), Fidelio, and Egmont; the symphonies from the Third through the Eighth; the Fourth and Fifth piano concertos; and Beethoven's only opera, *Fidelio*.

If Beethoven had stopped there, what difference would it have made? To the composers who have written since Beethoven's time, the difference would have been enormous. For the works of Beethoven's last period set the standards against which the most serious composers of our own time are still measuring themselves. Beethoven now confined himself to three instrumental situations: two lean ones, the solo piano and the

Sketches for the Fifth Symphony

string quartet, and one that is the richest of all, the combination of voices and orchestra. In this last medium he composed his two most gigantic works, the *Missa solemnis,* in D major, and the Ninth Symphony, in D minor. For the solo piano he composed his last five sonatas—Opuses 101, 106, 109, 110, and 111—the Bagatelles, Opuses 119 and 126, and the Variations on a Theme by Diabelli. For string quartet he wrote the quartets from Opuses 127 to 135; to these, his final testament, he devoted the last two years of his life.

These last works, beginning with the Piano Sonata in A, Opus 101, are among the most extraordinary achievements of mankind. They are all the more remarkable when one considers the state of the man who wrote them. For in the ten years during which they were produced, 1816–26, Beethoven was tried as sorely as any man ever was. Though a composer, he was completely deaf. Though honored as a leading citizen of Vienna, he was hard-pressed to pay the rent and keep himself alive. Though denied the joys of a marriage of his own, he had the thankless burden of caring for an irresponsible nephew who brought him no end of grief. And his health was poor.

It was from this torment that Beethoven brought forth some of the most sublime music ever written. It searches the depths of man's being. With such music the old Classical forms were left far behind; each work was created in a form of its own. Often the music is sparse; it is not music that just spins a beautiful, long melodic line, nor is it a succession of rich harmonies. Melodically it may merely move up and down a scale with effects that can be puzzling in their simplicity.

Beethoven never composed quickly and easily. When he improvised at the piano, his ideas flowed without effort—but when he sat down to write he always seemed to have a struggle. Throughout his life he wrote down sketches in a music notebook. The story of how he put his material together is all there in the notebooks—from the first crude beginning of a theme through its polishing to its final form. He hammered away with tones like a sculptor working in stone. He would spend months, even years, on one theme. He refused to use a theme until he had made it as nearly perfect as possible. In notebooks we see the theme of the slow movement of the Fifth Symphony starting out as a dull little minuet theme, then by stages becoming a musical utterance of unusual beauty (Ex. 23). Beethoven was a careful worker and a steady worker. In his lifetime he wrote thirty-two piano sonatas, seventeen string quartets, nine symphonies; five piano concertos; one violin concerto; a concerto for piano, violin, and cello; five sonatas for cello and piano; ten sonatas for violin and piano; an opera; a ballet; ten overtures; two masses; much chamber music for various combinations of instruments; cantatas; songs; and for the piano, innumerable occasional pieces, variations, and bagatelles. Beethoven had sworn that fate would never drag him down. With Beethoven for an opponent, fate hardly had a chance.

Ex. 23

BEGGAR'S OPERA, THE: the ancestor of all musical shows that combine singing, dancing, and talking. *The Beggar's Opera* opened in London in 1728, was immediately successful, and ran for a long time. (It is still revived from time to time.) The spoken dialogue and the words to the songs were written by John Gay. The music was a collection of English, Scottish, and Irish folk tunes plus a few songs by such composers as Purcell. The tunes were arranged by Dr. Christopher Pepusch, who also wrote an overture to the opera.

The Beggar's Opera was based on an idea by Jonathan Swift, the author of *Gulliver's Travels.* Swift suggested to his friend Gay that it would be a good joke to poke fun at the Italian operas—notably Handel's—that were popular in London in the early 1720's. Instead of presenting the noble heroes of the Italian operas, Gay wrote his opera about the thieves and beggars who lived in the slums of London.

The Beggar's Opera is about Captain Mac-Heath, a highway robber, and his love affair with Polly Peachum. Polly is the daughter of parents who rent crutches and tattered clothing to beggars. Practically all the characters in the opera are crooks. At the end of the opera Captain MacHeath is sentenced to be hanged, but before the sentence is carried out, he is pardoned and all the "villain-heroes" go free.

This work is a *ballad opera.* After its success, hundreds of ballad operas were produced in England and America. One imitation was translated into German. The Germans called the combination of singing and speaking *Singspiel.* Some of the greatest German operas, such as Mozart's *The Magic Flute* and Beethoven's *Fidelio,* are Singspiels. In 1928 Bertolt Brecht and Kurt Weill used *The Beggar's Opera* as a model for their popular *Three-penny Opera.*

At left: *John Gay*

Below left: *Act III of* The Beggar's Opera, *a 1790 engraving by William Blake after a painting by William Hogarth*
Below right: *American production of Marc Blitzstein's version of* The Three-penny Opera

Bells at Mafra, Portugal

BELL: a round or cup-shaped musical instrument that gives off a ringing sound when struck. Bells are used so much as signals in our homes and schools that they are not often thought of as musical instruments. Four thousand years ago, however, the Chinese had orchestras in which there were a great many bells, and bells are still used as musical instruments today.

Bells are usually made of iron, tin, and copper, but small ones can be made of clay or glass. Bells are both the smallest and the largest of musical instruments. Tiny sleigh bells are used in orchestras when the composer wants to suggest a ride in the snow. Big Ben in the tower of Parliament weighs over thirteen tons!

A bell is made to sound by hitting it with a hammer or a metal clapper. The clapper is a piece of metal that hangs inside the bell. When the bell is tipped off balance, the clapper strikes against the side of the bell. In a seagoing bell-buoy the action of the waves tips the bell. The bell in a church tower has a long rope tied to it so that a man far below can tip the bell by pulling the rope.

The sound of a large bell is very complicated. When it is struck it gives off its real pitch. This is followed by the tone an octave lower, called the "hum tone," and as many as five different pitches above its struck tone.

"Change ringing" is a kind of musical puzzle that uses five to twelve bells. The aim of change ringing is to play the bells in constantly changing order—but no bell is to be changed more than one place in its order: 1 2 3 4 5, 1 3 2 5 4, 1 3 5 2 4, and so on. Change ringing is practiced mostly in English churches.

A carillon is a group of bells made in different sizes so that a scale can be played. Melodies are played on a carillon by means of a keyboard like that of a piano. One of the largest carillons in the world is in the tower of Riverside Church in New York City. It has sixty-four bells and can be made to play complicated pieces of music.

Electronic carillons are being used in more and more church towers. These instruments have thin metal rods instead of large, heavy cast bells. The rods are vibrated by means of an electromagnet, and the vibrations are picked up, amplified, and fed to loudspeakers.

Orchestral bells are large metal pipes like the metal rods of a door chime. They are played by a member of the percussion group by means of a wooden or metal hammer. They can be heard in Wagner's *Parsifal* and near the end of Tchaikovsky's "1812" Overture.

The glockenspiel, a relative of the xylophone, sounds like a set of small bells.

In orchestral scores the bells are called *cloches* in French, *glocken* in German, and *campanelle* in Italian.

Chimes are a set of bells used in a clock to sound the quarter-hour, half-hour, and hour. The most famous bell sound is that of the Westminster Chimes (Ex. 24) in Cambridge, England.

Ex. 24— Westminster Chimes

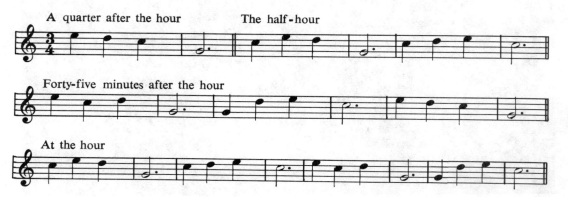

Ex. 25— "Casta Diva"

Andante sostenuto assai

BELLINI, VINCENZO (1801–35): a short-lived Italian composer who wrote several operas that have become staples in the repertoire of opera houses throughout the world. Bellini was born in Catania, Sicily, where his father and grandfather were organists. It was inevitable that Bellini would follow in their footsteps, and he started to compose while still a small child. Entering the Conservatory of San Sebastiano in Naples, he concentrated on studying the operas of earlier Italian composers.

Bellini's first opera, *Adelson e Salvina*, written in 1825, was successful. Commission followed commission. In the single year 1831 two of his most famous operas, *La sonnambula (The Sleepwalker)* and *Norma,* were given premier performances in Milan. Then, after the failure of *Beatrice di Truda* (1833), Rossini persuaded Bellini to move to Paris, where he wrote his last work, *I puritani* (*The Puritans,* 1835).

Bellini's operas call for great singers, particularly sopranos. They are "spectacle" operas, often weak in plot. From time to time the Bellini operas seem ready to be dropped from the repertoire—then the right prima donna comes along to breathe fresh life into them.

Bellini's music is primarily melodic. His harmony is simple, but above a routine accompaniment pattern he spins beautiful and often dramatic melodies.

In the last years of his life, in Paris, Bellini became a member of a group of young Romantic composers, poets, and painters. A likable, shy young man, he became deeply attached to Frédéric Chopin. Their elegant melodies are amazingly alike, as may be seen when the aria "Casta Diva" from *Norma* is played in a piano version (Ex. 25).

Recently the operas of Bellini have benefited from performances by Maria Callas and Joan Sutherland. Only such exceptional sopranos are able to supply the vocal virtuosity called for by Bellini.

Above: *Vincenzo Bellini*
At left: *Joan Sutherland in the sleepwalking scene from* La sonnambula

Portrait of Alban Berg by Arnold Schoenberg (c. 1900)

BERG, ALBAN (1885–1935): the composer of some of the most original, beautiful, and dramatic music of this century. Born in Vienna, Berg did not adopt music as his life's work until he was twenty-two years old. His teacher was Arnold Schoenberg, and like his teacher's, Berg's early works—such as his songs and his piano sonata in one movement—are highly Romantic in their use of restless chromatic harmony.

Berg and his fellow student Anton von Webern joined Schoenberg in experimenting with the technique of composition that became known as the twelve-tone, or dodecaphonic, technique. As an energetic champion of new trends in music, Berg lectured, wrote articles, and encouraged performances of contemporary works.

Berg was a slow, careful worker, so his total output was comparatively small. While following Schoenberg's example of organization of tones, Berg always felt free to use whatever was necessary for the complete success of his work. His *Concerto for Violin* is based on an arrangement of tones built on a series of intervals of thirds capped by three whole steps (Ex. 26). The final four notes of this tone row (see TWELVE-TONE TECHNIQUE) suggested the opening of the Lutheran chorale "It Is Enough," and Berg weaves Bach's harmony into the body of the concerto (Ex. 27). Berg was fond of quoting, and a bit later in the concerto introduces a little Viennese waltz (Ex. 28). The concerto, completed in 1935, was Berg's last finished work. It is

dedicated "to the memory of an angel," upon the death of Manon Gropius, young daughter of two of Berg's dearest friends. The concerto, *Lyric Suite* for string quartet (one of his most-played works), the *Concerto for Thirteen Instruments and Piano,* and the operas *Wozzeck* and *Lulu* are Berg's masterpieces.

Wozzeck was finished in 1921 and first performed in 1925. The story was a shocking one, the difficulties encountered by the singers and instrumentalists were great, and the opera took many years to gain full-scale performances and acceptance by the musical public who gradually came to the realization that this opera is a deeply moving work. The wide-leaping melodic lines, the rhythmic problems in the music, and the use of *Sprechstimme* (half-song, half-speech) posed problems for musicians forty years ago, but can be taken in stride by today's musicians. Not content with allowing the plot to be a frame on which to hang his music, Berg organized each scene of the opera in a musical form. There are a dance suite, a passacaglia with variations, a rhapsody, and several symphonic sections.

Berg's second opera, *Lulu,* was completed only through the second act. He interrupted work on it to write his violin concerto, and died before he was able to orchestrate his sketches for the last act. The plot and music of *Lulu* are more violent than anything in *Wozzeck.* As the work has been heard more frequently—in the incomplete version and in

A scene from the Hamburg State Opera's production of Lulu

Ex. 26

Ex. 27

Ex. 28

the version orchestrated by the American composer George Perle—music lovers have found it to be equally disturbing and fascinating.

Berg's music is always serious and always difficult to perform. Even his short pieces for clarinet and piano demand highly trained musicians. It is music that is dissonant but never dry; it is tightly organized but song-like and poetic. While his total number of works is small, each one is unique and has added something to the art of music.

Irving Berlin

BERLIN, IRVING (1888–): the composer of some of America's best-loved songs. He was born in Russia, but when he was a small child his parents moved to the lower east side of New York City. There the young man, whose name originally was Izzy Baline, started his career as a singing waiter in New York's Chinatown. Though he had no musical training, his great gift for writing singable words and tunes soon brought him success. First came "Alexander's Ragtime Band," in 1911. This was followed by a whole series of hits, including "Everybody's Doin' It," "A Pretty Girl Is like a Melody," "What'll I Do?," "All Alone," "Blue Skies," and many more.

While in the army in World War I, Berlin wrote a show called *Yip, Yip, Yaphank*. The hit tune voiced the feelings of all the soldiers: "Oh, How I Hate to Get Up in the Morning." In World War II, Berlin wrote another soldier show, *This Is the Army*.

Berlin has written songs for many Broadway musicals and Hollywood movies. His best-known shows were *As Thousands Cheer* (1933) and *Annie Get Your Gun* (1946).

Berlin's "Easter Parade," "There's No Business like Show Business," and "God Bless America" (written in 1917 but set aside until 1938) have become three of America's favorite songs.

BERLIOZ, HECTOR (1803–69): France's greatest symphonic composer and one of the leaders of the Romantic movement in music. Berlioz was also a brilliant critic, a masterful conductor, and the father of modern orchestration.

He was born in a village thirty miles from Grenoble in southeastern France. During his boyhood Napoleon was carrying the French flag all over Europe, but as Berlioz grew up, the conqueror's power was checked. The energy that had made the French Revolution and then been channeled into Napoleon's conquests was now dammed up and seeking new outlets. It was at this time that a whole generation of Frenchmen were swept up into the Romantic movement. Delacroix, who was to lead the Romantics in painting; Victor Hugo, who was to spearhead the Romantic drive in French literature; and Berlioz—all were born within a few years of one another.

It was not clear at first that the young Berlioz would become a professional musician. He played the flute and the guitar and enjoyed writing out musical arrangements. But his father was a doctor, and the boy was expected to follow in the father's footsteps. Accordingly, at nineteen he was packed off to Paris to study medicine. But he had an aversion for the dissecting room; what really interested him was the Paris Opéra. Within two years he had switched from medical school to the Paris Conservatory.

Berlioz at this time had not had much training in music, but he did have ideas about composition. He was a difficult student, always in rebellion against his old-fashioned teachers and particularly against the director of the conservatory, the composer Cherubini.

After several attempts at the Prix de Rome, Berlioz in 1830 won the first prize in composition with his *Sardanapale*. Under the terms of the prize he was to stay abroad for three years, but after eighteen months he became homesick, left Rome, and returned to Paris, where he took a job as music critic to support himself while composing. He organized and conducted concerts all over Europe, being greeted with enthusiasm in Germany, Austria, and Russia. The greatest composers of the time—Liszt, Wagner, Schumann, Mendelssohn—became his friends and learned

Ethel Merman in Annie Get Your Gun

Caricature of Berlioz by Grand-ville, 1846

Hector Berlioz in 1867

much from him. But in France, Berlioz met with all kinds of opposition. This was due partly to his outspoken manner as a critic: his critical blasts could be withering. Also, audiences were not used to the kind of music that Berlioz was writing; it was too violent for their tastes.

Berlioz was a restless experimenter. He demanded more instruments in his orchestra than any other composer before him. In a book on orchestration that he wrote at the height of his career, his ideal orchestra was set at 242 strings, 30 pianos, 30 harps, and hundreds of wind and percussion instruments! He was constantly searching for new combinations of instrumental colors and new tone qualities in each instrument. His melodies were long pictorial phrases with tempestuous accompaniments and rich harmonic backgrounds. His musical forms were based on established Classical ones, but were changed to fit his programs. In the *Symphonie fantastique* (1830) a theme is used to represent the "beloved one," and this theme (called *l'idée fixe*) comes back in every movement of the symphony, changing its character as the "beloved one" becomes less beloved.

Berlioz's music is always painting a picture or telling a story, and the greatest literary masterpieces were sources of his inspiration. He wrote symphonic works based on Shakespeare's *Romeo and Juliet, King Lear, The Tempest,* and *Hamlet.* He wrote a "dramatic legend," *La Damnation de Faust,* based on Goethe's drama. His last work, considered by many his masterpiece, was *Les Troyens (The Trojans),* based on the destruction of Troy and the flight of Aeneas and the Trojans. It is an opera on a colossal design—so huge in its cast and so

difficult in its scenic and musical demands that it was never put on in Berlioz's lifetime and even since then has rarely been given in its complete form.

Berlioz's religious works are planned on as large a scale as his other compositions. His Requiem and Te Deum call for a tremendous number of performers. Even his sweet and gentle oratorio *L'Enfance du Christ (The Childhood of Christ,* 1854) is built on a large plan.

Berlioz was as talented with words as he was with music. His *Memoirs* (1870) and his *Les Soirées de l'orchestre (Evenings in the Orchestra,* 1853) tell about European music in his time better than any other source. His *Traité de l'instrumentation (Treatise on Orchestration,* 1844) was the first book to show how a composer writes for the various instruments.

Near the end of his career Berlioz received honors, even in his native France, and his works now drew large audiences. In 1856 he was made a member of the French Institute and awarded a yearly sum of money that allowed him to give up his job as critic. In Russia more than twelve thousand people came to one of his concerts. The young Russian composers, particularly Mussorgsky and Rimsky-Korsakov, idolized him and modeled their music after his. By the time of his death, in 1869, he could finally be recognized as one of the founders of modern music.

BERNSTEIN, LEONARD (1918–   ): one of the most versatile of contemporary musicians, being a composer, conductor, and pianist of outstanding quality. Bernstein was born in Lawrence, Massachusetts. After graduation from Harvard, where he began composing, he studied conducting with Fritz Reiner and Serge Koussevitzky. He rocketed to fame when, as assistant conductor of the New York Philharmonic in 1943, he stepped in at the last minute to replace the ailing Bruno Walter and electrified the audience with his performance.

Dynamic and restless, Bernstein has found many outlets for his amazing talents. For a while he was co-conductor, along with Dimitri Mitropoulos, of the Philharmonic, and in 1958 he became music director. In the meantime he developed a series of musical television shows, through which he taught music to more people than any previous teacher had been able to reach.

As a composer Bernstein has been successful in ballet (*Fancy Free,* 1944); in symphonic composition (three symphonies—*Jeremiah,*

Above left: *dance scene from* West Side Story
Above right: *Leonard Bernstein conducting*

1944; *The Age of Anxiety,* 1949; and *The Kaddish,* 1963); in songs and chamber works; in choral works (*Chichester Psalms,* 1965); and in musical comedy (*On the Town,* 1944; *Wonderful Town,* 1952; and *West Side Story,* 1958). Several of his songs have become standard popular numbers. His most recent successes have been his theatrical *Mass* (1971) and the revision of his musical *Candide* (1973).

Bernstein is an eclectic composer, using whatever style of writing best suits his subject. Often the basis of his music is jazz, but there are echoes of other contemporary composers too. No matter what material he uses, Bernstein makes it his own by adding to it his driving energy, his melodic gift, and his passionate approach.

BILLINGS, WILLIAM (1746–1800): one of the earliest of American composers. He was a tanner by trade but gave up this work as soon as he had taught himself to read music and work out a few exercises in harmony. Most of his compositions were hymns, but he wrote also what he called fuguing tunes —simple exercises in counterpoint—as well as anthems. His music was popular until foreign musicians came to the United States after the Revolution. These musicians saw only the crudities in Billings' music—they missed its strength. For more than a hundred years Billings' music was sung only in rural churches, but he was recently discovered by serious musicians and has begun to assume his true role as one of the founding fathers of American music.

Billings' most famous composition is the militant "Chester," which became the fiery patriotic hymn of George Washington's soldiers. His beautiful canon "When Jesus Wept" is now a familiar work on choral programs. Three of Billings' tunes have been used by William Schuman as the bases for the three movements of his *New England Triptych,* written for orchestra.

BINARY FORM: a two-part musical form, usually with a strong cadence at the end of each section. Binary form was the most typical form of the dances written in the seventeenth and eighteenth centuries, as well as the form of most of the harpsichord sonatas by Domenico Scarlatti. While in the more popular ternary, or three-part, form there is often a contrast of musical material, the binary form features contrast of key (although both types of contrast may be found in some of the Scarlatti sonatas).

The short binary dance forms, such as those in Bach's "French" Suites, usually have a first part approximately eight measures in length followed by a second part that is approximately twice as long. A double bar and repeat marks are found at the end of each section.

In the first part of the form the music moves from the original key (the tonic) to the key three notes above (the relative major) if the tonic key is minor, or a fifth above (the dominant) if the tonic key is major. During the second part of the form the composer develops the material of part one, meanwhile working his way back to the original key by the end of the work.

Bach's saraband from his second "French" Suite is a clear example of a work starting in C minor, moving to a cadence in E-flat

Title page of William Billings' The New England Psalm Singer

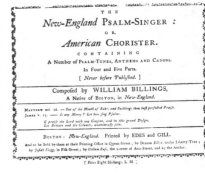

Ex. 29 — Saraband from "French" Suite No. 2 in C Minor, J. S. Bach

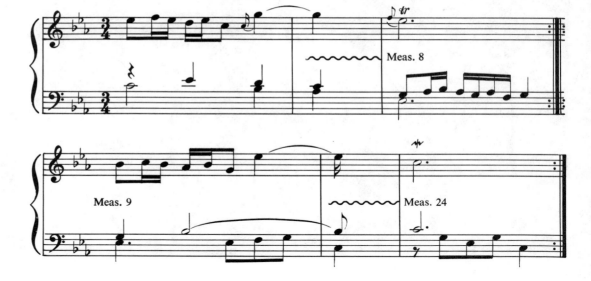

Ex. 30— "Barbara Allen"

major at the double bar, then developing the original material as the music moves back from E-flat major to the key of C minor at the final cadence (Ex. 29).

Large binary forms, such as those of Bach's "English" Suites and partitas and Scarlatti's sonatas, use the same principle, but each section of the form is greatly expanded.

Many short folk songs are in binary form (Ex. 30).

BIZET, GEORGES (1838–75): the composer of *Carmen,* was born in Paris. His parents taught him the elements of music from early years, and he was admitted to the Paris Conservatory before he was quite ten. He was a brilliant piano student but was more interested in composition and started to write operas at the age of sixteen. At nineteen he won the conservatory's big prize, the Prix de Rome. This prize, which Berlioz and Gounod had also won in their day, was designed to support a young composer for a few years at the French Academy in Rome to enable him to devote his full time to composing.

Bizet left for Rome in the last days of 1857. The stagecoach took him through Provence and in particular through the old city of Arles, which he was later to use as a setting for *L'Arlésienne.* In Rome, Bizet became a hard-working composer, turning out a steady stream of songs, piano pieces, and works for orchestra. But his main ambition was to write a successful opera. Time after time he tried, with no success; he burned some of his scores after hearing the works produced. But two of his early operas, *Les Pêcheurs de perles* (*The Pearl Fishers,* 1863) and *Djamileh* (1872), were moderately successful. Some of the compositions by which he is best known today were written as incidental and background music to the play *L'Arlésienne* (1872) by Alphonse Daudet. This music, not popular at the time, used traditional Provençal tunes as well as melodies Bizet had composed himself. Two orchestral suites drawn from *L'Arlésienne* (one by him and one put together after his death by his friend Ernest Guiraud) have become popular concert pieces. The first suite is especially known for its arrangement of the traditional "March of the Three Kings."

Bizet's most lasting impact on the musical world dates from March 3, 1875, when his opera *Carmen* opened at the Opéra-Comique. Many in the audience were offended by the boldness and passion of the story, which the soprano Galli-Marié, playing the role of Carmen, brought out with great dramatic effectiveness. Others felt that the music was too heavy, too much like that of Wagner. If the audience or the critics had been told that *Carmen* would go on to become one of the most popular operas ever written, they would have been unable to believe it. Bizet himself did not live to see its triumph. He died, at the age of thirty-six, three months after the first performance.

For many years after his death Bizet was known mainly for *Carmen,* the music from *L'Arlésienne,* and some pieces for piano four-hands, *Jeux d'enfants (Children's Games).* But in 1933 an old Bizet manuscript was discovered in the library of the Paris Conservatory: it was a symphony he had written at the age of seventeen. Now it is one of the more popular symphonies and has also been used by George Balanchine as the basis for a ballet, *Symphony in C.*

BLUES: a slow kind of song that became one of the strands woven into jazz music. No one knows exactly when or where this kind of music was born. The first published blues was W. C. Handy's "Memphis Blues," written in 1909. Before that the blues had been sung but never written down. Blacks in the cotton fields and cities of the southern United States made up blues just as all folk songs are made. The blues got its name because of the sadness of its words. Feeling "blue" meant feeling sad. A blues might be about a love affair gone wrong, a jail sentence, or being homesick.

The form of the blues is very simple. Each stanza of the words has three lines, of which the second line is a repetition of the first. Each line of words takes up four measures of music, so that the blues is twelve measures long. Usually there is room at the end of each line of words for the singer to stop for breath or to think of the next line. Sometimes a singer might put in a word or a phrase like a sigh or a comment. If there is a solo instrument playing along with the singer, the instrumentalist fills in the time at the end of the line with a melodic idea called a break.

The music of the blues is as simple as the form of the words. The three primary chords of the key are used—those based on the first (I), fourth (IV), and fifth (V) degrees of the scale. The pattern of the harmony is four measures of I, two measures of IV, two measures of I, two measures of V, two measures of I. Pianists often add a tone to the basic chord—the sixth or flatted seventh, for example. (A or B-flat to the C chord, D or E-flat to the F chord.)

A good blues singer does not stick too closely to perfect pitch. He wavers around the tone according to his feeling. There is often a simultaneous sounding of the major and minor thirds of chords. The accompaniment is usually just a simple four-beat repetition of the harmony (Ex. 31).

Blues singers
Top: *Billie Holiday*
Bottom left: *Ma Rainey*
Bottom right: *Bessie Smith*

Ex. 31

Almost every great jazz singer and instrumentalist has recorded blues. The harmony of the blues served as a plan for jazz players who got together in "jam sessions." Some of the best blues singing is to be heard on the records of Ma Rainey, a pioneer in blues singing, and Bessie Smith, the "Empress of the Blues." Louis Armstrong accompanied both of these singers with some of his most inventive trumpet playing. A fast, raucous style of blues is known as shouting the blues —a style heard in many records by Big Joe Turner. Another form of fast blues is the piano style of boogie-woogie, which developed in Kansas City.

Composers of concert music have drawn inspiration from the blues and have written it into their serious compositions. Some of the best examples are Gershwin's Piano Prelude Number 2 and his *An American in Paris*. Copland has written several "piano blues." But European composers have used the blues almost as much as American composers. The slow movement of Ravel's Sonata for Violin and Piano is a dissonant blues. Another French composer, Darius Milhaud, used the blues as a basis for his music for the ballet *La Création du Monde*, 1923.

BOHÈME, LA: an opera by Giacomo Puccini. It was first performed in Turin, in northern Italy, in 1896, under the young Arturo Toscanini. Within three months it became a tremendous success, making Puccini the successor to the aged Verdi as the outstanding composer of Italian operas.

The libretto of *La Bohème,* by Illica and Giacosa, was based on a book by the French writer Henri Murger. The book, *Scenes from Bohemian Life,* sketched incidents in the lives of persons Murger had known in the

1840's in Paris' Latin Quarter, a district of low rents that attracted young painters and poets. Murger's book popularized "Bohemian" (the French word for gypsy) as a word describing the happy-go-lucky life of struggling young artists. The Bohemian life mixed the gaiety of hopefulness with the tragedy of lack of food and warmth. This is the background against which Puccini tells the love story of Rodolfo and Mimi and that of Marcello and Musetta, who become the main characters of *La Bohème*. The opera does not actually give a continuous story of developing events, but rather it brings to life the moods and the passions of the characters.

The first of *La Bohème's* four acts takes place in the cold attic room shared by Rodolfo, Marcello, and two other young men —the Bohemians. There is much joking and a feast. When the landlord comes to collect his rent, the Bohemians get him drunk and throw him out. Three of the Bohemians then go out to a café, but Rodolfo stays to work. Mimi, a frail young neighbor who embroiders flower designs, comes in to get a light for her candle. Rodolfo falls in love with her, singing an aria (Ex. 32) about her frozen hands and beautiful eyes. The scene ends with a romantic love duet.

The second act is a colorful picture of Paris on Christmas Eve. The scene is a sidewalk café, where the Bohemians are celebrating. The streets are filled with children, soldiers, students, and people with things to sell. Musetta, a former girl friend of Marcello's, comes to the café with a rich old man. She becomes annoyed with Marcello because he pays no attention to her. She sings him a song—aided by a discreet orchestra—about her charm and beauty (Ex. 33). She sends the old man away on an errand

Blues are also sung by men
Top: *Jimmy Rushing*
Bottom: *Ray Charles*

Ex. 32

Ex. 33
Waltz tempo

Ex. 34

Allegro focoso (fiery)

Ex. 35

Allegro vivace

so that she can join the Bohemians. They all march away, following a troop of soldiers.

The third act takes place in a tavern near a tollgate, the time being early morning in late winter. Both pairs of lovers quarrel because of jealousy. The men accuse the girls of being flirts. But Rodolfo notices that Mimi is coughing a great deal. Afraid that she is desperately ill, he is too poor to help her. They decide they must separate forever.

The fourth act is set in the attic room of the Bohemians. The young men are trying to work, even though their hearts are sad. They try some dancing and dueling to cheer themselves. Musetta comes in to tell them that Mimi is on the stairs, too weak to come all the way up. She is dying and wants to see Rodolfo once more.

Mimi is carried up and tenderly put on a bed. She and Rodolfo sing of the earlier days of their love. Musetta sings a soft prayer while Mimi closes her eyes to sleep—and dies.

In spite of its tragic ending, *La Bohème* is one of the gayest and most charming of all operas. Puccini wrote music that is always beautifully melodic. The characters sing as though they were speaking the lines of a play. The arias are brought into the action naturally and never interfere with the drama.

La Bohème has no overture. Instead, Puccini wrote short orchestral openings that set the mood for each act. One memorable piece of musical stage setting is the opening to Act III, with its deft suggestion of snow falling on a bleak early morning in February. The revelry in the café, at the beginning of Act II, is suggested by a theme previously heard for a moment in Act I but now rendered boisterously by the whole orchestra (Ex. 34). Act IV, in which the solidarity of the group of friends is re-established, opens with the

theme one first heard on being introduced to them at the beginning of Act I (Ex. 35).

Each of these motives is used throughout the act it introduces, so that the music is knit together. Other motives are woven throughout the opera, the most important of these being Mimi's theme:

Lento

BOLÉRO: a proud and stormy Spanish dance. It probably came to Spain from North Africa. It is danced fairly fast, either as a solo or as a duet between a man and a woman. The meter is of three counts, with a basic rhythmic pattern that is repeated over and over (Ex. a or b):

(a)

(b)

This rhythm, played on castanets, starts the dance. Then a melody, usually played on a flute, comes in on top of the castanet rhythm.

The most famous of boleros was written for orchestra by Ravel in 1928. Ravel's *Boléro* has only one melody, which is played

Scenes from La Bohème. **Top:** *Act I.* **Bottom:** *the final scene, with Gianni Raimondi and Mirella Freni*

Dancing the boléro

over and over. Almost every instrument of the orchestra gets a chance to play it, except for those that are playing the repeated rhythm. The composition builds up from a whisper to one of the loudest orchestral tuttis.

BOOGIE-WOOGIE: a style of jazz piano playing, essentially a fast blues with a steady rumbling accompaniment. It started in Kansas City and Chicago as a feature of boisterous "rent parties" as well as honky-tonk night clubs. Boogie-woogie first became popular all over the United States about 1936, the greatest boogie-woogie pianists being Jimmy Yancey, "Pine Top" Smith, Meade Lux Lewis, Albert Ammons, and Pete Johnson.

The main feature of boogie-woogie is a repeated left-hand figure of eight notes per measure. This repeated rhythm gives boogie-woogie a powerful driving motion (Ex. a, b, and c):

Meade Lux Lewis

(a)

(b)

(c)

The harmony of boogie-woogie follows the twelve-bar plan of the blues: four measures of the tonic chord (I), two of IV, two of I; then two of V and two of I. Over the percussive accompaniment of the left hand the right hand plays syncopated melodic figures and sharply accented chords, the chords often being vibrated tremolo-fashion. A short group of fast grace notes is often played just before a melody tone or a chord; these are known as "crushed notes" (Ex. a and b):

(a)

(b)

BORIS GODUNOV: the greatest and most powerful of Russian operas, written by Modest Mussorgsky. The libretto, by the composer, was based on a tragedy written forty years earlier by Alexander Pushkin.

Mussorgsky's opera has come down to us in three versions, the first of which was finished in 1869. When it was refused performance by the Russian Imperial Opera, Mussorgsky rewrote large parts of it. The revised version, which included a love scene and a brilliant polonaise, was finally produced in St. Petersburg in 1874. After Mussorgsky's death his friend Rimsky-Korsakov produced still a third—and more refined—version of *Boris,* smoothing the rough edges of Mussorgsky's melodies, harmonies, and use of instruments and even changing the order of the scenes. For the entire first half of the twentieth century this doctored-up version was practically the only one performed. But in 1928 the Russian State Publishing House brought out Mussorgsky's original score and since World War II this version—in all its boldness and daring—has slowly been making its way into the opera houses of the world. Meanwhile, not satisfied with either Mussorgsky's or Rimsky's version, Dimitri Shostakovich in 1940 reorchestrated the work.

Boris Godunov, based on the lives of real historic persons, tells of the stormy period after the death of Ivan the Terrible. In the second, expanded version—the last version in Mussorgsky's own hand—the opera is in four acts with a prologue.

In the prologue Boris is being crowned Tsar of All the Russias before a crowd in a

Ex. 36 — Prologue, Scene 2

Andantino alla marcia

Martellato

Ex. 37 — Prologue, Scene 2

Moderato

square in the old fortified section of Moscow, the Kremlin. The people shout and sing praises of Boris. The bells of the two cathedrals set up a mighty din—first the great bells, then the smaller ones (Ex. 36).

At the announcement that Boris has accepted the crown, the people break out into a hymn of joy (Ex. 37)—an old Russian folk tune which Beethoven had worked into his String Quartet Opus 59, Number 2, dedicated to Count Rasoumovsky. Boris appears and asks the Lord's blessing and guidance.

In the first act the monk Pimen is seen in a candlelit cell, at work on his history of Russia. He tells the young monk Gregory how Boris came to the throne. There is a rumor that Dimitri, the young son of the former tsar, was murdered by order of Boris. Gregory, being of the same age as the murdered boy, decides to pretend to be Dimitri. He starts for Poland to raise an army to overthrow Boris.

When Gregory meets two monks drinking at an inn near the border, one of them, Varlaam, sings one of the few arias in the opera, "By the Walls of Kazan":

Act I, Scene 2

Allegro

Soldiers enter, looking for the false Dimitri. Boris has ordered that he be hanged. But Gregory escapes and makes for Poland.

The second act takes place in the cheerless palace of the tsar. Xenia, Boris's daughter, is sad because she has lost her lover. Xenia, Fyodor (the small son of Boris), and Fyodor's nurse play games and tell stories to cheer each other. Then Boris comes in to talk with his son. He is worried about the future because of the unrest in the country. Reports that the false Dimitri is about to march on Russia make him fear for the lives of his children. Gripped with terror, he imagines that he sees the prince who was murdered, and he cries out to God to forgive him. This episode, one of the most terrifying in all opera, is known as the "Clock Scene."

The third act is set in Poland, where the false Dimitri is using intrigue to get help for his march on Russia. He falls in love with Marina, the daughter of a Polish nobleman. She is interested only in the power that would be hers if she became the tsarina of Russia. While the orchestra plays a colorful polonaise, Dimitri and Marina plot the future.

In the deeply moving first scene of the fourth act, Boris has a heart attack and dies, surrounded by his family and his supporters. This act concludes with the so-called "Revolutionary Scene," in which amidst loud whistling and jeering a group of peasants tease a nobleman, the Boyar Kruschov, whom they have captured. There is a struggle between Roman Catholic and Orthodox priests. The false Dimitri comes in and leads the people into battle against the forces of

Chaliapin in the title role of Boris Godunov

Ex. 38 — Finale

Andantino

Ex. 39 — Act 1, Scene 1

Andante tranquillo

the tsar, and the sky in the background reddens with flames. A holy simpleton sings sadly, "Weep, weep, Russian folk, poor starving people," as the opera ends.

The disconnected story of *Boris Godunov* is not a pretty one, and Mussorgsky did not write pretty music for it. Instead, he wrote recitative-like melodies that suit the emotional meanings of the words; thus the music of *Boris* is different from all other music of its time. Mussorgsky blended together Russian folk tunes based on old modal scales (as the Kazan song) and melodies that are like dramatic, passionate speech. These melodies required a new harmony (Ex. 38) not at all like that of other composers of the nineteenth century. It keeps repeating the jangling sound of cathedral bells or goes off in unexpected ways (Ex. 39).

There is much choral singing in *Boris*. The chorus are the people of Russia, singing with the strength of those who know that no matter who rules, the people will live on.

Boris Godunov is one of the great landmarks in music. In writing it Mussorgsky became one of the prophets of the new music that was to flourish in the twentieth century.

BORODIN, ALEXANDER (1833–87): an important Russian composer; a member of "The Mighty Five" (see RUSSIAN FIVE). Like most of this group, Borodin was not professionally trained as a musician. He showed an interest in music as a boy, playing the piano and attempting composition, but his primary desire was to become a scientist. After sev-

eral years in medical school he began concentrating on the study of chemistry, and while still young became an authority in that field.

In the meantime, in 1862, Borodin met Mily Balakirev, an ardent advocate of Russian nationalism in music. Encouraged by Balakirev and the other members of "The Five," Borodin again turned to musical composition. His output was not large, since he worked slowly and had to steal time from his lectures and writings on chemistry. He managed to write two complete symphonies plus part of a third and two string quartets.

Below: *Alexander Borodin*
At right: *scene from the Bolshoi Theater's production of* Prince Igor

These works combine a typical nineteenth-century approach to Classical form with a tinge of Russian melodic qualities. The symphonic work *In the Steppes of Central Asia,* written in 1880, is more in line with the beliefs of "The Five."

Borodin was intensely interested in the exotic sounds of Asiatic Russia as well as in Russian history. These interests led him to the composition of his masterpiece, the opera *Prince Igor.* Finished by Rimsky-Korsakov and Glazunov after Borodin's death, this opera is based on a medieval Russian epic. The subject matter gave Borodin an opportunity to write music with a Slavic touch, spiced with oriental melodic and instrumental tone colors and charged with great rhythmic vitality. The well-known Polovtzian Dances from the opera were made into an orchestral suite by Borodin and performed in 1879.

Borodin was a gifted melodist (as shown in his eleven beautiful songs), an imaginative mixer of sharply contrasted orchestral colors, and a subtle and sensitive harmonist. While not so daring as his friend Mussorgsky, Borodin was one of the great original spirits of the nationalist movement that introduced Russian music to the world.

BOURRÉE: one of the liveliest of the French court dances. It is written in 4/4 or 2/2 time and begins with an upbeat (Ex. 40). The bourrée was a strong, vigorous dance, more suited to and more popular with the peasants than the nobility. Since the peasants danced it in their wooden shoes, the music had to be strong and rhythmic in order to be heard above the clatter. In the wine-making regions of France the bourrée was a kind of work dance, the men singing and dancing as they crushed the grapes with their feet.

Although the bourrée is French, some of the finest examples are by German composers like Bach and Handel, who found a place for this form in their suites, sometimes placing one or two bourrées between the saraband and the gigue.

BRAHMS, JOHANNES (1833–97): a late-Romantic German composer who wrote in a highly personal style developed from the styles of Haydn, Beethoven, and Schumann. Born in Hamburg, Brahms was the son of an all-round practical musician who played the double bass in a local theater orchestra. The boy started to play the piano at the age of seven. At ten he was fortunate in having as a teacher of piano and theory a fine musician named Edward Marxsen. Within a few years Brahms himself was a teacher of several younger children and had given his first recital.

Brahms's father had taught him how to play dance music on the violin, cello, and horn and how to arrange for brass bands. The young man helped his family financially by making arrangements of popular waltzes for a music publisher and by playing at taverns and theaters. His payment for a night of work was "two thalers and all the beer he wanted."

When Brahms was twenty, his virtuoso piano playing and his ability to read and transpose music at sight brought him to the attention of the Hungarian violinist Reményi. Reményi invited Brahms to be his accompanist and acquainted him with the style of Hungarian gypsy melodies that Brahms later used in his *Hungarian Dances.* Reményi also introduced Brahms to Joachim, the great violinist who was to become a lifelong friend of Brahms and the man to whom he dedicated his only concerto for violin.

Joachim, who knew most of the great musicians of the day, sent young Brahms to Franz Liszt and Robert Schumann. Liszt acknowledged the talent of Brahms, although he nodded drowsily as Brahms played one of his piano sonatas. Schumann took Brahms under his wing, advising him as to which works to have published first and proclaiming the genius of Brahms to the world via an article in the influential magazine *Neue Zeitschrift für Musik.* Schumann's wife Clara, a famous pianist, furthered the career of Brahms by playing his piano works at her recitals. More important, a close friendship

Dancing the bourrée

Ex. 40— Bourrée from Flute Sonata No. 5, Handel

Drawing of Brahms at twenty years of age

developed between Clara Schumann and Brahms—a friendship that was broken only by the death of Clara Schumann in 1896, a year before the death of Brahms himself.

Brahms's life was not a dramatic one. Between 1862 and 1869 he conducted choruses and orchestras in Vienna, Zürich, Hamburg, and Baden-Baden. Starting in 1869, he centered his life around Vienna and for a while conducted orchestral concerts there for the Society of Friends of Music. There were occasional tours of Germany, Austria, and Switzerland, involving both playing and conducting. Summers were spent in the country, where Brahms did much of his composing. He liked to take long walks in the beautiful country of the Alps and in the valley of the Rhine. During these summer walks he planned many of his large works, which seem to breathe of the great, spacious outdoors.

Brahms's music burst upon the musical scene of the 1850's in the form of three piano sonatas, some songs, and the rhapsodic first piano concerto, in D minor. It was vigorous, youthful music that seemed to bring thunder and lightning from the piano. Brahms was always a virtuoso writer for piano, reflecting his own tremendous technique. But the difference between Brahms and Liszt, another great virtuoso, was that Brahms never wrote difficult music merely for the sake of glittering effect. The music had to be difficult in order to express what Brahms wanted to say.

In the late 1850's Brahms ventured into the field of orchestral music, writing two serenades. These were followed a few years later by two piano quartets. Brahms liked to write in pairs: two pairs of symphonies (Numbers 1 and 2 in 1876 and 1877, Numbers 3 and 4 in 1883 and 1884); two overtures, in 1880 and 1881; two clarinet sonatas in 1894; and so on.

The 1860's saw the publication of his *Variations on a Theme by Handel* and, among the summits of piano virtuosity, the two volumes of his *Variations on a Theme by Paganini*. These were followed by two of his finest works, *Ein Deutsches Requiem (A German Requiem)* for solo voices, chorus, and orchestra, first performed in 1868, and the *Rhapsodie* for alto, male chorus, and orchestra presented in 1869. The *Requiem*—beautifully lyrical, deeply emotional, and masterfully written—is Brahms at his best and most characteristic. It is not based on the Latin text of the Requiem Mass, but uses various passages from the Bible in German. Although Brahms wrote music that was often personal, only the sorrowing *Requiem* can be traced to a definite inspiration—the death of his mother.

With the success of the *Requiem* (it was performed in almost every city in Germany) Brahms felt that he was at last ready to tackle the job of writing large symphonic works. He started with the orchestration of *Variations on a Theme by Haydn* (1873), originally a work for two pianos, as though to pledge allegiance to the composers of the Classical period. While other composers such as Berlioz, Liszt, and Wagner were saying that symphonic forms had become worn out and obsolete, Brahms proceeded to show that much could still be done with the musical forms developed by Haydn, Mozart, and Beethoven. For this he was bitterly attacked by such powerful critics as Hugo Wolf and Friedrich Nietzsche, the philosopher. Brahms never replied to the attacks, preferring to let his works speak for him. He was defended by Edward Hanslick, an influential critic, who used Brahms as a stick with which to beat Richard Wagner.

In the period 1876–87, Brahms composed his large-scale instrumental masterpieces: four symphonies in C minor, D, F, and E minor; a double concerto for violin and cello, and two overtures—the *Tragische Ouvertüre (Tragic Overture,* 1880) and the *Akademische Ouvertüre (Academic Festival Overture).* The latter, a wonderful example of Brahms's sense of humor, was written for the occasion in 1881 when the University of Breslau awarded Brahms the honorary degree of Doctor of Philosophy. Brahms was expected to write a typically solemn work for this solemn occasion. Instead, he surprised everyone by using as thematic material several jolly German student songs.

After 1887 Brahms wrote no more music for large instrumental groups, but concentrated on chamber music and songs. He wrote twenty compositions for piano: intermezzi, capriccios, a ballade, a romance, and a rhapsody (Opuses 116, 117, 118, and 119). In style they illustrate the wide spectrum of Brahms's approach to music, ranging from the passionate first intermezzo of Opus 118 (Ex. 41) to the almost mystic first intermezzo

of Opus 119 (Ex. 42), and from the march-like rhapsody of Opus 119 (Ex. 43) to the tender intermezzo of Opus 116 (Ex. 44).

In 1891 Brahms turned to the dark quality of the clarinet, using it in a trio with piano and violin; in a quintet, with string quartet;

Ex. 41 — Intermezzo, Op. 118, No. 1

Allegro non assai, ma molto appassionato

Ex. 42 — Intermezzo, Op. 119, No. 1

Adagio

Ex. 43— Rhapsody, Op. 119, No. 4

Allegro risoluto

Ex. 44— Intermezzo, Op. 116, No. 6

Andantino teneramente

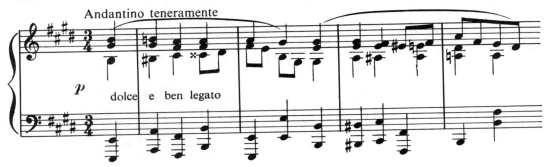

and in two sonatas, with piano. Last came *Four Serious Songs,* inspired by the death of his beloved friend Clara Schumann. They have a funereal quality, almost as though Brahms knew that the end of his own life was at hand. There remained time for only one more project, the eleven *Choralvorspiele* (*Chorale Preludes,* 1896) for organ. In these beautiful compositions Brahms, always a student of old music, went back to Bach and earlier German composers for inspiration. It was his statement of belief in the music of the past as opposed to the new "music of the future."

In his large works Brahms is serious, heroic, and autumnal. That he was not always solemn—he had, in fact, a robust sense of humor—is evident in the large number of light works he wrote: the *Hungarian Dances,* the sixteen charming waltzes for piano, and the two books of *Liebeslieder (Songs of Love)* waltzes—the latter being shyly sentimental

chamber music for a vocal quartet and piano four-hands.

Brahms's songs rank with those of the other great composers of lieder: Schubert, Schumann, Wolf, and Strauss. Many of them are based on folk songs, others are original but with a folk-song quality, still others are deeply passionate love songs. The accompaniments to the songs are woven in with the vocal melody, so that each song is a true duet for singer and pianist.

Brahms's style is difficult to analyze. It treads no new paths but rather follows many paths of the past. Yet Brahms did develop his own way of making music, and once we have heard several works by him, his unique way of saying things can easily be recognized. His harmony is that of an earlier period with some chromaticism and some dissonance resulting from the use of many pedal points (Ex. 45). His melodies outline a chord, sometimes in wide leaps (Ex. 46) and

Ex. 45— Sonata, Op. 5, No. 3

Ex. 46 — Waltz, Op. 39, No. 6

Caricatures of Brahms conducting

Brahms in his early thirties

Brahms (right) with Johann Strauss the Younger

sometimes gently (Ex. 47), or they center around one or two tones (Ex. 48). Brahms is fond of starting with a small germ motive that flowers into a cluster of themes (Ex. 49a, b, c, d, e, f). He likes to confuse his listeners, and sometimes his performers, by using complex syncopations or by writing so that the music does not seem to fit within the bar lines (Ex. 50).

In his large works Brahms used Classical forms but did not stick to Classical key relations. The keys of the movements of his First Symphony, for example, are C minor, E major, A-flat major, and C major (where Haydn might have had C, F, C, C). While other nineteenth-century composers were adding more wind and percussion instruments, Brahms was content to stay closer to

Ex. 47 — "Sapphic Ode," Op. 94, No. 4

Ziemlich langsam

Ex. 48 — Intermezzo, Op. 118, No. 6

Andante, largo e mesto

Ex. 49 — Symphony No. 2

Ex. 50 — Capriccio, Op. 116, No. 7

Allegro agitato

Ex. 51 — Symphony No. 2

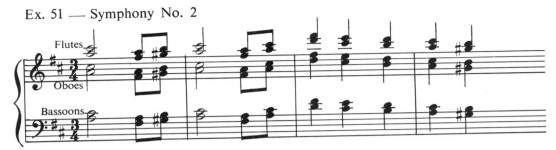

the Classical makeup of the orchestra. One characteristic of his instrumental writing is his doubling of a melody in parallel thirds and sixths (Ex. 51).

During his lifetime Brahms was accused of being old-fashioned. Today we see him for what he really was—a true Romantic composer who wrote poetic, emotionally charged music within the old forms he loved so much.

BRANDENBURG CONCERTOS: six concertos written by Johann Sebastian Bach in 1721 at the request of the Margrave of Brandenburg, a German prince who collected music the way many people collect stamps. There is no record of the concertos having been played at the margrave's court at Potsdam, nor of Bach's ever having been paid for them. At the margrave's death the manuscripts were sold for a few pennies apiece.

The style of the "Brandenburg" Concertos is that of the concerto grosso, in which a small group of instruments (the concertino) is contrasted with a larger accompanying group of strings and harpsichord (the ripieno). The two groups play sometimes in alternation and sometimes all at once, but never are more than some twenty instrumentalists involved. (The latter is a point worth keeping in mind, since performances of these concertos by large orchestras have sometimes muddied the interplay of Bach's contrapuntal lines.) The first movement of each work is a straightforward, athletic allegro; the last movement is usually fast and gay, and in between are slow movements with beautiful long melodies, and dances such as minuets. Each concerto has dazzling solo passages to show off the ability of the solo performers.

The First "Brandenburg" Concerto, in F, features two horns as the solo instruments. Bach must have had some extraordinarily accomplished horn players in mind, since even modern players, who have valves on their instruments, find these parts quite challenging. The solo horns dominate the opening movement with a cheerful fanfare. In the second movement, a mournful adagio in 3/4 time, the solos are taken by one of

three oboes and by a violino piccolo (a small violin usually tuned a fourth higher than the regular instrument but in this case tuned only a minor third higher). The horns return again in the third movement, a bustling allegro in 6/8 time, and play an in-and-out game in the final movement, an extremely complex minuet. Unlike the minuets that appear later in the symphonies of the Classical period, this one is quite contrapuntal and is constructed something like a super club sandwich: minuet, trio, minuet, polonaise, minuet, trio, minuet. The horns are featured in the minuet proper as well as in the final trio, in which they are accompanied by the oboes. The first trio is given to the traditional combination of oboes and bassoon, and the polonaise is given to the strings.

The succeeding concertos all show the same delight in the interplay of varied sonorities. The Second, in F, gives the solo status to four instruments: a trumpet, a recorder, an oboe, and a violin. The trumpet player, who must play in the highest clarino register, is given rest only in the second movement, which is a brief, lyrical andante in D minor.

The Third "Brandenburg" Concerto, in G, is the only one in the group that is not properly a concerto grosso—that is, it makes no attempt to distinguish between an inner concertino of soloists and the remainder of the orchestra. The first movement is a driving allegro, and the third and last movement a whirling perpetual-motion gigue. The middle movement consists of just two chords, on which the harpsichordist was expected to improvise embellishments according to prevailing eighteenth-century custom.

With the Fourth "Brandenburg" Concerto, also in G, we have again a true concerto grosso with a regular concertino—a violin and two recorders—and a ripieno played by the strings. Solo responsibilities are given to the first recorder in the second movement and to the violin in the third.

The Fifth "Brandenburg" Concerto, in D major, is easily remembered as the "harpsichord concerto" because of the harpsichord's virtuoso cadenza in the first movement. There are three solo instruments in this con-

The Margrave of Brandenburg

certo: flute, violin, and harpsichord. These three are given the second movement all to themselves, and in the third movement the flute and the violin finally get their chance to show off, in a dashing allegro.

In the Sixth and last "Brandenburg," Bach writes what amounts to a concerto for two violas. The accompanying ripieno consists of two violas da gamba and a cello, supported by a continuo played by the harpsichord and the double bass. For the first movement Bach writes what might be called an "endless melody" followed by a reflective adagio and a jubilant giguelike allegro.

BRASS INSTRUMENTS: today, the bugle, cornet, trumpet, flügelhorn, French horn, trombone, baritone horn, and tuba. All are made of tubes of metal that have a cup- or funnel-shaped mouthpiece at one end. The other end widens to form the "bell" of the instrument. Brasses differ in the design of the tube, which can be thin (trumpet) or fat (tuba) and in the tube length, which varies from four feet (cornet) to fourteen feet (trombone)—the tubes being made manageable by being bent back and forth or coiled over themselves. Brasses differ also in the shape of the long air tunnel within them. The shorter brasses (cornet, trumpet) are mostly cone-shaped, with a short, cylindrical middle section; the longer brasses (French horn, trombone) are cylindrical for slightly more than half their length. These varying shapes help to determine the overtones the instruments produce. Some brass instruments, such as the French horn, have mouthpieces that are small and deep. Others, like the trombone, have mouthpieces that are wide and shallow. The sound of each instrument depends on the length and circumference of its tube, its shape, and the kind of mouthpiece.

The player of a brass instrument produces a tone by blowing air through his compressed lips. The lips vibrate as they are pressed against the mouthpiece. (Pressing the lips against the slight opening at the thumb side of a clenched hand and blowing hard will show how this is done.) The vibration of the lips sets in motion a column of air in the tube of the instrument. The tightness of the lips and the length of the tube determine the pitch that is sounded. The tube also acts as a resonator—a kind of megaphone for the sound of the lips. The way a player uses his lips against a mouthpiece is called his *embouchure.*

Pitch on a brass instrument is governed by the harmonic, or overtone, series. When the lips of the player are as loose as possible, the tube will sound its lowest, or fundamental, tone. By tightening the lips and blowing a bit harder the player can sound the seven or eight higher tones in the harmonic series of the fundamental tone. The lowest series of the tenor trombone is:

The true fundamental tone, an octave lower than the low E, is impossible to play on the trombone. The E here is the first overtone.

If the player wants to play notes other than those in the overtone series, he must change the length of the tube. With the trombone, a part of the tube slides. On the other brass instruments, except for the bugle, there are three or four keys or valves. When a valve is pushed down, this lengthens the tube. As the tube gets longer, the fundamental tone gets lower.

During the time of Mozart and Haydn, brass players used "crooks" to change the fundamental tone of their instruments. A part of the instrument was taken out, and a longer or shorter piece of tube put in its place. If the composition was in the key of F, the player used a crook that made F the fundamental tone of the instrument. When the music went to another key, the player had to change his crook or wait until the music came to a key in which he could play. This limited composers to somewhat monotonous trumpet and horn parts. The use of crooks also led to the practice of writing one pitch and expecting to hear a different pitch. (See TRANSPOSITION.)

The ancestors of modern brass instruments were animal horns and conch shells. This is why brass instruments are still called horns. One of the oldest wind instruments still used is the shofar, made from a ram's horn. It is blown in the synagogue on Jewish holy days.

Brass instruments have gone through many changes since man first used them. Some early examples still exist, such as the long red horn blown by the lamas of Tibet and the giant alphorn used for signaling in Switzerland. Others, such as the beautiful, long, slim Siena trumpets and the members of the old cornett and zink families, have disappeared. (The cornett of 1600 was not like our present-day cornet; it was a wooden or ivory tube with finger holes, like a clarinet.) The last member of the cornett family to survive was the oddly shaped "serpent," the bass of the brass family until the invention of the tuba in 1835.

The first brass instruments used in opera

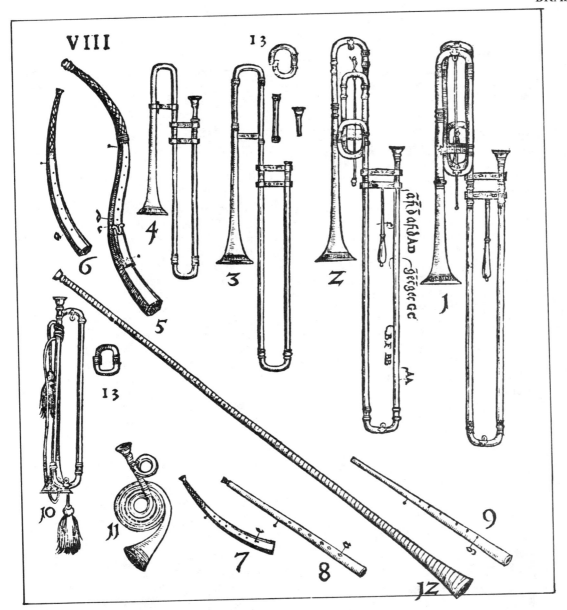

From Michael Praetorius' Syntagma musicum. *1–4: trombones; 5: cornett; 6–9: Zincken; 10–12: trumpets; and 13: a crook, to alter the tuning of a trumpet*

and concert orchestras were the trumpet and the French horn. The trombone was used in the opera orchestra, but not in the symphony orchestra until Beethoven's Fifth Symphony. When valves were added to the trumpet and the French horn, the instruments could do more, and composers immediately put them to work by giving them solo passages. Composers also discovered the majestic quality of brass instruments used as a choir. Various kinds of "mutes" were used to soften the tone, and this incidentally also changed the tone color and even the pitch.

The composers of the Classical period usually used horns and trumpets in pairs. In the nineteenth century composers added

the trombones and the tuba. Today there are usually ten to twelve brass instruments in the symphony orchestra, placed near the back in front of the double basses and the percussion. In the orchestral score the brass parts are written below the woodwind parts, in this order: French horns, trumpets, trombones. tuba.

The brass instruments, particularly the trumpet and the trombone, have been important members of the dance band since the birth of jazz. They are used as solo instruments or as part of the rhythmic background. In a big dance band the brass sometimes plays with a mellow tone, as in the Glen Miller Band, and sometimes with a

Ex. 52

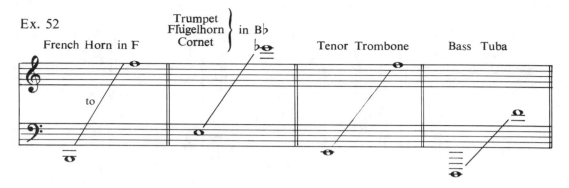

French Horn in F Trumpet Flügelhorn Cornet } in Bb Tenor Trombone Bass Tuba

driving, shrill tone, as on some of the Stan Kenton records. Some of the most experimental writing for brass has been done by Duke Ellington.

Among major works calling for a brass choir is Brahms's First Symphony (last movement). Wagner, one of the earliest composers to use a great deal of brass in the orchestra, did so in the prelude to *Parsifal* and the Funeral Music in *The Twilight of the Gods.* Ravel's arrangement of Mussorgsky's *Pictures at an Exhibition,* Hindemith's *Mathis der Mahler,* and Stravinsky's *Firebird* are other examples. Ex. 52 shows the ranges of the brass instruments.

BRITTEN, BENJAMIN (1913-76): the best-known English composer of our time. He was born in Lowestoft, England. At five he started to make up music, and his mother, a musician, helped and encouraged him. At twelve he began to study with the composer Frank Bridge, and four years later he won a scholarship in piano and composition at the Royal College of Music in London. On graduation from school he became an active professional composer, writing concert pieces as well as music for documentary films and for plays by his friend W. H. Auden.

Britten lived in the United States from 1939 to 1942. Returning to England, he played a great many concerts for war victims. Later he settled in Aldeburgh, a small fishing village, to compose and fish.

In 1945 his first opera, *Peter Grimes,* was produced. A great success in Europe and the United States, its strong, dramatic music established Britten as an outstanding composer. Four more operas followed: *The Rape of Lucretia, Albert Herring, Billy Budd,* and *The Turn of the Screw.* Britten has also written an opera for children, *The Little Sweep.*

Britten's gift for children's music appears also in his popular *The Young Person's Guide to the Orchestra.* Written originally for an educational movie, *The Instruments of the Orchestra,* it is based on a theme by Brit-

Below: *Benjamin Britten*
At right: *scene from Britten's opera* Peter Grimes

ten's favorite composer, the seventeenth-century's Henry Purcell.

In addition to his operas Britten wrote songs, choral works, concertos, and much chamber music, including two string quartets. His music, often sparse and lean, belongs to no one school of contemporary music. It is sometimes consonant, sometimes dissonant. His melodies can be as deceptively simple as folk tunes, or involved and dramatic in their wide leaps. In his fast music Britten often wrote nervous, syncopated counterpoint.

Britten's *Ceremony of Carols* is a favorite Christmas choral work. His "Four Sea Interludes" from *Peter Grimes* appears on many symphony programs. The major work of his later years is the *War Requiem*, given its first performance in 1962 at the consecration of the rebuilt cathedral of Coventry, which had been totally destroyed in World War II. This is a vast dramatic work in which Britten expressed his horror of war, alternating settings of the traditional words of the Mass for the dead with settings of poems about the ugliness of war by the English poet Wilfred Owen, who died in World War I. In March 1965, Britten was named by Queen Elizabeth II a member of the Order of Merit—the highest civilian honor in England.

BRUCKNER, ANTON (1824–96): composer of nine epic-length symphonies and grand choral works. Born in Ansfelden, northern Austria, Bruckner spent most of his life in Vienna, quietly teaching at the Vienna Conservatory and composing. He was devoted to the organ, and, although he made few concert tours, was acclaimed as a virtuoso performer on that instrument.

Bruckner was a deeply religious man, and a feeling of other-worldliness permeates his choral music as well as his symphonies. His thinking was on a large scale, as evidenced by the fact that he did not publish any small, short works. Although he admired Wagner, he was much more influenced by Schubert, whose Symphony in C Major he seemed to use as a model for its "heavenly length." Bruckner's music tends to be massive, with his orchestra often sounding like a symphonic band or organ as he employs a large number of wind instruments.

Bruckner's music has not been held in high regard outside of German-speaking countries until recently, when his three masses, choral Te Deum, and symphonies (particularly Number 4 and Number 8) have begun to receive performances in England and the United States.

BUGLE: a military instrument of the brass family. The simplest of wind instruments, it consists merely of a long, conical brass tube folded back on itself like a trumpet. It is one of the easiest instruments to play, having no valves or keys to press down. The player produces tones by tightening or loosening his lips. The average bugler can coax only five pitches out of his instrument:

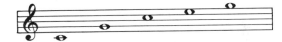

The bugle was used mostly to give signals to foot soldiers, having replaced the fife and drums in the early years of the nineteenth century. To the aristocratic trumpet went the task of giving signals to officers on horseback.

Because of its restricted number of pitches, the bugle is not a member of the orchestra. The only group in which it participates is the bugle-and-drum corps, often featured in parades. A single bugle is used at some race tracks to call the horses to the post, and at some camps to sound Reveille, Lights Out, and Chow Time.

At military funerals and on Veterans' Day it is the bugle that sounds Taps.

BUXTEHUDE, DIETRICH (1637–1707): a German-Danish organist and composer. At the age of thirty-one he became organist and music director of the Church of St. Mary in Lübeck, and his skill as both organist and composer was so great that he made Lübeck the music center of North Germany. Such musicians as Bach and Handel came to hear his music and learn his style of writing. Bach walked two hundred miles to hear Buxtehude, almost losing his own job because he stayed so long at Lübeck.

Buxtehude's brilliantly contrapuntal organ music served Bach as a model for his own toccatas, passacaglias, and fugues. Buxtehude also wrote many cantatas, full of religious and dramatic feeling. Some of these, such as *Ich suchte des Nachts (I Sought Thee Through the Night)*, are for solo voices; others, such as *Alles was ihr tut (All That Ye Do)*, are for chorus. These cantatas also were used as models by Bach.

After a period of great popularity, Buxtehude's music was overshadowed by that of Bach, but recently there has been a rediscovery of his works. Several cantatas have been recorded, and his organ music is a staple in the modern organist's repertoire.

Anton Bruckner

William Byrd

BYRD, WILLIAM (1543–1623): the greatest English composer of the Elizabethan period. Byrd was born in Lincolnshire. Little is known of his musical training, although it is possible that he studied with the famous composer Thomas Tallis. By the age of twenty Byrd was established as organist of Lincoln Cathedral, and in 1570 he was given the post of honorary organist to the Chapel Royal—a post he shared with Tallis.

In 1575 Byrd and Tallis were granted a monopoly on the printing of music and music paper in England—the first such grant. Evidently not many people wanted to buy printed music: the venture proved to be unprofitable.

Byrd's life was a busy one of playing, composing, publishing, getting involved in lawsuits, and avoiding persecution. He remained a Catholic when Catholics were being seized and jailed. Byrd was held in such high esteem as a composer that he was molested little, continuing to hold his place in the Chapel Royal.

Byrd wrote in all the styles of his day. His three masses—for three, four, and five voices—rank with the best of Palestrina and Lassus. They are written with a purity of melodic line completely suited to the Latin text. Byrd also became one of the first English composers to try his hand at the new light form of the Italian madrigal, just as he was one of the founders of the English virginal, or harpsichord, school. In such works as the variations on the tunes "The Carman's Whistle" and "The Earl of Salisbury's Pavane," Byrd anticipated many of the musical techniques of later composers. He was a master of counterpoint and harmony, creating many interesting sounds through the combined use of the old church modes and new major-minor scale system (Ex. 53).

Much of Byrd's keyboard music is contained in *My Lady Nevell's Booke,* the well-known *Fitzwilliam Virginal Book,* and *Parthenia,* the latter being a collection written in collaboration with John Bull and Orlando Gibbons.

It was in the field of religious music, however, that Byrd excelled. His devout Catholicism shines through his masses, the *Gradualia* (two books of motets, 1605, for the Catholic church year), *Teares or Lamentacions of a Sworrowful Soule* (his last published work), and his *Psalms, Sonetes and Songs of Sadness and Pietie.* In the foreword to the last of these he tells the reader—

Since singing is so good a thing,
I wish all men would learne to sing.

Ex. 53 — Galiardo

C: the tone sounded by the white key to the left of the two black keys on the piano. It is called *doh* in France and Italy; its old name in the musical scale was *ut*. The lowest string of the cello, and of the viola, is tuned to C. The black key on the piano immediately to the right of C is called C-sharp (*cis* in Germany). There is no black key between C and the white note below it, which is B; hence C-flat is the same key as B-natural. These are the C's on the staff (middle C is always written on its own line just below the treble staff or just above the bass staff):

The key signatures of the major and minor scales on C, C-sharp, and C-flat are:

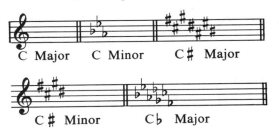

The keys of C major and C minor are used frequently. Great symphonies written in C major include Beethoven's First Symphony, Mozart's Forty-first (the "Jupiter"), Schubert's Seventh, and Robert Schumann's Second (Opus 61). The key of C minor, equally popular with composers, is the key of Brahms's First Symphony and Beethoven's Fifth.

Among the few large works written in C-sharp minor are Beethoven's Sonata Opus 27, Number 2 (the "Moonlight"), and Gustav Mahler's Fifth Symphony (the "Giant"). C-sharp minor was a favorite key of the piano pieces of the nineteenth-century composers Chopin, Liszt, and Brahms.

C-sharp major and C-flat major have been used rarely. In his *Well-tempered Clavier*, Bach included two preludes and fugues in C-sharp major but none in C-flat major.

The C clef, showing the position of middle C, can be placed on any of the bottom four lines of the staff:

Soprano Mezzo soprano Alto or viola Tenor

In old music all the C clefs were used. Today only the alto and tenor appear. Music for the viola is written in the alto clef. Music for cello, trombone, and bassoon is written in the tenor clef when the notes become too high to fit on the bass staff.

CADENCE: a place to breathe in musical composition. Just as words need to be formed into phrases, sentences, and paragraphs, tones in music need to be grouped into sections. This is done by planning rhythm, melody, and harmony so as to bring the flow of tones to various kinds of stopping points—sometimes for a long time, sometimes briefly. Cadences are therefore important in musical form, since they signal the end of large and small musical sections. Without cadences music would be like a long stream of words with no punctuation and no paragraphing.

Rhythm is the most important part of a cadence and, in fact, can by itself establish a cadence, as in the drum beat in Ex. 1. This particular cadence, ending on a strong beat, is sometimes called a masculine cadence. A cadence ending on a weak, or unaccented, beat (Ex. 2) is called feminine.

In early vocal music, cadences were determined by the lines of the text and the

Ex. 1

Ex. 2

Ex. 3 — *Liber Usualis*

Re -ctor Pot -ens, ve - rax De - us,_____ Qui tem -pe -ras re - rum vi - ces

Ex. 4 — "Servi Boni," Lassus

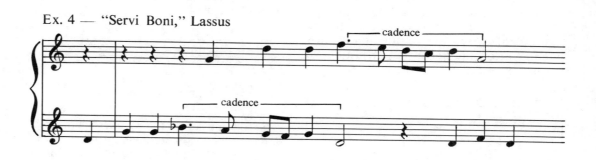

Ex. 5 — Invention No. 4, J.S. Bach

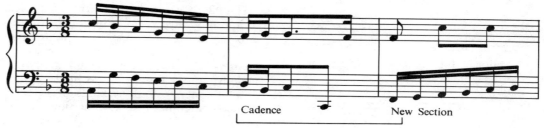

Ex. 6 — Sonata, Op. 31, No. 3, Beethoven

Ex. 7 — American Folk Song: "My Darling Clementine"

breath of the singer. A cadence coincided with the end of a line of poetry or a word phrase, although the composer always had to consider the breath capacity of the singer (Ex. 3).

Cadences are part of the architecture of music. Whether they are many or few, obvious or subtle, depends on the composer and the style or purpose of the music of the times. In dance music strong cadences come regularly, usually at intervals of four or eight measures. Here the function of the cadence is to tell the dancers where to end one dance figure and get set to begin the next. In contrapuntal composition there is often no place when all voices stop at the same time. Ex. 4, a section of a motet by Lassus, shows the upper voice coming to a cadence while the lower voice continues. In works such as Bach's fugues and inventions the final notes of a cadence often turn out to be the opening tones of a new section (Ex. 5).

In traditional music there are several kinds of cadence. A perfect cadence is found at the end of a composition or of a long section. In this cadence the fundamental tones of the chords used occur in the lowest vocal or instrumental part; the root of the final chord, usually the keynote, is in the soprano. One type of perfect cadence, called authentic (the most usual), is a chord built on the fifth tone of the scale (the dominant) followed by the chord built on the first tone of the scale (the tonic). Most of the symphonies and sonatas by Beethoven and Mozart end with perfect authentic cadences. The last two chords of Beethoven's Sonata Opus 31, Number 3, make an authentic cadence (Ex. 6). The other type of perfect cadence is the plagal cadence, in which the final tonic chord is preceded by the chord built on the fourth tone of the scale, the subdominant. The "Amen" sung at the end of a hymn is almost always a plagal cadence:

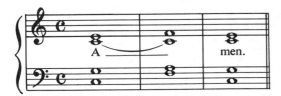

A cadence that takes the place of a semicolon—a pause but not a complete stop—is called a semicadence or half cadence. Such cadences occur in the middle of sections, phrases, and periods. The chord most often so used is the one built on the fifth tone of the scale, the dominant (Ex. 7).

A deceptive cadence occurs when, in a cadence progression, a composer leads the listener to expect one chord and gives him a different one:

Piano Sonata in E-flat, Haydn

Composers of the twentieth century add dissonant notes or chromatic tones to their cadence chords, as well as to their other chords, without disturbing the basic function of the cadence chords:

Prelude, Op. 74, No. 4, Scriabin

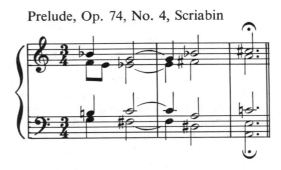

Even in music without a key center the composer can give a feeling of cadence:

Op. 19, No. 5, Schoenberg

CADENZA: a showing-off section of a musical composition. It is found most often in a concerto for solo instrument and orchestra. Just before the very end of a concerto movement, at the cadence, the orchestra comes to a stop. The soloist has the stage all to himself. He shows his skill by playing rapid runs, brilliant passages, showy swoops up and down the instrument, and dazzling chord passages. All these are built on themes from the concerto. The cadenza usually ends with a loud trill that tells the orchestra, "Get ready!" The music seems to be teetering at the top of a slide. Then the orchestra comes in with a loud, fast ending:

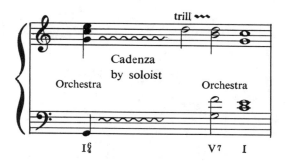

while the audience is still gasping with admiration for the soloist.

Cadenzas were first used in the 1600's by Italian opera singers, who at the end of each section of an aria sang an elaborate flourish. Since this happened at the cadence, it was called a cadenza. Violin soloists picked up the idea and used it in sonatas and concertos.

Until close to 1800 the composer did not write the cadenza for his concerto. The soloist was expected to make up a cadenza on the spot, often one for each movement. This was all right if the soloist was good at improvising, but so many soloists ruined the effect of concertos by long, tasteless cadenzas that composers began to write their own. Mozart was one of the first to do so.

Bach, Mozart, and Beethoven wrote short cadenzas in their keyboard music, even when the work was not a concerto. Liszt, in his *Hungarian Rhapsodies,* and Chopin, in his nocturnes, sprinkled short cadenzas throughout the compositions to give them color and glitter. Since Chopin and Liszt, composers have felt free to use a cadenza at any point in a composition.

As performers of the nineteenth century became less and less competent to improvise their own cadenzas, they began to rely on composed cadenzas. Among the best known of these composed cadenzas are the ones by Reinecke, Hummel, and Beethoven for Mozart's piano concertos and by Joachim for Beethoven's and Brahms's violin concertos. Brahms wrote some very Brahmsian cadenzas for piano concertos by Mozart and Beethoven.

CALLIOPE: keyboard instrument equipped with steam whistles that produce its tones. The voice of the calliope was the voice of the traveling circuses and the merry-go-round. It was loud and out of tune. Many persons did not think that it was a musical instrument at all, but its harsh tones cast a magic spell in spring and summer when the circus came to town.

The calliope is a noisy relative of the organ. It is an awkward instrument, requiring a boiler full of water which is heated to make the steam that blows through the pipes. In its standard form it is essentially a nineteenth-century instrument, having been developed by Josiah C. Stoddard, a New Englander, in 1855. Calliopes came in two sizes, the larger size having a keyboard of thirty-two keys, including a full set of sharps and flats. One reason why the instrument often sounded out of tune is that its pitch varied with the steam pressure from the boiler; the player had to control the valves as he played.

In the circus parade the calliope had its own gold-and-white wagon, pulled by two great Percheron circus horses. As long as it was a steam calliope, it was always accompanied by its boiler and firebox. The whole apparatus was rather unwieldy for parades and was gradually replaced by the pneumatic calliope, worked by compressed air. The steam calliope lived out its last years on showboats and excursion boats, where steam generation was no problem. Long after its sound had disappeared from circus parades,

A 20-whistle steam calliope

its shrill pandemonium could still be heard ranging over the valleys of the Mississippi and Ohio rivers.

One of the strangest aspects of this instrument is its name. *Calliope* in Greek means "beautiful voice." But Calliope, the muse of heroic poetry, was always pictured with a trumpet.

CANON: a type of counterpoint in which one or more voices imitate a leading voice. The simplest type of canon is the round, of which "Three Blind Mice" and "Frère Jacques" are the best-known examples. In these rounds each voice enters on the same pitch and sings the melody with no changes in rhythm or pitch. Such a canon is known as an exact canon at the unison. In a "free" canon the composer makes small changes in the pitch of the imitating voices.

The imitating voices in a canon can be written so that they come in at intervals other than the unison, above or below the leading voice. As a result there can be canon at the second, at the third, and so on (Ex. 8a, b, and c.)

The imitating voice does not even have to go in the same direction as the melody of the leading voice. Ex. 9 shows a canon with the second voice imitating in contrary motion.

Among other types of canon is the canon in augmentation, in which the note values

Ex. 8a — Motet: "Oculus non Judit," Lassus   Canon at the seventh below

Ex. 8b — "Goldberg" Variations, J.S. Bach
Canon at the second above plus an accompanying bass

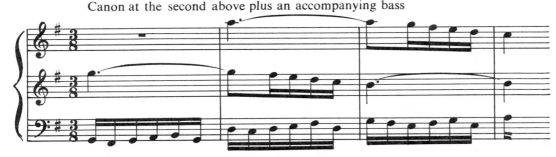

Ex. 8c — Motet:"Beatus homo," Lassus
Canon at the third

Ex. 9 — Motet: "Justi tulerunt Spolia," Lassus
Canon at the seventh below in contrary motion

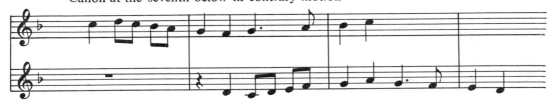

of the leading voice are doubled—in Ex. 10, in contrary motion.

There is the canon in diminution, in which the note values of the imitating voice are half those of the leading voice (Ex. 11). In the double canon, two canons are played or sung at the same time (Ex. 12). In the crab canon, sometimes known as the retrograde or cancrizans canon, the imitating voice is the leading melody, written backward from the end. Of course, composers often have combined several types of canon within the same work, as in Ex. 10 and 11.

Composers found, as early as the fourteenth century, that canon was a useful device to help them knit their compositions together. During the fifteenth and sixteenth centuries they explored all possible ways of making canons, including the writing of "puzzle" canons. In these sometimes playful

Ex. 10— Fugue No. 7 from *The Art of Fugue*, J.S. Bach
Canon in augmentation and contrary motion

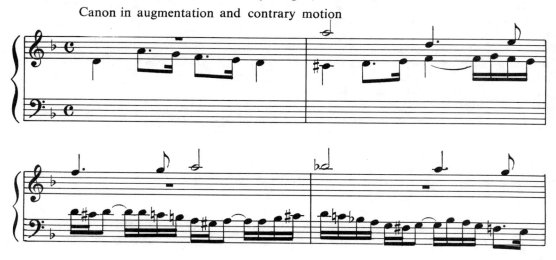

Ex. 11— Fugue No. 6 from *The Art of Fugue*, J.S. Bach
Canon in diminution and contrary motion

Ex. 12— Chorale Prelude for Organ: "In Dulci jubilo," J.S. Bach
Double canon

Note: the triplet eighth notes, written this way by Bach, would today be written as triplets of quarter notes.

works the composer would write only the notes of the leading voice. A few puzzling remarks, usually in Latin, hid the clues to the solution of the canon. The solver of the puzzle had to figure out where the imitating voice entered, what relation the rhythm of the imitating voice had to the rhythm of the leading voice, whether the music was meant to be read by means of a mirror, whether the second voice started at the end or sang the intervals of the melody in inversion—that is, upside down.

Canon at practically every interval is to be found in almost every phrase of a sixteenth-century motet, madrigal, or mass movement. The fugue, one of the most important musical forms of the seventeenth and eighteenth centuries, always starts with a form of free canon. Canon has remained as a basic form and texture of music throughout the centuries. It can be found in the twentieth-century music of Copland (near the end of *Appalachian Spring*) and the nineteenth-century music of Franck's Sonata for Violin and Piano (final movement) and Beethoven's Eighth Symphony (scherzando movement). Beautiful canons for unaccompanied voices were written by Mozart, Haydn, and Brahms. The finest examples of canons, with the imitating voice entering at every interval, are to be found in Bach's "Goldberg" Variations for harpsichord. In this stupendous work every third variation is a canon—progressing from canon at the unison to canon at the ninth.

Performance of a cantata in a South German church (from the frontispiece of Musikalisches Lexicon *by J. G. Walther, 1732). Note that the conductor is holding a roll of music in each hand*

CANTATA: a composition for voices, usually the setting of a religious text intended to be sung in church. The cantata normally has several sections, being longer than a church anthem but shorter than an oratorio. Cantatas with non-religious texts are called secular cantatas.

The earliest cantatas, dating from seventeenth-century Italy, are operalike settings of religious or secular poems and stories. The only forces needed for performance are one or two voices and one or more accompanying instruments. Many such cantatas, consisting of arias and recitatives, were written by the Roman organist Giacomo Carissimi, as well as by Handel and by Alessandro Scarlatti, who seems to have written over six hundred of them.

About 1700, Lutheran composers in Germany began to develop a distinctive form of church cantata based on texts of religious inspiration and incorporating the Lutheran chorale. This was sung by the choir, sometimes joined by the congregation. The finest cantatas in this style are those of Johann Sebastian Bach.

Bach wrote more than two hundred cantatas, some of them being numbered among his greatest works. In these he brought together the dramatic flair of the Italian composers and the devotional feeling of his North European predecessors, such as Buxtehude. Each of his church cantatas was written for a particular Sunday in the church year. Bach wrote also some cantatas that were not religious, such as his *"Coffee" Cantata* and his operalike *Phoebus and Pan*.

Bach's cantatas feature a great variety of moods—grieving, adoring, triumphant. In the course of expressing these moods musically, he developed the favorite melodic and rhythmic figures that characterize them. Some of the cantatas (such as Number 208, *Sheep May Safely Graze*) are written for a single singer and one or two instruments; others (such as Number 80, *A Mighty Fortress Is Our God*) call for soloists, chorus, and a large orchestra. In their incredible variety Bach's cantatas offer a wealth of expressive recitatives, tender duets, dashing orchestral interludes, and overwhelmingly dramatic choruses. Taken together they constitute one of the most compelling groups of masterpieces ever written.

The form and style of the cantata were not completely exhausted by the great composers of the Baroque period. Throughout the nineteenth century and up to the present, composers such as Debussy, Prokofiev, Stravinsky, and William Schuman have turned to the cantata as a vehicle for their own utterances.

CANTUS FIRMUS: literally, "fixed song" —the melody to which a composer or a student of counterpoint will add one or more melodies. In the Middle Ages the cantus firmus was a religious chant. To this another melody called the descant was added. At first the two melodies moved together note by note, but then composers began to make each note of the cantus firmus longer. This provided time to put many notes in the descant against each note of the cantus firmus. A long-breathed cantus firmus was played probably by an instrument, since no singer had the lung power to sustain tones for such a long time.

In the Renaissance, masses were composed with all sections based on the same cantus firmus. Sometimes this cantus firmus was a popular song such as the tune of "L'Homme armé" (The Armed Man), used by many composers in the fifteenth and sixteenth centuries:

"L'Homme armé," Dufay

The most famous of the "L'Homme armé" masses is that by Guillaume Dufay. Even

the melodies of love songs, such as "Kiss Me" or "Good-bye, My Love," were used as cantus firmi. If composers did this today, they would write a mass or anthem based on a tune such as "Tea for Two."

The technique of writing a melody against another melody is one of the most important things a composer must learn. Every time Bach, Beethoven, Tchaikovsky, or any other composer wrote a melody and then added counterpoint to it, he was using the cantus-firmus technique.

The cantus firmus used in teaching (traditionally marked CF) is usually simple and written in whole notes, as this one, by the great Baroque teacher Johann Joseph Fux:

Cantus Firmus by J.J. Fux

CAPRICCIO: the Italian name for a light instrumental work of a fanciful sort. (The French term is *caprice*.) It is usually written in several parts suggesting frequent changes of mood.

In the seventeenth and early eighteenth centuries a capriccio was a work written in counterpoint like a fugue. Its theme, or "subject," usually has special rhythmic interest (Ex. 13). The theme often has many fast notes, as does the counterpoint. Many more capriccios will be found in the music of Frescobaldi and Froberger than in that of later composers. This form did, however, continue to appear, as in Bach's *Capriccio on the Departure of His Beloved Brother*— a classic example of early program music.

In the nineteenth century "capriccio" came to mean a brilliant workout on a theme. The theme could be original or by another composer. Rimsky-Korsakov's *Capriccio espagnol* for orchestra is based on Spanish dance themes. Brahms gave the name "capriccio" to many of the fast piano pieces written in his last years.

Ex. 13— Capriccio for Organ, Froberger

A scene from Carmen *with Risë Stevens and Richard Tucker*

CARMEN: an opera by Georges Bizet—one of the most popular operas of all. Its libretto is based on a short story by Mérimée. The scene is Spain, with its colorful gypsies and bullfighters.

Carmen was produced for the first time in Paris in 1875. It was not immediately a complete success; many people found the story too violent, and others disliked the unhappy ending. Some musicians considered Bizet's music too heavy—the same music that was later used in textbooks to show students how to write light music for orchestra!

Carmen was given thirty-seven performances in its first season. Its fame spread rapidly, and within a few years it was being played in every opera house. Bizet, however, died only three months after the first performance—before the opera's world-wide success.

Although Bizet had never been to Spain, his music for *Carmen* was full of Spanish flavor. He took his inspiration from books of Spanish music that he found in the Paris Library. One authentic piece of Spanish music that did find its way into *Carmen* was the famous "Habañera," based on a song by the Spanish composer Sebastián Yradier.

Most of *Carmen* is bright, gay, and tuneful, but all through the opera Bizet weaves a menacing little motive (Ex. 14) that is sometimes called the "Carmen," or "Fate," motive. This is like a fortune teller's somber foreboding.

Carmen is a tragic story of jealousy. It has wonderful scenes with many singers, such as the chorus of the little boys who follow the soldiers, the chorus of the girls who work in a cigarette factory, the chorus of gypsies dancing and singing in a tavern. But the main story is about Don José and Carmen.

Don José, a soldier in the Spanish army, falls in love with Carmen, a wild gypsy girl. He deserts from the army to follow Carmen, who is a member of a gang of smugglers in the mountains. At the smuggler's camp Don José discovers that Carmen has fallen in love with Escamillo, a bullfighter. Insanely jealous, Don José wants to kill Escamillo. But Don José's young fiancée, Micaela, finds her way to the camp to tell Don José that his mother is dying and he must go to her. Don José leaves, assuring Carmen that they will meet again.

The last act is one of the most exciting in all opera. The scene is outside the bull ring in Seville. A gay crowd gathers and starts to go in through the gates, singing the "Toreador Song." Don José, hiding in the crowd, sees Carmen being escorted by Escamillo.

Ex. 14

Everyone enters the stadium except Carmen and Don José. Carmen has decided to end her romance with him. When he pleads with her to love him, she refuses, though afraid of the wild look in his eye. They argue while, inside the stadium, the bull ring echoes with cheers for Escamillo.

Carmen tries to get past Don José so that she can witness the triumph of her lover Escamillo. Taking off the ring that Don José gave her earlier, she throws it into his face. Once more she tries to get past him. But then, while inside the stadium the crowd is cheering wildly, Don José stabs Carmen. He cries out in grief as he realizes that he has killed the woman he loves. The crowd, having heard the commotion outside, streams out as Don José gives himself up to the police.

CAROL: today, a joyous song to be sung at Christmas. Actually, the singing of carols goes back to the Middle Ages, when they were sung at all times of the year. A carol was a song, on any subject, in which short stanzas (typically of four lines, sung by a soloist) alternated with a "burden" (usually two lines, sung by the group). These carols were danced as well as sung (that is why so many of the older carols are lively). Though the dancers might hold still during a stanza, they joined hands (sometimes in a chain, more usually in a ring moving clockwise) when they sang the burden.

Carols were composed in every country of Europe, starting in the fourteenth century. There are carols about the birth of Jesus —happy carols and sweet lullabies. There are carols about Mary and Joseph, about the Wise Men, about the shepherds, about the animals in the manger. Many of the songs, such as the "Coventry Carol," were composed to be sung in nativity plays.

About the middle of the sixteenth century the word "carol" came to be identified more and more with Christmas and less and less with danced songs in stanza-and-burden form. The Christmas tradition included tongue-twisting carols, such as "The Twelve Days of Christmas," sung at parties. Some carols, such as the wassail songs, were drinking songs with which to celebrate Christmas and New Year's Day. (*Waes hael* is an old drinking toast meaning "Good health to you!") In England groups of children went around singing carols for sweets or pennies; these carols came to be called "waits," because the custom had been started by the waits, or watchmen, who patrolled cities at night.

Many countries have contributed to the musical traditions of Christmas. The French call their Christmas songs *noëls,* and in English the word "noel" is often used interchangeably with "carol," though noels are quite unrelated to medieval carols and are actually more recent (by more than a century). The United States has given the world "O Little Town of Bethlehem" and the spiritual-carol "Go Tell It on the Mountain." From Austria has come the best loved of all carols, "Silent Night." These songs are far removed from the carols of the Middle Ages. The Pueblo Indians, on the other hand, who greet Christmas in full dance costume, beating drums as they dance and sing, celebrate Christmas in a way that would have delighted medieval carolers.

Sweet-singing carolers: the Vienna Choir Boys

CASTANETS: small instruments of the percussion family, identified with Spanish music. They are wooden or ivory clappers held in the fingers. The wood traditionally used to make them is chestnut, for which the Spanish word is *castaña*. The clappers are hollowed out to make their sound sharp and penetrating. The two parts of the castanets are held together by a string that fits tightly around the thumb and first two fingers. The other fingers are used to bring the two parts together. The player can click the castanets by tapping with all the fingers at the same time or can make a short roll by bringing down one finger after another rapidly.

Castanets have been used by Spanish dancers since the days of ancient Rome and possibly since the time of the Phoenicians, some of whom settled in southern Spain in the eleventh century B.C. A Spanish dancer

Ex. 15 — *Capriccio espagnol*, Rimsky-Korsakov

is judged by her playing of the castanets as well as by her dancing. She usually plays two pairs of castanets, one for each hand. The left-hand pair, called "the man," is large and plays simple beats. The right-hand pair, "the woman," plays the complicated Spanish dance rhythms. The castanets have no definite pitch and cannot play a melody; nevertheless, in the hands of brilliant Spanish dancers they seem almost to be carrying on conversations.

The percussion player in a symphony orchestra does not usually have time to fix the castanets to his fingers; instead he attaches them to a stick that he can pick up quickly and shake. Composers use the castanets mostly to suggest Spanish music. Rimsky-Korsakov uses them throughout the fandango movement of his *Capriccio espagnol*.

In an orchestral score the part for castanets is usually written on a single line. Ex. 15, above, is from Rimsky-Korsakov's *Capriccio espagnol*.

CELESTA: the instrument that produces the high-pitched, light, somewhat sugary sound one hears in the Dance of the Sugarplum Fairy in Tchaikovsky's *Nutcracker Suite*. It looks like a small piano (it does have a keyboard), but in the way it produces its sound it is more closely related to the xylophone, marimba, and vibraphone. When the player presses one of the keys, a small hammer strikes a steel plate and sets it vibrating. By itself the resulting tone would have a tinkly brittleness (like a toy xylophone) caused by a poor balance between its fundamental and its harmonics. To produce the pure, singing tone of the celesta, a resonator of carefully adjusted length is added under the vibrating plate to bring out the fundamental tone. Each tone of the scale has its own plate (the lower the tone, the longer the plate), and each plate has its resonator.

The celesta was invented in 1886 by the French instrument maker Auguste Mustel. Its new sound was welcomed by composers, and it was rapidly introduced into orchestral scores. For a small instrument it has a large range: from middle C to the top notes of the piano. Its part is written in two staves, like a piano part, but the notes it is usually called upon to play are so high that for ease of reading they are written one octave below their real sound (Ex. 16). The instrument's tone is soft and will not be heard if too many other instruments are playing at the same time. The celesta can be heard as a solo instrument in Bartók's *Music for String Instruments, Percussion and Celesta* (1936).

Lucero Tena, flamenco dancer, playing castanets

Russell Woollen playing the celesta

Ex. 16 — Dance of the Sugar Plum Fairy from *Nutcracker* Suite, Tchaikovsky

Andante non troppo
Sounds an octave higher

CELLO (VIOLONCELLO): the tenor-bass of the violin family. Its closest relatives are the violin and viola, but it is larger than these—so large that the performer must sit while playing it. A long spike at the bottom of the instrument holds the cello in place on the floor and makes it convenient to hold between the knees. Though it looks like a violin, it is not built in the same proportions: the length of the sounding box is curtailed and its depth is increased, so that the cellist does not obtain quite as much tonal support from the body of his instrument as does the violinist.

The violoncello (note the second "o"—not an "i") is usually called the cello. Its full name means "little bass viol," but somehow in contracting the name only the "little" was retained.

The cello is tuned like the violin, in a series of perfect fifths:

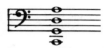

Its part is usually written in the bass clef unless the music goes too high, in which case the tenor clef, with middle C on the next-to-the-top line, is used. For a while in the early 1800's the high notes were written in the treble staff, an octave higher than they sound. Such high-looking cello notes can be found in Beethoven's string quartets.

The cello can play almost everything that the violin does—arpeggios, chords, harmonics, and so on. However, since the distances on the cello are larger than those on the violin, the cellist must develop a greater stretch in his fingers. In high passages the cellist uses his thumb on the strings, both to "stop" them and to help him find his correct position. The cello bow is a bit shorter, stubbier, and heavier than the violin bow. It is usually beautifully balanced, but it cannot play as many notes on one bow stroke as can a violin bow. The versatility of the cello is suggested by Ex. 17.

The pizzicato of the cello is one of its most useful sounds. The instrument is quite resonant in single notes and even richer in plucked chords. Hence it is most valuable in harmonic accompaniments, either to other strings or to woodwinds.

In the seventeenth and eighteenth centuries the cello was used in the orchestra to play just the bass notes along with the double bass. In Baroque music it played the continuo along with the organ or harpsichord. In early string quartets it served as the bass, seldom being given a melody to play. With Haydn and Mozart it was given running passages of its own. Finally, Beethoven brought out the singing quality of the cello in his orchestral works, chamber music, and five sonatas for cello and piano (Ex. 18).

Several composers of recent times have given the cello interesting roles. Richard Strauss used it to represent the Don in *Don Quixote*. Ernest Bloch used it to represent King Solomon in his *Schelomo*. Villa-Lobos scored one of his *Bachianas Brasileiras* for eight cellos and two for eight cellos and soprano. Concertos for the instrument have been written by Robert Schumann, Dvořák, Elgar, Hindemith, and Barber (who has also written a sonata for piano and cello).

The greatest works for the cello date from as far back as 1720. They are the six suites for unaccompanied cello by Johann Sebastian Bach—incredibly challenging pieces that rank among the masterpieces of the literature of music (Ex. 19).

Mstislav Rostropovich

Pablo Casals

Ex. 17 — *Lyric Suite*, Berg

Ex. 18 — String Quartet, Op. 59, No. 1, Beethoven

Ex. 19 — Saraband from Suite No. 3 for Unaccompanied Cello, J.S. Bach

Dancing the chaconne

CHACONNE: a slow processional dance in triple meter. The chaconne has a repeated bass melody, sometimes called a "ground bass" or a "ground." The harmonies suggested by the bass were used as a chordal pattern out of which the composer could invent an almost endless series of melodic variations. (This process is related to jazz, in which soloists improvise on a chordal pattern.) Almost every composer between 1600 and 1700 wrote variations over a chaconne bass, and opera composers used chaconnes for finales. The chaconne had a close relative called the passacaglia, which is also a series of variations over a ground bass. Because composers seem to have used these names interchangeably, it is often hard to detect any differences between the two forms.

A few chaconne basses were so effective that they were used by many composers. Ex. 20 and 21 show two of them. Their minor

key and the fact that they go down the scale slowly gave them a mournful quality. Basses like the second are used in "Dido's Lament" in Purcell's *Dido and Aeneas* and in the "Crucifixus" of Bach's B-minor Mass.

The greatest of all chaconnes is the one at the end of Bach's Partita Number 2 for unaccompanied violin (Ex. 22).

CHAMBER MUSIC: music written to be performed in a room of a private house or in a small hall. It has been written for voices alone, instruments alone, and combinations of voices and instruments.

In chamber music each player or singer has a part all his own; he does not play or sing the same part as other performers, as he would in a chorus or the string section of an orchestra. A chamber work may be for one person, as is a piano sonata, or for as many as twenty, as is a work for chamber orchestra or wind ensemble. Chamber operas, such as Richard Strauss's *Ariadne auf Naxos,* are operas written for just a few singers and a small orchestra.

The earliest chamber music was written to be sung. In sixteenth-century Italy and England small groups would get together to sing madrigals. These singers sang for their own entertainment, although there might be a few people who sat and listened. Other groups of music lovers would get together after dinner to play on the soft-voiced viols.

Noblemen of means liked to have music at dinner. Such "table music" was usually written for strings. In the seventeenth century composers began to write chamber music for two or more instruments, calling these works *sonatas.* The most common of these early forms is the trio sonata, performed on two soprano instruments, a bass, and a keyboard instrument. The keyboard instrument filled in the accompaniment

Ex. 20 — Bass

Ex. 21 — Bass

Ex. 22 — Chaconne from Partita No. 2 for Unaccompanied Violin, J.S. Bach

while the three others played the important melody lines. After 1750, when the keyboard instrument was replaced by the viola, the string quartet became the favorite form of chamber music, for both composers and listeners. This popularity was due to Haydn's eighty-two masterful string quartets. Since the time of Haydn almost every great composer has written at least one string quartet. Many composers, such as Mozart, Beethoven, Schubert, Brahms, and Bartók, poured some of their deepest thoughts into this mold.

Chamber music has been written for an almost unlimited number of vocal and instrumental combinations. Composers have written for families of instruments—trios for strings or woodwinds, for example, and quartets have been written for instruments of the same kind, as for four bassoons (by William Schuman) or four saxophones (by Henry Cowell). The piano has been used with the violin and cello in trios. It has also been used with the string quartet and many different combinations of wind instruments.

Brahms wrote his *Liebeslieder* waltzes for vocal quartet and two pianists. Villa-Lobos has scored two of his *Bachianas Brasileiras* for eight cellos and a soprano. Stravinsky, in his *In Memoriam Dylan Thomas,* has written for tenor voice, string quartet, and four trombones. Schoenberg wrote a serenade for clarinet, mandolin, guitar, violin, viola, and cello, and Berg has a chamber concerto for piano, violin, and thirteen wind instruments.

Jazz musicians join together in small chamber-music groups called "combos." A small combo may consist of piano, guitar, and string bass; or flügelhorn, vibraphone, and drums.

CHANTEY: a work song sung by sailors in the days of sailing ships. The rhythm of the song helped the sailors keep together as they hauled up the anchor or raised and lowered sail.

The singing of a chantey was usually started by a leader, who set the rhythm. He would sing out one line, which would be answered by another from the rest of the men. The leader was expected to improvise new lyrics, and good lines would be kept and passed from ship to ship. The melodies were often old tunes from Ireland, England, or America; sometimes the sailors adopted the melodies of black dockhands who sang as they loaded the ships.

There are four types of chantey. The "short drag," such as "Haul Away, Joe," was used for a series of short, strong pulls while rolling up a sail. The halyard chanteys, such as "Blow the Man Down," also were sung while adjusting the sail. Capstan chanteys, such as "Shenandoah," were sung while the men were working on a long, steady job, such as hoisting anchor by winding cable around the capstan. The forecastle chanteys were songs the sailors sang while sitting around after their work was finished. A forecastle chantey may be an old ballad, such as "The Golden Vanity," or a lively dance, such as "The Boston Come All-Ye."

A chamber music concert in a French salon (17th-century engraving by Duclos, after a design by Saint Aubin)

Chopin at age twenty-two

Portrait of George Sand by Charpentier

At right: *Chopin as painted by Eugène Delacroix, 1838*

CHOPIN, FRÉDÉRIC (1810–49): the Polish composer who has been called "the poet of the piano." No one has ever achieved more with the piano's capacity to create a world of color in sound. Chopin's rich harmonies, his bold or tender melodies, and his dashing arpeggios opened new vistas to all composers who came after him.

Chopin was born in a village near Warsaw, Poland. His father had come from France, and his mother was Polish. When Chopin was but seven he played a difficult piano concerto in a recital, at ten he wrote a march for band, and he was only fifteen and still in high school when a rondo he had written was published.

At the age of twenty Chopin left Poland to play in Germany, France, and Austria. He never went back to Poland. In 1830 the Russians had taken Warsaw, and Chopin never forgave them. He refused to play in Russia. For the rest of his life he filled his music with love for his native Poland.

Chopin was most successful in Paris, where he was welcomed by the greatest composers, painters, and writers of the day—Liszt, Balzac, Berlioz, Heine, and Bellini. He settled down to a life of writing and teaching, seldom playing in public. Somewhat of a dandy, Chopin was delighted to grace the salons of the aristocracy, where he was a great favorite. He had a famous love affair with a French woman who wrote novels under the penname of George Sand.

In 1848 a revolution in France sent Chopin to England. Long in poor health, he was now suffering severely from tuberculosis. He tried to give concerts but was in no condition to appear in public. After a collapse he went back to his beloved Paris and died there.

Almost everything that Chopin wrote involved the piano. The orchestra did not interest him, and in his two concertos, written in his twenties, he used it only to accompany the piano. He wrote few long works: three sonatas for piano, a sonata for cello and piano, and two piano concertos. He much preferred the shorter forms of music. Like a jeweler working on rare gems, he polished his pieces until they were as nearly perfect as he could make them.

Chopin could make the piano "sing." He played his melodies with a smooth touch, using the rhythmic freedom called rubato. In rubato the melody tones are not played exactly as written; they are hurried or slowed down while the accompaniment keeps on in accurate time.

For his dreamy nocturnes, in a form recently created by the Irish composer John Field, Chopin used a left-hand accompaniment (Ex. 23) that gave a rich background to the melody. It is necessary to use the pedal a great deal in playing Chopin, in order to blend the tones of the harmony and achieve the rich sonorities on top of which he floated his highly decorated melodies. Chopin was one of the first composers to exploit the possibilities of the piano's sustaining pedal. In his nocturnes, études, mazurkas, and ballades he often included short, colorful passages (Ex. 24) that are like small cadenzas.

Chopin brought into European music

Ex. 23— Nocturne, Op. 27, No. 2

Ex. 24— Mazurka, Op. 17, No. 4

Ex. 25— Mazurka, Op. 30, No. 4

Drawing of Chopin by George Sand

the dances of his native Poland. His mazurkas and polonaises are full of melodic and harmonic touches that were new to western Europe:

Mazurka, Op. 56, No. 2

His harmony, particularly in his mazurkas, astonished many people with its boldness and unpredictability (Ex. 25).

Chopin's music is not all dreamy. It can be stormy, as in the "Revolutionary" Étude and the polonaises. It can range up and down the keyboard, as in several of his études. It can be absolutely dazzling, as in his Étude in Thirds and the "Winter Wind" Étude. But Chopin could also be simple— not everything thunders or dreams. One of his most poignant works is the beautiful short Prelude in A Major, Number 7 of the twenty-four preludes, Opus 28, which can be played even by a comparative beginner.

Today, over a century after his death, Chopin's preludes, mazurkas, and waltzes probably are played more often than any other compositions for the piano.

flow of the melody give the chorale tunes a feeling of solidity and strength.

German composers began to arrange the chorales for voices, giving the melody to the sopranos and harmony to the other voices. This style of harmonizing a tune, with many harmonic changes in quick succession, called "chorale style," is still the foundation of much harmony study today.

The arrangements of the chorales became so complicated and dramatic that by 1700 the chorale had grown into a cantata, even serving as a basis for long oratorios. Organists decorated chorale tunes, and often wove them into lines of counterpoint. These chorale preludes and partitas for organ reach their highest point in the works of J. S. Bach.

Bach included arrangements of chorales in his cantatas and oratorios also. To express grief over the sufferings of Jesus, he used the chorale "O Sacred Head" five times, each time in a different setting or key, in his St. Matthew Passion. This popular chorale melody, incidentally, shows how things change in music: before it became a religious hymn it was a love song composed by Hans Leo Hassler.

Twentieth-century composers have not abandoned the chorale style. Stravinsky included two chorales in his little stage work *The Story of a Soldier* (1918), and Berg used Bach's arrangement of the chorale "It Is Enough" in his Violin Concerto (1936). More recently William Schuman began a movement of his Third Symphony with an instrumental chorale.

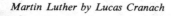

Martin Luther by Lucas Cranach

CHORALE: a simple hymn tune sung in Lutheran and other Protestant churches. After founding the Lutheran Church, Martin Luther felt a need for hymns that could be sung easily by his congregations. He wrote new words to melodies used in Catholic hymns and old German songs and dances. At first these chorales were sung in unison, without harmony or accompaniment. Luther chose melodies that move mostly from step to step within a scale. The rhythm is never complicated. The steady pulse and the smooth

CHORD: a combination of two or more tones that are sounded together or thought of as a group, as in an arpeggio or "broken" chord. The selection of chords and how they are used has much to do with making what is known as the "style" of a composer. Mozart, for example, used a fairly restricted vocabulary of consonant chords. Stravinsky, on the other hand, has used a wide range of chords, many of them quite dissonant.

Before the fifteenth century, composers thought of putting together intervals—not of building chords. From the fifteenth to the twentieth century, chords were built by putting intervals of thirds on top of each other—making triads, seventh chords, and ninth chords:

Triad Seventh Ninth
Chord Chord

Composers used primarily chords that were built on notes of the key in which a work was written. Within this limited number of chords, each was recognized to have certain characteristics and functions. These were dependent on the type of chord and its relationship to other chords, particularly to the keynote chord, the tonic. Each seventh chord, for example, usually "resolved" to a definite triad. Certain seventh chords, particularly the diminished seventh chord, were used for their dramatic effect. Bach seems to have attached special meaning to the diminished seventh chord, saving it for the climax of an invention or fugue, or using it on a dramatic word, such as the word "Death" in Cantata Number 4 ("Christ Lay in Death's Dark Prison"). Other composers, Mozart for one, used the diminished seventh to upset a harmonic progression, thereby extending a musical phrase (Ex. 26).

With the breaking down of conventional harmony in the nineteenth century due to the use of many chromatic, or "color," chords and with the new approach to harmony introduced by Mussorgsky and Debussy, the traditional sounds of triads and seventh chords have given way to many different kinds of chords. Since 1900, composers have experimented with chords in the following ways:

1. Adding tones to conventional triads:

Rigaudon from *Le Tombeau de Couperin*, Ravel

Ex. 26— Sonata for Piano K. 533, Mozart

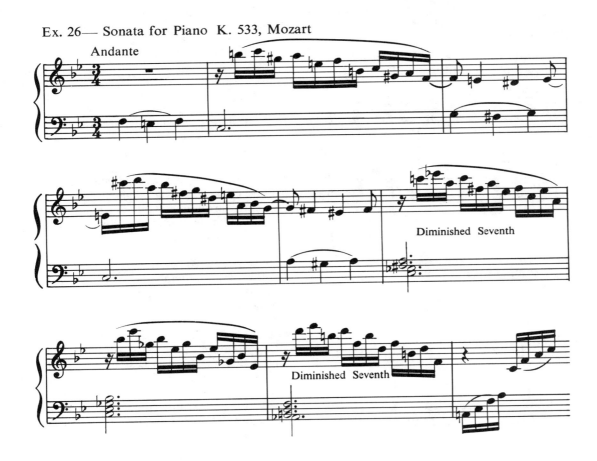

Ex. 27—Chanson for Chorus: "En Hiver," Hindemith

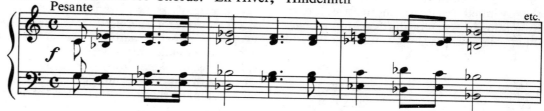

Ex. 28 — *Concord Sonata*, Charles Ives

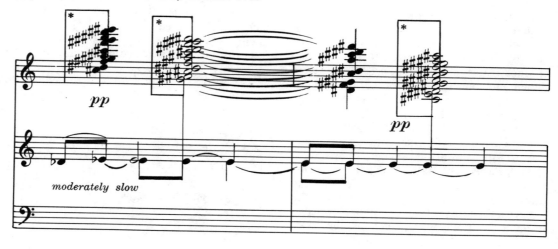

2. Using intervals of fourths and fifths to build triads instead of the usual interval of the thirds:

Chords Built in Fourths: *Saudades do Brasil* No. 9, Milhaud

3. Making chords of greater and lesser tension by experimenting with interval combinations of all kinds (Ex. 27).

4. Putting together two or more triads to make polychords:

Polychords: *Symphony for Strings,*
Schuman

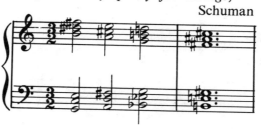

5. Making tone clusters by putting together a great many tones that lie next to each other (Ex. 28).

See TRIAD and HARMONY.

CHORUS: a group of singers, with more than one singer on each part; also, the refrain section of a song, where all join in, as opposed to solo sections. The chorus got its name from ancient Greece where, in plays, the *choros* was a group that danced and chanted comments on what was happening. Choir is the name given to a chorus that sings in church. Choral singing is the most popular way of making music: people sing in school choruses and glee clubs, church choirs, and community choruses. There are male choruses, women's choruses, and mixed choruses. In England and Wales there are festivals of choral singing that bring together thousands of singers. Strangely, there are very few professional choruses as contrasted with the number of professional orchestras.

Choral music has been written about every subject and for every occasion. A piece for chorus may be a simple arrangement of a folk tune, or it may be written in complicated lines of counterpoint. Most choral music is written to be sung in four parts—soprano, alto, tenor, and bass—but at times

Robert Fountain conducting the Oberlin College Choir

composers have divided each voice group into two or more parts, making eight- or twelve-part choruses. Music has been written for two or more choruses which answer each other in the style known as antiphonal singing, which reached its peak in the works of the Gabrielis in Venice around 1600.

Choral music has always been an important part of church services. Composers have written choral music based on the words of the Catholic Mass since the 1300's. Some of the greatest masterpieces of the world's music are the masses written by Machaut, Palestrina, Bach, Mozart, Beethoven, Berlioz, and Verdi. There is much wonderful music for chorus in the oratorios by Handel and the cantatas and passions by Bach. Beethoven brought the chorus into his Ninth Symphony. Since then other composers have used the chorus in symphonic works—Mahler in his Eighth Symphony (sometimes called the "Symphony of a Thousand") and Stravinsky in his *Symphony of Psalms.* Choruses have added excitement and color to many operas, such as Gluck's *Orpheo,* Purcell's *Dido and Aeneas,* Verdi's *Aida,* and Mussorgsky's *Boris Godunov.*

The word "chorus" is used in the musical form of "verse and chorus." The chorus is the section of music that keeps coming back after each new verse; sometimes it is called the "refrain." Most popular songs of today are written in the form of verse and chorus. The chorus is the part that is sung most often and is best remembered.

CHROMATIC: a melodic or chordal tone that is not in the key of the composition. Thus, in a piano work written in the key of C major, any black key is a chromatic tone. The word "chromatic" comes from a Greek word meaning "color." Chromatic tones are used by composers to add variety and color to their music. Although chromaticism has been used for hundreds of years, particularly by such composers as Gesualdo, Purcell, Bach, and Mozart, the nineteenth century is often called the "period of chromaticism" because Chopin, Schumann, Wagner, and others used it as an intrinsic part of their melodic and harmonic progressions (Ex. 29).

A chromatic scale is one that goes up

Ex. 29— Nocturne, Op. 37, No. 2, Chopin

Ex. 30 — Sonata in E-flat, Op. 7, Beethoven

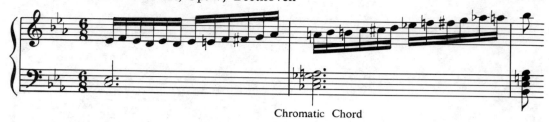

Chromatic Chord

Ex. 31 — Piano Concerto in C, K. 503, Mozart

or down in a series of half steps. When writing a chromatic scale, composers usually use sharps if the scale goes up and flats when the scale comes down, although they do not always adhere to this rule (Ex. 30 and 31, above). The signs for sharps, flats, naturals, double-sharps, and double-flats are called chromatic signs or accidentals.

CIRCLE OF FIFTHS: a melodic or harmonic progression in which tones or chords continually move to tones or chords a fifth lower. If the chords move in a series of perfect fifths, the progression will move through all twelve tones of the chromatic scale. This is a musical progression that is somewhat like going around the world: if

it keeps going long enough, it has to come back to its starting point:

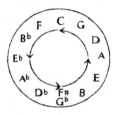

When the circle of fifths stays within a scale, it moves through seven tones before it arrives back at the starting point. In this diatonic circle of fifths not all the fifths will be perfect. This progression illustrates the natural movement of each chord within a key: I–IV–VII–III–VI–II–V–I (Ex. 32). To

Ex. 32 — Passacaille for Harpsichord, Handel

keep from running out of keyboard, one can play the circle of fifths zigzag, alternately down a fifth and up a fourth:

In this example we are able to see how a different kind of chord can be added to each bass note:

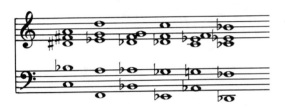

This entire progression is made possible by a tuning system known as "equal temperament." If a singer tried to get from C to C by singing twelve absolutely pure fifths in a row, he would end up a quarter of a tone too high. The carefully worked out compromises that prevent instrumentalists from getting into this situation are discussed under TEMPERAMENT.

In the period of music stretching from Bach to Haydn, the circle of fifths was an important part of musical form. Among other things it helped the composer get from one key to another and played a part in the development section of symphonies and sonatas.

By the nineteenth century, in the days of Chopin and Brahms, a circle of fifths in rapid motion showed up occasionally as an iridescent patch of color in the harmony (Ex. 33).

CLAQUE: a group of people who are given tickets and money to applaud a performer. The term comes from a French word that means "to clap one's hands." The idea of a claque goes back at least as far as ancient Rome: the emperor Nero had five thousand of his soldiers ready to cheer him when he performed.

Until quite recently claques were important in the opera houses of Europe and the United States. A singer who wanted to be a success had to hire the chief of the claque, who posted his men around the opera house. At a signal from the chief, the claque went into action. Their cheers and applause led the rest of the audience to add their applause. There are stories of many singers who were failures because they did not hire a claque to insure their success. Rival claques had wars in the opera houses to see which could get the greater number of encores and bows for their clients.

The managers of opera houses today do not favor claques. But in radio and television an announcer who holds up a card labeled "applause" is a contemporary *chef de claque.*

CLARINET: a single-reed member of the woodwind family. It is a nearly universal instrument: one can find it in orchestras, chamber-music groups, concert bands, and dance bands. The clarinet has a fairly narrow body, a tube about two feet long. Holes are bored in the tube so that its effective length can be changed to make the different notes. A system of keys and levers helps the player's fingers to cover the holes.

At the top of the tube is a mouthpiece that holds a single reed made from heavy cane. One side of the mouthpiece is cut at an angle. The reed fits on this side, leaving just enough space between the end of the mouthpiece and the reed itself for the player's breath to go through. The reed is held in place by a metal band that can be tightened

Ex. 33 — Intermezzo, Op. 116, No. 2, Brahms

Andante

on the bottom of the reed. The upper part of the reed is free to vibrate and make the tones. This is the part that is put between the lips of the player, without touching his teeth. The vibrations from the reed stimulate the air in the tube, which then produces a tone at a pitch determined by whatever holes are stopped. Opening the holes along the tube is a way of shortening the tube's effective length, producing tones of higher pitch.

The clarinet is an unusually expressive instrument. It can whisper a melody; it can swell from soft to loud and back again, like the human voice. It can play rapid arpeggios and passage work full of runs and leaps. Its lower tones are full and rich. (This register is called the chalumeau register in memory of a reed pipe, popular in many parts of France, that was an ancestor of the clarinet.) The middle tones are not as rich, but the higher ones are bright and clear. The very top tones are shrill and not much used.

Two kinds of clarinet are in regular use: the B-flat and the A clarinet. Both are transposing instruments—that is, the B-flat sounds a whole step lower than the notes the player sees in front of him, and the A clarinet sounds a minor third, or a step and a half, lower. The full range (and it's an unusually

Below left: *David Kalina playing the bass clarinet*
Below right: *Harold Wright playing the clarinet*

wide range) of the clarinet is shown here:

Range of the Clarinet

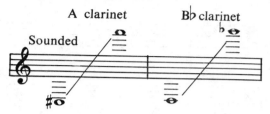

These are the notes one would hear. What the clarinet would be reading appears here:

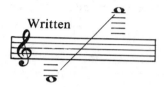

In concert work the player uses the B-flat clarinet for music that has flats in the key signature and the A clarinet for music that has sharps. For dance-band work and school orchestras and bands the B-flat clarinet is used.

The clarinet was invented about 1700 by Johann Christian Denner, a Nuremberg instrument maker. At first it sounded rough, a bit like a trumpet, and composers used it in pairs with the horns. Gradually it was improved, and composers (notably Gluck and Stamitz) ventured to use it in their orchestras, though its place was not secure until the time of Mozart. Mozart used it in the scores of several of his later symphonies, among them the Symphony Number 39 in E-flat, K. 543. He also wrote a concerto for clarinet and orchestra (in 1791, the last year of his life) and even trusted it to play chamber music along with a string quartet. But then he was great friends with Anton Stadler, a Viennese clarinetist whom he much admired.

The clarinet soon became a favorite instrument of composers, who prized its wide range and variety of tone colors. Solo works with and without accompaniments were written by Weber, Brahms, Bartók, Berg, and Stravinsky.

Today, in a full symphony orchestra there will usually be three clarinet players. The third player switches to the E-flat clarinet or the bass clarinet when these instruments are called for. Clarinets have become indispensable members of concert and marching bands, in which they take over many of the duties that in orchestras are given to the violins.

The E-flat clarinet, smaller than the B-flat, is not as mellow in tone and is saved for special effects. Its high register is a bit "nasty" in sound. Berlioz used it in the Witches' Sabbath section of his *Symphonie fantastique*. E-flat clarinet parts are written a minor third lower than the actual sound.

The bass clarinet is much larger than the regular instrument. Its bottom swells out into a large curved bell, so that it looks something like a curved smoking pipe. It reaches an octave lower than the regular clarinet, with low tones that are rich and dark—sometimes spooky. Its part is usually written in the treble clef, a ninth above the actual sounds:

Range of the Bass Clarinet

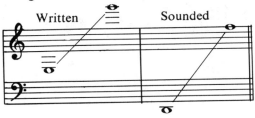

In spite of its size it can manage running passages and arpeggios. It can be heard by itself, in its lower range, in the Dance of the Sugarplum Fairy in Tchaikovsky's *Nutcracker* Suite. Tchaikovsky, fond of the dark sound of the clarinet and bass clarinet, often featured them as solo instruments.

Today one of the most familiar roles of the clarinet is in jazz and dance bands. Its squealing tones sounded in the earliest jazz bands in New Orleans as well as in the Original Dixieland Jazz Band, which made the first jazz records. In jazz the clarinet not only played rapid figures around the music of the other instruments but also had its bag of tricks, such as its "laughing" sound. The finest of the early jazz clarinetists was Jimmy Noone, whose style was the starting point for Jimmy Dorsey, Joe Marsala, Benny Goodman, Woody Herman, and others of more recent times.

CLASSICAL MUSIC: music written between 1750 and the early 1800's. "Classical music" also means, loosely, art music of any period as distinguished from popular or folk music. The greatest music of the Classical period came from Haydn, Gluck, and Mozart, although Beethoven's early works, too, are cast in Classical molds. Since so many of the outstanding composers of the period lived and worked in Vienna, the age is

sometimes referred to as the Viennese Classical period.

The Classical period was a time of change in feelings and ideas. Revolutions overthrew the social order in France and established American independence. Writers called for a return to the simple beauties of nature and for a reign of clear thinking over mysticism. The models held up to artists and architects were the severely uncluttered temples of ancient, Classical, Greece, as opposed to the highly decorated art of the Baroque period.

These changes were reflected in the music of the times. The wealthy aristocracy had replaced the church as the chief source of patronage for musicians, and what the nobleman wanted to hear was something elegant, polished, and tuneful. Such music already existed in the decorative harpsichord works of Couperin and the tuneful opera-buffa melodies of A. Scarlatti and G. B. Pergolesi.

The leaders in the search for a new musical style were two of J. S. Bach's sons, Carl Philipp Emanuel and Johann Christian. They turned away from the elaborate contrapuntal style of their father: instead of giving melodic parts equal importance, the younger Bachs wrote in a transparent style in which the soprano line is the most important voice. The melodies were set against the simplest of accompaniments, as for instance the Alberti bass. This music was expressive in a restrained, aristocratic manner but was also highly ornamented, like the costumes of the day.

Other composers, such as Giovanni Sammartini (1701–75) and Johann Stamitz (1717–57), took Alessandro Scarlatti's three-movement Italian opera overture and made it into the Classical symphony—to which a minuet was soon added, between the slow movement and the fast finale. To play this music, so full of contrasts and dynamic effects, Stamitz developed in Mannheim, Germany, the first virtuoso symphony orchestra. Music lovers came from all over Europe to hear the Mannheimers' carefully controlled crescendos and precise changes from loud to soft.

Contrast is the essence of Classical music. There is contrast of dynamics, with the music shifting back and forth from loud to soft; contrast of register, with wide-ranging melodies and wide spaces between bass and soprano; and contrast of mood, even within one movement of a work.

Much music of the preceding period, the Baroque, was based on the idea of a unity achieved by spinning a motive over a long harmonic plan or making repeated statements of a fugue subject as the music

Benny Goodman

Venetian orchestra and choir of the 18th century

moved from key to key. Once set in motion, the rhythm of a Baroque work runs like a motor, carrying through to the end with a minimum of breath-catching cadences.

Classical music has many starts and stops, its sections being fitted together like the pieces in a mosaic or a stained-glass window. The movements are put together by balancing one short phrase with another short phrase, one entire section with another entire section. Architectural thinking of this sort was one of the great concerns of the Classical composers.

The mold into which these composers poured their inspiration was the Classical sonata. Written in two, three, or four movements, the sonata was a perfect vehicle for contrasts and surprises. The movements were not all in the same key, and each had its own tempo and its own form. Characteristic of the sonata was its first movement, usually written in sonata-allegro form. Like a large aria da capo form, the sonata-allegro form features the return of the whole first section

of the movement after a middle section which is a free fantasia (later called the "development"). Particularly in the middle section, the composer could be as daring as he wished in terms of sudden key contrasts and the showing of different possibilities of his themes.

The new music reached its audiences through the medium of new instruments and instrumental combinations. Small wind ensembles grew out of the eight-piece regimental band of Frederick the Great. On oboes, clarinets, horns, and bassoons small groups performed their light, entertaining divertimenti, serenades, and cassations—at private parties or for the public, passing the hat for donations. Haydn was for a time a member of such a group and wrote many divertimenti that are sheer delights. Mozart, Beethoven, and Schubert are others who contributed to the literature for these ensembles.

The newly invented piano was greatly improved in the course of Haydn's lifetime,

December 1994

11 SUN _____
12 MON _____
13 TUE _____
14 WED _____
15 THU _____
16 FRI _____
17 SAT _____

18 SUN _____
19 MON _____
20 TUE _____
21 WED _____
22 THU _____
23 FRI _____
24 SAT _____

and by the last two decades of the eighteenth century it had just about replaced the harpsichord. Not only could it be played powerfully or softly at will, but the loudness could be varied from note to note in the shaping of a musical phrase. Glittering runs and arpeggios could be heard above the sound of the small Classical orchestra. The concerto for piano and orchestra became a favored vehicle for showing off the skill of the pianist, who as often as not was the composer himself. The twenty-five piano concertos of Mozart are supreme in their field and did for the concerto forms what Haydn's works did for the string quartet.

It was at this time that the string quartet came of age, replacing the trio sonata as the most popular form of chamber music. Haydn, who for good reason is often called "the father of the string quartet," discovered the possibilities of music produced by two violins, a viola, and a cello, and as he grew older he deepened these possibilities by assigning important roles to all four of the instruments, thus setting the style for what has remained the most popular form of chamber music.

The string group became the foundation of the symphony orchestra. Many early symphonies were written mainly for strings along with two horns or flutes and timpani. Gradually more and more instruments were added. The woodwind family was enriched by the addition of the clarinet, first used by Stamitz, and composers took percussion instruments from the popular "Turkish" music of the day—the snare drum, bass drum, triangle, and cymbals (see JANISSARY MUSIC).

Operas, which had degenerated, theatrically, into strings of beautiful, showy arias, now became coherent works of art at the hands of Gluck and Mozart. The music, while still of primary importance, had to help make dramatic truth and serve to bring the story to its highest pitch of excitement and meaning.

As the Classical period drew to a close, it became clear that its own tendencies had undergone changes similar to those of society. Rather impersonal to begin with, it ended with great expression of personal feeling. Symbolic of this change was the giving way of the highly formalized minuet, the queen of dances, to the romantic waltz. The charming, aristocratic, new music of 1750 was replaced by the deeper and more dramatic music of Beethoven. Rebellion, patriotism, and individualism became subjects for art. In fifty years music had changed its aim: it set out to entertain, but ended enriching man's mind and soul.

CLAVICHORD: a small keyboard instrument, popular in the seventeenth and eighteenth centuries. When closed it looks like a box made of beautifully finished wood, about five feet wide, two feet from front to back, and five inches deep. It is small enough to be carried about and is placed on a table or on a stand when it is to be played. Its keys are smaller than those of the piano, with key colors often reversed, each octave having seven black keys and five white keys.

The sound of the clavichord is made by small brass squares, called tangents, which move up to hit the strings. There are usually two strings for each key, each string being of fine wire (in early clavichords there was but one string per key, or even one string for two keys). The metal tangent and the key are on opposite ends of a piece of wood. The wood is balanced on a pin so that when the key is pressed down, the tangent goes up and hits a pair of strings, setting them in motion. The clavichord is a very delicate instrument: if the key is hit too hard, the tangent can break the strings. The range of notes is not large, being only four and a half to five octaves:

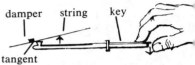

The Action of a Clavichord

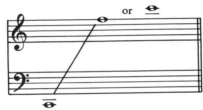

The sound of the clavichord is so light that it can barely be heard in one's living room, and the instrument is rarely used in concerts. Its great virtue is sensitivity: the tone can be given a vibrato by moving the

German clavichord of the early 18th century

Ralph Kirkpatrick playing the clavichord

key gently after the tone has been sounded *(Bebung)*, and the player can make crescendos and diminuendos. Since its expressive tone could not be matched on the bigger and more brilliant harpsichord, the clavichord was a favorite instrument of Bach and many other composers.

The clavichord is the oldest form of stringed keyboard instrument, with a history that goes back to the late Middle Ages. It was in great favor by the fifteenth century and again around 1780, particularly with C. P. E. Bach. By 1800 the piano, which was more versatile, had taken its place as an instrument for the home. But the clavichord has been rediscovered by musicians of today, and several instrument makers have begun making it.

CLEF: a sign placed at the beginning of each musical staff to indicate the pitches of the notes. Without a clef, a note on a staff has no meaning; this could be B, D. C, or A:

The clef is the key that opens the way to the reading of music.

There are three clefs: the C, the G, and the F clef. The G clef, or treble clef, centers around the second line of the staff and shows the G above middle C:

It is used for music that lies mostly above middle C. It is the clef used for soprano voices and instruments, and for the right-hand part in keyboard music.

The F clef, sometimes called the bass clef, curls around the fourth line of the staff and shows the F below middle C:

It is used for bass instruments and voices and the left-hand part in keyboard music.

The C clef can center on any line to show middle C. Only the alto and tenor clefs are in use today—the alto for viola parts and the tenor for bassoon, trombone, and cello when the music goes too high to be conveniently written on the bass staff:

Soprano   Alto   Tenor

CODA: an ending section designed to complete or round out a musical composition. (*Coda* is an Italian word meaning "tail.") It can be fairly short, as in the final cadence sections of many of Bach's fugues, or it can be quite long, as in many movements of Beethoven's symphonies and sonatas. Many of Beethoven's codas are, in effect, second large development sections that balance the earlier true development. The first movement of Beethoven's Third Symphony, the "Eroica," has a coda that is 140 measures long.

The coda comes at a point at which the composer has led the listener to believe the work is coming to an end. Then, with a spurt of new life, the music takes off in a series of new musical adventures. The coda, however, is not something that is simply plastered onto a work. It is something a composer feels is absolutely necessary to finish the architectural plan of his composition.

A *codetta* is a short coda, often to a part of a movement or work.

COL LEGNO: an Italian phrase that means "with the wood." With this phrase the composer instructs the violinist to play on the strings with the wooden back of the bow. The bow is usually bounced or tapped on the string, making a percussive sound rather than a stringlike sound. It is used for the effect of its color in Saint-Saëns' *Danse macabre*.

Modern composers utilize the col legno technique in string tremolos and melodic passages. The sound is rather eërie and glassy.

One of the most effective uses of this technique is to be found in the allegro misterioso movement of Alban Berg's *Lyric Suite*.

COLORATURA: a vocal melody decorated with trills, grace notes, leaps, and arpeggios. Though many coloratura arias are sung as concert pieces, these have usually been extracted from operas, such as those by Handel, Rossini, and Bellini, who wrote them for specific performers.

There are coloratura arias for all types of voice, including bass. The most famous coloratura soprano arias are "The Bell Song" from Delibes' *Lakme*, the Mad Scene from Donizetti's *Lucia di Lammermoor*, and the two arias for the Queen of the Night in Mozart's great opera *The Magic Flute*.

COMPOSER: someone who puts together sounds in a logical and meaningful way. The result may be a symphony, an opera, a popular song, or a percussion piece, depending on what the composer sets out to do. A composer must have both imagination and technique: imagination, to give him a vision of what he wants to write; technique, so that he can transform his vision into the reality of musical symbols. (Some composers, of course, cannot write down what they have composed. Many of the finest folk songs were sung for hundreds of years before anyone thought of putting them on paper. Their composers seem to have been born with an ability to create melodies.)

Most composers started their musical lives as performers. Many of them, Haydn for example, were boy sopranos in church choirs. As part of their musical education they studied music theory and learned to play one or more instruments. Usually their first works were imitations of the music they were performing. Under the guidance of a church organist or teacher of composition the young composer began to write more ambitious works. By the age of seventeen or eighteen he was a professional musician and composer.

Until 1800 the majority of composers were employed by churches or by wealthy noblemen who wanted music in their palaces. After 1800, following the example of Beethoven, composers earned their living partly by selling their works to publishers and partly by performing. Today, particularly in the United States, most composers are in the employ of colleges and universities.

Composers have approached their work in different ways. Some, like Mozart and Rossini, seem to have been able to compose as fast as they could write notes on paper. Others, such as Beethoven, toiled over every note, writing and rewriting until they had hammered each phrase into exactly the desired shape. A number of composers write at the piano, trying out each sound before committing it to paper. Others write away from the piano, hearing each sound accurately in their minds.

Many music lovers wonder how a composer hears in advance the sounds of an orchestra as he writes an orchestral score. The answer is that the composer has probably studied orchestration, either under a teacher or on his own. He has analyzed many orchestral scores and has a vivid memory of the sound of each instrument. Like a master chef who mentally combines ingredients as he invents a new dish, so a composer

Darius Milhaud

relies on memory and imagination to create orchestral colors.

Great composers through their large output have created a whole world of sound, ranging from light, short pieces to lengthy masterpieces. Bach wrote charming little "teaching pieces" for his children and his second wife as well as the monumental St. Matthew Passion. Wagner, who wrote almost nothing but operas, created tender, intimate scenes as well as those like the end of *Die Götterdämmerung,* in which flood and fire sweep everything away. Most of all, each great composer has given us a glimpse of the human spirit—at its tragic depths and its joyous heights.

John Cage

A concert at the old Gewandhaus, Leipzig (1845 woodcut)

Philharmonic Hall at Lincoln
Center

CONCERT: a program of music sung or played for an audience. (If there are only one or two performers, the program is called a recital.) So many concerts are presented today that it is hard to believe there was a time when there were none. For many centuries anyone who wanted to hear music had to play or sing it himself or go to church. A nobleman or wealthy merchant could hire musicians to perform for himself and his friends, or he might visit a court where there was an orchestra. In Italy opera houses were open to the public as early as 1637; but opera was a musical show, not a concert.

The first public concerts were given in London in 1672 by John Bannister, a violinist. After he died, the London concerts were continued for thirty years by a music-loving coal merchant, Thomas Britton. At first Britton did not charge for his concerts; later he sold yearly subscriptions. His audiences could buy coffee to drink as they listened to the music. The first concert hall to be built as such was raised at Oxford in 1748.

The idea of giving public concerts spread to Germany and France in the early 1700's. Vienna, the home of so many composers, did not have its first public concert until 1740.

In the United States there were concerts in Boston and in Charleston, South Carolina, as early as 1731. New York had its first public concert in 1736; it was given by Carl Theodore Pachelbel, son of a famous German composer. Pachelbel played on the harpsichord and was assisted by singers, a flutist, and a violinist. In 1744, concerts and chamber music were organized by the Germans who lived in Bethlehem, Pennsylvania.

Today so many concerts are given each year in the United States that no one has been able to give accurate figures on their number. In order to accommodate the audiences, concert halls have been or are being built as parts of cultural centers in every large city. Lincoln Center in New York City, containing, in part, Philharmonic Hall and several smaller halls, is the pioneer in this movement.

CONCERTINO: a concerto of modest dimensions. Often it is in one movement, and usually it is light in quality, as are the concertinos for piano by Piston, Honegger, and Françaix and for clarinet by Weber.

Concertino is also the name given to the group of soloists in the concerto grosso.

CONCERTMASTER: the leader of the first violins in a symphony orchestra. He sits directly to the left of the conductor, in the outside chair, and is a kind of assistant conductor with responsibilities of which the public is normally unaware. The concertmaster consults with the conductor as to the way in which the violin parts should be played. It is he who has the members of the orchestra tune to the oboist's A before the conductor appears on stage and who plays whatever violin solos occur in the course of the music.

The concertmaster is expected to be an outstanding musician; this tradition goes back to a time when he was, in fact, the conductor. Although a composer such as Haydn or Mozart led opera performances from the harpsichord, at an instrumental concert he was more likely to appear with a violin under his arm and lead the orchestra as a violinist. It is this sort of musicianship that has survived in the concertmaster's role to this day.

There are not many moments in symphonic literature that allow one to hear the concertmaster clearly. One score that does offer such moments is Rimsky-Korsakov's *Scheherazade.*

CONCERTO: an instrumental work, usually in three movements, which pits soloist against orchestra, small group against large, or instrumental family against the other instrumental families of the orchestra. The concerto gets its name from an Italian word meaning "to compete, or strive against." It was first used as a musical title around 1600 to describe a vocal work such as a madrigal which had instrumental accompaniment. The concerto has been a popular musical form for more than 250 years. Its lasting quality is due partly to the dramatic possibilities it offers to the composer, but even more to the fact that concertos are virtuoso pieces that challenge every outstanding instrumentalist.

The concerto for soloist and orchestra took shape in the hands of Corelli and Torelli in the late seventeenth century, and featured the recently perfected violin as the solo instrument. It was Vivaldi, however, who firmly established the Baroque style of the concerto, in the early eighteenth century, with his more than 400 works in this form.

Vivaldi's concertos were written for one to four violins, for flute, for bassoon, for two trumpets, and for various combinations of instruments. They followed, more or less, a three-movement pattern: a bustling first movement, a songlike slow movement, and a gay finale. The first movement was written in the ritornello form that first developed in the Italian opera aria. The orchestra of strings and keyboard instrument stated a bold, athletic theme—a kind of motto—that was easy to recognize. This theme was restated in various keys, with the soloist playing long virtuoso passages between statements. Sometimes the solo part is based on highly developed fragments of the ritornello theme; at other times it ignores the principal theme and brings in new material. The second movement was usually an aria or a series of variations over a ground bass. In this movement the soloist was expected to show his ability to embellish a melody, decorating the written notes with all kinds of fanciful patterns. The final movement was in a form similar to that of the first movement, but with a few more virtuoso fireworks to bring the work to a rousing finish.

Bach modeled his concertos on those of Vivaldi. As a matter of fact, he thought so highly of Vivaldi's concertos that he transcribed some of them for harpsichord solo and from others made concertos for from one to four harpsichords. Handel wrote concertos for oboe and for organ—those for organ to be played as interludes between sections of his oratorios.

About 1750 the piano began to replace the violin as the favorite solo instrument in the concerto, and the orchestra now included winds and timpani in addition to the strings. At the hands of Mozart, Haydn, and Beethoven the form of the concerto changed, particularly in its first movement, which was now written in Classical sonata-allegro form like the symphony and the sonata.

Mozart's concertos did for the Classical concerto form what Vivaldi's earlier concertos had done: they established the form and demonstrated its flexibility. The first movement, an allegro, has a double exposition, starting with an orchestral tutti in which the orchestra plays the whole exposition through, although remaining for the most part in the tonic key rather than modulating as would be customary in a sonata or symphony. The solo instrument then enters, usually with the first theme of the exposition but sometimes with a new but related theme. Solo and orchestra combine, answer each other, and alternately take over the center of the stage as the music follows the typical sonata-allegro form. The solo instrument is sometimes given the important thematic material; at other times it embroiders on the music of the orchestra. Just before the end of the movement the orchestra reaches a chord—the second inversion of the tonic—that seems to be leading to a closing cadence. Here the performer was originally expected to improvise a cadenza on the thematic material of the movement, showing off both his tech-

nique as a performer and as an improviser. (By the early 1800's the composer was usually writing his own cadenza, as a basic part of his work.) The cadenza ends in a long hammering trill to alert the orchestra, which then re-enters and finishes the movement. The second movement, usually in the subdominant but sometimes in the relative major or minor key, is usually slow and songlike in ternary, sonatine, or theme-and-variations form. The fast finale ends the concerto in a glittering display of the soloist's skills. It is most often in rondo form, although occasionally in sonata-allegro or theme-and-variations form, and, like the first movement, includes a cadenza.

The Classical concerto started as an elegant entertainment or display piece. Mozart and Beethoven deepened it, composing some of their noblest music in this form. Throughout the nineteenth century the concerto continued to be one of the most important of musical forms. Its first movement, although still following the sonata-allegro plan, often dispenses with the long orchestral tutti—as in Mendelssohn's Violin Concerto. The full-sized concert grand piano acquired the power to compete with the orchestra, as in the concertos of Schumann, Chopin, Liszt, Brahms, Grieg, Tchaikovsky, and Rachmaninoff. The violin was not ignored, and important concertos were written for it by Beethoven, Spohr, Paganini, Bruch, Wieniawski, Brahms, and Sibelius. Two mighty works for more than one soloist are Beethoven's Triple Concerto for violin, cello, and piano, and Brahms's Double Concerto for violin and cello.

Modern composers have added many significant works to the long list of concertos. Among them are Prokofiev's five concertos for piano and two for violin; Bartók's three concertos for piano and one for violin; Ravel's two concertos for piano (one of these for left hand alone); Berg's Concerto for Violin (his last completed work); Shostakovich's two concertos for piano; Stravinsky's Concerto for Violin, Concerto for Piano and Winds, and *Ebony Concerto* for clarinet and dance band. Bartók's, Piston's, and Gerhard's concertos for orchestra and Stravinsky's concertos for two pianos without orchestra are related to a seventeenth- and early eighteenth-century form of concerto, of which J. S. Bach's "Brandenburg" Concerto Number 3 is an example. Among the best-known concertos composed by Americans are the piano concertos by MacDowell, Gershwin, Barber, and Copland and the concertos for various other instruments by Schuman, Barber, and Copland.

An outstanding pianist, best known for his performances of piano concertos: Van Cliburn

CONCERTO GROSSO: one of the most popular instrumental forms of the Baroque period. In it a small group of instrumental soloists (the concertino) competes with and alternates with a larger group (the ripieno). Originating around 1700 in the writings of Corelli and Vivaldi, the concerto grosso had three to five movements. The first movement usually started with a slow, dignified opening like that of a French overture. This was followed by a muscular allegro in ritornello form in which the soloists alternated or joined with the large group. The other movements included an arialike adagio, several dances, and a closing allegro written in fugue or ritornello form.

The early solo group consisted of two soprano instruments, such as violins or flutes, and a bass instrument such as a cello or bassoon. The large group was made up of strings and a harpsichord which played a harmonic accompaniment realized from a figured bass. Vivaldi and Bach (in his "Brandenburg" Concertos) wrote for many different combinations of solo instruments.

The concerto grosso as a musical form was gradually dropped by composers in favor of the solo concerto, but in the twentieth century it was revived by Honegger and Bloch. Recently several interesting experiments have grown out of the old Baroque form, with a jazz group pitted against a symphony orchestra.

CONDUCTOR: one who directs an orchestra, chorus, or opera production. Conductors usually specialize in either orchestral or choral conducting and their tasks vary, but there are many elements in common.

The conductor has a difficult job—in fact, many jobs all rolled into one. He must study and memorize thousands of measures of music so that he can be free to turn from his score to look at his orchestra or chorus. (Someone has said that a conductor must have "the score in his head—not his head in the score.") He must drill his performers in rehearsal so that all the sounds become perfectly balanced. He must also be on the lookout for new works that he thinks his audience should hear. The orchestral conductor may be able to play only one instrument, but he is expected to know something about every instrument, so that he can make helpful suggestions to his players. A conductor must also be in good physical condition, like a well-trained athlete, because for several hours he will be moving about vigorously. He holds the baton at the height of his shoulder so that each member of the

orchestra can see him. The reader can get an idea of how this feels by waving a pencil held at shoulder height and seeing how long it takes for his arm to get tired.

The conductor keeps his musicians together by beating the pulse of the music with his baton or hands. Choral conductors usually give all signals with their hands, seldom using the baton, because though the baton is more precise, the hands are more capable of controlling the quality of voices. The first beat of a measure is always down, the last always up. The other beats are put in between the downbeat and the upbeat:

In slow music the beat is subdivided:

Leopold Stokowski

The conductor starts his music with a little warning beat to show the players exactly what the tempo is going to be. It is because of the warning beat that a conductor starts with an upward motion even when the music begins on the first beat of a measure. The size of the beat tells the players whether to play loudly or softly, a big motion calling for a big sound and a small motion calling for a soft one. There are crisp beats for music that needs precision and flowing beats for music the conductor wants to "sing."

The baton held in the conductor's right hand does only part of the work. The left hand gives all sorts of signals. The conductor may "shush" some instruments with his left hand while the baton is making big motions toward another group. The left hand or perhaps just a glance is used to warn a player to get ready. This "cueing" is one of the conductor's most important jobs.

The conductor must decide on his tempo and be able to hold it as though he had a metronome built into his mind and muscles. The conductor must discern what the composer was trying to say. Many different interpretations of the same work are heard, because each conductor sees each composition differently. He is like the director of a stage play who studies a play in advance until he is sure of its meaning, and only then decides how his actors and actresses must speak and move to make that meaning clear to an audience. Just as there are many different

Top left: *Arturo Toscanini*
Top right: *Sir Thomas Beecham*
Middle left: *George Szell*
Middle right: *Bruno Walter*

Bottom left: *Dimitri Mitropoulos*
Bottom right: *Herbert von Karajan*

ways of looking at Shakespeare's *Julius Caesar* and *Hamlet,* so there are different ways of looking at a work such as Mozart's Symphony in G Minor. For instance, one conductor will always keep the pulse steady; another will make retards and speed-ups in the music. One conductor will bring out all sorts of little melodies that are often overlooked; another will make the music build toward its high points. One will make the work sound tragic; another will make it elegant.

At the rehearsal every minute is precious. Big orchestras play a different concert each week for thirty or more weeks. The conductor has only ten or twelve hours to prepare a concert that will last for two hours. Difficult new works take a lot of time to learn. This is why conductors mix together new works and well-known ones.

If a composition is well known to the orchestra, at rehearsals the conductor may work only on tricky spots. If the work is new, he must be able to explain it to the performers so that they understand what they are to do. The conductor's ear must be so keen as to catch any mistakes in pitch, rhythm, or dynamics. He must listen carefully to be sure that an important melody in the flute is not smothered by the rest of the instruments. He must be able to spot the one instrument in a hundred that is flatting the pitch or coming in a tenth of a second too soon. He must be able to sing a phrase the way he wants it to sound. If there is a soloist in a concerto, the conductor must be able to follow him, no matter how much the soloist speeds up or slows down.

By the time of the concert the conductor has relatively little to do. He sets the tempo, beats the time, reminds players of things that were worked on at rehearsals, gives cues, and sparks the players with enthusiasm—playing on the orchestra as a good soloist plays on his instrument.

Different kinds of conducting present different sets of problems. The most difficult on-the-spot job is conducting an opera or a musical show. The conductor has to cue singers on the stage as well as the instrumentalists in the orchestra. (This is why opera singers usually stand so that they can see the conductor.) If there is dancing, the conductor must be able to play the music at exactly the right tempo. Ballet conductors "remember" in their muscles how fast or how slowly the dancers will move.

The great conductors in the past were usually composers also. Lully conducted his operas by pounding a big stick on the floor of the orchestra pit. Until the early 1800's the conductor was the concertmaster of an orchestra or the harpsichordist in the orchestra pit. Some conductors used a violin bow or a roll of music paper as a baton. Mendelssohn, Spohr, Berlioz, and Wagner, realizing that there was a technique to conducting, used batons and started the modern method of conducting. By the late 1800's conducting was so demanding that men no longer did it as a part-time job along with their composing or performing. The old idea of the conductor as just a time-beater died out. Such men as Von Bülow, Mahler, and Mengelberg made the conductor a true orchestra trainer and a music maker. In the 1920's and 1930's great conductors like Walter, Monteux, Beecham, Toscanini, Reiner, Koussevitzky, and Stokowski set the highest possible standards for their orchestras. Because of them the conductor has become the most important figure in music after the composer. The twentieth century is the age of virtuoso conductors, outstanding among whom are Szell, Von Karajan, Bernstein, and Steinberg.

Wilhelm Furtwängler

COPLAND, AARON (1900-   ): one of the first American composers to have his works played all over the world. Born in Brooklyn, New York, Copland did not begin to study music until he was thirteen, but once started he moved rapidly. His piano piece "The Cat and the Mouse" was published in 1921. That year he went to Paris and studied with Nadia Boulanger, becoming one of the first Americans to study in France rather than at a German conservatory.

Copland returned to the United States in 1924, and in 1925 wrote his *Music for the Theater.* This breezy, brassy work brought a fresh sound to music, using jazz as well as the "corny" sounds of a vaudeville orchestra. It is alternately boisterous and reflective. Greeted by musicians as the voice of a gifted young composer, it started Copland on his way to many successes, including the first Guggenheim fellowship for music in 1925, and many commissions and prizes.

In addition to composing, Copland leads a busy life as a lecturer, organizer of concerts to give hearings to other composers, conductor of new music by himself and others, and teacher of students from all over the world at the Berkshire Music Center. He has written four books: *What to Listen for in Music, The New Music, Music and Imagination,* and *Copland On Music.*

Copland has always felt that a composer should participate in and contribute to all aspects of music and society. He believes

An early portrait of Aaron Copland

A scene from Copland's Billy the Kid

Copland and Goodman at a recording session

Quartet (1950), *Piano Fantasy* (1957), and *Nonet* (1960) are masterful. The music is sparse and rugged, as though chiseled out of rock. The melodies move in large leaps (Ex. 34). They are often built from short motives. As the music moves along, the motives grow as more notes are added (Ex. 35). Copland's harmonies are dissonant, even when the chords seem to be simple:

Sonata for Violin and Piano

col 8va

His rhythm is jagged and nervous; he likes to change the meter of his music from measure to measure, and to pile up sounds from the bottom to the top of the piano:

Piano Fantasy

Copland's music is not always rock-hewn; it can be tender and intensely personal. He never does anything just to be different. Ruggedly honest in his music, he uses the sounds necessary to say what he intends.

composers should write for audiences of different kinds. For young performers he has created such works as his opera *The Second Hurricane* (1937) and his *Outdoor Overture* (1938) for high-school orchestra. He has written music that is tuneful, rhythmic, and colorful, and easy to follow, such as his *El Salón México* and *Four Piano Blues. Billy the Kid* (1938) and *Rodeo* (1942), his ballets, use melodies that are like cowboy and square-dance tunes. His *Appalachian Spring,* for which he received a Pulitzer Prize, is warm and flowing as it captures a bygone day in America's past. His setting of Lincoln's words in *A Lincoln Portrait* (1942), for speaker and orchestra, uses old folk tunes, such as "Springfield Mountain." His opera, *The Tender Land* (1954), is full of the flavor of the Midwest. In his music for movies, such as *Our Town* (1940) and *The Red Pony* (1948), Copland is most expressive and dramatic.

More difficult to understand and lacking the immediate impact of his more theatrical efforts are Copland's chamber music and symphonic works. His *Piano Variations* (1930), *Sextet* (1937), *Sonata for Piano* (1941), *Sonata for Violin and Piano* (1943), *Piano*

Ex. 34 — *Piano Fantasy*

Moderate tempo

Ex. 35 — *Sonata for Violin and Piano*

CORELLI, ARCANGELO (1653–1713): composer, and founder of the modern method of violin playing. Born in Fusignano, Italy, he studied violin playing and counterpoint in Bologna, and moved to Rome when he was eighteen. Here, except for trips to Naples, Modena, and Munich, he spent the rest of his life composing, playing, and teaching.

Corelli became a kind of composer-in-residence in the palace of his benefactor, Cardinal Ottoboni. He could have lived in the grand manner, but instead spent most of his money buying paintings, for which he had a passion. Handel, whose music was greatly influenced by that of Corelli, was shocked when he visited the master violinist, finding him dressed in shabby clothes and accustomed to walking everywhere instead of hiring a carriage.

Corelli conducted a regular series of concerts at the cardinal's palace. He also taught such important violinist-composers as Geminiani and Locatelli, but his greatest contribution was his music: forty-eight sonatas in groups of twelve; twelve concerti grossi (a form he brought into being); and twelve sonatas for violin, later arranged as concerti grossi by his pupil Geminiani.

Corelli's style of writing for the violin was directly related to his innovations in violin technique. His slow movements demand that the performer play with a beautiful singing tone and improvise elaborate decorations on the long notes. In passage work Corelli asked the performer to play several notes with one bow stroke; heretofore violinists had always played one note per bow. Corelli also established the playing of double and triple stops (playing two or three strings

Arcangelo Corelli

at the same time) as part of the violinist's basic technique.

His themes generally are tuneful and outline the basic harmony (Ex. 36). He uses counterpoint that is not tightly knit, like that of Bach, but serves to set off his principal melody (Ex. 37).

The music of Corelli influenced not only his students but also Purcell, Vivaldi, Handel, and Bach.

Ex. 36 — Giga from Sonata No. 9,

Ex. 37— Gavotta from Sonata No. 11,

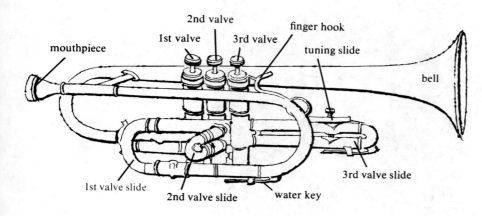

mouthpiece
2nd valve
1st valve
3rd valve
finger hook
tuning slide
bell
1st valve slide
2nd valve slide
water key
3rd valve slide

CORNET: a three-valved soprano member of the brass family, related to the trumpet (which is not short and fat) and the flügelhorn (which is fatter). The three instruments look so much alike that it is actually hard to tell the difference. The cornet has a deep mouthpiece, and its tube is one-third cylindrical and two-thirds conical; the trumpet has a shallow mouthpiece, and its tube is two-thirds cylindrical and one-third conical; the flügelhorn has a deep mouthpiece and an almost all-conical bore. In actual sound the cornet and flügelhorn are quite close, while the trumpet has a more brilliant sound than either. In practice many cornet players use a trumpet mouthpiece, making the sounds of these instruments almost identical.

The cornet, which is a B-flat transposing instrument, has the same range as the trumpet: from F# below the treble staff to about high E above the staff.

From the days of its origin in the early 1820's the cornet has been a favorite among brass virtuosos. It is very flexible and has a wide variety of tone colors. Runs, large leaps, high tones, and low tones—all the fireworks anyone would want are possible on the cor-

net. It is still the most popular solo instrument at band concerts, where it is used to play sentimental transcriptions of songs or show-off pieces such as Arban's "Carnival of Venice."

Most symphonic composers have preferred the aristocratic trumpet to the humble cornet, although in the band the cornet is given the solos and the trumpet merely fills in. French and Russian composers, however, have used the cornet to fine advantage: Stravinsky in his *Histoire du soldat* and *Petrouchka,* Tchaikovsky in his *Swan Lake,* Bizet in *Carmen,* and Franck in his Symphony in D Minor.

In music written between 1600 and 1800, composers used a family of instruments called *cornetts*—not related to the cornet of today. These were instruments with a shallow brass mouthpiece and a body made of wood or ivory. The body had finger holes like a recorder's. The cornett was used by Bach in his choral works to play along with the sopranos and altos of his chorus. The last member of the cornett family to be used was the strange-looking "serpent," which, shaped so that the player could cover all the holes with his fingers, served as the bass of the brass family until the invention of the tuba in 1835.

COUNTERPOINT: the weaving together of two or more melodic lines to make a tightly knit, complex musical texture. Not just any combination of melodies makes an acceptable counterpoint. The pitches of the melodies must be controlled by the composer so that at regular rhythmic points desired harmonic sounds, whether consonant or dissonant, occur. Rhythm, too, is controlled by the composer so that there is contrast between the various voices. One voice may hold a tone while the other voice runs along in quick notes (Ex. 38). The composer also controls the direction of contrapuntal melodies

Ex. 38— *The Musical Offering*, J.S. Bach

so that all the lines do not move in the same direction at the same time.

There are various types of counterpoint. A new melody can be added to an already existing melody, as when one sings a descant to a well-known tune. This cantus firmus technique is the basis of many great choral works. Composers also use this technique to give added interest to a melody on its repetition, as in many symphonies (Ex. 39).

Another way to make counterpoint is to write two or more melodies that fit together. Neither melody, perhaps, is complete in itself; as with a pair of scissors, both parts are needed. This type of counterpoint is often written so that the positions of the melodies can be exchanged: the top melody fits just as

well on the bottom. This is known as invertible or double counterpoint (Ex. 40a and b).

A third type of counterpoint is canon, or imitative counterpoint. All the voices sing or play the same melody, but each voice starts at a different time. Rounds are simple examples of this construction.

Counterpoint got its name from its mode of origin more than a thousand years ago. One note was placed above or below another note. The Latin phrase for this was *punctus contra punctum,* "note against note," and *contrapuncta* became counterpoint. At first the notes that were placed together made harmonic intervals of fourths, fifths, and octaves (see the second example in Organum,

Ex. 39 — Symphony No. 5, Tchaikovsky

Ex. 40 — Invention No. 6, J.S. Bach

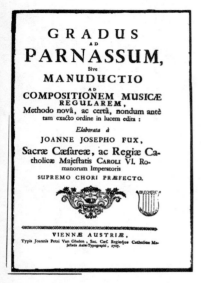

Frontispiece (above) and title page (below) of the first edition of Gradus ad Parnassum by J.J. Fux

page 393). By the fifteenth century the sweeter-sounding thirds and sixths were added (see the Rondeau under Harmony, page 230). The dissonant intervals of seconds and sevenths and the diminished and augmented intervals were used sparingly until 1600. Then composers discovered how the dissonant intervals could add expressiveness to their music. A dissonant interval was always followed by a consonant interval, leading from tension to relaxation. This is the type of counterpoint used by Bach, Mozart, and Beethoven. Modern composers use both dissonant and consonant intervals, but often string together a succession of dissonant sounds without resolving any of them to a consonance.

In many compositions of the eighteenth and nineteenth centuries counterpoint and harmony are mixed together. (It is almost impossible to write one without the other.) The composer writes what looks to be a simple chordal accompaniment, but if the important tones are played by themselves they form lines of counterpoint. A good performer makes his music sound interesting by searching for these melodies (Ex. 41).

Almost every composer has used counterpoint. Many musical forms, such as canon, fugue, motet, madrigal, and ricercar, have grown out of this practice. Landmarks in the development of counterpoint are the masses of Palestrina, the motets and madrigals of Lassus, the fugues of Bach, the late quartets of Beethoven, the finale of Mozart's "Jupiter" Symphony, the prelude to Wagner's *Die Meistersinger,* and the chamber music of Brahms. Most modern composers use counterpoint as a basic ingredient of their music. The music of Schoenberg, Webern, and their disciples is based almost completely on counterpoint. Hindemith's *Mathis der Mahler* and Stravinsky's *Symphony of Psalms* are as much based on the weaving together of melodic lines as was the music of the six-

teenth century. Some contemporary composers, starting with the American Charles Ives, have used masses of sound against each other—like two or three bands in a parade, playing different works in different tempos. The resulting counterpoint, while not always sweetly harmonious, is almost overpowering when well done, as in Ives's Fourth Symphony.

Counterpoint is often thought to be dry and scholarly. Until recently it was taught as a series of rules and drills, following an orderly progression based on the "species" of counterpoint found in the *Gradus ad Parnassum (Steps to Parnassus)* written by J. J. Fux in 1725. In species counterpoint the student learns all the rules relative to putting one note against another, two notes to one, and so on:

This pedantic approach has given way to a study of contrapuntal music itself, with the student deducing his own rules and writing not exercises but musical examples.

Ex. 41— "Thanks to the Brook," Schubert

COUPERIN, FRANÇOIS (1668–1733): one of the greatest composers of the Baroque period, and one of the subtlest and most musicianly minds France has produced. Couperin was born in a musical family that originally came from the county of Brie, east of Paris (today more famous for its cheese). His father was one of three brothers who had come to the attention of the harpsichordist Chambonnières, who had brought them to Paris and sponsored their entry into Paris musical life. One of the brothers, Louis Couperin, became organist at the old Paris church of St. Gervais. When he died in 1661, he was succeeded by his youngest brother Charles, who was François Couperin's father. When Charles Couperin died, young François was only ten; so the job at St. Gervais was saved for him until he was eighteen and ready for it.

In the early years of Couperin's professional life as an organist he wrote his first compositions: some organ masses and some sonatas in the manner of Corelli. But the big break in his career did not come until 1693, when he entered the king's service as one of the four organists of the King's Chapel. At this time Louis XIV was in trouble. The ministers who had been the most skilled at managing the country for him were dead and the neighboring European nations, against which his armies had made many victorious forays in former days, now had finally banded against him.

Music, Louis XIV suddenly discovered, meant a great deal to him, and Couperin's work pleased him especially. Within a year, Couperin was appointed harpsichord teacher to the royal children, and two years later he was raised to the nobility. In the early years of the 1700's, while Louis XIV was embroiled in the expensive and seemingly endless War of the Spanish Succession, Couperin dissipated the royal melancholy with motets and with programs of chamber music (the so-called *Concerts royaux*) and secular cantatas, presented at Sunday concerts over which he presided from the harpsichord. In the last years of the king's life (Louis died in 1715), Couperin composed an extraordinary series of Tenebrae psalms for the dark days preceding Easter. Three of these have survived. Intended for one and two voices, they are as highly stylized as anything any Baroque composer ever wrote, and yet they manage to be, at the same time, intensely personal and deeply moving.

The year 1713 saw the publication of the first volume of Couperin's harpsichord music: *Premier Livre de clavecin (First Book for the Harpsichord)*. Three further volumes ap-

peared in later years. Each was put together according to the same plan; that is, it was divided into a half dozen sets of pieces which most composers would call suites but which Couperin called *ordres*. Each *ordre* has its own key signature and contains stylized dances. Many of these individual dances have titles referring to pupils, dancers, his daughters, or the musicians' union, or portray such things as birds, a limping man, or even a goblin. Every aspect of the harpsichord is brought into play—the plucked attack of each tone, the transparency with which each voice allows the other voices to be heard through it, the contrast between the various registers, the vibrant richness of the full chords. Tense dissonances and elaborate decorations suddenly give place to moments of an apparent simplicity that hardly any other composer

Top: *Charles Couperin, father of François, by Claude Lefèvre*
Bottom: *François Couperin*

Ex. 42 — Chaconne: "La Favorite"

Ex. 43 — Passacaille from Ordre No. 8

could match—as in the chaconne, entitled "La Favorite," that appears in the First Book (see Ex. 42, above). But Couperin also had tremendous reserves of power, as one discovers in the B-minor Passacaglia of the Second Book, which brings out the majesty of the age of Louis XIV in its full splendor (Ex. 43).

The harpsichord suites have come down to us engraved with the greatest care. The neatness and orderliness of Couperin's mind also expressed itself in his instructions for the performance of his music. In 1716 was issued his *L'Art de toucher le clavecin (The Art of Playing the Harpsichord)* in which he shows the performer how to finger passages of various kinds and how to accompany, and also how to go about executing the fanciful ornaments that occur throughout Couperin's scores. It has become a bible to players of French Baroque music.

Couperin's harpsichord pieces are mostly short, and written for a single instrument. Yet, as one hears them, limitless perspectives seem to open out. Some special quality of mind—perhaps the combination of an irrepressible imaginativeness with an uncommon passion for clarity—must have enabled Couperin to achieve this effect. Whatever it was, it was fully appreciated by his contemporaries. Bach, for instance, had a tremendous respect for Couperin's artistry and used his work as a model for his "French" Suites as well as for many of his miscellaneous dance movements. It is known that Bach entered into correspondence with Couperin,

but his letters have not survived. Some not very farsighted members of the Couperin household used them, perhaps, to cover jam pots.

Couperin's last harpsichord collection came out in 1730, with a sad farewell in the preface: "I hope my family will find in my portfolios something that will cause me to be regretted, if regrets are of any use after death. . . ." He died three years later. His family never did publish the scores he left behind, and now they are lost.

Couperin belonged to the next-to-last generation of the Baroque period. When he died in 1733, Rameau, Bach, D. Scarlatti, and Handel were scaling the era's last great heights. They could look back on Couperin as a man whose subtlety, clarity, and unfailing professionalism set a standard for them all.

COURANTE: a favorite dance at the French court from 1550 to 1750. Its name is the French word for "running": the courante was originally a dance in which the dancers leaped and ran. But it did not start in France. It started in Italy (as the *corrente*) and did not appear in France till the time of Catherine de' Medici's arrival there in 1533; from France it spread to England and Germany. The music for the courante was in a meter of three; the tempo was fast, and the melody was filled with running eighth notes, as in Ex. 44, next page, a courante by Handel.

Ex. 44 — Harpsichord Suite No. 14, Handel

Ex. 45 — Suite No. 5, Purcell

Ex. 46 — Ordre No. 1, Couperin

Dancing the courante

A second type of courante, originally called the *branle de Poitou,* did come from France. In this form it did not have as much running and leaping: the dancers glided slowly while making gallant gestures, and there were not so many short notes in the melody. Ex. 45 is the beginning of a Purcell courante in this style. This courante is so serious in mood that at one time it was called *la danse des docteurs.* Its popularity lasted well into the time of the minuet, and a bitter rivalry smoldered between teachers of the two dances.

By the late seventeenth century, composers were making the slow variety of the courante so complicated in its rhythm that it could no longer be danced to. They would take two measures of 3/4 time and make them into one measure of 6/4 time; this might be followed by a measure in which the six counts would be divided into three sets of 2/4. (These meters as such are not indicated in the music. The performer has to discover how the composer meant each measure to be played.) This type of courante can be seen in the example above by Couperin, who wrote many courantes in this elegant and complicated style (Ex. 46). Bach, who greatly admired Couperin's style and workmanship, included

courantes of this type in his Fourth Partita and in his Third "French" Suite.

In suites and partitas, in which it was customary to follow slow dances with fast ones, the courante was placed after the allemande.

CRESCENDO: a term (Italian, "increasing") meaning "gradually getting louder." Any musical passage that increases in volume is called a crescendo. This is a device used by composers for dramatic and expressive purposes, having been first called for in Italian opera scores of the early 1700's.

Different instruments make crescendos in different ways. On percussion instruments, including the piano, several tones are needed to make a crescendo, each tone being struck a bit harder than its predecessor. (A timpani roll with a crescendo is one of the easiest and most effective means of achieving dramatic suspense.) Crescendo becomes most expressive with instruments capable of sustaining a tone for a long time—voices, strings, and winds. Here the effect of a crescendo is that of making the tone seem to topple into the next tone. A small crescendo followed by a diminuendo, as in Tchaikovsky's *Symphonie pathétique,* gives the suggestion of a musical sigh (see Ex. 6 on page 588).

Much of the fame of the first great orchestra, the Mannheim orchestra, came from its well-drilled and well-publicized crescendos. Musicians came from all over Europe to hear the "Mannheim crescendo." Rossini, too, was famous for this device in his overtures. But it was Beethoven who used the crescendo to erupt from calmness to tremendous vigor, as in the crescendo linking the end of the scherzo movement to the finale of his Fifth Symphony. A deafening thirteen-bar crescendo on the tone B-natural is a basic part of the drama in the third act of Alban Berg's *Wozzeck.*

The abbreviation for crescendo is "cresc." The "swell" sign, ———, also is used to show a crescendo. This allows the composer to show exactly where and how softly a crescendo starts and where and how loudly it ends:

p   *ff*

At right: small cymbals were known in Madrid, Spain—illustration from the 13th-century manuscript Cantigas de Santa Maria

CYCLIC FORM: a method of organizing a large musical work so that a theme appears and reappears in several or all movements. The best-known example of cyclic form is Berlioz's *Symphonie fantastique.* In this work a theme representing The Beloved—the "fixed idea," as Berlioz calls it—occurs in altered versions in each movement of the symphony. While Berlioz used his "fixed idea" for dramatic reasons, other composers have used cyclic forms to forge a unity between movements of a large work. The earliest examples of this approach are to be found in the cyclic masses by Dufay and other fifteenth- and sixteenth-century composers. In these works the same Gregorian chant melody or popular tune—"The Armed Man" was a favorite—was used as a basis for the counterpoint in each section of the mass.

Many composers of the nineteenth century adopted the principle of cyclic form, including Beethoven (Symphony Number Five), Schumann (Symphony Number Four), Franck (Symphony in D Minor), and Dvořák (Symphony Number Five, "From the New World"). Schoenberg's use of the same twelve-tone row throughout his *Suite for Piano,* Opus 25, is a contemporary version of cyclic form.

CYMBALS: round brass plates that have a special timbre, or tone color, but no particular pitch. The best ones formerly came from China and Turkey, where the exact composition of the brass was a closely guarded family secret. Basically it was a brass in which the copper was alloyed with tin rather than zinc. The finest cymbals today are those made by the Zildjians, an Armenian family with branches in Istanbul and Boston. The name Zildjian means cymbal maker.

Cymbals are played in several ways. The player can hold a pair, by leather straps passed through a hump in their centers, and clash them together—not crashing them head-on but bringing them together with a sliding motion so that each cymbal is free to keep on ringing after the contact. If the player rubs them together lightly they will make a soft *tsing,* but if he throws them against each other with all his strength they will produce a crash that will go on resounding for a long time. The player can always stop the sound by pressing the cymbals to his body ("choking" them).

Cymbals can be played singly rather than in pairs. In this technique a cymbal is hung from a stand and hit with timpani sticks, and the player chokes it by grabbing it with his hand. Composers sometimes use a soft, rapid roll on a hanging cymbal to create suspense, with a long crescendo to build to a climax. In marching bands one cymbal is fixed to the bass drum so that the drummer plays cymbals with one hand, the bass drum with the other.

In dance bands the drummer often plays the cymbals with his feet: two small cymbals are connected to a pedal, and the drummer presses his foot down to bring them together.

Cymbals came to Europe with the Turkish military bands in the late seventeenth and early eighteenth centuries. The first use of cymbals in a European orchestra has been traced to a German composer named Strungk and dates from 1680. Mozart, who lived during a great craze for Turkish Janissary music in Vienna, included a part for cymbals in his *Abduction from the Seraglio* (1782). By the 1800's cymbals were no longer felt to be specifically Turkish; composers valued them simply for their power and color. Berlioz prized their exhilarating noisiness, and Tchaikovsky used them to give an exuberant quality to the finale of his Fourth Symphony. It was only after their capacity for sheer noisiness had been satisfactorily established that their less obvious possibilities were explored: in the 1890's Debussy used them softly in *Fêtes,* and in 1936 Copland used a "choked" cymbal to bring out the syncopations of his *El Salón México.* Bartók, in the score of his *Sonata for Two Pianos and Percussion,* specified that the edge of the cymbal was to be touched with the blade of a penknife.

Modern cymbals have no fixed pitch, but those used in ancient Greece and Egypt were of a different sort. They were small, being held somewhat like castanets, and came in various sizes, each of definite pitch. Europe came to know them during the archaeological spree of the nineteenth century, Berlioz using them in his "Queen Mab" Scherzo and Debussy in *The Afternoon of a Faun.* They are called *cymbales antiques* in Berlioz's and Debussy's scores and *crotales* in Ravel's.

In orchestral scores the cymbal part is sometimes written on a single line:

Cymbal Part

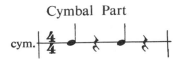

The part is often marked *piatti,* the Italian word for cymbals. Since the cymbal part is usually played by the percussionist who handles the bass drum, scores often show the two parts combined on one staff:

CZERNY, CARL (1791–1857): an Austrian composer of a thousand compositions, many of them large works such as sonatas and concertos; but, to piano students, the man who wrote the hundreds of études that must be practiced to develop technique in piano playing.

Czerny was born in Vienna, Austria. When nine years old he played the piano so well that his teacher took him to Beethoven, who became his teacher and later his friend. Czerny was nervous when he played in public, and at sixteen gave up the idea of a career as a concert pianist, becoming a teacher instead. He had great influence as a teacher, his most famous pupil being Franz Liszt. One by-product of his teaching was his complete edition of the keyboard works of J. S. Bach, the first ever published. Because of his admiration for Beethoven, he attempted to edit the pieces in accordance with his memories of the way Beethoven had played them. Since styles and instruments had changed between the time of Bach and the time of Beethoven, Czerny's edition of Bach was a distorted one.

Czerny's own music was popular while he lived. Publishers pleaded with him to turn out more and more music. He did. But all his works sounded alike and people tired of them. Today his big, serious compositions are played rarely. All that remains of his work is the études, such as those in his *Die Schule der Geläufigkeit (The School of Velocity).*

Carl Czerny

D: the white key between the two black keys on the piano. It is called *ré* in France and Italy.

The third string of the violin, the second string of the viola and cello, and the fourth string of the guitar are tuned to D. There are five D's on or near the staff:

The key signature for D major is shown in Ex. a, the key signature for D minor in Ex. b, for D-flat major in Ex. c, and for D-sharp minor in Ex. d:

Among the many famous compositions in D major are the violin concertos by Brahms and Beethoven, the Second Symphonies of Brahms and Beethoven, Mozart's "Haffner" Symphony, and Haydn's Symphony Number 101 and Symphony Number 104. Beethoven's Ninth Symphony begins in D minor and ends in D major.

Composers of virtuoso piano works, such as Liszt and Chopin, very often wrote in the key of D-flat major. For the expert pianist this key lies nicely under the hands and allows for rapid passage work. D-sharp minor is seldom used. In each volume of *The Well-tempered Clavier* there is a fugue in D-sharp minor. In Book II, the accompanying prelude is also in D-sharp minor. In Book I, Bach writes the companion prelude in the enharmonic key of E-flat minor. One of the most-performed piano works in D-sharp minor is Scriabin's rousing Étude Opus 8, Number 12.

Dancers of the New Stone Age (drawing found in the Hoggar Mountains of North Africa)

DA CAPO: an Italian phrase, appearing at the end of a musical movement, which tells the performer to go back to the beginning. Sometimes the phrase reads *da capo al fine* or, abbreviated, *D.C. al fine.* The performer is thereby instructed to go back to the beginning and play until the word *fine* appears. It is taken for granted that no section of the repeated part will be played twice, even if it contains repeat marks. To be quite sure

of this, the composer will sometimes write *D.C. senza repetizione*—"da capo without repeats."

It is an instruction composers first found to be convenient in the Baroque period, when many operatic arias were written in strict ternary, or A-B-A, form. After all, if part A reappears at the end of the piece, why go to the trouble of recopying and re-engraving it? It is simpler to put the instruction *da capo* (or *D.C.*) at the end of part B.

The D.C. sign is often found at the end of the trio section of minuets and scherzos, where the same conventions apply.

The aria da capo was a favorite musical form of the eighteenth century. It was usually a vocal solo in an opera or an oratorio. Most of the arias by Bach and Handel are da capo arias.

DAL SEGNO: an Italian phrase indicating a repeat, starting at the sign. The sign ∿ is usually placed after a short introduction that the composer does not want repeated. The music is repeated from the sign to the word *fine.* The abbreviation for *dal segno* is *D. S.* or *D. S. al fine.*

DANCE MUSIC: music composed to accompany movement. Its main characteristics are a fairly obvious pulse, regularly recurring accents, and strong cadences marking the ends of phrases.

There are four main types of dance music: ritual, social, exhibition, and concert. Of course, these categories are no more rigid that the dances themselves. A social dance form such as the waltz became an ingredient in the exhibition form of dance known as ballet. A composition written to be danced to, such as Ravel's *Daphnis and Chloé,* is most often heard as a concert piece.

Music owes more to dance than to any other influence. In fact, dance music is probably the oldest kind of music, going back to the time when both dance and music were part of primitive rituals. Man danced to the accompaniment of percussion instruments and voice as he prayed to the gods to make the crops grow, to give him victory in battle, or to restore him to health. Such ritual dancing relies greatly on the repetition of words or movement; thus the music for primitive dances is itself repetitive. It was to achieve the feeling of primitive ritual that Stravinsky used repetitive, percussive rhythmic patterns and snatches of melody in his music for the ballet *The Rite of Spring.* While certain contemporary composers have used primitive

ritual as a basis for music, however, the ritual dance itself has not been important in European history. It has been the social forms of dance that have served as the greatest inspiration to musicians. Such social dances as the medieval court estampies, the carol or chorale, and the various village dances whose names have not come down in history (if they were ever named) gave rise to forms of instrumental music and often provided a reason for instruments to develop. One thinks of the gigue, or fiddle, the pipe and drum, the many types of bagpipes and horns—all of which were used mainly to accompany dancing and all of which led to various modern instruments. From medieval dance music, too, came regularly phrased music. While composers of church music were writing a continuous flow of sound in their intricate polyphonic music, the composer of social dance music had to provide cadences in his music to signal the dancers at the end of one phrase and the beginning of the next. Dance music could not flow as church music could. It had to propel the dancers—and to some extent imitate the sound of the dancers' foot patterns. So from dance music came such important musical concepts as regular meter and balanced phrases.

The social dances of the Renaissance period—the bassedanse, a gliding dance; the pavane, a processional dance; the volta, a turning dance; and the galliard, a leaping dance—became the basis of many purely instrumental works for small ensembles, harpsichord, or lute. The combination of two dances—the slow pavane followed by the fast galliard, for example—became the basis of the first instrumental suite. Poets and composers such as Gastoldi and Morley took the rhythms of these dances and transformed them into madrigals and balletti. (See MADRIGAL.)

English keyboard composers, including Byrd and Bull, made dance melodies serve as foundations on which they spun elaborate variations. Dance musicians have always been partial to the making of variations. Rather than play the same eight- or sixteen-measure phrase over and over without changes, it was more interesting to retain the essence of a dance melody and still make something different of it on each repetition. Such improvisational practices among dance musicians led not only to the theme-and-variations forms of the English composers but to such important Baroque art-music forms as the chaconne and passacaglia—both of which were originally dances. In the twentieth century the essential ingredient of jazz is that it is a series of improvised variations.

Top left: *early Etruscan dancing girl*
Top right: *maenad in a Dionysiac dance*
Middle: *Etruscan dancers (drawing from tomb of the Triclinium, c. 470 B.C.)*
Bottom left: *a Renaissance dance (miniature from a French manuscript, Caroles et ménestrels)*

France under Louis XIII and Louis XIV became the dance capital of Europe. Here a whole new group of ballroom dances came into favor: first the allemande, courante, saraband, and gigue; later the minuet, gavotte, bourrée, rigaudon, and passepied. Of these, the minuet became the "queen of dances," holding sway until 1800, when it was replaced in popularity by the waltz.

Early French ballets were danced mostly by noble amateurs. But as ballets became staged works, in the ballets and operas of Lully in the late seventeenth century, the need was for technically trained professional dancers. For a while they danced to the same dance music that might be used in the ballroom. Then, as ballet became more expressive, choreographers demanded a new kind of dance music—one that was comparable to miming. This gestural music is found first in the ballets of the eighteenth-century composer Rameau and was developed further by Gluck, Beethoven, and other composers of the nineteenth century.

In the meantime many seventeenth- and eighteenth-century composers, following the lead of the German composer Froberger

Top left: *Irene and Vernon Castle, the dance team that popularized the fox trot and the tango*
Top right: *"La Valse" in 1840, after a lithograph by David*
Middle: *Valentino dancing the tango in* The Four Horsemen of the Apocalypse
Bottom right: *Dancing the frug, 1966*

(1616–67), turned to dance music for their purely instrumental works. One early branch of the sonata family—the sonata da camera, or chamber sonata—was actually a suite of dances. While these suites and sonatas used the dance rhythms of the allemande, courante, saraband, and gigue, the music was meant to be listened to rather than danced to. Among the great works that are dance-inspired are the suites and partitas of Bach and Handel and the charming keyboard works by Rameau and Couperin.

The Baroque period ended long before 1800, although a few of the old social dances such as the minuet and gavotte lingered on. Nineteenth-century Europe soon had its own popular dances, coming from middle Europe: the mazurka and polonaise from Poland, the polka from Bohemia, and, most important, the waltz from Austria. Musically, these dances too had their social forms (the waltzes of Lanner and Strauss), their exhibition forms (the waltzes of Tchaikovsky's ballets), and their art forms (the mazurkas and polonaises of Chopin).

As nineteenth- and twentieth-century composers looked to the dance music of their own and other countries for inspiration, ballet and concert music became increasingly exotic. One has only to think of Liszt's *Hungarian Rhapsodies,* Brahms's *Hungarian Dances,* and the Spanish dance rhythms used by Bizet, Rimsky-Korsakov, Albéniz, Debussy, Ravel, and Falla.

The Diaghilev Russian Ballet of the early twentieth century commissioned works for dance that have become acknowledged masterpieces in the realm of concert music: Stravinsky's *The Firebird, Petrouchka,* and *The Rite of Spring,* and Ravel's *Daphnis and Chloé.* Other ballet companies and American theater dance companies commissioned such scores as Stravinsky's *Agon,* Copland's *Rodeo* and *Appalachian Spring,* Shostakovich's *Golden Age,* and Prokofiev's *Romeo and Juliet.*

In social dance, the period of World War I saw first the South American tango, then the various dances performed to jazz music, sweep away the nineteenth-century dance forms, except the waltz. Jazz—which comes partly from dance, partly from folk song—has inspired much concert music (Stravinsky, Ravel, Copland, Milhaud) as well as ballets, musical comedies, and operas (Bernstein, Gershwin, Weill, Krenek). The latest social dances that have grown out of rock 'n' roll have not as yet called forth new ballets or concert works. If the past history of dance music is a good indicator, they might.

See BALLET MUSIC; JAZZ.

DEBUSSY, CLAUDE ACHILLE (1862–1918): one of the most original composers in the history of music. He was born in St. Germain-en-Laye, a suburb of Paris. His family moved to the big city when he was quite young, and at the age of nine he began to study the piano with a former pupil of Chopin. When he was eleven, he was accepted as a student at the Paris Conservatory, where he stayed for the next eleven years studying piano, theory, and composition.

At the conservatory, Debussy soon became known as a musical rebel. He did not believe in the unmusical rules of music theory that were taught; he spent his time searching for new chords and new kinds of melody. A trip to Russia in the employ of Mme. von Meck, wealthy patroness of Tchaikovsky, opened the ears of Debussy—then in his late teens—to the colorful Russian folk music, the wild music of the gypsies, and the startlingly different music of Borodin, Balakirev, and Mussorgsky.

Returning to the conservatory, he irritated his teachers more than ever with his dissonant harmonies and unusual chord progressions; even fellow students thought he went too far with originality. He won prizes in piano playing and in sight singing, but not in music theory.

Having decided to concentrate on composition, when not quite twenty-two he won the highest prize in that field, the Prix de Rome, with his rather sentimental cantata *L'Enfant prodigue (The Prodigal Son)*. The award gave Debussy three years in Rome, which were to culminate in a big public concert of his music. But Debussy was not happy there. When the authorities refused to allow his symphonic suite *Printemps (Spring)* to be programmed, he left Rome—before the end of his third year and without the concert of his works, which now included the cantata *La Damoiselle élue (The Blessed Damozel)* and a fantasia for piano and orchestra.

Returning to Paris, he joined forces with the poets Verlaine, Baudelaire, and Mallarmé and the Impressionist painters, particularly Monet, in advancing new techniques in the arts.

In 1889 Paris had a world's fair—the one for which the Eiffel Tower was built. Debussy spent many hours looking at the subtle paintings and elaborately decorated vases from Japan. He was fascinated by the strange, exotic sounds of the Javanese gamelan, an orchestra of delicately toned percussion instruments. The gamelan played highly complicated counterpoints in rhythm, full of syncopation and utterly unlike the rather square rhythms of European dance music. Sometimes the movement stopped and the long-held tones of gongs were heard, shimmering as though with many different parts of the same sound. Instead of the European succession of chords that might create a mood, here was a sound that was beautiful and evocative all by itself.

During this period of his life Debussy found his own style, starting with his settings of poems by Verlaine (*Ariettes oubliées*, 1888) and Baudelaire (*Cinq Poèmes*, 1890). A poem by his friend Mallarmé inspired Debussy to write his *Prélude à l'Après-midi d'un faune (Prelude to the Afternoon of a Faun)* for orchestra. In this dreamy summer idyl Debussy called forth a kind of quiet Greek paganism—a far cry from the deeply serious and more traditional works of the Germans, Wagner and Strauss. Later, in 1912, the famous dancer Nijinsky was to use *The Afternoon of a Faun* for a scandal-provoking—and successful—ballet.

To say things in a new way meant that Debussy had to invent a new musical vocabulary and a new grammar. Actually, his vocabulary consisted of much that was old but had dropped out of European music. He used the old, medieval scales, or modes, as well as the pentatonic (black-key) and whole-tone scales (C-D-E-F#-G#-A#-C, for example) that he had heard in Russia and at the Javanese concerts. He added notes to triads so that the triad sounded blurred (Ex. 1). He blended two chords together to

Claude Debussy by Nadar

Ex. 1 — "De Fleurs"

Ex. 2 —"Feuilles mortes" from Préludes, Book II

Lent et melancolique

pp

Debussy and his first wife, Rosalie Texier

make a new chord or found new ways to use seventh chords and ninth chords (Ex. 2).

His melodies are not the phrase-long melodies of Classical music, nor does he repeat and develop short motives as did the Romantic composers. Instead Debussy uses short melodic fragments which he fits together like pieces of stained glass. His rhythms tend to be free rather than regular. His chords do not at all follow the rules of traditional harmony. They go off in unexpected ways to unexpected places or they move in old medieval parallelism. Debussy was very much an aristocrat, disliking to do anything commonplace or routine. He once said that he had a horror of becoming a popular composer, although he was always happy when his work pleased sophisticated friends.

Debussy was a pianist, and much of his music was written for the piano—an instrument capable of a wide range of sonorities. From this basically percussive instrument he drew exquisite nuances, relying much on subtle uses of the pedals. He was a masterful composer for orchestra also, using a large number of instruments not for loudness but to give a variety of delicate combinations. The cool, low register of the flute, the "ping" of the muted horn, the rushing, soaring sound of the harp glissando, the lonely sound of the oboe, and the murmuring big chords that he could stretch over the divided string section—all these he loved. But he did not ignore the traditional instrument combinations: in 1893 he wrote a string quartet that, musically, looks both forward and backward.

Meanwhile he started to work on his opera *Pelléas and Mélisande,* basing it on a play by Maurice Maeterlinck. This is a play in which much of the action and feeling are submerged. Characters do not give vent to

their feelings directly, but hint at them. Much of what happens seems to be in the shadows or twilight; everything is subdued. The scenes are a forest, a dark castle, a cave. The story is of love, jealousy, and suffering.

Debussy worked on *Pelléas* for almost ten years. When produced in 1902, it was severely criticized. There were no arias, no ballet. The orchestra, while important, underscored the voice. Here, as in all of his vocal writing, Debussy paid great attention to the subtle rhythm and inflection of the French language, which made his vocal lines seem close to recitative. Everything was all of a piece. *Pelléas and Mélisande* comes closer to the original idea of opera—a drama in music—than any other opera does. In it Debussy seemed to have gone to the roots of music itself.

Maeterlinck wanted his wife to create the role of Mélisande. Debussy chose instead a young Scotch singer, Mary Garden, who was successful and justified Debussy's confidence in her. Gradually the opera made its way, although it is so difficult to produce in the correct style that it is not popular in the same way that *Aida* and *Carmen* are popular.

While composing *Pelléas and Mélisande,* Debussy worked on other things: several song cycles, the *Suite bergamasque* for solo piano (which includes the famous *Clair de lune*), and the *Nocturnes* for orchestra—*Nuages (Clouds), Fêtes (Fetes),* and *Sirènes (Sirens).* In these orchestral works Debussy was at his most evocative in giving his musical impressions of the shifting patterns of clouds, the excitement of groups of merrymakers, and the lovely but fateful song of those ancient enchantresses who lured sailors to destruction.

In 1899, having established himself as a

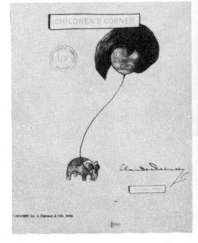

composer, Debussy felt it was time to marry and settle down. A young girl from the country, Rosalie Texier, became his wife, but this marriage ended in divorce in 1904. He then married a divorcee, Mme. Emma Bardac, the mother of his only child, a daughter. For this child, known as Chouchou, he wrote the charming *Children's Corner* for piano and a children's ballet, *La Boïte à joujoux, (The Box of Toys).*

Debussy's musical ideas caught the attention of young composers, who began to imitate him and his colleague Ravel. Although shy and sensitive, hating to appear in public, Debussy visited Italy, England, Belgium, and Hungary, playing and conducting his own works. A skillful pianist, he exploited the resources of the piano; thus his *L'Isle joyeuse (Joyous Isle,* 1904) and *Images* (1905–07) contain virtuoso piano writing. Fond of giving his works poetic titles, in the *Images* he included "Reflections in the Water" and "Goldfish" (inspired by some Japanese lacquerwork in his own collection). The *Children's Corner* (titled in English) contains the "Serenade for a Doll," "The Little Shepherd," and "Golliwog's Cakewalk"— the latter based on an American Negro rhythm. These works, plus his two books of preludes and études, served to make Debussy the most important composer of piano music in the twentieth century. Some of the études are among the most difficult pieces ever

written for piano; Debussy himself said of them, "They terrify your fingers."

He wrote words as well as music, and for several of his songs, such as his "Proses lyriques," he composed his own poems. Articles on music for leading French magazines and newspapers also came from his hand. Some of these essays were published in a book, *Monsieur Croche (Mr. Quarter Note).* Some of the articles are violent attacks on German composers who, Debussy felt, had been bad influences on French music. He admired the older French composers, such as Couperin, and in his later works tried to capture the delicacy and clarity of Couperin's music.

When World War I started, Debussy was in poor health. Of the series of six sonatas he planned for various small groups of instruments only three were ever finished: Sonata for Cello and Piano; Sonata for Flute, Viola, and Harp; and Sonata for Violin and Piano. He wrote "The Christmas of the Homeless Children," a beautiful song inspired by the stories of the German bombings in Belgium, but a large ode to France based on the life of Joan of Arc was never completed. He died during a bombardment of Paris; another bombardment jarred his quiet funeral.

Debussy's influence in music was tremendous. He shook the foundations of traditional harmony, form, and orchestration by his

Cover of La Mer, *1905, Durand &*
Fils

fresh look at every aspect of music. A sophisticated city man, he more than almost any other composer could portray the outdoors and even—as he did in his three-part *La Mer (The Sea)*—various moods of the ocean. Through just the sound of an unaccompanied flute, in *Syrinx,* he painted a woodland scene.

Like a magician he covered with glowing colors everything he touched. Full of irony and pungent wit, he could still write some of the tenderest pieces ever composed for children. His "Steps in the Snow" (Preludes, Book I) is as silent and lonely as a winter night. Seeming never to be carried away by feeling, he managed, as he said, "to arrive at the naked flesh of the emotion."

DECIBEL: A unit for measuring the intensity, or loudness, of sound. Decibel means "one-tenth of a bel." The original unit, the bel, was named after Alexander Graham Bell.

A sound that has an intensity of one decibel (1 db) can just barely be heard. One violin playing as softly as possible in an auditorium has a decibel rating of 1. A full orchestra playing fortissimo has an intensity of 85 db. Ordinary conversation has a db count of 65. When a sound reaches a decibel rating of 120, it produces a sense of pain in the ears of a listener. If this intense sound is continued, the ear can be damaged.

Decibels can be measured with an instrument known as a "sound-level meter," used by recording engineers and by acoustical engineers to study sounds in buildings.

Frederick Delius

DELIUS, FREDERICK (1862–1934): composer of operas *(Irmelin, Koanga, A Village Romeo and Juliet),* concertos, and large-scale choral works, but best known for his quiet orchestral tone pictures. Delius was born in Bradford, England, where his father, a well-to-do German merchant, had settled. He tried managing a Florida orange grove but, in 1886, having decided his future lay in music rather than business, Delius entered the Leipzig Conservatory. In Leipzig he met the composer Edvard Grieg, whose musical style and theories of nationalism appealed to him. Delius settled in France in 1890 and married the artist Jelka Rosen. Sir Thomas Beecham discovered Delius' music and performed it widely. Near the end of his highly productive life Delius became blind, but continued to compose by dictating his ideas to a younger musician, Eric Fenby.

Delius is known chiefly for his warm, sensitive mood pieces—such as the tone poems *On Hearing the First Cuckoo in Spring* and *Summer Night on the River,* and the *Walk to the Paradise Garden* and the orchestral interlude from his opera *A Village Romeo and Juliet.* His choral works, including *Sea Drift* and *A Mass of Life,* have gradually made their way into the concert repertoire, as have his orchestral pieces— *Paris: The Song of a Great City, Brigg Fair,* and two *Dance Rhapsodies.*

Delius' music is highly personal, poetic, and uncomplicated. It is often based on simple folklike themes that are harmonized with rich chromatic chords. His orchestral colors are warm as he contrasts the poignant sounds of oboe and flute with the glowing tones of the strings and the richness of the brass. More than any other composer, he has managed to portray in tone a sense of love for nature.

DESCANT: a new melody added to an old melody so that the two can be sung together. One of the oldest types of counterpoint in music, it was first added to the plainchant of the early church as a new, additional melody to be sung by the higher voices. (Originally the word was used interchangeably with "counterpoint.") Descants have been added to many hymn tunes and Christmas carols. Descant singing has been most popular in England, especially in English church music.

DEVELOPMENT: the modification of musical themes or motives for purposes of structure, of drama, or of a program. The second section of a SONATA-ALLEGRO form is often concerned chiefly with such manipulation, and hence is usually referred to as the development section.

Development depends on the disguised repetition of a musical idea. The original version of an idea or theme can be embellished, broken into fragments (FRAGMENTATION), repeated on higher or lower pitches (SEQUENCE), or played upside down (INVERSION) or backward (RETROGRADE). The melodic intervals may be expanded or contracted, or the rhythmic pattern played twice as fast (DIMINUTION) or twice as slow (AUGMENTATION). The pitches can be repeated and the rhythm changed, or the pitches changed as the rhythm stays the same. The musical idea can be tossed around from one register or instrument to another, or it can be combined with other ideas.

Short works of the Baroque period, such as many of the preludes in Bach's *Well-tempered Clavier,* have simple development as the basic structure of the piece. A motive is stated and then unfolded over a harmonic progression which is the ground plan of the work. As the motive is repeated, its intervals contract and expand to fit the chord of the moment. The device of sequence also is used as the motive is repeated on higher and lower pitches.

Development plays an important role in eighteenth- and nineteenth-century sonata-allegro form. While it is used in all sections of the form, it is in the second section, originally called the free fantasia section, that the thematic material first heard in the exposition is most fully explored.

The development section is often chromatic and episodic. It starts in a foreign tonality and takes the thematic material through many adventures as it steers toward the home key and the restatement that follows it. The adventures of the themes in the development might be likened to the wanderings of Homer's hero Ulysses as he attempted to return to Ithaca from Troy. In the development section of Beethoven's Fifth Symphony the familiar four-note motive here:

First Movement, Symphony No. 5,
Beethoven

passes momentarily through the keys of F-minor, C-minor, G-minor, F-minor again, and G-major before finally arriving at the tonic key of C-minor. The motive itself assumes the forms of Ex. a and b:

Sometimes the rhythm is hammered out on a repeated chord:

Beethoven could have developed his motive for a much longer time. But he used only enough development to balance the other sections of the movement, thus preserving the dramatic quality of the work.

Beethoven often used the coda of a composition for further exploration of the possibilities of his themes, so that the coda becomes, in fact, another development. In the coda of his Coriolanus overture he uses the development of a theme for programmatic purposes. The strong theme, conceivably representing the hero Coriolanus (Ex. 3), weakens as the theme seems to disintegrate rhythmically: Ex. 4.

This technique of using development for dramatic purposes is found in many nineteenth-century symphonic poems. The two main themes of Strauss's *Till Eulenspiegel* are developed throughout the work, always reminding the listener of the hero of the composition. As one hears Till's themes embark on various adventures, it is easy to imagine what is happening to him right through to the end, when his soul goes to heaven.

As early as the time of Haydn, composers of symphonies had begun to develop their musical ideas almost from the beginning of a work. This continuous development of thematic material is a mark of many contemporary composers. Other composers of today, following the lead of Debussy and Satie, do not develop material at any great

Ex. 3 — *Coriolanus* Overture, Beethoven

Ex. 4

length, preferring to bring in new ideas and make a mosaic pattern in which different musical ideas are placed next to each other.

Occasionally there is a confusion between the terms "variation" and "development." Every variation in a theme and variations uses the process of development, because the theme to be varied always undergoes some kind of change. But in a theme and variations, each variation follows, in strict order, the measures of the theme—from the first one through every measure in succession. In a development, however, only a portion of a theme might be used or the original theme might be extended. Each

variation is, in a way, complete in itself, whereas a development of an idea is part of a whole, incomplete in itself.

DIATONIC: a term that means staying, for the most part, within a key or scale. Diatonic music has a key signature, which can be that of any scale, usual or unusual. Any tones of the music that are not in the key of the composition are called chromatic tones.

Motives, melodies, and chords can be either diatonic (Ex. 5a, b, and c) or chromatic (Ex. 6a, b, and c).

Ex. 7 — Mazurka, Op. 33, No. 2, Chopin

Few musical compositions are completely without chromatic tones, which are used to add color and variety. Nursery tunes, Christmas carols, and folk tunes are usually diatonic. So, too, are many of the themes in the music written by the composers of the Classical period, such as Mozart and Haydn.

Nineteenth-century composers, such as Wagner and Chopin, turned more freely to chords and melodies with chromatic tones. But most of the leitmotifs from which Wagner built his *Ring of the Nibelungs* are still diatonic, as is Ex. 7, a mazurka by Chopin.

Much contemporary music dispenses with keys as such. This music cannot be discussed in terms of diatonic scales or chromatic tones.

DIDO AND AENEAS: one of the first operas written in English. It was composed by Henry Purcell around 1689, and although a dozen generations of English composers have come and gone since Purcell's time, *Dido and Aeneas* still ranks as the finest and most enjoyable of English operas.

Purcell wrote it for performance at a girls' school run by a London ballet master named Josias Priest. The libretto is by Nahum Tate.

The story begins at some time after the fall of Troy. A storm has driven Aeneas and his wandering Trojans to the shores of North Africa, where Dido, Queen of Carthage, has given them shelter. Dido and Aeneas fall in love. The fates have told Aeneas that he will not stay in Carthage, but he resolves to defy them. He has not reckoned, however, with the Sorceress, who with her witches in a cave has been hatching a plot to destroy Dido—her fame, her love, even her life. During a hunt (Act II) the Sorceress conjures up an image of Mercury, the messenger god, and has him instruct Aeneas to end his dallying in Carthage and to sail off and rebuild Troy. Aeneas, heart-broken, complies. After a wild dance with the witches (Act III) he and his sailors start for Troy.

Dido, crushed by a feeling of rejection, lies down to die. To her lady-in-waiting she

Scene from Purcell's Dido and Aeneas *at the Sadler's Wells in the 1950's*

An engraving by Abraham Bosse depicting "The Death of Dido"

sings her lament, a ground-bass air (Ex. 8) that is one of the most moving achievements in the entire world of opera. As she lies dying, a chorus of mourning Carthaginians gathers round her, singing

> *With drooping wings ye Cupids come,*
> *And scatter roses on her tomb.*

There is something modest about the whole production. It was written for young amateurs and lasts only about an hour. And yet everything about it is fresh, appropriate, and effective. The weird "Harm's our delight" chorus of the witches, the vivid and descriptive storm and hunting music played by the strings and harpsichord, the arias spun over their ground basses—all contribute memorable and telling effects. And certainly no one has ever set English words more beautifully.

Purcell wrote no other operas, although his incidental music to *King Arthur* and other dramas approaches opera. In the seven years that remained of his short life he wrote many times for the stage, in the form of incidental numbers. *Dido and Aeneas,* after its first stage performance in 1689, was not revived until 1895. It is now appreciated again, both for its own sake and for its value as an introduction to the works of one of England's greatest musicians.

Ex. 8 — "Dido's Lament"

DIMINISHED: literally, made smaller. A diminished interval is one that is a half step smaller than a minor or a perfect interval. Except for the diminished fifth, diminished intervals have no characteristic sound, but sound like other intervals. For example, the diminished sixth of Ex. a sounds like the perfect fifth of Ex. b:

Before 1600 the diminished fifth was considered so dissonant and so difficult to sing that composers rarely used it either harmonically or melodically. Other diminished intervals were difficult to sing not only because of the way they sounded but because of the way they read:

A *diminished triad* is made by combining the tones of two minor thirds so that the distance from the bottom tone to the top tone is a diminished fifth:

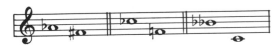

Triads built on the seventh tone of the major and minor scales and on the second tone of the harmonic and natural minor scale are diminished triads.

A *diminished seventh chord* is a four-note chord made by adding a minor third on top of a diminished triad:

The top tone is a diminished seventh above the bottom tone. The diminished seventh chord has been used by composers for centuries as a dramatic chord. Bach often uses a diminished seventh chord as the climax sound near the end of a composition:

Prelude in D from *The Well-tempered Clavier*, Book I, J.S. Bach

Mozart, Weber, Verdi, and Wagner used a diminished seventh chord as the single sound that could evoke a feeling of terror or suspense in the listener (Ex. 9).

In the nineteenth century, composers used diminished sevenths to modulate, or move from one key to another. When any tone of a diminished seventh is lowered a half step, the chord becomes a dominant seventh chord (Ex. 10). Each diminished seventh chord therefore can lead to four keys. There are only three different diminished sevenths. Each one can be written four ways: Ex. 11.

Ex. 9 — Wolf's Glen Scene from *Der Freischütz*, Weber

Ex. 10

Ex. 11

DIMINUENDO: an Italian word meaning "gradually getting softer." Different instruments make their diminuendos in different ways. On the piano and other percussion instruments several tones are needed to make a diminuendo, each tone being struck with a little less force than the preceding one. A most expressive use of diminuendo is possible on instruments capable of sustaining a long held tone—voices, strings, and winds.

The abbreviations for diminuendo are *dimin.* and *dim.* The sign for diminuendo is ══▶. A diminuendo can be made from any degree of loudness to any softer degree. If a composer writes *ff══mf* he means "start very loud and end medium loud." The notation *p══ppp* means "start softly and end with a tone that can barely be heard." This marking is often used together with the word *morendo* when the music is meant to die away to nothing.

Decrescendo and its abbreviation *decresc.* mean the same as diminuendo.

DIMINUTION: the use of a musical idea or theme with the rhythmic values decreased. They are usually shortened to one half, or possibly one third, or one fourth of what they were at first: whole notes become half or quarter notes; quarter notes become eighths, triplets, or sixteenths (Ex. 12).

Diminution is often found in music that is contrapuntal. It is also used by composers as a way of varying or developing a theme in a symphonic work. Diminution can be used dramatically, as in Wagner's overture to the opera *Die Meistersinger:* the solemn, heavy theme of the old mastersingers is repeated in shorter notes as the gay, playful theme of the young apprentices (Ex. 13 a and b).

At right: "Abstraction, 1923" by Wassily Kandinsky (color lithograph). Kandinsky's Expressionist art works have much in common with the highly dissonant music of Schoenberg

DISSONANCE: the effect of tension or disturbance made by certain combinations of musical sounds. Some intervals or combinations of intervals seem to be restful in quality; these are called consonances. Other combinations of tones have a tense, restless, or disturbing quality that seems to demand continued motion; these are dissonances. The concept of dissonance is always relative and always changing. A sound that is dissonant to one person might be considered consonant by someone else.

In traditional music theory the consonant intervals are the prime, perfect fifth, octave, and major and minor thirds and sixths.

Seconds, sevenths, and all diminished and augmented intervals have always been used as dissonances. The perfect fourth has been considered to be a consonance and a dissonance at various times in music theory.

There are many possibilities for dissonance. Some tonal combinations are less dissonant:

Ex. 12 — Fugue No. 9 from *The Well-tempered Clavier*, Book II, J.S. Bach

Ex. 13 — Overture, *Die Meistersinger*, Wagner

Some combinations are more dissonant:

The more complex the relationships of the intervals to each other, the greater the dissonance. Dissonance also depends on what instruments play the notes of the chords and how loudly or softly they are played.

The history of music can be traced partly by the way composers have used dissonance. Until 1600, dissonances were used very little, except for the suspension, where a tone which was part of a consonance was held over for a moment while the other tone moved on:

After 1600, composers discovered that dissonance added dramatic effect to their music. At this time the dissonant chord always resolved, or moved on, to a consonant chord. Gradually composers began to use several dissonant chords in succession before coming to a consonant chord (Ex. 14). Some composers of today use more dissonances than consonances in their music:

Op. 19, No. 3, Schoenberg

With composers exploring new means of producing sound, it is difficult for the average listener to distinguish between greater and lesser tensions; therefore, he probably no longer thinks in terms of dissonance and consonance when listening to this music.

Detail from "The Musical Entertainers" by George Bickman, 1737

DIVERTIMENTO: a set of short, light pieces to be played by a small group of wind instruments, stringed instruments, or combinations of these. A divertimento has from four to ten movements in different tempos. Divertimentos often combine features of both the suite and the short symphonic forms: they include gay allegros, light dances, and lyrical andantes. These sets of tuneful entertainment pieces were popular in Austria from 1750 to 1800. Mozart wrote at least 33 such works, and Haydn about 175. "Serenade" and "cassation" were other names given to the same kind of music.

DIXIE: the favorite popular song of the Southern armies during the American Civil War. It was written by a man from Ohio, Daniel Emmett, who was on the side of the North.

Emmett wrote the song in 1859 as a "walkaround" for the famous Bryant's Minstrels. The original title was "Dixie's Land." Negro

Ex. 14 — Fugue No. 24 from *The Well-tempered Clavier*, Book I, J.S. Bach

Daniel Emmett (portrait taken from the title page of Old Dan Emmit's Original Banjo Melodies, *1844)*

boys were often called "Dixie" after a play of 1850 had popularized the name. "Dixie's Land" was the southern part of the United States, but the song was as popular in the North as in the South. Emmett, along with Stephen Foster, was a writer of songs for minstrel shows. Two years after he wrote "Dixie" he sold it to a publisher for three hundred dollars.

Early in the Civil War, "Dixie" was sung by both armies, but more and more it became the song of the Southern soldiers. When Jefferson Davis was inaugurated as President of the Confederate States, the band played this song. A few days after the end of the war President Abraham Lincoln asked a band to play "Dixie"; he said it was a good song and now belonged to all Americans.

DOMINANT: the fifth tone in a major or minor scale. It is a perfect fifth above the keynote, or tonic, of the scale:

C Major

I   V

The dominant tone of the scale is next in importance to the keynote.

In both major and harmonic minor keys the triad built on the dominant tone is major. The dominant seventh chord is made by adding a minor third on top of the major triad (V7):

C Major Dominant Triad Dominant Seventh
V   V7

In the harmony used by composers between 1650 and 1850, the chord built on the dominant usually moved to the tonic, the chord built on the keynote. At the end of a composition or a section of it, this chord pattern is called an authentic cadence. Composers also used these two chords at the beginning of a composition to establish a key feeling in the minds of their listeners (Ex. 15). Many nursery tunes and short folk tunes, such as "Ach, du Lieber Augustin," use only the chords built on the dominant and the keynote.

The composers who wrote after 1850 added tones above the dominant seventh. The dominant ninth and thirteenth:

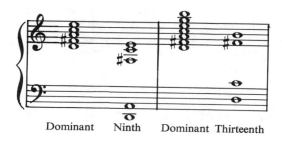

Dominant Ninth Dominant Thirteenth

were used by Debussy and Ravel in very free ways, not necessarily going to a keynote chord:

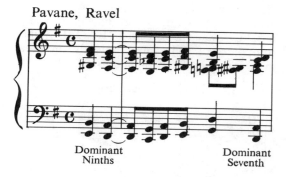

Pavane, Ravel

Dominant Ninths   Dominant Seventh

In harmony, any chord which is not the tonic can still have its own dominant chord placed in front of it. Such a chord is called a secondary dominant and is used by composers for coloristic effects or as a part of a long harmonic pattern involving the circle of fifths (Ex. 16—on the next page).

Ex. 15— Gigue from Suite for Harpsichord No. 1, Handel

I V I V   I V I V

Ex. 16 — Flute (recorder) Sonata in F Major, Handel

A Minor V7 ———— I   G Minor V ———— I

F Major V7 ———— I

DON GIOVANNI: Mozart's greatest opera, composed during the summer of 1787. *The Marriage of Figaro* had been a tremendous success in Prague the previous winter, and Pasquale Bondini, whose company had put on *Figaro,* was now eager to have a new opera from Mozart for the following season. Mozart turned to his *Figaro* librettist, Lorenzo da Ponte, who reworked an old Spanish play on the life and death of Don Juan, a play that had held the boards in one form or another since 1630.

The first performance of *Don Giovanni* took place on October 29, 1787. One of the Prague newspapers reported the event as follows: "On Monday the 29th the Italian opera company gave the eagerly awaited opera by Maestro Mozart, *Don Giovanni, or the Stone Guest.* Connoisseurs and musicians say the like of it has never been put on in Prague. Herr Mozart himself conducted, and when he stepped into the pit he was cheered three times: the same thing happened when he walked out of it."

The overture starts with an ominous, slow introduction in which Mozart pulls together various themes later heard near the end of the opera in the shattering moments in which Don Giovanni meets his fate. The main part of the overture is an allegro suggesting the driving passions of the hero, interspersed with a staccato five-note de-

Scene from Metropolitan Opera production of Don Giovanni: *Elisabeth Schwarzkopf as Donna Elvira, Cesare Siepi as the Don, and Geraint Evans as Leporello*

*Elisabeth Schwarzkopf as
Donna Elvira*

Ezio Pinza as the Don

Ex. 17

Molto allegro

Ex. 18

scending figure (Ex. 17 and 18, above) that
has something of a thou-shalt-not quality.

As the curtain rises on a garden at night,
Don Giovanni's valet Leporello (a part
taken by a basso buffo) is found singing
"Night and day I'm on the go" (Ex. 19) as
he is posted as lookout during one of the
Don's amorous escapades. Donna Anna
rushes by, trying to rouse the household.
She is the daughter of the Commander of
Seville and the latest victim of the unwel-
come attentions of Don Giovanni. The Commander (sung by a bass) appears on the
scene, engages Don Giovanni in a duel,
and is mortally wounded. As he dies, he
sings a trio with Don Giovanni (a baritone)

and Leporello that is one of the most beautiful moments in the opera. Don Giovanni
escapes, and Donna Anna and her fiancé
Don Ottavio swear revenge.

In the street the next day the Don meets
one of his former conquests, Donna Elvira,
who is out for revenge. He manages to break
away from her, leaving Leporello behind to
calm her boiling fury. This Leporello attempts in the famous "Madamina!" aria,
in which he proceeds to unreel for the hap-
less Donna Elvira a catalog of the love affairs his master has had in Italy, Germany,
France, Turkey, and Spain. The total is
2,065!

The scene changes to a country setting.
Don Giovanni comes across a group of villagers celebrating the forthcoming marriage
of the pretty Zerlina and Masetto, a country
boy. The Don tries to win away Zerlina
from Masetto—she's too good for the boy,
he tells her. Their flirtation culminates in
the "Là ci darem la mano" duet—"Put your
little hand in mine" (Ex. 20). Before they get
any further, Donna Elvira appears, whisks

Ex. 19

Molto allegro

Ex. 20

Andante

Zerlina away, and warns her that the Don is up to no good.

Don Giovanni sees a way of meeting Zerlina: he will invite the villagers to a party at his palace. He sings his orders to Leporello in the fast, bubbling "Champagne Aria" (Ex. 21). At the party Zerlina tries to calm the jealousy of Masetto; in an aria that begins *"Batti, batti"*—"Beat me, beat me"— she assures him of her love. The Don's party, which is also attended by Donna Anna, Donna Elvira, and Don Ottavio (all three masked and unrecognized), makes one of the most spectacular episodes in music. Three orchestras are on stage, playing a variety of dances suited to all the social groups represented among the guests. Each dance has its characteristic rhythm, but Mozart manages to fit them together. At the same time the characters on stage go on singing their dialogue.

Don Giovanni has led Zerlina away from the party. Suddenly, offstage, a woman is heard screaming for help. It is Zerlina. Donna Anna, Donna Elvira, and Don Ottavio run to her rescue. They confront Don Giovanni—who draws his sword and escapes.

Back in Seville (Act II), the Don and Leporello hide in a graveyard. By chance they are at the grave of the Commander whom the Don has killed; it is surmounted by a stone statue of the Commander. At one point, when the Don breaks into a raucous guffaw, the statue speaks out in low, majestic tones to reprimand him (the statue's voice is accompanied by trombones, which have not previously been heard). Leporello is scared out of his wits, but the Don laughingly invites the statue to supper.

The climax of the opera takes place in Don Giovanni's palace, where a table has been laid for a feast and a band of musicians has been assembled. The band plays tunes from operas that have recently been hits in Prague, including one from Mozart's own *Marriage of Figaro*. Donna Elvira rushes in to plead with the Don to change his ways. He refuses—he likes life as it is. The stone statue of the Commander appears. The Don orders Leporello to set a place at the table for the new arrival, but the statue points out that one who lives on celestial food does not partake of earthly repasts. This remark is chanted in a phrase that uses almost all the twelve tones of the

Cesare Siepi as the Don

chromatic scale—the remaining ones are heard in the cellos and double basses.

The statue will, however, sit down with Don Giovanni at the table if the Don will agree to join him. The statue offers its hand, and Don Giovanni screams in horror at the icy grip. The statue sinks out of sight. Flames appear on all sides, and voices from below proclaim the awful fate that awaits the Don. The ground opens, and Don Giovanni is swallowed up into hell.

Donna Anna, Donna Elvira, Don Ottavio, Zerlina, Masetto, and Leporello now take the stage and sing "Thus ends the life of evil."

Don Giovanni has been called "the perfect opera." The stage action keeps moving, and for each character—the noble Donna Anna, the agitated Donna Elvira, the rustic Zerlina—Mozart has managed to write exactly the right kind of melodic line. Even the slipperiness of Don Giovanni is rendered musically: he sings differently to each character—gallantly to Zerlina, cockily to Leporello, mockingly to the statue of the Commander. And the music is extraordinarily powerful. Mozart wrote it in the months following the death of his father, when all his emotional resources seem to have been mustered up.

Don Giovanni is one of the few operas written before 1800 that are still popular favorites. Its perennial appeal is a tribute to the stage sense of Da Ponte and to the musical genius of Mozart.

Ex. 21

Presto

DOTTED NOTES AND RESTS: signs (symbols) used to lengthen the time value of a note or rest by one half. The same can be accomplished by tying a note of one value to another note half as long:

(a)

(b)

A dotted note is the only way to show a ratio of 3 to 1:

In a meter of 6/8, which is 3/8 plus 3/8, the pulse note is a dotted quarter:

The rhythmic figure:

which is a 3-to-1 division of the beat, is a common one. Composers use it when they want a more nervous or bouncy feeling than they can get by using an even division of the beat. The performer must be aware of the time relationships of the notes:

so that the last note is always as short as it should be. The reverse of this pattern is used in the Scotch snap. Notice it in "Comin' Through the Rye":

In jazz the  is often used as an accompaniment figure. It is usually played with a lazy feeling, so that it sounds more like:

Strangely enough, this custom of writing

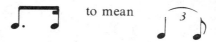 to mean

was prevalent in the time of Bach and Handel.

The *double dot* was invented as a way of lengthening the first note in a beat and further shortening the last note. The double dot lengthens the note it follows by three quarters of its original value:

The figure is often found in heroic, noble music.

DOUBLE BASS: the lowest-voiced string instrument. Known also as the bass viol, contrabass, or bull fiddle, it is six feet tall, and the bass player always has to perform while standing or sitting on a high stool.

Like other stringed instruments of the orchestra, the double bass has four strings. (A fifth string is occasionally added to extend either the upper or lower range.) These are tuned a fourth apart, on the tones shown here:

The other strings of the orchestra are tuned in fifths—but the size of the double bass presents a special problem to the player. The part of a bass string that actually sounds— the part above the bridge—is unusually long: 42 inches. If the strings were tuned in fifths, the player's left hand (as he played a scale) would have to span a fifth on each string; this would be one third of the string's length, or about 14 inches. If the string is tuned in fourths, the left hand need cover only a quarter of the string's length, or 10½ inches, before moving over to the next string. This is still quite a stretch, but bass players find it just manageable.

The tuning in fourths is not the only thing about the double bass that sets it apart from the other stringed instruments in the orchestra. Its low tones are produced by long strings, and the long strings require a large instrument—not only to support them physically, but to offer a good range of resonance to support the tone. If the double bass were an exact replica of the violin, but enlarged so that its body offered its best supporting resonance in the pitch region of the two middle strings (as in a violin), it would be an immense and quite unplayable machine. So certain compromises have been worked out over the years. The instrument's shoulders, or "bouts," are narrower than they would be in a true violin shape, and the back is usually flat rather than rounded. Though this makes it look somewhat like its cousins in the viol family, it is not a real viol. For instance, its finger board does not have frets across it to mark off the tones, its belly or front-surface has *f*-shaped holes rather than C-shaped holes, and the strings are kept at greater tension than they would be in a viol.

The music for the double bass is written an octave higher than the real sounds. The notes it plays are so low that many lines would otherwise have to be added below the bass staff.

The strings of the double bass are very thick, and the player must have large, strong fingers to press them down on the finger board. Two kinds of bows and methods of bowing are used. In the French system the player uses a short, stubby bow that looks like and is handled like a cello bow. In the German system the player uses a bow that has enough space between the hair and the stick of the bow for him to put his hand through, palm upward—and he looks as though he were sawing across the strings. Each system has its good points. Among the eight to ten players that usually make up the bass section of an orchestra, some will use the French system, some the German. Instead of producing their tone by bowing, the bass players often pluck their strings. This pizzicato is clear and resonant.

The voice of the double bass is deep. This makes it a good instrument to serve as a foundation for the rest of the orchestra. Before the time of Beethoven, the bass was rarely used for anything but the bass notes of the harmony. Beethoven had a friend, Dragonetti, who was a great performer on the double bass, and it was he who showed Beethoven what the big instrument could do. In his Fourth, Fifth and Ninth Symphonies Beethoven gave the double bass fast running passages and large leaping lines. After Beethoven's time, composers were no longer afraid to use the instrument for expressive purposes. Its deep tones, played pizzicato, were used for their ominous and dramatic color. In the opening of Tchaikovsky's Sixth Symphony the double basses provide a mournful support for the bassoons. Modern composers sometimes have the double bass play high notes in harmonics, making it sound like a breathy cello.

There are few concert solos written for the double bass. Dragonetti wrote some, as did Giovanni Bottesini (1821-89). So, too, did Serge Koussevitzky, the conductor, who started his career in music as a bass player. Schubert loved the double bass and let it sing the opening melody of his "Unfinished" Symphony, along with the cellos; he also made it a member of a chamber group in his "Trout" Quintet. Saint-Saëns wrote an awkwardly graceful solo for double bass in the elephant movement of his *Carnival of the Animals*. Stravinsky used the double bass as one of the eight instruments in the orchestra of his *Story of a Soldier*.

The most dramatic use of the double bass occurs in the ominous, brooding introduction to the last act of Verdi's *Otello* (Ex. 22).

The double bass replaced the tuba as the bass member of jazz bands in the 1920's. It soon became one of the favorite instruments in modern jazz. In large dance bands it is part of the rhythm section, along with the drums, piano, and guitar. In small jazz groups it is used to play both rhythm and melody. In both cases it is usually played pizzicato.

Serge Koussevitzky, virtuoso double-bassist

Ex. 22 — *Otello*, Verdi

DOUBLE STOP: the sounding of two tones simultaneously on the violin, viola, cello, or double bass. The term is often applied to any string part in which two, three, or four tones are played at the same time. Double stops, which allow the violin to play harmony as well as melody, must be written so that the tones lie on strings that are next to each other; then the bow can touch both strings. They must also be within the span of any two fingers. Certain intervals are easier to play than others, among them being the intervals of thirds and sixths, and also double stops in which one note is produced on an open or non-fingered string.

Double stops were used in the violin sonatas and concertos of Corelli and Vivaldi, in which they added harmonic richness to the violin part. The German composers Heinrich Biber and J. S. Bach (see Ex. 23) used double, triple, and quadruple stops in their sonatas for violin alone, thus allowing the instrument to play an accompaniment to its own melody or to suggest two-and three-part counterpoint. Biber tuned his violin to various intervals other than the usual series of perfect fifths. This process, called *scordatura*, made it much easier for him to play many of the double and triple stops.

In the nineteenth century the virtuoso violinist Paganini used fast double stops, among other technical devices, to dazzle his audiences (Ex. 24).

Close-up of double stopping

Ex. 23— Fugue from Sonata No. 1 for Unaccompanied Violin, J.S. Bach

Ex. 24— Caprice No. 4, Paganini

Ex. 25 — Ending of "Come Again, Sweet Love Doth Now Invite"

to see,   to heare,   to touch,   to kisse,   to die____

with thee a - gain   in sweetest sym — pa - thy.

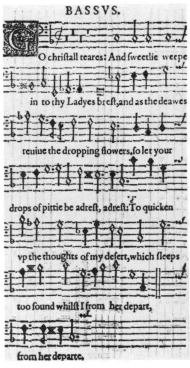

BASSVS.

O chriftall teares: And fweetlie weepe

in to thy Ladyes breft, and as the deawes

reuiue the dropping flowers, fo let your

drops of pittie be adreft, adreft: To quicken

vp the thoughts of my defert, which fleeps

too found whilft I from her depart,

from her departe,

Bass parts for "O Christall teares" from Dowland's First Booke of Songes or Ayres of foure partes, with Tableture for the Lute, *1597*

DOWLAND, JOHN (1562–1626): one of the first great songwriters. In his own day Dowland was best known as the greatest lute player in Europe. Born probably in Ireland, when young he went to Paris as a page to the English ambassador, returned to take a degree in music at Oxford, traveled to Germany, and later went as far as Italy to study under the madrigal composer Luca Marenzio. In 1597 he published his *First Book of Songs or Ayres,* with lute accompaniments, and in the following year he became lutanist to King Christian IV of Denmark at Elsinore. For the Danish queen he wrote his *Seven Tears, Figured in Seven Passionate Pavans* for an ensemble of lutes or viols. He lost his job at the Danish court because he did not take his teaching duties seriously.

In 1609 Dowland returned to England and published several more books of songs (his *First Booke,* of 1597, went through four editions during his lifetime). With his son Robert he wrote a "do-it-yourself" book on how to play the lute, and in 1612 he became one of the King's Musicians for the Lute.

Dowland's songs are gems. Some are happy and dancelike, but more of them sing of the sorrows of love. The melodies are flowing and always capture the spirit of the poem; the harmonies are often complex and unexpected, as are the rhythmic patterns. Dowland's accompaniments for the lute are more than just the strumming of supporting chords; each accompaniment suits the quality and mood of the song.

Dowland wrote eighty-seven songs. The best known are "Come Again, Sweet Love Doth Now Invite" (Ex. 25), "Flow My Tears," and "From Silent Night."

DRONE: a pipe or string that can play only one tone (it seems to derive its name from the buzzing of a bee). A bagpipe may have several drone pipes in addition to its chanter, or melody pipe. The drone pipes are usually tuned to the first and fifth tone of the chanter's scale.

The songs of the troubadours were often accompanied on the vielle, an ancestor of the violin. The vielle had a drone string in addition to its playing strings. A later form of the instrument, the hurdy-gurdy, had several drones.

Much of the charming sound of the Indian vina *is due to its three drone strings, which provide a rhythmic accompaniment to the melody played on the four other strings*

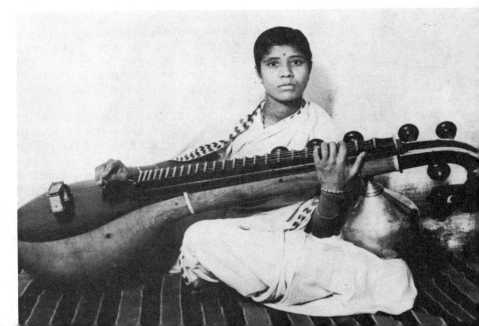

Ex. 26 — "Musette en rondeau," Rameau

Composers who have wanted to suggest the sound of a bagpipe while writing for regular concert instruments have simply accompanied their melodies with drone basses (Ex. 26). This effect is traditional in the musette, a French dance often used as the middle section of a gavotte.

DRUMS: the most used members of the percussion family of instruments. Drums are among the most ancient of all instruments and come in all sizes and shapes. Basically, a drum is a piece of material—animal hide or skin, or parchment—stretched over a hollow body made of metal, wood, or clay. The drumhead, the skin or hide, can be made to vibrate and give off a sound by striking it with fingers, hands, or beaters. The body of the drum, made from wood or metal, serves to amplify the drum sound and affect its quality, depending on the size and material of the body.

The drumhead must be kept taut. This is usually done by fitting a hoop around the part of the skin that overlaps the body of the drum. Another way of keeping the head taut is to attach to it ropes that can be fastened together at the bottom of the drum. Because the head absorbs moisture, humidity is often a factor for the drummer to overcome. As the head becomes flabby, the drum sound becomes a dull thud. The player who wants a clear tone must tighten the head, by means of ropes, screws, or a key like a skate key. Some drummers have used an electric light inside the drum in sticky weather.

The kinds of drums that exist in the world are almost unlimited in number. There are tiny bongo drums, held in the player's lap and sounded with the fingers. Some drums are so large that they must be hauled around on small wagons. There are square drums and round drums, long and narrow drums, and short, fat ones. There are drums that are partly filled with water. Chinese tom-toms are decorated with colorful pictures

Mounted musician, richly caparisoned, playing timpani

of dragons. Some tribes in Africa have huge drums that are played on by several men at the same time. Some drums, as in Africa, have been designed for sending messages rather than for making music.

In primitive societies drums have been sacred instruments, only chiefs or warriors being allowed to beat them. When timpani were first brought to Europe from Turkey, about 1500, only a king or high nobleman was allowed to own one. For many years drums were aristocratic instruments, used with trumpets to sound fanfares as the king entered a theater or a throne room. In many early instrumental scores the drum and trumpet parts are placed importantly at the top of the page, above the more lowly string, woodwind, and trombone parts.

Today the timpani player in the orchestra is usually the leader of the percussion section, partly because of the old honored position of the timpani and partly because among all percussionists the timpani player must have the keenest ear, since his drums must be tuned accurately to definite pitches. Although the other orchestral drums—the snare, or side, drum and the bass drum—can be tuned to slightly higher or lower pitches, these pitches are quite indefinite. Only the timpani and the newest form of drum, the steel drum from Trinidad, produce a definite pitch.

Steel drums are made from old steel barrels. The tops are made in sections, so that one drum can play as many as six different tones. A band of these drums can play melody and harmony with a haunting, sweet sound that reminds the listener of a band of marimbas.

For several hundred years the drums have been important members of bands and orchestras, but only jazz has allowed the drummer to show his real versatility. Surrounded by five or six types of drums of different sizes, he is often given long solo sections during which he improvises astonishingly complex rhythmic arrangements of the beat.

Top left: *strolling musicians, 17th-century Ming*
Top right: *Trinidad steel band*
Bottom left: *tribal dancers in Kenya*
Bottom right: *Gene Krupa*

W. A. Mozart at spinet with his sister Maria Anna ("Nannerl") and his father. (The portrait on the wall is of his mother)

Guilliaume Dufay (miniature from Champion des dames *by Martin Le Franc)*

are also quantities of duos by composers of Baroque times, who didn't always specify which instruments they had in mind, so that the music could be played about equally effectively on oboes, recorders, or violins; and there are duos that happen not to be called duos, like Ravel's Sonata for Violin and Cello (1922).

Duets between the hero and heroine are often the high points of operas and musical shows. Memorable examples are "Là ci darem la mano" in *Don Giovanni,* "O terra, addio" in *Aida,* and "Bess, You Is My Woman Now" in *Porgy and Bess.* Many equally fine duets are heard less often, notably the duets in Books VII and VIII of Monteverdi's *Madrigals* and the dozens of remarkable duets in Bach's cantatas.

DUET and DUO: compositions for two players or singers. The words have come to be used in certain traditional ways depending on the nature of the combination.

The most popular duets are written for piano. Known as "music for four hands," these are written for two players, who can be at one piano or at two pianos. The earliest four-hand piano duets were written around 1750 by J. C. Bach. The piano was then a new instrument and, in size and sonority, lent itself to such playing (the nine-year-old Mozart and his sister played duets for Johann Christian Bach on their visit to London in 1765). J. C. Bach was also the first composer to have his four-hand sonatas published, in 1775. Since his time, sonatas and other pieces for four hands have been written by Mozart, Beethoven, Schubert, Brahms, Poulenc, and Hindemith. Original duets to be played at two pianos include works by Mozart, Chopin, and Schumann. In addition to music originally composed as duets, duo-pianists also have many good arrangements of orchestral works and string quartets for one and two pianos. Playing these arrangements is a good way for pianists to get to know instrumental music.

The word "duo" is reserved for instrumental duets—traditionally for two members of the same family of instruments (two strings, two woodwinds, two brasses), but occasionally for more random combinations that the composer happens to think will work out. (On the other hand, the violin and piano combination—or the combination of any other instrument with a piano—is referred to as a sonata. Duos for woodwinds have been written by Wallingford Riegger, duos for tubas by Richard Goldman, and duos for violins by Mozart and Bartók. There

DUFAY, GUILLAUME (*c.* 1400–74): one of the first composers to become internationally known. Born in northern France, he started his musical life—as did so many other composers—by becoming a choirboy, in his case at the Cathedral of Cambrai. When nineteen he went to Italy, and for twenty-five years he alternated between singing there in the Chapel of the Pope and serving as choirmaster at Cambrai. Finally, in 1445, he settled in Cambrai as director of music at the cathedral.

As one of the leaders of the group of composers known as the Burgundian School, Dufay acted as a magnet, drawing many young composers to Cambrai to study with him. Burgundy provided both sacred and secular outlets for Dufay's talents. The rulers of Burgundy, Philip the Good and later Charles the Bold, were very much interested in the arts and encouraged Dufay to write his charming three-voice chansons and ballades. His music was sung on all great occasions—church festivals, noble marriages, celebrations, and coronations. When he died, he was mourned throughout Europe.

Dufay's compositions, like those of Beethoven, look back to the old and ahead to the new: his early works are closely related to those of the medieval period, and his later ones to the techniques and spirit of the Renaissance. Although his voices move along with great independence and in flowing melodic lines, Dufay placed greater emphasis than did his predecessors on the use of the harmonic intervals of thirds and sixths. The resulting sweetness of sound is much like the simple sweetness of Italian paintings of the period. Dufay was one of the first composers to use chords in the tonic-dominant sense of traditional harmony. A charming Gloria for voices and trumpets is almost completely based on the I-V-I progression.

In his religious music Dufay introduced popular songs, such as "L'Homme armé" (The Armed Man), using the melody as a cantus firmus around which he wove expressive melodies of his own. By using the same Gregorian chant or popular song in each movement of a mass, Dufay unified the work and helped to create the form of the "cyclic" mass.

Musicians neglected the music of Dufay for a long time after his death, but recently much of it has been published. Choruses have discovered its beauty, and there are now recordings of some of Dufay's masterpieces.

DULCIMER: an ancient stringed instrument of Persian origin brought to Europe by Crusaders returning from the Holy Land. It consists of a series of wire strings stretched across a wooden sound box. The strings are hit with sticks that have small knobs at the ends. The tone is soft and sweet. Since there is no way of dampening the strings, the tones of the dulcimer ring on and blur together, making a pleasant jangling sound.

The dulcimer became a popular instrument of peasants, particularly in Central and Eastern Europe, in the 1600's. In Germany it was called the *hackbrett,* or "board for chopping sausage meat," because of its shape. The dulcimer is still important in Hungarian and Rumanian gypsy music, being known as the *cimbalom.*

In 1697 a German musician, Pantaleon Hebenstreit, discovered that, by using hammers of different materials and by varying the amount of energy applied in playing the dulcimer, he was able to get a wide variety of tone colors and dynamics. His music was so expressive that it encouraged inventors to see if they could make the harpsichord equally expressive. Their work soon led to the invention of the piano.

The dulcimer, after hibernating for many years in the mountain region of the southeastern United States, has recently become popular accompanying folk songs.

Above left: Inamorato Cornelis, a 17th-century singer, playing the dulcimer
Above right: Jean Ritchie with her Appalachian dulcimer

DUPLE METER: meter characterized by two beats, or pulses, per measure. The common time signatures of duple meter are 2/4, 2/2, and 2/8. The polka, the galop, the march, and sometimes the tango are written in a meter of two.

Quadruple meter (4/4, 4/2, and 4/8) is basically a form of duple meter. Either it is a doubling of the note values of a duple meter:

or it is a compounding of two measures of duple meter with a primary accent on the first count of the measure and a secondary accent on the third:

$$1 \quad 2 \quad 3 \quad 4$$

so that the net result is a feeling of two main beats.

Duple meter is conducted simply with a downbeat followed by an upbeat:

The six-eight time signature represents a compound duple meter in which each beat has three subdivisions, as in Ex. 27.

Gigues, barcaroles, and many marches are written with a 6/8 time signature. Many of the final movements of Haydn's and Mozart's works are written in a fast 4/4 or 2/2.

Ex. 27 — Gigue, Rameau

Main Beats: 1   2   1   2   1   2   1

DVOŘÁK, ANTONIN (1841-1904): Czech composer of symphonies, operas, and chamber music, best known for his Symphony in E Minor, "From the New World." Dvořák was born in a small town near Prague, now the capital of Czechoslovakia. As a boy he loved music and had some lessons on the violin, although his father, a butcher and innkeeper, wanted him to carry on the family business. Instead, Dvořák at sixteen went to Prague and entered the musical world.

In Prague young Dvořák, while studying organ and composition, supported himself by playing the violin and viola in cafés and theaters. He wrote a great deal of music, but none of it was performed until he was more than thirty years old. Then several older composers—Brahms, Liszt, and Smetana—became interested in him and helped to get some of his music published. In 1874 a symphony won him a prize that provided him with a small pension, enabling him to give all of his time to composition.

Dvořák's home country was the old Slavic province of Bohemia, at that time a part of Austria. Following the lead of his fellow countryman Bedřic (Frederick) Smetana, Dvořák became interested in folk music and wrote his *Slavonic Dances* for piano duet. These were so successful that he arranged them for orchestra. Their brightness and tunefulness have made them popular on orchestral programs ever since. In 1876, in his grief over the death of his eldest child, Dvořák wrote one of his finest works, the *Stabat Mater*.

Dvořák was a hard-working composer. Pouring out large works and small, he wrote nine operas, nine symphonies, and concertos for cello, piano, and violin, as well as songs, piano pieces, and chamber works. All have a touch of the sweetly sad songs and dances of his Bohemian homeland.

In 1892 Dvořák went to New York to become the director of the National Conservatory of Music. There he wrote some of his best works, including the Concerto for Cello. He spent his summers in Spillville, Iowa, where there were many Czech farmers. In 1893 he wrote his Symphony in E Minor, "From the New World," in which he tried to catch the spirit of American folk songs and spirituals. The symphony (usually referred to as "Number 5," but actually his ninth and last) was immediately successful although there were great arguments as to whether or not he had used folk melodies in it. Thrilled with the United States, Dvořák also wrote a cantata to the American flag and offered to write a new national anthem. A great admirer of the work of Stephen Foster, he was one of the few trained musicians of his time to appreciate the talent of that American composer.

Among other works Dvořák wrote while in the United States are the String Quartet Opus 96 and String Quartet Opus 97, which are among his finest chamber works. After three years in America he grew homesick for his native land and arranged to return to his job as teacher of composition at the Prague Conservatory. Happy at the thought of going home, he wrote his little humoresques for piano. One of these, the seventh, became tremendously popular and has been arranged for various instruments. The version for violin is played more than any other.

Back in Prague, Dvořák settled down to a busy life, and was the first musician to become a member of the Austrian House of Lords. His symphonic poems, based on legends of Bohemia, and his opera *Rusalka (The Water Nymph)* established him as Czechoslovakia's most authentic musical voice.

Dvořák's musical style is not startlingly different from that of Brahms. His orchestration is a bit more colorful, relying on the individual timbres of the instruments. Like Schubert, he tends to weave back and forth between major and minor keys. His music is seldom complicated in rhythm or texture, being primarily songlike. Fond of putting sly little counter-melodies against his principal melody, he never does this to the point of obscuring the clarity of the music. Dvořák's musical form is mostly sectional— that is, balancing one phrase with another phrase, one section with another section. In his "New World" Symphony he uses a cyclic form in which material from one movement is carried forward to later movements.

Top: *Antonin Dvořák*
Bottom: *Dvořák's summer home in Spillville, Iowa*

DYNAMICS: gradations of intensity of sound in music. Few dynamic markings were written before 1700. The composer expected the performer to know how loudly a piece should be played. On the harpsichord there was no possibility of subtle shading; the music could get louder or softer all at once, but not gradually. Of the first composers to set down dynamic instructions many were Italian, and the markings they used were Italian words or their abbreviations. These are still in use today.

DYNAMIC MARKINGS

pianissimo	pp	very soft
piano	p	soft
mezzo-piano	mp	medium soft
mezzo-forte	mf	medium loud
forte	f	loud
fortissimo	ff	very loud
crescendo	cresc or ⟋	gradually louder
diminuendo	dim or ⟍	gradually softer
forte piano	fp	loud, then soft
sforzando	sfz	sudden strong accent

Once composers had seen the value of dynamic markings, they used them more and more. Eventually, by 1900, composers were using such extreme indications as *pppp* and *ffff* to make sure that their music would be played as softly or as loudly as possible. Modern composers, such as Bartók and Berg, put dynamic markings under almost every note.

The adoption of these refinements came at a time when acoustical engineers had established a standard unit of loudness called the decibel. But although numerical tempo indications have been used since Beethoven's time (see METRONOME), composers have not used decibel markings for loudness. They have kept in mind that a great deal depends on the size of the room in which the music is played, as well as on the individual instrument. Also, different people (one's neighbors, for instance) have different ideas of what "loud" and "soft" mean. To one listener a pianist might be banging loudly; to another he might be playing "just loud enough."

In orchestral writing, dynamic markings are used to balance the sounds of the various instruments. If a composer wants to blend a trumpet sound with a violin sound, he may mark a *p* under the trumpet part and an *mf* under the violin part—otherwise the trumpet would tend to cover up the violin.

Some contemporary composers treat dynamics as they do pitches and time values, organizing them as Schoenberg did in his tone row. In such a system of writing no two consecutive tones are sounded with the same intensity.

E: the pitch sounded by the white key immediately to the right of the two black keys on the keyboard of the piano. E is the top string of the violin, the top string of the guitar, the lowest written note in clarinet scores, the lowest string on the double bass:

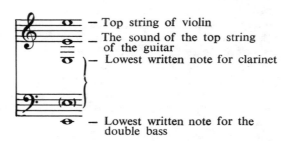

— Top string of violin
— The sound of the top string of the guitar
— Lowest written note for clarinet
— Lowest written note for the double bass

In France and Italy, E is called *mi*. The black key to the left of E is E-flat, called *Es* in Germany. (This allows German composers to use the note E-flat to represent the letter *s* when they want to make a theme by spelling out a name or word in notes, as Robert Schumann did in *Carnaval.*) There is no black key between E and F, so E-sharp is actually the same sound, enharmonically, as F.

Ex. 1 shows key signatures for the E and E-flat scales (there are no E-sharp scales). Except for the key of E-flat minor, in which little has been written (Prokofiev's Sixth Symphony; a few pieces by Chopin; the Brahms Intermezzo, Opus 118, Number 6; one prelude in *The Well-tempered Clavier*), the E keys are found in many musical compositions. E major has been used for piano sonatas by Haydn and Beethoven, for various short piano pieces, and for Beethoven's *Fidelio* overture and Haydn's Symphony Number 99.

E-flat major appears frequently in the piano works of Chopin, Schubert, Haydn, and Beethoven. Mozart wrote his Symphony Number 39, three piano concertos, and String Quartet K. 428 in this key, and Beethoven chose it for his "Eroica" Symphony (Number 3) and his Fifth Piano Concerto. The most sustained use of E-flat as a tonality is in Richard Wagner's prelude to *Das Rheingold,* in which an E-flat pedal is held for 136 measures.

E minor, the relative minor of G major with its signature of one sharp, was very much used by composers of the Baroque period. Among the large nineteenth-century works in E minor are Mendelssohn's Violin Concerto and three great symphonies: Brahms's Fourth, Tchaikovsky's Fifth, and Dvořák's "New World" Symphony.

EAR: the organ of hearing. Of its three parts, the outer ear is the part that can be seen. It connects with the eardrum, or tympanic membrane. Inside this is the middle ear, which consists of three small bones, and beyond these is the inner ear, which is so complicated that no one is sure how it works. It includes the vestibule, or entrance way; the semicircular canals, which give a person his sense of balance; and the cochlea. The cochlea is shaped somewhat like a snail. In it are various membranes, a liquid, many small hairs (cilia), and tiny bundles of thousands of nerves that eventually lead to the brain.

When a sound hits the eardrum, this vibrates. The vibrations are carried through the bones of the middle ear to the cochlea. This converts the vibrations into nerve messages that are sent to the brain.

The normal ear can hear as few as 20 vibrations per second and as many as 20,000. The number of sound waves per second that strike the ear determines the pitch of the sound. Having a "good ear" means being able to recognize small differences in pitch.

The ear is a sensitive instrument, and sound waves that are very powerful are likely to damage it. Gun crews use cotton in their ears to reduce the shock of the sound waves produced by firing.

Musicians often talk about the "inner ear." By this they mean the ability to hear music mentally while reading through a score. The brain stores up the memory of sounds, so that a composer who goes deaf, as Beethoven did, can still write music and know what it will sound like. A pianist who was deaf could still play the piano through the feel of his fingers on the keys. But a string player, who must use his ear to help him get the correct pitch, would be lost without his hearing.

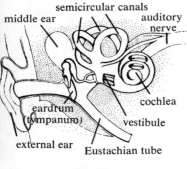

semicircular canals
middle ear   auditory
                    nerve
eardrum
(tympanum)   cochlea
                    vestibule
external ear   Eustachian tube

The Ear

Ex. 1

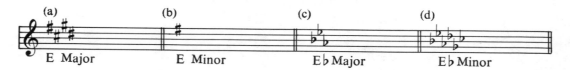

(a)   (b)   (c)   (d)
E Major   E Minor   E♭ Major   E♭ Minor

ELECTRONIC MUSIC: sound generated or altered by electronic means. Such sound may attempt to reproduce the timbre of already existing instruments or make available to composers a whole new world of tones.

The tone of any musical instrument can be analyzed just as a chemist can analyze a perfume. Scientists investigating the timbre of various instruments discovered that the difference between the sound of a trumpet and that of a flute is caused by the presence or absence of certain overtones in the harmonic series of each instrument's tone. They discovered that the recorded tone of a flute could be changed to that of a trumpet by adding certain overtones, much as new chemical compounds can be made by rearranging the molecular structure of an already existing substance. Having learned how to analyze tone, the scientist can now set up a series of tone generators—electronic vacuum tubes or transistors—and reproduce any instrumental sound or invent new ones.

This principle was applied first by the American inventor Laurens Hammond, who brought out his electronic organ in 1935. The Hammond organ was used as a substitute for the pipe organ because it occupied less space, but its possibilities were far greater in the eyes of the composer who was interested in new sounds. That development had to wait, however, as scientists and composers were drawn into participation in World War II.

Meanwhile other experimenters developed the electronic piano, which does not have the rich, percussive sound of a true piano. It has proved most successful in the classroom. Here twelve such pianos can be played at the same time, since the sound is heard only by the player and the teacher, who can tune in on any of the twelve players via earphones.

Many churches with bell towers too small for traditional carillons have installed electronic carillons. Instead of large cast bells weighing many tons, the electronic carillon uses thin metal rods vibrated by means of an electromagnet. The vibrations are picked up, amplified, and fed to loudspeakers.

Certain soft-speaking instruments, namely the guitar and double bass, have had their tones amplified electronically. The result has been not just equality of sound with other instruments of the dance band, but new playing techniques made possible by radical changes in the shape of the instrument itself.

The American composer John Cage has experimented with amplification of each string of the members of a string quartet. Controlling the amplifier himself, Cage has succeeded in making interesting and controversial accompaniments for the dances of Merce Cunningham.

A different approach to making what might be called "synthetic" sounds was that of the Canadian film maker Norman MacLaren. Studying sound tracks on films, MacLaren reasoned that sound, in this case, had its picture taken. He then proceeded to "paint" his own sound directly on the sound track itself. The labor of analyzing the almost imperceptible variations and differences of pitch and timbre, as they appeared on film, was so tremendous that MacLaren had to be content to use this technique only in the opening section of his films.

The development of the magnetic tape recorder during World War II led to a new form of electronic music. New sounds could be manipulated in many ways. They could be recorded at one speed and played at another. The sound could be played backward so that a piano tone, for instance, made a crescendo instead of a diminuendo, or its initial percussive beat could be cut

Norman MacLaren scraping emulsion from 35-mm film with various knives, styluses, and needlepoints. These strokes, when the film is projected, create percussive sound effects

Vladimir Ussachevsky, composer and professor of music at Columbia University, in front of some of his electronic equipment

Top: *Otto Luening*
Middle: *Karl Heinz Stockhausen at work*
Bottom: *the first electronic score to have been published—Karl Heinz Stockhausen's* Etude II, *Universal Edition, London, 1956*

off. Echo chambers reverberated sounds so that tones seemed to have pulsations. Natural sounds, such as surf or rain, could be mixed with the sounds of musical instruments and voices. Tape-recorder music of this kind first became popular in France, where it was called *musique concrète*. In the United States the most effective musique concrète has been created by Otto Luening and Vladimir Ussachevsky and by choreographer Alwin Nikolais for his dances. Musique concrète is, of course, an assemblage of sounds similar to the montage of movie film. Once assembled, the music will always sound the same, since no live performers are involved. Thus far it has been most successful as an accompaniment for dance or film.

But it was the development of pure electronic music itself, extending the principles of Hammond's electronic organ, that began to capture the interest of composers during the 1950's and 1960's. Scientists from the R.C.A. laboratories, working in conjunction with composers from Columbia and Princeton universities, perfected the "music synthesizer": a large-scale system of generators that could make any sound desired by a composer.

Of course, as with any musical instrument (and this is what the synthesizer is), the composer, who is also the performer, must decide what his vocabulary of sounds is going to be. He can set up his battery of generators to reproduce the sound of conventional instruments tuned to a traditional scale, or he can invent new sounds tuned to any scale known or unknown. A more recent development is the use of an electronic computer programmed for certain timbres and pitches. The sound can be made

to "decay," increase in intensity, or stay constant. The composer works as he would with any group of sounds: he plans a composition in his mind, but instead of writing notes on music paper he makes a graph or chart which can be translated into sounds. The music, once made, is permanently captured on magnetic tape and needs only a tape machine to perform it.

At present many composers are creating music through these new ways of sound generation. Since large equipment such as the synthesizer is prohibitively expensive, the composer who wishes to use such a device must go to the music center that houses it. Smaller tone generators and a group of tape recorders are still expensive and not found in many composers' homes. In the United States there are electronic studios at Yale, the University of Illinois, and U.C.L.A. Soon every school of music will probably have such a studio for its faculty and student composers. In Europe the studios are often run in conjunction with government radio stations.

Electronic music is still in its infancy, but many fine works have already been composed in this new idiom. Edgard Varèse, whose music in the 1920's and 1930's seemed to be bursting all conventional bounds, in his *Poème electronique* (1958) composed a work that is powerful and terrifying. Luening and Ussachevsky have composed short pieces that might be called Impressionist in quality. Milton Babbitt, Mario Davidowsky, Karl Heinz Stockhausen, Gerald Strang, A. J. Hiller, and Henk Badings have used electronic sounds by themselves or combined them with the sounds of live instruments and voices to create interesting works.

These composers are faced with the problem of not only inventing a new vocabulary but also developing a new grammar of music. Some of them believe that electronic music will be the "true" music of the future. Others believe that it will add new sounds to the traditional ones and that the new and the old will continue to coexist.

What of the audience? Listeners have already accepted electronic sounds accompanying dance and film, including television commercials. Will they come to concerts to look at a set of loudspeakers? Or will they buy records and have their concerts at home? Can musical traditions that have developed over thousands of years be replaced in a few decades?

Electronic music has opened up a whole new world of sounds. It has also raised a host of questions that can be answered only in the future.

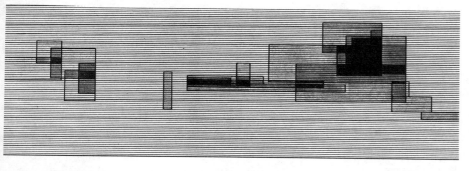

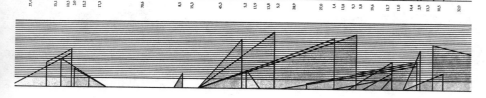

At left: *Edward VII's coronation parade, 1902*
Below: *Sir Edward Elgar*

ELGAR, SIR EDWARD (1857–1934): famous English composer. His musical education, like that of many other composers, was both practical and scattered. He learned much from his father, who was a music dealer, organist, and violinist in Worcester. Elgar at one time played the bassoon and picked up enough piano technique to act as a glee-club accompanist. For a while he worked as a clerk in a law office to support himself as he studied and composed. He took some violin lessons in London but decided that his playing would never be of concert caliber. For a while he was bandmaster in a Worcester mental institution and conductor of the local Amateur Instrumental Society.

At the age of thirty-two, when he married, Elgar was still an unknown and little-employed musician. England at the time was a good place for a composer only if he came from Germany or was named Sir Arthur Sullivan. Elgar persisted, however, and with his concert overture, *Froissart* (1890), achieved a small success. There followed six choral works that helped to build his reputation. When his *Variations on an Original Theme* for orchestra, generally known as the "Enigma" Variations, was played in 1899, English critics began to realize that a major talent was emerging in (of all places) England.

This work, which remains Elgar's most frequently performed orchestral composition, contains a series of fourteen variations, each dedicated to a friend except the final one, dedicated to himself. The "enigma" is the puzzle that many musicians have tried to solve: What is the unknown theme that Elgar said underlies the whole work?

The "Enigma" Variations was followed by his greatest choral work, the oratorio *The Dream of Gerontius* (1900). Based on a poem by Cardinal John Henry Newman, this work has a mystical and visionary quality that transcends everything else written by Elgar. Ironically, its beauty was not recognized on its first performance in Birmingham, England, and not until 1902, at a performance in Düssledorf, Germany, did it receive full critical acclaim.

While pursuing a career as a composer of large-scale choral works, Elgar wrote several instrumental compositions, which were destined to bring him more general fame than anything else he composed. In 1901 he wrote the concert overture *Cockaigne,* subtitled "In London Town"—a brilliantly scored description of the great English city. In the same year two marches for orchestra under the title *Pomp and Circumstance* were premiered at a promenade concert. These were the first of five marches composed by Elgar under that title, the other three being written in 1905, 1907, and 1930.

When asked to provide a ceremonial ode in honor of the coronation of Edward VII, Elgar used, in part, a strong singable melody from the first *Pomp and Circumstance* march. It was set to the words of "Land of Hope and Glory." Edward VII became ill and the performance did not take place as planned, but the melody became popular. Elgar was knighted in 1904 in recognition of his contribution to English music.

Elgar's music is generally conservative, in the great German tradition of Schumann and Brahms—a tradition most evident in his violin and cello concertos and his two symphonies. Endowed with a gift for creating melodies and with a fine ear for orchestral colors, Elgar wrote works that are warm, direct, and skillful. While living through a period when musical traditions of several hundred years were being questioned, Elgar remained secure in his own beliefs and concentrated on the job of the composer—actually writing music.

At **right:** *Duke Ellington's Band in 1929*
Below: *Duke Ellington*

ELLINGTON, EDWARD KENNEDY ("DUKE") (1899–1974): composer, arranger, pianist, and bandleader. Ellington composed some of the most colorful music of his time. He grew up in Washington, D.C., where he started to play the piano when he was seven. At seventeen he was torn between becoming a commercial artist or a musician and tried both: in the daytime he painted, at night he played the piano for dances.

In 1923 he moved to New York with several of his dance-band buddies, and within a few years the group had developed the Ellington "jungle" style. Ellington was extremely responsive to the individual abilities of his colleagues, an inventive group in their own right, and the Ellington style, with its distinctive line of new numbers and its wild-sounding arrangements, was something the whole band worked out together. They experimented with an odd variety of mutes for the brasses, the plumber's plunger being much favored for special effects, and after trumpeter James "Bubber" Miley joined the group, the Ellington band became noted for the way the brasses growled and grunted out its rhythm figures. The band's opening at the Cotton Club in 1927 created a sensation, with clarinets and saxophones wailing away in an evocative "jungle" style like nothing ever heard before. The rhythm section, with Ellington himself at the piano, kept a steady, danceable beat, punctuated every now and then by a stab of Sonny Greer's cymbal. Ellington's writhing theme song, the "East St. Louis Toodle-oo," soon became familiar from nation-wide radio broadcasts.

In 1930 Ellington became a national figure with his first big song hit, "Mood Indigo" (earlier tried out as "Dreamy Blues"). When the Depression years arrived, Ellington managed to keep his band together, but it seemed as good a time as any to take the band to Europe, and Ellington did, in 1933. The trip was a smashing success. This was also the year of two of Ellington's other great song hits, "Solitude" and "Sophisticated Lady."

Underlying Ellington's many achievements had been an irrepressible urge to experiment. He made use of daringly dissonant chords, producing original new combinations of sounds from his instruments, even including wordless singing blending with the instruments. Undaunted by the time limitation of the old 10-inch 78-rpm records, he let a single piece spill over two sides ("Crescendo and Diminuendo in Blue") or even four ("Reminiscing in Tempo"). In more recent years he had chafed over the barrier dividing jazz from symphonic music. In 1943 he deliberately blurred the line between the two in "Black, Brown and Beige," and in 1955 had the pleasure of hearing the combined sounds of his own orchestra and the Symphony of the Air in a performance of his *Night Creature* at Carnegie Hall. Ellington, a deeply religious man, wrote three Sacred Concerts to be performed in churches. In addition to his more than 6,000 compositions, he wrote an autobiography, *Music Is My Mistress*.

ENCORE: a French word meaning "again." It is shouted by English-speaking audiences at the end of a composition they want repeated, or at the end of a recital to urge the performer to play or sing more. In France and Germany audiences who want to hear something again shout *bis*, the Latin word for "twice."

An "encore piece" is a song or instrumental composition that suits the relaxed mood of the performer and the audience at the end of a recital. It is often shorter and lighter than the other works on the program.

Ex. 2 — Symphony in D Minor, Franck

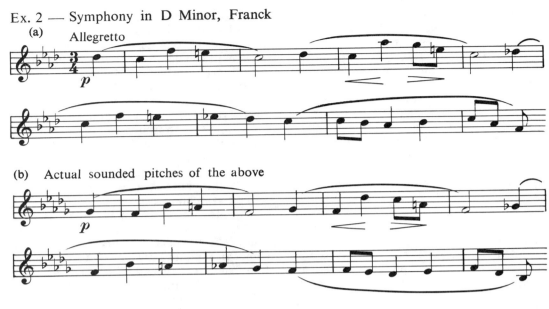

(a) Allegretto

(b) Actual sounded pitches of the above

Oboe   English Horn

ENGLISH HORN: an alto oboe. Doubtfully English and certainly not a horn, the English horn is an oboe with a bulb at the lower end. Its dark, mournful tone is remembered from the first theme of the Largo movement of Dvořák's symphony "From the New World" and the beautiful melody (Ex. 2a) in the slow movement of César Franck's Symphony in D Minor. The English horn (called *cor anglais* in French) is a transposing instrument sounding a perfect fifth lower than written, so that the actual sound of the Franck melody would be five tones below the written ones (Ex. 2b). Its range is about two and a half octaves:

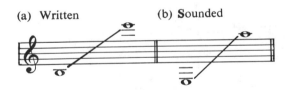

(a) Written   (b) Sounded

The ancestors of the English horn were the French tenor oboe and oboe da caccia. Originally curved like the bass clarinet, the English horn assumed its present straight form in 1839. It came into use first in the opera orchestras of the late eighteenth century—in Vienna and later in Paris, where it became a favorite of Gluck, Berlioz, Meyerbeer, and Bizet. Rossini in 1829 gave the English horn an important role in the overture to his *William Tell,* and since that time the instrument has been accepted as standard in the orchestra.

English horn players have had almost no compositions written expressly for them. Paul Hindemith in 1941 did write a sonata for English horn and piano. But generally performers have had to be content with isolated moments of glory in orchestral music. One such moment is the lonesome solo (see Ex. 56, page 617) Wagner gives the English horn at the beginning of the third act of *Tristan and Isolde.* The nearest thing to a concerto for English horn is Sibelius' *Swan of Tuonela.*

ENHARMONIC TONES: tones that sound alike but have different names. F-sharp and G-flat, C-sharp and D-flat, and E-sharp and F are examples of enharmonic tones.

Composers, particularly in the nineteenth century, often used enharmonic tones when they changed keys. By changing the spelling of a chord, the composer can make it go to an unexpected chord or a new key:

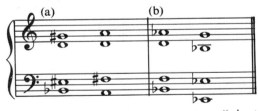

An enharmonic tone can act as a "pivot tone" in changing keys:

Key of G   Key of D♭

ENSEMBLE: a group of performers—instrumental, vocal, or both combined. The term is usually applied to groups of less than symphonic proportions, such as string quartets, madrigal groups, and chamber orchestras. Operatic ensembles often occur in final opera scenes when two or more singers perform together, sometimes with the addition of a chorus.

The term ensemble is more often used to describe the *ésprit* of a performance—its unity, its integrity, its totality. In true ensemble playing or singing each instrumentalist or vocalist uses his skill to achieve a unified blend, with proper phrasing and dynamic balance, in order to realize the music as the composer intended.

Ensemble music is probably as old as music itself. It existed in the ancient cultures and has been an important part of the history of music. At various times, particularly in the Baroque period, ensemble music has featured group improvisation—a practice carried on today by experimental composers as well as by jazz musicians. The improvisational ensemble can be a fine example of individualism and cooperation.

EROICA: Beethoven's Third Symphony, in E-flat, Opus 55. It was composed in 1803 and first performed in 1804. Beethoven was an admirer of Napoleon Bonaparte and originally wrote a title page dedicating the work to Napoleon, but when the work was published the title read: "Heroic symphony composed to celebrate the memory of a great man and dedicated to His Serene Highness Prince Lobkowitz." Many persons think Beethoven grew disgusted when Napoleon proclaimed himself emperor. But when Beethoven wrote to his publisher in 1804 he said, "The Symphony is really entitled Bonaparte . . . I think the work will interest the musical public." Whether or not the "Eroica" was dedicated to Napoleon, it is one of the grandest as well as one of the longest symphonies.

The first movement, in E-flat, starts with two loud chords that serve to get the attention of the audience. The first theme (Ex. 3) comes in right away. There is a long transition based on several ideas (Ex. 4). The transition takes the music to the key of B-flat and a calmer theme (Ex. 5). The music soon builds up to a heroic closing theme:

that is related to the first theme. In the development section Beethoven tosses bits of themes around and builds them up to a dissonant hammering climax (Ex. 6, top of next page). The music quiets down, and suddenly a new theme is heard (Ex. 7).

Title page of the first edition of the "Eroica" Symphony

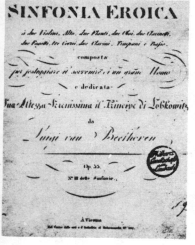

Ex. 6

Ex. 7

After this new theme Beethoven prepares to get back to his first theme and the key of E-flat. The music seems to unwind and to be awaiting something. The horns get impatient and come in "too soon":

There is a fast crescendo, and the first theme comes back as it was in the beginning. So do the other themes. There is a long coda in which several themes are put together:

The theme that was new in the development comes back and becomes important. Beethoven brings the movement to a brilliant close.

The second movement is a funeral march in the relative key of C minor. The violins play a sobbing melody while the double basses seem to shuffle along from note to note like mourners at a funeral (Ex. 8). There is a trio section in C major that has a feeling of hope in it:

After the trio the first theme returns and is developed. Next comes a short coda in which the violins play the first theme. But the theme is full of rests, like a voice that is choked with grief (Ex. 9).

After a wild scherzo in E-flat the symphony

Ex. 8

Ex. 9

Ex. 10

Ex. 11

ends with a fast finale. This starts with a rushing string passage and six loud chords, out of which creeps a little sketchy theme (Ex. 10) that, one senses, is a bass part to some theme. After some tentative melodies have been added to this, Beethoven brings in the theme (Ex. 11) that really fits it. On these two themes he writes one of the greatest sets of variations ever written. These were the same themes he had used for variations at the end of his ballet *Prometheus* and for a set of Variations for Piano, Opus 35.

The "Eroica" Symphony marks a great turning point in music. Longer and deeper in meaning than any previous symphony, the "Eroica" ends the Classical period and heralds the titanic and highly personal period of Romanticism. It stands in majesty as one of the great mountain peaks of music.

ÉTUDE: a technical exercise cast in musical form. (The word itself is French for "study.") It is usually based on a single playing problem, such as arpeggios, rapid passage work, crossing of hands on the piano, or bowing problems or double stops on the violin. Typically, the composer invents a musical idea that fits the problem, then uses the idea over and over with changes of key for variety.

Many études are written for practice purposes only; their musical interest is slight. Others are written in such an interesting manner that they are played in recitals. These are sometimes called concert études. Piano études often heard in recitals are those by Chopin, Liszt, Scriabin, and Debussy.

Études are almost as old as instrumental music, dating back to the sixteenth century. The first composer of études as they are known today was Muzio Clementi (1752–1832).

EXPOSITION: the term applied to the first part of a composition, in which the composer

introduces to the listener the thematic material on which the work or movement is to be based. The term is used particularly in reference to FUGUE and SONATA-ALLEGRO forms.

The exposition section of a fugue introduces the subject and the various voices that will be presenting the subject or its transposition, in which case it is known as the answer. The usual order of entrances in a four-voice fugue is: subject-answer-subject-answer, although this order is sometimes changed by the composer. As the second and succeeding voices take up the subject, the composer invents melodic lines that make interesting counterpoints to the subject or answer. Before the entrance of the third voice, and sometimes of the fourth, there is usually a transitional passage in which the composer gives a moment of anticipatory suspense to the listener. This passage also allows the composer to manipulate the harmonic rhythm of the work so that the entrance of the subject will come in on the correct chord. The opening of Bach's Fugue in G Minor, *The Well-tempered Clavier*, Book I, Number 16, shows a subject one and one-half measures long, followed by the answer, which is of the same length. Before the entrance of the third voice, Bach interjects a measure that serves to break the monotony of hearing the subject come in regularly every measure and a half. This fugue also shows voices entering in pairs: alto-soprano, bass-tenor (Ex. 12, on the next page).

The exposition, or statement, section of a sonata-allegro form is a bit more complex than that of a fugue. This is to be expected, since a sonata is generally much longer. Its exposition consists of three main sections: the first contains a theme, or group of themes, stated in the tonic key. Then comes a transition in which the composer usually moves toward the key of the dominant or the relative major. In this new key he states a second theme or group of themes, although he

Johann Baptist Cramer (1771–1858), author of the well-known 100 Progressive Études

sometimes repeats the first theme if the sonata or symphony is to be monothematic—based on one theme throughout. A closing section, introducing a new theme, is sometimes brought in to round off the exposition: this is basically a decorated cadence in the second key and might be followed by a brief codetta or ending. The end of the exposition is usually indicated by a double bar with repeat marks. At this point the composer usually writes a first and second ending, the first pointing the music back toward the beginning, and the second, toward the development section. The repeat is obligatory—yet many distinguished performers choose to ignore the repeat signs.

Ex. 12 — Fugue No. 16 from *The Well-tempered Clavier*, Book I, J.S. Bach

F: a mark that indicates dynamics, a clef, or a pitch. As *f* it stands for *forte,* an Italian word meaning "loud." The F clef, commonly known as the bass clef, is the one that curls around the fourth line of the staff and marks the position of the F below middle C:

F as a pitch name (it is called *fa* in France and Italy) is situated on the lines and spaces of the staves as shown in this example, a passage from Beethoven's Piano Sonata Opus 111, which contains only the note F:

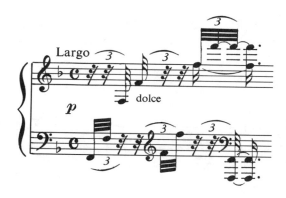

On the keyboard, F is the white key immediately to the left of the group of three black keys:

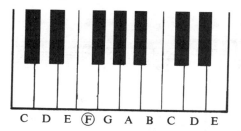

C D E Ⓕ G A B C D E

F-sharp is the black key to the right of F. Since there is no black key below F, F-flat is the same key as E. The scale produced by playing from F to F on the white keys is the medieval Lydian mode.

The key signatures for the various F and F-sharp keys are:

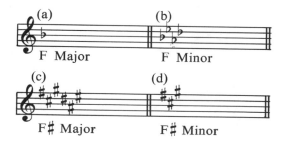

(a) F Major (b) F Minor
(c) F♯ Major (d) F♯ Minor

F major is the key of many well-known compositions. Among them are Bach's Invention Number 8, "Brandenburg" Concerto Number 1, *Italian Concerto* for harpsichord, and Toccata for Organ. Others include Beethoven's "Spring" Sonata for violin and piano, his Sixth ("Pastoral") and Eighth Symphonies, and his String Quartets Numbers 1, 7, and 16; Brahms's Third Symphony and String Quartet Opus 88; and Ravel's String Quartet.

The key of F♯ major is rarely used, possibly because of its forbidding key signature with six sharps. Bach wrote two preludes and fugues in this key for his *Well-tempered Clavier,* and the French composer Fauré used it for his *Ballade* for piano and orchestra, and Beethoven for his Piano Sonata, Opus 78.

F minor is the key of sonatas for piano by Schumann and Brahms; the Piano Concerto Opus 21 by Chopin; and the Fourth Symphony of Tchaikovsky. It is also the key of Beethoven's String Quartet Opus 95; a sonata for clarinet and piano by Brahms; and Chopin's *Fantasy,* Opus 21, and Études Numbers 9, 14, and 25.

One of the earliest large compositions in F-sharp minor is Haydn's Symphony Number 45, the "Farewell." Other works in this key are sonatas for piano by Brahms and Schumann.

FALLA, MANUEL DE (1876–1946): the composer of colorful operas, ballets, and shorter works that breathe the air of his native Spain. He was born in Cádiz, where his mother gave him his first lessons at the piano. After going to Madrid to continue his piano study, he began to compose. In 1905 his opera *La vida breve (The Brief Life)* won a prize, but it was not performed until 1913.

Falla lived in Paris from 1907 to 1914, becoming a friend and admirer of Debussy and Ravel. In his own music he tried to mix their styles with that of his own Spanish background. Returning to Spain, he founded a festival of *cante hondo,* the old type of southern Spanish folk song that is the ancestor of present-day flamenco music. He also did a great deal of teaching and conducting; many of the most gifted young Spanish composers came to study with him. In 1939, after the Spanish Civil War, Falla moved to Argentina. He lived there until his death, working on a vast cantata about Columbus, *La Atlántida,* which he did not live to complete.

Falla's best-known works are those for the stage: the puppet opera *El retablo de maese*

Pedro (The Show of Master Pedro), the ballets *El amor brujo (Love, the Magician),* which includes the popular Ritual Dance of Fire, and *El sombrero de tres picos (The Three-cornered Hat).* His settings of *Seven Spanish Folk Songs* are popular vocal works. His *Pour le Tombeau de Debussy,* in memory of his French friend, was originally written for guitar solo. Later Falla added three more parts to the work, making it the orchestral suite *Homenajes (Homages),* in which he paid his respects to Debussy, Arbos, Dukas, and Pedrell.

Falla was a pianist, and it is for the piano that he wrote his *Four Spanish Pieces.* The piano has the solo part in Falla's beautiful, descriptive *Nights in the Gardens of Spain.* Later in life Falla turned from Spanish folk music and took his inspiration from classic harpsichord music written by Domenico Scarlatti during a long stay in Spain. Inspired by Scarlatti, Falla wrote one of the first modern masterpieces for harpsichord: his Concerto for Harpsichord and Chamber Orchestra. Falla's work (Ex. 1) is full of musical wit and the vivid use of instrumental tone colors. His harmonies are mixtures of the rich chords of Debussy and the predictable chords of Spanish guitar music. Little counterpoint is used; mostly his music is melody and accompaniment—clear, direct, and to the point.

Falla at the harpsichord during the recording of his Concerto for Harpsichord and Chamber Orchestra

Ex. 1 — "Danza del terror" from *El amor brujo*

Manuel de Falla as drawn by Picasso

Ex. 2 — "Pantomine" from *El amor brujo*

Andante tranquillo

A scene from El amor brujo *(Op-éra Comique production, Paris, 1948)*

Much of it is based on Spanish dance rhythms, with the characteristic castanets and guitars. Spaniards say of Falla's music that it has in it the real Spain—not the flashy imitation of Spain that is so common (Ex. 2).

FANFARE: a musical announcement played on brass instruments before the arrival of an important person. Originally a fanfare heralded the entrance of a king into his great hall or into the royal box at the theater. Fanfares were also played on state occasions, such as coronations. In the England of Shakespeare's time they were often known as flourishes and sometimes as "tuckets" (a word related to *toccata*).

Fanfares were usually played on trumpets, which were historically the instruments of the nobility. The melody of the fanfare is often built from the notes of one major triad, although modern fanfares use a whole variety of brass instruments and move around from one triad to another. Heroic dotted-note rhythms predominate—first in long notes, then in shorter ones.

Composers are fond of writing fanfares, particularly in opera. Wagner includes many in *Tannhaüser* and *Lohengrin*. One of the best-known occurs in the former just before the famous Processional March (Ex. 3).

A most dramatic fanfare occurs in Beethoven's opera *Fidelio*. It is played offstage, at the very climax of the action, to announce the coming of the king's minister, who will rescue the hero (see Ex. 10, page 179). The same fanfare was used by Beethoven in one of his overtures to *Fidelio*—the one known as Leonore Number 3. A variant of the fanfare is heard also in Leonore Number 2.

Ex. 3 — *Tannhäuser*, Wagner

FANTASIA (FANTASY, FANCY): a composition in which the composer relaxes a bit from a strict musical form or allows his musical thoughts to change from moment to moment.

Among the earliest fantasias were those for keyboard instruments or lute in which the composer seemed to be writing out improvisations. The best-known fantasia of this type is Bach's *Chromatic Fantasy,* which starts with several scale passages and then switches to a section of broken chords, followed by a block of strange harmonies, snatches of recitative, a suggestion of a chorale melody, more passage work, arpeggios, and an ending that leads to a fugue. Bach's Fantasia and Fugue in G Minor for organ and Mozart's three Fantasias for Piano (K. 394, 396, and 397) are other outstanding works in this style.

Another kind of early fantasia was a predecessor of the fugue. It was related to the ricercar, a contrapuntal work in several sections, each based on a variant of a single subject. Ex. 4 shows the beginnings of each of the three sections of a fantasia by Johann Froberger (1616–67). In the first part the opening subject is answered by the second voice in contrary motion. In the second part the notes of the subject are in triple meter and the answering voice reverses the rhythmic pattern of the first voice. In the last section the subject, now in 4/4, is set off by a second idea, which recurs from time to time (Ex. 4a, b, and c).

The contrapuntal fantasia became a popular form of instrumental chamber music in late sixteenth- and seventeenth-century England. Often called fancies, these works were written for keyboard instruments or for groups, or consorts, of viols. The fantasias, or fancies, by Byrd, Gibbons, Jenkins, and Purcell are some of the finest instrumental compositions by English composers. In 1910 Vaughan Williams carried on the old English tradition by writing a fantasia on a theme by Tallis for string orchestra.

In the nineteenth century the term fantasia was used in several ways. Beethoven gave the name "Sonata Like a Fantasia" to both his sonatas Opus 27, Numbers 1 and 2, probably because neither follows the conventional form of a sonata. (Opus 27, Number 2, is popularly known as the "Moonlight" Sonata.) Similar large-scale fantasias are those by Schubert *(Wanderer-Fantasie),*

Ex. 4 — Fantasia, Froberger

Schumann (Fantasie, Opus 17), and Chopin (Fantasia, Opus 49). Brahms's Fantasias, Opus 116, are a set of short piano pieces that alternate between incisive capriccios and romantically longing intermezzos.

Another nineteenth-century form of fantasia is the highly decorated transcription of themes from opera written for piano, cornet, orchestra, or band. Many fantasias of this kind are virtuoso display pieces. Liszt's fantasias on works by Beethoven and Bellini and his *Don Juan Fantasia* are the most notable among them.

The middle section of a sonata, usually known as the development, is often called the "free fantasia" section.

FAURÉ, GABRIEL (1845–1924):

a French composer and teacher who was, in a quiet way, one of the most influential musicians of his time. Fauré was born in Pamiers, a small town at the foot of the Pyrenees in southern France. His father, an educator, recognized his son's musical talent and took him to Paris to study organ and composition. Fauré's teacher in composition was Camille Saint-Saëns.

Fauré became choirmaster at the Church of the Madeleine in 1877, and in 1896

Gabriel Fauré at the piano (1898)

finally became its organist. The same year he also became teacher of composition at the Paris Conservatory. His pupils there later included the composers Ravel, Enesco, Roger-Ducasse, and Florent Schmitt. Another pupil was Nadia Boulanger, teacher of many American composers.

As a composer, Fauré is best known through his vocal and chamber music. His violin sonatas, cello sonatas, and quintets for piano and strings contain some of his finest ideas. He wrote ninety-six songs, most of them gently flowing, often passionate, but rarely dramatic. The piano accompaniments are graceful and serve as a background for the voice. Many of Fauré's songs, such as "Après un Rêve," "Lydia," "Clair de lune," and the group known as *La Bonne Chanson,* have become widely known. His *Requiem Mass* and his *Pavane* for orchestra and chorus are also often performed.

The titles of Fauré's piano music—nocturnes, barcaroles, impromptus, waltzes—show that he was an admirer of Chopin. Most of these charming pieces are little known outside France.

In the world at large Fauré has been overshadowed by Debussy and Ravel. His music sounds simple, but it has the simplicity of a polished gem. It is always exquisitely done, full of gentle experiments.

Fauré was one of the first modern composers to use the medieval church scales or modes. These led him to harmonies which, with his poignant melodies, give his music a sense of nostalgia for the past.

FAUST:

an opera with music by Charles Gounod.

The legend of Faust, or Doctor Faustus, which has served as the basis for plays, operas, and symphonies, was based on the many stories that grew up about an early sixteenth-century astrologer and magician who lived in Germany. He was so skillful that people believed he had learned his black arts from the devil. As Faust's fame spread, so did the stories about his magical powers. All the old superstitions about men who sold their souls to the devil were added to the legends about Faust.

The English dramatist Marlowe wrote the first play about Faust around 1588. Many puppet plays performed by strolling players throughout Europe were based on the Faust theme. German writers in the 1700's discovered Faust and made of him a kind of national hero.

The greatest play about Faust was written by the German author Goethe. Goethe's work makes Faust the symbol of all men who search for truth, are betrayed by their desires, and find salvation through good deeds. It served to inspire operas by Berlioz, Gounod, Boito, Busoni, and Schumann. Wagner wrote a *Faust Overture* and Liszt a *Faust Symphony.* Of all these works based on the story of Faust, the opera by Gounod has been the most popular.

Gounod's *Faust,* based only on the first part of Goethe's drama, has a libretto by Jules Barbier and Michel Carré. At the beginning of the opera, Faust is an aging scholar and philosopher who has spent his days trying to solve the riddle of life. Weary, and waiting for death, he is visited in his lonely cell by Mephistopheles—Satan—in the disguise of a dashing nobleman. Mephistopheles promises Faust youth, riches, and love in return for his soul. He shows Faust a vision of Marguerite, a beautiful young girl, at her spinning wheel. Faust falls in love with the vision and hastily signs an agreement with the devil.

Transformed into a young man, Faust meets Marguerite at a *kermesse,* a kind of country fair. Thanks to Mephistopheles, Faust can offer her a box of jewels as well as his love—even though he realizes that Marguerite is doomed to a life of misery if she falls in love with him. He seduces Marguerite and she becomes a pathetic figure of scorn in the town. When her brother, Valentine, returns from war he is horrified to find that his noble, sweet sister is to become an unwed mother. Discovering that Faust was her lover, he challenges him to a duel. The unwilling Faust draws his sword and, with the help of Mephistopheles, mortally wounds Valentine.

Marguerite goes to church and prays for forgiveness at the altar while Mephistopheles mocks her and tells her that she is damned. The last scene of the opera takes place in prison where Marguerite is waiting to be hanged for the murder of her child. Faust, at the instigation of Mephistopheles, tries to persuade Marguerite to save herself by selling her soul. She refuses when her thoughts go back to the happy days of the past. As she prays to heaven for salvation, a choir of angelic voices assures her that her soul belongs to God because she has repented. Mephistopheles leaves, taking Faust with him.

In its first version *Faust* was an opéra comique—that is, its dialogue was spoken rather than sung. It was performed in this way during the first ten years after its première at the Théâtre Lyrique in Paris in 1859. Later, in 1869, for its performance at the Paris Opéra, the dialogue was set to music.

Left to right: Mirella Freni as Marguerite, Gianni Raimondi as Faust, and Giorgio Tozzi as Mephistopheles

Ex. 5 — Introduction

Ex. 6 — Waltz, Act II

Ex. 7 — "Jewel Song," Act III

*Cesare Siepi as Mephistopheles in
Faust*

Within a few years after its première, *Faust* had become one of the most successful of all operas, although Gounod at first had trouble finding a publisher for it. It was the first opera performed by the Metropolitan Opera Company at its home at 39th Street and Broadway.

Its popularity is easy to understand. Gounod had a fertile mind for inventing melody as well as a keen dramatic sense. The music ranges from highly chromatic sections, as in the introduction to the opera (Ex. 5), to a simple waltz (Ex. 6), the dazzling "Jewel Song" (Ex. 7), and the rousing "Soldiers' Chorus."

Gounod was a highly religious man who at one time considered becoming a priest. The religious music throughout *Faust* is especially fine, culminating in Marguerite's final outcry to heaven.

FIDDLE: a five-stringed instrument played by minstrels and jongleurs in the twelfth and thirteenth centuries. Another name for this instrument was *vielle*. One string was a drone, plucked with the thumb. The other strings were played by means of a bow, making the fiddle an important ancestor of the violin family.

The fiddle was one of the most popular instruments in medieval times, being used to play for dancing, to accompany the songs of the troubadours, and to double or replace voices in religious music.

The term fiddle is still applied to the violin of today.

FIDELIO: Beethoven's only opera. The libretto, by Joseph Sonnleithner, was based on a plot that had been used for several other operas and was typical of rescue operas in which the hero is saved in the nick of time. Such plots were popular around 1800, reflecting true experiences of people who had dramatically escaped death during the French Revolution.

The first performance of *Fidelio* took place in Vienna in November 1805—not an auspicious time, because Vienna had just fallen to the army of Napoleon. The Viennese who might have been attracted to this first opera by a popular young composer were afraid to venture out into the streets. Mostly the audience consisted of French officers and soldiers who neither understood the German words nor liked the music. After three performances *Fidelio* was withdrawn.

Beethoven's close friends who had seen the opera felt that it was too long, and they told him so during a long, grueling evening, in the course of which he argued over every point but finally agreed to shorten the work from three acts to two. He reworked much of the music, and this new version was presented in March 1806. This time *Fidelio* seemed to be a success, but Beethoven, always suspicious of those with whom he had business dealings, decided that he was being cheated, and he called the venture off after five performances.

In 1814 Beethoven revised *Fidelio* once more. When it was presented in May of that year, Beethoven conducted, although by this time he was so deaf that the musicians looked for their directions to an assistant conductor stationed behind the composer. The opera was a success notwithstanding, and soon it was produced in other opera houses in Germany, Italy, and England.

Since then *Fidelio* has joined the list of operas that, while not exactly staples, are permanent members of operatic repertoire.

Beethoven wrote four overtures for *Fidelio*. Three were called "Leonore," after the name of the heroine. Beethoven's instinct told him that the Leonore Overtures, particularly the third, overpowered the opera—telling the whole story like a symphonic poem. The Leonore Overture Number 3 is the one heard most often at symphony concerts. For the 1814 performance he wrote another piece which is more of a true overture—one that gives a sense of dramatic anticipation without giving away the plot. This *Fidelio* overture in E-major is the one that is played before the opera today.

The scene of *Fidelio* is eighteenth-century Spain. Leonora, the heroine, is searching for her husband Florestan, who has been put into a secret dungeon because he dared to oppose the wicked doings of Pizzaro, governor of the prison where the action takes place. Leonora dresses as a young man and, calling herself "Fidelio" (the faithful one), gets a job as helper to the jailer Rocco. Her disguise is so convincing that it fools everyone, including Rocco's daughter Marcelline, who falls in love with Fidelio and ignores her faithful lover Jaquino. The music throughout the opening scenes is light, in the style of the popular Singspiel of the day. (*Fidelio* is technically classified as a Singspiel because it combines singing with spoken dialogue.) The simple inno-

The minnesinger Reinmar playing a fiddle (from the Manesse manuscript, Heidelberg)

A scene from Fidelio *at the Vienna State Opera, 1955*

Aase Løveberg as Fidelio and Jon Vickers as Florestan in a Metropolitan Opera production of Fidelio

cence of Rocco, Marcelline, and Jaquino is established through Beethoven's light, almost folklike melodies in the arias, duets, and trios of the first scenes. Fidelio joins with them, but in asides to the audience expresses her fears and hopes.

Rocco tells Fidelio about one special prisoner who is never allowed to see daylight and who is being starved to death by order of Pizzaro. From the description, Leonora is sure that the prisoner is her husband. Pizzaro, having received a note warning him that the Minister of the Province is coming to investigate the prison, resolves to have Florestan put to death. At this point, where the true drama begins, Beethoven's style changes. No longer is it light chitchat. It becomes heroically dramatic, and scenes build to climaxes in the symphonic manner of which Beethoven was a master.

Pizzaro places a trumpeter in a watchtower to give a signal if the minister approaches. He tries to bribe Rocco to murder Florestan. When Rocco refuses, Pizzaro orders him to dig a grave in Florestan's cell. As Pizzaro and Rocco leave, Fidelio, who has overheard the plot, gives vent to her feelings in the aria that follows the agitated cry *"Abscheulicher!"* ("foul murderer"). The aria is in two sections, an adagio (Ex. 8a) and a resolute allegro (Ex. 8b).

Leonora persuades Rocco to let the prisoners enjoy some sunshine, hoping in this way to see her Florestan. As the prisoners shuffle from their cells into the sunlight, Leonora peers into their faces, but Florestan is not among them. The prisoners sing of liberty and freedom in a moving four-part chorus that is one of the musical highlights of the opera.

Pizzaro returns and, enraged, orders Rocco to return the prisoners to their cells. Slowly the men file off-stage, singing a sad farewell to the daylight as Leonora, Marcelline, Jaquino, Pizzaro, and Rocco each expresses his own hopes and fears.

The second act begins in the dungeon where Florestan is chained to the wall. The mood of the scene is established by the playing of a somber motive on the timpani. Florestan muses on the fate that has imprisoned him in the springtime of his life (Ex. 9). Rocco and Leonora enter and begin to dig Florestan's grave to the sound of a sinister contrabass figure heard under muted strings. The dialogue in this scene is spoken to the accompaniment of music— a technique that was called "melodrama." Leonora recognizes Florestan, although he does not recognize her in her disguise. Pizzaro, coming in to check on the progress of the grave digging, resolves to do away

Ex. 10

with Leonora and Rocco so that no witnesses will survive to tell of his evildoings. As Pizzaro raises his dagger to stab Florestan, Leonora runs to shield her husband, revealing herself as Florestan's wife. Pizzaro is about to kill them both when Leonora draws a pistol—and at that moment the offstage trumpeter plays the fanfare (Ex. 10) that signals the coming of the minister. Leonora and Florestan join voices in an exultant duet as Pizzaro leaves the dungeon. The prisoners are soon freed, and the minister, an old friend of Florestan's, condemns Pizzaro. Everyone, including prisoners, soldiers, and principals, unite in singing a final chorus in praise of the noble lady who saved her husband's life.

FIFE: a flutelike instrument made of metal or wood. Unlike the flute, it is made all in one piece, has the same diameter all through its length, and has mostly open finger holes (six of them) instead of the keys and levers that make the flute such an agile performer.

In the 1500's in Germany and Switzerland, the fife was used with a drum to play popular dance music. Its shrill tone also lent itself to giving signals to foot soldiers in maneuvers. Fife players were important members of both armies in the American Revolution. One of the three men in Archibald Willard's famous painting "The Spirit of '76" is playing a military fife, and in fact the man who posed for this figure was a Cleveland fifer named Hugh Mosher.

The fife is used very little today except in fife and drum corps, and even in these groups B-flat piccolos are sometimes substituted for the fifes.

FIGURED BASS: a form of musical shorthand, used by composers between the late 1500's and 1750, in which numbers written over the bass notes told a keyboard performer what chords to use. The procedure is comparable to present-day editions of folk songs in which chords for the guitarist are written as symbols, such as G7 or A min.

Figured bass came into being as composers turned from many-voiced music to the solo song, as in early opera. Rather than write out every note of an accompaniment, the composer discovered that he needed only to write his vocal line, a simple bass part, and indicate to the harpsichord player or organist what chord he wanted, leaving the distribution of the chord tones to the ingenuity of the player. From vocal works the idea spread to instrumental music, so that all works of the Baroque period —operas, cantatas, concertos, and sonatas— were written with figured basses.

The bass part itself was called the continuo, and was played by a cello or other bass instrument as well as by the keyboard player. Translating the figured bass numbers and symbols into an accompaniment was called "realizing the continuo." The keyboard player was expected to improvise an accompaniment that suited the style of the melody. He might play just a series of chords, arrange the tones into arpeggios, or invent one or more melodic lines that would fit the given melody.

When the art of playing from a figured bass died out, such works as Corelli's violin sonatas, Bach's cantatas, and Handel's sonatas for flute and violin were published with accompaniments added by editors. In good musical editions the notes added by the

"The Spirit of '76" by Archibald Willard

editor are printed in smaller type than the original notes of the composer.

One of the most important books on the subject of figured bass was written by C.P.E. Bach in 1753. It has been translated into English by William J. Mitchell, under the title *Essay on the True Art of Playing Keyboard Instruments.*

Figured bass works by very logical rules. Each number represents an interval made by the bass and the note to be supplied. A figure 5 over a C, for example, would mean that the tone G would be added to C. Actually, the knowledge of a few combinations of numbers covers most of the harmony used in the Baroque period. Only triads and seventh chords were used; and, knowing these, even a beginner can attempt to realize simple figured basses. The pitch of the realization can be placed in whatever octave seems best.

The most common figures are as follows:

Triads

In root position,
no number or 5
 3
or 5 below
the bass:

In first inversion,
6 or 6 below
 3
the bass:

In second
inversion,
6 below
4
the bass:

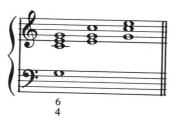

Seventh Chords

In root position, 7 below the bass:

In first inversion,
6 below the bass:
5

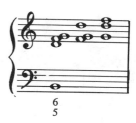

In second inversion,
(6)
4 below the bass:
3

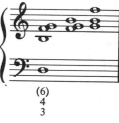

In third inversion,
(6)
4 below the bass:
2

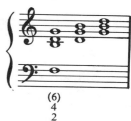

All tones are diatonic, in the key indicated by the key signature, unless a special sign is added. A sharp, flat, or natural sign by itself shows that the note which is at a distance of a third above the bass is to be sharped, flatted, or naturaled:

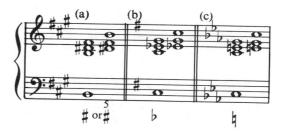

A flat in front of any number lowers that note by a half step (Ex. a and b). A sharp in front of any number or a line through the number raises that note by a half step (Ex. c and d):

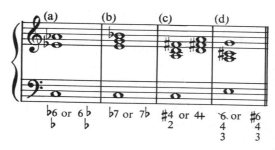

There are, of course, many figures that may be found in music. Some composers were so careful that they tried to account for every sound. Others did not figure every bass note, expecting the keyboard player to know which were the important notes.

The following are a few figured basses for the beginner to try to realize. They range from quite simple to moderately difficult (Ex. 11, 12, 13, and 14).

Ex. 11— "America"

Ex. 12— "Twinkle, Twinkle, Little Star"

Ex. 13— Menuetto from Flute Sonata in G, Handel

Ex. 14— Oboe Sonata, Handel

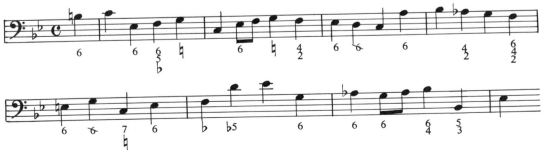

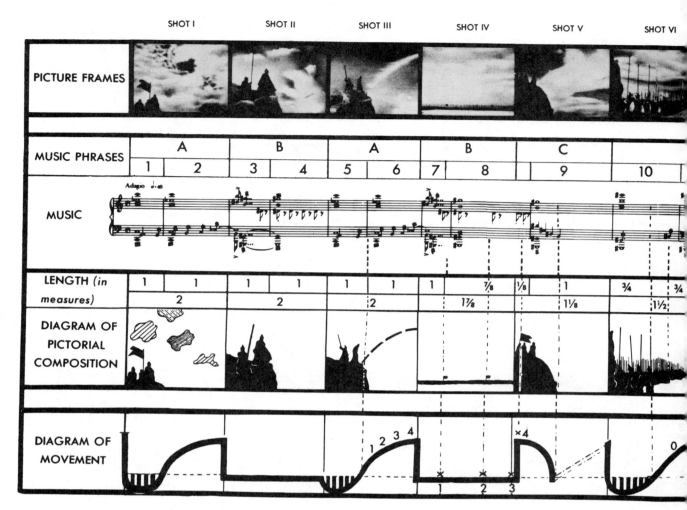

	SHOT I	SHOT II	SHOT III	SHOT IV	SHOT V	SHOT VI

Diagram by Sergei Eisenstein showing the audio-visual correspondences of 17 measures of Prokofiev's score and 12 frames of the "Battle on the Ice" sequence from Eisenstein's film Alexander Nevsky

FILM MUSIC: music written to accompany a motion picture. The music that film audiences hear today is a far cry from that of the pioneer days of the movies. Now the background music for films is written by well-known composers and recorded by some of the finest instrumentalists in the world. The sound track is an inseparable part of the film, so that no matter where the film is shown the same music will accompany it.

In the early days of silent films, a local pianist played anything that happened to come into his head, whether or not it had anything to do with the picture. Sometimes a wheezy player piano ground out ragtime or sentimental ballads. The owners of movie houses found that they needed music to keep the audience from being lulled to sleep by the steady whirring of the movie projector. The music also served to add interest and excitement to the flickering pictures.

As movie houses got larger, the music became even more important and theater or-

ganists replaced the pianists. Sometimes small orchestras played music which more or less suited the action of the films. Movie companies began to send out suggestions as to the type of music that could be used for a certain film. Collections of music were published expressly for movies, and this music had titles that told how it could be used. For example, Hurry #1, Hurry #2, and so on were for chases or other fast-moving parts, and lamentosos were for the sad sections.

The orchestra leader, usually a violinist, put the music in order on the stands of the players. At certain cues, the leader raised his violin and the orchestra stopped. When the violin was lowered, the orchestra began the next piece. There were no transitions from one key or mood to the next. The orchestra was hired for a certain number of hours a day, and at the end of that time the players packed up their instruments and left the theater. If the movie was a long one, the audience watched the end of it in

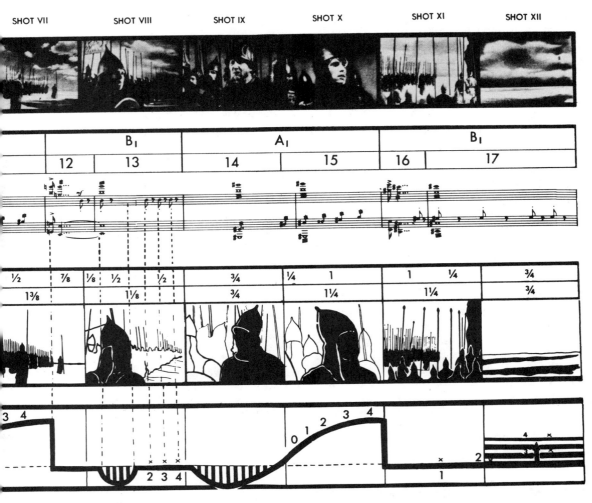

silence or a player piano would suddenly break forth under the guidance of an usher who played his own favorites.

Realizing the importance of the musical background, movie companies began to have music especially written for a film. One of the first of these scores was that written by Victor Herbert for *The Fall of a Nation* in 1916. An orchestra traveled with the film, which was shown like a stage show with reserved seats at higher prices.

When it was discovered how to record sound on film, a whole new field of music was opened to composers. Many theater musicians were thrown out of work, but the quality of music heard with films improved tremendously.

Today a composer for a film is chosen carefully. Film producers know how much the success of their films may depend on good musical scores. Music serves to tie film scenes together. It adds emotional meaning to a series of pictures which are not necessarily emotional in themselves, so that the audience is often stirred by the music rather than the film. If the film has a theme song, this can be played on the radio or sold on records, and so advertise the film.

Writing the music is the last part of making a movie, except for cartoon films, for which the music is sometimes written first. The composer is brought in when the film is almost finished. He and the director decide where there will be music and what kind it will be. The composer views the film in a projection room to get an idea of the whole story. Then he runs the film through a moviola, a machine he can control. He runs through a scene many times. Sometimes he looks at it frame by frame. The composer must be able to write music that not only will fit the mood of the film but will be timed absolutely right—to the tenth of a second.

The composer writes a complete musical sketch for a scene, but since he has such a short time in which to write his music— usually just a few weeks—his complete musical score is done by an arranger. As soon as the arranger has finished a page of full score he turns it over to a copyist, who does the laborious job of writing out a part for each instrument. The conductor begins to learn the score as fast as the copyist finishes it. Often the composer is writing the final minutes of his music while the orchestra is recording the opening minutes.

A film usually opens with "title" music. This is the music played while the title of the film, the cast of characters, and other screen credits are flashed on the screen. Title music is written so as to get the attention of the audience and give advance notice of the mood of the film. A gay film will have jaunty title music; a tragic film will have correspondingly sober title music.

Throughout the film the composer may write "mood" music, "neutral" music, or "Mickey Mouse" music. The composer may write a theme for each principal character of a film. Like a Wagnerian leitmotif the theme will tell the viewer what kind of person the character is. Mood music is tough, sentimental, heroic—or whatever the general action calls for. Neutral music is written as a background to speaking; it is almost no music at all. It must be sparse so that it does not interfere with the words that are spoken. "Mickey Mouse" music imitates exactly in sound what is happening in the film from moment to moment. If someone falls, the music also tumbles; a punch on the nose is accompanied by a thump in the music. "Mickey Mouse" music got its name from the kind of music written for cartoons, although the technique was used in opera as early as the middle 1700's by Rameau.

In musicals, the sound track of the song is recorded first and the singer mouths the words as the pictures are shot. This procedure gives the singers complete freedom of movement; they are not tied to a microphone. It also allows them to perform dances and other forms of physical activity without getting out of breath.

At the end of a film the music builds up to the "end title." Even before the end of the movie comes on the screen, the music has warned the audience that it is near.

Music for a movie is recorded on sound film or magnetic tape. In the final act of movie-making called a "mix," the film and sound tracks of the actor's voices, and the music and sound effects, are run at the same time. Sound engineers rehearse so that they know when to make the music soft or loud. Finally all the sounds are put together on one thin strip of film. As this film runs through a projector at the movie theater, the sound track passes a photoelectric cell. The cell converts what is recorded on the tape into an electric current, which is fed to a loudspeaker. The speaker converts the current into the sound of voices or music.

Outstanding film music has been written by many composers, including Max Steiner, Aaron Copland, and Alex North in the United States, Georges Auric in France and England, and Sergei Prokofiev in Russia.

Finale of Gilbert and Sullivan's The Gondoliers

FINALE: the last movement of a long work, such as a sonata or symphony, or the final scene in an act of an opera. The functions of a finale are to leave an audience in a cheerful or elevated frame of mind (Mozart's "Jupiter" Symphony) or to sum up the mood of the whole work (Beethoven's Ninth Symphony).

The most splendid operatic finales are those written by Mozart. Instead of the usual musical theater finales, which bring back the whole cast and fill the stage with movement, Mozart, as in the finale to Act II of *The Marriage of Figaro,* continues the dramatic action right up to the final moment. Within Mozart's opera finales there may be several arias, duets, and other ensemble numbers.

In early operas, such as those by Lully and Rameau, the finale consisted of a series of dances, celebrating the happy ending that was inevitable in French operas of the seventeenth and eighteenth centuries.

Left: *Carlos Montoya, flamenco guitarist*
Right: *Lucero Tena, flamenco dancer*

FLAMENCO: the style of music that comes from the gypsies of southern Spain. It is based on the *cante hondo,* or deep, tragic song, of old Spain. The name "flamenco" was first used in the middle 1800's, possibly referring to the bright, flamingo-colored costumes of the gypsies.

A flamenco singer is accompanied by a guitarist. The guitar starts with a prelude that is a flourish of running notes, full chords, arpeggios, and possibly a rhythmic pattern strummed on the wooden body of the guitar. The singer starts with a long-drawn melody, which is almost a wail, on the syllable *Ay!* As she gets to the highest point of the melody she holds the tone and then tears off an ending phrase. The audience applauds and shouts *"Olé!"* as encouragement. Then with a passionate, almost harsh tone, the singer utters the verses of the song. The guitar accompanies her and breaks into short cadenzas as the singer stops for breath. There is a quality of old Moorish music in the elaborate decorations performed by singer and guitarist.

The scales used in flamenco music are like the medieval modes, but with many notes slightly sharped or flatted. The guitar player uses one chord progression more than any other—this one:

Flamenco dancing is as passionate as flamenco music. The dancers, usually a man and a woman, whirl rapidly, strike dramatic poses, act out a love story, and make rapid heeltaps, known as *zapateados.*

The influence of flamenco music is felt in the works of Manuel de Falla who, after returning from Paris in 1914, founded a festival of *cante hondo* in his native Spain.

FLAT: the sign ♭ . When placed in front of a note, it lowers the pitch of that note by the interval of a semitone, or half step. On the piano it would mean playing the black key immediately to the left of the pitch note, except in the case of C-flat, which is the same note as B, and F-flat, which is the same note as E. A flat in front of a note applies only to that particular note, not to other notes of the same name that lie elsewhere on the staff, and only within the measure. Here, the top note is a B-natural, the bottom note a B-flat:

Flats are not used to lower the pitch of sharped notes. The natural sign (♮) serves this purpose.

The double flat (♭♭) lowers the pitch of a tone by the interval of a whole step: G-double-flat is the same pitch as F.

In tuning or performance, a tone that is lower in pitch than it should be is referred to as being flat.

Wallace Mann playing the flute

Johann Quantz

FLUTE: the soprano voice of the woodwind family. Along with its little brother, the piccolo, it is the only orchestral woodwind in which the tone is not produced by a vibrating reed. Instead, the flute player holds the flute *across* his face (hence the names "cross flute," *flauto traverso*) and blows across the mouth hole near the closed or "head" end of the instrument. And just as one can produce a tone by blowing across the top of a bottle, the flute player, by directing his breath to the far edge of the mouth hole, produces a tone by setting up a train of eddies in the air column within the flute.

Flutes are usually made of wood or silver. (Georges Barrère's, for which in 1936 Edgard Varèse wrote his *Density 21.5,* was of platinum.) For convenience in cleaning and carrying, flutes come apart in two or three sections. The instrument is about two feet long, producing as its soft, breathy bottom tone the middle C of the piano. From middle C its range stretches to the C three octaves above, sounding more brilliant with each successive octave:

Range of the Flute

The player holds the body of the flute to the right of his mouth, the left hand close to the mouth, with its knuckles facing away from him. When all the finger holes are closed, the tube of the flute has its longest effective length and gives forth its lowest tone. Successive tones of the scale are produced by lifting the fingers in order, starting with the little finger of the right hand. When all the fingers have been lifted (except the right thumb, which is reserved for support),

the player continues his scale by overblowing —that is, forcing air into the flute so as to raise the pitch.

The flute's ingeniously designed finger holes, keys, and levers have brought it close to mechanical perfection. Many of these features are due to the efforts of the Munich jeweler, flutist, and engineer Theobald Boehm, whose large-holed cylindrical model of 1847 has hardly been improved upon to this day.

Flutes are ancient instruments of the whistle family. Stone-age man made whistles from any material that lay at hand—wood, clay, or bone. The earliest flutes had no finger holes and sounded only one tone. Once holes were added, the player could produce a tune.

There is a pastoral quality in the sound of a solitary flute, and shepherds, in the loneliness of their long days, have always been partial to the instrument. Even today, in the mountains of eastern Europe, shepherds still pass the time carving beautifully decorated flutes and recorders, on which they can play duets all by themselves. Because of the spacing of the holes, their scales sound somewhat odd to our ears.

The flute family and their relatives, the recorders, are found throughout the world. The pastoral quality of the instruments appealed to the Indians of both North and South America, as well as to the natives of Africa, who used the flute as an instrument of magic.

A strange sort of flute is favored in Melanesia and in adjacent areas, notably Hawaii. This is the nose flute, blown by air from the nose rather than from the mouth; the player keeps one nostril closed by plugging it with cloth or by thumb pressure. The nose flute has few finger holes, but lends itself to the playing of astounding melodies, full of many wide leaps.

Flutes were among the instruments used in European orchestras of the early 1600's. Composers then had their choice between the soft-voiced recorder type of flute and the more brilliant cross or transverse flute. (In old scores *flauto* refers to the recorder, *flauto traverso* to the modern type of flute.) Developments taking place in other instruments finally settled the choice: by the second half of the eighteenth century, only the cross flute could hold its own against the other wind instruments as well as the full tones of the violins, and its continued use in the orchestra was assured. Today an orchestra usually has three flutes, the third player sometimes switching back and forth between flute and piccolo. The flute is also a member of the woodwind quintet along with the oboe, French horn, clarinet, and bassoon.

The flute is often given quiet, calm parts to play. But it can also be an acrobat. It can run up and down scales at breakneck speed and jump back and forth from high notes to low. Only long-held notes seem unsuited to it.

The flute has been held in esteem by many composers, but none rival Johann Quantz (1697–1773) in quantity of works written for the instrument. This virtuoso, who was Frederick the Great's favorite musician, turned out the almost incredible number of 300 concertos for the instrument, in addition to at least 200 other solo works for it. Other concertos have been written for the flute by Haydn and Mozart, and there are sonatas by Handel and Hindemith. Mozart combined the flute with the harp in one of his most charming concertos (K. 299). One of the most-heard works featuring the flute is Bach's Suite in B Minor for flute and strings, which almost amounts to a flute concerto. In many Baroque trio sonatas the title page read: "For two violins (or flutes) and bass."

Almost any orchestral score will illustrate the various uses of the flute—playing solo passages, doubling the oboes or first violins, or joining with the other woodwinds in sustaining the harmony. There are great moments for the flute in Beethoven's Leonore Overture Number 3, Mendelssohn's scherzo from his *Midsummer Night's Dream,* and Tchaikovsky's *Nutcracker Suite.* Debussy and Ravel were fond of the cool, low tones of the flute as well as its brilliant "top," Debussy giving the flute the opening solo of his *Afternoon of a Faun* and a totally unaccompanied role in his *Syrinx.* A more recent and very successful use of the flute is heard in the beautiful melody written for it by Kent Kennan in his *Night Soliloquy* (1938).

FOLK SONG: a song that has become so much a part of the heritage of a group or nation that there is a feeling of common ownership, whether or not the composer is known. A folk song usually deals with things of daily life. It may be a work song ("Blow the Man Down"), a storytelling ballad ("Barbara Allen'), a love song ("On Top of Old Smoky"), a dance song ("Pop! Goes the Weasel"), a religious song or spiritual ("Go Down, Moses"), a children's game ("Here We Go Round the Mulberry Bush"), or a patriotic song ("Yankee Doodle"). Impor-

tant social events such as the western migration in America and war, in general, have always inspired folk songs.

A folk song does not belong to any one composer or performer and so is often heard with slightly changed melody or words. Until recently such music lived by being passed on orally from one person or generation to another. In the process of being passed on it was changed—either deliberately, as when singers added their own decorations, or otherwise, as when someone had a faulty memory or a poor sense of rhythm or pitch.

Each country and locality develops its own style of folk song. The process can be seen today in the "new" songs that spring up as part of a social protest movement. The subject of the song depends on the way people live and work, the language they speak, the instruments they play. A group who have to work together, whose language has short explosive words, and whose favorite instruments are drums will have strongly rhythmic folk songs. A mother lulling her child to sleep will make up or use a quiet, repetitive rocking song.

The songs of sailors on the old whaling ships were rhythmic, sung as they hauled up the anchor—or freely phrased as they sat around thinking of home. The songs of the Venetian gondoliers were based on the slow, sweeping rhythm of rowing.

A conscious interest in folk music began in the nineteenth century as nationalism spread through the world. Each country became interested in its own past, and part of that past lay in its folk songs. Scholars began to collect and notate previously unrecorded songs. Publishers began to pay attention to this interest in folk music, as was evidenced in the commissioning of Beethoven

Cecil Sharpe and Maud Karpeles collecting folk songs in Kentucky mountains (c. 1917)

Grandpa Jones, a performer from "Grand Old Opry"

Joan Baez and Bob Dylan, contemporary folk singers

Top left: *Huddie "Leadbelly" Ledbetter, one of the great, authentic folk-song singers (1944)*
Top right: *Carl Sandburg*

to make arrangements of Irish and Scottish folk songs. In the twentieth century the concern of musical scholars with folk music has led to the establishment of a field of scholarship known as ethno-musicology. This study has been facilitated by the phonograph and, more recently, the tape recorder. Field recordings have rescued from oblivion many folk songs that were being superseded by American and European popular music. Among the earliest scholars in this field was Cecil Sharpe, who collected many old English songs in back-country England and in the Appalachian Mountains of America. Theodore Baker, Alice Fletcher, J. W. Fewkes, and Frances Dinsmore preserved music of the American Indian. Béla Bartók and Zoltan Kodály gathered the music of the Hungarian peasants, Kurt Schindler compiled a collection of Spanish and Portuguese folk songs, and Charles Pullen Jackson, Carl Sandburg, and John and Alan Lomax gathered together American folk music of all kinds, including black and white spirituals.

Not all folk songs are ancient. Many of the best-known French and German songs, such as "Au Clair de la lune" and "Die Lorelei," commonly regarded as folk songs, are as recent as the eighteenth and nineteenth centuries. Most American folk songs stem from the nineteenth century—many dealing with the settling of the West.

Folk songs have always been an important ingredient in art music. The great body of melodies known as Gregorian chant is, in a sense, folk music. These chants, along with folk songs that were transformed into Lutheran chorales, have been used literally by composers throughout the history of music. Composers have also used the idioms peculiar to a national folk literature. Russian composers such as Mussorgsky and Tchaikovsky incorporated actual Russian folk songs along with scales, rhythms, and melodic characteristics of Russian folk music into their operas and orchestral music. Spanish guitar harmonies and castanet rhythms have given a Spanish "flavor" to music by Russian and French composers as well as the native Spanish composers.

Among the earliest conscious uses of folk songs were the fifteenth- and sixteenth-century masses, based on the current popular song "L'Homme armé" (The Armed Man). Elizabethan composers used folk songs such as "The Carman's Whistle" (Byrd) and "Goe from My Window" (John Munday) as themes on which to make variations. Nineteenth-century music is full of folk-song and folk-dance influence, especially in the works of Chopin, Liszt, Brahms, Dvořák, Grieg, and Gottschalk. Russian composers, particularly "The Russian Five," made folk music their credo. In the twentieth century, folk influences have permeated the music of Bartók, Vaughan Williams, Percy Grainger, Copland, Falla, and Villa-Lobos.

FORM IN MUSIC: the design or shape into which musical materials are molded. Without some kind of form a musical composition would be just a jumble of sounds, making little if any sense. A composer is like an architect who plans a building. The musician plans not only the shape of his piece, but also what it will be made of—just as the architect must decide whether he is going to make a wooden building or one of glass or stone.

The composer must decide what instruments he is going to write for, whether the piece is to be fast or slow, whether it will have a long theme or a short theme, whether it will have thick chords or delicate sounds. Whatever materials go into the composition will give it its own particular flavor and quality.

An architect may be asked to design many different kinds of buildings—a church, a tall office building, a one-family house, or a one-room beach house. Each of these calls for a different kind of plan, or form. So, too, a composer might be asked to write a mass, a symphony, a suite for piano, or a short song. Each of these will have its own form. But just as no two beautiful churches are alike, so no two symphonies will be alike—even if they are built on the same general plan.

Certain forms are used over and over in music. Many of these are *sectional* forms, in which one section of music is added to another section. A cadence usually tells the listener when a section ends.

Popular songs mostly follow a set sectional plan. They start with a first melody that is eight measures long. That melody is repeated. Then comes a middle section, or "release," which has a slightly different theme. Finally the first melody returns. In letters the plan of this form would be: A–A–B–A. It is called three-part, or ternary, form and is one of the most common forms in music.

Other sectional forms are the two-part, or binary, form (A–B) and the rondo (A–B–A–C–A–D–A, etc.). The sonata-allegro form is a very large A–B–A. Variation forms, such as the passacaglia and the chaconne, repeat the original form of the theme (A–B, A^1–B^1, A^2–B^2, A^3–B^3, etc.— see THEME AND VARIATIONS). In the minuet (or scherzo) and trio forms, each section might be a small three-part form:

A	B	A
a–b–a	c–d–c	a–b–a

Some sectional forms, such as the toccata and fantasia, like the earlier motets and madrigals, might have no return to a first theme: A–B–C–D–E, etc. Opposed to sectional forms are such contrapuntal forms as the fugues, canons, and inventions. They are not easily divided into sections, since they keep going, without stopping for cadences, from beginning to end. This type of flowing form is also used by many modern composers. The music seems to grow out of itself like a skyrocket that keeps exploding into new forms and colors.

Musical form depends a great deal on repetition. A composer holds his composition together by repeating his ideas or by coming back to a home key, but if he has too much repetition the piece becomes dull. So he mixes in some variety to hold the listener's interest. The larger the composition, the more the composer has to try to repeat and still have variety.

There are many ways in which a theme can be repeated and still sound different. The theme might be made of just a few notes (Ex. 15). The composer can repeat it in sequence, starting each repetition on a higher or lower note (Ex. 16). He can play it twice as fast (DIMINUTION), as in Ex. 17, or twice as slow (AUGMENTATION), as in Ex. 18. He can play it in an opposite direc-

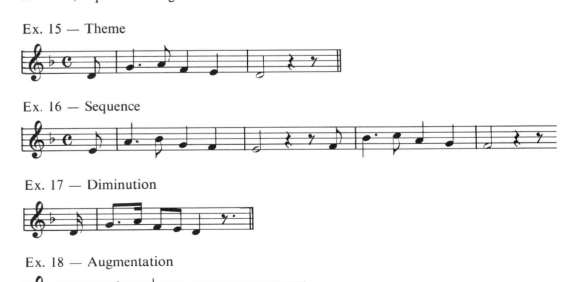

Ex. 15 — Theme

Ex. 16 — Sequence

Ex. 17 — Diminution

Ex. 18 — Augmentation

tion (INVERSION), as in Ex. 19, or backward (RETROGRADE MOTION), as in Ex. 20.

The theme can be broken into fragments which can be played in sequence (Ex. 21). The theme can be decorated (Ex. 22) or played with different chords (Ex. 23). The size of the intervals in the melody can be made larger or smaller (Ex. 24). A counter-melody can be added (Ex. 25, next page), or other voices can imitate the theme (Ex. 26).

There is almost no limit to what the composer can do with a theme as he develops it. He does not use every type of repetition, because that might wear out the patience of the listener. He chooses only what he needs for his general plan.

In a song or symphonic poem that tells a story, the composer may follow the plan of the story. Even so, he will try to hold his music together in purely musical terms through the use of repetition. Schubert's song "The Erlking" tells a dramatic story. Through most of the song Schubert uses the galloping rhythm of Ex. 27, next page.

The rhythm makes for excitement but also contributes a sense of form. Richard Strauss's *Till Eulenspiegel* and *Don Quixote* are biographies in music. *Till* is in the form of a large rondo; *Don Quixote* is a large theme and variations.

Composers sometimes make their musical forms very complicated. Certain works must be heard many times in order to be understood. Each time a listener hears such a work he will discover new things in it, just as new things can be seen as one comes to know a large building from different angles. A composition that is too clear or easy to listen to might end up by being a bore. A good composer plans his musical form so that the listener must give some of his own thinking to the work as he hears it.

Ex. 19 — Inversion

Ex. 20 — Retrograde Motion

Ex. 21 — Theme Fragment in Sequence

Ex. 22 — Decorated

Ex. 23 — With Different Chords

Ex. 24 — With Interval Changes

Ex. 25 — With Counter Melody

Ex. 26 — Imitation

Ex. 27 — "The Erlking," Schubert

FORTE: an Italian word meaning "strong" or "loud." In scores it is usually abbreviated to *f. Fortissimo (ff)* means "very loud," and *mezzo-forte (mf),* "moderately loud." Since the Romantic period, composers have taken to writing *fff* (or even *ffff*) when they want a passage to be played as loudly as possible.

Forte refers not to actual intensity of sound but to the feeling of loudness—it will mean different things to different people and in different situations. A violinist's intended forte may strike someone near him as an *ff,* but it would still produce less intensity of sound than a trumpeter's forte.

The word forte also occurs in *pianoforte* ("soft-loud"), one of the early (pre-1800) names of the piano.

FOSTER, STEPHEN COLLINS (1826–64): composer of many of America's best-loved songs. Born on July 4 in Lawrenceville, near Pittsburgh, Pennsylvania, Foster had almost no musical training although he did learn how to play the flute and harmonize simple melodies. He grew up listening to the sentimental songs sung by his sisters at home and to the spirituals sung in a nearby Negro church. His father and his brothers were businessmen who expected that Stephen would also become a businessman. But when he was fourteen he wrote his first composition, the *Tioga Waltz,* and at the age of eighteen he had his first song published.

In 1848 he sold a group of his songs, including "Oh, Susanna!" to a publisher for a hundred dollars. "Oh, Susanna!" became the favorite song of the Forty-niners in the California gold rush. When he heard that his publisher had made $10,000 on his songs, Foster decided that song-writing was to be his business. He left his job as a bookkeeper in his brother's office in Cincinnati and signed a contract with a New York publisher.

Foster wrote many of his songs for E. P. Christy, the head of Christy's Minstrels. For an extra $15 Christy was allowed to be known as the composer of "Old Folks at

Stephen Foster

Manuscript with lyrics to "Old Folks at Home" (often referred to as "Swanee Ribber" from its first line, which was originally, as shown here, "Way down upon de Pedee ribber")

Home," "Old Dog Tray," and other Foster songs. Foster was a bit ashamed to be known as the composer of what he called "Ethiopian songs."

Foster married in 1850 but the marriage was an unhappy one for his wife and daughter. Foster drank heavily and was always in debt, in spite of sizable amounts of money received from his publishers. When he was in need, he would sell all the rights to his songs for as much as he could get. "Camptown Races" and fifteen other songs were sold outright for $200. His wife left him several times. Finally, penniless, alone, and ill in a cheap New York hotel, he suffered a fall and cut himself so badly that he died soon after being taken to Bellevue Hospital.

In his short lifetime Foster wrote the words and music for almost two hundred songs. These are so singable, their moods so directly gay or sad and sentimental, that they have come to be thought of as folk songs rather than composed songs. American life and music is the richer for having such songs as Foster's "Old Folks at Home" (1851), "Camptown Races" (1850), "My Old Kentucky Home" (1853), "Old Dog Tray" (1853), "Jeanie with the Light Brown Hair" (1854), "Old Black Joe" (1860), "Old Uncle Ned" (1848), "Oh, Susanna!" (1848), and "Beautiful Dreamer" (1864).

FRAGMENTATION: the breaking of a theme into segments for purposes of development or structure. It is used in episodes or transitional sections of Bach's inventions and fugues where a part of the subject is repeated on a series of higher or lower pitches (SEQUENCE) as the music moves from one key to another. Ex. 28 shows the subject of Bach's Fugue in C Minor, Book I, of *The Well-tempered Clavier*. Ex. 29 shows a sequential use of a fragment of the original subject.

Eighteenth- and nineteenth-century composers depended greatly on the device of fragmentation in the transitions and development sections of their sonata-allegro forms. Ex. 30a shows a theme and Ex. 30b its subsequent fragmentation in the development section of a work.

Ex. 28 — Fugue in C Minor from *The Well-tempered Clavier*, Book I, J.S. Bach

Ex. 29

Ex. 30a — First Movement, Symphony No. 3, Beethoven

Ex. 30b

FRANCK, CÉSAR (1822–1890): Belgian composer who had a great influence on French music. He was born in Liège, Belgium, and studied music there at the Royal Conservatory. By the age of twelve he had given piano recitals throughout Belgium, and his family moved to Paris so that he could study at the Paris Conservatory. There, in five years, he earned prizes in piano, organ, counterpoint, and fugue. After several years back in Belgium, Franck and his family returned to Paris. Franck's family had hoped he would become a piano virtuoso, but his shyness did not fit him for the concert stage.

In 1848, Franck married the daughter of an actress. This shocked his strict, religious family—actresses were considered to be not quite decent. The young couple set up housekeeping on their own, and Franck settled down to a career as teacher and organist. He got up at half past five in the morning and worked on his compositions until half past seven. Then he started his day of teaching and playing the organ.

Franck was appointed professor of organ at the Paris Conservatory in 1872. The musical world of Paris—and the leading teachers at the conservatory—liked nothing in music at that time but opera. Franck, who loved the music of Bach and Beethoven, taught his pupils the greatness of instrumental music. Among his pupils were many of the most talented young composers—d'Indy, Chausson, Duparc, Pierné, Widor, and Vierne. Under the influence of Franck they turned from opera to songs, chamber music, and symphonies. After Franck's death, d'Indy

and several others founded the Schola Cantorum to carry on the teachings of Franck.

Franck had very little time to compose, and he was a careful worker; hence his output was limited. Most of his best compositions were written after he was fifty—his greatest after sixty. He wrote one symphony, one violin sonata, one string quartet, one quintet, and one concerto-like work—the *Variations symphonique (Symphonic Variations)*—for piano and orchestra. Each of these has taken its place in concert programs. He also wrote several symphonic poems, organ pieces, and choral works, including his oratorio *Les Béatitudes (The Beatitudes)*. His two most important piano compositions —the *Prelude, Chorale and Fugue* and the *Prelude, Aria and Finale*—are standard pieces in the repertoire of pianists.

Franck's music is very much his own. When one knows a work by Franck, it is easy to recognize his style in his other works. He loved rich, chromatic harmonies that could have resulted from improvisation at the organ, with the color of chords changed ever so slightly by modifying the shape of the chord at the keyboard. His melodies often seem to hover around one tone (Ex. 31). As much as possible he used counterpoint, as did his idol, Bach. The last movement of his Violin Sonata is a canon, with the violin repeating the melody of the piano and almost catching up to it.

In his large works Franck used CYCLIC FORM, tying different movements together by using some of the same themes throughout. When he wanted to, he could spin out

César Franck at the organ, from a painting by J. Rongier

Ex. 31— Symphony in D Minor

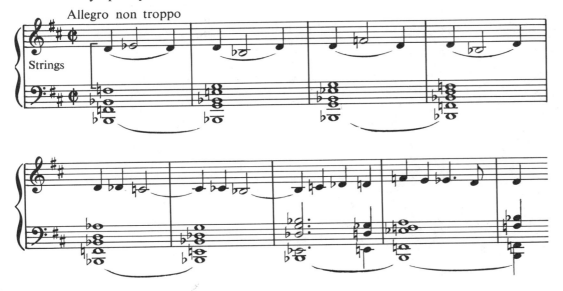

a beautiful long, melodic line, as in the slow movement of his Symphony in D Minor where the English horn sings to the accompaniment of the harp (see Ex. 2, page 165).

Franck had very little fame while he lived. His pupils worshiped him, but other musicians did not care for his music, and even walked out on it when it was performed. The few concerts of his works that were given were poorly rehearsed and poorly performed. Even this did not seem to worry the almost saintly Franck. His only real public success came from the performance of his String Quartet in the last year of his life.

FREISCHÜTZ, DER (*The Free Shooter* or *The Magic Bullet*):

the first German Romantic opera, written by Carl Maria von Weber. Premièred in Berlin in 1821, with its tremendous success it paved the way for the operas of Richard Wagner, and more than any other musical work it led to the Romantic period in German music.

The libretto, by Friedrich Kind, is based on an old German legend. Max, a young hunter and forester in the employ of the local prince, is in love with Agathe, the daughter of the chief forester, Cuno. If Max can win a shooting contest, he can marry Agathe and become the successor to Cuno. But Max has been shooting badly because of a spell cast on him by his rival, Caspar. Caspar has sold his soul to Samiel, the Black Huntsman, in return for seven magical bullets. By persuading Max to sell his soul, Caspar can have three more years of life. In the dead of night Max goes to the Wolf's Glen to meet Caspar, who will show him how to make the bullets. The Wolf's Glen is a terrifying place full of ghostly shapes, where an owl sits on a rotted tree and an

Above: *an 1841 costume sketch for a figure in* Der Freischütz
Below: *an engraving of the scene in the woods with Caspar and Max from* Der Freischütz

invisible chorus sings, on one note, a grisly tale. Max sees his mother in a vision, and she pleads with him not to go on with his plan, but Max also sees a vision of a distraught Agathe about to throw herself into a waterfall. He decides to go ahead.

Caspar shows Max how to cast the bullets, made from magical ingredients. As each bullet is cast, there are wild happenings in the Wolf's Glen. A wild boar runs across the clearing. A storm gathers force, and ghostly visions and sounds fill the dark sky. A frightful thunderstorm strikes. Rain pours down and trees are uprooted. Samiel appears and takes Max's hand. Lightning strikes Max and Caspar and they are knocked to the ground.

On the day of the contest Agathe is greeted by her bridesmaids. They sing a bridal chorus to a folklike melody (Ex. 32, next page). Agathe's cousin brings her the box containing the bridal wreath. When Agathe opens it, she finds a funeral wreath that has been put in by mistake. The cousin makes a wreath from a bouquet of white roses that have been given to Agathe by a holy hermit.

At the contest Max has only one more bullet—the seventh, which will be guided by Samiel. Max aims at a white dove just as Agathe appears. He shoots, and both Agathe and Caspar fall to the ground. Caspar dies, cursing Samiel. Agathe recovers. Max confesses to the prince his dealings with the Black Huntsman. He is forgiven but placed on probation for a year, at the end of which time, if he has proved himself worthy, he will be allowed to marry Agathe.

Der Freischütz is a SINGSPIEL—that is, the dialogue is spoken rather than sung. While there are "set" pieces such as choruses and arias, these flow in and out of the action, never stopping the drama. Through masterful use of the orchestra Weber paints many-colored pictures that portray the mood of the forest, the evil of the Wolf's Glen, and the gay life of the villagers. In the scene in the Wolf's Glen, Weber resorts to "melodrama" —dramatic words spoken to an instrumental accompaniment. The mysterious happenings at night are contrasted with the happy, folklike songs and dances of the country people. No previous opera had so captured the spirit of German Romanticism or given voice to the feelings of the German people.

Except in Germany, the opera is not performed regularly today, but its overture is often played on symphonic programs. This overture was one of the first to be based almost completely on themes from its opera. While still cast in sonata-allegro form, it is full of new ideas in harmony and in the colorful use of instruments. The clarinet and horns are given important melodies that bring out the unique tone color of each instrument (Ex. 33 and 34). The air of mystery in the scene in the Wolf's Glen is created by using an agitated tremolo in diminished sevenths in the strings against the ominous throbs of the timpani and double bass pizzicato (Ex. 35). (This sound is still used today during moments of suspense and horror in film and television music.) Agathe's aria, also used in the opera's choral finale, serves as the climax of the overture (Ex. 36, at the bottom of the page).

Ex. 32

Ex. 33

Ex. 34

Ex. 35

Ex. 36

FRENCH HORN: an important member of the brass family. Because it blends with the other brasses as well as with the strings and woodwinds, composers have used it in chamber music as part of brass or woodwind groups, and have combined it in trios with violin and piano. Familiarly referred to by musicians as just "the horn," it is called "Cor" or "Corno" in musical scores.

The French horn is easy to recognize by sight. The mouthpiece is deeper and narrower than that of the trumpet or trombone. From the mouthpiece the metal tube circles around in front of the player until it comes to an end near his right trouser pocket. The tube is narrow at the mouthpiece and gets gradually wider until it opens out to its end, which is called the "bell."

When the horn was first used in orchestras, the French thought it had come from Germany, so they called it the German horn. The English thought it had come from France, so they called it the French horn.

The French horn got its shape from its ancestor, the hunting horn. In medieval days huntsmen took a horn player with them. Throughout the hunt the horn player gave signals to the hunters, and at the finish he played a sprightly melody if the hunt was successful. But playing a long, straight horn while riding horseback was difficult. Some unknown genius solved the problem by winding the horn around his shoulder and under his arm. Later, when horns were used in orchestras, the tube was bent so that there were two or more loops instead of one. In this form the horn took up less room. The tube of the horn used today is from twelve to sixteen feet in length.

The hunting horn developed into the natural horn used by composers in the seventeenth and eighteenth centuries. The natural horn, like a bugle, could produce only six or seven tones above its fundamental tone. The horn player changed his tones by tightening or loosening his lips. He could also lower his series of tones a half step by putting his hand inside the bell, fingers first. But in order to get a completely different set of tones the player had to change the length of the tube. He did this by taking out part of the tube of his instrument, and replacing that part with a larger or smaller piece. These bits of tube were called "crooks," and the player was expected to carry nine of them.

When the music was in the key of F, the player used his F crook. If the music changed to a different key, the horn player either waited until the key of F returned or he scrambled to change the crook in his instrument. Sometimes the composer wrote

A primitive ancestor of the French horn—the conch shell

Dennis Brain playing the French horn

for two pairs of horns, so that he could avail himself of the horns even if the music went to different keys. This was done by Handel in his opera *Julius Caesar,* and by Haydn in his Symphony Number 31—a work which features the horns throughout.

Very little music was written for the horn before the eighteenth century, but once this instrument was introduced into orchestras and chamber groups it became popular almost immediately with composers, who realized its possibilities. Traveling horn virtuosos made careers for themselves by exploiting all the technical resources of the instrument. Soon Vivaldi, Bach (in his "Brandenburg" Concerto Number 1), and Handel (in his *Water Music* and *Julius Caesar*) were giving the horn an important role. The typical "horn call," based on the comparatively few tones the horn could produce, was imitated in vocal and keyboard music (Ex. 37, next page).

Haydn, always the innovator, used the horn effectively in his orchestral and chamber music. He and Mozart, who was also fond of the great variety of tone color the horn could produce, made the horn the workhorse of the orchestra—as background to hold the notes of the harmony and as reinforcement of the melody (Ex. 38 and 39). Beethoven, always demanding the utmost of performers, wrote scale passages and treacherous high notes for the horn (Ex. 40).

Ex. 37— Sonata in D, Longo 465, D. Scarlatti

Ex. 38 — Symphony No. 101 in D Major, Haydn

Ex. 39— Symphony No. 40 in G Minor, Mozart

Ex. 40— "Eroica" Symphony, Beethoven

Horns in E♭ sounding a sixth lower

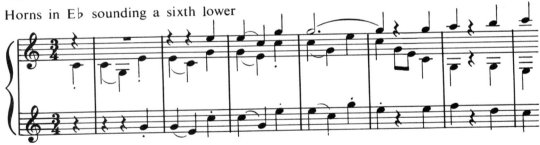

In the early 1800's three valves were added to the horn, replacing the crooks. Now the player changed the effective length of his tube simply by pressing down one or more valves, and with the valves he could produce all the notes of the chromatic scale. However, it took a long time for the valve horn to replace the natural horn with crooks. The French composer Halévy called for it in his opera *The Jewess* in 1835, but until 1900 composers wrote for horns pitched in E, D, and C as well as F. (When a horn player today comes across a part written for a horn other than the F horn, he mentally transposes the notes for his F horn.)

The French horn is very difficult to play well. Temperature and humidity affect the long metal tube and the player's lips. The player must always warm up his instrument, and even then he cannot always be sure of getting the right tone.

The horn has a very wide range. On the F horn, which is the one most used today, the written range is as in Ex. a, which sounds as Ex. b:

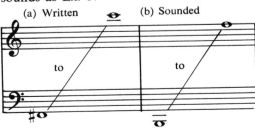

(a) Written   (b) Sounded

to   to

Because of its length and shape, the horn is not an especially agile instrument, although it is often given fast, far-ranging music to play. Its low tones are deep and solemn. Its middle register, which is the one most used, is rich and mellow, and its highest tones are brassy and brilliant. Most orchestras have four horn players who work in pairs. The first and third players are usually given the high notes, the second and fourth players the low notes. Modern composers use as many as eight horns, as in Stravinsky's *Rite of Spring*.

The horn can be played muted. This is done either with the hand of the player or with a wooden or cardboard mute. Played softly, this dampening gives a soft haunting tone, almost like a muffled echo.

If the hand is put so far into the bell of the horn that the tone is almost cut off, and if the player's lips are then tightened, the horn sound has an edge or a bite to it. When played fortissimo, this "stopped" sound, known as *cuivré* (meaning "coppered"), can be quite brassy and pungent. The composer indicates a stopped tone by writing a cross over or under tones to be stopped.

In loud passages the composer sometimes directs the players to hold the horn so that the bell is at the top and facing the audience. This is called *pavillons en l'air,* or "bells in the air," and is saved for big climaxes of sound. Loud lip glissandos, as used by Stravinsky in his *Rite of Spring,* make a whooping, sweeping rush of tones somewhat like those of a siren.

The horn truly came into its own in the nineteenth century. Its mystic, soft tones and heroic hunting calls became evocative symbols of the woodlands, legends, and sentiment of German Romanticism. From Weber to Mahler the horn was entrusted with key melodies. One need only remember the beautiful nocturne from Mendelssohn's *Midsummer Night's Dream,* Strauss's *Till Eulenspiegel* and *Don Juan,* Wagner's heroic theme associated with Siegfried, and Brahms's melancholy horn theme in his First Symphony to realize the colorful part the horn has played in music—Ex. 41, 42, and:

Siegfried's Horn Call

During the nineteenth century, German composers wrote low notes for the horn in the bass clef a fourth below the actual pitch instead of a fifth above, as illustrated in the Strauss excerpt.

Concertos have been written for the horn by Haydn (two concertos), Mozart (four), Strauss (two), and Hindemith. It has been used in chamber ensembles by Haydn, Mozart, Beethoven, and Brahms.

Ex. 41 — *Till Eulenspiegel*, Strauss

Ex. 42 — Symphony No. 1, Brahms

FRESCOBALDI, GIROLAMO (1583–1643): one of the first great composers of music for the organ. Born in Ferrara, in northern Italy, he studied music there with the cathedral organist, Luzzasco Luzzaschi, a fine composer of madrigals. As a young man he spent a year in Flanders and there published his first work, a book of madrigals, in 1608. In that same year he was appointed organist at St. Peter's in Rome, where 30,000 people flocked to his first performance, having been attracted by reports of his phenomenal skill. Except for six years spent in Florence at the court of the Grand Duke of Tuscany, Frescobaldi spent the rest of his life as organist at St. Peter's.

Frescobaldi lived at a time that was a turning point in music. Composers were just beginning to write music that was definitely for instruments rather than voices. Frescobaldi experimented in all the newly emerging musical forms—fantasia, ricercar, toccata, partita. His toccatas, which are among his greatest works, are filled with dissonances and syncopations that suggest the work of a composer closer to our own time (see Ex. 24, page 601). His tightly knit ricercars served later composers as models for fugues.

Frescobaldi's influence was extended by his activities as a teacher. His most famous pupil was Johann Froberger, who became a central figure in German organ and keyboard music of the Baroque period.

Girolamo Frescobaldi by Claude Mellan

FUGUE: one of the most important and exciting of contrapuntal forms. It is like a musical conversation, with three or more persons discussing one or two musical ideas. Fugue gets its name from a Latin word that means "flight," or "running away." In a fugue the theme, or subject, flees from one person, or voice, to another. No two fugues are exactly alike, but all have some things in common.

The composer decides in advance how many voices his fugue will be written for. In a four-voice fugue there will never be more than four voices sounding at one time, but there can be fewer. The first part of a fugue is called its exposition, which is somewhat like a canon. One voice announces, or states, the subject of the fugue. This is chosen carefully, because the success of the composition depends on whether or not the subject is interesting and whether anything can be "said" about it. The subject may be as short as four notes or as long as eight measures. After the first voice announces the subject, the second voice imitates it.

A portion of the "Toccata Prima" from the second book of toccatas by Frescobaldi (note the 8-line and 6-line staves)

Ex. 43— Fugue No. 1 from *The Well-tempered Clavier*, Book 1, J.S. Bach

Ex. 44— Fugue No. 8 from *The Well-tempered Clavier*, Book I, **J.S. Bach**

This imitation, called the answer, begins on a different note from that of the subject (Ex. 43). In this example, all the intervals between successive tones of the answer are exactly the same as the corresponding intervals in the subject, so that the two sound exactly alike. When the answer is designed in this way, it is called a "real" answer. If the answer is not *exactly* like the subject, it is called a "tonal" answer (Ex. 44).

The rest of the voices enter in their turn. As the second voice states the answer, the first voice goes on with a melodic line that fits the answer. This is called a countersubject. In many fugues the same countersubject is heard with every statement of the subject or answer. If the subject and the countersubject can change places, so that the upper voice becomes the lower voice, the composer has written invertible counterpoint:

Fugue No. 2 from *The Well-tempered Clavier*, Book I, J.S. Bach

When all the voices have entered, the fugue starts its second section, sometimes called the development section. Here the discussion gets hotter. The subject flies from voice to voice. Episodes, or transitions, move the subject from one key to another as though the discussion moved from one street corner to another. The episodes are usually based on a fragment of the subject, and the fragment is repeated a note higher or lower—a device called sequence.

Sometimes the voices are no longer polite. Instead of waiting until one voice has finished stating the whole subject, they pile in on top of one another. This method of imitating is called stretto (Ex. 45). In some fugues the whole second section is written in stretto. The composer can change the speed of his subject by making its notes shorter (diminution) or longer (augmentation). He can change the direction of its melody by making it move down where it originally moved up (inversion). He may even bring in one or two new subjects, develop them, and combine them with his original subject. Such fugues are called double fugues or triple fugues.

There are almost no stopping points, or cadences, in a fugue. Once it starts, it keeps going. It builds up to a climax at the end of its second section. Finally the music comes back to the original key. One voice may state the subject one last time. The discussion comes to an end with a final cadence.

Fugue writing started in the 1600's. It

Ex. 45— Fugue No. 16 from *The Well-tempered Clavier*, Book I, J.S. Bach

(Subject)

grew out of the sixteenth-century madrigals and motets for voices and ricercars and fantasias for organ.

Fugue composition reached its highest point in the hands of J. S. Bach. In his *Well-tempered Clavier* he included two preludes and fugues in every key, major and minor, of the chromatic scale. He also wrote fugues in many of his great choral works, some of these fugues being giant works for two choruses, orchestra, and organ. Bach died before he was able to finish his *Art of Fugue,* a vast set of fugues all based on the same subject. This work demonstrates almost every possible manner of treating a fugue subject.

After Bach's time the symphony and sonata replaced the fugue in popularity with composers and audiences. But when composers needed an exciting movement in their symphony, they very often wrote a fugue. There are fugues in Haydn's string quartets, and in Mozart's overture to *The Magic Flute* and the finale of his "Jupiter" Symphony. Beethoven, aware of the dramatic excitement the fugue gave to music, wrote fugues in his piano sonatas Opuses 101, 106, and 110. Some of the greatest fugues are in his string quartets—the three works of Opus 59, the quartet of Opus 131, and the *Great Fugue* of Opus 133.

Twentieth-century composers have continued to write in this form. Hindemith's *Ludus Tonalis,* for piano, is a series of fugues. The second movement of Stravinsky's *Symphony of Psalms* and the last movement of his *Symphony in Three Movements* begin with fugues. The third part of Erik Satie's *Three Disagreeable Sights* is a fugue.

A *fughetta* is a short fugue. It has an exposition like a regular fugue but little or no development section.

G: a clef and a pitch name. The G clef, also known as the treble clef, is a fancy form of the letter G that winds around the second line of the staff and indicates the G above middle C:

G as a pitch name (it is called *sol* in France and Italy) applies to the lines and spaces of the staves as here:

On the keyboard, G is to the right of the lowest of the three black keys:

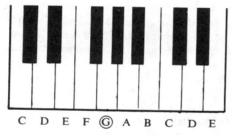

G-sharp is the black key to the right of G; G-flat is the black key to its left. The scale made by playing from G to G on the white keys is the medieval Mixolydian mode.

G is the pitch of the lowest string on the violin and the second lowest string on the viola and cello. It is the highest string of the four-stringed double bass. The alto flute, or G flute, is pitched in G. Its sound is a perfect fourth below the written note:

The key signatures for the G, G-flat, and G-sharp keys are:

(The keys of G♭ minor and G♯ major are not used.)

The key of G major has been quite popular with composers. Among the moderns, Ravel in 1931 wrote his Piano Concerto in this key. Haydn wrote no less than eleven symphonies in G major, including the well-known Number 94, the "Surprise." Beethoven wrote four piano sonatas, a String Quartet (Opus 18, Number 2), and his Piano Concerto Number 4 in this key, and Mozart used it for his charming *Eine kleine Nachtmusik,* as well as for several symphonies and concertos for violin and piano.

G minor is the key of some of Mozart's greatest works: the symphonies Numbers 25 and 40 and the String Quintet K. 516. It is also the key of piano sonatas by Beethoven and Schumann and piano concertos by Mendelssohn and Saint-Saëns.

The keys of G-flat major and G-sharp minor, with their array of flats and sharps, are nicely represented in some challenging études of Chopin: Opus 10, Number 5, the "Black Key"; Opus 25, Number 9, the "Butterfly"; and Opus 25, Number 6.

GABRIELI, ANDREA (*c.* 1520–86) and his nephew and pupil **GIOVANNI GABRIELI** (*c.*1557–1612): composers, organists, and pioneers in the writing of early instrumental music.

Andrea Gabrieli was born in Venice. He sang in the choir of St. Mark's Cathedral and studied there with the famous Flemish teacher and composer Willaert. After some years spent in the service of several German courts, Gabrieli returned to Venice, where he spent the rest of his life as organist at St. Mark's. Gabrieli wrote many works for voice—madrigals, motets, and masses—but is best known for his brilliant organ toccatas, ricercars, and canzonas. He also collaborated with his nephew in writing a group of concertos for voices and instruments which were published in 1587. (This was one of the first occasions when the word "concerto" was used, the term being here used to denote a vocal work—madrigal or motet—with instrumental accompaniment.)

The fame of Giovanni eclipsed that of his uncle, who was his first teacher. After some time spent at the splendid Bavarian court in Munich, where he worked with Orlandus Lassus, Giovanni Gabrieli returned to Venice as second organist at St. Mark's. When his uncle died, he became first organist—a post he held until his death. In his brilliant music for the services in the great cathedral, Giovanni Gabrieli was fond of using as many as four choirs of voices plus choirs of instruments. Each group was complete in itself and played in its own gallery.

Early engraving of the interior of St. Mark's Cathedral

The music is full of rich instrumental sounds, colorful dissonant harmonies, and lively little rhythmic figures. It is big, powerful music. Few composers have ever achieved such splendor and grandeur in musical tones.

Giovanni Gabrieli wrote many vocal motets and instrumental canzonas, but his most famous work is his *Sonata pian e forte.* Like the earlier concertos written with his uncle, this is an epoch-making work. It was one of the first to be given the title "sonata," and one of the first to specify the contrast between soft and loud—hence its name. It is also one of the first compositions in which the composer specified which instrument was to play which part. There are two choruses, or groups, of instruments.

Group 1 consists of a cornett and three trombones. Group 2 is made up of a violin and three trombones. Each group, when playing by itself, plays softly. When they play together, they play loudly. They echo little motives, finally combining in a forceful ending.

Giovanni Gabrieli's music pointed the way for the first great opera composer, Monteverdi. Through his pupil Heinrich Schütz, Gabrieli also started German music on the road that led to Bach.

The splendors of Giovanni Gabrieli's music are finding new audiences through stereophonic recordings. Only in this way or in live performances can the music of the many-voiced choruses be truly appreciated.

GALLIARD: a gay, athletic dance popular in the courts of Europe around 1600. Queen Elizabeth of England supposedly danced six or seven galliards each morning as a kind of "setting-up" exercise.

The galliard got its name from a French word that means "gay" or "lively." The dancers jumped, leaped, and ran as they went through the patterns of the galliard. It was the only court dance in which the men took off their hats as they danced. If they had not removed them, the hats would have fallen off.

The steps of the galliard took six counts of music, which are usually divided into two three-count measures. The galliard was often called the "fivestep" because the dancers jumped over the fifth count. This jumping was called "capering" or "cutting a caper." The rhythm of "America" ("God Save the Queen") is a perfect example of the galliard rhythm. The steps to fit this rhythm would be:

Run run run   leap and land.

The combination of a pavane and a galliard was the earliest form of the dance suite. The theme of the galliard was often the same as that of the pavane (Ex. 1a and b).

Steps from the galliard

Ex. 1 — Claude Gervaise (sixteenth century)

Pavane

(a) Slowly

Galliard

(b) Fast

Ex. 2 — Gavotte from "French Suite" No. 5, J.S. Bach

Ex. 3 — *Classical Symphony*, Prokofiev

Allegro non troppo

Dancing a gavotte

GAVOTTE: a dance popular in the French court in the sixteenth and seventeenth centuries. It was originally a peasant dance from the region around the town of Gap in the French Alps. The people from Gap were called *gavots*.

At first the gavotte was an energetic dance with much leaping. But, as with other dances of peasant origin, it became stiffer, more elegant, and sweetly sentimental when it reached the court. Its music is in a meter of four, beginning on the third beat with two light, lifting beats before the accented beat (Ex. 2). The dancers made two little springing jumps on the upbeats.

The gavotte is often found in the dance suites and sonatas of early eighteenth-century composers, such as Bach, Handel, Rameau, and Corelli. Many of these gavottes have a middle section called a musette, which is the French name for one form of bagpipe.

The modern Russian composer Prokofiev has written several gavottes, of which the best known is the third movement of his *Classical Symphony* (Ex. 3). The second movement of Schoenberg's Suite for Piano, Opus 25, is a gavotte (see Ex. 65, page 628).

GERSHWIN, GEORGE (1898–1937): one of the most irrepressibly creative figures to appear on the American musical scene. He was one of the few composers able to write demanding, serious music as well as song hits that could sweep the nation. A Brooklyn boy, he got his introduction into the world of music from Charles Hambitzer, a colorful and dedicated pianist from Milwaukee who gave him piano lessons. Gershwin brought great enthusiasm and concentration to his lessons, and Hambitzer, in turn, made Gershwin into an accomplished and resourceful pianist, seeing to it also that he got to know a wide range of piano music, including the very latest from Europe (which at that time meant the work of Debussy and Ravel). After a few years of study with Hambitzer, Gershwin went to work—he was now barely sixteen—as a Tin Pan Alley song-plugger for a publisher of popular music. His job was to pound out the latest songs for entertainers who came to the publisher in search of new material, and—occasionally—to make the rounds with his publisher's songs in New York and Atlantic City cafés.

By the time he was twenty-one, Gershwin had produced a musical comedy, *La, La, Lucille,* which had run for 104 performances, and had scored his first "smash" song hit with "Swanee." This song had been serviceable as a number in New York's Capitol Theater, but had not brought out any particular response from the audience. A bit later, Gershwin played it for the great vaudeville singer Al Jolson at a party one evening—and Jolson spotted a winner. He interpolated it in his next show, *Sinbad,* and it caught on like wildfire. Within a year, "Swanee" had sold over two million records and one million copies of sheet music. Gershwin was launched.

George Gershwin at the piano

A scene from George Gershwin's
Porgy and Bess

A string of successful musicals now followed from Gershwin's pen: *Lady Be Good* (1924), *Tip Toes* (1925), *Oh Kay!* (1926), *Funny Face* (1927), *Rosalie* (1928), *Strike Up the Band* (1930), and *Girl Crazy* (1930). Increasingly, as time went on, he relied on his older brother Ira for the lyrics of his songs, for Ira's way with words was prodigious. Together they wrote *Of Thee I Sing* (1931), a hilarious satire on a Presidential election. It ran for a record 431 performances and was the first Broadway musical comedy to win a Pulitzer Prize.

Gershwin was proud of his success on Broadway, but ever since his days with Hambitzer he had also had another goal—Carnegie Hall. In spite of his incredible success, however, he never was able to shake off a feeling of technical inadequacy. Popular songs he felt he could analyze himself—he had spent hundreds of hours playing over the songs of Irving Berlin, Jerome Kern, and Felix Arndt (chiefly known for his "Nola") and turning them over in his mind, until he could pretty well duplicate every trick they contained. But serious, traditional music was another matter, and here he envied the background of more traditionally trained musicians. And long after he had become famous he kept on going to them for lessons—in the late 1920's to Henry Cowell, in the 1930's to Joseph Schillinger. Plenty of European composers had integrated the folk music of their native land into their work. To Gershwin, America's folk music was jazz, and he was determined to master formal composition so that he could infuse jazz into it.

The first hint that he had succeeded came at a public concert in New York's Aeolian Hall on Lincoln's Birthday in 1924, when Paul Whiteman led his band in Gershwin's *Rhapsody in Blue,* with Gershwin at the piano. The *Rhapsody* turned out to be a combination of jazz sounds developed in the style of Liszt and Tchaikovsky. Because of the pressure of time, Gershwin turned over the job of scoring it for orchestra to Whiteman's master-arranger, Ferde Grofé (Gershwin himself orchestrated all his later works). It was a tremendous success, and Gershwin immediately found himself commissioned to write a piano concerto for the New York Symphony. The Concerto in F, with its hauntingly beautiful slow movement, was performed in 1925 and was followed in 1928 by *An American in Paris.* These works established Gershwin as one of the first American composers whose works were played regularly by symphony orchestras.

In 1934 Gershwin set to work on a full-scale opera, *Porgy and Bess,* based on the novel by his old friend Dubose Heyward. Heyward's novel was set in Catfish Row, a run-down area on the Charleston, South Carolina, waterfront. Gershwin spent several months in 1934 soaking up the musical idiom of the Charleston blacks—mostly offshore on Folly and James islands. Then he set to work on the opera, working with his brother Ira and Heyward.

Porgy and Bess opened in Boston on September 30, 1935, and in New York two weeks later. It was not an immediate success. The audiences were a bit ill-at-ease. Was it opera or was it musical comedy? But the great songs—"Summertime," "I Got Plenty o' Nuttin'," and "It Ain't Necessarily So"—caught on. And as they came to know it better, audiences over the years came to realize that *Porgy and Bess* is a remarkable piece of work. Black companies took it on tour throughout the world, and received ovations. (In 1955 it was a great success in Russia, and in 1959 it was made into a film.)

Gershwin now established himself in Hollywood, writing songs for the films. But he did not have long to live. In February 1937, while playing his Concerto in F with the Los Angeles Philharmonic, he experienced a brief loss of consciousness, but was able to resume playing. The following July, aged 38, he died of a brain tumor.

Gershwin brought to his show tunes a sophistication in melody, harmony, and rhythm far beyond that of his rival song writers. Aided and abetted by his brother Ira, he experimented with tricky syncopations, as in "Fascinating Rhythm," where the melody seems to be in a different meter from the accompaniment. His tunes tend to be brittle and complex, rather than sentimentally simple. They combine elements of blues, spirituals, and ragtime with the harmonies of Ravel. Gershwin was particularly fond of using "blue" notes in his melodies —the lowered third and seventh of the scale.

Since Gershwin's death, his music has continued to flourish, gaining in popularity as new millions come to know his work. The special quality of a Gershwin tune, with its fresh, personal melodic sense and tricky rhythm, will always be part of American life and music.

GIGUE: a fast, athletic dance popular in England and Italy around 1600. It was not a court dance but a dance of the common people, with a galloping rhythm of triplets somehow especially suited to the violin. As the "jig" of Scotland and Ireland, it has been a favorite down to the present time, usually being accompanied by a fiddler. An old German name for the violin is

Geige, and the Italians once used the word *giga* for an early form of this instrument.

The gigue reached its high point in music when it appeared as the last dance in the suites of Bach and Handel. Shakespeare, in *Much Ado About Nothing,* called the jig "hot and hasty." Its driving rhythm made it an exciting ending to a series of dances.

Except in a few odd specimens written for the lute by French composers, the meter of a gigue is always divisible by three. There are gigues in 3/8 time, in 6/8, 9/8, and 12/8—and even in 24/16. The tempo is fairly fast and the music begins with a short upbeat. Most gigues are built in two-part (binary) form, although Rameau wrote some in rondo form.

In a typical gigue each section begins with one voice, which is imitated by the second voice as in a fugue (Ex. 4). After a complete stop at a cadence, the second section then begins with an inversion—the first theme turned upside down (Ex. 5).

Ex. 4 — Gigue from "French" Suite No. 5, J.S. Bach

Ex. 5

After 1750, when composers had taken to writing sonatas rather than dance suites, they still used giguelike themes for their final movements. Mozart wrote one gigue for piano—a late work (K. 574) that follows the plan of the Baroque gigue, but is amazingly chromatic.

Beethoven's piano sonatas Opus 31, Number 3, and Opus 49, Number 1, as well as the sonatas Opuses 81a and 110, have gigues for their final movements—as do his *Kreutzer Sonata* for violin and piano and his Concerto for Violin. Among twentieth-century works ending with a gigue is Schoenberg's *Suite for Piano,* Opus 25, of 1925.

The first movement of Debussy's *Images* for orchestra is entitled "Gigues." It was inspired by Debussy's occasional short visits to England and the memories of the English music he had heard.

GILBERT AND SULLIVAN: the British duo that wrote the words and music for the series of famous popular comic operas including *The Mikado, The Pirates of Penzance, Iolanthe,* and *H.M.S. Pinafore.*

Sir William Schwenck Gilbert (1836–1911) as a young man spent several years in the army and then was trained as a lawyer—an experience later reflected in the fun he poked at courtroom procedures in his operas. Becoming interested in the writing of humorous verse, he published in 1869 a collection under the title *Bab's Ballads.* After working for a time as a drama critic, Gilbert found himself as a playwright, and this success led to his meeting with Sullivan in 1871. During the next twenty years this gifted pair turned out no less than fourteen comic operas, most of which had hundreds of performances. Gilbert was knighted in 1907.

Top left: *Sir William Schwenck Gilbert*
Top right: *Sir Arthur Seymour Sullivan*
Bottom left: *Henry Lytton and Eileen Sharp in* Iolanthe, *1924*
Bottom right: *a scene from* Pinafore, *1911*

Sir Arthur Seymour Sullivan (1842–1900) was one of the most talented English musicians of his time. His father was an Irish soldier who had come to England and had later become a teacher of clarinet at the Royal Military School of Music. The son began his study of music at an early age, and his first composition, an anthem, was written when he was thirteen.

After studying in Germany, Sullivan returned to England and started a career as composer and conductor. At various times he taught composition at the Royal Academy of Music, conducted the London Philharmonic Orchestra, and was the first director of the school that later became the Royal College of Music. Sullivan had great ambitions as a composer of serious music and tended to look down on his comic operas. Among his serious works are an opera, *Ivanhoe;* a cantata, *The Golden Legend;* and many songs, including "The Lost Chord." He was knighted by Queen Victoria in 1883.

Gilbert and Sullivan first collaborated on a rather unsuccessful comic opera, *Thespis* (1871). Richard D'Oyly Carte, an enterprising theater manager in London, brought Gilbert and Sullivan together again and eventually formed a company to produce their works. Starting with *Trial by Jury* in 1875, the team went on to write *The Sorcerer* (1877), *H.M.S. Pinafore* (1878), *The Pirates of Penzance* (1879), *Patience* (1881), *Iolanthe* (1882), *Princess Ida* (1884), *The Mikado* (1885), *Ruddigore* (1887), *The Yeomen of the Guard* (1888), and *The Gondoliers* (1889). Then came a quarrel, and for three years they worked independently. When they came together again in 1893, all England rejoiced, and two more works came from their hands—*Utopia Limited* (1893) and *The Grand Duke* (1896). Neither of these was very successful, and the team drifted apart again.

The Gilbert and Sullivan operettas are light and tuneful. Sullivan had a gift for writing simple, charming melodies. Gilbert's plots make fun of the plots of serious operas and also of the English nobility. Gilbert was a master of tricky rhymes and breathless, tongue-twisting "patter songs," and his rhythms often gave Sullivan the rhythm for the melodies. But Sullivan's music is more than just a series of melodies; it is full of skillful counterpoint and the clever use of instruments.

The Gilbert and Sullivan operettas are performed in England and the United States probably more often than any other musical stage works.

GLINKA, MIKHAIL IVANOVITCH (1804–57): the "father of Russian opera." Born into a well-to-do family, Glinka had a good education, including violin and piano lessons and vocal training. For a short time he studied piano with the composer John Field. From 1824 to 1828 he held a minor post in the Russian Government, but he gave this up to continue his musical and general education. For a while he studied in Italy, then spent the year 1833 in Berlin studying composition. He had been composing for most of his life, but only now did he feel adequately trained for the tasks he was to set for himself.

Mikhail Ivanovitch Glinka by Ilya Repin, 1837

Returning to Russia, he found that Russian writers, such as Pushkin and Gogol, were discovering a wealth of material in Russian history and life. Glinka, feeling the time was ripe for a truly Russian historical opera, set about writing one—*A Life for the Tsar.*

This opera tells how the Poles, in 1613, tried to capture the Russian Tsar and how the hero of the opera, the Russian Ivan Sussanin, led the Poles on a false trail, though aware that this would cost him his life.

When the opera was performed in 1836, it was an immediate success. Melodies like Russian and Polish folk tunes were used side by side with typical Italian opera arias. Glinka anticipated Wagner's use of the leitmotif by using some of the same thematic material throughout the opera. His colorful use of the orchestra was the beginning of a whole new approach to orchestration, which reached its peak in the works of Rimsky-Korsakov and Stravinsky. Like many other Russian operas, *A Life for the Tsar* features the chorus.

Glinka's second opera, *Russlan and Ludmilla,* had its first performance in 1842. It was not so immediately successful as *A Life for the Tsar,* but its influence on later Russian composers was considerable. In this opera Glinka used Persian melodies, daring harmonies, and brilliant orchestration. The whole-tone scale (C-D-E-F#-G#-A#-C), used to characterize an evil magician, appeared for possibly the first time in European music.

Glinka traveled throughout Europe all his life. He collected folk songs in Spain and used Spanish material in his successful orchestral works *Jota Aragonesa* and *Night in Madrid.*

Though Glinka's *Kamarinskaya* is often played on symphonic programs, the bulk of his piano music, church music, and songs is rarely heard.

Ex. 6 —— *The Afternoon of a Faun*, Debussy

GLISSANDO: a gliding or sliding from one note to another. The distance between the tones may be very small, as when a violinist shifts from one hand position to another; or the distance may be the whole range of the instrument, as in glissandos for harp. In scores, only the first and last notes of a glissando are written down. The intermediate notes are indicated by a slanting line (Ex. 6).

On the trombone and the members of the violin family there are no keys or valves to interfere with the glissando. The slide trombone glissando was popular in early Dixieland jazz music. Glissandos are difficult on woodwinds and on brass instruments with valves: they require great control of the lips, as in the slow clarinet glissando that opens Gershwin's *Rhapsody in Blue*. Glissandos appear frequently in vocal music, where they are known as portamentos.

It is in harp music that the glissando really flourishes. The harpist sets the pedals of his instrument so that the strings are tuned to a chord, then draws his fingers rapidly over the strings in a sweeping motion.

On the piano, glissandos are played on the white keys with the back of the thumb or third finger. Ascending chromatic glissandos using both black and white keys are possible, but trickier. Going up the keyboard, the second and third fingers of the right hand slide over the black keys, and the fourth and fifth fingers over the white keys. Coming down, the same fingers, this time of the left hand, are used.

A new sound in the music of our time is the glissando on timpani. Timpani used to be tuned by handles around the top of each kettledrum, and once tuned, the drum had a fixed pitch. Today timpani are equipped with pedals, so that the pitch, which depends on the tightness of the skin, can be changed either gradually or sud-

denly. This new and exciting sound is used by Bartók in his *Music for String Instruments, Percussion, and Celesta* (Ex. 21, page 599). Bartók was fond of strange glissandos and used pizzicato glissandos freely in his string writing (Ex. 62b, page 432).

The "instrument" whose basic sound is the glissando is the siren. Edgard Varèse used two sirens in his *Ionisation* (1931), along with forty-one percussion instruments. Since then, the wailing glissando of the siren has appeared in several modern scores.

GLOCKENSPIEL: a member of the definite-pitch group within the percussion family. The word in German means "play of bells." The musical instrument called the glockenspiel today, however, is fitted with thin steel bars rather than bells, so that it is a close relative of the xylophone. The bars are of different, exact lengths, each giving off a single high, bell-like tone. They are struck with a pair of hammers with wooden, metal, or plastic heads; sometimes the hammers are connected to a keyboard like that of a piano or celesta.

That the glockenspiel should have a name suggesting bells is a sign of its rather puzzling history. There is evidence that the Dutch in the seventeenth century started replacing cumbersome chimes with bars after seeing instruments brought back from the East Indies by sea-going merchants. The most famous use of the glockenspiel is by the character Papageno in Mozart's *Magic Flute* (1791), in which it is listed in the score as "steel instrument"—but exactly what Mozart had in mind is not clear. Earlier, in 1738, Handel in his oratorio *Saul* had called for a glockenspiel at the point where the Israelites welcome David after his victory over the Philistines. Again, it is not known exactly what Handel had in mind—possibly bells rather than bars.

Joseph Leavitt playing the glockenspiel

Ex. 7 — *Die Meistersinger*, Wagner

Ex. 8 — *Don Juan*, Strauss

Charles Jennens, Handel's librettist, referred to the instrument as a "tubalcain."

Today the glockenspiel is always made with bars. The tones are so high that the part for this instrument is usually written two octaves below the actual sound of the bars. (In the scores of Wagner and Strauss it still appears written only one octave below the sounding pitch.) The instrument is made in various sizes, with a range from a little more than two octaves to three octaves:

Range of the Glockenspiel

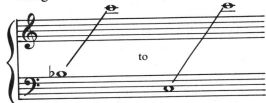

to

Wagner, in the cheery Waltz of the Apprentices in Act III of *Die Meistersinger,* gave the glockenspiel one of its finest moments (Ex. 7). In *Don Juan,* Richard Strauss uses the instrument humorously to mimic a heroic horn theme (Ex. 8). In both of these examples, the music has been written in the modern convention: two octaves lower than it sounds.

GLUCK, CHRISTOPH WILLIBALD (1714–87): best known as the composer of *Orfeo ed Euridice (Orpheus and Eurydice)* and one of the major reformers of opera.

Gluck was born in Erasbach, a tiny village in Bavaria about halfway between Nuremberg and the Danube. His father, a forester, was set on having him follow in his footsteps. When he saw that the boy had a talent for playing musical instruments, he tried to discourage him.

Gluck left home when he was eighteen. He spent several years in Prague, where he supported himself by playing for dances and singing in churches. Finally his father and several noblemen were persuaded to help Gluck so that he could go to Vienna and Italy to study. In 1737 Gluck took up studies in Milan with one of the first symphonic composers, Giovanni Sammartini. He went to hear as many Italian operas as he could, and four years later was ready with his own first opera, *Artaserse*. It was a great success and led to Gluck's receiving commissions for seven more operas during his Italian stay.

In 1745 he visited London, where he wrote two operas. There he came to know Handel, who liked him but remarked that his cook wrote better counterpoint than Gluck did. For the next fifteen years Gluck traveled all over Europe—to Hamburg, Leipzig, Dresden, Vienna, Copenhagen, Prague, Naples, Rome—conducting and writing new operas. These were written in the conventional Italian style of the time, with countless beautiful melodies but little dramatic sense. Most of these Gluck tossed off for celebrations such as royal weddings and the births of princes.

In 1760 an event took place that was to alter considerably the course of Gluck's work and style. It was the publication in Paris of the book *Lettres sur la danse et sur les ballets,* by the ballet master Jean-Georges Noverre. In opera and ballet, wrote Noverre, the most important elements are the story and the feelings of the characters. The theater had room for singing and dancing only if they contributed to the plot and to the understanding of the characters. According to Noverre, dancers who leaped about just for the sake of leaping and singers who decorated their arias just to show off their voices were the ruin of good theater.

Noverre's ideas had their first impact on Gluck through a ballet master named Gasparo Angiolini, who worked up a ballet scenario based on Molière's *Don Juan,* with dramatic rather than merely decorative dancing. Gluck wrote the music, and the ballet was put on in Vienna in 1761. Apart from its imaginative use of instruments (Gluck even included trombones, as Mozart would later in his *Don Giovanni*), *Don Juan* was revolutionary in its subordination

Christoph Willibald Gluck at the spinet by J. S. Duplessis, 1775

An outdoor production of the type for which Gluck often wrote

Kathleen Ferrier as Orfeo

of musical and dance elements in the interests of a unified dance-drama.

But 1761 was also the year in which a cosmopolitan dramatic critic, lottery organizer, and playwright, Ranieri di Calzabigi, arrived in Vienna. He was filled with Noverre's new ideas and itching to try them out. In 1762 the first opera along the new lines, with libretto by Calzabigi and music by Gluck, opened in Vienna. It was *Orfeo ed Euridice.* The tragic Greek legend (see ORPHEUS) gave Gluck the chance to write a grief-laden score of sustained power that went straight to the hearts of the audience. Responding to an unprecedented range of orchestral effects, the audience found itself carried from the feverish, lashing wrath of the Furies to the serene, unearthly calm of the Dance of the Blessed Spirits. Singing, dancing, and a whole rainbow of orchestral colors blended to tell the classic tale of Orpheus. Gluck did use arias, such as the heart-rending lament of Orpheus, "I Have Lost My Eurydice," but they were arias that fit the action.

Orfeo was a great success in Vienna. In 1774, when Gluck had established himself in Paris, he put it on again, but with a few changes. One of the peculiarities of the Vienna production had been the assignment of the part of Orpheus to a male alto; it was now adapted for a tenor. In its new version *Orfeo* was again a success. But rival composers were jealous, and when Gluck produced his next opera, *Armide,* he was set upon by a battery of French critics who championed the showy, conventional operas in the Italian style. A few

leading French musicians and commentators did come to his defense, and so did Queen Marie Antoinette, who had been his pupil.

Gluck knew exactly what he wanted to do. "I have tried," he wrote in the preface to *Alceste,* "to restrict music to its true role of backing up the poetry by means of expression and by following the situations of the plot, without holding up the action or stifling it with a useless superfluity of ornaments." He carried out his program during the 1770's in a succession of operas based on Greek legends—*Iphigénie en Aulide (Iphigenia in Aulis), Alceste* (a new French version of an earlier score), *Armide,* and *Iphigénie en Tauride (Iphigenia in Tauris).* These works established him as the greatest opera composer of his time.

Gluck's operas are among the oldest still performed. Part of their success is due to Gluck's gift for writing expressive dramatic music. But it is also because his daring and resourcefulness in the use of instruments often make his orchestra sound like that of Weber, Berlioz, or even Wagner. (When Berlioz wrote the first book on orchestration, in 1844, he used seventeen examples from Gluck's operas.) Gluck was one of the first composers to draw on clarinets, English horn, trombones, cymbals, triangle, and bass drum for special dramatic effects. Also, he did away with the harpsichord, whose twanging irrelevancies had accompanied solo singers in all earlier operas. Gluck did not start a school of composition, but his works served as the foundation for much of the music written in the century that followed.

GOD SAVE THE QUEEN: the national anthem of England. When a man is reigning, the word "Queen" is replaced by "King."

The words were written in the 1740's. Despite much musical detective work, the author of the words is unknown. But the tune is an old one, based on the rhythm of the galliard, a court dance popular about 1600, during the reign of Elizabeth I. Beethoven thought enough of the anthem musically to write a set of seven variations on it in 1804. This was an ambitious piece of work, foreshadowing his *Thirty-two Variations* of 1807 and his *Diabelli Variations* of 1823.

When the American colonies broke away from England, the colonists changed the words of the anthem to "God Save America" and "God Save George Washington." In 1831, for the occasion of a Fourth of July celebration in Boston, Samuel Francis Smith fitted the song with an entirely new set of words. It is these that are sung today as "America."

"GOLDBERG" VARIATIONS: a famous keyboard work by J. S. Bach, published in 1742. Its true title, translated, is *Keyboard practice consisting of an aria with different variations for the harpsichord with two manuals.* Prepared for the enjoyment of music lovers by Johann Sebastian Bach. . . .

The "Goldberg" Variations were written for Johann Gottlieb Goldberg, who had studied with Bach. Goldberg's employer, Count Kaiserling, had trouble sleeping and asked Bach to write some music that Goldberg might play for him—not to put him to sleep, but rather to entertain him on sleepless nights. Bach wrote thirty variations based on a saraband he had written for his second wife, Anna Magdalena. The count was delighted and rewarded Bach with a golden goblet containing a hundred gold pieces.

The variations are built on the bass melody (Ex. 9) of the saraband aria. This bass can be recognized in the low notes of all thirty variations, though at times it is highly disguised (Ex. 10). Every third variation is a canon over the bass. The first canon is at the unison, the second at the second, and so on up to a canon at the ninth. Other variations include a pastorale, a highly decorated aria, a fughetta, and many brilliant pieces written to show off a harpsichord with two manuals. The sixteenth variation is a French overture that begins the second half of the work. The last variation is a quodlibet—a mixing together of two German folk songs: "I've been away from you so long/Come closer, closer, closer, closer" and "Cabbage and red beets drove me away/Had my mother served meat I'd have managed to stay."

The "Goldberg" Variations are among the greatest examples of a complex art form in which complexities are disguised. Each variation is so charming or so moving that the listener is aware not of difficulty but of beauty. Rosalyn Tureck and Glenn Gould on the piano and Ralph Kirkpatrick on the harpsichord have become famous for their performances of this superb, enduring work.

Ex. 9

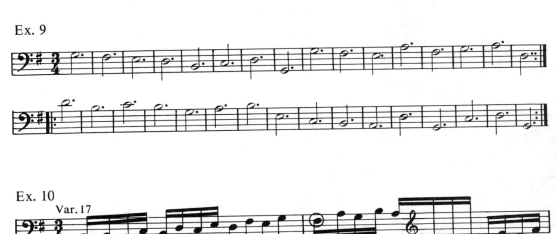

Glenn Gould at the piano

Ex. 10

GONG: a percussion instrument of no definite pitch. Gongs, which are made in many sizes, originated in China, Japan, and India. Basically, the design is that of a disk of bronze with upturned edges.

Large gongs are hung from a wooden stand. Small ones are often rested on a blanket on a bench or table. They are usually struck with a padded bass-drum stick but can also be sounded by rubbing them with a wet thumb.

The gong sounds best when struck gently and off center. It can be "crashed" with a heavy blow, but usually the tone is started softly and gradually gets louder. At its loudest the gong can overpower all other instruments of the orchestra. Its tone, which is long-lasting, can be solemn, terrifying, or mysterious. In eastern Asia the gong is believed to have strong magical powers, and perhaps this is why it is often part of a magician's act.

The gong is used by composers to add to the volume of sound at a climax and to provide dramatic color. Solemn repeated strokes on the gong are used throughout the beginning of the last section of Strauss's *Death and Transfiguration*. The gong can be felt rather than heard at the end of Tchaikovsky's Sixth Symphony, in which it serves as background for the deep, dark chords played on the trombones and tuba.

In orchestral scores the gong is often called the tam-tam. Its part is written on one line in the section of the score used for percussion instruments.

Charles Gounod by Nadar

GOUNOD, CHARLES (1818–93): a French operatic composer. Of his twelve operas, two were successful, *Faust* and *Roméo et Juliette* (Romeo and Juliet). Of his hundreds of other works only two are widely popular, "The Funeral March of a Marionette" and "Ave Maria." The latter is a melody Gounod added to the first prelude of Bach's *Well-tempered Clavier*.

Gounod was born in Paris. Like many other musicians he was first taught the piano by his mother. At eighteen he became a student of composition at the Paris Conservatory, and three years later he won the Prix de Rome. This prize, won in other years by Berlioz (1830), Bizet (1857), and Debussy (1884), gave the winner a fellowship toward study in Rome. Going to Rome, Gounod concentrated on the study of church music, particularly that of Palestrina.

On his return to Paris he became a church organist, and then for two years studied to become a priest. But he gave up this idea and, like most French composers, was drawn to the writing of opera.

In 1851 Gounod's first opera, *Sapho,* was produced. It was not a great success, but the composer continued to write operas while conducting and writing for a chorus. His fourth opera, *Faust,* produced in 1859, was a sweeping success. In the century since its debut it has been sung in twenty-four languages and has had more than 2,000 performances in Paris alone. Its sweet, melodious arias, passionate love duet, rousing "Soldiers' Chorus," and dramatic prison

Javanese gongs

Caricature of Gounod by L. Petit, 1867

scene are among the best-known pieces of operatic music.

Gounod wrote several hundred sacred songs and a great amount of religious choral music, including masses and oratorios. He also composed several symphonies and string quartets—unusual for a French operatic composer. His *Petite Symphonie (Little Symphony)* for wind instruments is played today by many bands and wind ensembles.

Today Gounod's music is often criticized for being too sentimentally tuneful. In his own day it was thought too heavy and "Germanic." In truth, his music is carefully composed and always melodious.

GREENSLEEVES: one of the most popular English folk songs. The tune is four hundred years old. When Shakespeare in *The Merry Wives of Windsor* had Falstaff cry out, "Let the skie raine Potatoes: let it thunder, to the tune of Greensleeves," he could be sure that his audience would recognize one of their favorite dance tunes. Later, during the English Civil War of the 1640's, the supporters of the king used the melody of "Greensleeves" as a sort of campaign song, fitting it with new words. In the seventeenth century it was used for a Christmas carol, "The Old Year Now Away Has Fled." A new set of words, "What Child Is This?" was written by William C. Dix in the nineteenth century. A beautiful orchestral setting of "Greensleeves" is one of Vaughan Williams' best-known works.

GREGORIAN CHANT (Plainchant or **Plainsong):** the collection of ancient melodies used in the Roman Catholic service. The melodies of the chant, which were sung in unison and without instruments, probably came originally from Hebrew and Greek music.

In the early days of the church each group of Christians developed its own set of chant melodies. There was also some improvisation during the service. A collection of melodies used in the Mass and in the Daily Hours of Divine Service was begun by several popes, and the organization of this material was completed during the reign of Pope Gregory the Great (540–604) and was given his name. To each Sunday of the church year and each saint's day, or other holy day, were assigned certain chants.

Pope Gregory established the Schola Cantorum, which later became the Sistine Choir, to train singers. The Gregorian chants became the official versions of the melodies, and as such they spread through Italy, France, England, and Ireland. Only a few churches, in northern Italy and in Spain, kept their own chants.

The chants were based not on major or minor scales but on a system of scales called *modes* (from D to D, E to E, F to F, G to G, and A to A on the white keys of the piano). The melodies moved mostly by scale step or at the interval of a third. Their rhythms were flowing and even, following the rhythm and accents of the words. A chant consists of as many phrases of music as there are phrases of words, each phrase being made up of groups of two- or three-note units. A syllable of a word might be sung to one note or to several notes, as in Ex. 11 at the top of the following page. The beginning of each unit is slightly accented. Important syllables in the words are usually stressed by stretching them out rhythmically or placing them on high tones. Gregorian chant is sung smoothly

Gregorian chant melodies formed the basis of many of the polyphonic works of the great Renaissance composers such as Johannes Ockeghem (1430–95). The picture below is presumed to be a portrait of Ockeghem among his singers

Ex. 11

Li - be - ra me, Dó _____ mi - ne, de mór - te ae - tér _____ na,

Ex. 12

Li - be - ra me, Do - mi - ne, * de mór - te ae - tér - na,

Pope Gregory the Great (miniature from a 10th-century Latin manuscript)

and evenly in phrases so that it sounds much like intoned speech.

Between the sixth and eighth centuries a method of notation was invented so that the chants could be sung the same way all over Europe. This notation used musical "shorthand" marks called *neumes* to show the direction of the melodic line. Square and diamond-shaped notes gradually replaced the neumes, but some of the old system was retained. By about the year 1000 these notes were being written on a four-line musical staff (Ex. 12).

As composers added counterpoint and harmony to the chants, the music became so complex that the chants themselves were covered up. The chant (called the *cantus firmus,* or "fixed melody") was sung in long notes by the tenor voices while the surrounding voices wove melodies around it. By 1600 the early, traditional method of singing Gregorian chant had almost disappeared.

In 1833 a group of Benedictine monks in Solesmes, France, started to revive the lost art of the chant. Through years of scholarly study they restored the purity of the chants and discovered how to perform them in their unaccompanied form. Under Pope Pius X, in the early 1900's, a Vatican edition of the chants was published. Today most of the chants are available in a book called the *Liber Usualis* and in authentic recordings by the monks of Solesmes.

Gregorian chant is the largest body of unaccompanied melody in the world. The purity of expression and the suppleness of the lines have been an inspiration to many composers, including those of today. The most used of all chants is the Dies Irae from the Mass for the dead. It has been introduced into such works as Berlioz' *Symphonie fantastique,* Liszt's *Totentanz,* and Saint-Saëns' *Danse macabre.*

GRIEG, EDVARD HAGERUP (1843–1907): the composer who brought to music the spirit of the songs and dances of his native Norway. Born in Bergen, he was taught the piano by his mother, from whom he learned also many of Norway's beautiful folk songs. At fifteen he was sent to study music in Germany, at the Leipzig Conservatory. There he started to write music in the Romantic style of Schumann and Mendelssohn.

After five years at Leipzig, Grieg returned to Norway. Feeling that the strong and colorful music of his own country should be better known, he formed music societies to help its cause. In 1869 he gave the first performance of his Piano Concerto in Copenhagen, and it was a great success.

A few years later Grieg wrote background music for Ibsen's play *Peer Gynt.* From this music he arranged two suites for symphony orchestra. "Anitra's Dance," "In the Hall of the Mountain King," and "Aase's Death" became popular throughout the world. The people of Norway were proud of Grieg, and their government gave him an annual income so that he could compose without financial worries. At his death he was given a state funeral, and all Norway mourned his passing.

Grieg was a shy little man. He traveled as little as possible, preferring to stay near his familiar fjords and write music that breathed the spirit of Norway. Although he wrote large works—three violin sonatas, a cello sonata, a piano sonata, and a string quartet—he felt more at home in writing short dances and melodious, quiet, lyric pieces for piano. He developed his own highly chromatic harmonic idiom, partly influenced by the shape of Norwegian folk melodies. Most of his songs were written for his wife, a concert singer. His "Ich Liebe Dich" (I Love You) is one of the most popular of concert songs.

Honored in his own country, Grieg won honors also in Germany, England, Sweden, and France. The freshness of his music was admired by Liszt, Brahms, and Tchaikovsky. It was to Grieg that the American composer Edward MacDowell dedicated his *Norse Sonata* for piano. Grieg's music is not world-shaking, but its charming tunefulness and colorful harmony have made him one of the best-loved of composers.

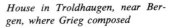

House in Troldhaugen, near Bergen, where Grieg composed

Edvard Hagerup Grieg

GROUND BASS: a musical form in which a bass melody is repeated while above it the melody or harmony is varied. The bass melody is usually four or eight measures long, with one or two notes per measure. Each variation over the ground bass contains one rhythmic or melodic idea, which is spun out over the whole phrase.

Between 1600 and 1750 the ground bass was one of the most popular musical forms. Many opera arias were built on ground basses, which served to hold the compositions together. The English composer Purcell was particularly fond of writing ground basses. They were, he said, the easiest form of music to write. "Dido's Lament," the great aria in Purcell's opera *Dido and Aeneas,* is an emotional cry over a ground bass that slowly and steadily moves downward (Ex. 13). The same type of falling ground bass also appears in the Crucifixus of Bach's B-minor Mass (Ex. 14).

Musicians in the 1700's often improvised on well-known ground basses, just as today jazz musicians improvise on the chord pattern of a well-known song. One way of working with a ground bass was to vary the bass line itself, rather than the melody. That is what Purcell does in Ex. 15.

A ground bass is sometimes called *basso ostinato* or "air on a ground." The passacaglia and chaconne are ground-bass forms that were originally slow processional dances. J. S. Bach's masterful "Goldberg" Variations, Passacaglia in C Minor for organ, and the chaconne from his Partita in D Minor for violin illustrate different varieties of ground bass.

GUIDO: (*c.*995–1050): a Benedictine monk and choirmaster who was one of the most important of music theorists. His full name is usually given as Guido d'Arezzo or Guido of Arezzo. He did teach at Arezzo, in Tuscany, for a time, but was not born there. Some historians think he was born in France.

More than nine hundred years ago he taught his singers to sight read by using syllables. He extracted his syllable names from a hymn to St. John—which was an eighth-century song sung on the feast of St. John the Baptist, June 24. In this song the beginning notes of each phrase move up the first six notes of the C-major scale. The Latin syllable that was sung with the note became the name of that note (Ex. 16, next page). Ut was later changed to doh, and si was added a century later to complete the scale.

Guido's series of six notes was called a hexachord. Hexachords could be built on C, G, and F (with a B♭). There was always a half step between the third and fourth

Ex. 13— Ground Bass for "Dido's Lament," from *Dido and Aeneas,* Purcell

Ex. 14— Crucifixus from B-minor Mass, J.S. Bach

Col 8s

Ex. 15— "A New Ground" from *Musick's Handmaiden* (a decorated bass), Purcell

Ex. 16

Ut que-ant la - xis Re-so-na - re fi - bris Mi - ra ges-to - rum Fa-mu - li

tu - o - rum, Sol - ve pol-lu - ti La-bi - i re - a - tum San-cte Jo-han-nes.

notes of the hexachord mi-fa. By shifting from one hexachord to another, the singers could go beyond the range of the six notes; they could also change key, as in the "movable doh" system that is taught in many schools today. Guido invented a complicated sketch of a hand—the Guidonian Hand—to help his pupils remember their hexachords. The lowest hexachord began on G; this note was called gamma and ut. In time the whole range of Guido's hexachords was called the "gamut."

Guido's other accomplishment was to set up the beginnings of a musical staff. Today a well-trained musician can usually sing any melody "at sight," whether or not he has ever heard it before; he needs only to follow the notes on the staff. But this has not always been so. In Guido's time musical notation took the form of *neumes.* These were little hooks and wiggles placed above the syllables of the text; they gave the shape of the phrase—such as up-and-then-down—but did not specify how far up or how far down. (Bits of visual shorthand of this sort survived into the eighteenth century as signs for ornamentation.) Neumes were sufficient to remind a singer of phrases in a chant he already knew, but they were not definite enough to direct him in one he had never heard before. Right around Guido's own lifetime, a few reference lines denoting an actual, fixed pitch began to be used—first a red line for the F just below middle C, then a yellow line for middle C. Later a third line, denoting A, was placed between them. Although it is not certain just what part Guido personally played in this development, it is known that he did recommend a staff of three or four lines (the three just mentioned and a fourth one, below them, for D). This four-line staff of Guido's, still used in books of Gregorian chant, is the direct ancestor of the five-line staff that we use today.

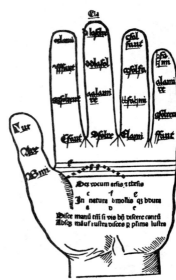

Above: *the Guidonian Hand*
Left: *Guido d'Arezzo, with monochord, and his pupil Bishop Theodal (from a 12th-century South German manuscript)*

It is not clear how many of the innovations that appear in eleventh-century music were actually the invention of Guido and how many he was merely adopting from musicians around him. In geometry, likewise, we don't know which propositions were Euclid's and which he was merely passing on. But Guido's main book, the *Micrologus,* contained all that was known about music in his time. The fame of the book reached the ears of Pope John XIX, who invited Guido to visit Rome. Guido explained the rules to the Pope and taught him to read a melody at sight. Pope John was soon won over to Guido's method, as were many musicians of later generations. Even if some of Guido's ideas were not his own, the clarity with which he presented them made them the foundation of all later music teaching.

"Leçon d'amour," an engraving after Watteau

George Harrison, a member of the Beatles

GUITAR: a member of the family of stringed instruments, played by plucking. It has curving sides, like a violin's, but a flat back. It has six strings made of gut or metal. Under these on the long finger board are small raised strips of metal called frets. The frets mark off intervals of half steps on the strings, helping the player to find the correct pitch. The fingers of the left hand (not including the thumb) press down on the strings just above the frets, while the fingers of the right hand strum across the strings, pluck them, or set them vibrating by means of a pick.

The strings are tuned as follows:

The guitar part is always written one octave above the real sounds:

Sometimes the part is indicated by written names of the chords to be used:

Guitar parts are also written in tablature to show the place of the fingers on the strings. Thus:

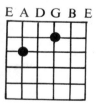

would show that the fingers are to stop the A string at the second fret and the G string at the first fret. This fingering makes an E7 chord.

The guitar has a history of 5,000 years, having been played first in the Egypt of the pharaohs. It was the Romans who brought it to Spain, where by 1500 it had become the national instrument under the name of "vihuela." One of Spain's first great composers, Louis Milan (1500-61), wrote a book of instructions for playing the guitar. The book contained sixty-eight compositions, some being stately pavanes, others fantasias with rapid running passages and rich harmonies.

After the time of Milan many other composers wrote music for the guitar. Domenico Scarlatti learned to love the guitar during his years in Spain, and though he did not write for it he used the guitar sound in many of his sonatas for harpsichord. Later, Boccherini and Paganini wrote chamber music for guitar and other strings. Manuel de Falla's tribute to his friend Claude Debussy— *Pour le Tombeau de Debussy*—was written as a guitar solo. Many composers of today have written for this instrument, particularly after hearing the virtuoso playing of Andrés Segovia.

The guitar came to Mexico with the first Spanish settlers. As early as 1526 a member of the army of Hernando Cortes set himself up in Mexico as a teacher of the guitar.

In American jazz the guitar replaced the banjo in the 1920's, the first great jazz guitarists being Eddie Lang and Johnny St. Cyr. In Europe, "Django" Reinhardt started a guitar style that influenced many Americans. His gypsy background added to jazz a free style of improvisation. The guitar used in jazz has changed its shape as it has become more and more an electric instrument.

The shapes and decorations of guitars have always attracted the attention of painters. During the last years of the reign of Louis XIV, in France, the painter Watteau frequently represented shepherds playing the guitar. The rage for playing the instrument had just hit the court of France, and Watteau took advantage of it. In our time the guitar appears in many paintings of the Spanish painter Picasso.

H: the German name for B-natural. Germans pronounce it *hah,* saving B for what we call B-flat. This came about because, in the early days of music notation, a round "b" was used for B-flat, later developing into the modern sign for flat. The B-natural was written as a square "b," which looks somewhat like an "H."

The German *H* allowed Bach to incorporate his "signature" in his last work, *The Art of Fugue:*

HABAÑERA: a popular Spanish social dance that came from Havana, Cuba, about 1850. It was danced in slow tempo by a man and a woman who moved their bodies more than their feet. The basic rhythm of its music (in two-beat measures) is like that of the tango:

On top of this rhythm, the melody often has eighth-note triplets followed by two regular eighth notes:

The best-known habañera is the song "La Paloma," by Sebastián Yradier (1809–65), the singing teacher of Empress Eugénie in Paris. The famous habañera in the first act of Bizet's *Carmen* is also a song by Yradier (Bizet mistook it for a folk song).

Debussy used the habañera rhythm in his piano preludes *La puerta del vino* (Ex. 1) and *La Soirée dans Grenade.* A habañera also appears in Ravel's orchestral work *Rapsodie espagnole.*

HANDEL, GEORGE FRIDERIC (1685–1759): the composer of the *Messiah,* and one of the towering figures of the musical world of his time. He was born in Halle, in central Germany, in the same year as Bach. Unlike Bach, who spent an entire lifetime in the same environment, Handel took a great interest in the world around him, traveled widely, and pursued a variety of musical experiences that enabled him, at the end of the Baroque period, to sum up in his work almost the entire musical experience of his time.

Handel's home town of Halle was a small Saxon community twenty-two miles from Leipzig. In the baptismal records of the local Lutheran church his name was entered as Georg Friederich Händel; in later life he half-Anglicized it to George Frideric Handel —as it stands in his will. His father, a barber-surgeon, was sixty-three years old at Handel's birth, and for the security of his family hoped the boy would enter the law. But young Handel was intent on music and musical instruments, and at seven played so well on the organ of the court chapel that the duke of the province persuaded his father to let him study music. And so for three years he received instruction in organ, harpsichord, violin, and oboe—and in counterpoint and composition—from Friedrich Wilhelm Zachau, the organist at Halle's Church of Our Lady. Zachau made a point of enlarging Handel's musical horizon, introducing him to the best music of his time, and Handel in turn was so enthusiastic that by the time he was eleven he was already composing his own sonatas and church services.

Zachau made Handel into a thoroughly professional musician, and in 1702, while enrolled as a student at the local university, Handel was appointed organist of one of Halle's Calvinist churches, a post he filled for one year. It was at the end of this year that Handel took the most important step of his lifetime: he left for the great cosmopolitan city of Hamburg, where he joined the opera orchestra as a violinist. This move,

Ex. 1 — "La puerta del vino" from Preludes, Book II, Debussy

Portrait of Handel by Sir James Thornhill

from the organ loft at Halle to the opera pit at Hamburg, turned Handel's sights away from the staid traditions of German counterpoint—the tradition followed by Buxtehude and Bach—and turned them instead toward the sunnier, more songful world of the opera.

What we know of Handel's life at Hamburg is what we find in the reminiscences of his friend Johann Mattheson, a Hamburg composer of the time. (Their friendship was firm but stormy: at one time they fought a duel over who was to play the harpsichord in certain parts of one of Mattheson's operas.) Within two years of his arrival in Hamburg —and before even reaching the age of twenty —Handel had an opera of his own produced, *Almira.* This was followed by three other operas and by a passion oratorio. According to Mattheson, Handel in those days was unusually skilled at counterpoint "but knew little of melody." Handel himself must have been aware of this, for by 1707 he had managed to get enough money together to take him to Italy, the home of opera.

For the next three years he lived in Florence, Rome, Venice, and Naples, immersing himself in the Italian operatic and concert world and getting to know the great style setters of the time, Corelli and Alessandro Scarlatti. He wrote operas and church mu-

sic during these years, and a great many chamber cantatas—all in the Italian style then in fashion. But he also became known as a performer, and at one point an instrumental "duel" was arranged between Handel and Domenico Scarlatti. In this affair, Scarlatti may have come out ahead in improvisations at the harpsichord, but on the organ Handel is reputed to have turned out a more resourceful and powerful performance.

By 1710 Handel was fully formed as a composer. He had learned theory and instrumental technique in Germany, and style in Italy. His competence was becoming known, and he was now offered a job at the court of the Elector of Hanover, in northwestern Germany. He took the job in June of that year, but with the understanding that he would be free to travel. And by November he was already on his way to London, where, shortly after his arrival, a new opera in the Italian style was announced —*Rinaldo,* by "Signor Georgio Frederico Hendel." Italian opera was becoming fashionable in London, and *Rinaldo,* written by a German who could beat the Italians at their own game, was a great success. Handel spent six enjoyable months in London, after which it was time for him to return. He reported back to his job in Hanover, where he set about writing chamber music and songs.

But Handel remembered how well his work had been received in London, and by the end of 1712, when a decent amount of time had elapsed, he asked the Elector of Hanover for a second leave of absence. The elector was rather fond of Handel, and agreed. And so Handel soon found himself back in London, writing for the English public. His first productions were operas, *Il pastor fido (The Faithful Shepherd)* and *Teseo (Theseus).* These were not as successful as *Rinaldo,* but his Te Deum to celebrate the Peace of Utrecht (1713) and his *Ode* for Queen Anne's birthday brought him a yearly pension that amounted to about $1,000.

London was a pleasant place, and Handel stayed on and on. After three years, he was probably afraid to return to Hanover and face the elector. But there was one thing he had not counted on. The elector was a greatgrandson of James I of England, and when Queen Anne died, in 1714, he became king of England, as George I. Handel would have to face him after all. Luckily, the king soon forgave him.

Handel now settled down to spend the rest of his life in England. Between 1717 and 1720 he lived on the estate of the Duke of Chandos not far from London, as master of the duke's chapel. It was here that he composed his first set of harpsichord suites, the eleven "Chandos" Anthems, and the pastoral masque *Acis and Galatea,* for soloists, chorus, and orchestra. The harpsichord suites (of which the fifth contains the variations known since the nineteenth century as the "Harmonious Blacksmith") were written for the king's granddaughters, the princesses Anne and Caroline, who were Handel's pupils.

After this interval in the country, Handel returned to London and for the next seventeen years not only wrote operas but helped manage the theater where they were produced. He went to Italy to hire singers, raised money when his theater needed it, and put in appearances at all sorts of social occasions—partly out of enjoyment, partly as roving press agent for his theater. He was both a businessman and a creative man. (Unlike Bach, who was a salaried appointee all his life, Handel had to make money from each venture as he went along.) More than two dozen operas came from Handel's pen during this period, including *Julius Caesar, Tamerlano, Sosarme,* and *Alcina.* These were produced as Broadway musicals are today. A "hit" would have a long run; a failure meant that Handel had to get another opera ready.

Handel wrote his operas at the exact peak of the London craze for the Italian style, and channeled their style to meet it. Once the fashion passed, the operas—for some two hundred years—were shelved, for later audiences grew to expect a real play with their music. Handel's operas have plots, but the plots are merely devices for maneuvering the main characters into the various moods recognized in Baroque times—at which points they burst forth with arias written in an appropriate rhythm and melodic pattern. So dramatic tension tends to run a bit thin in Handel's operas, and there is hardly any action, except in the music. No one had ever written more beautifully for the human voice, but Handel is hardly able to conceal, in his successions of recitatives and arias, his purpose of showing off the voices of his singers. It is only recently that Handel's operas have been revived, and many have been recorded. Listeners are now discovering that few composers can match Handel in the variety and effectiveness of his vocal writing.

The craze for Italian opera could not go on indefinitely, and beginning in the late 1720's there were signs of a reaction. A spoof of his grand style (in the form of *The Beggar's Opera*) was alarmingly successful, the decorum on Handel's own stage was broken by eruptions of jealousies among the singers, a rival opera company started up with backing from the Prince of Wales and, finally, Handel's middle-class audiences may have got a little tired of supporting a foreign art form catering to the tastes of a sophisticated nobility. In 1737 Handel closed his theater. Even his health had given out under the strain. In May of that year the London *Evening Post* reported: "The ingenious Mr. Handell is very much indispos'd, and it's thought with a Paraletick Disorder, he having at present no Use of his Right Hand, which, if he don't regain, the Publick will be depriv'd of his fine Compositions." Handel took a six-weeks steambath cure in Germany and returned at the end of the year, ready for work.

On his return Handel was not ready to give up opera completely—his *Sense* with its famous largo (actually a larghetto) was produced the following April—but his thoughts had begun to turn in a new direction. It was at this time that he turned to the oratorio. In January 1739 he produced *Saul* and ten weeks later *Israel in Egypt.* These massive choral epics had all the features of his Italian operas—arias, recitatives, choruses—but were based on inspiring passages from the Bible and from the Book of Common Prayer with which the London audiences could feel at home. Handel had now found the formula that allowed him to use the full resources of his technique and yet speak directly to the hearts of English audiences. In the space of twenty-four days in August and September 1741 he composed *Messiah.* He was just about to leave for Dublin, and took the score and the parts with him.

It was in Dublin, on April 13, 1742, that *Messiah* received its first performance. It was an instant success. In England, however, the following spring, it failed. But Handel, undaunted, kept right on turning out further oratorios—*Samson, Belshazzar, Judas Maccabaeus*—at the rate of sometimes one, sometimes two, a year.

Handel was troubled by *Messiah*'s lack of success in England, and after 1745 withdrew it. He brought it out again in 1749, and from 1750—when its cast was joined by the young male alto Gaetano Guadagni—it was firmly established in the hearts of English audiences.

Handel himself had now become England's favorite composer—and well he might, for he had given English audiences

Engraving of the great fireworks display in Green Park, London, on April 27, 1749, that celebrated the treaty of Aix-la-Chapelle—the occasion for which Handel wrote his Fireworks Music

Portrait of Handel by Thomas Hudson, 1749

music that in variety and interest rivaled anything they could remember. In addition to his operas and oratorios, he had produced a host of compositions of all sorts. They included several sets of harpsichord suites and some twenty organ concertos. Though audiences of today find a Handel oratorio quite long enough, listeners in Handel's time were delighted to have one or two lively organ concertos thrown in, perhaps one before the oratorio began and one during intermission. These were played by Handel himself, who was—along with Bach—one of the greatest organists of his time. (An organist, in those days, did not merely play the notes that were in front of him. Musicians looking at Handel's organ scores today find them a bit bare, but to Handel they were merely the foundation of his performance. As he played, he added all sorts of embellishments, variations, fugal passages, and cadenzas.)

Orchestral music also had attracted Handel's attention—right from his earliest years in England, when he produced his *Water Music* to be played from a barge as the king's party drifted down the Thames. Orchestral writing, for Handel, usually took the form of a concerto grosso, in which an

inner group of soloists is pitted against the remainder of the orchestra. His two main series of works in this vein are the six Concerti Grossi, Opus 3, featuring oboes, and the twelve Concerti Grossi, Opus 6, written for strings. Both groups date from the 1730's. Their soulful, arialike slow movements and skipping and rushing allegros contain some of Handel's most natural and effective counterpoint.

Side by side with this instrumental writing, Handel produced a great many compositions for voices—quite apart from his operas and oratorios. These were mainly written for special occasions: Te Deums for the Peace of Utrecht (1713) and for the English victory at Dettingen (1743), anthems for the coronation of George II, and an *Ode* —in the Purcell tradition—for the birthday of Queen Anne (1714) or for St. Cecilia's Day (1739). Though they don't reveal anything of Handel's powers not already evident in the great arias and choruses of his operas and oratorios, they give us a picture of Handel, the immigrant musician, bringing the best of his German and Italian gifts to the English crown and to the English people.

Handel's last years brought a rise in his

popularity but a decline in his ability to enjoy it. After a low point in 1745 (which had sent him to the spa of Tunbridge Wells for a water cure) he came out of his shell again in the late 1740's, producing the *Fireworks Music* (1749) and several oratorios, of which *Solomon* (1749) and *Jephtha* (1752) are perhaps the most notable. The *Fireworks Music* is a series of pieces written to celebrate the Peace of Aix-la-Chapelle; it includes an overture, an allegro, several dances, and some slow movements. The band that played it consisted of twenty-four oboes, twelve bassoons, nine trumpets, nine horns, three drums, and strings. Handel loved the loud tone of the oboe of his day, writing six concertos and several sonatas for it.

He paid a last visit to his relatives in Germany in 1750, then spent the remaining years in London. These were trying years for Handel, who lost the sight of one eye, then of both. In 1753 he conducted his oratorio *Samson* at Covent Garden, and few in the audience were unaware of the personal meaning that Samson's aria "Total eclipse! No sun, no moon!" held for the aging composer.

Handel played the organ at a performance of *Messiah* on April 6, 1759, and a week later he died. He was buried in Westminster Abbey.

Of the three great figures born in 1685—Bach, Handel, and Domenico Scarlatti—Handel was the one who best summed up the achievements and temper of his time. Disdaining the detailed counterpoint of Bach, Handel was like a painter who is at his best in huge mural paintings. Scarlatti, with his lean keyboard figurations and resolute harmonic independence, was very much ahead of his time. Bach, with the relentless march of his tight cantor's counterpoint, struck his own contemporaries as lost in the tradition of a former age. It was Handel, a professional concert musician determined to adapt the European techniques of his youth to the tastes of a new English public, who spoke the true language of the late Baroque.

HANDY, WILLIAM CHRISTOPHER (1873–1958): the American composer known as "the father of the blues." Handy was born in Florence, Alabama, where his father and grandfather were Methodist ministers. A graduate of the Agricultural and Mechanical College in Huntsville, Alabama, Handy was always interested in music. One day he bought, for $2.50, a battered old cornet, and soon he was playing in a band.

Handy taught school for two years, then worked in a factory. In 1893 the factory closed down, and Handy took to the road as a tenor in a quartet. The group worked its way north, spending some interesting but hungry days in St. Louis, Missouri. Joining the famous touring troups of Mahara's Colored Minstrels as cornet soloist and bandmaster, Handy stayed with them seven years, except for two years of teaching at his Alma Mater, the Agricultural and Mechanical College. One of Handy's interests during these early years was to listen to the songs of black laborers and the "country style" music of black guitar players, some of whom used a knife blade as a pick.

Handy settled down as a bandmaster in Memphis, Tennessee. Here, in 1909, he wrote his first great "blues," an election campaign song called "Mister Crump," supporting one of the mayoral candidates. Crump was elected, and Handy arrived as a composer. Changing the name of his tune to "Memphis Blues," he tried to get it published. It was in the usual twelve-bar form of the blues. New York publishers returned it to Handy, saying that it was four measures short. Finally he sold it to a local man who paid him $50 for all rights. For the first twenty-eight years of the copyright, Handy never received any more money for this piece—the first blues ever published.

In 1914 Handy wrote the blues that made him world-famous—the great "St. Louis Blues," then formed a publishing company with his brother to publish this and all his later works. The "St. Louis Blues" has since traveled around the world and been sung in almost every language. It has become a kind of national anthem of the world of jazz.

Handy spent the rest of his life writing other blues—"Joe Turner Blues," "Yellow Dog Blues," "Beale Street Blues," and many more. He also made many arrangements of black spirituals and compiled several volumes of blues and spirituals.

Handy lost his sight, recovered it, and lost it again. This did not stop his activities as an arranger, businessman, or churchgoer. He dashed around the country making speeches at schools and conventions, always pleading the cause of American music. Every now and then he dug out his old cornet and played some of his famous blues at concerts. Even in his late seventies he played nightly at a Broadway night club. Shortly before he died, the city of Yonkers, New York, named the street on which he lived "W. C. Handy Drive."

W. C. Handy

Scene from Act II of Hänsel and Gretel *(La Scala production)*

Engelbert Humperdinck

HÄNSEL AND GRETEL *(Hänsel und Gretel):* a favorite opera for children by Engelbert Humperdinck. As originally conceived by Humperdinck and his sister, Adelheid Wette, who wrote the libretto, *Hänsel and Gretel* was to be a little play for performance by children. But as they worked on the play it grew into a full-length opera.

Humperdinck (1854–1921) was an ardent follower of the opera composer Richard Wagner. In the last years of Wagner's life, Humperdinck acted as his musical assistant at Bayreuth, Germany, copying the score and parts of the opera *Parsifal,* and coaching the singers for the opera's first performance. Humperdinck learned much from Wagner, including how to develop musical ideas and how to get rich, full sounds from the orchestra.

Hänsel and Gretel was produced a few days before Christmas, 1893, at Weimar under the direction of the twenty-nine-year-old Richard Strauss (who had already composed a few tone poems but had not yet begun writing his own operas). No one except

Strauss and the composer expected *Hänsel and Gretel* to amount to much. But audiences throughout Germany were entranced by its music. Soon it became popular all over the world and took its place as a great favorite of young opera-goers.

The story of the opera is based on "Hänsel and Gretel" and "Little Brother and Sister"—two of the hundreds of German folk tales collected in the early 1800's by the brothers Jacob and Wilhelm Grimm. Hänsel and Gretel are children of a poor broom maker (The name Hänsel is a diminutive of Johannes, or John, and Gretel is a diminutive of Margarete.) While their parents are out, they sing and dance instead of doing their chores. When their mother comes home, she is angry with them and sends them out into the forest to pick strawberries for their supper. As Hänsel gathers strawberries, Gretel makes a wreath of flowers while singing an old folk tune (Ex. 2).

Darkness falls, and the children realize they are lost. The little Sandman, or Sleep Fairy, comes and makes them drowsy, but before they fall asleep completely they remember their evening prayer, which they sing together (Ex. 3).

In the opera's most beautiful moment, the fourteen angels of their prayer appear two by two, gathering silently around them as they sleep, and dancing a stately dance.

When the children awake they see a house made of candy, pastry, and gingerbread. The house is surrounded by a hedge composed of figures of children made out of gingerbread; on either side of it are a large oven and a cage. As the children start nibbling a piece of the goody house, the Witch, whose house it is, appears behind them, throws a rope around Hänsel's neck, and immobilizes Gretel with a magic spell. Hänsel is herded into the cage and Gretel is directed to get a little knife and fork, a dish, and a napkin for the Witch, who is planning to eat her. The Witch builds a

Ex. 2

Ex. 3

When at night I go to sleep, Four-teen an-gels watch do keep, fire in the oven and rides around on her broomstick, thinking of her forthcoming delicious meal. When she tries to get Gretel to poke her head into the oven, Gretel pretends not to understand and asks the Witch to show her how. As the Witch bends over the oven, Hänsel and Gretel push her in and shut the door. The oven gets hotter and hotter and finally crashes into bits as the Witch is baked into a gingerbread cake. The gingerbread figures are restored to life again as children and join Hänsel and Gretel in a dance of celebration. By this time the mother and father have appeared and, finding their children safe, give thanks. The father takes this opportunity to observe that the wicked are always punished. To the tune of the opening phrase of the "Children's Prayer," everyone joins in singing:

> *Heaven always comes to aid*
> *Just when hope is due to fade.*

The music of *Hänsel and Gretel* is charmingly and deceptively simple. Some of the melodies, notably the "Little Man in the Wood," are genuine folk tunes; most of them are Humperdinck's own invention but are in the spirit of German folk song. The "Children's Prayer" is like an old German chorale, and the Witch rides around on her broomstick to the music of a lively polka (Ex. 4).

Two extended portions of the score are especially worth listening to closely: the waltz following the liberation of the gingerbread figures and the prelude that precedes the opera (the one that is often played separately on concert programs). In their skillful weaving of melodies against one another, both show the work of a disciple of Wagner who learned much from his master.

Humperdinck wrote other music, but nothing quite as winning as *Hänsel and Gretel.* For much of his life he taught composition, and among his pupils was Kurt Weill, who later wrote *The Three-penny Opera.* When Humperdinck died, it was said that he left no enemies. Who could dislike the composer of *Hänsel and Gretel?*

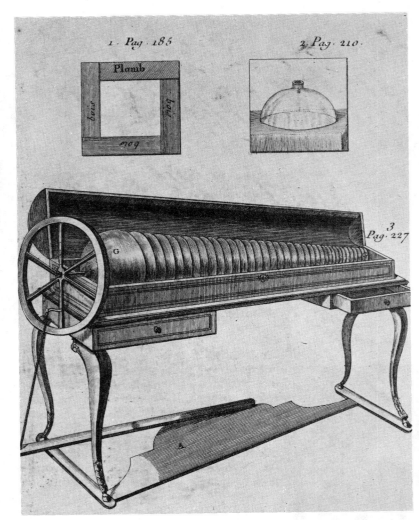

French engraving of Franklin's glass harmonica

HARMONICA: the name of two completely different instruments: the glass harmonica and the mouth organ.

The older of the two is the glass harmonica, known also as "musical glasses." It was popular in the late 1700's, and Mozart and Beethoven wrote pieces for it. At first the glass harmonica was a set of drinking glasses that were tuned by putting different amounts of water in each glass. A glass gave off a ringing tone when the player rubbed a moistened finger around its rim. About 1762 Benjamin Franklin, while in England,

Ex. 4

Right: *Borah Minevitch and his Harmonica Rascals, 1933*

Larry Adler playing the harmonica (with Dizzy Gillespie) at the Village Gate, 1959

improved this form of the glass harmonica (he spelled it "armonica") by putting together a series of glasses of varying sizes so that a scale could be played. The glasses were strung on an iron rod, and as the rod was turned by means of a treadle, the glasses passed through a basin of water. This kept them moist automatically, and the player no longer had to interrupt his performance to moisten his finger.

The glass harmonica was popular in England and Germany until the early 1800's. Then it died out, except as a curiosity.

Today's harmonica, the mouth organ, is a small relative of the harmonium and the accordion. It has a group of small metal reeds or tongues in a case. On one side of the case is a series of small holes, one for each reed. The player's breath, channeled through any one of the holes, makes the corresponding reed vibrate. Each reed gives two tones—one when the air is blown out through the hole, the other when air is sucked in. In playing the mouth organ, the player uses his tongue or index fingers to cover the holes of the reeds he does not want to sound.

Harmonicas are made in many sizes. Some are no bigger than the width of the mouth of the player. Others are large, with a great many reeds. Chromatic harmonicas have keys or buttons that are pressed to make sharps and flats.

The most common harmonica is the one with ten keys. In this instrument the fourth hole from the left is usually the keynote of a major scale, like the scale from C to C on the white keys of the piano:

Note:	C	D	E	F	G	A	B	C
Reed No.:	4b	4d	5b	5d	6b	6d	7d	7b

b means blow out breath
d means draw in breath

The harmonica is mostly an inexpensive "fun" instrument. Many schools have harmonica bands. The wizardry of Larry Adler on the harmonica has made him a popular soloist in concerts, and several composers have written music especially for him.

HARMONICS: a clear, flageolet-like sound on a stringed instrument that is produced by lightly stopping a string at its halfway, quarter, or other fractional point. The resultant sound will be an octave or more above that of the pitch of the string. Such harmonics are called "natural" harmonics and are indicated on a string part by a small circle above the note:

Harmonics Produced on the Open G String

The most used artificial harmonic on an instrument of the violin family is produced by stopping a string with two fingers spanning the distance of a perfect fourth. The

Ex. 5 — *The Sorcerer's Apprentice,* Dukas

lower finger stops the string completely, the upper finger barely touches the string. Artificial harmonics are written as a small diamond-shaped note a fourth above the bottom note:

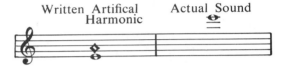

On the harp, harmonics are produced by plucking the string as the palm of the hand lightly touches the exact middle of the string. Such a harmonic, sounding an octave higher than the pitch of the string, is one of the most effective tone colors of the instrument. It can be heard in the opening of *The Sorcerer's Apprentice* by Dukas (Ex. 5).

"Harmonic series" is the name sometimes given to overtone series.

HARMONIUM: a keyboard instrument related to the harmonica, accordion, and organ; it is sometimes known as the reed organ. There are several varieties of harmonium (one is called the American organ), but all are based on the principle of a metal tongue or reed that is made to vibrate by air pressure. The air is supplied by a bellows, activated by means of foot pedals. The range varies from four to five octaves, depending on the size of the instrument.

The ancestry of the harmonium and its relatives goes back at least three thousand years to China and Japan, where the *sheng* and *sho*—both mouth-blown instruments—were important members of the royal orchestras. A contemporary relative is the *khaen,* played in the highlands of Thailand.

Instrument makers in Germany and France began to experiment with the free-reed principle in the early nineteenth century, and several men shared the invention of the European harmonium between 1810 and 1840. The American organ (which differs from the European harmonium in that air is drawn through the reeds rather than being forced through) was invented in Paris about 1835 but brought to the United States soon after.

The harmonium has been built with several stops, like the organ, but its basic sound is a reedy one. Very little music has been written specifically for the harmonium except for a few ensemble works by Percy Grainger. Its primary use has been to play hymns in church. A portable form of the harmonium is used by outdoor performers such as those of the Salvation Army.

HARMONY: the sound that results when two or more tones are played or sung at the same time. The study of harmony is the study of how chords are built, how they move from one to another, and how they have been used in the composition of music. There are no rules that say how chords *must* be used; there are only "rules" that say how chords *have* been used. At different times in the history of music, composers have used certain chords and avoided others. The way in which a composer builds and uses chords is an important part of his own unique style of writing.

The earliest harmony, known as *organum,* developed in Europe during the ninth century. As the tenor voices sang a chant melody, another group of voices sang the same melody at the interval of a fourth or fifth. (Two persons singing "America," one starting on C and the other on F, will give an idea of the sound of organum.) Composers and improvising singers used the basic intervals of organum—perfect fourths, perfect fifths, and octaves—as a series of pillars on which to string long, decorative melodic lines. (See ORGANUM.)

By the end of the twelfth century, organum had reached its highest point in Paris in the works of two of the earliest great composers, Leonin and Perotin. In the fourteenth century, composers began to turn away from the parallel sounds of organum; the imperfect consonances of thirds and sixths began to be used, and cadence formulas began to develop. The earliest of these cadences, called the Landini cadence and used extensively by Guillaume de Machaut, was arrived at by melodic movement that made the penultimate sound a three-note chord, or TRIAD:

Landini Cadence

Composers liked the sweet consonances of these triads and used them in a style known as *fauxbourdon,* making them move in parallel motion under a melody:

Rondeau, Binchois

The fifteenth-century composer Guillaume Dufay combined the sounds of fauxbourdon with a new kind of cadence—the dominant-tonic cadence that was to be the final cadence most used in music for the next several hundred years:

Agnus Dei from the Mass *L'Homme armé,* Dufay

By 1450 the triad had become the basic harmonic sound in music. Not every tone in every melody belonged to the harmony. Just as Leonin and Perotin had strung melodies from one perfect consonance to another, so later composers used tones that were not members of the triad of the moment. Such nonharmonic tones—neighboring tones, passing tones, and suspensions—gave the music its flow and the spice of slight dissonance.

One important result of the use of triads was that the bass, which was usually the root, or bottom tone, of the triad, became less free melodically and more functional. The upper voices were free to move around, while the bass became a support or foundation.

There were no set patterns in which triads were used, other than at cadence points. The line of the melodies, including the bass, determined the movement of the triads. An additional cadence—the plagal cadence, using triads based on the fourth and first tones of the scale—was added to the already existing authentic cadence. (See CADENCE.)

The dance music of the period exerted an important influence on harmony. While choral music flowed along in phrase-long rhythms, dance music needed to have definite meter so that the dancers could keep time. Composers discovered that by changing their harmonies with rhythmic regularity they could help the dancers feel the accents, and so "harmonic rhythm" came into the consciousness of composers. Harmonic rhythm has to do with the rate of speed with which one chord follows another. "America" has a fast harmonic rhythm, since the chords change with every beat. The folk song "Clementine" has a slow harmonic rhythm, because the chords change only once every three or four measures.

With the writing of dance music, composers discovered that harmony does not have to be the result of the weaving together of voices, but that chords could be used as blocks of sound, changing as necessary to mark accents (Ex. 6).

Experiments in writing for solo voice, as in the early operas of the late fifteenth and early sixteenth centuries, led to the use of harmony only as a support for the melody. Composers no longer bothered to write out all the notes of a chord but used a form of musical shorthand, FIGURED BASS, to tell the keyboard player what notes to play.

Ex. 6 — Lute Dance, Hans Neusiedler (1508-63)

As new instrumental forms developed, composers explored the field of harmony, adding chords such as the four-note seventh chord for the sake of variety and making their melodies more dependent on the movement of harmonies. By 1650 harmony was used in set patterns, and these patterns became the basis of most musical form until the nineteenth century. The musician who first deduced the "rules" of this "traditional" harmony was the French composer Jean Philippe Rameau, whose treatise on harmony, published in 1722, is one of the landmarks of music theory.

Traditional harmony is the kind that is studied by all music students—not necessarily to make them composers but to make them better able to analyze and understand the music of the past.

Each chord in traditional harmony is based on a root, which gives the chord its name (C major, G-seventh, and so on). Above the root any number of thirds may be added (Ex. 7). (A third is the musical interval from one tone to a tone two letter names away, as C–E or A–C.)

The name tells how far above the root the top tone is. Any tone of these chords may be raised (sharped) or lowered (flatted). Four kinds of triad and four kinds of seventh chord are the most commonly used chords. Each has its own quality of sound, depending on the sizes of the thirds used in building them. Only major and minor thirds are used. (A major third, M^3, is the distance of two whole steps: C–E. A minor

third, m^3, is the distance of a step and a half: D–F.)

Triads

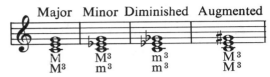

Seventh Chords

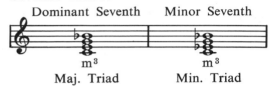

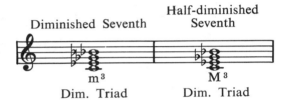

A chord may be built on each note of a major or minor scale. Each has its own name and number, based on its position in the scale (Ex. 8).

Chords are not always used in root position, and when a tone other than the root is in the bass, or lowest part of the music, the chord is said to be inverted (Ex. 9).

Ex. 7

Ex. 8

Ex. 9

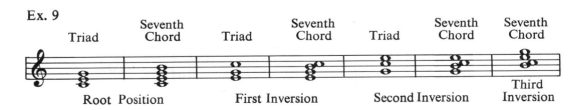

Ex. 10

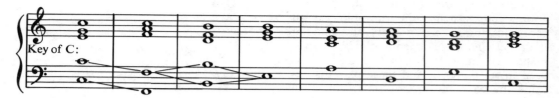

Ex. 11 — Invention in B-flat, J.S. Bach

The tonic chord acts as a sort of magnet to which other chords are attracted. The composers of the seventeenth and eighteenth centuries built up a pattern of chord movement toward the tonic based on the CIRCLE OF FIFTHS (Ex. 10).

Compositions usually opened with the harmonic pattern I-II or IV—V-I (Ex. 11). This established the key in which the piece was written. After the opening harmonic phrase the composer might gradually work toward another key. The move to another key, called MODULATION, gave variety to the harmony of the music.

A musical composition does not necessarily use all the possible chords in a key. Many pieces use only the three primary chords: I, IV, and V. A great many folk songs can be harmonized with these three chords alone. Among them are "Down in the Valley," "On Top of Old Smokey," "Camptown Races," "She'll Be Comin' Round the Mountain," and "My Darling Clementine." The Christmas carol "Silent Night," which is in a major key, can be harmonized on a piano or guitar as follows:

Silent night! Holy night! All is calm,
I   V
   all is bright
   I
Round yon Virgin Mother and Child,
IV   I

Holy Infant so tender and mild.
IV   I
Sleep in Heavenly peace, Sleep in Heavenly
V   I   V
   peace.
   I

Chords do not exist only in their block forms. They can become whatever a composer wishes to make of them. They can be made into the main motive of a work or can serve in many kinds of accompaniment. Composers think of chords as a sculptor thinks of a piece of modeling clay. They can be stretched into many different shapes. Ex. 12, next page, shows a few of the thousands of ways the C-major triad has been used.

The harmonic plan of Baroque and Classical compositions was a basic part of the structure of the work. From short dance forms to large sonata-allegro forms the composer planned his music so that it moved, in a long sense, from the tonic chord to the dominant chord and back again. An investigation of most of Bach's dance forms, Scarlatti's harpsichord sonatas, and Mozart's and Haydn's symphonies will show that the chord at the double bar, which ends the first section of the music, is a dominant chord. Because of this the form of such works, regardless of length, can be shown by the harmonic diagram I—V‖ V—I‖

Composers sometimes change the color of a chord by altering its notes. Such chords

Ex. 12

(a) Étude, Op. 10, No. 1, Chopin

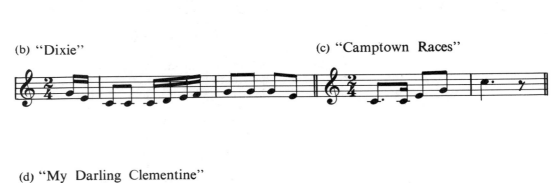

(b) "Dixie"

(c) "Camptown Races"

(d) "My Darling Clementine"

(e) Symphonies by Haydn

No. 32   No. 38

No. 82

(f) Accompaniment Patterns

Tango   Waltz

Alberti Bass   Boogie-woogie

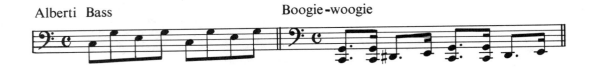

Ex. 13 — *Die Walküre*, Wagner

are called CHROMATIC. Thus C—E—G can become:

Chromatic chords are used either to help make a modulation or to evoke an emotional or dramatic reaction in the listener. Among the earliest chromatic chords were the Neapolitan sixth (see page 354) and augmented sixth chords (see page 27).

Bach, and later Mozart and Verdi, used the sound of the diminished seventh chord at moments of tension, suspense, or deep emotion:

Cantata No. 4: "Christ Lay In Death's Dark Prison," J.S. Bach

Bass: Death ⎯⎯⎯⎯⎯⎯

Weber, in the dark, magic-filled scene at the Wolf's Glen in *Der Freischütz,* used a shuddering single diminished seventh chord, accompanied only by the muffled sounds of drums and double basses, to create an atmosphere of terror. Wagner, the master psychologist in the use of musical materials, used a low-pitched chromatic chord to create a musical portrait of the evil Gibichungs in his *Ring of the Nibelungs.* The opening sounds of his *Tristan and Isolde* use harmony to set the stage for a story of desire and passion:

Tristan and Isolde, Wagner

Whenever a composer uses numerous colorful chords, his music is said to be chromatic. Bach and Mozart used chromatic harmony a great deal, but not until the nineteenth century did chromatic harmony begin to predominate. The works of Chopin, Liszt, and Wagner were so full of chromatic sounds that listeners often lost track of the original key of the music. Chords no longer moved in the circle of fifths, but led wherever the chromatic tones took them (Ex. 13).

Since 1900, composers have experimented with new ways of using the chords of traditional harmony as well as with new ways of building chords. (The Russian composer Mussorgsky had experimented in some of these ways as early as 1870.) Plain major and minor triads move freely without regard to key:

Free Use of Triads: "General Lavine," Debussy

8va. bassa

Two or three triads may be combined to make a sound known as a polychord:

Polychords: *Symphony for Strings*, Schuman

The French composers Debussy and Ravel used chords with added tones and also made free use of ninth chords. Scales such as the whole-tone scale, the pentatonic scale, and the medieval church modes gave new colors to harmony.

Ex. 14 — Menuett, Op. 25, Schoenberg

The Russian composer Scriabin built whole compositions from one chord. His "mystic chord" was built in a series of perfect, diminished, and augmented fourths. Schoenberg, Milhaud, and Hindemith experimented by building chords in perfect fourths rather than in thirds:

Chords Built in Fourths: *Saudades do Brasil* No. 9, Milhaud

Schoenberg's TWELVE-TONE music led to a whole new approach to harmony, in which chords could be made of any combination of intervals (Ex. 14).

To make a wall of sound, composers put together large groups of tones that were a whole or half step apart. These sounds were called tone clusters (see Ex. 28, page 106).

For the composer of today, the whole field of harmony is open. He uses whatever sounds he feels will best suit his purpose. His ear, not rules, decides what chords he will use and what chords he will not use. In many ways he has returned to the concept of music that preceded traditional harmony, in which melody is more important than chordal sounds.

HARP: one of the most ancient stringed instruments. Pictures on vases show that it was important in the ancient courts of Babylon four to five thousand years ago. A harp about 2,500 years old is exhibited in the Egyptian section of the Metropolitan Museum of Art in New York City. It was found buried in a tomb and still looks as though it could be played. Harps were known in both ancient Greece and Rome. In Ireland and Wales, where the harp is traditionally the national instrument, it was given the honor of accompanying the songs of the revered bards. A well-tuned harp was one of the three necessities for a Welshman in his home (the others were a virtuous wife and a cushion for the best chair).

The harp derives its shape from the fact that it is built to accommodate many strings of different lengths. The most primitive harp consisted mainly of several strings tied to a hunting bow. As the harp grew bigger, the strings were attached to two pieces of wood. The top piece, or neck, just holds the strings tightly; the bottom piece is larger and serves as a sounding board. A third part of the harp, called the pillar, connects the top and bottom pieces and, in a modern harp, serves as a pipe through which run the connections between the pedals and the mechanism that changes the length of the strings.

The harp of today has forty-seven strings and seven pedals. The player tilts it toward himself so that it rests on his right shoulder. The strings, which are plucked from both sides of the harp, are of different colors, so that the player can more easily distinguish one from the other. All the C strings are red; those that sound F are blue.

Until about 1810 each string of the harp could sound only one pitch, so that the harp was limited to the notes of one scale. When the French instrument maker Sebastien Érard introduced pedals to change the length of the strings, it became possible to play all the tones of the chromatic scale.

Each pedal can be depressed to either of two notches. When no pedals are pressed down, the harp is tuned to the key of C-flat major. Each pedal is connected to all the strings of the same pitch-name, so that pressing down the C-flat pedal raises all the C-flat strings to C or C-sharp, depending on the notch. Pressing all the pedals down one notch puts the harp in the scale of C major;

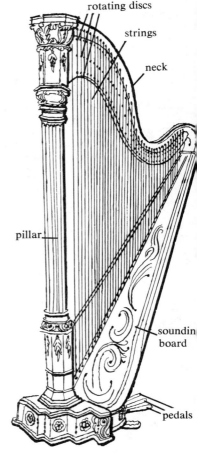

rotating discs

strings

neck

pillar

sounding board

pedals

Top left: *King David playing the psaltery, a predecessor of the harp (from an early English manuscript)*
Top right: *"Duet for Lute and Harp," a 15th-century engraving*
Middle: *primitive harp (an Obah) from the Tronbah tribe of Sierra Leone*

Bottom left: *a Burmese harp, or soung*
Bottom right: *Marcel Grandjany playing the harp*

pressing the pedals down to the second notch puts the harp in the key of C-sharp major.

By quick pedaling the harpist is able to set his harp so that it will play a chord instead of a scale. Often two strings are tuned to the same tone so that the seven strings will play a four-note chord:

Pedal No.:	1	2	3	4	5	6	7
Notch No.:	0	1	2	1	2	0	1
Note:	C♭	D	F	F	A♭	A♭	B (C♭)

The range of the harp is almost that of the piano:

Range of the Harp

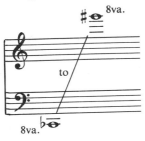

The most familiar sound made by the harp is the sweeping glissando. The setting of the pedals determines whether this rapid gliding over the strings will produce a chord or a scale. The harpist can play eight notes at one time (the little fingers are not used). In chords the notes are usually played in succession rather than plucked all together. This is so much a harp technique that when a piano or a violin is played to produce chords in this manner, the resulting sound is called an arpeggio, meaning "played like a harp." The harpist can produce a guitar-like sound by plucking the strings near the sounding board. One of the most delicate sounds in music is the harmonic of the harp, made by barely touching the midway point of the string with the palm as the string is plucked. The sound of the harmonic is so soft that it cannot be heard if too many other instruments are playing.

The harp is used as a solo instrument, as a member of a chamber music group, and as a member of the orchestra. Monteverdi was among the first to write for harp, using it most effectively in his opera *Orfeo*. Others who have written prominent parts for the harp include Mozart (Concerto for Flute and Harp K. 299), Beethoven (*The Creatures of Prometheus*), Debussy (orchestral music; Sonata for Flute, Violin, and Harp; *Danse sacrée*; and *Danse profane*), Ravel (*Introduction and Allegro* for harp, flute, clarinet, and strings), and the two great modern harpists Carlos Salzedo and Marcel Grandjany.

In 1830 Berlioz shocked his audiences by using two harps in his *Symphonie fantastique.* Since that time composers have used the harp freely, and there are usually two harpists in every symphony orchestra.

HARPSICHORD: a keyboard instrument in wide use from 1600 until shortly after 1750. It was used in opera and oratorio to accompany the recitatives, as well as to support the other instruments of the orchestra. It was a solo instrument and a member of chamber music groups. Its twanging tones formed a background for almost all types of music of the Baroque period.

The harpsichord (called *clavecin* in France, *clavicembalo* or *cembalo* in Italy) is a plucked-string instrument played by means of keys. Small picks made of birds' quills or of hard leather pluck the strings when the keys are pressed down. The plucking of the strings gives the harpsichord a tone somewhat like that of a guitar or mandolin.

No one knows exactly when the harpsichord was invented, but it probably first appeared in Italy in the 1400's. By the late 1500's it was a favorite in Flanders. The Flemish port of Antwerp was then the cultural center of the Low Countries, and it was in Antwerp that the great harpsichord-making family of Ruckers had its workshop. Between 1579 and 1645, Hans Ruckers and his sons brought the instrument to perfection. Even in the eighteenth century, Ruckers instruments were much sought after. Handel's favorite harpsichord was a Ruckers made in 1612.

Harpsichords, spinets, and virginals produced their tone in exactly the same way although their strings were stretched on frames of different shapes and sizes (see VIRGINAL). The word harpsichord is usually reserved for instruments in which the strings are laid out as on a modern grand piano—that is, running away from the player rather than across his line of sight.

Early harpsichords had one keyboard and one set of strings, with a range of not more than four octaves. The instrument, in its beautifully decorated wooden case, was light enough to be carried around. When it was to be played, it was set on a table. The tone of the harpsichord was bright, but could not be made softer or louder.

To get some variety of tone color, the builders added as many as three sets of strings above the original set. Two keyboards were needed to play these larger instruments,

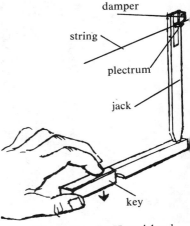

The Action of a Harpsichord

Wanda Landowska at the harpsichord

Roy Harris

music, and in more recent years Ralph Kirkpatrick's phenomenal control over the instrument has set a very high standard of performance. Composers such as Falla and Poulenc have written for it, and recordings have made its sound familiar to many listeners.

Modern harpsichords, patterned after some of the best instruments surviving in museums, are now being built at the rate of several hundred a year. Once again the masterpieces of Couperin, Bach, and Scarlatti are heard as they were meant to be heard two hundred years ago.

HARRIS, ROY (1898–   ): one of the outstanding composers of the United States. Born in Lincoln County, Oklahoma, on Lincoln's birthday, Harris was twenty years old before he decided to be a composer. His first composition, *Impressions of a Rainy Day,* for string quartet, was performed in 1926, the year he went to Paris to study with Nadia Boulanger.

In 1929 Harris returned to the United States to start a busy career as teacher and composer. He has taught at several American universities, organized festivals of modern music, set up summer schools to encourage young string players, and written and lectured about modern music.

Harris has written 11 symphonies, a great deal of chamber music, and many large choral works, including a *Symphony for Voices.* A distinctly American streak runs through many of his titles—for example, *When Johnny Comes Marching Home* (symphonic overture), *American Portraits* (for orchestra), *Gettysburg Address Symphony* (Number 6), and *Western Landscape* (ballet). Three of his large choral works are based on poems by Walt Whitman.

Harris' unique style is shown most clearly in his most-played work, the Third Symphony. His melodies are often long and spacious, at times suggesting Gregorian chant. His harmony combines the open sounds of perfect fourths and fifths with unorthodox treatment of major and minor triads.

The rhythms of Harris' music are often pulsating and driving, charged with the tensions of American life. In his choral works he has used the voice in nontraditional ways, always bringing out the dramatic meaning of the words. Harris' music breathes the air of the open spaces of the American Midwest. He has been an influence on many American composers, who have followed his lead toward an American kind of music.

which had a range of more than five octaves. Small knobs on the front of the harpsichord allowed the player to shift from one set of strings to another, to dampen the strings, or to couple the strings—that is, to make two tones an octave apart sound with one key. There was still no way to get a crescendo or diminuendo, but the harpsichordist could get contrasts of loud and soft into his music, often making echo effects to delight his listeners.

The harpsichordist who accompanied singers or violinists was expected to make up his own accompaniment. He was given the melody and a bass part with numbers over it—a figured bass. The numbers told him which notes above the figured bass were to be played. The kind of accompaniment—simple or complicated—was left to the player.

Music for the harpsichord reached its highest point between 1700 and 1760. Written during this time were the dazzling virtuoso works of Domenico Scarlatti; the short, delicate, graceful tone pictures of Couperin; the tuneful dances of Handel; Rameau's clucking *La Poule (The Hen)* and other fanciful works; and the mighty preludes, fugues, concertos, and suites of dances by J. S. Bach. The harpsichord lost favor with musicians after the invention of the piano, but in the twentieth century the beauties of the old instrument have been rediscovered. Arnold Dolmetsch and Wanda Landowska pioneered in playing concerts of harpsichord

HAYDN, FRANZ JOSEPH (1732–1809): great composer of the Classical period. When he was a small child, the world of music was nearing the end of the Baroque period. Handel, in England, was writing his operas and massive oratorios, and in Germany J. S. Bach was composing his complex contrapuntal works. In Spain, Domenico Scarlatti was writing his brilliant harpsichord sonatas, and in France Rameau was setting new styles in opera spectacles. By the time of Haydn's death, the world of the arts was getting ready for the outburst of personal feelings known as Romanticism, led in music by Haydn's one-time pupil Beethoven. It was between these two great periods that Haydn played a major part in establishing the style of music called Classical.

Haydn did not invent the Classical sonata, symphony, or string quartet, but the fertility of his ideas and his genius for musical construction brought these musical forms to such a peak that he is often called "the father of the symphony and the string quartet." He had taken the light instrumental music loved by the Viennese and made it into a style that could express the deepest emotions.

Unfortunately, only a small portion of Haydn's music is performed today. Chamber-music players know most of Haydn's eighty-three string quartets, but of his 104 symphonies only about ten are familiar. Pianists forever play the same four or five of his fifty-two piano sonatas. Few of his concertos for piano (fifteen), violin (three), horn (two), trumpet (one), flute (one), and cello (two) are heard in concerts. His delightful piano trios—thirty-five of them—and his more than 175 gay divertimentos are neglected. His masterful oratorios, *The Creation* and *The Seasons,* are occasionally performed by choral groups, but of his nineteen operas only one or two have been revived in recent years. Haydn wrote fourteen masses. Three of these, the *Lord Nelson Mass,* the *Mass in Time of War,* and the *Maria Theresa Mass,* are heard occasionally. His part songs and canons for voice are almost unknown.

Haydn's reputation has suffered because his music is so clear that even many musicians have thought it childishly simple. And yet this music served to inspire Mozart, Cherubini, Beethoven, Schubert, and Brahms.

Haydn was born in the small village of Rohrau, in Austria. His father was a wagon repairer as well as a minor town official. The Haydns were a music-loving family (Joseph's younger brother, Michael, became a well-known composer of religious works). Haydn showed such great musical talent

Franz Joseph Haydn

that at the age of six he was sent to live and study with a cousin of his father's, a choirmaster. He learned to play the harpsichord and violin, and on Sundays sang in the church choir.

When Haydn was eight, his beautiful singing voice was heard by the music director of St. Stephen's Church in Vienna. The director took Haydn to Vienna with him to sing in the choir at St. Stephen's. In Vienna Haydn attended the church school, studying the usual school subjects and harmony and counterpoint also. He spent his clothing money on music and books about music, and even though the choir director made fun of him, managed to teach himself how to compose.

At seventeen, his voice broke ("He sounds like a crowing rooster," the Empress Maria Theresa remarked). One of Haydn's many practical jokes—he cut off the pigtail braids of another singer—served as an excuse for the director to drop him from the choir. Now Haydn was without money, job, or a place to live.

A friend, who also was poor, let Haydn share his room, and Haydn set to work making a living by singing, playing, and teaching. A merchant lent him some money to set up a studio, and here the young musician practiced and studied the new keyboard sonatas by C. P. E. Bach. This was the music on which much of Haydn's later work was founded.

Through one of his pupils Haydn met a famous vocal composer of the day, Nicola Porpora. Haydn became Porpora's valet and accompanist in return for lessons in Italian and composition. For three months he shined shoes and took care of Porpora's clothes. Porpora not only taught Haydn but also introduced him to wealthy people who could help his career.

Haydn had by now written several serenades, his first string quartets, and a comic opera, *Der krumme Teufel (The Limping Devil)*. These led to his engagement as music director and composer for an Austrian count, Maximilian von Morzin. For the count's orchestra of sixteen players, Haydn in 1759 wrote his first symphony. It was in three movements, with no minuet. By good fortune, for the world as well as for Haydn, this work was heard by a wealthy Hungarian nobleman, Prince Anton Esterházy, who immediately offered Haydn the post of assistant music director. Haydn accepted.

When Prince Anton died in 1762, he was succeeded by Prince Nicholas, also a great music lover. Nicholas entertained lavishly and often, and the new castle he built rivaled in splendor the greatest of Europe. Near it was a theater that seated 400 spectators. Soon Haydn was in charge of all the music on the estate.

Here, at the Esterházy estate outside Vienna, Haydn poured out his symphonies, operas, and chamber music for almost thirty years. His orchestra at first consisted of five violins, one cello, one double bass, one flute, two oboes, two bassoons, and two horns; over the years it ranged from fourteen to twenty-two musicians. Extra singers were added for church services and operas. Each week Haydn presented two operas and two formal concerts, and every day he provided chamber music for the prince. The prince himself played the baryton, a complicated relative of the cello, and Haydn wrote more than 150 works for it.

Each day the composer met with the prince to plan musical events. Haydn was expected to write most of the music himself, particularly if some notable was to be a guest. In addition, he had to take care of his musicians, making sure that they wore clean white stockings, kept their uniforms neat, and did not get into mischief. So well did he treat them that they began to call him "Papa Haydn."

Haydn had been in love with one of his

View of Eisenplatz, Vienna, in 1779

Haydn at the harpsichord during a performance of his L'Incanto Improviso *in the Esterházy theater*

Prince Nicholas Esterházy

pupils in Vienna. When she became a nun he married her older sister, and this was one of the greatest mistakes of his life. His wife had no understanding that she was married to a man who was great. She had no love for music—she even used Haydn's manuscripts for hair curlers. In later years when Haydn was paying special attention to a young soprano, his wife's jealousy made her even more difficult.

Haydn built the orchestra and opera company of the Esterházy's so skillfully that their performances were among the finest in Europe. He soon began to try out all kinds of new ideas in musical form and harmony. No longer were his works light and frivolous. He began to develop his material so that one short motive served as the seed of a whole symphonic movement. His allegro movements could sparkle with witty rhythmic jokes or be passionately dramatic. To the symphony he added a fourth movement—the minuet. To the wind instruments, which in the past were used to reinforce the strings, he now gave a life of their own. His comic operas were the delight of the nobility.

Haydn was becoming a composer with a reputation. His works were played in the world at large. In 1766 a short article about his music described it as "charming" and "humorous," but by 1771 he had begun to compose pieces deeper in feeling than anything he had written so far. His Piano Sonata in C Minor is truly tragic, just as later works by Beethoven are.

In his experiments Haydn was encouraged by Prince Nicholas. The orchestra was there for Haydn to use in trying out startling harmonies and more complex ways of composition. He wrote in daring keys, such as C-sharp, F-sharp, and B major. The slow movements of his works were often like operatic recitatives and arias. Haydn even began to introduce little touches of Hungarian gypsy music into his writing.

In the 1770's Haydn's symphonies became more and more dramatic. The Symphony Number 44 laments the death of a hero. The Symphony Number 45, the "Farewell," one of Haydn's most beautiful works, has a different motivation. It ends with an adagio movement in which one instrument after another stops until finally only one first violin and one second violin are left to play. They end as softly as possible. It was a sweet-sad way of reminding Prince Nicholas that the men were anxious to have a little vacation.

In 1777 Haydn wrote a comic "space opera": *The World of the Moon.* A funny, bouncy, "loony" work, it showed that Haydn had not lost his sense of humor. It has recently been revived to show audiences of today how people of the eighteenth century thought of space travel.

In 1781 Haydn met the young Mozart, and this was a turning point in his life. Mozart admired Haydn's works, and Haydn recognized genius in this young man of twenty-five. He now took every opportunity to push Mozart's works rather than his

Haydn rehearsing with musicians at the Esterházy Palace

own. The two men learned from each other. Mozart opened Haydn's ears to new, delicate melodic writing. From Haydn, Mozart learned the craft of putting together symphonies and quartets. Whenever they could, the two men got together in Vienna and played chamber music.

Haydn's quartets became more intricate than before. All the instruments took part in the music on an equal footing. In his "Russian" Quartets of 1781, he wrote in a new style. Instead of stating a main theme and a second theme and then having a development section, Haydn now developed his ideas almost from the beginning of each movement. Each instrument had a chance to play with the principal motive of the work. There were no accompanying parts—everything grew out of the main themes. These quartets, Opus 33, were called "Russian" because they were dedicated to the Grand Duke Paul of Russia.

Haydn seldom gave a title to a composition beyond calling it a symphony or quartet, with an opus number. But to keep the individual works clear in people's minds, various nicknames have been adopted. The "Bear" Symphony was given this title because the last movement suggests a clumsy dance by a bear. The "Queen" was a symphony liked by Queen Marie Antoinette of France. The "Razor" Quartet was given to an Englishman in exchange for a new razor. In the "Lark" Quartet the first violin flies high above the three lower strings.

In 1790 Prince Nicholas died. His successor preferred paintings and statues to music, and one of his first acts was to cut Haydn's budget. Haydn remained an Esterházy employee but now he had a great deal of free time. He received offers from Italy and Eng-

land, and a German musician living in London, Johann Peter Salomon, persuaded Haydn that he could make his fortune in England.

Haydn went to England in 1791 and was greeted with cheers. His concerts, managed by Salomon, were smashing successes. The orchestra of forty men—a much larger group than Haydn was used to—gave inspired performances of his six new "London" Symphonies. Oxford University made him an honorary Doctor of Music. The Prince of Wales and other persons in society invited Haydn to dinners, parties, and dances. After a year and a half in England, he returned to Vienna with a small fortune. In 1794 he went back to England with six more new symphonies, and again his concerts were triumphs.

The "London" Symphonies are among his finest works. Each is different in its form and in the treatment of ideas. The "Surprise," Number 94, with its folklike slow movement which suddenly erupts into a fortissimo "surprise," also has a strange minuet which is more like a German country dance, or *Ländler*. The Symphony Number 100 got its nickname, "Military," from the use of cymbals, triangle, and bass drum—instruments that belonged in a military band rather than a symphony orchestra. The Symphony Number 101, the "Clock," features a "ticking" accompaniment in the slow movement. In this movement Haydn uses one of his favorite forms: the mixing together of a rondo form and a variation form.

The twelve "London" Symphonies and the "Oxford" Symphony were all written within a period of a few years. No composer except Mozart ever turned out so many great works in symphonic form in so short a time. Haydn's fund of ideas seemed to have no end.

Haydn's second London visit was as successful as his first. When he spoke of going home, all his English friends tried to persuade him to stay. Even King George III wanted Haydn to settle in London. But the pull of Vienna was too strong. Haydn returned, making a side trip to his home town, where a monument had been erected in his honor.

Back in Vienna, Haydn accepted as a pupil the young composer Ludwig van Beethoven. The hard-driving young man found Haydn too easy-going, and the lessons did not mean much—though the study of Haydn's music did.

In England Haydn had been moved by the patriotic feeling aroused when "God Save the King" was sung. He decided to write an Austrian national anthem. On the emperor's birthday, February 12, 1797, his new "Emperor's Hymn" was sung in almost every Austrian theater. It became his most popular composition. Haydn himself liked it so much that he later included a set of variations on the melody in his Quartet, Opus 76, Number 3.

While in England, Haydn had heard the great oratorios of Handel, and on his return he decided to try his own hand at large choral works. First he wrote a great many vocal canons in which he sharpened his skill at writing counterpoint. His "Thy Voice, Oh Harmony" can be sung forward and backward, then turned upside down and sung forward and backward again!

He wrote six masses between 1796 and 1802. They are big, dramatic works that use instruments as well as voices. There are fanfares of trumpets, rolls on kettle drums, and other almost operatic touches. In his *Mass in Time of War* one can feel the alarm of the Viennese over Napoleon.

In 1798 Haydn's *Creation* was performed at a private concert in Vienna and it was an instant success. Performances in Vienna, Paris, London, and the United States soon followed. The musicians of Paris had a large gold medal made for Haydn in honor of the occasion. Haydn had often written descriptive music previously, but in *The Creation* he produced some of the most vivid musical pictures ever written. The opening sounds of the Chaos out of which God made the Earth almost pass the bounds of music as then known.

Soon after finishing *The Creation*, Haydn started to work on his second oratorio, *The Seasons*. Baron von Swieten, who had written the libretto for *The Creation*, took the

Portrait of Haydn (1794)

series of poems by the Scottish poet James Thomson and made them into recitatives, arias, and choruses.

Haydn's health had begun to fail, but his strong peasant's body still resisted illness. (In his sixties, when he was persuaded to have a small operation on his nose, the sight of the doctor terrified him, and he screamed and fought his way out of the doctor's office.) He worked on *The Seasons* carefully, writing and rewriting. The oratorio sounds not a bit like the work of a sick man. It is fresh, and full of the love of life and simple pleasures. *The Seasons*, like *The Creation*, contains many musical pictures, such as one depicting the harshness of winter changing to the gentleness of spring. Crickets chirp, frogs croak, birds sing. And there are flashes of humor: in the Spring section Haydn has a flute play a theme from his "Surprise" Symphony to suggest what a working man whistled.

The Seasons was performed in April 1801, and it, too, was a great success. But it was his last big work. Haydn, then retired, drew up a catalog of his works, and received his many guests—composers, performers, music lovers. He showed them the medals that had been given him by kings and emperors.

In 1808 he attended a performance of *The Creation*. The strain was too much for him, and he had to be carried out before the end of the performance. He died in 1809 after his beloved city of Vienna was taken by the French troops of Napoleon—who, however, placed a protective guard around Haydn's house. His funeral was attended by many French officers as well as by the nobility of Vienna. The music was a Requiem by Haydn's favorite composer, Mozart.

Title page of Haydn's oratorio The Seasons

A 1903 production of Babes in Toyland

Victor Herbert

HERBERT, VICTOR (1859–1924): composer, concert cellist, and conductor. Herbert's serious music includes two cello concertos, two grand operas, and one of the first musical scores for a motion picture—*The Fall of a Nation* (1916). But he is best remembered for the songs from his more than forty gay operettas of which the best known are *The Fortune Teller, Babes in Toyland, Mlle. Modiste, The Red Mill,* and *Naughty Marietta.*

Herbert was born in Dublin, Ireland. His father died when he was three years old; when he was eight, his mother married a German doctor and the family moved to Stüttgart, Germany. Here he began to study the cello and in a few years became a professional musician. After several years of playing in various European orchestras, he decided to study composition, and in 1885 he wrote and played his first cello concerto. The following year Herbert and his wife, who was an opera singer, were hired by the Metropolitan Opera Company in New York.

Herbert played in the "Met" orchestra, as well as appearing as cello soloist with several American orchestras, including the New York Philharmonic. He became a bandmaster of New York's 22nd Regiment Band and from 1898 to 1904 he conducted the Pittsburgh Symphony Orchestra.

In 1893 Herbert started the career that brought him fame. He wrote *Prince Ananias* for a Boston light-opera group. When it was produced in New York in 1894, it was so successful that producers urged him to write more such works. He started writing one operetta a year, but soon doubled or tripled this output. He not only wrote the music of his stage works, he also did his own scoring for orchestra—something few present-day popular composers can do.

The lighthearted, romantic quality of Herbert's works and his gift for melody were very much in tune with the times, and in the years before World War I he was America's most popular composer.

Only two or three of Herbert's operettas are occasionally revived. But his sparkling and singable songs, such as "Kiss Me Again," "Ah, Sweet Mystery of Life," and "Just a Kiss in the Dark," have endured as light classics with recurrent popularity.

His cello works are played occasionally, but from his two grand operas, *Natoma* and *Madeleine,* only the stirring "Dagger Dance" from *Natoma* is sometimes played today. In 1914, disturbed about the plight of the composers who were receiving no royalties for the performance of their music, Herbert and a group of composers and publishers founded the American Society of Composers, Authors and Publishers (ASCAP). Herbert served as vice-president of the organization from the time of its founding until his death.

Herbert earned a great deal of money from his operettas. He also spent a great deal. He enjoyed being a generous host to his hundreds of friends, and probably overworked himself to provide this costly hospitality.

Herbert regretted that his serious music was neglected while the songs that he wrote so easily and quickly were popular. But at the end of his life even his lilting waltz tunes were being displaced by the sounds of the jazz age.

HINDEMITH, PAUL (1895–1963): one of the most prolific of modern composers, and perhaps the most complete musician of the twentieth century. In addition to writing hundreds of compositions and several books about music, he was a performer on the violin and the viola, a conductor, a teacher, and a musical scholar.

Hindemith was born in Hanau, Germany, a town ten miles from Frankfurt-am-Main. As a child he learned to play several instruments, and at eleven began to concentrate on the violin and composition. After graduating from the Conservatory of Frankfurt he became, at twenty, the concertmaster of the Frankfurt Opera House orchestra. In 1921 he became the violist in the Amar String Quartet, which made many successful European tours.

Hindemith always felt that a musician should not stay in an ivory tower, aloof from people. In 1926 he joined a musical "youth movement" in Germany, and for its groups of young music lovers he wrote many works, which he called "Music to Sing and Play." Some of these are songs for groups to sing, easy works for string players, arrangements of old German folk tunes for chorus and instruments, and a musical play for children—*Wir bauen eine Stadt (Let's Build a Town)*. His *Der Ploner Musiktag (A Day of Music in Plon)* has Morning Music for brasses, Dinner Music for winds and strings, a little cantata, and an Evening Concert with little pieces for orchestra, clarinet and strings, and a trio of recorders. *In Praise of Music,* for voices and orchestra, has a finale in which the audience joins in the singing.

In 1927 Hindemith was appointed professor of composition at the Berlin Conservatory *(Hochschule für Musik)*. When the Nazis seized power in Germany, they attacked him because he refused to change his style of writing or give up his Jewish friends. They then banned his music. In 1935 Hindemith went to Turkey, and there set up for the government a system of music education. In the course of this work he founded orchestras and conservatories.

Hindemith was in London in 1936 when King George V died. In one day he wrote his moving *Trauermusik (Music of Mourning)* for viola and strings, and played it the following day.

After living in Switzerland for a while, Hindemith came to the United States in 1939. The following year he became a professor of music at Yale University, where he taught young composers, organized concerts of old music, and even taught his students

Early portrait of Hindemith

how to play the old instruments, which he borrowed from museums.

When World War II ended, Hindemith returned to Europe and conducted many performances of his own works. German music lovers, who had not heard his music for more than ten years, greeted him warmly.

Hindemith had become an American citizen but liked the feel of Switzerland. For several years he alternated teaching at Yale and the University of Zürich. Finally, in 1953, he settled down in Zürich to compose and write books.

Notwithstanding his other activities, Hindemith managed to compose a large number of works. He believed a composer should write for all kinds of music lovers and performers, from beginners to the most accomplished professionals. He liked to think of himself as a composer of *Gebrauchsmusik,* "music for use," and made a point of writing at least one sonata for each instrument, including trumpet, trombone, harp, and bassoon. His stage works range from full-

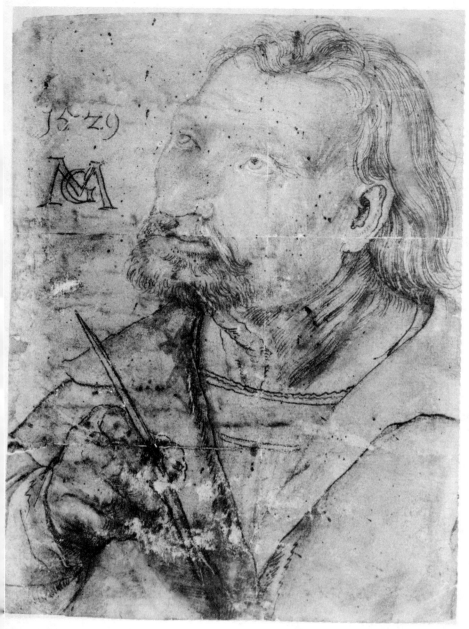

Self-portrait of the painter called Mathias Grünewald (Mathis der Maler), c. 1480–c. 1530

Hindemith's early work was wildly dissonant. Gradually he developed a style of writing based on theories about the greater and lesser feelings of tension given off by certain interval combinations. His music is at times highly chromatic but is almost never without a tonal center. Although he could invent imaginative melodies, he often seems, like Bach, to have taken seemingly insignificant motives and shown how they could be made into something of value. His study of old music led him to write in many of the old musical forms, such as the fugue, the sonata, and the theme and variations.

Hindemith's mastery of musical materials enabled him to write music that is full of compositional virtuosity. Thus the music and action of *There and Back* builds up to a certain point; then everything moves backward to the beginning. The postlude of his *Ludus Tonalis,* for piano, is the same as the prelude, but upside down and backward.

Hindemith's books are among the finest ever written about music. *The Craft of Musical Composition* explains his own style. His two books on traditional harmony have been published in German, English, Italian, Hebrew, Japanese, and Norwegian. In the scholarly, witty, and wise *A Composer's World,* a series of lectures given at Harvard, 1949–50, he summed up his views on the world of music.

HOMOPHONIC MUSIC: music that moves in harmonic blocks, as opposed to linear or contrapuntal music. Homophonic texture is basic to the harmonization of hymns and chorales, although it can also be found in Baroque dance music (Ex. 15, next page), in slow movements of Classical works (Ex. 16), in various types of nineteenth- and twentieth-century music (Ex. 17), and even in sections of otherwise polyphonic sixteenth-century choral works (Ex. 18).

Actually, homophonic music predates polyphonic music, the earliest form of which, known as organum, moves in solid homophonic blocks of sound:

Musica enchiriadis (c. 850)

Although applied in a strict sense only to chordal music, the term "homophonic" has been extended to include almost any music based on harmonic phrases and having frequent cadences (Ex. 19, next page).

length operas, such as *Cardillac, Mathis der Maler (Matthias the Painter), Neues vom Tage (News of the Day),* and the *Long Christmas Dinner,* to a twelve-minute opera, *Hin und Zurück (There and Back).* His ballets include *Hérodiade* and *St. Francis (Nobilissima Visione).* His *Das Nusch-Nuschi* is music for a marionette show. *Symphonic Metamorphosis on Themes by Weber* (a set of variations), *The Four Temperaments,* and his symphony *Mathis der Maler* are the orchestral works most frequently performed. Much of Hindemith's music is witty, but the symphony *Mathis der Maler,* like his song cycle *Das Marienleben (The Life of Mary),* is filled with deep emotional feeling.

Ex. 15— Saraband from Harpsichord Suite in G Minor, Handel

Ex. 16— Sonata in E-flat for Piano, Op. 7, Beethoven

Ex. 17— "From a Wandering Iceberg," MacDowell

Ex. 18— *Missa brevis*, Palestrina

Ex. 19— Piano Sonata in D Major, Op. 10, No. 3, Beethoven

HONEGGER, ARTHUR (1892–1955): one of the outstanding modern composers of France. His parents were Swiss, but Honegger was born in Le Havre, France, and had most of his musical training at the Paris Conservatory. He married a French pianist and took a leading role in French musical life.

In 1918 Honegger and five other young French composers shared a concert of new music. A Paris critic called the group "Les Six," and they became connected in the minds of many people, although each young composer went his own way thereafter. The other members of "Les Six" were Milhaud, Poulenc, Durey, Auric, and Mlle. Tailleferre.

In 1921 Honegger wrote incidental music, scored for an orchestra of fifteen pieces, for a Swiss playwright's Biblical drama, *Le Roi David (King David)*. The success of the work led Honegger to expand the music to an oratorio, or "symphonic psalm," as he called it. The revised work is scored for a large orchestra, a narrator, solo singers, and a chorus. Ranging in mood from barbaric to deeply mournful and tenderly lyric, it evokes all the splendor and pathos of the Old Testament story. Its performance in 1923 stamped Honegger as a powerful young composer.

Honegger achieved more widespread fame in 1924 when his symphonic poem *Pacific 231* was first performed. This piece of music suggests the sound of a large American locomotive as it starts, speeds on its way, and comes to a stop. The music for *Pacific 231* seems brutally dissonant and depends on rhythmic drive for much of its interest. It is one of the few lasting works that came from a period when artists were concerned with the new "machine age."

In 1928 Honegger's athletic symphonic poem, *Rugby,* was given its first performance between the halves of an international rugby match between England and France.

Among the many works written by Honegger, the best-known are his five symphonies, his ballet music, two operas *(Judith* and *Antigone),* a film score for a movie of Shaw's *Pygmalion,* and a concerto for flute, English horn, and strings. He wrote a great deal of chamber music: three string quartets, two violin sonatas, a cello sonata, and a sonatine for clarinet and piano. Honegger's oratorio, *Jeanne d'Arc au bûcher (Joan of Arc at the Stake),* written in 1934–35, has had many performances since its première in 1938.

Honegger's music is eclectic; that is, it follows no one school of contemporary composition. It is always well-made music, often contrapuntal. More than most French composers, Honegger was influenced by Wagner and Richard Strauss, as well as by Stravinsky. Like any other good composer, Honegger sounds like himself.

Above: *Arthur Honegger as a young man*
Right: *Honegger on the footplate of a locomotive*

HOPKINSON, FRANCIS (1737–91): lawyer, signer of the Declaration of Independence, and one of the first native-born American composers. Born in Philadelphia, Pennsylvania, he trained for the law and became a lawyer, but spent much time in the study and performance of music. A delegate to the Continental Congress, after the Revolutionary War he became a judge of admiralty, meanwhile continuing to play the harpsichord and write poetry.

In 1788 he published seven songs, dedicated to his friend George Washington. One of them, "My Days Have Been So Wondrous Free," has stood the test of time and is sung today. Hopkinson proclaimed it to be the first truly American song. It is a pleasantly melodic work in the style of earlier English composers such as Purcell and Arne.

Hopkinson's life was so busy that he had little time to compose. But along with Franklin and Jefferson he was one of the Founding Fathers who understood the value of music to mankind.

Hopkinson's son, Joseph, wrote the words to the patriotic song "Hail Columbia."

HORNPIPE: an ancient instrument which gave its name to several dances. It was exactly what its name suggests: one or two cows' horns into which were stuck one or two wooden musical pipes. The hornpipe was made in many different forms and was popular in Europe during the Middle Ages, particularly in England and Wales.

The hornpipe dance started as a stage dance in England in the middle 1700's, and was related to the Irish jig and the French *rigaudon,* or rigadoon. The music, originally in triple meter, later took on a fast two- or four-count form. It had many running notes and started on an upbeat.

The movement of the hornpipe features hopping and kicking of the feet. It became a favorite sailors' dance because it could be done in a small space and without a partner.

HURDY-GURDY: one of the most popular instruments of the medieval period, when it was known as the *organistrum.* It was a mechanical form of the stringed vielle, with a resined wheel which, turned by means of a crank, rubbed across the strings to make them sound. Several of the strings were drones, capable of sounding only one tone each. Two or three other strings, often tuned in unison, played the melody. The player changed the length of his strings by means of wooden keys which were attached to small wooden bridges under the strings. The bridges acted like the fingers of a violinist as they stopped the strings to produce tones of different pitches. Some hurdy-gurdies were so large that it took two persons to play them. The sound was like a mixture of a bagpipe tone and a rough string tone.

Early hurdy-gurdies were used in church services until the small portable organ drove them out of the church and into the hands of strolling minstrels and jongleurs. As a peasant instrument, the hurdy-gurdy lasted longest in France, where it finally died out about 1800. Haydn wrote five concertos and several nocturnes for two hurdy-gurdies and accompanying instruments. The hurdy-gurdies for which he composed them, known as the *lire organizzate,* combined the features of the old hurdy-gurdy and a small organ. These works were written for the king of Naples, who fancied himself a virtuoso on the instrument.

A nineteenth-century barrel organ—the instrument of the begging monkey—was erroneously given the name hurdy-gurdy because it, too, was operated by a crank.

Francis Hopkinson

Hurdy-gurdy player (an etching by Jacques Callot, 1626)

King David and minstrels (miniature from a psalter)

HYMN: a religious song of prayer, adoration, or praise sung by a congregation. Hymns of praise were sung in ancient Greece, and among the few pieces of Greek music of that era that have been preserved are two hymns to Apollo. The psalms of David were probably the hymns of the Jews in Biblical times.

The early Christians sang hymns together to proclaim their faith in God, and their steadfastness in this faith, and for cheer and encouragement. The Crusaders are reported to have sung hymns all across Europe as they made their way to the Holy Land, and martyrs sang as they were marched to the scaffold.

The leaders of the early Christian church, realizing the importance of hymn singing as a means of strengthening the faith and in some instances as a factor in counteracting heresy, took an active part in introducing hymns into divine service. After St. Ambrose (d. 397)—usually considered to have introduced the metrical hymn into the service—the use of hymns with poetic words or with meterized scripture was general in the service. The melodies of the earliest hymns were in plainchant. Because of the lack of a workable musical notation, we do not know exactly what the melodies were.

In 1589, the first great collection of Roman Catholic hymns *(Hymni Totius Anni),* arranged in fine polyphonic style for three, four, five, or six voices, was published by Palestrina. In it there is a hymn for every festival day of the Catholic church year.

Earlier in the same century, Martin Luther,

realizing the importance of congregational participation in the service, wrote new words in the language of the people to melodies that had been used for Catholic hymns. He also set new words to German folk songs, and for still other hymns he wrote original melodies. An interesting example of the development of a Lutheran chorale is the well-known, "O Sacred Head Now Wounded," used so effectively by J. S. Bach in his St. Matthew Passion. Starting as a love song composed by Hans Leo Hassler (1564-1612), the melody became both a chorale and a Catholic hymn. The Lutheran hymns, called chorales, were published in a hymnal (a collection of hymns) in 1524, arranged for voices by Johann Walter. Other settings of chorales were made by Schütz, Scheidt, Schein, and Praetorius. North German organists and choirmasters began to use the chorales as a basis for organ chorale preludes and vocal cantatas—musical forms brought to their highest peak in the works of J. S. Bach.

In the Protestant churches of England and France, the earliest hymns were settings of the Biblical psalms. The most famous collection was the *Genevan Psalter,* published over a period of years around 1542, some with melodies and some with text only. Louis Bourgeois, a Frenchman, is credited with the work. In 1612 Henry Ainsworth printed, in Holland, a psalm book written for the Puritans, who brought it to America. In 1640 the *Bay Psalm Book* was printed in Cambridge, Massachusetts, the first book to be printed in the English colonies in America. Only the words were printed in this book; the congregation sang the melodies from memory. Of all the hymns from the *Bay Psalm Book,* only the doxology, the "Old Hundred," is still sung today.

During the Revolutionary War several American composers wrote stirring hymns that are still sung. Among these are William Billings' "Chester" and Oliver Holden's "Coronation" ("All Hail the Power of Jesus' Name").

In England the first hymn writer to break down the tradition of basing hymns only on the psalms was Isaac Watts (1674-1748). His simple, folklike hymns led the way for many later hymn writers. With the beginning of each new sect of the Protestant church, a demand was created for new and special hymns. Recognizing the importance of singing to the Methodist movement, John and Charles Wesley wrote hundreds of hymns, many of them consisting only of new words set to old tunes.

In the nineteenth century new hymns

Below left: *John Wesley*
Below right: *Charles Wesley*

Top left: *Lowell Mason, American composer of hymn tunes*
Top right: *Homer Rodeheaver, choir leader for the revivalist Billy Sunday (1917)*
Below: *Vincent Persichetti, American composer of many hymns in a contemporary idiom*

grew out of the many revival meetings in America. At these revivals, notable for their camp meetings, the preacher used singing and dancing to arouse the religious fervor of his group. Out of these meetings in the 1840's came many fine "white spirituals," while on the plantations of the South the blacks contributed their own spirituals to the hymnody of America.

By the time of the Civil War, the revival hymns and black spirituals had given Americans a whole new set of religious songs. The revival hymn "Mine Eyes Have Seen the Glory of the Coming of the Lord" became the "Battle Hymn of the Republic"—the marching song of the Northern armies.

Most hymnals today include a wide variety of hymns. Each religious group publishes its own, but the various hymnals have many tunes in common. Numerous hymn tunes were given identifying names such as Windsor, York, and so forth. A single tune often serves more than one set of words, and in the same way the same set of words may be sung to more than one tune.

The remembered hymn is one of the strongest elements in our American musical heritage. Today, with so much of our music made for us by others, the singing of hymns is declining in our more sophisticated communities. Where vigorous congregational singing still takes place, it is probably as a result of enthusiasm for music by the clergyman. Even in Bach's time there were clerics who were not imbued with the need for the great ministry of music.

Many hymns and spirituals have been used by American composers. Ives's Fourth Violin Sonata is entitled *Children's Day at the Camp Meeting,* and uses the revival hymn "Shall We Gather at the River" as the basis for one movement. Aaron Copland used the Shaker hymn "Simple Gifts" in his ballet *Appalachian Spring.* Several of Billings' hymns are used by William Schuman in his *New England Triptych.* Black spirituals have served as inspiration for hundreds of works. A revival meeting is one of the most dramatic scenes in Floyd's popular opera *Susannah.*

IMITATION: the repetition by one or more different voices or instruments of musical material first stated by one voice or instrument. The imitation can be strict or free. A strict imitation is called a *canon*.

There are many kinds of imitation. It may start on the same tone as the original (imitation at the unison) or any other tone (imitation at the second, third, and so forth). The intervals of the imitation may move in the same direction as the original or they may be reversed so that an upward interval of a fifth is imitated by a downward interval of a fifth (imitation in inversion, or contrary motion). The time values may be the same, or they may be quickened (imitation in diminution) or broadened (imitation in augmentation). The original line

may even be imitated backward (retrograde motion), or several of these approaches may be combined. For example, an imitating part may be written in augmentation and in contrary motion (see CANON).

Imitation is an important structural device in most compositions written in counterpoint, such as the masses and motets of Lassus and Palestrina, and the instrumental and choral fugues by Bach and Handel. Composers of the Classical period, as well as of the nineteenth and twentieth centuries, use imitation in many of their instrumental and choral works, often resorting to a free type of imitation in which a fragment of a theme is tossed from instrument to instrument or from one register to another (Ex. 1 and 2).

Ex. 1 — Symphony in B Minor, Schubert

Ex. 2 — String Quartet No. 5, Bartók

IMPRESSIONISM: a term sometimes used to describe the musical style of the French composers Debussy and Ravel, the English composers Delius and Scott, the Spanish composer Falla, and the American composer Griffes.

Impressionism as an art movement started as an outdoor style of painting in France. In the hands of such painters as Monet, Manet, Renoir, Van Gogh, Sisley, and Turner, Impressionism reached its highest point in the 1880's. The Impressionists tried to give a sense of something seen just for a moment, rather than of something studied carefully and in detail. Many of their paintings were like improvisations in color—glowing, shadowy, and full of the contrasts between complementary colors. Shapes were often vague and outlines slightly blurred. Japanese art, new to Europe, showed the French artists fresh paths in the light and airy use of color and lines. French poets such as Mallarmé and Verlaine had their own version of Impressionism, using words for their sound as well as their meaning.

Both poets and painters influenced the greatest Impressionist composer, Debussy. He used fragments of melody, irregular patterns of rhythm, complex harmonies, scales other than the usual major and minor, and shimmering instrumental sounds to achieve his new kind of music. By avoiding harmonic and melodic patterns that had been traditional for several hundred years, Debussy broke down classical form and structure and opened the way for much of what is called modern music.

The Impressionist composers gave poetic titles to their compositions, although their music does not describe a thing as much as it gives the composer's impression of how that thing made him feel. Much Impressionist music, like painting, took its inspiration from nature. There are many compositions about clouds, the sea, gardens, fountains, and waterfalls.

Technically, Impressionist music is full of subtle contrasts. It speaks in whispers and uses short phrases. By adding tones to simple chords, the composers blur the outlines of their harmonies, making a series of slightly dissonant chords. Chords are used for their own unique sounds and move in unexpected progressions. In orchestral writing one hears the cool sounds of the flute and harp, the tang of muted trumpets and French horn, the melancholy sound of the English horn, the softly rich sound of the strings divided into many parts, and the exotic use of percussion instruments.

Impressionist music is concerned with subtleties of feeling and perception. Despite the highly personal vision of the composers, the music itself seems objective and reflective. It is music of the senses.

IMPROMPTU: a short musical composition, usually for piano, that has the feeling of an improvisation. The title was not used till the nineteenth century. After Schubert's death in 1828, his publishers issued some of his short, untitled pieces as "Impromptus," a title that was later used by Chopin. Chopin's famous *Fantasie-Impromptu* dates from 1834; three other pieces simply entitled *Impromptu* date from a few years later.

IMPROVISATION: a performer's invention on the spur of the moment. It can be as simple as someone's making up a little tune that he hums or whistles, or it can be as complex as a group of musicians improvising together at a concert.

As early as the twelfth century, singers in church choirs improvised melodies that fitted with the Gregorian chant being sung by the tenors. This early form of improvised counterpoint was called descant.

Improvisation was an important part of chamber, church, and opera music in the seventeenth and eighteenth centuries. Opera singers were expected to embellish their simple vocal parts with scale passages, trills, turns, and sobbing effects. Violinists would

The Kid Ory Band in a "jam session," 1949, with, from left to right: Ted Buchner, cornet; Kid Ory, trombone; Joe Darensbourg, clarinet; and Ed Garland, bass

decorate a slow melody with many fanciful embellishments. A church organist improvised preludes and interludes as part of his job. He was also expected to improvise between stanzas of a chorale or hymn—a practice that led to the musical form of the *choral prelude.*

The keyboardist of the Baroque period who accompanied instrumental or vocal music was expected to improvise his part from a *figured bass.* This device, a bass part with numbers above it, was a shorthand method invented by composers to tell the keyboardist what chords to use.

Many great composers were famous for their skill at improvisation. Bach amazed Frederick the Great of Prussia by the wonderful variations he improvised on a theme given him by the king. (Bach later wrote a set of variations, the *Musical Offering,* on this theme.) Mozart and Beethoven were noted for their improvisations; in fact, many thought Beethoven's improvisations were better and more exciting than his written compositions.

During the eighteenth century, composers began to write out their music in full. Improvisation disappeared except in the cadenzas of concertos. Here the soloist was expected to weave a glittering development of the themes of the concerto. Finally, in the nineteenth century, composers even began to write out their own cadenzas. Musicians continued to improvise, but only organists and dance musicians improvised in public.

Dance musicians have always been expected to improvise, and most of the great jazz performers have been inspired in this kind of expression, making up new variations on tunes night after night. Many people think jazz is at its best when improvised. Some of the most exciting "hot" records are the result of improvised "jam sessions" at a recording studio. The improviser of jazz operates much like his Baroque predecessor, but instead of using a figured bass, he improvises on the harmonic plan of a well-known popular tune. Because of its simple chord progression, which allows for great freedom, the blues pattern has always been a favorite of jazz improvisers.

Improvisation is of two kinds. The simpler kind, such as jazz or playing from a figured bass, calls for variations over a given harmonic plan. The more difficult kind is to take a theme and plan a form that the theme can be worked into. In no case does the improviser lose control of his musical materials—he is always aware of what he is doing and where he is going. Improvisation depends on a good ear and a knowledge of harmony. With these as a basis, the improviser can go as far as his imagination will take him.

INTERLUDE: a short musical composition often played between parts of a church service or a theater work. Interludes are often improvised by church organists between the verses of hymns. In Germany the improvised interludes between the verses or lines of a chorale led in the seventeenth century to the musical form of the *choral prelude.* Short movements of long musical compositions are sometimes called interludes.

In operas and plays, the music between scenes or acts may be called an interlude, an intermezzo, or an *entr'acte.*

INTERMEZZO: a piece of music played between acts or scenes of an opera. In sixteenth-century Italy it became customary to perform madrigals or elaborate musical spectacles between acts of a play. These intermezzi, or *intermèdes,* were important forerunners of opera. Later, in the 1600's and early 1700's, an intermezzo became a light story with music that was performed between the acts of a serious opera. The success of Pergolesi's light, witty intermezzo *La serva padrona* in 1733 led to the development of the *opera buffa,* or comic opera.

Composers have used the word intermezzo to mean a short instrumental composition played to show the passage of time between two scenes of an opera. (Usually the curtain is not lowered.) The French word for a stage intermezzo is *entr'acte,* which means "between the acts."

Brahms used the title "Intermezzo" for several of his short piano pieces.

INTERVAL: the distance from one pitch to another. A knowledge of intervals is important to musician and music lover alike, since two of the three important ingredients of music—melody and harmony—are based completely on intervals. It is partly through the hearing and analysis of intervals, for example, that one can identify a musical composition as coming from the fourteenth, eighteenth, or twentieth century. Composers, consciously or not, use some intervals as consonances, other as dissonances. In this sense the analysis of how a composer uses intervals—his intervallic controls—is one of the fundamental studies in musicianship.

Intervals are always measured from one

Table of Intervals

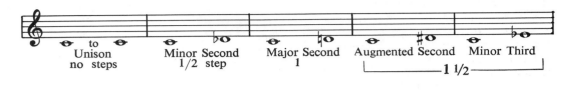

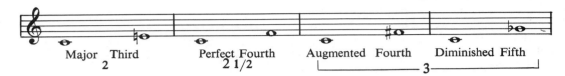

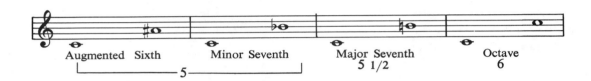

pitch designation to another. C (♯, ♮, or ♭) up to D (♯, ♮, or ♭) within the same octave is always called a second. The table above shows the intervals built above C.

Intervals larger than a tenth are usually referred to as though they were in the same octave: the interval from middle C to the A at the top of the treble staff, for example, is considered to be a sixth:

Each interval can have three or four sizes.

Fourths, fifths, and octaves can be perfect, diminished, or augmented. Seconds, thirds, sixths, and sevenths can be major, minor, diminished, or augmented.

A *perfect* interval can be made *diminished* by decreasing its size by a half step (Ex. 3a); a *perfect* interval can be made *augmented* by increasing its size by a half step (Ex. 3b); a *major* interval can be made *minor* by decreasing its size by a half step (Ex. 3c); a *major* interval can be made *augmented* by increasing its size by a half step (Ex. 3d); and a *minor* interval can be made *diminished* by decreasing its size by a half step (Ex. 3e).

Ex. 3

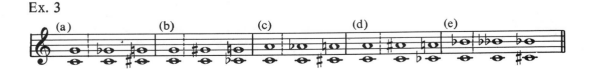

Intervals are sometimes classified as *perfect consonances* (unisons, perfect fourths, perfect fifths, and octaves), *imperfect consonances* (major and minor thirds and sixths), and *dissonances* (seconds, sevenths, and all diminished and augmented intervals).

There is a relationship between the table of consonances and dissonances and the table of interval ratios. In physics a musical interval is described in terms of the ratio between the frequencies of two tones. Thus the ratio between the tone A above middle C, whose vibration frequency is 440 per second, and the tone A below middle C, whose frequency is 220 per second, is 2 to 1. This ratio represents an octave. The simplest ratios are those of the perfect intervals; the more complex are those of the dissonances:

Interval	Ratio
Unison	1 to 1
Octave	2 to 1
Perfect fifth	3 to 2
Perfect fourth	4 to 3
Major third	5 to 4
Minor third	6 to 5
Major sixth	5 to 3
Minor sixth	8 to 5
Minor seventh	9 to 5
Major seventh	15 to 8
Minor second	10 to 9
Major second	9 to 8 (or 16 to 15)

Interestingly enough, the first four intervals were the basic sounds of harmony from the eleventh to the fifteenth centuries and the next four, from the fifteenth to the end of the nineteenth century. The last four intervals are the sounds much used in twentieth-century music.

When intervals are inverted (turned upside down), their size changes. The sum of an interval and its inversion always adds up to nine:

A unison inverted becomes an octave:

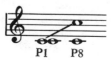

P1   P8

A second inverted becomes a seventh:

M2   m7

A third inverted becomes a sixth, and so forth:

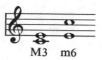

M3   m6

Also: When a perfect interval is inverted, it stays perfect:

P4   P5   P5   P4

When a major interval is inverted, it becomes minor:

M6   m3

When a minor interval is inverted, it becomes major:

m6   M3

When a diminished interval is inverted, it becomes augmented:

Dim.7 Aug.2

When an augmented interval is inverted, it becomes diminished:

Aug.4 Dim.5

Training one's ear to hear intervals is difficult but rewarding. One method is to play a tone on the piano, sing a given interval above it, and then test the ear by playing the tone. Another method is to concentrate on one interval at a time, recognizing it as it occurs during a composition. Gradually the small vocabulary of intervals will become known without one's thinking about it—just as one recognizes familiar faces.

INVENTION: a short contrapuntal composition based on one idea or invention. In 1723 Johann Sebastian Bach published a collection of thirty short contrapuntal pieces playable on the clavichord and other keyboard instruments. The first fifteen pieces—the two-part inventions—are written for two voices, one played by each hand. The second group—usually known as the three-part inventions—have an additional voice played sometimes by one hand, sometimes by the other. Bach called these three-part inventions "symphonies."

Both sets of Bach's Inventions are written in the following sequence of keys:

1. C major	9. F minor
2. C minor	10. G major
3. D major	11. G minor
4. D minor	12. A major
5. E-flat major	13. A minor
6. E major	14. B-flat major
7. E minor	15. B minor
8. F major	

(Bach carried out this experiment of using a variety of major and minor keys more completely in his *Well-tempered Clavier,* of which the first volume was written in the year 1722.)

Each invention begins with its subject or main idea. This may be a short motive played by itself and immediately repeated in another voice (as in Ex. 4 below). Or it may be two motives played together—in which case the voices soon exchange parts (as in Ex. 5 below).

Short episodes, usually based on a fragment of the subject, carry the music to different keys, in which the subject may be stated several times. The music reaches a modest climax, following which the subject usually reappears one last time in the original key. Many of the inventions close with a brief codetta.

Each invention has its own mood, depending on its main motive. Some are gay dance pieces (Numbers Four, Ten, and Fifteen of the two-part inventions and Numbers Three, Six, Twelve, and Fifteen of the three-part group).

Others, such as the F-minor inventions in both these groups, are wistful and even slightly sad. There are brisk allegros (Numbers Eight and Thirteen of the two-part

Ex. 4 — Invention No. 4, J.S. Bach

Ex. 5 — Invention No. 6, J.S. Bach

inventions) and decorative andantes (Number Fourteen of the two-part and Number Five of the three-part group).

Early versions of the Inventions appear in a *Little Keyboard Book* which Bach began putting together in 1720 for his nine-year-old son Wilhelm Friedemann. He thought they would help young Friedemann phrase voices independently at the keyboard, and would also serve as transparent demonstrations of how counterpoint is put together.

INVERSION: a change of the relative position of the notes of a harmonic interval, a chord, or a melody.

An interval is inverted by placing the lower tone above the higher tone:

The sum of the numbers of an interval and its inversion always equals nine: a third when inverted becomes a sixth; a second becomes a seventh, and so forth. Major intervals become minor, augmented intervals become diminished, and vice versa.

A chord is in an inverted position when any tone other than the root is in the lowest voice (see Ex. a and b at the top of the next column).

Chordal inversions are used to produce a more melodic bass part and to give variety to the music. Recitatives in operas and oratorios often begin with the playing of a major triad in its first inversion.

A melody moves in inversion, or contrary motion, when the direction of the melody is reversed on repetition (Ex. 6). In contemporary twelve-tone music the inversion of the original row of tones is one of the four ways in which the row appears (Ex. 7). In many compositions where voices imitate each other, the imitation often appears alternately in its original form and in inversion.

Counterpoint is said to be invertible when it is written so that the lower and upper parts can be exchanged. Most of the inventions and fugues of J. S. Bach are written in invertible counterpoint (see Fugue No. 2 on page 200).

Ex. 6 — *The Art of Fugue*, J.S. Bach

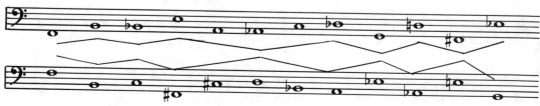

Ex. 7 — Duo for Tubas, R.F. Goldman

IVES, CHARLES EDWARD (1874–1954): an American composer who was one of the most original of the twentieth century. Born in Danbury, Connecticut, he studied music with his father, a bandmaster. By the age of thirteen he was a professional church organist, and soon he was trying his hand at composition. On graduating from Yale, where he studied composition with Horatio Parker, Ives knew that he wanted most of all to be a composer, but he also knew that a composer could not earn a living in the United States. He decided, therefore, to be an insurance man, and in time his abilities made him wealthy. He continued in the world of business until 1930, when his health began to fail. But throughout his life he reserved time for composing.

At first when Ives tried to have his works performed, the performers could not understand the strange music that this successful businessman was writing. It *was* strange music—far different from what was being written in Europe at the time. It was music that grew out of America—hymns, vaudeville ballads, village band concerts, barn dances, and folk tunes. Yet in Ives there was something deeper than the sounds of America. He believed in the American philosophy as expressed in the writings of Thoreau, Hawthorne, and Whitman. He reached out to the universe as did Emerson. Living a prosaic life during the day, he put the American dream on music paper at night and on weekends. Like the American pioneers, Ives opened new paths.

Long before Stravinsky, Schoenberg, and the other leading contemporary composers started breaking away from the old traditions, Ives was writing music in which lines of chords were treated like lines of single notes, piling up dissonance on top of dissonance, changing meters or doing away with regular bar lines. Sprinkled throughout an Ives score are musical quotations from hymn tunes and patriotic songs. In the midst of the greatest complexity one comes across a revival hymn; or a hymn bursts into a passage in which several rhythms go their own way.

The sound of several bands in a parade suggested to Ives the idea of polytonal music and polyrhythmic music. In a parade one heard two or three bands playing simultaneously in more than one key and at slightly different pulse rates. One also heard music coming at one from several sources. Thus Ives in his *The Unanswered Question* and *Central Park in the Dark* experimented with a subdivided orchestra—part on stage and part off.

Ives experimented in almost every medium, always pushing that medium a bit beyond where it was at the moment. The *Psalm 67* and *Three Harvest Home Chorales* still impress the listener by their inventive sounds for massed voices. The four violin sonatas—of which the Fourth, subtitled *Children's Day at the Camp Meeting,* is the most popular—combine the violin and piano in new ways. His two piano sonatas are tremendously difficult to play and to understand. New percussive sonorities are derived from the piano, and, in the Second Piano Sonata, Ives asks the pianist to play huge tone clusters by pressing on a board which is placed over the keys (see Ex. 28 on page 106).

Top: *a Fourth of July celebration (1859 lithograph)*
Bottom: *a camp meeting (lithograph c. 1830)*

Charles Ives

In 1919 Ives decided to publish at his own expense the Second Piano Sonata. He called it *The Concord Sonata* because in it he attempted to evoke the spirit of the great men who lived in that small Massachusetts town: Emerson, Hawthorne, the Alcotts, Thoreau. In 1922 he published, again at his own expense, a volume of 114 songs. These brought him to the attention of American musicians, most of whom had not even known of the existence of Ives. The songs range from watered-down German lieder, in the style of Schumann, to the dramatic setting of the legendary death of the cowboy Charlie Rutledge; from almost cheap vaudeville tunes to songs that are ecstatic and mystical.

By the late 1930's the world of music was becoming more and more aware of Ives—who, by this time, had stopped composing. Pianists such as John Kirkpatrick and William Masselos were playing the sonatas. Other pianists were performing the piano works, which had such odd titles as *Some Southpaw Pitching* and the *Abolitionist Riots*. Bernard Herrmann, Nicholas Slonimsky, and Anton von Webern were conducting his orchestral works. Within a comparatively short time Ives became known as one of the greatest composers America had produced. In 1947 a performance of his Third Symphony called him to the attention of the music critics, and the work was given a Pulitzer Prize.

One of Ives' last works to be heard in its entirety was his Fourth Symphony, played under Leopold Stokowski's direction at Carnegie Hall in April 1965. This sprawling, impressive work calls for a huge orchestra, two pianos, organ, a large group of percussion players, a distant group of strings, and a chorus. Two assistant conductors share with the principal conductor the job of bringing groups in at the right time and conducting one group at one tempo while the rest of the music is going on at another tempo. The performance took place approximately fifty years after the music was composed. Much of the material of the last of the four movements had to be pieced together from unnumbered pages of the manuscript found in a trunk after Ives's death. The reconstruction was done over a ten-year period by the musical scholar Theodore Seder and the composer Henry Cowell. The result of the Stokowski performance was tremendous, and the New York Music Critics' Circle awarded the work a special citation.

This symphony is remarkable music, sometimes murky, sometimes overpowering. It moves along sedately, then suddenly scoots off into a raucous square dance. While every other instrument is involved in complexities, the piccolo nonchalantly tootles "Yankee Doodle." "Marching Through Georgia" merges into "In the Sweet Bye and Bye," which in turn gives way to "Turkey in the Straw." The beautiful slow movement is a double fugue on themes from the hymn tunes "From Greenland's Icy Mountains" and "All Hail the Power of Jesus' Name." With this performance of his Fourth Symphony, Ives finally achieved recognition as one of the outstanding creative minds of the century.

JANISSARY MUSIC: music of the picked fighting men, mostly Christians, who made up the honor guard of Turkish sultans. These warriors drilled and fought to the sound of stirring music played by bands of flutes, oboes, and many percussion instruments, including bass drums, cymbals, triangles, and the "jingling johnny." This last instrument was a long wooden staff with a crescent-shaped piece of metal at the top. Small strips of metal strung along the crescent made a jingling sound as the staff was shaken or hit on the ground.

In the early 1700's Turkish bands began to tour Europe. Their wild rhythmic music and spectacular uniforms made such a strong impression on Europeans that the local bands adopted both instruments and costumes. The Turkish influences survive today in the uniforms and headpieces worn by American drum majors.

European composers began to add Turkish percussion instruments to their orchestras around 1760. Mozart set the scene for the Turkish locale of his *Abduction from the Seraglio* by using the triangle, cymbals, and bass drum in the overture. Beethoven used these instruments in his *Military Marches* and in the last movement of the Ninth Symphony. The symphony in which they were used for the first time was Haydn's Symphony Number 100, the "Military."

Composers could not find a use for the jingling johnny, and it dropped out of music. But the other Turkish instruments—triangle, bass drum, and cymbals—became permanent members of the percussion sections of European bands and orchestras.

The exotic sounds of Turkish music are suggested by Mozart in his Piano Sonatas in A Minor, K. 310, and A Major, K. 331. The finale of the A-major Sonata is marked *alla turca,* meaning "in the Turkish style." Beethoven's Six Variations for Piano, Opus 76, are based on the main theme of his Turkish March from *The Ruins of Athens.*

JAZZ: the American form of dance music which has branched out into so many different styles that it is difficult to define. It can be classified as Dixieland, ragtime, blues, barrel-house, boogie-woogie, swing, bop, or progressive jazz. It has been smoothed out to become "symphonic jazz," mixed with country "hill-billy" music to become "folk-rock," or given a Latin beat to become a rumba, conga, mambo, or cha-cha. Jazz can be "hot" or "cool." It can "swing" and "jump" or be a "businessman's bounce." Almost any kind of popular song in 2/4 or 4/4 time, played with a rhythmic accompaniment, is called jazz—whether it is a sweet ballad, a nonsense song, a musical-comedy love duet, or a deep-throated blues.

In the half century since 1910, jazz in its various forms and styles has conquered the world. To many people it is one of America's most important contributions to the world of the arts. Social dances based on jazz, such as the fox trot, have swept aside the waltz, just as the waltz in 1800 replaced the minuet. Other dances that have used jazz music have been the turkey trot, grizzly bear, bunny hug, one-step, Charleston, Peabody, big apple, rock 'n' roll, twist, frug, and a host of others.

Jazz is based on improvisation. The way a jazz musician plays is often more important than the tune he plays. The performer takes a basic idea from a composer and changes it to fit his own style of playing. The great jazz musician seems to speak directly to his audience through his improvisation.

Jazz uses rhythms, chords, melodies, and instruments like those employed in symphonic music. But the use of these musical elements is slightly different from that in art-music. Jazz speaks in the language of music but with its own special accent.

The heart of jazz is in its rhythm. Jazz rhythms have a bounce or swing because they are syncopated. Weak beats and weak parts of beats are stressed, as here:

A Turkish "jingling johnny" with horsehair pendants (German, 19th century)
At left: *a "jingling johnny" in an 1806 French infantry band*

This "misplacing" of accents, or syncopation, was not born with jazz. It had been used by European composers for hundreds of years, and is found in much of the music of Asia and Africa. But syncopation has been used in jazz so much as to become its most important rhythmic feature. Against the steady pulse of the measure (played by the rhythm section or the left hand of the pianist) the melody instruments accent the weak beats, or "offbeats," of a 2-count or 4-count measure. Weak parts of a beat are stressed or melody or chord tones are brought in just a bit early (Ex. 1).

In jazz the accents of one meter are pitted against the accents of another meter, as in the well-known "Twelfth Street Rag," in which a melody in 3/8 is played against a 4/4 accompaniment. Another form of syncopation found in jazz and Latin-American music is the division of eight notes unequally: instead of 4 plus 4 the pattern becomes 3 plus 3 plus 2. The result is rhythms like Ex. 2. The Charleston rhythm uses the unequal division of 8, as do a great many popular songs:

Jazz harmonies are basically simple. Chords follow the same patterns that are used in most folk songs and in the music of Bach and Mozart. These chords are often made more complex by adding one or more notes to each, so that they sound like the harmonies used by the French Impressionist composer Debussy. Recent jazz has added tones that make the chords quite dissonant, just as much modern symphonic music is dissonant.

The melodies of jazz are as varied as the melodies in any other style of music. They can be short, driving "riffs"—2-bar or 4-bar motives that are repeated. Or they can be long, curving lines, as in a saxophone solo in progressive jazz. Jazz melodies use many "blue notes"—notes that waver between a chord tone and the tone just below it (for instance, between E and E-flat over a C-major chord). The earliest blue notes in jazz were the lowered third and seventh of the major scale (E-flat and B-flat in the key of C). Such tones were called blue notes because they were much favored by blues singers. Gradually more and more blue notes were used, such as the lowered second, fifth, and sixth of the scale. Wind players and string players had no trouble in imitating the sliding blue notes. Pianists resorted to grace notes or both notes played at the same time to get the "blue-note" effect (Ex. 3).

Ex. 1

Ex. 2

Ex. 3

The musical form of jazz is a series of variations on a 12-bar or 16-bar blues song or a 32-bar popular song. The form of the 32-bar popular song is AABA—that is, four 8-bar sections. The first, second, and fourth parts are alike. The third part, known as the "release" or "bridge," uses different musical material. The variations, like the variations in symphonic music, usually keep the harmonic pattern of the original tune. But an inventive jazz musician will vary the melody so much that little of the original tune remains. Jazz players, for example, talk about playing some choruses based on the harmonic pattern of "I Got Rhythm." This means that the melody of "I Got Rhythm" will not be played; the players will merely use its chords as a basis for variations. The quality of the variations depends on the skill and imagination of the players.

Early jazz was always improvised. But in the 1920's, as dance bands grew larger, arrangers began to write out introductions and endings. Between the arranged sections, the musicians played solos or made background comments on the other solos. Fletcher Henderson, Don Redman, and Duke Ellington were the first arrangers to try to capture the spirit of improvisation in their written arrangements. Even in these arrangements there were spaces for solo improvisations for either the length of a chorus or a short one- or two-measure "break" (a kind of short jazz cadenza).

The difficulty with the arranging of jazz is that it is almost impossible to put everything down on paper. Many things are left to the feeling of the player, such as little melodic slides, "smears" (where the tone is ended with a short downward glissando), rhythmic freedom (rubato), the heaviness or lightness of the many different accents, the kind of attack (rough or smooth) given a tone, and the choice of a fast or slow vibrato in the tone. Usually each dance band has its own style, and the player is expected to fit his style into that of the band. For example, many bands play a rhythmic pattern exactly as written:

But more of them play the pattern as though it were triplets:

The three basic groups of instruments in a dance band are the reeds, the brasses, and the rhythm section. The reeds include the clarinet and the alto, tenor, and baritone (rarely the soprano or bass) saxophones. Performers are expected to play two or more of these instruments as well as flute, oboe, or bassoon. (This practice is called "doubling.") The brass instruments are the trumpet, cornet or flügelhorn, and trombone. For a while the tuba was used as a bass member of the rhythm section, but in the late 1920's jazz musicians retired the tuba and returned to the string bass.

The rhythm section of a dance band is really a rhythm and harmony section. It includes the drums, piano, guitar or banjo, and string bass. The drummer, with his steady beat plus his syncopations, has always been at the heart of good jazz. The piano, guitar, and banjo can play chords on the steady pulse of the music or can play solo passages. The first use of the guitar with an electronic amplifier—by Charlie Christian, in 1939—changed the quality and tone of the instrument. The string bass, played by plucking and slapping the strings, was used to accent the strong beats of the 4/4 measure, providing something for the rest of the instruments to syncopate against. Today's bass players, following the lead of Jimmy Blanton, play running melodic passages. Since 1930 the bass players have bowed their instruments as well as plucked them. Recently the string bass, like the guitar, has become electric.

Dance bands have made little use of the violin, because it lacks the percussive quality needed to bring out rhythmic accents. But they have welcomed the vibraphone, an electronic relative of the xylophone which can be played with great rhythmic drive and subtle melodic invention. At the hands of such virtuoso players as Red Norvo and Lionel Hampton the vibraphone has become one of the favorite instruments of jazz.

Jazz musicians are constantly seeking "new" sounds. Since 1940 they have used flutes, French horns, and oboes in their bands. In small groups, the electronic organ has sometimes replaced the piano. There have been bands without rhythm sections and bands made up only of percussion instruments. Arrangements have become so complex that some people fear jazz is in danger of losing its liveliness. It is true that jazz has changed; it has gone through many different styles, each based on an earlier form of jazz.

The beginnings of jazz are obscure. Starting in the South of the United States, it grew out of Scotch-Irish fiddlers' tunes, old Louisiana Creole dance tunes, black and

Top: *St. Louis Band, early 1920's (with Eugene Sedrie on clarinet; probably Marge Creath at the piano)*
Middle: *Original Dixieland Jazz Band, Chicago, before 1917 (left to right: Tony Spargo, Eddie ("Daddy") Edwards, Nick La Rocca, Alcide "Yellow" Nunez, and Henry Ragas)*
Bottom: *King Oliver's Creole Jazz Band, 1923*

white spirituals and revival hymns, black work songs, banjo solos in minstrel shows, folk-song "blues," and drum rhythms brought from Africa by black slaves. The cakewalk—a strutting, high-stepping dance with a syncopated accompaniment—was popular among the black slaves on Southern plantations in the middle 1800's. As early as the 1870's black musicians played syncopated dance music on the violin, banjo, and string bass at waterfront dance houses along the Ohio, Missouri, and Mississippi rivers.

New Orleans has been called the birthplace of instrumental jazz. There, in the 1880's and 1890's, bands of black musicians played for street parades and funerals. The bands improvised variations on marches, revival hymns, and Virginia reels. Each man tried to outdo the others in making up "hot" rhythms and bold melodies. Listeners added hand claps and finger snaps until the rhythm of the music so inspired them that they, too, began to dance.

By the 1890's small bands were playing for dancing in New Orleans. The "king" of the early jazz men was the barber-cornettist Charles "Buddy" Bolden. Bolden's Ragtime Band included clarinet, trombone, guitar, and string bass, plus the leader's cornet. In addition to Bolden's band there were the Olympia Band, led by Fred Keppard on cornet and featuring Sidney Bechet on clarinet and King Oliver on cornet; and the Eagle Band, which had William Bunk Johnson on cornet.

The 1890's saw also the start of the piano style known as RAGTIME. As this developed in cheap honky-tonk cafés the term came to be applied to any kind of "hot" syncopated music. The most famous ragtime pianist and composer was a black from Texas, Scott Joplin (1869–1917), whose best-known work, "The Maple Leaf Rag," was written in 1899. Laine's Ragtime Band, formed by a group of white musicians in New Orleans under the leadership of Jack "Papa" Laine, was the first to play in the style known as Dixieland jazz. Out of Laine's band came "Brown's Dixieland Jazz Band," which in 1915 gave Chicago its first taste of jazz, and the Original Dixieland Jazz Band, which came to New York early in 1917 and made the first records of jazz music. (Some early bands referred to themselves as "jass," rather than "jazz," bands.)

At the same time that instrumental jazz was developing in New Orleans and moving to Chicago and New York, another style of jazz was becoming known: a singing style called the blues. W. C. Handy, the "Father

Kid Ory's Original Creole Jazz Band, early 1920's

of the Blues," published "The Memphis Blues," his first effort in this style, in 1909. But, long before that, this kind of music had been sung in the cotton fields and cities of the South. Blues singers, making up their own words as they sang, wandered about, often living as beggars. The great blues singers Ma Rainey and Bessie Smith, "the Empress of the Blues," sang in black vaudeville houses and made records that were sold only in the black sections of cities. Their style of singing, as heard on "rhythm and blues" records, did much to influence instrumentalists as well as other singers. The most famous blues—Handy's "St. Louis Blues," published in 1914—soon became a kind of national anthem of jazz and has since been sung in almost every language. The simple harmonic pattern of the blues has served as a basis for many famous jazz improvisations.

By the end of World War I, in 1918, the world was ready for a new kind of excitement. People found it in jazz music and the dances that went with it. Jazz moved up the Mississippi River from New Orleans to Kansas City, Chicago, and the rest of the United States. King Oliver brought his New Orleans group to Chicago, which became the new headquarters of jazz. He was soon joined by trumpet player Louis Arm-

strong, who was to become the most famous figure in the history of jazz. From New Orleans came Jimmy Noone and Johnny Dodds to establish the basic style of playing jazz on the clarinet; Baby Dodds, one of the earliest jazz drummers; and Johnny St. Cyr, who set the pattern for jazz guitarists.

Kid Ory, composer of "Muskrat Ramble" and the finest of the early trombonists, moved with his band to California. Ory's band was the first black band to make jazz records (1921). In that same year James P. Johnson recorded the first jazz piano solo: "Carolina Shout." Two years before, Sidney Bechet had taken his clarinet and soprano saxophone to Europe. He became a great favorite in France, the first country in which jazz was taken seriously by composers and concert musicians.

The New Orleans Rhythm Kings, featuring Leon Rappolo on clarinet and George Brunis on trombone, played in Chicago. They made many early recordings of Dixieland jazz. Another New Orleans group, Morton's Red Hot Peppers, was led by Ferdinand "Jelly Roll" Morton. Morton was one of the earliest ragtime pianists as well as the composer of such standard items in the jazz repertory as "King Porter Stomp" and "Milenberg Joys."

New styles in jazz came thick and fast

"Bix" Beiderbecke (center) with The Wolverines, 1924, at their first appearance in Chicago

in the 1920's. Louis Armstrong left King Oliver's band and formed his Hot Five and Hot Seven. Armstrong's warm tone and driving rhythm on the trumpet, his effortless ability to play high tones, and his powerful personality made him the greatest influence in jazz. His "scat" singing, throaty and sly, using nonsense syllables, was imitated by many later singers. One of Armstrong's pianists, Earl "Fatha" Hines, adapted Armstrong's trumpet style to the piano, playing single notes in the right hand and using a tremolo to get the effect of a trumpet vibrato.

In 1923 Duke Ellington took his band to New York from Washington. Ellington's tunes and arrangements featured "jungle" sounds, for which the mute was much used. Already, brass players had experimented with all kinds of mutes. Almost anything that could be stuffed into or hung over the bell of the instrument had been tried. Ellington's trombone players, "Tricky Sam" Nanton and Juan Tizol, and the trumpet players, Cootie Williams and Bubber Miley, made their growling tones by using a plumber's rubber plunger. The saxophone, which had been discovered by jazz musicians in the early 1920's, was played in Ellington's band with rich, sweet-hot tones by Johnny Hodges and Harry Carney.

James P. Johnson, who started as a ragtime pianist in New Jersey, changed his style and in the 1920's became one of the first jazz pianists. He had influenced the playing of Duke Ellington and of his own pupil, Thomas "Fats" Waller. Waller developed his own style, with his right hand playing delicate and lacy patterns over a powerful beat in the left hand. Art Tatum,

the almost-blind pianist, carried Waller's style to a peak of virtuosity. Hines, Waller, and Tatum were the major influences on most jazz pianists of later years.

Fletcher Henderson, the first great jazz arranger, led a group that became the first large dance band to make records. His arrangements, which had the reeds playing in a block against the brasses, became the basis of most of the big-band arrangements of the 1930's and 1940's.

A symphony violinist named Paul Whiteman, and his arranger Ferde Grofé, tried to show the world how jazz could be made "symphonic." In 1924 the Whiteman orchestra played a concert of their version of jazz in New York. The featured work on the program was George Gershwin's *Rhapsody in Blue.*

Most of the finest early jazz players were black. But in the middle of the 1920's groups of young white musicians also began to be heard. Many of these new jazz players came from the Midwest, particularly around Chicago. Some were just high-school boys, such as the "Austin High" group. The outstanding white jazz musician was Leon "Bix" Beiderbecke, a trumpet player and pianist from Iowa. While other jazz musicians attempted to imitate Louis Armstrong, Beiderbecke went his own way, playing with a beautiful smooth tone, both sweet and "hot." His improvisations were among the most imaginative in jazz. Even the black musicians acknowledged his greatness.

There were many fine dance bands—Red Nichols and his Five Pennies, The Chicagoans, The Wolverines, Ben Pollack's Orchestra, Frank Teschemacher's Chicago Rhythm Kings, and the Canadian Casa Loma Band, which later became Glen Gray's Orchestra. These bands played in ballrooms in large cities and small towns, performed at college dances, made records, and played over the radio. With the invention of sound for motion pictures (1927) most of the big dance bands began appearing in movies, and large movie houses featured live dance bands. The period of the late 1920's and the early 1930's was indeed a Golden Age of Jazz for black and white jazz musicians alike.

The 1930's saw the rise of "swing" music, the introduction of "boogie-woogie" piano playing, and a revival of interest in Dixieland music. "Swing" is a style that combines the basic ideas of New Orleans jazz with the smoother and faster "Chicago" style. Swing uses a great many "riffs" (repeated short figures) and is continually on the move. Its syncopations are subtler and

"Fats" Waller

more complex than those of Dixieland jazz. Rhythmic patterns that move in even eighth notes are preferred to those using the earlier dotted eighth and sixteenth notes. Swing solos are worked out in great detail and show off the technique of the performer. Swing was sweeter than New Orleans jazz, but its fast tempo made it exciting for both musicians and dancers.

The big swing bands of the 1930's and early 1940's were those of the Dorsey brothers, Benny Goodman, Artie Shaw, Duke Ellington, Count Basie, and Glen Miller. Each big band developed its own style of arrangements, based mostly on the earlier styles of Fletcher Henderson and Duke Ellington. And within each band a small solo group was often featured. The Goodman Quartet, consisting of Goodman, Teddy Wilson, Gene Krupa, and Lionel Hampton, became the most famous small group.

The small groups within the large bands played as jazz musicians had played in private "jam sessions." Jam sessions took place originally after the musicians were through working for the night. They provided opportunities to try out all kinds of improvisations in a relaxed manner. Many well-known jazz ideas were first thought of in jam sessions and later tried out in public.

Swing music combined the best of the black and white traditions in jazz. It was now only natural that blacks and whites should be found playing together—for the first time in the history of jazz. The first "mixed" group was that of saxophonist Charley Barnet. The Goodman band, the most successful swing group, brought to national fame such black musicians as Teddy Wilson, Lionel Hampton, and Charlie Christian as well as such white musicians as Gene Krupa, Harry James, Bunny Berrigan, Jess Stacy, and Mel Powell. During the 1930's and 1940's almost every great jazz musician worked with Goodman, who became known as the "King of Swing."

In the middle 1930's a new style of jazz, called boogie-woogie, came from Kansas City and Chicago. It is based on playing the blues fast, with a steady, repeated left-hand rhythm. It was often used to accompany such "blues shouters" as Big Joe Turner. For many years it had been played at black "rent parties"—dances in an apartment to help the tenant raise his rent money. When the boogie-woogie pianists Meade Lux Lewis, Albert Ammons, and Pete Johnson appeared in 1938 at a jazz concert at Carnegie Hall in New York, they were a sensational success. The rough excitement of boogie-woogie with its driving left-hand

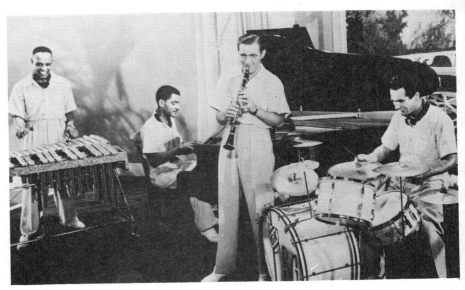

Top: *Paul Whiteman Band, c. 1930*
Middle: *Benny Goodman Quartet, 1937 (left to right: Lionel Hampton, vibraphone; Teddy Wilson, piano; B. Goodman, clarinet; and Gene Krupa, drums)*
Bottom: *Count Basie Orchestra, 1940*

Django Reinhardt

Thelonius Monk

rhythm and dissonant "riffs" in the right hand inspired many jazz pianists and amateur pianists to imitate the style that had been started by Jimmy Yancey and Clarence "Pinetop" Smith.

Jazz in the 1940's continued the period of swing. But it also saw the beginnings of the new sounds of "bop" and a revival of interest in Dixieland jazz. Many jazz musicians grew tired of playing the same style of music night after night. Such men as Charlie Parker and Lester Young on saxophone, Charlie Christian on electric guitar, Thelonious Monk and Bud Powell on piano, and Dizzy Gillespie on trumpet experimented with dissonant chords, unusual phrasing, and an attempt to get away from steady 4-beat rhythms. As they played they often used a phrase that sounded like the word "bebop." This was shortened to "bop" and used to describe the new jazz.

At the same time that bop was developing, musicians such as Eddie Condon in New York were reviving the Dixieland style. Old-time New Orleans musicians, such as Kid Ory and Bunk Johnson, were brought to recording studios in an attempt to recapture the early sounds of jazz. Businessmen and college students got together with professional jazz musicians to take part in large Dixieland "jam sessions."

By the end of World War II the era of the big swing bands had come to an end. Only Woody Herman's "First Herd" was able to sustain itself by playing at dances and doing radio shows. During the war so many jazz musicians were in the armed services that band leaders went broke trying to outbid each other for the few good ones remaining. Singers such as Frank Sinatra became the idols of popular music, whereas previously they had been considered simply as part of a dance band, not the main attraction. Billie Holiday, Ella Fitzgerald, Mildred Bailey, and Jimmy Rushing had sung with the great swing bands—as had such performers as Louis Armstrong, Fats Waller, trombonist Jack Teagarden, and trumpeter Roy Eldridge.

As the big bands disappeared and singers took the center of the stage in popular music, small jazz groups ("combos") playing "cool," "progressive" jazz set the pattern for jazz in the 1950's. This music was not meant so much for dancing as for listening. The pulsing rhythm of early jazz was replaced by rhythms that were syncopated so subtly that the accents were barely felt. Melodic lines were smooth and drawn-out. Harmonies were quite dissonant; the key of a piece often was not clear. The har-

monic pattern of the circle of fifths—which had come into music in the seventeenth century—was kept, but the chords were complex and filled with added tones:

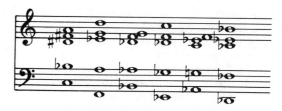

Gone were the shouting and brassiness of earlier jazz; progressive jazz spoke almost in whispers. Many of the arrangers and performers of progressive jazz, such as Dave Brubeck, Miles Davis, and Lenny Tristano, had studied music at conservatories. They attempted to make jazz something more than just an accompaniment to dancing.

Rock 'n' roll arose as a reaction against these new subtleties. Teen-age boys and girls responded with enthusiasm to rock 'n' roll as they heard it promoted on the radio by a few disc jockeys. Too often the disc jockeys were playing records that they had been paid to play, and there were abuses in rock 'n' roll music, such as pushing young singers to the top too quickly. But rock 'n' roll brought dancing back into jazz and probably led many young fans to discover the many forms and styles of jazz. Rock 'n' roll actually was not a new form of jazz, but combined elements of Dixieland jazz, fast blues, boogie-woogie, and American hillbilly tunes. Rather than featuring syncopation it featured heavy accents on the main beats of the measure—often emphasized by two drummers. Each beat of the measure was divided into steady triplets which gave a great feeling of motion to the music. Good rock 'n' roll is as vital as any good form of jazz; poor rock 'n' roll is as poor as watered-down jazz in a "commercial" arrangement. Rock 'n' roll reached its peak throughout the world in the late 1950's and since then it has declined slightly in popularity—following a pattern set by all styles of jazz. The raucous sounds of twist music and gentler qualities of folk music have been added to the rock-'n'-roll style, giving it a wider range of expressiveness.

Jazz has been far-reaching in its effects. In many parts of the world it is America's best-known export. Even in Communist countries when jazz was banned, young people managed to listen to it, collect records, and play it.

Good jazz performers have come from almost every European country. In France, where jazz was for the first time taken seriously as an art form, the Quintet of the *Hot Club de France* was started in the 1920's. The great French-gypsy guitarist Django Reinhardt brought his gypsy style to such a point that he became the first non-American to influence other jazz performers. His fellow-performer in the Hot Club Quintet, Stéphane Grappelly, was one of the few good jazz violinists. Fine jazz players have formed bands in England, the Scandinavian countries, and Japan. Even in Russia "forbidden" jazz is played in public increasingly.

Many composers have used jazz as part of their serious concert music. First to do so was the New Orleans composer Louis Moreau Gottschalk (1829–1869), who attempted to write piano pieces in the style of black musicians he had heard in Louisiana. His works, written in the 1850's, impressed such European composers as Franz Liszt.

Claude Debussy, whose Impressionist harmonies were used a generation later by jazz pianists, wrote in 1908 the first piece of jazz by a European composer: "Golliwog's Cakewalk." It was built on the most-used rhythm pattern of jazz:

This pattern goes back to such old Louisiana Creole tunes as "M'sieu Banjo" and to such minstrel-show tunes as the chorus of "Ol' Dan Tucker."

While living in France the Russian composer Igor Stravinsky wrote his musical comments on ragtime in his "Ragtime for Eleven Instruments" (1918) and "Piano Rag Music" (1921). In the 1940's when he had settled in the United States, Stravinsky wrote his *Ebony Concerto* for the band of Woody Herman.

By the 1920's there was much discussion among musicians as to the possibility of using jazz in concert music. In 1923 the French composer Darius Milhaud wrote a ballet, *La Création du monde (The Creation of the World)*, which used the blues as a basis. Almost every young French musician, as well as such German composers as Paul Hindemith, tried his hand at writing jazz. But American composers were slower to realize that a new kind of music was taking shape right under their noses. Among the first to awaken was George Gershwin, who turned from writing popular songs to writing large jazz works such as his *Rhapsody in Blue* and Piano Concerto in F. Aaron Copland wrote jazz effects in his *Music for*

the Theater (1925) and later wrote several charming blues for piano.

Many jazz performers since Gershwin have written symphonic works growing out of jazz. Duke Ellington's "Black, Brown and Beige," "Harlem," and "Deep South Suite" have been played and recorded by his dance band. Dave Brubeck's Quartet improvised against a background of the New York Philharmonic in Howard Brubeck's *Dialogue for Jazz Combo and Orchestra* (1959), while John Henry Lewis has written contemporary concerti grossi for his Modern Jazz Quartet and symphony orchestra. Gunther Schuller invented the term "third stream" to describe music of the 1960's that was part jazz and part avante-garde art-music, partly written and partly improvised.

Jazz has become respectable in its progress from the waterfront dancehouse to symphony hall. It has made many people happy and led to new forms of entertainment as well as new forms of serious music. Whether it will remain an art of improvisation, as it was when it started, or will become more complex and "progressive" remains to be seen.

Top: *the Modern Jazz Quartet with, from left to right: John Henry Lewis, pianist and musical director; Connie Kay, percussionist; Percy Heath, bass; and Milt Jackson, vibraphone*

Bottom: *Gunther Schuller*

Playing a jew's harp

JEW'S HARP: a simple, toylike instrument found all over the world. It consists of a small metal frame to which a thin metal tongue is fastened. The frame is held between the player's teeth. The metal tongue, which makes the tone, is plucked or snapped by one or two fingers. By changing the shape of his mouth, the player is able to get several different tones.

The jew's harp is an ancient instrument. In Hawaii and Southeast Asia it was made of bamboo. Its original name was "jaw's harp," but somehow it was misnamed "jew's harp," although it has nothing to do with Jewish history or music.

JONGLEURS: the professional entertainers in France and England during the Middle Ages. They sang; played the vielle, lute, or harp; told jokes; and performed tricks of magic (the term "jongleur" derives from the same Latin word as the English word "juggler"). A dancing bear was often part of a jongleur's act. No wedding, festival, tournament, or knighting of a page was complete without a jongleur to sing songs of chivalry. Jongleurs provided the music for the peasant dances on the village greens as well as for the dances of the nobles in their castles.

The jongleur traveled from place to place, going wherever he thought he might be rewarded by a bit of money or a meal. Some jongleurs had permanent jobs as companions to knightly troubadours and *trouvères* (the poet-musicians of northern France), wandering from castle to castle with their masters. The jongleur sang the songs composed by the troubadour or accompanied him on the vielle—the medieval fiddle. Sometimes he would set down on paper the words and music of the song, thus preserving it for the future.

Jongleurs who were content to stay in one place were thought of as household servants and were called minstrels.

There were no public entertainments during Lent. This was the time for the jongleurs to go to "school." The school was actually a convention of jongleurs where songs, jokes, and news were exchanged.

From the ninth to the fourteenth centuries, jongleurs performed the same services that radio and television do today. They not only entertained but brought news of the Crusades, of who married whom, and of who beat whom in a tournament. The traveling jongleurs did much to bring Frenchmen together as a nation by singing of the heroic deeds of Charlemagne, Roland, and other French heroes.

Jongleurs (from an 11th-century Latin manuscript)

JOSQUIN DES PRÉS (c. 1450–1521):

one of the great masters of the contrapuntal style of writing that flourished in the Netherlands in the fifteenth and the sixteenth centuries.

Born in the province of Hainault, in what is now Belgium, he learned music by singing in a church choir at St. Quentin. Later he became director of the choir. In his twenties he traveled to Italy, where he sang in a court choir in Milan. For eight years he was a member of the pope's choir in Rome.

Becoming court composer to Louis XII of France, Josquin dazzled everyone by his ability to write the most complicated music based on simple chants and folk songs. Martin Luther, an admiring friend and a good musician himself, said of him: "Josquin is the master of the notes, others are mastered by the notes." He became one of the best-known composers in Europe, and his style was much imitated.

Much of Josquin's music was written to be sung in church. It included thirty masses and many shorter religious works. But he also wrote hundreds of *chansons*—light songs for three, four, or five voices—that are gay and charming. The religious works are full of every known learned device of counterpoint, although the melodies that Josquin wove above the chant or folk song are spun out with marvelous freshness. In the chansons this composer used a lighter style with simple melodies and little touches of dance rhythms. He was fond of splitting four voices into different pairs, so that little duets are constantly taking place. At other times the master wrote chansons that move along in chords. These harmonic sections sound so much like music of a later period that Josquin has been called the "father of modern harmony."

Josquin was a good-humored man and fond of little musical jokes. When Louis XII forgot to give him a promised gift, Josquin wrote a motet to be sung in Louis's church. At the service Louis was embarrassed to hear the choir sing about those who broke their promises. On another occasion, noting that Louis was fond of singing but had a very poor voice, Josquin wrote a duet in which the king had but one long note to sing throughout the whole composition. Josquin also wrote a mass based on a pun. The melodic theme of the mass is: la sol fa re mi, suggesting, in Italian, *La ci fare mi,* or "Let me take care of it."

After all his worldly successes, Josquin settled down as provost of the cathedral in Condé-sur-l'Escaut, France. While he was alive his music was sung in all of the cities of Europe, but after his death people turned to the works of newer composers. The music of the one-time "Prince of Music" was almost unheard. But music lovers have recently discovered Josquin, and many of his works have been published in modern editions and recorded. (Ex. 4).

Josquin Des Prés

Ex. 4 — Motet: "Tu pauperum refugium"

"JUPITER" SYMPHONY: the name given by an unknown person to Mozart's forty-first, and last, symphony. It was written, along with his thirty-ninth and fortieth symphonies, in six weeks during the summer of 1788. In its beauty, nobility, and masterly workmanship it stands as one of the greatest of all symphonic works.

The first movement is in the key of C major, as are the third and fourth movements. The work begins with a main theme (Ex. 5) which contrasts the full orchestra with soft strings. A strong marchlike theme (Ex. 6) for full orchestra suggests that Mozart is leading toward a new theme, but instead he surprises us by bringing back his first theme softly, putting a gay, laughing theme on top of it in the flute and oboe (Ex. 7). The march theme comes back, and this time does lead to a new theme—in the key of G major. This delicate little theme (Ex. 8) is violently interrupted as the whole orchestra bursts in with a loud C-minor chord. A jaunty closing theme (Ex. 9) leads to the end of the first section of the movement (the exposition). Small bits of most of the themes are used in the development section. Near the end of the development the horn, then the bassoons, and finally the trumpets and timpani keep insisting on the tone of G. This pedal point leads back to the first theme and a shortened repetition of the exposition, with all themes now in the key of C major.

The slow movement, in the key of F major, is an andante cantabile in 3/4 time. Two songlike melodies are spun out, each having important dramatic rests. The first theme is softly sung by the strings, with punctuating loud chords from the winds (Ex. 10). The second theme, played by the strings and woodwinds, is built from a little rising figure that struggles upward only to fall back at the end (Ex. 11). After a short development section both themes are repeated, with added intricate embroidery.

Ex. 5 — First Movement

Allegro vivace

Ex. 6

Ex. 7

Ex. 8

Ex. 9

Ex. 10— Second Movement

Andante cantabile

Ex. 11

Ex. 12— Third Movement

Allegretto

Ex. 13

oboe

Ex. 14 — Finale

Allegro molto

The third movement is a happy minuetto in moderate 3/4 time. The first part is built on a sighing chromatic melody (Ex. 12). This is followed by a gay, rhythmic section like a German country dance (Ex. 13). The movement then finishes with a repeat of the first section.

The last movement of the "Jupiter" Symphony is one of the peaks of symphonic writing. It is an allegro molto in 2/2 time, the form being that of sonata-allegro mixed with the busy texture of a fugue. The movement starts with a simple theme (Ex. 14). More and more fragments of themes keep coming in, the music gets louder—and then comes to a complete stop. At this point there begins a fugue, based on the opening motive. In a whirlwind of contrapuntal writing, Mozart juggles five themes, tossing them upside down, making canons with them, putting two or three of them together, and joining part of one theme to part of another. The music sweeps along at such speed that the listener is not aware of the complexities of the music—only of its excitement.

This is the supreme example of Mozart's perfect sense of timing and balance.

K.: the initial of Dr. Ludwig von Köchel (1800–77), an Austrian botanist who was devoted to Mozart's music. In 1862 Köchel published his catalog of Mozart's more than 600 compositions, arranged more or less in the order in which Mozart wrote them.

Most composers give their compositions opus numbers as they are published. Since Mozart had little published in his lifetime, there are no opus numbers on his music. The K. (or K.V.) numbers given to Mozart's works, as cataloged by Köchel, make it possible to tell whether a certain work was written in Mozart's early, middle, or late period. They are useful also in differentiating between sonatas or symphonies written in the same key. For example, Mozart wrote three Piano Sonatas in B-flat Major: K. 281, K. 333, and K. 570.

The following table shows the approximate relationship between the Köchel numbers and the chronology of Mozart's life:

K. 1 to 100	1756–1770
101 to 350	1771–1780
350 to 626	1781–1791

In 1937 the music scholar Alfred Einstein brought out a revision of Köchel's catalog.

Ludwig von Köchel

KERN, JEROME (1885–1945): composer of many of America's best-loved popular songs, including "Ol' Man River," "Smoke Gets in Your Eyes," "Who," and "The Last Time I Saw Paris." Kern was born in New York City and, like so many other composers, was taught to play the piano by his mother. At the New York College of Music he had a thorough musical education, including the study of music theory and piano instruction under Paolo Gallico. Even as a student Kern was interested in popular music, and after becoming a piano player in the office of a music publishing company he graduated to the position of rehearsal pianist for Broadway shows.

In pre-jazz days Broadway musicals imitated Viennese operettas, and Kern adapted his own American background to the operetta style. In 1905 he wrote his first song hit, "How'd You Like to Spoon with Me?" Within a few years he was collaborating with Guy Bolton and P. G. Wodehouse on a series of shows that played in the old Princess Theater, an intimate place that seated only 250 persons. With *Sally* (1920), a large-scale musical show, Kern moved into the real "big time." This was followed by *Sunny* (1925), an all-star show the hit tune of which was "Who." In 1927 Kern wrote his finest

work, *Show Boat*, which ranks with Gershwin's *Porgy and Bess* and Rodgers' *Carousel* as top achievements in the American art form known as musical comedy.

Kern went on to write many more shows: *The Cat and the Fiddle* (1931), *Music in the Air* (1932), *Roberta* (1933, a show that featured a young actor named Bob Hope), and *Very Warm for May* (1937). For Hollywood he wrote movie scores for Fred Astaire and others—scores that included such songs as "I Won't Dance," "The Way You Look Tonight," and "A Fine Romance."

Kern was, in his day, a rarity: a composer of popular songs who had a solid musical training. This training may account for the many subtle melodic and harmonic inflections in his songs. But he could be out-and-out sentimental and simple, as in "The Last Time I Saw Paris," the song he wrote with Oscar Hammerstein II when Paris fell to the Germans in 1940. The best appraisal of Kern was written by his longtime collaborator, Oscar Hammerstein II, who said, "Jerry was a worker who would never stop polishing until he was satisfied that a melody had reached its destined and perfect shape."

At right: Jerome Kern at the piano

KEY, in *composition:* the tonality of a composition as defined by a particular major or minor scale. A work in the key of G major, for example, has a key signature of one sharp, and principally uses these tones:

Other tones—chromatic ones—may be introduced for color without necessarily changing the tonality.

The primary chords that help to define the key are those built on the first, fourth, and fifth tones of the scale. Of these the most important in establishing tonality is the tonic—the chord built on the first note, or keynote, of the scale. Very few compositions, and these mostly short, stay in one key throughout. For the sake of variety the composer usually makes his music move away from the basic tonality and then work its way back again. The key tone or key center acts as a magnet that draws all the other tones toward it.

In music of the seventeenth and eighteenth centuries, composers always made the listeners aware of the key at the very opening of a composition by using a series of chords that began and ended on the keynote (Ex. 1). During the nineteenth century, composers sometimes avoided the keynote at the beginning of a composition, starting at some distance away from the key tone and gradually working toward it (Ex. 2).

In some modern music, particularly that written by Arnold Schoenberg and his followers, the composer tries to avoid a tonal center by making all twelve tones equally important. Music without a key center is called atonal. Other modern composers use a series of shifting key centers or make their music pivot around one tone without using the major or minor scale built on the tone. Such a work is Stravinsky's *Serenade en la* for piano.

KEY, in *instrument construction:* a lever that activates a hammer, quill, or metal tangent on the piano, harpsichord, or clavichord, or that opens the pipes of an organ so that air can flow through them. On woodwind instruments the key is part of a mechanism that helps the player cover the finger holes in the instrument.

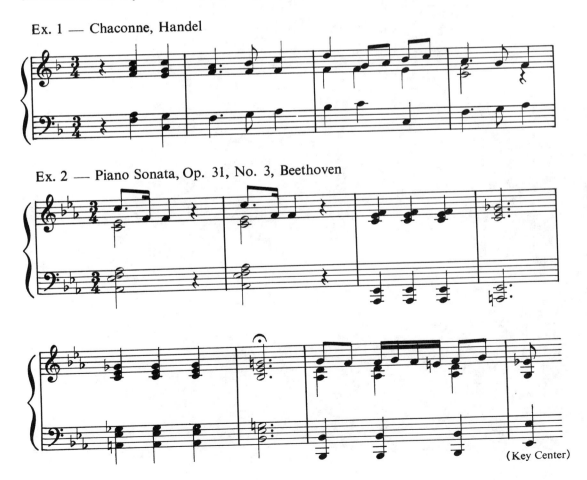

Ex. 1 — Chaconne, Handel

Ex. 2 — Piano Sonata, Op. 31, No. 3, Beethoven

(Key Center)

KEYBOARD INSTRUMENTS: the organ, piano, spinet, clavichord, harpsichord, harmonium, and accordion. By pressing a key, a keyboard player allows air to go through pipes (the organ, harmonium, and accordion), makes a small metal piece strike a string (clavichord), causes a quill to pluck a string (harpsichord and spinet), or makes a hammer strike a string (piano).

The earliest keyboard instrument was the organ. Some time in the twelfth century keys were used to open the valves which let air into the organ pipes. Before this, slides had to be pushed or pulled by hand in order to change the tones of the organ. Eventually organs were built with as many as seven keyboards played by hand (manuals) and one keyboard played by the feet (pedals).

Early organ keyboards were small and all the keys were the same color. As the keyboard grew larger in the fourteenth century, the black and white arrangement of keys was invented. For several hundred years keyboards had black keys for the notes of the C-natural scale. The sharp and flat keys were white—just the opposite of present-day keyboards.

The harpsichord was made with either one or two keyboards, depending on the number of sets of strings on the instrument. A piano with a double keyboard was invented in 1878, and many other different types of keyboard shapes and arrangements have been suggested. None of these has proved to be as usable as the standard keyboard.

The advantage of keyboard instruments is that they give the player command of a great many strings or pipes. They are the only instruments that can play many tones at the same time, like an orchestra. This wide scope made the keyboard instruments popular with composers, so that the literature for these instruments, with the exception of the harmonium and accordion, is much larger than for any other type of instrument.

Right: *spinet belonging to Mozart*
Below: *a cabinet organ made in Germany, 1598*

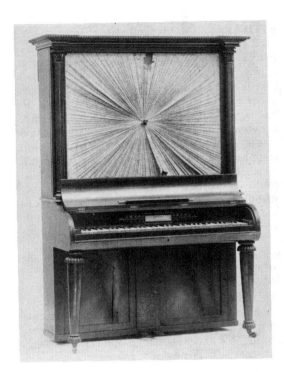

Top left: *18th-century piano, made in England by John Broadwood & Sons*
Top right: *Flemish harpsichord,* c. *1650*

Bottom left: *an early 19th-century "work-box" piano*
Bottom right: *Salvation Army member playing the harmonium*

Man playing kithara (drawing from an amphora)

KEY SIGNATURE: a group of sharps or flats (rarely, a mixture of both) placed at the beginning of a composition. It shows the performer which notes are to be played as sharps or flats throughout the composition, thereby saving the composer all the time and effort he would have to spend in writing each individual sharp or flat. The key signature usually is derived from the major or minor scale in which the composition is written. Composers do not use key signatures in modern music that has no true key.

Each key signature stands for two keys or scales—one major and one minor (Ex. 3). Contemporary composers have occasionally used a mixture of sharps and flats in their key signatures:

KITHARA: the plucked-string instrument used by the ancient Greek bards to accompany their songs about gods and heroes. It was a heavy wooden instrument of the lyre family, looking a bit like a guitar with two necks. Like all stringed instruments, it had a bridge to hold the strings away from the body of the instrument so that they could vibrate, a sounding board to add resonance to the tone, and a crossbar around which the strings were wound. The crossbar could be turned to tighten or loosen the strings in tuning the instrument. The kithara was played by means of a large plectrum which the player stroked across the strings.

The kithara was used for over a thousand years (in its earlier form it had five to seven strings; later, seven to eleven). Unlike the *lyra*—used by amateurs playing at home— the kithara was the instrument of professional musicians. It is to the accompaniment of a kithara that we must imagine Homer singing his epic poems of the Trojan War and the wanderings of Ulysses.

Ex. 3

| Major Key: | C | G | D | A | E | B | F-sharp | C-sharp |
| Minor Key: | a | e | b | f-sharp | c-sharp | g-sharp | d-sharp | a-sharp |

| | C-flat | G-flat | D-flat | A-flat | E-flat | B-flat | F |
| | a-flat (rare) | e-flat | b-flat | f | c | g | d |

LÄNDLER: an old Austrian peasant dance, the ancestor of the waltz. It got its name (pronounced "lendler") from Ländl, the mountain region of Austria. The music of the Ländler was in a meter of three, played at a moderate tempo, with a strong accent on the first beat of each measure. The melody usually contained large leaps, sometimes covering a distance of two octaves.

The dance was performed by couples gliding and turning in a large circle. The men sometimes let go of their partners and clapped in time with the music while the girls danced in a circle around them. In one favorite figure the girl circled beneath the raised hand of her partner, with the finger tips of both touching. In the closing figure the partners danced cheek to cheek.

Both Mozart and Beethoven wrote Ländler, but the most beautiful examples are the many composed by Schubert.

By the end of the eighteenth century, the Ländler began to replace the polished minuet at social dances and in the symphony. Haydn called the third movements of his symphonies "minuets," but as in the Symphony Number 94 in G, the "Surprise" Symphony, he really often wrote Ländler.

LARGO: an Italian word, meaning "broad" or "generous," which is used as a tempo mark. Music marked largo is to be performed slowly, at a broad, dignified pace. Slow movements of suites, sonatas, and symphonies are often marked largo, as in Handel's Twelfth Concerto Grosso, Beethoven's Piano Sonata in D Major (Opus 10, Number 3), and Dvořák's Symphony "From the New World."

The melody of a largo movement is usually rhythmically simple rather than highly decorated; however, it was the custom of the eighteenth-century singer to embellish these simple melodies at will. Many of Handel's most beautiful arias, such as the "Lascia ch'io pianga" (Let Me Mourn) of his early opera *Agrippina* (later used in *Rinaldo*) are largos. Strangely enough, his aria "Ombra mai fui" (Shade Most Dear) from the opera *Xerxes* is often called "Handel's Largo," but the tempo mark given it by the composer was *larghetto*. Larghetto means "a little largo"—not quite as slow as a largo.

LASSUS, ORLANDUS, also known as **ROLAND de LASSUS** or **ORLANDO di LASSO** (1532–94): the last of the great composers from the Netherlands who dominated musical Europe for more than a hundred years. He was born at Mons, now in Belgium, where he began to sing in church choirs at a very early age. His voice was so beautiful that, it is said, he was kidnapped several times to sing in certain choirs. At twelve he went to Italy, where he sang and directed choirs until he was twenty-three. His first collections of madrigals were published in 1555, the year he moved to Antwerp. In the following year he became composer to King Albert V of Bavaria. For the rest of his life he lived in Munich, turning out more than two thousand compositions and enjoying high honor.

Lassus wrote almost all his works for voice. Many of these were large sacred works such as masses, magnificats, and his famous *Psalmi Davidis poenitentiales (Penitential Psalms of David)*. For two or more voices he wrote hundreds of small, sacred motets, more than 500 of which were published by his sons under the title *Magnum opus musicum*. Lassus wrote many non-sacred works as well as church music. His French chansons, Italian madrigals, and German part songs are light, popular gems, melodic and dancelike.

Orlandus Lassus (1593)

Lassus (at the clavier) rehearsing in the Duke of Bavaria's private music chapel (a 16th-century miniature)

In his church music Lassus wove together beautiful, long, melodic lines. His mastery of counterpoint was so complete that even the most complex works sound free and effortless. The lighter works range from German drinking songs to the charming French love song "Bonjour, mon coeur" (Goodday, My Love) and the dark, colorful "La Nuit froide et sombre" (Cold and Sombre Night).

Lassus was called the "Prince of Music" in his time. Unlike the music of many composers of earlier days, that of Lassus has never dropped out of sight.

LEGATO: an Italian word meaning "bound" or "tied." In music it refers to the technique of connecting each tone smoothly to the next, with no break between the two. Musical phrases are much more interesting to listen to when some tones are detached and others tied together than when all the tones are articulated with a monotonous sameness.

Singers and wind players secure a legato effect by singing or playing successive tones on the same breath. The player of a stringed instrument achieves his legato by playing several notes on one bow stroke, and by continuous motion of the bow with no stopping at the end of a stroke. On keyboard instruments, such as the piano, an absolutely smooth connection of one tone to the next cannot be made; the player gets around this by holding one tone until the next one is sounded—producing an overlapping of sounds that suggests a true legato. The piano's sustaining pedal also helps to bind tones together.

In musical scores legato is indicated by a "slur"—a curved line over or under the group of tones to be connected:

Sonata in E flat, Op. 7, Beethoven

If the composer writes the word *legato* at the beginning of a musical passage, he wants the passage played as smoothly as possible.

LEGGIERO: an Italian word meaning "light" or "graceful." It is a direction from the composer to the performer not to press too hard on the keys or the bow. Leggiero passages are usually soft and fast.

LEITMOTIF or **LEADING MOTIVE:** a short musical idea used by a composer to represent a character, an object, or an idea. A leitmotif appears throughout a musical work each time a composer wishes to remind his listeners of the subject it represents. The leitmotif is primarily useful in operas and motion pictures, serving to portray a character quickly. For example, a nasty-sounding chord heard when a character appears tells that he is a villain.

The most thorough use of the leitmotif occurs in the operas of Richard Wagner—*The Ring of the Nibelungs, Parsifal, Die Meistersinger,* and *Tristan and Isolde.* In the four operas comprising *The Ring,* almost all of the musical material is made

Ex. 1

up of leitmotifs woven together. Wagner changed his leitmotifs and developed them as the character or object that they portrayed changed. The simple horn call of the hero Siegfried:

becomes heroic:

and finally triumphantly grand, as in Siegfried's Funeral March (Ex. 1). Wagner's motives are often musical pictures of the things they represent: for example, lightning, fire, and hammering on an anvil.

The term leitmotif was not used by Wagner himself. It first appeared in a book about Carl Maria von Weber written by F. W. Jähns in 1871. The term was popularized by Hans von Wolzogen (1848–1938), who wrote many essays about Wagner's music. Other composers have used leitmotifs, although not as extensively as Wagner. In his *Symphonie fantastique,* Berlioz portrays various aspects of his Beloved One with a motive which he calls an *idée fixe,* or fixed idea. In motion pictures and television shows a musical theme song is often used as a kind of leitmotif throughout the show.

LENT and **LENTO:** French and Italian tempo marks respectively, meaning "slowly." They come from a Latin word with a wide range of meanings, among them "flexible," "smooth," and "gentle." Lent and lento were used very little before 1800. Since then they have appeared frequently, notably in some of Chopin's nocturnes and several of Debussy's preludes for piano.

Lentando is an indication sometimes used in place of "ritardando." It means "slowing down gradually."

LIBRETTO: the text of the story of an opera or an oratorio. The term comes from the Italian *libretto,* a "little book." A libretto can be an original story (such as *The Medium)* or it can be based on a legend *(Orpheus),* a play *(Othello),* a novel *(War and Peace),* or a short story *(Carmen).* The form of a libretto depends on the style of opera the composer wants to write, since most librettos are written to the order of a composer. The composer tells the librettist what kind of story he has in mind, whether there should be poems that can be made into arias or set pieces, where to have dances, when to have crowd scenes—and even what kind of vowels or consonants to use.

Almost every type of story has been used as an opera libretto, the most popular material being the Orpheus myth and Shakespeare's plays. The earliest opera composers took texts of plays based on the legends of the gods and great heroes and set them directly to music. In the early 1700's the light Italian operas (opera buffa) and English ballad operas began to use librettos based on humorous events that happened to ordinary people. In the nineteenth-century German operas, the librettos were based on German romantic legends. The great opera composer Richard Wagner wrote his own librettos, inspired by German and Scandinavian myths.

Around 1800 many operas used stories in which the hero was saved from danger in the nick of time. These "rescue operas," such as *Richard the Lion Hearted* by Grétry and *Fidelio* by Beethoven, were popular not only because of their music but because many people had had the same kind of miraculous escapes during the French Revolution.

Many of Verdi's operas reflect the period of the nineteenth century when Italy was struggling for its freedom. Since Verdi's time Italian operas have featured plots full of violence and passion.

Debussy's *Pelléas and Mélisande* is one of the most experimental of all operas in its treatment of the libretto. Debussy set

Lorenzo Da Ponte (1749–1838)

Top left: *Hugo von Hofmannsthal*
Top right: *Puccini (right) with Luigi Illica, co-librettist with Giuseppe Giacosa for Puccini's* Tosca, La Bohème, *and* Madame Butterfly
Bottom: *Benjamin Britten (center) and librettists E. M. Forster (left) and Eric Crozier (right) working on Britten's opera* Billy Budd *(1949)*

Maeterlinck's play to music very nearly as Maeterlinck had written it. The result of the experiment came close to the original idea of opera: a play set to music, without arias or dances to stop the dramatic action.

The success of an opera is often due as much to the libretto as to the music. In many cases the only name associated with an opera is that of the composer, but the names of a few librettists have been outstanding in operatic history. Around 1600, Ottavio Rinuccini provided librettos for all the earliest opera composers. Quinault helped Lully establish the form of French opera. Metastasio, most famous of all librettists, wrote texts for Mozart, Gluck, and many others. Calzabigi's librettos helped Gluck reform opera. Da Ponte wrote the masterful librettos for Mozart's *Marriage of Figaro, Don Giovanni,* and *Così fan tutte.* Scribe, the busiest librettist of the nineteenth century, wrote for many composers, including Verdi, Meyerbeer, and Auber. Boito, himself a composer, wrote the texts of *La Gioconda* for Ponchielli and *Otello* and *Falstaff* for Verdi. Much of the success of Richard Strauss's *Elektra* and *Der Rosenkavalier* is due to the masterful librettos of the German dramatist Hugo von Hofmannsthal. The contemporary composer Gian Carlo Menotti has written librettos for his own operas as well as for Barber's *Vanessa.* In the field of light opera, the most famous librettist was the witty W. S. Gilbert, of the Gilbert and Sullivan team.

In a Broadway show the librettist often shares his work with a lyric writer. The librettist writes the "book" of the show—the story and dialogue—while the lyric writer provides the words for the songs. The greatest of Broadway librettists, Oscar Hammerstein II, wrote the words of his songs as well as the book. His collaborations with Jerome Kern and Richard Rogers resulted in such fine musical shows as *Showboat, Oklahoma!,* and *South Pacific.*

LIED, LIEDER: the German words for "song" and "songs," respectively. They are applied particularly to the art songs written by German composers starting with Haydn, Mozart, and Beethoven. In the lied the composer attempts to make a unity of the combination of words, melody, and accompaniment. The piano is often of equal importance with the voice. A folk song, on the other hand, is primarily a melody to which words are sung. Its accompaniment, if any, is hardly ever more than a simple background of harmony.

The greatest composers of lieder were Schubert, Schumann, Liszt, Brahms, Robert Franz, Hugo Wolf, and Richard Strauss. Schubert popularized the form of the art song with his more than 600 songs. His compositions are lyrical love songs, lullabies, dramatic ballads, or simple folklike songs. In his piano parts Schubert portrays such things as the rushing of a stream, the whirring of a spinning wheel, and the galloping of a horse. Some of his lieder are in strophic form; that is, the same music is repeated for a number of verses. Others change melody and accompaniments as the dramatic situation changes—a form sometimes called "through-composed." Schumann, Brahms, Liszt, and Wolf often make their piano parts the most important element of a song, while the voice declaims the words in short melodic lines. Wolf called his works "songs for voice and piano."

Collections of lieder on related poems are called SONG CYCLES. The most famous of these are Schubert's *Die schöne Müllerin (The Fair Maid of the Mill),* Schumann's *Dichterliebe (Poet's Love),* and Hindemith's *Das Marienleben (The Life of Mary).*

In many lieder the voice is accompanied by instruments other than the piano, so that the art song becomes a form of chamber music. In Gustav Mahler's beautiful song cycles the voice is accompanied by full orchestra.

Portrait of Liszt as a young man

LISZT, FRANZ (1811–86): composer, teacher, and the greatest of the piano virtuosos. He was born in Raiding, Hungary, and by the age of nine he had shown so much talent as a pianist that several wealthy Hungarian noblemen provided funds to enable him to continue his musical studies in Vienna. There he became a pupil of Czerny, studied composition, and was praised by Schubert and Beethoven. When Liszt was twelve his father took him to Paris, where he was refused admission at the Conservatory because he was a foreigner and because Cherubini, the director, disliked child prodigies. Liszt's piano lessons came to an end, but he continued the study of composition.

Paris became his home between his many concert tours. In Paris he became friends with all the young revolutionary writers and composers who were taking part in the new Romantic movement in the arts. During this period he came under the influence of the writer Victor Hugo, the composers Chopin and Berlioz, and the master violinist Paganini. The dazzling technical feats of Paganini spurred Liszt to try to achieve the same effects on the piano in his *Hungarian Rhapsodies,* concert études, and piano concertos, and in his many transcriptions of songs and orchestral compositions.

At left: *title page of Schubert's* Die schöne Müllerin

Caricature depicting the triumph of Liszt's style over "General Bass," 1842

Photograph of Liszt in later years

For a while, in the late 1830's, Liszt retired from concert life and seriously considered studying to be a priest. But he was persuaded to become a traveling concert pianist again, and soon set out on tours that were enormously successful. At his recitals (a term first used to advertise a Liszt concert in London in 1840) he played not only his brilliant arrangements of operatic scenes but improvised on themes given him by the audience. He also played with great understanding and feeling many of the sonatas of Beethoven. Liszt performed not only for his own profit but for any worthy cause—for example, to support benefits for flooded Hungarian towns and to raise money for a statue of Beethoven at Bonn, Beethoven's home town.

In 1848 Liszt became music director at the court at Weimar. He spent twelve years there, making Weimar the musical capital of Europe. He taught without fee all talented pupils who came to him and attracted music lovers from all over the world by the brilliance of the concerts he directed. And he helped struggling young composers—Wagner among them—by presenting their works to the public.

In the midst of his activity, Liszt always found time to compose, often in a daring style. He was the first to write symphonic poems for orchestra—compositions that told a story dramatically (for example, *Mazeppa*) or suggested a philosophical theme (*Les Préludes*). He also was a restless experimenter in new sounds, melodically and harmonically. Some of his piano pieces, such as "Au Bord d'une source" (Beside a Spring) and "Au Lac de Wallenstadt" (The Lake of Wallenstadt), paint charming nature scenes, and in these he showed the way, in many respects, for the Impressionist composers Debussy and Ravel. In many of his later works Liszt used so much dissonance that his music became almost atonal—without a key center, like much music of our own time. Instead of the traditional major and minor scales, he used a scale made up of whole steps (see WHOLE-TONE SCALE), as well as scales used by Hungarian gypsy musicians.

Liszt spent many of the later years of his life in Rome. Becoming increasingly religious, in 1865 he was received into a minor religious order, and from then on he was known as "Abbé Liszt." His long life, devoted to music and helping others, came to an end at Bayreuth, the great opera center built by his son-in-law Richard Wagner, who had married Liszt's daughter Cosima in 1870.

Many things for which Liszt had been best known in his lifetime—his piano transcriptions, his oratorios and masses, and his orchestral symphonic poems—are seldom played today. But his two piano concertos, his études, his three volumes of *Années de pèlerinage (Years of Pilgrimage),* his Piano Sonata in B Minor, and many of his *Hungarian Rhapsodies* are still concert favorites. Liszt's organ works, though few, rank with those of César Franck in originality of thought and expression. And musicians are finding in his songs and late piano compositions a deeper-feeling Liszt than the world has acknowledged in the past.

In his own day Liszt was a super-showman, dazzling everyone with his unbelievable technique. Today musicians regard him as one of the great innovators of the nineteenth century.

LOUDSPEAKER or **SPEAKER:** a device for reproducing in volume sounds that have been converted into electrical impulses. The impulses are amplified by means of electronic circuits using vacuum tubes and transistors; then they are fed into the loudspeaker, which reproduces the sounds. Today much of the music we hear comes from the loudspeakers of radios, tape recorders, phonographs—and electric guitars. In large concert halls amplifying equipment and loudspeakers may be used to boost the sound coming from the stage.

The first loudspeakers were no more than telephone receivers. When they transmitted speech, the result was recognizable but odd. Music was more than such devices could handle; all they could produce was a tinny screech. Curved horns fitted to early loudspeakers helped boost lower tones, but it was never practical to make the horns as

long (ideally, several yards) as they should be. Even long horns produced a great deal of distortion.

The solution came in 1925, largely through the efforts of two American engineers, Chester W. Rice and Edward W. Kellogg. Their new, simple design, the dynamic loudspeaker, gave a greatly improved tone and soon became standard for the reproduction of musical sound. Essentially it has three main parts: a strong magnet which in cross section looks like an E; a coil of wire wrapped around the middle bar of the E; and a paper cone with its apex glued to the coil of wire. Since the coil is suspended in a strong magnetic field, the least bit of oscillating current from the amplifier makes it vibrate. (Electric motors work on a similar principle.) This motion is transmitted to the cone, which can be of any size desired and will set a large mass of air into vibration.

Whatever its design, the speaker must introduce as little change as possible into the sound pattern it receives from the amplifier. It must allow low tones to be amplified as much as high tones; it must not "invent" harmonics of its own; it must not have local peaks of power at certain frequencies; and it must not keep "ringing" after a tone has stopped. Heard over a good speaker, percussion instruments sound crisp and "live," and a chorus singing a Handel fugue sounds clear enough for the various voices to be followed individually.

These are demanding ideals, and they have kept the engineers busy with some very ingenious schemes since World War II. Whatever the design, the goal is always the same: the speaker must behave in such a way that we are not aware that it is there.

See PHONOGRAPH.

LULLABY: a cradle song. The term comes from the syllables "la-la," which were sung over and over by mothers lulling their children to sleep. Brahms's *Wiegenlied* and Chopin's *Berceuse* (titles meaning "lullaby" in German and French, respectively) have a gentle rhythm that suggests the rocking of a cradle.

There are many beautiful folk-song lullabies. One of the finest is the well-known "Coventry Carol," "Lullay, Thou Little Tiny Child." This song originated in a scene of a fifteenth-century English miracle play in which the women of Bethlehem sang the lullaby to their children after hearing that King Herod had ordered his soldiers to slay all the young children.

Top: *engraving by Jean Lepautre of a performance of Lully's* Alceste *before King Louis XIV at Versailles (note that the scene is lit by thousands of candles from roof to ground)*
Bottom left: *Jean Baptiste Lully*
Bottom right: *portrait of Louis XIV by Hyacinthe Rigaud*

LULLY, JEAN BAPTISTE (1632–87): a composer who was the founder of French grand opera.

The son of a poor Italian miller, Lully learned to dance and to play the violin in Florence, Italy. At fourteen he was taken to France as a page boy. After becoming a violinist in the orchestra of Mlle. d'Orléans, he wrote an uncomplimentary poem about her and lost his job. Fortunately, however, he had become a friend of the fifteen-year-old "Sun King," Louis XIV. The king gave him a post as violinist in the royal band of twenty-four violins, the most famous orchestra in Europe at the time. Lully also danced in the royal ballets, often with Louis as a partner. Soon Louis made him the leader of a new orchestra, "the little violins of the king." Lully's ability as a leader, his high standards, and his great energy made the "little violins" superior to the older orchestra.

Lully meanwhile studied composition, and in a short time became the king's composer and the music master to the royal family. Interested in the theater, he now began to write ballet-plays with the great French playwright Molière. He also spent much time listening to the actors at the Comédie Française. By studying the sound and rhythm of the French language he mastered it so completely that when he began to write operas his settings of the words were close to perfection.

In 1672 the king gave Lully a monopoly on producing operas in France. In return, Lully gave France its own form of opera. He refused to follow the pattern of Italian operas, with their many arias and lack of glitter. Lully's operas—he called them "tragedies set to music"—with librettos by the dramatist Quinault were filled with lavish display, rich costumes, and large casts of dancers and singers. There were many choral sections, and the large orchestra had much colorful music to play. The flowing vocal melodies followed the natural rhythm of the French language; the dance music was more tuneful than any up to that time. Lully not only wrote the music but coached each singer in his or her part, and he conducted each performance by pounding a large cane on the floor of the orchestra pit. A musical tyrant, he made every singer and instrumentalist perform exactly as he wished. It is said that the infection which caused his death was due to the pounding he gave his foot during a performance.

The form of the eighteen operas Lully wrote during his last fourteen years was always the same. To open them he invented a two-part composition that became known as the "French overture." This starts with a slow, broad section filled with dotted-note rhythms. There follows a fast second movement in which the different voices of the orchestra imitate each other and toss around a light musical idea. The overture usually comes to a close with a few measures in a slow tempo.

The overture is followed by a long prologue, sung mainly by a chorus. The prologue usually praised the wisdom and virtues of a mythical king, whom everyone understood to be Louis. After the prologue came five acts that loosely followed a Greek myth, with very little dramatic action and much slow, beautiful music. Gods and goddesses came down from the skies on "cloud machines" seating a hundred people. The costumes were colorful and expensive, and so, too, were the many scenic effects, which were trundled on and off stage by elaborate machinery.

The most popular social dance during the reign of Louis XIV was the minuet. Its popularity was due in great part to Lully, who worked beautiful minuets into his operas. He usually grouped two of them together, with a repeat of the first after the playing of the second. The second minuet was often played by two oboes and a bassoon—a trio. The minuet-and-trio form was to become, by the time of the Classical composers, one of the most important musical forms.

Lully was one of the founders of the modern orchestra. Not content with the small string orchestra and harpsichord of the Italian opera house, he made effective use of woodwinds and horns, in addition to his strings. He was one of the first to use the newly invented oboe.

The success of Lully's operas set the pattern for French opera for many years. But as his audiences discovered the liveliness of light Italian opera, they turned away from the slow pageantry of Lully's works. Now, except for his ballet-plays, they are no longer given. But Lully's importance to music is reflected in the works of most French opera composers and in the French overture, grand and solemn, that survives in the opening movements of Bach and Handel.

LUTE: a long-necked stringed instrument played by plucking. Throughout most of western Europe in the sixteenth and seventeenth centuries, the lute was the favorite instrument for use in homes as well as in barbershops and taverns. It had originated in the Near East, probably somewhere between the Fertile Crescent and the Caucasus, and was known to the Arabs (as it still is) as the *'ud,* or *al'ud.* (The *l* of the article got transferred to the noun, so that we say *lute* instead of *ute*—just as we have come to say *a newt* and *a nickname* instead of the former *an ewte* and *an eke-name.*) Partly through contact with the Moors in Spain and partly through the interest of returning Crusaders, the lute entered western Europe toward the end of the thirteenth century; at that time it had four strings, tuned a fourth apart, and seems to have been plucked with a plectrum, traditionally a bird's claw or a quill.

By the fifteenth century each of the strings had been doubled. The two middle courses (as the doubled strings were called) were now tuned only a third apart; the other intervals remained fourths, and a single treble string had been added, tuned a fourth above the highest course. This is the classic Old Tuning of the lute, the form the instrument had in the Renaissance; it was no longer played with a plectrum but was plucked and strummed with the fingers of the right hand. European musicians were becoming interested in instruments that could play many-voiced music, and the lute was now taking part in ensemble or group music, accompanying singers and playing solos. Lute players (known as lutanists or lutenists) also played arrangements of songs originally meant for a group of singers, just as nineteenth-century pianists played transcriptions of orchestral music.

By the time of Shakespeare, around 1600, the lute was the favorite instrument of the English song writers. One of the finest composers of the time, John Dowland, was best known as a virtuoso lutanist, and his *Short Treatise on Lute-playing* is one of the best guides to the art. (Dowland and his songwriting contemporaries—Ford, Campion, and Robert Jones—are known collectively as the "lutanist school.") The music of the English lutanists has come down to us not in regular music notation but in tablature, a system in which finger positions, rather than tones, are set down. Something like tablature survives today in the little grids above the melody in sheet music: these are "tablatures" for ukulele players.

From the side, the lute looks like half of a pear. Its broad neck, which holds the fingerboard, ends in a pegbox (for tuning), which falls back at a sharp angle. The fingerboard is set with raised frets, as on a guitar; these mark out successive half tones for the player's fingers.

The whole instrument is extremely light, its flat belly little more than 1/16th inch

"A Lute Player" by Jean Louis Ernest Meissonier. (Instrument shown in painting is a theorbo)

*"The Concert" by Lorenzo Costa
(a lute player accompanying singers)*

thick. The most popular of the several ways of tuning it is shown here:

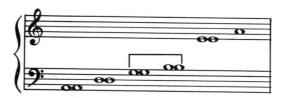

Another traditional tuning has the same intervals, but each string is one tone lower. All lute tunings, however, are characterized by a single interval of a third (above, from *g* to *b*) tucked in among the fourths. This is also a characteristic of the guitar.

Since there were always at least eleven strings to tune and keep in tune, lutanists had plenty to do. Handel's contemporary Johann Mattheson once remarked that an eighty-year-old lutanist would have spent sixty years tuning.

By the end of the sixteenth century the lute was being used increasingly to provide a bass for instrumental groups, somewhat as the string bass is used in jazz "combos" today. This may have been one of the reasons for the addition of especially deep-toned

strings to the instrument, sometimes necessitating a second neck, as in the so-called "archlutes," the *theorbo* and the *chitarrone*. The finest European lutes were made in northern Italy by makers with Austrian family backgrounds. Some of their descendants established themselves in France, where they were known as *luthiers*. In time these craftsmen also took up violinmaking, so that today, even in the United States, men who specialize in making and repairing violins quite often advertise themselves as luthiers.

Many beautiful compositions were written for the lute in the time of its greatest popularity. But as the harpsichord and the piano gained favor with musicians, the lute began to fade from the musical scene. One of the last composers to write for it was Johann Sebastian Bach, and within a few years after his death in 1750 the last works for the lute had been written.

Musicians of today have rediscovered the lute's delicate, muted beauty, and a few of them have revived it to accompany the songs of the English lutanists. It is played also in concerts with recorders, reminding us that it was an instrument for the home—not for the large concert hall.

LYRE: an ancient stringed instrument related to the harp. Its body was made of wood or tortoise shell. Two arms of horn or wood protruded from the body and supported a crossbar around which the strings, three to twelve in number, were wound. The crossbar could be turned to tighten or loosen the strings in tuning the instrument. The lyre was played by means of a plectrum which the player drew across the strings. Strings that the player did not want to sound were stopped by pressing on them with the fingers of the left hand.

Lyres were used in ancient Sumeria about 3000 B.C. and in Egypt about 1500 B.C. The form of lyre called the *kinnor* in ancient Israel was used for playing light, gay music. (The instrument is referred to as a harp in the King James Bible: "We hanged our harps upon the willows," Psalm 137.) When the Jews were forced into exile they left their *kinnorum* behind—there would be no gay music until the Exile was over. Scholars believe the kinnor to be the instrument played by King David.

The lyre reached its greatest importance in ancient Greece, and appears in many legends of Greek mythology. Some of these tell of its invention by the god Apollo and of its irresistible charm when played by Orpheus. Another tells how Amphion, son of Zeus and founder of the great city of Thebes, used his lyre to help build the walls of the city. As he played, huge stones that lay scattered around the plain gathered together and formed themselves into the walls.

Two types of lyres were used in Greece. The KITHARA was a large, heavy, wooden

Lyre players (painting from the outer surface of a Greek cup)

lyre used by professional musicians. This was the instrument used to accompany the epics of the Trojan War. The *lyra* was a smaller, lighter instrument used by amateurs playing at home. Its body was a tortoise shell, its arms were animal horns, and its sounding board was a piece of skin stretched over the shell.

Instruments of the lyre family were popular in northern Europe until the medieval period. The lyre finally vanished, displaced in public favor by the harp and the lute. One of the last surviving members of the lyre family was the Welsh *crwth,* or crouth.

MACHAUT, GUILLAUME DE (c.1300–77):

one of the greatest of French composers and one of the first composers whose life stories are known. Born in northern France, he was active not only as a composer but also as a poet and as a church court official. As secretary to King John of Bohemia, Machaut accompanied the king on campaigns and tours that took him all over Europe. For a while Machaut was at the court of Charles V of France. In 1337 he was made canon of the cathedral at Rheims, and this became his home for the rest of his life.

Machaut's music ranges in style from simple, folklike virelais to music of the most learned type. His virelais and ballades are full of the spirit of knightly chivalry. His rondeaux, for several voices and instruments, use all the complex devices known to composers at the time. In his rondeau "My End Is My Beginning and My Beginning My End," an instrument plays the tenor part backward while the lowest voice sings halfway through its part and then reverses itself (Ex. 1).

Machaut was one of the first to write in the style known as *Ars Nova*—the New Art. In this style music was becoming expressively free in harmony, melody, and rhythm. Machaut's sacred motets strike us as peculiar today—two voices singing French love songs while the third voice sings a sacred text. In the cadences of his works Machaut used a progression of sounds that has been given the name "Landini cadence," after a

Guillaume de Machaut (miniature from a 14th-century French manuscript)

later Italian composer who probably learned it from the works of Machaut:

Landini Cadence

Machaut influenced not only composers but, through his poetry, the great English poet Chaucer, also.

Machaut's crowning glory is his mass, sometimes known as the *Mass of Nôtre Dame*. Possibly written for the coronation of Charles V in 1364, though perhaps earlier, it is the first full setting of the Mass for four voices. It is still occasionally performed today. In inventiveness and rhythmic vigor it is one of the great landmarks of music.

MADRIGAL:

a type of vocal chamber music designed for two to nine singers, each having his own individual melodic part, like the players in a string quartet. Madrigals reached the height of their popularity between 1530 and 1630 in northern Italy and England, where they were sung by and for members of the upper classes.

The music of a madrigal closely follows the rhythm and meaning of a short poem,

Ex. 1 — "My End Is My Beginning and My Beginning My End"

usually no longer than twelve lines. The emotional feeling of the poem is exactly mirrored in the melody and harmony of the music. When the poem contains dramatic or colorful words such as "sigh," "weep," and "laugh," the music itself sighs, weeps, and laughs. Within one madrigal several emotions may be expressed; hence the form of a madrigal may consist of sections that contrast with one another as they follow the form of the poem.

Some of the sections might be homophonic, all the voices singing together in the same rhythm. Other sections might be contrapuntal, with one or two voices starting and the others imitating them. Poems with regular accents, such as those based on the popular galliard dance rhythm, would lead to madrigals in a steady three-count measure. Other poems were filled with subtle changes of accent so that while the music has a steady pulse it has no feeling of regular accent. The music itself was written without bar-lines so that each singer was aware primarily of the rhythm of his own part.

Much of the joy in singing madrigals comes from the freedom of each melodic line. The voices interweave, entering, dropping out, and reaching climaxes at different times. Madrigals can be easy to listen to but may be very complex and difficult to sing. Most of the poems were love poems, but almost any subject served as a topic: war, nature, sports, games, and even tobacco, which was new to Europeans when madrigals were popular.

An early form of the madrigal was sung in Italy in the 1300's, but the Renaissance madrigal was the joint product of Italian poets and Netherlands composers such as Arcadelt (c. 1505–c. 1560) and Willaert (1480–1562), who lived in Italy and taught many of the young composers there. Madrigals became an important part of Italian court festivities in the middle 1500's, being sung at marriage celebrations, on birthdays, and at intermissions between the acts of plays. In England, during the reign of Queen Elizabeth I, the composing and singing of madrigals became very popular, and English music reached one of its highest peaks in the tender, witty madrigals of Dowland, Morley, Weelkes, Wilbye, and Gibbons. The printing of books or collections of madrigals, which had started in 1533 in Italy, became an active business. Gentlemen prided themselves on their collections of madrigals, and brought them out after dinner so that their guests could make music together. A truly educated lady or gentleman was expected to be able to read a line at sight. If

The singing of frottole, *as here, was a popular form of music-making in 16th-century Italy*

there were not enough good voices, several of the parts might be played on a viol or a lute.

In the late 1500's and early 1600's, the madrigal became a more dramatic musical form at the hands of Monteverdi, Marenzio, and Gesualdo. These composers made their madrigals passionate and full of personal feelings. They introduced dissonant sounds to portray conflict or tragedy. Monteverdi added recitatives and other operatic devices. These madrigals became, in a sense, short operas. Orazio Vecchi (1550–1605), as a matter of fact, did compose "madrigal operas," in which several voices sing the same words rather than each character being portrayed by one voice. Such madrigals were too difficult for amateur singers and had to be performed by professionals. Even today they are a challenge to a group of well-trained singers.

Light and tuneful madrigals were called *frottole* (popular songs) or *balletti* ("dance songs") in Italy. In France such madrigals were known as chansons, and in England as canzonettas. Some of the balletti found their way to England. Here, with their refrain of nonsense syllables such as "Fa-la-la" or "Hey, nonny, nonny," they often were given a place in Shakespeare's plays. Many of these kinds of madrigals were solo songs for the soprano with the other voices or instruments acting as accompaniment.

Madrigals dropped from public favor about 1650, soon being replaced by the new-style solo cantatas and by instrumental chamber music such as the trio sonata. In recent years there has been a renewal of interest in the great treasury of music that exists in the madrigals of the sixteenth century.

Engraving of Emanuel Schikaneder as Papageno

Program for The Magic Flute *dated September 30, 1791*

MAGIC FLUTE, THE *(Die Zauberflöte):* the last of Mozart's great operas. Written in 1791 and produced the same year, a little more than two months before Mozart's death, it was composed for Emanuel Schikaneder, a theater manager, actor, and singer, and co-author of the libretto with Carl Ludwig Giesecke. Mozart was in ill health and in desperate need of money, but the immediate success of *The Magic Flute* came too late to help him.

It is a Singspiel, an opera with spoken dialogue—the favorite form of Viennese light entertainment at the time and much like the Broadway musical of today. Its plot is a mixture of love, comedy, courage, and magic that ends in praise of the moral ideas of Freemasonry, an institution then popular among artists, writers, and persons high in the Austrian government. (Mozart and Haydn were Freemasons, as were Austrian emperors and many Catholic churchmen.)

The story of *The Magic Flute* features two pairs of lovers—one high-born, the other low-born. Tamino, an Egyptian prince, falls in love with a portrait of the beautiful Pamina, daughter of the evil Queen of the Night. He and the comic Papageno, bird-catcher to the queen, set out to rescue Pamina from Sarastro, the High Priest of Isis and Osiris. The queen gives a magic flute to Tamino and a set of magic bells to Papageno to use when they are in trouble. Tamino and Papageno find the palace of Sarastro and learn that Sarastro has kidnapped Pamina to keep her away from the bad influences of her mother.

Tamino and Papageno agree to be initiated into the mysteries of Sarastro's faith, which is founded on the ideals of friendship, love, and reason. As part of the compact, each must face certain trials. Tamino undertakes his ordeals for love of wisdom and Pamina. Papageno agrees because he is promised Papagena, a pretty young girl who will be clothed in feathers, just as he is. Both young men take a vow of silence—they may not speak to any woman during the trials.

Meanwhile the queen finds her daughter, and in an aria full of hatred and vengeance gives her a dagger with which to kill Sarastro. The treacherous Moorish servant of Sarastro, Monostatos, snatches the dagger and threatens to kill Pamina if she will not give him her love. She is saved by Sarastro, who tells her that her mother will retire, defeated, if Tamino has the courage to overcome the obstacles that will be put in his way.

The oaths of silence taken by Tamino and Papageno are tested in various ways. Pamina, when Tamino will not talk to her,

thinks he no longer loves her. Papageno, who can never hold his tongue, is terrified into silence by thunder and lightning as he starts a conversation with an ugly old woman.

To the melody of an old chorale, two men in armor sing of the ordeals of fire and water that must be faced (Ex. 2). Pamina joins Tamino, and as he plays the magic flute they walk unharmed through the cave of fire and the cave of water. Papageno, who has found his Papagena but lost her because he talked, is all set to hang himself when three genii appear and tell him to play his magic bells. He does so, and Papagena is restored to him as they sing a delightful stammering duet, "Pa-pa-pa-pa-ge-na" and "Pa-pa-pa-pa-ge-no" (Ex. 3).

The Queen of the Night, three ladies of her court, and Monostatos, the evil Moor, appear near the Temple of Isis and Osiris. Lightning and thunder turn them away, vanquished forever by the forces of good. They disappear, and the priests sing a noble chorus of thanks to Isis and Osiris and a tribute to the courage of Tamino, who has won the eternal prizes of beauty and wisdom.

The Magic Flute contains some of Mozart's most inspired music and, in spite of his poor health and fortunes, some of his sunniest.

The overture, written two days before the first performance, on September 30, 1791, is often played at symphony concerts. It opens with the brass playing three solemn chords:

These chords, heard later in the opera from the trumpets of the priests, are thought by some to have a Masonic meaning. After a short, slow section, the true overture begins. It is in a combination of fugue and sonata style and is based primarily on a gay, bubbling motive (Ex. 4).

The vocal melodies in *The Magic Flute* demonstrate Mozart's genius at writing melodies completely typical of the character who sings them. Since Papageno is a simple fellow who wants just enough to live on, the melodies that Mozart wrote for him are almost like folk songs in their simplicity

Ex. 2 — Chorale: "Ach Gott, vom Himmel sieh' darein"

Ex. 3

Walter Berry as Papageno in a 1963 production at the Salzburg Festival

Ex. 4

Scene from The Magic Flute, *Act I*

(Ex. 5). Papageno always has with him his panpipes, on which he plays little flourishes:

Tamino and Pamina are given tender melodies (Ex. 6), while those of Sarastro are deep and noble (Ex. 7).

The part of the Queen of the Night, written for Mozart's sister-in-law, Josefa Hofer, is one of the most difficult ever written for a soprano. Her second aria, asking Pamina to murder Sarastro, ranges all the way up to an F above high C and demands great vocal agility, as well as dramatic power (Ex. 8).

There is a great deal of ensemble singing throughout the opera: duets, trios, and choruses. The long finale is one of the finest examples of Mozart's mastery of writing for the theater. Whereas in most operas the composer uses the finale only as a device to bring everyone on stage, in Mozart a finale serves as the climax of the whole work. It contains many sections and has in it much action. The finale of *The Magic Flute* includes the song of the men in armor, the ordeal of the caves of fire and water, Papageno's threat to hang himself, his duet with Papagena, the final defeat of the Queen of the Night, and the hymn to Isis and Osiris.

Mozart himself conducted the first two performances of *The Magic Flute*. He then turned his attention to the Requiem, which he never finished. When on his deathbed he longed to hear once more his *Magic Flute*.

Ex. 5

I — am the bird—catcher, gay am I, Always hap-py, hap-py, nev-er sigh

Ex. 6

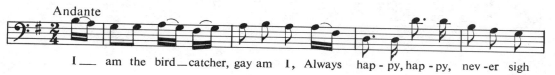

Ta - mi -no - mine! O luck-y fate! Pa - mi - na - mine, O luck-y fate!

Ex. 7

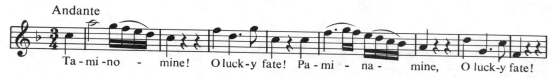

With - in these ho - ly, ho - ly halls, A man shall feel no rage

Ex. 8

more___

Two angels hold tablets on which are written the four parts of a Magnificat (Flemish engraving, c. 1600)

MAGNIFICAT: the song of Mary, Mother of Jesus. It appears in St. Luke's account of her meeting with Elizabeth in the house of Zacharias (1:46–55), beginning "My soul doth magnify the Lord." In Latin versions it is known as *Magnificat anima mea dominum*.

The Magnificat was one of the earliest texts to be sung in the church. At first it was sung to plainsong, or Gregorian chant, melodies. But as it became the most important part of the Vespers, or Evening Service, its settings by composers became long and elaborate, calling for soloists, chorus, and orchestra.

Before 1600 each of the great church composers wrote many Magnificats—Palestrina thirty-five, for example, and Lassus twenty-three. Later composers wrote fewer: Bach and Mozart each wrote only one, though Bach's has come down to us in two versions. In the earlier (E-flat major) version, written for his first Christmas at Leipzig, Bach had to interlard the numbers of the Magnificat proper with four hymns appropriate to the season; the work is still sometimes performed at Christmas. The later version, in D major, is more unified; built much like a cantata, it is one of Bach's most powerful compositions.

MAHLER, GUSTAV (1860–1911): late Romantic composer of lyrical symphonic works. Born in Kalischt, Bohemia (now Czechoslovakia), Mahler was for most of his working life an outstanding conductor of German opera, principally in Hamburg and Budapest, at the Metropolitan Opera in New York, and at the Vienna Court Opera, where for ten years he was artistic director in charge of all details of opera production. For the last two years of his life he conducted the New York Philharmonic Orchestra. His last concert, conducted while he was ill with a high fever, probably hastened his death, which occurred soon after in Vienna.

As a conductor Mahler was known for his attention to details and for his perfectionist aim to bring out everything that was in the music. It was said that he conducted "like a fanatic monk."

During vacations between opera seasons Mahler wrote nine symphonies and six song cycles, mostly with orchestral accompaniment. The themes in his symphonies are often songlike, while his song cycles, such as *Das Lied von der Erde (The Song of the Earth),* are symphonic. Fond of using voices in his symphonies, Mahler in his Second Symphony calls for soprano and alto soloists plus chorus, in the Fourth for a soprano soloist, and in the Eighth for eight soloists, a double chorus, and a boys' choir. The Eighth Symphony has been called the "Symphony of a Thousand" because of the large number of performers required. Although Mahler disliked giving names and programs to his music, several of his symphonies have been given titles: Number 1, in D—the "Titan"; Number 2, in C minor—the "Resurrection"; and Number 5, in C-sharp minor—"The Giant." (Mahler also sketched a tenth symphony. In the 1960's two performing editions were prepared, and the work has since been widely played.)

Mahler was a Romantic composer. His works are on a large scale, with long move-

Gustav Mahler

Silhouettes of Mahler conducting

ments and many performers, and are filled with Mahler's own personal feelings. His early works sing of nature and celebrate his love of the countryside. The later compositions are moody—full of longing, desolation, and loneliness. Like Beethoven and Mozart, Mahler yearned for a peaceful brotherhood of man.

Mahler was not an inventor in music. His melodies and harmonies follow in the Austrian-German tradition of Beethoven and Wagner. Sweet-sad Viennese waltzes and woodland hunting horns go in and out of the music. One of his most-played movements, the third movement of his First Symphony, is a funeral march based on a grave version of "Frère Jacques" played in a minor key. Mahler in his orchestration achieves a rich, glowing sound in which each instrument is heard in its own individual tone color.

Mahler's music has been popular in Vienna, where it influenced the early works of Schoenberg and Berg, but it has been slow to spread to other countries. Mahler wrote no short pieces through which music lovers could readily get acquainted with his style. The unusual length of this composer's sprawling works has tended to keep them off symphony programs and records. Starting in the 1940's, Mahler's music has been heard more frequently outside Austria and Germany. Under the leadership of Bruno Walter, one of Mahler's old friends, conductors have found that audiences appreciate the sensitive beauties that flow through Mahler's music.

MAJOR: a particular kind of interval, scale, or chord. Major means "greater" or "larger,"

as opposed to MINOR, meaning "lesser" or "smaller." The major form of an interval is always a half step larger than the minor form:

Major second: one whole step

Major third: two whole steps

Major sixth: one whole step larger than a perfect fifth

Major seventh: one half step *smaller* than an octave

Major ninth: one whole step larger than an octave.

The major scale, formerly called "the scale with the greater (major) third," is a pattern of whole steps and half steps starting from its keynote:

Major Scale

Counting up from the keynote of a major scale, all intervals except perfect consonances (perfect fourth, perfect fifth, and octave) are major intervals, comprising the major second, third, sixth, and seventh intervals shown below (see Ex. 9, at bottom of page).

Major chord forms include the major triad—a major third and a perfect fifth above the root, or bottom tone (Ex. a); the major seventh—a major triad plus a major seventh above the root (Ex. b); and the most common major ninth chord—a major triad plus a minor seventh and a major ninth above the root (Ex. c):

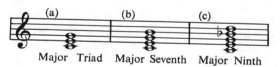

Major Triad   Major Seventh   Major Ninth

The major scale is sometimes called the cheerful or happy scale, as contrasted with the minor scale, which is supposedly the scale for sad music. But this idea is not accurate. Many "happy" pieces, such as the lively gigues and courantes by Bach and Handel, are in minor keys, while many "sad" compositions, such as "On Top of Old Smokey" and "Swanee River," are in the major.

In the church MODE system, the major scale was known as the Ionian mode.

Ex. 9— Intervals

Major Second   Major Third   Major Sixth   Major Seventh   Major Ninth

MANDOLIN: a stringed instrument that has been especially popular in and around Naples, Italy, and is the only surviving form of the Renaissance lute. Like the lute, it looks like half of a pear when seen from the side, but it has a deeper bowl that the lute, is smaller, and has a thinner neck. Its four sets of double wire strings are tuned like the strings of a violin:

Frets, like those of the banjo and guitar, guide the fingers of the player's left hand.

The instrument is played by means of a tortoise-shell plectrum, or pick, held in the player's right hand. The tone is weak. Except for short staccato notes, the player strums back and forth over a pair of strings to give the effect of a long, held tone. This produces the mandolin's characteristic tinkling trill.

In its Neapolitan homeland the mandolin is used to play folk songs and love songs. Mozart used it most effectively in *Don Giovanni*, in the scene in which the Don serenades Zerlina (Ex. 50, page 536). (The mandolin's tone is so delicate that in large opera houses its part is usually plucked on the violins.) Though Beethoven wrote a few short pieces for it, few composers have paid the instrument much attention. An exception is Weber, who loved to accompany himself on the mandolin, late in the evening, while singing for his friends. Mahler uses the instrument in his Sixth Symphony and the contemporary composer Carlos Surinach calls for three mandolins on stage in his ballet score *Acrobats of God*, written for Martha Graham. Schoenberg in his Serenade, Opus 24, includes a mandolin along with other strings, woodwinds, and a baritone voice.

MARCH: a form of music originally used to keep soldiers moving together in military formations. A march must have a strong rhythm, which is usually accented by drum beats. Most march music is written in a meter of two or four beats (2/4, 4/4, or 6/8).

As recently as 1800, armies marched into battle to the sound of drums, fifes, bagpipes, and trumpets. The music gave courage to the troops, and the marching formations, which showed the superb discipline of the soldiers, often were enough to frighten the enemy.

Shortly before 1600, march rhythms began to attract composers. Marches were written for wedding and funeral ceremonies and for processions of dignified officials of church

From left to right: mandolin, Naples, 1712; mandola (tenor mandolin), Naples, 1773; and a 19th-century Italian mandolin

and state. In 1591 the earliest concert marches were published in an English harpsichord collection, *My Lady Nevell's Booke*. It contained among other pieces "Marche before the Battell," "The Marche of Horsemen," and "The Marche to the Fight."

In the middle 1600's the French-Italian composer Lully wrote marches for the regimental bands of Louis XIV of France. These pieces, written for soprano, tenor, and bass oboes, are some of the earliest examples of music composed for band. Lully also introduced grand marches into his many operas, starting a fashion that was followed by Handel, Verdi, Meyerbeer, Wagner, and Prokofiev. Marches were included in numerous seventeenth- and eighteenth-century dance suites.

The slow, sad rhythm of the funeral march, played originally with muffled drums, attracted nineteenth-century composers. Beethoven wrote funeral marches for the slow movements of his Piano Sonata in A-flat, Opus 26, and his Third Symphony (the "Eroica"). Of all funeral marches the one in Chopin's Sonata in B-flat Minor is perhaps the most celebrated. Siegfried's Funeral March, like a flashback of his life, is one of the high points of Wagner's opera *Götterdämmerung*. It is often played at symphony concerts.

The two most familiar wedding marches

were written in the nineteenth century. "Here Comes the Bride" is from the Wedding Scene of Wagner's opera *Lohengrin*. Mendelssohn's Wedding March, played at the conclusion of the ceremony, is part of his incidental music to Shakespeare's play *A Midsummer Night's Dream*. It was first used as a wedding march in England in 1858 at the marriage of Queen Victoria's daughter, the Princess Royal, to the Crown Prince of Prussia.

Among processional marches used at school ceremonies throughout the United States, the most often played is Sir Edward Elgar's *Pomp and Circumstance Number 1*. Its dignified second theme is sometimes sung to the words of "Land of Hope and Glory." This piece was written in 1901 as the first of five marches for orchestra.

The most famous of all composers in this realm of music is John Philip Sousa, the American band leader who became known as the "March King." Of his many marches the best known are *The Stars and Stripes Forever, The Washington Post, American Patrol, Semper Fidelis,* and *High School Cadets.*

Sousa's marches usually follow a set plan: a flourish or fanfare introduction, a main section, and a trio section in the subdominant key. Instead of returning to the first section, as in a minuet and trio form, many marches end with the trio. Often, as in *The Stars and Stripes Forever,* the trio is more memorable than the first section.

MARIMBA: a deep-toned Mexican cousin of the xylophone. Its keys are strips of hard wood cut so that each one sounds a different tone of the scale. Under each strip is a sound box, or resonator, open at the top but closed at the bottom by a thin bladder. The resonator matches the tone of its key: the lower the tone, the longer the bar and the deeper the resonator. In Mexico and Central America one can hear entire orchestras of marimbas.

The North American marimba, which has become popular as a solo instrument, has a range of four octaves. The wooden keys are arranged like the keyboard of a piano but vary in size, ranging from the large bass keys to the small high keys. Since even the smallest key of a marimba is twice as large as the white keys of a piano, the marimba player cannot play chords that are widely spaced.

Two types of mallet are used for playing the marimba. Mallets made from hard rubber are used for brilliant, loud, percussive sound. Mallets wound with woolen yarn are used for mellow tones. For fast passage work the player uses two mallets, and when playing chords, four.

Many contemporary composers have become interested in the marimba for its diversity of tone colors. One of the most effective marimba parts occurs in Boulez' *Le Marteau sans maître.* Concertos for marimba have been written by Creston, Kurka, and Milhaud.

Marimba players at Panajachal, Guatemala

MARSEILLAISE, LA: the French national anthem. One of the most stirring of all patriotic songs, "La Marseillaise" was written in April of 1792 by Rouget de l'Isle (1760–1836), a military engineer in the French army along the Rhine. The song's original title was "Le Chant de guerre de l'armée du Rhin" (War Song of the Army of the Rhine). This title was changed to "La Marseillaise" when the revolutionary troops from Marseilles sang it as they entered Paris in the summer of 1792. Rouget de l'Isle himself was not a revolutionary, and when he refused to swear allegiance to the government that had overthrown the king, he was imprisoned.

"La Marseillaise" has come to be the musical symbol of France. As such it has been used by Schumann in his song "The Two Grenadiers" and by Tchaikovsky in his "1812" Overture.

MASS (*Missa* in Latin, *Messe* in German and French): the form of the Communion Service of the Roman Catholic Church and of many Anglican, or Episcopal, churches. The name comes from the phrase said by the priest at the end of the service: *Ite, missa est* (Go, [the congregation] is dismissed). In a Low Mass all the words are spoken, but a High Mass, or *Missa solemnis,* includes many sections that are sung. These sections are grouped into the Ordinary (the unchanging text) and the Proper (with changing text, depending on whether the service is for a special feast day, such as Christmas; a saint's day; or a funeral service, or Requiem Mass). In musical terms today, a mass is a setting of the Ordinary, the text of which has served to inspire more musical masterpieces than any other source.

The five parts of the Ordinary of the Mass are:

Kyrie (Lord, have mercy)
Gloria (Glory to God in the highest)
Credo (The Nicene Creed, beginning "I believe in one God")
Sanctus and Benedictus (Holy, holy, holy)
Agnus Dei (Lamb of God, who takest away the sins of the world)

The five parts of the Proper are:

The Introit (the introduction or beginning)
The Gradual (sung while the epistle is moved from one side of the altar to the other. Formerly sung from a step—*gradus*— of the pulpit)
The Alleluia or the Tract (a hymn of praise or verses from the Bible)

The Offertory (offering of bread and wine to God)
The Communion (the partaking of the consecrated bread and wine—the Eucharist)

In the early days of the church the parts of the Ordinary were sung by members of the congregation or auxiliary clergy. In the tenth century the Ordinary was given to a group of trained singers, the schola cantorum. These singers often improvised their own melodies on top of the Gregorian chant, which alone had been the music of the Mass. It was these improvisations that led directly to the development of counterpoint and harmony, the techniques of which have since been the basis of all European music.

In 1364 Guillaume de Machaut wrote a complete setting of the Mass for four voices —the first such work attributed to a single composer. Each section of Machaut's *Mass of Nôtre Dame* was based on a Gregorian chant sung in drawn-out notes by the tenors. For a while the importance of Machaut's mass went unrecognized, but by the middle 1400's many composers were writing in this form. Since then the text of the Mass has inspired many masterpieces.

Most of the masses of the fifteenth and sixteenth centuries were written in the cantus firmus technique. A Gregorian chant or a popular tune, usually with its rhythm changed, served as the thread around which a composer would spin three or four more melodic lines. In many cases a mass was known by the name of the chant or popular tune on which the work was built. The favorite popular tune "L'Homme armé" (The Armed Man) was used in masses by such great church composers as Dufay, Ockeghem, Obrecht, Josquin Des Prés, and Palestrina. Masses were sometimes named for a person (Palestrina's *Pope Marcellus Mass*) or for the scale tones on which a mass was based (Palestrina's *Missa ut re mi fa sol la—Mass on the Tones C,D,E,F, G,A*). Some masses were just called *Missa sine nomine (Mass Without a Name)*. Later masses received their names from the keys of their first movements (Bach's B-minor Mass) or because they were written for a special occasion (Haydn's *Mass in Time of War*).

The fifteenth- and sixteenth-century composers used in their masses all the newly discovered technical devices of music, particularly the devices of canon and of imitation in general. This led to writing of such complexity that a mass was more often a display of a composer's bag of tricks than a measure of his religious devotion and his

Painting by Isidore Pils, 1849, depicting Rouget de l'Isle singing "La Marseillaise" for the first time

Celebration of a mass (engraving from the 16th-century book En-comium Musicae)

inspiration. At the Council of Trent (1545–63) the assembled bishops declared that the music of the Mass should not be based on popular tunes, should not be too complex, and should not introduce material that was not a part of the service. The beautiful, flowing style of Palestrina seemed best to represent ideal church music. But other composers, interested in new dramatic uses of music, paid little attention to the style of Palestrina's ninety-three masses. Even in the twentieth century Pope Pius the Tenth's urging of church composers to imitate the smooth style of Palestrina brought little or no result.

The number of words in the different sections of the Mass influenced the handling of the text. Since the Kyrie, Sanctus, and Agnus Dei have few words, composers realized that these could be repeated like a musical motive; these sections lend themselves to the canon, with voice imitating voice. But the Gloria and the Credo have many words. These suggested a style in which all voices chant the words in chordal unison ("familiar" style). This difference in the settings of the words guided composers to a complete musical form that contained a great deal of contrast.

As music went through its many revolutionary changes around 1600, the music for the Mass also changed. The Protestant Reformation did away with much of the Latin form. The Lutheran Mass was reduced to two sections: Kyrie and Gloria. J. S. Bach wrote four such abbreviated masses. Composers, now in the employ of kings, dukes, and princes instead of the

church, added instruments to the voices of the choir. By 1700 the music of the Mass was written not so much for a solemn church service as for a festive performance at a court chapel or palace. Even dramatic echoes from the opera crept into it.

Bach's B-minor Mass, written during the 1730's, is one of the great landmarks in music. Using material from several cantatas, along with new music, he put together a dramatic and devout work for soloists, chorus, organ, and orchestra. The work takes more than two hours to perform. Each movement of the mass is broken into sections, and each section is a complete composition. In size and scope it is rivaled only by Beethoven's *Missa solemnis,* written almost a hundred years later.

The great Viennese masters Haydn, Mozart, and Schubert wrote some of their most glorious music in their masses. But they marked the end of an era. Composers of the nineteenth century no longer looked to the words of the Mass for inspiration. Only the dramatic text of the Requiem Mass appealed to the operatic instincts of Cherubini, Berlioz, and Verdi. Brahms's *German Requiem* is not a mass but a choral meditation on texts from Luther's Bible.

Contemporary composers have again taken the text of the Mass as a basis for some of their finest works, outstanding masses of this century being those of Poulenc and Stravinsky. The recent decision to allow the Mass to be celebrated in the language of each country offers new challenges to composers and has already resulted in jazz- and folk-based settings of the mass.

MAZURKA: a vigorous Polish social dance that is danced in a circle, usually by couples. More than fifty mazurka steps have been devised—plus such improvised steps as dancers have cared to invent. The most important characteristics of the mazurka are the stamping of the feet, the clicking of the heels, and the spinning turns of the couples, as in a Viennese waltz.

The mazurka was originally a folk dance, but before 1800 had already become a favorite ballroom dance in Russia. It spread westward in the first decade of the nineteenth century, and European ballrooms resounded with the precise stamping and heel-clicking of officers in the colorful uniforms of the period. Although it has now disappeared from ballroom dancing in the West, the form was guaranteed a long musical survival thanks to the fifty-eight mazurkas written for the piano by Frédéric Chopin. Chopin's mazurkas were written not to accompany dancers but rather to re-create the dance in the mind of the listener. They range from languid, sentimental daydreams (like the Mazurka, Opus 17, Number 4) to fast, stirring dances (Opus 56, Number 2). Some of them, like the first and third mazurkas of Opus 56, contain passages of extraordinary harmonic daring (for the 1840's), and it is probably in the mazurkas

more than in any other type of composition that Chopin's harmonic inventiveness is revealed in its greatest variety.

The mazurka has three beats per measure, with an accent on the second or third beat suggesting the stamping and heel-clicking of the dancers. Short notes in the first beat and a long note on the second help to bring out the accents:

Mazurka, Op. 68, No. 3, Chopin

In the Polish peasants' original mazurkas the melody was traditionally sung to the accompaniment of a drum or a drone bass, and echoes of this style can occasionally be heard in Chopin, as in the Mazurka, Opus 56, Number 2 (Ex. 10). In more recent generations Chopin's lead in writing mazurkas for the piano has been followed by Scriabin, Szymanowski, and Tansman. On a more popular level, variations of the mazurka have cropped up in South America (the *chacarura*) and, in the form of the *varsovienne,* in Mexico and the American Southwest.

Dancing the mazurka

Ex. 10 — Mazurka, Op. 56, No. 2, Chopin

MEDIANT: the third tone of the major and minor scales. The name comes from its position between the keynote, the first scale degree, and the dominant, the fifth scale degree. In Gregorian chants the mediant was the principal tone of phrases—other than the first and last.

The mediant is the tone that makes a scale major or minor. In the early 1600's, before the terms "major" and "minor" were used, scales were classified as to whether they had the "greater" or "lesser" third.

Compositions in a minor key often move quickly to the key of the mediant, which is the relative major of the original key. This close relationship is often seen and heard in the music of Bach and Handel:

"Air," Handel

Key: D Minor

Tonic   Dominant of →Mediant

The triad built on the mediant tone is minor in a major key, augmented or major in a minor key (Ex. 11). In music of the eighteenth and nineteenth centuries the mediant harmony usually progresses to the chord on the fourth or sixth tone of the scale (Ex. 12).

The tone midway between the keynote of a scale and the subdominant, or fourth scale degree below it, is called the submediant or undermediant.

MEDIEVAL MUSIC: music written during the medieval period (900–1450). This was the period during which musical notation began and developed, counterpoint was invented, composers discovered harmony, the earliest of modern musical forms began to appear, and ancestors of some present-day musical instruments were brought from Asia and Africa.

Music was an important part of all medieval life—in churches, taverns, castles, and village huts. Wandering entertainers and jongleurs sang their songs, which took note of all that was going on in the world. They played their stringed vielles and performed their tricks wherever they found a crowd that might pay them—at marriage festivals, tournaments, receptions for dignitaries, church holidays, and village celebrations. Learned church musicians copied the few manuscripts that were available and composed sacred works of their own. Knightly troubadours, trouvères, and minnesingers composed love songs to entertain their courtly friends. Wandering scholars—the goliards—made up songs of drinking and love and parodies of religious songs as they went back and forth from France to Italy in search of education. Pilgrims sang hymns as they walked hundreds of miles to visit holy shrines. Musicians accompanied soldiers into battle, encouraging them with warlike and patriotic music. Bells in the new Gothic churches added their clanging tones to the sounds of medieval cities as the people were called to their prayers. Waits, or musical night watchmen, played and sang as they sounded the hours of the night and proclaimed, "All is well."

Medieval music employed instruments of many kinds. In the churches the pipe

Ex. 11

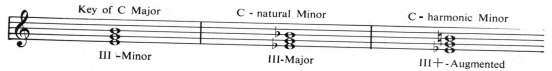

Ex. 12 — Chorale: "Nun lob', mein Seel, den Herren," harmonized by J.S. Bach

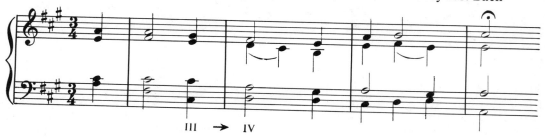

Left: *medieval music-making—*
"The Muses." In the foreground,
from left to right: a pipe and tabor
player; a cornett; and a dulcimer.
In the background, left to right:
a portative organ; a different type
of dulcimer; a shawm; a mandola
played with plectrum; and a flûte à
bec (miniature from a 15th-century
manuscript, Champion des dames,
by Martin le Franc)

Below: *woodcuts by Hans Holbein*
from his series depicting the "Dance
of Death"

organ grew from one octave with no keyboard to the splendid instrument, with several keyboards, that was needed to fill the immense spaces in the new cathedrals. A small portative organ was developed for use much as the accordion is used today.

Soldiers returning from the Crusades brought back new and wonderful instruments from the Near East: kettledrums, ivory horns, ancestors of the recorder and flute, and the rebec, or bowed lute, which was an ancestor of the viol family. The Moors in Spain contributed the lute, psaltery, and guitar.

The medieval bards recited their tales to the accompaniment of a lyre or harp. Bagpipes of many kinds were used to accompany dancing, singing, and marching. The one-man band of flute or trumpet and drum and cymbals was everywhere. By the thirteenth century there were so many wandering musicians that unions or guilds were organized in each city to keep them out. The guilds set standards of membership so that incompetent musicians were not allowed to work.

There was much dancing in medieval times. Much of it was in the nature of folk dances—caroles, or round dances, and estampies, or stamping dances. When the Black Death, or plague, raged through Europe in the middle 1300's, people crazed by fear danced the Dance of Death, or *danse macabre,* in which Death was often represented by dancers garbed as skeletons.

In the churches and monasteries a few great men were struggling with the problems of how to compose music and how to write it down. From their efforts came music as we know it today.

Until the medieval period, music was sung or played as a single line. The idea of harmony, or counterpoint, was almost unknown. Plainsong, or plainchant, melodies as in Gregorian chants, were sung by the priest and the choir in unison, without instrumental accompaniment. About the year 1000, singers began to experiment, some singing the chant on its correct pitches, others singing it a fourth, fifth, or octave higher. This style, called organum, led composers to experiment further in combining one or more melodies above the chant sung by the tenors. The art of composing organum was brought to a high peak in the twelfth century by the Parisian composers Leonin and Perotin, the great masters of the Notre Dame School.

The ancient Greeks had a system of musical notation, but the tradition was lost and the European musicians had to invent their own. A kind of shorthand, called neumes, came into use, showing whether the pitch of a chant went up or down, but it was often difficult to know just how far. A monk, Guido d'Arezzo, perfected a four-line staff about the year 1000. Now it was possible to place tones exactly in pitch. Guido also invented a way of teaching his singers sight singing by using the now familiar do, re, mi system.

As singers and composers discovered the delights of combining several melodies into

Miniature from the 13th-century manuscript Cantigas de Santa Maria, *compiled by Alfonso el Sabio*

The meistersinger Hans Sachs (a 1556 portrait)

counterpoint, they also encountered a new problem—that of keeping the voice parts together. A method of showing rhythmic relationships was invented by Franco of Cologne in the late 1200's.

At first the singers of organum sang the same words at the same time. Then the upper voices began to sing wordless melodies, called descants, as counterpoints to the tenor's chants. When words were added to the descant, one of the earliest musical forms developed—the motet (meaning "little word"). These added words might be in French rather than in the Latin of the chant, and might take the form of a love song within a religious work.

The greatest composer of the 1300's was Guillaume de Machaut who was also a poet and priest. His setting of the Mass for four voices was the first of a long line of masterpieces based on the service of the Mass. He also wrote motets and lighter works such as ballades in the style of the courtly trouvères. Machaut and later composers of the medieval period discovered how to use imitation in the technique known as canon. The Italian hunting song, or *caccia* (meaning "chase"), was among the first such canons. The old English round "Sumer Is Icumen In" dates from the 1300's.

Outside the churches the troubadours were composing their songs of chivalry. These songs in flowing rhythm were vocally much like later ones. The troubadours used regular accents, which church music did not, and they liked the major scale. Church musicians favored the other medieval scales.

The thirteenth-century trouvère, Adam de la Halle, wrote a little pastorale play with songs interspersed throughout. His *Play of Robin and Marion,* written about 1280, is the earliest-known short comic opera. Other works of this kind were undoubtedly written but, like much of the music of the medieval period, the manuscripts were lost or

destroyed. For hundreds of years musicians looked down on what they thought were the crudities of medieval music. Then, at the end of the nineteenth century, a search for new means of expression led the French composers Debussy and Satie to the discovery of such medieval sounds as organum and modal melodies. Musical scholars began an intensive study of medieval music. Today, a thousand years after they were written, many works of the medieval period are being deciphered, printed for the first time, and performed.

MEISTERSINGER: a German word meaning "mastersinger." The Mastersingers were a guild of poet-musicians who flourished in Germany in the fifteenth and sixteenth centuries. They were middle-class tradesmen and craftsmen who carried on many of the traditions of the aristocratic *Minnesingers,* the German poet-musicians of the Middle Ages. After church on Sunday the Mastersingers held a weekly meeting, during which they presented new poems or melodies.

The entrance examination for the guild was difficult. The candidate had to prove his knowledge of poetry and music. A "marker" presided and kept track of his mistakes. After admission as a *Schuler* (pupil), the new guild member could progress to *Schulfreund* (school-friend), *Singer* (singer), *Dichter* (poet), and finally *Meister* (master). *Dichter* was one who composed a new poem to fit an already existing melody, called a *Ton* or *Weise.* The *Meister* was one who had the privilege of composing new melodies.

The form of the song was strict. It consisted of a first part, the *Stollen,* which was repeated, and a contrasting second section, the *Abgesang.* Songs were usually named after their composers—*Brant-Weise,* for instance—or for some feature of the song or the occasion of its writing, as "Black-Ink-Melody." At times songs were even given a nonsense title, such as "Frog-tone."

The most famous mastersinger was Hans Sachs (1494–1576), who wrote more than 4,000 poems and composed many melodies. He is one of the main characters in Richard Wagner's opera *Die Meistersinger.*

With its strict form and rigid rules, the music of the mastersingers never achieved the flowing, expressive quality of many of the songs of the minnesingers. Despite their lack of musical importance, however, the mastersinger guilds, probably because of their social appeal, lasted until the eighteenth century.

MEISTERSINGER, DIE *(The Mastersingers):* Richard Wagner's gayest and most tuneful opera. Its full name is *Die Meistersinger von Nürnberg.* Originally (1845) planned as a small, "light" opera, it ended (1867) as an elaborate work calling for a large cast and orchestra.

The overture, which is often played as a concert piece, is based on themes to be heard later in the opera. One is the theme of the mastersingers (Ex. 13). Another is a fanfare that is an authentic mastersinger tune from the sixteenth century (Ex. 14). A third theme, from the finale of the opera, is in praise of German art (Ex. 15). There is the "Prize Song"—a passionate tenor aria, often sung as a concert work (Ex. 16). And

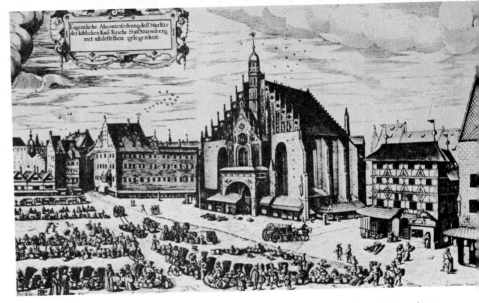

A 1599 engraving of Nuremberg

Ex. 13

Ex. 14

Ex. 15

Ex. 16

there is the lively theme of the young apprentices (Ex. 17). At the climax of the overture the themes of Ex. 13, 14, and 15 are combined in a masterful display of Wagner's skill in counterpoint (Ex. 18).

The opera tells the story of Walther, a young knight who falls in love with Eva, daughter of the mastersinger Pogner. She is to become the bride of the winner of a mastersingers' contest.

Walther is befriended by the shoemaker-mastersinger Hans Sachs and by Sachs's apprentice David. David tells Walther the bewildering array of rules that the mastersinger's guild uses in judging a song. At a preliminary trial Walther fails. His judge, or "marker," is old Beckmesser, town clerk and suitor for the hand of Eva. (In one of the original sketches for the libretto Wagner named this character Hans Lick after the Viennese music critic Hanslick, with whom Wagner was feuding.)

Beckmesser comes at night to serenade Eva. Sachs interrupts him by pounding with his hammer and singing a cobbler's song. Beckmesser objects, and Sachs agrees to hammer only when Beckmesser sings a wrong note. But the strange duet of hammer and florid song brings on young David, who thinks that Beckmesser is serenading Magdalena, David's girl. They begin to fight. The singing, hammering, and scuffling awaken everyone; lights appear at the windows and the neighborhood is in confusion. Finally things quiet down, and the night watchman sings his song as he walks down the narrow street under a full moon.

The next morning Sachs, thinking over the brawl of the previous night, sings his famous monologue, "The world is full of madness." Walther enters and tells Sachs of a wonderful dream he has just had. Sachs helps him put it into the proper form for a mastersinger's song and jots it down on paper.

Beckmesser then steals the song, but Sachs doesn't stop him—he knows Beckmesser will be unable to sing it correctly. Pleased with the way things are going, Sachs promotes David from apprentice cobbler to journeyman and baptizes Walther's song, calling it "The Morning Dream Song." Sachs,

Ex. 17

Die Meistersinger, *Act I (a Bayreuth* Festspielhaus *production)*

Ex. 18

Ex. 19

Ex. 20— "The Prize Song"

Die Meistersinger, *Act III*

Walther, Eva, David, and Magdalena sing a beautiful quintet and get ready to go to the song contest.

The whole population of the town assembles for the mastersingers' trial, each guild singing its own song. The apprentices dance with a group of girls to the gayest tune ever written by Wagner (Ex. 19).

At the contest Beckmesser attempts to sing Walther's song, but makes a hash of it and is laughed down. Walther then sings the song as it should be sung (Ex. 20) and everyone shouts that the prize is to be his. All then join Sachs in singing a final chorus in praise of German art.

In *Die Meistersinger* Wagner uses his usual system of leitmotifs to let the audience in on what is really happening. But in other ways this opera is completely different from Wagner's others. It is perpetually tuneful, with gay dances and bubbling counterpoints in the orchestra. The stage is filled with action as well as with the pageantry of the festive song contest. The music is sunny—mostly in a major key, with few chromatics. The hero is Sachs, the man wise enough to know when it is proper to break rules. Beckmesser is the rigid critic or teacher who prefers correct dullness to freshness and inventiveness.

Die Meistersinger is one of the few great satirical comedies ever written for the musical stage. At the time he wrote it, Wagner was depressed, his fortunes sinking. Yet no sadness or depression is conveyed in any part of the work.

MELODY: a series of tones of different pitches arranged in a rhythmic pattern. Melody is the most expressive element in music, possibly because the first melody instrument was the human voice.

There are as many varieties of melody as there are human emotions. For this reason it is almost impossible to classify melodies. Unlike harmony, about which thousands of books have been written, melody has been the subject of very few books. Fashions in melody change from time to time and from country to country. Thus the melody of Ex. 21, which occurs in a suite Schoenberg published in 1925, is acceptable today, but a hundred years ago it would not have been considered a melody at all.

Rhythm, harmony, scales, range of instruments—all these exert a powerful influence on melody. A simple major scale can be arranged in so many different rhythms that the possibilities seem endless. Some of the forms the scale can take appear in Ex. 22a, b, and c.

Rhythm is so important that it alone can suggest a melody, as it does in the musician's game of tapping out the rhythmic pattern of a melody that someone is to guess. The purpose of a melody determines its musical character. An heroic work, for example, calls for a melody whose pitch intervals and rhythmic patterns are decisive and bold. A lullaby, whose purpose is to soothe, should have an even, gentle rhythmic pattern and flow smoothly. A waltz melody must be written in triple meter with a strong emphasis on the first beat of each measure. A lament must be slow-moving; a scherzo, light and fast. Melodies can be made in various ways. Some center around one or two tones (Ex. 23), while others cover a great deal of distance (Ex. 24).

Ex. 21— Gavotte from Suite, Op. 25, Schoenberg

Ex. 22a — Slow Movement, Concerto for Two Violins, J.S. Bach

Ex. 22b— "Joy to the World," Handel

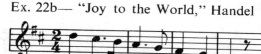

Ex. 22c— Mazurka, Op. 7, No. 1, Chopin

Ex. 23— Intermezzo, Op. 118, No. 6, Brahms

Ex. 24— *Don Juan*, Strauss

Certain kinds of melody, particularly in dance music, are built by repeating a short motive, sometimes starting each repetition on a higher or lower pitch (Ex. 25). Other melodies seem to flow on from the first couple of tones like a stream (Ex. 26).

Long melodies have a sense of direction—they seem to be moving toward a goal. This goal, or "climax tone," is a high or low tone near the end of the melody. It can be approached in a series of curves, each curve getting higher, or by a leap following a group of tones that act like a baseball pitcher's windup (Ex. 27, 28, and 29).

Ex. 25— "Air," Purcell

Andante

Ex. 26— Symphony No. 6, Schuman

Largo

Ex. 27— *Der Freischütz*, Weber

Ex. 28— Symphony No. 40 in G Minor, Mozart

Allegro

Ex. 29 — *Missa brevis*, Palestrina

San - ctus, San - ctus, San - - - - - - - - - - - - -

- - - - ctus

Ex. 30 — "Wohin?" Schubert

Ex. 31 — Chorale: Melody by Herman Schipp; used by J.S. Bach in the *Christmas Oratorio*

Ex. 32 — Sonata No. 1 for Unaccompanied Violin, J.S. Bach
Adagio

Ex. 33 — *Pastoral Symphony*, Vaughan Williams
Solo voice

to be sung freely

Some melodies are built on chord tones, as though a chord were being laid on its side (Ex. 30). Others move smoothly, step by step (Ex. 31). Triadic melodies—those built on chords—are typical of music of the Classical and Romantic periods. Scale-line melodies—those moving smoothly—are typical of the chorales sung in Lutheran churches and used in the music of the German composers of the seventeenth and early eighteenth centuries. Melodies written for instruments tend to skip around much more than melodies written for voice. It is easier for a violinist to jump his bow from string to string or a trombone player to tighten his lips and play a chord line than it is for a singer to jump his voice over large skips.

Apart from dance music, most compositions written before 1600 were for the voice. The old Gregorian chants, or plainsongs, are melodies meant to be sung without accompaniment. Their beauty lies in the balanced rise and fall of their lines. Mostly they move smoothly by steps or in small skips. When there are large skips, they are usually rising and are followed by a change of direction.

Most melodies written between 1600 and 1850 are in the major or minor scale system. They depend very much on a harmonic background and suggest the harmonic pattern of their accompaniment. After 1850, melodies became more chromatic as composers experimented with richer harmonies. As the major and minor scales gave way to a freer use of all twelve tones of the chromatic scale, the course of a melody became more and more unpredictable, as in Ex. 21, page 310. In some contemporary compositions, the melodic line jumps from instrument to instrument—a compositional device sometimes referred to as "pointillism."

"Melody" is often confused with "tune," which is a melody that is easy to remember and easy to sing. Folk songs and popular songs are almost always tunes, since they have been remembered by many people. But melody by definition includes many other types of musical expression. There are highly decorated lines and highly complex lines (Ex. 32, preceding page). Melody includes recitative—a line that follows the inflection of speech—and songs based on "breath rhythm," flowing along without any feeling of pulse (Ex. 33).

The ability to compose beautiful melodies is a great, unexplainable gift. But the gift is not enough; even a gifted composer works at his melody, whether it is a popular song or the theme of a symphony. He polishes it and tries different versions until he is satisfied that he can make it no better. In the examples on page 60 we can see how the beautiful theme of the slow movement of Beethoven's Fifth Symphony came into being.

MEMORY: an important element in the art of music. The role of memory in the work of composers is difficult to measure, but its importance for performers is obvious. Concert artists must be able to remember ten to twelve hours of solo music and ten or more hours of concertos. An opera singer must know ten or more operatic roles, each lasting several hours and including not only the words and notes but also the stage action. Opera singers usually have prompters at the front of the stage to help them, but the prompter can give only reminders—he cannot give the singer all the notes. A conductor must be able to recall all the standard works for orchestra plus a great many new works

that are not at all standard. He must know not only the notes but also which instruments play which notes, which instrument has not been playing and must be given a cue, and which instruments must be brought into prominence at a given point.

Players in a symphony orchestra do not memorize their parts. They must learn a new program each week, and they could not possibly memorize all the music they perform. Chamber-music players also usually do not memorize their parts, because of the risk of a memory failure that would disturb the whole group. String quartets memorize their programs only if they are going to play the same works many times on a concert tour.

Audiences, too, must use their memories. A composer expects us to remember the early themes of a work so they can be recognized when they reappear. He may even expect the audience to remember a theme from one movement of a work to another. If he quotes a well-known melody in his work—as Berlioz, Saint-Saëns, Liszt, and Rachmaninoff quote the melody of the plainsong Dies Irae—he expects the audience to recognize it.

Most musicians use a combination of the three main methods of memorizing. For *muscle memory* the performer plays or sings the composition so many times that it is remembered as muscular action. Persons who have a so-called *photographic memory* can memorize a page of music just by looking at it; their brain seems to take a picture of the page. In *analysis,* the third method of memorizing, the performer studies the work in great detail, often before playing it. He sees how it is put together, section by section; he learns the harmonic plan of the work and what the principal melody

Prompter at the Royal Opera House, London

tones are. Analysis calls for much musical experience, but once this method is mastered a performer can memorize long works in a short time. He also knows much more about the music.

It is always essential for the performer to memorize by ear, regardless of other methods he may use for committing music to memory. While playing one phrase, he is "hearing" the sound of the next phrase. An audience has a similar experience while listening to music, because in order to appreciate the design of a melody, one must remember the first part while the second part is being listened to.

For some people, memorization is no problem. Mozart, for instance, was able to hear a long work once or twice and then reproduce it from memory. Toscanini was forced, because of poor eyesight, to memorize all the operas and symphonies that he conducted. He remembered orchestral scores he had not looked at for twenty or thirty years. The Russian cellist Mstislav Rostropovitch has memorized every important work for cello plus its accompaniment.

A long musical work contains thousands of notes. It has instructions as to dynamics, tempo, and pedaling. It is full of subtle reminders of various types. What a complicated thing for the human brain to keep straight!

Felix Mendelssohn

MENDELSSOHN, FELIX (full name: Jacob Ludwig Felix Mendelssohn-Bartholdy; 1809–47): a brilliant composer of the early Romantic period. He was born in Hamburg, Germany, a son of well-to-do parents and grandson of Moses Mendelssohn, a famous philosopher. Having started to compose at the age of twelve, Felix within two years had written sonatas, two one-act operas, organ pieces, string quartets, and a cantata. His enthusiasm, intelligence, and intense love of Germany endeared him to the great German poet Goethe.

His first enduring work was the concert overture to *A Midsummer Night's Dream,* written in 1826. His other well-known incidental music for the play was written for a performance in 1843 at Potsdam.

Mendelssohn had a busy musical life as a composer, pianist, conductor, and educator. He traveled throughout Europe, but his favorite home-away-from-home was England, which he visited ten times. Trips to Scotland inspired him to write his descriptive overture *Fingal's Cave* (also known as the "Hebrides" Overture) and his Symphony Number Three ("Scotch"). A visit to Italy resulted in his Symphony Number Four, the "Italian."

In 1829 Mendelssohn conducted J. S. Bach's *Passion According to St. Matthew* in the first performance of a major work by

Bach since his death almost eighty years earlier. This performance led to a revival of Bach's music and to the formation of the Bach Gesellschaft (Bach Society) to publish his complete works.

Mendelssohn's brilliant conducting and ability to organize music festivals led to his appointment as director of music for the city of Düsseldorf. A few years later he became the conductor of the Leipzig Gewandhaus Orchestra, and in a short time made it the outstanding orchestra of its day.

An interest in the large choral works of Bach and Handel led Mendelssohn to write his oratorios *St. Paul* (1836) and, for presentation in England, *Elijah* (1846). The stirring solos and choruses of *Elijah* have made it one of the most popular oratorios.

After a brief and unhappy time as director of music for the king of Prussia in Berlin, Mendelssohn returned to Leipzig. In 1842 he organized the Leipzig Conservatory and soon made it the leading German music school. Here, where he acted as dean

and taught piano and composition, he was proud of the fact that he never neglected his pupils even when busy with his own composition and conducting.

When his *Concerto for Violin* was given its first performance in 1845, its passionate lyricism made it an immediate success. It has since become one of the best-loved and most-performed violin concertos (Ex. 34, 35, and 36). In the following year Mendelssohn finished his *Elijah,* performed busily as conductor and piano soloist, and found time to play with his four children. But his health, never robust, began to fail as he drove himself too hard. The death early in 1847 of his sister Fanny, a gifted composer and pianist, was a great shock to Mendelssohn, and he himself died a few months later.

In spite of his many activities Mendelssohn managed to write a great amount of music: two piano concertos, five symphonies, three sonatas, and many other works such as the *Variations sérieuses* for piano, six sonatas for organ, numerous charming songs

Top: *Mendelssohn's sister Rebecca*
Bottom: *Mendelssohn's sister Fanny (both drawings by Fanny's husband Wilhelm Hensel)*

Ex. 34— Themes from Violin Concerto

Ex. 35

Ex. 36

A watercolor by Mendelssohn

and vocal duets, and many chamber works.

Mendelssohn was a gifted artist as well as a musician. In his own way he translated sights and sounds into musical terms, believing music to be more descriptive than words. His eight books of *Lieder ohne Wörter (Songs Without Words)* are short works for piano that paint little tone pictures and have poetic titles such as "The Fleecy Cloud" and "The Sighing Wind." His style for a long time exerted an influence on German and English composers.

Mendelssohn's music was not revolutionary. It followed in the paths of Bach and Beethoven. In his scherzo movements he brought to music a lightness of touch that had never been there before. His music is always gracious—never violent or deeply tragic. It breathes goodness and happiness.

Gaetano Guadagni (at right)

MESSIAH: the best known and best loved of all oratorios, composed by George Frideric Handel. Throughout the English-speaking world many churches and choral groups have performed it every year for more than a century. Its text, taken from the Bible, was arranged by Charles Jennens, Jr., with whom Handel had previously collaborated on *Saul*. Handel wrote the music—the performance of which fills an entire evening—in twenty-four days.

Messiah (no *The* appeared in the original title) was performed for the first time on April 13, 1742, in Dublin, Ireland, where Handel was giving a series of concerts. It was an instant success. But when Handel gave it in London the following year it was received coolly. He presented it again, with a few changes, in 1745; it fared no better, and he withdrew it. It was not until four years later that he decided on a further performance, this time at London's Covent Garden, and it then went over well enough to encourage annual revivals. In 1750, Gaetano Guadagni, a young male alto, joined the cast, and the work really "caught fire." From then on, at the approach of Easter, Londoners flocked to hear it every year, and Handel himself conducted benefit performances at London's Foundling Hospital, his favorite charity.

All in all, *Messiah* was performed under Handel's personal supervision during fourteen concert seasons, each time with a few changes. At the first performance in Dublin his total vocal forces (including the soloists) numbered twenty-six; the voices were supported mainly by an organ and some violins, with trumpets and kettledrums joining in for the final choruses of Parts II and III. Later, at the Foundling Hospital performances, the singers numbered twenty-three and the orchestral players about thirty-three.

Handel was a working musician, with his eye on making the best of performance conditions as they happened to be at the moment. Preparing elaborate scores for posterity was hardly his concern. As it happened, tremendous changes of taste occurred in the eighteenth century. Handel's generation was followed by that of the sons of J. S. Bach, dedicated to Rococo sensitivity—and that generation, in turn, was followed by the early Classical generation of Haydn and Mozart. Ideas about how music "should" sound had changed, and when Mozart in 1789 was commissioned to reorchestrate Handel's *Messiah,* he greatly enriched the orchestral texture by the liberal addition of wind instruments. His skillful work has been the basis for most later editions of Handel's score because heavier orchestrations were necessary to support mammoth choruses of a size undreamed of by Handel. Twentieth-century conductors have occasionally tried to recapture the sound of Handel's original performances, but have been handicapped by a lack of reliable editions. After some careful detective work by English, Danish, and American scholars, an edition reflecting the changes Handel made over the years was finally produced by Alfred Mann in 1964.

Messiah is divided into three parts. Part I presents the prophecies of the coming of the Messiah and their realization in the birth and life of Jesus: it corresponds to the Advent and Christmas portions of the church year. Part II concerns the sacrifice of Jesus and the spreading of the Gospel corresponding to the Easter, Ascension, and Whitsun, or Pentacostal portions of the church year. With the end of Part II, the narrative portion of *Messiah* is over. Part III then presents the message of the work as a whole: the Resurrection of Christ gives man hope for his own resurrection—"We shall all be changed."

Part I begins with an orchestral overture in French style, a solemn opening in dotted-note rhythm being followed by a fugue (Ex. 37a and b). The orchestral fugue leads straight into the first section of the work (recitative, aria, and chorus), in which the promise is given of the coming of the Messiah: "Every valley shall be exalted. . . . And the glory of the Lord shall be revealed." A message of joy ("Behold, a virgin shall conceive") is followed by a reminder that "darkness shall cover the earth" before the arrival of the Messiah and the coming of light to the "people that walked in darkness." The gloom is broken by the radiant chorus "For unto us a child is born," a number much like a fast movement in any Handel concerto grosso.

We now approach the Christmas story, and to set the mood Handel gives us a gen-

The old Dublin Music Hall, where Messiah *had its first performance (in 1742)*

Ex. 37a

(Note: Handel wrote the opening rhythm as ♩. ♪ Some editions print the rhythm as it was played in Handel's time: ♩.. ♬)

Ex. 37b

A page from the original manuscript for Messiah *(the words shown are "King of Kings forever and ever. . . .")*

tle pastoral symphony to be quietly played by a few solo strings (Ex. 38). Its pedal points and lulling Siciliano rhythm set the scene for the angel to announce to the shepherds the birth of Jesus.

The vision of the shepherds and the angel's Christmas message make up the only stretch of storytelling based directly on one of the Gospels (Luke). Here, Handel was anxious to achieve directness and innocence, and so in the Dublin performance he gave "There were shepherds abiding in the fields," not to his Italian operatic star, but to an English woman with a plainer voice; and in later performances he had it sung by a boy soprano. Part I ends with a section on Jesus' pastorate on earth. Its most moving moment, the aria "He shall feed his flock," is a gentle Sicilian folk melody. Handel closes Part I not with a rousing final chorus but gently with the airy "His yoke is easy."

In Part II Handel tells the story of Christ's suffering and his sacrifice—not directly, as in German Baroque passions, but indirectly, through the visions of Isaiah and the Psalmist. Minor keys are used to express the dark moments of Easter week and the loneliness of Christ on the cross.

After Christ's ascension ("Thou art gone up on high"), the evangelists go out to spread the message. This is defiantly resisted by the world, as we learn in the bass's "Rage" aria, in Baroque opera style, "Why do the nations so furiously rage together?" But the rebellion is crushed ("Thou shalt break them"), and Part II concludes with a jubilant "Hallelujah!" This is Handel's most famous chorus, and the one for which George II rose from his seat, setting a precedent that audiences have observed ever since. It represents a masterly combination of two techniques of choral writing, with large blocks of sound (Ex. 39a, next page) alternating with stretches of fugal writing (Ex. 39b) and with the sounds of trumpets and timpani adding to the triumphant mood. With this emphatic close, Handel not only ends Part II but the entire storytelling portion of *Messiah*.

Part III is short. It has no story to tell but concentrates instead on the *meaning* of the Messiah's coming. It opens with a soprano solo, "I know that my Redeemer liveth," in which Handel expresses the certainty of faith, and ends with three choruses affirming that the Christ's sacrifice was not in vain.

It is difficult to pick outstanding sections of this work. Each aria, chorus, and orchestral part is a masterful example of Handel's genius and his ability to think on a large epic scale. The orchestra, which has an active part throughout, has two sections in which it has the stage to itself: the overture and the "Pastoral Symphony." It is the chorus, however, that overshadows soloists and orchestra. Like the voice of all people it comments on the soloists and sounds the triumphant and positive note of Christian faith, from its first entrance to the final fugal "Amen" chorus (Ex. 40).

Because listeners and choral singers have so loved Handel's *Messiah,* they have too often allowed themselves to stop there. There is only one *Messiah,* but an appreciation of its glories can also lead one to explore Handel's other great choral works—to come to know the drama of *Saul,* of *Israel in Egypt,* and of *Samson,* and the musical pageantry of *Solomon.*

Ex. 38

Ex. 39a

Ex. 39b

Ex. 40 — Final Chorus

Musical Instruments Through the Ages

BY Emanuel Winternitz   ILLUSTRATED BY Harry McNaught

"Pleasant to the ear as well as the eye" was a favorite motto painted on keyboard instruments of the Renaissance such as harpsichords and spinettinas. The main functions of a musical instrument could not be described more vividly. First, it is a tool: a mechanical contrivance made for producing organized sound—music. As such it has to obey the stern, immutable laws of acoustics. It must be made of certain materials and in certain shapes. Wind instruments —flutes, for example—must have a certain length, bore, thickness of walls, etc., and their finger holes must be exactly spaced according to certain proportions. Fiddles and lutes must be made of certain kinds of wood to make the fibers vibrate as freely as possible. The strings are stopped by fingers or keys at certain points to obtain the tones of a certain scale, and their spacing is again determined by mathematical ratios. Likewise, the tone of bells and drums depends on their material, shape, and the thickness of their walls, the tension of the skin, and many other factors. In short, the tool is determined and shaped by its function.

On the other hand, an instrument is more than a tool and an application of acoustical laws; it invites decoration, and, indeed, from the time of primitive societies up to our days, a wealth of decoration—carving, painting, inlay, gilding—was lavished on instruments wherever their functional shape permitted. But often enough the function itself created shapes so attractive and convincing that no surface decoration could improve them. An orchestral horn with its elegant coils is a feast for the eye, and the stunning beauty of a master violin is so perfect and logical that any accessory decoration, such as carved reliefs or inlays or painting, would hamper rather than enhance its visual appeal.

The visual beauty added to the functional shape is a heritage of times before the dawn of history when the magical importance of musical instruments for rituals and ceremonies was enhanced by their appearance—for instance, by their imitating the shape of totem animals. Later, in historic times, the visual aspect and appealing decoration added to the functional shape was determined by the use of instruments in processions, feasts, and stage plays, and by the fact that they were made as "works of art" (for instance, the treasure cabinets of the Renaissance).

Music, like the other arts, constantly changes its character throughout the centuries—sometimes slowly and almost imperceptibly; sometimes violently, in sudden revolutions against the established style. The instruments of the past—of the early and late medieval periods, of the Renaissance and Baroque orchestras, and of the Romantic era—were different in many regards because they served different purposes, different textures of music, and different predilections for tone color.

A few brief words on the problem of *classification* may help the reader to browse through the illustrations, as a compass through the amazing and confusing wilderness of shapes and sounds. The generally accepted classification distinguishes between:

1) Vibrating strings (stringed instruments or chordo-phones).   2) Vibrating air columns (wind instruments or aerophones).   3) Vibrating membranes, as in drums with skin heads (membranophones).   4) Matter vibrating without the aid of strings, air, or membranes (idiophones or autophones), as in bells, gongs, triangles, chimes, rattles, xylophones, musical glasses, and celestas.

Chordophones, or stringed instruments, are usually divided according to the way in which they are played (plucked, struck, or bowed strings), or according to shape, into four general groups:

a) Lutes, in the broad sense of this term, have a sound box terminating in a neck which serves both as a handle and as a device for extending the strings beyond the sound box. Against this neck, the strings are stopped by the fingers. There are plucked lutes such as the lute in the narrower sense of this word, the guitars, citterns, mandolins, and others; and bowed lutes such as violins, viols, violoncellos, and the like.
b) Harps are instruments whose strings are invariably plucked and do not run parallel to the sound board but vertically away from it towards the neck.
c) Lyres have strings which run parallel to the sound board and continue beyond it to the crossbar (or yoke) which is held by two arms that project from the sound box.
d) Zithers have neither neck nor yoke; the strings are stretched across the upper surface of a wooden box. Zithers have many forms, from small types placed upon the lap, up to large keyboard instruments including the pianoforte.

The wind instruments are usually divided into woodwind and "brass" instruments, a practical classification that suffices for the modern orchestra but does not do justice to the functional characteristics and the great variety of materials that have been used for making such instruments in various periods. A more scientific classification would divide the wind instruments into:

a) Flutes or flue-blown instruments—in which the air stream is shaped and directed by a "flue," either the lips of the player, as in vertical and transverse flutes, or a canal mouthpiece, as in recorders.
b) Reed-vibrated instruments—those pipes equipped with a double reed, such as the oboe and bassoon, or with a single reed, such as the clarinet and saxophone.
c) Lip-vibrated instruments—those in which the player's lips themselves function as vibrator, in combination with a special cup-shaped mouthpiece, such as trumpets and horns—in short, all instruments that are commonly called "brass."

The following selection of pictures is meant to invite the reader to ponder how, in many periods of European instrumental music and in many families of historic instruments, the visual appeal is integrated with the functional shape, and to understand the evolution through the ages.

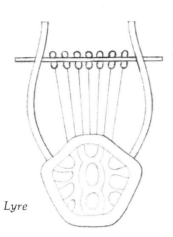

Lyre

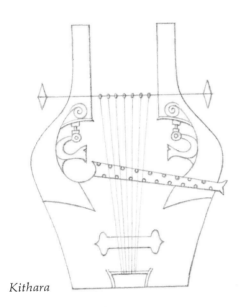

Kithara

The ancient Greeks had comparatively few string instruments. The most important by far were the lyre ("lyra") and the kithara. The lyra consisted of a shallow wooden bowl covered by a sound board made out of skin or a tortoise shell. Two wooden arms or animal horns were attached to the bowl. They carried a horizontal crossbar to which the upper ends of the strings were fastened.

The kithara was of a much more complicated build. It had a joined wooden body with front, back, and side walls, and broad, hollow arms.

Kithara player on oil flask,
Attica, 5th century B.C.

I

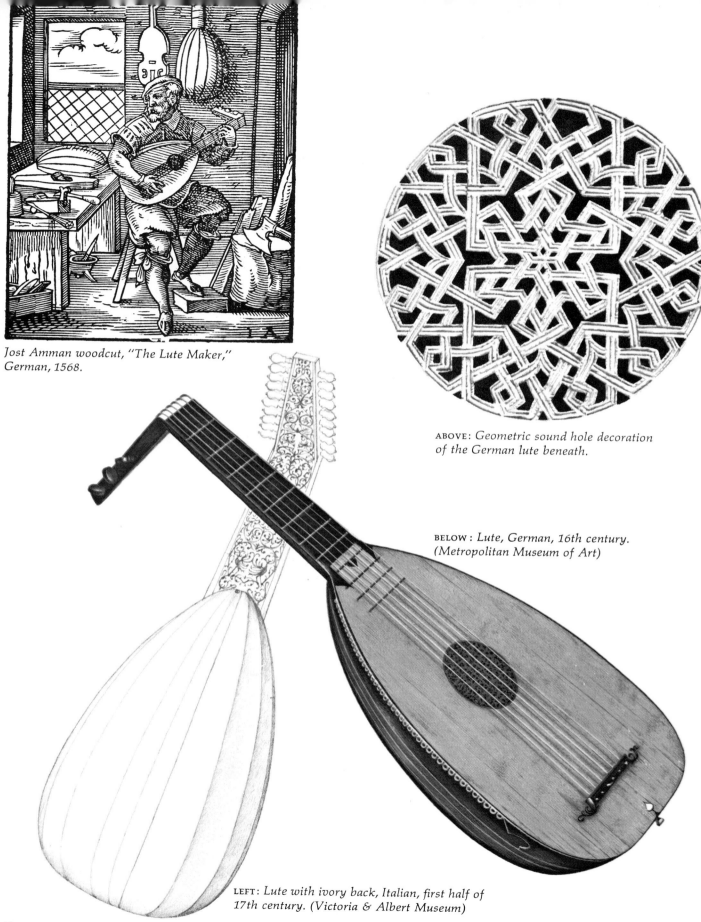

Jost Amman woodcut, "The Lute Maker,"
German, 1568.

ABOVE: *Geometric sound hole decoration
of the German lute beneath.*

BELOW: *Lute, German, 16th century.
(Metropolitan Museum of Art)*

LEFT: *Lute with ivory back, Italian, first half of
17th century. (Victoria & Albert Museum)*

II

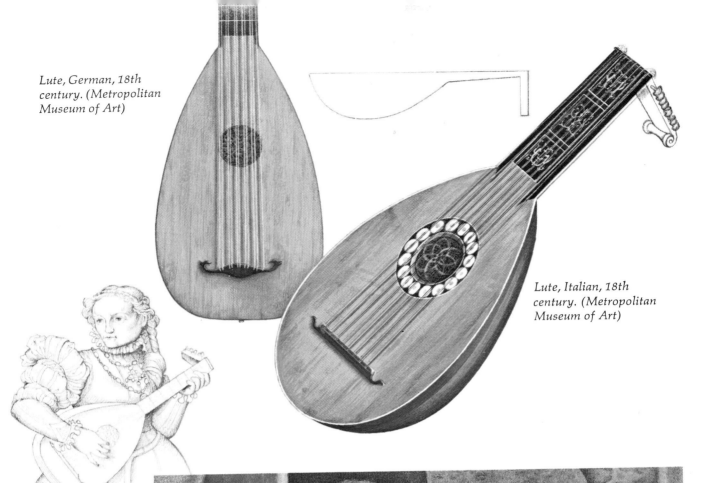

Lute, German, 18th century. (Metropolitan Museum of Art)

Lute, Italian, 18th century. (Metropolitan Museum of Art)

Woodcut of lady with lute, Tobias Stimmer, 1539-1585.

Lute-playing angel from "The Presentation of Christ," by Carpaccio, in the Accademia di Belle Arti, Venice, 1510.

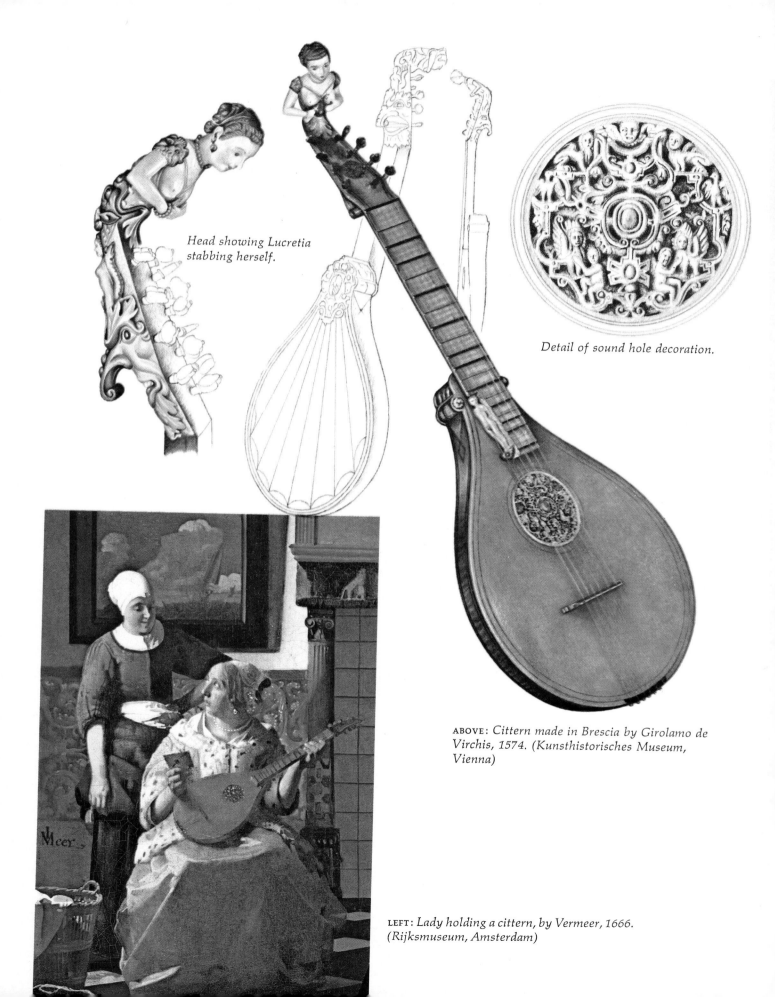

Head showing Lucretia
stabbing herself.

Detail of sound hole decoration.

ABOVE: *Cittern made in Brescia by Girolamo de Virchis, 1574. (Kunsthistorisches Museum, Vienna)*

LEFT: *Lady holding a cittern, by Vermeer, 1666. (Rijksmuseum, Amsterdam)*

Lady with theorboed lute and bass viol, by van der Helst, 1662. (Metropolitan Museum of Art)

Two archlutes (combining stopped gut strings with wire bass strings).
LEFT: *Chitarrone.*
RIGHT: *Theorbo, Italy, 18th century.* (Metropolitan Museum of Art)

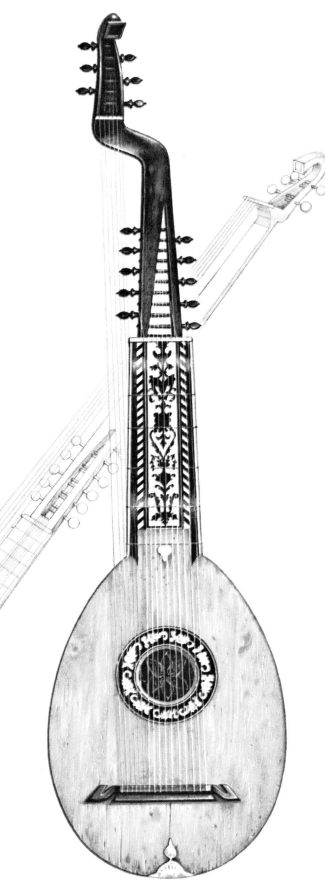

Lira da braccio, Italy, 16th century. (Musical Instrument Museum, Brussels)

Lira da braccio made in 1511 by Giovanni d'Andrea, Verona (5 melody strings, 2 drones). (Kunsthistorisches Museum, Vienna)

BELOW: *Viol diagram (front elevation and right-hand side view).*

VIOLA DA GAMBA: The viol was the principal bowed instrument from the end of the 15th century until far into the 17th century. It differs from the violin by its sloping shoulders, deep ribs, broad neck, its "c" or flame holes, its numerous strings (6 or 7), its inner construction, and its tuning.

High treble viol, France, 18th century. (Metropolitan Museum of Art)

Viola da gamba (bass viol), France, 18th century. (Metropolitan Museum of Art)

Alto or small tenor viol, German, 17th century. (Metropolitan Museum of Art)

VII

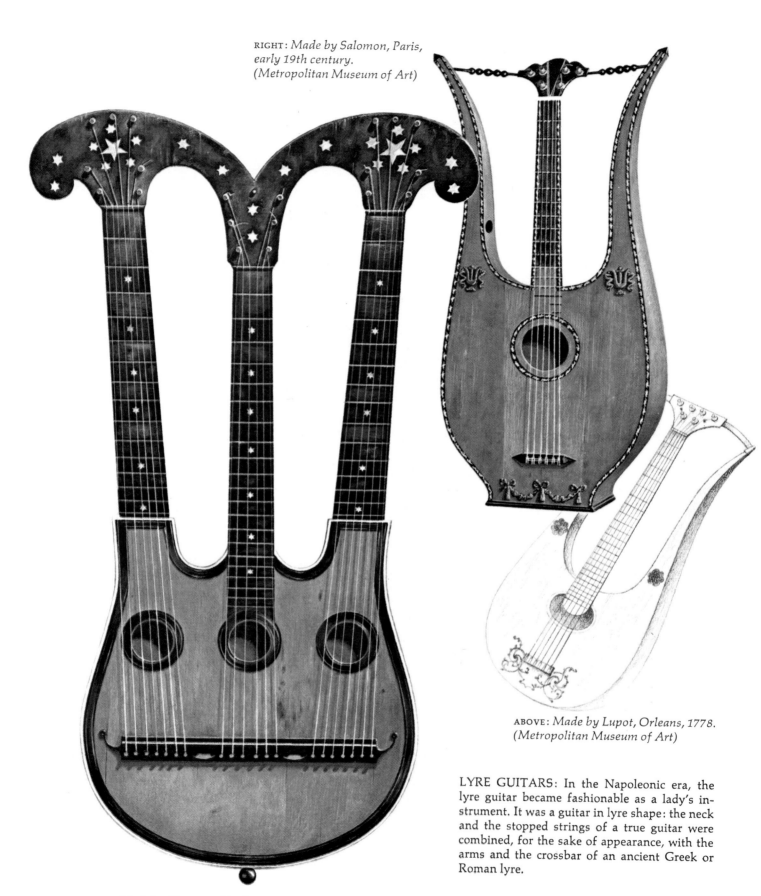

LYRE GUITARS: In the Napoleonic era, the lyre guitar became fashionable as a lady's instrument. It was a guitar in lyre shape: the neck and the stopped strings of a true guitar were combined, for the sake of appearance, with the arms and the crossbar of an ancient Greek or Roman lyre.

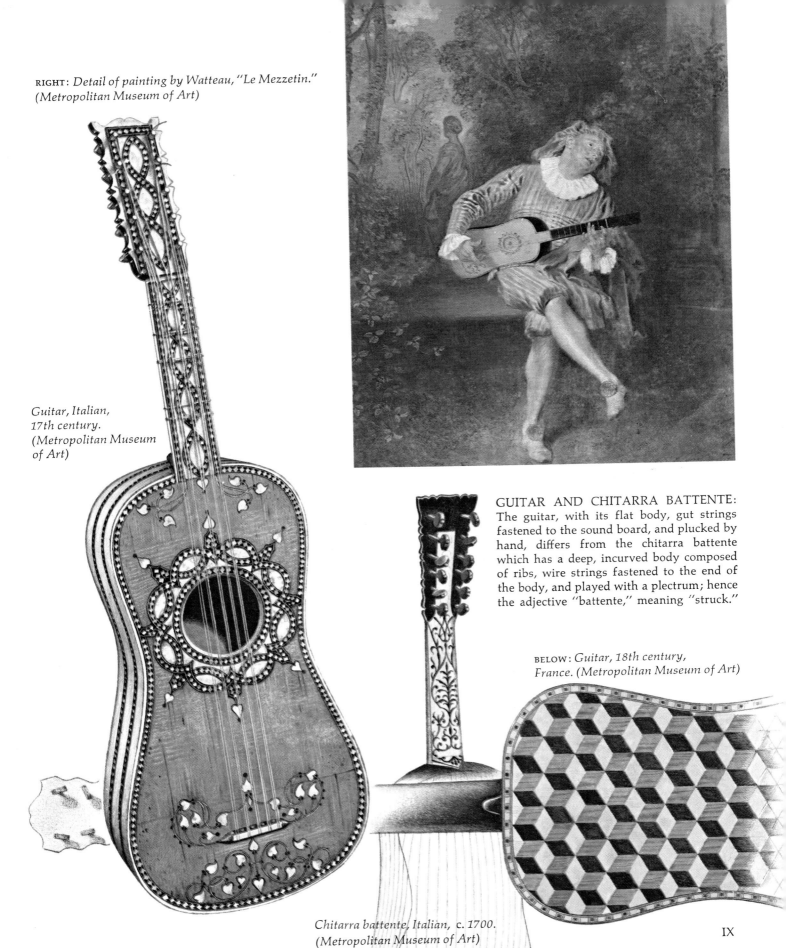

RIGHT: *Detail of painting by Watteau, "Le Mezzetin."* (Metropolitan Museum of Art)

Guitar, Italian, 17th century. (Metropolitan Museum of Art)

GUITAR AND CHITARRA BATTENTE: The guitar, with its flat body, gut strings fastened to the sound board, and plucked by hand, differs from the chitarra battente which has a deep, incurved body composed of ribs, wire strings fastened to the end of the body, and played with a plectrum; hence the adjective "battente," meaning "struck."

BELOW: *Guitar, 18th century, France.* (Metropolitan Museum of Art)

Chitarra battente, Italian, c. 1700. (Metropolitan Museum of Art)

IX

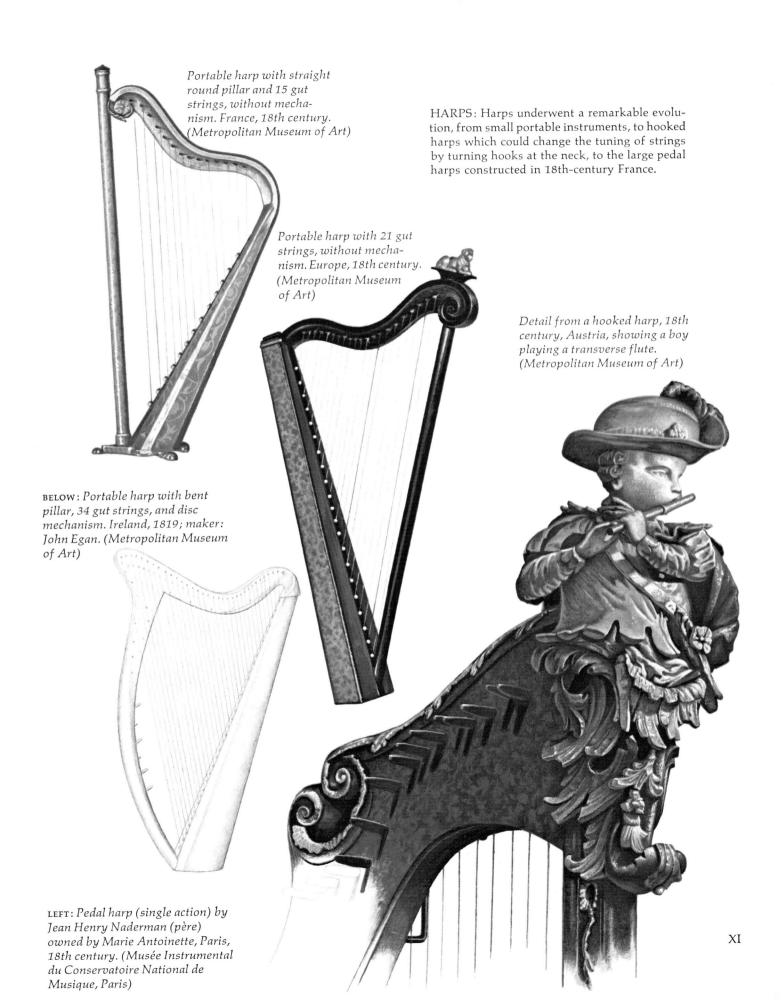

Portable harp with straight round pillar and 15 gut strings, without mechanism. France, 18th century. (Metropolitan Museum of Art)

HARPS: Harps underwent a remarkable evolution, from small portable instruments, to hooked harps which could change the tuning of strings by turning hooks at the neck, to the large pedal harps constructed in 18th-century France.

Portable harp with 21 gut strings, without mechanism. Europe, 18th century. (Metropolitan Museum of Art)

Detail from a hooked harp, 18th century, Austria, showing a boy playing a transverse flute. (Metropolitan Museum of Art)

BELOW: *Portable harp with bent pillar, 34 gut strings, and disc mechanism. Ireland, 1819; maker: John Egan. (Metropolitan Museum of Art)*

LEFT: *Pedal harp (single action) by Jean Henry Naderman (père) owned by Marie Antoinette, Paris, 18th century. (Musée Instrumental du Conservatoire National de Musique, Paris)*

XI

KITS (*Pochettes, Taschengeigen*): Kits were miniature fiddles, used by dancing masters, which could be accommodated in a pocket when not being played. Their narrow form with a long neck, often terminating in a carved or sickle-shaped head, stemmed from the Renaissance rebec, which was also used to accompany dances. Since the appearance of the kit was often more important than its tonal quality, it could and did assume many playful and even grotesque forms.

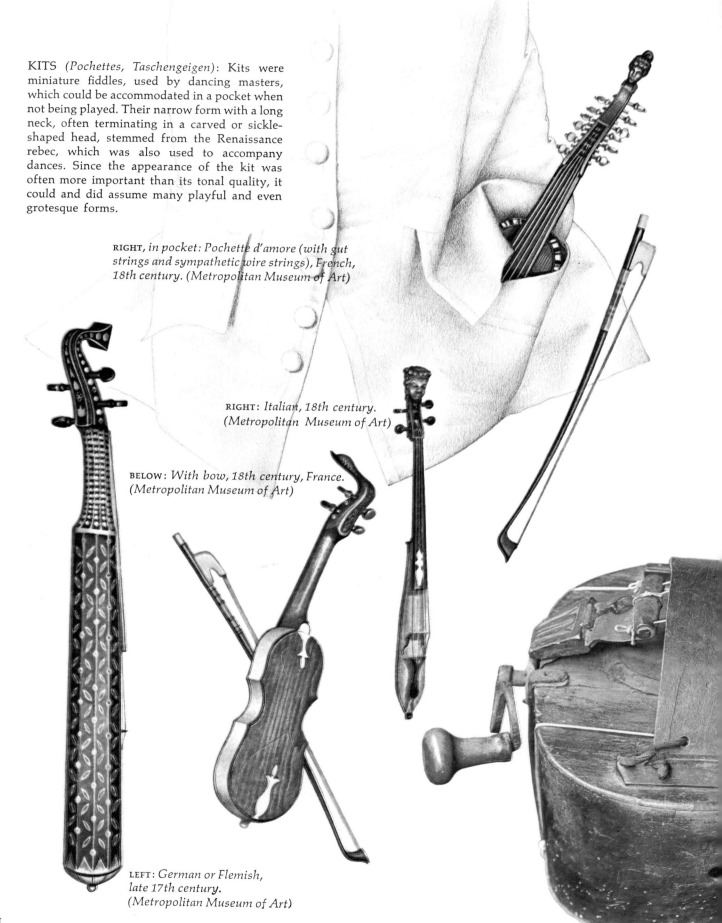

RIGHT, *in pocket: Pochette d'amore (with gut strings and sympathetic wire strings), French, 18th century. (Metropolitan Museum of Art)*

RIGHT: *Italian, 18th century. (Metropolitan Museum of Art)*

BELOW: *With bow, 18th century, France. (Metropolitan Museum of Art)*

LEFT: *German or Flemish, late 17th century. (Metropolitan Museum of Art)*

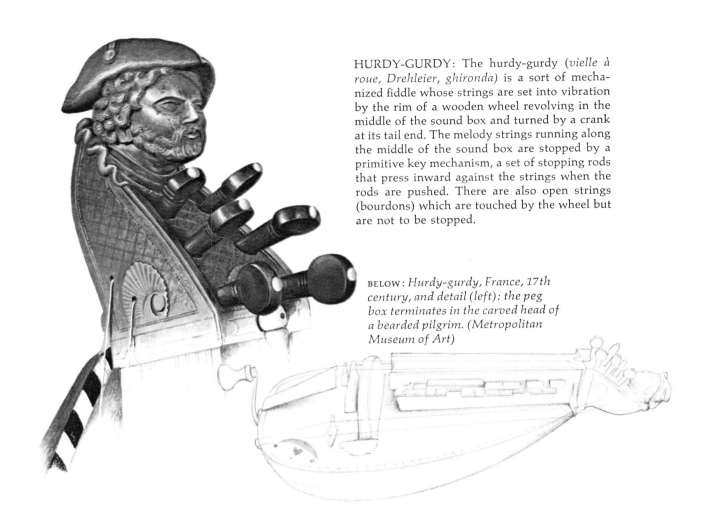

HURDY-GURDY: The hurdy-gurdy (*vielle à roue, Drehleier, ghironda*) is a sort of mechanized fiddle whose strings are set into vibration by the rim of a wooden wheel revolving in the middle of the sound box and turned by a crank at its tail end. The melody strings running along the middle of the sound box are stopped by a primitive key mechanism, a set of stopping rods that press inward against the strings when the rods are pushed. There are also open strings (bourdons) which are touched by the wheel but are not to be stopped.

BELOW: *Hurdy-gurdy, France, 17th century, and detail (left): the peg box terminates in the carved head of a bearded pilgrim. (Metropolitan Museum of Art)*

Hurdy-gurdy, Spain, 17th century. (Museo Municipale di Musica, Barcelona)

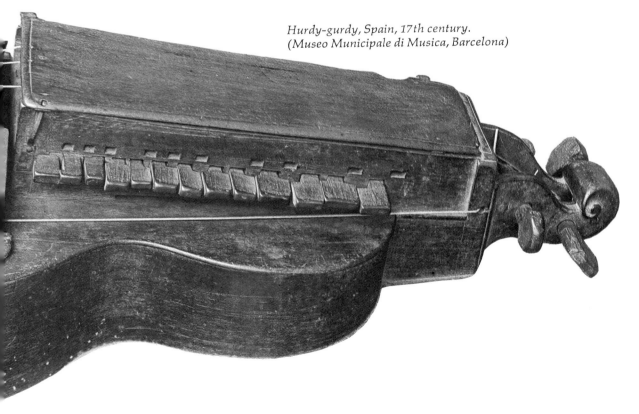

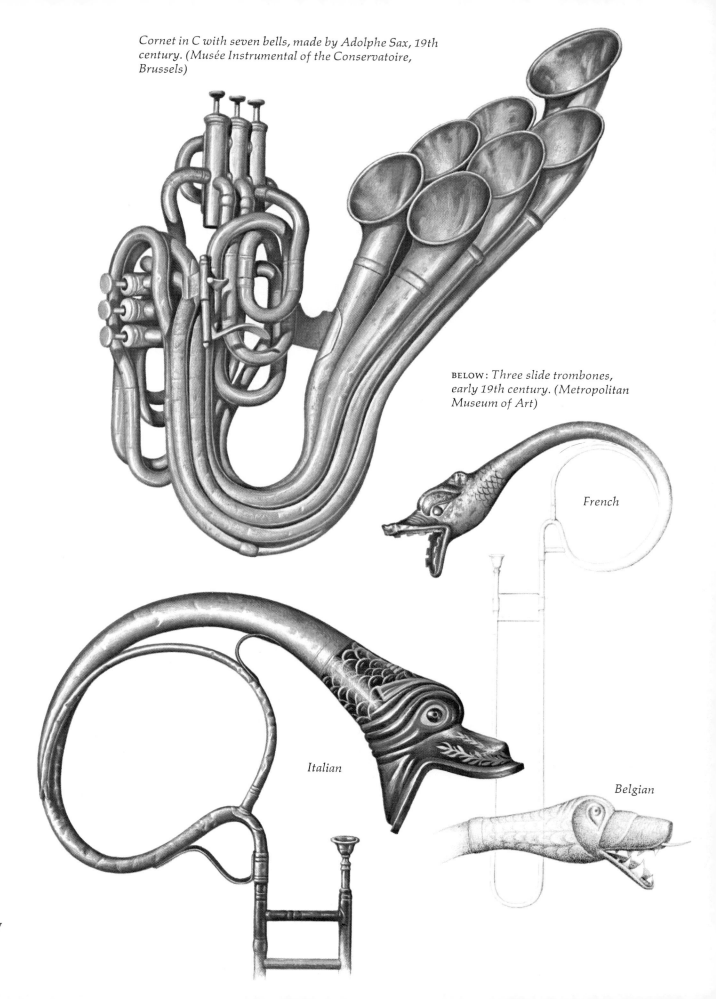

Cornet in C with seven bells, made by Adolphe Sax, 19th century. (Musée Instrumental of the Conservatoire, Brussels)

BELOW: *Three slide trombones, early 19th century. (Metropolitan Museum of Art)*

French

Italian

Belgian

XIV

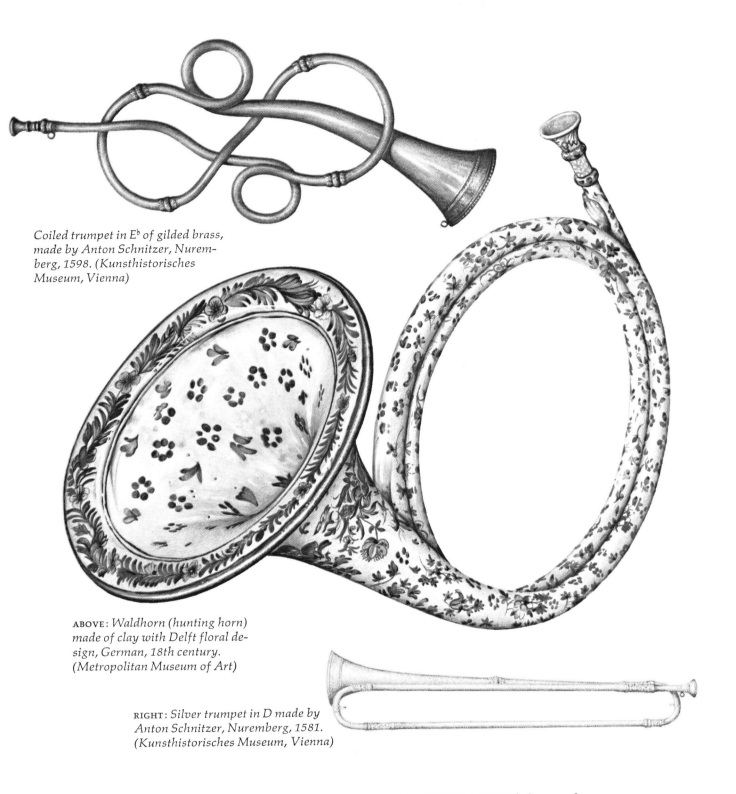

Coiled trumpet in E♭ of gilded brass, made by Anton Schnitzer, Nuremberg, 1598. (Kunsthistorisches Museum, Vienna)

ABOVE: *Waldhorn (hunting horn) made of clay with Delft floral design, German, 18th century. (Metropolitan Museum of Art)*

RIGHT: *Silver trumpet in D made by Anton Schnitzer, Nuremberg, 1581. (Kunsthistorisches Museum, Vienna)*

FANFARE TRUMPETS belong to the most exquisitely decorated instruments which have come out of that famous center of brass instrument makers, Nuremberg. Anton Schnitzer was a member of a family outstanding in this craft.

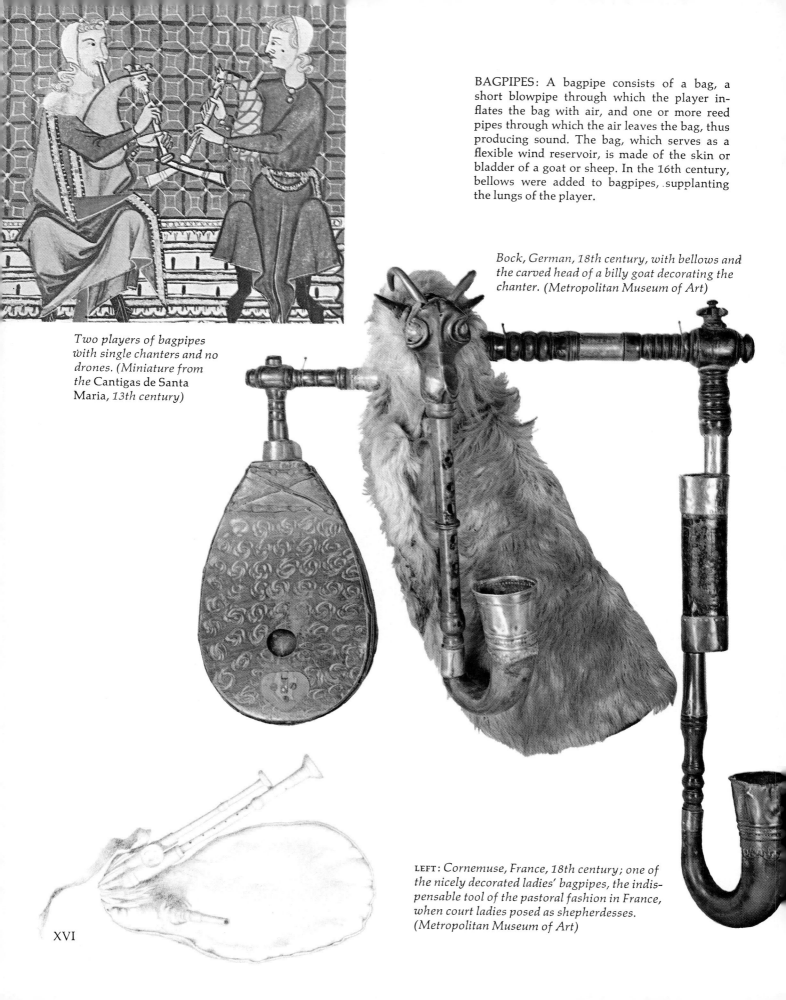

BAGPIPES: A bagpipe consists of a bag, a short blowpipe through which the player inflates the bag with air, and one or more reed pipes through which the air leaves the bag, thus producing sound. The bag, which serves as a flexible wind reservoir, is made of the skin or bladder of a goat or sheep. In the 16th century, bellows were added to bagpipes, supplanting the lungs of the player.

Bock, German, 18th century, with bellows and the carved head of a billy goat decorating the chanter. (Metropolitan Museum of Art)

Two players of bagpipes with single chanters and no drones. (Miniature from the Cantigas de Santa Maria, *13th century)*

LEFT: *Cornemuse, France, 18th century; one of the nicely decorated ladies' bagpipes, the indispensable tool of the pastoral fashion in France, when court ladies posed as shepherdesses. (Metropolitan Museum of Art)*

XVI

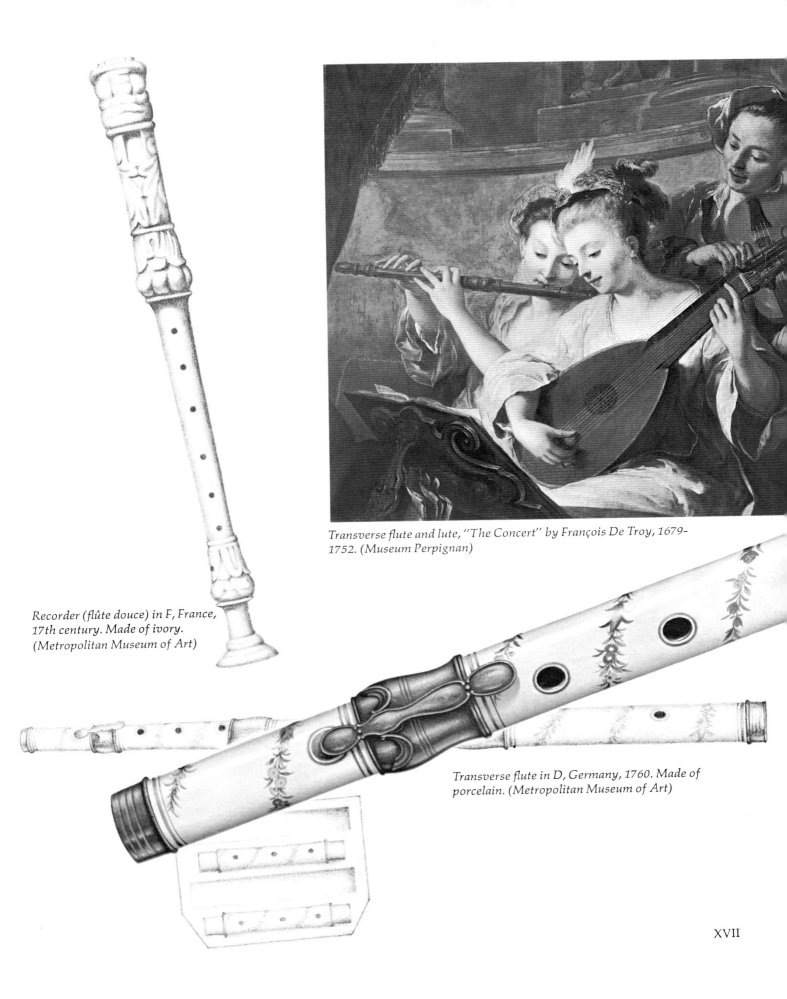

Recorder (flûte douce) in F, France, 17th century. Made of ivory. (Metropolitan Museum of Art)

Transverse flute and lute, "The Concert" by François De Troy, 1679-1752. (Museum Perpignan)

Transverse flute in D, Germany, 1760. Made of porcelain. (Metropolitan Museum of Art)

XVII

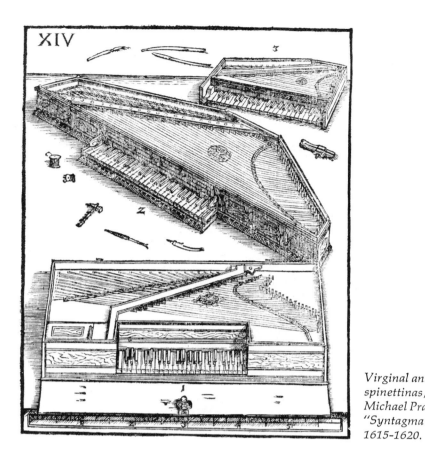

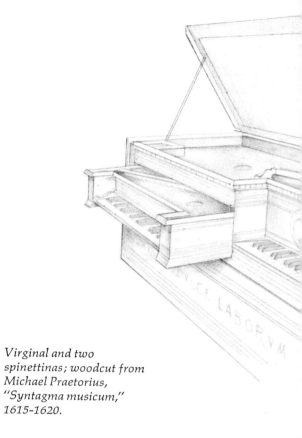

*Virginal and two
spinettinas; woodcut from
Michael Praetorius,
"Syntagma musicum,"
1615–1620.*

*Painting from the inside of the lid of the
Ruckers double virginal. There are depictions
of open air games, entertainments, and concerts.
(Metropolitan Museum of Art)*

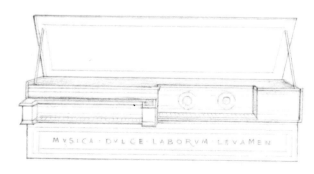

Double virginal

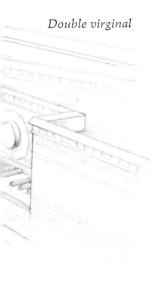

THE VIRGINAL was an instrument with a receding keyboard and a mechanism plucking the strings by quills cut from bird feathers or little pieces of buffalo leather.

This example, made by Hans Ruckers in Antwerp, 1581, a double virginal with two keyboards, is one of the earliest specimens known. The second smaller instrument—an "ottavino," is placed in a drawer so that both keyboards appear side by side. It can be removed and placed on top of the sound board of the large instrument for combining the sound of both sets of strings.

Clavicytherium, Italian, early 17th century. "Clavicytherium" was an old name for an upright harpsichord, used as early as 1511. (Metropolitan Museum of Art)

Lady playing a harpsichord, by Jan Steen, 1626-1679. (National Gallery, London)

Harpsichord supported and flanked by allegorical figures, Italy, mid-17th century. (Metropolitan Museum of Art)

XX

Harpsichord, Rome, mid-17th century. (Metropolitan Museum of Art)

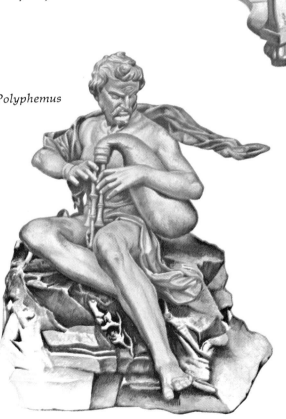

RIGHT: *Harpsichord with two keyboards, made by the famous maker Joannes Couchet, Antwerp, 1650. (Metropolitan Museum of Art)*

Allegorical figure of Polyphemus playing the bagpipe.

Calcant (man working organ bellows). Detail from Michael Praetorius, "Organographia," 1618.

Interior of church of the Monastery of Saint Florian; organ begun in 1770 by F. X. Chrismann.

"The Concert," detail from tapestry, early 16th century. (Musée des Gobelins, Paris)

THE ORGAN: The queen of the instruments had a long history, from ancient Roman times when it was used as an instrument in the circus, up to its glorious role as the church instrument par excellence in the Renaissance, the Baroque, and still today.

RIGHT: *Detail from the famous organ in the Grote Kerk, Haarlem, Holland, by Christian Mulder, 1735-1738.*

Pianoforte made by Erard & Co., London, c. 1840. One of the most beautifully decorated pianofortes ever made, quite different from the small, black, and inconspicuous first instruments with a hammer mechanism invented by Bartolommeo Cristofori in Florence, about 1706. (Metropolitan Museum of Art)

MESTO: an Italian word meaning "sad" or "woeful." It is not so much an indication of tempo or dynamics as an indication of mood. Béla Bartók's Sixth Quartet opens with a solo statement by the viola marked "mesto."

METER: the measure of the number of pulses from the first beat of one measure to the first beat of the next. There are two basic meters: duple and triple. From these all other meters—4, 5, 6, 9, and so on—can be made. The meter of a composition is usually indicated by a time signature at the beginning of the work.

Meter is not something superimposed, defined only by bar-lines. It happens because melodic and harmonic accents recur regularly. Satie wrote his *Gnossienes* without bar-lines because he wanted the performer to feel the flow of the music; yet the repeated patterns in both melody and harmony represent an unmistakable organization of the music in units of four beats (Ex. 3, page 501). A Chopin mazurka, on the other hand, could have a bar-line after every four counts, and yet the "threeness" of the music would emerge in performance.

Meter is one means by which types of musical works can be identified. An important characteristic of waltzes and sarabands is that they are written in triple meter. Marches, polkas, and tangos owe much of their quality to their duple meter. The liveliness of gigues and tarantellas derives to a large extent from their 6/8 meter.

Meter is, then, an organizing factor in music. A composer can set up a meter and work strictly within it, or he can exploit it in other ways. Cross-rhythms and syncopations, which add interest to the rhythmic design of music, can be made by putting a musical idea into a meter different from that of the time signature. Brahms in many of his works seems to delight in throwing the listener off-balance by using syncopations and contrasting meters together. In the following example the opening phrase clearly defines the triple meter of the time signature, but soon both melody and bass have taken on the feeling of a two-count meter which syncopates against the established triple meter (Ex. 41).

Now notice how Beethoven in his "Eroica" Symphony moves toward a dramatic climax by shortening measure lengths from three counts to two (Ex. 42, page 322).

Meter probably has always been associated with dance music, in all periods of time and in all parts of the world. Vocal music, on the other hand, is more likely to be thought of in terms of the singer's breathing. Vocal music of the Renaissance was measured in sentences and phrases, like prose, rather than in the regular flow of accented and non-accented words, like poetry. But as composers became interested in poetic meters, their music came more and

Ex. 41— Capriccio, Op. 116, No. 1, Brahms

Ex. 42 – First Movement, Symphony No. 3, Beethoven

Ex. 43 – "Revercie du printemps," Claude Le Jeune

Ex. 44 – First Movement, Piano Sonata, Copland

more under the dominance of meter. By faithfully following the heavy (long) and light (short) pattern of a poem, a composer could arrive at a melodic line with constantly changing meters, as did Claude Le Jeune (1528–1600) in Ex. 43.

Composers of our own time have changed meters and used the "uneven" meters of 5, 7, and 11 to achieve restless, nervous effects and to avoid what they have felt to be the "square" meters of Classical music. When writing a work in changing meters, the composer also changes the time signature as necessary (Ex. 44).

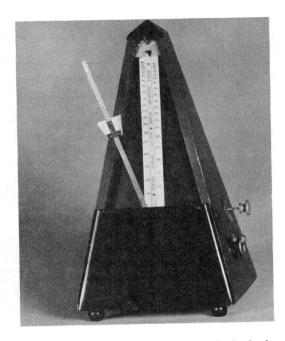

METRONOME: a kind of musical clock, used to set the rate of speed of a musical composition.

For hundreds of years composers had no way of telling performers how fast to play or sing. They could just hope that a fast dance would not be played like a lament, or a lament like a fast dance. About the year 1600, composers did begin to write tempo directions on their music. Since the composers were Italian, they used such Italian words as *allegro, adagio,* and *presto.* But even these indications were not very accurate. One performer's idea of fast might be another performer's medium-fast.

Finally, after many experiments, a machine known as the metronome came into use. Two men invented it between 1813 and 1817—a Dutch inventor named Winkel and Johannes Maelzel, a friend of Beethoven. Maelzel patented his invention and had the help of Beethoven in making its value known to other composers. Beethoven was the first composer to use the metronome to give an accurate indication of tempo.

A metronome is a device that has a short metal or wooden pendulum with a fixed weight on the bottom and a sliding weight on top. As the pendulum moves, a small wheel at the base of the device also moves, making a click at the end of each swing. By moving the top weight downward, one can make the pendulum go faster. The pendulum is calibrated for clicks per minute. Until recently it was kept in motion by means of a spring that was tightened by winding, like a clock spring, but today most metronomes are electric.

The metronome mark appears at the beginning of a piece of music. It reads something like this: M.M. ♩ = 120. This means that the pendulum will make 120 clicks per minute. M.M. ♩ = c. 100 means *circa,* or around, 100 beats per minute. A metronome marking of M.M. ♩ = 112–128 gives the performer a certain amount of latitude within the range of these tempo marks. In today's scores the M.M. is usually omitted.

MEYERBEER, GIACOMO (1791–1864): composer of highly theatrical operas that helped establish the style of French grand opera. Meyerbeer was born in Berlin. A child prodigy as a pianist—he was a pupil of Clementi's—he turned to the study of composition with Abbé Vogler. Deciding to learn more about writing operas, he went to Italy. Modeling his style on Rossini's, he met with success. Paris was the opera center of Europe and it was there that Meyerbeer found his own dramatic style. From 1831 until his death in Paris, he dominated the European opera theater. His *Robert le Diable* (1831), *Les Huguenots* (1836), *Le Prophète* (1849), *Dinorah* (1859), and *L'Africaine* (1865) combined spectacle, slightly shocking story, strong long-line melodies, and colorful orchestration which stirred the Parisian audiences and brought them in large numbers to the opera. His vivid Romantic approach to opera, and his great public success, did much to influence the work of Wagner and Berlioz. Wagner later repudiated Meyerbeer, even though Meyerbeer encouraged the young man by producing his *Rienzi.*

Meyerbeer wrote little other than operas. His four *Frackeltänze* (dances) for band are occasionally performed, but Meyerbeer was the master of the grand statement, for which he needed the vast resources that only the opera could provide.

Giacomo Meyerbeer

MEZZO: an Italian word meaning "middle" or "half," used ordinarily in combination with other words.

Mezzo forte (mf) and *mezzo piano (mp)* are marks of dynamics, indicating "halfway between loud and soft."

A *mezzo-soprano* or "mezzo" is a woman whose voice has a range almost as high as a soprano's and almost as low as an alto's. Mezzo-soprano voices are usually rich in quality and suitable for big dramatic roles in opera. The part of Carmen in Bizet's opera is written for a mezzo-soprano, although it is often sung by sopranos who have a wide range.

The *mezzo-soprano clef* is a C clef on the second line. It is found in old music for voices.

Mezzo voce means "with only half the power of the voice"—almost a croon.

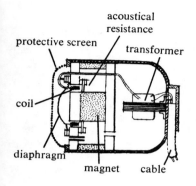

A Coil Microphone

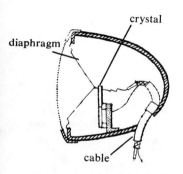

A Crystal Microphone

MICROPHONE: a device that transforms sound waves into electrical energy so that they can be sent out by telephone or radio, or stored on magnetic tape, sound film, or records.

All microphones contain a thin sheet of metal, or diaphragm, that vibrates when hit by sound waves. The vibrations exert pressure on a box of carbon granules (in the telephone), a crystal such as Rochelle salt (in the crystal microphone), a coil of wire (in the electrodynamic microphone), a metallic ribbon (in the velocity microphone), or a simple condenser (in the condenser microphone). The changing pressure of the diaphragm on the material causes a greater or lesser flow of electric current through the material. This varying current represents the original sound waves. It can be fed to an amplifier for conversion back into sound, as in a public-address loudspeaker, or it can be used to make a recording on tape, film, or disc.

Some microphones are one-directional: they will pick up only the sounds that hit the diaphragm from the front. This type is often used in radio and TV interviews on the street, since it will keep out much of the background noise. Other microphones are omni-directional: they will pick up sound from all angles. In recordings, a sound engineer will use one or more omni-directional microphones for over-all sounds of an orchestra and possibly add one or more directional microphones to pick up special instruments, particularly soft-sounding ones such as the flute.

MILHAUD, DARIUS (1892–1974): a prolific and highly original French composer. Born in Aix-en-Provence, Milhaud left home at the age of seventeen to enter the Paris Conservatory. Soon discovering that his talents were compositional rather than violinistic, he threw himself into creative work with the incredible energy that was to result in a large catalog of works in every form. These ranged from colossal operas such as *Cristophe Colomb* (1928) to operas lasting only eight minutes; from experimental works using films and electronic

sounds to tuneful works such as the popular *Suite provençale* (1937) and *Scaramouche* (1937); from the conventional chamber-music forms of the string quartet (of which he has written fifteen) to *Cocktail*, for voice and three clarinets (1921). Milhaud's seeming ability to write under almost any conditions is shown in his *Une Journée* (1946), a collection of delightful piano pieces, all written in one day. His *Concertino d'hiver* (1953) for trombone and string orchestra was composed during a five-day crossing of the Atlantic.

Milhaud's wide-ranging tastes have been influenced by the many places in which he has lived and worked. Following his graduation from the conservatory he spent two years in Brazil, with light duties as secretary to the French minister, Paul Claudel. As poet and librettist Claudel supplied Milhaud with texts for songs, cantatas, and operas. Milhaud reveled in the exotic popular folk music of Brazil, later capturing his impressions of Brazilian music in his *Saudades do Brasil* (*Souvenirs and Memories of Brazil,* 1921).

Returning to Paris, Milhaud became a member of the creative group headed by Satie, Cocteau, and Picasso that was setting the artistic world on its ear. Anti-Romantic and anti-German, this active collection of artists emphasized youth and audacity. Milhaud was hailed as a member of "Les Six"—the six young French composers which included Honegger, Poulenc, Durey, Tailleferre, and Auric.

Some of his earliest successes were in the field of ballet, particularly *Le Boeuf sur le toit* (*The Ox on the Roof,* 1920) and *La Création du monde* (*The Creation of the*

World, 1923). This last work, one of the first to use the jazz idiom, partly resulted from Milhaud's visit to New York, where, in Harlem, he heard superior black jazz musicians.

Until the outbreak of World War II, Milhaud centered his activities in Paris, with occasional trips to other European cities. In 1940 he came to the United States to teach composition at Mills College in Oakland, California. (Although Mills is a college for young women, Milhaud taught many young men at the graduate level.) Despite the crippling onset of arthritis in his hip Milhaud continued to compose at his usual rapid rate and conduct concerts of his music—which he did with a minimum of motion while seated in a chair.

After the war Milhaud returned to his native land, where he was welcomed with great warmth. From then on he taught in alternate years at the Paris Conservatory and at Mills College. Many of his summers had been spent at the music school in Aspen, Colorado, which he had helped to make one of the outstanding summer music gathering-places.

Milhaud's music, while dissonant, is always tonal. Early in his career he wrote an article that pointed to the choice the contemporary composer had to make: between the atonality of Schoenberg and the tonality of traditional music. Milhaud chose the latter path, often intensifying his belief in tonality by putting two tonalities together—an effect known as polytonality. Milhaud's music is strongly rhythmic. His melodies are built in phrases and, depending on subject matter, can be classical or folklike, or complex and full of large leaps. He handled instruments in a virtuoso fashion and seemed able to solve any technical problem in composition. (His fourteenth and fifteenth string quartets are written so that they may be played singly or combined to make an octet.) His output includes at least twelve operas, more than twenty concertos, a large number of choral works and songs, five symphonies for chamber orchestra, eight symphonies for full orchestra, plus many chamber-music works and scores for films, ballets, and plays.

MINOR: a particular form of interval, scale, or chord. Minor means "lesser" or "smaller," as opposed to MAJOR, which means "greater" or "larger." The minor forms of intervals are a half step smaller than the major forms:

The minor scale, formerly called "the scale with the lesser (minor) third," developed in the seventeenth century from the Aeolian and Dorian modes. There are three forms of minor scales: the harmonic, natural, and melodic. They differ from each other only in their sixth and seventh tones. The first five tones of all minor scales follow the pattern, in whole and half steps, of 1-½-1-1. The harmonic minor continues, ½-1½-½; the natural minor continues, ½-1-1; and the ascending form of the melodic minor continues, 1-1-½; the descending form of the melodic minor follows the pattern of the natural minor (Ex. 45).

Minor chords and their interval patterns include the minor triad—a minor third and a perfect fifth above the root; the minor seventh—a minor triad plus a minor seventh above the root; and the minor ninth—a minor seventh chord plus a minor third or a dominant seventh chord plus a minor third:

The key signature of a minor scale is the same as that of its relative major scale a minor third above. C minor, for example, uses the signature of E♭ major; A minor uses the signature of C major, and so forth. Occasionally, in old music, the key signature for a minor scale with flats is printed with one less flat than called for.

Ex. 45 —

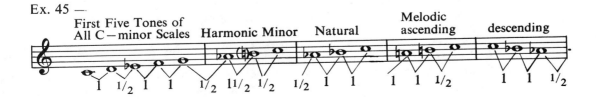

19th-century posters for minstrel shows

MINSTREL SHOW: the most popular form of theatrical entertainment in the United States in the middle 1800's. For it were written such beloved songs as "Dixie," "Oh, Susanna!" "Old Folks at Home," and "Camptown Races." Though minstrel shows were often called "banjo operas," the great American poet Walt Whitman saw in them the beginnings of American grand opera. Actually, the minstrel show was a combination of vaudeville acts and burlesques of plays. It usually featured black-faced white men impersonating blacks, although there were indeed a number of famous black minstrels.

The first white man to blacken his face and perform a memorable black song-and-dance was Thomas Dartmouth ("Jim Crow") Rice (1808–60). In 1828 he acted the part of a black field hand in the play *The Rifle*. Between acts Rice sang "Jump Jim Crow" and danced as he had seen a limping black dance. His act was an immediate success, and the fame of his songs reached as far as Europe.

Rice's success led Daniel Decatur Emmett (1815–1904) to organize in 1842 the first real minstrel troupe, the Virginia Minstrels. Emmett knew the genius of black music, dancing, and humor from watching and listening to the runaway slaves who came through his father's house, an Ohio station of the Underground Railroad. Emmett later joined the most famous of all minstrel troupes, Bryant's Minstrels, for

which he and Stephen Foster supplied most of the musical hits. Emmett was particularly good at writing rousing "walk-arounds," such as "Dixie." The walk-around was the high point of the minstrel show. It featured complicated marching patterns and dancing contests such as the high-stepping cakewalk and foot-tapping songs, often with shouted choruses such as "Doo-dah."

The early minstrel shows soon set a pattern that became tradition. The cast marched in singing. They stood in front of their chairs, arranged in a semicircle, until the master of ceremonies—the "interlocutor"—said, "Gentlemen, be seated." The interlocutor sat in the middle, trading jokes with the comic end men, Mr. Bones and Mr. Tambo. Mr. Bones and Mr. Tambo earned their names by playing the castanetlike "bones" and the tambourine.

There were two acts to a minstrel show. Act I was a mixture of jokes, songs, and dances. Act II was the "olio," made up of vaudeville sketches or a burlesque of a popular play or familiar opera. At the end came a walk-around and singing and dancing by the entire cast.

The minstrel show remained popular until the arrival of jazz and the movies, around the time of World War I. In its later years it came to include Irish jigs and reels and Irish, German, and Jewish dialect stories.

The minstrel show was one of the first uniquely American art forms. It was based on the music and dances of the plantation slaves and the black riverboat workers. The sound of its bones, tambo, and banjo was an ancestor of ragtime and jazz. The show was sentimental but mocking, and by today's standards, minstrel shows would be labeled racist. The caricaturing of blacks and lampooning of their music has, fortunately, become obsolete in the musical theater.

The songs of Rice, Emmett, and Foster were unlike anything being written in Europe at that time. It was to be fifty years before serious composers, such as Debussy and Stravinsky, saw the musical values in the syncopated rhythms of the cakewalk and other features of the minstrels' "Ethiopian melodies."

MINUET: from the middle 1600's to 1800, the most popular court dance. Starting among peasants in the province of Poitou in western France, it became the most fashionable dance at the court of Louis XIV, the "Sun King." Louis himself, in the daily ceremonial, led the dancers through many of the steps of a minuet before withdrawing to his throne. No lady or gentleman could be a member of court society without knowing all the steps and patterns of the different minuets, and dancing masters made a good living keeping their pupils up to date on the newest figures. Many books were written on how to dance the minuet, one of these running to 1,200 pages.

This dance is graceful and formal. The man pays homage to his partner by bowing deeply. Then he guides her through the intricate gliding and bending motions. Hand in hand, smiling dutifully, the dancers perform their dainty retreats and approaches. It is the small steps and movements that give the dance its name, for "minuet" derives from a word meaning "small" or "minute."

The music of the minuet has three beats per measure, with two or three changes of harmony in each measure (Ex. 46). The dancers sometimes moved in a rhythmic pattern that covered two measures. This is the rhythm used in the minuet of Mozart's Symphony Number 40 in G Minor (Ex. 47). Authorities differ on how fast the dance went, some saying it was fast, others only moderately fast. Most minuets begin on the downbeat, although Beethoven's famous Minuet in G breaks the rule.

The earliest concert minuets were written by the founder of French opera, Lully. Lully's minuets occur in pairs, the first being repeated after the playing of the second. The second was quite different from the first, and Lully emphasized this contrast by using a different group of instruments to play each part. For the second minuet he used a trio of two oboes and a bassoon. This trio of instruments gave its name to any musical form in which, regardless of the number of instruments, the second part contrasts strongly with the first part.

It was Haydn who introduced the minuet and trio into the symphony, making it a third movement, between the slow movement and the finale. His example was fol-

Ex. 46 — Minuet from Suite in G, Purcell

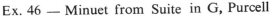

Dancing the minuet

Ex. 47 – Symphony No. 40 in G Minor, Mozart

Dancers:

Louis XIV and his queen dancing the minuet (a 17th-century French engraving)

MODERN MUSIC: music written according to new techniques that have been developing since the early 1900's. The twentieth century has been one of experiments in science and revolutions in politics. Music, too, has been involved in experiments and revolutions.

Why do composers want to experiment? Mostly because they want to find new ways to express ideas. In their minds they hear new sounds that no one has used before, or they think of new ways of using old sounds. Each generation of composers feels that it must carry on where the older composers left off. It feels the need to reflect the life of its own time.

Modern composers, like modern painters and writers, are interested in machines and in the quick, nervous tempo of modern life. They are intrigued also by music from Africa, Asia, and other faraway places. Even in the folk songs of their own countries and in popular music they have discovered a freshness that can be brought into music of the concert hall. Jazz and electronic instruments have stimulated composers to try new ways of making musical sounds.

Revolutions and experiments are not new to music. All through the history of European and American music there have been changes in style. Single-voiced chant gave way to complex polyphony, which in turn gave way to the melody and accompaniment of early opera. The instrumental trio sonata replaced the vocal madrigal as a form of chamber music in the 1600's and was itself replaced by the string quartet of the 1700's. The invention of the piano in the early 1700's led to the eclipse of the harpsichord as the most popular keyboard instrument.

The symphony orchestra grew from the few strings and winds of the 1700's to the large orchestra of Wagner, Liszt, and Berlioz in the 1800's. For a thousand years European music has been constantly changing.

Each change depends on some form of experimentation and a certain amount of revolution. Modern composers have revolted against a tradition of music that has held sway since the early 1600's. This tradition was based on the major and minor scale systems, rhythm that grew out of a regular metric plan, and harmony that was a vocabulary of chords built by piling up intervals of thirds. Harmony was arranged in patterns whereby each chord had its own particular function within a key and all chords led, by regular progression, to the chord based on the keynote of the scale, the tonic. Dissonant sounds were allowed

lowed by Mozart and Beethoven. Some symphonic minuets of the Classical period got faster and faster, until they were no longer like court dances. Others, such as the one in Haydn's Symphony Number 103 in E-flat, became *Ländler,* the Ländler being the ancestor of the waltz. Beethoven's minuets were so slight and so fast that he called them scherzos—musical jokes. They kept the form and meter of the minuet but seemed to be making fun of the delicate court dance.

The popularity of the minuet as a social dance lasted until the period of the American and French revolutions. Then, like the French court itself, the minuet disappeared. Its place was taken by the waltz.

Almost every composer who wrote between 1650 and 1800 composed at least one minuet; there have probably been more minuets written than anything else in dance form. And even such recent composers as Ravel, Debussy, Prokofiev, and Schoenberg have paid their respects to the old "Queen of Dances."

Some composers of the 20th century
Top left: *"Les Six"—Darius Milhaud, Georges Auric (in picture by Cocteau), Arthur Honegger, Germaine Tailleferre, Francis Poulenc, and Louis Durey (Jean Cocteau is at the piano)*
Top right: *Pierre Boulez*
Middle left: *Elliot Carter*
Middle center: *Henry Cowell*
Middle right: *Alberto Ginastera*
Bottom left: *Roger Sessions*
Bottom right: *Gian Carlo Menotti*

Top row *(left to right): Alan Hov-haness; Luciano Berio*
Second row: *Edison Denisov; Luigi Dallapiccola*
Third row: *Olivier Messiaen; Hans Werner Henze*
Bottom: *(from left to right) "The new Russians"—Volkonsky, Gra-bovsky, Silvestrov, Gadyatsky, and Blashkov*

only if they resolved to more consonant sounds. Musical form was based on repetition and balancing of phrases. The most important musical forms were those of the Baroque fugue and the Classical sonata, both of which depended on the setting up of a basic tonality or key feeling, the going away from that tonality (modulation), and a return to the first tonality.

Modern composers have sometimes used the old ingredients but mixed them in new ways so as to create fresh sounds. Satie, Debussy, Ravel, and Prokofiev added tones to the chords built in a series of thirds. They used simple chords but took them out of any key relationship. They often avoided the major-minor scales and substituted the old church modes, the pentatonic scale, or the whole-tone scale.

Other composers—Milhaud, Copland, Schuman—have used simple triads, and in fact have piled together two different triads to make polychords. Hindemith evolved a style that had its roots in Baroque counterpoint but often used dissonant sounds rather than traditional harmonies.

Folk music, with its dance or speech rhythms and its use of the old church modes, started Stravinsky and Bartók on their experimental paths. Both of these composers use rhythms that are jagged, meters that change from bar to bar, and harmonies that have little in common with Classical chord structure or chordal progressions. Stravinsky's ballet *The Rite of Spring*, at its first performance in 1913, shocked the musical world. Its brutal primitivism, its unexpected orchestral sounds, its lack of tonality and melody in the traditional sense—these opened a new age in music. With this ballet Stravinsky became the musical leader for many modern composers.

The other important leader of modern composers was Arnold Schoenberg. He and his pupils Berg and Webern threw away all old ideas of tonality, rhythm, melody, and harmony. They based their music on an arrangement of the twelve tones of the chromatic scale, making a "tone row." By manipulating the tone row they found new types of melody and harmony. The resulting compositions are often most expressive and disturbing. The twelve-tone system, or serial technique, is now used by many composers, often in combination with other modern devices. Webern carried the new technique into his writing for instruments, breaking melodies into small bits and giving no instrument more than a few notes in succession, much as a painter makes a line from a series of dots.

The American composer Henry Cowell discovered the unusual sounds that could be made by playing directly on the strings of the piano or by hitting the keys with the fist or forearm to produce "tone clusters." The French-American composer Edgard Varèse, experimenting with orchestral instruments, built his music by contrasting one instrumental sound with another quite different sound regardless of key, scale, or harmony.

Varèse was also a leader in the field of electronic music. The discovery of electronic sounds, including those of the tape recorder, opened up new areas for experimentation. On the tape recorder natural sounds can be played slowed down, speeded up, or even backward, in a style known as *musique concrète*. The resulting change of pitch and direction is as startling as the appearance of a drop of water under a high-powered microscope. Radio tubes give forth sounds that no known instrument could possibly make. The earliest electronic instrument was the electronic organ, but even that complex instrument is a child's toy compared to the new electronic sound generators or computers programmed to compose music.

Among the newest experimenters are the American John Cage, the German Karl Heinz Stockhausen, and the Frenchman Pierre Boulez. Some of their music is based on the laws of chance. Some of it is drawn on graph paper, and some of the scores let the performers decide what sounds to make and when to make them. These experimental composers sometimes combine the twelve-tone technique with electronic sounds and the sounds of chance. Of all composers writing today, this group has most consistently turned their backs on the musical past.

Every country has its quota of innovative composers: England—Humphrey Searle, Peter Racine Fricker, Roberto Gerhard; France—Olivier Messiaen; Italy—Luigi Dallapiccola, Luigi Nono, Luciano Berio; Poland—Witold Lutoslawski, Krzystof Penderecki; United States—Carl Ruggles, Wallingford Riegger, Gunther Schuller, Elliot Carter, George Rochberg, Ralph Shapey, Otto Luening, Vladimir Ussachevsky, George Crumb, Lukas Foss; Russia—Andrey Volkonsky, Valentin Silvestrov, Vladimir Zagortsev, Edison Denisov; Argentina—Alberto Ginastera.

Not all composers of today are experimenters. Barber, Menotti, Shostakovich, Britten, and Poulenc all have written works that contain little experimental technique. When these men have used something new, they have incorporated it in a basically traditional technique.

Many persons resent experiments. They would like all music to sound like Bach or Brahms. They forget the lesson of music history—that to some degree, music is always changing. Other persons like all new things for their newness. They forget that the history of music is strewn with experiments that failed.

Good composers write good music. No trick ever makes a composer's work enduring. Once the novelty wears off, the audience listens for what lies behind it. If nothing is there, the composer is unlikely to achieve lasting fame.

Good music is always a part of its own age, even though this might not be evident during the composer's own lifetime. If the age is one of strife, space probes, unsureness, experimentation, and political upheaval, the music that best expresses human experience among these conditions is the music that will endure.

MODES: the scales in which all medieval and Renaissance music was written. After 1600 two of these modes—known today as the major and minor modes—were used almost exclusively as the basis of music until the late 1800's.

The organization of tones into modal patterns began in ancient Greece. A Greek mode was made up of two tetrachords (four note groups) connected by a whole step. Each tetrachord contained two whole steps and one half step, but the way the whole and half steps were distributed varied from one mode to another. Each mode had its own *ethos*—a moral value or inner meaning. Plato, the philosopher, suggested that male students play and hear music only in the Dorian mode, which was manly and warlike. The Lydian mode was considered suitable only for girls. The tendency to give meaning to a scale still exists today; thus many persons think a composition in a major key must be happy, and one in minor, sad.

Since the chant of the medieval church was derived from the eastern Mediterranean, it too was organized in modes. These modes gathered their own traditions around them, and the Greek interpretations were soon lost. The Greek names of the modes were adopted but were not used for the same scale designations. These modes are the seven different scales that can be played on the white keys of the piano.

Certain tones within the scale are of special importance: the final tone (or keynote), on which a mode usually begins and always ends; the dominant (or reciting tone), around

Ex. 48 — "A solis ortus cardine," a Christmas Hymm

Ex. 49a — Authentic Modes

Ex. 49b — Hypo Modes (* is placed over keynote)

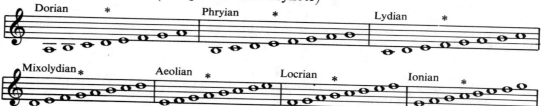

which much of the chant is sung; and the mediant, which serves as the first and last tone of the internal phrases of a chant—that is, of the phrases other than the opening and closing ones. (The mediant is named for its place between the final tone and the reciting tone.) The dominant was not always the fifth note of the modal scales. In the Phrygian mode, for instance, it is the sixth tone of the scale (Ex. 48).

Each medieval mode has two forms—authentic and plagal, depending on the range of the melody. A chant is in the authentic mode if its melody lies between the keynote and its octave above; it is plagal if it lies in the octave four tones below the keynote and five above. The plagal modes were also called hypo modes, from the Greek *hypo,* "below," since they lay below the keynote (Ex. 49a and b).

While the modal scales can be analyzed in terms of their whole-step and half-step structures, and may be built starting on any note, it is sometimes easier to think of a transposed mode as it relates to the key of C major. In transposing a mode, it is merely

necessary to remember the note of the C scale on which the mode begins. The Dorian mode, which is the white key scale from D to D, can be thought of as beginning on the second tone of the C scale. To begin a Dorian on F, it is possible to think, "D is the second tone of C, F is the second tone of E♭." The Dorian on F, therefore, is like playing the scale of E♭ starting on the second tone:

A Dorian Mode Starting on F

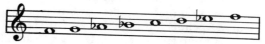

In the Middle Ages and the Renaissance the modes most used in church music were the Dorian, Phrygian, Lydian, and Mixolydian. (The Locrian mode was almost never used—in or out of church.) In the songs and dances of the people, the Ionian and Aeolian modes were the favorites, and about 1600 these began to be used more and more for all types of music. The Ionian mode became the major scale and the Aeolian became the natural minor scale.

Many folk songs are modal—for example, "The Drunken Sailor," "I Am a Poor Wayfaring Stranger," and "God Rest You Merry, Gentlemen." The revival of interest in folk songs has reinstated modal music as part of the popular music of today.

As musicians of the nineteenth century became increasingly aware of the folk music of their own countries, they began to introduce modal melodies into their compositions. Among the first composers to rediscover the beauties of modal music were Beethoven (Quartet, Opus 132) and Chopin (Mazurka, Opus 24, Number 2). It was the Russian composers of the late 1800's, however, who used the modes extensively—a natural outgrowth of their interest in Russian folk music, which was predominantly modal. Since then many composers, including Satie, Ravel, Debussy, and Vaughan Williams, have turned to the modes for both melodic and harmonic inspiration.

MODULATION: the change from one key, or tonal center, to another. A musical work, particularly a long one, needs variety. Composers use modulation as part of the basic form of their compositions to vary the tonality, just as they change from one chord to another for harmonic variety.

If the music stays in a new key for a short time, the modulation is called a transient modulation. True modulations occur in long works, such as symphonies and sonatas. Beethoven's "Eroica" Symphony, for example, starts in the key of E-flat. Later it modulates to the key of B-flat and stays there for seventy-two measures.

Modulation is an old device in music. It became an important part of music in the 1600's and early 1700's, when Bach and his contemporaries made it basic to the form of every composition. The modulations of these Baroque composers rarely carried their music far from the original key and the listener was led gradually from one key to another (Ex. 50). But Haydn, Mozart, Bee-

Ex. 50 — Prelude in D Minor from *The Well-tempered Clavier*, Book I, J.S. Bach

Key of D Minor

Pivot Chord   Pivot Chord

Key of F

Ex. 51 — Nocturne in G, Op. 37, No. 2, Chopin

thoven, and Schubert, as if to keep the listener off balance, used startling modulations or suggestions of modulations that went far from the original key and were dramatic in effect.

Composers of the 1800's, especially Chopin, Liszt, and Wagner, sometimes used a constant series of modulations to make the music more colorful (Ex. 51). Many composers of today write music that is keyless. They do, however, sometimes use one tone as a center around which the music is built. By changing from one tonal center to another they are able to achieve the same kind of variety that earlier composers achieved through change of key.

The most common way of modulating in traditional music is by the use of pivot chords or pivot tones. After first making the listener aware of the original key of the music,

the composer chooses a chord or a tone that is in the scale of the original key as well as in the scale of the key to which he wants the music to move. Landing on a pivot tone or chord is like coming to an intersection of two streets. One can continue on the same street or turn off on the new street. If the composer turns off on the new street, or modulates, he usually confirms it by making a cadence in the new key and stating a theme in the new key (Ex. 52).

Modulations occur most often in the transitional sections of large works. The listener is not always aware of what is happening but feels that the music is going somewhere. A transition may be just a few measures in length or it may be as long as forty measures, as in Beethoven's "Eroica." Usually the longer the composition is, the longer the transition, or modulating section.

Ex. 52

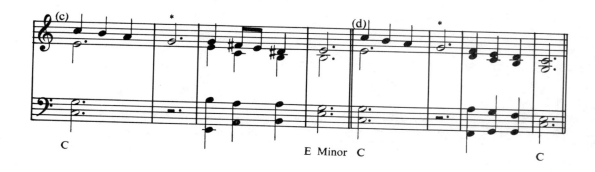

MONTEVERDI, CLAUDIO (1567–1643): the first great composer of operas, the first composer to use the instruments of the orchestra for dramatic effects, and also the composer who brought the vocal madrigal to its highest point. Monteverdi's compositions are turning points in the history of music. His early works, written before 1600, are based on musical styles that had been developing for several hundred years. In later works he explored musical territory along paths that were followed by many later composers.

Monteverdi was born in Cremona, Italy, the home of the great violin-makers. He sang in the choir of the cathedral, where he learned to read music, to sing, and to play the organ and viol. His choirmaster, Ingegneri, was a well-known composer who recognized the talent of Monteverdi and taught him counterpoint and composition so that by the age of sixteen Monteverdi had written a book of religious madrigals *(Madrigali spirituali)* for four voices. These were soon published, as was his book of graceful canzonettas for three voices. In 1587 Monteverdi published his first book of madrigals for five voices. Even these early works show his bold and original way of setting poems to music, portraying in musical tones the dramatic and emotional feeling of the words.

In 1590 the Duke of Mantua, in northern Italy, hired Monteverdi as a violinist and singer. Whenever the duke went to war, as he did in Hungary, or to visit, as he did in Belgium and Holland, his court musicians went with him, and so Monteverdi heard the music of many lands. He saw battles and ballets, and all that he saw and heard influenced his later music.

By 1602 Monteverdi had written his second and third books of madrigals. He had also become the director of music for the court of Mantua. Here he wrote music, taught young singers, and rehearsed and directed performances for the court.

His fourth book of madrigals was published in 1603. In these compositions Monteverdi, seeking ways to make his music more expressive, used dissonances previously unheard in music.

At this time in Italy several composers were experimenting with the style of musical declamation that was later called recitative. The rhythms in Monteverdi's madrigals came close to being recitatives. When critics attacked him, Monteverdi answered by saying that dramatic words need a dramatic, passionate—even violent—musical setting.

In his fifth book of madrigals (1605) Monteverdi continued his revolutionary

Claudio Monteverdi

experiments by adding an instrumental part to the voices. The old idea of flowing lines in each voice part was replaced almost completely by the jagged rhythms of recitative. Dissonances such as the dominant seventh chord were sounded without preparing the ears of the audience. Harmonic patterns gave a major-minor key feeling instead of staying within the scales of the old church modes. Monteverdi's last books of madrigals (the sixth in 1614, seventh in 1619, eighth in 1638, and ninth in 1657) are more like cantatas and chamber operas than madrigals.

The eighth book, the *Madrigali guerrieri et amorosi (Madrigals of War and Love),* sings of love and the cruelties of war. The most famous composition in this book is the pantomime chamber-opera *Il combattimento di Tancredi e Clorinda (The Combat of Tancred and Clorinda).* The narrator of this work sings the story of two lovers dressed in armor who meet but do not recognize each other. They duel, and the maiden Clorinda, wounded, dies as she sings of the peace she will find in heaven.

To bring out the drama of *The Combat*, Monteverdi used several new sounds in his orchestra. The strings are given a rhythm that gallops along like the horses of the knights. The players are instructed to make a tremolo (a fast-bowed repetition on one tone) and also to use pizzicato, the plucking of the strings. These new ideas and others were so used that throughout the work the orchestra set the mood of the action. No composer had done that previously.

In 1607 Monteverdi wrote his *Orfeo (Orpheus)*, a "drama in music," for the court at Mantua. It was not the first opera. Almost twenty years earlier composers had been trying to recapture the wedding of music and poetry as it had existed in ancient Greek dramas. Peri and Caccini had each written music for a drama based on the myth. But Monteverdi's *Orfeo* surpassed all these works by older composers.

Orfeo calls for a large orchestra, chorus, solo singers, and dancers. The music is joyful, sad, dramatic, triumphant, according to the story. The choral music shows Monteverdi's mastery of vocal writing as it portrays grief, joy, and terror. From the beginning fanfare toccata for brass instruments to the happy chorus that is sung as Apollo takes Orpheus to heaven, Monteverdi manages to make the music always interesting and full of contrast. Throughout the work there runs a ritornello—a recurring theme. Its noble style epitomizes the tragic quality of the legend (see Ex. 41 on page 484).

Orfeo was immediately successful. After its first performance in the royal palace for the duke and his close friends, the opera was given for all the noblewomen of the city. The fame of *Orfeo* spread, and it was performed in many other cities.

After Monteverdi's wife died in 1608, he poured out his grief in the moving "Lament of Arianna," the only section of his opera *Arianna (Ariadne)* that still exists. The "Lament" is sung today either as a solo or in the arrangement for five voices made for it by the composer. It was also in 1608 that Monteverdi composed his great ballet, *Il ballo delle ingrate (The Ballet of the Ungrateful Women)*.

In 1613 Monteverdi became music master at St. Mark's Cathedral in Venice, the church that could boast of a long list of great composer-directors, including Willaert and the Gabrielis. At St. Mark's Monteverdi composed many religious works and found time to write ballets and short dramatic pieces. Shortly after the first public opera houses were established in Venice in 1637, Monteverdi wrote several operas for them: *Il ritorno di Ulisse in patria (The Return of Ulysses)* and *Le nozze di Enea con Lavinia (The Marriage of Aeneas)*.

The final masterpiece of this Italian composer was *L'incoronazione di Poppea (The Coronation of Poppea)*, produced in 1642. For this Monteverdi had no large orchestra. The manager of the theater, thinking of expense, allowed him only a few strings and a harpsichord. The text of the opera is based on history—the love intrigues of the Roman emperor Nero—rather than the myths of the earlier Monteverdi operas. Out of the wisdom of his many years he produced a musical masterpiece full of love, comedy, jealousy, tragedy, and intrigue.

When Monteverdi died, the city of Venice mourned him, but his music was soon forgotten and Monteverdi became merely a name in the pages of the history of music. Composers who had learned from Monteverdi took music into new paths. Not until the middle of the 1800's did musicians begin to rediscover the bold, expressive sounds of the old master.

Many of Monteverdi's works were lost, and only in the past few years have all his known works been published. Singers, conductors, and recording companies have done much to rescue this great composer from obscurity. Music lovers, hearing his passionate utterances, have begun to realize that he was the greatest creative musician of the 1600's and one of the greatest of all time.

MORENDO: an Italian word meaning "dying away." It is used by a composer, usually at the end of a score, to tell the performer to let the music get gradually softer until it can barely be heard. The same effect may be indicated by a decrescendo mark:

The morendo marking is usually found at the end of a slow composition, as the first movement of Tchaikovsky's Sixth Symphony. The effect is most important in string and vocal music, because here the performer can at will reduce his tone to almost nothing. On the piano each tone gradually dies away regardless of the composer's wishes.

MORLEY, THOMAS (1557–1602): one of the most active composers and musicians in England during the time of Queen Elizabeth I and Shakespeare. After studying with the great religious composer William Byrd and taking a music degree at Oxford, Morley became a favorite organist of the queen. Later he was honored by being made a Gentleman of the Chapel Royal.

Morley's best-known compositions are his light, tuneful canzonettas, his melodious madrigals, and his gay "balletti"—dancelike works for five voices, often with a "fa-la-la" refrain. One of Morley's *Aires or Little Short Songs,* "It was a lover and his lass," appears in Shakespeare's *As You Like It.*

Toward the end of his life Morley was given a monopoly to print music in England. As a publisher, he helped to popularize the new Italian madrigals. He assisted English composers by publishing their works in a collection of instrumental music and in *The Triumphes of Oriana,* a book of madrigals for five and six voices.

Perhaps Morley's greatest contribution was his *A Plaine and Easie Introduction to Practicall Musicke* (1597). Like many other early textbooks, it is written as a dialogue between a master and a pupil. It starts by teaching the student how to read and perform music, takes him through all kinds of counterpoint, and leads him to the point where he is able to compose in all vocal and instrumental forms popular at the time. It was the first important music book written in English.

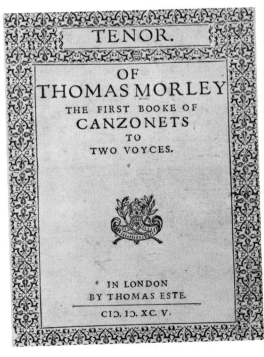

Motets have been written in many contrapuntal forms; here, the contratenor part of a motet "canonique" written for Henry VIII

MOTET: a vocal composition with a sacred text, usually in Latin, and without accompaniment. One of the oldest and most important musical forms, it originated in the thirteenth century, when composers customarily wrote one or two counter-melodies above the melody of a church plainsong chant. At first the added melodies were sung without words. When words were added, they were called "the little text" or, in Latin, *motetus.* The plainsong in the lowest voice was sung by the tenor. The upper voices were called the duplum and the triplum.

Motets of the fourteenth century were built by weaving melodies over the plainsong, which was sung or played to a repeated rhythmic pattern. Such motets were called isorhythmic. Above the tenor part the duplum might sing a Latin hymn while the triplum sang words of a popular love song in French. This not-very-religious form of music was changed by the English composer John Dunstable (*c.* 1370–1453). In his motets all voices sing the same sacred text, although not at the same time. Dunstable was followed by the Burgundian and Netherland composers—Dufay, Josquin Des Prés, Ockeghem, and Obrecht—in bringing the motet to a high point of musical beauty and display of compositional techniques. Every possible form of contrapuntal writing was used (see CANON).

The great composers of the late 1500's were fond of the motet form: Palestrina wrote more than 250, and Lassus over 500. The number of voices normally ranged from two to six. In general there were two main parts to a sixteenth-century motet and as many sections as there were lines or sentences in the text. Each section began with a melodic line in one voice that was imitated by the other voices as they entered. The musical line followed the meaning of

At left: the title page of Thomas Morley's First Booke of Canzonets to Two Voyces (London, 1595)

Ex. 53 — "Qui Sequitur Me" (Who Followeth Me), Lassus

Original a third lower

the text—changing as the text changed—so that no main theme or motive runs through a whole work. Composers aimed at thematic variety rather than at unity.

Each section of a sixteenth-century motet ended with cadences, but some voices dropped out for a breath and began again while other voices held. This overlapping continued the smooth flow of the music, which had a steady pulse but irregular accents. Composers often illustrated in music certain words in the text. There might even be a touch of humor in this word-painting, as in Lassus' motet "Who Follows Me": here the text is set in such a way that the second voice follows closely on the heels of the first (Ex. 53).

When composers began to write purely instrumental music, in the late 1500's, they adopted the sectional form and polyphonic style of the motet. Hence the motet is considered an ancestor of the fugue. After 1600 the cantata for voice and instruments began to replace the motet in composers' affections. The German composers Schütz, Bach, Schubert, Mendelssohn, and Brahms wrote motets that are among their greatest works for chorus. But these motets were many fewer than those of Lassus and Palestrina. Bach wrote only six motets and Brahms seven.

MOTIVE: the smallest unit of musical form. It can be as short as two notes (as in the "cuckoo" motive used by composers) and is rarely longer than six notes. A motive usually has a clear rhythmic pattern as well as a clear melodic outline. In some cases it is a harmonic pattern of two or three distinctive chord sounds.

A motive is a musical seed from which a long composition might grow. The four tones that form the motive at the beginning of Beethoven's Fifth Symphony are used as the basis for the whole first movement of the work:

Symphony No. 5, Beethoven

Wagner's operas are built from a number of motives, each one representing an idea, a person, or an action. (See the article on LEITMOTIF.)

A motive might be a short rhythmic pattern, as in Mozart's Symphony Number 40 in G Minor, which through repetition on different pitches becomes part of a long melodic line (Ex. 54). Handel's famous Saraband in D Minor repeats a two-measure

Ex. 54 — Symphony No. 40 in G Minor, Mozart

Ex. 55 — Saraband, Handel

An unfinished portrait of Mozart by his brother-in-law Joseph Lange

pattern on rising pitches, as though the composer were piling brick upon brick in making a building (see Ex. 55). Chopin's Prélude in C Minor uses a one-measure rhythmic motive throughout, achieving variety and expressiveness by means of constantly changing chromatic harmony. Many popular songs, such as George Gershwin's "I Got Rhythm" and Vincent Youman's "Tea for Two," are based on short rhythmic motives which are repeated on various melodic pitches.

A motive has little or no meaning by itself. Like a newborn baby, it cannot be judged. Only after it has "lived" in a musical composition can its possibilities be seen and appreciated.

MOVEMENT: a section, complete in itself, of a large work such as a symphony, sonata, string quartet, or suite.

The name "movement" comes from the fact that various sections of a large work are performed at different rates of speed. A movement is known by its tempo mark (such as "the slow movement") or else by its position in the work (such as "the second movement").

The idea of putting together complete pieces in contrasting tempos started in the late fifteenth century. In the sixteenth century a slow dance, the pavane, was followed by a fast dance, the galliard. The dance suite and the opera overtures of J. B. Lully and Alessandro Scarlatti led to the Classical symphony and sonata in three or four movements.

Recently composers have experimented with the one-movement symphony made up of contrasting sections, none of which is complete in itself. Among such works are Sibelius' Seventh Symphony, Barber's First Symphony, Harris' Third Symphony, and Schuman's Sixth Symphony.

The German word for movement is *satz,* as in the *Quartettsatz,* a single movement Schubert wrote for a quartet he never completed.

MOZART, WOLFGANG AMADEUS (1756–91): of all composers, the most complete genius. Opera was his favorite form, but he also poured out an incredible number of great works for piano, voice, orchestra, and chamber groups. He was a gifted and active pianist, violinist, and conductor. He taught off and on, to add to the pitifully small income received from his compositions. Despite a busy life, he found time to be a dutiful son and a loving husband and father. Somehow he also found time for his favorite pastimes of dancing, bowling, and billiards.

Mozart loved the gay city of Vienna but was at home in most of the capitals of Europe. He was a truly democratic man, equally at ease with royalty or sitting around a table with his non-courtly drinking companions. Almost everything Mozart wrote was commissioned by someone; he could hardly bear to write except to order. No commission was too large or too small, whether it was an opera for the coronation of an emperor or a short work for a musical clock.

Mozart's music is a true picture of the man himself. It ranges from a mood of simple, almost slapstick, humor to a mood of noble tragedy; from peasantlike simplicity to elegant brilliance; from dance tunes to the most complex of musical forms, and from dainty court music to heroic works that are full of the spirit of freedom and the brotherhood of man.

Mozart's short life—he died at the age of thirty-five—began in the Austrian town of Salzburg. His father, Leopold Mozart, a violinist in the orchestra of the Archbishop of Salzburg, was a famous teacher and composer, whose *Versuch einer gründlichen Violinschule (Essay on the Fundamentals of Violin-playing)* is one of the most important music books of the eighteenth century and whose *Toy Symphony*—for a long time wrongly ascribed to Haydn—is one of the best-loved musical works for children. Mozart's sister Maria Anna was a talented pianist who participated in the first tours made by Mozart and his father.

Top left: *Mozart in court dress at 6 years of age. The costume was given to him by Empress Maria Theresa after a concert at Schönbrunn (the Imperial Palace in Vienna), Oct. 30, 1762*
Top right: *Mozart at 11*
Bottom left: *excerpts from a music book kept by Mozart when he was 8*
Bottom right: *Mozart at 21, wearing the order of "The Golden Spur" awarded him by the pope*

Mozart began to study music at the age of four, and in two years was a skilled performer on harpsichord, organ, and violin. His father took him on a series of tours that were all triumphs: to Vienna in 1762 (when he was six), to Paris in 1763, to London in 1764, and to Italy in 1769. In each country Mozart was greeted as a "wonder child." His improvisations and compositions, as well as his ability to read anything at sight, astounded all who heard him. The rulers of Austria, France, and England received him royally. In each country he heard and absorbed the music of the leading composers. In England he discovered the singing, melodious style of Johann Christian Bach, the youngest son of the great Johann Sebastian Bach. It was here that Mozart wrote his first symphony.

In Italy, Mozart was decorated by the Pope and given instruction in counterpoint by the "grand old man" of music in Italy at that time, Padre Martini. At Rome's Sistine Chapel the boy performed one of his great feats of memory in writing out the whole score of a nine-voice *Miserere* after hearing it twice. At Milan he first tasted operatic success when he conducted his *Mitridate, rè di Ponto (Mithridates, King of Pontus)* for twenty performances; he was then not quite fifteen years old. Italy and its music made such a strong impression on him that forever after his music retained much of the lyric quality of the Italians.

In 1771 Mozart returned to Salzburg to take up his post as concertmaster of the archbishop's orchestra. For the next few years his base was Salzburg, although he took as many leaves of absence as possible, particularly after the music-loving archbishop died in 1772 and was succeeded by Hieronymus, who cared little about music. On the occasion of a trip to Vienna with his father in 1773, Mozart discovered the beauties of the string quartets of Haydn. He was so moved that he sat down and wrote, within a month, six quartets of his own (K. 168–173). Mozart at the age of seventeen was now the mature composer.

Despite lack of encouragement from the new archbishop, Mozart was highly productive at Salzburg. Between 1773 and 1776 he wrote his first group of piano sonatas, five violin concertos, his first five piano concertos, some sacred music, many serenades and divertimentos, and five symphonies, including the "Little" Symphony in G Minor.

Seeing no future at Salzburg, in 1777 Mozart set forth with his mother on a tour of Germany and France to seek a position equal to his genius. But there were no commissions for operas in Munich, Augsburg, or Mannheim. In Paris the opera lovers were quarreling over the merits of Gluck and the Italian Piccini. Since there was no chance for another composer to break through, Mozart settled down there to a career of teaching and composing instrumental works, including his Concerto for Flute and Harp. On commission he wrote a symphony in D, the "Paris" Symphony, "to please the tastes of the Parisians," as he said. He also wrote a ballet, *Les Petits Riens (The Little Trifles),* for the great ballet master Noverre.

In Paris, in 1778, Mozart's mother died. Sorrowfully he started home, giving concerts along the way and always hoping for a commission for an opera. For the next few years he performed his duties at Salzburg for the archbishop.

The year 1781 was a turning point in Mozart's life. He finally received a commission to write an opera—one in the Italian style for the carnival at Munich. This work, *Idomeneo,* was Mozart's first big, serious opera. It was not a popular success but it established his reputation. He now settled down in Munich to enjoy life among music lovers who appreciated him. But almost immediately he was called back to his post as concertmaster at Salzburg. The archbishop, having no idea of Mozart's greatness, expected the composer to behave like the rest of his upper-class servants. Mozart, in turn, went out of his way to insult the archbishop. When he finally resigned, the archbishop had him kicked out of the palace.

With no more duties at the archbishop's court, Mozart now made his home in Vienna, throwing himself into an active career as a composer, performer, and teacher. He took part in a series of concerts, bringing a new piano concerto to each concert. He met his idol Haydn, and the older composer came to love Mozart like a son. To Mozart's father he said, "I consider your son to be the greatest composer I have ever heard." Haydn did everything he could to advance the young man's fortunes. The two men played chamber music together, and learned from each other.

Joseph II, Emperor of Austria, commissioned Mozart to write *Die Entführung aus dem Serail (The Abduction from the Seraglio),* a comic-romantic opera. It was Mozart's first large-scale opera in his native German language. When he conducted it in Vienna in 1782, it was an immediate success.

Top: *Mozart's wife Constanze, whom he married in 1782*
Bottom: *Mozart's two sons, Karl (1784–1858) and Franz Xavier (1791–1844)—also known, later, as Wolfgang Amadeus*

Mozart now felt that good fortune was on its way and that he could begin to have a family of his own. Some years earlier he had been in love with Aloysia Weber, one of a family of singers and a cousin of the composer Carl Maria von Weber. After she married an actor, Mozart turned his attention to her younger sister, Constanze. He married her soon after the performance of *The Abduction*. For a while they lived in gypsy fashion, moving from house to house. At one time they had an apartment with violinists above and below, a singing teacher next door, and an oboist down the hall. At night, when the house had quieted down, Mozart composed. It was a gay, carefree life, except that Constanze always seemed to need more money than Mozart could earn.

In spite of the success of *The Abduction*, Mozart did not receive another opera commission for three years. During that time he wrote many of his finest works for voice and instruments—the "Haffner" Symphony, the Mass in C Minor, and the Piano Concerto in D Minor K. 466. Out of his love and admiration for Haydn, he dedicated six string quartets to the older master. Among these is the famous C-Major Quartet K. 465, the "Dissonant," whose strange opening puzzled many musicians (Ex. 56).

Mozart's music for *Der Schauspieldirektor (The Impresario)*, a one-act satire on the life of an opera manager, and a revival of his *Idomeneo* brought him once more to the attention of Joseph II. The emperor gave his consent to Mozart and the librettist Lorenzo da Ponte to make an opera based on Beaumarchais' *Le Mariage de Figaro*, a gay comedy that had biting things to say about the ruling class. After much censorship Mozart's *Le nozze di Figaro (The Marriage of Figaro)* received its first performance in Vienna in 1786. At first the audiences were enthusiastic, but soon their fancy was caught by new works of other composers.

The Opera House in the city of Prague decided to put on *Figaro* and invited Mozart for the opening. When he arrived, he found the whole city *Figaro*-mad. Never had the young composer been happier. Besides the acclaim for *Figaro*, his new symphony, Number 38 in D, K. 504, now known as the "Prague" Symphony, was a success. And when the Prague opera director asked him for a new opera, Mozart was delighted. He returned to Vienna, and with da Ponte began work on *Don Giovanni (Don Juan)*. From the popular legend Mozart made what was to be his greatest theater work. *Don Giovanni* has been called "the perfect opera." From first to last it tells a dramatic story—swiftly, mockingly, at times comically—a story carried by voices and instruments to its inevitable tragic ending.

Don Giovanni was a success when produced in Prague. But the Viennese, six months later, thought it "too heavy"—mostly because Mozart had used the orchestra to underline the drama. Later composers, notably Wagner, were to do just that, but in Mozart's day the proper function of the orchestra was considered to be mostly background support for the singers.

The small amount of money that came to Mozart for *Don Giovanni* was soon spent. The emperor appointed Mozart to the post of court composer (mostly of dances) to take the place of Gluck, who had recently died. But for this job with its high-sounding title Mozart was paid only a few hundred dollars a year—less than half the amount given to Gluck.

To make ends meet, Mozart, who was now a father, threw himself into a frenzy of composing. In the summer of 1788 he wrote his three greatest symphonies: Number 39 in E-flat, Number 40 in G Minor, and Number 41 in C Major, known as the "Jupiter." During this period also he wrote his charming *Eine kleine Nachtmusik (A Little Night Music)*, his masterful string

Ex. 56 — Quartet, K. 465

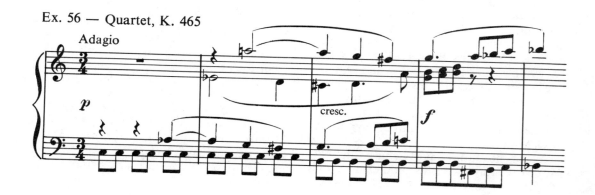

quintets—including the Quintet in G Minor K. 516, one of his most hauntingly beautiful works—and a quintet for clarinet and strings, K. 581, written for his clarinet-playing friend Anton Stadler. Along with these glowing works, Mozart found time for his *Ein musikalischer Spass (A Musical Joke)*— a parody of his own Classical style, done as a simple-minded, dull composer might have gone about it. The *Musical Joke* is one of the few successful pieces of musical wit and low comedy. It is full of meaningless dissonances, cadenzas that backfire, and musical forms that stutter—and it ends in four keys at the same time!

A commission to add wind parts to *Messiah* and other choral and operatic works by Handel led Mozart to a new study of the contrapuntal works of Handel and J. S. Bach. Out of this study came Mozart's most adventurous style of harmonic writing. The Adagio in B Minor, the Rondo in A Minor, and the Gigue in G Major for piano are so daring harmonically that they seem to be years ahead of their time. Preludes, fugues, and dance suites testify to the influence of Handel and Bach at this point in Mozart's career.

A tour of various German cities in 1789 led Mozart to write three of his finest string quartets, on commission from the king of Prussia. When Mozart returned to Vienna, the emperor asked him to write another opera, light enough for the tastes of the court. The charming comic opera *Così fan tutte,* with libretto by da Ponte, was the result. Its full title is *Così fan tutte; osia La Scuola degli amanti (Thus Do They All; or The School for Lovers).*

The last year of Mozart's life, 1791, was one of his most productive. He composed his Concerto for Clarinet and his Concerto for Piano in B-flat K. 595, the last of his piano concertos. Both are among his noblest works. But the two adagios for combinations of clarinets, basset horns, and bassoons give an indication of Mozart's inner sadness.

In March of 1791, Emanuel Schikaneder, the manager of a theater in a Viennese suburb, asked Mozart to write a "magic" opera. At first the composer thought himself not in the mood for something light and frothy, but as he began work on the opera in the little summer house that had been placed at his disposal, his enthusiasm waxed. *Die Zauberflöte (The Magic Flute),* starting as light clowning, gradually became transformed into Mozart's testament to the brotherhood of man. It reflects the many-sidedness of Mozart himself, being a mix-

A scene from The Marriage of Figaro

ture of slapstick comedy and folklike melodies, of brilliant arias and noble choral ensembles.

Mozart's work on *The Magic Flute* was interrupted several times. In July a messenger from an anonymous patron appeared with a commission for Mozart to write a Requiem mass. The commission was to be kept secret so that the nobleman, who fancied himself a composer, could have the work performed under his own name. As Mozart started work on the mass, his second son was born.

Then came a "command" commission to write an opera for the festivities attending the coronation of Emperor Leopold II as king of Bohemia in Prague. Without much interest in the project, Mozart tossed off *La clemenza di Tito (The Clemency of Titus),* an old-fashioned opera in the Italian style, and traveled to Prague to conduct it. It was hardly listened to, and its creator, sad and exhausted, returned to Vienna and *The Magic Flute.*

The first performance of his opera was conducted by Mozart on September 30. At first but a moderate success, the opera soon became a great favorite of the Viennese. Meanwhile Mozart resumed work on his Requiem. Ill and depressed, he became convinced that the Requiem was for his own death. On December 4 he gave his pupil Süssmayr instructions for the completion of the work, and that night the great Mozart died. He was given a pauper's funeral, attended by only a few friends, and a sudden storm drove even these away. The body was buried in an unmarked grave, in silence and unattended.

Mozart's home in Salzburg

Crayon drawing of Mozart

he wrote forty-two arias, twenty canons, nineteen masses and litanies, several cantatas, and thirty-four songs.

Mozart's compositions are often identified by the letter K. followed by a number, such as K. 467 or K. 503. The K. stands for Ludwig von Köchel, who issued in 1862 a catalog listing Mozart's compositions as nearly as possible in the order in which he thought they were written. The K. number not only is a clue to whether a piece is early or late Mozart but also helps in another way. Where two or more Mozart works are in the same key, the Köchel numbers help to tell them apart. For instance, Mozart wrote two piano concertos in C major in his later years; one is known as K. 467, the other as K. 503. (Some of the numbers were changed by the musical scholar Alfred Einstein in a revised catalog issued in 1937.)

Mozart was not a great innovator. Like J. S. Bach, he brought together all the musical ideas of his time and welded them into his own personal way of making music. His earliest works are graceful and charming. Melodies are beautifully balanced in phrases, and are often supported by a simple Alberti bass.

His earliest piano concertos are written in the *style galant*—they are brilliant, showy, and a bit superficial, since they were meant as entertainment.

As Mozart matured, his melodies sing more expressively (Ex. 57), while his accompaniments throb with dramatic agitation

In his short life Mozart managed to write an amazing number of musical works—with the exact number of works in any category always open to question. Many of his compositions were arrangements of his own or other composers' works. There are many incomplete compositions—movements of sonatas and symphonies, for example—and the problem is whether or not to include them in adding up totals. In any event, Mozart's output includes eighteen operas, a ballet, at least forty-one symphonies, twenty-six string quartets, twenty-five concertos for one or more pianos, ten instrumental quintets, nineteen piano sonatas, forty-two violin sonatas, close to forty divertimentos and serenades for various combinations of instruments, six violin concertos (plus concertos for bassoon, horn, clarinet, flute, and flute and harp), twenty-three sets of dances, and many miscellaneous works for all kinds of instrumental groups. For voice, in addition to his operas,

Ex. 57 — Quintet for Strings, K. 516

Ex. 58 — Piano Concerto in D Minor, K. 466

Ex. 59 — Slow Movement, "Jupiter" Symphony

(Ex. 58). His harmonies, which had been uncomplicated in the early works, now become more chromatic and even dissonant as he strives to say with eloquence what is in his heart (Ex. 59).

Mozart's youthful works follow the strict patterns of the early Classical period. Dances, sonatas, rondos, and variations are clear-cut. As his music becomes more a personal ex-

pression of his feelings, his forms become more complex. At times they are tightly knit as he weaves counterpoint into his symphonies, chamber works, and operas. Then again his forms sprawl, as though he were thinking out loud.

In many ways Mozart was a composer of the Romantic period, born fifty years ahead of his time. Like the composers of the nine-

Left: *Mozart's sister Maria Anna ("Nannerl") shown in a court costume given to her by Empress Maria Theresa*
Right: *Leopold Mozart, father of the composer*

teenth century, he was interested in the different musical colors possible through the use of the orchestral instruments. In concertos and chamber music, he showed off the possibilities of the clarinet and the horn, and helped to establish the clarinet as a legitimate member of the symphony orchestra. In Mozart's instrumental works, wind instruments, instead of merely supporting the strings, are allowed to carry sections of a work by themselves. Brasses, particularly the horns and trombones, are used in whole scenes of his operas for dramatic purposes. For color he used the so-called "Turkish" percussion instruments—triangle, bass drum, and cymbals—as well as the shrill piccolo. Mozart's earliest symphonies use the simple Classical groups of instruments: strings plus a pair of horns and a pair of flutes or oboes. In his last works, particularly the operas, the modern symphony orchestra with its balance of string and wind instruments has arrived on the scene.

Although Mozart's favorite musical form was opera, the instrument he loved to play and to write for was the piano. The instrument itself was just coming into favor, especially in Vienna, and Mozart's concertos and sonatas did much to establish the basic styles of pianistic writing. Even in his earliest sonatas, written in 1774, Mozart had discovered the suitability of the piano for playing big chords, for rapid passage work, and for singing melodies. Long before Chopin,

he played with the free and expressive treatment of rhythm known as rubato. He took pride in the fact that his left hand strictly kept the beat while his right hand was able to take the subtle rhythmic freedoms.

The piano used by Mozart was much smaller than the piano of today:

Range of Mozart Piano

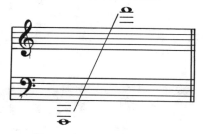

But even with a smaller range of tone, inadequate sustaining power, and fewer keys, Mozart made the piano sing, glitter, and thunder.

Mozart's handling of the voice has never been surpassed. He usually wrote with specific singers in mind, knowing which voices were high and brilliant, or sombre, or caressing, or capable of rapid-fire patter songs. But when he wrote for the voice, Mozart not only showed it off—he used it as the highest form of expression. Each aria and ensemble in a Mozart opera helps to complete the portraits of the characters on stage. Perhaps this is why Mozart's operas have held the stage longer and more thoroughly than those of any other composer.

The Mozart family was a tightly knit unit. Although they were often separated, they kept in touch with each other by writing many letters. Fortunately most of these letters have been saved and published. They give a remarkably complete picture of the life of a musician in the late eighteenth century. More than this, they give better than any other biographical material a clear image of Mozart, the great composer and warm human being.

MUSETTE: a small French bagpipe especially popular at the courts of Louis XIV and Louis XV. Originally a peasant instrument brought to France by the ancient Romans, the musette was adopted by French courtiers who were taking part in a make-believe back-to-nature movement. Dressed in lavish shepherd and shepherdess costumes, the courtiers wandered through the manicured gardens playing musettes whose bags were highly ornamented with exquisite needlework and precious stones. Like all bagpipes, the musette consisted of one or two chanter pipes on which a melody could be played, several drones (tuned to the tonic and dominant tones of the scale) which provided an accompaniment, and a set of bellows, pumped by the arm, which supplied air to the pipes. Many of the finest musettes were made by Jean Hotteterre (d. c. 1690), co-inventor of the oboe, who perfected the instrument's drones.

The vogue for the pastoral tone quality of the musette carried over into musical compositions. Its droning accompaniment could easily be imitated on the harpsichord or orchestral instruments. Sometimes a musette was written as an independent piece. More often it appeared as a contrasting section of a gavotte or occasionally a bourrée or minuet. Clear examples of such musettes are to be heard in the gavotte from the "English" Suite Number 3 of J. S. Bach and the gavotte from Prokofiev's *Classical Symphony* (Ex. 60).

MUSICAL COMEDY: the form of popular musical theater in the United States, where it is referred to also as the "Broadway musical." The composers whose music has highlighted musical comedy include Herbert, Cohan, Friml, Romberg, Kern, Berlin, Rome, Gershwin, Porter, Youmans, Rodgers, Weill, Bernstein, Duke, Loesser, Arlen, and Loewe. The often-neglected librettists and lyricists, whose creative use of words has done so much to establish the uniquely American tone of musical comedies, include Harry B. Smith, Otto Harbach, Guy Bolton, P. G. Wodehouse, Ira Gershwin, Oscar Hammerstein II, Lorenz Hart, Howard Dietz, E. Y. Harburg, and Alan Jay Lerner.

Each country, it seems, develops its own popular theater form—a form that grows out of the spirit of a people as expressed in its folk tales and its songs and dances: the zarzuela in Spain, the ballad opera in England, the Singspiel in Germany, opera buffa in Italy, and operettas in France and Austria. In the United States the minstrel show emerged in the middle of the nineteenth century. With its mixture of Negro and white humor, music, and dancing, it might have become the basis of a truly national form of folk theater. Unfortunately, its basic values were neglected, and as it became cheapened with dialect jokes and tasteless parodies, it degenerated into something suitable only for amateurs. Meanwhile the romantic operetta had established itself, particularly in melodic works such as Victor Herbert's *The Fortune Teller* (1898), *Babes in Toyland* (1903), *Mlle. Modiste* (1905), *The Red Mill* (1906), and *Naughty Marietta* (1910).

Charging into the marshmallow world of operetta came George M. Cohan (1878–1942), the "Yankee Doodle Boy," who had grown up in the hard-hitting song-and-dance world of vaudeville. His shows, for which he wrote both words and music, were fast-paced, extravagantly patriotic odes to America and show business. His tunes—"Give My Regards to Broadway," "You're a Grand Old Flag," "Over There"—were easy to remember, and they punched hard in their march-

Ex. 60 — *Classical Symphony*, Prokofiev

Top: *a scene from* The Red Mill *by Victor Herbert*
Middle: Blossom Time *by Sigmund Romberg*

Bottom: 45 Minutes from Broadway *by George M. Cohan (pictured on the left)*

like syncopated rhythms. His first "hit" show, *Little Johnny Jones* (1904), set the pattern for future Cohan shows as well as the pace of the fast-moving musicals.

Broadway, after World War I, found two sources for its inspiration. One was the Viennese form of operetta, based on highly romantic plots and featuring waltzes and marches; the other was the revue with its successor, the musical comedy.

The two most important suppliers of operettas to the Broadway scene were Rudolf Friml (1879–1972) and Sigmund Romberg (1887–1951). Friml, who had studied composition with Dvořák, is best known for his *Rose Marie* (1924) and *The Vagabond King* (1925). Romberg, a Vienna-trained composer, is remembered for his *Blossom Time* (1921), *The Student Prince* (1924), *The Desert Song* (1926), *The New Moon* (1928), and *Up in Central Park* (1945). Both men had a gift for composing full-throated arias, duets, and rousing choruses which were skillfully introduced into the sentimental libretto.

It was Jerome Kern who brought to Broadway the idea of writing shows based on stories about believable people rather than romantic characters from never-never land. In such early works as *Very Good, Eddie* (1915) and *Oh Boy!* (1917) his principal collaborators were the highly literate Guy Bolton and P. G. Wodehouse. Together they produced shows in which plot, lyrics, and music were equally important.

Kern contributed songs to the *Ziegfeld Follies* of 1916. The *Follies,* of which there were almost annual editions through 1936, represented another form of musical theater —the storyless revue. Everything about the *Follies* was spectacular. There were opulent settings, top comedians such as Fanny Brice, W. C. Fields, and Eddie Cantor, and music by such men as Kern, Herbert, and Berlin. Most important were the queenly *Ziegfeld Follies* girls, who did little but make entrances in exquisite gowns, stroll around the stage, and pose in tableaus to the "national anthem" of the *Follies*—Berlin's "A Pretty Girl Is Like a Melody."

The revue form dominated the Broadway stage of the early 1920's. A theater—The Music Box—was built for a series of *Music Box Revues* written by Berlin. There were also *George White's Scandals* (1920, 1921, 1922, 1923, 1924), with music by Gershwin, and *Earl Carroll's Vanities* (1930, 1931), which featured girls rather than music, and body rather than costume. Most important of the revues, because they brought to light two great talents, were the *Garrick Gaieties* of 1925 and 1926, which established the

Broadway team of Richard Rodgers and Lorenz Hart.

The revue form was a fast-paced alternation of romantic or topical songs, bright and often satirical comic sketches, and dances that combined elements of tap, ballet, and ballroom dancing. *The Little Show* of 1929, for example, featured such stars as Libby Holman, Fred Allen, and Clifton Webb; songs by Arthur Schwartz and Howard Dietz, Kay Swift and James Warburg, and Ralph Rainger; and sketches by Fred Allen, Marya Mannes, and George S. Kaufman. In the many intimate revues the accent was on performance rather than the eye-catching spectacle. What show needed girls if it had Fred Astaire, Fred Allen, Frank Morgan, Libby Holman, Imogene Coca, Bea Lillie, or Bert Lahr?

The period of the 1920's served to bring together the men who were to dominate the American musical stage: the Gershwins, Rodgers and Hart, Cole Porter, Vincent Youmans, Kern, and Oscar Hammerstein II. It was these last two who brought musical comedy to its maturity in 1927 with their memorable *Show Boat,* based on a novel by Edna Ferber. It featured blacks—not as caricatures but as real, suffering persons. All its characters, white and black, were believable, three-dimensional figures. And there was the musical score, studded with such songs as "Ol' Man River," "Make Believe," "Why Do I Love You?," and "Bill."

Show Boat brought out the best in Oscar Hammerstein II (1895–1960), the most talented writer of books and lyrics for American musical theater. Before *Show Boat* he had collaborated with various composers in such lightweight shows as *Tickle Me* (1920) and *Daffy Dill* (1922) and romantic operettas such as *Rose Marie* (1924) and *The Desert Song* (1926). Later, teamed with Richard Rodgers, Hammerstein opened his heart and gave full reign to his concern with human beings in works that have become modern classics: *Oklahoma!* (1943), *Carousel* (1945), *South Pacific* (1949), *The King and I* (1951), *Flower Drum Song* (1958), and *The Sound of Music* (1959).

The period of *Show Boat*—the late 1920's —was also the period of such Gershwin shows as *Funny Face* (1927) and *Girl Crazy* (1930). It was a time of sophisticated humor and music as well as a time of uneasiness for Broadway. Sound had been added to the image of the heretofore silent movies. The movies moved in on the spectacular revue and outdid Ziegfeld. The United States was hit by a great, sobering depression. Prohibition, with its encouragement of gangsters

From the Ziegfeld Follies *of 1928*

and the flouting of law, produced a nationwide cynicism. In the musical theater the Gershwins' *Strike Up the Band* (1930), *Of Thee I Sing* (1931), and *Let 'Em Eat Cake* (1933) satirized war and national politics. (*Of Thee I Sing* won a Pulitzer prize in drama, not for its music but for its script by George S. Kaufman and Morrie Ryskind!) Irving Berlin's *Face the Music* (1932) and *As Thousands Cheer* (1933) were concerned with topics of the day, as was the revue *Americana* (1932), with its "Brother, Can You Spare a Dime?" (by E. Y. Harburg). *Americana* was the first large-scale musical show to include dances by serious American choreographers—Doris Humphrey and Charles Weidman. The show-stopping music of *As Thousands Cheer* was "Heat Wave," sung by Ethel Waters and danced to by Letitia Ide and José Limon.

A scene from Ziegfeld's production of Show Boat *by Kern and Hammerstein*

Top: As Thousands Cheer, *with Ethel Waters flanked by dancers Letitia Ide and José Limon*
Middle: Pins and Needles, *the original I.L.G.W.U. production, 1937*

Bottom: *the original cast of* Oklahoma!

With the change to adult musical shows, Broadway was ready for its closest approach to true American opera—Gershwin's *Porgy and Bess* (1935). This work, with its recitatives linking its arias, and its orchestration carefully worked out by Gershwin, remains a landmark of the American musical theater. Its complete interdependence of story, action, lyrics, and music—all fully realized by a brilliant all-Negro cast—and its tragic overtones added a dimension to Broadway that had been approached only by *Show Boat.*

Musical comedy had grown up. In its adolescence it had depended on romantic love as its chief ingredient. The 1930's was a time of maturing. Not that all musicals were tragic—far from it. Musicals could now feature spoofs on ballet with choreography by a real ballet choreographer—George Balanchine (*On Your Toes,* 1936). There were antiwar satires (*Johnny Johnson,* 1936, by Kurt Weill), songs of social significance (*Pins and Needles,* 1937, by Harold Rome—a revue originally staged by members of the International Ladies Garment Workers' Union), and the love life of a cheap hoofer (Rodgers and Hart's *Pal Joey,* 1940, based on short stories in letter form by John O'Hara), and psychoanalysis (*Lady in the Dark,* 1941, by Moss Hart and Kurt Weill).

Writers of musicals discovered that there was truly no limit to subject matter. In 1938 the playwright Maxwell Anderson wrote an ode to freedom, *Knickerbocker Holiday,* based on the earliest days of New York, for Kurt Weill. To this Weill contributed one of the most poignant of all his songs: "September Song." Shakespeare's *A Comedy of Errors* was tapped for Rodgers and Hart's *Boys from Syracuse,* also in 1938.

During World War II musical comedy dealt with wartime themes, as in Irving Berlin's *This Is the Army* (1942) and in Cole Porter's *Let's Face It* (1941), which starred Danny Kaye, and *Something for the Boys* (1943). But the important shows of the period dug into America's past, combining history with an integration of music, words, and dance in a most complete way.

Oklahoma!, the first collaboration of Rodgers and Hammerstein, set the style for the musical comedy of the next several decades. Lynn Riggs's play *Green Grow the Lilacs* was the basis of *Oklahoma!*—a play about the old West. Songs and dances (staged by Agnes de Mille) flowed naturally out of the dramatic situation. The story gave Hammerstein a chance to compose lyrics that had warmth and friendliness. For it Rodgers wrote one of his finest scores, and de Mille's dances were designed for a group of dancers who could combine swift-moving folk dances with ballet. *Oklahoma!* was a supreme achievement, and the public responded by supporting its New York run for more than five years and its touring company for ten.

Three shows of 1944 illustrate the wide range and rich possibilities of the Broadway musical. *The Seven Lively Arts* contained an overture by William Schuman, a ballet score by Igor Stravinsky, and paintings by Salvadore Dali to be looked at during intermission. *Bloomer Girl,* on the other hand, was a Civil War period piece with score by Harold Arlen and dances staged by de Mille.

Both *Oklahoma!* and *Bloomer Girl* were orchestrated by Robert Russell Bennett. He had become the man who did most to change the sound of the pit band from that of routine orchestrations (good enough for vaudeville) to sparkling and inventive scores that could be listened to with pleasure. Except for Gershwin and later Bernstein, most composers rely on someone like Bennett to arrange their tunes for orchestra.

The third show of 1944 was *On the Town,* a work that brought together a new team consisting of composer Leonard Bernstein, choreographer Jerome Robbins, and writers Betty Comden and Adolph Green.

By the middle 1940's all musical comedies were strong in story, expressive in music and dance, and intellectually tolerable—or else they were destined to fail. The story might be whimsical (*Finian's Rainbow,* 1947; *Brigadoon,* 1947; *Greenwillow,* 1960), or have an exotic flavor (*The King and I; House of Flowers,* 1954; *Flower Drum Song*), or be based on a well-known play or story (*Kiss Me Kate,* 1948; *Where's Charley?* 1948; *Gentlemen Prefer Blondes,* 1949; *Candide,* 1956), or even be biographical (*The Sound of Music,* 1959; *Gypsy,* 1959; *Fiorello,* 1959).

The two most important shows of the recent past have been Lerner and Loewe's *My Fair Lady* (adapted from Shaw's *Pygmalion*) and Bernstein and Stephen Sondheim's *West Side Story.* Strangely enough they close this short history of American theater by illustrating the two strands that have been woven together to make musical comedy. *My Fair Lady,* which opened in 1956 and broke the record set by *Oklahoma!* for number of performances, is related to the operetta by its opulent settings and romantic story. But its charming, varied songs and its lively dances, choreographed by Hanya Holm, made *My Fair Lady* a work of today—intelligent, tuneful, and believable.

West Side Story (1957) was as topical as the newspaper headlines in a great city.

A scene from My Fair Lady

Based on Shakespeare's *Romeo and Juliet,* it is set in a slum; its conflict is gang warfare. *West Side Story* is as tough as it is sentimental. It was directed by one of the new breed of choreographer-directors, Jerome Robbins. Perhaps *West Side Story* points the way to the new forms of musical theater that seem to be in the offing.

MUSIC BOX: a mechanical instrument related to the barrel organ. In the box is a metal plate from which a row of metal tongues project, somewhat like the teeth of a comb. These tongues are graded in size so that when plucked they vibrate to produce the various tones of the scale. Next to the row of tongues is a cylinder studded with metal points or pins. When the cylinder is rotated, the pins or points pluck the tongues one after another, causing them to sound. The tune that is produced is determined by the positions of the points on the cylinder. The cylinder is turned by a clocklike spring mechanism.

Practically all music boxes are made in Switzerland, where they were invented in the early 1800's. Most music boxes are tiny and play but one tune. There are, however, larger ones that can play several dozen melodies or a movement of a symphony.

The high tinkling sound of the music box has been imitated on the piano and in the orchestra by many composers, including Liadov and Stravinsky.

Portrait of Mussorgsky as a young man

A scene from Boris Godunov *(Paris Opéra production, 1962)*

MUSSORGSKY, MODEST PETRO-VITCH (1839–81): the most daring and most talented member of the group of composers known as "The Russian Five." Born in Karevo, in northwestern Russia, Mussorgsky had little musical training other than some lessons on the piano. Most of his life was spent in government service, as an officer in the Imperial Guard and as a clerk in the communications and forestry departments.

The turning point in Mussorgsky's career came in his early twenties. He had been content to play the piano at dances and compose polkas in the popular style of the day. A group of young Russian musicians, including Rimsky-Korsakov, Borodin, Balakirev, and Cui, persuaded Mussorgsky to join them in establishing a style of music based on Russian folk music and stories. Mussorgsky was encouraged to throw away German and Italian models and invent his own musical language.

Mussorgsky completed only one large work: his powerful opera *Boris Godunov.* In this work, based on Russian history as dramatized by Pushkin, he mixed together folk melodies, sometimes dissonant harmonies, and vocal lines that follow closely the rise and fall of emotional speech, and made colorful use of the instruments of the orchestra. Since much of the music of *Boris* was thought to be too crude and rough, Mussorgsky's friend Rimsky smoothed it and polished it. Not until many years after Mussorgsky's death did the world hear the masterpiece as he had intended it; in fact, the original score was first performed in the United States in Boston in 1965. Mussorgsky's other operas were finished after his death: *Khovanshtchina* by Rimsky in 1886 and *The Fair at Sorotchinsk* by Cui in 1917.

Mussorgsky was at his best when writing for the voice. He ranges from the tenderness of children's songs, as in *The Nursery,* to the many guises of death, as in his *Songs and Dances of Death.* That he could be bitterly satiric is proved by his songs "The Seminarian," "The Classicist," "The Peep Show," and his well-known "Song of the Flea."

Mussorgsky wrote no sonatas, concertos, or symphonies. His instrumental works are primarily musical paintings, such as *Night on Bald Mountain* for orchestra and *Pictures at an Exhibition* for piano, written in 1874. These piano pieces, later orchestrated by several musicians, including Maurice Ravel, are completely original—unlike anything else written at the time. They come as close as music can to making a listener "see" what he is hearing.

Mussorgsky's life was a tragic one. Torn between his composing and his government work, he worked briefly as a professional accompanist, but this job gave him even less time to compose. The lack of musical training that made him so inventive musically also made him unsure of himself and his work. He began to drink heavily, and this undoubtedly led to his early death.

Many composers, in the years since 1900, have followed the musical paths first opened by Mussorgsky. He influenced not only Russian composers but many French, Spanish, and American men of music also: Debussy, Ravel, Satie, Falla, Copland. *Boris Godunov* showed the way to the young Italian composers Mascagni and Leoncavallo in their search for operatic realism. No composer with so little musical education ranks with Mussorgsky in influence upon other composers.

MUTE: a device temporarily added to an instrument to soften or dampen its tone. In most cases a mute also changes the instrument's tone color.

Violins are muted by means of a small comb-like attachment whose prongs grip the bridge of the instrument and stop some of the vibrations that are carried from the strings to the body of the violin; the result is a thinner, wispier tone. There are several kinds of violin mutes. The newest can be clamped onto the strings behind the bridge when not in use, and so does away with the frantic searching in pockets for the old-fashioned mutes. Muted violins were called for as early as 1686 by Lully in his opera *Armide et Renaud.* Like most other novel instrumental sounds, those produced by muted instruments were used in theater orchestras long before they were used in concert orchestras.

Mutes for the viola, cello, and stringed bass did not become common until after 1800. Since then, many composers have made use of mutes on the whole string section. A beautiful example of the veiled tone of muted strings occurs near the beginning of Debussy's *The Afternoon of a Faun.* Here the strings play a trembling accompaniment to the flute, oboe, and horns.

Composers have been putting mutes into brass instruments since the seventeenth century, possibly as early as 1607, when Monteverdi in his opera *Orfeo* called for a *tromba sordino.* Early brass mutes were made of cardboard, leather, or papier-mâché; they not only softened the sound but also raised the pitch so the performer had to play his note a whole step lower to have it sound as intended. The modern brass mute, cone-shaped and made of metal or wood, is designed so that its use does not affect pitch. A muted trumpet played with a sharp attack makes a soft brassy "tang." A long passage for muted trumpets, horns, and violins occurs in Richard Strauss's tone poem *Till Eulenspiegel.*

Trumpets and trombones are more often muted than the horns and tubas. The horn player can get a muted effect simply by stuffing his fist into the bell. Mutes for the horn and tuba are so large that they are somewhat unwieldy, and composers call for them only when they want very special effects, as in Strauss's *Don Quixote,* where the muted brasses are made to sound like bleating sheep.

Jazz brass players have tried almost every possible kind of mute, from derby hats to a plumber's plunger. Opening and closing the throat of the trumpet by means of "the plumber's friend" made possible the trumpet's familiar "wah-wah." The early records of Duke Ellington abound in muted brass sounds.

Woodwinds are rarely muted. For special effects a player occasionally stuffs a piece of cloth into the end of his instrument. An oboe fitted with its pear-shaped mute makes a mournful sound that has been called for by composers only rarely.

Drums are muffled or muted in several ways. In bass drums the head is sometimes loosened. For timpani a piece of cloth is placed on the drumhead. The sound of snare drums in funeral processions is changed by loosening the snares or placing a cloth between the snares and the drumhead.

The piano is muted when the composer writes *una corda,* meaning "one string." Muting is done by means of a pedal. On a grand piano the hammers move to the right so that they hit only one string instead of two or three. On an upright piano the pedal moves the hammers closer to the strings so that they hit with less force.

When the composer wants an instrumentalist to put the mute on his instrument, he writes *con sordino, gedämpft,* or "mute." When the mute is to be removed, he writes *senza sordino, ohne gedämpft,* or "mute off."

NATURAL: the sign (♮) used to cancel a flat or a sharp. The C-major scale contains nothing but natural tones—that is, there are no sharped or flatted tones. In music written with bar-lines, the bar-line itself will normally cancel any chromatic signs that have occurred in the previous measure. However, in highly chromatic music the natural sign is often used as a reminder:

Mazurka, Op. 17, No. 4, Chopin

Since the function of the natural sign is purely negative, it is rarely found in key signatures, and then only when there is a change of key within a composition with a resultant reduction in the number of sharps or flats.

The natural sign took its shape from ♭, which stood for the tone B as distinguished from b or B-flat. For a while the natural sign was used to signify the raising of a tone—a function later taken over by the sharp (♯) sign. It was not until the beginning of the eighteenth century that the natural sign assumed the role of neutralizing both sharps and flats.

NEAPOLITAN SIXTH: one of the earliest chromatically altered chords. Traditionally thought to have a sombre quality, the Neapolitan sixth was popular with the opera composers of seventeenth-century Naples. It is usually used in music written in minor keys, where it can be thought of as the first inversion (a) of a major triad (b) whose root is the lowered second degree of the scale (c):

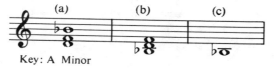

It is called a sixth because its figured-bass symbol is $\frac{6}{3}$:

Neapolitan Sixth in A Minor

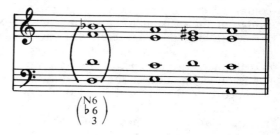

At first the Neapolitan sixth was used most frequently just before a cadence:

Neapolitan Sixth in C Major

Later composers used the chord for its dark harmonic color, as in Mozart's Quintet for Strings K. 516 (Ex. 1).

Some music theorists explain the chord as derived from the Phyrgian mode:

Phrygian Mode

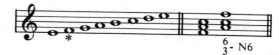

NEIGHBORING TONE: in music theory, a non-harmonic tone that returns to its generating tone. The trill consists of a principal tone alternating with its neighboring

Ex. 1 — Quintet in G Minor, K. 516, Mozart

tone. An upper neighboring tone is usually diatonic; a lower neighboring tone is often just a half step below the principal tone and can be chromatic. (The second tone of "Silent Night" is an example of an upper neighboring tone. The fourth tone of "O Little Town of Bethlehem" is a chromatic lower neighboring tone.) The primary function of a neighboring tone is to embellish its principal tone, as in the case of the trill and the turn ∾ :

The neighboring tone is usually found in a spot that is weak rhythmically:

"Skye Boat Song"

but it can also be placed in a position of prominence, in which case it assumes thematic importance:

Sonata for Piano, Op. 2, No. 3,
Allegro con brio   Beethoven

NINTH: an interval which is a half step (minor ninth) or a whole step (major ninth) larger than an octave:

A ninth chord is a five-tone chord arranged in a series of intervals of a third. The top tone of such a chord is a major or minor ninth above the root, or bottom tone, of the chord:

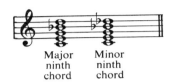

Major   Minor
ninth   ninth
chord   chord

Ninth chords were hinted at in the music of Mozart and Beethoven, where they were built on the fifth tone of the scale—the dominant. Dominant ninths were used freely for their harmonic color by Wagner, Debussy, and Ravel:

Pavane, Ravel

Dominant   Dominant
Ninths   Seventh

Four-tone chords built on the seventh degree, or leading tone, of the major and minor scales contain the upper four tones of dominant ninth chords. For this reason they are sometimes called "incomplete dominant ninths":

VII7 of F Major   VII7 of F Minor

In traditional harmony, ninth chords are used mostly in root position. Except for the third inversion, all other positions of the ninth chord become dissonant and lose their rich flavor.

NOCTURNE: a night piece or night song, usually of a calm nature. The piano style of nocturne, brought to its highest point by Chopin, originated with the Irish composer John Field (1782–1837). The nocturnes of Field and Chopin are written with long melodic lines, often highly decorated, played with rhythmic freedom over a chordal ac-

Ex. 2 — Nocturne, John Field

Ex. 3 — "Nachtstück" from *Suite 1922*, Hindemith

companiment. The beginning of one of them is shown in Ex. 2.

The gentleness of the nocturne appealed to the Romantic composers of the nineteenth century. Chopin wrote nineteen nocturnes; Fauré, the French composer, thirteen. The "Nachtstück" (Night Piece) from the contemporary composer Hindemith's *Suite 1922* (Ex. 3) is brooding and less calm than the nocturnes of the nineteenth century.

The beautiful slow movement of Mendelssohn's music for *A Midsummer Night's Dream* is a nocturne whose melody is played on the French horn. Debussy wrote three nocturnes for orchestra: *Nuages, Fêtes,* and *Sirènes.* Nineteenth-century painters such as Whistler carried the musical term nocturne over into some of their evening scenes.

The *notturno,* an early form of nocturne, was a favorite of the eighteenth-century composers. Designed for evening entertainment, it was a series of short, light pieces like a serenade, usually meant to be performed outdoors. Mozart's Notturno K. 286 was written for four small orchestras, each consisting of a string quartet and two horns. Haydn wrote a curious set of seven notturnos for several instruments and two *lire organizatte* (see HURDY-GURDY) for the king of Naples in 1790.

NOTATION OF MUSIC: the use of signs and symbols in the writing of music. Music is a form of language with its own ABC's— notes. Each note tells how high the musical sound should be *(pitch)* and how long it should last (musical *timing*).

Pitch. The pitch of a note is shown by its position on a group of five horizontal lines

Ex. 4

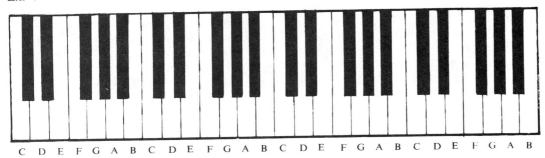

C D E F G A B C D E F G A B C D E F G A B C D E F G A B C D E F G A B

called a *staff.* The notes are given the names of the first seven letters of the alphabet: A-B-C-D-E-F-G. After G the alphabet starts again from A. The letters are the names of the white keys of the piano. The black keys, in alternate groups of twos and threes, sound tones that lie midway between the notes of the white keys. The black keys also serve as guideposts to the performer; without them, the keys would all look alike. The distance from one tone to the next tone of the same name, above or below, is called an octave. Middle C, the C in the middle of the piano keyboard, is a useful point of reference (Ex. 4).

At the beginning of each staff is a sign called a *clef.* The clefs give each staff its name and show the position of three notes: the G above middle C, middle C, and the F below middle C.

The G clef, or treble clef, curls around the second line (from the bottom) of the staff. It shows the place of the G above middle C:

The F clef, or bass clef, curls around the fourth line of the staff. It shows the place of F below middle C:

The C clef shows the place of middle C on the staff. It can be centered on any of the bottom four lines of the staff:

Soprano   Mezzo-soprano   Alto   Tenor

Of these various forms of the C clef, only the alto and tenor clefs are used today—the alto clef in viola parts, the tenor clef in parts written for cello, trombone, and bassoon. (In the tenor parts of some vocal music the C clef is centered on the third space—a more

accurate way of writing the tenor part than the usual method of writing it in the treble clef to be sung an octave lower.)

The treble and bass staves are used in all piano music and in most vocal music printed today. They are combined in the *grand staff:*

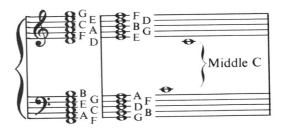

Middle C

Since there is no place in the treble and bass staves for middle C, a line is added for it below the treble or above the bass staff. Such added lines, called *leger* (or *ledger*) *lines,* are used whenever a note lies too high or too low for the staff being used:

To avoid using too many leger lines, the composer can write his music at the next lower octave in the treble or the next higher octave in the bass. The instruction *8va (ottava—* "play these notes an octave higher") or *8va bassa* ("play these notes an octave lower") is then written above or below the notes:

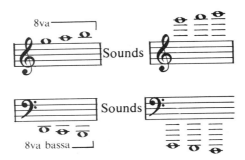

8va

Sounds

Sounds

8va bassa

Special signs called *accidentals* are used for raising or lowering the pitches of notes. A *sharp* sign (♯) placed in front of a note raises the pitch of that note by the interval of a semi-tone, or half step. On the piano it would mean playing the black key immediately to the right of the pitch note except in the case of B♯, which is the same as C, and E♯, which is the same as F:

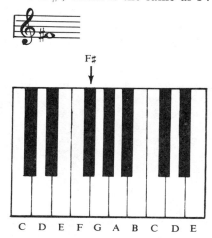

A *flat* sign placed in front of a note lowers the pitch of that note by the interval of a semi-tone, or half step. On the piano it would mean playing the black key immediately to the left of the pitch note, except in the cases of C♭, which is the same note as B, and F♭, which is the same note as E:

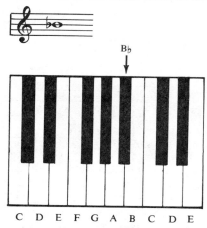

An accidental applies only to the particular line or space on which it is written:

 F Natural
F Sharp

It lasts until the next bar-line unless it is cancelled by a natural sign:

A B♭ C B nat.

A *double sharp* (✕) tells the performer to play the key next above a sharped key; thus F✕ is the same as G. A *double flat* (♭♭) tells the performer to play the key next below a flatted key; thus B♭♭ is the same as A. All the black keys and several of the white keys have two names:

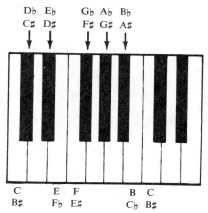

A *key signature* is placed right after the clef sign when a composer is going to use the same sharps or flats throughout a composition. The signature:

tells the performer that all Bs are to be played as B-flats.

Tablature is a system of notation that tells the performer where to place his fingers on an instrument. It was used especially in old music for the lute, but is still used today for the guitar and ukulele and for teaching beginners on woodwind instruments:

Conversion of Tablature

Guitar

 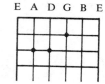

Timing. The timing of notes is written and counted much as money is counted. A whole dollar equals two half-dollars or four quarters. In music a whole note (○) equals two half notes (♩), four quarter notes (♩), eight eighth notes (♪), or sixteen sixteenth notes (♬). These five kinds of note values are the ones used most often. Rests, which correspond to notes in time values, are necessary because a musical pulse keeps going even when there are no sounds—much as the pulse of the blood keeps going during sleep. Rests show how much "silent music" there is.

Ex. 5

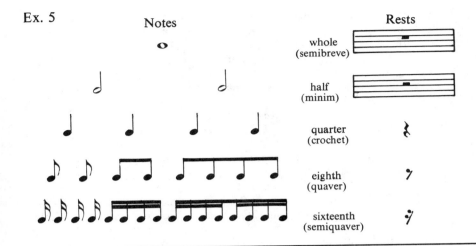

Notes   Rests

Music takes place in time. In counting note values the performer is measuring the time (Ex. 5).

When notes are written on a staff, the stems are turned up when the note heads are below the middle line. The stems are turned down when the note heads lie on or above the middle line:

When two voices are written on one staff, one voice is written with all stems up, the other with all stems down. This holds true even when voices cross:

Two signs are commonly used to lengthen a note. A *tie* connecting two notes of the same pitch adds the time value of the second note to the time value of the first:

A *dot* after a note adds a time value half again as long as the note. It can be thought of as tying a note of the next smaller note value to the first note:

A *double dot* adds a time value half again as large as the dot:

Each composition has a pulse note whose rate of speed determines whether the music will be fast or slow. A *metronome mark* (♩ = 120), or a word such as allegro, tells the performer the tempo of the pulse note. Thus ♩ = 120 means that the quarter notes should be played at the rate of 120 per minute. From the pulse note the rate of speed of the other note values can be figured out. Unless they are tied or dotted, these notes will be two or four times faster or slower than the pulse note.

Pulses are combined into larger units called *measures,* which are regular combinations of strong and weak pulses. The strong pulse, called the measure *accent,* occurs on the first beat of each measure. The distance from one measure accent to another is called the *meter* of the music. The *bar-line* placed in front of the first beat of each measure helps the eye keep track of the measures.

The *time signature* at the beginning of a composition tells the performer how many pulses there are per measure (the upper figure) and which note value the composer has chosen as his pulse note (the lower figure). 2/4 as a time signature shows that every measure will have note values equal to two quarter notes:

There are two basic *meters* in music: the meter of two pulses and the meter of three pulses. Composers group these basic meters into compound meters. A meter of 5 is 2 plus 3; 6 is 3 plus 3, and so on. One of the largest meters is in a prelude by J. S. Bach (Ex. 6). Its time signature is 24/16 (24 is 8x3).

In many folk songs such as "Shenandoah" and modern compositions such as Stravinsky's *Rite of Spring* the meter changes from time to time. A new time signature is used every time the meter changes (Ex. 7).

History of Musical Notation. The musical notation used today developed in Europe over a period of a thousand years. The ancient Chinese, Japanese, Hindus, and Greeks used letters or signs over the words of a song to show the rise and fall of pitch. None of these systems was precise, and all needed the aid of performers' memories.

The earliest form of European notation, developed in the sixth or seventh century, was a system of marks called *neumes*. These were placed over the words to be sung to show whether pitch was to rise or fall—but not precisely how much.

The first staff was a red line which showed the pitch of F below middle C. Soon a green or yellow line was added to show middle C.

Around 1026, Guido d'Arezzo showed the advantages of placing the neumes on a four-line staff. By the thirteenth century the five-line staff with clefs had been proved the most practical for many-voiced music (though to this day the Roman Catholic Church still uses the four-line staff and neumes for Gregorian chant).

Guido had invented a system of six-note scales called *hexachords*. One hexachord needed a B-flat, while the others needed B-naturals. From the two forms of writing the letter B—*b* and ♮—came the flat and natural signs of the present day. The sharp sign was not used until the 1400's, although singers had sung sharped tones when their ears told them to do so.

Musical timing came into being in the thirteenth century, when the writing of many-voiced music made it necessary. An early way of showing time values was to write the notes in red or black ink. Dots were used in the thirteenth century; the tie was not known until the fifteenth. But by the fifteenth century the present system of black and white notes and their corresponding rests had become fairly standardized. The bar-line, modern time signature, tempo marks such as "allegro," and dynamic marks such as "forte" were introduced in the sixteenth and seventeenth centuries. The double dot, first used by Leopold Mozart, became in the middle 1700's the last important element of musical notation to be accepted. (In the Baroque period a dotted quarter note in a slow tempo was performed as if it were doubly dotted. Some present-day editions of Bach and his contemporaries have added double dots in the music.) Many expression marks were added in the eighteenth and nineteenth centuries, but no basic changes were made in notation. In our own century, certain composers have experimented with new forms of notation, including the use of graph paper, elaborate drawings, and even complex signs that are like contemporary neumes—almost as though music were repeating its history.

Below left: *an example of neumatic notation from 11th-century French manuscript*
Below right: *portion of a page from an illuminated antiphonary (from a 15th-century Italian manuscript)*

Ex. 6 — Prelude No. 15 from *The Well-tempered Clavier*, Book I, J.S. Bach

Ex. 7

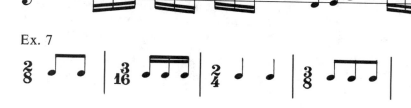

Above left: *the "Snowflakes" scene*
Above right: *Suzanne Farrell in the "Dewdrop" scene (both from a New York City Ballet production of* Nutcracker*)*

NUTCRACKER: a ballet with music by Tchaikovsky. It contains some of his gayest tunes and most colorful orchestration. Strangely enough, just about the time he was finishing the *Nutcracker*, Tchaikovsky started sketching out the somber *Symphonie pathétique.*

The scenario for the *Nutcracker* (*Casse noisette* in French), based on a story by E. T. A. Hoffman, was written by Marius Petipa, ballet master at the Russian Imperial Theaters. Together with his assistant Ivanov, Petipa also composed the dances for the ballet. This work was first performed in Leningrad (then St. Petersburg) in 1892. From its final scene Tchaikovsky had, a few months earlier, made a suite for orchestra that has since become one of the most popular of light orchestral works. It contains an Arabian Dance, the Dance of the Sugarplum Fairy, a Russian Dance, a March, a Chinese Dance, a Dance of the Reed Flutes, and—as the finale of the ballet—the Waltz of the Flowers. The quality of each dance is delightfully brought out by Tchaikovsky's skillful use of instruments: the newly invented celesta in the Dance of the Sugarplum Fairy, the three flutes swirling in the Dance of the Reed Flutes, and the grotesque combination of piccolo, flute, and bassoon in the Chinese Dance.

In the *Nutcracker* story two children, Clara and Fritz, are given a Christmas party, to which a magician named Drosselmeyer brings an assortment of amazing toys and dolls that dance. The magician presents a nutcracker to Clara, and she and her brother Fritz quarrel over it. Later it is thrown aside when they go to bed. But Clara cannot sleep for thinking of her nutcracker. She sneaks downstairs to the dark living room and finds it leading a troop of toy soldiers in battle against an army of mice. Clara hits the King of the Mice with her slipper. The toy soldiers win the battle, and the nutcracker is transformed into a handsome prince.

The prince rewards Clara for her help by taking her to the Kingdom of the Sweets. On their way they cross a country where they see snowflakes dancing together. When they reach the Kingdom of the Sweets, they are greeted by the Sugarplum Fairy, who provides Arabian, Chinese, and Russian dances as entertainment. After a dance by the Sugarplum Fairy (see CELESTA) the ballet ends with the famous Waltz of the Flowers.

OBOE: the soprano member of the double-reed family of woodwinds. With its high nasal twang the oboe is the most expressive of the woodwinds. The name comes from the French *hautbois,* meaning "high" or "loud" "wood." The body of the oboe is cone-shaped, being narrowest at the mouthpiece and widest at the bottom, or "bell." For convenience in carrying and cleaning, it is made in three sections, usually of hard, shiny ebony or rosewood.

The oboe's tone is produced by the flow of the player's breath between two strips of reed. (The two strips make it a "double-reed" instrument, like the bassoon—and unlike the clarinet.) Oboists are very particular about their reeds, which are cut from cane that grows in southern France and Italy. The oboist trims and shaves his reeds to the thinness and narrowness he prefers (generally, the softer and thinner the reeds, the sweeter the tone). He then binds them with thread and fits them into the holder. Before a concert, an oboist can often be seen sucking on the reeds to moisten them and make them more flexible. At the last minute he will plug the holder into the oboe and be ready to play.

The oboe is not an easy instrument to play. It has fifteen or more keys or levers for the fingers to work. One of them, the octave key, is used in combination with others to produce the high tones. The complete range—the smallest for any of the woodwinds—is shown here:

The real difficulty in playing the oboe is controlling one's breath. The oboist does not blow into the instrument, but rather lets air escape through the mouthpiece, all the while breathing in fresh air and expelling extra air from his lungs. It has been said that playing the oboe is like swimming underwater.

There are two main styles of oboe playing. The French style tends to make the tone colorful and expressive, the German style to make it warm and mellow. This difference results in part from the fact that in the French tradition the reeds are cut thinner and narrower.

The modern oboe is three hundred years old, but some instruments like it are quite ancient. The Egyptians, Greeks, and Hindus all used instruments that had double reeds. The Greek oboe, called the *aulos,* was popular but took great strength to play; the player's cheeks were strapped in a leather belt so that they would not burst. In Turkey,

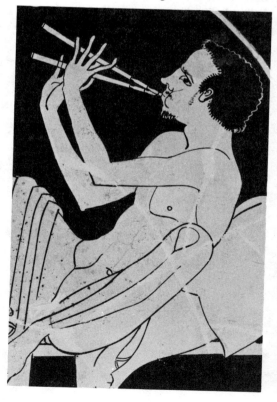

Left: *man playing a Greek aulos (from an early 5th-century* B.C. *kylix)*
Right: *Ernest Harrison playing the oboe*

Ex. 1 — Second Movement, Symphony No. 7 in C Major, Schubert

Ex. 2 — Second Movement, Symphony No. 4 in F Minor, Tchaikovsky

an instrument like an oboe was used in the military bands. Since the bands played during battle, the Turkish oboe must have been loud enough to be heard along with drums, cymbals, and trumpets.

The modern oboe was developed in Paris in the late 1650's by Jean Hotteterre, a bagpiper in the court ballet orchestra. Hotteterre, who was also a woodworker, was attempting to improve the *shawm*—a medieval double-reed instrument then still used in bands. Hotteterre narrowed the body of the shawm, divided it into three sections, improved the mouthpiece, and added finger holes for tones in the higher register. This new "hautbois" was first used by Lully in his opera orchestra. Its expressive tone gave the woodwinds something to pit against the popularity of the voices and strings. In fact it fit all situations—it could hold its own with the trumpets or blend with the soft recorders. Within a short time two oboes became standard instruments in every good orchestra, and in Baroque chamber music they were used interchangeably with violins and flutes.

All the great composers have delighted in writing for the oboe. Handel wrote six concertos for it, as well as six sonatas for two oboes and bass. Bach gave the oboe eloquent melodies—often in his cantatas as duets with a soprano soloist. Symphonic literature abounds in expressive melodies written for oboe, among the best known being those in Schubert's C-major Symphony (Ex. 1) and Tchaikovsky's Fourth Symphony (Ex. 2).

It is the oboe, in today's orchestra, that gives the "A" for the other instruments to tune to. This is because the oboe's pitch cannot be altered without resorting to actual carpentry. A large orchestra usually has three oboes, the third oboist sometimes switching to English horn—which is, in fact, an alto oboe.

Two older forms of the oboe, familiar in the 1700's but rarely heard today, are the *oboe d'amore* and the *oboe da caccia*. The former (oboe of love) is pitched three tones lower than the regular oboe. It was a particular favorite of Bach, who gave it soulful melodies in his cantatas, expressing heartfelt longing. One of the rare uses of the oboe d'amore by a modern composer is in Ravel's *Boléro*. The oboe da caccia, or "oboe of the hunt," was an alto instrument (actually used for a time on hunts) with a curved shape and a range that extended five tones lower than the oboe. By the nineteenth century it had straightened out and become the English horn we know today.

OCARINA: a plaintive-sounding relative of the woodwind family made of clay. Often called "sweet potato" from its shape, it has a mouthpiece of a simple whistle type, so that the tone is easy to produce, and it has eight finger holes—four for each hand—underneath which are two thumb holes and a "voicing" hole from which the air issues. The range of the ocarina is three tones larger than an octave; it comes in different sizes,

Playing the ocarina

each pitched in a different key. The larger the ocarina, the deeper the tone.

The ocarina, developed in the nineteenth century in Italy and Austria, is made in two halves, glazed and baked together. It is a later relative of the primitive whistles, the old Chinese *hsüan,* or "goose-egg," and an Italian carnival whistle.

The ocarina has not been used in concert music. For a while it was popular in vaudeville but at present seems restricted to home use. Its low tones are breathy and mellow, somewhat like those of the recorder. Its upper tones tend to be shrill.

OCTAVE: the distance from one tone to the next tone of the same letter name. It takes its name from *octo,* the Latin word for "eight," because if the bottom note is called the first note, the octave interval lands on the eighth note above it:

When the tones are exactly alike, the interval is called a perfect octave. Other forms of the octave are the augmented octave, which is a half step larger than a perfect octave:

and the diminished octave, a half step smaller than a perfect octave:

Most scales have a compass of one octave:

The perfect octave is the most perfect consonance, since one tone duplicates the other at a higher or lower pitch. The perfect octave is the first interval above the fundamental tone in the overtone series. In acoustics the ratio of the tones in an octave is 2 to 1. In other words, the higher tone vibrates at a speed (vibrations per second) exactly twice as fast as that of the lower tone:

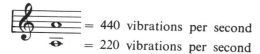

= 440 vibrations per second

= 220 vibrations per second

In early medieval music the melodies were often sung in octaves. This is called "magadizing," from the name of a Greek lute, the *magadis,* whose strings were grouped in pairs tuned an octave apart. Later composers avoided the simultaneous duplication of melodies at the octave, and in the study of traditional four-part harmony such duplication is considered to be incorrect, even for short stretches. In piano, organ, and orchestral scores, however, melodies are often made to sound louder by being reinforced in octaves. In piano music the composer writes the indication *col 8va* below the notes he wants played in octaves:

col 8va

OCTET: a chamber work to be played by eight solo instruments. Any combination of instruments may be used, depending on the tone color the composer has in mind. The best-known octets are those by Beethoven (Opus 103, for oboes, clarinets, horns, and bassoons), Schubert (Opus 166, for strings, clarinet, bassoon, and horn), Mendelssohn (Opus 20, for strings), and Stravinsky (for wind instruments). The *Bachianas Brasileiras,* Number 1, by the modern Brazilian composer Heitor Villa-Lobos is for eight cellos.

The German composer Ludwig Spohr (1784–1859) was intrigued by the possibilities of the octet and wrote one for violin, two violas, cello, string bass, clarinet, and two horns. He also experimented in writing four double string quartets that are actually octets. The modern French composer Darius Milhaud wrote his fourteenth and fifteenth string quartets in such a way that they can be played either separately as quartets or together as an octet.

OFFENBACH, JACQUES (1819–1880): the favorite operetta composer of Paris in the 1860's, who wrote more than a hundred works for the musical stage. He was born in Cologne, Germany, where his father sang as cantor in a synagogue. After some training as a cellist Offenbach entered the Paris Conservatory, but soon left to try his luck as a cellist in the orchestra of the Paris Opéra-Comique, then as a touring soloist, and also as the conductor of a theater orchestra.

The light, romantic operetta was just becoming a popular form of entertainment in Paris when, in 1855, Offenbach wrote his first successful stage work. His gay, witty music matched the irreverent plots that he chose. In a short time he was the king of popular music in Paris, with a theater of his own, the Bouffes-Parisiens, where he first produced his *Orphée aux Enfers (Orpheus in the Underworld)* in 1858.

In the 1860's he joined forces with a team of librettists of great skill, Meilhac and Halévy, to produce many of the operettas for which he is best remembered—*La Belle Hélène (Fair Helen,* 1864); *La Vie parisienne (Parisian Life,* 1866); *La Grande Duchesse de Gérolstein* (1867); and *La Périchole* (1868).

In 1877 Offenbach toured the United States to build up his fortunes, which were low at the moment. His concerts were not received with enthusiasm, but he returned to Paris with $20,000 and material for a book: *Offenbach in America.* The last years of his life were spent working on his single serious opera, *Les Contes d'Hoffmann (The Tales of Hoffmann),* by which he hoped to be remembered. He died four months before the first performance of this complex masterpiece, which has since become standard operatic repertory.

Offenbach's music remains popular today because he was able, with the simplest means, to write music that is clear and direct. In his works languishing melodies alternate with music that bubbles and crackles gleefully. A lilting waltz gives way to an impish galop; a long, flowing melody bursts into a breath-taking presto. When he wanted to, Offenbach could write music that was excitingly dramatic, as in sections of *The Tales of Hoffmann.*

In 1938 music from several of Offenbach's works was arranged by Manuel Rosenthal as the score for Massine's ballet *Gaité parisienne.*

Offenbach surrounded by his family

Can-can dancers as portrayed by Toulouse-Lautrec in a lithograph poster, 1896

OPERA: a drama in which the moods and emotions are heightened by combining the singing of the words with orchestral accompaniment, stage action, and scenic effects. The text of an opera—that is, the words that are sung and occasionally spoken—is called its libretto.

There are many kinds of opera. "Chamber" operas, requiring only a few singers and instrumentalists, may be only a half hour in length; some of the longest operas take five hours to perform and involve hundreds of singers and dancers. In most operas all the words are sung, but in some there is spoken dialogue. Some operas are primarily successions of arias connected by the declaimed type of speech-song known as recitative. In others the flow of dramatic action is not interrupted by any set piece such as an aria. Operas can be tragic or gay; superficial in meaning or deeply philosophical; witty and sophisticated in tone or unrestrained in passion. Musically an opera can be composed primarily of straightforward vocal melodies, with the orchestra playing the simplest kind of accompaniment, or it can be highly complex in melody and harmony, with the orchestra equal in importance to the voice. Really, then, there is no such thing as a "typical" opera.

Because of the expense of producing it, opera more than any other form of music has reflected the social conditions among which it has grown and flourished. Depending on its audience, opera at different times in its history has featured the witty or noble words of the librettist, the spectacular effects devised by the scenic designer, the virtuosity of the singers, the pageantry invented for the corps de ballet, or inspired directing by the conductor, who from his position in the orchestra pit functions like a field marshal as he takes charge of all the on-stage and off-stage forces.

Even the opera house itself has often been designed with the wishes of the audience in mind. The horseshoe-shaped interior of most opera houses allows everyone in the boxes to see and be seen. Opera-going has often been a form of social entertainment accompanied by the fun of gossiping, eating, drinking, and even gambling. Interestingly enough, the horseshoe shape has been perfect for acoustics, even if it has prevented many in the audience from seeing the whole stage.

Opera has been cluttered with so many trappings that one wonders how it ever reached artistic heights. Its success has been due to its composers; it has survived only because it has offered great music. The inventiveness of a long line of geniuses has continually refreshed the whole field of opera: Monteverdi, Lully, Handel, Alessandro Scarlatti, Gluck, Mozart, Rossini, Bellini, Weber, Meyerbeer, Wagner, Verdi, Mussorgsky, Strauss, Debussy, Puccini, Berg.

More than any other type of composer, the creator of opera has always had to experiment and invent. Dramatic situations have called forth new sounds and new forms. Instrumental effects, such as string tremolos and the pizzicato, were first used in a dramatic work by the first great opera composer, Monteverdi. The clarinet, piccolo, trombone, cymbals, bass drum, and triangle were used in the opera orchestra before they became members of the symphony orchestra. From opera came such new musical ideas as the recitative and the da capo aria. The short instrumental interludes between stanzas of a song—the ritornello—directly influenced the form of the first movement of Baroque concertos and concerti grossi. The very essence of Classical musical style has its origins in the melody and rhythm of eighteenth-century Italian opera overtures, arias, and sinfonias. The form of the Classical symphony, with its movements in contrasting tempos of fast-slow-fast, can be traced to the Italian opera overtures of Alessandro Scarlatti. The history of opera is, in fact, a major part of the history of European music since 1600.

The practice of combining song with instrumental music and movement is ancient and world-wide. Each culture has invented its own form of what might be considered to be opera. In ancient Greece the plays of Aeschylus and Sophocles were declaimed or sung to the accompaniment of plucked strings and flutes.

Music and drama were combined in the thirteenth-century *pastourelles*—little plays about shepherds and shepherdesses which contained short songs and dances. The combination appeared also in the sixteenth-century *mascarades,* which were pageantlike Italian court entertainments given at carnival time. The *intermedie,* or intermezzo, featured a group of vocal madrigals or instrumental compositions performed between acts of plays. As such productions became more and more popular at the sixteenth-century Italian courts, they became more elaborate, using dramatic action as well as orchestral sinfonias and large-scale choruses. By the end of the 1500's the new musical style that was to shake the foundations of European music was ready to emerge as "drama in music"—and later, under the name of "opera," to sweep the world.

Top left: *a gala performance at the San Benedetto Theater, Venice, in 1782*
Top right: *"L'opera seria," an 18th-century Venetian painting*
Bottom: *a performance in the open-air theater at Grosser Garten, Dresden, in the late 18th century*

The founders of opera were like the explorers and inventors who have sought one thing and found something different—and more important. A patron of those founders was the wealthy nobleman Giovanni de Bardi (1534–1612), who gathered about him in Florence, Italy, a group of poets, philosophers, and musicians. They talked about reviving the ancient Greek method of performing drama, and under the leadership of Vincenzo Galilei (d. 1591), father of the great astronomer, this group (the *Camerata di Bardi*) invented a kind of single-line vocal music midway between speech and song. The Camerata called this style *recitativo*. It was directly opposed to the many-voiced style of music which had held sway for almost two hundred years and of which Lassus and Palestrina were the greatest living masters in the late 1500's.

The Camerata had no knowledge of what kind of music was used in the performances of Greek drama, since they were unable to decipher the few surviving fragments of Greek music. But by reading about drama, poetry, and music in the works of Plato and other Greek writers they arrived at certain theories, which they put into practice. The melodic line must follow the emotional meaning of the text, rising and falling as the pitch of an actor's voice rises and falls while he declaims the words. The rhythm must be free—now hurrying, now slowing—depending on how the words would have been spoken in a play. The words must be heard clearly; therefore a solo voice with a very simple accompaniment was preferred to many voices often singing different words at the same time.

Galilei used the new *stile recitativo* in setting a section of Dante's *Inferno* in 1582. The first complete "drama in music" was *Dafne*, written by Jacopo Peri (1561–1633) in 1597. *Dafne* was performed as a private entertainment at the home of Count Corsi, another Florentine nobleman who had become the patron of the Camerata after Count Bardi left Florence. Unfortunately only two fragments of *Dafne* have survived.

Opera can be said to have become firmly established in the year 1600. At this time two musical settings were made of Rinuccini's poetic drama *Euridice*. The first was by Peri, with a few additions by Guilio Caccini (*c.* 1546–1618). It was performed in celebration of the wedding of Henri IV of France and Marie de' Medici in Florence. The score was published in 1601. Meanwhile Caccini had composed his own version of *Euridice,* published in 1600, although the opera itself was not performed until 1602.

These versions of *Euridice* by Peri and Caccini are quite similar. Neither has an overture. Both have happy endings; the poet merely left out Orpheus' pledge not to look back as he brings Eurydice out of the underworld. In both versions the recitative style, now called *stile rappresentativo,* predominates. There are occasional short songs and rhythmic, tuneful choruses, often accompanying dances. The instruments, a harpsichord and several members of the lute family, merely support the voices with chordal accompaniment written in the musical shorthand known as figured bass.

Obviously, at such an important social event as the wedding of a king of France and a princess from Italy's greatest family, the production of Peri's *Euridice* would have used all the resources of the scenic designer and the costumers. When heard today without the sumptuous and opulent settings of its first performance, *Euridice* is a bit monotonous. The noble recitativo is often dramatic and affecting, but it is also full of starts and stops because of the constant cadences in the music. It remained for another composer to show the true possibilities of music drama.

Monteverdi's *Orfeo (Orpheus),* first performed at Mantua in 1607, is based on the same legend as Peri's and Caccini's *Euridice.* It also uses a great deal of the Florentine recitative style. But from its brassy toccata before the curtain opens—the first true opera overture—to its happy closing ballet, *Orfeo* is a complete theater piece, holding its audience by the beauty and boldness of its creator's ideas. Monteverdi's *Orfeo* is still performed in opera houses for general audiences. Peri's *Euridice* is given for special audiences—as an historical rarity.

Orfeo contains passionate recitatives, charming and moving songs, choruses which are sometimes gay dances and sometimes tragic laments. There are orchestral sinfonias, probably written to accompany stage action or a change of scene, and ritornellos—that is, recurring themes played between stanzas of a song. The whole work is unified not only by the plot but by the use of a ritornello which is heard at various moments throughout the opera. In his handling of the orchestra Monteverdi showed how the proper choice of instruments can help the composer to establish a mood. The large orchestra of almost forty instruments (undoubtedly some players doubled on several) allowed Monteverdi to use high-pitched recorders and small violins for some scenes, while saving a choir of trombones, organ, and double bass for a somber scene in the underworld.

Title page of Rinuccini's libretto for Euridice

L'EVRIDICE
D'OTTAVIO
RINVCCINI,
RAPPRESENTATA
NELLO SPONSALITIO
Della Chriſtianiſſ.
REGINA
DI FRANCIA, E DI
NAVARRA.

IN FIORENZA. 1600.
Nella Stamperia di Coſimo Giunti.
Con licenza de' Superiori.

A production of Cesti's Il Pomo d'oro, *1667*

Rarely in the history of music has any composer, in one work, shown so many paths to the future as did Monteverdi in *Orfeo*.

The success of *Orfeo* opened Italian eyes to the many possibilities of "drama in music." The Barberini family, with a 3,000-seat theater in their Roman palace, gave their guests operas that featured large choruses and splendid scenic effects. But the great surge of opera's popularity came in 1637 when the first public opera house was opened in Venice. Before this time opera had been an entertainment for the privileged and invited few. Now anyone who could pay the small admission charge could be an opera-goer. Soon there were sixteen opera houses in Venice alone. The mushrooming of early opera houses was much like the rapid spread of movie theaters in the early 1900's.

The original thought of recapturing the style and spirit of ancient Greek tragedy was soon abandoned. Even Monteverdi in his last opera, *L'incoronazione di Poppea (The Coronation of Poppea)*, written in 1642 for an opera house in Venice, used Roman history rather than Greek mythology for his plot. Monteverdi's followers in Venice, Pier Cavalli and Marc' Antonio Cesti, wrote 140 operas between them, developing a graceful,

flowing type of song which grew out of the flow of the Italian language. This *bel canto* ("beautiful song") style of melody lent itself to tuneful arias rather than to free, dramatic recitative.

Audiences demanded not only good tunes but gaudy spectacles. Stages were filled with sumptuous scenery. Gods descended from on high, by means of creaking "cloud machines," to unravel plots that were hopelessly tangled. Battles, shipwrecks, and erupting volcanoes were thrown into the story, whether or not the plot demanded them. In 1680 an opera was produced that advertised, in addition to the singers, one hundred horsemen in armor, two lions, two elephants, chariots and cars drawn by several dozen horses, and a forest in which roamed wild deer and bears!

Gradually the singers began to replace the scenic designers as box-office drawing cards. They dictated to the composer, telling him exactly what kind of arias to write. They did not hesitate to add numerous embellishing notes to a melody. They even added their favorite arias from other operas. The temperamental and pampered *castrati*—men whose voices had a quality and range somewhere between that of a boy soprano and a contralto—became the darlings of the

Caricature of Gaetano Donizetti.

audiences and therefore of the opera impresarios. This form of singers' opera was carried by Italian opera troupes to Austria, Poland, Germany, England, and France.

The French were mildly interested in Italian opera but preferred their own court ballets and the plays by such great writers as Molière, Racine, and Quinault. It was an Italian-born Frenchman, Jean-Baptiste Lully (born Giovanni Battista Lulli), who changed the attitude of the French court toward opera. This he did with his first opera, *Cadmus et Hermione (Cadmus and Hermione),* in 1673. Lully had succeeded in working his way up from teen-age kitchen worker and dancer to musical dictator of France. When the Royal Academy of Music went bankrupt after producing several unsuccessful operas, Lully took it over, tightening his control of musical life in France and thereafter becoming France's first great composer of operas. In fifteen years he wrote and produced fifteen operas, and through his genius influenced music for several generations.

Lully had prepared himself for his career in opera. He had studied the French language for its musical possibilities, having listened day after day to the finest actors in France, the members of the Comèdie Français, noting the rhythm of the language, its rising and falling inflections and its accents. Working with some of France's finest writers, Lully devised a stately form of opera that featured large choruses, charming dances, elegant costumes, and lavish scenic effects. The operas themselves were noble and heroic in tone, slow-moving, and not very dramatic. There were usually five acts plus a prologue, which was actually a hymn of praise to Louis XIV, although ostensibly sung to a god such as Apollo.

Lully's recitatives and arias established a melodic style that was exactly suited to the subtle rhythms of the French language. His forty-piece orchestra of strings, flutes, oboes, bassoons, trumpets, and drums provided colorful contrasts of instrumental timbres. The singers were rehearsed in every note and gesture by Lully himself—and woe betide the singer who dared to add an embellishment to the carefully written melodies. Lully, not trusting anyone else, conducted his operas himself, pounding a heavy pole in the orchestra pit to give a strong beat.

Lully set the pattern for French opera for many years to come. He popularized the minuet, was the true father of the modern orchestra, the first dictator-conductor, and the inventor of the French overture. For almost fifty years after Lully's death his

operas held sway in Paris. Then, in 1733, Jean-Philippe Rameau's *Hippolyte et Aricie (Hippolyte and Aricie)* was produced, and despite the outcries of Lully's admirers Rameau became the acknowledged master of French opera. Rameau, famous as a theorist and composer of chamber music, was interested in all forms of theatrical music—opera, ballet, and incidental music for plays. His musical background was richer than Lully's, and his music is more varied in harmony, rhythm, and instrumental color. A revival of a Lully opera today is almost unthinkable, whereas Rameau's works are produced often.

Rameau was a master of "gestural" music—music that suggests actual movements, such as those of rushing winds and descending gods. His descriptive music, accompanying stage earthquakes, storms, and battles, introduced a style of writing that culminated in the many musical storms in nineteenth-century operas and symphonies. Rameau wrote many charming dance pieces for his operas, and his *Pygmalion* contains a fairly complete catalog of the popular dances of the mid-eighteenth century.

While opera was finding its own forms in France, the Italian impresarios, librettists, and composers were not idle. They competed with each other in devising splendid scenic effects and in trying to attract star singers to their opera houses. Given virtuoso singers, such composers as Marc' Antonic Cesti (1623–1669) and Alessandro Stradella (c. 1645–82) developed many different kinds of arias to show off different styles of singing. Among these were the graceful, tender airs; long, flowing lines that called for the utmost in breath control; rapid bass airs, depending on the use of large intervals for humorous effects; coloratura solos and duets for sopranos; and saucy, folklike airs sometimes based on dance rhythms. By the beginning of the eighteenth century the opera world was ready for two of its greatest composers: Alessandro Scarlatti and George Frideric Handel.

Most of Alessandro Scarlatti's 115 operas were *opera seria*—that is, operas based on serious themes. For these he wrote expressive as well as coloratura arias, so many of which were in the da capo form that he is often thought of, wrongly, as the inventor of this form. What he did invent was the Italian overture. This immediate ancestor of the symphony had three clearly defined movements: an allegro opening, a contrasting slow section, and a fast, dancelike finale. Although many of Scarlatti's operas have good dramatic plots, some of his stories were merely pegs on which to hang a succession of arias. Such works are sometimes called "numbers" operas. Each aria, complete in itself, contributed little to the action, which was carried on in *recitativo secco* (rapid speechlike dialogue accompanied by an occasional chord on the harpsichord) or *recitativo stromentato* (dramatic declamation accompanied by dramatic chords and tremolos in the orchestra). The aria itself was a kind of aside to the audience in which the singer disclosed his inner feelings.

Scarlatti wrote several comic operas based on farcical plots dear to the hearts of his Neapolitan audiences, and often ended the acts of his operas with comic duets. Eventually such comic scenes were played between the acts of serious operas and given the name *intermezzi*. Of these the most famous example was Pergolesi's *La serva padrona (The Serving Maid Who Became Mistress)*.

The intermezzo developed into *opera buffa,* an operatic form featuring ordinary persons whom one could make fun of, rather than heroes, gods, and legendary figures. The music for an opera buffa was lyrical and tuneful, with simple melodies mostly in major and with rapid solos for the always-present basso. The orchestra joined in the fun with light, bubbling accompaniments. Both acts ended with long finales using all the principal characters. The success of *La serva padrona* in Paris in 1752 led to the War of the Buffoons, a violent argument that split French society into two camps, one preferring the noble style of Lully and Rameau and the other the naturalness and wit of the opera buffa. The balanced phrases, primary harmonies, and general lightness of the music of the opera buffa did much to influence the style of the early Classical symphony.

Handel started his career writing for the opera house in Hamburg, Germany. Established in 1678, this was the first public opera house outside Italy. The early German composers of opera, of whom the best known was Reinhard Keiser (1674–1739), had not attempted to strike out in new directions but developed a style that combined elements of Italian and French opera with the serious vocal style of the German church composers.

Handel learned his trade at Hamburg, then took a kind of post-graduate course in Italy, where he heard and absorbed all that was happening in the home of opera. In 1712 he settled in England, a country that seemed ripe for good Handelian Italian music.

England had been slow to accept opera as such, having much preferred the pageant-like masques and plays with many musical interludes. Strangely enough, the Puritans who controlled England from 1649 to 1660 encouraged opera—by forbidding the presentation of plays. An opera was judged to be a musical concert, and so a musical play, *The Siege of Rhodes,* with music by several composers, was allowed production in 1656. Even after the Restoration in 1660 English operas were primarily plays with incidental music. Many such plays were provided with music by Henry Purcell, the great English composer, who wrote but one true opera, *Dido and Aeneas.*

When Handel arrived on the London scene, he brought with him his background of opera from Hamburg and Italy. In England he heard many of the choruses and songs of Purcell and added these to his sources of inspiration. His own operas were written for a public opera house in London, which at various times he managed. The plots of his operas were large-scaled and serious, drawn from history or legend. While the action was not always highly dramatic, most of the plots moved along at a good pace. The scores were put together in episodic fashion like many of Shakespeare's plays. The operas featured many arias that are so moving—even breathtaking—that almost every Handel opera is well worth listening to. The scenes often include marches and choruses, so that there was on the stage a certain amount of spectacle.

The overtures to Handel's operas are mostly of the French type. He had a fondness for the noble opening adagio followed by the fast, contrapuntal movement; he used

Title page of Pergolesi's La serva padrona

Giovanni Battista Pergolesi

Caricature of a scene from an opera by Handel showing two castrati and a prima donna. From left to right: Gaetano Berenstadt (a German born in Italy, and one of the few non-Italian castrati); soprano Francesca Cuzzoni; and Francesco Senesino

The castrato Carlo Broschi, called Farinelli

this form not just in his operas but also in his oratorios and instrumental music. The arias are for the most part in the aria-da-capo form, which gave the singer a chance to display his vocal virtuosity as he embellished the repetition of the principal melody. The singers also brought from Italy the idea of the *cadenza,* consisting of vocal fireworks added just before the final cadence in a work. The cadenza eventually found its way into the instrumental concerto.

Handel wrote and produced operas until 1741. Then, as the opera house proved more and more unprofitable, he gradually switched his activities to the field for which he is most famous: the oratorio. In England as in Italy, where the big opera seria was giving way to the light opera buffa, the serious opera was being replaced by the tuneful *ballad opera.*

The English had never quite accepted the unreal quality of opera librettos. Spurred on by Jonathan Swift, John Gay (1685–1732) and Dr. John Pepusch (1667–1752) put together an opera in which all the characters were anti-heroes: members of the London underworld of criminals, fake beggars, and bribe-taking law enforcers. This work, *The Beggar's Opera,* was produced in 1728. Its dialogue was spoken and the melodies of the songs were either folk songs or airs taken from works by well-known composers. *The Beggar's Opera* was a tremendous success and was soon followed by a whole swarm of ballad operas. The ballad opera

was imported by the Germans, who called it the *Singspiel.* For a hundred years it was one of the most popular entertainment forms in Austria and Germany. Combining earthy and sometimes vulgar humor with romance, the Singspiel appealed to both workingmen and nobility. A national theater for the sole purpose of producing Singspiels was established in Vienna by Emperor Joseph II in 1778. Some of the most famous German composers turned to this form when they wrote for the stage: Mozart (*The Abduction from the Seraglio* and *The Magic Flute*), Beethoven (*Fidelio*), Weber (*Der Freischütz*), Schubert, and Haydn. *Fidelio* and *Der Freischütz* also include elements of the *melodrama,* a theatrical form popularized by Georg Benda (1722–95), in which spoken words are accompanied by descriptive music.

In Paris, the War of the Buffoons was but one aspect of the struggle between those members of the court who liked opera as it was and those who thought it was an artificial form that could be improved. The popularity of *La serva padrona* crystallized the thinking of the latter group. Led by Jean-Jacques Rousseau (1712–78), whose *Le Devin du village (The Village Seer)* was produced in 1752, French composers of the new persuasion invented the operatic form called *opéra comique.* This combined a romantic story with spoken dialogue and songs that were like popular French vaudevilles. It encompassed not only comedies but almost every other kind of story, from a setting of *Tom Jones* by François Philidor (1726–95) to the 1784 production of *Richard Coeur de Lion (Richard the Lionhearted)* by Grétry. Grétry (1741–1813), one of the most celebrated and prolific opera composers of his day, started the new trend of the *rescue opera,* the greatest example of which is Beethoven's *Fidelio.*

Christoph Willibald Gluck (1714–87), who was destined to become one of opera's great reformers, started his career inconspicuously enough as a writer of operas in the Italian style. As court conductor and composer in Vienna, he came into contact with a few examples of opéra comique. He set several French texts and was impressed with the economy of means in the French style. Always on the alert for new ideas, Gluck discovered the theories about theater expressed by the dancer Jean-Georges Noverre (1727–1810), who in 1760 had written a book in which he said that each element in a theatrical work exists only to contribute to the total drama. An aria, for example, must grow out of a dramatic situation and not impede the action. Dance must be introduced not for entertainment but because it adds something to the plot or mood of the work.

In *Orfeo ed Euridice (Orpheus and Eurydice),* first produced at Vienna in 1762, Gluck and his librettist Ranieri di Calzabigi (1714–95) composed a new form of opera in which there was no showing off of voices or irrelevant use of chorus or dance. The ending was happy, because the Austrian court would not have accepted a complete tragedy. Otherwise the drama moves logically from the opening lament to its noble finale. Dance is brought in to portray expressively the Furies and the Blessed Spirits in the underworld. This dignified, moving work was unlike any other opera since Monteverdi's *Orfeo.* Orchestra, chorus, dance, soloists—all combined to make a complete work of art.

Gluck continued his career with *Alceste* (1767); *Iphigénie en Aulide (Iphigenia in Aulis,* 1774); *Armide* (1777); and *Iphigénie en Tauride (Iphigenia in Tauris,* 1779). In this last opera Gluck even dispenses with a formal overture, substituting a stormy prelude that leads directly into the opening scene. Throughout his operas Gluck often did away with the formal aria, evolving instead a vocal form that grew out of the drama. Gluck's ideas were slow to make their way in the musical world; his works were too noble, too Classical, perhaps too true, to appeal to audiences that preferred entertainment to real drama. Orchestrally, Gluck was an innovator who chose each instrument carefully for its expressive value. He retired the harpsichord from the opera pit, where it had held sway for 175 years. In the nineteenth century two important composers followed the lead of Gluck: Wagner in theory and Berlioz in style.

During the period when arguments were still rife in Paris about the virtues of opera buffa versus opera seria, there was born a composer who was destined to take all operatic forms to their highest peak. In his youth Wolfgang Amadeus Mozart (1756–91) had the advantage of hearing in Salzburg and Vienna all the currently fashionable types of opera, from opera seria to the sunny Singspiel. By the age of twelve he had composed an opera buffa and a Singspiel. Trips to Italy led, at the age of fourteen, to commissions for his first two big operas; then followed a period in which he wrote only a few dutiful works. But his eye was on Paris or, failing that, Munich. It was the latter city that had the honor of hearing Mozart's first truly mature opera, the serious *Idomeneo* (1781), in which he showed that he had absorbed some of Gluck's theories

and style. He was to write only one more opera seria, *La clemenza di Tito (The Clemency of Titus),* done for Prague in the last year of his life. Meanwhile he took the popular Singspiel form and used it in two of his finest works: *Die Entführung aus dem Serail (The Abduction from the Seraglio,* 1782) and *Die Zauberflöte (The Magic Flute,* 1791).

Three of Mozart's greatest operas use elements of opera buffa: *Le nozze di Figaro (The Marriage of Figaro,* 1786); *Don Giovanni (Don Juan,* 1787); and *Così fan tutte (Thus Do They All,* 1790). All three show the typical Mozartian wit and skill at depicting characters through the melodies they sing. The orchestra is almost as important as the singers, for it makes comments on what the singers are singing, sketches in an expressive background, and in general sets the mood of the scene. Most remarkable are Mozart's ensemble finales, which are not just series of duets and quartets but actually are symphonic in the way in which the action builds to a climax at the end.

Opera as we know it might be said to begin with Mozart. He demonstrated that a composer could bring out the dramatic situation in a plot and yet write beautiful, even coloratura, arias. The arias, in fact, do not stop the action, as they did in the earlier "numbers" operas, but contribute to its momentum.

Mozart's old friend Haydn wrote many operas, mostly light ones, to entertain the guests at the Esterházy estate. The other great symphonic composer, Beethoven, wrote but one opera, *Fidelio.* This, while not completely satisfying theatrically, is full of great music and is the most expressive of all rescue operas—the type that started with Grétry's *Richard Coeur de Lion* in 1784 and became immensely popular during the dramatic upheavals of the French Revolution. Such works signaled a change in opera —from works of pure entertainment to those that could treat serious matters in a serious way.

During the reign of Napoleon Bonaparte, French opera returned to its magnificent standards of the past, and Paris became the magnet that attracted the leading composers of Italy (Cherubini, Rossini, Spontini, Bellini, and Verdi) and of Germany (Meyerbeer and Wagner). Cherubini's *Médée (Medea,* 1797) and *Les Deux Journées (The Two Days,* known also as *The Water Carrier,* 1800) were tremendously popular and exerted great influence on Beethoven. One of the few French composers who achieved any kind of success during this period was

Costume sketch for Orpheus in the first Paris performance of Gluck's Orfeo

André Grétry

Three great sopranos
Top: *Wilhelmine Schröder-Devrient, German soprano who created leading roles in Wagner's early operas*
Middle: *Maria Jeritza in the title role of Massenet's* Thaïs
Bottom: *Rosa Ponselle in Ponchielli's* La Gioconda

Étienne Méhul (1763–1817), whose greatest contribution was to show how the form of opéra comique could handle serious subject matter. He also experimented with an opera, *Joseph* (1807), in which all the characters are men, and in *Uthal* (1806) wrote for an orchestra without violins.

Napoleon's favorite composer was Gasparo Spontini (1774–1851), who like himself was not a Frenchman. Spontini established the style known as *grand opera* with his *La Vestale* (*The Vestal Virgin*, 1807) and *Fernand Cortez* (1809). Musically not especially gifted, Spontini had an eye for spectacles that filled the stage and plots that were exotically theatrical.

Spectacular and serious operas were just what the newly emerging upper middle-class audiences in Paris responded to. Sumptuous to look at and stirring to hear, such operas as Rossini's *William Tell* (1829), Halévy's *La Juive* (*The Jewess*, 1835), Bellini's *I puritani* (*The Puritans*, 1835), and *Les Huguenots* (1836) of Giacomo Meyerbeer (1791–1864) provided both entertainment and food for thought.

Hector Berlioz (1803–69), the outstanding Romantic composer in France, wrote several operas, ranging from the slight, lyrical *Béatrice et Bénédict* (1862), based on Shakespeare's *Much Ado About Nothing*, and humorous *Benvenuto Cellini* (1838) to one of the most monumental of all operas, *Les Troyens* (*The Trojans*). This mighty work was given in part in Paris in 1863 but had to wait until after the death of the composer for its first complete production.

While the Paris Opéra was featuring opera on the grand scale, the Italians were developing opera buffa as well as their own style of grand opera. Opera buffa reached its peak in the works of Gioacchino Rossini (1792–1868). In his early years he wandered through Italy providing a new opera every six or eight weeks for various impresarios. Rossini had a natural gift for writing for the voice. His study of the works of Mozart, whom he idolized, is most evident in *Il barbiere di Siviglia* (*The Barber of Seville*, 1816), his first great comic opera.

Rossini's arias are almost all coloratura arias. The embellishments and cadenzas were written by Rossini himself in an attempt to curb the freedoms taken by the singers. A master of the orchestra, he developed the so-called Rossini crescendo, heard in almost all his overtures. It consists of a phrase repeated with growing intensity to build up excitement.

Other Italians of the early nineteenth century who contributed masterpieces to the operatic repertoire were Gaetano Donizetti (1797–1848) and Vincenzo Bellini (1801–35). Donizetti's *L'elisir d'amore* (*The Elixir of Love*, 1832) and *Lucia di Lammermoor*, (1835) remain in operatic repertoire primarily because they are full of good tunes and display pieces. Bellini's operas *La sonnambula* (*The Sleepwalker*, 1831), *Norma* (1831), and *I puritani* hold the stage today because of the superior quality of the music as well as the opportunities they provide for outstanding coloratura sopranos.

Rossini, Donizetti, and Bellini were succeeded in Italy by a composer who was to share with Richard Wagner the European world of opera: Giuseppe Verdi (1813–1901). Verdi brought to Italian opera a virile style that appealed to all classes. He chose plots that, in addition to being violent, were calculated to arouse the patriotic feelings of his countrymen. At Verdi's insistence the stories were cut to their very essence. Violent action followed violent action, making good theater and providing opportunities for passionate arias, stirring choruses, and ensembles that expressed conflicts of emotions.

Even in his earliest operas—*Nabucco* (1842); *Ernani* (1844); *I Lombardi alla prima Crociata* (*The Lombards on the First Crusade*, 1843); *Giovanna d'Arco* (*Joan of Arc*, 1845); and *Attila* (1846)—Verdi displayed an ability to write strong elemental music that could stir the emotions of audiences deeply. As he progressed through *Rigoletto* (1851); *Il Trovatore* (*The Troubadour*, 1853); *La Traviata* (1853, based on *The Lady of the Camelias*); and *La forza del destino* (*The Force of Destiny*, 1862), some of the rough edges of his style were made smoother, but without sacrifice of intensity. *Aida*, finished in 1871, represented a turning point for this composer. Themes representing Aida and other characters run through the opera like the leitmotifs of Wagner. Harmony, melody, and orchestration are pushed beyond Verdi's former limits, partly because of the exotic nature of the subject material and partly because Verdi was always extending his technique.

For his last two works Verdi turned to Shakespeare. *Otello* (1887) and *Falstaff* (1893) are his greatest masterpieces. In both works there are set pieces—arias, duets, and choruses—but the listener is hardly aware that they are set pieces. There are masterful strokes of orchestration, but again, the listener is aware only that the mood of the orchestra matches the mood on the stage.

The tide of nationalism on which Verdi rose was an important element in the rise of opera in Germany also. The German

Five great opera houses
Top left: *interior of the Bayreuth Theater (the* Festspielhaus), *showing the sunken orchestra pit*
Top right: *the Staatsoper, Vienna*
Middle left: *La Scala, Milan*
Middle right: *interior of the new Metropolitan Opera House at Lincoln Center, New York*
Bottom left: *interior of the old Metropolitan (1938), with Erich Leinsdorf conducting a performance of* Lohengrin *for a student audience*

Top: *Nellie Melba as Rosina in Rossini's* Barber of Seville

Middle: *Giovanni Martinelli and Rosa Ponselle in* William Tell
Bottom: *Joan Sutherland and Sandor Konya in* La Traviata

Romantic poets of the late eighteenth and early nineteenth centuries searched for symbols of the German spirit, and found them in the medieval legends, in the German forests and the Rhine, and in the folk tales of the peasants.

Out of this movement came German Romantic opera. Carl Maria von Weber (1786–1826) had written several Singspiels, or comic operas, before he came upon the story of *Der Freischütz (The Free Shooter),* which contrasted evil magic with the solid virtues of the good German life. In vocal and orchestral writing Weber evoked the beauty of the forest and the warmth of the domestic hearth as well as the horrors of the baleful Wolf's Glen. When *Der Freischütz* was first performed in 1821 it was greeted enthusiastically by the German people, who saw in it an idealized reflection of themselves. Ignored by the German nobility, who clung to Italian opera, *Der Freischütz* established Weber as a national hero. Unfortunately he did not live long enough to produce a full body of German operatic works. That task fell to Richard Wagner (1813–83), who was possessed of the genius needed for the fulfillment of German operatic destiny, although other German composers, among them Heinrich Marschner (1795–1861), Otto Nicolai (1810–49), and Friedrich von Flotow (1812–83), wrote operas that were highly successful.

Wagner, who started out by emulating Meyerbeer in his first opera, *Rienzi* (1842), became the most powerful influence in music during the second half of the nineteenth century. Imbued with the spirit of German nationalism, Wagner turned away from Classical Mediterranean subject material and based his librettos on stories from northern European history and legend. But Wagner's music, more than the locale of his plots, was what differentiated him from other composers of his time. Starting as a musical conservative, he later pushed far beyond the boundaries of traditional tonality. He abandoned the formal aria in favor of a dramatic form of melodic recitative, thus reverting to the original idea of music drama as formulated by the early Florentines, in which the text was of primary importance. For each opera Wagner invented a goup of themes, later named leitmotifs, each of which represented a person, a thing, or an idea. By weaving together various leitmotifs Wagner achieved a remarkable unity in each opera, making it a small world of interwoven themes. Wagner had ideas about almost every aspect of opera or, as he preferred to call it, music drama. These ideas were

codified in his theory of the *Gesamtkunstwerk,* the "total art work," similar to the ideas expressed almost a hundred years earlier by Noverre and Gluck. Unlike many other theorists, Wagner carried out his theories in his operas: *Die Meistersinger (The Mastersingers), Tristan und Isolde (Tristan and Isolde),* and the monumental *Der Ring des Nibelungen (The Ring of the Nibelungs).* A restless innovator, philosopher, conductor, and critic, Wagner was most of all a master psychologist who through his manipulation of text, music, and staging, played directly on the emotions of his audience. Better than any other composer he knew how to handle harmony, instruments, and melody so that they evoked a particular feeling. The orchestra became the truest voice in his opera, since it let the audience know what was really happening, regardless of what was being said or done on stage. By avoiding harmonic cadences, his music had a seemingly endless flow, thus ensuring a continuity that no "numbers" opera could achieve.

Wagner helped design his own theater in Bayreuth. Here the orchestra is out of sight, and there are no boxes arranged in horse-shoe fashion so that the audience can look at itself. Everything is planned so that all attention must be focused on the stage. The audience was welcome, but on the composer's terms. It was welcome not to be entertained but to be spiritually moved and mentally enlightened.

Wagner's music was referred to as the "music of the future," and he himself wrote voluminously about his theories. To some extent he did influence the future, but not necessarily in the way he intended. Although many composers paid him homage by imitating his works, others like Satie and Debussy reacted violently against all Wagnerianisms.

Meanwhile it was in the form of opera that the pent-up creative forces of Russia burst upon the European musical scene. Following the lead of the writer Pushkin, Russian composers concentrated on various aspects of Russian life and legend. First, in 1836, came *Zhizn za Tsara (A Life for the Tsar)* by Mikhail Glinka (1804–57). This was followed in 1842 by his *Russlan y Lyudmila (Russlan and Ludmilla).* While influenced by Italian opera buffa and containing some traces of Weber, Glinka's music did have a flavor of Polish and Russian melodies. There was even a bit of romanticized Asian music, as if to remind the world that Russia existed on two continents.

By the middle of the nineteenth century there were two schools of Russian composers. One, led by Anton Rubinstein (1829–94), who wrote nineteen operas, used the same musical techniques as the French and German composers. The other group, the so-called "Russian Five" (Cui, Balakirev, Borodin, Mussorgsky, and Rimsky-Korsakov), believed in a style that would have its roots in the folk music of Russia. Mussorgsky carried out his ideas most completely in the episodic *Boris Godunov* (1874), with a libretto based on Pushkin's play, telling the story of the rise to power—and subsequent fall—of a Russian tsar at the end of the sixteenth century and the beginning of the seventeenth. The music of *Boris* broke away almost completely from western European concepts of harmony and melody. Melodies that are actual phrases of folk songs, jagged declamatory vocal lines, unclassical orchestration, avoidance of the usual love scenes, stark and psychologically true portrayal of characters, and the use of a chorus which, representing the Russian people, takes an active part in the drama—all combine to make *Boris Godunov* unique in the history of opera.

Neither of Mussorgsky's other operas, *Khovanshtchina (The Khovansky Affair)*, and the unfinished *Fair at Sorotchinsk*, came close to the intense and whole-hearted Russianism of *Boris*. Nor, for that matter, did the exotic *Prince Igor* (1890) of Borodin, the colorful *Sniegurotchka (The Snow Maiden*, 1882), *Sadko* (1898), and *Le Coq d'or (The Golden Cockerel*, 1909) of Rimsky-Korsakov, or the lyrical *Eugene Onegin* (1879) and *Pique Dame (The Queen of Spades*, 1890) of Tchaikovsky. Although each was based on Asian or Russian subject material, their musical idioms combined eastern and western European harmony and melody. The two outstanding Russian composers of the twentieth century, Sergei Prokofiev (1891–1953) and Dimitri Shostakovich (1906–), continued the tradition, adding to it some spice of dissonance and their own highly personal styles. Their most successful works have been the fanciful *Love for Three Oranges* (1921) and the large-scale *War and Peace* (1946), by Prokofiev, and the witty *The Nose* (1930) and *Katerina Ismailova* (originally the government-censored *Lady Macbeth of Mtzensk*, 1934), by Shostakovich.

The same combination of Slavic and Germanic techniques is characteristic of the operas by the Czech composers Bedřich Smetana (1824–84) and Antonin Dvořák (1841–1904). Of the fourteen stage works by these men only Smetana's sparkling *Prodaná nevěsta (The Bartered Bride)*, written in 1866, has made its way outside Czechoslovakia. Recently the works of Leoš Janáček

(1854–1928) have begun to find receptive audiences in Europe and America.

France had provided the stimulus and the place for grand opera in the Napoleonic and post-Napoleonic periods. Paris, always hospitable to foreign composers, in the middle of the nineteenth century welcomed another outsider with a different brand of opera: Jacques Offenbach (1819–80). Offenbach came from Germany and, in a short time, had all Paris singing his praises—as well as singing the melodies from such gay works as *Orphée aux enfers (Orpheus in the Underworld*, 1858); *La Belle Hélène (Fair Helen*, 1864); *La Vie parisienne (Parisian Life*, 1866); and *La Grande Duchesse de Gérolstein* (1867). His great serious work, *Les Contes d'Hoffmann (The Tales of Hoffmann*, 1881), has proved to be one of the most durable nineteenth-century "French" operas. Offenbach's influence spread from Paris to Vienna, where his operettas served to inspire the popular works by Franz von Suppé (1819–95) and Johann Strauss the Younger (1825–99).

Meanwhile, in Paris, French composers of the mid-nineteenth century developed a style based on the lyrical quality of the French language combined with Italian bel canto and some traces of Wagnerian chromaticism and rich orchestration. The locale of the operas ranged from Spain (Bizet's *Carmen*, 1875) to India (Delibes' *Lakmé*, 1883). Subject matter came from Goethe (Gounod's *Faust*, 1859) and the Bible (Saint-Saëns' *Samson and Delilah*, 1877). The most popular French operas of the late nineteenth and early twentieth centuries were those by Jules Massenet (1842–1912). Completely theatrical and possessed of a great lyrical gift, Massenet pleased his Parisian audience with a long list of melodius works, among them *Manon* (1884), *Le Cid (The Cid*, 1885), *Thaïs* (1894), and *Le Jongleur de Nôtre-Dame*, (1902).

It remained for that unique and original genius, Claude Debussy, to write the greatest of French operas: *Pelléas et Mélisande* (1903). Based on a play by Maurice Maeterlinck, *Pelléas et Mélisande* comes closest of all operas to the original idea of a drama set to music. There are no arias, no spectacles, no rousing climaxes, no appeal to the indifferent spectator. It is an opera in which much happens in the shadows and in the hearts of its characters. The vocal lines are like lyrical recitatives, with the orchestra subtly underscoring the symbolic meaning of the words. Each scene is in effect a mood piece, and even the orchestral interludes between scenes serve to fill the time needed

Kirsten Flagstad and Lauritz Melchior acknowledging ovations after a performance of Wagner's Tristan and Isolde *(Metropolitan Opera production, 1937)*

Margarete Matzenauer and Karl Braun as Brünnehilde and Wotan in Wagner's Die Walküre

Top: *Enrico Caruso as Nemorino in Donizetti's* L'elisir d'amore

Middle: *Edouard De Reszke as Mephistopheles in Gounod's* Faust
Bottom: *Luisa Tetrazzini, coloratura soprano, in Thomas'* Mignon

for scenic changes with sounds that keep the audience in the dream-world atmosphere of the opera. The harmony consists of soft Impressionist chords, or medieval sounds moving in parallel motion. The whole-tone scale, which Debussy used extensively, serves —because of its absence of a keynote—to intensify the unsettled emotional life of the main characters. The settings are subdued and gray: a shaded forest, a dark and dank castle, a dusky grotto.

Pelléas has never been a popular opera, nor did Debussy intend it to be such. It was written to be appreciated by those who react to art of great restraint and sensitivity. By its very nature it was a protest against full-blown German Romantic music, particularly that of Richard Wagner, although in a sense *Pelléas* illustrates Wagner's theories better than Wagner's own operas do.

Debussy was followed in his opposition to Wagnerianism by his countryman Maurice Ravel, whose two stage works, *L'Heure espagnole* (*The Spanish Hour,* 1911) and *L'Enfant et les sortilèges* (*The Child and the Sorceries,* 1925), are witty and sophisticatedly simple. *L'Enfant* is not even called an opera or drama, but a *fantasie lyrique*—a term that describes precisely what the work is: a fantasy with imaginative sounds drawn from the orchestra by a master of instrumental sounds. *L'Heure espagnole* is a one-act satire with an underpinning of Spanish dance music.

Spain, which had produced primarily composers of the popular zarzuelas and tonadillas, entered the operatic scene on a wave of musical nationalism fostered by the scholar-composer Felipe Pedrell (1841–1922). Among his followers were Enrique Granados (1867–1916), whose *Goyescas* was successful when it was first produced at the New York Metropolitan Opera House in 1916, and Manuel de Falla (1876–1946), whose *La vida breve* (*The Brief Life,* 1911) reflects the exotic qualities in Spanish music while his *El retablo de maese Pedro* (*The Show of Master Pedro,* 1919)—for puppets, singers, and chamber orchestra—goes back to classic Spanish tradition.

In South America both light and serious operas have filled the beautiful, large opera houses of the major cities. While many South American composers have written operas, until recently only one, the Brazilian Antonio Carlos Gomes (1836–96), had been internationally successful. His *Il Guarany,* which has elements of native Brazilian music, has been played in many opera houses throughout the world, although only its overture survives today, mostly in an arrangement for

band. In 1966 the Argentinian composer Alberto Ginastera (1916–) received acclaim for his *Don Rodrigo* when it was performed by the New York City Opera Company.

In Germany the triumph of Wagner's theories and music was so overwhelming that for a while it seemed German musical talent would be stifled. Wagner had many imitators who, like second growths, lacked the stature of the original. One of the few works that came out of the "music of the future" was a little fairy-tale opera, Humperdinck's *Hänsel und Gretel* (*Hänsel and Gretel,* 1893). Germany had to wait until the twentieth century for Wagner's successor, Richard Strauss (1864–1949). Strauss had written many of his tone poems—including *Till Eulenspiegel* and *Don Juan*—before he wrote his first successful opera, *Salome* (1905). This sensational work, which caused much controversy when first produced, is much more dissonant than anything written by Wagner. *Elektra* (*Electra,* 1909) has many exciting sounds in it, and harmony far in advance of its time, but it suffers from a too-lurid text, which is matched by Strauss's equally lurid music. In the opinion of most music lovers, Strauss's greatest opera is his charming, tuneful comedy *Der Rosenkavalier* (*The Cavalier of the Rose,* 1911). Built on waltzes, featuring delightful ensemble scenes, *Der Rosenkavalier* is an enchanting work from beginning to end— and a most welcome change of pace after Strauss's earlier tragedies. The move away from the influence of Wagner continued with *Ariadne auf Naxos* (*Ariadne on Noxos,* 1912– 16), a virtuoso chamber opera. Strauss never again achieved the success of his earlier operas, although *Die Frau ohne Schatten* (*The Wife Without a Shadow,* 1919), *Intermezzo* (1924), *Arabella* (1933), and *Die Schweigsame Frau* (*The Silent Woman,* 1935) get an occasional performance.

While Germany had to wait a while after the death of Wagner for a new opera composer, this was not true of Italy, where Verdi's successors became competitors while the old master was still on the scene. In between Verdi's *Otello* and *Falstaff* came two passionate one-act operas that heralded the new operatic movement of *verismo,* or realism. *Cavalleria rusticana* (*Rustic Chivalry,* 1890) by Pietro Mascagni (1863–1945) and *Pagliacci* (*The Clowns,* 1892) by Ruggiero Leoncavallo (1858–1919) became opera's most famous double bill, known as "Cav-Pag." Both are well-written operas, deserving of their popularity, but neither composer was ever able to write anything as successful again. The verismo composers were, in a sense, "trumped" by their fellow-Italian, Giacomo Puccini (1858–1924).

Puccini brought to opera an infallible sense of theater, a genuine gift for writing expressive melody, a talent for orchestration, and a searching mind that was aware of all that was happening musically in his time. His most famous operas are *La Bohème* (1896); *Tosca* (1900); *Madame Butterfly* (1904); *Turandot* (completed after his death by Franco Alfano); and three one-act operas known as *The Triptych: Il tabarro (The Cloak), Suor Angelica (Sister Angelica),* and *Gianni Schicchi* (all 1918). At one time many musicians looked down on Puccini as a composer whose direct playing on the emotions of his audience was unfair, but in the perspective of history the audience that took Puccini's music to its heart was right.

Like composers in any country where one or two geniuses have dominated the musical scene, young Italian composers have had to find ways to get out of the shadow of Verdi and Puccini. Most successful have been Luigi Dallapiccola (1904–   ), Luigi Nono (1924–   ), and Luciano Berio (1925–   ). Dallapiccola's best work has been his score for *Il prigioniero (The Prisoner,* 1950), in which contemporary techniques are fused with a Verdi-ish sense of theater to make a moving stage work. Berio and Nono are experimentalists. Nono's *Intolleranza* (1961) calls for the use of almost every musical and theatrical device of the day, including electronic sounds and a closed television circuit.

Of all the operas of the past fifty years, the most provocative are those from Germany and Austria. Foremost is *Wozzeck,* by Alban Berg (1885–1935), finished in 1922 and first performed in 1925. Like a tragic *Beggar's Opera* it presents people who are the downtrodden, the unfortunate, and the bitter poor. The music of *Wozzeck,* alternately brutal and tender, always has a hyperemotional quality that hides its tight organization. Every scene, every act, is based on a musical form. The vocal line is sometimes sung, sometimes declaimed in *Sprechstimme* (a cross between song and speech). Sometimes there is a tonal center, often not. In his other, later opera *Lulu* (1937), Berg adopted Schoenberg's tone-row method of organization.

Arnold Schoenberg himself had composed several operas. His *Erwartung (Expectation,* 1909) and *Die glückliche Hand (The Lucky Hand,* 1913) use one soloist and three respectively, and are nightmarishly dramatic. Schoenberg finished only two of the projected three acts of his *Moses and Aaron,* a

vivid Biblical drama containing spectacular theatrical effects in staging and in music. This great work is just beginning to make its way in the opera houses of the world.

Contemporary composers have searched many avenues for operatic forms that can be used to convey contemporary ideas and feelings. Some have gone back to the old "numbers" opera, with its set-piece arias, as in Stravinsky's *The Rake's Progress* (1951) and Hindemith's *Cardillac* (1926). Darius Milhaud (1892–   ) has written for a large number of singers in his *Les Euménides* (1922) and *Cristophe Colomb (Christopher Columbus,* 1930). Francis Poulenc (1899–1963) ranged for subject matter from the devout *Les Dialogues des Carmélites* (1957) to the delicious wickedness of *Les Mamelles de Tirésias* (1947). Ernst Krenek (1900–   ) in his *Jonny spielt auf (Johnny Strike Up,* 1927) experimented with jazz, as did Kurt Weill (1900–50), who used jazz in a bitter and exaggerated form in his successful *Threepenny Opera (Die Dreigroschenoper,* 1928) and the *Aufstieg und Fall der Stadt Mahagonny (The Rise and Fall of the City of Mahogany,* 1930). Weill left Nazi Germany in 1933 and came to the United States, where he wrote successful Broadway shows and a popular folk opera, *Down in the Valley* (1948).

Birgit Nilsson and Richard Tucker in a Metropolitan Opera production of Puccini's Turandot

Beniaminio Gigli as Des Grieux in Puccini's Manon Lescaut

Maria Callas in Bellini's Norma

In England and America opera has been until quite recently an art form imported from Italy, France, Germany, and Russia. A form of English opera might have come to maturity in the eighteenth century as an outgrowth of the theater music of Purcell and his contemporaries, but instead the more highly developed Italian opera was imported with great success, and it flourished until it in turn gave way, in the 1730's, to the more topical and typical English "ballad opera." For almost two hundred years English composers were more successful with light opera forms than with more pretentious types. Even Sir Arthur Sullivan, whose romantic lampoons of English social and political life, written with W. S. Gilbert, were tremendously popular, failed when he turned his hand to a "grand" opera, *Ivanhoe.*

During this time Italian and German operas became standard fare in England and, later, in the United States. It is interesting to note that in these countries operas have usually been performed in their original languages. In most European countries opera is heard in the language of the country in which it is being performed. Perhaps the inability to understand what was happening on stage has contributed to the lag in support of opera, particularly in the United States.

The breakthrough in England started with Frederick Delius (1862–1934), whose *A Village Romeo and Juliet,* first performed in 1907 in Berlin (of all places), achieved moderate success. Delius was followed by Ralph Vaughan Williams (1872–1958), whose *Hugh the Drover* (1924) and *Riders to the Sea* (1937) are concerned with English and Irish subject matter and, more because of this than their theatricality, do receive occasional performances.

The first English composer whose operas show promise of becoming standard repertoire is Benjamin Britten (1913-76). His *Peter Grimes* (1945), *The Rape of Lucretia* (1946), *Albert Herring* (1947), *Billy Budd* (1951), and *The Turn of the Screw* (1954) give evidence of a composer who, like Verdi, wrote operas not to prove aesthetic theories but to hold the attention of the listener, using whatever contemporary or traditional means are necessary. Britten has been successful in producing for young people works such as *The Little Sweep* (1949), in which the audience takes part, and *Noye's Fludde (Noah's Flood,* 1958), a form of modern miracle play with music that includes many parts for children to sing.

In the United States the opera composers of the nineteenth and early twentieth centuries were content to imitate European models. Among the most successful of these were Walter Damrosch (1862–1950) with his *The Scarlet Letter* (1896), Horatio Parker (1863–1919) with *Mona* (1912), and Deems Taylor (1885–1966) with *The King's Henchman* (1926, libretto by Edna St. Vincent Millay) and *Peter Ibbetson* (1931).

When writing operas, American composers seem to create best with American subject matter. Mostly the musical idiom is conservative, as in *Merry Mount* (1934) by Howard Hanson (1896–1981), *Ballad of Baby Doe* (1956) by Douglas Moore (1893–1969), *Vanessa* (1956) by Samuel Barber (1910–   ), and *The Crucible* (1961) by Robert Ward (1917–   ). A few works suggest the development of a form of American opera that combines so-called serious opera with the more popular and indigenous musical comedy. Among these works the most prominent are *The Cradle Will Rock* (1937) and *Regina* (1949) of Mark Blitzstein (1905–64); the witty and deceptively simple *Four Saints in Three Acts* (1934) and *Mother of Us All* (1947) of Virgil Thomson (1896–   ); and the *Mighty Casey* (1953) of William Schuman (1910–   ). Others in this group are *Porgy and Bess* (1935) by George Gershwin (1898–1937), *West Side Story* (1957) by Leonard Bernstein (1918–   ), and *Susannah* (1957) by Carlisle Floyd (1926–   ). One of the few operatic works by an American composer to become popular in Europe is Gunther Schuller's (1925–   ) *The Visitation,* premièred in Hamburg in 1966. A recent revival of Scott Joplin's *Treemonisha* (1911) proved the work to be the earliest successful American opera.

Opera has not been an art form that goes on quietly repeating itself. It has always changed in response to changing social conditions, taking on whatever new shape is necessary. Today it is finding new audiences all over the world, as completely new groups of people are being attracted to cultural events. Many of these people will want to explore the great treasure-trove of operas already written. New opera companies will come into existence, some performing "live" and others on television. Faced with new audiences and equipped with new technological resources, the opera composer of the future will undoubtedly find new forms of musical theater that will fit the cultural needs of his public. These new forms will disturb many people who think that opera means only "Mozart," "Wagner," or "Verdi," forgetting that throughout music history there has never been a simple answer to the question "What is opera?"

OPERETTA: a gay, tuneful "little opera." Its story is usually a sentimental one with a happy ending, although some operettas are comic or satirical. The dialogue is always spoken, so that an operetta is much like a play with vocal solos, duets, and choruses added in.

Except for the witty works of Gilbert and Sullivan in London and of Offenbach in Paris, the home of the operetta was Vienna, where the form originated in the works of Franz von Suppé (1819–95). It was there that Johann Strauss, Oscar Straus (1870–1954), and Franz Lehár (1870–1948), wrote such favorites as *The Bat, The Gypsy Baron, The Merry Widow,* and *The Chocolate Soldier.* Since Vienna was the home of the waltz, the most important musical ingredient in an operetta became the waltz-song.

After 1900 some of the most popular operettas written in the United States were by two composers from central Europe: Rudolf Friml *(Rose Marie, The Vagabond King)* and Sigmund Romberg *(The Student Prince, Blossom Time, The Desert Song).* Among Americans, the most prolific writer in this vein was Victor Herbert. The most memorable of his forty-one operettas are *Babes in Toyland, Naughty Marietta,* and *Mlle. Modiste.*

Operettas flourished from the middle 1800's until the 1920's. By this time the waltz had been replaced in popularity by jazz, and the operetta gave way to the musical comedy.

Above left: *a waltz from* The Merry Widow
Above right: *Franz von Suppé (an 1851 lithograph)*
Bottom left: *a scene from* The Desert Song, *with, from left to right, Pearl Regay, Edmund Elton, Vivienne Segal, and Robert Halliday*

OPUS: a term (Latin, "work") used by composers and music publishers to identify compositions; often abbreviated to *Op.* and followed by a number. The practice of using opus numbers started in the 1600's but did not become customary till the early 1800's—the time of Beethoven. In the middle 1700's, the word was usually reserved for a collection of works of the same kind. Handel's London publisher, for instance, included twelve of his concerti grossi in Opus 6.

Sometimes opus numbers indicate which of two compositions a composer wrote first. Unfortunately, many opus numbers of the nineteenth century were assigned by the publishers for their own convenience, without regard to when a piece was actually written. Opus numbers that are chronologically out of order, and hence meaningless, abound in the works of Mendelssohn and Schubert. Thus Schubert's Sonata Opus 122 was written nine years *before* his Sonata Opus 78. Numerous compositions—of Beethoven, among others—have no opus numbers at all. In our own time, many composers have given up using a single series of opus numbers for their work and instead number their works by type—Symphony Number 5, Quartet Number 2, and so on.

To make up for the unreliability of opus numbers, musical scholars have sometimes renumbered the entire output of a composer, assigning numbers in a single series progressing from his earliest to his last compositions, strictly in the order in which he is thought to have written them. These modern renumberings are indicated by letters, such as K. for Mozart's works and L. for Scarlatti's works, placed in front of the numbers.

Façade of the Oratory of St. Filippo Neri, founder of the Congregation of the Oratory (from which use of the word "oratorio" evolved to describe a large-scale form of sacred music)

ORATORIO: a dramatic but unstaged telling of a Biblical or religious story. Like an opera it requires solo singers, a chorus, and an orchestra, but unlike an opera it is performed in a church or a concert hall. It uses no scenery or costumes, and there is no dramatic action.

An oratorio starts with an overture by the orchestra. The story is then unfolded by a narrator, who sings in a style of melodic speech called recitative. Solo singers sometimes represent characters in the story; in other instances, as in *Messiah,* they reflect the emotional color of the text. The chorus plays an important part, sometimes as the crowd in the story, taking part in the action, and at other times as spectators of the action, making comments on it as it is told by the narrator. The libretto is usually based on a Biblical story or on the life of some inspiring figure; if it deals with the crucifixion of Jesus, it is called a passion.

The oratorio gets its name from the sixteenth-century religious meetings held in the small chapel, or oratory, of Filippo Neri in Rome. These meetings featured the singing of hymns, or *laudi spirituali,* at various points during the telling of a Biblical story.

A variety of sacred music dramas, some with elaborate scenery, costumes, and even dancing, were produced in Italy in the early 1600's. But the first true oratorios were those written toward the middle of the century by Giacomo Carissimi in Italy and Heinrich Schütz in Germany. Carissimi (1605–74), whose *Jeptha* (c. 1665) is still sung today, wrote in a vocal style that combined the practices of sacred music with that of early Italian opera. Schütz, in his *Die sieben Worte (The Seven Last Words)* and his passions, was able through his genius to express passionate and dramatic feelings in a style that was austerely religious.

Oratorio reached its highest peak in the works of the German composers of the 1700's. Bach poured forth his intense religious fervor in his passions and in his *Christmas Oratorio,* and Handel, in his more than twenty oratorios, explored almost every possibility of the form, producing religious dramas of great sweep and grandeur. Devout arias alternate with dramatic choruses, as in Handel's most famous work, *Messiah.*

After Haydn's *Die Schöpfung (The Creation,* 1797), the great tradition of the oratorio was carried on during the nineteenth century in such works as Beethoven's *Christus am Öelberg (Christ on the Mount of Olives),* Mendelssohn's *Elijah,* and Berlioz's *L'Enfance du Christ (The Childhood of Christ).* It is these works, along with the oratorios of Bach and Handel, that form the basic repertoire of most choirs and choral societies today. Many of them are given in annual festivals throughout the world.

Modern composers are still drawn to the grand scale of the oratorio form. The best-known oratorios of our time are William Walton's *Belshazzar's Feast,* Honegger's *Le Roi David (King David)* and *Jeanne d'Arc au bûcher (Joan of Arc at the Stake),* Stravinsky's opera-oratorio *Oedipus Rex,* and Kodály's *Psalmus Hungaricus (Hungarian Psalm).*

ORCHESTRA: a large group of musicians performing on stringed, woodwind, brass, and percussion instruments. The word "orchestra" once meant the semicircular area of a classical Greek theater, between stage and audience, in which the chorus danced. The corresponding space in European opera houses of the 1600's seemed an excellent spot for the musicians; and eventually the name of the space was given to the men who played in it. Today the word refers to any large group of musicians that includes string players; if there are no strings, the group is called a band.

Several kinds of orchestras participate in our musical life today: the chamber orchestra, a group of from ten to thirty instrumental soloists; the theater orchestra, with from ten to fifty musicians, which plays in the pit at musical shows; the dance orchestra or dance band, a variety of chamber orchestra that plays dance music; and finally the opera orchestra and the symphony orchestra, which are the largest and are quite similar in their make-up.

Modern symphony orchestras vary in size from sixty players to about a hundred, depending mostly on how many strings they can afford. The distribution of instruments in a modern orchestra is shown on page 384.

Each wind or percussion player has his own part to play, but members of each string section play together in unison, like sopranos, altos, tenors, and basses singing in a chorus. A large number of strings is needed to balance the power of even a small number of wind instruments.

The orchestra is usually so arranged that the larger and louder instruments are at the back. Each section of an orchestra has its leader, or principal, who leads his group so that they all attack their tones at exactly the same time; he also plays the solo passages written for his instrument. The conductor stands on a small platform, or podium, so that he can be seen by every member of the orchestra. Every player, even while reading music, is expected to watch the movement of the conductor's baton out of the corner of his eye.

An important and often unseen member of the orchestra is the librarian. Before each rehearsal and each concert he arranges the music, or "part," for each player and puts it in a folder. Each folder is then placed on the correct music stand, or "desk." String players usually share their parts, two by two; elsewhere in the orchestra each player reads from his own part.

Orchestral musicians usually warm up their fingers, lips, or instruments for about a half hour before a concert, mostly backstage. The first members to appear are usually the percussion players, string bassists,

and harpists, whose instruments are kept on stage. When all the members are on hand the concertmaster asks the first oboe player to sound his "A," and the other instrumentalists tune to this note. After the tuning the conductor walks on stage, lifts his baton, and the concert begins.

The modern symphony orchestra is a complex music-making machine. In its present form it came into being just about two hundred years ago, but its history goes back to the earliest cultures, in which percussion groups accompanied religious songs and dances. Several thousand years ago there were orchestras at the courts of Egypt and India. The Emperor of China had an orchestra of more than 500 musicians playing stringed instruments, woodwind instruments, drums, bells, and gongs. The Old Testament (in the Book of Daniel, describing events of the sixth century B.C.) tells of the Babylonian King Nebuchadnezzar's orchestra of strings, brasses, and woodwinds.

The earliest European orchestras were those that played for court entertainments—ballets, masquerades, and so forth—in the late 1500's. These orchestras were varying assortments of strings and wind instruments plus organs, guitars, and harpsichords. The composers did not write parts for specific instruments but allowed each player to perform whichever part best suited the range of his instrument. The first composers to allot parts to definite instruments were Giovanni Gabrieli in his *Sonata pian e forte* (about 1600) and Monteverdi in his opera *Orfeo* (1607).

The first of the modern orchestral instruments to be perfected were the violin family, in the seventeenth century. The strings,

Greek amphitheater at Epidaurus during the summer festival of 1961. Members of the chorus are standing in the orchestra of the theater

A Renaissance orchestra (miniature from a 15th-century psalter)

The Cleveland Orchestra, with Dr. George Szell conducting

Distribution of Instruments in a Modern Orchestra

WOODWINDS:

2 to 4 flutes and piccolo
2 to 4 oboes and English horn
2 to 4 clarinets
2 to 4 bassoons

PIANO: 1 (occasionally used as an
orchestral instrument)

BRASS:

2 to 8 French horns
2 to 4 trumpets
2 to 3 trombones
1 to 2 tubas

STRINGS:

12 to 16 first violins
12 to 16 second violins
8 to 12 violas
6 to 10 cellos
4 to 9 double basses

PERCUSSION:

2 to 5 timpani (played by one player)
cymbals, triangle, snare drum,
bass drum, gongs, xylophone, etc.
(played by 2 to 3 players)

HARP: 1 to 2

therefore, supported by a harpsichord, became the basis of the orchestra. Flutes, oboes, and bassoons were used to give variety, usually playing along with the strings rather than by themselves.

Until the late 1700's the musicians in many orchestras, bewigged and often wearing swords, played while standing. The conductor was usually the composer himself, who led either from the harpsichord or, as concertmaster, with his violin. Opera conductors led from the harpsichord or, like Lully at the Paris Opéra, beat time by pounding a wooden pole on the floor.

In the 1700's every nobleman with a court had an orchestra of his own. Many of the players were part-time musicians and part-time gardeners, cooks, or general servants. The court orchestras played on all kinds of occasions. They performed in the theater for operas and in ballrooms for dancing. When their employers entertained guests at dinner, they made "table music," and after dinner they played concert music. In nice weather they put on outdoor concerts, like the summer band concerts of today, and on Sunday they played in church at all special services.

The most famous of the early symphony orchestras was that of Mannheim, Germany, in the middle 1700's. Drilled to perfection by its conductor, the composer Johann Stamitz (1717–57), it became the standard by which other orchestras were judged. It was made up of sixteen violins, four violas, two cellos, two double basses, three flutes, three oboes, two clarinets, four bassoons, and five horns. Trumpets and drums—from the military band of Duke Carl Theodore— were added to the orchestra when needed. The Mannheim orchestra was noted for its soft pianissimos, sudden fortissimos, and exciting crescendos. Music lovers traveled from all over Europe to hear the Mannheimers and to marvel at their skill. In due course, members of the orchestra were lured to other courts, where they built orchestras modeled on the one at Mannheim.

The greatest of the early symphonic composers, Haydn, wrote most of his works for the orchestra of his employer, Count Esterházy. This orchestra never had more than twenty-five members. Haydn was overwhelmed by the size of the London orchestra that played his works in 1790—it had forty players!

Until the early 1800's, orchestras for special concerts (except at a court) were got together only for the occasions at hand, and then disbanded. Made up partly of professional musicians and partly of amateurs, they did little or no rehearsing and were often unable to cope with scores of the slightest difficulty.

As the composers of the 1800's demanded more tone and more ability, the orchestras grew larger in size and became completely professional. Berlioz, in his *Symphonie fantastique* (1830), in a note in the score, specified that at least sixty string players were necessary. The brass and woodwind choirs of the orchestra were enlarged throughout the 1800's. Mammoth orchestras were needed to produce the grand sonorities Wagner, Strauss, and Mahler had in mind. Debussy and Ravel called for orchestras with a great variety of instruments to enable them to manipulate the tone color of the music in the way they imagined it. One of the largest orchestras was required by Stravinsky in his *Rite of Spring* (1913), which is scored for four flutes, four oboes, six clarinets, four bassoons, eight horns, five trumpets, three trombones, two tubas—plus the usual strings and a large percussion group. Since that time composers (led by Stravinsky himself) have in general been more modest in their demands, sometimes calling for as few wind parts as Haydn.

The first permanent *professional* orchestra was the Royal Philharmonic, founded in London in 1813. This was followed, in 1828, by the orchestra of the Paris Conservatory. Two of the most famous symphony orchestras of today were started in 1842: the New York Philharmonic and the Vienna Philharmonic. Another American orchestra with a long history is the Boston Symphony, which dates from 1881.

Today almost every important city in the world has a symphony orchestra. Many cities (Vienna, Paris, Tokyo) maintain two or more. In some of the smaller cities the orchestras are only partly professional.

A symphony orchestra is an expensive organization. A financial loss is normally incurred during every orchestral season. In many parts of Europe it is customary for the orchestras to receive a subsidy from the government; in the United States the deficit is made up by private individuals and philanthropic foundations, although local, state, and federal agencies have recently made some funds available to symphony orchestras.

In spite of the expense, symphony orchestras have sprung up all over the United States. A recent survey reported more than 1,400, each giving from two to over a hundred concerts a year. These figures reflect not only the need of musicians to make music together but also the satisfaction audiences get from listening to fine, live music.

ORCHESTRATION: the art of arranging the notes of a composition among the instruments of the orchestra. It is sometimes called "scoring," since the composer writes out all the notes of his orchestration in full orchestral score.

Although a composer may sketch his composition in an abbreviated score, he invariably has certain instruments in mind as he writes a melody, a series of chords, or even a rhythmic pattern. The orchestral colors, in fact, are so important that a composer might have a clear idea of the instrumental sounds before he knows the actual notes he will write. He might be thinking, "The piece will start with low rumbling sounds in the strings. These will be interrupted by jagged chords in the brass, out of which will come a long string melody, on top of which there will be comments by the woodwinds." Having established the orchestral color scheme, he then sets about finding the notes he wants to use.

The kind of music that a composer wishes to write determines to a great extent the kind of orchestration he will use. He might want primary colors, in which each instrument has its own line, or in which a family of instruments, such as the oboes and bassoons, plays by itself. The composer might want an element of contrast, in which case he will give a melody to a solo instrument—the flute, for example—while the strings play a soft accompaniment. At all times the composer must keep in mind the characteristic sound of each instrument, its range, and its change in quality as it is doubled by one or more instruments of other families. Much of a composer's ingenuity goes into the mixing of instrumental tone colors. By combining different colors he is able to tint and shade his music, just as a painter achieves subtle effects by mixing his colors. There are thousands of ways in which instrumental tone colors can be blended or contrasted. When all the instruments of the orchestra are used together, the result is called a *tutti* (which means "everybody.") Ex. 3 shows a

Ex. 3

C-major chord as it has been orchestrated by Mozart, Beethoven, Berlioz, Wagner, Brahms, and Stravinsky.

Throughout the history of European music, fashions have been changing in the use of instruments. Some of these changes have been due to the introduction of new musical forms and styles. Others occurred when new or improved instruments gave composers fresh sounds to work with. During the medieval and early Renaissance periods instruments were used primarily to double the voice parts and had no independence of their own. As families of viols and recorders were developed they were used in groups, usually in five parts, paralleling the typical madrigal distribution of voices.

Giovanni Gabrieli, in his *Sacre Symphoniae (Sacred Symphonies),* 1597, was one of the first to specify the exact instrumentation to be used. His famous *Sonata pian e forte* calls for two choirs: one consisting of a cornett and three trombones: the other of a violino and three trombones. Another work

in this collection uses viol, cornett, and nine trombones. (The trombone of this period was a much softer instrument than the modern trombone and came in sizes ranging from soprano to bass.)

That there was great interest in musical instruments in the early 1600's is proved by the fact that Michael Praetorius (1571–1621) devoted Volume II of his three-volume treatise on music to a description of every known instrument, its range, and its tone color. But the first composer who seems to have been aware of the unique expressive quality of each group of instruments was Claudio Monteverdi. In his opera *Orfeo* (1607) he used plucked strings to accompany Orfeo's arias and a group of trombones to depict the underworld. In his *Il combattimento di Tancredi e Clorinda* (1624) Monteverdi used two of the most colorful devices in music—the pizzicato of strings and the dramatic string tremolo.

Throughout the Baroque period there were several approaches to the problem of

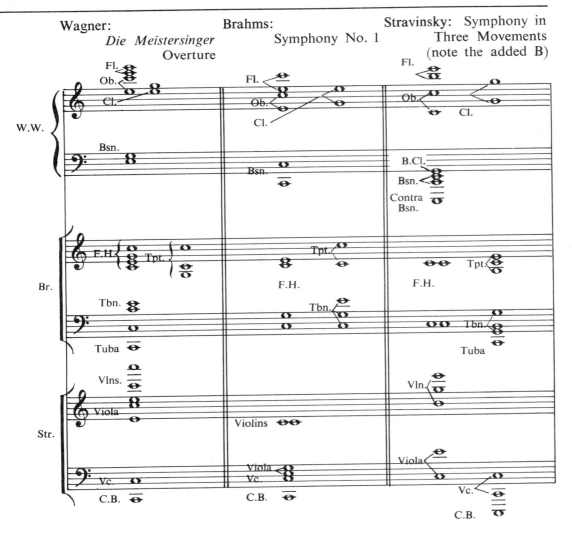

orchestration. Lully and Rameau, in their French operas, increased the size of the orchestra. Lully combined flutes, oboes, horns, and bassoons with his basic string group. Rameau added the clarinet to his orchestra and in general used his instruments for their unique tone colors: the flutes in swirling passages, the horns in fanfares suggestive of the hunt, and so on.

The Italian composers who were developing the concerto and concerto grosso forms depended primarily on the string group plus harpsichord. The sound of wind instruments was used for contrast as in J. S. Bach's "Brandenburg" Concertos Numbers 1 and 2. In their concertos composers learned how to balance small groups against large, or write light accompaniments that did not overwhelm the soloist.

In his cantatas and passions Bach used an ever-changing group of instruments for contrast with the basic string and harpsichord or organ sound. He chose his obbligato instruments—the ones that carried on duets and trios with his vocal soloists—with great care, matching a dolorous alto solo with the mournful sound of the oboe d'amore or a joyful soprano solo with ecstatic flutes. For accompanying the full chorus Bach piled up sonorous tuttis that had weight and provided support, leaving the color to the singers.

The Classical symphony orchestra consisted of a body of strings, one or more pairs of woodwinds, a pair of horns, and a pair of timpani. The strings play most of the time; the woodwinds are given occasional solos, while the brass and timpani play in climactic tuttis. Mozart was one of the first composers to let his woodwinds sound out in the open, playing all by themselves or underneath the solo part in piano concertos.

The opera house was usually the place where composers experimented with new instruments and new sounds. Gluck and Mozart, in their operas, added to the conventional instruments the then-exotic or dramatic sounds of the trombone, piccolo, bass drum, cymbals, triangle, and snare drums. To Gluck also goes the credit for removing the twanging sound of the harpsichord from the orchestra.

In the Classical period was developed one of the most important devices of orchestration: the orchestral "pedal." As strings made busy accompaniment patterns or as fragments of themes were tossed from one instrument to another, the music sometimes did not seem to hold together. As a remedy composers began to give long held notes in the middle register to the bassoon or the horn. These continuous pedal sounds seemed to fuse all elements of the music together. The orchestral pedal is still used, although contemporary composers, seeking clarity of line rather than blend, often dispense with it (see Ex. 48 on page 535).

Beethoven added orchestral color by giving new freedom to such former drudges as the French horn, double basses, and timpani. Weber, too, investigated new orchestral sounds in his opera *Der Freischütz,* particularly in contrasting the romantic German countryside with the terrifying atmosphere of the mysterious Wolf's Glen. He invented the shuddering string tremolo against which pizzicato bass tones and timpani strokes suggest a frightening and eërie situation, a device of orchestration still much in use today.

Berlioz was the great innovator in orchestration in the nineteenth century. As the first serious student of the subject, he produced the earliest book on orchestration— the famous *Traité de l'instrumentation,* published in 1844—and his *Symphonie fantastique* was a sounding of a declaration of independence for all instruments. In it he specified that the work could not be played with less than thirty violins. He asked for four timpani, tuned to various chords. The percussion instruments were treated as a choir and given important tones and passages to play—a process that had been inaugurated by Haydn and Beethoven.

In his imaginative use of all elements in the orchestra Berlioz paved the way for the rich scoring of Wagner, Liszt, and Rimsky-Korsakov. Wagner added new brass instruments to the orchestra so that a full brass choir could provide a resonant background for the other instruments as well as building weighty climaxes.

The symphonic poems and operas of Richard Strauss demanded large orchestral forces, modeled on those of Wagner. Strauss wrote parts that demand virtuoso playing on every instrument as he spun active contrapuntal lines out of his often luxuriant harmonies. A Strauss score always looks very "busy," and, in truth, each instrument has much to do.

Rimsky-Korsakov took Berlioz's ideas of scoring and developed them to achieve a variety of lush and luminous sounds that are always colorful. There is much dependence on woodwind sounds and percussion effects. Such orchestrating, sometimes referred to as the "Russian" style, can be heard in works by many later composers, as in Stravinsky's *Firebird* Suite.

Tchaikovsky used great subtlety in dealing with the orchestra, bringing out the particular colors of the solo woodwinds and showing the great varieties of string sounds that can be achieved by the composer who knows string bowing and phrasing. The music of the *Nutcracker* Suite is full of inspired orchestration. Almost every instrument, including the newly invented celesta, gets a chance at a solo, and each section of the suite appears in a different set of orchestral colors.

Gustav Mahler and Claude Debussy brought to the art of orchestration their own original approaches. Mahler called, at times, for a large number of performers. In his Eighth Symphony winds are used in groups of fours and fives, there is an enlarged percussion section, and in addition to the strings, two choruses plus a boys' choir and soloists. On some occasions Mahler used his orchestral resources for effects that almost overwhelm the listener, but there are other instances in which the orchestra is treated like a group of soloists, achieving a sense of large-scale chamber music.

Debussy used a large orchestra not for massive sounds but for delicate refinement of instrumental timbres. His orchestra can glow when necessary, but most of the time it is used as the Impressionist painters used color—for subtle contrasts and speaking in hints rather than outright statements. Debussy's fellow-countryman Ravel scored in a virtuoso fashion, as in his *Bolero,* in which a single melody holds the audience's attention as it keeps reappearing in fresh colors.

New contributions to orchestration have been made in more recent times. With the gigantic orchestra called for in *The Rite of Spring* (1913), Stravinsky produced sounds that were sometimes percussive, sometimes more in the orchestral manner of Debussy. In his later works Stravinsky led the way in the revolt against the lush sounds of the nineteenth-century orchestra—a revolt that is still in progress.

Anton von Webern wrote sparsely for the orchestra, breaking up the melodies so that no instrument plays more than a few notes in succession and few instruments ever play together. The effect is like that of hearing a chamber orchestra possessing a large palette of colors.

Edgard Varèse, a great innovator in pure sound, contrasted blocks of sound, often using only the extreme ranges of the instruments. Varèse was one of the first to combine electronic sounds with those of conventional instruments. It is probable that the addition of electronic sounds will affect orchestration at least as much as did the perfection of the string and woodwind instruments, and the addition of valves and pistons to the brass.

ORGAN: a wind instrument played by means of a keyboard. The organ has been called "the king of instruments," and no other can compare with it in range of tone or in loudness. It is like a whole orchestra or band in the varieties of tone color it can produce. Although one of the oldest-known instruments, going back at least 2,000 years, it was also the first instrument to be powered by electricity and, in a new form, the first of the electronic instruments.

In its long career the organ has been associated with Roman gladiators, medieval monarchs, the Christian church, silent movies, and radio and television "soap operas." It has been the favorite performing instrument of such great composers as Gabrieli, Frescobaldi, Buxtehude, Handel, Bach, and Franck. Also, it has inspired many important musical forms, among them the fugue, the toccata, the theme and variations, the partita, and the chorale-prelude.

The organ is a wind instrument—or group of wind instruments. Its tones are made by forcing air, under pressure, through a variety of pipes. Some of the pipes are square and made of wood, and operate like whistles or recorders. Others are round and made of metal, and at their lower ends have small metal tongues that vibrate like the reeds of woodwind instruments. Air is fed to the pipes from a large windchest, which, much like the bag of a bagpipe, stores the air until it is needed. In former times the air was forced into the windchest from a series of large bellows; today a pump is used, like the small pump that circulates air in a tropical fish aquarium.

An organ will have from a few hundred to several thousand pipes, varying in length from a few inches to thirty-two feet. Some are just pencil thin in diameter; others, large enough for two men to crawl through side by side. No two organs are exactly alike. A small chapel will not need as large an organ as a big cathedral or auditorium. Each organist will have his own individual preferences for certain tone colors and will have these sounds built into his instrument.

The organist plays the instrument while seated on a bench which allows him to move freely. His fingers play on one or more keyboards, called manuals. Most organs have from two to four of these, although organs have been built with as many as seven. With his feet the organist plays a set of large wooden pedals arranged like a huge keyboard. Beside or above the manuals are groups of stops—knobs, keys, buttons, or levers. There is a set of stops for each manual and one for the pedals. Each stop controls a

Panpipes

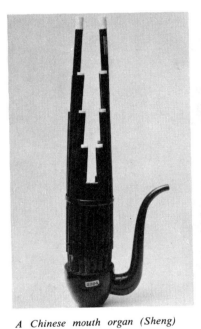

A Chinese mouth organ (Sheng)

Boy holding portative organ (from the cantoria of Luca della Robbia in the Cathedral of Florence, 15th century)

Ex. 4 — Fugue in D Major, J.S. Bach

Fast

group of pipes of the same quality, and since there are as many pipes to a given stop as there are keys on the manual, each stop is in itself a complete organ.

The tone quality of each stop depends on the material, shape, and type (whistle or reed) of the pipes. The typical "organ-like" sound is that of the *diapason*—a round metal pipe that gives a reedy, sweet tone. Other stops give the sound of flutes, trumpets, strings, oboe, and piccolo. The *vox humana* makes a vibrato like that of the human voice.

The principal manual on an organ is called the great organ, and usually it has the largest number of stops. Above it is the swell organ, its pipes enclosed in a box. Shutters along one side of the box can be opened and shut by means of a swell pedal for crescendo and diminuendo effects. Other manuals are the choir organ, the solo organ, and the echo organ. The pedal organ serves as the rich, strong bass of the organ. It has many large pipes—sixteen or thirty-two feet in length—and in its lowest register gives off a rumbling sound that is felt as much as it is heard.

The tone of an organ sounds only when one or more stops are opened to allow air into the sets of pipes controlled by the stops. When the organist presses down a key, with finger or foot, he makes a tone that will sound only while that key is held. There is nothing like the sustaining pedal of the piano to keep the tone sounding while something else is being played. Also, the way in which the player attacks the key has nothing to do with the actual sound—it is as loud or as soft as the stops that are open. The organist is thus unable to make accents as a pianist can.

To build up the full sound of an organ, the player can couple two manuals together. In this way he makes available all the sounds

of both manuals. He can also put together combinations of stops so that he gets mixtures, or doublings, of tones. By mixing together pipes of different length he can play one key and get sounds an octave lower and higher than the note he is playing. He can even add stops that will play five notes higher than the basic note; a melody will then sound as if played by two instruments playing a fifth apart. The organist must work quickly to change the stops, or registrations, between phrases of his music. To hasten this process he can arrange a series of pre-set groups of stops each of which is put in action by one button or lever.

The organ is the perfect instrument for music made up of strands of independent voices—the use of a different manual for each hand allows each melody to be heard clearly. The pedal keyboard can carry a melody of its own, freeing the hands of the player for intricate passage work. Of course the feet of the organist can also play rapid passage work, as in Ex. 4, a fugue theme by Bach.

In any complex machine, many things can go wrong. On the organ, the most common difficulty is the cipher—a note that continues to sound after the key is released. Many an unlucky organist has had to finish a performance with a steady unexpected tone sounding through the music.

The organ developed from the early Greek panpipes, a series of cane tubes arranged in a scale. The player blew across the tubes to make a melody. A complicated version of Greek panpipes is still popular in Thailand, where it is known as the *khaen*. When the Greeks, about 250 B.C., invented a way of sending compressed air through the panpipes, to make the instrument called the *hydraulus*, they had the first real organ. When large pipes came to be used, the sound was loud enough to fill a whole arena. It was

Playing the positiv organ. Two people were needed to play this chamber instrument: one to pump the bellows and one to play the keyboard (a German engraving of the late 15th century by Israhel Van Mechenem)

Top left: *Baroque organ loft in the Wallfahrts Church in Moravia (part of Czechoslovakia)*
Below: *diagrams showing two forms of organ action: tracker and electro-pneumatic. The inset in the center shows some of the variety of pipes used in organs. An organ pipe is not unlike a penny whistle. Basically, the wind enters the foot and exits through a narrow flue at the mouth. The splitting of this air column on the upper lip causes the air column to vibrate. The length of the body or resonator gives the pipe its pitch in the musical scale*

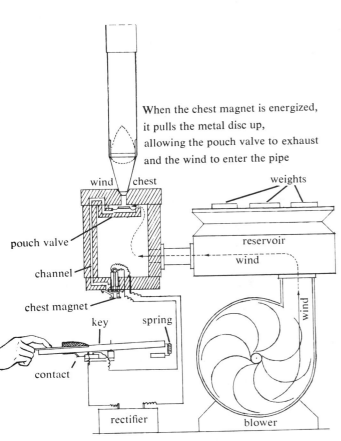

When the chest magnet is energized, it pulls the metal disc up, allowing the pouch valve to exhaust and the wind to enter the pipe

Electro-pneumatic Action
Contemporary (Used Since c. 1900)

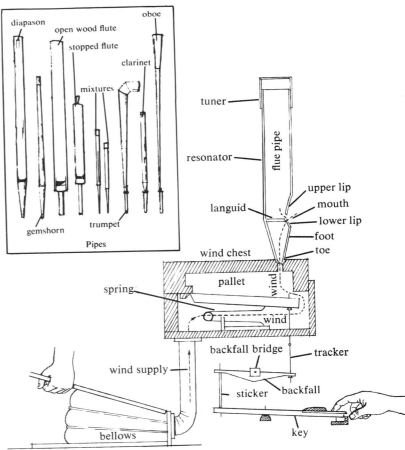

Pipes

Tracker Action
Dating from Biblical Times and Still Widely Used Today

Console of the Wurlitzer organ in Radio City Music Hall, New York

the hydraulus that became the accompaniment to the Roman circuses with their battling gladiators and raging wild animals. When the Christians came to power in Rome, the hydraulus was banned because of its pagan associations.

In the meantime bellows, pumped by hands or feet, replaced the hydraulic method of supplying air to the organ pipes. The bellows, or pneumatic, organ was used in churches to aid the congregation in singing, and organs became favorite gifts for one monarch to send to another. By A.D. 980 an organ with twenty-six bellows and two keyboards was in use at Winchester, England. The keyboard was just a series of wooden strips which the organist pulled out to allow air to go into a pipe—and pushed back when he wanted the sound to stop. Fast passage work was out of the question.

In the thirteenth century the keys were attached to valves that opened the pipes so that air could come through. Several pipes could be attached to each key; the voice of the organ was now loud enough to fill the large cathedrals that were being built all over Europe.

Meanwhile, around the twelfth century, the *portative organ* had become popular. The player carried it around his neck on a strap, much like an accordion of today.

Later organs took on many of the features we associate with organs today. New stops were added during the fifteenth and sixteenth centuries, and pedal keyboards also had by that time been invented. Composers began to see new possibilities in the instrument. One thing they wrote for it was dance music. Another was the ricercar, which, in imitating the many-voiced music of the day, gave the composer a chance to weave together several strands of melody, try rapid scale passages, and even use big chords. Cabezón in Spain, Merulo and the Gabrielis in Italy, and Sweelinck in Holland were the founders of the great schools of organ music, writing variations, canzonas, fantasias, and toccatas. The organ had become a solo instrument capable of playing brilliant as well as serious music.

A small reed organ, the *regal,* was a popular instrument in the sixteenth-century home. It probably sounded somewhat like the modern harmonium. Some persons thought its tone was sweet, but others found it too harsh, and by the early 1700's it had fallen out of favor.

The highest peak in the history of organ music is the Baroque period, from the early 1600's to the middle 1700's. It was at this time that Italian composers such as Frescobaldi wrote their display pieces—toccatas and ricercars. German composers, meanwhile, based their organ music on the Lutheran chorales, on which they developed skillful variations or chorale-preludes. The two greatest composers of this time—Bach and Handel—were both outstanding organists. Bach's chorale-preludes, fugues, and partitas soar above all other organ music and have become the organist's "Bible."

After 1750 the organ was neglected by most composers. Mozart, Mendelssohn, Liszt, and Brahms wrote some compositions for it, but Germany, once the center of organ music, now gave way to France and Belgium. Franck, Widor, and Guilmant used the organ in many colorful ways, helped by the invention of new stops, better air supply, and—starting in 1868—the new electric action from key to pipe.

In 1917 the largest organ in the world was installed in the Wanamaker store in Philadelphia. It had 232 stops and 18,000 pipes. Fifteen years later the organ in the Convention Hall at Atlantic City became the world's largest. It has 1,233 stops and more than 32,000 pipes.

During the early 1920's many motion-picture theaters installed organs to provide musical background for films, which in those years were silent. These organs were not on the same scale of development as the organs in large churches. Many of them had "dummy" manuals—keyboards not connected to any pipes, but intended merely to impress. Their special features were the "fancy" stops—imitations of drums, cymbals, and other percussion instruments—and as a rule the builders avoided making them sound like church organs. When sound films became common, the theater organs began to disappear. For a while the organist did short pieces between shows and played while the audience sang songs, following the bouncing ball on the screen. But soon the theater organ practically vanished.

Recently the instrument has moved in two directions, both backward and forward. It became in 1934 the first instrument to become completely electronic, with electrical circuits and amplifiers taking the place of the bulky pipes. This compactness has popularized the Hammond organ, making the organ once more an instrument for the home. The electronic organ is capable of almost limitless tone possibilities, although to many listeners it will never sound quite like a pipe organ.

Numerous churches and schools have rediscovered the beauties of the Baroque organ of the period of Bach and Handel. Old organs in Germany, Denmark, and France have been studied and reproduced. Modern organ builders in Europe and the United States have been able to combine the best of the old ideas with the newest in techniques and materials. The modern organ is capable of producing the clear sounds of Baroque music as well as the brilliant and colorful sounds of the more recent French composers.

ORGANUM: a word (pronounced with the stress on the first syllable) referring to an old way of singing in parts. Organum is hardly ever heard today, but it is important as the ancestor of all harmony and counterpoint. It results when two singers perform the same melody, one starting on C and the other on F. The intervals between the two voices then form a string of perfect fourths or fifths:

"America," as it would sound in organum

Organum started in the ninth century, when singers used it in simple parallel form in performing Gregorian chant. In the course of the next few centuries freer forms developed—first an "oblique" form in which the upper voice sang a succession of fourths, fifths, and octaves:

Cunctipotens genitor

Cun · cti · po · tens ge · ni · tor de · us

and later a "melismatic" form, in which the upper voice sang a highly decorated line against the slow-moving chant (Ex. 5). The two earliest composers of whom anything is known, the twelfth-century Frenchmen Leonin and Perotin, wrote in organum of as many as four parts.

By the middle of the thirteenth century, composers had grown tired of the sound of unrelieved fourths and fifths. They were building their harmony on the sweeter sound of the third, and were letting melodies move against each other. Organum had dropped out of music. It was not to be heard again till the 1880's, in the music of Debussy and Satie. Other composers have used organum since.

Ex. 5 — *Cunctipotens genitor*

Cun - - cti - po - - tens

ORNAMENTATION: the simple or elaborate embellishment of musical tones. An ornament may be indicated by grace notes (printed smaller than the principal notes) or by signs such as *tr* ~ or ~ . On the other hand, embellishments may be written out, as in some of the ornate passages in Bach's slow movements, or they may be left completely to the musical taste of the performer.

The ornamentation of tones is probably as old as music itself. Certainly much so-called primitive music is highly embellished—a fact that led Stravinsky to compose such a melody (see Ex. 34, page 483) for the opening section of his *Rite of Spring*.

Singers have long been the leaders in musical ornamentation—and they still are today in popular music. In early polyphonic music the singer was expected to improvise "diminutions" or embellishments—a custom that prevailed even in the performance of religious works, such as those by Lassus and Palestrina in the sixteenth century. Giulio Caccini, in the preface to his *Nuove Musiche* of 1601, goes into great detail about the various types of ornaments that were expected of singers to make their performances more expressive.

As composers transcribed vocal works for keyboard instruments, they wrote out the embellishments that singers had used. During the seventeenth century many of the ornaments had become formalized, and a composer could write a sign which replaced the tonal figuration. But there is confusion about seventeenth-century ornamentation. In England and in France (where ornaments are known as *agréments*) different systems of indicating the ornaments arose. The English composers wrote slanted lines through the note stems or above the notes, while the French used various kinds of wavy lines. Often two composers from the same country did not agree in their manner of showing agréments.

During the Baroque and Classical periods a few types of ornamentation were considered essential (Ex. 6): the mordent, inverted mordent, appoggiatura, turn, and trill.

Singers and even many instrumentalists continued to add embellishments, often on top of those already written. Rossini did much to stop the excessive ornamentation of his melodies by writing such florid passages—including embellishments—that the singers had as much as they could handle without adding further complexities.

Nineteenth- and twentieth-century composers, seeking to leave nothing to chance, have written out most of their ornamentation. An additional type of ornament that appeared in the nineteenth century was the so-called "grace" note (Ex. 7), the only ornament that is played before the beat.

Ex. 6

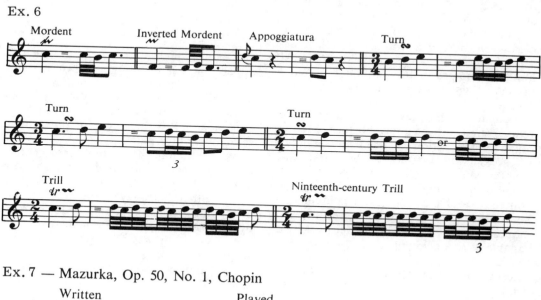

Ex. 7 — Mazurka, Op. 50, No. 1, Chopin

"Orpheus among the Thracians" (from a Greek krater of the middle 5th century B.C.*)*

ORPHEUS: the sweet-singing hero of a Greek legend. The story of Orpheus and his love for his wife Eurydice has been used as the plot of more than thirty operas. Two of these, both entitled *Euridice,* are the earliest operas for which the music is still in existence. They were written in 1600 by two of the founders of opera, Peri and Caccini. Other important operas on the subject of Orpheus are those by Monteverdi (1607) and Gluck (1762). A witty operetta, *Orpheus in the Underworld,* was composed by Offenbach in 1858.

According to legend, Orpheus was the son of the muse Calliope and the king of Thrace. From his mother he received the power to make music that could move rocks, tame wild beasts, and change the courses of rivers.

The opera stories begin after Orpheus has married Eurydice. Soon after their wedding she is bitten by a poisonous snake and is taken to the home of the dead, the underworld. Determined to get her back, Orpheus sings his way to her, and his music softens even the hard heart of Pluto, god of the underworld, so that Eurydice is allowed to leave. But she does not know that Orpheus is to walk in front of her and never look back until they have reached the safety of the upper world. In Gluck's opera Eurydice pleads with Orpheus and doubts his love for her because he does not look at her; in Monteverdi's opera Orpheus thinks he hears pursuers. In both operas he looks back—and Eurydice sinks lifeless to the ground.

Early operas were performed for kings and the nobility—audiences that did not want stories with unhappy endings. So, in opera, the story of Orpheus is usually changed. In Monteverdi the god Apollo reunites the lovers by taking them with him to heaven. In Gluck it is Venus, goddess of love, who takes pity on Orpheus and restores Eurydice to life. These changes allow both operas to end with dancing and rejoicing.

OSTINATO: a short bass melody (*basso ostinato,* "obstinate bass"), that is constantly repeated. In the seventeenth and eighteenth centuries composers wrote variations over ostinatos, calling such works "Air on a Ground Bass." The form of a passacaglia or a chaconne was most often a set of variations over a ground bass.

Recently the term ostinato has been applied to any short musical idea that is repeated many times, not necessarily in the bass part. It is a favorite device of many modern composers, who use it sometimes as an accompaniment to a melody, sometimes to help build a climax. Stravinsky is especially fond of piling several ostinatos, in different meters, on top of each other:

Symphony in Three Movements, Stravinsky

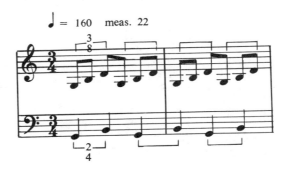

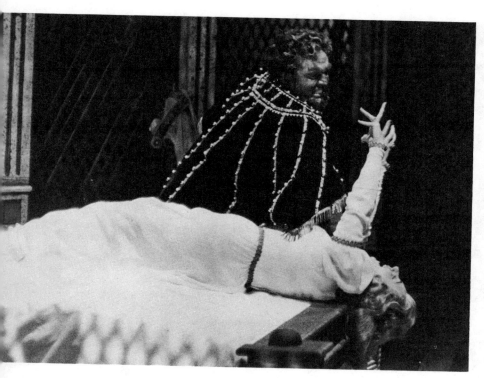

Final scene of Otello *with James McCracken in the title role and Renata Tebaldi as Desdemona (Metropolitan Opera production, 1962–3 season)*

OTELLO *(Othello):* Giuseppe Verdi's next-to-last opera. It was first performed in Milan, Italy, in 1887, sixteen years after Verdi's previous opera, *Aida.* The libretto, by Arrigo Boito, was a tightened version of Shakespeare's *Othello,* which in turn had been based on a sixteenth-century Italian short story.

Othello (in Italian, *Otello*), a heroic black Moor, is the duke of Venice's general in charge of the island of Cyprus. His wife is the gentle and noble Desdemona. Iago, the central character of the opera, is an envious and bitter officer serving under Othello. Iago plots to destroy Othello by leading him to believe that Desdemona is in love with another officer, Cassio.

Iago gets Cassio drunk and into a fight, and Othello dismisses Cassio from his service. As Desdemona pleads with Othello to forgive Cassio, she drops her handkerchief to the ground. It is no ordinary handkerchief, but one of the first tokens of love given to her by Othello. Emilia, Desdemona's maid

and Iago's wife, picks it up, and Iago later snatches it from her to use it in his plot.

The jealous Othello discovers that Cassio has the handkerchief, but does not know it was left with him by Iago. In front of messengers from Venice and many of his friends, Othello in a rage throws Desdemona to the ground. That night he creeps into her room after Emilia has bid her good-night. He kisses his wife and then smothers her. In the tumult that follows, Othello learns that Iago has been behind the whole tragedy. He starts out after him, then changes his mind and stabs himself in the heart.

To many listeners, *Otello* contains some of the most beautiful, most dramatic, and most poignant music in all opera. There are exciting choruses at the beginning as Othello's ship fights its way through a storm. A rollicking drinking song runs throughout the scene that leads to Cassio's fight. A love duet, as Desdemona greets the return of Othello, ends with the beautiful "motive of the kiss" (Ex. 8), which returns at the end of the opera.

Although the opera has no set recitatives and arias in the traditional sense, two of its dramatic scenes, or arias, are sometimes sung as concert numbers. One of these is Iago's "Credo," in which he bitterly tells the audience his cruel philosophy of life. The other is Desdemona's singing of Verdi's hauntingly beautiful setting of the old English ballad "The Willow Song."

Much of the dramatic effectiveness of *Otello* is due to Verdi's skill in using the instruments of the orchestra to set the mood of each scene. The love duet of Othello and Desdemona is accompanied by four solo cellos sighing in ecstasy. Desdemona's "Willow Song" is introduced by bassoons breathing desolation and doom. And as Othello prepares to commit murder, a snake-like melody is heard in the double basses.

This opera, finished in the composer's seventy-fourth year, proved Verdi was indeed the master of dramatic music. His crowning glory, *Falstaff,* was still six years in the future.

Ex. 8

Ex. 9 — Fundamental tone and the overtone series produced on a tuba eight feet in
   length:

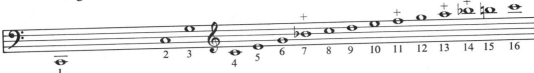

Fundamental Tone
   Note: Numbers 7-11-13-14 are "out of tune" in terms of the tempered (piano) scale.

OVERTONE SERIES: the series of tones given off by a vibrating body, such as a string or the column of air in a wind instrument, in addition to its basic or fundamental tone. These tones, which lie above the fundamental, are also called harmonics, or upper partials. Overtones result from the fact that a body vibrates in sections as well as along its total length.

For brass players in particular, a knowledge of the overtone series is of great importance. One fundamental tone will give off only its own set of overtones. These always follow the same pattern: the first tone above the fundamental is an octave, next comes a perfect fifth, and so on (Ex. 9). Within a set of overtones a brass player produces a particular pitch by changing the tension of his lips as he blows. In order to get pitches that do not lie in the original overtone series, the length of the vibrating body must be changed. The trombone player does this by means of his slide. On the horn, cornet, trumpet, and tuba the tube length is changed by means of a set of valves or pistons.

The timbre or tone color of any instrument depends on how many overtones, and which ones, are present in the complex composite tone of the instrument. The tone of a flute, for example, has very few overtones. The rich sounds of the cello and the trumpet are due to an abundance of overtones.

Contemporary composers experimenting with computers and electronic sound generators can set up their own specifications as to the overtones they choose to work with. Interesting sounds, unlike those of conventional instruments, are often the result. They open new areas of tone color to the experimental musician.

OVERTURE: the musical opening played before the curtain goes up at the beginning of a play or an opera. The term can also refer to a concert work, often of a dramatic or programmatic nature, for orchestra.

The earliest known overture is that to Monteverdi's opera *Orfeo,* written in 1607. Before that time instrumentalists announced the beginning of a theater piece by playing an improvised fanfare or flourish. Monteverdi's overture was little more than a written-out fanfare, which he called a toccata.

The first important formal overtures are those devised in Paris by Lully to open his ballets and operas of the 1670's. These "French overtures" started with a slow introduction (usually in a meter of 2 or 4) and used many dotted-note rhythmic patterns. A fast, sprightly allegro, with much imitation of themes in the different instruments, followed the solemn and heroic introduction. At the end of the allegro a few slow chords brought back the mood of the introduction.

The French type of overture, popular for many years, was used not only in operas but also in oratorios, cantatas, and instrumental suites. The overtures to Purcell's opera *Dido and Aeneas,* Handel's oratorio *Messiah,* and Bach's Orchestral Suite Number 2 in B Minor all follow the pattern established by Lully.

Italian opera overtures followed a different path. Called *sinfonia avanti l'opera* ("symphony before the opera"), they were in three movements: fast-slow-fast. This form was established by Alessandro Scarlatti in the late 1600's.

Both French and Italian types of overture influenced other forms of music. The French overture was used as a first movement in instrumental suites or partitas, particularly those of German composers such as Bach and Telemann. The Italian overture helped composers to settle on the fast-slow-fast movement plan used in the early Classical symphonies. Until the late 1700's many symphonies, including Haydn's "London" Symphonies, were called Overtures or Grand Overtures.

Neither Lully's nor Scarlatti's overtures had tried to do anything other than announce to the audience that the show was about to begin. Gluck's overture to his *Alceste* (1767) was the first to set the mood for the opera that was to follow; in fact, the overture to *Alceste* flows into the opening scene of the opera.

By the late 1700's many opera overtures were being based on the same form as that of the first movement of classical symphonies: the sonata-allegro form. Mozart added another dramatic element when, in his overture to *Don Giovanni,* he used thematic material from the last scenes of the opera, thus giving the audience a taste of the tragedy that was to come.

Beethoven and Weber, following Mozart's example, also used themes from their operas in the overtures. They also made the overture a dramatic work that foretold the story completely, in sonata-allegro form. Beethoven's three Leonore Overtures, originally written for his opera *Fidelio,* were so complete and powerful in themselves that Beethoven put them aside and wrote a fourth piece, the *Fidelio* overture, for the opera itself. The Leonore Overtures, as well as Beethoven's overtures to the plays *Egmont* and *Coriolanus,* are now favorite concert works.

Descriptive and programmatic music, which reached its height of popularity in the symphonic poems of the nineteenth century, was an important feature of many overtures of the early 1800's. Nature painting fills the overtures to Weber's *Der Freischütz* and *Oberon,* Wagner's *Flying Dutchman,* and Rossini's *William Tell.*

Rossini, who wrote many operas and thus had to write many overtures also, often followed the practice of other composers in making one overture serve for several operas. The overture to *The Barber of Seville* was borrowed from an opera he had written the year before—*Elisabetta.* Rossini's overtures—gay, tuneful, and cleverly orchestrated—can be counted on to feature a "Rossini crescendo." Toscanini, in the course of his ca-

reer as a conductor, made many of these Rossini works popular as concert pieces.

Mendelssohn's overtures—*A Midsummer Night's Dream, The Hebrides,* and *Calm Sea and a Happy Voyage*—were written as dramatic concert works. As such they served as models not only for later symphonic poems but also for such later concert overtures as Brahms's *Tragic Overture* and *Academic Festival Overture;* Tchaikovsky's *"1812" Overture, Hamlet,* and *Romeo and Juliet;* and, in our own time, William Schuman's *American Festival Overture;* and Copland's *An Outdoor Overture.*

After Weber and Rossini, nineteenth-century opera overtures developed in several directions. In some cases, as in the operas *Carmen* and *Faust,* the composer wove together several themes from the opera. Wagner, in *Die Walküre* and other operas of *The Ring of the Nibelungs,* composed a PRELUDE (*Vorspiel*) that carries right into the opera. But for *Die Meistersinger* and *Tristan and Isolde* he built symphonic overtures that can hold their own as independent concert works.

Verdi and Puccini often did away with the overture. A few dramatic chords serve as a signal for the curtain to rise.

Modern composers follow no particular pattern. Berg's *Wozzeck* has no overture, but Hindemith's *Mathis der Maler* has a long one. In the field of musical comedy most overtures serve to give the audience a taste of the "hit" tunes that will be heard. They are usually brightly orchestrated to put the audience in a festive mood.

Most movies have an overture, the "title music," which is played as the title of the film and the names of the makers and the cast are being shown. In television the "theme," which in the space of a few seconds identifies a dramatic program and sets its mood, is—in its own way—an overture.

p: a musical direction (an abbreviation for "piano") that tells a performer to play or sing softly. *pp* means *pianissimo*—"very softly"; *mp* means *mezzo piano*—"moderately softly."

P. or *Ped.,* printed under the lower staff of a composition for piano, is an abbreviation for "pedal," indicating that the sustaining pedal is to be used.

PAGANINI, NICCOLÒ (1782–1840): the wizard of the violin. His tall, thin body and black, wavy hair hanging down to his shoulders, and his burning dark eyes, suited the stories about him. It was said that he had sold his soul to the devil; that he had been in prison for murder; that sparks exploded as he touched his bow to the strings of his violin. It is little wonder that he was the most famous musician of the early 1800's.

He was born in Genoa, Italy, where his father first taught him to play the mandolin and violin; he later took lessons from neighborhood teachers. At the age of eleven he started his concert career, and by the time he was sixteen he had written his twenty-four *Capricci (Caprices)*—some of the most difficult music ever written for the violin.

In 1805, the year after Napoleon crowned himself emperor, Paganini became director of music at the court of Princess Elisa, one of Napoleon's sisters, in northern Italy. At this time he composed his *Dialogue for Two Lovers,* using only two of the violin's four strings. The high string was the girl's voice; the low string, the man's. This work was followed by the "Napoleon" Sonata, which required only one string.

Court duties bored him, and in time Paganini resumed his career as a touring virtuoso. In Vienna, London, and Paris he was a sensation: poems were written about him, pastry was named after him; he was showered with jewels and medals, and crowds followed him in the streets. The greatest writers and musicians went to hear him. Liszt modeled his études, fantasies, and rhapsodies on Paganini's brilliant style, and it was Paganini for whom Berlioz wrote his viola concerto *Harold in Italy.*

Paganini had led a wild life as a youth, and his health was poor in later years. Between concerts he mostly lay in bed. He never practiced, but said, "I did all my practicing when I was a boy." If he read a newspaper, it was to see what it said about him. He never learned arithmetic, but his own ways of keeping his accounts worked well enough. When he died, he left his son almost half a million dollars.

Paganini's favorite violin, made by Giuseppe Guarneri, had been lent to him one day by a wealthy French music lover. After hearing it played by Paganini, the owner decided that it should never be played by anyone else, and gave it outright to Paganini. After the great violinist's death it was placed in a glass case in Genoa, and no one has played it regularly since. Known as "Paganini's widow," it has been played on in recent years only by Zino Francescatti and Ruggiero Ricci—by special invitation.

Paganini played mostly his own music, which he studded with dazzling double-stops and high, brilliant harmonics. By playing on one string with the bow while plucking another string with his left hand, he gave the audience the sensation of hearing two instruments at once. Living in fear that his secrets might be ferreted out by rival violinists, he allowed only a handful of his many compositions to be published during his lifetime. Among these were the twenty-four *Caprices,* six duets for violin and guitar, and six quartets for violin, viola, cello, and guitar. Several sets of variations, a few independent movements, two concertos, and a concert allegro were published after his death; the rest of his music has been lost.

Paganini's works have served as inspiration for other composers. Liszt and Schu-

Drawing of Paganini by Ingres (1819)

mann made piano transcriptions of some of his *Caprices*. Brahms wrote two books of variations on a single caprice, and Rachmaninoff used the same caprice in his *Rhapsody on a Theme by Paganini* for piano and orchestra.

More than any other musician, Paganini set styles of playing and living. He was the first of the great nineteenth-century virtuosos. His romantic looks and deeds, his passion for gambling, his artistry and genius as a performer—all have made the name "Paganini" a symbol of the Romantic period.

PALESTRINA, GIOVANNI DA (c. 1525–94):

the greatest master of Roman Catholic church music. His name was originally Giovanni Pierluigi. Palestrina, the name by which he became known, is a small town near Rome where he was born.

Palestrina began his musical training at the age of seven. Like many other composers he was a choirboy in the local cathedral. Going to Rome, still as a member of a choir, he continued his study of music there. In 1544 he returned to his home town as organist and choirmaster of the cathedral. When the bishop of the cathedral became Pope Julius III, he brought Palestrina to Rome as choirmaster of the Cappella Giulia.

Palestrina's first book of masses, printed in 1554, was dedicated to the pope, and the pope in turn rewarded Palestrina by making him a member of the Sistine Choir in the Vatican. But Palestrina was a married man, with two sons. This, with the fact that he was not a priest, was reason enough for the next pope to remove him from his post.

Palestrina served as music director of several churches in Rome and for a while was in charge of music at the Roman Seminary. When offered posts at several courts of music, he demanded such a high salary that he was not hired. In 1571 he returned to the Cappella Giulia and stayed there as music director for the rest of his life.

After his wife died in 1580, Palestrina for several months considered becoming a priest, but finally decided that the priestly life was not for him. He married the widow of a wealthy merchant and became a part-time businessman as well as a musician. When he died he was buried in old St. Peter's Church in Rome. The inscription on his coffin called him "Prince of Music."

Palestrina wrote in, and perfected, a musical style that had started in the Netherlands in the fifteenth century. It was smoothly written for voices. It was polyphonic—many-voiced—and full of canons, in which one voice part imitated another. In a time when many of the younger Italian composers filled their madrigals with dissonances and anguished outcries, the voices in Palestrina's music moved serenely in an angelic world of their own.

Palestrina's melodies show his genius at its height. They are long and flowing. At times they float gently down from high to low, and at other times soar gradually upward to their goals (Ex. 1 and 2). In many of his works Palestrina used the old church modes, or scales. He also used the modern major scale, which was becoming popular in his day. Not all of his music is based on the polyphonic weaving of voices; for contrast he often stops the flow and writes chantlike blocks of chords for his four- to twelve-voice choir.

Palestrina's beautifully clear works, such as the *Missa Papae Marcelli (Pope Marcel-*

Palestrina

Ex. 1 — "Ave Maria"

Ex. 2 — Christe Eleison from the Mass *Dies sanctificatus*

Palestrina presenting his first Book of Masses *to Pope Julius III (engraving from the title page, 1554)*

lus Mass), did much to quiet the criticism of many of the church fathers who felt that complicated music—some of it based on popular tunes—interfered with the sacred text. Palestrina was held in such high esteem that he was given the job of revising the old Gregorian chants that were the basis of the Mass. His work—finished by other composers after his death—was used for 300 years. Then the monks of Solesmes brought out an edition of the chants that was closer to the medieval originals.

Palestrina wrote ninety-three masses, almost 200 motets, and more than a hundred hymns and offertories. Like many of his contemporaries he wrote madrigals also, but he felt more at home in church music.

Palestrina was not an experimenter. He was content to compose in a style which seemed to sum up all that was good in music. After his death, music went in new directions—to opera, the symphony, and chamber music. But Palestrina's music was still sung, and, more important, it became the basis of the study of counterpoint. In 1725 Johann Joseph Fux published his *Steps to Parnassus,* a textbook of counterpoint based, more or less, on the style of Palestrina, and generations of composers have been taught from this book. As recently as 1903 Pope Pius X recommended the style of Palestrina as the finest model of church music.

For four centuries now, Palestrina's music has been sung in church services and in concerts. The complete works of Palestrina in thirty-three volumes were published in Germany between 1862 and 1894. A new edition of his complete works, to take thirty-

four volumes, is being published at the present time. Oddly enough, the most popular work with his name attached to it, *O Bone Jesu,* was written by someone else. Among the many books that have been written about Palestrina, the most thorough study of his style is *Counterpoint,* by the Danish musical scholar Knud Jeppesen.

PARSIFAL: Richard Wagner's last opera, first produced in 1882—within a year of his death—in his own theater at Bayreuth. Wagner had first begun to think about the medieval legend of Parsifal and the Holy Grail in 1845, and had written the libretto for it between 1865 and 1877, in intervals between work on other operas. He completed the music in 1882.

For many years *Parsifal* was given in no opera theater other than Bayreuth. The Metropolitan Opera Company of New York City first performed it in 1903. Since then it has had yearly performances at Easter time, as befits its religious subject matter. (Wagner called *Parsifal* a "religious festival stage work," meaning it to be an act of faith rather than theatrical entertainment.) As at the performance of other religious works, no applause is allowed.

The scene of *Parsifal* is Monsalvat, in the mountains of Spain. There in a castle live a brotherhood of knights dedicated to guarding two of the most precious relics of Christianity: the spear that pierced Christ's side and the Holy Grail. The latter is the cup from which Jesus drank at the Last Supper and which later was used to catch His blood when He was on the cross.

The knights are served by Kundry, a strange woman who is dedicated to them but who also, at times, comes under the magic power of Klingsor, a knight who has been rejected by the brotherhood and whose passion for revenge will be satisfied only by its destruction. Kundry, who is present in almost every scene of the opera, lives in a nightmare of agonized guilt. When not under the power of Klingsor's enchantment she devotes herself to whatever service she can do for the knights. In a sense, she personifies the temptress who longs for holiness.

As the opera opens, the knights are sorely troubled. Their leader, Amfortas, has been wounded in the side by the holy spear, which he lost in a struggle with Klingsor. The wound can be cured only if a pure and innocent youth will recover the spear and touch it to Amfortas' side.

Parsifal, a youth of great purity of heart, follows some Knights of the Grail to Monsalvat. He watches the ceremony of the knights' Love Feast—a re-creation of the Last Supper—and the beauty of the ceremony and the agony of Amfortas leave him spellbound. The old knight Gurnemanz, who at first befriends the youth, does not understand his speechlessness and puts him out of the castle.

Determined to find the spear so that he can heal Amfortas, Parsifal finds his way to Klingsor's castle. Klingsor, with the power of the holy spear, is able to conjure beautiful gardens out of the desert, peopled with beautiful maidens who tempt the knights away from their lives of purity. Here at the castle Parsifal meets Kundry, now under the influence of Klingsor, and she attempts to get Parsifal to fall in love with her, appealing to his pity and his kindness. He scorns her. Enraged at Parsifal's devotion to his quest, Kundry calls on Klingsor to destroy him. The magician hurls the spear—but it hangs in mid-air. Parsifal seizes it and makes the sign of the cross. Klingsor, his castle, and his magic gardens disappear, and only the desert remains.

Parsifal wanders for many years, searching for Monsalvat. Finally he finds the hut of Gurnemanz, now a hermit. Kundry in her misery is there too, acting as servant to Gurnemanz. When Gurnemanz recognizes Parsifal, he also realizes that to him has been given the power to heal Amfortas. Gurnemanz baptizes Parsifal, who in turn baptizes Kundry. Together they go to the castle, Monsalvat. There, during a burial service for Amfortas' father, Titurel, the knights plead with Amfortas to take the Grail from its shrine, as the ceremony requires. But his agony is too great—he cannot perform the ritual. Parsifal, whose presence has been unobserved, now touches the spear to Amfortas' wound and heals it. He then ascends the altar and kneels before the glowing Grail. The knights acknowledge him as leader. Kundry, cleansed of her sins, dies—joyously repentant.

Parsifal has few dramatic moments. Its action is generally slow, but the opera is filled with colorful spectacles, magnificent choral writing, and some of Wagner's most poignantly beautiful music. As in all his later operas Wagner uses leitmotifs to underline the action and emotion of the opera. These are so artfully composed that within a few measures he is able to create a complete musical portrait or suggest the deepest feelings.

The themes of holiness—the Communion (Ex. 3), the Holy Grail (Ex. 4), and Faith (Ex. 5)—are solemn, at times hymnlike. (The Grail theme is the "Dresden Amen" used in the Dresden Royal Chapel.) Parsifal's theme (Ex. 6) is boldly heroic and positive. The motive of the enchanted Flower Maidens is gracefully dancelike (Ex. 7).

The prelude to *Parsifal* is often played at symphonic concerts. Based on the motives of Ex. 3, 4, and 5 it builds slowly to a peak of mystical fervor. Another excerpt, the Good Friday Music, also is played separately. Based on a songlike motive (Ex. 8), it is the gently ecstatic music that follows the baptism of Parsifal and Kundry.

Scene from Act I of Parsifal *(a Bayreuth Theater production)*

Ex. 3 — The Communion

Ex. 4 — The Grail

Ex. 5 — Faith

Ex. 6 — Parsifal

Ex. 7 — The Flower Maidens

Leicht bewegt

Ex. 8 — Good Friday Music

Ex. 9 — Passacaglia and Fugue in C Minor for Organ, J.S. Bach

PARTITA: a set of variations on a theme; or a group of court dance forms. The name comes from a Latin word meaning "divisions," here referring to divisions of notes into shorter notes—that is, embellishments. (English keyboard composers of the early seventeenth century often called their variations "Divisions on a Ground [Bass].") Among the earliest variation partitas are those of Frescobaldi, written in the early 1600's.

Best known are the six keyboard partitas by Bach. Each consists of a long prelude followed by a group of dances. A seventh partita was given the title *French Overture in B Minor*. Of the six works for unaccompanied violin by Bach, three—each consisting of a prelude and a set of dances—are called partitas. The other three are called sonatas. To add to the confusion about the names of musical forms, Bach called his six works for unaccompanied cello "suites," although they are similar to his violin par-

Doris Humphrey's Passacaglia, *danced by the José Limon Company (with Chester Wolenski in the foreground)*

titas. Bach also used the old form of the partita in three sets of variations for organ on chorale tunes.

Since the time of Bach the name *partita* has almost dropped out of music. Composers prefer to call their works either suites or variations. Among the few partitas of our day is Irving Fine's Partita for Woodwind Quintet.

PASSACAGLIA: a slow Spanish dance in 3/4 meter, popular about 1600; later, an important variation form. The word in Spanish means "street song"; originally it referred to a serenade played on the guitar.

Performed at a deliberate pace, the passacaglia required many repetitions of the melody, usually only eight measures in length. Musicians, probably tired of playing the same notes over and over, began to weave decorations and embellishments over the melody, much as jazz musicians improvise variations on well-known tunes of today. Eventually the musical form of the passacaglia became that of variations over a ground-bass melody. Many composers of the seventeenth and early eighteenth centuries —Handel, Buxtehude, Couperin, Pachelbel, Bach—wrote beautiful passacaglias for organ and harpsichord. Bach's Passacaglia and Fugue in C Minor for organ is the best known (Ex. 9).

Although the passacaglia is traditionally in triple meter, composers have written passacaglias in 4/4 meter (Handel's Passacaglia in G Minor for harpsichord) and 5/4 meter (Walter Piston's Passacaglia for piano). The difference between the passacaglia and the chaconne also has been uncertain. Most musicians distinguish between them as follows: the passacaglia has variations over a repeated bass melody; the chaconne has variations built on a repeated series of chords.

The passacaglia dropped out of favor in the nineteenth century, but contemporary composers have revived interest in the old form. Copland and Piston have written passacaglias for piano. The opening movement of William Schuman's Third Symphony is a freely treated passacaglia for orchestra. Alban Berg used the passacaglia form for the fourth scene in the first act of his opera *Wozzeck*.

Ex. 10 — Passepied from *L'Europe galante*, Campra

PASSEPIED: the gayest and lightest of the court dances. Coming from Brittany, in northern France, as a folk dance, in the middle 1600's it became a favorite dance at the court of France. Its main feature was a series of gliding steps and the crossing and recrossing of the feet. It was from the crossing of the feet that it took its name, *passepied*, "passing of the feet."

The passepied remained a popular court dance for a hundred years—until the middle 1700's. Many composers of the time wrote charming passepieds in their operas and in their instrumental music. Among the best known are those by Bach (in his Fifth "English" Suite and Fifth Partita), Handel, Couperin, Rameau, and the French opera composer Campra.

The court passepieds were written in a fast 3/8 or 3/4 meter, beginning on an upbeat. There were two or four sections in the music, each eight or sixteen measures in length. Cadences at the end of sections were often syncopated by putting accents on every other beat (Ex. 10)—a rhythmic device used in triple meter and called a *hemiola*.

Like many court dances the passepied was ignored by composers for the hundred years after 1750. Since then several composers, among them Delibes and Debussy, have written lively examples. The modern passepieds are written in 2/4 meter—the meter of the old peasant dance of Brittany.

PASSING TONE: a non-chordal tone that is approached and left by step. Passing tones may be diatonic and single, as here:

"Swanee River," Foster

or chromatic and in groups, as in Ex. 11. Passing tones are as old as the twelfth

Ex. 11 — Rondo, K. 494, Mozart
* = Passing Tones

Ex. 12 — Sonata in C, K. 309, Mozart

Ex. 13

* = Passing Tones

century. They were used then to decorate the principal tones in works written in organum. They may be unaccented or accented, as in Ex. 12; such accented passing tones are sometimes called *appoggiaturas.*

Whenever a diatonic or chromatic scale is played while one chord is held throughout, the result is a series of passing tones. Ex. 13 shows the C-major scale played against the two primary chords with the passing tones indicated.

Since passing tones can be confirmed only in relation to the more or less traditional chords, they are not to be found in twelve-tone, serial music, nor in electronic music, although in the latter something like passing tones may evolve.

PASSION: the story of Jesus from the time of the Last Supper through the Crucifixion. Musical settings of the Passion began in medieval times with the short chants and choral responses used in church services during Holy Week to dramatize the sufferings of Jesus. By the sixteenth century the whole Gospel story was being sung in the splendid, many-voiced settings of Tomás Luis de Victoria and Orlandus Lassus.

In the course of the seventeenth century, German composers expanded the setting of the Passion so that it became, in effect, a dramatic oratorio. To the story of the Passion, told in recitatives of great purity and

severity, were added inspirational religious verses in aria or chorale settings. The greatest passion music of this period is to be found in the three versions of the story composed by Heinrich Schütz (1585–1672).

The German oratorio form of the passion was what J. S. Bach drew upon as he set out, in the 1720's, to compose his passions for the Church of St. Thomas in Leipzig. His St. John and St. Matthew Passions, performed on Good Friday of the years 1723 and 1729, are among the crowning achievements of the Baroque era. They call for solo singers, a large chorus, and orchestra, and in the St. Matthew a separate boys' choir also is used. The story is told by the Evangelist, who is a tenor. A bass voice (accompanied in the St. Matthew Passion by stringed instruments) represents Jesus. The chorus sometimes represents all the faithful, sometimes the crowds of Jews and Roman soldiers. At many points throughout each of the passions the chorus sings Lutheran chorales—slow, beautiful hymns that Bach harmonized in such a way as to bring out, during the story of Christ's suffering, the feelings of the faithful (Ex. 14).

Bach's son Carl Philipp Emanuel also wrote two settings of the Passion. Since then the form has practically died out. Two of the few modern examples are colorful scores by the contemporary composers Bernard Rogers and Krzystof Penderecki.

"The Three Crosses," an etching by Rembrandt (1653)

Ex. 14 — "Passion Chorale" from the St. Matthew Passion, J.S. Bach

Ex. 15 —Concerto Grosso, Op. 6, No. 8, Corelli

Largo

PASTORALE: a gentle piece of music suggesting the calmness of the countryside, usually in a slow 6/8 or 12/8 meter. It gets its name from *pastor* (Latin for "shepherd"), and its melody is often accompanied by long, held bass notes that suggest the drone of the shepherd's bagpipe.

Short instrumental movements with a pastoral feeling often occur in longer works having to do with Christmas. Here they are used to suggest the shepherds in their fields watching the Christmas star. The last movement of Corelli's Christmas Concerto Grosso, Opus 6, Number 8, is a pastorale (Ex. 15). A pastorale serves as the opening to the second part of Bach's Christmas Oratorio. The famous "Pastoral Symphony" in Handel's *Messiah* sets the mood for the shepherd's scene which follows it.

The aria "He Shall Feed His Flock" in *Messiah* is a pastorale based on an old Sicilian folk song, "The Carol of the Bagpipers." The pastorale is closely related in meter, tempo, and feeling to a dance known as the siciliano.

Beethoven gave the title *Pastoral Symphony* to his Sixth Symphony in F Major. Its five movements describe Beethoven's feelings about being in the country: his happiness, a scene at a brook (with the calls of the nightingale, quail, and cuckoo heard in the orchestra), a peasant dance, a thunderstorm, and a shepherd's song and the general rejoicing after the storm. The "Pastoral" title given to his Piano Sonata in D Major, Opus 28, on the other hand, was merely the inspiration of his publisher.

Country life has been a popular subject with poets and dramatists since the days of ancient Rome. In the thirteenth century short plays with music about knights, shepherds, and shepherdesses were called *pastourelles.* The most famous pastourelle is Adam de la Halle's *Robin and Marian,* written in the early 1280's. Handel's opera *Il pastor fido (The Faithful Shepherd)* is based on a pastoral play.

PATHÉTIQUE: a descriptive French word that occurs in the titles of two of the best-known of all concert works, Beethoven's "Pathétique" Sonata and Tchaikovsky's *Symphonie pathétique.*

It was Beethoven himself who gave the title *Grande Sonate pathétique* to his Sonata Number 8 in C Minor, Opus 13, when it was published in 1799. This was the first time Beethoven gave such a descriptive title to a sonata; it was his way of calling attention to the deep emotion of the music.

The slow, dramatic introduction to the first movement is a kind of motto (Ex. 16) that sets the mood of the work. It returns twice (unusual for an introduction), first at the end of the statement of the themes, and again just before the very end of the movement. The main themes of the allegro section of the first movement are an uprushing melody that slowly falls back (Ex. 17) and a short motive that first appears in the unexpected key of E♭ minor (Ex. 18). The main theme of the second movement is one of Beethoven's most beautiful singing melodies (Ex. 19). There is drama in this movement, but only in short flashes. The last movement is a fast rondo—not jolly, as rondos often are, but resolute. Each return of the main theme (Ex. 20) is preceded by a rushing scale passage.

Tchaikovsky's *Symphony pathétique (Pathetic Symphony)* of 1893 was not so named by Tchaikovsky himself, to whom it was a symphony in B minor, his sixth. But when his brother Modeste suggested the descriptive title, Tchaikovsky approved of it. It was his last work and his masterpiece. He died nine days after conducting the St. Petersburg orchestra in its first performance.

The symphony opens slowly with a dark theme (Ex. 21) sung by the bassoon to the accompaniment of divided double basses. This theme is whipped up into an excitement that leads to a wonderful curving melody such as only Tchaikovsky could write (Ex. 22, on page 410).

Ex. 16

Ex. 17

Ex. 18

Ex. 19

Ex. 20

Ex. 21

Ex. 22

Andante

Ex. 23

Allegro con grazio

Ex. 24

Allegro molto vivace

Ex. 25

Adagio lamentoso

José Limon and Betty Jones in Limon's The Moor's Pavane

The second movement is waltzlike, but with five counts in a measure instead of three (Ex. 23). Almost happy, this movement ends with fragments of the theme in the winds over solemn-sounding string chords and a repeated note in the cellos and basses that throbs like a beating heart.

The third movement is a wild scherzo-march. Its main theme (Ex. 24) is heralded by scurrying strings and woodwinds, snatches of the theme in the brass, and pizzicato strings emphasizing the interval of a fourth which is so important in the theme itself. Scorching scale passages flash from strings to woodwinds, the theme is stated by the whole orchestra, and everything builds to a loud climax. All is ready for the finale, whose main theme (Ex. 25) is a sigh, a lament, a last and pathetic song of suffering.

The *Symphonie pathétique* was successful from the start—almost too successful. It was played too much and became too familiar. After a while, listeners tired of it. It has now returned to public favor, taking, at last, its rightful place among the masterworks of music.

PAVANE: a slow, dignified court dance that came from Spain (*pavo* is the Spanish word for "peacock") or from northern Italy (*paduana* means "from Padua") in the 1500's. The dance itself consisted mostly of walking, bowing, and curtsying—never any jumping or fast movement. At times one gentleman moved majestically alone down the middle of the ballroom, strutting like a peacock. Slowly and ceremoniously, he bowed to the lady opposite him. Then, equally slowly, he moved back to his original place and bowed to his partner.

The music for the pavane was always solemn and steady, with two or four beats per measure. It was usually in two large sections, with heavy cadences at the middle and the end. The melody of the pavane was simple, almost hymnlike. Its harmony was solid and chordal, its rhythm clear and uncomplicated (Ex. 26).

The pavane often was followed by a fast galliard, called an "after-dance" or "Nachtanz." Such a grouping of two dances, possibly using the same melody, was the ancestor of the later dance suite.

Ex. 26 — Pavane from Arbeau's *Orchésographie* (1589)

The pavane was a popular instrumental form used by many composers of the late 1500's and early 1600's. The most famous pavanes of this period are those by Milán, Byrd, and Dowland. But the pavane was succeeded by the allemande in the dance suite, and it dropped out of music until the French composer Fauré revived it in his "Pavane" for orchestra in 1887. The best-known pavanes of more recent times are those by Ravel: "The Sleeping Beauty" from the *Mother Goose* Suite and the "Pavane for a Dead Princess."

PEDAL POINT: a tone that is held, or continually sounded, while the harmony around it keeps changing. Since it is at times quite dissonant with the harmony, its musical effect is of something insistent and unyielding.

It gets its name from its early use on the organ, where a tone was held on the pedal keyboard while the two hands played melodies or shifting harmonies above it (Ex. 27). Long pedal points based on the tonic, or keynote, of the scale are often found at the endings of Bach's fugues (Ex. 28).

Ex. 27 — Toccata for Organ, Pachelbel

etc. for 14 meas.

Ex. 28 — Fugue No. 2 from *The Well-tempered Clavier*, Book I, J.S. Bach

Ex. 29 — *Hungarian Rhapsody* No. 2, Liszt

The pedal point on the dominant, the fifth tone of the scale, is often used to lead back to the restatement section of a work written in a sonata-allegro form. In an orchestral work, such a pedal point often appears in the middle register, sounded by the bassoons or horns (see Ex. 48, page 535). Pedal points, originally in the bass, are now used in any register—high, middle, or low (Ex. 29).

The drone bass, imitating bagpipes or drums, is related to the pedal point.

PELLÉAS AND MÉLISANDE (*Pelléas et Mélisande*): an opera by Claude Debussy. The libretto is from a play by Maurice Maeterlinck, which also inspired—under the same title—incidental music by Gabriel Fauré (1898) and a symphonic poem by Arnold Schoenberg (1905). But it is Debussy's opera—the only one he wrote—that is the best-known work under the title.

This opera, one of Debussy's masterpieces, was ten years in the writing. At the first performance in Paris, in 1902, the role of Mélisande was sung by Mary Garden, a Scottish opera singer. The scandal caused by this choice, added to Debussy's unusual style of writing, made the opera a subject of numerous arguments. It has never been a great, popular success—and Debussy did not intend it to be. He deliberately shied away from rousing choruses and crowd-pleasing scenic effects. There are seldom more than two persons on the stage. The scenery and lighting are shadowy, almost dreamlike. There are no arias—just the flowing, poetic text, set to a recitative-style melody that follows the rhythm and emotion of the words. *Pelléas and Mélisande* is close to the ideal of opera, or music drama, as it was first established in Florence over three hundred years ago.

The opera tells, often in symbolic language, of a royal family in medieval times whose life is disrupted by the appearance of Mélisande, a strange, beautiful girl who is found weeping in a forest by Golaud, grandson of the king of Allemonde. Golaud, a widower with a young son, Yniold, marries Mélisande and takes her to the family castle, a dark and joyless place.

Pelléas, the younger half-brother of Golaud, falls in love with Mélisande. As Mélisande nurses her husband, who has met with an accident, she tells Golaud that she is not happy in the gloomy old castle. She feels a tragedy building up around her and pleads with him to take her away. Golaud now notices that a gold ring he has given her is missing. Mélisande cannot bring herself to tell him that she lost it in a well in the garden where she was walking with Pelléas; instead she says she lost the ring in a cave by the sea. Golaud insists that Mélisande and Pelléas find the ring at once, even though it is night. They visit the cave and are frightened away by seeing three sleeping, starved peasants.

Golaud begins to be suspicious of his brother and his wife. Finding Pelléas outside Mélisande's window, he warns him to avoid her. Golaud tries to find from Yniold if the child has seen or heard anything that would confirm his suspicions. The child's answers, though innocent, become twisted in Golaud's mind, and when the jealous man meets Mélisande, he becomes half-crazed and drags her around by the hair.

Later, Pelléas, having decided to leave, meets Mélisande at a fountain in the garden. At this last leave-taking they passionately

Scene from a 1947 Paris Opéra production of Pelléas and Mélisande

Ex. 30

Ex. 31

etc. col 8va

Ex. 32

Très modéré

Mary Garden as Mélisande

declare their love for each other. They are overheard by Golaud, who kills Pelléas with his sword.

Some time later, as Mélisande is seriously ill after giving birth to a child, Golaud comes to her. He wants to be forgiven, but he must know whether the love of Pelléas and Mélisande was an innocent one. Mélisande grants him forgiveness and tells him that she did love Pelléas, but innocently. Now the servants in the castle slowly file into the room, sensing the end of the tragedy. A bell tolls slowly, and Mélisande dies as the music comes to a murmuring close.

Pelléas and Mélisande is a series of moods —mysterious, tender, shy. The music, at times breathtakingly beautiful, never takes the center of the stage but remains in the background, commenting on the words and the action. Orchestral interludes connect the scenes and make transitions from one mood to another. Debussy uses a large or-chestra, not for overpowering effects but for many subtle contrasts of tone color.

The music is built in melodic fragments and motives rather than on long, melodic lines. One motive appears throughout the opera (Ex. 30). It is not a leitmotif, as in a Wagnerian opera, but a kind of motto that appears in many colors.

The audiences that first heard *Pelléas and Mélisande* were shocked by the style of the work. In it Debussy abandoned traditional scales and chord progressions, using instead medieval modes, the whole-tone scale, and rich progressions of seventh and ninth chords (Ex. 31). Open fifth intervals and parallel motion of chords give a medieval quality to the music, aurally underlining the medieval setting of the play (Ex. 32).

This opera has never achieved the popu-larity of *Aida* or *Pagliacci*, but it has made a place for itself as one of the most unique and important operas of all time.

PENTATONIC SCALE: a scale consisting of five notes. Its most familiar form is that made by the black keys of the piano. Any one of the five tones may serve as the tonic, or keynote:

The pentatonic scale is world-wide, being the basis of folk music in the Orient, North and South America, Africa, and the British Isles. Many American folk songs, stemming from Scotland or Ireland, derive from the pentatonic scale, as do many Negro spirituals (Ex. 33, 34, and 35). Some medieval Gregorian chants are primarily pentatonic (Ex. 36). Because the scale was used in countries outside Europe, there has been no pattern for the harmonization of the tones of the scale. In fact, because of the lack of half steps in the scale, any combination of tones can be sounded together.

In their search for scales other than the conventional major and minor, both Debussy and Ravel lighted on the pentatonic scale and used it in their compositions (Ex. 37). Since then, many other contemporary composers have incorporated this scale in their music.

Ex. 33 —American Indian (Chippewa)

Ex. 34 —Negro Spiritual: "Nobody Knows the Trouble I've Seen"

Ex. 35 —American Folk Song: "Pretty Saro"

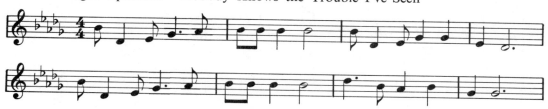

Ex. 36 —Gloria

Ex. 37 — "Laideronette, Empress of the Pagodas" from *Mother Goose* Suite, Ravel

A peculiar kind of pentatonic scale, containing half steps, is found in Japanese music:

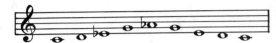

PERCUSSION INSTRUMENT: an instrument whose tone is produced by hitting, scraping, rubbing, shaking, or whirling.

These make up the largest family of instruments and, after the human voice, the oldest. It is the family of drums, bells, cymbals, gongs, rattles, triangles, and many more. The family constantly grows as players and composers think up new things to hit. Some of the recent additions are automobile brake drums and the popular Trinidad tuned oil drums. Even the piano, in which the hammers hit strings, is often considered to be a percussion instrument and has been used as such by many contemporary composers. Percussion instruments range in size from tiny orchestral sleighbells and finger cymbals to huge bells such as Big Ben in London.

Musical scholars classify percussion instruments as *idiophones* and *membranophones*. Idiophones, or self-sounding percussion instruments, are those whose main body makes the sound—cymbals, gongs, and so forth. Membranophones are those, such as most members of the drum group, whose sound is made by hitting a stretched skin or membrane.

Percussion instruments are also classified into those with definite pitch and those with indefinite pitch. The instruments that can be tuned to give a definite pitch include kettledrums (timpani), xylophone and marimba, bells, chimes, glockenspiel, and celesta. Those that cannot be tuned to definite pitches include the bass drum, snare drum, triangle, cymbals, wood blocks, rattles, and many primitive instruments.

Percussion was much used by primitive man. At first he slapped his body, stamped his feet, and clapped his hands to make a rhythmic accompaniment to his dancing. Next he hung animal hooves, shells, and jingling pieces of metal around his ankles, arms, and neck. Rattles were made from

Left: *a Balinese orchestra*

Below: *Yoruba tribal drums, from Western Nigeria*

The Manhattan Percussion Ensemble with conductor Paul Price

gourds filled with pebbles; drums from hollow logs—sometimes with an animal hide stretched over one end. Scrapers were made from tortoise shells, bones, or bumpy pieces of wood. The bull-roarer, whose roaring sounds supposedly provided powerful magic to frighten away evil spirits, was a piece of wood swung rapidly on the end of a strip of rawhide. Xylophones were made from a few slabs of wood or stones of varying sizes.

Several thousand years ago the Chinese organized the first orchestras, made up primarily of gongs, bells, and drums. The oldest form of orchestra still in existence today is the gamelan, or percussion orchestra, of Java, Bali, Burma, and Malaya. Gamelans range in size from eight instruments to fifty or more.

Of all the percussion instruments used in the orchestras of today, the earliest to be introduced were the kettledrums. Imported to Europe from Asia in the thirteenth century, they were first paired with trumpets as instruments of the nobility. In the late 1600's Lully made them members of the opera orchestra. In the late 1700's Gluck and Mozart added the bass and snare drums, cymbals, and triangle to their opera orchestra—for "Turkish" music effects.

Nineteenth-century composers used the percussion family for color effects and to reinforce climaxes. They also searched for new kinds of percussion sounds, trying everything from anvils (Verdi, *Il Trovatore*) and wind machines (Strauss, *Don Quixote*) to live cannons (Tchaikovsky, *"1812" Overture*).

Modern composers have experimented with percussion orchestras of many kinds. Hi-fi and stereo recordings have created much interest in the percussion music of such composers as Cowell, Varèse, and Harrison. Varèse's *Ionisation,* written in 1931, uses two sirens plus regular percussion instruments.

The percussion section in the symphony orchestra is often called the "battery." There is usually one player for the kettledrums and two or three players for all the other percussion instruments. In an orchestral score the percussion parts are written just below the brass parts.

Sonny Greer, well-known jazz drummer (1940)

PETER AND THE WOLF: one of the most popular musical works composed for children. Written by the great Russian composer Sergei Prokofiev in 1936, it was an instant success and has been recorded many times.

The story is a simple one. On a beautiful morning little Peter opens a gate and goes for a walk in a green meadow near his home. He sees his friends—the bird who greets him with a chirp, and the duck who follows him into the meadow and goes for a swim in the pond. Peter notices a cat creeping stealthily on her velvet paws. "Look out!" he shouts to warn his friends. The bird flies up to a branch of a tree; the duck quacks from the safety of her pond.

Peter's grandfather comes out and tells Peter, "The meadow is a dangerous place. Suppose a wolf comes out of the forest?" Peter is not afraid, but his grandfather takes him home and locks the gate. No sooner has Peter gone away than a gray wolf does come out of the forest. The cat climbs the tree, but the duck, quacking in excitement, loses her head and jumps out of the pond. She runs, but the wolf catches her and, in one gulp, swallows her. Then the wolf walks around the tree, eyeing the bird and the cat greedily.

Peter, alerted by the commotion, gets a strong rope and climbs up the high stone wall that surrounds his home. From the wall he can climb onto the tree. He makes a lasso with his rope, and as the bird flies low to distract the wolf, Peter carefully drops the lasso and catches the wolf by the tail. He ties the rope tightly to the tree.

A group of hunters who have been trailing the wolf appear. Peter pleads with them not to shoot the wolf. He wants to give it to the local zoo. The hunters agree and all march off in triumph, with the poor duck quacking away inside the wolf's stomach.

Each character in the story is represented by a theme and a certain instrument in the orchestra: Peter by the strings (Ex. 38), the bird by the flute (Ex. 39), the duck by an oboe (Ex. 40), the cat by low notes on the clarinet (Ex. 41), Peter's grandfather by the

Ex. 38 — Peter
Andantino

Ex. 39 — The Bird
Allegro

Ex. 40 — The Duck

Ex. 41 — The Cat

Ex. 42 — Peter's Grandfather

Ex. 43 — The Wolf

Ex. 44 — The Hunters

Nijinsky in the title role of Petrouchka

bassoon (Ex. 42), the wolf by three French horns (Ex. 43), the hunters by a march theme with much percussion (Ex. 44).

Prokofiev hoped that through his little musical fable children would learn to recognize the sounds of most of the orchestral instruments.

PETROUCHKA: a ballet with music by Igor Stravinsky, first performed in Paris in 1911 by the most famous of all ballet companies, the Diaghilev Russian Ballet. Stravinsky had originally planned to write a concert piece for piano and orchestra, with the piano representing a puppet struggling and squirming against the power of the full orchestra. Diaghilev suggested that Stravinsky and Benois, an artist who designed stage sets, map out a story based on Petrouchka, a traditional Russian puppet character; and this gave us *Petrouchka* as we know it. The choreography was by Michel Fokine; the dancers were the two greatest ballet stars of the day: Nijinsky as Petrouchka and Karsavina as a ballerina. The ballet was an instantaneous success and has been in the repertoire of most ballet companies for the past fifty years.

Pétrouchka is the French spelling for a Russian boy's name corresponding roughly to Peterkin. If the ballet had had its première in New York City instead of Paris, the title would probably be spelled Petrushka—as it sometimes is.

The scene of the ballet is St. Petersburg (now Leningrad) during the carnival week before Lent, some time around 1830. Crowds of celebrating people mill about, taking in the sideshow attractions, and they dance to the music of a strolling organ-grinder. A drum roll calls attention to a puppet show in a booth at the center of the stage. The showman plays his flute and the curtain goes up on his show. Three puppets—the beautiful ballerina, the muscular Moor, and pathetic little Petrouchka—perform a Russian dance together, introducing the actors of the show (Ex. 45). The curtain comes down and the story of the puppets begins.

Petrouchka, in his room, rages at the fate that has made him a sensitive clown instead of a strong hero. He is in love with the ballerina, but she prefers the Moor. In the Moor's room the ballerina does a flirtatious dance while playing a toy trumpet (Ex. 46). She and the Moor dance a mechanical little waltz (Ex. 47). Petrouchka enters and, in a fit of jealousy, attempts to fight the Moor (Ex. 48). The Moor chases him away to end the puppet play.

The final scene is like the opening. The crowds go back to their strolling dance. There are dances by groups of nursemaids, coachmen, masqueraders, and gypsies. A peasant brings in a dancing bear. There is much noise from the puppets' booth. Suddenly Petrouchka runs out, pursued by the Moor, and the sword of the Moor slashes the little clown. He falls—dead. The showman now appears and demonstrates to the crowd that Petrouchka is indeed only a puppet, filled with sawdust. Slowly he drags the puppet away, wonderingly. There is shrieking laughter—and the ghost of Petrouchka appears above the booth. The showman, terrified, runs away as the ghost collapses and hangs over the booth.

Petrouchka was Stravinsky's second ballet (his first was *The Firebird*). It is brilliantly colorful—in the dizzying piano arpeggios that represent Petrouchka, in the swirling atmospheric music for the crowd scenes, and in the orchestration of the puppet play. Stravinsky proved himself a master of

"gesture music"—music that describes action. In the music the listener can almost "see" the mechanical dance of the ballerina and the Moor, the rage of Petrouchka, the lumbering gait of the trained bear, and the cocky manner of the coachmen. The music becomes puppetlike in the opening Russian dance and the waltz. Petrouchka's rage and despair are portrayed in the orchestra with biting dissonance. The melodies of the ballet are often just short fragments, repeated with subtle changes of rhythm. Some of them, like the ballerina's waltz, are deliberately almost too sweet and too simple. In every scene of the work there is the great vitality

Ex. 45

Ex. 46

Ex. 47

Ex. 48

of the young composer who would go on to become one of the greatest creative figures of the twentieth century.

In 1921 Stravinsky made a piano transcription of three movements from *Petrouchka*. They are brilliant virtuoso pieces, often heard at piano concerts.

PHONOGRAPH: a machine designed to reproduce sound that has been "stored" on a record. The phonograph has done more than anything else since the invention of printing to make available to many people the music of their choice. Some phonographs of today are complete in themselves; others consist of a record player which is a part, or component, of a "hi-fi" set that includes a radio, tape recorder, amplifier, and one or more loudspeakers.

Thanks to the miracle of recording, the performance of music by great singers and instrumentalists can be preserved, so that future generations can hear what music was like in the 1900's. Through the medium of records, a person can choose whatever music and performer he wishes to hear, and can listen to them whenever and as often as he wants. The listener can also hear performances of great plays; or he can hear great poets reading their own poems. "Talking books" have been a great boon to the blind, enabling them to hear readings of complete classics as well as recent best-sellers.

Like the inspiration of many other inventions, the idea of capturing and storing sound occurred to several men at about the same time. In 1877 the Frenchman Charles Cros wrote a scientific paper describing a theoretical way of recording sound vibrations on glass covered with lampblack. Cros tried to raise money to build a model of his machine,

A Mathew Brady portrait of Thomas Alva Edison, 1878

which was christened "phonograph" (a term, derived from Greek, meaning "writing sounds"). No one believed in the idea, so no model was built.

In the same year the American inventor Thomas A. Edison was working on a method of recording the dots and dashes of Morse code on a roll of paper. As he ran the paper through his machine, he noticed that the slight dents in the paper made sounds as they rolled over the end of a steel spring. Edison was quick to see what was happening, and he made a primitive but practical machine to record and play back sounds. Although he knew nothing about the Frenchman Cros, Edison hit on the same name for his machine—the phonograph.

Edison's first record was a metal cylinder wrapped in tin foil. It was mounted on a screwlike rod so that the record moved past the cutting needle or the playback needle. The sound vibrations from a voice speaking into a small horn exerted varying pressures on a carbon diaphragm. The diaphragm transmitted the varying pressures to a stylus, or needle, which made corresponding dents in the grooves of the tin-foil record as it turned. The up-and-down pattern of the dents caused this method of recording to become known as the "hill-and-dale" system.

The record was played back by means of a different needle, with its own diaphragm, which retraced the steps of the cutting needle. It translated the hill-and-dale patterns back into sound vibrations. These were not loud but were clear enough to form distinguishable words. Edison himself was the first recording artist; he recited "Mary had a little lamb" into his machine. By February 1878 he had secured a patent for his phonograph—his "talking machine," as the newspapers named it.

The first crude phonographs were sent around the country to perform for paying audiences. The machine was made to speak, sing, sneeze, and reproduce a cornet solo. For a while audiences were amazed by the fact that sound could be stored at all. But the quality of the sound was so poor that, once the novelty wore off, people stopped coming.

In 1885 a pair of Americans, Alexander Graham Bell and Charles S. Tainter, patented the "graphophone," a machine that reproduced sound more clearly than Edison's phonograph. The tin-foil cylinder was replaced by a cardboard cylinder covered with hard wax. The reproducing needle was lighter and freer than Edison's. Best of all, the record was turned at an even speed by a foot pedal or an electric motor.

Two famous pianists, Josef Hofmann and Hans von Bülow, made the first recordings of serious music at Edison's laboratories in 1888. But mostly the phonograph was rented to business and government offices as a dictation machine, or it was rented to small stores as an early form of jukebox. For a nickel, a listener heard about two minutes of music or storytelling through his ear tubes.

The first commercial records were those of whistlers, singers, storytellers, and bands, including the United States Marine Band directed by John Philip Sousa. There was no mass production of records. A band could make ten records at a time, playing into the horns of ten recording machines. Soloists, who were not so loud, could make only two or three records at a time. An order for a hundred records meant that the performer must repeat the same composition thirty to fifty times!

Emile Berliner, who left Germany to seek his fortune in the United States, changed the whole approach to recording and thereby laid the foundation for the growth of the recording industry. In 1887 he invented the "gramophone," which used for a record a flat disc instead of a round cylinder. The recording needle moved from side to side, instead of up and down as in the hill-and-dale method. Berliner also found a way of making a master record from which hundreds of duplicates could be produced.

Phonographs, as the machines continued to be known in the United States, were equipped with wind-up spring motors. Horns were added to the machine so that whole families could listen. Prices came down, widening the market for "talking machines." Several large companies, including Edison, Columbia, and Berliner Gramophone, competed with each other in offering wider selections of records at lower prices.

In 1899 an English artist, Francis Barraud, painted a picture of his dog, Nipper, listening to a phonograph. He called the picture "His Master's Voice." The picture was bought for the Gramophone Company in England and was used in advertisements for this company and its American offshoot, the Victor Talking Machine Company (formed in 1901). Barraud's picture became one of the best-loved of all pictures, and its popularity helped to make Victor one of the giants of recording companies.

Improved methods of recording, using shellac and wax discs, made it possible to record serious music with greater fidelity of sound. The Gramophone Company started its Red Label celebrity discs, featuring famous opera singers. In 1902 the world-famous

tenor Enrico Caruso made ten records, for which he was paid about $500. Soon all record companies were pouring out recordings of opera arias as sung by the great singers of the day.

Complete symphonies were not brought out until 1913. In that year a German company, Odeon, released uncut versions of Beethoven's Fifth and Sixth Symphonies. (Tchaikovsky's *Nutcracker* Suite had been recorded as early as 1909, but in a series of short pieces, not as a full-length work.) Between them the two Beethoven symphonies occupied eighteen record sides—certainly an unwieldy and bulky package to store and handle!

The old shape of the phonograph, with its jutting horn, changed in 1906 with the

An early recording session, with Rosario Bourdon conducting the Victor Orchestra

Lauritz Melchior and "Nipper" in a scene depicting the first Victor recording session (from the movie Two Sisters from Boston)

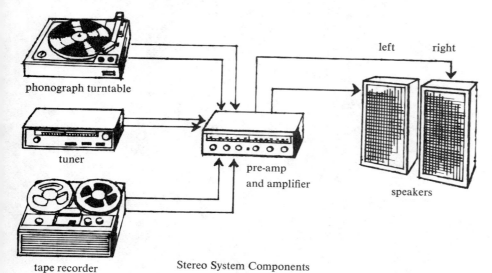

phonograph turntable

tuner

tape recorder

Stereo System Components

left   right

pre-amp
and amplifier

speakers

appearance of the Victrola. This had the horn inside a console. Furniture designers began to disguise the machine in various ways. More important, however, were the development of electrical recording and the growth of interest in jazz.

From 1919 to 1924 engineers and scientists worked to improve recording methods, using the newly discovered microphone and amplifying tubes. The Bell Telephone Laboratories succeeded in recording high and low sounds that were previously missing in records. Musicians no longer had to huddle in front of the large horn which fed their sounds to the record. Orchestras and choruses could record in concert halls and so achieve a fuller sound. In 1925 Victor and Columbia released the first electrical recordings, the first record being Victor's—a mild jazz piece played by Meyer Davis and his orchestra.

The first jazz record had been made for Victor in 1917 by the Original Dixieland Jazz Band. So much interest was aroused by this new form of dance music—and the dancing that went with it—that record sales boomed to all-time highs.

Early records, seven inches in diameter, had a playing time of only two minutes. As records got larger, the playing time became longer. But even the large twelve-inch record played for only four minutes and twenty seconds. Victor had experimented in 1931 with a long-playing record which rotated at 33⅓ revolutions per minute instead of the usual 78, and on which the grooves were cut a bit thinner, so that the record could play up to fourteen minutes per side. But lack of proper materials for the disc, and the great expense of new turntables, delayed the adoption of any such long-playing product.

In 1948 Columbia unveiled a new long-playing record which, like the earlier Victor disc, played at 33⅓ rpm. It was made of an unbreakable plastic vinylite. On these records large works, such as symphonies, were less expensive, tended to sound better, and took up much less space.

Victor countered by issuing small microgroove records that played at 45 rpm. These seven-inch records had fine tone quality, but their playing time was considerably shorter than the 33⅓-rpm discs. For a while, record companies put out discs at all three speeds—78, 33⅓, and 45 rpm. But issuing every work in three speeds was impractical, so the old 78's—which in fact were already outdated—were discontinued; single short works, mostly popular, were issued on the 45's, while the 33⅓'s were used for symphonies and collections (albums) of popular songs and dances. With microgroove records came also refinements in the pickup arms and amplifying systems.

Many phonographs today are equipped for stereophonic sound. Twin channels of sound are engraved in a single record groove and reproduced by means of a specially designed stylus and cartridge that feed the sound to separate loudspeakers. The listener hears the sound coming from different directions, as he might if he were sitting in a recording studio.

Most recordings are now done originally on magnetic tape or on sound film, which have several advantages over the old master record. A greater range of highs and lows can be recorded, and the recordings can be edited more carefully. One wrong note does not spoil a whole work, since the sound engineer can remove the wrong note and substitute the right one, without repeating the whole piece. A soprano who has trouble singing a high note on the correct pitch can sing the note several times, and whichever version is best can be spliced onto the tape.

A record catalog of today, such as Schwann's monthly guide to long-playing records, shows a tremendous range of offerings. The long-playing record has opened vast new areas of music for the listener: music from centuries before 1600, music from remote parts of the world, music from the pens of the most modern and experimental composers. It has preserved the voices of great historical figures, as well as those of unknown folk singers and country fiddlers. The phonograph and record industries sell over a billion dollars' worth of equipment and records in the United States each year. A cultural giant has grown from Edison's original tin-foil cylinder.

PHRASE: the smallest complete unit of musical form, containing about as much music as can be sung on one normal breath. Depending on the tempo of the music and the number of beats per measure, a phrase may be as short as two measures or as long as eight measures (Ex. 49–53).

Each phrase has its own shape or form, rising or falling in a curved or terraced line:

"Au Clair de la lune":

Brahms's "Lullaby":

"The Star-Spangled Banner":

"My Darling Clementine":

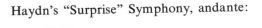

Haydn's "Surprise" Symphony, andante:

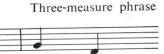

Ex. 49 — Symphony No. 6, Tchaikovsky

Two-measure phrase

Ex. 50 — Minuet from Symphony No. 40 in G Minor, Mozart

Three-measure phrase

Ex. 51 — Soldier's March, Schumann

Four-measure phrase

Ex. 52 — Scherzo from Sonata, Op. 42, Schubert

Five-measure phrase

Ex. 53 — "Britons Strike Home" from *Bonduca*, Purcell

Six-measure phrase

Brit - ons strike home, re - venge, re - venge your coun - try's wrongs

Ex. 54 — "Au Clair de la lune"

Ex. 55 — Symphony No. 2, Brahms

Ex. 56 — Symphony No. 2, Brahms

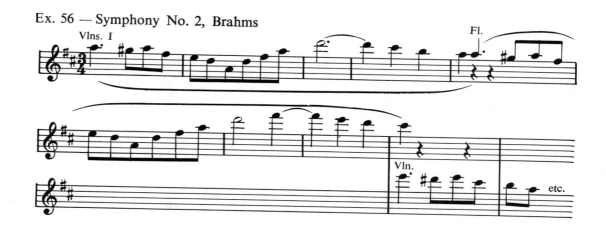

Ex. 57

Ex. 58 — March Rhythm for Drums

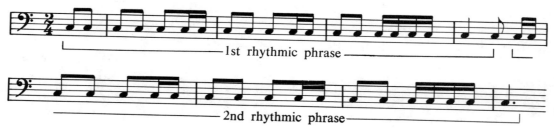

The ending, or cadence note, is often a long one, so that there is time in the music to take a new breath for the next phrase.

The phrase is an important part of musical form. In a sense it is a basic building block of musical structure. By putting phrases together, a composer can make a long composition or a section of a composition, just as a writer puts together sentences to make a paragraph. "Au Clair de la lune," for example, consists of a first phrase, a repeat of that phrase, a new phrase, and a repeat of the first phrase (Ex. 54). Many folk songs follow such a pattern.

Two phrases are sometimes put together as though the first phrase were asking a question which is answered by the second phrase. Pairing of phrases gives the listener a sense of balance and symmetry. Such a combination of phrases is sometimes called a musical period. The opening of Brahms's Second Symphony shows such phrase groupings (Ex. 55). Later in the same work Brahms shows another method of dealing with phrases. Here one phrase begins as another ends, so that there is a series of overlapping five-measure phrases (Ex. 56).

Phrases can be made by means of harmony and rhythm as well as melody. A series of chords can give the feeling of a harmonic phrase (Ex. 57), just as a drum pattern can give a sense of rhythmic phrase (Ex. 58). In both cases there is a distinct feeling of cadence at the end of each phrase.

Clear-cut phrases are to be found in most songs and in dance music. Dance music needs to be regular in phrasing, so that the dancers can feel the right moment to change step patterns or direction. Vocal music based on poems with regular meter usually has a series of phrases all equal in length. Songs based on irregular poems, or on prose, have phrases of varying lengths, as in many Gregorian chants.

Phrases are not so easily heard in complex polyphonic music, in which the interweaving of the different voices gives the listener the impression of a continuous flow of sound. In the music of the Classical period the phrase is always clearly apparent.

The basic phrase length in eighteenth- and nineteenth-century music is usually four measures. The great composers, such as Haydn, Mozart, and Beethoven, however, vary the length of their phrases to avoid the "squareness" that results from having all phrases equal in length. They add an extra measure to throw the listener off balance or disguise the phrase pattern so that the listener is not always certain of where he is in the music. A series of nothing but four-measure phrases can become dull in a long work. In folk songs such regularity is important, because a song is easier to remember when all the phrases are equal. When phrase lengths vary, there is more likelihood of uncertainty among the singers.

Phrasing is the art of performing so that the shape of each phrase is made clear to the audience. It also means rounding off and ending one idea before beginning the next. It means the bringing out of important tones and the playing down of less important tones. Phrasing also means that the relation of each phrase to all other phrases is made clear, so that the audience hears the composition as a whole rather than as a series of individual notes. There are many theories about phrasing, but the truest guide to a well-phrased performance is a thorough understanding of the structure of a musical work.

Phrasing is sometimes confused with articulation—the connecting of tones, as in a legato passage, or the separation of tones, as in a staccato passage. Phrasing in this sense is usually indicated by the composer, who puts slurs over the notes he wants to have connected or dots over those he wants to be played staccato.

PIANO: the keyboard instrument invented in 1709 by Bartolommeo Cristofori, curator of musical instruments for the wealthy Medici family in Florence, Italy. He called his invention a *gravicembalo col piano e forte*—a "keyboard instrument that can be played soft and loud."

The piano is one of the youngest of musical instruments, but in spite of its youth it has already outstripped all other instruments in the number of solo compositions written for it. Its popularity in the home and in the concert hall results from its versatility. Its range of more than seven octaves is greater than that of any other instrument except a large pipe organ. It can produce a range of sound from the faintest pianissimo to the loudest fortissimo. It allows melodies and accompaniments to be played at several different levels of loudness—and at the same time. Ten-note chords can be played, or several melodies at the same time, or whirlwind arpeggios, percussive and drumlike rhythms, sharp accents, rapid repeated notes, a melody in long sustained tones, and fast scale passages. The piano can suggest a whole orchestra—and many orchestral works have been transcribed so that they can be played on the piano.

The piano is played by means of a key-

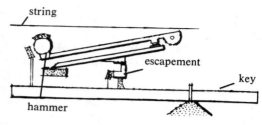

Cristofori Action

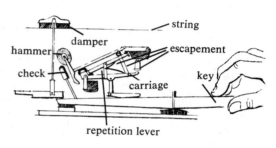

repetition lever

Modern Grand Action

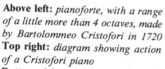

Above left: *pianoforte, with a range of a little more than 4 octaves, made by Bartolommeo Cristofori in 1720*
Top right: *diagram showing action of a Cristofori piano*
Bottom right: *the action of a modern piano*

board consisting of eighty-eight keys—fifty-two white keys and thirty-six black ones. The black keys, arranged in two's and three's, serve as guideposts to the fingers of the pianist. One can imagine trying to find one's way on a keyboard of eighty-eight white keys all alike!

When the player strikes a key, a felt hammer is thrown at a string or group of strings, and a felt damper is lifted so that the sound of the string can ring out. Resonance is provided by a sounding board under the strings. An escapement allows the hammer to fall back so that it is ready to play again, even though the key is still being held down. The wedge-shaped damper remains off the strings until the key is released, at which time it clamps down on the strings and cuts off the sound. The tone of the piano can be varied in intensity, or loudness, by varying the amount of force used on the keys. A concert pianist can produce about twenty shadings between his loudest and softest tones.

The strings of the piano, like those of the harp, vary in size. The shorter the string, the higher the tone. All the strings are made of steel, and each must be strong enough to withstand a tension of several hundred pounds when tuned. From the lowest A to the G above it there is one thick string, wound with wire, for each key. The next tones, up to the C below middle C, have two strings per key, each also wound with wire. For

each of the rest of the keys there are three strings made of solid steel wire. (The use of two and three strings per key makes for greater richness of sound but presents a problem to the tuner. He must not only match one tone with other tones, but within each tone he must tune three strings so that they sound as one.)

The strings are suspended over a steel frame capable of sustaining a pull of several tons. One end of each string is wound around a metal tuning pin that fits firmly into a strong, multilayered wrest plank (at the front of grand pianos, at the top of uprights). The other end is looped around a metal pin driven into the far side of the frame.

Grand pianos have three pedals; uprights usually have two.

The pedal to the right is the sustaining, or "loud," pedal. When pressed down it lifts all the dampers, allowing the strings to continue sounding until the pedal is released. In music scores the use of this pedal is indicated by *Ped . . . . . .** or └──┐ . The use of this pedal is an art; incorrect pedaling can make music messy and blurred.

The pedal on the left is the "soft" pedal. When pressed down it moves the hammers so that the tone is softer than normal. (On a grand piano the hammers move to the right and hit only one or two strings instead of three; on an upright they move closer to the strings.) The use of this pedal is indicated by the phrase *una corda. Tre corde* means "three strings"—or "release the soft pedal."

The middle pedal, the *sostenuto*, is found on most grand pianos but not on all uprights. It lifts the dampers only on the strings of certain keys—the ones that are held down when the pedal is applied. This allows the player to sustain a note or a chord that will not be blurred by the addition of other tones played after the pedal is pressed down.

The piano came into being out of necessity. In the early 1700's many instrument makers of Europe were trying to invent a keyboard instrument that could match the power and expressivity of the violin. The harpsichord was not powerful, nor could it make subtle changes in loudness or softness. It could play one phrase loud and the next soft, but within the phrase it could make no crescendos or diminuendos and could produce no melodic accents. A traveling virtuoso on the dulcimer, Pantaleon Hebenstreit, had shown European music lovers how the most delicate varieties of tone could be produced by varying the amount of force used in hitting strings with a soft leather hammer. It remained only for Cristofori to figure out the escapement—a device for releasing the hammer after it has struck the string—and the piano was born.

After Cristofori produced his first piano, in 1709, other instrument makers became piano manufacturers: Silbermann and Stein in Germany, and Broadwood in England. Performers and composers discovered the advantages of the piano. Interest in the harpsichord began to decline, although until 1800 music was printed "to be played on harpsichord or piano." Beethoven's first eight sonatas bore this motto.

C. P. E. Bach, at the court of Frederick the Great, was one of the leaders in the writing and performing of piano music. His younger brother, J. C. Bach, is credited with performing in 1768 the first public solos on the piano. Before this, in 1765, he had introduced the nine-year-old Mozart to the instrument—and Mozart promptly wrote the first pieces for four hands at one piano. Mozart became in fact one of the piano's first virtuoso players. His sonatas and concertos, along with those by Haydn and C. P. E. Bach, were the beginnings of the great literature for the piano.

The early pianos were small, their action and tone light and delicate. For public recitals, larger pianos were demanded—for bigger tone and increased range. Mozart's piano had a range of not quite five octaves. A piano built by Broadwood in 1817 for Beethoven had a range of six octaves. (It was for such a comparatively small instrument that Beethoven wrote his thirty-two sonatas and five concertos, thought by many to be the summits of piano literature.) In the middle 1800's Liszt's piano covered a span of seven octaves.

The keyboard of the early piano had been placed so that the performer's hands were partially hidden. Broadwood brought his keyboards forward so that the audience could watch the soloist's fingers work.

Piano makers experimented with varying shapes, materials, and mechanisms. The square grand, often outfitted with drawers and bookshelves, became more popular than the harp- or wing-shaped grand. The grand was tipped on its side and placed on a support to make a giant upright, seven to nine feet tall—a design known as the "giraffe." Eventually piano makers discovered that the strings could be strung from the bottom of the instrument, at floor level—and so the upright took on its present shape.

Composer-virtuosos, such as Clementi, Hummel, Czerny, and Moscheles (who in 1837 gave the first complete solo piano recital) demanded faster action and bigger sounds. In 1821 the French piano maker Sébastien Érard invented a double escapement, in which the hammer did not drop all the way back. This made possible quicker repeated notes and a generally faster action. In the 1820's Alpheus Babcock, of Boston, made cast-iron frames that permitted greater tension on the strings than did the old wooden frames. This frame not only gave the piano a more brilliant sound but also protected it against severe changes in weather. Other piano makers discovered cross stringing—that is, placing one set of strings over another. In this way most of the strings passed over the middle of the sounding board, and the sonority of the tone was increased.

Audiences, and the many young ladies who played the piano at home, loved program music—particularly battle pieces. To please them, the piano makers added pedals that worked triangles, cymbals, and drumsticks. Composers of today who call for strange noises inside the piano are merely following the custom of a hundred years ago.

As piano makers extended the resources of the instrument, composers took advantage of the improvements. The magic and trickery of the violinist Paganini were transferred to the keyboard by Liszt, Thalberg, and Schumann. With sensitive fingers and skillful use of the sustaining pedal, Chopin showed

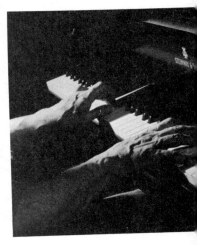

Artur Schnabel's hands

Top left: *caricature of Anton Rubinstein*
Top right: *Ignace Paderewski*
Bottom left: *Leopold Godowsky*
Bottom right: *Josef Hofmann*

how the piano could "sing." And Liszt, with his brilliant technique, brought about another important change. Before him the pianist had sat on a low seat, his forearm making a level line with the knuckle of the second finger joint. Liszt, using a high seat and a sloping forearm, ranged up and down the keyboard with unprecedented facility.

In the 1800's piano factories sprang up all over Europe, the United States, and Japan. Among hundreds, a few became internationally famous: Knabe, Steinway, Mason and Hamlin, and Chickering in the United States; Bechstein and Blüthner in Germany; Érard and Pleyel in France; Broadwood in England; and Yamaha in Japan.

Composers such as Brahms, Tchaikovsky, Scriabin, Debussy, and Ravel carried piano techniques forward from Liszt and Chopin. Their compositions, particu-

larly those of Debussy and Ravel, brought out new pianistic colors. Low, middle, and high sounds were blended through deft use of the pedals. Pure speed and brilliance gave way to subtle contrasting sonorities.

Liszt and Chopin in the middle 1800's had begun the great age of piano playing. Pianists such as Anton and Nicholas Rubinstein, Clara Schumann, and the American Gottschalk attracted large audiences on their concert tours. But it was the Polish pianist Ignace Paderewski (1860–1941) whose romantic presence and lyrical playing—aided by a great deal of publicity—captured the imagination of music lovers all over the world. To this day a fine pianist is often hailed as "another Paderewski."

From Poland and Russia also came a whole group of virtuoso pianists specializing in the music of Chopin and Liszt: the child prodigy Josef Hofmann, Rachmaninoff, Josef Lhévinne, Leopold Godowsky, Vladimir de Pachmann, Moritz Rosenthal. They achieved international fame as they played with brilliance and sensitivity.

Music lovers who could not hear enough of their favorite pianists in person could hear them by means of a player piano, invented in various forms in France and the United States in the 1860's. By 1900 the player piano was becoming popular, and by 1919 more than half the pianos made in the United States were of this kind. With the early ones the player pumped on pedals like those of a harmonium, and as he pumped, a roll of paper with holes punched into it unwound over a cylinder with tubes leading to the hammers. Air going through the holes set the hammers in motion. Various attachments allowed the operator to make crescendos, bring out the left hand, and otherwise improve on the performance of his favorite pianist. When an electric motor was substituted for the foot pedals, all the music lover needed to do was push a button, sit back, and listen to the music. Player pianos in ice-cream parlors and saloons had slots to receive nickels, and thus were ancestors of the present-day jukeboxes. Most of the famous pianists of the time made player-piano rolls, and it is because of the player piano that we today have samples of Debussy and Grieg playing their own compositions.

The player piano died out, being replaced by the phonograph and the radio. Since 1930 there have been several experiments with electronic pianos, in which microphones and amplifiers replace the sounding board, but nothing of this sort has yet become popular. The newest type of piano is the small spinet, convenient for the small apartment.

Modern concert pianists play on a nine-foot grand with fast action and a booming—but slow-to-speak—bass. Dame Myra Hess, Artur Rubinstein, Vladimir Horowitz, the Casadesus family, Sviatoslav Richter, Van Cliburn, and a host of other fine pianists have used the modern grand as soloists in recitals, with orchestras, and as recording stars. They have, in effect, put the fully developed resources of modern technique in instrumental design and piano playing in the service of a repertoire composed mostly of works written before 1900.

The audiences of these pianists have yet to discover an entire new continent of the musical world—the works written for piano by composers of our own century. Works by these composers have explored new techniques and new sonorities on the piano. Ives, Bartók, Prokofiev, Stravinsky, Boulez, and Copland have used the piano as a mighty percussion instrument, full of gonglike reverberations. Some of these composers have found a place for the piano as a member of the symphony orchestra, supplying a powerful rhythmic part in the bass. In the 1920's the experimentally minded Henry Cowell played whole clusters of sound with his forearms on the keyboard. At other times he struck the strings directly, achieving weird effects. Cowell's experiments were carried forward by John Cage, who placed nuts, bolts, and rubber erasers on his piano strings. Cage's "prepared piano" sounds like a tinkly Javanese percussion orchestra.

The piano has been an important member of jazz groups since the ragtime of the 1890's. Such great early pianists as Scott Joplin, James P. Johnson, and "Jelly Roll" Morton led the way for Earl "Fatha" Hines, Duke Ellington, "Fats" Waller, and Art Tatum. These men set jazz styles that have been expanded by Teddy Wilson, Errol Garner, Nat King Cole, and many others. With its ability to play a solo as well as to furnish harmonic and rhythmic accompaniment, the piano has established itself as a versatile member of dance bands large and small.

The history of the piano is short in years but filled with testimonials as to the key role it has played. Its story has been told in two interesting and scholarly books: *The Pianoforte,* by Rosamond Harding, and *Men, Women and Pianos,* by Arthur Loesser.

Errol Garner

Richard Townsend playing the piccolo

PICCOLO: the small brother of the flute; its full name is *flauto piccolo,* "little flute." In orchestral scores it is also called *ottavino* and *kleine Flöte.*

Made of wood or metal, the piccolo is about half the size of the flute—so small that the third flute player, who usually plays the piccolo, can carry it in his jacket pocket.

The piccolo is the highest-pitched orchestral instrument. Even its lowest note is nine notes above middle C:

The piccolo part is written an octave below its real sound, so that the flute player who has to switch suddenly to the piccolo does not have to adjust to a new set of fingerings. The player also avoids becoming dizzy from reading the many leger lines that would result if the piccolo part were written at its true pitch.

In the upper part of its register the piccolo's tone is penetrating and even shrill; hence composers have used it to add a brilliant top to the rest of the orchestral sound. In its lowest register the piccolo's tone is soft and breathy, and a bit plaintive. It can be heard only if the rest of the orchestra is playing very softly or if its tone is amplified in the recording studio.

Before the 1800's the piccolo was used only in theater orchestras in such works as Mozart's *Abduction from the Seraglio,* where it is combined with the triangle, bass drum, and cymbals to give a "Turkish" touch to the music. A charming use of the piccolo occurs in the Spring section of Haydn's ora-

torio *The Seasons* (1801), where it is given a little solo to represent the farmer whistling as he works.

Beethoven helped the piccolo establish itself in the symphony orchestra by using it in the last movements of his Fifth and Ninth Symphonies. Berlioz was fond of the instrument, using it effectively in the first and last movements of his *Symphonie fantastique.* It remained for Tchaikovsky, however, to bring out all the possibilities of the instrument, particularly in his music for the *Sleeping Beauty* and *Nutcracker* ballets. Stravinsky's score for *The Rite of Spring* calls for two piccolos.

The most familiar piccolo solo is the tootling obbligato in the trio section of Sousa's famous march, "The Stars and Stripes Forever."

PITCH: the highness or lowness of a sound. Pitch is determined by the frequency of vibrations—that is, how many times per second the sound-making material (string, reed, or whatever)—vibrates. The more vibrations per second, the higher the pitch.

The human ear has a normal hearing range of 16 to 20,000 cycles of vibration per second. Some persons can hear higher pitches; others, particularly older persons, are limited to a top of 10,000 to 15,000 cycles per second.

Some high-fidelity systems are said to have a range of 2 to 160,000 cycles per second. Their upper frequencies would not be heard by the human ear, but would reproduce the upper harmonic tones of instruments and thus enrich the fundamental tones that do lie within the ear's range.

Animals can hear tones above the 20,000-cycle range. Certain dog whistles are pitched in this high area so that they can be heard by a dog but not by a human being.

The basic pitch to which instruments are tuned is the A above middle C. In the seventeenth century this "A" had several pitches, ranging from 373.7 to 402.9. By the middle of the eighteenth century, concert "A" was pitched to 422.9—but "A's" as high as 461 were also used. The variations in basic pitch have led some historically minded people to suggest that the music of the 1600's and 1700's should be played in a lower key today.

The first attempt to standardize pitch occurred in 1834 when a group of German physicists advocated an "A" of 440. In 1859 France adopted an "A" of 435, and this pitch was used for most instruments until recently, when the "A" of 440 was adopted

Ex. 59 — *Capriccio espagnol*, Rimsky-Korsakov

in the United States. The Bureau of Standards broadcasts this pitch several times daily on station WWV in Washington, D.C. Some orchestral conductors require that their players tune to an "A" higher than 440, to achieve a more brilliant sound.

An electronic device, the Stroboconn, is now being used to tune instruments. It enables one to compare visually the vibrations of an instrumental "A" with a standard "A" of 440. By means of the Stroboconn an instrumentalist can tell immediately if he is sharp or flat. Previous to the coming of electronic instruments, an instrumentalist had to depend on his own ear.

Some persons have a more highly developed sense of pitch than others. A few have the gift of perfect pitch memory, or absolute pitch: they can name with complete accuracy any tone or group of tones that they hear. Others have what is known as relative pitch: they can tell that one tone is a fifth above another, for example, but they cannot tell the exact names of the pitches. Relative pitch is what is developed in classes in sight singing and ear training, and it is entirely adequate for most musical purposes.

The ability to hear slight differences between tones that are practically identical is necessary in a great variety of musical situations. A conductor must be able to tell one player that his tone is just a bit higher or lower than that of the other instrumentalists playing the same tones, and singers and instrumentalists performing duets and trios must also have a keen sense of pitch so that they can adjust to each other. In a large orchestra or chorus, slight deviations may not be heard. The piano tuner, whose ear is trained through experience, can hear differences of one-fiftieth of a half step.

Tuning forks, which give off exact pitches, have been used since the early 1700's to test the tuning of instruments. The small pitch pipe, which is only fairly accurate, is used to give pitches to choruses.

PIZZICATO: an Italian word meaning "pinched" or "plucked." It is an indication to string players to pluck their strings rather than play them with their bows. *Pizz.* is the often-used abbreviation for pizzicato. *Arco* tells the players to resume playing with their bows.

One of the earliest uses of the pizzicato was in Monteverdi's dramatic madrigal *The Combat of Tancred and Clorinda* (1624). Since then many composers have used pizzicato string tones and chords as a harplike or guitarlike accompaniment (Ex. 59) and for light arpeggio figures (Ex. 60). The ominous repeated, deep tones of double basses played pizzicato, used by Weber in the overture

Ex. 60 — Symphony No. 2, Brahms

Ex. 61 — Symphony No. 4, Tchaikovsky

Cellos and Brasses pizz.

Ex. 62a — String Quartet No. 5, Bartók

Ex. 62b — String Quartet No. 5, Bartók

to his opera *Der Freischütz,* are heard a great deal in modern background music for suspense movies:

Overture, *Der Freischütz,* Weber

The wizard of the violin, Paganini, discovered a way of combining a left-hand pizzicato accompaniment and a bowed melody:

Caprice, Paganini

Tchaikovsky was particularly fond of the sound of plucked strings. The scherzo of his Fourth Symphony, which is played pizzicato throughout, is the most famous pizzicato movement in a symphony (Ex. 61). The modern composer Bartók achieved a strange effect by making a glissando on a plucked tone (Ex. 62a and b).

In jazz the double bass is traditionally played pizzicato. The resonant jazz pizzicato is often alternated with the slapping of the strings in the effect known as "slap bass."

POLKA: a popular social dance since the 1830's. Starting as a peasant dance in Bohemia (now a part of Czechoslovakia), it soon gained great success in Prague, Vienna, and Paris, spread over Europe and the United States, and for a time threatened to dethrone the waltz as "queen of the dances." Other relatives of the polka, the fast galop and *Rutscher,* or sliding dance, also became favorite nineteenth-century social dances.

The polka is a moderately fast dance in 2/4 time. It is danced by couples who turn

Dancing the polka

as they circle the dance floor. Its foot pattern follows this plan:

Hop - step - close - step

The music for the polka is usually written in four-measure phrases. The melody is gay, usually in a major key, and the harmony simple.

Bedrich Smetana (1824–84), the great Bohemian composer, used the polka to give a Bohemian flavor to his string quartet *From My Life* and to his best-known opera, *The Bartered Bride* (Ex. 63). He also wrote three sets of polkas for piano solo. Other Bohemian composers, among them Dvořák and Weinberger, have used the rhythm of the polka in their works. The polka from Weinberger's opera *Schwanda the Bagpiper* is often played on programs of popular light symphonic works.

In the United States the polka has managed to keep its popularity despite the competition from jazz and Latin-American music. In the middle 1930's the "Beer Barrel Polka" even became a top-selling song. In a recent catalog of long-playing records, more than seventy polka albums were listed, in addition to those recorded by the popular bandleader Lawrence Welk.

POLONAISE: an old Polish court dance—dignified, stately, and ceremonious. It was performed by couples who proceeded around the ballroom in a processional fashion. Its basic movements were two gliding steps followed by a third step with the supporting knee bent and the free leg extended.

Ex. 63 — *The Bartered Bride*, Act I, Scene 5, Smetana

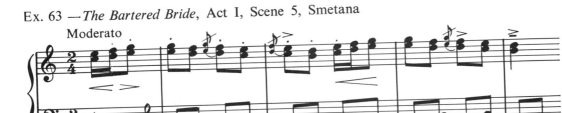

Ex. 64 — Polonaise from *Boris Godunov*, Mussorgsky

The music for the polonaise was in a moderate 3/4 meter. Each beat is often subdivided, as in these examples:

so that the music has a heroic, triumphal quality. Polonaises are found in the music of J. S. Bach, W. F. Bach, Mozart, Beethoven, and Schubert. Chopin raised the polonaise to its highest musical form in his noble—often tragic—twelve polonaises for piano. Into these Chopin breathed longing for his homeland, grief for its fate under the conquering Russians, and hopes for its eventual independence. But Poland, as a kingdom, had come to its end by 1795. With no court, there was no reason for the polonaise to survive, and, with a few exceptions, after Chopin it died as a musical form. One of the exceptions is the brilliant polonaise in the Polish scene in Act III of Mussorgsky's opera *Boris Godunov* (Ex. 64).

POLYPHONY: the result of combining two or more equally important melodic lines. (The opposite of polyphony is *homophony*.)

The musical period from the twelfth century through the sixteenth is often referred to as the Polyphonic period, since the main texture of music written at this time was many-voiced.

Polyphonic music uses the techniques of counterpoint. The terms contrapuntal and polyphonic are therefore often used interchangeably, although with the distinction that "polyphonic" describes the primarily vocal music of the medieval and Renaissance periods, while "contrapuntal" is used to denote the texture of many-voiced music written since 1600.

Many important musical forms developed in the Polyphonic period: the polyphonic setting of the Mass, the motet, the rota (or round), the ballade, the caccia, and the early madrigals and chansons. All the various types of imitative writing, or canon, were discovered in the early period of polyphony.

See COUNTERPOINT; MEDIEVAL MUSIC; CANON.

POLYTONALITY: the simultaneous use of two or more keys. Occasionally polytonality is found in works of the Baroque period as two different forms of a scale clash briefly. The first deliberate use of polytonality occurs at the end of Mozart's *Ein musikalischer Spass* as a humorous device to poke fun at village-band musicians (Ex. 65). The tonal conflict that is a basic ingredient of polytonality was used most effectively by

Richard Strauss in his *Ein Heldenleben* to characterize the bickering and niggling of his critics.

Composers since 1900 have turned to polytonality as a source of new sounds. It was used by Debussy and Scriabin to blur the outlines of cadences or to give a feeling of unrest to their music. Polytonality has been an important feature of the music of Prokofiev, Stravinsky, Honegger, Milhaud, Bartók, and Schuman.

The simplest form of polytonality occurs when a melody in one key has an accompaniment in a different key (Ex. 66). Sometimes the composer writes a work in which there are two melodies, each having its own key and its own key signature, as in Bartók's *Bagatelles*, Opus 6, Number 2. In another form of polytonality there is a common key center for two different scales. Ex. 67 shows the keys of A major and A minor scrambled together.

Ex. 65 — "A Musical Joke," Mozart

Ex. 66 — *Saudades do Brasil* No. 7, Milhaud

Ex. 67 — *Saudades do Brasil* No. 8, Milhaud

Above: *a scene from* Les Dialogues des Carmélites *(Paris Opéra production, 1957)*
Below: *Francis Poulenc*

POULENC, FRANCIS (1899–1963): outstanding French composer. Born in Paris, Poulenc studied composition there with the composer Koechlin. In 1917 his music was played at a concert along with that of five other young French composers who were rebelling against the Germanic tradition in music. Nicknamed "Les Six," the group followed the artistic credos of Satie and Cocteau rather than those of Schoenberg and Debussy.

All through his career Poulenc wrote music that is witty, crystal-clear, and smoothly tuneful. In a satirical way, it seems to give a knowing wink as it sheds a sentimental tear. At times Poulenc's music sounds like that of a sophisticated, slightly modern Chopin.

Poulenc composed in almost every musical form, from short piano works (he was himself an exceptionally fine pianist), such

as his "Mouvements perpétuels" (Perpetual Motions) and his nocturnes, to concertos for one and two pianos and orchestra. He wrote much chamber music, including sonatas for two clarinets, for clarinet and bassoon, and for trumpet, horn, and trombone; a sextet for piano, four woodwinds, and horn; and a string quartet. Some of his finest music was written for chorus: a mass, *Un Soir de neige (A Snowy Night),* and a *Stabat Mater.*

Poulenc's vocal works range from children's songs and an accompaniment for the *Histoire de Babar, le petit éléphant (Story of Babar, the Little Elephant)* to extremely expressive songs and song cycles. His theater works include several ballets; a one-character, one-act tragedy, *La Voix humaine (The Human Voice);* a comic opera, *Les Mamelles de Tirésias (The Breasts of Tiresias);* and his most popular theater work, the religious opera *Les Dialogues des Carmélites (The Dialogues of the Carmelites).*

PRELUDE: a short piece that prepares the way for a longer work or constitutes a composition complete in itself. The earliest preludes (from the 1500's) were improvised solos for a lute or keyboard instrument consisting of several, often contrasting, sections.

In the seventeenth and eighteenth centuries the introductory movement of a dance suite tended to be given the form of a free improvisation. Such a movement was called a prelude, sinfonia, or toccata. Sometimes in the works of Couperin, Rameau, and Handel, only the pitches of the notes were written. The rhythm was to be free, as in an improvisation (Ex. 68).

Ex. 68 — Prelude from *Pièces de clavecin,* Book I, Rameau

Another type of prelude, which usually preceded a fugue for organ or harpsichord, was used by Kuhnau, Bach, and other German composers of the eighteenth century. In these short, complete pieces a single musical idea was developed throughout the work. This is the form of most of the forty-eight preludes in Bach's *Well-tempered Clavier.*

Sets of independent piano preludes, many of which follow Bach's plan, have been written by Chopin, Scriabin, Rachmaninoff, and Shostakovich. (Some of these preludes, such as Rachmaninoff's popular Prelude in C-sharp Minor, also are written in the three-part A-B-A form.)

Debussy wrote two books of preludes for the piano, each book containing twelve preludes. Some of these are among his most popular works—for example, "The Maid with the Flaxen Hair" and "The Engulfed Cathedral." All have individual titles.

At the height of the Romantic era, opera composers turned to the word "prelude" to describe what had previously been called an overture. They wanted to emphasize that the music heard before the rise of the curtain was no longer a set piece (traditionally, in sonata-allegro form) but a preliminary portion of the opera itself. Wagner, in 1840, opened his *Lohengrin* with a prelude, and by 1853 Verdi, too, was using a prelude—to open *La Traviata.*

Les Préludes is the title Franz Liszt ultimately gave to a symphonic poem worked up in the 1850's from an overture he had written for a choral work in 1848. He had in the meantime come across a poem by the French Romantic writer Lamartine: it gave him his new title and suggested a philosophical vision he hoped would also be suggested by his music—that life is a series of preludes.

PRESTO: an Italian word meaning "quick" or "lively." It is used in music as an indication for a tempo faster than allegro. *Prestissimo* means "as fast as possible." *Più presto,* within a movement, means "more quickly."

PRIMITIVE MUSIC. Nobody knows how or when music started. Primitive man was singing and dancing long before he discovered how to write words or notes. He discovered that he could make sounds that expressed his emotions, including pleasant sounds, by using his voice. He felt some strange power in him as he clapped his hands or stamped his feet in a repeated

rhythm. Probably it was in such simple ways that man discovered the joys of music. He also felt that singing and playing had some magical effect on himself, and believed they would probably have a magical effect on his gods. He invented songs and dances designed to insure victory in battle, success on a hunt, and recovery from illness. Music became part of life's important events—marriage, birth, initiation rites, and death. Men doing hard or monotonous labor discovered that singing together made work lighter. Mothers made up lullabies to put their children to sleep, the children made up singing games, and lovers made up love songs. Long before history was written, man had discovered all the basic reasons for making music.

The first musical instrument was man's own body. As he became more and more aware of sounds, he began to construct simple instruments. Bunches of jangling shells, deer hoofs, and seeds were hung around his neck, legs, and arms. The rattling sounds added excitement to the slapping, clapping, and stamping sounds made by his hands and feet.

The earliest drum consisted merely of a hollow log or a piece of wood placed over a hole in the ground. "Slit drums" were made by hollowing out logs through longi-

Top: *an African "kissar," which functions as both a drum and a lyre (made from animal horns and a skull)*
Bottom: *even in contemporary society some primitive instruments survive: here a man of Jos, in Northern Nigeria, plays a modern-day version of a primitive horn*

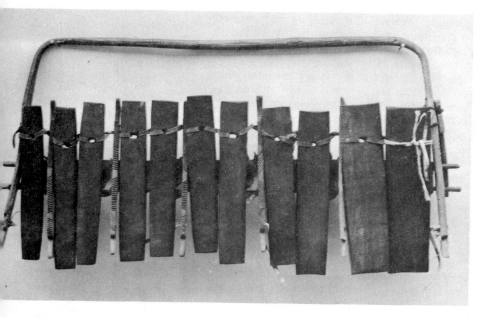

Above: *a primitive precursor of the marimba*
Below: *a wooden drum*

vention of the horn and brass instruments. The wind blowing through tall marsh grasses or across the end of a hollowed cane led to the whistle, and to the many families of pipes, flutes, and woodwind instruments.

No music has come down to us from very early times. Scholars have, however, studied the music of people who still follow a primitive way of life. This music is often a simple drum rhythm, repeated many times. If there is a melody, it may be in a three-note scale or a five-note scale similar to the scale made by playing on the black keys of the piano (Ex. 69). At times a melody is highly decorated, often by tones just a bit above or below the main tones of the melody (Ex. 70). In some songs the singer jumps from a high falsetto to low, sharp grunts (Ex. 71).

As remote places gradually succumb to civilization, so, too, will the few primitive people who inhabit them. Primitive songs and dances will also recede into history. But the inventions and discoveries of early man will always be with us: vital necessities such as the wheel, fire, and—music.

tudinal slits; the drummer hit the hollowed-out wood with sticks. Finally, when animal hides were stretched over the ends of hollow logs, the ancestors of present-day drums came into being.

Drums of all sizes, shapes, and materials became sacred objects. Only chiefs and warriors were allowed to play them. Drums were worshiped as though they were gods. Animals and produce were given to them as sacrificial offerings.

Another primitive instrument consisted of several stones, of varying sizes, that were placed in a row and struck. This was the forerunner of the xylophone and the marimba. The twanging bow of the hunter led to the making of the lyre and the various families of stringed instruments. Shouting or singing through a hollow tube or blowing into a conch shell or animal horn led to the in-

PROGRAM MUSIC: music that attempts to paint a picture, describe an action, or tell a story in sound, without using words. Such music may suggest a battle, drifting clouds, a steam engine, a storm, or the quiet countryside.

Some sounds of nature are easy to imitate in musical tones. The hooting of an owl, the clucking of a hen, the two-note call of the cuckoo, even the puffing of a locomotive—these have been portrayed many times by composers. If the listener has ever heard

Ex. 69

Ex. 70

Ex. 71

grunt

such sounds in reality, he recognizes them in the music.

Other sounds are used to suggest a certain scene or action because the sound of a particular instrument recalls them by association. Composers use drumbeats to suggest soldiers marching, horn calls for the feeling of a chase, trumpet calls for a battle, the droning of a bagpipe for the shepherd on a quiet mountainside.

The composer of program music usually helps the listener by giving his music a descriptive title. Instead of calling his work just Symphony Number X, he calls it perhaps *Bullfight* or *Winter Storm*. If it is a story that he is telling—*The Life of Hercules,* for example—he hopes that his audience will know the story and get the same reaction from the music that they would from reading the story. The danger here is that the audience, in fact, may *not* know the story. The music must then stand on its own as interesting music—and be complete in musical form. If it tries to describe every little thing that happens in a story, the music will sound like the background music of a cartoon film, but without the cartoon to make the references clear.

Program music is probably as old as music itself. Bird calls, the barking of dogs and foxes, and the sound of wind in the trees are heard in the songs of many primitive peoples.

Sixteenth-century vocal music is full of imitations. The French Renaissance composer Janequin (*c*.1485–*c*.1560) wrote long choral works depicting battle scenes and bird calls. Word painting—dwelling on a word and attempting to portray it in music —was popular among the madrigalists. On a word such as "laugh," the melody runs up the scale, happily; on "death" or "I die," it falls slowly downward.

Composers of the seventeenth and eighteenth centuries suggested heroic emotion through a military march, or the feeling of waves or of being on water by music with an uneasy, rocking motion, or, in an opera, the descent of a god by a falling melodic line.

Kuhnau (1660–1722) wrote six sonatas that tell Biblical stories. One of these, the *Combat of David and Goliath,* describes Goliath's challenge, the fear of the Israelites and their prayer to God (a chorale on *De Profundis*), David's courage, the fight between David and Goliath (featuring the slinging of the stone and the fall of Goliath), the flight of the Philistines (with the Israelites in pursuit), and the final rejoicing of the Israelites at their victory.

J. S. Bach wrote much programmatic music, in his cantatas and his autobiographical *Capriccio on the Departure of His Beloved Brother.* Rameau, Gluck, and Mozart composed highly descriptive storm scenes for their operas—anticipating such nineteenth-century storms as those in Rossini's *William Tell* and Wagner's *Die Walküre* and *The Flying Dutchman.*

Program music came into its own in the 1800's. Beethoven gave his Sixth Symphony the added title of "Pastoral" Symphony, making clear in the program of its first performance that he was attempting to describe his feelings about nature rather than nature itself. But the effect of bird calls and a rousing orchestral storm is to make the symphony programmatic.

Berlioz in his *Symphonie fantastique* gave each movement a title—"Reveries," "A Ball," "Scene in the Country," and so on, rather than the mere tempo indication that had been customary.

After these major works, pieces of program music were composed in considerable numbers. Mendelssohn wrote for the piano eight books of *Songs Without Words.* Some of these have only the name of an emotion as a title: "Passion," "Consolation," and so on. Others have titles such as "The Spinning Wheel" and "The Hunt."

Schubert had used suggestions of program music in the accompaniments to his songs. Each of his songs is, in fact, a short dramatic scene in which the piano accompaniment provides background music that sets the mood. The whirring of the spinning wheel is heard in "Gretchen at the Spinning Wheel" and the sound of the street barrel organ in "The Organ Grinder," while the rushing sound of the brook occurs at many points in the song cycle *Die schöne Mullerin.*

Later composers of the nineteenth century were not content to write works in which such things as storms or spinning wheels were incidentally suggested. Liszt invented a whole new musical form, the symphonic poem, in which the music told a story (as in *Mazeppa*) or even preached a philosophy (as in *Les Préludes*). Liszt's symphonic poems were built to follow the form of the story rather than a purely musical form, such as a symphony. His theories were adopted by Richard Strauss and Saint-Saëns, whose *Danse macabre* is one of the most popular of all symphonic poems.

Strauss carried program music to its highest point in such tone poems as *Don Juan, Death and Transfiguration, Don Quixote, Till Eulenspiegel, A Hero's Life, A Domestic Symphony,* and *An Alpine Symphony.* He managed to unite descriptive music, such

Sergei Prokofiev

as the baa-ing of the sheep in *Don Quixote,* with musical form: *Don Quixote* is an ambitious theme and variations, *Till Eulenspiegel* a large rondo, *A Hero's Life* a vast symphony.

A few of Strauss's contemporaries, including Paul Dukas *(The Sorcerer's Apprentice)* and Jean Sibelius *(A Saga, The Swan of Tuonela, Finlandia),* also wrote successful symphonic poems, but by the twentieth century the musical world was moving away from musical storytelling.

The French composer Claude Debussy attempted to give the same feeling in music that one might have while viewing a scene, but without trying to paint a specific musical picture. The "Clouds" section of his *Three Nocturnes* suggests one's impressions as fleecy clouds move slowly across the sky. The three symphonic sketches in *The Sea* portray the composer's feelings about the sea. Debussy's most famous piece of program music, *The Afternoon of a Faun,* matches the lazy mood of the poem by Mallarmé, but does not offer more than fleeting impressions of the faun's daydreams.

In his *Pacific 231* (1923), the Swiss composer Arthur Honegger started composers thinking about the music of machines. The puffing start and the clatter of a train running at full speed exhilarated audiences, and soon the mechanical repetitions that suggest machinery were being experimented with by other composers. The Russian composer Alexander Vassilievitch Mossolov wrote in 1927 a ballet entitled *The Factory,* and an excerpt from this work, "Soviet Iron Foundry," became a popular concert-hall noisemaker during the 1930's.

By 1930 composers were shifting their attention to new musical forms, new sounds, and new instruments. The composer who might have written program music for concerts had a new outlet for his ideas in background music for movies and for radio and, later, television.

In one form or another program music will probably always survive. Composers will continue to be attracted to the sounds of nature and attempt to imitate them—as Rimsky-Korsakov did in "The Flight of the Bumblebee" and Bartók in "The Fly." But the new experimental music, such as *musique concrète,* or electronic and taped sounds, has reversed the formula of program music. Instead of nature being imitated in music, the sounds of nature are being used as pure sounds in themselves and treated like a C-major chord in Mozart or Bach. The sounds that inspired program music have now become the basic stuff of abstract, non-programmatic music.

PROKOFIEV, SERGEI (1891–1953): one of Russia's greatest and most productive composers. He was born in the village of Sontzovka in the region of Ekaterinoslav (now Dnepropetrovsk) in southern European Russia. His mother taught him to play the piano and encouraged him to make up his own pieces. By the age of nine he had written a three-act opera, *The Giant,* and had started on another one. After his family moved to Moscow, Prokofiev studied composition there with the composer Glière. At thirteen he became a student at the conservatory in St. Petersburg (now Leningrad) and here studied composition with Rimsky-Korsakov, as well as piano and conducting with other teachers.

The short piano pieces that Prokofiev wrote while still a student were disturbing to his teachers. His dissonances were biting; his melodies darted off in unpredictable ways. His music seemed to be making fun of everything serious. But in spite of his reputation as a rebel, no one doubted his talent. When he graduated from the conservatory, in 1914, he played his own brilliant First Piano Concerto. His playing was dazzling, and he easily won the first prize— a grand piano.

With his piano pieces *Sarcasms* and *Visions Fugitives* and his first big orchestral work, the *Scythian Suite,* Prokofiev quickly established himself as a composer of the front rank. In 1917 he wrote his charming *Classical Symphony*—"as Haydn might have written it," he said, "had he lived in our day."

The Russian Revolution upset Prokofiev's life. In 1918 he left Russia to tour Japan and the United States, and then made his home in Paris. He supported himself by giving concerts; by composing the ballets *Chout (The Buffoon), Le Pas d'acier (The Age of Steel),* and *L'Enfant prodigue (The Prodigal Son)* for Diaghilev's famous Russian Ballet in Paris; and by writing an opera, *Love for Three Oranges,* for the Chicago Opera Company.

In 1933, after fifteen years in exile, Prokofiev returned to Russia. Musicians and government officials there greeted him with open arms, and he became one of his country's most honored—and highly paid—men.

The return to his native land seemed to mellow Prokofiev. His music became more lyrical, his humor less biting and mocking. He even wrote a work for children—the popular *Peter and the Wolf,* a fairy tale for symphony orchestra and speaker. He composed music for the films *Alexander Nevsky, Lieutenant Kijé,* and *Ivan the Terrible.* From the music for *Nevsky,* Prokofiev later made

Ex. 72 — *Visions fugitives* No. 5

Ex. 73 — Sonata No. 5 for Piano

Ex. 74 — Concerto No. 3 for Piano and Orchestra

Prokofiev at the piano at age 11

a dramatic cantata. From the other films he made popular orchestral suites.

During World War II Prokofiev wrote marches, songs, cantatas, and symphonic works full of patriotic fervor. After the war, however, Soviet officials and critics attacked his music as "formalistic" and tried to make him change his style. He resisted and continued on in his own way.

Prokofiev was an unceasing worker. He wrote eight operas, seven ballets, seven symphonies, five piano concertos, two violin concertos, two cello concertos, plus suites from ballets, films, and operas. For soloists or small chamber groups he wrote ten piano sonatas; two violin sonatas; two string quartets; an *Overture on Hebrew Themes* for clarinet, strings, and piano; sonatas for various small combinations of instruments; and many songs.

In style Prokofiev's music is always clear —never thick or complex. Often it is a melody with a simple but interesting accompaniment. He was fond of straightforward rhythms—dances and marches—and had a great gift for writing singing, melodic lines that alternate with bold, athletic melodies or scurrying, humorous figures. His harmony is sometimes dissonant, particularly in his early works. Most often it is simple and tonal, although he was fond of sudden, unsettling key changes (Ex. 72, 73, and 74).

Prokofiev was one of the great masters of the orchestra. He used orchestral colors in sharply contrasting ways—from massive deep walls of sound to thin, bright flute and clarinet duets. He was not a truly revolutionary composer; his style was based on music of the past. But everything Prokofiev wrote was touched with a unique vision.

Giacomo Puccini

PUCCINI, GIACOMO (1858–1924): Verdi's successor as the leading composer of Italian opera. He was born in Lucca, Italy, where his family, starting with his great-great-grandfather, had been leading musicians. His father, the local organist and head of a conservatory, died when Puccini was five. The boy did not want to be a musician—he much preferred bird-catching and practical jokes. But his mother, determined that he should follow in the family tradition, placed him with her brother, who taught him to play the organ and to sing, and incidentally was given to kicking him in the shins when he sang a wrong note. By the age of ten Puccini was a choirboy; at fourteen he was the church organist. For cigarette money (he was a heavy smoker all his life) he played the piano in local taverns.

When Puccini was eighteen he walked twenty miles to hear Verdi's *Aida*—and now he knew what he wanted to do. As he said, "I felt that a musical window had opened for me." He began to write music, preparing for the Milan Conservatory, which he entered at the age of twenty-two.

In Milan he lived a penniless, carefree life, not far removed from that of the young artists he would one day describe in his opera *La Bohème*. For a while his roommate was Mascagni, who later composed *Cavalleria rusticana*. In these years Puccini lived mostly on soup and beans, saving whatever money he had to go to operas.

For his graduation piece, in 1883, Puccini wrote his only orchestral work, a *Capriccio sinfonico*. It was a success, but Puccini's goal was still opera. He wrote a one-act opera, *Le Villi (The Willi),* for a prize competition. Partly because the manuscript was messy and unreadable, *The Willi* did not even get an honorable mention. Nevertheless he got it produced in a small theater in 1884, and the powerful Italian publisher Ricordi heard the work, liked it, and decided to back Puccini. Ricordi commissioned him to write a full-scale opera, *Edgar,* which was produced in 1889 at La Scala in Milan, the greatest opera house in Italy. *Edgar* was received with lukewarm applause and in its first year had only three performances.

It was Puccini's next opera, *Manon Lescaut,* that established him as a success. Five librettists helped him mold the story to the proper form. With this work, put on at Turin in 1893, Puccini found his own style. He then became associated with two librettists who understood the kind of passionate scene that was needed to inspire him. These men, Illica and Giacosa, provided the librettos for Puccini's next three works, which were his greatest successes: *La Bohème, Tosca,* and *Madame Butterfly.*

La Bohème was given its première in Turin in 1896, with a young conductor named Arturo Toscanini in charge of the music. The tender story of the young Bohemian artists and their love affairs drew from Puccini a flowing, passionate kind of music—and bustling and tragic music, too. The audience loved it. In spite of critical attacks, *La Bohème* had twenty-four sold-out performances within a month. It became a success first throughout Italy, then in Paris, and finally in the whole operatic world.

Tosca, a darkly dramatic tale, had its first performance in Rome in 1900. There was a bomb threat on opening night—the work of Puccini's rivals. But *Tosca,* too, became a world-wide favorite.

While searching for a story for his next opera, Puccini saw an English production of a play by David Belasco, *Madame Butterfly.* This work, based on a short story by John Luther Long, appealed to him, and so he set to work on an opera that told the story of the little Japanese girl who was deserted by her lover, an American naval officer.

At this time Puccini's work suffered a severe interruption. From the moment he had begun to make money with his operas, he had been living expensively. He had country estates, complete with waterfowl shooting, and he enthusiastically pursued the hobby of fast riding—first on a bicycle, then in cars, and finally in speedboats. And now, while in one of his cars, he had an accident. For eight months he was a convalescent, recovering from broken bones. But during

this time he worked on *Madame Butterfly.*

Its first performance (1904), at Milan's La Scala, was turned into a musical scandal. Puccini had been too successful to suit his rivals, and had disdained certain parties in high society. To make sure that *Madame Butterfly* would fail, these people hired a claque—a crowd who would whistle and howl insults—to attend the performance. So it was that the tender music and tragic story were greeted with groans, growls, and laughter. During one moving interlude the claque whistled bird calls, and at the sad ending they hooted and laughed.

Despite this rough christening, *Madame Butterfly* soon made its way into opera houses throughout the world. Once again Puccini could look down upon his enemies with scorn. And from *Madame Butterfly* came Puccini's most-sung aria "Some Fine Day" (Ex. 75, on page 444).

In 1907 Puccini visited New York to hear the first Metropolitan Opera Company production of *Madame Butterfly.* While there he saw another play by Belasco, *The Girl of the Golden West,* a story of life among the gold miners of California. Puccini liked the story and wrote an opera based on it, completing the work in 1910. The opera, *La fanciulla del west (The Girl of the Golden West),* was produced that year at the Metro-

A scene from Act I of Puccini's Madame Butterfly *with, from left to right: Calvin Marsh as the High Commissioner, Antoinetta Stella as Butterfly, and Eugenio Fernandi as Lieutenant Pinkerton*

Ex. 75 — "Some Fine Day" from *Madame Butterfly*

Ex. 76 — *La Bohème*

Andante calmo

Ex. 77 — *Tosca*

Andante molto sostenuto

Ex. 78 — Opening of Act III, *La Bohème*

Ex. 79 — *Turandot*

Ex. 80 — *Turandot*

Lento

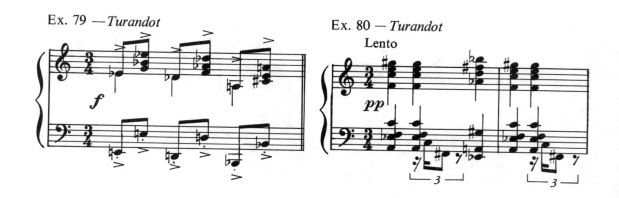

politan Opera House in New York. It has never been as successful as Puccini's other big operas, possibly because the composer was not quite at home in the story. Puccini then tried his hand at a light work, *La rondine (The Swallow)*, but the public did not take to it.

Puccini now turned in an entirely different direction for his next venture: a set of three one-act operas—*Il trittico (The Triptych)*. Of these, *Il tabarro (The Cloak)* is a violent and somber tragedy; *Suor Angelica (Sister Angelica)* is the moving story of a nun who sins; and *Gianni Schicchi* is a comedy with characters out of old Italian plays. *The Triptych* has slowly become a success since its first performance at the Metropolitan Opera House in 1918. *Gianni Schicchi* is often given by itself.

For what was to be his last opera Puccini turned to a Chinese tale, *Turandot*. Originally *Turandot* was a play by an eighteenth-century Italian playwright, Count Carlo Gozzi. Its oriental setting appealed at one time or another to at least five composers other than Puccini, who spent four years working on it. He studied Chinese music and introduced many Chinese melodies into his opera, and for it invented a new style—dissonant, complex in orchestration, full of choral writing.

Unfortunately Puccini did not live to finish this "heroic-comic-fantastic" work, as he called it. The last scene was written by Franco Alfano, who used Puccini's sketches. The first performance of *Turandot* was given at La Scala in 1925. The conductor—Toscanini again—led the work up to the point that Puccini had reached, then turned to the audience and put down his baton. "Here," he said, "Giacomo Puccini broke off his work. Death was stronger than art." The next night the opera was performed with Alfano's ending.

Turandot puzzled audiences, who expected the music of the Puccini they knew. It did not have the immediate success of his earlier works, but its popularity has grown through the years. It may well turn out to be his masterpiece.

Puccini's music is "theater." It goes directly to the dramatic point and makes use of whatever style of harmony and melody Puccini feels is right. Sometimes he uses leitmotifs to bind the musical framework together, but never lets them become all-important. His melodies are beautifully written for the voice. Few composers have achieved the pathos and tenderness of Puccini's mostly stepwise vocal lines (Ex. 76). Puccini's operas open with a brief splash of color in the orchestra—there are no full-fledged overtures. The opening sounds set the scene or the mood. A few triads, often moving in non-traditional progressions, or a succession of a mere few notes, are all Puccini needs to set the scene. The opening of *Tosca* depicts the brutal forcefulness of Scarpia, the chief of police (Ex. 77). The opening of the third act of *La Bohème* portrays the chilling winter by means of open fifths played on flute and harp, suggesting falling snowflakes (Ex. 78). In *Turandot* Puccini uses, besides his open fourths and fifths, sounds made up from the Chinese pentatonic scales, from whole-tone scales, and from combinations of scales (Ex. 79 and 80).

He was a true theater composer, using every means available to move the emotions of an audience. His aim was dramatic truth.

Puccini (in the side seat) and a friend

PULSE: the steady beat that is present in almost every musical composition. The pulse of the music may be clearly defined, as in marches and dances, or may be disguised so as to be barely discernible, as in a slow, songlike work.

The pulse note is the type of note chosen by the composer to represent one beat. It may be any type—from a whole note to a thirty-second note. Rhythmic patterns are made by subdividing the pulse note or using one note equal to several pulses. The rhythmic pattern of the chorus of "Camptown Races" shows how this is done:

In the time signature at the beginning of a musical work, the pulse note is shown by the bottom figure (except in compound meter): in 2/4 time the quarter note is the pulse note; in 3/8 time the eighth note is the pulse note.

The speed of the pulse note is indicated at the beginning of a work by a tempo mark (allegro, adagio, and so forth) or by a precise metronome mark (♩ = 120).

In music of the fifteenth and sixteenth centuries, the pulse was called the tactus.

See also RHYTHM; TIME SIGNATURE; METER.

Portrait of Henry Purcell by J. Closterman

A portion of Purcell's song "Pious Celinda" (from the collection of songs Deliciae Musicae by Henry Playford, 1695)

PURCELL, HENRY (1659–95): one of England's greatest composers. Strangely enough, little is known of his life, even though he was one of the busiest men in England's musical life during his time. The month of his birth is unknown, and there is even a dispute as to the identity of his father. He was the son of either Henry or Thomas Purcell, both musicians in the Chapel Royal, where he himself became a choirboy at the age of ten. Here he received enough musical instruction for his future work as assistant repairer of the king's instruments, composer to the king's band, organist at Westminster Abbey, and harpsichord player to James II. For the last ten years of his life Purcell was England's most sought-after composer of incidental music for plays and theatrical spectacles.

In his short lifetime Purcell wrote a large body of work, ranging from earthy rounds for a men's glee club to more than forty church anthems. His chamber music, which is among his most distinguished work, contains both music in contemporary style—for example, his trio sonatas for two violins, bass, and harpsichord—and in that of the previous century, such as his fantasies for strings in three, four, or five parts. One of his most famous works is his *Fantasy upon One Note*, in which the viola plays nothing but middle C—while the other four instruments weave melodies around it. For harpsichord Purcell wrote several sets of *Lessons*, or suites. These contain tuneful marches, minuets, and airs,

as well as pieces in his favorite form—variations over a ground, or repeated, bass. Purcell used this form in his vocal works as well as his instrumental pieces. The famous "Dido's Lament" from his opera *Dido and Aeneas* is built on a ground bass.

As court composer, Purcell wrote many odes for chorus, soloists, and orchestra. These royal "Welcome Songs," birthday odes, and odes for St. Cecilia's Day are noble and powerful works that influenced the later choral work of Handel.

Purcell's genius was at its peak in his songs and dramatic works. He wrote but one opera, *Dido and Aeneas,* but his other stage works—*Dioclesian, King Arthur, The Fairy Queen, The Indian Queen,* and *The Tempest*—contain so much vocal and instrumental music that they are often classified as operas. In these, as well as in the incidental music for many other plays and the more than one hundred songs, Purcell wrote colorful music that was both dramatically exciting and quite singable. Many composers have had difficulty in setting English words to music, but Purcell's songs show how the rhythm of English poetry can be captured in musical phrases.

The most distinctive feature of Purcell's vocal works is the way in which he illustrates the meaning of a word or a dramatic situation (Ex. 81 and 82). *King Arthur* has a frost scene in which a bass sings with a shivering sound on every note—indicated by Purcell with a wavy line over the notes

Ex. 81 — "Air" from *The Tempest*

Ex. 82 --- "Air" from *Bonduca*

Ex. 83 — Frost Scene from *King Arthur*

Ex. 84 — A New Irish Tune: "Lilliburlero" from *Musick's Handmaiden*

(Ex. 83). Sometimes Purcell's melodies are flowery; at other times they are almost as simple as folk songs (Ex. 84).

Purcell was appreciated in his lifetime; only after his death did the popularity of his music go into a decline. The English music lovers preferred the music of German composers to that of their native son. In the nineteenth century some of Purcell's works were finally published, but often with many changes. His bold harmonic progressions and unusual melodic lines were smoothed out, and some of his choral works were reharmonized. Many of the works performed were among his least interesting compositions, and he became known as a composer of dull music!

In 1876 the Purcell Society was formed to publish all of Purcell's works in their authentic form. The final volume, Number 32, was brought out in 1962. As the music became available, performers began to sing his songs and play his chamber music. Many of Purcell's masterpieces have since been recorded on long-playing records. By a strange freak of fate, the most popular work associated with Purcell's name is the *Trumpet Voluntary*—written not by Purcell but by Jeremiah Clarke.

Purcell was buried in Westminster Abbey, where England inters her great. As one of his friends, the writer Roger North, said, "A greater musical genius England never had."

QUARTET: a musical composition for four vocalists or instrumentalists. The string quartet, consisting of two violins, viola, and cello, has been the favorite form of chamber music since the middle 1700's. Starting with Haydn (who wrote eighty-three string quartets) and continuing through Mozart (twenty-six) and Beethoven (seventeen), almost every major composer has written at least one string quartet.

The string quartets of the Classical period had four movements much like the symphony—in fact, many of the earliest symphonies were hardly more than string quartets with an added pair of horns, flutes, or oboes. The early string quartets of Haydn featured the first violin, which soloed to the accompaniment of the other three instruments. In his later works, all four of the instruments share equally in the music, discoursing on the intriguing thematic material invented by Haydn. Mozart, whose first quartets were inspired by those of Haydn, brought to the string quartet a beautiful sense of lyricism and a great intensity of expression.

Beethoven carried the string quartet to its loftiest peaks, particularly in his last quartets—Opuses 127, 130, 131, 132, 133, and 135. While the early Classical quartets were meant to be pleasant to listen to and easy to perform, the Beethoven quartets present tremendous difficulties to the performers and are meant to stir the deepest emotions of the listeners. Daring in their form and harmony, they are to many musicians the greatest of all instrumental works.

Many beautiful string quartets were written by composers of the nineteenth century: Schubert wrote fifteen, Schumann three, Mendelssohn seven, Dvořák sixteen, and Brahms three. The violinist-composer Ludwig Spohr (1784–1859) wrote thirty-four string quartets and invented a new form—the double string quartet, of which he wrote four. Spohr also wrote a concerto for string quartet and orchestra.

The idiom of the string quartet has continued to intrigue contemporary composers, starting with Debussy and Ravel, each of whom wrote one. Outstanding quartets have also been written by Schoenberg (four, with a part for voice added to the Quartet Number Two), Berg (two, including his famous *Lyric Suite*), Webern (three, including his six brief bagatelles), Hindemith (seven), Milhaud (fifteen, of which Numbers Fourteen and Fifteen may be played together), Bartók (six—among the most-played of all contemporary works), Britten (two), Schuman (four), and Carter (three).

Quartets for vocal soloists occur in many operas, often as a closing section to a scene or an act. Vocal quartets are also a feature of many oratorios and cantatas. In the field of true chamber music are the vocal quartets by Schumann *(Spanisches Liederspiel—Spanish Songs)* and Brahms's two sets of *Liebeslieder (Love Songs),* in the form of waltzes for singers and piano, four hands, and Brahms's *Gypsy Songs,* Opus 103.

Quartets have been written for almost every combination of instruments. Among the most popular are the quartets for piano and three stringed instruments by Mozart (two), Beethoven (four), Schumann (one), Brahms (three), and Copland (one). Mozart wrote a quartet for oboe and three strings; Rossini, a theme and variations for flute, clarinet, bassoon, and horn; and Webern, a quartet for piano, violin, saxophone, and clarinet. Composers have been intrigued by the homogeneous sound of four identical instruments—a musical form exemplified by Beethoven's three *Equali* for four trombones, Elliot Carter's suite for four alto saxophones, and works for quartets of bassoons by Prokofiev and Schuman.

Various combinations of four instruments have been used in jazz groups. Probably the most successful jazz quartets are those of Benny Goodman, Dave Brubeck, and the Modern Jazz Quartet. As the big dance bands of the 1940's began to disband in the 1950's, their places were taken by the more intimate small "combos," such as a quartet of piano, drum, guitar, and string bass. These groups often have had the pleasant quality of the early Classical string quartets and are as entertaining to their listeners as the quartets of Haydn.

The Juilliard Quartet: Robert Mann, violin; Raphael Hillyer, viola; Claus Adam, cello; and Robert Koff, violin

QUINTET: a musical work for five singers or instrumentalists. The earliest quintets were the five-voice madrigals composed in Italy in the sixteenth century. These were written for three women's and two men's voices or the reverse combination.

The string quintet became an important musical form in the late 1700's, along with its more popular relative the string quartet. The usual string quintet is written for two violins, two violas, and one cello; like the symphony and string quartet, it is usually in four movements. For this combination of instruments Mozart wrote seven works, Beethoven three, and Mendelssohn and Brahms two each, while Schubert wrote his Quintet in C for two violins, one viola, and two cellos.

Other quintet combinations are piano and string quartet (Schumann, Brahms, Harris); horn and string quartet (Mozart); piano and four winds (Mozart, Beethoven); piano, violin, viola, cello, and double bass (Schubert, *Die Forelle—The Trout*); clarinet and string quartet (Mozart, Brahms, Hindemith); oboe, clarinet, violin, viola, and double bass (Prokofiev); five winds (Hindemith, Schoenberg).

Many vocal quintets occur in opera. Among the best known are the two in Mozart's *The Magic Flute* and the one in the third act of Wagner's *Die Meistersinger*.

QUINTUPLE METER: music that has five beats per measure: 5/4, 5/8, 5/16, and so on. Its restless, asymmetrical quality, with accents on the first and third or first and fourth beats of a measure, did not appeal to the composers of the Baroque and Classical periods, who preferred the simple meters of two and three, plus their even compounds of four and six. In the nineteenth century only a few compositions, such as Chopin's Sonata in C Minor (third movement), Tchaikovsky's *Symphonie pathétique* (second movement), and sections of Mussorgsky's *Pictures at an Exhibition,* were written in a meter of five. Contemporary composers, beginning with Erik Satie, have been attracted to the quality of the five-beat measure, and its use has become more general.

In Ex. 1 the composer emphasizes the unevenness of quintuple meter by putting an accent on the first note of each group. In Ex. 2 he writes so that the five beats flow without much feeling of accent.

Ex. 1 — Sonatina for Piano, Lloyd

Ex. 2 — Symphony No. 6, Tchaikovsky

Ex. 3 — *Carnaval* No. 5, Schumann
Adagio

There are various methods of conducting quintuple meter. Many conductors beat alternate two's and three's. Others beat a true five with a sideward accent on count three or four, depending on the placement of the accent:

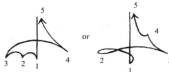

In a fast quintuple meter the conductor often beats a meter of two, with one beat lasting longer than the others.

QUINTUPLET: a group of five equal notes —the result of dividing a certain space of time into five equal parts. The type of note used in the quintuplet is the same as that used to divide the same amount of time into four equal parts:

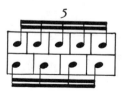

The quintuplet is found mostly in music of the nineteenth and twentieth centuries, although an example of it is included in Morley's *A Plaine and Easie Introduction to Practicall Musicke* (1597). A quintuplet often occurs when a composer writes out a melodic turn, as in Ex. 3.

QUODLIBET (Latin, "what you please"): a kind of musical joke in which several melodies—usually popular tunes—are played or sung at the same time. The writing of quodlibets was popular among German composers of the sixteenth and seventeenth centuries, since it allowed them to show their compositional skill by combining as many as five tunes.

The singing of quodlibets can be a kind of competition, as it was in the annual get-togethers of the Bach family. J. S. Bach wrote a quodlibet based on two folk songs as the last of his "Goldberg" Variations.

One of the most amazing quodlibets occurs in Louis Moreau Gottschalk's *L'Union,* in which "Yankee Doodle" is combined with "Hail to the Chief," even though they don't quite fit together (Ex. 4).

Ex. 4 — *L'Union*, Gottschalk

RACHMANINOFF, SERGEI (1873–1943): Russian composer, pianist, and conductor. He was born on a family estate near Novgorod, about 100 miles south of St. Petersburg (now Leningrad). His father and grandfather were good amateur pianists, and Rachmaninoff was given piano lessons at an early age—although he was expected later to enter the elite military college for officers. But Rachmaninoff's father was a poor businessman and lost the family fortune; even the family estate had to be sold at auction. Since a military career without money was unthinkable, when the family moved to St. Petersburg the boy—now nine years old—was entered as a scholarship student at the conservatory.

Rachmaninoff was not a good student. He wandered about the city instead of attending classes, sometimes spending his carfare at a skating rink. His grandmother took him to church services, where he loved to listen to the singing and to the tolling of the bells. But the teachers at the conservatory saw no future for him in music.

His twenty-two-year-old cousin, Alexander Siloti, was already a concert pianist. He advised the family to send Rachmaninoff to Moscow to study with the famous, eccentric, and strict teacher Nicolai Zverev. Rachmaninoff moved to Moscow and lived at the home of Zverev, who supervised every detail of his students' lives. Here Rachmaninoff met and played for many of the top Russian musicians, including Tchaikovsky, who became his musical idol.

At the age of fifteen Rachmaninoff entered the Moscow Conservatory. To his piano studies he added composition (with Arensky and Taneyev), and he became ambitious to graduate early and to win the Great Gold Medal for composition, which had been awarded only twice in the history of the conservatory. In spite of a serious illness, he achieved his purposes, graduating as pianist in 1891, the year he completed his First Piano Concerto, and as composer in 1892 (a year ahead of his class), and winning the Great Gold Medal for his opera *Aleko.*

A publisher offered him 200 rubles (about $100) for five short piano pieces. Among them was the Prelude in C-sharp Minor, destined to become his first popular work. Rachmaninoff thought so little of the piece that he did not bother to copyright it and thus lost a fortune in royalties. None of Rachmaninoff's twenty-three preludes written later, except the marchlike Prelude in G Minor, achieved comparable fame, although each is a gem.

When his First Symphony was given its première in St. Petersburg in 1897, the critics tore it and its composer to shreds. Depressed, Rachmaninoff stopped writing for several years. A psychiatrist named Dahl hypnotized him into writing again, and in the fall of 1901 he played the first performance of his Second Piano Concerto. Its success launched Rachmaninoff on a busy career. In 1904 he became conductor of the Bolshoi Opera in Moscow.

After several years he began to wander—to Italy, to Germany, to Paris. He was in great demand as a pianist and conductor of his own works. For his United States tour in 1909 he composed his Third Piano Concerto. From 1910 to 1917 he lived off and on in Moscow. Then, while he was working on his Fourth Piano Concerto (which he was not to finish until 1928), the Russian Revolution broke out. Rachmaninoff left Russia with his wife and two daughters, never to return, even though his music remained popular with Russian audiences.

Rachmaninoff became a touring virtuoso, specializing in the music of Chopin in addition to his own. His home, when he was not touring, was Switzerland. Finally, in 1935, he made the United States his permanent home, living first on Long Island and later in the suburbs of Los Angeles. A few weeks before he died he became an American citizen.

Rachmaninoff is best known for his piano works: the preludes, the four concertos (the first of which he revised in 1917), and the *Rhapsody on a Theme by Paganini.* As a master pianist, he knew how to bring out all the nuances and sonorities of the instrument—how to make scale passages and arpeggios glitter and how to make melodies sing (several of his themes were made into popular tunes). Like his idol Tchaikovsky, he wrote nostalgic and even melancholy music—he worked the funereal Dies Irae (Day of Wrath) chant into several of his works. He was fond of broad, singing melodies that move mostly step by step as they surge up and down (Ex. 1). Around the singing melodies of his concertos, Rachmaninoff wove rhapsodic piano parts. At times the piano takes over completely and sings the melody to its own accompaniment (Ex. 2).

Rachmaninoff worked irregularly. His exhausting months of touring interfered with composition throughout much of the year. Even so, he turned out a large number of works in addition to those for piano: seventy-nine songs; a choral symphony, *The Bells;* a symphonic poem, *The Isle of the Dead;* three symphonies; a set of *Symphonic Dances;*

Sergei Rachmaninoff

Rachmaninoff at the piano

Ravi Shankar

Ex. 1 — Theme from Piano Concerto No. 2

Ex. 2 — Theme from Piano Concerto No. 2

and many small pieces for one or two pianos. Chamber music did not interest him—he wrote only a few works for violin and cello, and those when he was young. He did like to make concert transcriptions: of Kreisler's "Liebesfreud" and "Liebeslied," Mussorgsky's "Hopak," Rimsky-Korsakov's "Flight of the Bumble Bee," and his own songs, "Lilacs" and "Daisies."

Rachmaninoff was a great figure among twentieth-century pianists. Audiences flocked to hear the powerful and original interpretations of this giant with the stern Mongolian features. As a composer, he was content to follow in the style of Tchaikovsky, while adding his own brand of personal songfulness. Fortunately for music lovers of the future, Rachmaninoff made many glorious records of his own works and of other music that he loved. From these one can recapture his poetic approach to piano playing—an approach that combined breathtaking virtuosity with marvelous control of all the nuances.

RAGA: an arrangement of the tones of one of many scales, which serves as the basis for melodic improvisations in the music of India. There are thousands of ragas, each associated with a time of day, a being from Hindu mythology, a season of the year, or an important formal event. In India, pictures illustrating certain ragas are painted, much as a European artist might paint his impression of Beethoven's *Pastoral Symphony.* The theory is that if one listens intently to a fine musician improvising on his stringed *vina* or his *sitar,* there will flash into one's mind a vivid picture associated with the raga being used. The improvisations feature glidings between tones, grace-note decorations, and the use of microtones smaller than the European half step. While a stringed instrument or the oboe-like *shahnai,* or *surnai,* is playing melodically, a series of exciting, syncopated cross-rhythms is usually being played on the *tablas,* or hand drums. The drum rhythms are based on rhythmic units known as *tāls,* or *talas.* (A tala—there are several hundred of them—is a rhythmic framework on which one or more drummers can improvise.)

In the early twentieth century, the ancient music of India was in danger of being wiped out by the strong influence of European music. Recently, both North Indian (Hindu) and South Indian (Carnatic) music have had a remarkable rebirth, due to the interest of such men as the poet Rabindranath Tagore, the dancer Uday Shankar, and the musicians Ravi Shankar, Ali Akbar Khan, Yehudi

Ex. 3 — "Golliwog's Cakewalk," Debussy

Ex. 4 — "Maple Leaf Rag," Joplin

Not too fast

"Jelly Roll" Morton

The cover of Scott Joplin's famous "Maple Leaf Rag"

Menuhin, and the Beatles. The raga has become an important ingredient in American jazz music, and many jazz musicians now base their improvisations on ragas as well as on more traditional "blues" harmonic patterns.

RAGTIME: a style of piano jazz that was played in honky-tonk cafés in the 1890's. It grew out of the banjo solos that had been features of minstrel shows in the United States in the middle 1800's. Pianists imitated the jangling sound of the banjo solos by weaving fast, strongly accented syncopated patterns over a steady, strong beat in the left hand. The jerky rhythms made much use of the pattern here:

This pattern had been used much earlier in old Creole dance tunes such as "M'sieu Banjo," and in minstrel tunes such as the chorus of "Old Dan Tucker." The French composer Debussy also used it to give a ragtime flavor to his "Golliwog's Cakewalk" (Ex. 3).

The most famous ragtime pianist and composer was Scott Joplin (1869–1917), a black pianist from Texas. He wrote thirty-nine piano rags, an instruction book, and two ragtime operas. His best-known work, "The Maple Leaf Rag," was written in 1899. It was named after the Maple Leaf Club in Sedalia, Missouri, where Joplin was playing (Ex. 4).

Other ragtime pianists were Tom Turpin in St. Louis, "Jelly Roll" Morton in New Orleans, and James P. Johnson in New Jersey. Ragtime swept the United States in the early 1900's and was heard in Europe as played by John Philip Sousa's band. The raucous sounds of ragtime inspired Igor Stravinsky to write his *Ragtime* for eleven instruments (1918) and *Piano Rag-Music* (1920).

Ragtime was, for a while, the name for any kind of jazz. Classical melodies were given the ragtime treatment in a style known as "ragging the classics." The earliest jazz bands in New Orleans were called "ragtime bands." Ragtime music was popular on player pianos; it was used to accompany early silent movies, and it provided part of the noisy atmosphere of the old-time saloons. But by 1918 ragtime had been swept aside by the jazz bands and blues singers who came north from New Orleans. In a few short years true ragtime was heard and played only as a memory of the past—although there has recently been a revival of interest in it.

Top: an 18th-century French engraving depicting "The Triumph of Rameau" in the feud between his supporters and those of Lully, the former "ruler" of French opera
Bottom: *Jean-Philippe Rameau*

RAMEAU, JEAN-PHILIPPE (1683–1764): an outstanding French composer, organist, and theorist in the time of Bach and Handel. Rameau was born at Dijon, France, of a musical family, and began the study of keyboard instruments and the violin when quite young. For a short time he played the violin in the orchestra of a traveling opera company, but in 1702, at the age of nineteen, he followed in his father's footsteps and became a church organist in Avignon. For the next thirty years he was an organist in various French cities, including Paris. His first book of pieces for the harpsichord, a suite of dances, was published in 1706. In the meantime he worked on his revolutionary textbook on harmony *(Traité de l'harmonie)*, published in 1722.

Rameau's harmony system established principles that are still in use today: the derivation of the major triad from the overtone series, the relation of chords to a tonal center, the building of chords in a series of thirds, and the theory of chordal inversions (see HARMONY). Rameau asserted that melody grows out of harmony and that therefore harmonic progressions are the basis of musical form. His theories of fundamental basses (chord roots not necessarily in the bass part) and of the importance of the chords built on the primary tones of the scale (the first, fourth, and fifth tones) were

attempts to explain the new kind of music that was replacing the old counterpoint. Many musicians of the time, including J. S. Bach, attacked his work because it seemed to make melody less important than harmony. But Rameau's theories have been taught to all generations of music students since his time.

Rameau achieved recognition as France's greatest organist and theorist. It was in opera, however, that a French composer could be truly successful, and so at the age of fifty Rameau started a new career—that of composer of stage music.

A wealthy pupil used her influence to get him a libretto. She persuaded the great writer Voltaire to produce one, but the result—a Biblical opera, *Samson*—was refused by the Paris Opéra. Rameau's first real opera, *Hippolyte et Aricie (Hippolyte and Aricie),* was produced in 1733, and was followed by twenty-two more dramatic works. Many of these were ballets or opera-ballets which combined singing and dancing. One of the most lavish of all ballets, *Les Indes galantes,* established Rameau as a composer for the theater when it was produced in 1735. One reason was that it satisfied the French public's love of big dance spectacles, providing dance scenes on an Indian Ocean island and a Peruvian mountaintop, at a Persian court, and in an American Indian forest. Its scenic effects included a storm at sea and a volcanic eruption.

The success of Rameau's stage works was due not only to the colorful scenery and costumes but also to the expressive music that helped to knit the ballets together with dramatic unity—a new idea at the time. Rameau's tuneful dance music swept Europe and was used as interludes in many Italian operas. In his descriptive works Rameau anticipated many of Wagner's ideas about "gestural" music, which describes action in terms of sound. For example, descents of the gods (Ex. 5) and the swirling motions of dancers portraying zephyrs are brightly mirrored (Ex. 11, page 43). In writing for the voice, Rameau carefully considered both the meaning and rhythm of the words, often underlining a dramatic phrase with startling

Ex. 5 — Descent of Mercury from *Platée*

chromatic harmonies (Ex. 6). His arias are quite free and his recitatives often come close to being ariosos. Throughout his operas there are many magnificent choral effects.

Rameau's theories and his music caused many arguments. At first the admirers of Lully, the founder of French opera, criticized Rameau because he refused to follow Lully's style slavishly. The critics disliked his dance music because it made the dancers jump about instead of gliding smoothly across the stage. But eventually Lully's followers realized that in his own way Rameau was continuing the tradition of French opera. The king gave him an annual pension and the honorary title of royal chamber-music composer.

In the 1750's Rameau became the center of attention in the battle of musical philosophies known as the War of the Buffoons. His music was attacked as being unnatural by lovers of light Italian operas and by the anti-royalist group of writers called the Encyclopedists. Rameau defended his position by writing essays, but his best defense was his music. His comic opera-ballet *Platée* showed that French music, too, could be light and gay.

Most of Rameau's music was written for the stage. He composed some motets and cantatas and a few chamber works for harpsichord, flute, violin, and viola. Little of this is heard today. The works that are played include some orchestral dance-suites arranged from his operas and ballets, and his keyboard music.

Rameau wrote three sets of keyboard pieces *(pièces de clavecin)*. They are full of delightful musical ideas, often illustrating titles such as "Le Rappel des oiseaux" (The Call of the Birds) and "Les Tourbillons" (The Whirlwinds). There are little jokes such as "Les Tricotets" (The Knitters), in which the player's hands make motions like those of a knitter, and "Les Trois Mains" (The Three Hands), in which the left hand crosses back and forth over the right hand (Ex. 7). Most famous of all is "La Poule" (The Hen), cackling and clucking in musical tones (Ex. 8).

Except for occasional revivals of *Les Indes galantes* and the opera *Castor et Pollux (Castor and Pollux)*, Rameau's stage works are rarely performed. His greatest continuing effect on music is that of philosopher-theorist and keyboard composer.

A costume sketch for one of the characters in the ballet Les Indes galantes *(1735)*

Ex. 6 — "Where are you fleeing to, miserable one? Tremble—shudder with horror," from *Hippolyte et Aricie*

Ex. 7 — "Les Trois Mains"

Ex. 8 — "La Poule"

A young girl from Thailand performing with bamboo rattles

RATTLE: a container of seeds or pebbles which, when shaken, gives off a series of sharp percussive sounds. The rattle is among the oldest of musical instruments.

Primitive man made rattles with bunches of thin stones, animal teeth or hooves, and nutshells. Tied to his ankles or around his neck, they made sharp, exciting noises as he danced. Later rattles were made from large dried seed pods, gourds, baskets, and clay pots containing seeds, pebbles, or any other small hard objects. Handles were then added for ease in shaking.

Rattles have been associated mostly with dancing. One of the most popular rhythm instruments in Latin American dance music is a rattle called the maraca. Maracas are usually played in pairs.

RAVEL, MAURICE (1875–1937): master of the orchestra and one of the greatest of modern French composers. Ravel was born in the small town of Ciboure in southwestern France, near the Spanish border. His father was a Swiss and his mother a Basque. It was probably the influence of his mother's Spanish background that led Ravel so frequently to seek his inspiration in Spanish stories and ideas.

Ravel's family moved to Paris when he was a small child, and here, at the age of six, he started to play the piano. His father encouraged him by paying him to practice. At twelve he began to study theory and composition, and at fourteen he entered the Paris Conservatory to study composition and piano as well. He stayed at the conservatory for sixteen years, trying unsuccessfully in his last years there to win the Grand Prix de Rome. While still a student, Ravel wrote his only string quartet, his *Shéhérazade* for voice and orchestra, and many piano pieces—including his popular "Pavane pour une infante défunte" (Pavane for a Dead Princess), "Jeux d'eau" (The Fountains), the five pieces that make up his *Miroirs (Mirrors),* and a sonatine.

The failure to award Ravel the Grand Prix in his last year at the conservatory caused such a scandal that the head of the institution was forced to resign. After all, Ravel had shown himself to be the outstanding young composer of France and the only rival of Debussy, who was thirteen years older. The Durand publishing company offered Ravel a subsidy of 12,000 francs a year against royalties. Ravel decided to accept only half that amount, so that he would not have to turn out music in great quantities. All his life he worked carefully and slowly, polishing each composition like a jewel.

In the nine years between his conservatory days and the outbreak of World War I in 1914, Ravel turned out a series of fine works: a piano trio; the three fantastically difficult piano pieces of *Gaspard de la nuit;* many songs, including beautiful settings of traditional Greek and Hebrew songs; the delightful *Ma Mère de l'oye (Mother Goose* Suite) for four hands at one piano; a short, witty opera, *L'Heure espagnole (The Spanish Hour);* and the ballet *Daphnis et Chloé,* written for Diaghilev's Russian Ballet and later made over by Ravel into two orchestral suites.

When the war started Ravel tried to enlist as an aviator, but looked so frail that he was turned down. Becoming an ambulance driver, he came under fire in battle, then was hospitalized because of poor health. His war services ended, he again became a composer. He finished *Le Tombeau de Couperin,* a set of piano pieces written in honor of François Couperin and based on late seventeenth-century musical forms and dances. These pieces, like many others of his works for piano, were later arranged by Ravel for orchestra.

After the war, Ravel felt he must seek new paths. His old rival, Debussy, had died, and a whole new group of young French composers, "Les Six," was beginning to take over the musical leadership of France. Ravel, now "the old master" in his middle forties, set to work to regain his position. A shy man, he held no official position and did no teaching. His life was one of composing and living well. He still labored slowly, averaging about one work each year.

First came one of his few works written directly for orchestra, *La Valse (The Waltz)* —music that evokes the swirling dancers at the Viennese court of the middle 1800's and at the same time has an undertone of sadness that hints of the decay and downfall of the glittering Austrian Empire. *La Valse* was followed by Ravel's orchestral transcription of Mussorgsky's *Pictures at an Exhibition,* commissioned by the conductor Serge Koussevitzky.

While orchestrating *Pictures,* Ravel was writing one of his masterpieces: the Sonata for Violin and Cello, which he finished in 1922. In this sonata Ravel turned his back on the rich harmonies that had previously filled his music. He relied on long, wiry, melodic lines and driving rhythms. At times the two instruments are made to sound like a full string quartet. With this work Ravel

Portrait of Maurice Ravel by Nadar

showed his young colleagues that there were still a few tricks left in him.

Between 1922 and 1928 Ravel toured Europe and the United States, conducting and playing his own music. In Paris he had become fascinated by the black jazz musicians who were finding an appreciative audience there. When he came to New York he insisted on spending as much time as possible in Harlem night clubs, listening to the improvisations of the many fine black jazz musicians of the 1920's. Jazz melodies, harmonies, rhythms, and orchestral sounds began to creep into his music.

Between tours Ravel managed to turn out a strange little opera, *L'Enfant et les sortilèges (The Child and the Sorceries),* which he called a "lyric fantasy." He also wrote a sonata for violin and piano, with a curious slow movement that is a "blues" in two keys, and the exotic-sounding *Chansons madécasses (Madagascar Songs)* for voice, flute, cello, and piano.

In 1928 Ravel completed his most famous work: the *Boléro* for orchestra. Commissioned by the French dancer Ida Rubinstein, the *Boléro* is based on a Spanish dance rhythm. Ravel chose an eight-measure theme which is repeated over and over, always with different orchestral colors, reaching a huge, convulsive climax. Fond of talking down his own accomplishments, Ravel referred to this work as "seventeen minutes of orchestra without any music." But the *Boléro* became his most popular work, presenting, as it does, one of the most masterful displays of instrumental sounds ever conceived by a composer.

Ravel's health, never robust, began to fail. He did manage to finish two piano concertos: one for the left hand alone, and the other the often-played Concerto in G Major. The left-hand concerto was written for Ravel's friend Paul Wittgenstein, a German concert pianist who had lost his right hand in the war. Ravel's last work was a set of three songs for voice and orchestra for a movie—never made—based on the story of Don Quixote. The finale is a joyful drinking song: "I drink to the joy of life."

Ravel's music has many sides. Early in his career he was linked with Debussy as an Impressionist composer. Both men wrote music with colorful titles and used some of the same musical techniques—the medieval church scales; the oriental five-note, or pentatonic, scale; rich chords; and chords with vibrant dissonances. Both men were masters of orchestral sounds. But where Debussy's music consists of small fragments fitted together, Ravel's sweeps on in phrases that are almost Classical in form. Ravel's

Above: *a scene from the* Mother Goose *ballet (Opéra Comique production, 1948)*

Below: *Michel Renault and Madeleine Lafon in* Daphnis et Chloé *(Paris Opéra production, 1947)*

Ex. 9 — **Forlana** from *Le Tombeau de Couperin*

Allegretto

Ex. 10 — *Valses nobles et sentimentales* No. 3

Modéré

harmonies are often more complex in construction, but traditional in usage, as in the forlana—an Italian dance—from *Le Tombeau de Couperin* (Ex. 9). Debussy drew much of his inspiration from nature; Ravel, from dances of the past and present, from faraway places, from Spain. Debussy was always searching for new, vague forms, but Ravel could in his own very modern way be severely Classical.

Ravel's music is rarely emotional. It sounds, rather, as though he stood aside and looked at a waltz, a minuet, a sonata with amusement and affection. His music is often witty, usually elegant and polished. It is always colorful, always fresh and inventive (see Ex. 10 above).

RECITATIVE: a type of dramatic writing for voice that lies between ordinary speech and pure singing. It is usually sung, or declaimed, by a solo voice or as dialogue for several solo voices. The rhythm of a recitative is quite free, following the rhythm of the words of the text as they would be spoken rather than the regular rhythm of a song or aria. The melodic line of a recitative is most elementary—rising and falling as the voice would do in speaking the same words. There is usually one note for each syllable of the text.

Recitative is found in operas, oratorios, and cantatas, where it is used for dialogue or to explain or narrate the action, or to tell the story of the work. In early oratorios the recitative was called the *testo,* or text, of the story. A recitative is usually followed by an aria that comments on the action or tells something of the emotion of the character singing the aria.

The two types of recitative are the *secco* ("dry") and *stromentato,* or *accompagnato.* In *recitativo secco* the primary interest is in the words; the accompaniment consists only of an occasional chord played as background by a harpsichord or piano. *Recitativo secco* is an important part of Italian comic operas (opera buffa). The dialogue is fast and often funny, and the accompaniment is as sparse as possible, so that the audience can follow the words (Ex. 11).

Recitativo stromentato calls for an accompaniment of strings or even a full orchestra. It is used at highly dramatic points in an opera or oratorio, with the orchestra providing an agitated accompaniment as a comment on the words (Ex. 12, page 460). In expressiveness *recitativo stromentato* often comes close to being a dramatic aria.

The recitative style was one of the revolutionary musical developments of the late 1500's. Called *stile rappresentativo* ("theater style"), it grew out of an attempt to recapture the expressive style in which ancient Greek plays were thought to have been performed—the actors declaiming their lines instead of speaking them. Recitative was

Ex. 11—*Don Giovanni*, Act III, Scene 3, Mozart

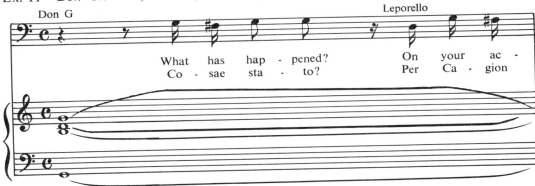

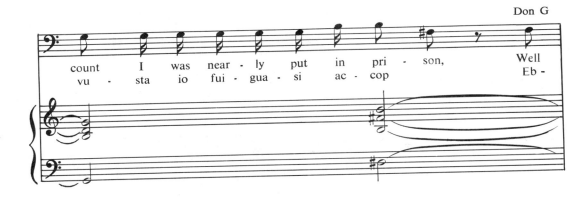

Ex. 12 — *Fidelio*, Beethoven

Ex. 13 — Piano Sonata, Op. 31, No. 2, Beethoven

Ex. 14 — Symphony No. 9, Beethoven

also partly a revolt against the non-dramatic and many-voiced church music and madrigals of the time. The early operas of Peri and Caccini and Monteverdi consist of many slow, noble recitatives, accompanied by chords indicated by the newly invented system of musical shorthand known as figured bass. Each line of verse ends with a cadence —an effect that makes for a certain amount of monotony, since the music is constantly starting and stopping. Once composers realized this, they began to alternate arias and choruses with their recitatives.

The French type of recitative was established in the late 1600's by Lully, who modeled it on the speech of the best actors in France. Lully's recitatives are often accompanied by orchestra and at emotional moments become ariosos, or little arias.

In nineteenth-century operas, as the orchestra began to play a larger role, the vocal melodies came closer to being recitatives. Wagner called the vocal writing in his operas *Sprechgesang*, or "speech-song"—a style that combines aria and recitative. Debussy, in his *Pelléas and Mélisande*, gives his singers almost nothing but recitative—thus coming back to the original sixteenth-century ideal of a declaimed play.

A modern type of recitative is that which Arnold Schoenberg used in his *Pierrot lunaire.* Schoenberg called this style *Sprechstimme,* "speech-voice." The reciter speaks the words approximately on the pitches and rhythms written by the composer.

Composers have used the jagged, dramatic rhythms and broad melodic range of recitative in instrumental works also. Beethoven was particularly fond of instrumental recitative, introducing it in piano sonatas (Ex. 13) and in his Ninth Symphony (last movement, before the entrance of the voices—Ex. 14).

RECORDER: an easy-to-sound but hard-to-master member of the flute family. It differs from other woodwind instruments in that the player blows through a whistle-type mouthpiece.

The recorder is made in three sections that fit tightly together. The upper part contains the mouthpiece, which can be adjusted to tune the instrument. Pushing the mouthpiece in raises the pitch; pulling it out lowers the pitch. The middle section contains six small holes on top and a hole for the thumb at the back. The small bottom section, the foot-joint, turns so that its one

Right: *an engraving showing the finger positions for the recorder*
Below: *a family of 18th-century German recorders made of wood, metal, and ivory*

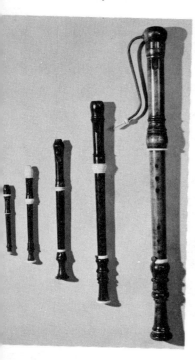

Each recorder has a range of about two octaves above its lowest tones:

Descant Treble Tenor Bass

The tones in its higher octave are produced by overblowing while half-closing, or "pinching," the thumb hole.

Well known in the medieval period, during the 1500's and 1600's the recorder became one of the most useful members of large and small orchestras. Shakespeare referred to it in several of his plays. Wealthy households had "chests" or "nests" of five to twenty-two recorders.

The medieval instrument was improved in the middle 1600's by Jean Hotteterre, the same man who invented the modern oboe and bassoon. He made the recorder in three sections so that it was easier to tune and to play. His instrument, called *flûte à bec* (mouthpiece flute) or *flûte douce* (sweet flute) in France, *flauto dolce* in Italy, and *Blockflöte* in Germany, became one of the favorite instruments of the great composers of the Baroque period. It could play long, singing melodies, as well as nimble bits of passage work (Ex. 15). Handel and Telemann wrote sonatas for it, and Bach gave it important solos in his cantatas and in his "Brandenburg" Concertos Numbers 2 and 4. Then, about 1750, the great days of the recorder came to an end. It was replaced by the more brilliant-sounding modern flute (called *flauto traverso* in old scores). The recorder, whose cool tones had blended so well with those of the soft viols and the small harpsichord, was unable to hold its own against the powerful new violins and the piano.

hole can be reached easily by the player's little finger. Four fingers of each hand are used in playing; the little finger of the left hand has nothing to do. The thumb of the right hand serves as the main support for the instrument.

At present recorders are made in four main sizes: the small descant, or soprano; the treble, or alto; the tenor; and the bass. In addition to these, there is also a small descant recorder called a sopranino, or, in Bach's scores, a *flauto piccolo*. The bass recorder is about three feet long—too long to have its top section put in the player's mouth. Instead it has a curved pipe through which the player blows. The holes on the bass recorder are widely spaced, so that large hands are needed to stretch from hole to hole. The smaller recorders are the most popular.

Ex. 15 — "Brandenburg" Concerto No. 2, J. S. Bach

For more than one hundred fifty years the recorder was out of sight and sound, although a relative of it survived in such places as the mountainous country of Spain and southern France. This was the three-hole pipe played by the pipe-and-drummer at village dances. He played with his left hand, keeping his right hand free to beat the drum.

In 1919 an Englishman, Arnold Dolmetsch, became interested in playing old music on the instruments for which the music was written. He began to make recorders based on Hotteterre's model. Along with a revival in home music-making, people discovered the beauties of the recorder—its sound, its ease of playing, and its low cost. Factories began to turn out quantities of recorders. Publishers once more issued music for the instrument, and schools started classes in recorder playing. Groups of music lovers have formed recorder societies, and many contemporary composers have written solos and chamber music for this venerable instrument.

REGISTER: a part of the total pitch range, or compass, of an instrument or voice that has qualities distinct from the other parts of this range. On the clarinet, for example, the bottom octave, with its rich, deep tones, is referred to as the *chalumeau* register. Above that lie the *middle* register, where the tones are mellow but not quite so resonant, and the *top* register, where the tones are bright and penetrating.

Voice registers are referred to as *head* (high) and *chest* (low).

The *tessitura* of a vocal or instrumental part relates to the register or part of a register in which most of the notes of the part are written. The tenor line in the choral part of Beethoven's Ninth Symphony, for example, has a high tessitura—meaning that the tenors are almost always singing near the top of their range.

Register also refers to the set or series of pipes controlled by one organ stop. The "registration" of an organ sound is the combination of stops selected by an organist or indicated by the composer.

RELATIVE: describes the affinity that exists between a major and a minor key which have a common key signature. Relative keys lie at a distance of a minor third from each other. The minor key that shares the key signature of a major key is called its relative minor. Conversely, the major key can be called the relative major of a minor key. The relationship depends on which key is stated first. E-flat major and C minor, for example, have a common key signature of three flats. If C minor is stated first, then E-flat becomes its relative major; when the first key is E-flat, then C minor is its relative minor.

The relationship between one key and its relative major or minor has been an important factor in musical form. During the Baroque period, many compositions started in a minor key and moved quite soon to the relative major. Having the tonal resources of two keys at his disposal, the composer was able to achieve a great deal of harmonic variety. Ex. 16 shows the opening of a saraband by Handel—it starts in G minor and moves to B-flat major at the end of the first section. During the Classical

Ex. 16 — Saraband from Suite No. 7 for Harpsichord, Handel

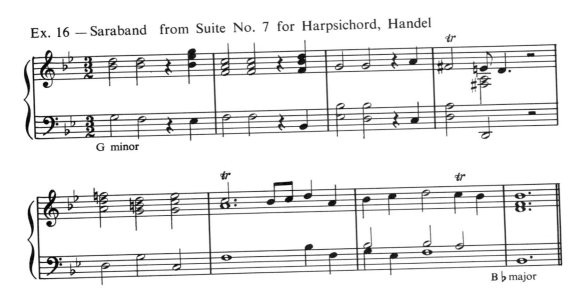

Ex. 17 — Sonata in B Minor, Haydn

period a sonata-allegro movement that began in a minor key almost invariably moved to the relative major for its second theme and key area (Ex. 17). The relative major-minor association declined in importance in the nineteenth century as composers searched for new and different key relationships.

The term "related keys" refers to the relationship that exists between a tonic key and the keys built on the first six notes of the tonic scale. In the first movement of Bach's "Brandenburg" Concerto Number 4, for example, the tonic key is G major. During the course of the movement the related keys of D major, E minor, A minor, C major, and B minor—all tones of the original scale of G—are touched on.

RENAISSANCE MUSIC: music of the period in history between medieval and Baroque times, about 1450 to 1600. The word *renaissance* is French for "rebirth." Renaissance scholars and artists took pride in recovering a level of achievement which they associated with the most glorious moments of Classical times.

But the Renaissance is much more than its name would suggest. In music, as in science and painting, it was a period not only of revival but of discoveries and beginnings —an age of pioneers. Columbus and Magellan gave men a new picture of the earth, with a vision of new lands beyond the seas. Copernicus, discovering that the earth revolved around the sun—not the reverse— created a new view of the universe and of man's place in it. In painting, a new sense of space appeared, achieved through the discovery of perspective. Pictures were now multiplied by means of woodcuts and engravings, as were texts by the invention of movable type. A lay culture came into being, independent of the Roman Catholic Church, and the church meanwhile was split by the Reformation and weakened by the establishment of the Church of England.

The great surge of faith that had raised the spires of cathedrals on the horizons of medieval Europe was now ebbing, and the vision of an afterlife was fading. A new age had begun. Man was discovering himself as the center of things. In the new philosophy, called humanism, the artists, writers, and composers were giving free rein to their curiosity and enthusiasm about all that was immediate, earthly, and human. When artists such as Leonardo da Vinci and Michelangelo did treat religious themes, they brought to them a concern for the human body and human emotion hardly known to the Middle Ages.

Music played an important part in Renaissance life. There was music in the cathedrals, where it fulfilled its traditional role in the liturgy. There was music in the halls of the nobility—and many of the provincial courts rivaled the church in the splendor of their musical establishments. There was music—of a do-it-yourself variety—in homes and wherever a few voices and a lute could be gathered around one of the new songbooks the printing presses were now turning out. German tradesmen and craftsmen joined together in forming guilds of mastersingers, carrying on the musical tradition of the earlier knightly minnesingers. And there was music even in the streets, where—continuing a medieval tradition—wandering minstrels, pipe-and-drummers, singing peddlers, and bagpipers brought their tunes to even the poorest of the citizens. Catholic congregations heard the flowing polyphony of the masses and motets of Dufay, Josquin Des Prés, Lassus, and Palestrina. Venetians thronged to St. Mark's to experience the crossfire of sound from the two organs and the multiple vocal and instrumental choirs as they gave forth the glorious music of Andrea and Giovanni Gabrieli.

In the Lutheran churches the congregation sang the new chorales—the stepwise melodies in even rhythm which were sometimes new tunes and sometimes old chants and folk tunes. The chorales would ultimately serve as the basis of new choral and instrumental forms in Germany.

Following the lead of the English composer John Dunstable (c. 1370–1453), the Roman Catholic religious music of the Renaissance took on a style that was brought to its highest point by a succession of composers from northern France, Belgium, and Holland. Known as the Netherlands School, it included Dufay, Ockeghem, Obrecht, Josquin Des Prés, Willaert, and Lassus. As these Netherlanders traveled, they taught composers of other countries how to weave the contrapuntal lines which they spun out so beautifully. One of the last of the Netherlands School was an Italian—Palestrina. His expressive music, breathing great purity of religious feeling, set the standard by which Roman Catholic church music came to be judged.

In the music of the Netherlands School the main interest lay in the weaving together, in different voices, of long melodic lines. These lines were so constructed that the ear heard a succession of consonant harmonies. Even though the emphasis was on musical lines, the three-tone triads that resulted along the way became more and more important. To fill out the triad, the bass part gradually gave up its share of the melodic line and in time became what it has remained—the foundation of the harmonies above it. The music of the early Renaissance is polyphonic—many-voiced. By the end of the period, composers had become interested in writing a single melody with blocks of chords accompanying it—a style known as homophony.

The masses and motets were full of learned devices of composition. The newly discovered art of writing canons, in which all voices repeat the same melody, grew into art-

Renaissance musicians practicing on their instruments (woodcut by Hans Burgkmair)

fully mystifying puzzles. These "puzzle canons" were prefaced by a riddle that had to be solved before the canon itself could be sung. The puzzle canons were not so much to be heard by an audience as they were to be enjoyed by the composer and whichever of his friends could figure them out. Ockeghem, Obrecht, and Josquin Des Prés particularly delighted in canons of every conceivable type.

It was also at this time that secular melodies found their way into church music. Masses in the Renaissance period were written on a cantus firmus—a melodic line that ran through the work like a thread. Originally the cantus firmus was a Gregorian chant sung in long notes by the tenor. But when composers discovered that a popular melody served just as well, they produced masses on such popular tunes as "The Armed Man," "Good-bye, Lover," and "Kiss Me." The tunes were disguised by changing the note values and by covering them with so many other melodies that no one really heard much of the tune.

As composers came to be employed by kings and nobility rather than by the church, they began to break away from the Netherlanders' involved style. Music for entertain-

ment—listening or dancing—could not be so complex. Italian and French composers developed the madrigal, a song for four or five voices. In some sections of a madrigal counterpoint would be used; in others, the voices sang together in the same rhythm, making a series of chords. Harmony thus came to be used as a new expressive element in its own right.

Throughout the latter part of the Renaissance composers had become more and more concerned with expressing the literal meanings of words. They made their music suggest the emotion that lay in such words as *suffering, joy, crying, laughing. Run* and *fall,* for example, were sung to melodies that ran in fast notes or fell down the scale; *suffering* called for a chromatic, almost wailing, melodic phrase. The French composer Janequin (*c.* 1485–*c.* 1560) wrote choral works that were pieces of program music—based on bird calls, street cries, hunting sounds, and even the sounds of battle.

The early madrigals by Arcadelt (*c.* 1505–*c.* 60) were beautiful love songs. Those by the later composers, Lassus and Marenzio (1553–99), were filled with strange harmonic and melodic progressions. They pointed the

way for Gesualdo (*c.* 1560–1613) and Monteverdi, whose madrigals reached such a pitch of dramatic intensity that they were in fact short music dramas. Gesualdo's melodies and harmonies are so wild and unpredictable as to seem like music written in the twentieth century. Monteverdi's madrigals, from his Fourth Book on, are filled with melodies exactly like early operatic recitatives.

Light madrigals were called canzonettas or balletti. The balletto was a dance song, often with a phrase of nonsense syllables or a string of "fa-la's" that keeps coming back like a refrain. The gayest balletti were those by the Italian Gastoldi (*c.* 1550–1622); it was under his influence that the English composers came to write the "fa-la's" and "Hey, nonny-nonnies." Playwrights of the period, including William Shakespeare, often threw in a "fa-la" song at a light moment.

English music reached its greatest heights in the late-Renaissance period of Elizabeth I. Byrd, Morley, Weelkes, and Gibbons wrote many beautiful choral and instrumental works, while Dowland and Campion turned out subtle and charming songs with lute accompaniment. The lute had become the most popular home instrument. Systems

that taught one how to play it were published in great numbers, like the how-to-do-it books of today. A method of notation called tablature told the player which finger to put on which fret of the fingerboard; the method is still used today for chords on the ukulele.

The spread of music was greatly furthered by the invention of the printing press. Books of religious songs were published as early as 1476. In 1501 the Venetian printer Ottaviano dei Petrucci published the first book of part songs: the *Harmonice musices odhecaton.* In these early publications the paper was sent through the presses three times: once for the staff lines, once for the note heads and stems, and once for the words. Not until 1525 did a printer invent a way of printing everything at once.

The printing press contributed tremendously to the growth and spread of music. No longer was it necessary to copy everything by hand. Small singing groups could gather together and from their part books sing music from all over Europe. It was part of a gentleman's and a lady's training to be able to pick up a part book and read a madrigal at sight. Each book contained only one part. Complete scores, with the parts aligned one below the other, were just coming into use at the end of the Renaissance.

Instrumental music, which had been ignored by the monks who did much of the copying of music, could now be printed and sent around. Dance music, which had always been in existence but seldom written out, now became a legitimate part of musical culture.

The instruments of the Renaissance were related to the same string, woodwind, brass, percussion, and keyboard families that exist today. In general the tone quality of Renaissance music was softer. The instruments were far from perfected, and not too many technical difficulties were put in front of the players. The primary instruments were the viols, trumpets, trombones, and cornetts (woodwind instruments with a cup-shaped mouthpiece like that of the trombone). Shawms, recorders, and cromornes *(crumhorns)* were the woodwinds. The organ had reached a high state of development, as had the clavichord and the harpsichord. The zither and the bagpipe were popular, along with the lute and its guitarlike Spanish relative, the *vihuela de mano.*

The instruments on this page, from left to right, are: a straight trumpet, a folded trumpet, a portative organ, a harp, and a vielle

In the early Renaissance the instruments played along with the voices, doubling them or replacing them. Tuneful songs, called *chansons* in France, *frottole* in Italy, and *Lieder* in Germany, were written with a melodious upper voice part that was accompanied by less interesting lower voices played by instruments. They were love songs, story songs, drinking songs, and dance songs. Written in the major-minor system rather than in the old church scales, or modes, these songs were close to dance music, with their regular accents and repeated rhythmic patterns.

As composers began to write music for instruments alone they modeled their works on the vocal music of the day. The ricercar was like the motet; the canzona was like the chanson. Both forms ultimately developed into important musical forms of the seventeenth century—the ricercar into the fugue, and the canzona into the early sonatas.

Renaissance composers based much of their instrumental music on popular dances, just as Bach, Chopin, and Gershwin used dance forms in many of their works. The dances were often composed in pairs, a fast following a slow one: pavane-galliard, allemande-courante, passamezzo-saltarello. The saraband, later to become stately, was beginning its career in Europe as a rather wild dance, frowned on by the authorities. The pairings of the dances would lead, in the seventeenth century, to the groups of dances known as suites or partitas.

Musicians in all periods have improvised. Sometimes the written improvisations of the Renaissance performers were quite free. A piece might start with a series of chords, go on to rapid running notes, and end with a lot of imitative, or canonlike, writing. Such works were given various names: fantasia, prelude, and toccata.

Other improvisations were built on themes that already existed—a song, or the bass of a slow dance. Composers realized that they had hit on a new instrumental form: the variation. The earliest variations that have come down to us are those for the keyboard by the Spanish composer Antonio de Cabezón (1510–66).

English composers at the end of the Renaissance were particularly fond of keyboard variations. For the small harpsichord, known in England as the virginal, composers such as Byrd, Bull, Farnaby, Morley, and Gibbons wrote variations as well as dance tunes, fantasies, and preludes by the hundreds. Most of these show how much music had changed since 1450. The music is measured off by bar-lines, the major-minor scales are used practically always, and involved counterpoint has given way to harmony that moves in relation to its tonal center, or tonic. Melodic interest, once distributed equally among the voices, now has centered on a simple, tuneful melody carried by the top voice. A good way to come to know this music is through the *Fitzwilliam Virginal Book*—currently available as a two-volume paperback—which contains close to three hundred keyboard pieces of this period.

Instrumental music, which came of age during the Renaissance, undoubtedly reached its peak in St. Mark's Cathedral in Venice. Here the Gabrielis wrote glorious and splendid music for as many as five choirs of voices and instruments. It was Giovanni Gabrieli who wrote the famous *Sonata pian e forte*, an instrumental work for two choirs of instruments. One choir consisted of cornetts and trombones, the other of a viol and trombones. The sonata has glowingly contrasting instrumental colors as well as the "echo" effect with which many composers were experimenting. The score of this earliest sonata (1597) is important not only for the music itself but also because it was the first time any indication was being given as to how fast or how loud a musical work was to be played. It also pioneered in the specifying of instruments by the composer.

The wealth of many Italian families allowed them to put on elaborate entertainments. Always seeking novelties, they encouraged composers to work in new forms. Out of these entertainments came, in 1581, the first ballet—*Le Ballet comique de la reine,* based on the legend of Circe. And from the *intermedie* (musical interludes in plays), from the madrigal operas (in which actors mimed while singers sang the text), and from attempts to produce plays in the style of the ancient Greek tragedies came a whole new approach to music, taking the form of opera.

By 1600 the world of music was ready for its next style period, that of the Baroque. But no later period would ever surpass the Renaissance as the highest point in many musical forms. Its music still lives today—much of it recently reprinted for the first time since 1600. Singing groups are discovering the beauties of the vocal writing of Josquin Des Prés, Lassus, and Palestrina. Brass groups have discovered the rich, stirring sonorities of the works of the Gabrielis, and keyboard players have taken up many works by the English virginalists. Singers include solo songs by Dowland and Campion on their recital programs. Today Renaissance music is having its own rebirth.

Ex. 18a

Ex. 18b — Gregorian Notation

REQUIEM MASS (*Missa pro defunctis* in Latin; *messe des mortes* in French; *Totenmesse* in German): the solemn Mass for the dead sung in Roman Catholic churches at funeral services, on the anniversaries of deaths, and on All Souls' Day, November 2. The chief characteristics are its opening section, the Introit "Requiem aeternam' (from which the Mass gets its name), and the Dies Irae. The Gloria and Credo of the Ordinary of the Mass are omitted from the Requiem Mass, probably because of the conflict of their joyful words with the somberness of the occasion.

The sections of the Requiem Mass, then, are:

1. Introit (*Grant them eternal rest, Lord*)
2. Kyrie (*Lord, have mercy*)
3. Dies Irae (*Day of wrath, day of judgment*)
4. Offertory (*Lord Jesus Christ, King of Glory*)
5. Sanctus (*Holy, holy, holy*)
6. Benedictus (*Blessed is he who comes in the name of the Lord*)
7. Agnus Dei (*Lamb of God, who takest away the sins of the world*)
8. Communion (*Eternal light, shine on them*)
For absolution after the Mass:
9. Responsory (*Deliver me, O Lord*)

While composers had written settings of the Requiem Mass as early as the sixteenth century (Palestrina, Lassus, and Vittoria), its dramatic quality was not fully exploited until the late eighteenth century. Since that time there has been a long list of vivid and even theatrical settings by Mozart, Cherubini, Berlioz, Dvořák, Verdi, and Fauré. Brahms's *German Requiem* is not a Requiem Mass but a large vocal and orchestral work, based on selections from the Bible, written in memory of his mother.

The Dies Irae, a thirteenth-century addition to the Requiem Mass, is quite long. In musical settings, as in Mozart's Requiem, it is often broken into sections: Dies Irae, tuba mirum, Rex tremendae, Recordare, Confutatis maledictus, and Lacrymosa. More than any other section of the Requiem Mass the dramatic words and doomful Gregorian chant melody of the Dies Irae have appealed to the imaginations of composers (Ex. 18a and b). It has been used as a theme by Berlioz (*Symphonie fantastique*), Liszt (*Totentanz*), and Rachmaninoff (*Rhapsody on a Theme by Paganini, The Isle of the Dead, Symphony Number 3, Symphonic Dances*).

RESTS: signs used to indicate silence in music. For dramatic purposes and practical ones too (singers and wind players need time to breathe), a method to measure silences had to be invented as soon as rhythmic notation came into being. The earliest rests were vertical ⌐ or ⌐, or the letter S, an abbreviation for *sine*, meaning "without (sound)." At some time in the thirteenth century each type of note was given a comparable rest symbol. In modern notation the most usual rests and their equivalent notes are:

A rest may have a dot after it to add half again the value of the rest:

𝄽 · = 𝄽 + 𝄾 = 1/4 rest plus 1/8 rest

Composers use more rests in orchestral music than in piano music. A large group of performers must phrase their playing so that they will all release a note at exactly the same time. This timing can be indicated more accurately by rests than by phrasing marks:

Piano Version

Orchestral version of the same rhythm:

Instrumental parts often have rests of several measures duration. When there are no changes of meter within the rest time, and regardless of the number of beats in a measure, they are indicated by a whole rest with a number above it to show how many measures of rest there are:

(a)

or, in manuscript:

(b)

RETROGRADE: literally, going backward. In music the term refers to a composition or part of a composition that can be played or sung backward as well as forward. Ex. 19 shows a minuet *al roviesco* ("in reverse") from a sonata by Haydn in which the second part is the exact reverse of the first. It is doubtful whether any listener would recognize the second part of this minuet as the reverse of the first part. Retrograde motion is not meant to be heard as such but is, rather, a method used by a composer to organize his music.

As early as the fourteenth century, composers delighted in writing and solving musical puzzles containing retrograde motion. Retrograde canons, called crab canons or cancrizan canons, were used by Bach in his *Musical Offering*, but for more than one hundred fifty years thereafter few composers were interested in the old polyphonic devices. Today, however, modern composers have rediscovered them. Composers of twelve-tone music—Schoenberg, Berg, and Webern—used retrograde motion and retrograde inversion (backward and upside down) —as two of the four forms of their tone-rows (Ex. 20). They also used retrograde motion in the form of their music, as in Schoenberg's *Pierrot lunaire,* in one section of which the music goes forward to a midway point and then works its way exactly backward.

Ex. 19 —Piano Sonata in A; also Sonata for Violin and Piano No. 4, Haydn

Ex. 20 —A Twelve-tone Row

Retrograde Inversion of the Above

Ex. 21 — *Ludus Tonalis,* Hindemith

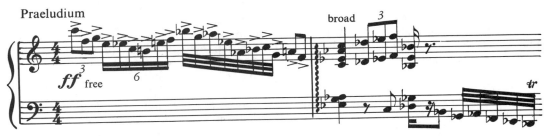

In Hindemith's piano work *Ludus Tonalis,* the Postludium is, with the addition of a final chord, the Praeludium to the same work, but upside down and backward (Ex. 21). Hindemith also used retrograde motion in his little opera *Hin und Zurück.* Here not only the music but also the stage action moves backward from a center point.

RHAPSODY: a composition in free form, particularly popular in the late nineteenth century. The form was used for compositions that were heroic in feeling, full of broad, sweeping melodies and brilliant passage work. In form a rhapsody has an improvisational quality, at times being like a medley of themes stitched together and decorated. The word comes from ancient Greece, where a rhapsody was an epic poem, or section of one, recited with dramatic passion and intensity.

Among the earliest examples of this musical form are Liszt's *Hungarian Rhapsodies,* based on gypsy themes, and Brahms's two *Rhapsodies* for piano, Opus 79, which date from the 1850's. Brahms's *Rhapsodie* for alto, male chorus, and orchestra dates from 1869. Since these, many rhapsodies have been written for various instruments: Debussy's *Rapsodie* for clarinet and orchestra, Ravel's *Rapsodie espagnole* for orchestra, and Bartók's two *Rhapsodies* for violin and orchestra. Gershwin's famous *Rhapsody in Blue,* for piano and orchestra, was written for the first concert of jazz music given by Paul Whiteman's orchestra in 1924. It follows the free plan of Liszt's rhapsodies but uses jazz themes. Gershwin wrote a second rhapsody which has not achieved the success of the first. Rachmaninoff's *Rhapsody on a Theme by Paganini,* for piano and orchestra, is a true rhapsody—singing, passionate, glittering—even though its form is a theme and variations. Berg called the second scene of his opera *Wozzeck* a rhapsody, although it is a tightly knit form based on a progression of three complex chords.

RHYTHM: the organization of musical tones in time. It includes the factors of beat (pulse), meter, tempo, and metronomic accuracy as well as patterns of long and short note values. It is rhythm that gives life and form to musical sounds. The word comes from a Greek word meaning "to flow."

Time, in a musical sense, must flow as a river flows—not always at the same rate of speed but always with motion. The composer Stravinsky has said, "Rhythm and motion, not the element of feeling, are the foundations of musical art."

Rhythm, then, has to do with *all* musical timing. For a whole musical composition it determines where the climax occurs, how fast the harmony changes, where the music breathes at cadences, and how one section balances another in terms of time. The great masters of music—Bach, Beethoven, Haydn, Mozart—were masters of timing. They knew that the right note must come at the right time; otherwise it is not the right one.

Despite the importance of rhythm, very little has been written about it. Mostly this is so because rhythm must be felt; it cannot be seen or heard. No one has ever seen time; one sees or hears only the effect of time *on* something. Even the clock ticking off its minutes cannot account for the fact that some minutes pass more quickly than others.

There are many ways in which rhythm is a part of life. Blood is driven through the arteries rhythmically. A person breathes at more or less regular intervals, at a rate which depends on how calm or excited he is. The earth spins on its axis, making night and day. The moon waxes and wanes in about twenty-eight days, and the seasons change at regular intervals.

Music, too, exists in terms of different time spans. The pulse of the blood is like the pulsing of the fundamental beat of a musical work, and in fact most musical tempos are related to the average human pulse rate ($\quarternote$ = 60, 90, 120, etc.). Just as a person's pulse speeds up and slows down, so does musical pulse have flexibility. A musical phrase is like breathing—longer and slower than the pulse but related to it. In music that suggests excitement, the phrases are often shorter, just as breathing gets faster with excitement or exertion. A whole composition might be compared to the twenty-four-hour cycle of day and night, for within that cycle many things happen, and the pulse and the breath speed up and slow down many times.

Rhythm is a common factor in all cultures. Dance music usually has an obvious pulsing beat. Vocal music tends to depend more on long breath-rhythms.

In western European music of the medieval and Renaissance periods there was a great variety of rhythmic pattern in the same work. The flow of the words often determined the rhythm of the music. Even so, a certain rhythmic form developed in the works of Palestrina and Lassus. A sense of momentum was achieved by starting a work with long note-values, gradually decreasing the length of the notes, while saving the greatest amount of rhythmic activity for cadence points. The effect is that of a stream which starts slowly and gathers speed as it tumbles downhill.

As instrumental music grew in importance in the seventeenth and eighteenth centuries, it posed new problems of rhythmic organization for the composer. Corelli and Vivaldi, among others, solved the problem by inventing "motor rhythms" which, once set in motion, drove through a whole allegro movement on sheer momentum.

As instrumental works increased in length from two- or three-minute movements to those lasting fifteen to thirty minutes, the composer was faced with even greater difficulties. One of the great achievements of Haydn, Mozart, and particularly Beethoven was their architectural treatment of time. Such planning in the abstract realm of rhythm depends on a superb sense of timing—on the ability to know just how long to carry on a musical idea before bringing in an element of contrast. The composer must mentally balance one phrase against another, one long section with a later section, as Beethoven builds a weighty coda to balance a lengthy development section in a symphony.

It was Beethoven more than anyone else who broke away from previous concepts of rhythm and forced his performers and listeners to think of rhythm in its larger aspects. Particularly was this true in his last string quartets. His approach to rhythm, however, was not understood by many of his successors. It remained for twentieth-century composers, especially Debussy and Stravinsky, to make use of some of Beethoven's findings.

Composers of the nineteenth century were more intent on stretching out their harmonic phrases so that their works existed over a long time span. They exploited the dramatic possibilities of rests—the dramatic silence of rhythm. Wagner, whose rhythm followed the ebb and flow of his emotionally charged words, almost succeeded in doing away with cadences through the adroit handling of his "endless" harmony. This was based on continuity rather than predictable resolutions.

Rhythm in the twentieth century has been treated variously. Schoenberg and his followers, particularly Webern, avoided rhythmic patterns that had any relationship to the past. Meters and tempos changed constantly, so that it is often difficult for the listener to feel any pulse—although he is much more aware of the irregular phrases that stop and start like unrelated thoughts. Following the lead of Webern, composers "serialized" rhythm, treating time values as they did pitches, so that there is practically no repetition. The result is kaleidoscopic in its ever-changingness.

Stravinsky, of all twentieth-century composers, was most aware of the impact of rhythm. There is in his music a rhythmic interplay from one block of sound to another. Some of these blocks last a few seconds, others a half minute. Within each there is often a propelling ostinato that holds the unit together. Stravinsky was concerned (as were Mozart and Beethoven in a different way) with contrast: the making of a musical form by juxtaposing seemingly unrelated elements. (Many people speak of contemporary music as being "disjointed," forgetting that more often than not music has been built in patterns of starts and stops. They have accustomed themselves to the stops and starts of the composers of the Classical period, but have heard too little contemporary music to adjust to its rhythmic form.) Such an approach to rhythm is also typical of the long-time experimenter Edgard Vàrese. American composers and some European composers have been influenced by the syncopations of jazz. In Gershwin's and some of Copland's music, the jazz element is immediately apparent. Related to jazz are the nervous rhythmic patterns of much of the music of Copland and Schuman. Elliot Carter has focused his attention on rhythm and has developed a type of "rhythmic modulation" in which the length of the beat is subtly lengthened or shortened.

The new medium of electronic music has posed its own problem of rhythmic organization. No rhythmic pattern, or combination of patterns, is too complex to be handled electronically. As yet, however, no aesthetics of rhythm has arisen to dominate the thinking of the composers writing electronic music. Composers have been more concerned with experimenting in timbre than in time. The situation is much like that of the seventeenth century when new instrumental idioms ultimately led to new rhythmic forms.

Another group of avant-garde composers, following the lead of John Cage, has left rhythm to chance—along with pitches. Music, they argue, is a slice of life. Events happen in haphazard fashion; therefore it is all right for rhythm to be equally haphazard.

Charles Ives, who was also concerned with the way sounds coincide, either in harmony or as clashes, composed music in which two, three, or even four seemingly non-related rhythms are played at the same time. The resultant sound is as exhilarating as it is complex.

While tonality, traditional ideas of melody, and conventional instruments often seem to be disappearing, rhythm remains as the most important factor of musical organization. Above all else, music exists in time.

RICERCAR: a contrapuntal instrumental work especially of the sixteenth and early seventeenth centuries. The earliest ricercars (the name means "to seek out") date from about 1500 and are written for lute. They are "free" forms in several sections—much like a toccata or fantasia—consisting of alternating scale passages and series of chords. Because of the character of the lute, these early ricercars contain only suggestions of counterpoint.

Later in the sixteenth century, the ricercar took on the sectional form and the polyphonic texture of the vocal motet (whose sectional form depended on the number of lines in the text that was set). As in the motet, the themes or subjects usually started with long notes, giving a dignified character to the ricercar. There are occasional exceptions, as in Andrea Gabrieli's "Ricercar del 12 tono," written for viols; here the themes are sprightly (Ex. 22).

Ex. 22 — "Ricercar del 12° tono," Andrea Gabrieli

Ex. 23 — Ricercar in E, Froberger

(a)

(b)

(c)

Froberger used the title of Ricercar for organ works that are based on imitative counterpoint and are like a succession of fugues on the same subject. Ex. 23 shows the beginnings of three sections of Froberger's Ricercar in E. Part I is in duple meter; Part II, with a slight rhythmic change in the theme, is in triple meter; Part III is in duple meter again, with the principal theme in augmentation while a second theme provides rhythmic motion. One main difference between Froberger's ricercars and Bach's fugues is that Froberger almost always restricts his statement of the theme to two keys, whereas Bach goes much further afield. Also, the element of suspense built up by Bach in a fugal episode is lacking in Froberger, who mostly confines himself to restating the theme. Froberger achieves variety—and surprise—through his inventive handling of contrapuntal lines.

Bach included a ricercar in his *Musical Offering.* Then, for two hundred years, the form was ignored, but it has been rediscovered by contemporary composers in their search for old forms that could be adapted to new techniques. Among those recently written in the form are three ricercars for piano and orchestra by Norman Dello Joio (1913–   ) and a ricercar for piano by Gian Carlo Menotti (1911–   ) on themes from his chamber opera, *The Old Maid and the Thief.*

Dancing the rigaudon

RIGAUDON: a lively dance that first came to general notice when it became popular at the court of Louis XIII of France around 1630. Its music is written in 2/2 or 4/4 time, is trippingly light in quality, and begins on the fourth quarter note of the measure—the quarter note usually being divided into two eighth notes:

Ex. 24 — Rigaudon from *Pièces de clavecin*, 1724, Rameau

The dance featured running, hopping, and turning movements that were ideal to show off nimble feet. By the late seventeenth century the rigaudon had become a favorite dance form in French ballets and operas. It was also used by composers in their instrumental suites or dance collections, as in Ex. 24 from a piece for harpsichord by Rameau.

Scholars do not agree on the origin of the rigaudon. Some say it came from Italy; others, from southern France. (In France several different kinds of folk dances are called *rigaudons*.) The form was popular in England around 1700, where its name became "rigadoon," and it was very much like the hornpipe danced by English sailors. Few composers have written rigaudons since 1750. Among the few are Saint-Saëns, MacDowell, Prokofiev, Grieg, and Ravel.

As a composer Rimsky believed, as did the rest of "The Five," in using Russian stories as the basis of symphonic poems and operas. His melodies are based on Russian folk tunes, using ancient modal scales and oriental scales. His harmonies, while not as startling as Mussorgsky's, are often boldly dissonant and highly spiced. His orchestration, rich and varied in sound, uses the instruments uniquely. Many of the orchestral sounds of Debussy, Ravel, and early Stravinsky are modeled on the glowing orchestration of Rimsky-Korsakov.

Rimsky-Korsakov's most popular orchestral works are the colorful *Scheherazade, Capriccio espagnol, Russian Easter Overture,* and the suite from the opera *Tsar Saltan* (which includes the famous "Flight of the Bumblebee"). His fifteen operas are popular in Russia but seldom performed outside Slavic-speaking countries. The best known

Above: *Nicolai Rimsky-Korsakov*
Below: *scene from a 1959 Russian production of* Sadko

RIMSKY-KORSAKOV, NICOLAI (1844–1908): the most prolific of the group of Russian composers known as "The Russian Five." Like the others, Rimsky-Korsakov was not trained as a professional musician. He studied the piano as a child, but his early career was that of a naval officer. While still a cadet he met Balakirev, leader of "The Five," who encouraged and helped him in composition. After a two and one-half year tour of duty as an officer Rimsky-Korsakov settled in St. Petersburg (now Leningrad). Here, at the conservatory, he became in 1871 a teacher of composition and orchestration, having largely taught himself these subjects. His Opus 1 was a symphony—the first full-fledged one by a Russian composer. For a while he held the post of inspector of bands and orchestras in the Russian navy, and thus was able to learn much about the use of wind instruments.

Rimsky's self-teaching helped him to become one of the best teachers of composition. Among his students were Glazunov, Liadov, Arensky, Ippolitov-Ivanov, Gretchaninov, and Stravinsky. His writings included a book on harmony, another on orchestration, and an autobiography—*The Chronicle of My Musical Life.*

of his operas are *Pskovityanka (The Maid of Pskov), Maiskaya Notch (May Night), Mlada, Sniegurotchka (The Snow Maiden), Sadko, Tsar Saltan, Pan Voyevoda (The Commander),* and *Le Coq d'or (The Golden Cockerel).*

Rimsky-Korsakov revised and re-orchestrated the works of many of his friends: Dargomyzhsky's *Kamennyi Gost (The Stone Guest);* Borodin's *Prince Igor;* and Mussorgsky's *Night on the Bald Mountain, Khovanshtchina,* and *Boris Godunov.* These labors of love caused much criticism of Rimsky-Korsakov, because he tampered with the melodies and harmonies, but it was through his efforts, and in his versions, that these masterpieces gained acceptance in the musical world.

RING OF THE NIBELUNGS, THE *(Der Ring des Nibelungen):* a cycle of four operas by Richard Wagner; one of the monumental achievements in the whole field of music. The first opera, *Das Rheingold (The Rhine Gold),* is relatively short; the other three—*Die Walküre (The Valkyrie), Siegfried,* and *Götterdämmerung (Twilight of the Gods)—* are quite long. Wagner called the complete cycle "A festival stage work for three days and an introductory evening." *The Ring* was dedicated to Wagner's patron, King Ludwig II of Bavaria. It was first performed in its entirety at Wagner's theater in Bayreuth, Germany, in 1876.

The writing of the words and music for *The Ring* occupied Wagner for twenty-six years—with time out for writing *Tristan and Isolde* and *Die Meistersinger.* The libretto is based on the old German and Scandinavian myths of the gods. The stories were changed by Wagner, partly for dramatic effect and partly to fit Wagner's philosophy that most of the evils of the world are due to man's striving for gold and the power that gold will bring. Throughout the operas the gods and demigods cheat, lie, and murder in their attempts to win the ring made from the gold of the Rhine. Love, to Wagner the most important thing in life, is the only challenge to the corruption of power, and love must be given up by those who seek only power.

Wagner worked on the libretto for five years. He started with the story of the death of Siegfried in *Götterdämmerung.* Feeling the need for preparatory explanation, Wagner worked backward, writing *Siegfried,* then *Die Walküre,* and finally *Das Rheingold.* To knit the gigantic work together the composer relied on a large number of leitmotifs: short, vivid themes used to represent persons, things, or ideas. The leitmotifs, usually heard in the orchestra, serve various purposes in addition to being used as symphonic themes that can be developed. They often tell what is going on in the mind of a character, even if the words seem to be saying something different. They also tell the audience things that are not known to the characters on stage, as when Sieglinde tells Siegmund of the wandering old man who has thrust a sword into the ash tree—and the orchestra lets us know that the old man was the god Wotan. At times the motives are developed and woven together as though the music were the synopsis of a story, as in "Siegfried's Funeral March." Wagner substituted preludes for the traditional overture and built the preludes on motives, setting the scene for what was about to happen or giving the audience a sense of the action before the rising of the curtain.

With the comparatively few notes of a motive Wagner was able to portray the inner essence of a character or of a situation. The motives range from the heroic, straightforward "Sword":

to the writhing "Dragon" (Ex. 25); from the tenderness of "Love" (Ex. 26) to the tragedy of "Death" (Ex. 27). No human emotion is left out of Wagner's vocabulary of motives. He is the master psychologist among composers, overwhelming his audience as he plays on their emotions.

Scene from Das Rheingold *(Bayreuth production, 1963)*

The music of *The Ring* is given largely to the orchestra. It is the leading voice as it comments on every word, every action. It tells the truth to the audience and at times cries out in anguish at the unfolding tragedy.

The orchestra for *The Ring* was the largest ever used up to that time. Wagner demanded three or four of each wind instrument, including bass trumpets and trombones plus eight horns, two sets of timpani, six harps, and a full body of strings. To fill out his brass section, on which he relied so heavily, Wagner invented the Wagner tuba —a cross between the tuba and the French horn. He also asked for eighteen anvils to hammer out the rhythm of the Nibelung forge. With such a large array of instruments Wagner was able to achieve a tremendous variety of sounds, from the merest murmur to the most thundering climax. The full brass, by itself, gives massive sounds, majestic and solemn as befits the gods. The woodwinds sing beautiful solos or chatter away in their own group. The strings, freed from being a support to the winds, soar and are ecstatic or heartbreakingly sad.

Harmonically the music of *The Ring* is almost always restless, making a kind of "endless harmony" to support Wagner's "endless melody." There are few final cadences throughout the work. Just as the listener feels an ending approaching, Wagner slides off with an unexpected chord that sets up a wholly new musical section. In order to achieve dramatic effects he used highly chromatic chords, or chords in unusual progression (Ex. 28), mixing his harmonic colors like a painter getting unusual tints and shades from his palette.

Ex. 25

Ex. 26

Ex. 27

Ex. 28 — *Die Walküre* (Magic Sleep)

The usual operatic arias are missing from *The Ring*. The music flows on, following the dramatic line of the libretto. The singers, who need large voices and much strength to be heard above the large orchestra in the pit, have few long, lyrical lines. For the most part they sing in a declaiming fashion—a style which Wagner called *Sprechsingen*, "spoken song" or "singing speech." The vocal sections that come closest to being arias are Siegmund's impassioned love song in *The Valkyrie* ("Winter storms give way to the blissful spring") and Brünnhilde's Immolation Scene—the last scene in *The Ring*. These excerpts plus a few orchestral scenes—"The Ride of the Valkyries," "Siegfried's Funeral March," and "The Magic Fire Music"—are often performed at orchestral concerts. Most of the music of *The Ring* is too much a part of the dramatic action to be played or sung by itself.

Staging *The Ring* presents many problems. Wagner called for scenic effects which are almost impossible to produce. The Rhine must seem to flow across the stage while the Rhine maidens swim and dive in it. The Valkyries must ride their horses through the air from mountaintop to mountaintop. Men must become invisible or turn into giant serpents. At the end of *The Ring* the Rhine must flood across the stage while Valhalla, the home of the gods, goes up in flames. In most opera houses the poor quality of the scenic effects interferes with the enjoyment of the opera. Recently several scenic designers, including Wagner's grandson Wieland, have experimented with stages that do not attempt to be realistic.

More books and articles have been written about *The Ring*—its music and its philosophical meanings—than about any other musical stage work. Such respect, in addition to the many performances of the cycle, is a tribute to the many-sided genius of Richard Wagner.

THE STORY OF THE RING

I. *Das Rheingold (The Rhine Gold)*

The prelude suggests the surging waters of the Rhine (Ex. 29). For 136 measures only an Eb-major triad is heard as it builds up to the motive of the Rhine. On a rock in the center of the Rhine is the Rhine gold, guarded by three Rhine maidens. Alberich, a member of the dark, dwarfish Nibelung clan, tries to make love to the maidens, who mock him and repulse him. They tell him what power the gold would have if it were made into a ring—the power to conquer the world if one gives up hope of love. Alberich curses love, grabs the gold, and disappears.

Meanwhile the gods admire their new castle, Valhalla, even as they worry about paying its builders, the giants Fasolt and Fafner. Wotan, chief of the gods, has promised the giants that they would have Freia, the goddess who keeps the gods eternally young by supplying them with golden apples from her garden. The crafty Loge, god of fire, tells the giants and the gods how Alberich has made himself all-powerful by fashioning a ring from the Rhine gold. Greedy for the treasure, the giants agree to give Freia back if they are given the gold.

Wotan and Loge descend deep into the earth to the home of the Nibelungs. There Alberich has enslaved his fellow dwarfs, who quarry treasures from the earth and hammer out the precious metal (to the accompaniment of a motive whose rhythm Wagner wanted sounded on eighteen anvils). Loge tricks Alberich into showing off the powers of the Tarnhelm, a metal helmet which allows the wearer to become invisible or to assume any shape he desires. First Alberich becomes a huge serpent; next he becomes a toad, whereupon Wotan and Loge seize him and tear the Tarnhelm from him. To ransom himself, Alberich gives up all his treasure. Furious with rage, he puts a curse on the ring—a curse of death and sorrow to whoever wears it.

The giants are given all the gold, including the Tarnhelm and the ring, and immediately the curse starts its evil work. The giants, brothers though they are, quarrel about the division of the loot, and Fasolt is killed. Fafner puts the gold in a sack and departs as the gods proudly march across a rainbow bridge to their new castle, Valhalla.

Wieland Wagner

Ex. 29

Ex. 30

Ex. 31

Ex. 32

II. *Die Walküre (The Valkyrie)*

This second opera in *The Ring* takes place some years after the end of *Das Rheingold.* Out of a driving storm, dramatically painted in the prelude (Ex. 30), comes Siegmund, a member of the Wälsung race. His father was Wotan, who hoped by marrying a mortal woman to raise a hero who would recover the ring from Fafner and return it to the gods. By chance, Siegmund stumbles exhausted into the house of his enemy, Hunding. Siegmund is allowed to stay the night but is warned by Hunding that in the morning, even though defenseless, he will have to protect himself. Siegmund has fallen in love with Sieglinde, Hunding's wife, not knowing that she is his long-lost sister. In one of the few arias of *The Ring* he pours out his passionate love for her (Ex. 31).

Sieglinde gives Hunding a sleeping potion. She shows Siegmund a sword that has been thrust into an ash tree by a wandering old man. (The orchestra at this time lets the audience know that the old man was Wotan.) No one yet has been strong enough to draw the sword from the tree, but Siegmund, with a mighty effort, succeeds. He names it Nothung (Needful). Then the lovers flee from the sleeping Hunding.

Meanwhile Fricka, Wotan's wife and goddess of marriage and the home, accuses Wotan of helping Siegmund break Sieglinde's marriage vows. Wotan promises that in the oncoming fight between Hunding and Siegmund he will aid Hunding. Brünnhilde, one of the nine Valkyries (the warrior maidens whose job it is to bring fallen heroes to Valhalla), is Wotan's favorite daughter, and she knows how much he had counted on Siegmund to recover the ring. In spite of Wotan's warning she attempts to shield Siegmund in the fight with Hunding, but her efforts are in vain. Wotan splinters Siegmund's sword, and Siegmund is mortally wounded by Hunding.

To the galloping motive (Ex. 32) of the Valkyries in the orchestral prelude known as "The Ride of the Valkyries," Brünnhilde's sisters gather round her. Knowing that she has disobeyed her father, they refuse to help her. Brünnhilde gives Sieglinde the pieces of Siegmund's sword and prophesies that to Sieglinde will be born a glorious hero whose name shall be Siegfried. She sends Sieglinde off to a forest and steels herself to meet her father.

Wotan, torn between love for his daughter and anger at her disobedience, sentences her to the loss of her godhood. She is to be put into a deep sleep, and whoever wakens her can take her as wife. To insure that only a great hero will do so, Wotan calls on Loge to encircle with fire the mountaintop which will be Brünnhilde's resting place. The opera ends as the flames leap around the sleeping Brünnhilde.

Birgit Nilsson as Brünnhilde and Jerome Hines as Wotan in Die Walküre, *Act III (Bayreuth production, 1960)*

A scene from Act I of Siegfried (Bayreuth production, 1966)

III. *Siegfried*

Siegfried, whose mother Sieglinde died as he was born, has been brought up to young manhood by one of the Nibelungs—Mime, brother of Alberich. The treasure of the Rhine has been stored in a cave by Fafner, who by means of the Tarnhelm has transformed himself into a dragon. Mime attempts to forge a sword from the broken fragments of Siegmund's weapon, hoping that somehow he can get Siegfried to use the sword to kill Fafner, thus securing the treasure for him— Mime. Mime is told by Wotan that only one without fear can forge the sword. Siegfried, tested by Mime and found to be fearless, takes on the job and does it. After testing the sword by shattering an anvil with it, he sets forth to slay the dragon. Fafner sets himself to pounce on Siegfried, but the boy plunges the sword into the dragon's heart.

A drop of Fafner's blood has fallen on Siegfried's hand. Tasting it, Siegfried is suddenly able to understand the chattering of a bird which has been flying around him. The bird tells Siegfried of the treasure, and particularly of the Tarnhelm and the ring. Mime now tries to force on Siegfried a drink with a sleeping potion, so that he can kill him. But the dragon's blood enables Siegfried to read Mime's thoughts, and, furious with Mime, Siegfried slays him.

The bird that has been so helpful to Siegfried now tells him of the sleeping Brünnhilde and the fire surrounding her. Only one without fear shall awaken her—and Siegfried knows that he is without fear.

Joyously he follows the bird until they meet Wotan, who tests the youth by barring his way with his spear. The magic sword shatters the spear of the god, who then points the way to the mountaintop. Siegfried braves the fire and awakens Brünnhilde with a kiss.

The opera ends with a rapturous love duet filled with some of Wagner's most glowing and passionate music.

IV. *Götterdämmerung (Twilight of the Gods)*

A scene in which the Norns, the weavers of Fate, see the end of the gods serves as a brooding, doomful overture.

Siegfried, having placed the ring of the Nibelungs on Brünnhilde's finger as a symbol of his love, rides out into the world. His journey takes place in the minds of the audience as it listens to the long orchestral piece known as "Siegfried's Rhine Journey." He is welcomed at the castle of the Gibichungs by King Gunther, Gunther's sister Gutrune, and their half-brother Hagen, whose father was Alberich.

Before Siegfried's arrival, Hagen plots to get the ring through Siegfried. He tells Gunther, who is unmarried, about the beautiful maiden asleep, surrounded by fire, who would make him a great queen. Since Gunther, knowing fear, cannot penetrate the fire, Hagan persuades him to use Siegfried as his emissary. Siegfried, to whom Hagen had given a magic potion that wipes out all memory of Brünnhilde, falls in love with Gutrune and swears blood-brotherhood with Gunther. Then Siegfried, wearing the Tarnhelm and taking the form of Gunther, returns through the magic fire to Brünnhilde. He takes the ring from her finger and forces her to return to the castle of the Gibichungs. There she is to become the bride of Gunther while Siegfried is betrothed to Gutrune.

At right: Götterdämmerung, *Act I (Bayreuth production)*

The wedding celebration is the one "crowd" scene in *The Ring*—the only place where choral singing occurs. During the festivities, Brünnhilde tries to make Siegfried understand that she is his wife, but the magic potion has worked too well. In her despair and bitterness, she desires vengeance and tells Hagen—who needs the information for his plan—of the one place where Siegfried can be harmed: in the back.

A woodland hunting scene opens, with the Rhine maidens playing and singing in the water. When Siegfried enters alone, they tease him to give them his ring. When he offers it, they insist that if he were to keep it his death would occur that very day. Siegfried, unable to know fear, keeps the ring.

Hagen, Gunther, and the rest of the hunting party arrive for the midday rest, and when Hagen asks Siegfried to tell him the meaning of the bird's sounds, Siegfried offers to tell him the story of his life instead. While Siegfried is telling his story, Hagen puts a drug into some wine and offers it to Siegfried. As Siegfried drinks, his memory is restored, and he tells of his finding of Brünnhilde. As he is transported by the memory of their love, Hagen asks him to read the runes of two ravens flying overhead. Siegfried turns to look at the birds, and Hagen stabs him in the back with his spear. Siegfried dies.

The body is brought back in funeral procession. The orchestra reviews the history of the Wälsungs and the life of Siegfried in one

Götterdämmerung, *Act II (Bayreuth production, 1963)*

of Wagner's most magnificent scores, known as "Siegfried's Funeral March." Brünnhilde asks that a funeral pyre be prepared. She takes the ring from Siegfried's finger as his body is lifted onto the pyre. Then she mounts her horse and leaps into the blaze.

The Rhine pours over everything. Hagen rides into the water still after the ring, but the Rhine maidens drag him down into the flooding river. The ring has returned to its home.

In the distance Valhalla and all its gods crash and blaze to destruction. The orchestra sings the beautiful motive (Ex. 33) of "Redemption through love" as the curtain comes down.

Ex. 33

RITE OF SPRING, THE *(Le Sacre du printemps):* an epoch-making ballet with music by Igor Stravinsky. Its first performance, by Diaghilev's Russian Ballet in Paris in 1913, set off one of the greatest uproars in the history of music and theater. Many in the audience screamed themselves hoarse trying to get the curtain to come down. An equally noisy group demonstrated in favor of the work.

The causes of the furor were the primitive choreography by Vaslav Nijinsky and the equally primitive-sounding music by the young composer Igor Stravinsky. The dancers used heavy, earthy, turned-in movements—far removed from the customary pretty ballet steps. The music was percussive, dissonant, rhythmically unbalanced. The instruments shuddered, screamed, and pounded.

Since this first performance a half century ago, the music has become a standard work on orchestral programs. It is still exciting, even though the novelty of its sounds has worn off. Musically it influenced a whole generation of composers and stands as one of the great landmarks of contemporary music. As a dance, however, it has not fared as well. Expense for the large number of dancers and the tremendous orchestra has limited the number of performances, although the ballet has been revived successfully several times. One of the revivals, in Philadelphia and New York City in 1930, featured Martha Graham.

Martha Graham in The Rite of Spring, *1930*

The ballet was based on a scenario by Stravinsky and the scenic designer Nicholas Roerich. Rather than a plot the ballet is built on a series of dances which praise the fertility of the earth. It reaches a violent climax with the frenzied sacrificial dance of a chosen virgin. The ballet is set in pagan Russia, more than a thousand years ago. It is in two parts: The Adoration of the Earth and The Sacrifice.

The ballet begins with a soft introduction. The bassoon in its highest register plays a long, halting melody which has primitive embellishments of grace notes (Ex. 34). This builds up to mysterious flutterings in the winds and strings, and then dies down. A group of adolescents dances to the steady pounding of combined F-flat and E-flat major chords in the strings. A battery of eight horns punctuates the steady rhythm with syncopations (Ex. 35). Out of this grows a folklike tune (Ex. 36), to which is added an important slower theme (Ex. 37). Around these themes Stravinsky weaves ostinatos, or repeated patterns—his favorite compositional device. Fanfarish music, with constantly changing meters, accompanies a game of abduction by rival groups of boys and girls. This is followed by a Spring Dance, using thematic material as in Ex. 37, in a slow and heavy version over a lumbering ostinato in the bass instruments. Rival groups try to outdo each other while the orchestra alternates between boiling over with activity and singing a small-interval theme (Ex. 38). Into the rivalry march the ancient sages, accompanied by a pompous theme in the tubas and by nervous ostinatos. After a short silence, a wild running dance ends the first section.

Part II opens with an introduction which is an Impressionist piece suggestive of the mysterious sounds and feelings of night. Soft, subdivided strings, sometimes in high harmonics, play a lyrical motive accompanied by constantly shifting chords in the oboes (Ex. 39). A group of young girls dances in a magic circle, as though in a trance. A wild dance, glorifying the chosen virgin, has much motion in all the instruments—and little actual thematic idea. It is followed by a strange ritual dance performed by the old men of the tribe. The music builds on top of a shuffling, snaking idea. The old men surround the Chosen One and dress her in the sacrificial garments. She begins to dance convulsively as the orchestra plays short spasms of motives. The meter changes from bar to bar (Ex. 40). The Chosen One trembles with ecstasy and hysteria; her irregular, jerky movements build to a frenzy. A sudden spasm—and she is dead.

Ex. 34

Ex. 35

Ex. 36

Ex. 37

Ex. 38

Ex. 39

Ex. 40

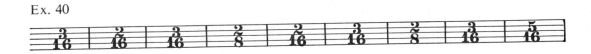

Ex. 41 — Prologue, *Orfeo*, Monteverdi

RITORNELLO: a musical phrase that keeps returning. In early operas an instrumental ritornello came at the beginning of an aria and, like a long, dramatic form of punctuation, between sections of an aria. The most famous ritornello is the noble theme heard in Monteverdi's opera *Orfeo*. It occurs before and after each of the four verses of the prologue of the opera and is heard also in later scenes (Ex. 41).

Since 1600 the ritornello has been used in almost all forms of music both vocal and instrumental. The "vamp till ready" of vaudeville songs and the recurring flourish of the country fiddler between the calls of a square dance are both related to the ritornello.

Composers of the Baroque period, starting with Torelli (1658–1709), based many of the allegro movements of their concertos and concerti grossi on the ritornello principle. The full orchestra, the tutti, states the main theme, which will be the ritornello. Then follows a section by the soloist which leads to a statement of the ritornello theme in a new key. This alternation of soloist and ritornello in various keys continues until the ritornello theme finishes in the key in which it originally started.

Richard Rodgers

RODGERS, RICHARD (1902–1979): America's most prolific writer of outstanding popular songs. Born in New York City, he studied the piano and attended Columbia University and the Juilliard School of Music. From the age of sixteen, when he met his first collaborator, Lorenz Hart, Rodgers wanted to be a song writer. When "Manhattan" and other

Rodgers and Hart songs became hits of the lively *Garrick Gaieties* of 1925–26, Rodgers gave up his alternate career of selling children's underwear and went on to become the most successful of popular song writers.

The team of Rodgers and Hart turned out hit after hit: "Blue Room," "My Heart Stood Still," "With a Song in My Heart," "Lover," "Blue Moon," "Small Hotel," "Johnny One-Note," "Falling in Love with Love," "Bewitched," and hundreds more. Hart's clever and impudent words were matched by Rodgers' melodies. Seemingly straightforward and simple, these contained subtle harmonic shifts, sophisticated rhythmic patterns, and all avoidance of anything routine. They ranged in feeling from sentimental ballads to satirical patter songs; in style, from lilting waltzs to sophisticated jazz rhythms.

Along with the Gershwin brothers, Rodgers and Hart changed the form of the Broadway musical show. They made the song grow out of the dramatic situation, instead of the reverse. The show was all of a piece, including semi-serious ballet when necessary. *On Your Toes* (1936), for example, was about ballet, government, and gangsters, and included the long ballet "Slaughter on Tenth Avenue." With *Pal Joey* (1940), based on a character out of stories by John O'Hara, the team produced a new kind of dramatic musical—one with a "heel" for a "hero."

After the death of Hart in 1943, Rodgers turned to another collaborator, the already well-known Oscar Hammerstein II. Between them they continued the revolution of Broadway to the point where the American musi-

Richard Rodgers (center) with two of his early collaborators: Herbert Fields and Lorenz Hart

cal became more important than the serious drama.

Two of the long-running Rodgers and Hammerstein shows received Pulitzer prizes: *Oklahoma!* in 1944 and *South Pacific* in 1950. Other shows by the team ran for several years—*Carousel* (1945), *Allegro* (1947), *The King and I* (1951), *Flower Drum Song* (1958), and *The Sound of Music* (1959). Even after their Broadway runs ended, the Rodgers and Hammerstein shows continued to be performed all over the world.

For a while after the death of Hammerstein in 1960, Rodgers worked without a partner, writing both words and music for the successful *No Strings*, produced in 1962.

In 1952 Rodgers wrote the thematic material for one of the most popular television film series: *Victory at Sea.* These themes were developed and arranged by Robert Russell Bennett, who also made a symphonic suite from the material.

Of Rodgers' music his long-time partner, Oscar Hammerstein, has said: "Each melody adheres to the purpose for which it was put into a play. It is romantic, funny, or sad according to the situation for which it was written and the character required to sing it."

Rodgers' early songs were tuneful hymns to his beloved Manhattan. Later his songs deepened, taking their inspiration from the whole world. In return, the world loves and admires his songs.

Yul Brynner and Gertrude Lawrence in a scene from The King and I

ROMANCE or **ROMANZA:** a quiet, tender work for instrument or voice. It is usually songlike in quality and seems to give voice to the tender sentiments of the composer. A romance is not a musical form but rather a musical mood. As the title of a musical work, it was most popular with nineteenth-century composers.

Among the earliest romances (the French form of the word), or romanzas (the Italian form), are the slow movements of Mozart's Piano Concerto in D Minor, K. 466, and Beethoven's two "Romances" for violin and orchestra. The poetically minded Robert Schumann was fond of the title and wrote three romances for oboe and piano, three for piano solo, twenty-nine romances and ballads for mixed chorus, and twelve romances for women's chorus. The beautiful slow movement of his Symphony in D Minor is called (by the German form of the word) "Romanze."

ROMANTIC PERIOD: the years between the late 1700's and 1900, which saw the emergence of highly individual musical styles. The age was one of great contrasts—in musical literature and musical esthetics. It was the epoch of such diverse forms as the short, intimate preludes of Chopin and the thundering concertos of Liszt and Rubinstein; the fresh, lyrical love songs of Schumann and the bitter, satirical songs of Mussorgsky; the dazzling orchestral works of Berlioz and the dark-hued symphonies of Brahms; the light-hearted operettas of Offenbach and Sullivan and the monumental, brooding *Ring of the Nibelungs* by Wagner.

Romanticism takes its name from the medieval "romances," which were stories and poems about heroic figures written in the language of the people—Italian, French, or Spanish—rather than in the classical Latin of scholars. Romanticism represents an approach to life and to art completely different from that of Classicism. Whereas Romanticism tends to be personal and subjective, stressing freedom, Classicism is impersonal and objective, operating within discipline. No one period or individual is completely Romantic or Classical, but the personal element in creative expressions of the nineteenth century was so strong that the whole century has been called the Age of Romanticism.

The Romantic period started with a literary movement in Germany in the late eighteenth century. During the next thirty or forty years Romantic ideas spread from Germany over the rest of Europe, becoming the credo not just of poets but of dramatists, painters, dancers, and composers. Possibly because of the literary origins of Romanticism there was some poetic inspiration at the root of all the arts of this time. Musical compositions were often given descriptive titles or conformed to literary programs, just as paintings often attempted to portray stories.

Romanticism can be regarded as a subconscious revolt by sensitive, creative persons against the onrushing Industrial Revolution and its mechanization of work, which seemed to threaten the dignity of man. The artist, turning away from the present, sought his inspiration in legends of faraway places and times, or he looked to Nature and idealized the quiet, idyllic life of the rustic village or the beautiful, yet mysterious forest with its wandering stream. For drama he looked to the vast and untamed sea or the unleashed powers of the storm. Not content with his lot, the Romantic poet and composer seems always to be yearning through his work for something just beyond his grasp—the love of an unattainable woman, the swashbuckling career of a hero-warrior, the supposedly simple, untroubled life of the savage or the tiller of the soil. His desires were always unfulfilled, his dreams unrealized.

The Romantic artist was involved with the somewhat contradictory ideas of nationalism and the universal brotherhood of man. He longed for freedom—political and social. His music, dances, poems, and paintings symbolized an era that saw first the American and French revolutions, then the unification of Germany and Italy by zealous patriots, the abolition of slavery in the United States, and the freeing of the serfs in Russia.

The Romantic age was one that prized individuality. Each man sang, like Walt Whitman, a song of himself. The popular idea of the composer as the long-haired Bohemian who, between love affairs, writes works that no one can understand comes from this period. It is true that Paganini and Liszt wore their hair long, but so did many of the politicians of the time. Some composers did have love affairs, as did bankers and merchants. A few composers, notably Berlioz and Wagner, met resistance to their works, but on the whole the composer of the nineteenth century did find an audience for his music. The composer as a man living in his mental ivory tower apart from the rest of the human race—the Artist with a capital A—was just another myth that the Romantic helped to popularize, just as he popularized older myths and folk tales.

But along with the myths there were certain real differences between the nineteenth-century composers and those of previous centuries. Almost without exception the earlier ones had been trained from early youth to be professional musicians, skilled in all branches of performance and composition. Many composers of the nineteenth century, such as Berlioz, Wagner, Schumann, and Mussorgsky, came to music comparatively late in life. Wagner and Berlioz were professional conductors, representing a new branch of performance in which musical understanding was needed more than technical skill.

The Romantic composer took himself and his art with great seriousness. For him, music was not mere entertainment but a passionate expression of personal thoughts and feelings. Earlier composers had been content to let the musical content of a work speak for itself; they had called their compositions simply "fugues," "sonatas," or "symphonies"—titles that told only the form of their works. The Romantic composer wanted to be sure that his listeners were hearing in his music exactly what he intended, so he gave his music specific titles and sometimes even prefaced a work with a short poem. He wrote essays or stories to explain his musical beliefs, so that if his musical message was not clear the words would make it so. In doing this the composer was not downgrading his audience; he wrote the explanations because he knew he was dealing with an audience different from that of earlier composers, who wrote for a knowing few. No longer in the employ of the church or a court, the composer now depended for his livelihood on sales of his music or, if he was a performer, on admissions paid to his concerts.

The audience did indeed have much to do with changing the musical styles of the nineteenth century. It was made up of newly affluent members of the rising middle class who were attracted to an art event by showmanship as much as by artistic merit. They thronged to hear such artists as Paganini, the "wizard" of the violin; Liszt, the most dazzling of all pianists; and Jenny Lind, the "Swedish nightingale." They supported a host of virtuoso pianists, violinists, and singers who happened to be the sensations of the moment. It was during this period that the solo recital came into being.

But music was not performed solely in the concert hall, salon, and opera house. There was much home music-making, helped by the popularization of such newly invented instruments as the accordion and the harmonium. Each well-to-do family demonstrated its devotion to culture by owning a

piano, placed in the parlor, there to be played on by the young ladies of the household. The great increase in the numbers of amateur performers prompted the writing of many short, not-too-difficult works as well as the composing of many glittering fantasies on operatic arias which sounded more difficult than they were. While most of the young ladies aspired no higher than to play such works as "The Dying Poet" or "The Maiden's Prayer," others realized that a concert career was open to them. For the first time women appeared as professionals, and one of them, Clara Schumann, became an outstanding concert artist.

The demands made on virtuoso performers led to the writing of exercises and études that young pianists could practice in their drive for technical mastery of the instrument. The earliest of these "methods" were those of Johann Baptist Cramer (1771–1858), published in 1815, and Muzio Clementi (1752–1832), in 1817. These études became the daily fare of generations of aspiring pianists. They were followed by the well-known and musically dull studies by Czerny, and by the difficult but beautiful études of Chopin and Liszt.

The eagerness for training in music resulted in the establishment of conservatories throughout Europe and the United States. Conservatories had existed in Italy since Renaissance times, but these had been simply orphanages that stressed music. In France the Conservatoire National de Musique was formally established in 1795. This was followed by the setting up of similar institutes in Prague (1811), Brussels (1813), Vienna (1821), London (the Royal Academy of Music, 1823), and Leipzig (1843). The Leipzig Conservatory, founded and directed by Mendelssohn, became the model for many other conservatories in the world, particularly in America, where the Oberlin (1865), New England (1867), and Cincinnati (1867) were among the earliest.

Many permanent choral and orchestral societies came into being in the nineteenth century. Singing societies consisting of amateur singers led by a professional conductor were especially popular in Germany, England, and the United States. Of these groups the Handel and Haydn Society is the oldest, having been started in Boston in 1815. The need for new choral music led to the writing of many fine secular works by such composers as Brahms and Schumann. But church music, hitherto accounting for a large part of most composers' output, was not neglected. Monumental sacred works for chorus and orchestra were composed by Beethoven,

Salon concerts, such as depicted in this painting of Franz Schubert at the piano, were quite popular in the Romantic period

Mendelssohn, Berlioz, Verdi, Dvořák, and Brahms.

Except for the Leipzig Gewandhaus Orchestra, which was formed in 1743, symphony orchestras before 1800 were either small groups of musicians in the steady employ of a wealthy nobleman or bands of instrumentalists gathered together for a specific concert. But in the nineteenth century, orchestras were established to give a number of concerts each year for subscription audiences. Among the earliest of these were the London Philharmonic Society (1813), the orchestra of the Paris Conservatory (1828), and the Vienna and New York Philharmonic orchestras, both dating from 1842.

Musical culture was spread, meanwhile, by the appearance of new music journals such as Robert Schumann's *Neue Zeitschrift für Musik* and the founding of many publishing houses, including Peters and Schött in Germany, Novello in England, Ricordi in Italy, Durand in France, and G. Schirmer in the United States. The earliest permanent music publishing house was that of Breitkopf and Härtel, established as the firm of Breitkopf in Leipzig in 1719.

Scholars of the nineteenth century, following the lead of the scholars of the last part of the eighteenth century, were intensely interested in the past—in art history, in archaeology, even in the origins of man himself. In music this preoccupation with the past took several forms. Mendelssohn, in the 1830's, revived the great choral cantatas and passions of J. S. Bach, which had been forgotten for more than eighty years. Many scholars, beginning with Johann Gottfried von Herder (1744–1803), had begun to collect folk songs, and composers started to use folk melodies in their works. Musical scholarship based on a rigid, Germanic, scientific approach led to the establishment of the discipline of musicology—the study of the history of music based on textual evidences rather than on hearsay and possibly faulty traditions.

The musical forms and styles of the nineteenth century grew out of those of the preceding Classical period. Works called "sonata," "quartet," "concerto," and "symphony" were related to works with similar names by Mozart and Haydn in over-all plan. But starting with Beethoven's Third Symphony, the "Eroica," the nature of these large forms changed considerably. Movements became longer and thematic contrast became greater. Composers wrote fewer works in these larger forms because each work was now a major one. The total number of symphonies written by Beethoven, Schubert, Schumann, Mendelssohn, Brahms, Bruckner, and Tchaikovsky combined was far less than the 104 composed by Haydn. The concerto now was a piece to be performed only by a great virtuoso. Since the virtuoso was primarily a performer rather than a composer-performer, the cadenzas which the soloist had previously improvised were now written out for him by the composer.

Chamber music, while continuing as an intimate form of music-making, also became a form of concert music, often dominated by the increasingly powerful piano. The size and sonority of the piano itself increased as the virtuosos played in larger halls and as technical demands by the composers called for a quicker action and a greater range of tone-color. At the hands of a Liszt or Brahms the piano became, in effect, a kind of one-man orchestra. Likewise the string quartet, which originally provided a delightful pastime for four musicians, now became a medium that demanded the utmost skill and much re-rehearsal time for the proper performance of Beethoven, Schubert, Schumann, and Brahms.

The true chamber music of the period was the art song, or lied. The art song, as opposed to the operatic aria, had disappeared since the days when the Elizabethan composers in their lute songs had brought the form to a high peak. The Romantic composer saw the art song as the perfect vessel into which he could pour out his soul. He conceived it as a duet for singer and pianist, the accompaniment being at least as important as the vocal line and, often, providing the dramatic background that gave the song its essence. The art songs of Haydn and Beethoven inspired the writing of more than 600 songs by Franz Schubert. At his hands each song became a miniature drama, and the song cycle—itself a nineteenth-century idea —became a complete dramatic tapestry. The art songs of Schubert, along with those of Schumann, Liszt, Berlioz, Wolf, Brahms, Mussorgsky, and Fauré, make up one of the greatest treasuries of the Romantic period.

In their emphasis on the literary and pictorial aspects of music, composers wrote many short piano pieces under descriptive titles as specific as "Child Falling Asleep," "Witches' Dance," and "The Spinning Wheel," or as general as "Bagatelle," "Nocturne," and so on. Such short pieces were often grouped together into larger works, which also carried such titles as *Carnival, Scenes from Childhood,* and *Pictures at an Exhibition.*

The orchestra gave composers great opportunities to "paint" musical scenes in an almost realistic manner. Storms were conjured up in musical tones by Beethoven, Rossini, and Wagner. The motion as well as the sound of the sea was suggested in orchestral colors by Mendelssohn, Wagner, Debussy, and Rimsky-Korsakov. The use of tone to "paint" a picture was part of the Romantic's idea of the fusion of the arts. Poets tried to achieve musical values in their poems, and Impressionist painters aimed at the fluidity of music. Wagner thought of his operas as *Gesamtkunstwerken*—works that were all-encompassing. From simple nature painting it was a small step to the symphonic poems of Liszt, Saint-Saëns, Strauss, and Franck, which told a story or even projected a philosophy.

Orchestral composers benefited from the many new or improved instruments that became available. Tonal freedom came to the trumpets and the French horns, which, thanks to the addition of valves and pistons, were now able to play the chromatic scale throughout their entire range instead of being restricted to the overtones of one fundamental tone. The woodwinds were improved so that their players could surmount almost any technical difficulty. Even the stringed instruments were changed by increasing the height of the bridge and by lengthening the strings, so that the resulting tone was brilliant and powerful enough to hold its own in the ever-growing orchestra.

The invention of the tuba gave the brass a true bass that provided a richly resonant fundamental tone for the trombones, horns, and trumpets. The creative mind of the fine instrument-maker Adolphe Sax (1814–94) gave to composers the saxhorns (a whole family of brass instruments) and the saxophones, which were to become such important members of the jazz band. The dainty-sounding celesta was welcomed into the orchestra almost as soon as Mustel invented it. The addition of all these instruments, plus the bringing of the piccolo, trombone, bass drum, snare drum, triangle, and cymbal from the opera orchestra, gave the composer of the middle and late nineteenth century greatly heightened orchestral resources, which have continued in use—with increasing numbers—until today.

The art of dance, to which music has been so closely allied, underwent revolutionary changes in both social and theatrical forms in the early nineteenth century. The waltz reigned supreme in the worlds of ballet and ballroom. As a social dance it scandalized some who saw it as a symbol of a breakdown in morality. Here were men and women dancing together as a couple rather than as two members of a formal pattern. But as other couple dances came into society from eastern and middle Europe—mazurka, polka, and polonaise—such dances became the usual thing rather than the exception. Group dances did not die out, but they took the form of the folksy, gay quadrille. Meanwhile Lanner and the Strausses turned out lovely, danceable waltzes while other composers idealized this form, Chopin stressing its poetic lilt, Tchaikovsky its sensuous, long line, Brahms its tenderness, and Mahler its nostalgic memory of an earlier, happier time. To Berlioz goes the honor of introducing the waltz into the symphony, which he did in his *Symphonie fantastique.*

The Romantic "white" ballet, such as *La Sylphide* (1832), flourished in Paris. In the

Adolphe Sax

Caricature of Berlioz, 1891

Caricature of Rossini, 1867

The "great ones" often gathered together: a painting by J. Danhauser showing Liszt at the piano in Rossini's home. George Sand sits behind Liszt (dressed as a man) and Alexander Dumas père sits next to her. Victor Hugo, Paganini, and Rossini stand, from left to right, behind Liszt. Marie d'Agoult sits at his feet

last third of the nineteenth century Russia challenged Paris, as did the Royal Danish Ballet. Unfortunately the music of many of the earlier ballets of the period was routine and uninspired. It took the genius of Delibes in Paris and Tchaikovsky in Russia to elevate ballet music to a high level.

In the early part of the nineteenth century, opera had different appeals in different countries. Italy was partial to the light buffa operas of Rossini; Vienna took all forms to its heart; and Paris, responding to the grandiose ideas of Napoleon, developed spectacular grand opera. As in so many aspects of the Romantic movement, the audience and the composer interacted to create new forms.

The serious audiences that attended performances of opera in Paris were interested in the "rescue" operas, in which plots were

as suspenseful as those of a dramatic film today, with the forces of good triumphing over those of evil and injustice. From rescue opera it was an easy transition to grand operas based on truly serious subjects, such as Rossini's *William Tell,* Halévy's *The Jewess,* and Meyerbeer's *The Huguenots.* Meyerbeer was the German-born master of operatic effects. His works were theatrical, colorful, and masterfully designed for both orchestra and voice. Meyerbeer exerted a powerful influence on Richard Wagner, the genius who was to carry German opera to its loftiest heights.

German Romantic opera had emerged full-fledged with the first performance of Weber's *Der Freischütz* in 1821. The way had been paved by many light Singspiels that were based on folk tales and contained folklike melodies. *Der Freischütz* contrasts cozy, homey scenes with those of evil and dark magic. It was from the strange combination of *Der Freischütz* and the serious spectacle operas of Meyerbeer that the weighty, myth-laden operas of Wagner were born.

Wagner summed up almost all aspects of Romanticism. He was the poet-philosopher-musician who saw the totality of opera—or music drama, as he called it—in the bringing together of words, action, scenery, and music. Opera was the perfect vehicle for his artistic theories and personal beliefs. His use of leitmotifs made each opera a large-scale cyclic form. The bases of the librettos, which he wrote himself, were the Nordic myths and the medieval German legends.

Wagner was a master psychologist in his use of musical effects to persuade, manipulate, and overwhelm his listeners. His daring innovations in harmony and melody influenced the future of music. For several hundred years harmony and melody had contained some chromatic tones—that is, "color" tones which lay outside the key of a work. But this chromaticism never disturbed the listener's sense of key center, even in the highly chromatic works of Bach, Mozart, and Schumann. In Wagner, however, key centers changed so rapidly that they were hard to find. Thus the way was opened for the non-tonal composers of the twentieth century. Many musicians think of Wagner's *Tristan and Isolde,* his most thoroughly chromatic work, as the beginning of one mainstream of modern music.

Wagner was such a monumental figure that he dominated his time as few composers have ever done. Other major opera composers, including Bizet and Gounod, were drawn into Wagner's orbit. Later French composers such as Satie and Debussy reacted to Wagner by consciously setting forth in new directions.

Among all the Romantics, Brahms reigned supreme in the non-theatrical fields of music. Some critics saw him as the challenger to Wagner's supremacy, but his symphonies, concertos, chamber works, and songs existed in a different realm from that of Wagner's operas. Although they were completely of the nineteenth century, their roots were in the past. Brahms's contemplative works sum up Classicism; Wagner's operas summed up the nineteenth century and possibly pointed the way to the twentieth.

But not all composers of opera followed the lead of Wagner. Verdi and Mussorgsky were strong enough to stand their ground against the German master. Verdi, who always wrote with the voice in mind, was Wagner's antithesis. He did not aspire to reform the world or intellectually change the art of music. Whereas Wagner wrote essays about the complete fusion of the arts, and composed music that overwhelmed the drama, Verdi said little about his aims and wrote operas that held the stage dramatically as well as musically. Both men in their music sounded the depths and scaled the heights of the human spirit.

Mussorgsky, following the lead of his countryman Glinka, brought to music a different strength. He represents the composer who lets his musical personality emerge from a background steeped in folk music rather than art music. Writing operas based on Russian history and using Russian folk melodies, he was to a great extent an outgrowth of the new concepts of nationalism that swept through Europe in the nineteenth century.

For a long time music had been almost exclusively the creation of the Germans, Frenchmen, Austrians, and Italians. But in the Romantic period the creative talents of the musically undeveloped nations, like a dammed-up stream, broke through whatever barriers had been holding them back. Brilliant composers appeared from all parts of Europe and America: Chopin from Poland, Liszt from Hungary, Glinka and Tchaikovsky and "The Russian Five" from Russia, Grieg from Norway, Smetana and Dvořák from Bohemia, Pedrell from Spain, Gottschalk and MacDowell from the United States, and Balfe, Sullivan, and Elgar from England. Most of these men were steeped in the old traditions of western European music but they brought fresh concepts of harmony, melody, rhythm, and instrumentation to the established forms of writing. They introduced dances such as the mazurka, the polonaise, the polka, and the czardas—and even a hint of jazz. They restored to music old scales that had been hibernating for centuries, and they introduced new scales from exotic places. Without meaning to they contributed to music certain ingredients which, when mixed with Wagner's colorful harmony, were to make a potion that would eventually transform most of the old traditions on which European music had been based.

By the end of the nineteenth century, composers were ready to move in several new directions. Instead of yearning and dreaming about life, talents such as Strauss, Mascagni, and Leoncavallo tried to capture its realism. The French composers Fauré, Satie, and Debussy turned their backs on the passionate outpourings of Wagner and tried to achieve in their compositions a feeling of balance and control. Their music was aristocratic, or at least sophisticated; it was for

Caricature of Richard Wagner conducting

the few rather than the many; it was elegant and ironic rather than exuberant and unself-conscious.

Wagner's music had led to the beautiful lieder of Hugo Wolf (1860–1903) and the monumental symphonies of Anton Bruckner (1824–96) and Gustave Mahler (1860–1911). These composers are just now becoming well known. Their compositions contrast strangely with the music of the early Romantics. What started in Germany and Austria as a youthful, ecstatic utterance about life and love gave way to a brooding, nostalgic mood in these later figures, as though they realized that a whole way of life in the world was coming to an end—an end signalized by the outbreak of World War I.

Musical audiences of the twentieth century are still, on the whole, strongly Romantic. They respond not so much to the music of their own time as to the thousands of beautiful works of the nineteenth century. This music is direct in its emotional appeal, uncomplicated and reassuring rather than disturbing. Amid the machinery and terrifying realities of the twentieth century it is comforting to hear the poetic music of those who affirm the importance of human feeling and the good life.

Below left: Galina Ulanova and Alexander Lapauri in a Bolshoi Theater production of Prokofiev's Romeo and Juliet
At right: Rudolf Nureyev and Merle Park in a Royal Ballet production

ROMEO AND JULIET: a play by William Shakespeare based on Porto's sixteenth-century story of the tragic love between children of two feuding Italian families. It has inspired many musical works, including operas by Bellini (1830) and Gounod (1867) and a dramatic symphony in seven movements for orchestra, chorus, and vocal soloists by Berlioz. The Berlioz work is dedicated to Paganini, who gave Berlioz money so that he would have free time to compose. The work is seldom performed except for the fourth movement, the virtuoso section known as the "Queen Mab" Scherzo.

Tchaikovsky's overture-fantasia, *Romeo and Juliet,* on which he worked from 1869 to 1880, is one of his most-played works. The music was used by Sergei Lifar for a successful ballet produced at the Paris Opéra in 1942. The story formed the basis of the libretto for a full-length ballet, with music by Prokofiev (1940), which has been produced by the Leningrad, Bolshoi, and Royal Danish Ballet companies. Variations of the story are used for Delius' opera *A Village Romeo and Juliet* and in Leonard Bernstein's *West Side Story.*

RONDO: one of the most important musical forms. As in the refrain or chorus form of songs, the rondo allows a single main idea to alternate with new ideas brought in as the piece develops. These new ideas are called "episodes," or "digressions," from the theme. With the letter A representing the main theme, the form of a rondo might look like this: A B A C A D A. A rondo is sometimes a complete work, as in Mendelssohn's *Rondo capriccioso,* or it may be a single

movement of a larger work, as in the finales of many sonatas by Haydn, Mozart, and Beethoven.

The rondo is one of the oldest musical forms. Its ancestor was the *rondeau,* a type of fourteenth- and fifteenth-century French poem in which the first and last lines were the same, giving the feeling of something going a-*round* in a circle until the starting point is reached. Musical rondos, or rondeaux, in this form were written by French trouvères as well as by such composers as Machaut and Dufay.

Instrumental rondos were popular with composers of the seventeenth and eighteenth centuries, who used the form for movements of their suites and sonatas. These rondo movements were often dances, such as the gavotte in Bach's unaccompanied Violin Partita in E and the chaconnes by François and Louis Couperin. In the rondos of these composers, the main theme alternates with a number of couplets—other themes not too different in style from the main one (Ex. 42).

The composers of the Classical period developed the rondo by mixing it with the

Ex. 42 — Chaconne: "La Favorite," Couperin

Ex. 43 — Piano Sonata in B-flat, K. 33, Mozart

Main Theme

2nd Theme - key of F

Main Theme

3rd Theme - key of G minor

Main Theme

2nd Theme - key of B-flat   Main Theme

sonata-allegro form of the first movement. The first and third digressions are similar, but in different keys. The first digression might be in the key of the dominant tone of the scale; the third would be in the key of the tonic. The plan of such a rondo would be A B A C A B¹ A, as in Ex. 43.

Another plan used by the Classical composers was the division of the rondo into three sections—like the statement, development, and restatement of the sonata-allegro form. The statement would contain the main theme and the digression (in the dominant key). The development would contain the main theme and a development of either or both themes. The restatement would have the main theme, the digression (this time in the key of the tonic), and a final statement of the main theme. The total form—sometimes called sonata-rondo or rondo-sonata—would be: A B A C (Development) A B A.

Such rondos, as well as the simpler variety,

are found mostly as the final movement of a sonata, symphony, or concerto, but are occasionally used for slow movements as well. In many cases the composer writes a coda, or ending, to round out the form. Good examples of rondos may be found in the last movements of Mozart's Piano Sonatas in B♭ (K. 333) and D (K. 311) and Beethoven's Piano Sonatas in E♭ (Op. 7), D (Op. 10, No. 3), C minor (the "Pathétique," Op. 13), and D (the "Pastorale," Op. 28).

The rondo idea has continued throughout the nineteenth and twentieth centuries as a popular form for composers to work in. Many pieces in rondo form occur in the works of Schubert, Mendelssohn, and Brahms. Richard Strauss used the rondo form to hold together his musical story of *Till Eulenspiegel*, with the main theme representing Till himself. In our own century composers used the rondo idea quite freely, as in the final scenes of Acts I and II of Berg's opera *Wozzeck*.

ROSSINI, GIOACCHINO (1792–1868): an Italian composer, best known for his operas, particularly the light *Il barbiere di Siviglia (The Barber of Seville)* and the heroic *Guillaume Tell (William Tell).*

Rossini was one of music's men of mystery. At the height of his fame, after the success of *William Tell* in 1829, he retired completely from the field of opera and almost completely from music. Over the last thirty-nine years of his life he wrote almost nothing —only some sacred works and collections of short pieces for piano, other instruments, and voice. Although there have been many guesses, no one knows for sure why one of Europe's greatest opera composers turned away from the theater. Possibly he was tired; he had written thirty-eight operas in nineteen years. Possibly he saw that the future of opera was turning away from the style that he knew. Possibly he just wanted to live to enjoy the fame and fortune his composing had brought him. He liked to eat and compose new recipes for tasty dishes and sauces. He liked to entertain and to take part in social gatherings. But the grinding life of a composer would interfere with these pleasures. Certainly he had come a long way from his knock-about childhood days.

Rossini was born in Pesaro, Italy, on Leap-year Day, February 29. His parents were wandering musicians. His father played the trumpet, his mother was a singer, and while they were performing on the road Rossini lived with a butcher's family in Bologna. As a child he became known for his beautiful voice. He always liked to sing, and in later years his knowledge of what the voice could do would endear him to singers.

In addition to singing he learned to play the harpsichord, and by the age of ten he was a professional musician. Entering the Bologna Conservatory, he studied theory and also picked up some playing knowledge of the horn and the cello—instruments for which he later wrote so well. After he won a prize for a cantata, his teacher told him that he had sufficient knowledge of music theory to write an opera. The teacher never dreamed that this information would lead Rossini to leave school, but it did. Opera was his goal. His first one, written at the age of eighteen, was a moderate success—enough to launch Rossini on a whirlwind career.

He wandered around Italy, composing an opera for any producer who desired a new work for a festival. Sometimes the whole process took place within six weeks—finding a libretto, writing the music, rehearsing the singers, and putting on the show. At one

Gioacchino Rossini

point the young man wrote fifteen operas within four years. He made a contract with a manager in Naples to write two operas a year for a salary (a little more than $100 a month) and a percentage of the profits from the manager's gambling house.

Rossini had developed great facility. He could compose in the middle of a party, or while fishing or carrying on a conversation. Caring little for the words, he is reported to have said, "Give me a laundry list and I will set it to music." Occasionally he would spend too much time in gaiety. Disliking to write a new overture for each opera, he fell into the habit of using the same overture for several. (The overture to *The Barber of Seville* originally served as an

A scene from Rossini's Cenerentola *(La Scala production, 1963–64 season)*

overture for *Elizabetta*.) Sometimes a desperate manager would lock Rossini in a room, under guard. Manuscript would be thrown out the window to the waiting copyist.

Amazingly enough, Rossini managed to write wonderful music. His great idol was Mozart, and Rossini, like Mozart, could make his orchestra bubble with excitement or sigh with sadness. His overtures, on which he spent so little time, are today played as concert pieces. Full of bright melodies and colorful instrumentation, they reach dramatic climaxes by way of what has been called the Rossini crescendo—a musical phrase repeated many times, each time getting louder. For the singers Rossini wrote melodies that brought out all the brilliance and expressive qualities of their voices. Disliking the way in which singers took liberties with melodies, putting inartistic embellishments in the wrong places, Rossini decorated his own melodies so thoroughly that there was no place for the singer to add anything.

Rossini turned from comedy to tragedy quite easily. The opera buffa *L'Italiana in Algeri (The Italian Maid in Algiers)* followed right on the heels of the dramatic grand opera *Tancredi (Tancred)*. Both written in 1813, they established Rossini, age twenty-one, as a master. Two of his best works, *The Barber of Seville* and the setting of Shakespeare's tragic *Otello,* and a minor work, *La Gazzetta,* were written in 1816. The charming *Cenerentola (Cinderella)* and three others date from 1817.

Tiring of the Italian public, which was critical of his *Semiramide* (1823), Rossini moved on. First he went to England, where he received many honors and made more than $20,000 in a few months. Next he went to Paris, at this time the opera center of Europe. For a while he was the music director of the Théâtre Italien in Paris, conducting new versions of his old operas and contributing one new work. He also directed the first Paris performance of an opera by Meyerbeer—the Meyerbeer who was to replace Rossini as the favorite opera composer of the French.

To keep Rossini in France, the government gave him a yearly pension and the titles of Royal Composer and Inspector General of Singing. He continued the new productions of his early works and, for the Paris Opéra, wrote the sparkling *Le Comte Ory (Count Ory)*. Tiring of his official duties, Rossini made a new arrangement under which the government guaranteed him a yearly sum in return for a new Rossini opera every two years. The composer now planned a series of five operas, of which only one was written—*William Tell,* in 1829. In the heroic, exciting, and tender music of *Tell,* Rossini reached his peak. To achieve a dramatic flow he discarded the speechlike *recitative secco,* replacing it with dramatic melodies, always with dramatic accompaniment. It is a long opera, difficult to produce and difficult to sing, but it remains one of the masterworks of its kind.

A revolution in France in 1830 ended Rossini's pension. For five years he fought his case in the courts, and he won. During this time he wrote his last large-scale work, a *Stabat Mater.* Moving to Italy, he became honorary director of his old conservatory in Bologna, and worked to improve the standards of singing. But in 1855 he moved back to Paris for good. Here he lived and entertained generously. Fat and amiable, he spent his time inventing recipes and being kind to young composers—Saint-Saëns and Wagner among many others. Later it would be Wagner who would write a eulogy, calling Rossini the first great man he had met in the world of the arts.

When Rossini felt like writing, he turned out short pieces, referring to them as "sins of my old age." Many of these were arranged for orchestra by Respighi for the ballet *La Boutique fantasque.* In the last year of his life Rossini was honored on the occasion of the five-hundredth performance of *William Tell.* Soloists, chorus, and orchestra of the Paris Opéra serenaded the old composer, who responded with his expected wit.

After his death, Rossini's music had its ups and downs, but it has always managed to maintain itself on the stage. *The Barber of Seville* is standard fare in all opera houses. *William Tell* is revived from time to time, as are *Cinderella, Count Ory,* and *Otello.* Most familiar are the many tuneful overtures which were brought to the attention of modern audiences by the great Italian conductor Toscanini.

ROUND: a tuneful song made up of sections of equal length which can be sung simultaneously. One person sings the first section, and as he starts the second section, the second singer starts the first section, and so on. Each person sings the melody, but starts at a different time. Favorite examples of rounds include "Three Blind Mice" and "Frère Jacques." Because the melody can be sung over and over again a round was called a *rota*, or "wheel," in medieval England.

Rounds (which are simple forms of canon) may be sung so that each voice goes through the melody several times and then drops out—so that only one voice is singing at the end. They may also be performed so that all voices stop on a given signal or at a given place. Such rounds usually have a fermata sign (⌒) to show the stopping place (as in Ex. 45).

Rounds have been most popular in England, where clubs such as the Round, Catch, and Canon Club provided gathering places for men to get together to sing. The earliest known composition constructed as a round is the well-known "Sumer Is Icumen In," written in England about 1300. It calls for four voices singing a round over a repeated little melody for two other voices. Many collections of rounds were printed in seventeenth- and eighteenth-century England. The earliest of these were Ravenscroft's *Pammelia* and *Deuteromelia*, both printed in 1609.

A playful type of round is the *catch*. Catches usually have humorous words and a melody full of stops and starts to make the rhythm tricky. The English composer Purcell wrote more than fifty of them.

Rounds are fairly easy to compose. The harmony is simple—often consisting of only two chords. The phrases of the melody are written so that any number of the voices always make harmony with each other. Ex. 44 shows how the phrases of "Frère Jacques" fit together.

Rounds are printed in two ways: the whole melody is written out, with numbers or a sign where the voices enter (Ex. 45), or the round is printed with all the voices lined up so that the eye can see which notes are to be sung together, as in Ex. 44.

The term *round* is also used for a dance in which the dancers form a circle—as opposed to a "square" dance or a "longways."

RUBATO: a way of playing or singing in which some melody tones are slightly hurried while others are slowed down, while the underlying pulse remains steady. The effect of rubato is a free-flowing expressiveness as opposed to a mechanically correct but stiff interpretation. Much of the fame of Mozart's and Chopin's piano playing was due to their exquisite use of rubato.

Rubato is most effective in slow music such as adagios and poetic nocturnes and romances. Music of the nineteenth century in particular was written to be played with a certain rhythmic freedom, but rubato has always been an important part of musical performance. As early as the seventeenth century, Johann Froberger asked that a lament be played "without a steady beat." The composer usually leaves it to the performer to decide whether or not to play his music with rubato. If he wants to be sure, he writes "rubato," "molto rubato," or "very freely" at the beginning of a composition or section of a work.

Many jazz singers and instrumentalists use a great deal of rubato. To achieve a relaxed feeling or one of intense emotion they drag the early notes of a phrase, then hurry —while the accompanying instruments play a steady beat. Such rubatos come under the heading of "styling"—singing or playing a popular tune in a unique manner.

Ex. 44

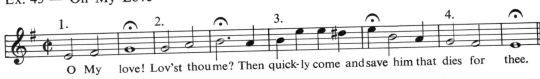

Ex. 45 —"Oh My Love"

O My love! Lov'st thou me? Then quick-ly come and save him that dies for thee.

Above: *Mily Balakirev by Léon Bakst*
Below: *César Cui*

RUSSIAN FIVE: a group of Russian composers—Balakirev, Borodin, Cui, Mussorgsky, and Rimsky-Korsakov, sometimes known as "The Mighty Five" or "The Five." In the latter part of the nineteenth century they developed a musical style based on the melodies, rhythms, and harmonies of Russian folk music. Mily Balakirev (1837–1910) was the leader and the only thoroughly trained musician of the group. Arriving in St. Petersburg from the provinces, where he had come to know Russian folk music intimately, Balakirev at the age of eighteen set about to preach the nationalist ideals that were inspiring Michael Glinka (1804–57) and Alexander Dargomyzhsky (1813–69) to compose operas based on Russian subject matter.

Russian musical life had been dominated until the middle of the nineteenth century by western European composers and native composers trained in the western European style. Balakirev, fired with tremendous energy and an almost fanatical zeal, attracted the four other talented young men and infected them with his own enthusiasm.

Alexander Borodin (1833–87) was one of the leading chemists of his day. César Cui (1835–1918), trained as a military engineer, became a professor at the Russian Artillery School and Military College. Mussorgsky (1839–81) was a cavalryman and civil-service employee. Rimsky-Korsakov (1844–1908) was a naval officer until, in his late twenties, he chose music as his career.

"The Five" met regularly, performing and discussing both the musical classics and the new music of the Romantic composers. They also brought in their compositions—whatever they happened to be writing—for criticism, suggestions, and encouragement. Basing their works on Russian folk songs and exotic Asian melodic ideas, "The Five" were forced to invent a harmonic style that fitted the modal patterns of the melodies; a type of orchestration colorful enough to portray the vivid scenes they had in mind; and musical forms in which the song-phrase, rather than the motive, was the basic building block.

Somewhat narrow in their outlook, "The Five" sneered at the less nationalistic compositions of Anton Rubinstein and Tchaikovsky. These men were great enough to ignore the sneers of "The Five" and even to encourage performances of their music.

Once having established the principles of what they felt to be truly Russian music, the members of "The Five" quickly asserted their individualities. Balakirev concentrated on symphonic poems and overtures on folk themes (although his best-known work now is the difficult *Islamey* fantasia for piano). Cui, who managed to compose a large number of works—including operas, symphonic suites, and many short works for piano—is remembered chiefly for his songs. He was also the essayist-critic who informed the Russian and western European world of the theories and deeds of "The Five." The lives and works of Borodin, Mussorgsky, and Rimsky-Korsakov are treated in separate articles elsewhere in this book.

SAINT-SAËNS, CAMILLE (1835–1921): one of France's leading musicians for almost seventy years.

Born in Paris, he showed such interest and talent in music that his great-aunt began to give him piano lessons when he was five. At six he started to compose, and at eleven he played a Mozart and a Beethoven piano concerto at his first public concert. A few years later he entered the Paris Conservatory, where he studied organ and composition. He became an organ virtuoso, famous for his sight reading and his improvisations. One of his feats consisted of playing at first sight the full, complex orchestral score of a Wagner opera—a deed that astounded Wagner himself.

Saint-Saëns started on his professional career as organist at the Church of St. Merry in Paris in 1853. Going on to the much-coveted post of organist at the Madeleine, also in Paris, in 1858, he remained there till 1877. In the meantime he continued to compose prolifically, and by the end of his life his output totaled 169 opuses.

Under the influence of Franz Liszt, Saint-Saëns wrote several symphonic poems, of which the *Danse macabre* and *Le Rouet d'Omphale (Omphale's Spinning Wheel)* are the best known. He followed the lead of Berlioz in championing the cause of instrumental music in France, where the public preferred opera and ballet to symphonies. He organized a society to promote French orchestral music. Like Berlioz he wrote symphonic and chamber works that are cyclic in form: themes are carried over from one movement to another, or—as in his Third Symphony—one main theme is used throughout the whole work.

Almost no area of music was ignored by this man of tremendous energy. He taught for a while, numbering among his pupils the future composers Messager and Fauré. Throughout his life he toured as a pianist, organist, and conductor. He toured the United States at the age of eighty, at eighty-one he went to South America, and at eighty-five he attended a concert of his works in Greece. A few months before his death in Algiers he played a complete program of his piano compositions.

Saint-Saëns received many honors, both in France and throughout Europe. Besides music he wrote twelve books, mostly of essays about music and musicians, and several volumes of poetry.

This French genius combined German technical thoroughness with French wit and tunefulness. His music is lyrical and polished, not passionate or emotional. At times it suggests a French Mendelssohn in its easy-going clarity. The orchestration is rich, and often—as in the *Danse macabre*—colorful. A modernist in his early days, Saint-Saëns as he grew older found fault with the younger and more radical Debussy.

To the end of his days, Saint-Saëns continued to write fluent and most agreeable music. Of his large output, the works that are still most played today include the first of his two cello concertos, the second of his five piano concertos, his symphonic poems, and his third and last symphony, in C minor with organ. The *Carnaval des animaux (The Carnival of the Animals)*, which he wrote as a series of musical satires in 1886, was one work he would not allow to be published during his lifetime. In recent years the American poet Ogden Nash has written a series of short, witty poems to go with this music. One of Saint-Saëns' most interesting works is his orchestral *Suite algérienne (Algerian Suite)*, in which he painted a musical picture of a land he had enjoyed visiting.

Saint-Saëns wrote a great deal of chamber music, more than 100 songs, several large choral works—notably the *Oratorio de Noël (Christmas Oratorio)* and *Le Déluge (The Flood)*—and twelve operas. Only one of the latter, the Biblical *Samson et Dalila (Samson and Delilah)*, was a success—and that in Germany before France. Still given occasional performances, it is best known for the aria "My Heart at Thy Sweet Voice."

Saint-Saëns with his dog in 1906 (portrait by Nadar)

Caricature of Saint-Saëns done in 1907

SARABAND: one of the most beautiful of the court dances of the seventeenth century. Slow and elegant, in a meter of three, the saraband has been the inspiration to composers in some of their most expressive music.

The origin of the saraband is obscure. It came to Spain either from Central America or from the Near East shortly before 1600. As a dance it was neither slow nor beautiful at that time. Its sensual movements caused it to be banned in many places. Like many Spanish dances the early saraband was accompanied by the castanets.

When the saraband was brought to the French court of Louis XIII (1601–43) its character changed. It became noble and serious, much like a slow minuet. By 1700 it was losing its popularity as a court dance but was gaining favor among composers. It became a permanent member of the dance suites of Froberger, Bach, Handel, and Couperin, usually as the third movement.

The saraband of the dance suite was in

Dancing the saraband

Ex. 1 — "Lascia ch'io pianga," Handel

Largo

Las - cia   ch'io pian-ga   mia cru - da   sor - te,

a two-part form, with eight to sixteen measures in each part. The melody is always songlike, sometimes highly ornamented. Not all sarabands carry the name of the dance. Some are called "airs," or "arias." Others are preludes, as in Bach's Prelude in E-flat Minor from the first book of *The Well-tempered Clavier.* Many slow eighteenth-century operatic arias, such as Handel's "Lascia ch'io pianga," from the opera *Rinaldo,* are built on the most typical saraband rhythm (Ex. 1). The slow tempo gave the composer time to use many expressive chromatic harmonies, as in Couperin's *La Lugubre.* The saraband like the chaconne was often used as a theme on which variations were made; Bach's "Goldberg" Variations is a monumental example.

For a while after 1700 the saraband died out, even though many slow movements by later composers have the characteristics of the dance. In 1887 Erik Satie revived interest in the saraband by writing a set of three sarabands for piano. Sparse and harmonically strange, Satie's sarabands were among the earliest reactions to the passionate music of Wagner and other Romantic composers. Since Satie other composers, including Debussy, Honegger, and Dukas, have written in this form.

Erik Satie

SATIE, ERIK (1866–1925): a French composer whose music had more influence on other composers than on audiences. He was noted for his unconventional behavior, his jokes, his eccentric titles *(Three Pieces in the Form of a Pear; Desiccated Embryos),* and the even wilder directions and explanations that he wrote throughout his music ("Light as an egg," "Like a nightingale with a toothache," "Here comes the lantern"). Most important was his attempt to free French music from what he considered German heaviness. "We want our own music, and—if possible—without kraut."

Satie was born in Honfleur on the coast of Normandy. His first training in music was at the age of eight, when he studied the organ. When he was thirteen his family moved to Paris, where his father became a music publisher. The son entered the Paris Conservatory but stayed there only for one year—its rigid requirements made it seem like a jail. He then became a cabaret pianist in the Bohemian section of Paris, among artists, writers, and musicians in Montmartre.

Satie's first published works were three sarabands for piano (1887). In contrast to the passionate, romantic works that were fashionable in music at the time, Satie's sarabands were quiet blocks of chords that moved slowly and strangely (Ex. 2).

His next pieces for piano also were in sets of three—*Gymnopédies* and *Gnossiennes.* Their strange titles and long melodic lines pulling against simple accompanying chords suggest the slow athletic dances of ancient Greece and Knossos. Instead of major or minor scales Satie used scales more like those of ancient music. In the *Gnossiennes* he even abandoned bar lines (although the music is in regular meter), to try to achieve a flowing unaccented rhythm (Ex. 3).

Satie went through many phases in his career. For a while he was a mystic—a Rosicrucian—and his music at this time had a medieval feeling. He met Debussy and tried to draw him to his ideas. Debussy's opera *Pelléas and Mélisande,* written in the 1890's, has some of Satie's medieval mysticism in it, but for the most part Debussy continued on the path of Impressionism. It was this Impressionism, with its vagueness and poetic titles, that Satie was later to make fun of.

All through his life Satie was the foe of art that takes itself too seriously. He became interested in French vaudeville songs and American ragtime. The future of music, he felt, lay in the direction of simplicity—of melody rather than involved harmonies and counterpoint. Serious composers, he thought, could learn much from music-hall ditties. He himself composed songs for a nightclub singer.

Satie lived the life of simplicity that he preached. His house was a one-room apartment far from the cabaret where he played, and he walked to and from work. When a publisher offered him a certain sum of money to write a series of piano pieces to illustrate a series of watercolors, *Sports and Diversions,* Satie refused until the publisher agreed to pay him less money. Then, at the lower fee, he wrote a long set of piano pieces—charming ones.

By the time of World War I, Satie had become the leader of all the young rebels in the arts—Picasso, Cocteau, Picabia. With Picasso doing the set and Cocteau writing the scenario, Satie composed *Parade* for Diaghilev's Russian Ballet. To get sounds of modern life into his music he introduced into his orchestra a typewriter, an airplane engine, and other noisemakers. *Relâche,* a ballet by the painter Picabia, was meant to shock its audience, and Satie helped— partly with his music and partly by gravely riding around the stage in a baby Citroën car.

Not all of Satie's music is witty. He felt strongly about the mean way in which the working-class people of Arcueil, his home district, lived. For them he wrote one of his most beautiful works, *Messe des pauvres (Mass for the Poor).* One of his last works was *Socrate,* which Satie called a "symphonic drama." In quiet music for voices and chamber orchestra it tells the story of the death of Socrates. The music, never rising to a climax, is as simple as Plato's report of Socrates' death.

The influence of Satie has been enormous. He encouraged many of the young French composers of his time, among them Poulenc,

Milhaud, Auric, Honegger, and Sauguet. And it is from his music that many younger American composers, notably Aaron Copland and Virgil Thomson, learned the art of simplicity when they were studying in Paris. Later, Satie's influence was to be felt in the early music of the experimental composer John Cage. Satie taught composers that music does not have to shout or beat its breast to be heard.

"Le Tango," one of the watercolor drawings from Sports and Diversions *for which Satie composed piano pieces*

Ex. 2 — Saraband No. 1

Ex. 3 — *Gnossienne* No. 2
Avec étonnement

SAXOPHONE: an instrument with a cone-shaped body made of brass and a mouthpiece containing a single reed like that of a clarinet. As a result of its mixed parentage the saxophone blends well with either the woodwinds or the brasses. It is played by means of padded keys that make it easy to close the fingerholes. Easy to play passably, the saxophone like any other instrument is difficult to play really well.

There are seven sizes of saxophone, including the almost never used contrabass. The highest sounding—the rare sopranino in E-flat and the soprano in B-flat (made famous by Sidney Bechet)—are straight in form, like a clarinet. All the others—the alto in E-flat, the tenor in B-flat, the baritone in E-flat, and the bass in B-flat—are curved, with a flaring bell at the end. All saxophone parts are written within the following range:

The music for all types of saxophones is written as above in the treble clef, although the actual pitch produced will depend on which size of instrument is being played. The fingering for each written note is the same on all saxophones, making it easy for a player to switch from one size of saxophone to any other without learning a new fingering for each instrument. The actual sound of the lowest note of each saxophone is as follows:

Sopranino   Soprano   Alto   Tenor   Baritone

The saxophone is now over a century old, having been invented by the Brussels-born clarinetist Adolphe Sax in 1846. (Sax also invented the baritone horn and the tenor horn and perfected the tuba.) The saxophone soon became popular in France, where entire choirs of saxophones appeared in military bands. Bizet gave the saxophone a charming melody in his *L'Arlésienne* Suite Number 1. Debussy composed a

Above: *members of a military band playing "the new instruments of Mr. Sax"*

Bottom left: *Coleman Hawkins, about 1955*
Bottom middle: *Gerry Mulligan*
Bottom right: *John Coltrane*

Rapsodie for saxophone and orchestra, and Jacques Ibert gave the instrument a solo part in his *Concertino da Camera.*

In the United States, alto and tenor saxophones became standard members of the wind band starting in the 1870's. In the band the saxophone is used as a melody instrument, sometimes with bassoons or clarinets. Although the saxophone is particularly prized for its ability to sing cello-like lines in the middle register, its sustaining power and ability to blend have also made it useful in holding chords as a harmonic background.

It is from the wind band that the saxophone moved to its greatest triumph as a virtuoso instrument in the world of jazz. Since the early 1920's a dazzling list of jazz greats—Johnny Hodges, Harry Carney, Barney Bigard, Jimmy Dorsey, Adrian Rollini, Charlie Parker, Lester Young, Benny Carter, Coleman Hawkins, Gerry Mulligan, John Coltrane—have devoted their talents to the perpetual renewal of the possibilities of the instrument.

In the symphony orchestra and in chamber music the saxophone has still not found a permanent place for itself. Its rich, tremulous tone overpowers the sound of the strings. It has had to be confined to the role of a color instrument, and as such has been put to work by Strauss *(Symphonia domestica),* Honegger *(Joan of Arc at the Stake),* Vaughan Williams (Sixth Symphony), Milhaud *(La Création du monde),* and Ravel *(Boléro).* Other than works for saxophone groups, such as Henry Cowell's "Sailor's Hornpipe for Four Saxophones," not much has been written for the saxophones in chamber music. The true chamber music of the saxophone is that of the small jazz group.

SCALE: a series of tones arranged in a set pattern from low to high or high to low. (In Western European music the scales run from low to high. Ancient Greek scales, or modes, went from high to low.) The word "scale" comes from a Latin word meaning "ladder" or "a series of steps." The successive tones of a scale are called degrees and today are usually numbered from lowest to highest. The first degree of a scale —the tonic, or generating tone—may be of any pitch. To find the tones of a given scale one starts with the tonic and lays out the scale pattern like a stencil over the other notes. Some scales, such as the *melodic minor,* go up one way and come down another; see MINOR.

A scale is somewhat like a tonal alphabet from which melodies and harmonies can be made. Within a musical composition the scale out of which the music is built might never be heard in its basic pattern—just as in a book the alphabet never appears in order from A to Z. Ex. 4a and b shows how a theme can be rearranged to yield its scale. On the other hand, many melodies are just scales with rhythmic life given to them (Ex. 5a and b). Scale runs often turn up in the course of musical compositions, usually in transitional sections or as embellishments to a melody.

Most scales are divisions of the octave, although some contemporary composers—Bartók for one—have made scales that span more than an octave.

In European music the smallest interval within a scale is the semitone, or half step. Other civilizations, particularly in Asia, use *microtones*—intervals smaller than the semitone.

The number of tones in a scale may vary from primitive two-tone and three-tone scales

Ex. 4a — Symphony No. 3, Harris

Ex. 4b

Ex. 5a — "Joy to the World," Handel

Ex. 5b — Mazurka, Op. 7, No. 1, Chopin

to the forty-three-tone scale invented by the American composer Harry Partch. A composer can make up any new scale he wants; such scales are called synthetic. In his opera *Mlada* (1892) the Russian composer Rimsky-Korsakov uses a scale of alternating semitones and whole tones:

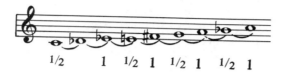

The most common forms of scales are those with five tones (pentatonic), six tones (whole tone), seven tones (modes, major, minor, Hungarian gypsy—the example here), and twelve tones (chromatic).

SCARLATTI, ALESSANDRO (1660–1725):

the most important opera composer of his day. Born in Palermo, Sicily, Scarlatti as a boy showed such talent that he was taken to Rome to study with Carissimi (1605–74), then the dominant figure in the musical world (he is remembered today as one of the first writers of oratorios). By the age of twenty Scarlatti had written his first opera. For several years he was music director to Queen Christine of Sweden, who had a palace in Rome.

In 1694 Scarlatti moved to Naples, the largest city in Italy at that time. Here, except for brief periods in Rome and Florence, he settled down to an active life as composer, performer, conductor, and teacher. Scarlatti had come to Naples at just the right time. Opera in Naples was a form of popular entertainment, much as Broadway musicals are today. The city had several opera houses, where the Neapolitans came to hear their favorite singers—meanwhile playing chess, eating, or gambling in dull stretches of the performance. This audience demanded a new kind of opera—something other than the stiff, heroic productions of Rome and Venice.

Scarlatti developed a style to suit himself, his singers, and his audience. Each of his operas contained few choruses and few duets, but many beautiful arias. In this Neapolitan style, sometimes called "numbers opera," the three-part aria da capo became the es-

tablished form—a form that would be used by many later composers, notably Bach and Handel. Instead of the French overture, which had a solemn beginning followed by a fast contrapuntal section, Scarlatti developed a form, called *sinfonia* at the time, that followed the tempo plan of fast-slow-fast. (It is known today as the Italian overture.) Its themes were short and dancelike, its phrases evenly balanced. Eventually the sinfonia, or Italian overture, became the pattern for the Classical symphony.

Most of Scarlatti's operas were *opera seria,* based on serious subjects but with comic relief. There was, however, a theater in Naples that produced straight comedies. It was for this theater that Scarlatti wrote one of the first light operas, or *opera buffa* —a little gem called *Il trionfo dell'onore (The Triumph of Honor).* Ironically, this untypical production was for many years the only Scarlatti opera available on records. In this opera, as in many others, Scarlatti developed the style of rapid patter known as "dry recitative," or *recitativo secco.* He also experimented with a dramatic recitative in which the strings or the whole orchestra accompanied the singer.

By the end of his life Scarlatti had by his own count some 115 operas to his credit. Only thirty-six of these are still in existence. But Scarlatti did not confine his writing to opera. Much of his greatest music is found in his hundreds of chamber cantatas. Six hundred of these are for solo voice accompanied by harpsichord and viola da gamba; another sixty have full string accompaniment. The solo cantatas contain some of Scarlatti's most expressive music, and it was in these more intimate works that he apparently felt free to pour forth his feelings.

Scarlatti also wrote many motets and masses, oratorios, and madrigals. Primarily a composer for the voice, he wrote for it with tremendous skill. He did, however, write twelve sinfonias, or concertos, for orchestra, chamber music for flutes and violins, and several works for harpsichord. Among these last is a set of variations on the popular tune "La Follia." It is one of the finest sets of variations ever written for a keyboard instrument—and almost completely neglected by pianists today.

Such neglect is true of almost all of Scarlatti's works. He was one of the greatest composers and innovators in the history of music, yet is one of the least played. In some measure, this is because he was overshadowed in the later part of his life, partly by his own son and partly by Corelli, Vivaldi, and Handel.

Alessandro Scarlatti

SCARLATTI, DOMENICO (1685–1757):

Italian composer and harpsichordist. Scarlatti brought to the harpsichord the same dazzling virtuosity that Liszt brought to the piano a hundred years later. More than any other composer of his time, Scarlatti explored every possibility of the instrument in his more than 600 sonatas, half of them written in the last five years of his life.

Scarlatti was born in Naples, Italy, in the same year that gave the world Bach and Handel. He was trained in music by his father, Alessandro Scarlatti, famous as an opera composer, and later by Francesco Gasparini. At the age of sixteen Scarlatti was a professional musician performing as organist at the royal chapel in Naples. For the next eighteen or nineteen years he wrote sacred music and operas, following the style of his father—and not producing anything very distinctive. Most of this time was spent in Rome, where Scarlatti held the positions of music director to a former queen of Poland and head of music at the Julian Chapel of St. Peter's.

In 1709 Scarlatti had a friendly contest with Handel on the organ and the harpsichord. The two became lifelong mutual admirers after Handel emerged as victor at the organ and Scarlatti at the harpsichord. The possibilities of the harpsichord had always intrigued Scarlatti, but in Italy patrons and audiences preferred violin music and opera. When offered the post of music director at the Portuguese court in Lisbon, he jumped at the chance, knowing that the young Princess Maria Barbara was musically gifted and interested in the harpsichord.

When the princess married the heir to the Spanish throne in 1729, Scarlatti moved with her to Madrid. Here he spent the rest of his life teaching music and performing and composing his harpsichord sonatas for the princess, who later became queen of Spain.

The only collection of harpsichord pieces Scarlatti ever published during his lifetime appeared in 1738. These *Esercizi per gravicembalo,* a collection of thirty "exercises," as the composer referred to his sonatas, show many of Scarlatti's characteristics.

Instead of being in detailed counterpoint, like Bach's fugues, they are usually in just two or three voices. This thin texture allows Scarlatti to cover great distances in each hand:

K. 7; L. 379

The hands often cross over each other—a keyboard technique which Scarlatti was one of the first to use:

K. 96; L. 465

Harmonically, Scarlatti is daring in his use of chromatics, leaving the listener bewildered as to where the music is heading (Ex. 6).

Most of the sonatas follow the same structural pattern. The work is usually divided into two sections, with a double bar and repeat sign at the end of each section. In this two-part sonata form, the piece starts in the tonic key and moves so that it is in the dominant key or the relative major by the time the music arrives at the double bar. The second section moves through various keys and arrives back at the original tonic key. Most of the material of each sonata is announced at the beginning of the work. When Scarlatti is moving to his second key, he often takes a colorful and

Domenico Scarlatti

Ex. 6 — K. 3; L. 378

Ex. 7 — K. 133; L. 282

Ex. 8 — K. 119; L. 415

Ex. 9 — K. 96; L. 465

Ex. 10 — K. 308; L. 359

The Spanish Royal family—Ferdinand VI and Maria Barbara. The group of musicians to the left of the royal couple includes Scarlatti

roundabout route—in one case (Number 41 in the Kirkpatrick edition) from C major to G major by way of F minor and E-flat minor and D-flat major. A large part of each section consists of cadence material announcing that the section is coming to an end. Here Scarlatti is fond of repeating measures, building up suspense (Ex. 7).

In his later sonatas—most of which were not published in his lifetime—Scarlatti became more and more inventive. A harpsichordist cannot make a crescendo by striking the keys more heavily, but Scarlatti achieved much the same result by adding notes to his chords, often making these increasingly dissonant with "crushed" notes (Ex. 8).

The sound of the Spanish guitar suggested to him strummed chords and rapidly repeated notes (Ex. 9).

Many of Scarlatti's sonatas are whirlwind prestos; others are solid marches or moderate minuets. Some are lyrical pastorales. Other slow sonatas suggest a Mozartean song movement (Ex. 10).

In many ways Scarlatti was one of the most advanced composers of his time, pointing the way to music's future and away from its recent Baroque past. His use of musical material was close to the methods of Haydn and Mozart. His opening out of keyboard technique laid the foundation of later virtuoso writing for the piano.

Scarlatti's keyboard works were not known in his native Italy, nor in Germany, during his lifetime, though some of his writing in other media did reach England and France. It was in Spain that his influence was most immediate. Here Scarlatti taught and influenced many young composers, setting up a Spanish school of composition. One of his students, Padre Antonio Soler (1729–83), wrote many keyboard works following the style of his master.

Scarlatti's harpsichord works were discovered in the late 1800's by virtuoso pianists, who arranged them for the piano. The first fairly complete edition, including some 545 items, was published by Ricordi in 1906. The editor of this edition was Alessandro Longo, who assigned numbers to the various sonatas. Today the Longo numbers are gradually giving way to those assigned by Ralph Kirkpatrick, an American harpsichordist who has made an exhaustive study of Scarlatti's works and life. Kirkpatrick's biography of Scarlatti was published in 1953. It was Kirkpatrick who proved that most of Scarlatti's sonatas were originally grouped in pairs—making them sonatas in two movements, both in the same key.

Scarlatti's crystal-clear works, sparkling with rhythmic drive, are becoming more and more popular with pianists and harpsichordists. Many recordings have made them available to enthusiasts whose own pianistic technique is not up to the demands of the scores. Amazingly enough, these works of some two hundred years ago are today as fresh and as vital as they were when they were new.

Ex. 11 — Sonata in A Minor, Op. 42, Schubert

SCHERZO: a title given to certain light, often humorous compositions. The earliest scherzos were Monteverdi's charming little vocal trios with instrumental accompaniment, published in 1607 as *Scherzi musicali.* Based on dance rhythms, these "musical jokes" are delightful pieces for two sopranos and a bass. In style they are important ancestors of the Baroque trio sonata.

The scherzo came into its own at the hands of Haydn and Beethoven, who used it as a rapid third movement in a sonata, quartet, or symphony to replace the minuet and trio. The scherzo kept the triple meter of the minuet as well as its basic form of A-B-A—a first section being repeated after a contrasting section. Beethoven included scherzos in all but his first and eighth symphonies. His scherzos covered a wide range of meaning—from the fortissimo, peasantlike laughter of the Ninth Symphony to the lightning-fast chuckles in the Seventh. In the Third, Fifth, and Ninth Symphonies the scherzo is no longer just a joke, but a welcome relief from the high emotional pitch of the other movements.

Schubert, an ardent admirer of Beethoven's music, brought a more songlike feeling to his scherzos, as in his great C-major Symphony. In the scherzo of his Sonata in A Minor, Opus 42, there are sudden accents, shifts of register, and landings on unexpected chords—all of these making for a kind of playfulness (Ex. 11).

Many composers of the Romantic period discarded the scherzo in their symphonies, substituting for it a waltz, as in Berlioz's *Symphonie fantastique,* or a march, as in Tchaikovsky's Sixth Symphony. Berlioz made a glittering orchestral work in the "Queen Mab" Scherzo movement of his *Romeo and Juliet* Symphony. Schumann in his Third ("Rhenish") Symphony has a scherzo which is a flowing melody, suggesting a smile of contentment rather than a joke. Brahms's scherzos suggest a mixture of Beethoven and Schumann.

Something new was brought to the scherzo by Mendelssohn: the dancing, fairylike lightness of his *Midsummer Night's Dream* music and his "Scotch" Symphony. Chopin introduced a dramatic quality, sometimes mysterious, sometimes gay, into his large-scale scherzos for piano.

Contemporary composers often write scherzos, sometimes calling them that (as Bartók does in his Suite for Piano, Opus 14, and his Fifth String Quartet) and sometimes not (as in Copland's Sonata for Piano and Shostakovich's Fifth Symphony). But such works are no longer necessarily in triple meter or in the three-part form of the Classical scherzo.

SCHOENBERG, ARNOLD (1874–1951): the composer who, through his composing, teaching, and books, did more to change the sound of music in the twentieth century than any other musician.

Born in Vienna, Schoenberg studied the violin and, before he was nine, had started to compose little pieces for that instrument. He had already decided that he would be a musician, but his family was poor and unable to afford lessons for him in music theory or composition. A friend, Oscar Adler, taught him a little about harmony and ear training, and another friend, Alexander von Zemlinsky, gave him some instruction in counterpoint. The rest Schoenberg learned on his own.

He played chamber music, at one time playing the cello part on a viola fitted with zither strings. He studied the music of Beethoven from the few scores of symphonies and string quartets that he could afford to buy. From an encyclopedia he learned about sonata form—and promptly wrote the first movement of a symphony. No composer ever started with so little formal training and ended with so much theoretical perception. Even when he was a teacher he was humble about what he knew. In his *Harmonielehre (Theory of Harmony),* published in 1911, he acknowledged this by saying, "This book I have learned from my pupils."

Schoenberg's early works, which he began to write in his twenties, were Romantic in feeling, modeled on the passionate, glowing music of Mahler and Strauss. His first successful work was *Verklärte Nacht (Transfigured Night),* for string sextet of two violins, two violas, and two cellos. (Schoenberg later arranged the work for string orchestra, including double basses.) The work has a program: as two lovers wander in the moonlight, the woman confesses that she has been unfaithful, and her lover forgives her and by this act becomes a better man—transfigured by his goodness. The music of *Verklärte Nacht* is close in style to the chromatic music of Wagner's *Tristan and Isolde.* It is built from short motives which are developed at length, with climax piling on climax as the feeling of the poem grows more intense.

Verklärte Nacht has become Schoenberg's most-played work—as a sextet, as an orchestral piece, and as the music of Antony Tudor's ballet *Pillar of Fire.* His Romantic style was continued in his symphonic poem *Pelleas und Melisande,* based on the same play as Debussy's opera, and written in 1902, the year of the opera's first performance. He then began his *Gurre-Lieder (The Songs of Gurre),* a huge choral composition for five solo singers, a narrator, an eight-part mixed chorus, three male choruses, and an immense orchestra. This mammoth work, which required special manuscript paper big enough to hold all of the score, was started in 1901, finished in 1911, and given its first performance in 1913. More romantic in feeling than any work by Wagner, Strauss, or Mahler, *The Songs of Gurre* marked the end of Schoenberg's writings in the style of the nineteenth century.

For several years Schoenberg lived in Berlin. He arranged and conducted music for cabaret shows and operettas. But the pull of Vienna was too strong, and he returned. A group of students gathered round him, including his two outstanding pupils, Berg and Webern. Mahler, the most influential musician in Vienna, championed Schoenberg's music. In 1904 Schoenberg started the first of his societies for the performance of new music.

In the meantime Schoenberg had been experimenting. In his compositions he turned away from traditional harmony and melody. The melodies in his first two string quartets (the second of which adds a soprano voice in the last movement) became more wide-spaced, with large intervals replacing stepwise motion. By 1909 he had done away with traditional ideas of consonance and dissonance; his music now lacked a key center—it became atonal. His *Three Piano Pieces,* Opus 11, the song cycle entitled *The Book of the Hanging Gardens,* and his first *Kammersymphonie (Chamber Symphony)* shocked most of their listeners, who heard only dissonance and missed the emotional intensity of the music.

Schoenberg was exploring the world of fears and dreams—the deeply hidden world that men and women keep to themselves, the world that was explored by another Viennese pioneer, Sigmund Freud, in psychoanalysis. From being a Romantic composer, Schoenberg became an Expressionist. Expressionism—an approach best known from the visual arts—called on the artist not to render the world about him or even (as with the Impressionists) to render fleeting images of it as caught by his senses; instead, it called on him to project his personal feelings into his work. (Painting, as a matter of fact, did interest Schoenberg, and he studied it with Kandinsky, one of the leading Expressionist painters.) In music, Schoenberg came to believe that he could not possibly express his own feelings through the building blocks—the chords, the intervals, the rhythms—used by other composers. To express his own world of feelings he would, he was sure, have to make up his own sounds.

Schoenberg's music became more night-

Arnold Schoenberg

A scene from the American première of Moses and Aaron (1966 production by the Opera Company of Boston)

marish in his two works for the stage: *Erwartung* (*Expectation*, 1909) and *Die glückliche Hand* (*The Lucky Hand*, 1910–13). *Erwartung* is a "monodrama"—a work for one character (a soprano) and orchestra. It concerns a woman who wanders into the woods at night, seeking her lover, and finally finds him—dead. It is a vivid work, quite beautiful in its strange way. Like most of Schoenberg's works, it is filled with compassion and warmth.

Even more experimental were the *Five Orchestral Pieces* (1909) and the song cycle *Pierrot lunaire* (1912) for female singer-reciter and chamber orchestra. The *Five Orchestra Pieces* has titles for each movement: "Forebodings," "The Past," "Summer Morning by the Lake": "Colors," "Crisis," "The Obligatory Recitative." They call for a large orchestra, used by Schoenberg for a great variety of color rather than for sheer bulk of sound. Rather than blending, the instruments seem to play *against* each other. The score of the last movement is so complicated that Schoenberg invented a system—carried out in all his later works—of marking the principal part at the moment with an **H** for *Hauptstimme* (principal voice).

Pierrot lunaire is based on a series of poems about a moonstruck Pierrot, the white-suited lover in the pantomime tradition. The singer declaims the poem in a speaking voice that glides from pitch to pitch in strange rhythmic patterns. Schoenberg called this technique *Sprechstimme*, "speaking voice." Its effect in *Pierrot lunaire*, in which it goes its own way while the instruments go theirs, is eerie and romantically moon-mad. The Berlin audience that heard it in 1912 did not like it any more than the Paris audience liked Stravinsky's *Rite of Spring* in the following year.

After a few more works, including the *Six Little Piano Pieces*, Opus 19, and the *Four Songs with Orchestra*, Opus 22, Schoenberg stopped composing for seven years

(1914–21). Part of this time he was busy with World War I military duties. After the war he returned to Vienna to continue his teaching. There he organized, with Webern, a Society for Private Musical Performances. But most of all he took stock of himself and his music. He had ventured so far away from any previous musical theories that he felt the need to set up some way of organizing tone. There was no longer in his music any major-minor scale system, nor any traditional system of making chords or chord progressions; there was no feeling of any key center or tonic. To give himself some boundary, some framework, he set up for himself the twelve-tone technique. In 1921 he gave a lecture on his new theory, calling it "Method of Composing with Twelve Tones."

From that time on Schoenberg was known as "the twelve-tone man." People strained to penetrate his system instead of listening to his music as music. He himself, much later, said bitterly that audiences were interested not in "What did he say?" but in "How did he say it?" The result was that of all leading composers of his time, Schoenberg has had the fewest performances. And the man who said, "I write what I feel in my heart . . ." was attacked as an unromantic intellectual.

Schoenberg's first work completely in the new system was his Suite for piano, Opus 25. The method had been used in some sections of his *Five Piano Pieces*, Opus 23, and his Serenade, Opus 24, for seven instruments (including mandolin and guitar) and baritone. For a time his works were almost Classical rather than programmatic. He wrote as though the restrictions of his system had given him freedom of ideas. His music is difficult to play, requiring the performer to shed almost all his habits relating to rhythm, harmony, and melody. It split performers into a majority that would have nothing to do with it and a dedicated minority (the pianist Eduard Steuermann, in particular) who made it their specialty.

In spite of his revolutionary theories, Schoenberg was appointed in 1925 to a professorship at the Prussian Academy of the Arts in Berlin. He held this post until 1933, when he was dismissed by the Nazis. His crime consisted of coming from a Jewish family; in fact he was a convert to Catholicism.

Schoenberg emigrated in 1933 to the United States and settled in California. There he taught first at the University of Southern California and then, until his retirement, at the University of California in Los Angeles.

Meanwhile he returned to the Jewish faith. In 1938 he made a setting of the Jewish prayer *Kol Nidre* for speaker, chorus, and orchestra. He wrote both words and music for a cantata, *A Survivor from Warsaw,* as a memorial to those who had died in Nazi prison camps. He became an American citizen and symbolized this act by changing his name from Schönberg to Schoenberg.

After coming to the United States, Schoenberg wrote many of his largest works: the Fourth String Quartet, a String Trio, a Fantasia for violin and piano, a Concerto for Violin and Orchestra, the second *Chamber Symphony,* and the *Ode to Napoleon* for speaker, strings, and piano.

In most of the later works Schoenberg used his new language of twelve-tone music. But in his Suite in G, for school orchestra, and his *Theme and Variations for Band,* Opus 43a, he used more traditional means.

A Biblical opera, *Moses and Aaron,* had long engaged Schoenberg. He finished the first two acts in 1932 and attempted to finish the third act in 1951, but this was never completed. It remains one of the strangest masterworks of our day and is gradually making its way on the opera stages of the world.

Schoenberg was one of the most thoughtful composers. His lectures and writings about music and musicians contain much wisdom. Many of these essays were gathered in his book *Style and Idea,* published in 1950.

Schoenberg died in 1951, but the controversy he started has gone on. His twelve-tone method has influenced almost every contemporary composer. Many, such as Stravinsky, who originally opposed him have come around to his method (often through the influence of his pupil Webern). But Schoenberg foresaw this. "Time," he said, "is a great conqueror. He will bring understanding to my works."

SCHOTTISCHE: one of the popular social dances of the nineteenth century, performed particularly in England and the United States. It was a group couple-dance much like the American square dance, except that the basic formation was a circle rather than a square. The calls, also, were like many heard in American square dances: "Ladies forward and back, gents the same. . . . All balance at corners and turn. . . . Grand right and left. . . ."

The dance was called *Schottische*—German for "Scottish (dance)"—because it grew out of a real Scottish dance, the *écossaise,* to which had been added a series of turning waltz steps in 2/4 time. The music of the schottische is usually in 2/4 time but is occasionally written as 4/4. The tempo is an easy-going allegretto. It was first danced in the middle 1800's in England, where it was sometimes called the "German polka."

In the early 1900's the schottische became a popular couple-dance with American cowboys. They speeded the tempo a bit and made the movement a little more athletic (Ex. 12).

Ex. 12 — "Flying Cloud"

Franz Schubert

SCHUBERT, FRANZ PETER (1797–1828): great Austrian composer who has been called "the last of the Classical composers and the first of the Romantics." He wrote symphonies, sonatas, and string quartets following Classical patterns, but changed these patterns to suit his own purpose and nature. He established a new form of chamber music in his songs. His waltzes, *moments musicaux,* and impromptus set the pattern for the many short pieces by such later composers as Chopin, Schumann, and Mendelssohn. Although Schubert lived a shorter life than any other great composer, in his fourteen or fifteen active years he turned out an incredibly large number of masterworks: more than 600 songs, at least eight symphonies, a vast body of chamber music, operas, masses, and choral works, and innumerable piano pieces for two or four hands.

Sadly enough, in spite of his subsequently recognized greatness, Schubert never achieved fame or fortune while he lived. He was admired and appreciated by a large circle of musical friends but never by the larger world of music—or even by the general public of his home town, Vienna. His works had many performances, but these were mostly at private musical evenings, called "Schubertiades." He had one hundred opus numbers published during his life, but many of his greatest works remained in manuscript form for a long time. His two greatest symphonies had to wait many years for their first performances. The Symphony in C Major, called the "Great" to distinguish it from an earlier "little" symphony in the same key, was not performed until 1839, eleven years after his death, and the Symphony in B Minor, the "Unfinished," not until 1865. Even today some of his works have not reached print.

Schubert's life was not known in detail until quite recently. The early biographies depended on anecdotes told by friends. Many of these anecdotes, since shown to be not completely true, have served to form a distorted image of the man. He has long been known as the composer who dashed off songs in a beer garden, who lacked musical training, who lived a dissolute life—a kind of musical "nature boy." None of these ideas could be further from the truth as it has been traced by two musical scholars: Otto Erich Deutsch and Maurice Brown. Deutsch put together the documents that attest to the real facts of Schubert's life and reconstructed a catalog of Schubert's music in the order in which it was written. Brown published an authoritative biography of Schubert in 1958.

Schubert was a true son of Vienna, the home of the waltz and the symphony. He was born in the Leichtenthal section, where his father was a schoolmaster, and except for brief excursions to the country he never left the city. His early training in music, up to the age of eleven, consisted of lessons on the violin and organ and some training in singing and music theory. Then, at eleven, Schubert was accepted as a member of the choir of the imperial Court Chapel, known as the *Konvict.* Here he had one of the best educations available in Vienna, in regular school subjects as well as in music. The school's orchestra was a good one; audiences were known to gather outside the building to listen to the rehearsals. Schubert started as a second violinist in the orchestra, but his talents soon won him the post of assistant to the conductor.

In 1811 he began to study theory and composition with Salieri, who was famous as a composer, music director at the court, and sometime teacher of Beethoven. During the first of his five years with Salieri, Schubert wrote his earliest song, "Hagars Klage" (Hagar's Lament). This was followed by some chamber music, part of an opera, some piano solos and duets, and a few church anthems. During school vacations Schubert played the viola in a family string quartet, thus absorbing the music of the great Classical composers.

When his voice changed, in 1813, Schubert was dismissed from the choir and faced the problem of his future. He was exempt from military service, being only about 5 feet 1½ inches tall. Unable to play any one instrument very well (this was to hold back his success), he could not become a professional virtuoso. Schubert therefore decided to become a schoolteacher, like his father. He lived at home and attended a teachers' college, but meanwhile continued to write, producing his first symphony, an opera, and various string quartets.

In 1814 he became an assistant teacher at his father's school, instructing beginning students in the ABC's. At this time his first mass, in F, was performed and warmly received. In October of 1814 he wrote one of his finest songs, "Gretchen am Spinnrade" (Gretchen at the Spinning Wheel). This, with its whirring accompaniment, on top of which floats a melody filled with longing, was the first of a new kind of art song. In it, words, melody, and accompaniment created a short musical drama. The song was not just a vocal melody supported by an accompaniment, but a creation in which the two performers merged as equals.

In the next few years Schubert gathered round him three friends who throughout his lifetime encouraged him, helped him financially, found poems for him to set to music, and labored to make his works known. Josef von Spaun and Franz von Schober were young law students who loved music and made Schubert's cause their own. Johann Vogl was a singer whose career at the opera house was drawing to a close, and who now found a new career in being the first to present Schubert's songs to the public. These three men did everything they could to push the works of their friend, whose greatness they realized. Spaun, for example, sent a collection of Schubert's musical settings of Goethe's poems to the poet himself, hoping that Goethe, an extremely influential man, would help the young composer. Goethe never acknowledged receipt of the songs.

Refused a job as music instructor in a teachers' college, Schubert settled down to the life of a schoolteacher, composing in his spare time. In 1815 he wrote no less than 150 songs, an operetta, and choral pieces. It seemed as if almost every poem Schubert came across ended up as a song. Among the songs of 1815 was the ballad of *Der Erlkönig*—the tragic ride of a father trying to outdistance the Erlking, Death. The three characters of Goethe's poem are portrayed in the voice part: the child who sees Death, the father who tries to give him courage, and the enticing voice of the Erlking. Suggesting rapid hoofbeats and a pounding pulse, the piano accompaniment keeps an exciting rhythm going throughout (Ex. 13). Only at the end, on a dark chord—the Neapolitan sixth, a favorite of Schubert's—does the motion stop. The singer gasps the final line, "In his arms the child was dead," and the song is over.

Ex. 13 —"The Erlking"

A "Schubert Evening," showing Schubert at the piano and Johann Vogl singing

"The Erlking" was an instant success within Schubert's circle of admirers. Together with "The Wanderer" (1816), it was the first of Schubert's songs to make its way outside his own circle.

Within the two years 1815–16, Schubert wrote four symphonies, including his now popular Number 5 in B-flat. The works were tried out by an amateur orchestra that had grown out of the Schubert family string quartet. It was also during this time that Schubert started to write the first of his many dance pieces for piano—waltzes, écossaises, and Ländler.

In 1817 he moved to Schober's house and gave up teaching for a while. There was a piano in the house (Schubert almost never had his own), and he began to write the series of piano sonatas which are ranked by many musicians with those of Haydn, Mozart, and Beethoven. During this period Schubert discovered the gay overtures of Rossini, whose music was the rage of Vienna. He also wrote his four violin sonatas, including those which the publishers later called "Duos" and "Sonatinas." And as usual he wrote songs, including some of his best: "Die Forelle" (The Trout), "Der Tod and das Mädchen" (Death and the

Maiden), and "An die Musik" (To Music).

The year 1818 saw the first publication of any of Schubert's works: two of his songs were printed in a magazine. He had by now resumed teaching, but continued to write, sketching new works, revising sketches, and polishing almost-finished compositions. Appointed music master to the household of Count Johann Esterházy, he left Vienna —for one of the few times in his life. Esterházy was a member of the wealthy Hungarian family for which Haydn had worked for many years. On the Esterházy estate Schubert gave piano lessons to the children, wrote vocal exercises for the mother, and accompanied the count, who loved to sing. For the children Schubert also wrote some four-hand duets. He was fond of this medium, which was a popular form of music-making at the time.

Life in the country bored Schubert. He missed the stimulation of his friends and disliked private teaching. Saying that he would rather get along by eating only stale bread, he returned to Vienna. There he wrote some operettas, or Singspiels, which were only moderately successful. Schubert had in fact little feeling for the stage and tended to choose undramatic librettos. What little drama there might be in a story was usually stopped in its tracks by some beautiful song or choral piece that Schubert could not resist putting in.

Schubert now composed more piano duets, since publishers seemed to be more interested in these than in string quartets or symphonies. One duet, a set of variations, was dedicated to Beethoven by his "admirer and worshiper, Franz Schubert." The two composers lived in the same city but apparently never met. Schubert was too shy to force his attention on the great Beethoven, and Beethoven was too preoccupied to think of inviting the younger man. In 1827, a few weeks before he died, Beethoven was shown some of Schubert's songs and sent a complimentary word about them back to the composer.

A wealthy cellist, who held musical evenings in Vogl's home town in Upper Austria, asked Schubert to contribute a new work. The result was the famous "Trout" Quintet for piano, violin, viola, cello, and string bass. This beautiful work gets its name from the slow movement, a string of variations on Schubert's song "The Trout." The "Trout" Quintet received one performance; then it was not heard of until after the composer's death.

Schubert's friends got together and backed the publication of "The Erlking" and "Gretchen at the Spinning Wheel." The songs were immediate successes: 600 copies of each were sold. The publishers Cappi and Diabelli now began to publish Schubert's songs, waltzes, duets, and part songs. During this time Schubert also wrote one of his finest works: the *Quartettsatz*, or Quartet Movement, in C minor. As with his "Unfinished" Symphony, no one knows

why he never got around to completing this quartet. It stands by itself as one of the earliest (1820) of Schubert's deep works.

Things seemed to be going well, and Schubert decided to try the stage once again. He spent much time and effort on a most ambitious opera, *Alfonso and Estrella,* but no one would perform it. He sketched out three movements of a symphony in B minor, but orchestrated only the first two movements. This, his "Unfinished" Symphony, was written in 1822.

The first movement, in B minor, starts with a deep, questioning phrase (Ex. 14) in the cellos and basses. This is followed by a trembling string figure over which the oboe and clarinet sing a plaintive song (Ex. 15). A new theme in G major, played by the cellos, is one of Schubert's best-known melodies (Ex. 16). The themes are developed most skillfully. The music smolders, then builds to climaxes. There are no spare notes, no "padding." The movement is as concise and well planned as is any symphonic movement by Haydn, Mozart, or Beethoven, with counterpoint brought in whenever necessary. Schubert was criticized, particularly in the nineteenth century, as lacking training in counterpoint, but actually his counterpoint is quite skillful—it just happens not to call attention to itself. It does what it is supposed to do—contribute to the composition as a whole.

Schubert was not a showman. His music does not glitter; it is sincere, warm, and friendly—and deceptively simple. It sings along so naturally that the listener is hardly aware of the skill with which the composer makes his themes grow, develop, and flower. His harmony is filled with colorful chords, placed just at the right moment, under-

Ex. 14

Allegro Moderato

col 8

etc.

Ex: 15

col 8

Ex. 16

Schubert and friends, setting out for an excursion to the country surrounding Vienna

lining a word or bringing in a new mood. His key changes, often unexpected, serve to open whole new territories into which his themes can venture. Schubert was fond of the sudden shift from major to minor and back again—an effect like a smiling face clouded over by a moment of seriousness. His forms are long. His building block is the phrase of four, five, or six measures, rather than the one-measure motive. Naturally this leads to larger proportions as Schubert balances this phrase with other phrases.

In 1822 Schubert came closest to writing a virtuoso work: the piece was his *Wanderer-Fantasie* for piano solo. This work, a set of variations, gets its name from Schubert's song "The Wanderer," on which it is based. It is like a sonata in that it has four movement-like sections. It concludes with a fugue, in which Schubert shows his ability to write counterpoint when necessary. The *Wanderer-Fantasie* makes terrifying demands on the performer. With its publication, in 1823, it became one of Schubert's most admired works. Schumann said of it, "Schubert would like, in this work, to condense the whole orchestra into two hands. . . ." Many years later, Liszt arranged it for piano and orchestra—and that is as near as Schubert ever came to writing a concerto.

After a few more attempts at writing for the theater, Schubert stopped. His last try had been the incidental music for the play *Rosamunde.* But publishers were now seeking him out, asking for little pieces for piano. Schubert obliged with whatever he could to eke out his meager living.

Schubert meanwhile turned to the musical form known as the song cycle—a group of songs using the poems of a single poet and often having a single idea running through the whole. Müller's *Die schöne Müllerin (The Fair Maid of the Mill)* furnished Schubert with a set of poems that tells the story of a shy young miller who falls in love with the daughter of a mill owner, becomes jealous of a hunter, and dies of heartbreak. The music of the cycle portrays the flowing of the brook beside the mill, the exuberant happiness of the young man, his jealousy and pride, and his final despair. Some of the songs are as simple and as tuneful as folk songs. These are written in "strophic" form, the same music being repeated for each verse of the poem. Other songs in the cycle are more dramatic, following the changing moods of the poem in a form that has been called "through-composed." This form was another of Schubert's contributions to the world of music.

In 1824 Schubert concentrated for a while on chamber music, writing, as usual, several works in the same medium. The results were his beautiful String Quartet in A Minor and String Quartet in D Minor ("Death and the Maiden"—based on his song of that name), plus an octet for clarinet, horn, bassoon, string quartet, and string bass. The A-minor Quartet, the first of Schubert's quartets to be presented at a public concert, was greeted as though it were his first effort in the form, whereas he had written twelve others before it. The "Death and the Maiden" Quartet, revised by Schubert in 1826, is considered by many to be his greatest achievement in chamber music. Yet it had but one performance during Schubert's lifetime; it was then put away and not published until after his death.

In the summer of 1824 Schubert once again went with the Esterházy family to their Hungarian estate. On his previous visit he had been put up in the servants' quarters; now, better known, he was given a room in the castle. He wrote more piano duets for the children, who now played better. Schubert accordingly made greater technical demands on them, as in his "Grand Duo" in C. When he got back to Vienna he continued to write piano works, including marches for four hands and one of his most beautiful piano sonatas—the Sonata in A Minor, Opus 42.

Schubert tried to obtain the post of assistant music director at the court, but was refused here as well as at several other places where he applied. Meanwhile he continued to turn out masterpiece after masterpiece, such as the Shakespearean songs "Hark! Hark! the Lark" and "Who is Sylvia?"; the song cycle *Die Winterreise (Winter's Journey);* the eight Impromptus for piano; and the Piano Sonata in G Major, sometimes called the Fantasy in G.

Schubert was ill, now—too ill to take part in the social events he loved so much. He saved his energy, for he had long been thinking of his next symphony, which was to be a big one.

In March 1826 a first public concert consisting solely of his own works took place in Vienna. His friends packed the hall and there was much applause for the composer. Excellent reviews appeared in the Leipzig, Berlin, and Dresden papers. The Vienna papers ignored it.

In the last year of his life Schubert wrote his crowning works: the Symphony in C Major; the F-minor Fantasy for piano duet; more songs, including the popular "Serenade"; and the three last piano sonatas—in C minor, A major, and B-flat major.

Schubert worked on his C-major Symphony for several years. He did a great deal of rewriting on it, and finally it became his greatest symphonic achievement. Long it is, but Schumann—who first discovered it and had Mendelssohn conduct it in 1839—called it "the symphony of heavenly length."

The introductory andante of the symphony opens with a horn call (Ex. 17) whose first eight measures all grow out of the first two measures. The opening ideas build to an allegro, the opening theme being based on two contrasting and overlapping motives, each of two measures. This phrase of four measures is balanced by another phrase of four measures (Ex. 18). The second theme (Ex. 19), a little dance, is in E minor—the distance of a third away from

Ex. 17

Ex. 18

Ex. 19

Ex. 20

Ex. 21

Ex. 22

Allegro vivace

Ex. 23

the original key. This device of shifting from one key to another key three notes away is a favorite one of Schubert's. The themes are developed through many keys, bouncing from flat keys to sharp keys. After the return of the themes in their original aspect, Schubert tacks on a long coda at a faster tempo. Near the end of the coda, the introductory horn theme emerges triumphantly in augmentation— that is, the notes are played twice as slowly as before.

The second movement is an andante con moto in the key of A minor. After a preliminary seven measures, which establish a strange little march rhythm, the oboe sings the main theme—also a march, slightly sad (Ex. 20). As in the introduction, Schubert avoids the usual phrasing of four measures plus four measures by building his main theme as a three-measure phrase answered by a six-measure phrase. The main theme alternates with another little march idea (Ex. 21). The themes are tossed around the orchestra, with the oboe getting the biggest workout.

The third movement is a scherzo in A minor. Unlike many scherzos, this one is not a witty joke but rather an amiable, good-humored waltz (Ex. 22).

The finale, an allegro vivace, seems to gather together everything that has gone before. A triplet figure and a dotted-note figure are spun out as only a master could spin them. They lead to a second theme that marches along on top of the triplets (Ex. 23). All this material is developed and transformed as though a magician were at work making something great and wonderful out of very little. The excitement never lets down, even though the movement is 1,154 measures long. In this C-major Symphony, Schubert showed that he was a musical giant. Yet, as we have seen, he never heard the work, which had its first performance only in 1839.

Schubert died in November 1828, only one and one half years after his idol, Beethoven. On his deathbed he read James Fenimore Cooper's *Last of the Mohicans* and asked for more stories about the redskins. He was buried, as he had requested, near Beethoven, and in 1863 the remains of both composers were reburied side by side. The Vienna papers, which had steadfastly ignored Schubert alive, now printed memorial poems about Schubert dead. And a public subscription was launched for a suitable tombstone with a bust of the composer.

During his lifetime the number of Schu-

The house in Vienna where Schubert was born (his rooms have become the Schubert Museum)

bert's published works had reached Opus 100. After his death, many works were turned up, sometimes in odd places, and were given opus numbers as published, not as written. Confusion resulted. Not until Deutsch's thematic catalog of 1951—which did for Schubert what Köchel's catalog had done for Mozart—were Schubert compositions listed according to date of composition. For example, the Piano Sonata in A Minor, Opus 42, was written in 1825, whereas an earlier sonata in A minor was given the opus number 164, although it was written in 1817, eight years before Opus 42.

By 1897, the centennial of Schubert's birth, the twenty-first volume of his complete works was published. Today there are still songs that have not appeared in print. Also, Schubert's sketchbooks have not been published. When they are, they will help to change the minds of those who think of Schubert as careless. He was, in fact, a tireless worker, always striving for perfection.

Schubert's reputation suffered for many years. He was dismissed as only a composer of songs. As his symphonies, sonatas, and quartets have become better known, the world of music has begun to realize what a rich treasure was given to it by the son of Vienna's Schoolmaster Schubert.

William Schuman

SCHUMAN, WILLIAM HOWARD (1910–
): a leading contemporary American composer. His works include nine symphonies, four string quartets, a violin concerto, and a large work for cello and orchestra. He has also written works whose inspiration came from baseball (*Casey at the Bat,* an opera), the American Revolutionary War (*New England Triptych,* based on works by the eighteenth-century composer Billings), a high-school chorus ("Holiday Song," for the chorus of the New York City High School of Music and Art), a familiar New York sight ("George Washington Bridge," for band), and the Bible (*Judith,* a ballet for Martha Graham). He has received practically every award that an American composer can be given, including the first Pulitzer Prize in music.

Schuman was born in New York City. He learned to play the violin acceptably, and with it he led a dance band while in high school. After high school Schuman enrolled as a student in the School of Commerce at New York University, but hearing his first live symphony concert excited him so much that he immediately left college and plunged into the study of harmony and counterpoint with all his energy. His academic training was completed later in spare time at Teachers College of Columbia University. Two years of composition study with composer Roy Harris gave Schuman confidence and technical equipment, and his study and friendship with Harris encouraged him in his vision of the music he wanted to write—big, forceful, American in its vigor.

He wrote two symphonies as warm-ups, and Serge Koussevitzsky, who conducted the second one with the Boston Orchestra, invited Schuman to write more for him. The result was *American Festival Overture* (1939). This lively composition was followed by a steady stream of works, large and small, despite Schuman's teaching responsibilities at Sarah Lawrence College and his work as an administrator—as president of the Juilliard School of Music and, after 1961, president of New York's Lincoln Center for the Performing Arts.

Schuman firmly believes that a composer not only puts notes together but also plays an active role in his society. He has served on government commissions and artistic boards that further the cause of music. At Juilliard he and Norman Lloyd introduced a new approach to the teaching of music theory which has done much to change the teaching of music in the United States.

Schuman's music suggests the power and the nervous energy in American life. He does not use American folk music or jazz as such, although typical jazz rhythmic figures constantly pop up in his music. His melodies are at various times athletic, oratorical, tender, or brooding. They are treated in counterpoint that builds up to a high tension before driving on until the music is allowed to relax. The melodic and harmonic tension is increased by his exuberant orchestration, which features bursts of brass, wonderfully noisy percussion, and strings playing with bite and forcefulness. Instrumental choirs answer each other in blocks of sound; but every work also has virtuoso solo passages.

Harmonically, Schuman bases his music on triads or combinations of seconds and fourths, not in a key relationship but in a melodic relation to each other. Melodic lines are spun out of, and on top of, the triads (Ex. 24). The triads themselves are often clustered with added tones to give greater tension. The triads sometimes include both a major and a minor third, a sound that is tense as it "pulls" in two directions (Ex. 25).

Schuman is most of all a rhythmic composer. The toccata finale of his Third Symphony, for example, starts with a long perky rhythmic pattern stated by the snare drum. This pattern is picked up by the bass clarinet, which gives a good-humored melodic line to the rhythm (Ex. 26a and b). By this means Schuman has arrived at a complex theme which can be thrown around, taken apart, and given a good workout by all the instruments.

Ex. 24 —Second Movement, *Symphony for Strings*

Ex. 25 — Symphony No. 6

Ex. 26a — Toccata from Symphony No. 3

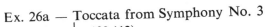

Ex. 26b —Same rhythm as picked up by the bass clarinet

Schuman writes contrapuntally, and it is natural that the old contrapuntal forms appeal to him. The Third Symphony consists of Baroque forms—Passacaglia, Fugue, Chorale, and Toccata—and he treats these forms quite freely. As his writing progresses, the structures become more complex. His Sixth Symphony is in one movement, consisting of many sections full of contrasts in color, dynamics, and methods of treatment.

Schuman's music is jubilant, nervously impatient, and compassionate. In it the composer states his deep-felt and sincere vision of what has been called "the American dream."

Robert and Clara Schumann in a daguerreotype portrait made in 1850, Hamburg

SCHUMANN, ROBERT: (1810–56): outstanding German composer and music critic of the early nineteenth century. Son of a bookseller who was a minor author, Schumann was born in Zwikau, Germany. There was little or no musical atmosphere in Schumann's home or in Zwikau generally. He studied with a town musician who could give him hardly more than the rudiments of music, but Robert soon began to improvise his own pieces. By the time he was ready to attend the University of Leipzig he was torn between music and poetry as possible creative careers. But his father had died, and his mother was insisting that he study law. So Schumann went to Leipzig as a law student, though he spent most of his time reading the Romantic poet-writer Jean Paul Richter.

By a happy quirk of fate, Schumann encountered in Leipzig a well-known teacher of piano, Friedrich Wieck, who revived his interest in music. Schumann started to study again, practicing under the supervision of Wieck. But some inner compulsion drove him to compose, and rather than seek a teacher of composition he chose to immerse himself in the works of Bach. Still a student of law, he moved to the more congenial city of Heidelberg, where he alternated between composing and practicing the piano for seven or eight hours a day and living a wandering social life. On a trip to Italy he managed to hear the great violin virtuoso Paganini—an experience which he was never to forget and which resulted in his arranging several of Paganini's Caprices for piano.

Now twenty years old, Schumann had to make a final decision between law and music. A "cram" course in law, which he found dull, and a long discussion with Wieck led to Schumann's decision to become a musician. Trying to make up for lost time, the young man crippled the ring finger of his right hand by using a mechanical device that was supposed to give it independent motion—a physical impossibility. His projected career as a pianist ended, Schumann now threw all his energies into the study of composition with Heinrich Dorn, a composer and prominent conductor.

Dorn allowed his gifted pupil to study in his own way—which had little resemblance to a traditional course in composition. Perhaps this is why there is in Schumann so little suggestion of any other composer. Schumann even in his earliest works has freshness and complete originality.

He tried to write a symphony, but two

Ex. 27 — Sonata in G Minor

years of study were hardly enough to enable him to cope with this large form. Since he had little or no experience with instruments other than the piano, his student symphony was unsuccessful. He fell back to writing for the piano, the instrument that was always closest to his heart.

The bold opening (Ex. 27) of Schumann's Sonata in G Minor announced the arrival of a new, masterful composer, age twenty-three. But who was to recognize him? There was at the time not a single paper or magazine in Germany or Austria that carried any critical weight in the field of music. So Schumann and a few friends in 1834 founded the *Neue Zeitschrift für Musik*— a periodical that would fight for the highest standards in musical criticism. Schumann edited it for ten years, writing criticism that he signed Florestan or Eusebius —depending on whether the tone was stormy or gently poetic. He wrote about an imaginary group of Davidsbündler, who were ready to tear down all that the Philistines in the arts—those who were against new ideas—believed in.

Schumann's magazine called attention to the new group of composers that were coming onto the musical scene—Berlioz, Chopin, Mendelssohn, Heller, Franz, and later Brahms. His work as editor seemed to spur him into great musical activity, and he wrote—during these years of his twenties —some of his finest music for piano: *Carnaval, Symphonic Études,* the mighty Fantasie, Opus 17, and a host of shorter works—the *Scenes from Childhood, Humoresque,* and romances. Other musicians were a bit puzzled by this tempestuous young man; only Franz Liszt recognized his genius and wrote about him.

Schumann and Mendelssohn became close friends. Schumann appreciated the talents of Mendelssohn, although Mendelssohn was somewhat puzzled by the untraditional music of his friend. To Mendelssohn, Schumann dedicated his three string quartets, written in 1842.

In his articles in the *Neue Zeitschrift,* Schumann might be said to have originated the modern style of music criticism. He wrote about music and musicians in an informed manner. He bullied, coaxed, and harangued his readers until they accepted

The piano used by Clara Wieck in her first concert appearance, at the Leipzig Gewandhaus, in 1828

the new music of the day. His concept of the critic's role was a lofty one: to stimulate and improve the artistic tastes of an apathetic public.

Schumann thought that by moving the offices of the magazine to Vienna, the former musical capital of Europe, he might attract a wider audience. But musical culture in Vienna had petrified; it had not evolved beyond Mozart, Haydn, Schubert, and Beethoven. It was not ready to accept any new musical styles or the magazine that advocated such styles.

After a half year Schumann retreated. But he came away with ideas for a musical work that became the charming *Faschingsschwank aus Wien (Viennese Carnival)* and he had uncovered Franz Schubert's great C-major Symphony, which had never been performed. Returning to Leipzig, he started to rebuild his magazine's influence. He also asked Wieck, his former piano teacher, for the hand of his daughter —the gifted, already-famous Clara. When Wieck objected strenuously, Schumann took the matter to a court of law. Finally, in 1840, the court decided in Schumann's favor and the two were married.

Throughout the year of waiting Schumann could think of little else than his love for Clara. Musically this resulted in an outpouring of his feelings in more than a hundred songs—fresh, new approaches to the *Lieder,* or art songs, that placed him on a level with Franz Schubert.

The marriage was an idyllic one. Clara became the foremost interpreter of her husband's works, playing them all over Europe. Their eight children did not seem to stop Robert and Clara from traveling as far as Russia, where she was a great success and he conducted his First Symphony in B-flat, which he called his "Spring"

Symphony. The composition of this work was followed immediately by the D-minor Symphony, which was published much later and called Number 4.

More than most composers, Schumann would explore one medium, write many works in it, and then move on to something else. Before 1840 he wrote almost nothing but pieces for piano. Then came his song period, followed in 1841 by several symphonic works and the beginning of his piano concerto. In 1842 he wrote chamber music—three string quartets, and a quintet, a quartet, and a trio for piano and strings. In these compositions that use the piano Schumann, as in his songs, gave the piano the featured role.

The year 1843 saw a new medium explored—that of choral music, principally the large work *Das Paradies und die Peri (Paradise and the Peri)* for chorus, orchestra, and soloists. The success of this work led to the settings of Goethe's *Faust,* also for chorus, orchestra, and soloists.

Schumann helped his friend Mendelssohn start the famous Leipzig Conservatory and even taught there for a while. But teaching was a hard chore for Schumann, and his health began to suffer. With his family he moved in 1844 to Dresden, there devoting his time to the study of Bach's works—a study that resulted in several sets of fugues of his own. He also found time to write his Symphony Number 2 in C Major and become a friend of Richard Wagner, who was conducting in Dresden. Perhaps it was Wagner's *Tannhäuser,* which he admired, that led him to make his own libretto for his only opera, *Genoveva.* Schumann as an ardent nationalist was one of the first to use German tempo and dynamic markings instead of traditional Italian ones, and he wanted to invent his own style of German opera. *Genoveva* has no recitative, and the music sounds like a succession of large and small arias; it was not a success.

The last period of Schumann's life was an alternation of triumphs and disappointments. He decided to become a conductor, first of choruses and then of the orchestra in Düsseldorf, but he had neither the temperament nor the training for such work and eventually was forced to relinquish the posts. Meanwhile, however, he wrote a number of choral works, the Symphony Number 3 in E-flat (the "Rhenish" Symphony), a concerto for violin, and one for cello. He was invited to conduct concerts of his own music, and in general Germany was beginning to acknowledge his greatness as a composer.

In 1853 the twenty-year-old Brahms came to play for Schumann and show him his compositions. Schumann was so impressed by Brahms's music that he dashed off his first article in years for his old magazine the *Neue Zeitschrift,* and arranged for the first publication of Brahms's works. But this generous act toward a young composer was one of Schumann's last public deeds. The intense schedule of work he had followed for over twenty years took its toll in the form of a mental breakdown. Schu-

mann spent the last two years of his life in an institution.

Schumann made a strong contribution to the musical life of his times through his discerning and appreciative criticism, but his greatest contribution to the world was his fresh and youthful music. Working in traditional forms, he managed to transform them through his originality. Sonata and symphony form gained new freedoms, as in his D-minor Symphony, a non-programmatic work in which themes reappear from one movement to another. In its use of pedal points and its slightly thick orchestral sounds, the D-minor sounds like a forerunner of the symphonies of Brahms—and, in a sense, it was. Its slow second movement is a romance featuring a shimmering violin solo. A hearty scherzo gradually leads to a vivace final movement, which opens with the wide-spaced chords of which Schumann was so fond (Ex. 28).

Much of Schumann's orchestral writing sounds as though it had been tried out at the piano. And certainly that instrument was always at the back of his mind. He was particularly fond of the rich, singing middle register, with the thumbs playing a duet and the other fingers playing an embroidery on either side of the melody (Ex. 29). Schumann was one of the first

Clara Schumann (an engraving after the painting by Eduard Bendemann, 1859)

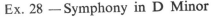

Ex. 28 — Symphony in D Minor

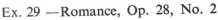

Ex. 29 — Romance, Op. 28, No. 2

Robert Schumann (an engraving after the painting by Eduard Bendemann, 1859)

Ex. 30 — Sonata in F-sharp Minor

Ex. 31 —"Préambule" from *Carnaval*

composers to take real advantage of the sustaining pedal, which allowed him to play a sonorous bass, accompanying chords in the middle of the piano, and a singing melody on top (Ex. 30).

Harmonically Schumann was not excessively chromatic, but he had learned from his study of Bach how a good bass line could, in combination with a melody, suggest unusual chords. Counterpoint in Schumann's music is not of the academic kind but rather a natural product, providing a solid bass line, for example, against which melodies could soar or dip and pivot capriciously (Ex. 31).

Much of the Romantic yearning that characterizes Schumann's music is due to his avoidance of the prosaic resolution of tones. He preferred to jump to the other side of the resolution tone, making the listener wait for the eventual fulfillment:

"Valse noble" from *Carnaval*

There is a rhapsodic quality to much of his music—it surges with passion, as in the opening of the Fantasie, Opus 17 (Ex. 32). He was especially fond of a toccata-like rhythm, sometimes filling in every sixteenth note in a measure. At times this motor-rhythm is divided between hands while he floats a melody on top and provides a sturdy bass below (Ex. 33).

Schumann was interested in rhythmic experiments, especially those using cross-rhythms or syncopations (Ex. 34). His music seems to alternate, like the Florestan-and-Eusebius side of his nature, between good, solid square rhythms and those with subtly disguised basic pulses.

Schumann's songs are, along with Schubert's, the greatest German art songs. His two song cycles, the *Dichterliebe (Poet's Love)* and *Frauenliebe und Leben (Woman's Love and Life)*, are standard recital works. In many of the "atmosphere" songs the piano part is almost like a solo, with the voice singing short phrases over the accompaniment (Ex. 35, page 528).

When the song is a folklike melody, however, Schumann tones his accompaniment down to the simplest basic support (see Ex. 36, on page 528). In his lovely *Spanische Liebeslieder (Spanish Gypsy Love Songs)*, for mixed voices and piano (four hands), he invented a form of vocal chamber music

Ex. 32 — Fantasie, Op. 17

Ex. 33 — Arabeske, Op. 18

Ex. 34 — "Des Abends," Op. 12, No. 1

Ex. 35 — "Der Nussbaum" (The Nut Tree)

Ex. 36 — "Volksliedchen"

that was to serve Brahms as inspiration for his *Liebeslieder* waltzes.

There is little pure display in Schumann's music—even in his concertos. Virtuoso passages occur in the *Symphonic Études,* the studies on the Paganni Caprices, and the Toccata, but the difficulties for the performer are intrinsic in the music.

Because Schumann wrote in traditional forms, such composers as Wagner looked down on him as being slightly old-fashioned. Now, after more than a hundred years, we see Schumann as one of the most romantic of the Romantics. His music is youthful, exuberant, springlike. It holds out to mankind a message of joy in life and love.

SCHÜTZ, HEINRICH (1585–1672): a great German composer of the early Baroque period who brought to music a depth of feeling that would not be equaled until the works of Bach, who was born exactly a hundred years later. Schütz began his career as a choirboy in the court chapel of Kas-sel, Germany. Later he went to Marburg University to study law, but the Margrave of Hesse, himself a composer, recognized Schütz's talent and persuaded the young man's parents to withdraw him from the university. The margrave sent Schütz to Venice to study with the great master Giovanni Gabrieli. In Venice, Schütz heard not only the glorious, many-choired music of his teacher but also the dramatic new madrigals and operatic recitatives of Monteverdi.

Returning to Kassel, Schütz worked for several years as court organist and in 1617 was appointed music director to the Elector of Saxony at Dresden. He held this post for the rest of his life, except for several leaves of absence, spent mostly in Copenhagen, during the upheavals of the Thirty Years' War. In 1628 Schütz made another pilgrimage to Italy, now as a successful composer, to study with the man he called "the wise Monteverdi."

Most of Schütz's music is religious, but he wrote an opera and a ballet for court wedding celebrations. The opera, *Dafne,* was the first in German. Unfortunately the

Engraving showing Schütz, with both arms extended, surrounded by the members of his chorus at the Schlosskirche in Dresden

Ex. 37

Tenor

Organ

Mein ____ Gott, ____ Mein ____ Gott, Mein ____
My ____ God, ____ my ____ God, my ____

____ Gott, Mein Gott, wa - rum, wa - rum hast du Mich ver - las - sen,
____ God, My God, why ____ why ____ hast thou Me for - sa - ken

music for both the opera and the ballet have been lost.

Schütz was one of the first German composers to study the rhythms of his native language and use them in music. These efforts, with his skill at bringing out the dramatic meaning of words, made for a new, powerful style. As a good Lutheran he often used chorale tunes in his big works, but always changed the melodies to suit the needs of his music.

The works of Schütz are full of startling melodic and harmonic progressions. The use of German speech rhythms led him to treat musical rhythm quite freely. A beautiful example of this occurs in his oratorio *Die Sieben Worte (The Seven Last Words)*. The words of Jesus have the rhythm of a sob as he asks, "My God, why hast Thou forsaken me?" (Ex. 37). In this work the utterances of Jesus were given to a solo singer accompanied by strings, whereas the tradition was to have the words sung by a quartet. Hearing a voice representing Jesus the person is a deeply moving experience.

Schütz wrote no purely instrumental music. He did use instruments with voices quite regularly, following the Venetian manner of Gabrieli. Most of his works were in style somewhere between the new Florentine opera recitative and Gabrieli's massive choral-instrumental works. His *Psalms of David* is for solo vocal ensembles, choruses, and an accompaniment of one or more organs.

Schütz's masterpieces are the *Symphoniae Sacrae (Sacred Symphonies)*, published in three installments from 1629 to 1650. In these his restless, inventive mind found new sounds that are amazing even today. "Da-

vid's Lament for Absalom," for bass voice and four trombones, is one of the great dramatic works in all music. In "Saul" the words of Jesus—"Saul, Saul, why do you persecute me?"—are sung by a solo sextet and two four-part choruses accompanied by two violins and organ. In Schütz's setting, the words of Jesus seem to fill the whole air with the question. One of the most imaginative scenes in music, it must be heard live or in full stereo to be fully experienced.

Schütz's other works include a Christmas Oratorio, an Easter Oratorio, and three passions. These last—written when Schütz was eighty years old—are austerely religious, as though Schütz had found new depths in the old style of unaccompanied recitative and chorus. Gone are the color and the drama of his earlier works. Schütz's passions are the final works of an old man who no longer allowed his music to be governed by surface effects.

Schütz at 85 years of age

SCORE: the arrangement, one above the other, of all the parts that are to be sung or played together in a musical performance. The part of each instrument or voice is shown on a staff of its own (or sharing a staff with similar instruments). The notes are spaced in such a way that all sounds meant to be heard together appear lined up so that a vertical line could pass through all of them.

It would be quite impossible for a conductor to read a score of this sort as fast as necessary unless each part had a traditional place. Woodwinds are usually placed at the top, followed by brasses; then come the percussion and various special instruments (like the harp), the part for the soloist (in a concerto), and the vocal parts; and at the bottom are the strings. Within each group the high-pitched instruments are placed near the top, the low-pitched ones near the bottom. The exact sequence usually followed is shown at the right.

Within each instrumental group bar lines are drawn from top to bottom. These bar lines are interrupted as one goes from one group to the next, to help organize the page so that it can be taken in at a glance. Parts for similar instruments are usually connected at the beginning of each line by a brace { or a heavy double rule [

As a conductor studies a new orchestral score he sometimes takes it to the piano and plays all the parts (or the most conspicuous ones) together. This is known as "reducing" a score. To do it skillfully takes a great deal of practice. Not only does one have to follow twenty or so parts, but these parts are written in as many as four different clefs. Furthermore, some instruments —the French horns, trumpets, English horns, and clarinets—are transposing instruments; that is, their music is written a few notes higher or lower than the actual sounds produced on the instruments. Anyone using a full score has to take all this in his stride.

For those people who do not want to wade through a complicated full score, there is sometimes available what is known as a "reduction," a "short score," or a "condensed score." A reduction of this sort is usually written to be played on one or two pianos. Singers usually use a vocal score—the full score of an opera or oratorio so arranged that the voices are on separate staves but all orchestral sounds are reduced for piano. Some composers write their music first in short-score form, saving the orchestration for a later stage. This orchestration is sometimes called scoring, though on Broadway and in Hollywood "scoring" often means the entire procedure of writing the background music for a show or for a film.

The writing of music in score dates from about 1600. Before that some vocal and keyboard music was occasionally written in score. More generally music was written in part-books, each of which contained only the music for one performer.

The word "score" comes from the name given to the process of drawing lines through the music: "scoring" or "marking off." A score is a *partition* in French, a *partitur* in German, and a *partitura* in Italian.

WOODWINDS

- Piccolo
- Flute
- Oboe
- English horn
- Clarinet
- Bass clarinet
- Bassoon
- Contra-bassoon

BRASS

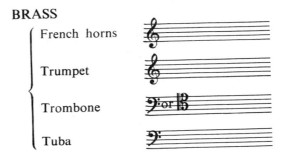

- French horns
- Trumpet
- Trombone
- Tuba

TIMPANI
and
PERCUSSION

Harp
or
Piano

SOLOISTS
CHORUS
STRINGS

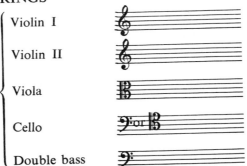

- Violin I
- Violin II
- Viola
- Cello
- Double bass

Alexander Scriabin in 1914

SCRIABIN, ALEXANDER (1872–1915): one of the trail-blazers of modern music. New paths in sound were opened by his invention of new ways of building chords, his abandonment of any feeling of scale, and his rhythmic freedom, which broke down many old concepts of rhythm.

Scriabin was born in Moscow, Russia, and after some early piano lessons with an aunt and some private lessons in composition with Sergei Ivanovitch Taneyev, he entered the Moscow Conservatory. A classmate of Rachmaninoff, Scriabin graduated as a brilliant pianist. He stayed on at the conservatory to study fugue, but failed an examination and left school. Already, however, he had written some piano pieces, very much in the style of Chopin. These attracted the attention of Belaiev, a wealthy amateur who had his own musical publishing house. Belaiev gave Scriabin a contract for his music and backed him in a concert tour of Europe.

For a few years thereafter Scriabin taught piano at the Moscow Conservatory, then he gave up the position to gain more time for writing and performing. In 1906 he made a concert tour of the United States. Several years later he met the conductor-publisher Koussevitzky, who gave him a good yearly fee for his music and took him on an orchestral tour down the Volga by boat. In his last years Scriabin appeared in many recitals of his own music in England and Russia.

Unlike most Russian composers, Scriabin showed in his works no feeling for the tradition of Russian folk music. Instead he became more and more involved in theosophy —a mystical search for direct union with an immanent Supreme Being. In his music he attempted to portray the ecstasy and rapture of his beliefs. The early Chopin-like compositions gave way to rhapsodic works more in the manner of Liszt. Finally, unable to express himself through conventional sounds, he broke into a new world of chords and rhythms. He sprinkled his scores with directions such as "languidly," "imperiously," "deliriously," "mysterious-ly," "fantastically," and "with light." No longer were his piano works mazurkas, preludes, and études—they became short tone poems for the piano with titles such as "Desire," "Toward the Flame," "Satanic Poem," "Enigma," and "Languid Poem." In his use of the piano Scriabin achieved ravishingly tender sounds that alternated with hammered, vibrant tremolos. Birdlike trills and swooping runs occur side by side with somber rumblings in the bass.

The demands Scriabin makes on the pianist are fantastic in their coverage of keyboard space and their rhythmic complexity. His parts for the left hand are probably more difficult than those of any other composer. They dart up and down the keyboard, playing complicated rhythmic patterns against equally complicated patterns in the right hand. Scriabin's own left-hand technique was outstanding. One story is that he hurt his right arm, and sooner than stop practicing he worked for days with just the left hand. He did write several works for the left hand alone.

In the field of harmony Scriabin moved from the comparatively simple chords of Chopin to more dissonant chords vaguely based on the whole-tone scale. From there he moved to chords built up with intervals other than the traditional thirds. Many of his later works are built on one sound from which the whole work grows. The sound may be a series of changing intervals or a combined major-minor triad—a restless sound he used in his Prelude, Opus 74, Number 4 (Ex. 38). His most famous chord is his so-called "mystic" chord, made by piling up different kinds of fourths. This chord is the basic harmony underlying his *Prometheus,* or *The Poem of Fire,* for orchestra, which he wrote in 1909–10.

This work, like his earlier Third Symphony, *The Divine Poem,* and his symphonic *The Poem of Ecstasy,* was an attempt by Scriabin to express his religious exaltation —his joy of creation—in music. But in *Prometheus* there was to be the added use of colors played on a "keyboard of light," the colors changing with the mood of the work.

Ex. 38 — Prelude, Op. 74, No. 4

Ex. 39

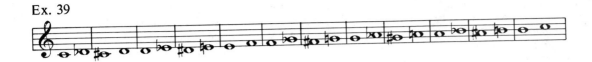

Ex. 40

Ex. 41 — Introduction, *Tristan and Isolde*, Wagner

Scriabin died before he could begin what was to be his masterpiece—a mystic drama to be performed by a cast of 2,000. This visionary project was to combine music with poetry, dancing, colors, and perfumes. Through this work Scriabin hoped to unite mankind in a search for a future of beauty, joy, and religious contentment.

In the early 1900's Scriabin's fame rose like a meteor. He became the center of a group of disciples, particularly in Russia, and his music was treated as a revelation. In the minds of his followers, it would displace all other music. After his death he suffered a decline in popularity, but in recent years he has been rediscovered. Pianists have found a wealth of beauty in his many short pieces and in his ten sonatas.

SEMITONE: in European music, the smallest difference in pitch heard between two tones. On the piano it is the distance from one key to the next closest key, black or white (the keyboard of the piano is completely divided into semitones). B to C and C to C# are semitones. Each octave contains twelve semitones, and each of these may be written as a minor second (Ex. 39) or as an augmented prime (Ex. 40). In the major scale a semitone occurs between the third and fourth and the seventh and eighth scale degrees:

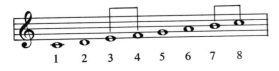

The presence of semitones and their placement determine the form of a scale. In the Dorian mode, for example, semitones occur between the second and third and the sixth and seventh scale degrees:

Much of the music written in the nineteenth century depends for its expressiveness on the use of the semitone, as in the opening motives of *Tristan and Isolde* (Ex. 41).

SEMPLICE: an Italian word meaning "simply." A composer uses semplice as a direction when he wants his music to be played in a straightforward, unaffected manner, with no liberties in tempo or dynamics. The term occurs most often in music of a moderate tempo and with a singing melody that the performer might be tempted to make too much of. Beethoven uses it in the "arietta," or "little aria," of his Sonata for Piano, Opus 111. The beautiful theme of these variations is marked *Adagio molto semplice cantabile*—"very slowly, in a singing, simple manner."

SENZA: an Italian word meaning "without." In music for string or brass instruments, the phrase *senza sordini* means that the mutes are to be removed from the instruments. *Senza misura* or *senza tempo* was used by Verdi, Schumann, and Chopin to indicate a very free tempo. *Senza repetizione* means "without repeating." *Senza rallentando* is a reminder to the performer not to slow down.

SEPTET (SEPTETTE): a work for seven instruments. No one particular combination of seven instruments has interested composers more than another. Septets for combinations consisting of piano, strings, and wind instruments have been written by Hummel, Spohr, Stravinsky, and Schoenberg. Other instrumental septets have been written by Beethoven (Opus 20, for strings clarinet, bassoon, and horn); Ravel (*Introduction and Allegro* for harp, string quartet, flute, and clarinet); and Schoenberg (Serenade, Opus 24, for clarinet, bass clarinet, mandolin, guitar, violin, viola, and cello).

SEQUENCE: the repetition of a musical idea at a lower or a higher pitch. The idea may be just a few notes (Ex. 42) or a whole phrase (Ex. 43). Although sequences are to be found in music written before 1600 they are rare, usually occurring as the music approaches a cadence (Ex. 44).

The sequence became a most important ingredient in the structure of music in the Baroque period (1600–1750). It could be an element in the construction of a fugue subject or concerto theme (Ex. 45) or the compositional device used in making an episode or transition from one key to another (Ex. 46). In many cases both melody and harmony have a sequential pattern (see Ex. 32 on page 108).

In the Classical period sequences continued to be a valuable structural device. In the opening of Mozart's Symphony Number 40 in G Minor the second phrase is a sequence of the first phrase (Ex. 47). Later, at the end of the development section, a chromatic sequence, based on a fragment of the first theme, leads gently back to the restatement (Ex. 48).

During the nineteenth century composers discovered the expressive and dramatic possibilities of sequence. Wagner and Tchaikovsky built their music to emotional climaxes by piling sequence on sequence. Chopin employed sequences both structurally and coloristically (Ex. 49).

Contemporary composers rarely use sequences, preferring a varied or an exact repetition of a theme. In popular music, however, melodic sequence is an important part of most songs. Harmonic sequence, using the circle of fifths and colorful chords, often serves as the basis for improvisations by members of small jazz combinations.

"Sequence" is also the name given to a form of chant that was added in the eighth century to the Alleluia of the Mass. By the twelfth century the sequence had become separated from the Alleluia and existed on its own. Hundreds of such sequences were in use until all but four were abolished from the Catholic service by the Council of Trent in the 1560's. The sequences

Ex. 42

Ex. 43

Ex. 44 — Two-part Motet: "Expectatio Justorum," Lassus

Ex. 45 — Fugue in G from *The Well-tempered Clavier*, Book I, J.S. Bach

Ex. 46 — Fugue in B-flat from *The Well-tempered Clavier*, Book I, J.S. Bach

Ex. 47 — Symphony No. 40 in G Minor, Mozart

Ex. 48 — Symphony No. 40 in G Minor, Mozart

Ex. 49 — Mazurka in B Minor, Op. 30, No. 2, Chopin

allowed to remain were *Victimae paschali laudes* for Easter, *Veni Sancte Spiritus* for Whitsunday, *Lauda Sion Salvatorem* for Corpus Christi, and *Dies Irae* in the Mass for the Dead. In 1727 a fifth sequence was added to the service—the *Stabat Mater*.

SERENADE: a calm piece to be sung or played at evening, usually outdoors. In its vocal form it goes back to the medieval period, when the serenade was a favorite way for a troubadour to pay homage to his loved one. This form of serenade, the lover singing outside the window of his lady-love, is that of Mozart's "Deh vieni alla finestra" from his *Don Giovanni*. The accompaniment suggests the traditional sound of a plucked instrument such as the guitar, mandolin, or lute (Ex. 50).

Hugo Wolf's "Italian Serenade" in one movement for string quartet, and the two movements entitled "Nachtmusik" (Night Music) in Mahler's Seventh Symphony, are instrumental versions of the vocal serenade. Another form of vocal serenade is the eighteenth-century *Serenata* (the Italian form of serenade), which was a modestly mounted opera to be performed at such festive occasions as royal weddings and birthdays. Gluck's *Le nozze d'Ercole e d'Ebe* (*The Marriage of Hercules and Hebe,* 1747) and Handel's *Acis and Galatea* (*c.* 1720) are typical examples of the theatrical serenata.

As an instrumental form, popular during the Classical period, the serenade was similar to the divertimento, cassation, and notturno, in that it consisted of many short movements such as minuets and marches plus movements that might have been used in a light symphony. The serenade never contained "heavy" music, but charming and appealing melodies. Befitting its light nature, the serenade was played by a small group of strings and winds or by strings or winds alone—as in Mozart's Serenade for Thirteen Winds and *Eine kleine Nacht-musik (A Little Night Music)* for strings alone. Mozart wrote more than a dozen serenades, including the famous "Haffner," composed to celebrate the marriage of the daughter of the mayor of Salzburg.

Many nineteenth-century composers wrote instrumental serenades, preferring this term to "suite" for a work of less than symphonic proportions or weightiness. Among the best known of such works are Beethoven's Fifth String Trio, Opus 8, and Serenade for Flute, Violin, and Viola, Opus 25; Brahms's earliest works for or-

Ex. 50 — *Don Giovanni*, Mozart

Count Almaviva (right) serenades Rosina in the opening scene of The Barber of Seville. *The singers are, from left to right: Robert Merrill as Figaro, Roberta Peters as Rosina, and Ceasare Valetti as Almaviva (Metropolitan Opera production)*

chestra, his Serenades in D Major and A Major; Strauss's early Serenade for Thirteen Wind Instruments; and Tchaikovsky's *Sérénade mélancolique* for violin and orchestra and his melodious Serenade for String Orchestra.

Twentieth-century composers have not ignored this form. Sometimes they have blended the vocal and instrumental types, notably in Schoenberg's Serenade, Opus 24, for clarinet, bass clarinet, mandolin, guitar, violin, viola, cello, with baritone voice in the fourth of the seven movements (1923). Other examples are Stravinsky's elegant neoclassic *Serenade en la* for piano (1925) and Copland's *Ukulele Serenade* for violin and piano (1926).

SEXTET (SEXTETTE): a work for six instruments or voices. (It is called *sextuor* in French, *sestetto* in Italian.) Vocal sextets are usually found in operas; for example, the finale of Mozart's *Don Giovanni* and the sextet at the end of the second act of Donizetti's *Lucia di Lammermoor*.

The string sextet, consisting of two violins, two violas, and two cellos, is the most popular form of instrumental sextet. Its rich middle-register sounds have appealed to many composers: Brahms (Opus 18 and Opus 36), Tchaikovsky *(Souvenir de Florence)*, Dvořák (Opus 48), and Schoenberg *(Verklärte Nacht)*.

Sextets have been written for other instrumental combinations by Beethoven (Opus 71 for clarinet, bassoons, and horns; Opus 81b for strings and two horns), Cowell *(Tall Tales* for six brass instruments),

Villa-Lobos (*Mystic Sextet* for flute, clarinet, saxophone, celesta, harp, and guitar), Poulenc (Sextuor for piano and winds).

Some divertimentos by Mozart (K. 247 in F, K. 334 in D, K. 287 in B♭, K. 522 in F—"A Musical Joke") are all scored for two violins, viola, bass, and two horns. When there is one player per part, these works are true sextets; otherwise they become works for chamber orchestra.

SHARP: a sign (♯) placed in front of a note to raise its pitch by the interval of a semitone, or half step. On the piano it means playing the black key immediately to the right of the pitch note, except in the case of B♯, which is the same as C, and E♯, which is the same as F.

A sharp in front of a note applies only to that particular note, not to other notes of the same name that lie elsewhere on the staff. In this example the bottom tone is an F-sharp, but the top tone remains an F-natural:

Sharps are not used to raise the pitch of flatted notes. The natural sign (♮) serves this purpose.

The double-sharp (✕) raises the pitch of a tone by the interval of a whole step: F-double-sharp is the same pitch as G.

In tuning or performance, a tone that is higher in pitch than it should be is referred to as being "sharp."

Dimitri Shostakovich in 1965

Scene from a Russian production of Katerina Ismailova

SHOSTAKOVICH, DIMITRI, (1906-75): an outstanding Russian composer. Born in 1906 in St. Petersburg (now Leningrad), he began to take piano lessons at the age of nine and by the age of eleven had begun to compose. The Russian Revolution of 1917 stirred him to write a symphonic poem, *Funeral March in Memory of Those Who Fell in the Revolution.* When he entered the St. Petersburg Conservatory as a piano student, his talent at composing was noticed by Glazunov, then the dean of Russian composers. On Glazunov's recommendation Shostakovich began the study of composition with Steinberg, a composer and former pupil of Rimsky-Korsakov. While Shostakovich was still a student his father died, and to help with family finances, he worked as a pianist for silent movies.

At the age of nineteen Shostakovich wrote his First Symphony, as a graduation piece. It proved to be quite successful, first in Russia and later in the United States and western Europe. The dry, brittle style of the fast movements showed an exceptional sense of melody and instrumental color; the slightly sorrowing slow movement showed that Shostakovich was a composer who could write from the heart. Within the next few years he established himself as Russia's leading serious composer, rivaled in reputation only by the older, wandering Prokofiev. The success of the younger man's First Symphony raised great expectations about his next works, but the three symphonies that followed disappointed everyone—including Shostakovich. Of these, only the Fourth Symphony has subsequently been performed.

In the meantime he had written his charming twenty-four Preludes for Piano, Opus 54, and his Concerto for Piano, Trumpet, and Strings, a glittering virtuoso work. He had also written two operas: *The Nose* and *Lady Macbeth of Mtzensk.* The latter was successful in its first performance in 1943, but after a two-year run was attacked in *Pravda,* the Communist Party newspaper, as being "coarse." The music, according to *Pravda,* "quacks, grunts and growls . . . love is smeared all over the opera in the most vulgar manner." The performances of *Lady Macbeth* stopped, not to be resumed until 1963, when Shostakovich introduced a new version of the opera under the title *Katerina Ismailova.*

Shostakovich accepted criticism of his work and took time out to think. He was encouraged by the success of his ballet *The Golden Age,* with its well-known polka. His song for the film *Counterplan* had become a favorite national song. He could dig into composition with a better idea of what he should do. By 1937, with his Fifth Symphony, he was hitting his compositional stride.

This symphony, in four movements, contains the composer's typical mixture of nineteenth- and twentieth-century musical styles. The first movement is in the sonata-allegro form. The themes are developed, as in a nineteenth-century symphony, by being torn to fragments and presented with various changes of character. The piano, not ordinarily included in symphony orchestras, is used for its dry, percussive quality in this work as well as in Shostakovich's First Symphony. At the end of the development section the music builds powerfully to a broad march that grows out of the second part of the first theme. The snare-drum beat under the theme is an example of Shostakovich's favorite rhythmic device♩♫, which he uses to give motion to his music. The movement ends with a re-statement of the original themes, with the order of the keys reversed.

The second movement is a scherzo. Dancing little themes presented by solo woodwinds or strings are interrupted by a hearty beer-hall waltz in the horns. The form of the movement is roughly like Bee-thoven's scherzo form of A-B-A.

The third movement is a slow one. Spun out of simple material, it builds to an emotion-packed climax that falls away at a final fade-out.

The finale is in one of Shostakovich's favorite styles—the triumphal march. It starts with a bold main theme blared out by the trumpets, trombones, and tuba over the steady beat of the timpani. Material from other movements is brought back, a lyrical section intervenes, and the music then drives on to a furious finish in D major.

The Fifth Symphony has taken its place as a standard orchestral work, and has been followed by ten more. Among the later ones the Seventh is perhaps the best known. Shostakovich wrote it during World War II, when he was serving as a fire warden in besieged Leningrad. It was his tribute to the courage and determination of his fellow-Russians.

Shostakovich was an ardent patriot. Love of his homeland runs through many of his works in spirit, although he did not often use actual Russian folk songs. Among his patriotic works are the large choral works *Song of the Forests* and *The Sun Shines Over Our Homeland*, and his background scores for the movies *The Young Guard*, *Meeting on the Elbe*, and *The Fall of Berlin*.

This composer alternated between theater or program music and concert music. In addition to his fifteen symphonies, he wrote thirteen string quartets, two piano concertos, a cycle of twenty-four preludes and fugues for piano, two concertos for cello and one for violin. He received many honors from his own government as well as from organizations in England, Sweden, Italy, and East Germany. In 1940 his Quintet for Piano and Strings earned him the Stalin Prize of 100,000 rubles. Interested in the peace movement in his country, he had also attended various conferences in other parts of the world and had twice visited the United States—in 1949 and 1959.

In 1954 the World Peace Council awarded him a Peace Prize. On his fiftieth birthday, in 1956, he was awarded the highest honor that the Russian government can bestow—the Order of Lenin.

SIBELIUS, JEAN (1865–1957): Finnish composer of symphonies and symphonic poems. The son of a doctor, he was born in Tavastehus, in southwest Finland. He was interested in music from early childhood, studying first the piano, then the violin. For a short while he was a law student at the University of Helsinki, but the pull of music was too great and he left to enter the Helsinki Conservatory, where he concentrated on the study of violin and composition.

When several of his works were played in 1889, they were received so favorably that Sibelius was given a government grant to study in Berlin and Vienna. Returning to Finland in 1891, he threw himself into the patriotic movement to free Finland from Russia. His role was to portray in musical language the spirit of Finland, particularly as expressed in the great Finnish epics and legends. His music, breathing of the land and waters of Finland—of its dark pine forests, its thousands of lakes, its long winter nights, and its isolation—served to remind his fellow countrymen of their national heritage.

Soon after the first performance of his early tone poem *En Saga (A Saga,* 1893) and the four legends based on the epic *Kalevala* (1893–95), Sibelius was given an annual government subsidy that allowed him to devote all of his time to composition. He settled in a country house close to his beloved forests and lakes. From here he ventured forth to Germany, England, and the United States, where in 1914 he conducted his *Aallottaret (The Oceanides),* commissioned by the Norfolk (Connecticut) Festival. But mostly he stayed home with his wife and five daughters, and composed.

In the middle 1920's, Sibelius stopped writing. Over a thirty-year period he had produced seven symphonies, thirteen tone poems, a violin concerto, and a host of songs and chamber works. Perhaps he was tired out or written out. In any case, for his remaining thirty years Sibelius lived a non-creative life, receiving admirers from abroad (many of whom brought presents, such as the big black cigars he liked), accepting the honors his country heaped on him (including the issue of a postage stamp bearing his portrait to celebrate his eightieth birthday), and listening via radio to the new music coming out of Europe and the United States.

A nationalist composer, Sibelius did not use Finnish folk songs in his works, but rather contributed to his country's folk-song lore. The eloquent chorale from his popular

Jean Sibelius in 1940

Lake Saimaa, in the eastern lake region of Finland

A modal quality in his music is as far as he strayed from the vocabulary used by Dvořák and Tchaikovsky. Only in his Fourth Symphony (1911), which is built on the sound of the tritone (C-F#), is there anything even slightly daring in his harmony and melody.

Outside Finland, Sibelius' music has been successful only in the United States and England. In these countries, which were late in developing their own twentieth-century composers, Sibelius is a staple in the repertoires of all symphony orchestras. His *Valse triste* for orchestra and Romance for piano are popular salon pieces. In some musical circles of today Sibelius is not held in high regard. On the other hand, he has been called "the only true symphonic composer of the twentieth century." Regardless of musical fashion, it is certain that he did create works that are significant. At least one symphony, the Fourth, is a contemporary classic. The tone poems brought new, dark-hued colors into music. Through Sibelius the voice of the north was heard, sometimes brooding and tragic but often sunny and warm.

Finlandia (1900) became so strongly associated with the Finnish independence movement that the Russian tsar ordered it not to be performed during political crises.

Sibelius' early style contains many hints of nineteenth-century German music mixed with some elements of Tchaikovsky. As he matured, his works became stamped with his own individual genius. His symphonic forms, at first a bit sprawling, became tighter, reaching a peak of effectiveness in his Fourth Symphony.

Sibelius was a master of orchestral tone color. Woodwinds chatter or sing long, often mournful melodies, as in *The Swan of Tuonela* (1893), which is practically a concerto for English horn. Strings rustle and scurry, while above them solo woodwinds toss thematic fragments about and the brasses bite into chords that are thrown into the general turmoil.

A master builder of symphonic structure, Sibelius adhered only in a general way to traditional sonata form. He developed his own technique, in which fragments of motives evolved into full-blown themes. There is a sense of continuous growth and variation of thematic material as the music mounts to a climax. The climaxes are powerful and triumphant—a bringing-together of all that is important in the works.

Melodically, Sibelius was fond of using one tone that grows in intensity until it lashes out to another long tone or ends in silence. Then again he sets up a kind of perpetual motion that gives momentum to a whole movement.

Harmonically, Sibelius was highly conservative compared to his contemporaries Debussy, Schoenberg, Bartók, and Stravinsky.

SILENT NIGHT: a favorite among Christmas songs the world over. For a long time it passed as a folk song; then an inquiry in the 1850's turned up the full story of its humble beginnings. "Silent Night" (in its original version, *Stille Nacht*) was first performed on Christmas Eve, 1818, in the church of St. Nicola in the Austrian village of Oberndorf in the Tyrolian mountains. The two soloists would normally have been accompanied by the church organ, but since the organ's bellows had been gnawed away by mice, they were accompanied by a guitar. The words had been written by Josef Mohr, a priest of the local parish, and the music by Franz Gruber, the thirty-one-year-old organist of a neighboring town.

That the song should have appealed to the congregation is easy to believe, but how did it spread to the outside world? When the organ came to be repaired the following year, the organ builder, Mauracher by name, took a copy of the score with him. Some years later, two brothers named Strasser learned the song from Mauracher and sang it at a Catholic service in Leipzig. From Leipzig it spread through the world at large.

The villagers of Oberndorf display Gruber's original score every Christmas, as well as the guitar used in the first performance. They are rightly proud of the song that is now cherished throughout the world.

Sibelius and his wife at their villa 20 miles outside of Helsinki

SINGSPIEL: a German comic opera with spoken dialogue rather than sung recitative. In its earliest form, it consisted of translations of English ballad operas—plays with interpolated popular songs. The Singspiel clearly filled a need; within a short time it became the favorite form of theatrical entertainment in Germany and Austria. During the middle and late eighteenth century many theaters were built to house productions of Singspiels. Emperor Joseph II even went so far as to establish in Vienna, in 1778, a National Singspiel Company. It was for this company that Mozart wrote *The Abduction from the Seraglio.* For a different company he composed *The Magic Flute.* Schubert, Dittersdorf, and Haydn also contributed to this first form of German opera.

The Singspiel had started as light, at times even farcical, entertainment. But as early as 1770 Johann Adam Hiller (1728–1804) had composed Singspiels that were close to being folk operas in their simple melodic style and their sentimental portrayal of the life of the common man. From this type of Singspiel developed German Romantic opera: first Beethoven's *Fidelio* (1805) and then Weber's *Der Freischütz* (1820).

In 1928 Kurt Weill and Berthold Brecht revived the form of the Singspiel in their bitter *The Three-penny Opera,* based on the first English ballad opera: *The Beggar's Opera.*

SMETANA, BEDŘICH (1824–84): the patriot-composer whose operas and symphonic poems became the foundation of the Czech nationalist school of composition.

Smetana (the name is pronounced with an accented, long first syllable) was born in Leitomischl, a small town in southern Czechoslovakia which, in 1824, belonged to Austria. In spite of haphazard music study, Smetana's talents were so great that he began to build a reputation as a virtuoso pianist. To further his career he moved to Prague, where there seemed to be greater opportunities to study and perform. For a while he was music teacher to the family of Count Leopold Thun, but, encouraged by Franz Liszt, who became a lifelong friend, he resigned this post to establish a music school.

From 1848 to 1856 Smetana and his wife struggled to make a success of the school. But Prague, torn between those who wanted to set up an independent Czech state and those who were content under Austrian rule, was no place for a Czech composer to be happy. When the chance came, Smetana moved to Sweden to become director of the Göteborg Society of Classical Music. Here he conducted a series of orchestral programs, introducing audiences to the "new" music of Mendelssohn, Liszt, and Wagner. Smetana lived in Sweden for five eventful years—a period during which his wife died, he remarried, and he wrote his first long orchestral works: the symphonic poems *Richard III, Wallenstein's Camp,* and *Hakon Jarl.*

By 1861 political conditions in Prague had improved and Smetana returned, becoming the musical leader of the Czechs. When a Czech theater was opened in 1862, Smetana began to think of writing operas. His first, *The Brandenburgers in Bohemia,* which celebrated Czech resistance to the Germans, was completed in 1863. He immediately started on his masterpiece—the warm, vivacious, tuneful *The Bartered Bride.* Strangely enough, the work was not an instant success when it was first produced in 1866. Gradually, however, its melodies, gay choruses, and rhythmically infectious polkas won the public, and the opera eventually became a kind of Czech musical shrine.

Smetana wrote six more operas, most of them serious. *Dalibor* (1868) and *Libuše* (1872) are strongly patriotic, breathing the spirit of liberty and freedom for the Czechs. *The Kiss* (1876) is more in the vein of the light-hearted *Bartered Bride.* It was so immediately popular that special trains were run to bring its audiences in to Prague from surrounding areas.

The year 1874 was one of great achievement and great personal trial. Smetana brought to the attention of the Czechs a young composer, Antonin Dvořák, whose Symphony in E-flat Major he conducted. He also started his cycle of six symphonic poems: *Má Vlast (My Country).* First came *Vyšehrad,* the name of the castle of the kings of Bohemia, and *Vltava (The Moldau),* the most popular of the series. But, as with Beethoven, deafness cast a shadow over Smetana's life. It ended his appearances as a performer and forced him to withdraw into himself. The result was alternating periods of depression and of highly productive inspiration. In following years he completed the rest of *My Country: Šárka, From Bohemia's Meadows and Groves, Tábor,* and *Blanik*—the last two based on legends of the Hussite's struggle for religious freedom. Also from Smetana's last ten years came two string quartets, both subtitled "From My Life," some fine choral works, and the ten brilliant *Czech Dances* for piano.

Bedřich Smetana

Smetana's work is related to the general style of the middle nineteenth-century Romantic composers. It is not distinctive, in the sense that Wagner put his musical signature on every measure, but it is highly individual in its tunefulness and colorful instrumentation. His use of perky polka rhythms elevated that Czech dance form to major importance. Smetana became the nationally loved composer of the Czechs—partly for the warm personality that shines through his music and partly because he expressed the finest patriotic spirit of a proud people longing for freedom.

SNARE DRUM: the most important drum used in marching bands; and, in the symphony orchestra, the drum next in importance after the timpani. The snare drum has many more names: side drum, military drum, *tambour militaire* (France), and *kleine Trommel* (Germany). It is a two-headed drum, with four to twelve metal or catgut strings on the outside of the bottom drumhead. When the top drumhead is hit, these strings make a buzzing, rattling sound. But the snare drum can also be made into a high-pitched straight drum by turning a lever that loosens the snares. When the snare drum is not being used, its snares must be loosened; otherwise it makes a buzzing sound that is disturbing. Whether used with or without snares, the drum is played with two sticks of hard, polished wood; these are thin, with a small knob at the end that looks like an olive. In dance bands the snare drum is often played with two fan-shaped wire brushes. When drumsticks are used, the drum is

The proper way to hold drumsticks for the snare drum

played by bouncing each stick, the drummer playing two lefts, two rights, and so on. The drummer first finds the place between center and rim on his drumhead that gives him the best rebound, then makes sure that both sticks hit the head at the same distance from the rim.

The most important drum strokes are:

the *flam* (a), which sounds *ba-DUM,*
the *drag* (b), which sounds *brr-r-UM,* and
the *roll* (c), which sounds *B-r-r-r-r-r-r.*

The drummer practices a roll, his most difficult stroke, by alternating R-R-L-L in a rhythm known as "Daddy Mama":

Among the other strokes on the snare drum are the *rim shot* and playing on the rim. The rim shot is done by holding the end of one stick against the drumhead and hitting that stick hard with the other stick. The result is a sharp-toned accent, like a gunshot. Playing on the rim gives a light, clicking sound somewhat like the old minstrel show "bones."

In parades the snare drum often plays alone for long stretches. Its basic "cadence," as notated by Beethoven, is shown in Ex. 51. In dramatic moments of suspense in theatrical performances, such as a high-wire balancing act of a circus, composers use nothing but a solo snare-drum roll. It is one of the most effective theatrical devices ever discovered. After a long military history the snare drum came into the orchestra by way of the opera house. Gluck and then Rossini used it for dramatic purposes. Berlioz, always on the lookout for new instrumental colors, used it in his *Symphonie fantastique.* Since then it has continued to be a valuable member of the percussion section of the orchestra. Modern composers have used it for important solo roles in concert works; thus Copland has it start off his *Music for the Theater* with a rush, and Schuman

Ex. 51

lets it play the long opening rhythm of the Toccata of his Symphony Number 3 (see Ex. 26a on page 521).

SONATA: an instrumental form usually consisting of three or four complete movements in contrasting tempos. Like many other musical terms the word "sonata" has meant different things throughout its more than three-hundred-fifty-year history. In recent times a sonata has meant a work for one or two solo performers; sonatas for three instruments are called trios, those for four instruments quartets, and so on. A symphony is a sonata for orchestra, while a concerto is a sonata for soloist with orchestra.

The term sonata (from the Italian *suonare,* "to sound") was applied first to instrumental works as distinguished from vocal works. The earliest sonatas were contrapuntal pieces in one movement, much like the vocal motets and chansons of the time. One of the first such sonatas was the famous *Sonata pian e forte,* written for brass instruments and viol by Giovanni Gabrieli in 1597.

The home of the early sonatas was Italy. This was also the place where the master-makers of stringed instruments turned out their newly perfected violins. It was only natural that the Italian composers would turn to the violin as the instrument for which to write sonatas. The violin could sing, but it was also agile, and its very agility suggested new kinds of melodic lines to the composers. As early as 1629, Biagio Marini composed a sonata for violin that made use of the violinistic technique. The sonata for two violins, a bass, and a keyboard or lute accompaniment—known as the trio sonata—developed along with the solo sonata as an important instrumental form of the early Baroque period.

The sonata that grew out of the old vocal contrapuntal forms was called *sonata da chiesa,* a church sonata originally written to be performed in churches. The sonata da chiesa started with a slow movement, this being followed by a fast fugal movement, a slow air, and for a finale, a rapid and rather gay contrapuntal movement. All movements were usually in the same key.

A lighter type of sonata, the *sonata da camera,* or chamber sonata, was composed of court dances such as the allemande, the saraband, and so on. Both types of sonata were written by Arcangelo Corelli, who established the Baroque solo sonata and the trio sonata as Haydn later established the Classical sonata. Corelli, who was one of the first to truly exploit the resources of the

violin, led the way for Purcell, Bach, Telemann, and Couperin, all of whom wrote sonatas for one or two violins.

Among the earliest keyboard sonatas were those written by Johann Kuhnau (1660–1722), Bach's predecessor at St. Thomas' Church in Leipzig. Each of Kuhnau's second set of sonatas, six in number, told in pictorial fashion a story from the Bible: David and Goliath, Saul and David, and so on. Similar program sonatas, based on the life of Jesus, were composed by Heinrich Biber (1644–1704) for unaccompanied violin. A difficult form to write as well as play, the unaccompanied violin sonata was primarily cultivated by Biber, Johann Jakob Walther, and J. S. Bach. Bach brought the art of writing for unaccompanied violin and cello to its peak in his three sonatas (da chiesa) and three partitas for violin and his six suites for cello.

The harpsichord and then the piano began to rival the violin as the favorite instrument of performers and composers in the middle of the eighteenth century. It was at this time that Domenico Scarlatti wrote his more than six hundred sonatas for harpsichord, one of the great treasures of the late Baroque period. These sonatas are apparently one-movement works, but some scholars, including the eminent contemporary harpsichordist Ralph Kirkpatrick, believe many of them were meant to be grouped in sets of two and three.

Scarlatti's sonatas, covering a wide range of styles, include virtuoso works, slow airs, pastorales, and marches and dances, often with a Spanish flavor. Almost every one is based on a two-part form or plan. In the first part several motives, often quite contrasting, are stated. Meanwhile the tonality shifts from the tonic, or home key, to the key of the dominant or the relative major. The first part has a double bar and a repeat, after which the second part starts in a key other than the tonic. Most of the material heard in Part I is repeated, but with changes, because the composer is now plotting his harmony so that he will eventually arrive at an ending cadence in the tonic key.

During the Classical period the form and content of the sonata changed. The keyboard sonatas of C.P.E. Bach, Haydn, Clementi, and Mozart generally consist of two or three movements, of which one is in sonata-allegro form, usually the first movement.

The slow movement, in a different key from the first movement, may be a two- or three-part lyrical aria, a theme and variations, or a sonatina. The last movement is

Heinrich Biber

Muzio Clementi

usually in a quick tempo form—a rondo, sonata-allegro, or theme and variations. Throughout the Classical period, however, many sonatas were written that do not follow this plan. In some two-movement sonatas the second movement may be in sonata-allegro form. Often a minuet—the only court dance carried over from the Baroque suite and sonata—served as the closing movement. The composer chose the pattern that best suited his purpose; he did not rely on formulas.

In his sonatas for piano, for violin, and for cello, Beethoven remolded the Classical sonata to fit his own dramatic purposes. Movements became longer; there were violent contrasts of themes, dynamics, and registers. Episodes or transition sections were made to contribute to the over-all dramatic pattern rather than serving only to move the music from one key to another. Fugues sprouted in finales; recitatives and cadenzas interrupted an otherwise smooth rhythmic flow.

The highly dramatic style of Beethoven's sonatas was continued by such nineteenth-century composers as Schubert, Weber, Schumann, Chopin, and Brahms. Liszt in his B-minor Sonata for Piano endeavored to create a new type of sonata—one many-sectioned movement that suggests a program, although he gave no clue to the meaning of the work.

Organ literature, which languished after Mozart's death, received a new impetus from the six organ sonatas by Mendelssohn. The clarinet had its literature enriched by Brahms, who wrote two sonatas for clarinet and piano in his later years.

Since Brahms a steady but small stream of sonatas has been written for piano and various instrumental combinations. In general the form of the Classical sonata is kept, loosely. The material and its manipulation are in keeping with the many changes that have happened in modern music. Among the important sonatas of the twentieth century are those by Debussy, Ravel, Scriabin, Prokofiev, Copland, Stravinsky, Berg, Bartók, Hindemith, Barber, Ives, Carter, and Persichetti. Hindemith has written a sonata for each orchestral instrument plus piano, thus providing recital pieces for performers who otherwise have little solo literature.

The sonata for four hands at one piano has intrigued composers—and has been welcomed by performers—since Mozart wrote his first such sonatas in 1764. The best known of the four-hand sonatas are by Mozart, Beethoven, Schubert, Hindemith, and Poulenc.

SONATA-ALLEGRO: the large structural plan that was the most important instrumental form of the Classical period. Developed originally as a form used for the first part of a sonata, symphony, concerto, or string quartet, the sonata-allegro form is sometimes referred to as "first movement" form or even just as "sonata" form. Its use soon spread to the slow movement, the final movement, and even to the opera overture. As with any musical form, the structure of sonata-allegro form has little or nothing to do with the kind of musical material used in the work or with the emotional response evoked in a listener. There are heroic, gay, or lyrical sonata-allegro movements, and in a long movement many contrasting moods may be present. A sonata-allegro may be a few pages in length (in which case it may be called a sonatina) or it may last a half hour.

Basically, a sonata-allegro is a three-part form whose sections are called the *exposition,* or statement; the *development,* or free fantasia; and the *recapitulation,* or restatement. Before the exposition there is often a slow, free introduction, and, after the recapitulation, an ending *coda,* which serves to round off the composition.

The exposition is concerned with the establishment of the tonic key and a move to a related key such as the dominant or relative major. Within the exposition the composer presents most of the material to be used in the movement. Each key may have its own theme or set of themes, or one theme may be used throughout. The exposition usually ends with a slight theme, called a closing theme, that is basically a decorated cadence or ending. Within the exposition there are usually several modulatory or transitional sections. These serve to move the music from one key to another, to afford contrast, and to build up a certain amount of suspense or anticipation as the listener is made aware that a thematic statement is in the offing. At the end of the exposition there is a double bar with a repeat sign, or a first and second ending.

The development section—it was originally known or thought of as the free fantasia—is the place where the composer moves to other keys, discourses on fragments of thematic material which are manipulated in various ways, brings in new thematic material (often quite striking, as in Beethoven's "Eroica" Symphony), and builds to an eventual return of the original key.

In the recapitulation, or restatement, the tonic key is re-established. In general, there are no modulations to any other key, so that the tonic key, once it returns, lasts until the end of the movement. Occasionally, as in Mozart's well-known Sonata in C Major K. 545, the restatement begins in the subdominant key and moves to the tonic, making a tonal scheme parallel to the exposition: C-G; F-C.

The coda, which comes when the recapitulation has seemingly ended, can be a brief afterthought or, as in the case of Beethoven, a long second development in several sections.

The sonata-allegro form developed out of the two-part sonata form of early eighteenth-century composers such as Domenico Scarlatti. C. P. E. Bach and Johann Christian Bach contributed to its growth by emphasizing thematic contrasts and by showing the dramatic possibilities in the transition sections. Haydn in his numerous sonatas, quartets, and symphonies was the first composer to realize fully the dramatic values and compositional flexibilities in the form. Since the 1750's sonata-allegro form has been *the* large musical form. Often a dramatic idea has been placed on top of it, as in Beethoven's Leonore Overture Number 3. It was crossed with rondo form to create a hybrid form, the sonata-rondo, as in Mozart's Sonata in B-flat K. 333. Mozart, who, like Beethoven after him, seemed determined to stretch sonata-allegro form in various ways, mixed it with fugue, as in the last movement of his "Jupiter" Symphony and the overture to *The Marriage of Figaro*.

During the nineteenth century many composers used the sonata-allegro form as a framework on which to superimpose a poetic or programmatic form. Others let musical sense dictate their approach to the form. Chopin, in his piano sonatas in B-flat minor and B minor, does not restate the first theme in the restatement section, feeling either that he had used the material enough or that it did not lend itself to restatement. Even later, when composers began to abandon rigid tonality, they kept many of the structural features of sonata-allegro form, modifying them as necessary. Bartók, for example, in the first movement of his Fifth String Quartet, devised what has been called the "arc" principle, in which the order of sections is as follows:

Exposition	Development	Restatement
Parts I		Parts II
and II		and I

Many contemporary composers, such as Prokofiev, Ravel, Stravinsky, and Hindemith, have utilized the form in their instrumental music. Berg wrote the first scene of the second act of his opera *Wozzeck* in sonata-allegro form. The old Classical structure has proved most flexible, and chances are good that it will adapt itself to whatever course music takes in the future.

SONATINA: a short sonata, usually light in character. Ordinarily it has three movements, each being a miniature. The first movement is likely to be in sonata-allegro form, with each part—statement, development, and restatement—much shorter than that of a regular sonata-allegro. In some cases the development section is omitted or is as short as a few chords. Such a modified version of sonata-allegro form is often referred to by music theorists as "sonatina form." It characterizes many slow movements of works of the Classical period.

Most sonatinas are fairly easy to play, although those by Ravel and Busoni are quite difficult. The best-known sonatinas for piano are those by Beethoven, Clementi, Gretchaninov, Kabalevsky, and Persichetti. The eccentric French composer Satie wrote a *Bureaucratic Sonatina* for piano. Sonatinas for instruments other than the piano are uncommon, among them being Milhaud's Sonatina for Two Violins and Sonatina for Violin, Viola, and Cello. Schubert's sonatinas for violin and piano were called "sonatas" by the composer, "sonatinas" by the publisher.

SONG: the musical setting of a poem. Singing comes from man's own musical instrument—the voice. Having this source of music always with him, man has spontaneously called on it to express every emotion from the deepest sorrow to the greatest joy. In song he has celebrated every event in his life from birth to death, and to song he has turned to express himself in worship, to teach his children, to lighten his labor, and to make his relaxation enjoyable.

Songs are often classified as folk, popular, and art songs. A folk song is one that has become so much a part of the heritage of a group that there is a feeling of common ownership, whether or not the composer is known. For the most part, a folk song has no composed accompaniment; in fact, the accompaniment changes from one performer to another. Even folk melodies and texts are known in various versions.

An art song is a form of chamber music in which a composed accompaniment is usually an integral part of the song. Every musical detail of the art song is written by

Title page of Deliciae Musicae, *a collection of songs published in London, in 1695, by Henry Playford*

A late 15th-century engraving of a singer and lute player by Israhel Van Meckenem

the composer, and the song must be performed as written.

Between the art song and the folk song is the area of popular song. Popular songs are like art songs in that their composers and authors are known. Unlike the art song, the popular song may be arranged or "styled" to fit a performer's tastes. Many songs that started out as popular songs achieve such affection in the hearts of a people that they become, in effect, folk songs. This is exactly what happened to Emmett's "Dixie" and Foster's "Swanee River"—both popular songs written to be performed by minstrel troupes.

To make a song, the composer chooses a set of words which he happens to like. In the case of a folk song, both words and melody may pop into his head at the same time. In an art song a line of poetry may suggest a melody or a descriptive accompaniment above which a melody could be placed. The composer finds the words or syllables that would be stressed or accented when spoken. These may be placed on strong beats in the music. The composer also looks at the rhythmic pattern of the poem, and decides whether or not he will follow that pattern exactly. He may decide that he can make a more interesting pattern by holding certain syllables and running others together.

In writing an accompaniment, the composer chooses from among several possi-

bilities. He can make an accompaniment which is merely a series of harmonies to support the melody, or he can write out an elaborate accompaniment for piano, string quartet, or even full orchestra. Such an accompaniment may be dramatic, adding more emotional impact to the melody. It may make a duet between the piano and the voice, as in the songs of Schubert and Schumann. The accompaniment may set a scene against which the singer performs the melody, as where the piano suggests a whirring spinning wheel in Schubert's "Gretchen at the Spinning Wheel" (see Ex. 1 on page 11).

Throughout the history of European music, art songs have taken many different forms. The earliest were those written by the traveling troubadours and trouvères of France and the minnesingers in Germany. These knightly musicians wrote songs of love, of nature, and of God. They did not bother to write out any accompaniment, but it was expected that their minstrels would play along with them on the vielle, an ancestor of the violin.

French composers of the fifteenth and sixteenth centuries wrote many charming chansons, usually for a solo singer with several accompanying instruments. Serious composers, among them Josquin Des Prés and Lassus, wrote light chansons as a relief from their more serious church works. Their songs are about love, good companionship, and human nature, good and bad.

Among the earliest pieces of published music are the fifteenth- and sixteenth-century Italian songs known as *frottole*. A collection of these gay songs, arranged, like madrigals, for several voices, was published in 1509 by Ottaviano dei Petrucci, the first music publisher.

The first published collection of true solo art songs, with a simple accompaniment, was Dowland's *First Booke of Songes or Ayres* (1597). The solo song with lute accompaniment was a favorite with English composers in the days of Elizabeth I. Composers such as Byrd, Campion, Dowland, and Danyel poured out a flood of songs and airs (the Fellowes collection of songs by English lutanist composers, published in 1920–32, fills thirty-two volumes). Most of the lutanist songs were love songs, but there were also philosophic songs (Hume's "Tobacco Is Like Love"; Dowland's "The Lowest Trees Have Tops") and songs of sadness.

During the 1600's each leading country developed its own type of song as its language fell into certain rhythms which influenced the composers. The use of many short words or long words, and of many accents or few—all these contributed to the difference between the smooth *bel canto* of Italy, the flowing ariosos of Lully's French operas, and the dramatic and rhythmically free songs of Henry Lawes and Purcell in England. The Italian opera brought into being two new types of song: the speechlike recitative and the regularly phrased aria.

During the Baroque period, from 1600 to 1750, composers often wrote songs as parts of long vocal works—operas, cantatas, or oratorios. The solo songs in Bach's cantatas consist of melodies for voice intertwined with melodies for violin, flute, or oboe—almost as though the voice were another instrument. Handel, in his operas and oratorios, spun out his melodies at such length that they test the breath control of any singer. It was Handel, more than any other composer of the early 1700's, who showed off the voice to its best advantage. It is interesting to note that he set his melodies to an Italian text mostly, using a flowing language, whereas Bach's sturdy and often angular melodies are set to a German text.

Germany, which had lagged behind Italy, France, and England in the development of song, now began to take its place as a leader.

Both Haydn and Mozart turned to solo songs for expression—songs that were not parts of larger works but were complete in themselves. Beethoven composed many songs, of which the best known are "Adelaide" and those in his song cycle, the first of its kind, *To the Distant Beloved.*

It was Franz Schubert who brought the art song, in the form of the German lied, to its highest point of perfection. In the melody and structural conception of a Schubert song, the meaning and emotion of the original poem find their perfect counterpart. His piano accompaniments add a subtle dramatic touch lacking in previous songs. With Schubert, a song becomes a complete art work as a result of the wedding of words, melody, and accompaniment. Whether the song is the big and dramatic ballad of "The Erlking"; the simple, almost folklike "Hedge Rose"; or the leadenly empty "Organ Grinder"; Schubert manages to find exactly the right kind of background to suit the mood of the song (Ex. 52 and 53. Also see Ex. 27 on page 191). The form of Schubert's songs is either strophic, with the same music repeated for many verses, or *through-composed*, with the music changing mood and style as it follows the meaning of the words.

Ex. 52 — "Heiden Röslein" (Hedge Rose)

Ex. 53 — "Der Leiermann" (The Organ Grinder)

Hugo Wolf

Schubert's song cycles, *Die schöne Müllerin* and *Die Winterreise,* set the pattern for the Romantic composers who followed him, for whom the lied became a favorite medium. It was through the lied that they expressed their love of their homeland and its countryside, their passionate longings, and their deepest feelings and emotions. The lieder of Mendelssohn, Schumann, Liszt, Robert Franz, Hugo Wolf, Brahms, and Strauss make up a unique treasury of song. Many singers of today, such as Dietrich Fischer-Dieskau, give recitals that consist entirely of German lieder.

The tradition of German song writing was carried over into the twentieth century by Mahler, who combined in his songs an almost folklike kind of melody with a haunting, darkly colored orchestral accompaniment. Hindemith's *Das Marienleben* is a beautiful and devout song cycle that tells the story of the mother of Jesus. Even the more revolutionary German and Austrian composers of recent times—Schoenberg,

Berg, Webern—manage to fill their songs with the nostalgia and longings of the nineteenth-century lied. Their melodic lines are often awkward, with their wide leaps and difficult rhythmic patterns (Ex. 54), but once the singer learns the pitches and rhythms, he sings such a song much like any other lied. These composers have also experimented with a different kind of singing, *Sprechstimme,* in which the singer *speaks* the words, but on definite musical pitches. The effect is strange and often quite moving.

Not all art songs of the nineteenth century were written in Austria or Germany. Grieg wrote lovely songs based on Norwegian turns of melody, with accompaniments rich in colorful harmony. In Russia such composers as Glinka, Borodin, and Tchaikovsky used Russian folk tunes as models for their art songs. One of the greatest of all songwriters was the Russian Mussorgsky, whose songs range from tender melodies for children to songs of the bitterest realism. Among his targets are the art lover who recoils from anything modern; the mumbling, empty-headed divinity student; and the scholar who is a warped "grind."

French composers of the nineteenth century followed their own national traditions in their art songs. Berlioz, Gounod, Franck, Fauré, and Duparc wrote songs that have great beauty and subtlety of feeling. The songs of Fauré, in particular, breathe an unusual lyrical beauty. Unlike the German and Austrian composers, the French did not pour out all their innermost feelings in song—or, if they did, they tried to disguise them. This does not mean that there is no passion, no great ecstasy, in French songs—the works of Fauré, and Duparc prove otherwise—but the emotion is always under control.

In the twentieth century the most important French songs have been those of Debussy, Ravel, and Poulenc. Debussy's songs are Impressionist word-paintings: delicate, lyrical, and full of rich harmonies in the

Ex. 54 — "Wie bin ich froh!" from *Drei Lieder*, Op. 25, Webern

piano part. Ravel's songs are like his instrumental works: clear, witty, and suggestive of faraway places. Poulenc's works range in style from almost cheap vaudeville ditties to sophisticated and polished songs of great beauty.

In England both Vaughan Williams and Benjamin Britten have contributed many songs that have achieved a place in the recital repertoire.

Before the 1920's American song was represented by Francis Hopkinson's sweet melodies (which were much like those of his contemporary Haydn), by the minstrel songs of the gifted Stephen Foster (whose tunes could be as simple as folk music and as fine as art songs), and by the sentimental songs of Ethelbert Nevin ("The Rosary") and Carrie Jacobs Bond ("I Love You Truly"). The American art song has often been obscured by the works of the gifted composers of popular tunes—Gershwin, Rodgers, Kern, Arlen, and Berlin. But since 1920 American composers have written so many art songs that publishers and performers can hardly keep up with them. Among the finest American art songs are those by Ives, Copland, Barber, Paul Bowles (1910–   ), Ned Rorem (1923–   ), and Vincent Persichetti (1915–   ).

SONG CYCLE: a group of songs by one composer based on poems all written by the same poet. The theme of the cycle may be a story, as in Schubert's *Die schöne Müllerin (The Fair Maid of the Mill)* or Hindemith's *Das Marienleben (The Life of Mary)*, or it may be simply a mood, as in Mussorg-sky's *Songs and Dances of Death* or Mahler's *Kindertotenlieder (Songs on the Death of Children)*.

The earliest example of a song cycle is Beethoven's *An die ferne Geliebte (To the Distant Beloved)*, written in 1816. It set the pattern for the many nineteenth- and twentieth-century composers who have written song cycles. Among the finest of these later cycles are Schubert's *Die Winterreise (The Winter Journey)*; Schumann's *Dichterliebe (The Poet's Love)* and *Frauenliebe und Leben (Woman's Love and Life)*; Fauré's *La Bonne Chanson*, based on nine love poems by Paul Verlaine; Debussy's three *Chansons de Bilitis*, delicate poems about the loves of a Greek girl in ancient times; Ravel's *Histoires naturelles*, settings of Jules Renard's slyly humorous poems about animals; Schoenberg's settings of Stephen George's *Book of the Hanging Gardens;* and Vaughan Williams' *On Wenlock Edge*, based on poems by A. E. Housman. One of Schoenberg's most revolutionary works is the song cycle *Pierrot lunaire*, for voice and chamber orchestra, in which the singer uses *Sprechstimme*, the cross between speaking and singing. Two recent song cycles of importance are Poulenc's *Tel Jour telle nuit (As Day, So Night)*, on poems by Paul Éluard; and Aaron Copland's *Twelve Poems of Emily Dickinson.*

Song cycles are held together by mood rather than a set of key relationships, although songs within some cycles do have key or thematic relationships. The songs of a cycle are meant to be sung as a group, but songs are often taken out of the cycle for recital purposes.

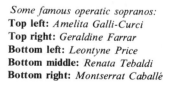

Some famous operatic sopranos:
Top left: *Amelita Galli-Curci*
Top right: *Geraldine Farrar*
Bottom left: *Leontyne Price*
Bottom middle: *Renata Tebaldi*
Bottom right: *Montserrat Caballé*

SOPRANO: a voice of the highest pitch, ranging upward from around middle C to the F two and one-half octaves higher:

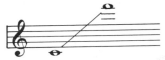

Soprano voices, including those of young boys, girls, and women, are of great variety. Some are lyric—light and sweet, and at their best when singing melodies of simple beauty. Others, like those of Flagstad, Callas, Tebaldi, and Nilsson, are dramatic—big, rich, and at home in the nineteenth-century operas of Verdi and Wagner. Rarest of all is the coloratura, such as that of Joan Sutherland. The coloratura voice must be able to sing the most embellished melodies of Bellini, to trill like a bird in Donizetti, to be agile as a flute in Rossini. It was for such a voice that Handel wrote many of his finest arias, and Mozart wrote the fantastically difficult music for the Queen of the Night in *The Magic Flute*. Boy sopranos, heard in many church choirs, usually have a smaller range than the mature female soprano. The purity of sound of the boy soprano, however, has exactly the right quality for the serene church music of the sixteenth century.

The highest-pitched member of an instrumental family is often referred to as a soprano instrument—for example, the soprano saxophone and soprano recorder.

The soprano clef, with middle C on the bottom line:

was used for soprano parts in published music and for some keyboard music until 1750. Today the clef is not published in music, except for scholarly editions. It is learned, however, by musicians, who can use it to help them in orchestral transpositions.

SOSTENUTO: an Italian word meaning "sustained." Originally it was used by composers to warn the performer that each tone was to be held for its full value. In the nineteenth century composers began to use the term to mean "slightly slower."

The sostenuto, or sustaining, pedal is the middle of the three pedals found on many pianos. Its function is to sustain, or keep sounding, whichever tones are being held by the player's fingers as the pedal is pressed down.

SOUND: the medium in which music exists. The science of sound is called acoustics.

Sound consists of waves produced in air by the vibration, or rapid back-and-forth motion, of an object, such as a string or a piece of metal. Waves of air move out from the vibrating object in all directions, much as waves of water spread in ever-widening circles when a stone is tossed into a pond. As the air waves strike the listener's eardrum, corresponding nerve impulses are sent to the brain, and thus the listener "hears" the music.

The number of waves per second produced by the vibrating object is called the frequency of the sound. The greater the frequency, the higher the pitch that is heard. The lowest pitch that the human ear can hear represents a vibration of about sixteen times per second—so low that it is a rumble which is felt rather than actually heard. When the pitch gets above 20,000, the human ear fails. Dogs, as well as many other animals and insects, can hear much higher frequencies, and that is why dog whistles can be heard by dogs but not by human beings.

Not all possible frequencies are used in music. Most musical instruments—except for the voice, sirens, trombones, and members of the violin family—can produce only a fixed number of frequencies. So instead of approximately 20,000 different musical tones, only about 120 are actually used in ordinary music. Instruments are considered to be "out of tune" when they wander outside the fixed number of tones that make up the musical scale.

Pitch is determined by the material that is vibrating and by its length, thickness, and tightness. In the piano, all the strings are made of steel. The strings on the left are longer, fatter, and looser than the strings on the right. The long strings vibrate slowly, giving off deep tones, while the small strings vibrate fast, making the higher tones.

Some instruments have a different sounding part for every tone to be produced. The piano has eighty-eight strings, or sets of strings, for its eighty-eight tones, and a xylophone has as many wooden bars as it has tones. Other instruments have just a few sounding parts, which the player shortens to get his different pitches. The violin has only four strings, but the player can produce tones extending over a wide range by shortening them. The trombonist has only one tube, which he shortens to various lengths by means of his slide. The woodwind player likewise has one tube, but this has holes which are covered or uncovered to produce various pitches.

VNICA CHORDA QVA SONI CVIVSLIBET CONSONANTIÆ SIMVL AVDIRI POSSVNT .

Man playing a monochord (a woodcut from Musica theorica *by Ludovico Fogliani, Venice, 1529)*

Hermann von Helmholtz, the German scientist whose work became the basis of the science of acoustics

Each different musical instrument has its own way of making sound. In percussion instruments a drumhead or metal bar is struck to start it vibrating. In stringed instruments a string is plucked or bowed to set it in motion, whereas wind instruments contain an object that interrupts a steady stream of air. This object in woodwinds is a reed, in brass instruments the lips, and in the voice, the vocal cords.

After a tone is produced it must be amplified—that is, made louder. This is done by building up the energy of vibration in a larger object, called a resonator, much as a child's swing is pushed higher and higher by small pushes given at just the right intervals. Most stringed instruments use a hollow body of wood for the resonator. Wind instruments use a wooden or metal tube—which, if too long, may be coiled. The voice is resonated by the cavities of the throat, mouth, and nose. Among percussion instruments, the xylophone and its relatives have resonating tubes under the wooden or metal bars which the player strikes; and in drums the body of the instrument increases the amount of sound made by the skin drumhead. The body of the drum also gives the head of the drum freedom to continue vibrating— otherwise the sound would stop.

Members of the violin and guitar families have a bridge which serves to keep the strings away from the body of the instrument. Without the bridge, the vibration of a string would stop almost immediately. This principle can be demonstrated by stretching a rubber band lengthwise around a ruler. When plucked it only makes a "plop," but if a finger is held under it, this allows the vibration to continue and the rubber band will sing out. Pitch can be changed by changing the position of the finger.

Instruments of the violin and guitar family have another device to help their tone: the S- or F-shaped sound holes, or *f* holes, on each side of the bridge. These regulate the amount of air that is contained within the body of the instrument. Scientific experiments have proved that the air in the body must vibrate with a frequency of 512. All great violins, since the days of Stradivarius, have been made in this way. Experiments have shown that any shape other than the S or F shape diminishes the amount of sound. Even covering one hole with paper makes a tone which is softer and also flatter in pitch.

The shape and size of each instrument, the material of which it is made, and the method of making the sound all help to determine the unique sound of each instrument—its quality, or timbre. This is a most complex quality. Any musical tone consists of a fundamental tone, which is the basic one that is heard, plus a number of higher tones or overtones that blend with the fundamental. The quality of an instrument depends on how many, and which, overtones are present. The flute, for example, has very few overtones; its sound is called "pure" or "cool." The human voice has the most overtones—one of the reasons for its warmth of sound.

Each musical tone has not only pitch and timbre but also intensity, or degree of loudness. A big stone thrown into the water makes a bigger splash and bigger waves than a small stone makes. In music a tone is made louder because a string is plucked or bowed with more force, a drum is hit harder, or a wind player blows harder.

The final element of musical sound is duration: how long the tone lasts. With wind instruments this depends on how long the lungs can provide air. With bowed strings it depends on how long the player can continue smooth bowing. With plucked strings and percussion instruments duration depends on how long the vibrating surface continues to sing out. With electronic instruments the only limit to duration is the electrical supply.

SOUSA, JOHN PHILIP (1854–1932): America's favorite and best-remembered bandmaster. For more than twenty-five years, from 1892 until about 1920, Sousa's Band was the most popular musical group in the United States—probably in the world. His more than a hundred marches, including such favorites as "The Stars and Stripes Forever," "King Cotton," "The Washington Post," "El Capitan," and "Semper Fidelis," earned him the title of the "March King."

Born in Washington, D.C., Sousa was trained as a violinist, although he had a playing knowledge of the piano and of various wind instruments. He was inducted as a member of the United States Marine Band when he was but thirteen. After a five-year hitch with this band, Sousa played the violin in theater orchestras, including that of the touring French composer Offenbach. At the age of twenty-six, in 1880, he was appointed leader of the Marine Band.

What Sousa took over was an ordinary service band—the oldest of such bands and the official one of the President of the United States. Within a few years Sousa made the Marine Band the finest in the country. Drilling and rehearsing his players to perfection, he ordered new music from Europe and wrote his own pieces to enlarge the band's repertoire. By 1892 his reputation had risen so high that he decided to form his own concert band.

Sousa's Band, usually numbering about sixty players, was made up of the finest wind players in the country. It toured Europe four times, introducing Sousa's marches as well as the "new" American ragtime music. In 1910 it went on a world tour.

Sousa was a superb showman. He demanded military bearing in his men. Uniforms, including his own white gloves, were spot-

Cover of "The Stars and Stripes Forever"

less. Sousa believed in giving people what they wanted to hear, but he also managed to give many people—in days when the phonograph was primitive and radio nonexistent—their first hearings of Wagner, Tchaikovsky, and Dvořák. His programs always provided variety, such as arrangements of operatic overtures (from Rossini, Suppé, Verdi, and Wagner), soprano solos, show-off pieces for his cornet and trombone soloists, and always some Sousa marches and excerpts from his own eleven light operas.

Sousa was a highly intelligent man of wide interests. In addition to the marches for which he is famous, he wrote waltzes and other light music to play at dances, a symphonic poem (The Chariot Race, based on Ben Hur), and suites for band and orchestra. He inspired the invention of the sousaphone, a type of tuba whose bell can be turned to aim its sound in any direction. A book of his writings, Through the Years with Sousa, published in 1910, was followed in 1928 by his autobiography, Marching Along.

Sousa's marches are still the most popular items in any band's repertoire. They are tuneful, forceful, and beautifully written for the full band sound. Each of them illustrates Sousa's belief that a good march should "make a man with a wooden leg step out."

SOUSAPHONE: a tuba of the helicon type with a wide "bell," or end, that can be turned to throw the sound of the instrument in any direction. The idea for such an instrument was suggested by the American bandmaster John Philip Sousa, and the instrument, first made in 1908, was named in his honor.

At left: John Philip Sousa

The nine members of the first group of Fisk Jubilee Singers (from a daguerreotype, c. 1871)

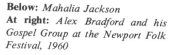

SPIRITUAL: a revival hymn, often strongly rhythmic, based on folk tunes from the British Isles and from Africa. As with much other folk material, the origins of black and white spirituals are unknown because when they were new no one—except those singing them—paid any attention to them. The late George Pullen Jackson, an authority on spirituals, found the earliest publication of white revival spirituals to have been in Boston in 1842. This was followed by the publication in 1844 of the famous *Sacred Harp* collection in Hamilton, Georgia. The earliest collection of black spirituals dates from the middle 1860's. Obviously both white and black spirituals had been sung long before the tunes and words were collected and published. One problem in tracing origins is due to the fact that both white and black spirituals tend to be based on the pentatonic scale (the scale made

by playing the black keys of the piano), and this scale is found in folk songs of Africa as well as those of England, Scotland, and Ireland. However, the largest body of spirituals are those developed by the blacks in the South of the United States.

The most popular form of spiritual, often used in the telling of a Biblical story, is that of leader and chorus. The leader "lines out" a phrase which is answered by a shout, such as "Glory Hallelujah!" In the black spirituals various interjections, such as "O Lord!" are thrown in along the way.

Spirituals are often sung to the rhythmic accompaniment of hand-clapping and dancing or marching. The revival meetings from which the spirituals sprang became highly charged with emotion as the preacher exhorted his listeners to avoid the damnation and hell-fire that would be the fate of sinners.

Many of the black spirituals grew out of the despair of slavery. They told of a better world ahead—in heaven or in a new society where the slave would become free. (The contemporary spiritual by Pete Seeger, "We Shall Overcome," expresses this same drive for freedom.) Other spirituals served as signals and warnings in a code that was not understood by the white slave-owner or overseer.

Black choirs such as the Fisk Jubilee Singers, in the late nineteenth and early twentieth centuries, were the first to bring the beauty of the black spirituals to the attention of American and European audiences. Trained black musicians such as J. Rosamond Johnson and R. Nathaniel Dett arranged the spirituals so that they became accessible to all music-lovers.

Below: *Mahalia Jackson*
At right: *Alex Bradford and his Gospel Group at the Newport Folk Festival, 1960*

STACCATO: an Italian word meaning "separated," or "detached." The signs for staccato are used by a composer who wants a slight pause between the melodic tones—either for the dry, light effect of such tones or for a contrast with a series of notes played in a legato, or held, manner. If a whole passage is to be played staccato, the composer indicates this by writing *sempre staccato* above or under the part. Otherwise he puts one of the three staccato markings above or under the note heard. For absolute precision, many contemporary composers avoid staccato marks, preferring to write out the exact lengths of notes and rests:

Slightly Staccato

Ordinary Staccato

As Staccato as Possible (Staccatissimo)

Staccatos are made on the piano by making the fingers and wrist bounce back from the key as quickly as possible. Violin staccato is made by bringing the bow to a stop before attacking the next tone or by bouncing or springing the bow against the string. The use of pizzicato—plucking the strings—is another way of achieving staccato sounds on stringed instruments. Staccato on a wind instrument is made for a single tone by blowing just a short burst of air into the mouthpiece; for a series of tones, it is made by "tonguing"—stopping the mouthpiece with the tongue.

STAFF (plural *staves*): a set of five lines—and the spaces between them—on which notes can be placed to show the pitches of musical tones. The lines and spaces are numbered, starting at the bottom. Additional lines and their spaces are used when tones go above or below the staff. Such added lines are called leger (or ledger) lines.

The notes on the lines and spaces of the staff correspond to the white keys of the piano. To show pitches exactly, a clef is put at the beginning of the staff. The three different clefs show where middle C (Ex. a), the F below middle C (Ex. b), and the G above middle C (Ex. c) are placed:

At one time all the clefs were considered movable and might be found on any line. Now only the C clef is movable, the F and G clefs being confined to the positions above.

The C clef is used in any of the positions shown here:

Music for keyboard instruments and the harp is written on two staves connected by a brace or bracket:

The staff developed around the year 1000. Before this time an inexact system of notation, called neumes, showed whether tones went up or down—but not how far up or down. A single red line was drawn to show F below middle C. Then a green or yellow line was drawn above the red line to show the C above the F. Guido d'Arezzo is credited with adding two more lines, making the four-line staff—still used in Catholic Church plainsong chants.

The five-line staff came into use sometime in the thirteenth century. But until it became established, sometime in the seventeenth century, there were all kinds of experiments with the number of lines comprising a staff, as many as twenty-five being used for some choral music. Keyboard music of the sixteenth and seventeenth centuries was often written on a six-line staff, and some Italian composers wrote organ music with a six-line staff for the right hand and an eight-line staff for the left hand and the feet. Anyone who has trouble reading music today should be thankful there are only five-line staves to worry about. (See: NOTATION.)

STAR-SPANGLED BANNER, THE: the national anthem of the United States. "The Star-Spangled Banner" was written in 1814 during the war between Britain and the United States. The author of the poem was Francis Scott Key, a young Baltimore lawyer. He had come aboard a British warship lying off Baltimore to arrange for the release of an American doctor who had been

Francis Scott Key

The British bombardment of Fort McHenry on September 13–14, 1814 (aquatint by John Bower)

Label from a violin made by Stradivarius, and the Stradivarius violin known as the "Antonius," made in 1717–21 (the bow was made later by Xaver Tourte)

Antonius Stradiuarius Cremonenſis
Faciebat Anno 1719

captured. The British detained Key for fear that he might warn the Americans of a coming attack. During the night, British gunboats fired shell after shell at Fort McHenry, which guarded Baltimore. Key spent a sleepless night as the guns roared. He wondered whether the Americans could hold out.

When the sun came up, Key saw that the American flag was still flying over the fort. The words of "The Star-Spangled Banner" came to him in a rush, and he jotted them down on the back of an envelope. The words were set to the melody of an English drinking song, "To Anacreon in Heaven." Key had the song printed, and it became an immediate success.

Throughout the years the rhythm and melody of the tune have been changed slightly, but attempts to make its range smaller have not been successful. In 1943 Igor Stravinsky was prevented from conducting his unconventional arrangement of the song in Boston.

"The Star-Spangled Banner" was made the national anthem of the United States by act of Congress in 1931.

STRADIVARIUS (STRADIVARI), ANTONIO (c. 1644–1737): the greatest of all violin makers. He was born in Cremona, Italy, where the violin family of instruments reached their height of perfection at the hands of the Amati, Guarneri, and Stradivarius families.

Stradivarius started as an apprentice-pupil of Nicolo Amati, the grandson of the man who started the art of violin making in Cremona. After an apprenticeship of about seven years, Stradivarius set up his own workshop. He was a prodigious worker, turning out in his lifetime more than 1,100 violins, violas, cellos, and guitars, of which some 600 survive. He married twice and had eleven children, several of whom became violin makers. Stradivarius lived at a time when all of Europe seemed to be clamoring for violins. He amassed such a fortune that "rich as Stradivarius" became a proverbial expression in Cremona.

At first Stradivarius' instruments were patterned after those of his master Amati, but by the 1690's he realized that musicians wanted violins of greater power. Then he created the "long Strad" (14 3/16 inches long, 8 inches wide), and he continued to experiment, shortening the body and making it fuller, so that no two Strads are ever quite alike. He worked on every part of his instruments—the pegs, the finger boards, the curve of the body. No detail was too small. He tried various types and sizes of wood, using different kinds of varnishes, ranging in color from a soft dark red to a brighter orange. There is controversy about the basic varnish used by the master. Stradivarius supposedly wrote the recipe for it in the family Bible, but this was lost and the formula is today uncertain.

Stradivarius made his greatest instruments after 1700. These still sing today with a big, rich tone. Many have been given distinguishing nicknames, such as "Viotti" (1709), after a famous owner, and the "Dolphin" (1714), because of its iridescent varnish. For their beauty, rarity, and musical tone Stradivarius' instruments are very valuable, especially his cellos and violas, of which he made comparatively few. There are at present several quartets of matching "Strads" that bring great delight to chamber-music players who are allowed to use them.

Each year hundreds of people get excited when, rummaging through an attic, they find a battered violin with the Stradivarius label in it. Their hopes are usually dashed, however, when they consult an expert. It is easy to duplicate the Stradivarius label; it is almost impossible to duplicate the Stradivarius violin.

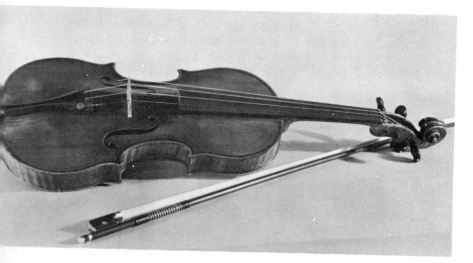

STRAUSS, JOHANN SR. and **JOHANN JR.:** the "Waltz Kings." Father and son ruled the social dance life of Vienna in the 1800's as the Hapsburg royal family ruled the empire. To several generations of Viennese, the Strausses represented the true soul of the city. Even the great composers who called Vienna their home—from Beethoven and Schubert to Brahms and Mahler—took their coffee, beer, and sausages at cafés or outdoor gardens where the Strauss music held sway.

Johann Senior (1804–49), sometimes called the "Elder" or "The Father of the Waltz," dreamed from childhood of being a coffeehouse musician. Instead he was apprenticed to a bookbinder, from whom he promptly ran away. Somehow or other he managed to study the violin and a bit of music theory. At the age of fifteen he joined the café quartet of Joseph Lanner (1801–43), himself an outstanding waltz composer. Between them they became the most fashionable dance musicians of Vienna. Strauss split with Lanner, formed his own group, and by his middle twenties was playing in the largest outdoor gardens.

Strauss's reputation spread, and he toured most of the capital cities of western Europe. His orchestra became the official dance orchestra for Austrian court balls. When Queen Victoria was crowned in England, it was Strauss's orchestra that played at the coronation ball. His compositions, which were published complete in seven volumes after his death, include more than 150 waltzes plus galops, polkas, and other popular dance forms of the day. Berlioz compared him favorably to Beethoven and Gluck. Others called him the "Austrian Napoleon." Everywhere he went, audiences reacted with almost delirious delight.

Johann Junior (1825–99), sometimes called the "Younger" or "The Waltz King," gave Vienna its musical immortality with his *An der schönen blauen Donau (By the Beautiful Blue Danube)*, most loved of all the many waltzes that came from Vienna, the city of waltzes.

His father did not want him to be a musician, and would have liked him to be a businessman or civil official. The son had to study the violin and music theory on the sly. He had started to make up waltzes when he was only six. He dreamed of waltzes and of playing in front of an orchestra like his father.

When Johann Senior deserted his family, the younger Strauss no longer had any opposition to his dreams. At nineteen he started his first orchestra and played in competition

Above left: *Johann Strauss the Elder*
Above right: *Johann Strauss the Younger*

with his father. Vienna was split into two camps. When the father died in 1849, the younger Strauss took over his orchestra. His popularity became even greater than that of his father, and he toured as far as Russia and the United States.

In 1867 Strauss wrote his famous *Blue Danube* waltz. Its swaying melodies, suggesting the flowing river, are typical of Strauss's style. The melodies curve over the simplest of accompaniments, and the little connecting interludes give just enough harmonic color to set off the simple harmony that supports the melodies. The orchestration was equally simple and equally just right. It is no wonder that Brahms, who loved the waltz and wrote many beautiful ones himself, autographed Mrs. Strauss's fan by writing the opening melody of *The Blue Danube*, followed by the comment, "Unfortunately not by Johannes Brahms."

Strauss wrote many more waltzes, all beautiful and graceful: *Roses from the South; Tales from the Vienna Woods; Wine, Women and Song; Artist's Life;* and hundreds more. There were also the polkas, galops, quadrilles, and marches with which he regaled his audiences. Strauss's orchestra, one of the finest in Europe, played not only his own music but concert music, too. As early as 1853, when Richard Wagner was still fighting for success, Strauss played portions of Wagner's *Lohengrin* and *Tannhäuser*.

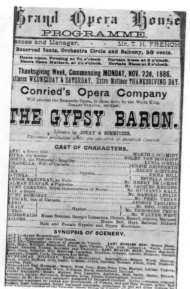

Program for a performance of The Gypsy Baron *on Nov. 22, 1886, by Conried's Opera Company*

Strauss, living in an expensive villa near the royal palace, toured less and less. A suggestion from his friendly rival in the field of light music, Offenbach, started Strauss off on a new trend. In 1871 he wrote his first operetta—*Indigo und die vierzig Räuber (Indigo and the Forty Thieves).* This was followed by *Die Fledermaus (The Bat),* whose combination of romantic, improbable story and beautiful music still holds the stage today. He wrote thirteen more operettas, of which the best known is *Der Zigeunerbaron (The Gypsy Baron).*

In 1894 all Vienna honored the fiftieth anniversary of Strauss as a conductor. He had dreamed of becoming a coffee-house musician and had instead become one of the world's best-loved composers. When he died, a whole era came to an end—the era of dancing Vienna.

STRAUSS, RICHARD (1864–1949): a great German composer, best known for his symphonic poems and his operas. Strauss was born in Munich, Germany, the son of a famous player of the French horn—an instrument for which Strauss later wrote superbly. He started to study music at the age of four and two years later wrote his first work, a polka. His *Festmarsch (Festival March),* composed when he was twelve, was published when he was only fourteen.

Strauss attended the University of Munich for two years, studying law and philosophy. He was encouraged to become a conductor by Hans von Bülow, the great conductor, who even secured a post for him. Strauss had

by this time written several symphonies, a serenade for thirteen wind instruments, and a concerto for violin and orchestra. His music was well composed but a little too safe and sound to arouse much excitement.

A friendship with a young poet-musician, Alexander Ritter, changed Strauss's ideas about music and set him on his future career. Ritter convinced Strauss of the truth in the ideas of Berlioz, Wagner, and Liszt: that music must say something definite; should have a program, a literary idea, or a philosophy; and above all, that music must be poetic and always expressive of the composer's emotion.

Strauss started his long career as a conductor at Meiningen, Munich, and Weimar. He became one of the finest conductors in Europe, both in the opera house and in the symphony hall. In the meantime he began to write the symphonic poems that were to make him famous. He was twenty-five when he conducted the first performance of his *Don Juan,* based on a poem about the legendary lover. From its first rushing surge of notes (Ex. 55), *Don Juan* flames with the spirit of the bold adventurer. This work brought Strauss to the forefront of young German composers, and is still one of his most-played works.

Don Juan was followed by *Tod und Verklärung (Death and Transfiguration,* 1889), the story of a dying man who in a delirious fever remembers the struggles of his childhood, youth, and manhood, and through death is transformed so that in heaven he will have a life of happiness.

In 1895 Strauss brought out his most suc-

Richard Strauss

Ex. 55 — *Don Juan*

cessful work: *Till Eulenspiegels lustige Streiche (Till Eulenspiegel's Merry Pranks)*. Till was a legendary German character (his surname means "owl's mirror")—a scamp, a rogue, a practical joker. Till represents the side of man that makes fun of solemn, pompous people. The danger to someone like Till is that the people who cannot take a joke often control laws and justice.

Till Eulenspiegel begins with a beautiful little string phrase that suggests someone telling a story by beginning with the magical words, "Once upon a time . . ." (Ex. 56). Till's theme comes in, played on the French horn and covering the entire range of the instrument (Ex. 57), just as Till's adventures range the whole spectrum of life. Strauss usually thought of each theme in connection with a specific instrument. His themes are used like the leitmotifs in Wagner's operas to represent a character, a thing, or an idea. In *Till Eulenspiegel* the audience can follow the hectic career of the little fellow by means of his theme as he gets entangled in many adventures. He rides his horse into a crowded marketplace, upsetting everything. He disguises himself as a monk. He has a love affair. For a long time he manages to escape from the danger that threatens him—a danger constantly suggested by the sounding of his theme. Strauss realized that even program music must have musical form in addition to its story: only in this way can it stand on its own as a piece of music. The reiterations of Till's theme make the musical form of the work a large-scale rondo.

Finally Till is brought to a court of justice. His theme seems to plead, "But I was only

having a little fun." The whole orchestra thunders, "Guilty!" Till's theme pleads once more. Again the orchestra, like a stone wall in sound, is unmoved. There is a moment of suspense, a shuddering in the strings. With two ominous notes played by the bassoons, horns, trombones, and tuba, Till is beheaded. His theme, played on an E-flat clarinet, flutters upward, like a soul going to heaven. The orchestra plays the "Once upon a time . . ." theme, and the work ends.

After *Till Eulenspiegel,* Strauss wrote sev-

A scene from Act II of Der Rosenkavalier, *with Annelise Rothenberger as Sophie and Sena Jurinac as Octavian (Salzburg Festival production, 1963)*

Ex. 56 — *Till Eulenspiegel,* Strauss

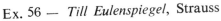

Ex. 57 — *Till Eulenspiegel,* Strauss

Ex. 58 — *Don Quixote*

eral more tone poems. *Also sprach Zarathustra (Thus Spoke Zarathustra),* performed in 1896, is an attempt to give a listener the same feeling he would get from reading the book by Nietzsche on which the work is based. In *Don Quixote* (1897) Strauss chose another form: that of the theme and variations. Don Quixote, the hero, is characterized by a solo cello; Sancho Panza, the don's faithful squire, has a theme which is heard first in the bass clarinet and tuba, to give it the proper peasant, down-to-earth quality; thereafter the viola becomes the voice of Sancho Panza. The don's ideal woman, Dulcinea, is given one of Strauss's most beautiful motives, played on the oboe above muted strings and harp (Ex. 58).

Each episode in the adventures of *Don Quixote* is a free variation of the themes of Don Quixote and Sancho Panza. The don attacks a windmill with disastrous results. He thinks that a herd of bleating sheep (muted horns and tuba) is a hostile army. He imagines a group of religious pilgrims to be a gang of ruffians. When he attacks them, they knock him senseless. Seeing an ugly peasant girl, he thinks she is his Dulcinea made ugly by a sorcerer. He rides through the air in his imagination, aided in the music by a "wind machine." His return to sanity is shown by a succession of harmonies that change from vague and muddled chords to clearer and simpler ones. Thus, in *Don Quixote,* Strauss wrote some of his most beautiful, most colorful, and most descriptive music. As in most of his tone poems, his scoring gives little solos to almost every instrument. Strauss was fond of sub-dividing his string section to make it a rich, twenty-voiced, smooth-as-silk choir.

After *Don Quixote,* Strauss wrote one more great tone poem, *Ein Heldenleben (A Hero's Life),* premièred in 1899. The hero is Strauss himself, and he describes in music his beliefs and his struggles to overcome his critics. Going beyond the Wagnerian harmonies that had served him so well, he ventured into dissonance and polytonality, at one time using three keys simultaneously. After *Ein Heldenleben* there came the *Symphonia domestica (Domestic Symphony)* of 1903, which pictures a day in the Strauss household. This work was written for Strauss's American tour in 1904. With it he seemed to have exhausted the possibilities of the symphonic poem and became increasingly interested in opera (he had already written two operas, *Guntram* in 1894 and *Feuersnot,* or *Fire Famine,* in 1901).

Strauss now turned to the Bible to make an opera based on the story of Salome, who danced for Herod in return for the head of John the Baptist. The libretto was a translation of Oscar Wilde's play *Salome.* The combination of Strauss's violently passionate music and the shocking story led to both praise and protests at the first performance in 1905. At the Metropolitan Opera House, in 1907, the sensuous "Dance of the Seven Veils," Salome's song to the Baptist's head, and the killing of Salome by Herod's soldiers was too much for the scandalized audience. The work was removed from the Metropolitan repertoire and was not revived for many years. It has since taken its place in operatic repertoire as a masterpiece of great dramatic force. The "Dance of the Seven Veils" is often performed on orchestral programs.

In *Salome* and his next opera, *Elektra* (1909), Strauss again went beyond the style of Richard Wagner, using even more biting dissonance. The music flows continuously, avoiding cadences. Leitmotifs, representing the different characters, are piled up and developed in the orchestra. The vocal line is much like recitative, following the ups and downs of a dramatic speaking voice. At times there are arialike passages—long, free lines that follow the changing mood of the words. Both operas are in one act, allowing Strauss to build straight through to powerful climaxes.

Elektra has been called "an opera of horror." Hugo von Hofmannsthal, who wrote many librettos for Strauss, based this one on the ancient Greek play by Sophocles. *Elektra* allowed Strauss to push his dissonance almost to the breaking point as the music keeps pace with the brutality and violence of the plot. At times there is no key and at other times several keys are suggested. One sound, the "Elektra chord," serves to generate the harmonic tension that is always present in the work:

Like *Salome*, *Elektra* horrified and fascinated audiences. The title role is one that is attempted by very few dramatic sopranos. The vocal and emotional demands made on the singer are almost overwhelming.

After *Elektra*, Strauss seems to have turned away from shocking subjects or anything that was deeply stirring or emotional. His next opera was the light, frothy *Der Rosenkavalier* (*The Cavalier of the Rose*, 1910), elegant and much closer to the old Italian opera than to the works of Wagner. It has become the most popular of Strauss's operas. The enchanting waltzes, with their melting harmonies, are often played as orchestral pieces.

Strauss continued to write operas—*Ariadne auf Naxos* (*Ariadne on Naxos*), *Intermezzo*, *Arabella*, *Die Frau ohne Schatten* (*The Woman Without a Shadow*), *Die ägytpische Helena* (*The Egyptian Helen*), *Die schweigsame Frau* (*The Silent Woman*), *Friedenstag* (*Peace Day*), *Daphne*, and *Die Liebe der Danae* (*The Love of Diana*). All contain some wonderful music but, except for *Arabella* and *Ariadne*, they have never been completely successful. Much

Scene from Strauss's Ariadne auf Naxos *(Salzburg Festival production, 1964)*

of their lack of success is due to the fact that Strauss continued to write in a style that was closer to the eighteenth and nineteenth centuries than to the twentieth.

Compared to the newer composers, Strauss began to seem old-fashioned. Aside from his tone poems and operas, only a few of his other works have made their way permanently into the concert repertoire. Some of his many songs appear frequently in recitals. Of his purely instrumental works only the Serenade for Winds, the Burleske for piano and orchestra, the concertos for horn and for oboe, and the orchestral suite from *Le Bourgeois Gentilhomme* (*The Would-be Gentleman*) are still played.

When Hitler and the Nazis took over Germany, Strauss became the official head of German music. He held this post for a year and a half, and was criticized bitterly for doing so. After the war he was put on trial for working with the Nazis but was found not guilty of any wrongdoing.

Many composers seem to have lived too short a life and never to have savored the fullness of their success. Strauss lived long enough to see his fame, which had been high, flicker lower and lower. It was a sad ending to a career that has flamed so brilliantly for twenty years. Strauss was a master of description in musical tones, a magician at conjuring up new sounds from the orchestra. At best he was a genius in the field of musical drama. His three or four best symphonic poems and his three or four best operas continue to gain new audiences. His place in music history is secure.

Igor Stravinsky

STRAVINSKY, IGOR (1882–1971): the leading spirit in modern music for more than fifty years. He lived long enough to see his early works, particularly *Le Sacre du printemps (The Rite of Spring),* which caused a near-riot at its first performance, become accepted parts of the standard literature of music.

More than any other composer, Stravinsky had changed his style of writing to suit the idea on which he had been working. This changeability had often bewildered and baffled audiences who, expecting to hear one kind of Stravinsky, often heard something quite different. At various times Stravinsky tried to recapture the spirit of ancient Greece, seventeenth- and eighteenth-century Italy, primitive Russia, and the days of the Old Testament—always in musical terms of the present. He wrote music for many different media—ballet, opera, symphony orchestra, church, circus, dance band, and player piano. Yet through all his style changes he always remained himself, like a man who constantly changed his costume but not his inner nature. No matter what this composer wrote, each measure bore his unmistakable signature in sound. Of all those who have written for instruments, he was possibly the most inventive. He was the greatest master of musical timing since Beethoven. For most of his life he had been the composer with the greatest influence on his contemporaries.

Stravinsky was born in Oranienbaum, near St. Petersburg (now Leningrad), Russia, where his father was a leading bass singer at the Imperial Opera. Stravinsky started to study the piano at the age of nine, but he preferred improvising and reading through his father's opera scores to practicing his lesson. He was taken to many concerts and operas, gaining a wide musical background, but not until he became a law student at the St. Petersburg University did his study of music theory begin. He was given harmony lessons by a private teacher, but counterpoint, the subject he liked most, he studied on his own.

At the university, Stravinsky had a classmate who was the son of the leading Russian composer and teacher, Rimsky-Korsakov, and Stravinsky was introduced to this older composer. After hearing some of Stravinsky's early attempts at composition, Rimsky-Korsakov suggested that he needed a great deal of study in theoretical subjects. Rimsky-Korsakov also felt that at the age of twenty Stravinsky was too old to start at the conservatory, and offered to give him private lessons in composition and orchestration. His method was to point out the relations between musical form and instrumental color. For example, he assigned Stravinsky the task of orchestrating several pages of the piano version of one of his operas, then showed him, with explanations, how he had orchestrated it himself.

Stravinsky wrote a symphony and a short suite for mezzo-soprano and orchestra *(Le Faune et la bergère).* Rimsky-Korsakov arranged to have the suite played at a public concert in St. Petersburg in 1908. The success of the work encouraged Stravinsky to write an orchestral *Scherzo fantastique* and to begin an opera, *Le Rossignol (The Nightingale).* A brilliant orchestral work, *Feu d'artifice (Fireworks),* was sent to Rimsky-Korsakov, but too late—the old master had died.

Diaghilev, the impresario of a newly founded Russian Ballet Company in Paris, was looking for fresh talent. After hearing Stravinsky's two orchestral works, he engaged the young composer to orchestrate two short piano pieces by Chopin for a new ballet, *Les Sylphides.* Pleased with the quality of Stravinsky's work, Diaghilev commissioned a score for a ballet based on a Russian fairy tale, *L'Oiseau de feu (The Firebird).*

The work had its first performance in Paris in 1910. Its brilliant, glittering score was a perfect setting for the colorful costumes and dancing. In style the music of *The Firebird* resembled that of earlier Russian composers, Borodin and Rimsky-Korsakov. There are melodies like folk songs (Ex. 59 and 60). The Infernal Dance of the subjects of Kastchei, the magician, is savage, with its heavy syncopated theme, first heard over a rumbling drumbeat (Ex. 61). Splashes and swirls of orchestral tone color are thrown into the driving rhythm of the music. There are glissando swoops on the trombone, harp, and piano. A short motive rattles out of the xylophone. There are active passage work and big leaps in the brass, and virtuoso writing for the strings. All these combine to make a truly "infernal" sound.

The Firebird was Stravinsky's apprentice work. It proved that he could write against a deadline and could follow a scenario. Ready now to strike out on his own, he started to write a concert piece for piano and orchestra. When Diaghilev, by now one of his best friends, heard part of the music, he insisted that Stravinsky turn it into a ballet. The result was *Petrouchka,* one of the most famous of all ballets. Here Stravinsky cast aside the style of writing he had used in *The Firebird.* He used short motives instead of long melodic lines, and avoided sweet, lush sounds. The music itself almost tells the story as it shrieks and reels like the puppets on the stage. At times it is as busy as the crowded square where the action takes place. Both as a ballet and as an orchestral suite, *Petrouchka* has been a favorite with audiences ever since its first performance in 1911.

Stravinsky's *Rite of Spring* was first performed in 1913, by Diaghilev's ballet company. The biting dissonance, primitive repetitions of short motives, completely new orchestral sounds, and savage rhythms with constantly changing time signatures, combined with Nijinsky's unorthodox choreography, caused an uproar. The work established Stravinsky as the most adventuresome composer of the day.

After finishing his opera *The Nightingale,* begun years before, Stravinsky moved with his family to Switzerland. World War I and the Russian Revolution prevented him from returning to his native land until his visit of 1962. For many years—until the death of Stalin in 1953—Stravinsky's works were not played in Russia. But this composer had moved on to become a citizen of the world —writing, conducting, and playing his own piano works.

His next ballet, *Les Noces (The Wedding),* was scored for four pianos, a large number of percussion instruments, a chorus, and vocal soloists. It is based on the customs of Russian peasants as they celebrate a village wedding. *Les Noces* was not produced until 1923, four years after he had returned to France, where he became a French citizen. In the meantime Stravinsky had written *L'Histoire du soldat (The Story of a Soldier),* a little theater piece based on an old folk

Ex. 59 — *The Firebird*

Drawing of Stravinsky by Picasso, 1920

tale. A soldier returning to his native village after a war meets the devil and trades his soul—in the form of a violin—for a magic book that will bring him wealth and happiness. The story is told by a narrator who gets so involved that he steps out of character to advise the soldier. Other characters are the devil, the soldier, and the princess, with whom the soldier falls in love. The small orchestra of violin, double bass, clarinet, bassoon, trumpet, trombone, and percussion plays on stage. The music has a devilish, satirical quality. Everything is cut to the bone in Stravinsky's attempt to be economical with notes. There are a little march, a tango, a waltz, a piece of ragtime, and several hymn-tune chorales harmonized quite dissonantly. With this work Stravinsky began to move away from Russian-inspired works, although later he did do two short comic operas, *Mavra* and *Renard*, on Russian themes. Stravinsky relaxed by writing two sets of easy, short four-hand piano pieces. Later he orchestrated these compositions, making them into two orchestral suites that include a Spanish dance, a polka, a march, a galop, and a waltz. The jagged, nervous rhythms of American ragtime, by then pervading Europe, appealed to Stravinsky and resulted in *Ragtime* for eleven instruments (1918) and *Piano Rag-Music* (1920). He became intrigued by the mechanical player piano and wrote an Étude for Pianola.

For his friend Diaghilev, he wrote the music for the ballet *Pulcinella* (1920). This time Stravinsky costumed his music in the light, graceful style of the eighteenth-century composer Pergolesi, using, in fact, much thematic material from this Italian master.

There followed one of Stravinsky's strongest works, the *Symphonies of Wind Instruments*, dedicated to the memory of the French composer Debussy. It puzzles many listeners because it is unlike any other composition by Stravinsky. Its dissonant harmonies move gradually from great tension to a feeling of calm triumph. In it there is none of Stravinsky's nervous rhythm or brilliant use of instruments. He has described the piece as "an austere ritual." Of all Stravinsky's works, it is the most moving and, unfortunately, one of the least played.

In the middle 1920's Stravinsky entered what has been called his "neoclassic" period, going back to the musical forms of the seventeenth and eighteenth centuries for inspiration. In 1925, the year of his first visit to the United States, he wrote a sonata and a *Serenade en la*. In the serenade he tried to capture the feeling of eighteenth-century entertainment music, and the result was elegant, refined, and graceful. The tone A is the tonal center around which the music develops, but there is no feeling of eighteenth-century chord progression. Thus the music may be a charming little dance, as in the rondoletto (Ex. 62), or a slightly sentimental piece such as the cadenza finale (Ex. 63). This freely dissonant but tonal music has been called pan-diatonic.

Ex. 62 — *Serenade en la,* Rondoletto

Ex. 63 — Cadenza

Other works from Stravinsky's neoclassic period are a Capriccio for piano and orchestra; a Concerto for piano and wind instruments, double basses, and timpani; and the ballet-pantomine *Apollon Musagète (Apollo, Master of the Muses).* Next Stravinsky turned to the tragic Greek legend of Oedipus, out of which he made an opera-oratorio, *Oedipus Rex,* for chorus, vocal soloists, and orchestra. In this he used a Latin text because of its dignified and formal sound. It is a powerful dramatic composition, usually performed as a kind of staged concert work.

The weightiness of *Oedipus Rex* was balanced by Stravinsky's next ballet, *Le Baiser de la fée (The Fairy's Kiss),* based on the Hans Christian Andersen fairy tale *The Ice Maiden,* and produced in 1928. The light, tuneful score of this ballet uses themes by one of Stravinsky's favorite composers, Tchaikovsky.

The year 1930 saw the birth of a new Stravinsky masterpiece, the *Symphony of Psalms,* dedicated to "the glory of God and to the Boston Symphony Orchestra on its fiftieth anniversary." This reverent, deeply felt work is for chorus and an orchestra without violins, violas, or clarinets but including two pianos. In style it combines Stravinsky's rhythmic drive and sense of orchestral color with a new quality of melody, harmony, and counterpoint. Many of its melodies are chantlike, moving up or down in small intervals. The second movement consists of two fugues in progress at the same time—one for orchestra and one for voice. The subject of the orchestral fugue is wide-spaced (Ex. 64). The voices sing a line that is more flowing (Ex. 65). The third movement, the high point of the work, moves from a soft cry of "Alleluia, laudate Dominum" (Praise the Lord) through a syncopated, driving rhythm to a lofty emotional plane. At this point the chorus breaks into a slow hymn of praise. Underneath the chorus the timpani, harp, and pianos play a solemn, majestic ostinato, or repeated figure (Ex. 66). The work ends softly with a repetition of "Alleluia, laudate Dominum" on widely spaced C's and E's.

During the 1930's Stravinsky continued to write large works which combined his own rhythmic and dissonant harmonic style with the musical forms of the seventeenth and eighteenth centuries. Among the most important of these works are *Perséphone,* a ballet with recitation and chorus; a Violin Concerto; a sonata for violin and piano (entitled *Duo concertant);* a concerto for

Ex. 64 — *Symphony of Psalms*

Ex. 65

Ex. 66

A scene from the Metropolitan Opera première (1953) of The Rake's Progress, *with Blanche Thebom as Baba the Turk*

Stravinsky conducting at a recording session

chamber orchestra (the "Dumbarton Oaks" Concerto); and a "ballet in three deals" called *Jeux de cartes* (*Card Party,* 1937).

As more and more of Stravinsky's commissions came from the United States, it was only natural that in 1939 he should move to America. He bought a home in Hollywood and became an American citizen in 1945. Enjoying American life, he took part in it in many ways. He wrote a *Circus Polka* for the elephants in Ringling Brothers' Circus; *Ebony Concerto* for "Woody" Herman's dance band; and ballet music for the Broadway show *Seven Lively Arts.* He even made a new arrangement of "The Star-Spangled Banner," but after one performance was not allowed to conduct it again in Boston because of its unusual harmonization, which was regarded as "mutilation" of the national anthem. In 1962 Stravinsky was lured to write a work for television, *Noah and the Flood.*

Not all Stravinsky's works written in America are of a commercial nature. There is the light Symphony in C and the immediately popular Symphony in Three Movements. Other works include a mass for boys' and men's voices and ten instruments, and an opera, *The Rake's Progress,* produced at Venice in 1951. The latter is an old-style opera with tuneful set-pieces such as arias and ensemble scenes. For his friend the choreographer Balanchine, Stravinsky wrote the successful ballets *Orpheus* (1948) and *Agon* (1957).

During the greater part of his life Stravinsky criticized the twelve-tone method of composition used by Arnold Schoenberg and his followers. Stravinsky's disciples were much surprised, therefore (though they should have been used to such things), when Stravinsky himself began to use the serial techniques of Anton von Webern. The idea of the tone row and the sparse, fragmented sounds of which Webern was so fond are found in several of his later works, such as *Agon;* the *Canticum sacrum ad honorem Sancti Marci nominus* (Sacred Song in Honor of the Name of Saint Mark) for tenor, baritone, chorus, and orchestra; and *Threni—* the *Lamentations of the Prophet Jeremiah.* But as with all his works, Stravinsky managed to make his twelve-tone music sound like himself. It is as though he had marched into the enemy camp and come home with the spoils of the warfare—new sounds.

Stravinsky authored several books, which explain his often-changing views of music and musicians. The autobiography (1935) was followed in 1946 by *Poétique musicale* (English version, *Poetics of Music,* 1948)— a series of lectures given at Harvard University. Since then his ideas have appeared in several books of interviews by Stravinsky's American disciple, the conductor Robert Craft.

Ex. 67—Fugue in B-flat Minor from *The Well-tempered Clavier*, Book I, J. S. Bach

A banjo used in the West Indies and Central America

Ex. 68

STRETTO: an Italian word meaning "close." In music it is applied to the entrances of compositional themes, usually in fugal works where the different voices do not wait for each other to finish stating the fugue subject but pile in on top of each other. The device of stretto is used in some fugues for most of the composition after the opening section, in which each voice has its full allotted time to state the subject. Because the effect of stretto is exciting, like a lively conversation or argument, the composer often saves it for the climax of the work.

Ex. 67 shows the opening of Bach's Fugue in B-flat Minor from *The Well-tempered Clavier*. The second voice does not enter until after the full two-measure statement of the subject by the first voice. Ex. 68 shows the stretto section of the same work near the end. Here the voices wait only half a measure before coming in.

The term stretto is sometimes used in a musical composition to indicate a gradual speeding up of the tempo, usually near the end.

STRINGED INSTRUMENTS: instruments on which tones are produced by vibrations of taut strings. The strings are stretched across a hollow wood or metal body which acts as a resonator to increase the volume of sound. In order to vibrate freely, a string must be free of obstructions. In instruments where the strings lie close to the body, as in the violin family, this freedom is achieved by passing the strings over a bridge, which elevates them above the instrument's body. Stringed instruments are of many shapes and sizes and are played in different ways.

The largest group of stringed instruments is that in which the sound is made by plucking the string. It includes the banjo, guitar, harp, lyre, lute, mandolin, balalaika, ukulele, zither, and harpsichord. (In the harpsichord the player presses a key but the mechanism inside the instrument plucks the string.) These instruments are usually played as solo or accompaniment instruments, and except for the harp and sometimes the harpsichord, they are not regular members of the orchestra.

A second group of stringed instruments consists of those whose tone is produced by drawing a bow across the strings. This group includes the various instruments—violin, viola, cello, and double bass—that have for many years provided the foundation of the symphony orchestra, in which there are usually fifty or sixty stringed instruments. The viol family, popular in the sixteenth and seventeenth centuries, but no longer in general use, were also bowed instruments.

In one small group of stringed instruments the strings are struck by a hammer (piano), metal tangent (clavichord), or beater (the Hungarian gypsy cymbalon). On the piano and clavichord, the hammer and tangent are activated by means of a keyboard.

The keyboard stringed instruments have a string or group of strings for each playable tone. Most of the others have a few strings which must be shortened by the player's

An Indian fiddle, or sarangi

Top left: *Burmese stick zither, shaped like a crocodile*
Top right: *students in a music class in Calcutta, working on the sitar and vina*
Bottom: *a mariachi band in Puebla, Mexico*

fingers to produce all the required tones. On these instruments a fingerboard under the strings serves as a brace for the fingers to press against. On bowed instruments, such as the violin, this fingerboard is smooth; the player, aided by his ear, must judge how far apart his fingers must be placed to get the desired tones. On the plucked instruments there are small pieces of metal, called "frets," placed across the fingerboard in such a way that they guide the fingers to the correct place to stop the string. The harp has many strings, but in order to produce all the tones of its chromatic scale some of its strings must be shortened by means of pedals.

One end of each string of a stringed instrument is fixed to a permanent tailpiece; the other end is attached to a device that can be adjusted to tune the string to its proper pitch. This device may be a peg, as in the case of the violin and guitar, or a small metal pin in the frame of the instrument, as in the piano.

The shapes and sizes of the stringed instruments have come about as the result of experiments by makers who, throughout history, have worked to perfect and enhance the peculiar quality of each kind of instrument. Thus the fat body of the guitar contributes to its mellow tone, while the skin drumhead stretched over the body of the banjo gives it its plunking, jangling sound. Instruments with a great many strings, such as the harp and piano, have assumed shapes that follow the graduated changes in the lengths of the strings, from longest to shortest.

Stringed instruments have existed since the days of primitive man. Perhaps the earliest was the hunter's bow. Its twanging sound as an arrow was released probably led to experiments with other types of stringed instruments. Soon man discovered that when the bow was placed in a pot or a gourd, the volume of sound made by the string was increased. As more strings were added, the instruments took on new shapes. Stringing bits of material from a crosspiece between two animal horns led to the lyre, the instrument honored by the ancient Greeks as the invention of the god Apollo. Instruments of the lyre and harp families were used in ancient countries as early as 2000 B.C.

Bowed instruments seem to have been invented in the Near East. From there they spread to Europe, where they became ancestors of the violin and viol families. For a time during the sixteenth and seventeenth centuries, the thinner-sounding viol held its own with the more brilliant-sounding violin. By 1700 the violin had won out and had become the most important stringed instrument in European music.

During the Renaissance, about 1450 to 1600, the most popular stringed instruments were the lute and its relatives of the guitar family. Much of the first instrumental music was written for the lute, and the earliest solo songs are sometimes called "lute songs" because a lute accompaniment was provided for them. Europeans and Americans have recently discovered, through recordings and live performances, the exotic sounds of the Japanese stringed instruments, the samisen and the koto, and the Hindu stringed vina and sitar.

Some members of the string family have benefited from electronic amplification. The most important of these is the electric guitar, whose sound can now be made loud enough to match that of jazz trumpets and saxophones. This change in sound has been accompanied by a change in shape, since the amplifier of the modern electric guitar does away with the need for a resonant body. Electronic pianos have been used in schools for several years. As yet, however, no one has been able to make an electronic violin that has the warmth of tone produced by string and wood. Perhaps the personal touches and the loving care put into violins by the great violin makers, Stradivarius, Amati, and Guarneri, can never be duplicated by an electronic tube.

Two musicians playing the samisen (woodcut by Kiyonaga, Japan)

STRINGENDO: an Italian word meaning "pressing" or "tightening." A composer uses it to tell the performer to step up the tempo, or accelerate. It usually signals the approach of a climax, as when Beethoven uses it in the finale movement of his Ninth Symphony. There, over a short connecting phrase leading to the final prestissimo, Beethoven wrote *Poco allegro, stringendo il tempo, sempre più allegro*—"a bit fast, tightening up the pace, always faster."

SUITE: a musical term, derived from the French *suite* ("series" or "set"), with various meanings. An early use of the term referred to a collection of court dances of the Baroque period (1600–1750). Since the early 1800's the term has been applied also to a number of compositions held together by a story, mood, or idea—for example, Ravel's *Mother Goose* Suite.

The earliest type of suite was written in the late sixteenth century when composers paired two kinds of court dances—a slow, stately pavane and a gay, fast galliard. The pavane and galliard dropped out of favor and were replaced by the flowing allemande and the running courante. Gradually other court dances, such as the saraband, gigue, minuet, and gavotte, were added to the original pair of allemande and courante. The group of dances was called a suite or partita in Germany, a chamber sonata (*sonata da camera*) in Italy, and an *ordre* by the French composer François Couperin. The first suite for harpsichord was written about 1650 by the German composer Johann Jakob Froberger (1616–67).

The dances in the Baroque suite were usually arranged in alternating tempos: allemande, courante, saraband, gigue. All dances within a suite were usually in the same key, although occasionally one movement might be put in a related key for variety. The dances all had the same two-part form, with a double bar and a repeat at the end of each section of the piece (AA-BB). Optional dances, such as the gavotte, minuet, and bourrée, often written in three-part form, were usually placed after the saraband.

This form of suite, sometimes with a short improvisational prelude, was one of the most popular instrumental forms of Handel, Rameau, and most of the other composers of the Baroque period. It was most fully developed by J. S. Bach, who wrote sets of French and English suites plus a set of partitas for harpsichord. Bach's suites for unaccompanied cello and unaccompanied violin are considered the greatest of their kind. He himself used the term "overture" for each of the four orchestral works now known as suites. They take the form, set by Lully in his opera ballets, of a full French-style overture followed by a series of dances.

Couperin's *Ordres* are collections of short pieces for harpsichord. The individual movements have descriptive, fanciful titles, such as "Le Petit Moulin à vent" (The Little Windmill), "La Lugubre" (The Sad-faced One), and "La Majesteuse" (The Majestic One).

After 1750 the suite of court dances disappeared. The term returned in the middle 1800's as a title for a collection of concert works drawn from the theater. Among the best-known of these suites are Grieg's *Peer Gynt*, Bizet's *L'Arlésienne*, Tchaikovsky's *Nutcracker*, Ravel's *Daphnis and Chloé*, Stravinsky's *Petrouchka*, and Copland's *Billy the Kid* and *Rodeo*.

By the late nineteenth century the word suite came to refer to a group of works held together by story, mood, or idea. Such suites are Rimsky-Korsakov's *Scheherazade*, Debussy's *Suite bergamasque*, Grofé's *Grand Canyon*, and Ellington's *Harlem*—one of the first jazz suites.

Contemporary composers have gone back to the old Baroque idea of the suite in such works as Schoenberg's Suite for Piano, Opus 25; Bartók's Suite for Piano, Opus 14; Berg's *Lyric Suite* for string quartet; and Honegger's *Suite archaïque* for orchestra.

SUMER IS ICUMEN IN ("Summer Is A-coming In"): the oldest known round—the ancestor (or great-uncle) of "Frère Jacques," "Row, Row, Row Your Boat," and the hundreds of other rounds that are favorites of singers of all ages. It is a round, or canon, for four voices singing over a little, repeated duet in two lower voices, making it a six-part work.

For many years it was believed that "Sumer is icumen in" was written as early as 1240, but music scholars of late have decided that it was more probably written in the early 1300's. It stands by itself as a musical work. Its melody is like many other happy, dancelike English melodies of the 1200's and 1300's, but no other composition of its time used so masterfully the device of imitation, which is what a round is based on.

"Sumer is icumen in" is often called the "Reading Rota," since Reading Abbey is the place where the manuscript was found and *rota* was the old name for a round or canon. It is not known whether the work was composed by a monk in the abbey or was copied from an earlier manuscript. In the manuscript that has come down to us, a Latin text was written under the old English words.

SUSPENSION: a dissonance produced by holding over one or more tones of a chord as the other voices move on to a new chord. The pull exerted by the suspension gives music a great deal of forward motion, like water which is dammed up and then released. In the vocal works of Lassus, Palestrina, and other composers of the sixteenth century, the suspension occurs at cadence points where it serves to bring the music to a point of tension and climax. Sixteenth-century suspensions were often decorated and used in a series or chain (see Ex. 44, page 534).

The suspension can also have a pathetic quality, particularly in slow music. Bach uses this sadness of the falling suspension to set the mood of the Crucifixus of his

Early 14th-century manuscript of "Sumer is icumen in"

B-minor Mass (Ex. 69). In this case the suspension is sounded rather than held. Bach also liked to pile up dissonance by suspending a whole chord—a practice found also in the works of many later composers, such as Mozart, Beethoven, and Brahms (Ex. 70).

In traditional harmony and counterpoint, there are three parts to a suspension: the preparation (p), in which the tone that will become the suspension is a consonant, or chord, tone—usually on an unaccented beat; the suspension (s), where the tone held over is dissonant in relation to the other tones being sounded—usually on an accented beat; and the resolution (r), where the suspended tone moves downward to become a consonance—usually on an unaccented beat:

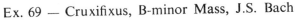

Preparation Suspension Resolution

A suspension that resolves upward is sometimes called a *retardation*:

Sonata in D Major, Op. 10, No. 3, Beethoven

Suspensions may occur in any voice. Although they are characterized by the use of the tie, not all tied notes are suspensions. Contemporary music does not depend on the suspension as much as earlier music did, partly because contemporary composers do not think of one sound as being more dissonant than another. It does occur occasionally, as in the slow movement of Schuman's *Symphony for Strings* (Ex. 71).

Ex. 69 — Cruxifixus, B-minor Mass, J.S. Bach

Ex. 70 — Sonata in F, Op. 10, No. 2, Beethoven

Ex. 71 — *Symphony for Strings*, Schuman

Larghissimo

Above left: *pas de deux from a 1955 Bolshoi production of* Swan Lake

Above right: *scene from Act II,* Swan Lake

SWAN LAKE *(Le Lac des Cygnes):* a ballet with music by Tchaikovsky—probably the most famous of all ballets. It is done as a full-length, four-act ballet, as a one-act ballet, and as a duet—the Black Swan *pas de deux,* or dance for two. *Swan Lake* was the first of Tchaikovsky's three ballets (the others being *Sleeping Beauty* and *Nutcracker*). When it was presented for the first time at the Bolshoi Theater in Moscow in 1877, it was a failure. Later, in 1895, the work was redone for the Maryinsky Theater in St. Petersburg (now Leningrad). The new choreography by Petipa and Ivanov made *Swan Lake* a success, but unfortunately the composer had died before seeing his greatest ballet succeed.

Like many other ballets of the 1800's, *Swan Lake* is based on a romantic tale. Siegfried, a youthful prince, has been told by his mother that he must choose a bride at a ball she is giving. The prince, sad because he must give up his carefree bachelor existence, organizes a shooting party. At the shore of a lake they see a group of swans. The prince is just about to shoot the leader of the swans when it turns into a beautiful girl, the Princess Odette. She tells the prince that she and her fellow swans have been cast under a spell by Rothbart, a magician who lives in a nearby castle. The spell can

be broken only if she finds a man who swears to love no one but her. Siegfried pledges his love to Odette and they dance until daybreak; then she once more becomes a swan.

That night, at his castle, Siegfried watches the dancing of the girls his mother has assembled for him to choose from. Rothbart, the magician, enters with his daughter Odile. She has been disguised to look like Odette, and Siegfried rushes to greet her. They perform a long duet, known as the "Black Swan duet" because Odile wears a black ballet costume instead of Odette's white one. Siegfried asks for the hand of Odile, upon which both father and daughter disappear.

Siegfried realizes that he has been made the victim of Rothbart's magic. He hurries to the shore of the lake where he first saw Odette. He finds her, but cannot stop her from grieving over his unfaithfulness. Odette plunges into the lake, followed by Siegfried. This sacrifice for love breaks Rothbart's evil spell, and his castle tumbles down in ruins as Siegfried and Odette are reunited.

Swan Lake contains some of Tchaikovsky's most beautiful music. The theme of the swan, a plaintive yet graceful song on the oboe, appears throughout the work (Ex. 72). Much of the music was taken by

Ex. 72

Andante

Tchaikovsky from an earlier opera of his, *Ondine,* which had been unsuccessful. It is a romantic ballet, underlain by a yearning sadness.

The most important dance sections are the duet between Odette and Siegfried; the beautiful, formal patterns of the swans moving in their unearthly grace; the quartet for the four little swans, a pert little dance requiring the utmost in rhythmic precision; the Black Swan duet between Odile and Siegfried; and the finale in which love finally triumphs.

The parts of Odette and Odile are performed by one dancer. It is a role that demands everything from great technical virtuosity to tragic simplicity. Most of the great ballerinas have appeared in the leading part, including Karsavina, Pavlova, and Ulanova in Russian companies, and in English companies, Markova and Fonteyn.

For many years *Swan Lake* in its full-length version was produced only in Russia. Finally, in 1934, it was added to the repertoire of the Royal Ballet of England, and since then it has been produced also by companies in Sweden, Canada, and the United States. Outside the Soviet Union, *Swan Lake* is often seen as a one-act ballet (the second act of the full production).

SYMPHONIC POEM (or **tone poem,** as it was called by Richard Strauss): an orchestral work in which the composer attempts to give, in musical sounds, the feeling that a listener might get from looking at a painting or a landscape, reading a poem, seeing a drama, or discussing an idea. It is program music in that the audience has to know the title, the story, and often the poem on which the composer bases his composition to fully appreciate and understand the work.

A symphonic poem may be a mood piece —vague in meaning, as in Debussy's "Nuages" and *The Afternoon of a Faun.* It may be descriptive, as in Strauss's *Don Quixote,* where the sound of a wind-machine portrays the hero riding through the air, or in Liszt's *Mazeppa,* where a galloping horse stumbles. The basis of the symphonic poem may be a philosophy, as in Liszt's *Les Préludes,* and Strauss's *Thus Spoke Zarathustra.* It may be a myth or legend, as in Liszt's *Prometheus* and Sibelius' *Swan of Tuonela,* or it may be a fanciful landscape, as in Liadov's *Enchanted Lake.*

Once the composer has decided on the literary or pictorial theme of the work, he invents musical motives that not only can be identified with the story but also are capable of musical development. In *Till Eulenspiegel's Merry Pranks,* Strauss, who brought the tone poem to its highest development, uses two musical ideas to represent the two sides of Till's nature. As Till gets entangled in his pranks, so, too, do his motives. When he is hanged for his misdeeds one of his motives soars higher and higher, as though Till's soul were flying up to heaven. In Dukas' *The Sorcerer's Apprentice,* the motive of the magic broomstick bringing water, originally stated by the bassoon, finally spreads over the whole orchestra to suggest the flooding of the room.

The form of the symphonic poem may be a free one, unlike any particular musical form as it follows the course of the story. Sometimes, however, the composer chooses a musical form that happens to fit the subject matter. In *Don Quixote,* Strauss chose to write a theme and variations, each variation representing an adventure. *Till Eulenspiegel* is a very free kind of rondo form in which Till's themes weave their way in and out of trouble.

The first composer to use the term "symphonic poem" was Franz Liszt, around 1850. His thirteen symphonic poems set the pattern which was followed by many composers of the late nineteenth century. Each work usually consists of one movement, which can be fairly short. The freedom of form of the symphonic poem appealed to composers who were trying to break away from the Classical forms of Haydn and Mozart.

Composers of the nineteenth century tended to be literary-minded, and the symphonic poem provided them with a musical way of expressing literary themes in tone. They also wanted to be sure that their audiences knew exactly what their music meant. Into the symphonic poem could be poured all the Romantic feelings of the composer:

Don Quixote and Sancho Panza (wash drawing by Honoré Daumier)

Two woodcuts of Till Eulenspiegel from a German book of 1567 entitled Noctuae Speculum

his patriotism, love of nature, yearning for the past, admiration for the heroic figure, or passion for life.

Hundreds of symphonic poems were written in the sixty years between 1850 and 1910. In addition to the works already mentioned the best-known symphonic poems are Sibelius' *Finlandia* and *Night Ride and Sunrise;* Strauss's *Don Juan* and *Death and Transfiguration;* Rachmaninoff's *The Isle of the Dead;* Scriabin's *Poem of Ecstasy;* Smetana's *My Country*—a set of six symphonic poems of which *The Moldau* is the best known; Franck's *Les Eolides* and *Les Djinns;* and Schoenberg's *Pelleas und Melisande.*

Contemporary composers have ignored the symphonic poem, preferring to write symphonies or other non-literary forms.

SYMPHONIE FANTASTIQUE *(Fantastic Symphony):* a symphony by Hector Berlioz —one of the most important works of the nineteenth century. It was first performed in Paris in 1830, only three years after the death of Beethoven. With its defiance of Classical traditions, it was like the opening shot of the Romantic revolution. Almost everything about it was new and different. It has a story, or program. One theme is used throughout all the movements—Berlioz called it an *idée fixe,* or obsession. The symphony has five movements instead of the Classical four, and its harmony is highly chromatic. Its orchestration uses every orchestral group to the fullest extent. The strings soar up above the winds, free of their bread-and-butter job of holding down the harmony. Even the percussion instruments (usually restricted to marking accents) are given solo passages, or help to hold harmony. Berlioz had the audacity to specify that the work needed "at least thirty violins."

The *Symphonie fantastique* received an enthusiastic welcome at its first performance at the Paris Conservatory. Among the most enthusiastic members of the audience was the nineteen-year-old Franz Liszt. In the course of the nineteenth century the symphony led to such works as Liszt's and Strauss's symphonic poems. The *idée fixe* was used later by Schumann, Tchaikovsky, Dvořák, and many others. It undoubtedly influenced the young Richard Wagner, showing him how a theme can undergo dramatic change as a character changes.

There are many stories about the program of the *Symphonie fantastique,* which was subtitled "Episode in the Life of an Artist." These stories usually involve Berlioz's love for an Irish actress, Harriet Smith-son (whom at the time of writing he barely knew). All that Berlioz himself ever said to explain the symphony was ". . . a young man . . . in despair caused by unhappy love . . . has drugged himself. . . . He plunges into a heavy sleep accompanied by weird visions. His sensations . . . are transformed into musical images and ideas. The beloved one herself becomes to him a melody, a returning idea *(idée fixe)* which haunts him everywhere."

The movements of the symphony are:

I. *Reveries, Passions.* A slow introduction is followed by a sonata-allegro form of which the *idée fixe* is the most important theme (Ex. 73).

II. *A Ball.* At a ball the young man finds his loved one again. The *idée fixe* appears in the middle of a delicately scored waltz (Ex. 74). Two harps are given an important place in the orchestra—for the first time in a symphony.

III. *In the Country.* On a calm summer's night two shepherds call to each other (Ex. 75). For this episode Berlioz uses two Swiss alpine-horn melodies, known as *ranz des vaches* (traditionally, a call by herdsmen to their scattered cows). The loved one appears to the young man in his mind, disturbing the calm evening. He wonders, "What if she is not faithful to me?" The *idée fixe* appears in a rhythmically shortened form (Ex. 76).

IV. *March to the Scaffold.* The young man dreams that he has killed his loved one. He is condemned to death and marches toward his execution. Just before he is beheaded, the *idée fixe* appears, played by a clarinet. It is like a last thought of the loved one.

In this movement Berlioz wrote some of his most colorful orchestration. At the very beginning the timpani are tuned in a G-Bb-D-F chord—a most unusual thing at that time. The double basses play a pizzicato G-minor triad all by themselves. The movement is built on two themes— one like heavy, plodding footsteps (Ex. 77); the other, a triumphant march (Ex. 78):

V. *Dream of a Witches' Sabbath.* In the midst of unearthly groans and cries, the young man hears the theme of his beloved. But now it is nasty. It cackles, for his beloved has come to join the witches (Ex. 79). The solemn Dies Irae (Day of Wrath), from the Mass for the dead, is burlesqued. Bells, six pianos (not always used), and two tubas provide a macabre background against which the *idée fixe,* in its bewitched form, dances. The movement builds, by way of a fugue, to a brilliant climax and ending.

Ex. 73

Ex. 74

Ex. 75

Ex. 76

Ex. 77

Ex. 78

Ex. 79

SYMPHONY: a work for orchestra usually consisting of three or four separate movements. The number has ranged from one (Sibelius, Harris, Schuman) to seven (Anton Rubinstein). A symphony may be for strings alone or winds alone but as a rule calls for full choirs of strings, winds, and percussion. In certain symphonies by Beethoven, Berlioz, Liszt, Mahler, and Stravinsky, voices have been added to the instruments. In its two-hundred-year history the symphony has ranged from the elegance and good-natured humor of the eighteenth-century works through the passionate, stormy, romantic examples of the 1800's to the nervous and energetic symphony of the present. Like a novel in its large scope, the symphony still holds its place as the most popular form for the composer with serious things to say.

Though the symphony arrived at its full growth in the period of Haydn and Mozart in the latter half of the 1700's, its beginnings go back to the early 1600's. The *Sacrae symphoniae* of Giovanni Gabrieli and Heinrich Schütz were works for voices, with instrumental interludes. In Monteverdi's opera *Orfeo* (1607) the sinfonia was a piece of instrumental music that accompanied action on the stage. The term sinfonia was used also for a prelude to a suite of dances or to a large vocal work or section of a vocal work, such as Handel's "Sinfonia Pastorale" in *Messiah*. It was also used by J. S. Bach as the title for his keyboard works now known as Three-part Inventions.

The true ancestor of the symphony of the Classical period was the Italian opera overture form popularized by Alessandro Scarlatti. The Italian overture, called by Scarlatti "sinfonia before the raising of the curtain," consisted of two fast compositions separated by a slow movement. By the 1730's instrumental works having nothing to do with opera were being written in this form. For want of a better word they were called "symphonies." Their style was much closer to the tuneful Italian opera style of melody supported by harmony than it was to the tightly knit fugues being written by J. S. Bach at the same time. For a long time the symphony, as written by the earlier eighteenth-century symphonists, G. B. Sammartini, Georg Matthias Monn, Johann Christian Bach, and Johann Stamitz, had three movements, the last of which was often a minuet. Many of the early symphonies of Haydn follow this plan.

The first movement of the Classical symphony was based on the newly developed sonata-allegro form. Material was presented in an *exposition,* or opening statement, then was tossed around in a free fantasy, or *development,* section, and finally was brought back in a *recapitulation* section. The second movement, in a key different from but related to that of the first movement, was written in various forms including the da capo aria (A-B-A), theme and variations, and a small sonata-allegro (sonatina) form. The minuet movement remained what it had been in the dance suite of the early 1700's—a first minuet, a second minuet or trio in contrast to the first, and a repeat of the first minuet. Composers soon saw the need for a rousing final movement and added a rondo form or another sonata-allegro form after the minuet.

The early symphonies were sonatas for a small group of instrumentalists—often only a string quartet and a pair of French horns, flutes, or oboes. Trumpets, timpani, and bassoons were added gradually until the modern symphony orchestra had come into being. The full orchestra gave the composer a varied set of colors with which to work. It allowed him to spin longer movements as he contrasted a theme played by strings with the sound of the same theme as played by the woodwinds; he could repeat and still have variety in his sounds.

The first of the great symphonists was Haydn, who wrote more than a hundred works in this form. Although they follow a pattern, as far as movements and forms within the movements are concerned, they show tremendous range of content, from gay, bubbling works to compositions that are deep in feeling and filled with dramatic contrasts. Mozart brought his singing, melodic lines to the symphony and his genius to the various forms of the movements, as in the last three symphonies—Numbers 39, 40, and 41 (see "JUPITER" SYMPHONY), written within six weeks in the summer of 1788. Between them, Haydn and Mozart made Vienna the home of the symphony—a position it held for a hundred years.

Beethoven wrote only nine symphonies, setting a pattern of fewer but bigger works that was adopted by composers who followed. In his Third Symphony, the "Eroica," he broke away from the Classical pattern. The first movement is still in the traditional sonata-allegro form, but each of its sections is enlarged. Seven themes are stated and developed, making the movement a masterpiece of complexity in form and of clarity in its heroic quality. In the second movement Beethoven defied tradition by composing a funeral march instead of the more usual slow, songlike movement. This is followed

Giovanni Battista Sammartini

Johann Stamitz (from the title page of L'Art du violo by Jean-Baptiste Cartier, Paris, 1798)

An open-air orchestra close in size to that for which Haydn's early symphonies were written (note the accompanist at the harpsichord, with bass player near him)

by a scherzo—strange, scurrying pianissimo figures in the strings and woodwinds which erupt *fortissimo* in the ninety-third measure with the full force of the whole orchestra. Beethoven had abandoned the usual minuet as a third movement in his Second Symphony, replacing it with a scherzo—a musical joke. With the scherzo of the "Eroica," Beethoven showed new possibilities in the third movement, which had formerly been a slight interlude between the slow movement and the fast finale. In the finale of the "Eroica" he continued to break new ground, constructing a huge theme and variations, almost 500 measures in length.

After the "Eroica" there was no turning back to the small-scale symphony of the Classical period. Beethoven continued his remaking of this musical form in his Fifth Symphony, which develops entirely from an opening four-note motive. To give more power to his orchestra, Beethoven added trombones, piccolo, and a contra bassoon. The forcefulness, power, and vigor of the Fifth have made it the best known of all symphonies.

In his Sixth Symphony, the "Pastoral," Beethoven added another element to the new form: a program or title for each of the movements. The Classical pattern of movements is kept, with a "storm" movement added between the scherzo and the finale. In the last movement of his Ninth Symphony, Beethoven wrote for vocal soloists, chorus, and orchestra. The work ends with a sublime "Ode to Joy"—a vocal and instrumental poem in praise of the brotherhood of mankind.

Beethoven's explorations were continued by the composers who came after him. Schubert, who wrote eight symphonies, alternated between the smaller Classical form and the large. His Eighth Symphony in B Minor, the "Unfinished," is both songlike and concise. His Seventh in C Major—written in the last year of his life—has been called "the symphony of heavenly length."

Berlioz's *Symphonie fantastique* of 1830 is held together both by a story and by the use of a theme that appears in each movement—a theme Berlioz called an *idée fixe*. He termed his *Romeo and Juliet* Symphony for voices and orchestra a "dramatic symphony."

Throughout the nineteenth century the symphony followed the patterns set by Beethoven and Berlioz. In some works, such as Schumann's Fourth, Franck's Symphony in D Minor, Dvořák's "From the New World" Symphony, and Tchaikovsky's Fourth, the whole work is tied together by the recurrence of one or more themes throughout. Some composers, particularly Mahler and Bruckner, made each movement huge; and Mahler used voices along with the instruments. Mendelssohn used descriptive local color in his "Scotch" and "Italian" Symphonies. Brahms, in his four symphonies, came closest to retaining the Classical idea of a symphony and the feeling of timing that played such an important part in the works of Haydn, Mozart, and

Beethoven. Borodin, Tchaikovsky, Dvořák, and Sibelius wrote symphonies that manage to be both personal and national in feeling.

For a while, in the nineteenth century, the symphony form fought for its place with Liszt's descriptive symphonic poems and Strauss's tone poems. The fact that the symphony was adaptable enough to take in some of the freedom and color demanded by Liszt and Strauss helped it survive. The symphony of today follows no one pattern, except that it is a large work requiring a full orchestra for performance. The Classical forms of the various movements are no longer followed, but the idea of a variety of tempos remains.

Almost every major composer of the modern period has written at least one symphony. Among the best known are those by Prokofiev (seven), Hindemith (two), Shostakovich (fifteen), Honegger (five), Vaughan Williams (nine), Stravinsky (three), Schuman (nine), Piston (eight), Harris (eleven), and Copland (three).

SYNCOPATION: the accenting of a beat or part of a beat that is not normally given such emphasis. The accenting of weak beats occurs in exciting dance music all over the world. It can be heard, or felt, for example, in African, Indian, Israeli, Arabian, and southeast Asian music—but most of all in American folk songs and jazz.

Syncopation has been a basic part of European music from the fourteenth century on. It can happen in any form of music, from a symphony, such as Mozart's "Little" G-minor Symphony (Ex. 80a), to a sixteenth-century religious work.

For its full effect a syncopation must always be felt against the normal beat or accent. A pattern such as that in Ex. 80b feels like a steady series of staccato quarter notes, with no feeling of syncopation. As soon as the other voices are added they show where the normal accent is, and the pattern can be felt as a syncopation (Ex. 80c). It is for this reason that most jazz has a steady four-count pulse under the rest of the patterns, which are syncopated.

The subtle shifts in accent in jazz melodic figures cannot be taught. Only the basic idea of *not* accenting the heavy beats—the first and third beats of the measure—can be explained. Beyond this the player must depend on his physical sensitivity to the true nature of rhythm.

In the simplest type of syncopation the composer puts accent marks over notes on weak beats or writes chords only on the weak beats (Ex. 81). Another way of making a syncopation is to omit any sound on a strong beat of a measure or a strong part of a beat. This can be done with rests or with the use of tied notes (Ex. 82). Syncopation based on the omission of strong beats happens, for example, when a group singing

Jazz musicians playing in Preservation Hall, New Orleans

Ex. 80a — Symphony No. 25, Mozart

Allegro con brio

Ex. 80b — Fantasie, Schumann

Ex. 80c

Ex. 81 — Sonata in A Minor, Op. 164, Schubert

Allegretto

Ex. 82 — Sonata in G Minor, Op. 14, No. 2, Beethoven

Ex. 83 — "Camptown Races"

Ex. 84 — Symphony in D Minor, Franck

Ex. 85 — Sonata, Op. 31, No. 1, Beethoven

Allegro vivace

a highly rhythmic song clap their hands on the second and fourth beats of the measure (Ex. 83).

One of the most common syncopations occurs when a beat or a measure is broken apart in such a way that a long note is placed between two short ones. The longer note by its very length makes an accent where no accent should be. This short-long-short pattern can be written three ways:

(a)   (b)   (c)

The first of these figures is found in many American folk songs, such as "Turkey in the Straw." The second and third patterns are the basis of many popular tunes, such as "Blue Room," "I Want to Be Happy," and symphonic themes (Ex. 84).

A slightly more unusual syncopation occurs when a note seems to be brought in just a bit too soon. This syncopation-by-anticipation is used a great deal in Beethoven's Sonata for Piano, Opus 31, Number 1 (Ex. 85). It is also a basic figure in American jazz. Ex. 86 shows a measure with a steady beat in quarter notes followed by a

Ex. 86

Ex. 87

Ex. 88

measure in which the right-hand chords are syncopated by being brought in early.

One of the most interesting ways of making a syncopation is the putting of one meter on top of another, with the resulting combination of accents. Beethoven and Brahms were particularly fond of this device, bringing a melody in 2/4 or 6/8 time, for example, into a piece that is mostly in 3/4. A great deal of Latin-American folk music depends on this form of syncopation, which is based on a shift in groupings of beats (Ex. 87). A similar shift of accent that takes advantage of the fact that six beats may be broken into two sets of three or three sets of two may be found in music as early as the fifteenth century. Known as the *hemiola,* it occurs often at cadence points in such dance forms as the galliard and passepied, where the meter changes from 3/4 to 3/2, and in Latin American folk dances (Ex. 88).

TABLATURE: a form of musical notation that, in its simplest form, tells the player where to place his fingers on a stringed or woodwind instrument. Used from the fifteenth to the eighteenth century, tablature survives today in some editions of popular music, in which the ukulele part is indicated above the melody as in Ex. 1, here:

Ex. 1   A7

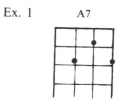

In this example each vertical line represents a string; the horizontal lines show the frets, one for each semitone. A dot indicates where the string is to be stopped; if there is no dot, the string is an open one. Of course, the ukulele tablature would be meaningless if one did not know how the strings were to be tuned. This problem is one that confronts the musical scholar who deciphers or transcribes much of the instrumental music of the Renaissance and early Baroque periods, since there were various ways of tuning the stringed instruments for whose music tablature was given.

Music for the lute and vihuela (an ancestor of the guitar) was written on a five- or six-line staff, each line representing a string. Numbers or letters showed the performer which frets to put his fingers on. A "0" or "a" represented an open string, "1" or "b" the first fret on a string, and so on.

Other forms of tablature were used in Spanish and German organ music. The Spanish used numbers to represent scale degrees (C = 1, D = 2, and so forth) for each melodic part; the Germans, a combination of conventional notation and letter names. The German system was used as late as the time of J. S. Bach.

Lute tablature, Italian, 1517 (music of Vincenzo Capirola)

Ex. 2 — *Pièces de clavecin*, 1724, Rameau

TAMBOURIN: a French dance of the seventeenth century. Its name comes possibly from the *tambourin du Bearn* or *tambourin de Gascogne,* a kind of two-stringed zither tuned to sound the first and fifth notes of the scale, or from the *tambour de Provence,* a long, narrow drum played with one hand while the other hand fingers a small recorder. The dance was in a lively 2/4 meter. The best-known tambourins are those by the eighteenth-century composer Jean-Philippe Rameau, who wrote several for orchestra and for harpsichord. In Ex. 2 Rameau suggests the two-stringed tambourin instrument of southern France by sounding the first and fifth notes of the scale in the left hand.

TAMBOURINE: a small, single-headed member of the drum family. Its shell consists of a wooden hoop clamped around the drumhead and containing holes at regular intervals. In the holes thin, round pieces of metal, or "jingles," are hung in pairs and act like miniature cymbals. The tambourine is played by rapping the knuckles on the drumhead, tapping the drumhead lightly with the fingertips, rubbing the thumb around the drumhead, or shaking the instrument to make the metal disks jingle.

The history of the tambourine goes as far back as ancient Mesopotamia and Egypt. By Old Testament times it had appeared in Israel as the *tof,* or English "timbrel" ("Then Miriam, the prophetess . . . took a timbrel in her hand"—Exodus 15:20). For centuries it was used principally to accompany dancing. In the eighteenth century the tambourine entered European bands and orchestras, along with the cymbals, triangle, and bass drum, during the vogue for Turkish Janissary music.

Since the time of Carl Maria von Weber, the tambourine has been used in the orchestra for its exotic color or to mark accents. Its part in scores is written on a single line (or sometimes in the treble clef, though the instrument has no definite pitch). Tchaikovsky gave it an important part in the "Danse Arabe" of his *Nutcracker* Suite.

TAM-TAM: a large bronze gong of indeterminate pitch used in symphony and opera orchestras (not to be confused with the tom-tom, a kind of drum commonly beaten with the hands). The tam-tam is used sparingly, either softly to provide a mysterious sound or loudly at a climax.

This instrument is hung by ropes from a metal stand. The percussionist strikes it with a felt bass-drum stick or a timpani stick, choosing his striking point carefully, for the gong is several feet across and its tone changes greatly from center to rim. The tam-tam gives an exotic flavor to the scores of Spontini's *La Vestale* and Puccini's *Madame Butterfly*—as befits an instrument that originated in the Orient.

Lithograph of girl dancing with a tambourine

A member of the National Symphony playing the tam-tam

Joan Crawford and Monroe Owsley doing the tango (from the movie This Modern Age)

The tango features smooth, slow, gliding steps interrupted by sudden stops and haughty poses like those in Spanish gypsy dancing. The music is in a moderate 2/4 meter. It combines the accompaniment pattern of the Cuban-Spanish habañera dance:

with a syncopated melody line. The melody is usually in units of two measures, with a long note at the end of each unit. A heavy downbeat opens each two-measure unit. A group of "crushed" tones or a glissando is often used to slide into the accented downbeat.

The most famous tango in concert music is Isaac Albéniz' little Tango in D (Ex. 3).

Other composers who have written tangos include Igor Stravinsky *(The Story of a Soldier)*, Kurt Weill *(The Three-penny Opera)*, and Enrique Fernández Arbós (Tango for Violin and Orchestra).

TANGO: the most popular social dance form of the period around World War I. It had originally been danced in Central America and Argentina, where it was quickly adopted as the favorite dance of the gauchos. The sensuous dancing of a tango by Rudolph Valentino, playing the part of a gaucho in *The Four Horsemen of the Apocalypse* (1921), helped to make him a great star in silent films. The tango paved the way for the fox trot, Charleston, rumba, samba, and other jazz and Latin-American dances that have been popular since 1920.

After World War I the tango became such a craze that dance halls named "tango palaces" were built to accommodate the millions who wanted to try it. The craze reached its height in Argentina, Germany, and to some extent the United States.

TAPE RECORDER: a machine that "stores" sound on magnetic tape. Developed for non-musical purposes on the eve of World War II, tape recorders have gone on to become one of the major means by which music is preserved and transmitted. They have taken their place among the other great devices—musical notation (developed in Classical and Byzantine times), the printing of scores (begun during the Renaissance), and the phonograph—that have enabled music to be carried beyond its own time and place.

When the first tape recorders were made commercially available around 1950, it became possible to record music in any hall, house, or apartment that had electric current; and with the later development of genuinely portable recorders (powered by batteries and using transistors instead of radio tubes) it became possible to record absolutely anywhere.

Ex. 3 — Tango in D, Albéniz
Andantino grazioso

The tape recorder represents a great advance over the phonograph. Tape reproduces sound more faithfully than a phonograph record and has the advantage of allowing for corrections. In disc recordings, an orchestra could play magnificently, then see its whole "take" ruined by an odd hiccup from the French horn a few bars from the end; the whole recording then would have to be done over—and for the rerun the orchestra as a whole might not do as good a job. But tape offers a better solution: the passage with the "fluff" is done over by itself, and the new passage is merely spliced in. (There are stories of a singer who sang her final high tone four times, then chose the one that came off best.)

The tape recorder has not always been as satisfying a piece of equipment as it is today. In its original form (as invented in 1898 by Valdemar Poulsen, a Danish telephone technician), it used steel wire instead of tape and produced a great deal of background noise during playback. In the 1920's new electronic circuits were designed that eliminated the background noise, and in the 1930's a German engineer, Fritz Pfleumer, brought about the use of plastic tape with a special coating that could be magnetized. Many of the details of present-day tape recorders were worked out by a young Chicago engineer, Marvin Camras, during World War II.

In its present form the tape recorder consists of an erasing head (which erases any previous recording that may have been made on the tape) and a recording head. A reel of tape is driven past them at an even speed—first past the erasing head, then past the recording head. The tape moves at speeds of 3¾, 7½, or 15 inches per second. The higher speeds prevent the pitch from wavering and make possible greater faithfulness to the original sound.

The sound to be recorded is received by a microphone, in which the pressure waves are transformed into electrical impulses that control the magnetism of the recording head. As the tape passes by, its coating picks up a varying sequence of magnetization from the recording head; this sequence of patterns, which matches the sound waves originally received by the microphone, remains in the coating of the tape, unless some day it is purposely erased to make way for a new recording.

For listening, the process is reversed. As the tape is played back, the erasing head is automatically cut out of the circuit and the recording head functions as a reproducing head. Varying patterns of magnetization on

A stereo tape deck, Ampex model 750

the tape are converted by the reproducing head into variations in the electric current reaching the loudspeaker. These in turn are converted by the speaker into variations in sound.

Radio listeners can now make their own recordings by plugging a tape recorder into a radio and taping a performance off the air, and hi-fi rigs are designed to make this possible. All that is needed is a "tape deck" that uses the amplifier and speaker of the hi-fi system, though a full tape recorder with its own amplifier and speaker can also be used. Pre-recorded tapes can also be bought, featuring musical performances of the sort already obtainable on phonograph records, but with a broadened frequency range that allows for a closer reproduction of the original performance.

Once the tape recorder came onto the market, musicians seized on its capacity for producing novel sounds. They realized that sounds from non-musical sources could be assembled in musical ways (with or without the addition of sounds from traditional instruments), and that a novel sort of composition would result—called by the French *musique concrète*. Or the sounds produced by conventional instruments could be recorded on tape and revised afterward. For example, they could be played backwards, so that a piano tone, instead of beginning percussively and then dying out, would build up and *end* with an accent. Or the tape could be run the regular way but with the percussive attack snipped out of it and only the remaining part of the tone used. Sounds recorded at one speed could be played back at another, with interesting results. Sounds from widely different sources could be manipulated as elements of a sort of mosaic, or made to alternate in rhythmic patterns. Some of the effects are strange and unearthly; some are quite amusing.

Tape-recorder music has been used with great success as background accompaniment for movies, dramatic works, and ballets.

Ex. 4 — Sonata in E Minor, Weber

TARANTELLA: a rapid dance in 6/8 or 2/4 meter whose whirling rhythms and legendary background inspired many composers of the nineteenth century. The tarantella, danced in southern Italy, took its name from the town of Taranto, after which a kind of spider, the tarantula, also was named. According to legend, the bite of the spider could be cured only by dancing the tarantella. Out of this grew one of the dance madnesses that swept across Europe in the fifteenth and sixteenth centuries. Many people thought they could be cured of their illnesses only by dancing the tarantella, and wandering musicians traveled from town to town acting as healers, playing the dance for ten to thirty-six hours at a stretch. The dancers often accompanied the music by playing the tambourine and castanets. They jumped, turned, and improvised various figures until they sank exhausted to the ground.

Among the best-known tarantellas are those for piano by Heller, Chopin, Liszt, and Weber (Ex. 4). The finale of Mendelssohn's Symphony Number 4, the "Italian" Symphony, is a light form of tarantella.

The tarantella: a scene from the ballet L'Étoile de Messine, *produced in 1861*

TCHAIKOVSKY, PETER ILYITCH (1840–93): one of the outstanding composers of the late nineteenth century and the best known of all Russian composers. His genius for creating melodies, his mastery of musical structure, and his highly developed sense of musical drama enabled him, probably more than any other composer, to reach directly to the hearts of his listeners.

Tchaikovsky was born in Votkinsk, in the Ural Mountains of European Russia, where his father was a government inspector of mines. He began the study of piano at the age of seven but did not show evidence of great musical talent. When he was ten his family moved to St. Petersburg (now Leningrad), where he went through traditional schooling, studied law, and at nineteen became a clerk in the Ministry of Justice.

At this point in life, Tchaikovsky realized that he really wanted to be a musician. For a while he studied music theory and composition at a music school founded by Anton Rubinstein, although still continuing with his job. Then, to the surprise of everyone, he resigned to concentrate on music. In 1865 he graduated from the music school (which had become the St. Petersburg Conservatory), winning a prize for a cantata.

Nicholas Rubinstein had just established the Moscow Conservatory. Needing a professor of music theory, he hired Tchaikovsky —an act that took both courage and a belief in the young composer's talent, since Tchaikovsky had only a minimum of theoretical training. For twelve years Tchaikovsky retained the post; he even wrote a most pedantic book on harmony, as though to prove that he was, indeed, a true professor.

Tchaikovsky's aims, however, were compositional rather than pedagogical. At first he tried his hand at symphonic poems and opera. Influenced by Berlioz and Liszt, his music, while Russian, was not nationalistic enough for "The Russian Five," composers and critics who were declaring Russia's musical independence. Led by critic César Cui (1835–1918), "The Five" sniped at Tchaikovsky although he, as a music critic, was generous in his estimation of them.

Strenuous work as composer, critic, and teacher brought Tchaikovsky to a state of nervous collapse. Fortunately, help came in the form of a yearly subsidy paid to him for thirteen years by a wealthy widow, Nadezhda von Meck. She was the mother-in-law of Tchaikovsky's niece and a great music lover, with a gift for singling out interesting composers. (In the 1880's she hired Claude Debussy as a music teacher for her children during summer vacations.) The relation between the benefactress and the composer was a strange one. They never met, although they did carry on a continuous correspondence.

Mme. von Meck's generosity came to Tchaikovsky in one of the darkest of his many dark periods. In 1877 he had married a music student much younger than himself. Completely unsuited for marriage, and finding himself wed to an emotionally unstable young woman, Tchaikovsky became utterly despondent. He tried to catch pneumonia by throwing himself into the Moskva River, but succeeded only in catching cold. After nine weeks the couple separated for good. Tchaikovsky reacted by becoming morbid and melancholy. At this point Mme. von Meck gave him enough money to spend some time in Switzerland, France, and Italy. During these difficult days he wrote some of his gayest music—his Piano Sonata in G Major; much of his most successful opera, *Eugene Onegin;* and his Fourth Symphony, which he dedicated to Mme. von Meck.

Tchaikovsky settled down to a fully creative life, spending part of the year in Moscow but the rest of the time in the country. Each day he wrote something—that was his credo as a composer. The remaining time he spent with friends, dining, going to the theater, or playing cards. He was a voracious reader of books and musical scores. A warm, sensitive human being, he was not afraid to express his feelings in his music or his personal diary.

Yet for a composer whose music is now so well loved, Tchaikovsky met with many bitter disappointments. In 1877 the first performance of *Swan Lake*—originally a short work to be danced by his sister's children—was a failure. The music for *Swan Lake* was too symphonic for the tastes of the balletomanes, but it is hard to see what fault could be found with *The Sleeping Beauty* (1889) and the *Casse-noisette (Nutcracker,* 1891-92). These, too, were not completely successful at their first perform-

Peter Ilyitch Tchaikovsky in 1863

ances. And there was his now-famous Piano Concerto in B-flat Minor, written for Nicholas Rubinstein—who refused to perform it because he considered it "unplayable." (It was premièred in Boston in 1875 by Hans von Bülow.) The same response greeted the Violin Concerto in D, intended for and rejected by Leopold Auer.

Fortunately, not all was lost. Tchaikovsky came into demand as a conductor of his own works, and made several tours of Europe. In 1893 Cambridge University awarded him an honorary music doctorate. His reputation spread to America, and in 1891 he was invited to conduct several of his works during the dedication in New York City of Carnegie Hall. He shared four concerts there with conductor Walter Damrosch, encountering more enthusiasm than he had ever experienced in Russia. He conducted his works in Philadelphia and in Baltimore, where his co-conductor was Victor Herbert. Like most other European celebrities, he was taken to visit Niagara Falls and Washington, D.C., but the more he traveled the more he became homesick for his homeland and friends. Unlike many other European celebrities, however, Tchaikovsky treasured his American experiences and wrote glowingly of them in his diary.

On returning to Russia, Tchaikovsky plunged into two completely different kinds of compositions—the gay *Nutcracker* ballet and the melancholy Sixth Symphony, the *Symphonie pathétique (Pathetic Symphony).* He conducted the first performance of the symphony at St. Petersburg on October 28,

Tchaikovsky in 1888

1893. Within a little more than a week he was dead—the victim of a cholera epidemic.

Tchaikovsky wanted most to be successful as a composer of opera, yet of his ten operas only two, *Eugene Onegin* and *La Pique Dame (The Queen of Spades),* have made their way into the world's opera houses.

Tchaikovsky revitalized ballet music, giving it stature and dignity. Except for the works of Minkus (1827–1890) and Delibes (1836–91; *La Source, Coppélia,* and *Sylvia*), most ballet music was a series of mediocre tunes strung together in the flimsiest manner. With *Swan Lake, The Sleeping Beauty,* and the *Nutcracker,* ballet music was raised to its highest level, so that since 1900 fine composers have not thought it beneath them to write in this medium.

Dance was never far from Tchaikovsky's thoughts, and many of his most beautiful melodies are waltzes—whether in ballets, symphonic works, or operas (particularly *Eugene Onegin*). In general, his waltz melodies are slower and more surging than the Viennese waltzes of the Strausses. His harmonic backgrounds, too, are more sophisticated, so that the melodies can be spun out over a longer time.

Tchaikovsky thought in terms of tone colors. Although he wrote many works for piano, only the B-flat Minor Concerto, the *Humoresque,* and *En Traineau,* with its sug-

gestion of a Russian sleigh ride, are played much today. He loved the deep register of the clarinet and bass clarinet, the melancholy sound of the oboe (to which he gave lovely melodies to sing), and the military gusto of brass fanfares. To the French horn he gave inner melodies that move slowly up or down the scale, and passionate themes that might have been written for the voice (Ex. 5). Even the humble bassoon, usually given only a supporting role, sets the somber mood of the Sixth Symphony, in the opening measures of which it sounds with a rising sequential melody that sinks back at the end of each short phrase (Ex. 6).

Tchaikovsky's editing, with the careful marking of each measure, is typical of the painstaking effort he took with his music. Few composers have been so precise in their indications of bowings and phrasings. A detailed study of a Tchaikovsky score makes one of the best lessons in orchestration.

The strings are never neglected by Tchaikovsky. Cellos sing the opening phrases of the second movement of the "Pathétique," a long melody in the unusual meter of 5/4 (Ex. 7). The violins, over the barest of accompaniments, dance the Valse which is the third movement of the Fifth Symphony (see Ex. 39, page 125).

Tchaikovsky makes his music come alive

Ex. 5 — Symphony No. 5

Ex. 6 — Symphony No. 6

Ex. 7 — Symphony No. 6

by using little figures that dart from one instrument to another and swirling passages that are tossed from winds to strings and back again. Choir answers choir, often in preparation for the moment when all forces join together to state a theme.

Tchaikovsky's genius at merging form and tone color is seen at its best in the scherzo of the Fourth Symphony. The opening section is played only by the pizzicato strings (see Ex. 61 on page 432). This is followed by a trio in which the winds alone play a Russian dance (Ex. 8). The brasses enter with a little march which manages to combine with the Russian dance. There is a return to the pizzicato strings, and the whole movement dies out as fragments of all the themes make their final bows.

Always looking for new sounds, Tchaikovsky was one of the first composers to see the possibilities in the newly invented celesta, using it in the Dance of the Sugar Plum Fairy of the *Nutcracker* ballet.

In comparison with his younger contemporaries, Debussy and Richard Strauss, and with his fellow countryman Mussorgsky, Tchaikovsky was fairly conservative in his approach to music, but never routine. He relied for the most part on a harmonic vocabulary not much different from that of Schumann and Liszt. Structurally, his music is always well made. His orchestral overtures, fantasias, and tone poems—such compositions as *Romeo and Juliet, Marche Slav,* the "1812" Overture, and *Francesca da*

The ball scene from Eugene Onegin

Rimini—are not just pictorial pieces but follow a musical logic. His symphonies and concertos, on the other hand, show how freely and dramatically symphonic form can be treated. The Fourth Symphony, for example, opens with a thematic motto (Ex. 9) representing Fate, which returns in the final movement to interrupt a joyous celebration.

Because of his habit of writing something

Ex. 8 — Symphony No. 4

Ex. 9— Symphony No. 4

every day, Tchaikovsky, in a comparatively short period of about twenty-five years, managed to compile an impressive list of works. In addition to the operas, symphonic works, and concertos, he wrote the fiendishly difficult *Variations on a Rococo Theme* for cello and orchestra; the beautiful Serenade for String Orchestra; four orchestral suites, of which the last is titled *Mozartiana* in honor of Tchaikovsky's most beloved composer; a piano trio; three string quartets, of which the first contains the hauntingly melodic "Andante Cantabile" that moved Tolstoy to tears; several large choral works; and approximately one hundred songs, of which the best known is the setting of Goethe's "Nur wer die Sehnsucht kennt" (None But the Lonely Heart).

Much of Tchaikovsky's music has been described as being "too sentimental," "too morbid," and "not really Russian." Often such opinions are heard after a performance led by a conductor who sees only the obvious elements in Tchaikovsky's music. Unbiased musicians probe deeper and understand the imagination and skill that went into each work, acknowledging that here was indeed a gifted composer.

Was he a truly Russian composer? In the same sense that Russian culture of its day was a mixture of Russian, German, and French ideas, Tchaikovsky was Russian. He did not parade his nationalism—any more than he really paraded his personal feelings. Yet the spirit of Mother Russia pervades his music, from first to last. Igor Stravinsky did much to revive interest in Tchaikovsky by conducting his early symphonies and basing his ballet *Le Baiser de la fée* on themes by Tchaikovsky. It was Stravinsky who said of Tchaikovsky, "He was the most Russian of us all."

Georg Philipp Telemann (a 1750 engraving)

TELEMANN, GEORG PHILIPP (1681–1767): the prolific contemporary of Bach and Handel. Telemann was born in Magdeburg, Germany. Largely self-taught in music, he managed to become a good enough performer to hold down a job as organist while attending Leipzig University. Here he organized a "Collegium Musicum"—a society where music lovers could come together to perform or listen to music. After holding various posts as organist and music director, Telemann in 1721 was placed in charge of the music at the largest church in Hamburg. Here he stayed, with occasional trips to Paris and Berlin, for the rest of his life. In 1722 he was offered the post of cantor at St. Thomas Church in Leipzig. Only after

his refusal was the position offered to J. S. Bach.

In spite of—or possibly because of—Telemann's lack of musical training, he managed to absorb all the musical styles of his day. His facile ability enabled him to please all musical tastes and he became the most popular composer in Germany. He turned out an incredible number of works, including forty operas, hundreds of orchestral suites, forty-four passions, twelve cycles of cantatas for the church year, concertos, ceremonial pieces, trio sonatas, and keyboard works.

After Telemann's death his music soon lost favor with the public. It is only during the past few decades that performers and audiences have discovered the musical treasure left by this man who was an important link between the Baroque and early Classical periods.

TEMPERAMENT: the term used for systems of tuning. One of the peculiarities of music is the fact that keyboard instruments with fixed, non-adjustable pitches are slightly out of tune—scientifically. To tune such instruments it is necessary to relate one tone to another. Since the time of Pythagoras (about 550 B.C.) the perfect fifth has been used as a basis for tuning. But if one started on the note C and continued in a series of perfect fifths until C was reached again, that C would be slightly higher than the tone which resulted from a true series of perfect octaves above the original C. To accommodate all the variations in pitch that would result if acoustically perfect fifths were used would mean hundreds of additional keys on the piano.

In the Baroque period harpsichords and clavichords were tuned to play only in sharp keys or in flat keys. This is one reason why music of this period did not usually have more than three sharps or flats in the signature, nor modulate to far-removed keys. As early as the sixteenth century, musical theorists advocated slight alteration in the size of intervals so that the twelve semitones could be fitted into each octave. Fifths were to be made slightly smaller and major thirds a bit larger. This *equal temperament* meant that music in any key could be played without changing the tuning of the instrument. It was partly to prove the value of equal temperament that J. S. Bach wrote his *Well-tempered Clavier,* which contains preludes and fugues in all major and minor keys.

Acceptance of equal temperament was a

long time in coming, being adopted in Germany in the early 1800's and in France and England in the middle 1800's. One reason for hesitance in using equal temperament was that when a keyboard instrument tuned in this way played with stringed instruments it sounded out of tune. Orchestral instruments, for example, can differentiate between F# and Gb—both of which are identical in equal temperament.

In choral music the singers adjust to the tuning of the piano if that is the accompanying instrument. A cappella singing, on the other hand, allows the singers to modify their pitch so that they can produce acoustically true triads which are slightly larger and brighter than those obtained through equal temperament.

Actually our ears accept the "out-of-tuneness" of the piano, and after we have heard much piano music it is the strings, as in a string quartet, that sound out of tune.

TEMPO: the rate of speed at which a musical composition is to be played or sung. Choosing the right tempo for a work is one of the most important parts of a fine musical performance. The performer can be partly guided by a tempo mark or a metronome mark placed at the beginning of a work. Tempo marks such as allegro or andante can give considerable freedom to the performer. (Certain performers are known for their predilections for faster or slower tempos than those usually accepted as normal.) A metronome mark, designating the number of beats per minute, is more exact, but many composers have found that the selected metronome mark is often too fast or too slow. Every good performer or composer knows that many things can affect the tempo chosen for a work. A big hall or a small hall, a lively audience or a sleepy audience, even the way the performer happens to be feeling—any of these things can make a performer decide on a tempo slightly different from the tempo chosen the night before. Composers, knowing this, often write their metronomic marks so that there is leeway for the performer. They will, for example, write " ♩ = 132 – 144" or " ♩ = c. 132" (c. standing for the Latin circa, "around").

The tempo of a work may vary throughout the course of the composition. A new tempo is indicated by a new tempo mark, and in some modern music this may happen as often as every measure, as the composer tries to get a feeling of flexibility and free-

dom in his music. If the old tempo is to return, the composer writes "Tempo 1" or "Tempo primo" in the music. Gradual changes in tempo are shown by the directions ritardando (slower) and accelerando (faster). After such a change, the composer writes "a tempo" when he wants a return to his basic tempo.

Before the invention of the metronome, in 1816, a performer was expected to know how fast a certain style of music would be played, with only the Italian tempo mark to guide him. Most tempos were related to the pulse rate of the human body at somewhere between sixty and eighty beats per minute. This was also the rate of speed of the *tactus*—the even beat given by a conductor in music written before 1600.

The most familiar Italian tempo indications are, from fastest to slowest: presto, allegro, andante, adagio, largo.

TENOR: the highest natural adult male voice. The term comes from the Latin *tenere*, "to hold," and dates back to medieval music, in which the tenor was the voice that carried, or "held," the cantus firmus—the theme around which the other harmonies were written.

The tenor voice has a range of about two octaves, starting from the C below middle C. The part is written today in the bass, the treble, or tenor clefs (the tenor clef is also used for trombone, bassoon, and cello parts). The G below middle C in a tenor part can be written in three clefs, as shown here:

Bass Clef   Treble Clef   Tenor Clef

Tenor voices, which in operas usually portray the hero's role, are sometimes classified as lyric (light and agile) and robust (rich and sonorous). The few tenors who have the power to sing above the sound of the large orchestra in Wagner's operas are called *Heldentenore,* or "herotenors." Among the famous tenors of recent times have been Caruso, Gigli, McCormack, and Melchior. Countertenors sing above the usual tenor range and have the light quality of a male alto. Much music written about 1700 for countertenors has been revived and recorded by the two outstanding countertenors of today—Russell Oberlin and Alfred Deller.

In music for male quartet, such as barbershop quartets, there are two tenor parts.

Caricature done by Caruso of himself (New York City, 1901)

Franco Corelli, one of the leading operatic tenors of today

The second, or lower tenor, usually carries the melody.

Several important instruments are the tenor members of their instrumental families. They have the same relationship to their relatives that the tenor voice has to the soprano, alto, and bass voices. The tenor trombone is the most common trombone in use today. The tenor saxophone is one of the three most-used saxophones. The tenor drum, between the bass and snare drums in size, and somewhat hollow-sounding, is used mostly in bands. The tenor horn, used in bands, is related in range and in tone quality to the baritone horn and the euphonium.

TERNARY FORM: a three-part musical form created by repeating a first section, more or less exactly, after a contrasting section. It is sometimes called the A-B-A form. Almost every popular tune, such as Gershwin's "I Got Rhythm," is in ternary form. So is almost every minuet and scherzo (the middle section being called a trio).

To save time and space, composers write D.C., an abbreviation of *da capo* ("from the beginning"), at the end of the second section to show that the first part of the music is to be repeated exactly. From this practice came the term da capo aria, the most popular form for an aria in seventeenth- and eighteenth-century Italian operas, as well as in many of the vocal solos of Bach and Handel.

A ternary form may be comparatively short as in many folk songs, such as "Drink to Me Only with Thine Eyes." But it can also be quite large, as in the SONATA-ALLEGRO, with its statement-development-restatement sections.

THEME AND VARIATIONS: a musical form consisting of a theme which is repeated with changes in melody, harmony, rhythm, or texture. The theme itself may be a well-known melody or an original melody invented by the composer. It can be just a bass line over which varying harmonies and melodies occur, as in the ground bass and passacaglia. It may be merely a progression of chords out of which a composer spins many strands of melody, as in a seventeenth-century chaconne or in contemporary jazz where a "chart" shows the performers the chords on which they are to improvise. The job of the composer is to show the many possibilities that lie hidden in the theme.

Making a variation on a theme is relatively easy. Almost everyone has sung a melody and put in a few extra tones as embellishments. Any good musician can play a melody with chords different from the usual ones. Both of these methods show basic elements of variation. In a variation either the melody, the harmony, or the rhythm can be changed—but one of these elements must be kept while the others are varied. If all elements were varied, the listener would no longer be able to recognize any relation between the variation and the original theme.

Building a whole set of variations poses for a composer the same problems that arise in the writing of any large musical form. Each variation must be thought of relative to previous variations and to those that are to come. The series as a whole must make a complete musical structure. Only the greatest composers have been able to master the extended variation form.

The theme used for a set of variations is usually quite simple in melody, harmony, and rhythm. The melody has a clear sense of direction, moving up or down in a graphic pattern. Sometimes this sense of direction is all that can be recognized in a variation. The theme must have definite beginnings and endings to its phrases so that the form is clear. Its harmony must be simple enough so that it does not act like a strait-jacket on the inspiration of the composer. In the ground bass of a passacaglia and of some chaconnes the theme is often stated just as a melodic line without accompanying chords. Ex. 10–14 show how simple a theme for variations can be. Each of these themes has been made into a musical masterpiece. Some offer such challenges that they have been used by several composers.

Each variation usually follows a theme through its full course. If the theme is eight measures in length, every variation will be eight measures long. The composer does not stop on one measure and work only on this; such a process is called development rather than variation. A variation starts with a main idea or figure which has grown out of the theme, and that idea or figure is carried throughout the whole variation. If, for example, the variation starts with running notes, these running notes will be heard throughout.

A set of variations must have variety. One method is to change from a major key to a minor one, or vice versa, as in Bach's Chaconne in D Minor for unaccompanied violin, in which a large section in D major brightens a work that is primarily in D minor. For a change of pace a group of slow variations might be contrasted with a group

Ex. 10 — "The Carman's Whistle," Byrd

Ex. 11 — Passacaglia in C Minor for Organ, J.S. Bach

Ex. 12 — 33 Variations on a Waltz by Diabelli, Beethoven

Ex. 13 — "La Follia," Corelli

Ex. 14 — Nursery Tune, Variations by Mozart, Dohnanyi, etc.

of fast ones. A variation with slow, colorful chords might give relief after several variations with driving rhythm. Short interludes are sometimes thrown in to break the possible monotony that happens when a succession of equal-length phrases is played. The interlude might be a kind of development of the theme. It might be a fugato, or short fugue, in which part of the theme is imitated in different voices. At the end of a set of variations the composer sometimes writes a coda, which is an ending that serves to round off the piece in brilliant fashion. Some themes and variations end with a big fugue based on the theme, as does Brahms's Variations on a Theme by Handel. In any case the task of the composer is to build his variations into a worthy piece of music.

Ex. 15 (Variations 1 through 7) shows in a small way how a theme-and-variations form is built. Only the first two measures of the theme and of each variation are shown. The work is a set of variations, written by Beethoven in 1804, on the well-known tune "America" (known to Beethoven and Englishmen as "God Save the King"). In the variations the melody tones are circled so that it is easy to see what Beethoven added.

In the first variation the accompaniment is changed. Next, the melody is embellished and starts in the left hand. The third variation shows how Beethoven opened out the repeated C's of the theme to make a broken chord figure followed by off-beat melody tones. In the fourth variation the melody, which jumps from one octave to another, is harder to find. The fifth, in the minor mode, is marked *con espressione*—"with expression." Here the melody is decorated quite simply and the mood has become sweetly sad. It is followed by a variation which shows how "America" would sound as a march in 4/4 time. The seventh variation is a kind of perpetual-motion duet, leading to a coda that contains a short adagio which suggests a change of key from C to F major. The theme is harmonized with color chords. The coda finishes with a fast, brilliant variation.

The idea of making variations on a theme is very old. It was started probably by singers or instrumentalists who had to perform the same musical phrases over and over. To get a bit of variety into the music they began to improvise little decorations. Composers, looking for ways to build larger musical forms, hit on this device.

The earliest written instrumental variations were composed by several Spanish composers. Luis de Narvaez, in 1538, published a set of variations for lute—*Diferencias,* he called them—on the melody "O Gloriosa Domina." Antonio de Cabezón, a famous sixteenth-century organist, wrote a set of *Diferencias* on a Spanish folk tune. In both sets the variations consist of slight embellishments on the melodies, changing them from voice to voice as different contrapuntal lines are placed against them.

Various types of variation forms developed around 1600. English keyboard composers, such as William Byrd, Dr. John Bull, and Orlando Gibbons, embellished tuneful melodies, some of which were popular songs of the day, with flowery running passages and many trills and ornaments. Italian composers such as Caccini, Monteverdi, and Frescobaldi used short, repeated bass patterns over which they wrote their vocal arias. Many of these patterns, which are called ground basses, were used by several composers. The most famous ground-bass melody was that of the Portuguese dance *La Follia*. It is the bass theme underlying Corelli's variations for violin and harpsichord, and Alessandro Scarlatti's variations for harpsichord.

Related to *La Follia* were the ground-bass dance forms of the chaconne and the passacaglia. These slow, three-count dances were written in four-measure or eight-measure phrases. The basses, particularly in the chaconne, were simple—often only a note on the first beat of each measure. Some of the chaconne basses were straight lines down the scale. Others used a repeated interval pattern. Most colorful of all were the basses that descended slowly by half steps (Ex. 20 and 21 on page 100). The chromatic falling bass was used by Purcell for his beautiful aria "Dido's Lament" from the opera *Dido and Aeneas*. It was used also by Bach in the Crucifixus section of his B-minor Mass. Purcell was fond of the ground bass form, using it in vocal as well as instrumental works.

A form of variation developed in seventeenth-century France was that of the court dance followed by its "double." The "double" was exactly what the name suggests: there were at least twice as many notes in the double as in the same number of measures of the dance. This method of making a variation became especially common for melodies other than dances. It is the way Handel's well-known "Harmonious Blacksmith" variations are built: the rhythm goes from eighth notes to sixteenths and eventually to thirty-second notes.

German composers of the seventeenth century originated their own style of variations in the course of making their choral preludes for organ which were based on

Ex. 15 Variation 1

Ex. 16

chorale hymn tunes. The form was brought to its highest point in the eighteenth century by J. S. Bach, who in his choral-preludes used almost every technique of variation, not only ornamenting the chorale or making a fugue of it but managing to find matching melodies that reveal the emotional character of the chorale melody. Ex. 16 shows the melancholy touch given to the chorale tune "The Old Year Is Gone" by the chromatic tones of Bach's added melodies.

Bach was, with Beethoven and Brahms, a great master of the variation form. His Passacaglia in C Minor for organ, Chaconne in D Minor for unaccompanied violin, and "Goldberg" Variations for harpsichord are among the supreme masterpieces of music.

The composers of the Classical period were not as fond of the ground-bass variation form as were their predecessors. They preferred to decorate a melody gracefully and elegantly in keeping with the spirit of the times. Haydn and Mozart wrote many themes and variations as movements of their sonatas, string quartets, and symphonies. Mozart's variations tend to be songlike and poetic, as in the A-major Sonata for Piano. Haydn's variations were often like developments and were full of contrasts. He liked to make variations on pairs of themes, alternating them, putting interludes between them, and in general trying to avoid the monotony that sometimes creeps into the theme-and-variation form.

The nineteenth century is full of variations designed to dazzle the audience. Many of them sounded much like the kind of variations that a present-day cocktail-lounge pianist makes on popular tunes. The virtuoso made no attempt to dig deeply into a theme for its possibilities. He merely tried to see how many notes he could play on his piano or violin, or what theatrical effects he could come up with.

This method is far from that used by Beethoven and those who followed him—Schubert, Schumann, and Brahms. With Beethoven each variation revealed a new glimpse of the theme, as though the theme were a person and each variation a different side of his character. He used variations in his sonatas, quartets, and symphonies (the finale of the "Eroica" is a giant variation form). He also wrote sets of variations that are as monumental as those by Bach: the Variations on a Waltz by Diabelli, for example, and the Thirty-two Variations in C Minor.

Several of Schubert's finest chamber-music works have movements in the variation form. He used his own songs as themes in the "Trout" Quintet and the "Death and the Maiden" Quartet in D Minor. Schumann wrote many variations, the best known of which are the *Symphonic Études,* in which variations and études are mixed together.

Brahms's variations are among his greatest and most-played works. His keyboard variations include those on an original theme of Handel, and on a theme of Paganini. The Paganini variations, in two books, are based on a caprice for violin; they are challenges

Ex. 17 — Symphony No. 4, Brahms

to the technical ability and strength of any pianist. The same caprice was used for variations by Liszt and Rachmaninoff (in his *Rhapsody on a Theme by Paganini*). One of the most glorious variations is the final movement of Brahms's Fourth Symphony in E Minor, which is a giant chaconne (Ex. 17, page 596). Brahms also wrote a beautiful set of variations for orchestra on a theme attributed to Haydn.

Composers of the late nineteenth century used the variation form in their otherwise programmatic pieces. Strauss's tone poem *Don Quixote* is a very free variation form. Elgar's "Enigma" Variations for orchestra is a series of musical portraits of his friends. One of the strangest theme and variations is d'Indy's "Istar" Variations. The work begins with the most complex variation; each succeeding variation becomes simpler until finally the theme is revealed.

The theme-and-variations form has interested many modern composers. Among the outstanding examples are those by Webern (variations for orchestra and for piano), Britten (*The Young People's Guide to the Orchestra* on a theme by Purcell), Copland (*Piano Variations*), Schoenberg (Theme and Variations for Band, Opus 43a), Hindemith (*The Four Temperaments*), Schuman (*Song of Orpheus* for cello and orchestra). Even experimental composers use the theme-and-variations form. Luening and Ussachevsky have written *Rhapsodic Variations* for tape recorder and orchestra. The variations form is central to all jazz. Every arrangement of a popular theme, whether written or improvised, is a set of variations.

TIE: a curved line connecting notes of the same pitch, indicating that the second note is not to be played again but that its time value is to be added to that of the first note. The tie (also referred to as a "bind," "liaison," or "Bindung") is used to denote a musical

time-length that cannot be shown in any other way, such as the value of five sixteenth notes:

seven quarter notes:

and so on. The tie can be used to bind a tone over many measures, as in bassoon and horn parts in the scores of Mozart and Haydn:

Symphony No. 103, Haydn

The tie is used also to bind together notes on both sides of a bar-line, in which case it sometimes serves the purpose of making a form of syncopation (Ex. 18).

The tie can easily be confused with the slur sign for legato, which is an indication of phrasing or articulation. To indicate that tones are to be sounded rather than tied, the composer usually writes dots over the note heads:

The tie is usually drawn to connect the note heads rather than the stems:

In musical works where several voices are written on one staff, a tie in one voice is placed so that it does not interfere with the other voices.

The tie came into use during the early part of the sixteenth century; thus it is one of the most recent devices of musical notation. It is a most valuable device for the

Ex. 18 — Sonata in C Minor, K.457, Mozart

Molto Allegro

Ex. 19a — *Faust*, Gounod

Ex. 19b — *Madame Butterfly*, Puccini

Ex. 19c — Symphony No. 3, Schumann

Fast

composer, giving him a method of achieving rhythmic fluidity and momentum. Ex. 19a, b, and c show how the tie has helped in the making of interesting thematic material. Singing or playing the themes with and without the tie is most instructive.

TIMBRE: the tone color, or quality of sound, of an instrument. Each type and size of musical instrument has its own unique timbre; that is why we are able to recognize it when we hear it.

No instrument can produce a sound that contains only a fundamental tone. Rather, a tone on any instrument is complex, being made up of a fundamental tone and a certain number of overtones. The number and kind of overtones are influenced by the size and shape of the instrument as well as by its method of tone production; thus the timbre is determined. The "cool" tone of the flute, for example, contains very few overtones, while the cello has an abundance. The lower register of an instrument is its "richest," because the ear can hear more of the overtones in the low notes; in the top registers many of the overtones are beyond the range of hearing.

Knowledge of instrumental timbres is a necessary part of the composer's equipment. As he writes a work, he must be aware not just of the range of instruments but also of their tonal coloring. A melody that is exactly suited to the pungent sound of the oboe, for example, might sound ludicrous if played by the tuba. The task of combining these timbres requires the composer mentally to blend tone colors much as a painter blends primary colors to get various hues and shades.

TIME SIGNATURE: a sign that looks like a fraction placed at the beginning of a piece of music to tell the performer how many beats there are in a measure and to identify the pulse note. The upper figure, showing the number of beats, is a 2, a 3, or a multiple or combination of these (see METER).

Any type of note can be the pulse or beat note. It has nothing to do with tempo, which is determined by the tempo mark or the metronome mark. (Many persons believe that 2/8 is played faster than 2/4, but such is not necessarily the case. The 2/8 may be marked adagio—slowly; the 2/4 may be marked presto—very fast.) The quarter note is the most-used beat note. It can be divided easily into eighth notes and sixteenth notes or several can be added together to make half notes and whole notes.

In most music the time signature carries throughout the whole composition. Occasionally (frequently in many contemporary compositions) the time signature changes, sometimes with every measure. Usually the pulse note stays the same and the note values relate to each other, as in Stravinsky's *Rite of Spring,* in which the signature changes from 2/8 to 3/16 but the sixteenth note in either measure takes up the same amount of time. In Elliot Carter's method of "rhythmic modulation," however, the actual pulse note changes its tempo. When this happens the indication is as in Ex. 20.

Symbols are sometimes used in place of

Ex. 20 (♩ =120)

the regular time signature: **C** is used for 4/4 time; **¢** for alla breve time—that is, 2/2.

TIMPANI: large drums that can be tuned to definite pitches. They are commonly called "kettledrums" because their gleaming copper bodies look like large cooking kettles. (In German scores they are called *Pauken;* their French name is *timbales.*) The drumhead is made of calfskin stretched across the top of the copper shell. It can be tightened to raise the pitch, or loosened to lower the pitch, by means of large screws. Each of these screws was formerly turned by hand—until a chain mechanism was developed that allowed the timpanist to adjust them all by turning one. A similar improvement is the pedal by means of which the timpanist can change the pitch of his drums while playing. This has allowed composers to write short scale passages for one drum or to make a glissando—a sound that Bartók used in his *Music for String Instruments, Percussion, and Celesta* (Ex. 21).

Fred Begun playing the timpani

The timpani rest in cradles of crossed sticks or on metal stands with four arms. They are played by means of a pair of wooden sticks with striking ends of hard or soft felt—the composer usually specifies which. The drumhead is struck not in the center but at a spot midway between the center and the rim (the calfskin is usually not of the same thickness all over, and it is up to the drummer to find the most resonant spot). The timpanist strikes the drums with a smart staccato stroke, since if the felt is in contact with the head for too long, the tone is damped and does not ring out. He produces shades of loudness and softness by increasing or decreasing the force of the stroke. One of the timpanist's most-called-for sounds is the "roll," a tremolo achieved by rapid alternations of the two beaters and written:

The timpanist usually arranges his three or four drums around him in a curve so that he can move quickly from one to the other. He is placed at the back of the orchestra or concert band, where he has room in which to move around. It is the timpanist who acts as leader of the percussion section; usually he is not required to play any other percussion instrument. He must have a keen sense of pitch so that he can retune his drums even while the rest of the orchestra is playing. (The timpanist is one of the busiest members of the orchestra even when he is not playing. He is constantly leaning over with his ear close to the heads to check on the pitch of his drums or prepare them for the next tones he is to play.) Warm, moist weather during outdoor summer concert seasons makes life difficult for the timpanist: the drums become limp and the timpani do not hold their tuning. One famous timpanist has rigged his drums with small electric lights inside to keep the heads taut.

Timpani come in three standard sizes, each with a range of about six tones:

In addition there are small timpani *(piccoli timpani)* that can be tuned to the F above middle C. The timpani parts are written on their own bass staff at actual pitch. (In old scores timpani were sometimes treated as transposing instruments—they were tuned to the first and fifth tones of whatever scale the composition was written in, their parts being always written on C and G.)

Timpani originated in India long ago.

Ex. 21 — *Music for Strings, Percussion, and Celesta,* Bartók

Two Turkish timpanists (detail from Turkish illustration of the Shah-namah, *late 16th century)*

Small timpani, called "nakers," were the first to be brought to Europe—about 1300. Crusaders came across them when fighting the Turks in the Holy Land. The Turkish armies were equipped with timpani, played by men on horseback, as part of the bands used to encourage their troops in battle.

When timpani were introduced to Europe they belonged to kings or nobles and were considered part of the military establishment. For many years—until about 1750—timpani were used with trumpets primarily to play fanfares, providing the bass tones of the two chords played by the trumpets.

In the Classical period the timpani became members of opera and symphony orchestras. There were usually two of them, tuned to the first and fifth tones of the scale of the composition. When the music went to other keys, the timpani had to rest until the original key returned. The timpani were used in tutti passages, where they marked accents or played little rhythmic figures with the winds. One of their first solo uses was by Haydn in his Symphony Number 103 in E-flat. The effect was so startling that the symphony was nicknamed the "Drum-roll" Symphony.

Beethoven was the composer who first fully explored the possibilities of the timpani. He tuned the instruments to intervals other than those made by the first and fifth scale degrees. He began his Violin Concerto with a timpani solo and used a timpani roll to represent thunder in his "Pastoral" Symphony. In the scherzo of his Ninth Symphony, timpani tuned in octaves play an important bit of the theme (Ex. 22).

In the nineteenth century, composers called for three or four timpani in their scores. Berlioz started a trend in his *Symphonie fantastique* by tuning his four timpani to a chord:

He also indicated where the player was to use a softer, spongier beater for a muffled effect.

The invention of the pedal mechanism allowed composers to call for frequent changes of tuning, even as the player was using his hands to play. Long solos have become fairly common in contemporary music, an example being that in William Schuman's Sixth Symphony (Ex. 23). Stravinsky uses five timpani (one of them of piccolo size) in his *Rite of Spring*. To play them, at least three players are required (the composer asks for five), and the drums are tuned to match the dissonant sounds being played by the rest of the orchestra.

Ex. 22 — Symphony No. 9, Beethoven

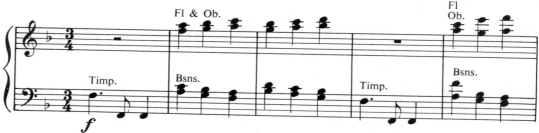

Ex. 23 — Symphony No. 6, Schuman

TOCCATA: a very free musical form, usually in several sections. Each section is built on a single idea, such as big chords, running passages, arpeggios, or imitations of a short motive (as in a fugue). In the sixteenth century the toccata took various forms. One was a short, often improvised fanfare by wind instruments, played as a prelude to a play, ballet, or opera to let the audience know that the entertainment was about to begin. The most famous of these wind toccatas is the one that opens Monteverdi's opera *Orfeo*.

Another form of sixteenth-century toccata was written for the lute. Consisting of scale passages and chords strung together rather loosely, this form was one of the first types of instrumental music to be written. (The same type of piece might also be called a ricercar or a prelude; composers were not very precise about what they named a work.)

The best-known type of toccata, and the true "touch-piece" (the term comes from the Italian *toccare,* "to touch"), was developed around 1600 by the Italian organists Andrea and Giovanni Gabrieli, Claudio Merulo (1533–1604), and Girolamo Frescobaldi. The toccata became a work to be performed in church. Sometimes it accompanied an action in the service of the Mass; sometimes it served as a short prelude either to set the pitch for singers or to be an introduction to a larger work. It also developed into a long work which was like a patchwork quilt in form.

Many of Frescobaldi's toccatas are quite short. They open with majestic, often tense and slightly dissonant harmonies that finally resolve into flowing passages in which a short melodic idea is repeated in sequence. Note this in Ex. 24—excerpts from Frescobaldi's

"The Organ," an engraving by Martin Engelbrecht

Ex. 24 — "Toccata quarti toni," Frescobaldi

"Toccata quarti toni," which is only fifteen measures in total length.

The toccata was adopted by the German organ composers of the seventeenth and eighteenth centuries. One of the earliest of these was Johann Froberger, whose toccatas are sometimes like a short suite, with the movements connected. After a solemn opening (Ex. 25), a section follows in which one musical idea is imitated in various voices (Ex. 26), and then comes a final section like a gigue—again with an idea tossed from voice to voice like a fugue (Ex. 27).

Johann Pachelbel (1653–1706) created brilliant toccatas which served to show off the technique of the organist. They are full of rapid passage work, fast repeated notes, and broken chords that scamper up and down the keyboards.

J. S. Bach's toccatas for harpsichord and for organ combine all that had previously been done in the toccata form. His organ Toccata in D Minor, which serves as a prelude to a fugue, is probably the best known of all toccatas. It has been recorded many times, both in its original form for organ and as transcribed for orchestra.

The toccata as a musical form disappeared during the Classical period. In the 1800's composers such as Robert Schumann gave the title to fast, brilliant, and technically showy—and difficult—works for the piano. Modern composers have revived the toccata and have written in this form for piano, chamber ensembles, and orchestra. Among many such works are those by Ravel *(Le Tombeau de Couperin)*, Prokofiev (Toccata for Piano, Opus 11), Stefan Wolpe (Toccata in Three Movements for piano), Irving Fine (*Toccata Concertante* for orchestra), and William Schuman (the final movement of his Third Symphony).

TONIC: the keynote, or first note, of the scale in which a composition is written. The tonic chord is the triad built on the tonic tone of the scale. In traditional harmony the tonic triad was the "home" chord toward which all other chords moved. In a composition in E-flat, for example, the tone E-flat is the one toward which all other tones seem to be attracted. Likewise, the triad built on E-flat would be considered the tonic chord of the composition. In music written between 1600 and 1900, the tonic chord is usually the final chord of a work.

Ex. 25 — Toccata No. 13, Froberger

Ex. 26

Ex. 27

TRANSCRIPTION: an arrangement of a musical composition for a medium other than that for which it was originally composed. *The Blue Danube* waltz, for example, which is usually heard as an instrumental work, was written by Johann Strauss, Jr., for voices.

Transcriptions are made for various reasons—for example, to enlarge the repertoire of an instrument for which little original material has been written, as in the case of the accordion or the concert band; or to show a composition in new colors, as in Ravel's transcription of Mussorgsky's *Pictures at an Exhibition;* or to make works written for large performing groups more accessible to the student of music, as when orchestral works are transcribed for piano.

Works are often transcribed by the composers themselves. Beethoven rearranged his Piano Sonata in E, Opus 14, Number 1, for string quartet. Schoenberg reversed the usual procedure and made an orchestral transcription of his band work, Theme and Variations, Opus 43a. Ravel transcribed his *Mother Goose* Suite from its original four-hand version to orchestra.

In transcription, notes are usually added or subtracted. In transcribing a piano work for orchestra, for example, the arranger must add notes that sustain the harmonies—a job done by the damper pedal on the piano. The piano transcription of a full orchestra work may leave out some of the ornamental secondary lines. Some transcribers try to make the transcription sound as much as possible like the original, so that an orchestra sounds like an organ, a band like an orchestra, or a chorus like a string choir. Others possibly more imaginative, such as Ravel, bring out wholly new colors in a work.

Transcriptions did not enter music history until composers began to specify whether voices or instruments were to be used in performances of the music. Before the sixteenth century and during it, many vocal lines were played on instruments. As lutes and keyboards came into favor, the performers on these instruments needed things to play, and one of the simplest solutions to this problem was to make transcriptions of songs. Out of these early transcriptions grew important musical forms such as the canzona and the theme and variations.

J. S. Bach was particularly fond of transcribing violin concertos by Vivaldi and others, and he arranged sixteen such works for one or more harpsichords. The greatest transcriber was Franz Liszt, who made dazzling transcriptions of songs, orchestral works, and operatic scenes. Liszt's transcriptions did much to popularize the instrumental and vocal music of Schubert, Mendelssohn, and Wagner.

Today there is a tremendous market for transcribed music to satisfy the needs of performing groups of many kinds, especially vocal and instrumental combinations for which little music has been written specifically. Present-day arrangers and transcribers have exploited the music of all periods and styles. In some instances the results are gratifying and pleasurable to listen to; in others the distortion has made the original work unrecognizable.

To a listener who has become attached to a particular piece of music in its originally composed form, the idea of transcription of that work is likely to be offensive. A transcription, however, never really harms a work in its original form. A great work remains a great work despite anything that may be done to it.

TRANSPOSING INSTRUMENT: an instrument for which music is written at a higher or lower pitch than the actual sound. These instruments are mostly members of the woodwind and brass families: the clarinets, saxophones, English horn, French horn, and trumpets. Instruments whose parts are written an octave higher (double bass) or an octave lower (piccolo) for convenience are not true transposing instruments.

Transposing instruments offer definite advantages. In the case of the woodwinds, a player can learn the fingering on one instrument and switch to another instrument of the same family without learning a completely new fingering. A saxophonist who learns to play an alto saxophone can with slight adjustments switch to any other saxophone. The same is true of the English horn, which is played with the same fingering as the oboe and sounds a fifth lower. With brass instruments, transposition is a holdover from the times when a trumpet or horn player could play only a restricted number of tones in one key. In order to change the key of the instrument, a piece of tubing was inserted into its main body. The player's part, however, was always written in the key of C, and the length of the added tube, or crook, determined the actual sound of the written notes.

The pitch name of the instrument always tells what note will sound at actual, or concert, pitch when the instrument plays a written C. For example, when a performer on a trumpet in B-flat plays the written note C, the resulting sound will be the tone B-flat. This means that the instrument's part is al-

Harry Carney with two saxophones, 1930

Ex. 28 — Symphony No. 3, Schumann

Ex. 29 — Symphony No. 6, Tchaikovsky

Ex. 30

ways written a whole tone *higher* than the sound it will produce. The French horn in F sounds a tone which is five notes lower than its written tone. Ex. 28 and 29 show the written and sounded notes of musical excerpts for trumpets and horns.

Ex. 30 shows the actual sounds on the transposing instruments as they play the written note C above middle C.

TRANSPOSITION: the changing of the pitch of a musical work or part, either in writing or in performance. Sometimes the melody of a song lies too high or too low for a particular singer or group of singers. (A soprano who wants to show off her high tones might have whole operatic scenes or arias transposed to a higher key.) When transposition of a song is necessary, the accompanist is expected to make the required adjustment—that is, to play it in a higher or lower key than written. The singer has no problem, since he merely sings his melody by ear. The pianist, however, must develop skill at transposition—skill that results from practice, a knowledge of music theory, and a good ear.

In transposing a work up or down a semitone—from C to C#, A to Ab, and so on—the player mentally changes the key signature—from no sharps to seven sharps, from three sharps to four flats, and so on—and reads the notes as written. Chromatic changes and modulations make the job more difficult.

If the harmony of a composition is simple enough, as is the case with most folk tunes, the transposition is done by means of harmonic analysis. A tonic chord, on the first degree of one scale, is changed to the tonic chord of the new key. For example, in the key of C the three primary chords are built on C, F, and G. In the key of Eb, these chords become Eb, Ab, and Bb.

The composer or arranger must be adept at transposition. Unless he writes for strings only, he will be writing parts for transposing instruments (see preceding article) in his orchestral scores. Some composers, to save time, write clarinet, trumpet, and horn parts at their actual or concert pitch, leaving the job of transposition to the person who copies out the individual parts.

TRAPS: the name given to the tremendous variety of percussion instruments and assorted noisemakers used by a drummer in popular music, particularly in musical shows. In addition to his regular drums and cymbals, the trap drummer (the name given to one who performs such a job) plays on bells, whistles, rattles, and whatever else the performer needs as a musical help. The traps are used to their fullest extent in slapstick or knockabout comedy. (The term "slapstick" comes from the sticks that are slapped together by the drummer as one comedian smacks another.) The trap drummer must switch from instrument to instrument so quickly that his actions led to the saying "as busy as a trap drummer with the hives."

TREMOLO: a rapid repetition of one or more tones for as long a time as the note value indicates (on drums a tremolo is called a roll). One of the most common sounds made by members of the violin family, it has been used also on almost every other instrument, including the voice.

In string music there are two kinds of tremolos. In the *bowed tremolo* the performer draws the tip of his bow back and forth

across the string as fast as he can. When this is done softly in the low or middle registers, the effect can be mysterious or even ominous, and the sound is often heard as background music in suspense movies. Played with an accented attack, the bowed tremolo can suggest excitement or turmoil. Played softly, high up, it can seem angelic, or eërie. The bowed tremolo is written as here:

usually with three dashes through the stem of the notes. If the note is a whole note, the dashes are written above or below it:

Whole chords are often played as tremolos by all members of the string family. Such agitated chords are commonly used in accompaniments to the voices in opera. One of the earliest bowed tremolos—used to suggest the excitement of a duel—occurs in Monteverdi's *Combat of Tancred and Clorinda* (1624).

Another kind of tremolo is the *fingered tremolo:* the rapid alternation of two tones, usually on the same string. The bowing is done in long, slow strokes while the fingers of the left hand make the rapid changes in pitch. The tones of a fingered tremolo are so rapid that both tones are imagined to sound at the same time. In the score, each note is therefore given the full time value of the tremolo (Ex. 31).

On most other instruments the tremolo is like the violinist's fingered tremolo—a fast alternation of two or more tones. If the tones are on adjacent pitches, the result is called a *trill*. On the piano whole chords can be agitated:

Tremolos are common in woodwind parts, being used in accompaniments or for special effects. On brass instruments the tremolo is rarely executed, because its sound is so unnatural that the effect is likely to be humorous.

Spike Jones, surrounded by the noisemakers of a trap drummer: bells, cymbals, washboard, and so on

Ex. 31

The wavering vibrato in a voice is sometimes called a tremolo. If done too slowly or over too wide an interval, it is not pleasant, becoming what critics call a "wobble." A true tremolo, resembling the bowed tremolo of the violin, was used in vocal parts by Purcell in *King Arthur* where he wanted to suggest an icy shivering (see Ex. 83 on page 447).

Most organs have a tremolo stop. It activates a vibrating valve placed in the wind channel. Used discreetly, it can give a warm blend to the sound of the organ.

TRIAD: a three-note group of tones of different pitches—not counting octaves or unisons. In traditional harmony, triads are built by placing the interval of a third on top of another third: C-E-G. The bottom tone of the triad is called the *root,* the middle tone the *third,* and the top tone the *fifth* (the interval from top to bottom takes in five letter names: C-D-E-F-G).

When the root of a triad is in the lowest voice, the triad is said to be in *root position,* with a figured bass symbol of 5 or $\frac{5}{3}$. With the third of the triad in the lowest voice, the triad is in its *first inversion,* with the figured bass symbol 6 or $\frac{6}{3}$. If the fifth is in the lowest voice, the triad is in its *second inversion,* with the figured bass symbol $\frac{6}{4}$.

Triads are made up of combinations of major thirds (two whole steps: C-E) and minor thirds (a whole step and a half step: C-Eb). There are four types of triads:

Type	Example	Types of thirds, starting at bottom
Major	C-E-G	Major third plus minor third
Minor	C-Eb-G	Minor third plus major third
Diminished	C-Eb-Gb	Minor third plus minor third
Augmented	C-E-G#	Major third plus major third

The tones of the triad can be arranged in many different ways and with duplication of tones (Ex. 32, page 607). When all tones lie within an octave, the triad is said to be in closed position:

Chopin

If the tones lie beyond the octave, the triad is said to be in open position:

Chopin

Triads may be built on every tone of the major and minor scales. Major triads are found on the first, fourth, and fifth tones in the major scale; and on the third, fifth, and sixth tones of the minor scale. Minor triads are found on the second, third, and sixth tones of the major scale; and on the first and fourth of the minor scale. Diminished triads are found on the seventh tone of the major scale; and on the second and seventh tones of the minor scale. The augmented triad is found only on the third scale degree in the harmonic form of the minor scale. It is also the only traditional type of triad to be found in the whole-tone scale. As such it was used at times by Debussy (in *Pour le Piano,* for instance).

Triads became in the 1400's the basic building blocks of harmony. Before that they were used only occasionally. In the type of harmony called *fauxbourdon,* triads in first inversion moved up and down in parallel motion, as in the fifteenth-century music of Dufay:

Throughout the fifteenth and sixteenth centuries composers wove their melody lines in counterpoint, so that the ear of the listener heard a steady succession of triad sounds.

Seventeenth-century composers began to introduce more complex and more dissonant chords, made by adding another third on top of a triad. These were called *seventh chords.* Triads and seventh chords began to be used in definite patterns, always moving toward the triad on the first degree of the scale. A triad other than that on the first degree usually moved to a triad whose root was five tones

Ex. 32 — Different Ways of Using a C-major Triad

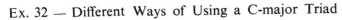

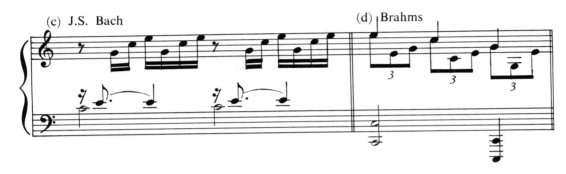

(e) Beethoven

Ex. 33 — "General Lavine" from Preludes, Book II, Debussy

In the style and tempo of a Cake-walk

lower: A to D, D to G, and so on. The movement of triads and seventh chords by fifths is part of the system known as "traditional harmony." Its usage lasted from about 1650 until 1900 in concert music. In general, triads have been used almost exclusively in root position or in first inversion, the second inversion being saved for cadences.

The triad has been the single most important harmonic sound in music for the past 600 years. It is still a basic part of the harmonic vocabulary of many contemporary composers—with modifications. Since Debussy's time triads have been used as blocks of sound without too much regard for key (Ex. 33). Sometimes one triad is superimposed on another to form a polychord:

No. 10 from *The Little Piano Book*, Persichetti
Adagio pesante

Ex. 34 — *Tanzstücke*, Op. 19, Hindemith

Ex. 35 — Violin Concerto, Berg

8va bass

F. Sinatra playing the triangle

Angel playing a triangle (border detail from the "Apocalypse Tapestries" of Angers, France, late 14th century)

Composers have built triads using intervals other than thirds (Ex. 34). In twelve-tone, or serial, music the triad as a harmonic entity is almost totally abandoned, although Alban Berg makes the old traditional triad an integral part of his Violin Concerto (Ex. 35).

TRIANGLE: a member of the percussion family of instruments that consists of a slim steel rod bent into a three-sided shape, with a gap left at one corner. Each side of the triangle is about seven inches long. It is played by means of a thin wand, also made of steel.

In order not to damp its vibrations, the player suspends the triangle from a string held in his left hand or hung from the stand that holds his music. He can tap the triangle with the beater to make a rhythmic pattern, or he can make a tremolo by shaking the beater back and forth on an inside corner of the instrument.

The triangle vibrates at so many different frequencies at the same time that its tone has no definite pitch, but it seems to fit with any orchestral sound. It has a great range of dynamics—pianissimo to fortissimo. And in spite of its small size, its tone can cut through the sound of the whole orchestra playing at its loudest.

Although the triangle appears to have been known throughout the Renaissance, evidence of its use is hard to come by because it was never one of the "regular" instruments in common use. It is clearly shown in the Apocalypse tapestries at Angers, France, which date from about 1380, and this may be the earliest known picture of it. But it did not join the orchestra till the eighteenth century when, in the craze for "Turkish" or Janissary effects, composers (notably Gluck) used it along with the cymbals and bass drum in operas with a Near-Eastern setting. Mozart used it in this way in his *Abduction from the Seraglio.* It was not till later—in the works of Spontini, Rossini (overture to *The Thieving Magpie*), and Wagner *(Siegfried* and *Die Meistersinger)*—that the triangle became a regular member of the percussion group. Liszt gave it a little solo bit in the scherzo of his Piano Concerto in E-flat.

In scores the triangle part is written either in the treble clef or on a single line. In manuscript the triangle is indicated by a △.

TRILL: the rapid oscillation, or seesawing, between a principal tone and the tone immediately above it in a scale. The trill is both an embellishment and a dramatic device used for moments of suspense or climax. It is indicated by: *tr*, *tr*⁓, ⁓, or T.

The trill began, like many embellishments, as a vocal ornamentation of the next-to-last note of a cadence in sixteenth-century music. (One of the earliest opera composers, Guilio Caccini, describes two forms of trill in his *Le nuove musiche,* or *The New Music:* one a bleatlike sound on one tone, the other the trill as it is usually known.)

The main characteristic of the trill in the seventeenth and eighteenth centuries was that it began with and emphasized the dissonant tone above the principal tone (Ex. 36a, b, and c). This rule is often broken if the main tone is approached by step from below (Ex. 37a and b), or if a small note appears before the principal note (Ex. 38a and b). According to the tempo or the length

of the tone, the performer would put in as many notes as possible—never less than four.

In the nineteenth and twentieth centuries the trill begins with and emphasizes the principal tone, unless the composer writes a small note to show that the trill is to begin above the principal note (Ex. 39; Ex. 40).

As a dramatic device, a trill in the low bass, as in Beethoven's Sonata in C Minor, Opus 111, where the trill is written out, suggests a suspenseful drumroll (Ex. 41). Beethoven, particularly in his late works, was fond of using soaring trills which moved up the chromatic scale or hovered ecstatically above melody and accompaniment (Ex. 42).

When the note above the principal tone is to be chromatically altered, the flat or sharp or natural sign appears with the trill sign, as in Ex. 42, where the flat sign above the trill in the lower voice of the right hand part signifies that the trill should consist of D and E-flat.

Bach often uses a long trill as a kind of

Ex. 36

Ex. 37

Ex. 38

Ex. 39 — Étude, Op. 10, No. 8, Chopin

Ex. 40 — Piano Sonata, No. 4, Weber

Ex. 41 — Sonata, Op. 111, Beethoven

Allegro con brio ed appassionato

Ex. 42 — Sonata, Op. 111, Beethoven

Ex. 43 — Invention in D Minor, J.S. Bach

pedal point on the harpsichord. The tone of the instrument could not sustain for long, and the trill adds excitement to what is usually the climax of the work (Ex. 43).

The trill, often suggesting the warbling of birds, is an important ingredient in the music of Scriabin, who uses its agitation for his music of mystical tremblings and exaltations.

TRIO: a term which may mean a work for three performers, a group of three performers, or a part of a musical form, as in "minuet with trio."

Vocal trios occur in many operas, cantatas, and oratorios. They have no set form, merely arising out of the immediate dramatic situation. They can be sad, like the farewell of Fiordiligi, Dorabella, and Don Alfonso to the departing officers in Mozart's *Così fan tutte;* satirical, like the trio "Jimmy's Going to Eat His Hat" in Kurt Weill's *Mahagonny;* or dramatic, like the "handkerchief trio" (Iago, Otello, and Cassio) in Verdi's *Otello.* Another type of vocal trio is the light madrigal written for three voices—typically, three women's voices—around 1600. Such a madrigal was usually called a canzonetta for three voices, or a *terzetto.*

One of the most popular forms of instrumental trio is the piano trio—a sonata in several movements for piano, violin, and cello. Among the earliest composers of such trios were Haydn, who wrote thirty-five (like piano sonatas with accompaniments), and Mozart, who wrote seven. Beethoven, in his nine trios for piano, violin, and cello, gave each performer an interesting part, raising the trio to a high form of chamber music. Composers of the nineteenth century—notably Schubert, Schumann, Mendelssohn, Brahms, Dvořák, Tchaikovsky, and Arensky—each wrote one or more trios that are still played today. Ravel's Piano Trio in A Minor, written in 1914, is one of the few twentieth-century works in this form that have achieved a permanent place in chamber-music repertoire.

One established form of trio is the string trio: for violin, viola, and cello. Haydn wrote numerous charming works for this combination. Mozart wrote only one—but an especially fine one, his Divertimento K. 563. Beethoven wrote five string trios, then forsook this form for the string quartet. Among the few string trios written since 1900 are two by Hindemith and one by Schoenberg.

Many trios include one or more wind instruments. Haydn wrote trios for three flutes as well as for flute, violin, and bass. Mozart wrote one for piano, clarinet, and viola. Beethoven wrote a trio for flute, violin, and viola, and another for two oboes and English horn. Beethoven and Brahms each wrote a trio for piano, clarinet, and cello. Among the most popular items in Brahms's chamber music is his Trio for violin, horn, and piano, Opus 40. Two notable trios date from our own century: Debussy's Sonata for flute, viola, and harp and Bartók's *Contrasts,* written in 1938 for Benny Goodman and Joseph Szigeti, which is for piano, violin, and clarinet.

As a musical form, the trio is the second section of many minuets, scherzos, and marches, where its function is to contrast strongly in musical idea, key, and style with the first section. It is traditionally referred to as a trio because, in French Baroque music, it was originally assigned to two oboes and a bassoon—after a first section played by the strings or by the orchestra as a whole. Every Sousa march has a trio section, and the trio is also a feature of the Classical sonata and symphony, in which it occurs as a contrasting section in the minuet or scherzo movement.

The title "trio" is sometimes given to organ works (by J. S. Bach, Josef Rheinberger, and others) in which three contrapuntal lines are woven together. Such trios are related to the trio sonata.

The Beaux Art Trio: Daniel Giulet, violin; Menahem Pressler, piano; and Bernard Greenhouse, cello

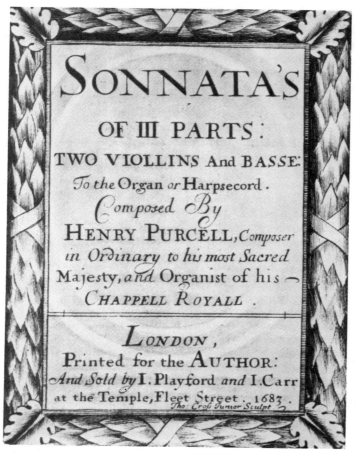

Title page of Henry Purcell's Trio Sonatas; *the first in this form to be published in England*

TRIO SONATA: one of the most popular forms of chamber music in the seventeenth and early eighteenth centuries. It was written to be played by two soprano instruments, usually violins or recorders, accompanied by a bass part called the continuo. The continuo was played by a bass instrument, such as cello or bassoon, and by a keyboard instrument—harpsichord or organ. The keyboard player improvised a part for his right hand, derived from a form of musical shorthand called figured bass. In spite of its title, therefore, a trio sonata was usually played by four performers.

There are two types of trio sonata. One, the *sonata da camera,* or chamber sonata, consisted of a group of dance forms—allemande, courante, saraband, gigue, and so on—all in the same key. The other, the *sonata da chiesa,* or church sonata, consisted of alternate slow and fast movements, the fast movements usually being fugal. At times composers mixed the two forms, ending a church sonata with a dance form or beginning a chamber sonata with a dignified prelude.

Trio sonatas were written by Corelli, Purcell, Telemann, Vivaldi, Couperin, Bach, and Handel. Bach's sonatas for violin and harpsichord are really trio sonatas in which the right hand of the harpsichord part takes the place of the second violin.

With the beginning of the Classical period of music, around 1750, composers and listeners came to prefer the sound of the string quartet to that of the trio sonata. Since that time practically no trio sonatas have been written.

TRIPLE METER: music that has three beats, or pulses, per measure. The most common time signatures of triple meter are 3/16, 3/8, 3/4, 3/2, 9/8, and 9/4. Many dances throughout the history of music are in triple time: the galliard, saraband, courante, minuet, Ländler, waltz, mazurka, and polonaise. The variation forms of chaconne and passacaglia are usually in a triple meter of 3/4 or 3/2.

At a moderate or a slow tempo, triple meter is conducted so that the conductor's baton makes a triangle in the air:

At a fast tempo, it is often conducted as though it had one beat—a downbeat with a bounce back up. Some conductors also conduct a fast triple meter as a circle, with the first count at the bottom of the circle. This brings out the "roundness" of triple meter, caused by the two weak beats which follow the strong beat.

TRIPLET: a group of three notes to be played in the time of two notes of the same value. It is formed by the division of a beat or part of a beat, or a measure or part of a measure, into three equal parts (Ex. 44). (In arithmetic 3/4 never equals 2, but in music that is just what happens when a triplet is written or played.)

Ex. 44

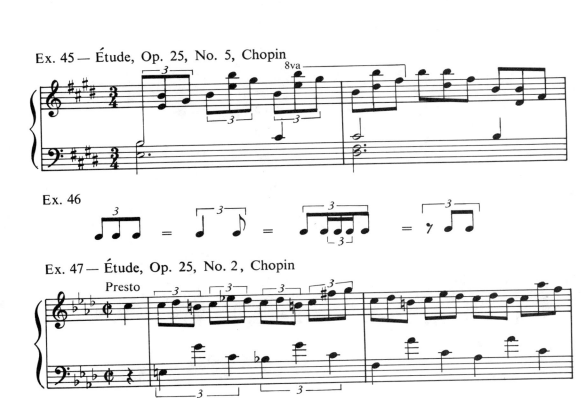

Ex. 45 — Étude, Op. 25, No. 5, Chopin

Ex. 46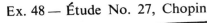

Ex. 47 — Étude, Op. 25, No. 2, Chopin

Ex. 48 — Étude No. 27, Chopin

A triplet is written by placing the figure 3 over or under the notes; if the triplet is repeated a number of times, the 3 is often omitted after the first few triplets (Ex. 45). (When the pulse of a composition is always to be divided into three parts, the composer usually writes the music in 6/8, 9/8, or 12/8 meter. This shows that there are two, three, or four basic pulses, each divided into three parts.)

A triplet may be subdivided as long as the rhythmic pattern is always equal to the three notes of the triplet (Ex. 46). (A triplet may even occur within a triplet.) Triplets of one kind are sometimes written to be played against triplets of another kind, as in Chopin's Étude in F Minor (Ex. 47).

Many composers have written music in which a triplet in one part is played against the two tones of the same value in another part, as in Chopin's Étude in A-flat (Ex. 48). This is sometimes called "playing three against two." In order to make each part

absolutely even, the performer practices the music by counting as here:

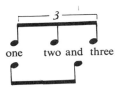

one   two and three

Music students often have trouble playing triplets accurately. They tend to hurry the beginning of the triplet, so that instead of playing Ex. a they would play Ex. b:

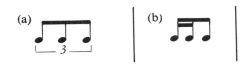

This mistake can be corrected by holding back slightly on the second tone.

A scene from Tristan and Isolde, *Act I, with Kirsten Flagstad and Lauritz Melchior*

TRISTAN AND ISOLDE (*Tristan und Isolde*): an opera by Richard Wagner, based on a romantic Celtic legend of the Middle Ages. Wagner planned the work as an easy-to-produce little opera—an interlude in his project of writing *The Ring of the Nibelungs,* which was to take twenty-six years. Wagner himself wrote the libretto as well as the music for *Tristan and Isolde* between 1857 and 1859. Three years later the opera was scheduled for performance in Vienna, but the "easy little opera" proved too difficult for singers and orchestra. After fifty-four rehearsals it was taken off the opera schedule, being called impossible to perform. Finally, in 1865, after many more rehearsals and disappointments, *Tristan and Isolde* received its first performance in Munich, under the patronage of King Ludwig of Bavaria.

There were several reasons for the opera's difficulties in the 1860's. Although the music was tonal—always in a definite key—there were so many chromatic tones and unusual harmonic progressions that many musicians were bewildered. As in all of Wagner's mature works, the harmony is "endless," rarely stopping at cadence points. Restless chords moving to other restless chords combine with surging rhythmic figures in the orchestra to underline the ardent passions of the two lovers. There is much use of the leitmotif—a short melodic figure or harmonic progression that represents a character or idea. Leitmotifs, as they are developed throughout the work, bind its parts together musically.

Tristan and Isolde is one of the foundation works of modern music. In it traditional harmony and chromaticism were pushed to such extremes that many composers after Wagner felt compelled to seek new directions. Some, notably Satie and Debussy, turned to a simpler style. Others, such as Strauss and Schoenberg, pushed on to the realm of atonal music. In both its beauty and its influence on later music, *Tristan* stands as one of the great landmarks of nineteenth-century Romantic music.

The opera's prelude (often played on concert programs) sets the mood of tragic longing for love and death that is the dra-

Ex. 49

Slowly

Ex. 50

matic theme of the entire work. It begins slowly with sighing phrases that end with long rests. The harmony is restless; chords resolve unexpectedly and deceptively. Wagner makes use of sequence, repeating phrases at higher and higher pitches to create increasing emotional impact. The opening motive of grief or sorrow, played only by the cellos, is overlapped by a four-note figure and two chords that symbolize desire, or Isolde's magic (Ex. 49, page 614). A bit later two more motives are heard: the theme of Tristan, the hero:

and the theme of the "Look" that passes between Tristan and Isolde:

These are followed by the motives of the love potion:

and of death (Ex. 50). All the motives build to a climax, at which point the motive of the longing for death appears. The prelude unwinds down to a soft passage for cellos and basses. The curtain rises and the opera begins.

King Mark of Cornwall has sent Tristan, his nephew and heir-to-be, to Ireland to bring back the Princess Isolde, who is to become the king's bride. On the return voyage Isolde recognizes Tristan as the one who, years earlier, killed the man she was to have married. At that time she held the life of the weak and wounded Tristan in her hands, but rather than kill him she nursed him back to health. Moved by her compassion, Tristan swore everlasting gratitude to her.

Isolde, having resolved to die rather than marry King Mark, tells Brangaene, her attendant, to prepare a death cup. When Tristan comes to tell Isolde to get ready for the landing in Ireland, she tells him that he has broken his oath of gratitude and will be forgiven only if he drinks a peace cup with her. Brangaene brings the cup; but she has mixed a love potion—not a death potion. Tristan and Isolde drink, and instead of death they find the love that they have felt for each other from the beginning.

The second act opens with a short, fast prelude based mostly on motives of Isolde's impatience (Ex. 51, page 616), her desire to see Tristan (Ex. 52), and on a theme of ecstatic love (Ex. 53). King Mark has gone on a hunting trip. The hunter's horns are heard again and again in the orchestra (Ex. 54), reminding the listener of both the absence and the nearness of the king. The music is in the key of Bb major—and yet the chord of Bb is almost never heard as the harmonies revolve around it.

Brangaene warns Isolde of the knight Melot, a false friend of Tristan's. Isolde, impatient, bids Brangaene give the signal to Tristan. He comes, and the pair sing a

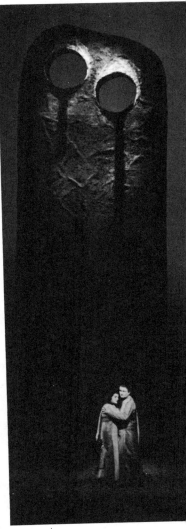

Tristan and Isolde, *Act II (1962 Bayreuth Theater production)*

Ex. 56

Ex. 57

long, glowing love duet. Thoughts of love are mingled with a longing for death, represented by one of Wagner's most beautiful motives (Ex. 55).

The duet is interrupted by a shriek from Brangaene as King Mark and Melot appear and face the lovers. Tristan and Isolde confess their overpowering love for one another. Melot, also in love with Isolde, challenges Tristan and they fight. Tristan, dropping his own sword, is run through by Melot's. He falls, badly wounded, into the arms of his trusted old retainer, Kurvenal.

The short prelude to Act III merges into the lonely, desolate sound of a shepherd's melody, played by an unaccompanied English horn (Ex. 56). Tristan, lying in his garden at his castle on the coast of Normandy, to which he has been brought by Kurvenal, knows that he is dying. Isolde, whom he awaits, will not be able to cure him this time. As her ship approaches, Tristan feverishly tears off his bandages and rushes to meet her. He dies in her arms

as King Mark appears with Melot, whom Kurvenal then kills in combat. King Mark announces sadly that he has come to forgive, not to punish. Isolde, mindful only of the dead Tristan, sings the great dramatic aria known as the "Liebes Tod" (Love Death) (Ex. 57). The music builds to an ecstatic climax, then dies down as Isolde sinks to the ground, joined with her lover in death. In the legend, a rose and ivy spring from the graves of the lovers and intertwine their branches.

TRITONE: the interval consisting of three whole steps that occurs between the fourth and seventh degrees of the major scale. The tritone divides the twelve half steps of the octave exactly in half. Its inversion is therefore the same size as the tritone itself, regardless of how the interval is placed: B-F is three whole steps; F-B is three whole steps. Its notation depends on which way the interval is going to resolve. If it moves

Ex. 58 — Suite for Piano, Op. 25, Schoenberg

in, it is the diminished fifth:

If it moves out, it is the augmented fourth:

The tritone was avoided in music before 1600. It was often called "the interval of the devil," possibly because it was difficult to sing in tune melodically or harmonically. Even two adjacent major thirds were avoided because their outer voices made the interval of a tritone:

In time, musicians became used to the sound of the tritone as they grew familiar with dominant seventh and diminished seventh chords which contain tritones:

Dominant Seventh   Diminished Seventh

Since 1900 the tritone has come into frequent use, not just as an interval which would resolve, but as a basic sound in music. Compositions in the whole-tone scale contain many tritones, since the interval from any tone to a tone four steps away is a tritone.

Tritones   etc.

Many harmonic sounds in twelve-tone music emphasize the ambiguous quality of the tritone (Ex. 58).

TROMBONE: the mellow tenor and majestic bass of the brass choir. It is a large relative of the trumpet (*trombone* is Italian for "big trumpet"). In Germany it is called *Posaune*. Its old English name, "sackbut," came from two French words that meant "pull-push"—which is just how the trombonist plays his instrument.

The tube of the tenor trombone—the type mostly used—is in three sections measuring nine feet in total length. The deep, cup-shaped mouthpiece is on the end of one section. The *bell,* or flaring part of the tube, is at the end of another section, which is U-shaped and rests on the player's left shoulder. The parallel arms of this section are connected by a metal piece which the player holds with his left hand to steady the instrument. The middle of the tube, the *slide*, is also U-shaped. It fits over the open ends of the other two parts and is moved from position to position by the player's right hand.

There are seven basic tones, each produced by moving the slide downward to the seven successive basic positions:

The highest of these tones is produced when the player's right hand is closest to his mouth. As he pushes the slide away from him, he lengthens the tube and lowers the pitch. The trombonist must have a keen ear—there are no keys to guide him to the correct notes. His arm must remember how far to push the slide in going from one position to another.

Tones that lie above this basic series of seven are produced by tightening the lips and blowing a bit harder, thus producing higher overtones of the harmonic series. The full set of these overtones allows the trombone to produce a full chromatic scale for about three octaves:

The trombone part is written on the bass clef or on the tenor clef, with middle C on the next-to-top line.

Several additional tones, called pedal tones, lie below the basic series. These are, in fact, the true fundamentals of the trombone:

Since they are difficult to produce and cannot always be counted on, composers have learned to use them sparingly.

The downward reach of the bass trombone is shown here:

This is such a large, cumbersome instrument that its place has been taken by a modern tenor-bass trombone, which is only slightly larger than the regular model. It is fitted with a valve that allows the player to fill in the tones that lie between his low E and the pedal tones.

The trombonist produces his tone by blowing air through tightened lips. His tongue helps him to attack a tone: for fast, repeated tones he double-tongues as if to say "tu-ku" or triple-tongues a "tu-ku-tu." The trombone can play almost any kind of scale passage or arpeggio, although legato passages are difficult in the low register. Composers and arrangers are careful not to give the trombonist rapid alternations of the low E and B-flat, because fast shifts from first to seventh to first positions make the trombonist look as if he were priming a pump. Some trombones have been made with valves replacing the slide, thus giving the instrument some of the agility of the trumpet.

The trombone was the first brass instrument to be perfected—at some time in the early 1400's. For the next several hundred years it was a favorite instrument in church music and "tower music." The tower band originally played music signals that told the hour. In the middle 1500's they played chorale tunes from the towers, as well as providing entertainment for the townspeople. In church the trombone, aided by the cornett—an ivory or wooden instrument with keys—accompanied the congregational singing of hymns. It got this job because valveless trumpets and horns could not play melodies that moved up and down by steps. Four sizes of trombones were used, one for each kind of singing voice. The soprano and alto trombones were gradually discarded.

Trombones began to be called for by composers from around 1600. Giovanni Gabrieli and his pupil Heinrich Schütz used trombones in their sacred music for several choirs. Schütz's lament of David for his son Absalom (*Ach, mein Sohn Absalom*)— one of his most beautiful works—starts with a dark-colored passage for four trombones. The somber effect of trombones also appealed to Monteverdi, who used five of them to accompany the chorus of underworld spirits in his opera *Orfeo*.

The trombone was neglected for a time in the early 1700's as composers became interested in newer instruments—violins, oboes, and clarinets. Bach used trombones only with the voices in his choruses. The trombone dropped out of favor even in military bands until almost 1800.

It was the opera composer Gluck who brought the trombone back into music. In

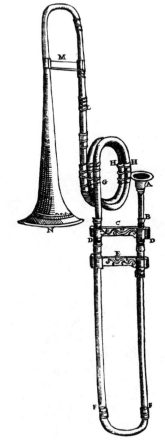

A sackbut (woodcut from Harmonie universelle *by Marin Mersenne, Paris, 1636–37)*

Men on horseback playing trombones (wood engraving from "The Triumph of the Emperor Maximilian" by Hans Burgkmair)

Jack Teagarden playing the trombone with his band, c. 1944

his search for orchestral sounds that would match a dramatic mood, he rediscovered the trombone and used it in his operas *Orfeo* and *Alceste*. Mozart followed Gluck's lead by using three trombones to give a solemn, fateful quality to the graveyard scene in the second act of his *Don Giovanni*.

It was in 1808 that the trombone was first used in a symphony orchestra: when Beethoven called for three trombones in the finale of his Fifth Symphony. Since that time the trombone choir has been used often in orchestral works. Brahms, Wagner, and Strauss were particularly fond of its rich sound. They gave it weighty, chorale-like passages:

Symphony No. 4, Brahms

Allegro energico

or used it to provide a harmonic background, often combined with trumpets. When the tuba was invented, in the 1830's, it became the bass to the trombone choir. In orchestral scores the parts for the third trombone and the tuba are often written on the same staff.

Because of the nature of the instrument, there is not a large repertoire of solo or chamber music for trombone. Hindemith and other modern composers have written sonatas for trombone and piano; Rimsky-Korsakov and Milhaud have contributed concertos. Among the few works that feature combinations of trombones are Beethoven's three *Equale* for four trombones and Stravinsky's *In Memoriam Dylan Thomas*

for tenor, string quartet, and four trombones.

The trombone was one of the earliest members of the jazz band. It was one of the mainstays of the New Orleans bands that played for funerals and rode on advertising wagons. The trombonist, who needed room for his slide, rode on the endpiece of the wagon—the tailgate. So a "tailgate trombonist" became the name for one who played the trombone in the New Orleans style. Jazz trombonists explored all the possibilities of the instrument, using their slides to make swooping glissandos from note to note. Out of this came such novelty works as "Slidus Trombonis." (The glissando has also been used by composers of concert music; thus Stravinsky calls for a trombone glissando in the uproarious Dance of the Infernal Kastchei in his *Firebird* Suite.) Jazz trombonists developed a sobbing vibrato tone to use in playing solos of sentimental ballads. George Brunis, not one to neglect an opportunity for clowning, managed to play the slide with his foot. Joseph "Tricky Sam" Nanton, another memorable technician, pioneered in using a rubber plunger as a mute when he played with Duke Ellington's early band. Many of the great names in jazz are those of trombonists: "Miff" Mole, Kid Ory, Tommy Dorsey, Jack Teagarden, J. C. Higginbotham, and J. J. Johnson. Johnson at one time teamed up with another trombonist, Kai Winding, in a small combo to play progressive jazz based on the sounds of two trombones—one of the few uses of the trombone in chamber music.

In concert and marching bands, the trombone is one of the most useful instruments, playing bass, tenor, solo, or fill-in parts.

TROUBADOUR: the poet-musician who was the voice of the Age of Chivalry—from the twelfth to the fourteenth century—in the old region of Provence in southern France. The troubadour was an aristocrat, for the most part, who had a talent for writing courtly poems. Melodies for the poems were usually composed by a professional musician, or jongleur, who copied the music and often performed the song. If the troubadour was himself a singer, a jongleur played the melody with a drone accompaniment on the medieval stringed instrument called the vielle. In rare cases the troubadour was such a good musician that he not only composed the melodies to his songs but also played his own accompaniment.

Many of the troubadour songs were dance songs—the medieval estampies danced by nobles as well as villagers. Other dance songs were the ballade and rondeau. They were written so that a verse sung by a soloist would be answered by the whole group as a chorus. All troubadour songs were monophonic; that is, they were melodies without any accompaniment other than the drone of the vielle. While some songs sounded like the chants of the medieval church, others were quite different. They were often in the major scale, whereas church music was written in the church modes. They were quite regular in form, often in four-measure phrases like much later dance music, instead of the irregular phrases of church music of the time.

In addition to dance songs, the troubadour sang polished lyrics about courtly love and in praise of women, as well as religious songs to the Virgin Mary and Crusaders' songs in praise of valor. Of the troubadour songs, only about 260 melodies have been found, while about 2,600 poems without music survive. Many of the poems were written to already-existing melodies, just as new lyrics are sometimes given to popular tunes today.

The earliest-known troubadour (the term comes from a Provençal word meaning "to find or compose in verse") was Guilhem VII (1071–1127), Count of Poitiers, who later became William IX, Duke of Aquitaine. Among the most famous troubadours was Raimbaut de Vaqueiras (d. 1207), whose "Kalenda maya" is one of the most beautiful medieval love songs.

The art started by the troubadours soon spread to northern France, where the noble poet-musician was known as a *trouvère*. The trouvères developed additional types of songs—ballads, pastorales, and "dawn songs,"

sometimes called *aubades* or serenades. The ballads were usually about a beautiful lady and her noble husband, who was sometimes a villain, sometimes a laughing stock. The pastorales were in some instances songs about spring and the newly blossomed trees, or little song stories about a knight who roams the countryside and meets a young shepherdess. He makes love to her, but she—often with help from an indignant father or fiancé—sends him back to the ladies of his own class. Such a pastorale story is the basis of the *Play of Robin and Marion*, a drama with music by one of the few trouvères not of noble birth, Adam de la Halle (*c.* 1240–87).

The dawn song told of a meeting of lovers under cover of dark. A friend is posted to keep watch for the coming of dawn, at which time the lovers must part. The German

Heinrich von Meissen (called Frauenlob), a 13th-century German minnesinger, who established a school for poet-musicians. "Minnesinger" was the German equivalent of the French "troubadour." (Miniature from the Manesse manuscript, Heidelberg)

Adam de la Halle (miniature from a late 13th-century French manuscript)

troubadours, called minnesinger, were particularly fond of the dawn song. The second act of Wagner's opera *Tristan and Isolde* is a nineteenth-century version of an aubade.

The most important trouvère songs were the long epics—the *chansons de geste*, or songs of action—that told of the bold deeds of French heroes such as Charlemagne and Roland. Such songs did much to give the French people a feeling of patriotism, pulling them together in a difficult period in the history of France. Two of the most important trouvères were the famous composer Machaut (*c.* 1300–77) and England's gallant King Richard I (the Lion-hearted, 1157–99). The story of Richard's imprisonment, the wandering of his minstrel Blondel—singing a song known only to him and to Richard—and of Blondel's rescue of his king is one of the best-known legends of the Age of Chivalry. Both troubadours and trouvères did much to open the path to the new kind of music that was to emerge in the late sixteenth century—a path obscured for a while by the new art of polyphonic music that started in the fourteenth century.

TRUMPET: the soprano member of the brass family. The modern trumpet, a B-flat transposing instrument, is four to five feet in length. Its cylindrical body, which flares out into a "bell," is looped for ease in handling. Before 1500, trumpets—some as long as seven feet—were straight and thus rather awkward for the player. The mouthpiece of the modern trumpet is shaped like a shallow goblet.

Until the early 1800's, the trumpet was a natural horn, much like the present-day bugle, which could produce only a limited number of tones. The addition of three piston valves allowed the player to change the length of the tube so that he could produce all the tones of the chromatic scale. The player uses the middle three fingers of his right hand to press down the valves. The left hand is used to help hold the instrument steady and to adjust a small tuning valve which helps to keep certain notes in tune.

On a regular trumpet the lowest tone that can be played without using valves is the written middle C, sounding B♭. This is called the trumpet's "open sound." By using the valves the player can lengthen the tube so that he can produce the written F♯ below middle C. The order of use of the valves and the notes they produce below middle C are:

Second valve	B
First valve	B♭
First and second valves	A
Second and third valves	A♭
First and third valves	G
First, second, and third valves	F♯

The player produces tones higher than these fundamentals by tightening his lips and blowing harder. The muscular control of the lips is called the player's "embouchure." The practical range of the trumpet is shown here:

Range of Trumpet in B♭

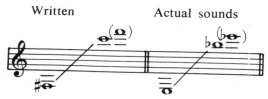

The trumpet can play almost any kind of melodic passage: arpeggios, rapid scale runs, fast-repeated note patterns, and so forth. In fast passages the player resorts to double- or triple-tonguing. In double-tonguing, the tongue is used as if to make the sound "tu-ku"; in triple-tonguing, "tu-ku-tu." Orchestral scores sometimes ask for a "flutter tongue," a rolling movement of the tongue that produces a buzzing sound useful for certain dramatic effects.

The trumpet is very good at singing long slow melodic lines, as in Copland's *Quiet City*. Sometimes these passages are played with the open horn; often they call for the use of a mute. The mute softens the tone and can also change its quality. The regular trumpet mute is a pear-shaped block of wood or thin metal which fits into the bell of the trumpet. It can make the trumpet sound like an echo, or, when the tone is

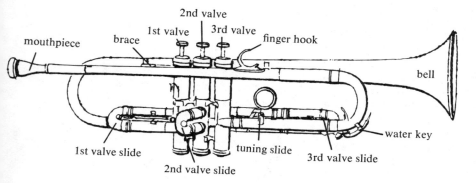

Detail from "Christ in Glory" by Fra Angelico, c. 1430

A pair of 18th-century Tibetan trumpets

accented, can produce a biting tone. Jazz trumpet players have tried various ways of muting their instruments, some putting hats across the bell and others using a plunger mute which can be opened and closed so that the trumpet seems to be saying "wah-wah." In old jazz records of Duke Ellington's band the trumpet as played by "Bubber" Miley and "Cootie" Williams growls, bubbles, and cries in a virtuoso display of the many tonal qualities of this instrument.

For centuries the trumpet was the aristocrat of instruments. The ancient Egyptians credited the god Osiris with its invention. In primitive tribes only warriors were allowed to play it. The conquering Roman legions under the Caesars were proud of their war trumpets, which they called "tubas." In Europe in the Middle Ages only a nobleman could employ a trumpeter. As late as 1700 the trumpets were part of an army, giving signals and sounding alarms. Actually two types of trumpet player developed: those who were members of the military establishment and those who were town musicians. The military trumpeters did not need to know how to read music; they played well-known fanfares and flourishes. The town trumpeters were better musicians, able to play "clarino" trumpet parts. These parts used the highest register

of the natural trumpet—so high that scale melodies could be played. The trumpet they used was larger than the regular one of today, being from six to nine feet in length. Because the instrument was so long, its fundamental tones were lower, which meant that in the high register the tones of the overtone series lay close together, so the player could play scale passages ranging around the high C above the staff. It was for such an instrument that Bach wrote his brilliant high trumpet parts (Ex. 59). The Bach trumpet passages are often played today on a small valve trumpet which gives a brighter and less mellow sound than the old instruments.

In the early 1700's the king of Poland and King Frederick the Great of Prussia each had two bands of trumpets and timpani (the timpani played the part of the bass instrument). These bands were used only on ceremonial occasions. They played a salute as the monarchs entered a theater and a farewell fanfare when they left. Fanfares usually served as overtures to theatrical entertainments in the 1500's, at which time they were called "toccatas." Monteverdi's opera *Orfeo* starts with the first written-out brass toccata.

In many early scores of the 1600's and 1700's the trumpet parts were printed at the

Ex. 59 — "Brandenburg" Concerto No. 2, J.S. Bach (as written for a trumpet sounding a perfect fourth higher)

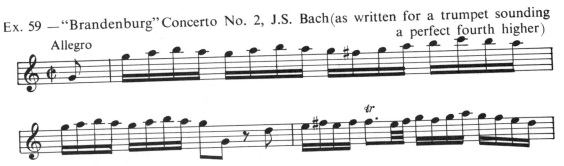

top of the page, along with the timpani parts, as befitted their noble rank. Trumpets in the Classical symphonies were used sparingly, usually in pairs. They were brought in to supply weight at tutti sections, to make accents at climaxes, and to hold long tones as background for the rest of the orchestra. Like the French horn, the natural trumpet could produce only the limited set of tones in which the instrument was pitched. To play in other keys the player replaced a section of his trumpet tubing with a section of different size, called a "crook." The use of a crook, of course, meant that one limited set of tones was replaced by an equally limited set of different tones. There were many experiments using a sliding mechanism like that of the trombone. Finally the invention of the valve system in Germany, about 1815, allowed the trumpet player to begin to regain his importance in music.

For various reasons the virtuoso trumpet playing of the clarino parts became a lost art. But the valve trumpet gave the instrument agility and the ability to play all the tones of the chromatic scale. Soon composers began to give the trumpet important melodies, although for many years they treated it rather gingerly. Wagner, always on the lookout for new instrumental sounds, used the trumpet extensively in his operas, particularly *Parsifal*. Wagner even wrote parts for bass trumpet, pitched an octave lower than the standard instrument, in his *Ring of the Nibelungs*. Strauss, Debussy, and Ravel (especially in his *Daphnis and Chloé* Suite for orchestra) exploited the many different tonal features of the trumpet. Symphonic composers of today usually write for three trumpets, although exceptionally, as in Stravinsky's *Rite of Spring*, as many as five are called for.

The trumpet is an important member of the concert band, where anywhere from two to ten will be found. Strangely enough, and possibly because of its former limitations when used as a military instrument, the trumpet is used in these bands to play "filler" parts, while the cornet is given the solo passages.

Jazz has used the sound of the trumpet throughout its long history. Leading jazz trumpeters, of whom Louis Armstrong is the most durable and influential, have extended the possibilities of the trumpet both in range and in tone quality. In addition to Armstrong, Miley, and Williams, the most important jazz trumpeters have been Bix Beiderbecke, Roy Eldridge, Dizzy Gillespie, Charlie Shavers, and Miles Davis.

Above: *Gottfried Reiche, the famous German trumpet player who played Bach's florid solos under the composer at Leipzig*

Bottom left: *Bubber Miley, 1930*
Bottom right: *Cootie Williams*

TUBA: the lowest-pitched and youngest member of the brass family. It is best known as the instrument that provides the "oom-pah" beat for the marching bands, but is used in a much more valuable way in orchestras and concert bands, in which its rich, full tone is blended with the trombones to make a solemn-sounding brass choir. In spite of its size, it has a wide range of tone —from velvet to thunder. In the hands of a good player it is surprisingly nimble.

The actual "tube" of the tuba is from twelve to eighteen feet long. The instrument's body, consisting of many coiled parts, is cone-shaped and ends in a wide "bell." The mouthpiece is deep and cup-shaped. The player works from three to five valves, placed to lie under the fingers of the right hand. As with other members of the brass family, the tuba's low tones make up a group of fundamental tones. From each fundamental tone the player can coax a limited number of overtones by changing the tension of his lips (or "overblowing"). To switch from one fundamental to another, the player works one or more of the valves, thus changing the length of the tube. By adjusting his lips and using the valves, the player can perform any tone in the chromatic scale.

The tuba comes in various sizes, the smallest being the B♭ tuba with the range shown here:

Deeper than this are the E♭ tuba:

and the big contrabass, or BB♭ ("double B♭), tuba:

The baritone horn, euphonium, and tenor horn are relatives of the tuba; they have about the range of the small B♭ tuba.

The tuba is the result of many experiments in the 1820's and 1830's. Musicians at that time felt the need for a brass instrument to replace the old wooden serpent (see BRASS INSTRUMENTS), whose tone was

William Lewin playing the tuba

not a match for those of the other brass instruments. The tuba was first used in Prussian military bands in 1835. Soon after, a Russian inventor improved the tuba by coiling it around the player's body so that its weight would rest on his shoulders. The coiled tuba, found mostly in bands, is called a helicon. (The American bandmaster John Philip Sousa suggested it be given a movable bell, and the sousaphone resulted). The tuba family was brought to its present form in 1843 by the Belgian instrument maker Adolphe Sax, who united the cornet, flügelhorn, baritone, euphonium, and tuba all together in one family—the saxhorns.

Richard Wagner, looking for new tone colors to be used in his opera cycle, *The Ring of the Nibelungs,* suggested a new kind of tuba that would be a cross between a French horn and a tuba. Such instruments, called Wagner tubas, are made in two sizes, tenor and bass. Since Wagner's time Bruckner and Richard Strauss have scored for them.

There is usually but one tuba in a symphony orchestra. The part is written on the same staff as the part for the bass trombone.

Ex. 60 — Overture, *Die Meistersinger*, Wagner

Ex. 61 — *Don Quixote*, Strauss

Most of the time the tuba's job is to provide a mellow bass, as in the ending of the first movement of Tchaikovsky's *Symphonie pathétique*. At other times it doubles the bass trombone part:

Symphony No. 4, Tchaikovsky
Bass Tbn. & Tuba

Wagner was fond of the instrument and gave it an important place in his scores, even allowing it to perform an unusual trill in the overture to *Die Meistersinger* (Ex. 60). One of the trickiest of all tuba parts is in Strauss's symphonic poem *Don Quixote,* in which the tenor tuba has several solos representing the Don's squire and companion, Sancho Panza (Ex. 61).

The tuba was a member of the rhythm section of early dance bands but was later replaced by the string bass, which provided a crisper beat. It can be heard in many old jazz recordings, marking off a square two-count beat. In some of the big bands of the 1930's and 1940's it was occasionally used as the bass of widespread, juicy brass harmonies.

TUNING: the matching of a tone on one instrument with the same tone on another instrument or a tuning fork (though for pianos and organs, tuning involves a great deal more). Tuning is done by changing the length or tension of a string or the length of a wooden or metal tube. Once one tone is matched or tuned on an instrument, all other tones of that instrument can be adjusted to the matched tone. On woodwind instruments the holes in the tube are cut so that the tones will be in the right scale relationship. Small adjustments in pitch on a woodwind instrument are taken care of by the lips of the player.

On brass instruments there is a tuning slide which allows the player to adjust his pitch. Woodwind instruments can be lengthened or shortened by adjusting the mouthpiece section so that it fits into the body of the instrument tightly or loosely. But this is impossible to do on the oboe; therefore all other instruments in the orchestra must tune to the sound of the oboe's "A."

The pitch of a certain tone is not standard at all times and in all places (see PITCH). Today "A" is set at 440 cycles of vibration per second—and in some cases orchestral conductors have their players tune "A" even higher. Their theory is that the higher the "A," the more brilliant the music will sound—but it also means that music is sometimes being played as much as a whole step higher than the composer intended.

String players match their A string to the pitch of the oboe. Then on the violin, viola, and cello they tune their other strings in the intervals of perfect fifths above or below the A string. The string bass tunes his strings in a series of perfect fourths up from the lowest tone, E: E-A-D-G.

The piano (with its relative the harpsichord) and the organ are the most difficult instruments to tune, since they have so many pipes or strings. Organ pipes are tuned by pulling out or pushing in a metal tongue at the top of a pipe, by moving a wooden slide to make an opening at the top of a pipe smaller or larger, or by adjusting some device that shortens or lengthens a pipe. The piano is tuned by adjusting the tension on each string; this is done by turning a metal pin around which the string is wound. Small rubber wedges that look like erasers are inserted between two strings of each set of three to stop them from sounding while the tuner concentrates on bringing the third string to the correct degree of tension.

Once the tuner has adjusted one string to the A or the C of his tuning fork, he tunes the other two strings of the same pitch to that tone. From there he moves on to make an octave and then a series of perfect fourths and fifths over the whole range of the instrument. (There are several ways of tuning in intervals. Some tuners use one set and some another.) Since all twelve half tones of a piano cannot be perfectly in tune (see TEMPERAMENT), the tuner must make small adjustments in pitch all the way up and down the keyboard.

The tuner listens for clear tones, watching out for pulses or "beats" that tell him whether or not the strings are in the correct pitch relationship to each other. (Learning to hear these "beats" is one of the most difficult parts of his training.) An octave is tuned so that it has no beats; a perfect fifth so that it gives off one beat per second. Modern electronic instruments have been invented to help the tuner, but most tuners prefer to rely on their own ears and judgment.

TUNING FORK: a two-pronged metal fork that gives off a clear, pure tone when struck against a solid object. It gets its shape from the fact that the prongs of a fork (even a table fork) continue to vibrate, or ring, for a longer time than would a single metal bar.

The tuning fork was invented in 1711 by John Shore, Handel's favorite trumpet player. Today it is used primarily by piano tuners (see TUNING). From the one tone on the piano that matches the tone of the tuning fork—usually A above middle C—the tuner can tune all the other notes. The tuning fork is tuned to the required pitch by filing the ends of the prongs or filing between the prongs where they join the shaft of the fork.

The sound of the tuning fork is not a loud one. To amplify it, the fork is held against a wooden box or a part of the piano.

TUTTI: an Italian word meaning "all." It is used to mean the whole orchestra in contrast to a soloist or a group of soloists. In the Classical symphonies of Haydn and Mozart the composers made much use of the contrast of strings or winds alone and the tutti of the full orchestra. In concertos the word is used to show that the orchestra is on its own and does not have to keep its tone down while accompanying the soloist.

TWELVE-TONE TECHNIQUE: a compositional technique that changed the course of music in the first half of the twentieth century; also known as "dodecaphonic," or "serial," music. The twelve-tone technique is a way of organizing a musical composition so that all its melody, harmony, and counterpoint grow out of a single arrangement of the twelve different tones within the musical octave. It does away completely with previous ideas of major-minor scales, a tonal center, and chords built in thirds. (Because of the absence of tonality, twelve-tone music is sometimes called "atonal" music—although not all atonal music is constructed on the twelve-tone principle.)

Arnold Schoenberg was the first composer to turn to the "method of composing with twelve tones," as he called it. In his own music he was developing a style that grew farther and farther away from the highly chromatic—yet tonal—music of Wagner and Richard Strauss. It seemed to Schoenberg, about the time of World War I, that music could not possibly go much farther in this direction without undermining the unity of each composition—its ability to hang together. In turning to the twelve-tone technique he saw a way of securing both freedom and order. By coincidence another Viennese composer, Josef Matthias Hauer, was working along the same lines during these years, but the magnetism and creativity of Schoenberg—as well as his relentlessness—caused his version of the new technique to win out.

In writing a piece in this fashion the composer makes a tone row, or series, by arranging the twelve tones of the chromatic scale in a certain order (Ex. 62, page 628). He usually tries to avoid any suggestion of tonality in the old sense by avoiding any series of tones in which tones could make triads when played together. The tone row shown is the one on which Schoenberg based his Suite for Piano, Opus 25 (1925).

The tone row has four forms: the original (O); the original backward, or retrograde (O-R); the original upside down in inversion (I); and the inversion in retrograde (I-R). If we were dealing with letters of the alphabet instead of with tones, the four forms of the tone row would look something like this:

O QUESTIONABLY   O-R YLBANOITSEUQ
I ÕᑎƎ⅃ꓕIⵑOꓦᗺ⅃ꓤ   I-R ⴋ⅃ᗺⱯNOIꓕⵑƎⵑÕ

In addition, each form of the tone row may be transposed, starting on any of the other eleven tones of the chromatic scale, so that we end up with a total of forty-eight possible series of tones built on the original row. These forty-eight series constitute the composer's thematic material—he is free to vary it and develop it with the

Ex. 62

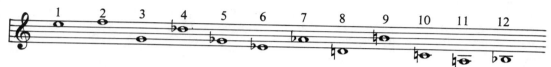

Ex. 63a — The above, inverted

Ex. 63b — Row transposed down a diminished fifth

Ex. 64 — Praeludium, Op. 25, Schoenberg

Ex. 65 — Gavotte, Op. 25, Schoenberg

Ex. 66 — Gigue, Op. 25, Schoenberg

help of all the traditional devices of composition that he can muster. There is one restriction: once a tone (which may appear in any octave) has been sounded and left behind, it may not be repeated until all the eleven other tones of the row have been used.

Scale passages are usually avoided. Tones next to each other are thrown into different octaves; the interval of a second, say from B to C, becomes a seventh **(a)** or ninth

(a)   B

   C

(b)   C

      B

(b) . Most twelve-tone music is contrapuntal rather than harmonic; that is, the listener is aware of separate strands of voices rather than progressions of chords. In line with this reaction against nineteenth-century practice, repetitions and sequences are avoided and the old contrapuntal devices of imitation are brought to the fore. The forms are terse and condensed rather than drawn out, and within them the themes are constantly varied and developed; they are seldom heard the same way twice. The result is music charged with great emotional feeling packed into a short listening span. To listeners not accustomed to it, it seems like concentrated orange juice before the water has been added.

Ex. 63a and b shows what happens to Schoenberg's tone row when he inverts it and transposes it.

We can now examine the beginnings of several of the pieces that make up Schoenberg's Suite for Piano. Numbers here refer to the positions of the tones in the original tone row (Ex. 64, 65, and 66).

There is so much a composer can do with a tone row that he can make of it whatever he has imagination enough to think up, just as in Beethoven's time a composer could use the tones of a major scale to make a fast dance, a soulful melody, or a dramatic series of chords. Schoenberg and his pupil Alban Berg used twelve-tone construction as a foundation for darkly romantic music; Schoenberg's pupil Anton von Webern, on the other hand, used the technique to build highly condensed compositions showing a great concern with tone color. Twelve-tone technique has been used to write music of every imaginable sort, including background scores for films that range from cartoons to serious psychological productions.

Twelve-tone music met with great animosity on the part of musicians and audiences when it first appeared in the 1920's. Since then it has become, sometimes in combination with more traditional techniques, part of the craft of such composers as Copland, Barber, Sessions, Dallapiccola, and Schuller. Even Stravinsky, who once violently opposed the twelve-tone technique, finally succumbed to its lures, starting with his cantata *Canticum sacrum* (1956) and his ballet *Agon* (1957).

UKULELE: a small four-stringed guitar, originally from Portugal, which became the favorite stringed instrument of the Hawaiians. Brought to the United States in the early 1900's, by the 1920's it had become a popular instrument for strumming accompaniments to jazz ballads. Its small tone prevented it from making a place for itself in dance bands, but this was no bar to its adoption for picnics, canoe parties, and front-porch serenades.

The ukulele is tuned as shown here:

The fingering is helped by a system of frets (small metal bars set across the fingerboard) which guide the player's fingers on the string. The string is pressed down behind the fret to secure the best tone. All strings are strummed with the fingers of the right hand or with a felt pick.

Ukulele chords are written in tablature—a system of notation that shows at which frets the fingers are to be placed. Each fret raises the pitch of its string by a semitone, and a player soon learns to figure out chords by ear. The example below shows some of the more usual chords. The strings are numbered in the first tablature to correspond to the tuning shown above. String 1 is at the top when the ukulele is held in playing position:

Cliff Edwards, better known as "Ukulele Ike," playing the ukulele

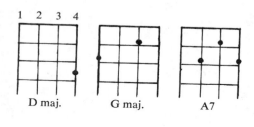

D maj.   G maj.   A7

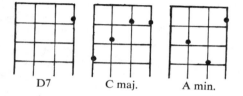

D7   C maj.   A min.

Ex. 1 — Sonata, K. 282, Mozart

UPBEAT: a part of a measure that precedes the first measure accent, setting up a rhythmic pattern that is generally carried on throughout the remainder of the composition. It is related to the iambic meter in poetry, in which an unstressed syllable is followed by a stressed one. An upbeat might be as short as a part of a beat (as in Ex. 1 below), or it might be almost as long as a full measure, as in this example:

"La Bandoline" Couperin

The effect of the upbeat is to throw the music into the following downbeat—like the windup of a pitcher before he throws the baseball, or the whirl of the discus thrower before he releases the discus. At the end of a composition, or section of a composition, the value of the upbeat is subtracted from the final measure as in the ending of Couperin's "La Bandoline":

A main characteristic of several court dance forms—the gavotte, rigaudon, and bourrée—is that each begins with a slightly different kind of upbeat (Ex. 2, 3, and 4). The most dramatic use of an upbeat occurs in the introduction to the final movement of Beethoven's First Symphony. Here a series of upbeats, starting with two notes, adds one more note with each repetition, until the upbeat seems to get so heavy that it plunges the music into the boisterous theme that follows (Ex. 5).

An upbeat is sometimes called an "anacrusis" or "pick-up."

Ex. 2 — Gavotte from "French Suite" No. 5, J.S. Bach

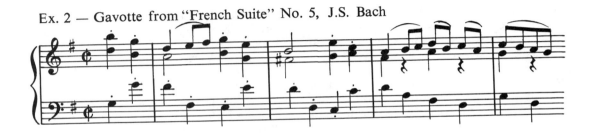

Ex. 3 — Rigaudon from *Pièces de clavecin*, 1724, Rameau

Ex. 4 — Bourrée from Flute Sonata No. 5, Handel

Ex. 5 — Symphony No. 1, Beethoven

VARÈSE, EDGARD (1883–1965): a French American composer of many controversial works. Varèse was born in Paris where, in his teens, he was torn between his father's desire that he become an engineer and his own desire to become a composer. Music won out, and Varèse studied with d'Indy and Roussel at the Schola Cantorum, and with Widor at the Paris Conservatory. An interest in choral music took the young man to Berlin, where he organized a symphonic choir and came under the influence of the composer-philosopher Ferruccio Benvenuto Busoni (1866–1924).

Varèse spent the first year of World War I in the French Army, from which he was discharged in 1915 because of ill health. He then came to the United States and settled in New York City, where he played an important role in musical life until his death. One of his first acts was to found an orchestra, the New Symphony, for the performance of new music. In 1921 he and the harpist Carlos Salzedo started the International Composers' Guild, which presented works by the men who were changing the face of music: Stravinsky, Schoenberg, Webern, Berg.

During the 1920's Varèse, whose early works were conventional in character, began to bring forth his own new conceptions of tonal organizations. Possibly influenced by the Italian Futurists, who envisioned music as "organized noise," and to some extent by Busoni, Varèse experimented in new sonorities and a new method of rhythmic organization. Sometimes his music is almost primitive, as one block of sound is succeeded by another, contrasting block. Traditional harmony is abandoned and with it traditional concepts of melody. Varèse developed a new vocabulary and a new musical syntax. His work was expressive in ways new to music, cutting through the listener's past experience to arrive at the inner essence of music itself.

At times Varèse called for large orchestral forces, as in *Amériques* (1926) and *Arcana* (1927). Then again he wrote for smaller but novel groups, as in *Hyperprism* (1923), which is for two woodwinds, seven brasses, and sixteen percussion instruments, and *Octandre* (1924), which is for seven winds and a double bass. Unafraid of new instruments, he used the electronic *ondes martenot* in *Equatorial* (1934).

Varèse's titles are somewhat mystifying and usually testify to his earlier interest in science. His *Density 21.5,* written for Georges Barrère, refers to the specific gravity of the platinum flute owned by Barrère. *Ionisation* (1931), which on its first performance became one of Varèse's most controversial works, showed remarkable insight into the future, when the atom would control much of man's destiny. It is scored for thirty-five different percussion instruments to be played by thirteen musicians. The instruments include Afro-Cuban gourds and rattles and a dominating pair of sirens. One of the most unsettling musical works of the twentieth century, *Ionisation* was the culmination of Varèse's non-electronic period.

For almost twenty years Varèse produced nothing. A combination of poor health and an uninterested public (only Leopold Stokowski had championed him) led Varèse to withdraw from the world. For some of this time he went back to his early love—the conducting of amateur choruses. He also kept in touch with what scientists in their laboratories were achieving in electronics.

In 1954 he wrote his first electronic score, combining wind instruments, percussion, and taped sounds. Then in 1958 came the *Poème électronique,* written to be played in a pavilion designed by Le Corbusier at the Brussels World Fair. He combined natural sounds, distorted through filters, and electronically generated sounds that were played through 400 loudspeakers. *Poème électronique* is possibly the first masterpiece using the electronic idiom. Hearing it is a harrowing, moving, exhilarating experience. When Varèse translates into music the sounds of the future (or the non-future) of the world, the audience is compelled to sit up, take notice, and contemplate.

In the last years of his life Varèse was accorded the honor and veneration he so richly deserved. Impatient with traditional musical sounds, ever youthful and dynamic, he became an acknowledged leader for a large cadre of young composers.

Above: *Edgard Varèse in 1961*
Below right: *Edgard Varèse with Heitor Villa-Lobos in Paris, 1929*

VAUGHAN WILLIAMS, RALPH (1872–1958): the greatest English composer of the first half of the twentieth century. Born in a small town in Gloucestershire, where his father was a minister, he studied at the Royal College of Music, at Cambridge University (where he received his doctorate of music), and in Germany with the composer Max Bruch (1838–1920). Later, after having written many works he went to France and studied with his younger contemporary Ravel.

Equally important with his musical studies was Vaughan Williams' membership in the society of scholars who were collecting and studying English folk songs. Also, on his own, he became acquainted with the great English choral music of the late 1500's. Out of this combination of folk and contrapuntal music Vaughan Williams forged a style uniquely his own. His melodies are often like folk tunes, but with breadth and a long line like those of the old English composers of the time of Queen Elizabeth I. In his harmony he often used only simple major and minor triads, moving in parallel motion. Particularly in his early works he turned his back on the rich harmonies of Wagner and Debussy.

The feeling of English countryside was captured in his *Norfolk Rhapsody* for orchestra and *Hugh the Drover,* an opera. The spirit of old England breathes through his best-known work, *Fantasia on a Theme by Tallis,* for string orchestra. *On Wenlock Edge,* written in 1909 for tenor, string quartet, and piano, was Vaughan Williams' first work to become known outside of his own country. It has kept its place on recital programs.

After World War I, in which he served as a lieutenant in the artillery, Vaughan Williams became professor of composition at the Royal College of Music. Settling down to a long career, he wrote nine symphonies, concertos for violin, piano, oboe, tuba, and harmonica, and many beautiful choral works based on the Bible and on poems by Walt Whitman and George Herbert. Almost no area of music was ignored by Vaughan Williams. Among other things he wrote six operas, of which *Riders to the Sea* is most often performed. Of his three ballets *Job,* "A Masque for Dancing," has proved most popular. In the 1940's he wrote music for six films.

Vaughan Williams' early symphonies are slightly programmatic. His second, *A London Symphony,* paints a picture of the bustling, foggy city awakening, going about its business, having fun in the evening, and finally quieting down for the night. Many of the

Left: *Ralph Vaughan Williams in 1951*
Below: *a scene from* Hugh the Drover *(British National Opera Company production, 1924)*

Ex. 1 — Second Movement, *London Symphony*

Ex. 2 — Fourth Movement, *Pastoral Symphony*

Ex. 3 — Symphony No. 4

themes are like folk tunes (Ex. 1). At times Vaughan Williams quotes the sound of Big Ben and the street cry of the lavender seller.

A Pastoral Symphony is, as its title suggests, a portrait of the English countryside. It is also a musical portrait of the English countryman: slow of speech, fond of old folk songs, and full of quiet humor—a man dear to the heart of the composer (Ex. 2). Written in 1922, it was immediately popular, and Vaughan Williams himself conducted it on various occasions, including a festival at Norfolk, Connecticut. But when his next symphony—the Fourth—was performed, in 1935, it shocked those who expected to hear another foggy or folksy work, because it is full of sharp dissonances. It is a tight, highly dramatic work. Instead of being built on a jaunty folk-style melody the first movement has a four-note motive related to the B-A-C-H (B*b*-A-C-B) motive used by many other composers (Ex. 3).

The Fourth Symphony was a turning point in Vaughan Williams' work. First-night audiences could no longer predict what a new Vaughan Williams work would be like. He experimented in the use of dis-

sonance, combining it with strong, athletic melodies used in counterpoint. His orchestration, which had used subdued colors in his early works, became vivid and at times sparklingly light. His Eighth Symphony, written in 1956 when he was eighty-four, is one of his finest and also one of his most experimental works. Like Verdi, Vaughan Williams was a composer who continued to grow in spirit and venturesomeness throughout his life.

He received many honors, including the Order of Merit from King George V. His belief in the power and strength that a composer gets from the folk music of his own country was eloquently stated in a series of lectures later published as *National Music.* Lectures delivered at Cornell and Yale in 1954 were published in *The Making of Music,* a book filled with the wisdom of a thoughtful man.

Vaughan Williams was not a composer like Schoenberg or Stravinsky, whose music and theories about music always made headlines. But it is possible that in its own quiet yet strong way his work will last as long as any other music of its time.

Left: *Giuseppe Verdi (portrait by Nadar)*
Right: *Giuseppina Strepponi, Verdi's second wife*

VERDI, GIUSEPPE (1813–1901): the greatest of Italian opera composers. He was born in the small village of Le Roncole, near Busseto, in north-central Italy. His family was poor, but when he showed an early interest in music, they bought him a battered old spinet. The village organist gave him lessons and soon made him his assistant.

At the age of twelve, Verdi went to live in Busseto, staying with the family of Antonio Barezzi while studying with Ferdinando Provesi. Barezzi was a shopkeeper who loved music, and often a group of local musicians would gather at his house to play and sing. Verdi copied parts for the players and began to write short pieces for them. He began to think about furthering his musical education.

Barezzi agreed to finance him in his studies in Milan, and Verdi applied for admission to the conservatory there. But he was eighteen—too old to be accepted by a school which usually accepted no one over fourteen. The authorities did, however, stretch the rule enough to give Verdi an examination. He failed, both in piano and in music theory.

But Verdi was a tough-minded young man who did not easily accept defeat. Backed by Barezzi, he settled down to the study of counterpoint with Vicenzo Lavigna, a member of the musical staff of La Scala, Milan's famous opera house. Verdi heard as much opera as he could, meanwhile analyzing music by earlier Italian composers, particularly Palestrina.

Between 1834 and 1838 he spent most of his time back at Busseto, teaching and performing but continuing his studies with Lavigna. Then in 1836, amid great rejoicing, he married Margherita Barezzi, the daughter of his benefactor.

Soon Verdi's persistence began to pay off. His first opera, *Oberto,* was accepted for performance at La Scala. After months of postponement it was finally produced in 1839, and was successful enough to be bought for publication by Giovanni Ricordi, the Italian music publisher whose company eventually made a fortune from Verdi's music and, later, Puccini's.

La Scala commissioned Verdi to write two more operas. The first was to be a comic opera, *Un giorno di regno (King for a Day).* Verdi set to work on the libretto. But the household had little money, and at one point Verdi's wife pawned her jewels to buy food. Then tragedy struck. Within two months in 1840 the composer's infant son, daughter, and wife died. Verdi meanwhile struggled to finish his comic opera, and it was produced in 1840—a failure. The audience rudely, cruelly, booed and hissed the cast and the composer.

Verdi emerged from the episode with a bitterness toward the opera-going public that he never lost. Never again until *Falstaff,* near the end of his life, did he attempt to write a comic opera. Cynical and disheartened, he thought of giving up opera

A scene from Act I of Il Trovatore
(Metropolitan Opera production,
1959)

Verdi's choice of subject matter—often violent and revolutionary—struck a responsive chord in the souls of his fellow-Italians. Italy, which had been torn apart for more than a thousand years, was filled with aspirations for national unity. The Risorgimento movement was fighting against the tyranny of Austria. Even Verdi's name was a rallying point for Italians, to whom it suggested "*Vittorio Emanuele Re D'Italia.*" When Italy did achieve independence under Victor Emmanuel, Verdi was made a member of Parliament and later a senator. He attended the Senate only once—when he was installed. A fighter for democracy, Verdi knew that his time could be better spent in music than in debates.

Verdi's next opera after *Don Carlo* was *Aida,* a work commissioned for performance in Cairo to celebrate the opening of the Suez Canal. In this opera he started to break away from his old patterns of set arias and ensembles. These set pieces are still there but they come out of the drama itself, so that the action continues straight through a scene instead of being interrupted. Verdi still loved spectacles, and *Aida* is filled with triumphal processions, choruses, and dances. The opera shocked many listeners, who complained that Verdi was trying to write like Wagner. They pointed out that *Aida* contained themes which could be identified with some of the characters, like Wagnerian leitmotifs. Verdi smiled at the accusations, saying that he was an Italian who wrote Italian operas, and Wagner was a German writing German operas.

By now Verdi was rich and famous. He settled down to enjoy the good life with his second wife, Giuseppina Strepponi, a soprano whom he had married in 1859.

The death of Rossini in 1868 led to a proposal that a group of Italian composers honor the dead man by writing a Requiem Mass, each doing a portion of it. Verdi wrote his assigned text, "Libera me," but the plan for the whole work collapsed. Then when the Italian poet Manzoni died in 1873, Verdi alone composed a complete Requiem Mass in his honor. This Requiem has come to be recognized as one of the great choral-orchestral masterpieces, ranking in popularity with Mozart's Requiem and Brahms's *German Requiem.* When first performed it was attacked bitterly for its theatricality, but few questioned its beauty or effectiveness. And when so eminent a composer as Brahms came to its defense, much of the criticism quieted down.

Now, after a long and honorable career, Verdi felt that he need no longer turn out

entirely. But the manager of La Scala persuaded him to look at a new libretto based on the biblical story of Nebuchadnezzar, and the story caught his fancy. He plunged into writing the music, and when *Nabucco* was produced, in 1842, it was an immediate success.

During the next eight years Verdi wrote more than thirteen operas. Of these, *I Lombardi alla prima crociata (The Lombards on the First Crusade,* 1843); *Ernani* (1844); *Giovanna d'Arco (Joan of Arc,* 1845); and *Macbeth* (1847) were popular. The rest were at least moderately successful.

In 1851 Verdi began to compose the operas that were to make him world-famous. First came *Rigoletto* and, in 1853, *Il Trovatore (The Troubadour)* and *La Traviata* (based on *The Lady of the Camelias*), which was at first a fiasco. Then almost every other year yielded a masterpiece: *Les Vêpres siciliennes (The Sicilian Vespers),* for Paris (1855); *Simone Boccanegra,* for Venice (1857); *Un ballo in maschera (A Masked Ball),* for Rome (1859). The original version of the last-named opera, dealing with the assassination of Gustav III of Sweden, was considered so inflammatory in text that the authorities forbade its performance until the setting was changed from Sweden to Boston, Massachusetts, with a new cast of characters. These operas were followed by two of his most powerful scores: *La forza del destino (The Force of Destiny),* for St. Petersburg (1862); and *Don Carlo,* for Paris (1867).

an opera every other year. He even allowed himself the luxury of writing a string quartet—as non-theatrical a musical form as could be imagined. Perhaps, many thought, Verdi is through; maybe he is an old man who is too tired to put himself through the strenuous work of writing another opera.

But Verdi fooled everyone. His great literary and dramatic hero had always been Shakespeare. When Ricordi, the publisher, suggested an opera based on *Othello*, Verdi became interested. The brilliant young composer-librettist Arrigo Boito (1842–1918) fashioned a script that pleased him, and he set to work on what was to be his next-to-last opera.

Otello was premièred at La Scala in February, 1887. It was a great success, much to the relief of Verdi, who in composing the work had not so much discarded his earlier approaches to opera as refined and intensified them. His use of the orchestra showed his ability to evoke almost every shade and nuance of color that the instruments are capable of. But the orchestra never interferes with the voices, and so every word is heard clearly. Verdi's harmony in *Otello* is much more subtle and evocative than the harmony of his earlier operas. As for the melodies, they are, as always, superbly written for the voices. But they are not so clearly categorized into recitatives and arias, although Iago's "Credo" and Desdemona's "Salce" are true arias. Actually the music is written so that it flows naturally, following and underlining the expressive plan of the work. Much of the vocal writing is declamatory, like Mussorgsky's *Boris Godunov* and seventeenth-century French and Italian operatic recitatives before they became stilted.

After *Otello*, the world of music wondered again whether there would be any more Verdi operas. He himself had always thought about making Shakespeare's *Merry Wives of Windsor* into an opera, but his experience in the field of comic opera had been searingly bitter. Boito won him over when he showed his condensation of Shakespeare's play. Verdi went to work and the result was *Falstaff*. This, the greatest of all comic operas, is an ensemble work that sparkles with invention from start to finish. It is not produced as often as other Verdi operas, because it cannot be pulled together in the usual amount of rehearsal time that is allotted to an opera production.

Falstaff was premièred at La Scala in 1893, when Verdi was within a few months of his eightieth birthday. It was Verdi's operatic farewell to the world. With his typical ironic humor, he ended the opera

Verdi, in the garden of his Villa Sant' Agata, Milan, with his wife Giuseppina and friends

with a fugal setting of the words *Tutto nel mondo è burla* ("All the world's a joke").

But all was not finished for Verdi. In his last years he composed a group of four sacred choral works that were performed in Paris in 1898. These are puzzling, chromatic pieces, one of which, the "Ava Maria," is based on what Verdi called an "enigmatic scale": c, db, e, f♯, g♯, a♯, b, c. These choral works show that Verdi was still busily exploring new musical areas.

The composer was now eighty-five. His wife had died in 1897. In her honor Verdi had established in Milan a house of rest—the Casa di Riposo per Musicisti—for retired musicians, with money to maintain it for thirty years. When he died in 1901, he was buried next to his wife at the Casa in a simple ceremony that, following his wishes, contained no music.

A highly articulate man, Verdi was also shrewd. His letters to his friends and his librettists are full of wise comments about life and theatrical affairs. Unlike his great rival Wagner, Verdi did not go in for writing essays to explain his theories, but was content to let his works speak for themselves. He knew the stage as few composers or playwrights ever do. He rode herd on his librettists to give him dramatic texts, not literary masterpieces. He explained to them how one colorful word was worth more than an elegant stanza. He supervised the casting of his operas and haggled over details of production, always aiming for perfection.

Giuseppi Verdi, c. 1897

As for the public, Verdi looked on it with scorn. When he needed kindness at the time of the death of his first wife, the public gave him taunts. Therefore he wrote first to satisfy himself, and secondly for his audience.

In his earliest operas Verdi showed his genius for inventing melodic lines. Some of these were so simple, so artless, that they seemed always to have existed. "La donna è mobile," in *Rigoletto,* was hummed all over Italy after it was first performed (Ex. 4). He always seemed able to come up with a rousing march, as in *Aida* and *Il Trovatore.* Was it his village band experience in Busseto that had taught him how to achieve the proper martial effect? Or was it his innate sense of the theatrical—as when he based a whole scene of *La Traviata* on a brittle waltz that points up the tragedy-to-be?

Verdi's melodies have infinite variety. He can take a melodic line that is almost like that of his idol, Palestrina, and imbue it with great passion, as in *La Traviata* (Ex. 5).

There is always a carefully placed high note which serves as a "climax tone" (Ex. 6). Ends of phrases do not die out, but often take on new life as they propel the music into the next phrase. The composer is fond of writing melodies in which a key interval gradually gets smaller or larger (Ex. 7). In his early operas, the melodies are direct and almost brutally forceful. It is interesting to contrast them with most of the writing in *Otello,* which, except for Iago's "Credo," is just as direct but more sensitive and filled with more subtle nuances.

Verdi was one of the great men and great composers of the nineteenth century. For a while, some of this greatness was obscured by the wave of Wagnerianism that swept Europe, and by the popularity of the new Italian opera composer Puccini. Only a handful of his most popular operas stayed in the repertoires of the opera houses of the world. Gradually, one by one, the great Verdi operas have since been revived, and the genius of the man has been revealed.

Ex. 4 — *Rigoletto*

Con brio

Ex. 5 — *La Traviata*

Ex. 6 — Drinking Song from *La Traviata*

Ex. 7 — *La Traviata*

Lionel Hampton playing the vibraphone

VIBRAPHONE: a young relative of the xylophone, consisting essentially of thin metal bars made in different sizes so that they give off a chromatic scale when struck in order. Underneath each strip is a metal pipe that acts as a resonator. Inside each pipe is a thin metal fanlike disk which revolves on an axle activated by electricity. The revolving disk opens and closes the upper opening of the pipe, producing a vibrato. The rapidity of the vibrato can be controlled to suit the needs of the music or the style of the player.

The vibraphone is played with two or four soft beaters. Its tone is rather sweet, vibrating like a human voice. Its range is the same as that of the xylophone. Because of its newness the vibraphone has not been used much in concert music, although many contemporary composers, such as Boulez, have called for it in their scores. It is used much more in music for television and movies, in which its ability to hold tones for a long time makes it a perfect instrument to connect the end of one scene with the beginning of the next.

Red Norvo and Lionel Hampton brought the vibraphone, or "vibes," to a high position in jazz music, in which it is one of the most versatile of instruments.

VIBRATO: a slight wavering in the pitch of a tone. It is used more in slow, expressive music than in fast music, and is especially used in the playing of stringed instruments. A cellist, for instance, will produce a vibrato by rolling his left hand, putting pressure on different parts of the finger that is stopping a string; this alternately shortens and lengthens the vibrating portion of the string, thus changing the pitch. String players like to use a vibrato because it makes for a sweeter

tone; but they also depend on it to help them adjust their pitch ever so slightly as they go along.

A vibrato tone was cultivated by violinists as early as the sixteenth century, but the technique did not become essential in violin playing until the nineteenth. We have now come to expect violin tone to carry a vibrato deviating as much as an eighth of a tone above and below the pitch the violinist *thinks* he is playing. But if a vibrato is too slow and covers too wide a pitch interval, the effect is sentimental and annoying. This is especially true of a singer's vibrato, which throbs at very much the same rate as a violinist's, but which covers a wider variation in pitch—in opera singers it amounts to half a tone. The slow, ample vibrato favored by some singers would more accurately be termed a "wobble."

With wind instruments vibrato is used more in sentimental jazz ballads than in concert music. When playing in a group, wind players are careful to adjust their vibratos to produce a uniform effect. Part of the distinctive sound of such dance bands as that of Guy Lombardo lies in the extensive—but synchronized—use of vibrato. In the most complex wind instrument of all, the organ, vibrato-like effects are obtained in several ways. One way is to introduce a vibrating valve in the wind channel; this is known as a tremolo. Since the pitch is not varied, it is not a true vibrato. Another effect can be produced by resorting to the *vox humana* register, in which reed pipes tuned very slightly off pitch can produce a slow throbbing that can be particularly expressive—or obnoxious—depending on one's point of view.

Apart from the organ, only one keyboard instrument can produce a slight vibrato, and that is the clavichord. Players cultivate a trembling change in pressure—known by the German word *Bebung*—which they can apply either as they first touch a key or while the key is held down. This is a genuine vibrato (though a faint one), since the varying pressure on the key, though it does not change the *length* of the vibrating portion of the string, does succeed in changing its *tension*—and an increase in tension produces a rise in pitch.

Composers do not ordinarily write an indication for vibrato. In fact, the practice of playing with vibrato is now so widespread that they usually direct the player *not* to use vibrato when what they have in mind is a pure, "white" tone, as in the opening clarinet passage of Copland's *Appalachian Spring.*

VIOL: any of the family of six-stringed bowed instruments, related to the violin and guitar family, that flourished from the sixteenth century through the eighteenth. The viol was a flat-backed instrument with frets like those on the guitar. It had sloping shoulders as opposed to the violin's rounded ones. (An ancestor of the viol was the *vihuela de arco*, the bowed guitar of fifteenth-century Spain.)

In its earliest period the viol was held in the lap, like a guitar, and was bowed in a manner almost opposite that of the violin. Later it became larger, and players found it easier to hold between the legs, so that the name of the family became *viola da gamba:* the leg viol. Even its smallest member, the treble viol, was played in this fashion.

Three sizes of viols were developed: the treble, tenor, and bass. Their tuning was related to that of the guitar, consisting of a series of perfect fourths with a major third as the third interval from the bottom instead of being next to the top, as in the guitar:

Major
Third

The viols originated in Spain, moved to Italy, and then found their most congenial home in Tudor England. Here a repertoire for groups of viols, called "chests of viols," was written by Gibbons, Jenkins, and later Pur-

cell. The latter's fantasias for viol are among his finest works.

Strangely enough, the bass viol, similar in range to the cello, was the most durable member of the family. At first its function was to provide a bass to the higher instruments, and for a long time it was used in trio sonatas along with two violins and harpsichord, in preference to the cello. Also, at the hands of virtuoso players, it was used to play variations, or divisions, on a ground bass. It was for the bass viol—not to be confused with the double bass—that Bach wrote his three viola da gamba sonatas.

The voices of the viols were soft. Played as a consort, or family, they were perfectly suited to the restrained contrapuntal lines of late Renaissance music. They also combined well with other soft instruments such as the lute and the portable organ. But the very sweetness and softness of the viol led to its abandonment. By the late seventeenth century the violin family had proved itself much more able to hold its own in chamber music and in orchestras. Audiences demanded brilliance, and this the violin could provide much better than the viol. The last composers to write for the viols were Bach and Rameau.

As contemporary musicians have become more interested in hearing old music in its original instrumentation, there has been a revival of viol making and playing. The revival was generated by Arnold Dolmetsch (1858–1940), a French-Swiss musician and instrument maker who settled in England and started festivals of Renaissance and early Baroque music.

Above: *portrait of Johann Schenck playing the bass* viola da gamba
Below right: *the Carl Dolmetsch family playing a consort of viols*

The Juilliard String Quartet with, from left to right: Robert Mann, Isidore Cohen, Claus Adam, and Raphael Hillyer

VIOLA: the alto member of the violin family, known in French as the *alto,* in German as the *Bratsche.* It is longer and larger than the violin, so that ideally the violist should be long-armed. The viola's relation to the violin can be seen in the way the instruments are tuned:

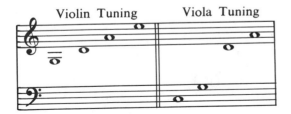

Violin Tuning   Viola Tuning

Since a violist usually plays in the region around middle C of the piano keyboard, his part is usually written in the alto clef, in which middle C is placed on the middle line of the staff:

When the part ranges too high, it is written on the treble staff.

Today we know that the viola can do almost anything the violin can do, and we especially value the distinctive sound of its lower register, a bit veiled and thick but capable of very warm tones. For many years the viola was given little to do except double the bass and cello parts an octave higher.

The man who freed the viola was Gluck, who gave it an important voice among his strings. Haydn continued this encouragement of the viola in his quartets, allowing it an active role in the give-and-take with the violins and the cello. Mozart was fond of the instrument and played it himself in quartets in his later years. He used two violas in his string quintets and wrote two beautiful duos for violin and viola as well as a *Symphonie concertante* for violin, viola, and orchestra.

Berlioz gave the viola the solo voice in his *Harold in Italy* Symphony. In Strauss's *Don Quixote* the instrument represents the character of the Don's attendant Sancho Panza. But it is in the work of contemporary composers that the viola has found the most dependable employment. Schoenberg features it in several of his chamber works; Hindemith (himself a fine violist) has written several sonatas for the instrument; and it was to the viola that Bartók turned for his last work—the Viola Concerto which was finished by his friend Tibor Serly.

From an orchestral drudge played by not-so-good violinists, the viola has gone on to become a distinctive voice with a demanding repertoire. Bartók's concerto was dedicated to William Primrose, a violist whose career has done much to establish the instrument in the eyes of the world. In more recent years accomplished instrumentalists such as Milton Katims and Walter Trampler have further secured the viola's vital role in musical life.

VIOLIN: the soprano member of the bowed string family. It is one of the most popular of all instruments, and more solo works have been written for it than for any other instrument except the piano. In large numbers the violin and its relatives—viola, cello, and double bass—form the backbone of the symphony orchestra. The greatest chamber-music works have been written for the string quartet—two violins, a viola, and a cello. The only place where the violin is not at home is in the wind band. Even dance bands have featured its singing tone.

The violin is made from about seventy carefully shaped pieces of various kinds of wood—maple, sycamore, ebony, pine, and pearwood. The pieces are glued together and then varnished. Much of the quality of tone of a violin depends on the types of woods used and on the formulas from which the glue and varnish are made. Other factors that affect it are the dimensions of the air enclosure within its wooden body, the shape of its curves, the size of its *f* holes, the quality of wood used in its sound posts— and, of course, the performer.

The length of the violin was determined by the average length of the human arm from the shoulder to the palm of the hand— between 23 and 24 inches. Smaller sizes of violin—3/4, 1/2, and even 1/16 lengths— are made for children. The strings are made from pig gut, sheep gut, steel, nylon, or gut wound with a thread of silver or aluminum. The four strings are tuned in a series of per-

Jascha Heifetz playing the violin

fect fifths, starting with the G below middle C:

The strings stretch the whole length of the instrument, from the tailpiece to a set of pegs by means of which the strings are tuned to the correct pitches.

A thin wooden bridge, which is curved, is placed on top of the body midway to the *f* holes. The bridge, which holds up the vibrating part of the strings, has small grooves cut in it to keep the strings in place. An ebony fingerboard lying under the strings at the peg end provides a hard surface against which the player presses the strings with his fingers—an action called "stopping" the strings. The part of a string that vibrates is the part between the finger and the bridge.

The violin bow consists of a wooden stick strung end to end with many strands of horsehair. The player holds the bow with the thumb on the bottom and the other four fingers balancing on the top. The bow is held at the "frog" end, which has a screw that can be turned to tighten the hair of the bow. When not using his bow, the violinist loosens its tension so that the horse hair is not permanently stretched out of shape. Resin is rubbed on the hair of the bow so that it will bite into the string rather than glide over it without making a sound.

It is the control of the bow that makes a fine violinist. The bow is held at an angle so that not all the hair is in contact with the string (the hair side faces the player). By changing the amount of pressure on the bow, the violinist can dig into the string or caress it. He can draw the bow smoothly across the strings, making connected legato tones, or he can bounce the bow for a detached staccato. He can make a tone start softly, gradually get louder, and then soften again. He can play one tone on each upstroke or downstroke of the bow, or he can play a great many notes with the left hand while the bow makes one trip across the strings. The composer or an editor indicates the direction of the bow by using the symbols ⊓ for down-bow, ∨ for up-bow. When two or more tones are to be played with the same bow stroke, the composer writes a slur over or under the notes:

Ex. 8 — The Seven Positions

(a) On the G string

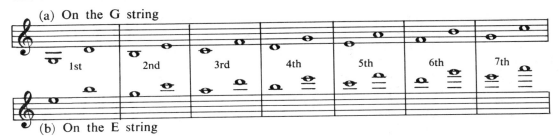

(b) On the E string

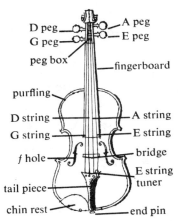

Front View

The violin is held between the left shoulder and the chin. The left hand cradles the neck of the instrument but must be free to slide from one position to another. (Violins are occasionally strung so that they can be played by left-handed violinists—the most famous of whom is Charlie Chaplin.) A string produces its lowest tone when open—that is, untouched. The violinist makes the notes of the scale by pressing his fingers down on the string in order, starting with the index finger. (The thumb is not used to stop the strings of the violin or viola.) This procedure gives the player the notes within the interval of a perfect fifth on each string in the first position. To achieve higher tones than are possible in the first position, or to facilitate the playing of certain passages, the violinist shifts to higher and higher positions by sliding his hand toward his shoulder (Ex. 8).

The violinist must have a keen sense of pitch, because he has no set of keys or valves to help him produce the correct note. There are no frets to guide his fingers, as there are on the guitar and ukulele. His hand and fingers must remember how far it is from one tone to another, and his ear must know if a tone is too high or too low. The use of a vibrato—a rocking vibration of the hand while the finger is pressed down—allows him to make small adjustments in pitch. It also gives the throbbing tone which can be so beautiful on the violin.

The violin is capable of so many things that it is almost impossible to list them all. Among the most important are the possibilities of double-stopping: the playing of two, three, or even four tones at the same time. One can play opened-out chords or arpeggios across the strings (Ex. 9a). Pizzicato can be achieved by plucking the strings. Bowed tones *(arco)* can be combined with plucked tones to produce a melody and its accompaniment simultaneously (Ex. 9b). The agitated sound called tremolo results from drawing the bow back and forth rapidly:

Romeo and Juliet, Tchaikovsky

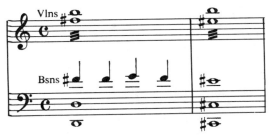

Above all, the violin comes closer than any other instrument to the sound of a beautiful human singing voice.

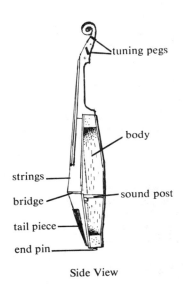

Side View

Ex. 9a — Violin Concerto, Mendelssohn

Ex. 9b — Violin Concerto, Berg

Back View

One of the special sounds of the violin is in its harmonics. These are the soft and fluty sounds the Germans call *Flageolett-töne* and the Italians *flautando*. They are produced by barely touching an open string exactly at its middle, which gives a tone an octave higher than the open string, or on the fifth note of the string (D on the G string), which sounds the octave and a fifth above the open string. The harmonics on the open strings are called natural harmonics and are limited. There is almost no limit to the number of artificial harmonics that can be produced; hence they can be used to play whole melodies. In the artificial harmonic the player barely touches a string with his little finger while stopping the string with his first finger. The resulting tone sounds two octaves higher than the stopped tone, carrying the range of the violin up to the top of the piano. The composer writes the artificial harmonic by means of two notes: the bottom shows the stopped note, and the top—which is diamond-shaped —shows the note the little finger plays. Ex. a shows a short passage written to be played as artificial harmonics; Ex. b shows the actual sound of the passage:

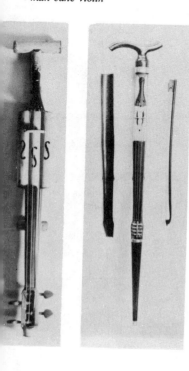

Another special effect available to violinists is given by the mute, a little comb-like device that can be clipped onto the bridge, increasing its mass. Thus weighed down, the bridge still transmits the lower vibrations from the strings to the body of the violin, but discriminates against the higher overtones. The resulting tone is both weaker and somewhat less brilliant.

No one knows who invented the violin, since it was the result of gradual changes in the many bowed stringed instruments used in Europe in the Middle Ages. Among its ancestors were the "fiddle" or *vielle,* the bottle-shaped Near-Eastern instrument that was a favorite of the minstrels and troubadours, and the *rebec,* a thin Arabian instrument that shrank to become the pocket violin—the *pochette*—of French dancing masters. In Germany the violin is called the *Geige,* a word related to gigue, or "jig"—a reminder that one of the earliest jobs for the ancestors of the violin was to play for dancing.

During the sixteenth century two types of bowed stringed instruments developed, both being called viols. One was held on the knee or between the legs; such instru-ments were called *viole da gamba,* or "leg viols." The other type was held in the arms; these were *viole da braccio,* or "arm viols." Each family developed a particular shape and a certain number of strings. Then, as larger and smaller members of the family appeared, they took the name of the family; thus the violin is the treble, or soprano, arm viol.

The earliest violin makers were Italian. (Many of them had been trained as lute makers, so that any maker or repairer of stringed instruments became known as a *luthier.*) It was in northern Italy, in Cremona, that the highest peak of violin making was attained. There the Amati family, Stradivarius, and Guarneri turned out hundreds of beautiful instruments. They experimented with sizes, shapes, wood, glues, and varnishes —usually keeping their secrets to themselves. Over a period of 150 years these men made the greatest violins the world has ever heard. They never repeated a design exactly, but always introduced little changes in design or material. Unlike other instruments, violins seem to improve with age. Concert violinists today pay large sums of money—anywhere between $20,000 and $400,000—for a violin made by one of the old masters of Cremona.

Since the death of Stradivarius, in 1737, the violin has changed very little. The bridge has been made higher to get a more brilliant tone from the strings. The strings have been wound with silver wire or even made completely from metal. The bow, in which the wood curved away from the string, as with a hunter's bow, was changed so that it curved inward, giving the violinist better control and allowing more brilliant playing. The modern bow came into being through the work of the greatest bow maker, François Tourte (1747–1835). The art of violin making has never died out, and there have been many fine instruments made in recent generations. Some concert violinists prefer an exceptionally good modern violin to one of the lesser old Italian makes.

For the first hundred years of its existence the violin family struggled with the viols for supremacy. The violin was used as early as 1581, in the orchestra that played for the first ballet, and for a while its main employment was in the theater. Its stronger tone made it a match for the wind instruments, while the viols were soft and better suited to chamber music. By the middle 1600's the violin had become firmly entrenched in opera-house orchestras; then, as the symphony orchestra grew out of the opera orchestra, it was natural to make the members of the violin family the principal performers. The Classical orchestra, for which the early symphonies were written, consisted of a string group to which were added pairs of oboes, flutes, horns, bassoons, timpani, and eventually clarinets.

The first famous instrumental group consisted of members of the violin family—the twenty-four violins of the court of Louis XIII (the *Vingt-quatre violons du roi*). This band played for court dances, entertained the king and his friends at concerts, and when called upon appeared in plays with music. The musicians wore elaborate costumes, much as bands of today have their distinctive uniforms. Charles II of England had a great admiration for all French fashions, and one of the first things he did on being crowned was to set up his own band of twenty-four violins—the "King's Musicke." This group was the "four and twenty fiddlers all of a row" of the old nursery rhyme.

The violin was brought to its high point of development in Italy, and it was natural that Italian composers should be the first to write for it. Marini and Rossi wrote works for one and two violins between 1617 and 1623. The instrument inspired a wholly new kind of music, no longer written as though for voices but containing large skips, and arpeggios, which are not difficult on the violin. Sonatas, dance suites, concerti grossi, and eventually solo concertos developed for the violin. The works of Corelli and Vivaldi explored the many different technical things that could be done on the instrument. Monteverdi had already used the effects of the pizzicato and the tremolo in his *Combat of Tancred and Clorinda* in 1624.

In Germany a different approach to the violin led to the unaccompanied sonatas and suites by Biber and J. S. Bach. Heinrich Biber (1644–1704) wrote a set of violin sonatas that attempted to portray happenings in the life of Jesus. He was among the first to experiment with different ways of tuning the violin, a process called *scordatura,* so that chords could more easily be played.

Bach's three sonatas and three partitas for unaccompanied violin are among the summit peaks of music. The violinist, all by himself, must perform incredibly difficult feats of double- and triple-stopping, play two or three melodies at the same time, and—in spite of the difficulties—always make music.

Since the time of Corelli almost every important composer has written music for the violin. New technical demands were made by such violinist-composers as Tartini, Geminiani, and Locatelli. A famous book on playing the violin—one of the great reference works for music of the 1700's—was Leopold Mozart's *Treatise on the Fundamentals of Violin-playing,* published in 1787. Leopold's son, Wolfgang, contributed six concertos for the violin and much chamber music that features the instrument, including sonatas for violin and piano—with the piano having the major share of the work.

The nineteenth century saw the more nearly equal use of violin and piano in the sonatas of Beethoven, Schubert, Schumann, Brahms, and Grieg. But in the meantime the world of violin playing had received its greatest boost in the fireworks displayed by the great Paganini. His brilliant bowing, his use of artificial harmonics, his fast double stops—all became part of the concert violinist's equipment. But not all improvement in violin technique came from Italy. A whole school of fine violin playing developed in Paris in the late 1700's. Such men as Viotti, Rode, and Baillot, less showy than Paganini, improved on the Classical, noble Italian style, emphasizing beauty of tone and expressiveness rather than the technical tricks of Paganini. It was for this style of playing that Spohr wrote his fifteen concertos, which formed the basic literature for the French school of performers. Spohr was followed by De Bériot (1802–1870) and Vieuxtemps (1820–1881), who combined

Above: *Ludwig Spohr*
Bottom left: *Eugène Ysaÿe, famous Belgian violinist*
Bottom right: *Fritz Kreisler, outstanding 20th-century violinist*

some of the virtuoso display of Paganini with more songlike melodies. Other important violinists of the nineteenth century were Ferdinand David (who gave the first performance of Mendelssohn's Violin Concerto), Joseph Joachim (friend of Mendelssohn, Schumann, and Brahms), and Leopold Auer (teacher of Heifetz, Elman, Zimbalist, and Milstein).

As violinists explored the technical features of their instrument, composers accepted all the advances and put them into their compositions, not for show but for musical reasons. Beethoven, Mendelssohn, Schumann, Brahms, Tchaikovsky, Sibelius, Elgar, and Dvořák each wrote a concerto for violin and orchestra. These concertos form the staple diet of the concert violinist. But contemporary composers have not neglected the instrument, for which fine sonatas and concertos have been written by Bartók, Honegger, Prokofiev, Stravinsky, Copland, Schoenberg, and Berg. In recent years the violin seems to have kept pace with the piano in the number of works written for it. The sounds that can be made by four fingers and a bow on four strings have not been exhausted.

VIOLONCELLO: See CELLO.

VIRGINAL: the name given to the small harpsichord in the fifteenth, sixteenth, and early seventeenth centuries. The instrument, which was also called *spinet,* could be square or rectangular, and sometimes even came in the shape of an oblong pentagon. It was often highly decorated on its lid, on the front portion of the keys, and on almost every other area that could be seen. The origin of its name has been the cause of dispute among scholars, some believing that the name came from the fact that the instrument was played mostly by young ladies, while others say the name comes from Elizabeth I, England's "Virgin Queen." Curt Sachs in his *History of Musical Instruments* traced the word back to 1463, long before the time of Elizabeth. He surmised that "virginal" came from the Latin *virga* —a jack, which is an important part of the instrument's mechanism.

The virginal was particularly popular in England around 1600. A collection of pieces for it, containing music by Byrd, Bull, and Gibbons, was published as *Parthenia* in 1611. The most famous collection of music for the virginal is the *Fitzwilliam Virginal Book,* a group of manuscripts containing tuneful dance pieces and virtuoso variations and fantasias by Byrd, Morley, and other English composers of the Elizabethan period.

A double virginal, Flemish, made by Hans Ruckers, 1581

VIRTUOSO: a performer, either instrumental or vocal, who has exceptional technical mastery of his instrument. Every great artist must have the capability of a virtuoso, but not every virtuoso is necessarily a great artist. The great artist uses his technical skill to present the inner meaning of a musical composition to his listeners. The performer who is only a technician uses his skills to show off in front of an audience, by playing or singing faster or louder than is necessary, disregarding the true spirit of the music.

Throughout the history of music the virtuoso has revealed to composers the technical resources of an instrument. In many cases the performer and composer have been one and the same. Each period of music has seen the rise of virtuosos in different fields. Among the first, in the early 1600's, were the keyboard virtuosos such as Frescobaldi, who attracted 30,000 people to his first performance in Rome, and Dr. John Bull, whose harpsichord technique was outstanding. A bit later Corelli, a violin virtuoso, founded the modern school of violin playing by his experiments in bowing and his playing of several strings at the same time. Domenico Scarlatti opened up a new world of the keyboard by writing dazzling harpsichord sonatas in which the melodies covered great ranges and demanded that two hands do the work of three.

One of the strangest and most influential virtuosos was Panteleon Hebenstreit (1669–1750). So marvelous were the effects he produced with his beaters on a dulcimer that many inventors started searching for a way to make a keyboard instrument which could also make such effects. The result was the piano.

During the early 1700's the most prominent virtuosos were singers. They dominated opera to the extent that composers were forced to write according to the singers' whims. Audiences came not so much to hear the music as to hear what a great performer such as Farinelli would do in decorating the melodies with elaborate ornaments. Virtuoso singers such as coloratura sopranos of the nineteenth century and on into our own day have continued to amaze and delight audiences with their artistry.

During the last part of the seventeenth century and the early part of the eighteenth, a school of virtuoso brass players was developed. It was for these men that Purcell, Bach, and Handel wrote their brilliant trumpet parts. In the early 1800's the technical abilities of Dragonetti, the foremost double-bass virtuoso, led Beethoven to give this instrument more to do than just support the orchestra. Dragonetti had shown in his concertos that the double bass could be almost as agile as the cello. The clarinetists J. S. Hermstadt and Karl Barmann inspired Weber, Spohr, and Mendelssohn to write works that are important foundations of clarinet literature.

Mozart's early fame was as a keyboard virtuoso. He put many brilliant passages into his piano concertos because his audiences expected such display from him. He was followed in the early 1800's by a large number of piano virtuosos: Clementi, Cramer, Hummel, Dussek, in addition to Beethoven and Weber. Chopin and Mendelssohn brought to piano playing a form of virtuosity in terms of tonal control, drawing from their instrument a wide range of poetic expression. But it was the brilliance of Franz Liszt that did the most to change the technique of piano playing. He and Paganini—the "wizard" of the violin—led the way in devising sounds on their instruments that had not been heard up to that time. Many of Liszt's and Paganini's tricks were for display only. They knew this themselves but gave audiences what they seemed to want. It was their followers, less talented, who perfected tricks that had no musical reason for being. One pianist, for example, made a career for himself by playing Chopin's *Revolutionary Étude* with the difficult left-hand part in octaves—a trick that he worked countless hours to perfect.

The end of the nineteenth century and the beginning of the twentieth saw large crops of virtuosos appear, many from Russia and Poland: Hoffman, Godowsky, Rosenthal, De Pachmann on the piano; Sarasate, Kreisler, Heifetz, Elman, and Zimbalist on the violin. The most recent field for the virtuoso is that of conducting. Such men as Toscanini, Koussevitzky (who started his career as a virtuoso double-bass player), Reiner, Ormandy, Stokowski, Karajan, and Szell have made audiences aware of the virtuoso conductor. Of course, such a conductor must have a virtuoso orchestra. Such are the Philadelphia Orchestra, the Boston Symphony Orchestra, the Cleveland Orchestra, the New York Philharmonic, and the Chicago Symphony.

Today every fine performing artist must necessarily be a virtuoso. It is expected that he will be able to dash off a difficult showpiece as well as give a beautiful performance of a Bach fugue or a slow movement of a Mozart sonata.

A portrait of John Bull done in 1589, when he was 27

Caricature of Vivaldi by Ghezzi, 1723

A view of Venice showing the Hospitale (Ospedale) della Pietà, the music conservatory in which Vivaldi worked

VIVALDI, ANTONIO (*c.* 1675–1741): Italian composer, one of the most prolific and inventive of the Baroque period. Born in Venice, he received his earliest music lessons probably from his father, a violinist in the orchestra at St. Mark's Cathedral. Later he studied with Giovanni Legrenzi (1626–90), noted composer and leader of the orchestra of St. Mark's. Ordained as a priest—he was called the "Red Priest" because of the color of his hair—Vivaldi served only a short time in the church. In 1703 or 1704 he became a teacher, and later conductor and director of music at the music conservatory of the Ospedale della Pietà in Venice.

This conservatory, like others in Italy, was a home for orphan girls. The talented ones were given thorough instruction in music, and in return performed at important church services. In cities where musical attention was centered around opera, performances at the charity schools fulfilled purposes much like those of present-day choirs and symphony orchestras. Many of the most famous Italian musicians were associated with the conservatories at one time or another.

It was for an orchestra of young girls that Vivaldi turned out his more than 400 concertos. He was always trying to keep up with the demand for new material just as Bach did in writing his weekly cantatas.

But Vivaldi often took leaves of absence from the conservatory, and he managed to write more than forty operas for Venice and other cities in Italy and Germany. In the last year of his life he moved to Vienna, hoping to capitalize on his talents at one of the richest courts in Europe. Unfortunately things turned out badly for him and he died poor.

Vivaldi was best known in his lifetime for his operas, oratorios, and cantatas, but his present fame is due to his instrumental music. While his concertos used many of the idioms and formal ideas of his immediate predecessors, Corelli and Torelli, his fertile mind carried the Baroque concerto style into new realms. At times his music suggests the early works of Haydn and Mozart, and undoubtedly it influenced the Classical symphony and concerto.

Most of Vivaldi's concertos were written for from one to four solo violins. He experimented with many other solo instruments, too, including flute, trumpet, and bassoon. Always looking for new sounds, he was one of the first composers to make use of the newly invented clarinet.

Vivaldi's concertos follow a three-movement plan. First comes a bustling allegro written in ritornello form. In this movement the orchestra of strings and a keyboard instrument states a short, clear theme based on the primary chords of the

A presumed painting of Vivaldi owned by the Music Conservatory of Bologna

key or on a scale passage outlining the tones of the key. This theme is restated in various keys, with the soloist playing long virtuoso passages between the statements. Sometimes the solo part is based on fragments of the ritornello theme; at other times it ignores the principal themes and brings in new material. There is counterpoint primarily between the soprano and bass parts, and the counterpoint is never so complex that it obscures the prima-donna role of the soloist.

The second movement is a slow adagio, an aria that allows the soloist to play in a highly expressive manner and to show off his ability to improvise decorations on the melody—decorations similar to the embellishments introduced by singers.

The final movement is in a form similar to that of the first movement but with more virtuoso passages.

Some of the importance of Vivaldi's concertos is due to their influence on J. S. Bach, who not only studied them carefully but also arranged six of Vivaldi's violin concertos for solo harpsichord. Bach also arranged four of Vivaldi's concertos for organ, and another (orginally for four violins) for four harpsichords.

Vivaldi was interested in program music, and one of his most popular works is a group of four concertos, *Le quattro stagione (The Four Seasons),* in which he portrays his feelings about spring, summer, autumn, and winter.

Most of Vivaldi's music remains unpublished. A society was organized by the American conductor Max Goberman to record and publish all of Vivaldi's instrumental music, but Goberman died in 1963 before completing this most important and ambitious undertaking.

VOICE: the first, and still the most important, musical instrument. More music has been composed for this instrument than for any other. It is the richest in timbre, having the greatest number of overtones in its composite tone. It is the easiest instrument to use, as even a newborn baby soon learns, and perhaps the most difficult to master.

Vocal sounds are made by forcing air from the lungs through a set of muscles in the throat: the "vocal cords." By tightening or loosening the vocal cords a singer can achieve higher or lower tones. All children have high voices, but as boys reach the age of puberty a change in their vocal cords deepens their voices.

The quality of a singer's voice depends on what happens to the sound after it leaves the vocal cords. Cavities in the head and body act as resonators, just as the body of a brass instrument amplifies and modifies the tone produced by the action of the lips against the mouthpiece. A good singer uses his lips, his jaw, his throat, his tongue, and his ribs to make the desired kind of tone. Because most of the tone-producing mechanism of the voice is hidden from view, vocal teaching is the most difficult and most misunderstood area of musical training. The difficulties are increased by the fact that it is hard for anyone to hear himself as others hear him.

The kind of vocal sound that is admired varies thoughout the world. In European cultures the smooth-sounding "bel canto" is most in evidence, although in popular music certain kinds of shouting tones or nasal twangs have been favored. Some peoples like "pinched" or high thin tones (Eastern Asia); others use grunts and falsettos (certain American Indian tribes). Spanish gypsy flamenco singers seem to "orchestrate" their voices, going from somewhat harsh low tones to smoother lyrical passages. Much depends on the language being used; bel canto, for example, is perfectly suited to the liquid Italian language, with its many open vowels. A language that uses many consonants or "i" or "ee" sounds will naturally favor a form of vocal production different from bel canto.

Voices are classified in terms of their

Detail from the 15th-century cantoria of Luca della Robbia, Florence

ranges and their quality. There are three ranges in women's voices and three in men's, thus:

Soprano   Mezzo-soprano Alto

Women

Tenor   Baritone   Bass

Men

Not every voice can achieve all the tones within a given range. On the other hand, a few singers, because of training or natural ability, can sing far above or below the normal range. A coloratura soprano, for example, might be able to produce tones that lie an octave above the top of the usual soprano range. A *basso profundo* might be able to sing an octave below the usual bass level. Falsetto tones are used by male singers to add another octave to their top limits, making what is, in effect, the sound of a male alto or male soprano.

Singers have always played important roles in history, from the time of Orpheus and the Sirens in Greek mythology to the Carusos and Flagstads of recent times and the Callases, Sutherlands, and Fischer-Dieskaus of the present. Equally important in contemporary life are the voices that have entertained tens of millions: the Mermans, Sinatras, Crosbys, and Beatles.

WAGNER, RICHARD (1813–83): the German composer whose music and ideas, as expressed in his operas and essays, made him one of the most important and controversial men of the nineteenth century.

Wagner was born in Leipzig, Germany. Unlike most great composers, he had very little training in music. His father, a clerk in the local police court, died when the boy was less than a year old. Shortly thereafter the widow married Ludwig Geyer, an actor, and the family moved to Dresden. Wagner had a few lessons at the piano when he was twelve years old and, being quite ambitious, immediately tried to play his favorite opera score, Weber's *Der Freischütz.* Six years after the death of his stepfather, in 1821, the family moved back to Leipzig. Here Wagner was strongly influenced by his scholarly uncle Adolph. At fourteen Wagner, whose literary fare was Shakespeare, Goethe, Dante, and the Greek myths, wrote a tragic drama, *Leubald and Adelaïde,* full of violence, ghosts, witchcraft, and love. Deciding to make an opera out of his drama, he started to study music theory on his own. He had a few lessons with a local organist and began to compose.

Wagner's sisters and a brother were already involved in opera and theater. The mother, aware of the difficulties and uncertainties of theatrical life, tried to keep Wagner away from the arts. His urge was too strong, however, and he threw himself into the study of Beethoven's scores, going so far as to make a piano arrangement of the Ninth Symphony and even trying to play the violin. By 1830 Wagner had written an Overture in C, a Piano Sonata, and an Overture in B-flat. This last work, featuring a solo kettledrum beat every five measures, was performed on Christmas eve, 1830, much to the amazement and merriment of the audience.

For a while Wagner was a student at the University of Leipzig, being particularly interested in philosophy. There he had, for the only time in his life, the discipline of a course in music theory. His teacher was Theodore Weinlig, the gentle musical director of St. Thomas' Church—the church served so well by J. S. Bach. Weinlig made Wagner promise to forget composition while devoting himself to rigorous exercises in harmony and counterpoint for a period of six months. Eventually, having mastered counterpoint and fugue to Weinlig's satisfaction, the student was freed and told to write a sonata (which Weinlig subsequently had published), a fantasia, and three orchestral overtures. The success of these works led Wagner to write a Symphony in C, which was performed in Prague in 1832.

Deciding that it was time to start earning his living, Wagner became the choirmaster at the theater in Würzburg—a job obtained for him by his brother. Feeling ill-equipped for his post, Wagner devoted himself to the study and performance of scores by Marschner and Meyerbeer. Publicly he disliked the music of the latter composer; privately he learned much from him, theatrically and orchestrally.

The year 1833 was an important one for Wagner. It was the year of his first job and the completion of his first opera: *Die Feen (The Fairies).* The latter had to wait fifty years for its first performance, but its completion was a great success for the young composer.

Wagner now launched himself on a career as conductor, first at the Magdeburg theater, then in Königsberg, and finally in Riga. In Königsberg he married the actress Minna Planer. During the years 1834 to 1839 he managed to compose *Das Liebesverbot (Forbidden Love),* a frothy Italian type of opera based on Shakespeare's *Measure for Measure,* and he started on *Rienzi,* a big work in five acts calling for a large cast and a large orchestra.

Rienzi was in the new style of grand opera which, at the hands of Rossini and Meyerbeer, had proved so successful in Paris. Deciding that his greatest opportunity lay in that city, Wagner took his wife and set sail from a Prussian port in a small passenger boat. The first part of the voyage, to London, was a stormy one, lasting three weeks instead of the scheduled eight days. The storm-tossed waters made a great impression on Wagner, who had already begun to think about writing an opera based on the legend of the Flying Dutchman, in which the captain of a phantom ship roves the world seeking the woman who, through love, can free him from the curse under which he must wander forever.

Wagner went from London to Boulogne, where Meyerbeer gave him letters to people who might help him in Paris. Finally arriving in that city, Wagner set about seeing these people. Desperate for funds, he supported himself and his wife by doing all sorts of odd jobs, such as making piano arrangements of Donizetti's and Halévy's operas and writing music criticisms for a German music journal. For a while he arranged cornet solos based on popular operatic airs.

While busily trying to eke out a living and arrange for a production of *Rienzi,*

Minna Wagner

Top: *a scene from* The Flying Dutchman, *Act II (1965 Bayreuth Theater production)*
Bottom: The Flying Dutchman, *Act I (1959 Bayreuth Theater production)*

At right: *Richard Wagner, c. 1872*

Wagner went ahead with other projects. He wrote the first movement of. a *Faust* symphony, which later, on the advice of Franz Liszt, became the *Faust Overture*. Obsessed with the Flying Dutchman legend, Wagner wrote a libretto on the subject, hoping to get a commission to write the score for the Paris Opéra. The director of the Opéra forthwith bought the libretto—and gave the commission to a composer named Dietsch. Wagner, distressed about the whole matter, decided to go ahead with his own version of the Flying Dutchman, and he finished it in less than two months.

In 1842 fortune began to smile on the young composer. *Rienzi* was accepted for performance at Dresden and, when it proved to be a success, *Der Fliegende Holländer (The Flying Dutchman)* also was performed. Wagner was appointed conductor of the opera in Dresden in 1843 and filled the post with distinction for the next six years. In addition to conducting the operatic masterpieces of Gluck, Weber, Mozart, and Beethoven, he directed a choral group and worked on his next opera, *Tannhäuser*.

Through his study of Grimm's German mythology, Wagner had begun to delve more and more into medieval German history. From the medieval period came the story of Tannhäuser, the noble poet-musician who reveled with the goddess Venus, distressed his friends by extolling her delights in a contest of song, then in penance joined a group of pilgrims going to Rome, and was given salvation through the death and prayers of his saintly loved one, Elizabeth. The first performances of *Tannhäuser*, in Dresden in 1845, were only partially successful—but more so than the Paris production of 1861. In the latter Wagner extended the wild bacchanal with which the opera opens, giving more opportunities to the dancers, who were indispensable to Paris productions. He hoped by so doing to forestall criticism from the Parisian opera-public, which expected a ballet in the second act of any opera regardless of dramatic necessity. When the Parisians discovered that their ballet came at the beginning, they caused a series of uproars that resulted in the withdrawal of *Tannhäuser* after only three performances.

After *Tannhäuser* Wagner worked on the libretto and music of another opera based on a medieval German legend, the story of Lohengrin. In this Wagner used leitmotifs much more extensively than in his previous operas. *Lohengrin* was finished in 1848 but was not produced until two years later, at Weimar, under the direction of Liszt.

Meanwhile Wagner had become involved in the political revolutions that swept over much of Europe in 1848 and 1849. To avoid arrest and possible imprisonment he fled from Dresden, first to visit Liszt in Weimar and then to Zürich in Switzerland.

With *Lohengrin* Wagner had arrived at a turning point in his life. He realized that opera had now become a form of spectacular entertainment, not something to be taken seriously. The lofty ideals of serious drama, to be lifted to even greater heights through music, had disappeared. Yet he believed this great art form should express ideas of the deepest significance. Accordingly Wagner began taking a fresh look at the forms of opera and their possibilities, dealing with them in his essays and books— *Art and Revolution, Opera and Drama, The Artwork of the Future*.

Wagner's thoughts crystallized into a philosophy that he resolved to express in his works. He did not call these works operas, but rather music dramas—with emphasis on "drama." Clearly, no one else could properly put into words what Wagner felt, and he set about writing the series of poems that would become the libretto for *Der Ring des Nibelungen (The Ring of the Nibelungs)*. These poems were based on old Scandinavian and Germanic legends, which Wagner changed when necessary to fit his dramatic purpose. The words of the poems were carefully chosen for sound, with much use of alliteration. The first poem was begun in 1848; the entire project was to take twenty-six years, with time out for the operas *Tristan und Isolde* and *Die Meistersinger von Nürnberg (The Mastersingers of Nuremberg)*.

Only a man with complete faith in himself could have undertaken an opera that would take four evenings to perform. Wag-

Leone Rysanek as Elsa in the bridal procession, Act II, of Lohengrin *(1958 Bayreuth Theater production)*

Mathilde Wesendonck

ner probably did not realize the magnitude of his undertaking when he started his libretto for the opera that was to be called *Siegfried's Death*. But as he worked he realized that much had to be explained, and the result was four operas: *Das Rheingold (The Rhine Gold); Die Walküre (The Valkyrie), Siegfried,* and *Götterdämmerung (Twilight of the Gods).*

After finishing the libretto for *The Ring* in 1852, Wagner tried once more for success in Paris—and met with the same rebuffs as before. Again he retired to Zürich to work on his poems and the *Rheingold* score, and to be visited at intervals by Liszt, who brought the news from the world of music. Discovering the works of the philosopher Arthur Schopenhauer, and inspired by the mood of his speculations, Wagner began thinking of an opera based on the story of the ill-fated love of Tristan and Isolde.

In 1855 Wagner went to London to conduct a series of concerts by the London Philharmonic Society. These were successful, but to Wagner the most important part of his London stay was getting to know Berlioz, a composer whom he admired in an uneasy and grudging way.

In 1857 Wagner and his wife Minna went to live on the estate of Otto Wesendonck, a wealthy silk merchant in Zürich. Wagner had fallen in love with his host's wife, Mathilde. Dropping his work on *The Ring* (*Das Rheingold* had been completed in 1854 and *Die Walküre* in 1856), he poured his love for Mathilde into the libretto for *Tristan and Isolde,* finishing it early in the year. He also wrote five songs in the "Tristan" style to poems written by Mathilde.

Minna, for whom life was increasingly difficult, left Wagner and did not become reunited with him until 1859 in Paris. In 1861 she left him for good and returned to Dresden, where she died in 1866.

In 1858, Wagner went to Venice and devoted himself to the music of *Tristan,* writing part of it in Venice and completing it in Lucerne in 1859. The next job was to find an opera house that would produce it. Fortunately for Wagner, in 1860 his political activities were forgiven and he was free to travel and live once more in Germany, except in the area of Dresden, from which he was barred until 1862.

After several visits to Vienna, Wagner convinced the authorities at the opera house that *Tristan* was a work they should produce. The cast and the orchestra set to work on the score but found it, for them, unsingable and unplayable, and after fifty-four rehearsals the production was called off. Not until 1865, in Munich, was the composer to hear his work presented.

Wagner interrupted his work on *The Ring* to devote his thoughts to another opera that had been germinating in his mind for many years. This was to be a light little work based on the song contests of the sixteenth-century mastersingers. The libretto and music occupied much of Wagner's time from 1861 to 1867. The result was his one sunny opera, *Die Meistersinger,* which contains some of his most inspired music. Actually it is not a "little" thing but an opera calling for a large cast, large orchestra, and considerable scenic effects.

In 1864 Wagner was in desperate financial plight, not knowing where to turn for help. At this point, one of the many benefactors who helped him throughout his life came to the rescue. Young King Ludwig II, who had just become ruler of Bavaria, was full of romantic notions about becoming the greatest patron of the arts in Europe. Ludwig invited Wagner to join him in Munich, and there in the next few years a series of Wagnerian works were given their first performances: *Tristan and Isolde* (1865), *Die Meistersinger* (1868), *Das Rheingold* (1869), and *Die Walküre* (1870).

But Wagner's stay in Bavaria was comparatively brief. He ran into trouble with political and musical groups who accused him of exerting too much influence on the king. His proposals for a great music school and a new kind of theater were abandoned when their probable costs became known. Socially, Wagner was unpopular because he and his wife had separated and he was infatuated with Cosima von Bülow, the daughter of Liszt and the wife of one of Wagner's best friends.

Like the Flying Dutchman, Wagner could find no place to stop. King Ludwig, under much pressure from Wagner's enemies, was forced to ask the composer to leave Bavaria, although he was allowed to visit Munich from time to time. In the spring of 1866 Wagner moved to Triebschen, on Lake Lucerne in Switzerland, to settle down and finish the operas of *The Ring*. There he began work also on the libretto for another opera he had been contemplating, based on the teachings of Jesus. This was put aside for a libretto, in sketch form, based on the ideas of Buddhism; but the latter too was abandoned in favor of *Parsifal,* which was to be his final opera.

Success now began to crown Wagner's operatic projects. Triebschen was a haven where he could work without becoming involved in non-creative affairs. In 1870 he solved a long-standing problem by marrying Cosima. On Christmas day of that year, Wagner surprised her with the playing of the *Siegfried Idyll,* written in honor of their son Siegfried and performed to celebrate her birthday.

For a long time Wagner had been thinking of establishing his own theater, where his operas could be performed under the best possible conditions. In 1872 an offer of land came from the city of Bayreuth, and plans based on ideas of an architect named Sember were drawn up by Wagner for the Bayreuth *Festspielhaus.* Money came in from private contributors and from the many Wagner societies that were springing up all over Europe and America. In this theater of his own, in 1876, Wagner had the satisfaction of seeing *The Ring of the Nibelungs* performed in its entirety.

The *Festspielhaus* was built so that Wagner's operas could be heard and seen to the best advantage. There are no balconies or boxes—only one floor of seats, which rises and opens out in a fan shape. The stage seems to be a continuation of the auditorium, because the orchestra pit is submerged and hidden from the view of the audience. (Singers like this plan because they can hear the orchestra much better than with the conventional orchestra pit.) The fan-shaped theater has gradually become accepted as a practical design and has been used in many later auditoriums.

Wagner also built for himself in Bayreuth a "dream house": Wahnfried. In this house—destroyed in World War II—he and Cosima planned productions and raised their family. *Parsifal,* the "holy" opera,

was finished and performed at Bayreuth in 1882. For Wagner it was an act of faith, a religious work not to be thought of in the same terms as other operas. Its performance outside Bayreuth was forbidden until the expiration of its copyright in 1913.

All Wagner's projects seemed to have been pulled together at last. *The Ring* and *Parsifal* were complete, his theater had become a reality, his family life was on an even keel, his prose essays had been published in an authorized version, and he was honored in all parts of the world. His many exertions, however, had undermined his health. To recuperate, he returned in 1882 to his favorite vacation place, Venice. There he suffered a heart attack and died on February 13, 1883. His body was buried in the garden of Wahnfried.

The arguments and discussions about Wagner's music did not cease with his death. He was attacked by the supporters of Brahms, although not by Brahms himself. He was hailed by many younger musicians, who flocked to the banner of the "Music of the Future." Books about the man and his music began to pour from the printing presses. Music theorists analyzed his harmonies, philosophers dissected his ideas, and friends wrote their reminiscences. Guidebooks telling the stories of the operas and listing the leitmotifs appeared in many languages. The performances of Wagner's works increased until they matched in number those of his great contemporary Verdi.

Wagner's achievements were stupendous. His concept of opera, or "music drama," as he preferred to call it, went beyond that of any previous composer. His genius elevated opera to an art form in which the deepest ideas could be expressed. His plans were so vast that only he could write the librettos, and for the music he had to burst the traditional bonds of melody and harmony, add new instruments to the orchestra, and train a new type of singer who could project above the large orchestra in the pit.

Wagner's stage works, particularly after *Lohengrin,* combine narrative form with the symphonic. Leitmotifs gave his work rich connotations as well as a strong, diversified structural fabric. The introduction to the second act of *Tristan,* for example, gives a hint of the tragedy to come, yet has a restless, impatient section that rises to a seething climax of ardor and ecstasy, then subsides as the curtain rises. All is accomplished through the use of four short motives that are manipulated in sequence—one of Wagner's most-used compositional devices. The form is not traditional; the music seems to

The Festspielhaus at Bayreuth

Cosima Wagner

Cosima and Richard Wagner, 1870

arch from an enigmatic beginning up to a climax and down again.

The music in the later operas flows continuously from the beginning of a scene to the end. "Set" pieces are very rare, and there are no recitatives and arias in the usual sense. For each opera Wagner invented a slightly different style. Thus *Tristan* had to be highly chromatic to suit the passionate, emotional quality of the story. *Parsifal* is alternately diatonically "pure" and sensuously chromatic. *Die Meistersinger* is squarely tonal and harmonically diatonic, as befits its subject matter. *The Ring,* which ranges over all the darker and more intense emotions, is harmonically complex as well as chromatic.

Wagner was probably the greatest psychologist who ever wrote music. He knew exactly which chord or chord progression would touch off the proper emotional response in his listeners. Not only were his harmony, melody, and words used in telling fashion, but the potentialities of the instruments were fully exercised. The passion and longing of *Tristan and Isolde* are brought out by glowing string sonorities and the melancholy sounds of the low woodwinds such as the clarinet and English horn. In *Die Meistersinger* the orchestral colors are brighter as Wagner uses sonorous chords in the brass, string lines that weave a continuous web of counterpoint, and perky little themes for the woodwinds.

The four-opera *Ring of the Nibelungs* was a large musical mural, painted with many instrumental colors. The leitmotifs were given to instruments that brought out the full character of the themes: dark registers of winds for dark themes, and the brass as solo instruments, or as a choir, for heroic themes. Each group was divided in many ways. Mixtures of instruments from different choirs offered almost endless possibilities. The use of full woodwind and brass choirs freed the strings for soaring, surging climaxes, for expression boiling with excitement, for short themes darting from section to section. In tender passages the strings could become an eight-, ten-, or twelve-voiced choir spread over slowly changing chromatic harmonies.

The brass sometimes served as background, holding chords in long notes, but Wagner's use of the brass choir is most noticed as the music builds in a long crescendo. Climax piles on top of climax, stirring the pulse of the listener with increasing intensity. To fill out his brass choir of trumpets, horns, trombones, and bass tuba, Wagner added a quartet of "Wagner tu-

bas," which in tone color were somewhere between the conventional tuba and the French horn.

Wagner was most inspired in the field of harmony. The type of chord, how long it was to last, and how it was spread over the instruments—all this was determined by the dramatic situation. Rich seventh and ninth chords, often in strings and woodwinds, accompany tender moods. Heroic ideas are portrayed by solid, almost traditional harmonies. Evil or "dark" situations call for seventh or ninth chords that are distorted with flatted fifths or ninths. His "endless melody" is based on "endless harmony" in which chords resolve, not traditionally but unexpectedly.

Like many other outstanding persons Wagner touched off arguments and furors with everything he did—in his thirteen operas, in his many volumes of essays, in his autobiography, in his way of life. Although many of his ideas now seem conventional, a century ago they were revolutionary, precipitating arguments for and against Wagner that last to this day. In both his works and his life Wagner summed up Romantic music and thought, so that after him music had to find new directions altogether. His music, particularly *Tristan and Isolde,* led to later music in which a sense of key is done away with. Reacting against the passionate emotional quality of Wagner's music, many composers, especially the French Debussy and Satie, went to the opposite extreme of coolness and sparseness.

Wagner has been the subject of more books and more articles than any other composer. He has been called both "monster" and "genius." His ideas and his music have motivated books by such famous authors as Shaw, Mann, Nietzsche, and Baudelaire. Only Wagner, of all composers, is much discussed in college philosophy and literature classes as well as in music classes. Even now, more than eighty years after his death, he remains controversial, although his works are well established in the opera houses and concert halls of the world.

Today Wagner's works form the backbone of German opera. Bayreuth has been perpetuated as the great Wagnerian center, first under the supervision of Cosima Wagner, then under their son Siegfried, and later under a grandson. The scenic designs and lighting have changed, but the music is still presented under the conditions Wagner himself laid down. The arguments about the man and his theories will gradually die away, but his music has a secure place in history.

WALTZ: a lilting dance in fast triple meter. In the nineteenth century, its swinging motion so expressed the Romantic spirit of the times that it dominated the ballroom and the minds of many composers. The music for the waltz is uncomplicated and direct, being principally a songful melody over a simple accompaniment. The sections of the music are usually sixteen measures in length.

The waltz came into popularity at the end of the eighteenth century, as the highly formal minuet and other French court dances were, like the French monarchy itself, swept aside. The new spirit of freedom in the world called for a social dance that could express the character of the times. The freshness and gracefulness of the waltz appealed especially to young couples who, despite the objections of their elders, delighted in holding each other in their arms as they yielded to the intoxicating, exhilarating rhythm of the dance.

The ancestors of the waltz were the moderately paced turning and gliding dances of Germany and Austria: the *Drehtanz* and the *Ländler*. These peasant dances were lusty and somewhat heavy; the men accented the rhythm with their hobnailed boots. The true home of the waltz was Vienna, where as early as 1776 Vicente Martín y Soler wrote a waltz in his opera *Una cosa rara*. Ländler and slow waltzes began to appear in the music of Haydn, Mozart, and Beethoven, but it was Schubert who, in the early 1800's, brought the music for these dances to its first high point.

As the dancers became less restrained in their movements, the tempo of the waltz quickened. The three strong beats per measure gave way to a strong downbeat and two faint afterbeats, so that actually the Viennese waltz is conducted as though it had one beat per measure. The effect of this is a lightness that appealed both to dancers and to choreographers. During the nineteenth century many Romantic ballets featured waltzes done by the corps de ballet.

As the waltz swept the ballrooms of Europe, it also kindled the imaginations of composers, and many wrote waltzes in their concert music. Among the first was Carl Maria von Weber, whose *Invitation to the Dance* remains one of the most evocative series of waltzes. Berlioz boldly wrote a waltz movement instead of the traditional minuet or scherzo in his *Symphonie fantastique*. Chopin's waltzes combine the tender passion of the dance with the composer's own poetic style.

Waltzing couple (an 1844 lithograph)

The spirit of the Viennese "waltz kings" —Schubert, Lanner, and the Strausses— suffuses the music of many composers who lived and wrote in that beautiful city on the Danube. One thinks of Brahms's nostalgic *Liebeslieder* waltzes for vocal quartet and piano, four hands, as well as his sixteen waltzes for piano solo or duet, and of Richard Strauss's waltzes in his operas *Der Rosenkavalier* and *Arabella*. And naturally the waltz dominated the Viennese operettas of Lehár, Friml, and Romberg.

The waltz, however, knew no boundaries. It spread out from Vienna to the whole world, appealing to composers of many lands. Among these was Tchaikovsky, whose lyrical waltzes in his ballets, operas, and instrumental music are among the loveliest of all. There was Offenbach, whose waltzes in his Parisian operettas are sparkling and at the same time sentimental. Ravel, looking regretfully at the fading glories of Vienna, wrote *Valses nobles et sentimentales* for piano and a choreographic poem for orchestra, *La Valse*.

The waltz has had a varied career in America. Here its popularity came late in the nineteenth century, particularly in a slow version know as the "Boston." During the 1890's such waltz songs as "East Side, West Side" and "In the Good Old Summertime" dominated the popular music of the day. America's favorite composer of operettas, Victor Herbert, turned to the rhythm of the slow waltz for such song hits

Joseph Lanner

as "Kiss Me Again" and "Just a Kiss in the Dark."

With the growing popularity of the tango and fox trot as dances in the 1920's, the waltz as a social dance was on its way to becoming a rarity. Gradually, however, its popularity has been reasserted, particularly through the waltz songs of Irving Berlin ("All Alone"), Jerome Kern ("The Touch of Your Hand"), and Richard Rodgers ("Falling in Love with Love").

WEBER, CARL MARIA VON (1786–1826): one of the first of the German Romantic composers. He was successful in opera, chamber music, and concertos.

Weber was born in Eutin, northwestern Germany, where his father was a pretentious but mediocre violist and double-bassist. A cousin of Weber's having married Mozart, Weber's father looked at his three sons, hoping to find a prodigy within his own family. The two older boys did have talent and were placed under the tutelage of Haydn in Vienna. Carl Maria, however, seemed destined not to be a musician, and the father tried to make him a painter.

The father started a traveling theater company, and young Carl Maria grew up backstage—an experience that was later to be of much benefit to him. When he was ten years old, his father settled for a while in Hildburghausen, where the boy had les-

Carl Maria von Weber

sons in piano and composition with an excellent local musician, J. P. Heuschkel. It was Heuschkel who convinced the father that Carl Maria had great musical talent.

In 1798 the Webers moved to Salzburg, where Carl Maria sang in the cathedral under the direction of Michael Haydn, brother of the great composer. Haydn was so impressed with Weber's talent that he gave him free lessons in composition. The boy wrote six short fugues, and his father immediately had those published. But the restless man decided to move to Munich, and so the lessons with Haydn came to an end.

In Munich, Weber continued to study piano and voice, meanwhile writing his first opera, sonatas, and variations—most of which he later burned. He met Aloys Senefelder, the inventor of lithography, and became proficient enough to lithograph his Opus 2, a set of variations. He and his father decided to set up their own lithography shop in Freiberg. But here Weber lost his interest in lithography, for he was given an opera libretto to set to music. The opera, *Das Waldmädchen (The Forest Maiden)*, was produced in Freiberg in 1800, six days after Carl Maria's fourteenth birthday, and later it had a modest success in Vienna, Prague, and St. Petersburg.

In 1801 the Webers moved back to Salzburg, where in the same year another opera by Carl Maria, *Peter Schmoll und seine Nachbarn (Peter Schmoll and His Neighbors)* was produced, with only moderate success. Once again the family moved, this time to Hamburg, where Weber discovered the world of music theory through study of C. P. E. Bach's *Essay on the True Art of Playing Keyboard Instruments*. The young musician, now sixteen, began to think of writing a dictionary and a history of music.

A return to Vienna in 1803 resulted in a meeting with the Abbé Vogler, a famous theorist and composer. Vogler put Weber to work analyzing intensively the works of the great masters. In return for lessons, Weber made piano scores of the Abbé's operas.

Convinced of the youth's promise, Vogler secured a job for him as conductor at the Breslau theater. But things were difficult. The eighteen-year-old conductor had trouble with his orchestra and singers, all of whom were much older than he. Weber made many friends, but an opposing faction made the situation unbearable, and in 1806 he resigned.

For a while Weber lived at the castle belonging to Duke Eugen of Württemberg.

Here he was in charge of musical affairs, and for the duke's excellent little orchestra he wrote two symphonies (both in C) and a concerto for horn. Weber tried to arrange a piano concert tour, but the Napoleonic Wars upset his plans, and after giving a few concerts he took a post as secretary to Duke Ludwig of Württemberg at Stuttgart. This job included managing the duke's shaky budget and stalling off creditors. But Weber enjoyed an active social life and improved his education by reading philosophical works he found in the duke's library. He even found time to write several works for piano, including a set of six pieces for piano duet as well as thirteen songs and solo works for various instruments.

Accused of accepting a bribe to keep a wealthy young man out of the army, Weber was thrown into jail by the king of Württemberg. His opera *Das Waldmädchen,* revised and called *Silvana,* had been scheduled for a performance early in 1810, but the king canceled it. Weber was released from jail but banished from Württemberg.

Much chastened, Weber moved to Mannheim and then on to Darmstadt, where he was reunited with his old teacher Abbé Vogler. He helped Vogler revise and "correct" J. S. Bach's harmonization of chorales. Also he found a friendly group of young intellectuals with whom he planned to found a musical journal whose motto would be "musical criticism by musicians." Much of the activity of Weber and his group was like that of Robert Schumann's *Davidsbündler* some years later.

In Darmstadt, Weber came across the story of *Der Freischütz* and began to think of making it into an opera. Meanwhile he wrote a comic opera, *Abu Hassan,* a Singspiel which had some success when produced in Munich and Darmstadt.

Ever restless, Weber set out on another piano concert tour. During five months in Munich he became a close friend of Heinrich Bärmann, the first clarinetist of the court orchestra and the outstanding one of his day. It was for Bärmann that Weber wrote his concertino and two clarinet concertos.

In 1813 Weber was made conductor of the opera theater in Prague. This once-excellent theater had gone downhill since Mozart wrote *Don Giovanni* for it, and Weber's first job was to reorganize the company completely. Now his early theatrical background came to his aid. He supervised and directed all aspects in the staging of twenty-five operas within a half year. Among the singers he hired was a young soprano, Caroline Brandt, who was to become his wife.

The battle of Waterloo excited Weber's patriotic feelings and spurred him to write a cantata, *Kampf und Sieg (Battle and Victory).* This and several songs on German subjects made him a hero with German university students.

In 1816 Weber resigned from the Prague theater, having done all that he could to revitalize it. Accepting an appointment as conductor of the opera theater at Dresden, he stayed there nine years, making it the leading musical theater in Germany.

In 1817, the year of his marriage with Fräulein Brandt, Weber commenced work on the opera that was to be his masterpiece and the foundation of German national opera—*Der Freischütz (The Free Shooter).* Completed in May 1820, it was premièred a year later at the opening of a new opera theater in Berlin. The opera was an immediate success. Riding the crest of the growing tide of nationalism in Germany, it was produced in all the leading opera houses there and in Austria—although six months went by before it was produced in Dresden. The inhabitants of that city never quite realized Weber's importance as a composer.

In 1823 Vienna saw the production of Weber's opera *Euryanthe,* with the composer conducting. This had only a moderate success in spite of its beautiful music. Weber meanwhile had been suffering from tuberculosis, and his physician had advised him to take a year of rest. The composer, however, wanting to make money for his family, accepted a bid to write a new opera for London. He began work on it and, despite several periods of severe illness, finished this opera, *Oberon,* in the British capital in April 1826. It was produced at Covent Garden Theater shortly thereafter, with Weber conducting the first twelve performances, and was a partial success. But Weber unwisely tried to give several piano concerts also. His health failed rapidly, and he died in London in June. England honored him with a ceremonial funeral. In 1844 his body was moved to Dresden, where, at another ceremonial funeral, Richard Wagner delivered the eulogy.

Weber's fame is due chiefly to *Der Freischütz,* which had a profound influence on many later German composers of the nineteenth century. Weber was one of the first master instrumental colorists, anticipating in certain ways the orchestral techniques of Hector Berlioz. In combining instrumental and harmonic effects dramatically to produce

Above: Spectre de la Rose, *here danced by Nijinsky and Karsavina, is based on Weber's piano solo "Invitation to the Dance," arranged for orchestra*
Below: *"Carl Maria von Weber," a drawing by Aubrey Beardsley, 1893*

a definite emotional response in his listeners, Weber opened the way for Wagner and many other composers.

Weber was one of the first composers, along with Beethoven and Schubert, to exploit the possibilities of the piano. His four sonatas, two concertos, and *Konzertstück* in F major explore many new technical devices. They include wide-ranging leaps combined with passage work (Ex. 1), delicate figuration reminiscent of his own and Mendelssohn's fairy music (Ex. 2), athletic melodic figures over wide-spread chords (Ex. 3), and octave passages that heralded the com-

ing virtuoso pianists, such as Liszt and Brahms.

Weber's piano sonatas are works that do not deserve their neglect by pianists. The Fourth Sonata has a dramatic plan that has been explained by Sir Julius Benedict (1804–85), the English composer who studied with Weber. This plan is interesting to compare with the program of Berlioz's *Symphonie fantastique*. The first movement, according to Benedict, "portrays in mournful strains the state of a sufferer from melancholy and despondency, with occasional glimpses of hope, which are always dark-

Ex. 1 — Sonata No. 1

Ex. 2 — Sonata No. 1

Ex. 3 — Sonata No. 2

ened and crushed." The second movement, a dramatic *menuetto,* "describes an outburst of rage," while the following *andante consolente* is "of consolatory nature" as his friends endeavor to calm the sufferer. The final prestissimo is "a wild tarantella with only a few snatches of melody, finishing in exhaustion and death."

Is such an interpretation too literary, too Romantically poetic? Weber, it must be remembered, had a fertile, imaginative mind. For a while he worked on a musical novel. He was truly a forerunner of those other great nineteenth-century composer-authors: Berlioz, Schumann, Wagner, and Debussy.

WEBERN, ANTON VON (1883–1945): one of the most original and influential composers of the twentieth century. Born in Vienna, Webern prepared for life as a musical scholar by earning a Ph.D. in musicology in 1906 at the University of Vienna. There he studied under the noted musicologist Guido Adler. In the meantime he had begun to study composition with Arnold Schoenberg and Egon Wellesz.

For a while Webern conducted theater orchestras in and around Vienna and Prague and in various German cities. After World War I, in 1918, he settled in a suburb of Vienna and worked with Schoenberg in organizing the "Society for Private Musical Performances," which gave a series of concerts of new music from which critics were excluded.

After several years spent in conducting a workers' chorus and orchestra, Webern began to withdraw from public life, although he occasionally emerged from his teaching and composing to conduct concerts of new music. Webern was one of the first to recognize the genius of the American composer Charles Ives, and he conducted some of the first performances of Ives's works.

Webern's music, with its advanced idiom, was banned by the Nazis, and he had difficulty in teaching his few students, giving a few lectures, and continuing with his composition. During a bombardment of Vienna his son was killed. To escape future bombings, he fled with his wife to Mittersill, a suburb of Salzburg. Here, several months after the end of the war, Webern was fatally shot by a United States sentry when he disobeyed, perhaps unintentionally, the curfew rules.

Webern is both the most concise and the most romantic composer of his time. Even more than his teacher Schoenberg and his fellow-student Alban Berg, Webern wrote

Anton von Webern

music which is tightly organized and intellectually conceived. Yet the result, to the listener, is as though highly romantic music were distilled to its very essence. As Schoenberg said of it, "Every glance is a poem; every sigh, a novel."

Webern's music does not depend on any traditional method of composition. There is no key, nor are any conventional chords used. A melodic line is split among many instruments, as though it were a series of points rather than being continuous. Transitions, modulations, and all other aspects of conventional form are done away with, so that what remains is a series of varied statements of thematic material. The compositions are very brief, often lasting less than one minute. The early *Five Pieces for Orchestra,* Opus 10, lasts less than five minutes, the fourth movement taking only nineteen seconds. Webern's life's work is now contained on four long-playing records —although in recent years many previously unknown compositions have been found.

In his early pieces, such as the *Five Movements for String Quartet* and the *Six Bagatelles for String Quartet,* Webern went far beyond the realm of traditional sound. He had an ear for the exquisite in tone-color, and in the *Five Pieces for Orchestra* used a chamber group featuring mandolin, guitar, celesta, glockenspiel, harmonium, strings (usually muted), horn, and trumpet. Later, adopting Schoenberg's twelve-tone principle of organization—in which a tone is not repeated once it has been left—Webern carried the process several steps further, using the serial technique to organize both his rhythmic structure and his orchestration.

Ex. 4 — Variations for Piano

Sehr Mässig (♪.=ca.40)

pp

Webern was fond of all kinds of compositional devices. The opening of his Variations for Piano, Opus 27, shows the statement of his tone row through the first note of measure four and its immediate repetition backward (Ex. 4). This brief example also shows Webern's fondness for large intervals and augmented and perfect fourths and fifths.

Not confining himself to instrumental works, Webern wrote seven song cycles with instrumental accompaniment. He also composed two cantatas for chorus and instrumental groups. The sound of Webern's orchestration, as in his Symphony, Opus 21, is like the splitting of sunlight by a prism. Whole new concepts of tone colors result from his completely individual use of the orchestra.

Webern has had many imitators. None has matched the vision of this unique, modest Austrian genius.

Below left: *Kurt Weill*
Below right: *Lotte Lenya as Polly in the 1955 production of* Three-penny Opera *in New York City*

WEILL, KURT (1900–50): a composer best known for his music for *Die Dreigroschenoper (The Three-penny Opera).* Born in Dessau, Germany, he started to compose when eleven years old, his composition teachers being Humperdinck and Busoni. After writing a violin concerto and a symphony in highly dissonant style, Weill became interested in theater music and composed several operas, of which *Aufstieg und Fall der Stadt Mahagonny (Rise and Fall of the City of Mahagonny)* is the most performed. Weill, feeling that modern composers were getting too far away from their audiences, deliberately set about using various kinds of popular music as his vocabulary. Like many French composers in the 1920's, Weill used American jazz forms, tangos, and the style of music-hall ballads, mixing the ingredients together in such a way that the language became his own.

Germany in the late 1920's was full of bitterness. There was a ruinous inflation. Corrupt businessmen and some government officials were the targets for Weill and playwright Berthold Brecht as they wrote *The Three-penny Opera.* The work was modeled on an old English ballad opera, *The Beggar's Opera,* by John Gay. Its main characters are thieves and fakes, the words and thoughts are bitter, and the music as venal as the characters. As a portrait of a period in German history *The Three-penny Opera* is a masterpiece. A revival of the work in New York in 1955 ran for more than five years.

When Hitler came to power in Germany, Weill felt that he was not free to compose. He and his wife, the actress-singer Lotte Lenya, moved to Paris, where Weill wrote the music for the stinging, provocative ballet *Die sieben Todsünden (The Seven Deadly Sins).* From Paris the Weills moved to the United States, where the composer became completely committed to American ideals and cultural resources.

Weill always felt that as an artist he needed to be concerned with all aspects of life. His collaborators were such serious theater men as Berthold Brecht, Maxwell Anderson, and Elmer Rice. Of his several Broadway musical shows, the most successful were *Knickerbocker Holiday* and *Lady in the Dark.* He also wrote a musical version of the play *Street Scene;* an American "folk opera," *Down in the Valley;* and *Lost in the Stars,* a serious musical based on Alan Paton's novel *Cry, the Beloved Country.*

Weill's best-known songs, "Mack the Knife" from *The Three-penny Opera* and "September Song" from *Knickerbocker Holiday,* prove the composer's ability to say something serious in the most conventional forms and to add a note of bitterness or sadness that makes his so-called "popular" songs true art songs.

WHOLE-TONE SCALE: a six-tone scale associated with the music of Claude Debussy, who used it more than any other composer. Consisting of a succession of whole steps, this scale has neither a tonic, nor a dominant, nor a leading tone. The lack of key center gives the scale a feeling of vagueness and restlessness—factors that undoubtedly led to Debussy's adoption of the scale as part of a vocabulary suitable for Impressionism (see Ex. 30 on page 413).

On the keyboard there are basically two whole-tone scales: one using the two black-key group, the other the three black-key group (Ex. 5a and b).

Among the peculiarities of the whole-tone scale is that the only traditional triad available is the augmented triad, heard in Debussy's *Pour le Piano* (see Ex. 19 on page 27). On the other hand, because of the lack of dissonant half steps, any or all tones of the whole-tone scale may be combined to form chords, of which the tritone (C-F#, D-G#, and so forth) is the most characteristic interval, as in Ex. 30 on page 413.

Since the whole-tone scale is outside the major-minor key system, there are no rules of harmonic progression. The main concern of the composer using this scale is to avoid monotony, which he does by switching from one whole-tone series to another or by combining the whole-tone scale with other tonal organizations (Ex. 6).

The earliest use of the whole-tone scale is to be found in the Russian composer Dargomyzhsky's opera *The Stone Guest* (finished by Rimsky-Korsakov in 1872 after the death of the composer), based on the Don Juan legend. Dargomyzhsky chose this scale on which to build the leitmotif of the opera.

Mussorgsky made use of the scale, as did Busoni, Scriabin, and Ernst Toch. The American composer Wallingford Riegger (1885–1961) experimented with the two whole-tone series by making them two halves of a twelve-tone row. Otherwise, since its use in the early 1900's, the whole-tone scale has ceased to interest composers.

Walter Huston in Knickerbocker Holiday

Ex. 5a   Ex. 5b

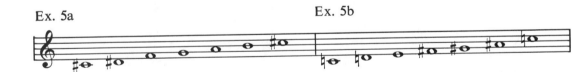

Ex. 6 — "Les Tierces alternées" from Preludes, Book II, Debussy

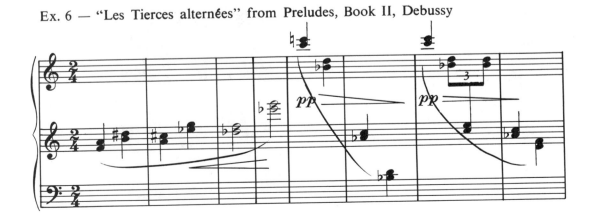

WOODWINDS: the large family of orchestral instruments that consists of the piccolo, flute, oboe, English horn, clarinet, bassoon, and saxophone. Closely related to these are the recorder, harmonica, bagpipe, accordion, pipe organ, and the humble whistle and ocarina, or "sweet potato."

The woodwind family has two main branches, which can be described very simply. In one group (flutes and recorders) the sound is made as the player directs his breath across the tip of a tube, as in blowing across the top of a bottle. In the other group, including all other woodwinds, the tone is made by setting one or more reeds in motion, as when one makes a squawking or whistling noise by blowing hard at a blade of grass held tightly between the thumbs. Although all members of the family are called "wood" winds, the instruments have been made of many materials besides wood: clay, metal, glass, ivory, and plastics.

The shape and length of the body of a woodwind instrument, the size of the finger holes, and the method of tone production determine the timbre of the instrument, as well as the pitches it can produce. The differences between the clarinet and the oboe, for example, are due to the fact that

the clarinet is a single-reed cylindrical instrument while the oboe is a double-reed instrument with a conical bore. Conical instruments such as the oboe require "over-blowing" at the octave; that is, to extend the higher range of the instrument the player uses his breath and a "speaker key" to produce overtones exactly an octave above the original fingering. On the clarinet and other cylindrical instruments, the over-blown note is an interval of a twelfth above the note in the bottom range.

The lowest pitch of a woodwind is produced when all the holes in the body are covered. As the length of the air column in the tube is shortened by opening the holes successively, the pitch is raised. Because of the difficulty of completely covering every hole with the fingers, the orchestral woodwinds have been fitted with sets of pads that fit securely over the holes. The pads are manipulated by means of keys and levers. The improved mechanism, in addition to completely stopping the holes, includes extensions that permit the use of holes which would otherwise be beyond the span of the hand.

Woodwinds have appeared in various forms in all parts of the world. Flutes and whistles made from cane, wood, bone, and

Left: *some 18th- and 19th-century woodwinds. Top row, from left to right: basset horn in F (tenor clarinet), German, late 18th century; basset horn (tenor in F), English, 19th century; basset horn in F (tenor clarinet), German, c. 1800; basset horn in F (tenor clarinet), German, early 19th century; clarinet in B-flat, French, c. 1800; clarinet d'amour in G, French, 18th century. Middle: clarinet (tenor in E-flat), Belgian, 19th century. Bottom: clarinet (bass in C), Italian, early 19th century*
Right: *a Belgian clarinet (B-flat) made of ivory and brass, c. 1830*

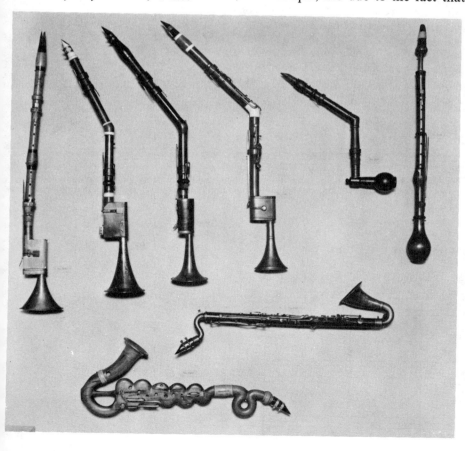

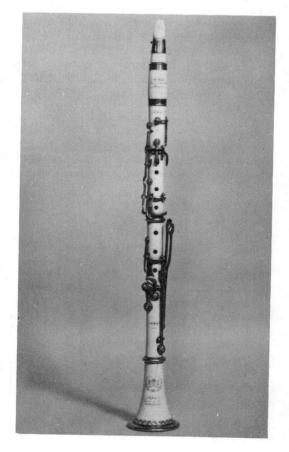

stone were among the most primitive instruments. Among the North and South American Indians and certain African tribes the flutes were considered potent forces for good or bad magic. Instruments with single and double reeds—sometimes even with twin bodies—were popular in the eastern Mediterranean several thousand years before the Christian era. The Chinese *sheng,* known at least as early as 1000 B.C., was a group of "free reeds," with bamboo-pipe resonators, blown by mouth. A free reed is a thin strip of metal secured at one end and set in motion by the breath, as in the harmonica, or by air forced from bellows, as in the accordion. It is "free" because it cannot be controlled, as by a player's lips.

In Europe during the medieval and Renaissance periods whole families, or *consorts,* of woodwinds developed: the recorders, cromornes (crumhorns) and shawms (predecessors of the oboe), bombardons or pommers (bass shawms which became the fagotto and then the bassoon), and the chalumeau (which, when improved, became the clarinet).

As orchestras became established in Europe in the mid-seventeenth century, the use of pairs of flutes and oboes became customary. Bassoons were soon added to provide a bass. With the invention of the clarinet by Johann Christopher Denner, of Nuremberg, in the late seventeenth century, the woodwind section of the symphony orchestra was complete.

As the early instruments improved, they could be played with more agility and control. New ones such as the oboe d'amore and basset horn, or tenor clarinet, came into being in the eighteenth century and were used by Bach and Mozart respectively. Theobald Böhm (1794–1881) and Adolphe Sax (1814–94) perfected, redesigned, and (in the case of Sax) invented new instruments of the woodwind family. During the eighteenth century small groups of woodwinds were used for the playing of the outdoor serenades and divertimentos that were so popular in the Classical period.

In the symphony orchestra today there are usually three of each type of woodwind. The players sit in the center of the orchestra, just in front of the conductor. Woodwinds constitute the largest family in the modern concert band. Fifes and bagpipes were used in military bands of the sixteenth and seventeenth centuries—to provide marches for the foot soldier. Later the bagpipes were replaced by oboes, which were louder then than now.

The saxophone and clarinet have been

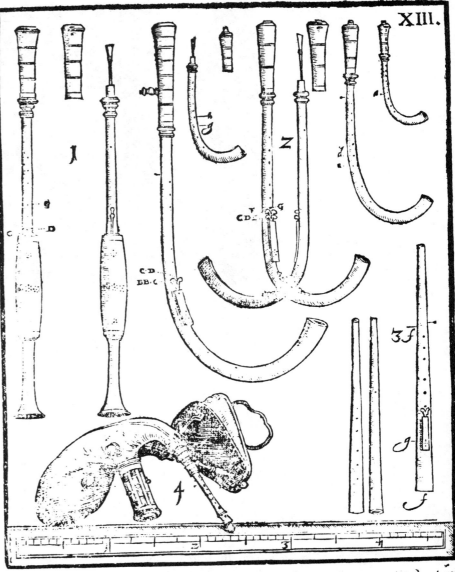

1. Baſſett: Nicolo. 2. Krumbhörner. 3. Cornetti muti: juue Zincken.
4. Sackpfeiff mit dem Blaßbalg.
B iij

important members of jazz groups since the earliest days of Dixieland jazz. Recently the flute and oboe have been used. Only the bassoon has been ignored, the more resonant tones of the tenor and baritone saxophones being preferred.

There is no standard style of woodwind playing; each country seems to prefer one kind of sound to another. The French, German, English, and American tones for the various instruments have been markedly different. In recent years, however, as music has become more truly international, the tendency has been to agree on a sweet and multi-colored tone quality.

Plate XIII from Michael Praetorius' Syntagma musicum, *published 1618–20*

Scene from a 1966 Paris Opéra production of Wozzeck *with Erika Wien as Marie and Walter Berry as Wozzeck*

WOZZECK: one of the most important twentieth-century operas, composed by Alban Berg. The libretto was put together by Berg from an unfinished play by Georg Büchner (1813–37), whose most famous work was *Danton's Death.* Of Büchner's twenty-five scenes Berg chose fifteen, grouped into three acts of five scenes each. Berg started work on the libretto in 1914 and finished the music in 1921. The first performance of *Wozzeck,* in 1925, created a furor and catapulted Berg into international prominence. Although *Wozzeck* became one of the best-known and most controversial operas of modern times, Berg did not consciously set out to reform opera. His primary aim was to write music that would illuminate Büchner's drama, at the same time turning a spotlight on a society that cruelly allowed man to inflict indignities and sorrows on his fellow man.

Wozzeck—an orderly in the army, his loved one Marie, and their child are symbols of the world's poor and oppressed. Other characters are an overbearing captain, a coldly scientific doctor, and a callous drum major. Both the doctor and the captain treat Wozzeck as a kind of soulless animal. Marie flirts with the drum major, then has an affair with him. The captain and doctor taunt Wozzeck about the unfaithfulness of Marie. Insanely jealous, Wozzeck fights with the drum major and is badly beaten. Marie has been praying to God for forgiveness, but Wozzeck, no longer able to reason, murders her. He tries to wipe out the memory of his evil deed but cannot. He throws the murder knife into a pond—thinks it is too close to shore, wades out to it, and continues wading until the water

closes over his head. In the final scene the child rides his hobbyhorse, unconcerned with the tragedy that has overtaken his parents. As the curtain falls he slowly rides off singing "Hopp, hopp," and the music comes to a despairing pianissimo close.

The score of *Wozzeck* contains some of the most poignant, inspired music ever written. The orchestration glows. It is fearsome, wild, murderous, tender, catastrophic. The vocal line is at various times declamatory, in the style of Wagner, or melodic in the traditional sense. Much of it is written in *Sprechstimme*—half speaking, half singing. At times Berg uses spoken words accompanied by music—a style of dramatic word-setting known as *melodrama.*

Wozzeck is written basically in the atonal style of Berg's teacher, Schoenberg, but Berg was not content to limit his vocabulary. At times the harmony and melody are written in the twelve-tone idiom, yet there are also suggestions of Wagner, of Mahler, and of Debussy. Perhaps the most amazing thing about *Wozzeck* is its great emotional impact, particularly in view of the fact that the opera itself is one of the most highly organized and intellectually conceived works in the whole realm of music. Each of the three acts has its own musical form. To connect the many scenes of the opera, Berg wrote important interludes that serve as codas to the previous scenes or as preludes to those that follow.

Act I consists of five scenes, or character sketches. The first is a suite, consisting of a prelude, pavane, gigue, and gavotte that set forth the characters of Wozzeck and the captain. The climax of this scene is Wozzeck's tormented "aria" in which he cries out at the fate of the poor folk like himself (Ex. 7). Scene 2, taking place outdoors, is a rhapsody based on a progression of three strange chords:

Scene 3 starts with a military march, which is followed by one of the most beautiful sections of the opera—Marie's lullaby, which she sings to her child (Ex. 8). Scene 4 is a passacaglia with twenty-one variations based on a twelve-tone theme (Ex. 9), during which the cold, egocentric character of the doctor emerges. The final scene of the first act is a brief *andante affettuoso* (tenderly) in rondo form.

Act II is a symphony in five movements: a sonata-allegro form, during which Wozzeck becomes suspicious of Marie; a fantasia and fugue as the doctor and the captain torment Wozzeck; a *largo* as Wozzeck accuses Marie and threatens her; a strange scherzo consisting of a Ländler, a song by a workman, and a waltz, as Marie dances with the drum major in a tavern while Wozzeck's jealousy builds up; and a martial rondo for the scene in which the drum major fights and defeats Wozzeck.

Act III, the catastrophe, has the form of six inventions—a series of pieces each based on one short musical idea: a theme, a tone, a rhythm, a six-tone chord, a tonality, and a perpetual motion. This act with its tragedy piled on tragedy is brutal, shocking, and haunting. It is possibly one of the greatest examples of a highly organized art form in which every compositional device is used only to further the total purpose of the work. In the second scene, for example, the tone B is heard obsessively throughout—as a fundamental pedal point that eventually spreads out over the whole orchestra, as though the instruments themselves were frozen in horror.

The subject matter and the difficulties of performance for a while held back general acceptance of *Wozzeck* in the opera houses of the world. Gradually, however, it has assumed its place as one of the great landmarks of operatic history.

Ex. 7

Sehr breit

Ex. 8

Ex. 9

XYLOPHONE: a tuned percussion instrument whose history goes back to the days of primitive man. In its oldest forms it was just a few slabs of wood or pieces of stone of different sizes. Later it became flat pieces of glass which were tuned to make a scale. The pieces of glass were laid on a bed of straw—and that is why one of the German names for the xylophone is *Strohfiedel,* or "straw-fiddle."

The present-day xylophone consists of thirty or more pieces of hard wood which are held to long crosspieces by means of screws. Under each wooden bar there is a tube which is called a resonator. The resonators, which are tuned like the wooden bars, slightly amplify the sound of the vibrating wooden bars.

Turned on its side, the xylophone looks like a ladder, with its longest wooden bars making the lowest tones. The wooden bars, arranged like the white and black keys of the piano, are tuned to make a chromatic scale:

Morris Goldenberg playing the xylophone

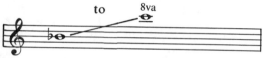

The xylophone part is often written an octave lower than it sounds. The instrument is played with wooden, spoon-shaped beaters or sticks that have a small metal knob at the end.

Ex. 1 — *Danse macabre,* Saint-Saëns

The tone of the xylophone is hollow and dry, since the instrument has no way of sustaining a tone. Saint-Saëns, one of the first composers to realize the possibilities of the instrument, used it to represent dancing skeletons (Ex. 1) in his orchestral work *Danse macabre* (1874). The xylophone is at its best when it plays fast running notes, repeated notes, and nimble jumping arpeggios. There are interesting parts for the instrument in Bartók's *Music for Strings, Percussion, and Celesta;* Surinach's *Ritmo Hondo;* Shostakovich's Fifth Symphony; and Copland's *Music for the Theater.*

YANKEE DOODLE: the first American patriotic song. Originally it was a song the English soldiers sang to make fun of the Americans, shouting it with great glee outside the Puritan churches. They sang it as they marched toward Lexington, Massachusetts, in April 1775. After the Minutemen beat the British at Concord they took "Yankee Doodle" as their own, fitting new words to the old tune. Someone made a verse that describes it very well:

It suits for feasts, it suits for fun;
And just as well for fighting.

When the British surrendered at Yorktown, it was "Yankee Doodle" that the American band played.

ZARZUELA: a Spanish form of opera, now roughly comparable to the musical comedy or operetta. The zarzuela's history is a venerable one, being almost as long as that of Italian opera.

The Spanish royal court of the seventeenth century vacationed in a country palace known as La Zarzuela—a former hunting lodge which had been transformed into the sort of place where royalty could rough it in luxury. Life being occasionally a bit dull at La Zarzuela, professional entertainers were brought in to perform music and short theatrical works. The first unified theater piece, combining music, dance, and spoken dialogue, was performed at the palace in 1657. Its text was by the famous Spanish writer Calderón de la Barca (1600–81), who singlehandedly established the form that was to be known as a zarzuela.

Calderón's *El Laurel de Apolo* (1657) introduced a novel element—in addition to the spoken dialogue—into an operatic form: the folk-dance form known as the *seguidilla*. This use of popular material in the zarzuela happened long before such folk material was interpolated into the English ballad opera and the German Singspiel.

For a while zarzuelas were based on mythological stories, as were early Italian and French operas. Then, in the middle 1700's, at the hands of the lyricist Ramón de La Cruz (1731–94) plots became concerned with ordinary beings. In *Las labradoras de Murcia (The Working Women of Murcia)* there occurs a scene in which, during an off-stage storm, the working people rush in with typical Spanish musical instruments and perform the Spanish dance known as the *jota*.

The popularity of the zarzuela was broken for a while by the *tonadilla*, a topical and often satirical short play set to music. A tonadilla, which ran for just a few performances, was a popular form of Spanish theater, and so used the most representative Spanish dances and songs. It was from the music of tonadillas that many non-Spanish composers, such as Bizet, got their inspiration for Spanish color.

The tonadilla, which played to the crowd, and Italian opera, which played to the upper classes, put the zarzuela in the shadows. It re-emerged in the 1830's to become once more the most popular form of musical theater in Spanish-speaking countries. The outstanding composer of zarzuelas in the nineteenth century was Francisco Asenjo Barbieri (1823–94), who wrote no less than seventy-seven zarzuelas and, incidentally, influenced the Spanish composers Albéniz and Falla.

The zarzuela has always been a form that draws its inspiration from various sources, including Italian opera as well as folk music. In its South American version it has continued to absorb other elements of the twentieth century—Latin American dances and ballads as well as North American jazz. A look at the record catalog and the long lists of zarzuelas available on long-playing discs will testify to the modern interest in this musical form.

A scene from the well-known zarzuela La Verbena de la Paloma

Austrian zither player Karl Jancik

ZITHER: a stringed instrument popular in Austria. Related to the guitar, dulcimer, medieval psaltery, and Greek kithara, the zither consists of as many as forty-five strings stretched over a shallow wooden body. Five of these are melody strings that lie over a fingerboard equipped with frets to guide the fingers of the player. The other strings are open, each being tuned to a single tone. The player uses his left hand to stop the melody strings, which he plucks with a plectrum attached to his right thumb. With the other fingers of his right hand he plucks the open strings to make a harmonic accompaniment. The haunting tone of the zither was heard all over the world when this instrument was used to provide the background music for the movie *The Third Man* (1950).

SIGNS AND SYMBOLS USED IN MUSIC

Asterisks indicate those terms which also appear as articles within the body of the encyclopedia.

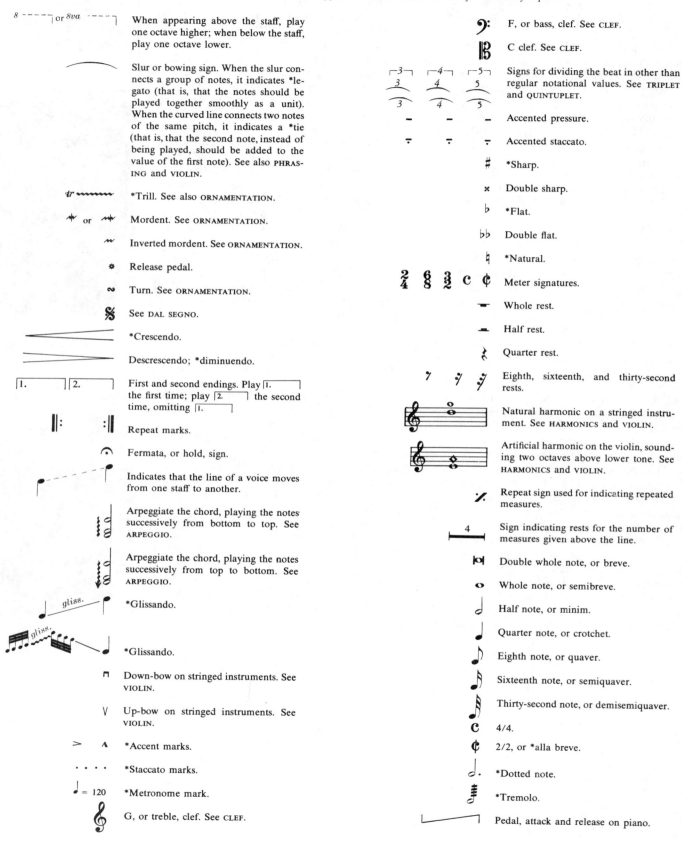

8 ----- or 8va ----- When appearing above the staff, play one octave higher; when below the staff, play one octave lower.

Slur or bowing sign. When the slur connects a group of notes, it indicates *legato (that is, that the notes should be played together smoothly as a unit). When the curved line connects two notes of the same pitch, it indicates a *tie (that is, that the second note, instead of being played, should be added to the value of the first note). See also PHRASING and VIOLIN.

*Trill. See also ORNAMENTATION.

Mordent. See ORNAMENTATION.

Inverted mordent. See ORNAMENTATION.

Release pedal.

Turn. See ORNAMENTATION.

See DAL SEGNO.

*Crescendo.

Descrescendo; *diminuendo.

First and second endings. Play the first time; play the second time, omitting.

Repeat marks.

Fermata, or hold, sign.

Indicates that the line of a voice moves from one staff to another.

Arpeggiate the chord, playing the notes successively from bottom to top. See ARPEGGIO.

Arpeggiate the chord, playing the notes successively from top to bottom. See ARPEGGIO.

*Glissando.

*Glissando.

Down-bow on stringed instruments. See VIOLIN.

Up-bow on stringed instruments. See VIOLIN.

*Accent marks.

*Staccato marks.

*Metronome mark.

G, or treble, clef. See CLEF.

F, or bass, clef. See CLEF.

C clef. See CLEF.

Signs for dividing the beat in other than regular notational values. See TRIPLET and QUINTUPLET.

Accented pressure.

Accented staccato.

*Sharp.

Double sharp.

*Flat.

Double flat.

*Natural.

Meter signatures.

Whole rest.

Half rest.

Quarter rest.

Eighth, sixteenth, and thirty-second rests.

Natural harmonic on a stringed instrument. See HARMONICS and VIOLIN.

Artificial harmonic on the violin, sounding two octaves above lower tone. See HARMONICS and VIOLIN.

Repeat sign used for indicating repeated measures.

Sign indicating rests for the number of measures given above the line.

Double whole note, or breve.

Whole note, or semibreve.

Half note, or minim.

Quarter note, or crotchet.

Eighth note, or quaver.

Sixteenth note, or semiquaver.

Thirty-second note, or demisemiquaver.

4/4.

2/2, or *alla breve.

*Dotted note.

*Tremolo.

Pedal, attack and release on piano.

FOREIGN TERMS AND PHRASES USED IN MUSIC

Compiled by Ruth Lloyd

Asterisks indicate those terms which also appear as articles within the body of the encyclopedia.

Abdämpfen (Ger.). Muted.

Abgemessen (Ger.). In strict time.

Abnehmend (Ger.). Gradually softer.

Abschwellen (Ger.). Gradually slower.

*****Accelerando** (It.). Gradually faster.

Achtel (Ger.) Eighth note; *quaver.*

Adagietto (It.). Slightly faster than *adagio.*

*****Adagio** (It.). Slowly and smoothly.

Ad libitum (Lat.). As you please; freely.

Affettuoso (It.). Expressively; tenderly; lovingly.

Agilité (Fr.). Quickness.

Agitato (It.). Agitated.

Agité (Fr.). Agitated.

Al; Alla (It.). At the; to the; in the style or manner of.

Al fine (It.). To the end.

À la mesure (Fr.). In strict time.

*****Alla breve** (It.). With the half note as the beat indicated by 2/2 or ₵ .

Allant (Fr.). Moving on.

Allargando (It.). Slowing and broadening.

Alla turca (It.). In the Turkish style.

Allegretto (It.). Fairly lively; not as fast as *allegro.*

*****Allegro** (It.). Lively; fast.

Allmählich (Ger.). Gradually.

Al loco (It.). At the written—that is, normal—pitch.

A mezzo voce (It.). With half the voice.

Andächtig (Ger.). With devotion.

*****Andante** (It.). Going; moving; at a moderate rate.

*****Andantino** (It.). Usually means slightly faster than *andante.*

Anfang (Ger.). Beginning.

Anhang (Ger.). Coda; supplement.

Animato (It.). With spirit; animatedly.

Animé (Fr.). Animated.

Anmutig (Ger.). *Grazioso;* with charm.

Anwachsen (Ger.). Gradually louder.

Appassionato (It.). With passion.

Assai (It.). Very; very much.

Assez (Fr.). Enough; sufficiently.

A tempo (It.). At the preceding rate of speed.

Attacca (It.). Play what follows without pause.

Aufgeregt (Ger.). Agitated.

Ausdruck (Ger.). Expression.

Ausdruckslos (Ger.). Without expression.

Ausdrucksvoll (Ger.). With expression.

Ausgabe (Ger.). Edition.

Avec (Fr.). With.

À volonté (Fr.). At will; as you please.

Beaucoup (Fr.). Very much.

Bedeutungsvoll (Ger.). Meaningfully.

Belebt (Ger.). Lively.

Bestimmt (Ger.). With decision.

Betont (Ger.). Accented.

Bewegt (Ger.). With motion.

Breit (Ger.). Broad.

Breve (Eng.). A note equal to two whole notes.

Breve (It.). Short.

Brio (It.). Spirit; animation.

Calando (It.). Gradually softer.

Calme (Fr.). Serene; quiet.

Cantabile (It.). Songlike; singingly.

Caressant (Fr.). Tender; caressing.

Cédez (Fr.). Go slower.

Col, Coll', Colla (It.). With the.

*****Col legno** (It.). With the wood—that is, with the wooden back of the violin bow.

Comodo (It.). Easily; leisurely.

Con (It.). With; by; to.

Con fuoco (It.). With fire.

Con moto (It.). With movement.

Corda (It.). String.

Corde (Fr.). String.

Coulé (Fr.). Slur.

*****Crescendo** (It.). Gradually getting louder; increasing the volume.

Crotchet (Eng.). Quarter note.

*****Da capo** (It.). Repeat from the beginning.

*****Dal segno** (It.). Repeat from the sign.

Dämpfer (Ger.). Mute.

Début (Fr.). Beginning.

Decrescendo (It.). Lessening in loudness; *diminuendo.*

Demisemiquaver (Eng.). Thirty-second note.

Deux (Fr.). Two.

Diligenza (It.). Carefully.

*****Diminuendo** (It.). Gradually getting softer.

Divisi (It.). Divided.

Dolce (It.). Sweetly.

Dolorosamente (It.). Sadly; grievingly.

Doppelt (Ger.). Double; twice as fast.

Doppio movimento (It.). Twice as fast.

Doucement (Fr.). Gently; softly.

Doux (Fr.). Sweet.

Drängen, Drängend (Ger.). Pressing; hurrying.

Droite (Fr.). Right.

Dur (Fr.). Harsh.

Dur (Ger.). Major.

Éclatant (Fr.). Brilliant.

Également (Fr.). Evenly; equally.

Eilen (Ger.). Hurried.

Ein (Ger.). One.

Einfach (Ger.). Simple.

Einleiten (Ger.). Introduce; begin.

Élargi, Élargissez, en élargissant (Fr.). Broadening; *allargando.*

Eleganza (It.). Grace; elegance.

Empfindung (Ger.). Feeling.

Emphase (Fr.). Emphasis.

Emporté (Fr.). Fiery; passionate.

Enchaînez (Fr.). Go on; connect.

*****Encore** (Fr.). Again.

En dehors (Fr.). Make prominent.

Energico (It.). With energy.

Énergie (Fr.). Energy; power.

Energisch (Ger.). Forceful; vigorous.

Enserrant (Fr.). Contained.

Erst (Ger.). First.

Etwas (Ger.). Some.

Facile (Fr., It.). Easy; flowing.

Fastoso (It.). Pompous; stately.

Feierlich (Ger.). Ceremonial; solemn.

Fermata (It.). Pause sign; prolong time value of note so marked.

Feròce (It.). Fiercely.

Feurig (Ger.). Fiery.

Filer la voix (Fr.). Prolong a tone swelling and diminishing.

Fine (It.). End.

Fliessend (Ger.). Flowing; smooth.

Flott (Ger.). Smart; snappy.

Flüchtig (Ger.). Fleeting.

Flüsternd (Ger.). Whispering.

Folgend (Ger.). Following.

*****Forte** (It.). Loud; strong.

Fortissimo (It.). Very loud.

Forzando (It.). Forcefully.

Frei (Ger.). Free.

Frisch (Ger.). Vigorous.

Fröhlich (Ger.). Gay.

Früher (Ger.). Earlier.

Fuoco (It.). Fire.

Furioso (It.). Furious; violent.

Gai, Gaiement (Fr.). Gaily; briskly.

Ganz (Ger.). All.

Gauche (Fr.). Left.

Gebunden (Ger.). Tied or *legato*.
Gedehnt (Ger.). Slow; stately; studied.
Gefühl (Ger.). Feeling.
Gehalten (Ger.). Sustained; held.
Gehend (Ger.). Going; *andante*.
Gemächlich (Ger.). Easy going.
Gemessen (Ger.). Measured.
Genau (Ger.). Accurate.
Geschwind, Geschwindt (Ger.). Swiftly.
Getragen (Ger.). Solemn; grave.
Giocoso (It.). Playfully.
Giusto (It.). Strict; exact.
Glühend (Ger.). Ardent.
Gracieusement (Fr.). Gracefully.
Grandioso (It.). With grandeur; majestically.
Grave (It.). Slow; heavy; solemn.
Gravemente (Fr.). Solemnly.
Grazioso (It.). Elegantly; gracefully.

Halbe (Ger.). Half note.
Hastig (Ger.). Hasty; hurried.
Hauch (Ger.). Breath.
Haupt (Ger.). Head; main.
Heftig (Ger.). Vehement.
Heimlich (Ger.). Secret; mysterious.
Heiter (Ger.). Serene; bright.
Herzlich (Ger.). With heart.

Immer (Ger.). Always.
Innig (Ger.). Ardently tender.
Intimo (It.). Intimate; personal.

Joyeux (Fr.). Merry.

Kurz (Ger.). Short.

Lamentoso (It.). Mournfully.
Langsam (Ger.). Slow.
Languido (It.). Languidly.
Larghetto (It.). Somewhat less slowly than *largo*.
*****Largo** (It.). Broadly and slowly.
Lebendig (Ger.). Alive; vivacious.
Lebhaft (Ger.). Lively.
*****Legato** (It.). Smoothly and connectedly.
Léger, Légèrement (Fr.). Lightly.
*****Leggiero** (It.). Light; airy; graceful.
Leicht (Ger.). Light.
Leidenschaftlich (Ger.). Passionate.
Leidenschaftlicher (Ger.). More passionate.
Leise (Ger.). Soft.
Lent, Lenteur (Fr.). Slow; slowing.
Lento (It.). Slow.
Librement (Fr.). Freely.
Lié (Fr.). Tied; connected.
L'istesso (It.). The same.
Loco (It.). Place; play notes as written (usually follows 8va).
Lointain (Fr.). Remote; distant.

Luft pause (Ger.). Breath pause; momentary suspension of rhythm.
Lunga (It.). Long; prolonged.
Lustig (Ger.). Merry; gay.

Maestoso (It.). Majestic; stately; grand.
Main (Fr.). Hand.
Mano (It.). Hand.
Ma non troppo (It.). But not too much.
Marcato (It.). Marked.
Marqué (Fr.). Marked.
Mässig (Ger.). Measured; *andante*.
Même (Fr.). Same.
Men, Meno (It.). Less.
Mesuré (Fr.). Measured; moderate.
*****Mesto** (It.). Sad; mournful; woeful.
*****Mezzo** (It.). Half; middle; medium.
Minim (Eng.). Half note.
Misterioso (It.). With mystery.
Mit (Ger.). With.
Moderato (It.). Moderately; at a moderate rate.
Modéré (Fr.). Moderate.
Möglich (Ger.). Possible.
Moins (Fr.). Less.
Moll (Ger.). Minor.
Molto (It.). Much; very.
*****Morendo** (It.). Dying away.
Mosso (It.). Moved; agitated; lively.
Moto (It.). Motion; movement.
Mouvement (Fr.). Motion.
Munter (Ger.). Lively; gay; *animato*.

Nachdenklich (Ger.). Thoughtful.
Nach gefallen (Ger.). Freely; *ad libitum*.
Nachlassend (Ger.). Gradually slower.
Naïvement (Fr.). Simply.
Nicht (Ger.). Not.
Noch (Ger.). Still; yet.
Non (It.). Not.

Ohne (Ger.). Without.
Ossia (It.). Or; or else; an alternate reading or fingering.
Ou (Fr.). Or.

Perlé (Fr.). Pearly.
Peu (Fr.). Little.
Piacere (It.). To please.
Piacevole (It.). Pleasant; agreeable.
Piangevole (It.). Mournfully.
Piano (It.). Soft.
Pianissimo (It.). Very soft.
Più (It.). More.
Placido (It.). Calm; tranquil.
Plus (Fr.). More.
Poco (It.). Little.
Pomposo (It.). With dignity; pompously.
Positif (Fr.). Choir organ.
Preciso (It.). With precision.

Près de la table (Fr.). Play near the sounding board (harp).
Presque (Fr.). Almost.
Pressante (It.). Pressing on; getting faster.
Pressez (Fr.). Accelerate.
Prestissimo (It.). As fast as possible.
*****Presto** (It.). Very fast; lively; quick.
Primo (It.). First; upper part in piano duets.

Quaver (Eng.). Eighth note.

Ralentissez (Fr.). Slow down.
Rallentando (It.). Gradually slower.
Rapide (Fr.). Swift.
Rapido (It.). Rapidly.
Rasch (Ger.). Fast.
Récit (Fr.). Swell organ.
Religioso (It.). In a devotional style.
Reprenez (Fr.). Repeat.
Reprise (Fr.). Repeat.
Retenant, Retenu (Fr.). Hold back.
Revenez (Fr.). Return.
Revenez au mouv. (Fr.). Return to original tempo.
Rien (Fr.). Nothing.
Rigeur (Fr.). Precisely; strictly.
Rinforzando (It.). Sudden crescendo; make prominent.
Riposo (It.). Calm; repose.
Risoluto (It.). Resolute; determined.
Ritardando (It.). Gradually slower.
Ritenuto (It.). Held back; slower.
Robusto (It.). Firm; vigorous.
*****Rubato** (It.). A way of playing or singing with regulated rhythmic freedom.
Ruhig (Ger.). Calm; quiet.
Rythme (Fr.). Measured.

Sagement (Fr.). Steadily.
Sanft (Ger.). Gentle; easy.
Sans (Fr.). Without.
Satz (Ger.). Movement.
Schleppend (Ger.). Dragging.
Schluss (Ger.). Close cadence.
Schnell (Ger.). Fast.
Schwer (Ger.). Heavy.
Schwermütig (Ger.). Melancholy.
Schwungvoll (Ger.). Buoyant; spirited.
Sec (Fr.). Dry.
Sécheresse (Fr.). Dryness.
Secondo (It.). Second or lower part.
Segno (It.). Sign.
Segue (It.). Follow; continue without pause.
Sehr (Ger.). Very.
Semibreve (Eng.). Whole note.
Semiquaver (Eng.). Sixteenth note.
*****Semplice** (It.). Simply.

Sempre (It.). Always.

*****Senza** (It.). Without.

Serioso (It.). Seriously.

Serrez (Fr.). Hurry.

Sforzando (It.). With accent.

Silenzio (It.). Silence.

Simile (It.). Perform what follows in the style already established; for example, a pattern of pedaling or of arpeggiating chords.

Smorzando (It.). Dying away.

Sopra (It.). Above; over.

Sordino (It.). Mute.

*****Sostenuto** (It.). Sustained.

Sotto (It.). Under; beneath.

Sourdine (Fr.). Mute.

Soutenu (Fr.). Sustained.

Spiritoso (It.). Witty; humorous.

*****Staccato** (It.). Detached; separated.

Steigern (Ger.). Intensify; heighten.

Stimme (Ger.). Voice.

Straffer (Ger.). Tightened.

*****Stretto** (It.). Close; a gradual speeding-up of tempo.

*****Stringendo** (It.). Hurried; accelerated.

Subito (It.). Suddenly.

Suivez (Fr.). Follow; continue on.

Tacet (It.). Silent.

Takt (Ger.). Beat; pulse; measure.

Teil (Ger.). Part.

*****Tempo** (It.). Rate of speed.

Tendrement (Fr.). Tenderly.

Tenuto (It.). Held.

Tirasse (Fr.). Coupled (organ manuals).

Toujours (Fr.). Always.

Traîne (Fr.). Spin out; drag.

Tranquille (Fr.). Quiet.

Tranquillo (It.). Peaceful; calm.

Très (Fr.). Very.

Triste (Fr.). Sad.

Troppo (It.). Too much.

Ugualmente (It.). Evenly; smoothly.

Und (Ger.). And.

Unmerklich (Ger.). Imperceptible.

Unruhig (Ger.). Restless; agitated.

Veloce (It.). Rapid.

Verlangsamen (Ger.). *Ritardando;* slow down.

Verschwind (Ger.). Dying away.

Viertel (Ger.). Quarter note.

Vif (Fr.). Quick.

Vigoroso (It.). With energy.

Vite (Fr.). Quickly.

Vitement (Fr.). Quickly.

Vitesse (Fr.). Speed.

Vivace (It.). Brisk; lively.

Vortrag (Ger.). Performance.

Weich (Ger.). Soft.

Wenig (Ger.). Little.

Wie (Ger.). Like.

Wieder (Ger.). Again.

Wiederholen (Ger.). Repeat.

Wuchtig (Ger.). Hefty.

Zart (Ger.). Tenderly; delicately.

Zeitmass (Ger.). Tempo.

Ziemlich (Ger.). Somewhat.

Zögernd (Ger.). Hesitating.

Zu (Ger.). Too.

Zurückgehen (Ger.). Return to a preceding tempo.

Zurückhalten (Ger.). Hold back; *ritardando.*

ABBREVIATIONS USED IN MUSIC

accel.	accelerando	ff	fortissimo	Ob.	oboe	smorz.	smorzando
ad lib.	ad libitum	Fl.	flute	Op.	opus	sost. } sosten. }	sostenuto
arp.	arpeggio			Ott.	ottava (octave)		
		Gd.	grand organ			stacc.	staccato
c. } ca. }	circa	G.O. } G. Org. }	great organ	P.	positif	string.	stringendo
				p	piano	sub.	subito
cal.	calando	G.P.	grand pause	Ped.	pedal (engage)	Sw.	swell organ (récit)
cant.	cantabile	Gt.	great organ	Pfte.	pianoforte		
c.f.	cantus firmus			Picc.	piccolo	Tbn.	trombone
Ch.	choir (organ)			pizz.	pizzicato	ten.	tenuto
Cl. } Clar. }	clarinet	L.	left hand	Pos.	positif	Timp.	timpani
		leg.	legato	pp	pianissimo	Tpt.	trumpet
Cnt.	cornet	L.H. } l.h. }	left hand			Tromb. } Trb. }	trombone
Cor } corno }	French horn			R.	récit (swell organ); right hand		
cres. } cresc. }	crescendo	m.	hand; manual (organ); metronome	rall.	rallentando	unis.	unison
		Man. } man. }	manual (organ)	rf. } rfz. }	rinforzando		
Dal. S.	dal segno	marc.	marcato	R.H. } r.h. }	right hand	Va.	viola
D.C.	da capo	M.D. } m.d. }	right hand	rinf.	rinforzando	Var.	variation
decres.	decrescendo			rit.	ritardando; ritenuto	Vc. } Vcl. } Vcllo } Vlc. }	violoncello
dim. } dimin. }	diminuendo	mf	mezzo-forte	ritard.	ritardando		
div.	divisi	M.G. } m.g. }	left hand	riten.	ritenuto		
D.S.	dal segno	mor.	morendo			Vibr.	vibraphone
		mp	mezzo-piano	sf. } sfz. }	sforzando	vl.	violin
f	forte	M.S. } m.s. }	left hand	sim.	simile	vla.	viola
Fag.	Fagott, fagotto (bassoon)					Vln.	violin

FAMOUS NAMES IN MUSIC

The aim here is to briefly identify various famous people in the field of music—composers, conductors, performers, publishers, instrument makers, and so forth. (Those having separate articles within the body of the encyclopedia are not listed here.) Dates of birth and death follow the name. Uncertain dates are preceded by a *c.* notation. The country or region of birth is in parentheses; if a second country is given, it indicates another country with which the subject is associated (usually the country in which a musician did most of his work or where he settled). Since further information on many of the subjects listed here will be found elsewhere in the encyclopedia, the interested reader may also wish to consult the index.

Abbreviation Key: Aus.—Austria. **Belg.**—Belgium. **Czech.**—Czechoslovakia. **Eng.**—England. **Fr.**—France. **Ger.**—Germany. **H.**—Hungary. **It.**—Italy. **Mex.**—Mexico. **Rus.**—Russia. **Scot.**—Scotland. **Sp.**—Spain. **Switz.**—Switzerland. **U.S.**—United States.

A

Abravanel, Maurice, 1903– (Greece; U.S.) Conductor (Utah Symphony).

Abt, Franz, 1819–85 (Ger.) Composer of songs.

Adam, Adolphe-Charles, 1803–56 (Fr.) Composer of ballets *(Giselle)* and operas.

Adam de la Halle, *c.* 1240–87 (Fr.) Trouvère; composer of vocal works and the pastoral play with songs *Le Jeu de Robin et de Marion.*

Addinsell, Richard, 1904– (Eng.) Composer of theater and cinema music *(Warsaw Concerto).*

Adler, Peter Herman, 1899– (Czech.; U.S.) Conductor (N.B.C. Opera; Baltimore Symphony).

Albanese, Licia, 1913– (It.; U.S.) Operatic soprano.

Albéniz, Isaac, 1860–1909 (Sp.) Composer of Spanish nationalist school.

Alberghetti, Anna Maria, 1936– (It.; U.S.) Soprano.

d'Albert, Eugène, 1864–1932 (Scotland; Ger.) Pianist and composer (opera: *Tiefland*).

Albert, Prince Consort of Queen Victoria, 1819–61 (Ger.; Eng.) Composer of works for chorus and orchestra.

Alberti, Domenico, 1710–*c.* 40 (It.) Composer of keyboard music using Alberti bass.

Albinoni, Tomaso, 1671–1750 (It.) Violinist; composer of concertos and sonatas.

Albrechtsberger, Johann Georg, 1736–1809 (Aus.) Theorist and composer of organ works.

Alda, Frances, 1883–1952 (New Zealand; U.S.) Operatic soprano.

Alfano, Franco, 1876–1954 (It.) Composer; completed Puccini's last opera, *Turandot.*

Alkan, Charles-Henri Valentin, 1813–88 (Fr.) Pianist; composer of virtuoso works for piano.

Amram, David Werner, 1930– (U.S.) Composer of chamber works and incidental music for theater and films.

Anderson, Leroy, 1908–75 (U.S.) Composer of popular, light orchestral works.

Anderson, Marian, 1902– (U.S.) Contralto.

Ansermet, Ernest, 1883–1969 (Switz.) Conductor (Diaghilev's Russian Ballet; Orchestre de la Suisse Romande).

Antes, John, 1740–1811 (U.S.; Eng.) Composer of string trios considered the earliest chamber music written by a native American.

Antheil, George, 1900–59 (U.S.) Composer of avant-garde music of the 1920's *(Ballet mécanique)* and film scores.

Applebaum, Louis 1918– (Canada) Composer whose work has been mostly for film and stage.

Arbós, Enrique Fernández, 1863–1939 (Sp.) Violinist and conductor.

Arcadelt, Jacob, *c.*1505–*c.*60 (Flanders) Composer of madrigals.

Arel, Bülent, 1918– (Turkey) Composer.

Arensky, Anton Stepanovitch, 1861–1906 (Rus.) Teacher; conductor and composer of operas, symphonies, and chamber music.

Arlen, Harold, 1905– (U.S.) Composer of popular music ("Stormy Weather"; "Blues in the Night").

Arne, Thomas Augustine, 1710–78 (Eng.) Composer of songs and incidental music for plays.

Arnold, Malcolm, 1921– (Eng.) Composer of symphonic and chamber works.

Arrau, Claudio, 1903– (Chile) Pianist.

Aschaffenburg, Walter, 1927– (Ger.; U.S.) Composer of orchestral works and operas *(Bartleby).*

Ashkenazi, Vladimir, 1937– (Rus.) Pianist.

Atterberg, Kurt, 1887– (Sweden) Composer of symphonies and operas.

Auber, Daniel-François-Esprit, 1782–1871 (Fr.) A founder of French grand opera tradition; composer of both light and dramatic works *(Masaniello; Fra Diavolo).*

Auric, Georges, 1899– (Fr.) Member of "Les Six"; composer of film music *(Moulin Rouge),* ballets *(Les Matelots);* director of Paris opera houses.

B

Babbitt, Milton, 1916– (U.S.) Theorist and composer; pioneer in electronic music.

Babin, Victor, 1908–72 (Rus.) Pianist and composer; director of Cleveland Institute of Music.

Baccaloni, Salvatore, 1900–76 (It.) Operatic bass (specialist in comic roles).

Bachauer, Gina, 1913– (Greece) Pianist.

Backhaus, Wilhelm, 1884–1969 (Ger.) Pianist and teacher; Beethoven specialist.

Bacon, Ernst, 1898– (U.S.) Composer, teacher, and theorist.

Badings, Henk, 1907– (Java; Holland) Composer of orchestral and chamber works, including many that combine traditional instruments and electronic sounds.

Balakirev, Mily Alexeyevitch, 1837–1910 (Rus.) Composer; member of "The Russian Five."

Balfe, Michael William, 1808–70 (Ireland; Eng.) Composer of operas *(The Bohemian Girl).*

Ball, Ernest R., 1878–1927 (U.S.) Composer of popular songs ("Mother Machree"; "When Irish Eyes Are Smiling").

Bampton, Rose, 1909– (U.S.) Concert and operatic soprano.

Banister, John, 1630–79 (Eng.) Violinist; organized first concert series in England.

Bantock, Sir Granville, 1868–1946 (Eng.) Teacher; composer of a wide range of symphonic, operatic, and chamber forms, often based on exotic themes.

Barbirolli, Sir John, 1899–1970 (Eng.) Conductor (New York Philharmonic; Houston Symphony; Hallé Orchestra).

Bärmann, Heinrich Joseph, 1784–1847 (Ger.) Clarinetist for whom Mendelssohn's and Weber's clarinet works were written.

Barraqué, Jean, 1928– (Fr.) Composer of coloristic, experimental works.

Barrère, Georges, 1876–1944 (Fr.; U.S.) Flute virtuoso. Varèse wrote *Density 21.5* for him.

Basie, William ("Count"), 1904– (U.S.) Jazz pianist and bandleader.

Bauer, Harold, 1873–1951 (Eng.; U.S.) Pianist and editor.

Bax, Sir Arnold, 1883–1953 (Eng.) Composer of 7 symphonies, chamber and choral works.

Beck, Conrad, 1901– (Switz.) Composer of 7 symphonies, choral music, and chamber music.

Becker, John J., 1886–1961 (U.S.) Teacher and composer; early member of American musical avant-garde.

Beecham, Sir Thomas, 1879–1961 (Eng.) Conductor (Royal Philharmonic Orchestra).

Beeson, Jack Hamilton, 1921– (U.S.) Composer of chamber works and operas *(Lizzie Borden).*

Beiderbecke, Leon Bismark ("Bix"), 1903–31 (U.S.) Jazz trumpet player with warm personal style; composer of piano piece: *In a Mist.*

Beinum, Eduard van, 1901–59 (Holland) Conductor (Amsterdam Concertgebouw Orchestra).

Belaiev, Mitrofan Petrovitch, 1836–1904 (Rus.) Publisher of works by Russian composers.

Belcher, Supply, 1751–1836 (U.S.) Composer of early American hymns.

Benda, Georg, 1722–95 (Bohemia) Composer of melodramas (spoken dialogue with orchestral accompaniment).

Benedict, Sir Julius, 1804–85 (Ger.; Eng.) Conductor; composer of operas and symphonic works.

Ben-Haim, Paul, 1897– (Ger.; Israel) Composer of symphonies and chamber music.

Benjamin, Arthur, 1893–1960 (Australia;

Eng.) Composer of operas and instrumental works *(Jamaica Rumba)*.

Bennett, Richard Rodney, 1936– (Eng.) Composer in dissonant idiom of a successful opera *(The Mines of Sulphur)*, symphonies, chamber music, and film scores.

Bennett, Robert Russell, 1894– (U.S.) Outstanding arranger and orchestrator of Broadway musicals; composer of operas, instrumental works, and film scores.

Bennett, Sir William Sterndale, 1816–75 (Eng.) Conductor; composer of symphonic works and 4 piano concertos.

Berezowsky, Nicolai, 1900–53 (Rus.; U.S.) Violinist; composer of symphonies and chamber works.

Berger, Arthur, 1912– (U.S.) Composer, known chiefly for his chamber music.

Berger, Jean, 1901– (Ger.; U.S.) Composer of choral and orchestral works.

Bergsma, William, 1921– (U.S.) Composer of instrumental works and an opera.

Berio, Luciano, 1925– (It.; U.S.) Composer of experimental instrumental and dramatic works *(Passaggio)*.

Bériot, Charles de, 1802–70 (Belg.) Violinist and composer (7 violin concertos).

Berkeley, Lennox, 1903– (Eng.) Composer of works in all forms.

Bernac, Pierre, 1899–1979 (Fr.) Baritone; recitalist with Frances Poulenc.

Berners, Lord (Gerald Tyrwhitt-Wilson), 1883–1950 (Eng.) Composer, best known for witty ballets and instrumental music.

Biber, Heinrich Ignaz Franz von, 1644–1704 (Bohemia) Composer of violin sonatas, often with programmatic titles.

Biggs, Edward Power, 1906–77 (Eng.; U.S.) Concert organist.

Binchois, Gilles, c. 1400–60 (Burgundy) Early Renaissance composer, best known for his chansons.

Birtwistle, Harrison, 1934– (Eng.) Composer of instrumental and vocal works.

Björling, Jussi, 1911–1960 (Sweden) Operatic tenor.

Blacher, Boris, 1903–75 (China; Ger.) Composer of operas and instrumental music; director of the Hochschule für Musik in West Berlin.

Blackwood Easley, 1933– (U.S.) Composer of symphonies and chamber works; virtuoso pianist specializing in 20th-century music.

Bland, James A., 1854–1911 (U.S.) Composer of songs ("Carry Me Back to Old Virginny").

Bliss, Sir Arthur, 1891– (Eng.) Composer of operas, orchestral and choral works, ballets *(Miracle in the Gorbals)*. Named Master of the Queens Musick in 1953.

Blitzstein, Marc, 1905–64 (U.S.) Composer of theatrical works *(The Cradle Will Rock; Regina;* English version of *Three-Penny Opera)*.

Bloch, Ernest, 1880–1959 (Switz.; U.S.) Composer of vocal *(Sacred Service)* and instrumental works *(Schelomo* for cello and orchestra; 2 concerti grossi; chamber music).

Blomdahl, Karl-Birger, 1916–1968 (Sweden) Composer of symphonies, chamber music, and operas *(Aniara)*.

Blow, (Dr.) John, c. 1648–1708 (Eng.) Composer of choral music, songs, and a masque *(Venus and Adonis)*.

Boccherini, Luigi, 1743–1805 (It.; Sp.) Cellist; composer of chamber music and many orchestral and choral works in the style of Haydn.

Bochsa, Robert-Nicolas-Charles, 1789–1856 (Bohemia; Eng.) Harpist (one of the first virtuosos on the instrument, which he improved technically); composer of many compositions for harp.

Bodansky, Artur, 1877–1939 (Aus.; U.S.) Conductor of German opera at Metropolitan Opera; director of the Society of Friends of Music (1916–31).

Bohm, Karl, 1844–1920 (Ger.) Pianist; composer of piano pieces and songs ("Still wie die Nacht").

Böhm, Karl, 1894– (Ger.) Conductor of German opera.

Böhm, Theobald, 1794–1881 (Ger.) Flutist; inventor of the Böhm system of woodwind construction.

Bohnen, Michael, 1886–1965 (Ger.) Operatic bass.

Boieldieu, François-Adrien, 1775–1834 (Fr.) Composer; one of the founders of the 19th-century school of French opera *(Le Calife de Bagdad; La Dame blanche)*.

Boito, Arrigo, 1842–1918 (It.) Librettist (Verdi's *Otello* and *Falstaff*) and opera composer *(Mefistofele)*.

Bolcom, William, 1938– (U.S.) Composer of instrumental and theatrical works *(Dynamite Tonight)*.

Bond, Carrie Jacobs, 1862–1946 (U.S.) Poet and composer of songs ("A Perfect Day"; "I Love You Truly").

Bononcini, Giovanni, 1670–1747 (It.) Opera composer who, around 1720, was a rival of Handel in the London operatic world.

Borge, Victor, 1909– (Denmark; U.S.) Pianist and humorist.

Bori, Lucrezia, 1887–1960 (Sp.) Operatic soprano.

Bos, Coenraad Valentyn, 1875–1955 (Holland; U.S.) Pianist; noted accompanist; co-author with Ashley Pettis of *The Well-tempered Accompanist*.

Bottesini, Giovanni, 1821–89 (It.) Double-bass virtuoso; conductor; composer of operas and works for double-bass.

Boulanger, Nadia, 1887– (Fr.) Teacher of many contemporary composers: Berkeley, Copland, Françaix, Harris, Markevitch, Piston.

Boulez, Pierre, 1925– (Fr.) Conductor; composer of colorful, complex experimental works (3 piano sonatas; cantata, *Le Marteau sans Maître; Figures, Doubles, Prismes* for orchestra).

Boult, Sir Adrian Cedric, 1889– (Eng.) Conductor (B.B.C. Symphony; London Philharmonic).

Bourgeois, Loys (Louis), c.1510–c.61 (Fr.) Composer and arranger of many of the hymn melodies in the *Genevan Psalter*.

Bowles, Paul Frederic, 1910– (U.S.) Author; composer of instrumental and stage works (opera and ballet).

Boyce, William, 1710–79 (Eng.) Organist and composer of sacred works, instrumental works (8 symphonies), incidental music for plays. He completed a 3-volume

collection of church music by many English composers of the 16th and 17th centuries.

Brailowsky, Alexander, 1896– (Rus.) Pianist specializing in works of Chopin.

Brain, Dennis, 1921–57 (Eng.) Outstanding horn player for whom Benjamin Britten wrote his *Serenade* for tenor, horn, and strings.

Brant, Henry Dreyfus, 1913– (Canada; U.S.) Composer of much avant-garde music for interesting instrumental combinations, using unorthodox spatial groupings.

Bream, Julian, 1933– (Eng.) Guitarist and lutanist.

Breitkopf & Härtel: German music publishers; founded in Leipzig in the mid-18th century by Bernhardt Christoph Breitkopf (1695–1777).

Bridge, Frank, 1879–1941 (Eng.) Composer of chamber music, often based on English subjects and folk tunes (4 string quartets, plus treatment of "Cherry Ripe").

Broadwood & Sons: English manufacturers of keyboard instruments, founded in 1728.

Brown, Earle, 1926– (U.S.) Composer in experimental media, including electronic.

Browning, John, 1933– (U.S.) Pianist; premièred piano concerto by Samuel Barber in 1962.

Brownlee, John, 1900–1969 (Australia; U.S.) Baritone with the Paris Opéra and the Metropolitan Opera; director of the Manhattan School of Music.

Brubeck, David, 1920– (U.S.) Jazz pianist and bandleader.

Bruch, Max, 1838–1920 (Ger.) Teacher and composer of operas, 3 violin concertos, *Kol Nidrei* for cello and orchestra.

Brumby, Grace, 1937– (U.S.) Operatic soprano.

Bull, John, c. 1562–1628 (Eng.) Virtuoso organist and composer of idiomatic works for virginal, many printed in the *Fitzwilliam Virginal Book*.

Bull, Ole Bornemann, 1810–80 (Norway) Violin virtuoso; composer of violin works based on Norwegian and American subjects.

Bülow, Hans Guido von, 1830–94 (Ger.) Pianist and conductor; conducted first performances of *Tristan and Isolde* and *Die Meistersinger;* as pianist, he premièred Tchaikovsky's first piano concerto (Boston, 1875).

Burkhard, Willy, 1900–55 (Switz.) Composer of opera, oratorios, and instrumental works.

Burleigh, Henry Thacker, 1866–1949 (U.S.) Baritone and composer of songs; arranged many Negro spirituals.

Burney, Charles, 1726–1824 (Eng.) Composer and keyboardist (organ and harpsichord); best known for his 4-volume *General History of Music*.

Busch, Adolf, 1891–1952 (Ger.) Violinist and composer; founder of the Busch Quartet.

Busch, Fritz, 1890–1951 (Ger.; Eng.) Conductor (Dresden State Opera; Glyndebourne Opera; Metropolitan Opera). Brother of Adolf Busch.

Busoni, Ferruccio Benvenuto, 1866–1924 (It.; Ger.) Composer of operas *(Turandot; Arlecchino),* piano works, and numerous transcriptions—particularly of Bach's organ works; author of influential essay: "Toward a New Aesthetics of Music."

Bussotti, Sylvano, 1931– (It.) Composer of avant-garde school.

C

Cabezón, Antonio de, 1510–66 (Sp.) Organist and composer of early keyboard variation forms.

Caccini, Guilio, *c.* 1546–1618 (It.) Singer and composer; one of the first to write vocal solos in the then-new recitative style ("Amarilli") and operas *(Euridice).*

Cadman, Charles Wakefield, 1881–1946 (U.S.) Composer of music based on American Indian themes, operas *(Shanewis, or The Robin Woman),* and many songs ("At Dawning").

Cage, John, 1912– (U.S.) Pianist and composer. Used 'prepared' piano (changing the tone quality and pitches of the instrument by placing assorted objects on the strings); aleatory music (sounds by chance); many scores for dance, especially for Merce Cunningham; author of *Silence* (1961) and *A Year from Monday* (1967).

Callas, Maria, 1923–1977 (U.S.) Coloratura and dramatic soprano.

Calloway, Cab, 1907– (U.S.) Jazz singer with unique style based on fast flow of nonsense syllables.

Calvé, Emma, 1858–1942 (Fr.) Operatic soprano; created roles in several operas by Massenet; famous for her singing of Carmen.

Campion, Thomas, 1567–1620 (Eng.) Poet and composer of several books of *Airs* for voice and lute.

Campra, André, 1660–1744 (Fr.) Composer of operas and ballets produced in Paris.

Canteloube de Malaret, Marie-Joseph, 1879–1957 (Fr.) Pianist and composer; collector and arranger of folk songs *(Chants d'Auvergne).*

Carey, Henry, *c.* 1687–1743 (Eng.) Writer of ballad-operas; words for "Sally in Our Alley." Often credited, incorrectly, as the author of "God Save the King."

Carissimi, Giacomo, 1605–74 (It.) Organist and composer of early oratorios *(Jephte)* and solo cantatas.

Carmichael, Hoagy, 1899– (U.S.) Singer, pianist, and composer of outstanding popular songs ("Stardust").

Carpenter, John Alden, 1876–1951 (U.S.) Composer ("jazz pantomime," *Krazy Kat;* ballet, *Skyscrapers).*

Carreño, Maria Teresa, 1853–1917 (Venezuela; U.S.) Singer, conductor, composer, but best known as concert pianist.

Carrillo, Julián, 1875–1965 (Mex.) Composer of many works utilizing microtones, subdividing the octave into as many as 97 tones.

Carte, Richard d'Oyly, 1844–1901 (Eng.) Impresario of Gilbert and Sullivan operettas.

Carter, Elliot Cook, 1908– (U.S.) Composer with highly individualized approach to melody and rhythm (2 string quartets; Variations for orchestra; Double Concerto for piano, harpsichord, and 2 small orchestras; 8 Études and a Fantasy for woodwind quartet; Concerto for Piano and Orchestra).

Caruso, Enrico, 1873–1921 (It.) Operatic tenor; one of the first great singers to record; best known for his roles in *Pagliacci* and *Tosca.*

Carvalho, Eleazar, 1912– (Brazil) Composer of operas, symphonic poems, chamber music; conductor (St. Louis Symphony, 1963–68).

Casadesus family: Robert (1899–1972), **Gaby** (1901–), and **Jean** (1927–1972) French pianists noted for performing individually and in twos and threes.

Casals, Pablo, 1876–1973 (Sp.; Puerto Rico) Cellist, conductor, and composer; founder of Prades Music Festival; noted for Bach interpretations.

Casella, Alfredo, 1883–1947 (It.) Pianist, critic, and composer of many orchestral and choral works in mildly dissonant style (3 symphonies, concertos, stage works, chamber music, short piano pieces, and songs).

Castelnuovo-Tedesco, Mario, 1895–1968 (It.; U.S.) Composer of stage works, concertos, and other instrumental works, plus scores for Hollywood films.

Caturla, Alejandro García, 1906–40 (Cuba) Composer who used Afro-Cuban rhythms, contemporary techniques, and dissonance in a highly original style.

Cavalieri, Emilio del, *c.* 1550–1602 (It.) Composer sometimes referred to as the father of the oratorio because of his *La rappresentazione de anima e di corpo*—a morality play with music first performed in the oratory of St. Filippo Neri in Rome.

Cavalli, Pier Francesco, 1602–76 (It.) Organist, and one of the first composers to write operas emphasizing aria rather than recitative.

Cesti, Marc' Antonio, 1623–69 (It.) Composer of important early operas *(Il Pomo d'oro)* and cantatas.

Chadwick, George Whitefield, 1854–1931 (U.S.) Music educator (director of New England Conservatory); prolific composer in all forms.

Chambonnières, Jacques Champion, *c.* 1602–72 (Fr.) Composer; founder of French keyboard school which culminated in François Couperin.

Chaliapin, Feodor Ivanovitch, 1873–1938 (Rus.) Bass singer, outstanding in his dramatic interpretation of Boris Godunov and Méphistophélès in *Faust.*

Chaminade, Cécile, 1857–1944 (Fr.) Composer, best known for her songs and light piano pieces ("The Flatterer"; "Scarf Dance").

Charles, Ray, 1930– (U.S.) Blind jazz musician who performs in an inventive combination of blues, gospel, and rock 'n' roll style.

Charpentier, Gustave, 1860–1956 (Fr.) Composer of many works, but best known for the opera *Louise.*

Charpentier, Marc-Antoine, 1634–1704 (Fr.) Composer of theatrical and sacred vocal works in grand style.

Chausson, Ernest, 1855–99 (Fr.) Composer in highly chromatic style; best-known work: *Poème* for violin and orchestra.

Chávez, Carlos, 1899– (Mex.) Conductor and composer of works for orchestra and choral groups *(Sinfonia India; Xochipilli Macuilxochitl;* Toccata for percussion).

Cherubini, Luigi, 1760–1842 (It.) Composer of influential operas *(Les Deux Journées),* church music, and chamber music; director of Paris Conservatory (1821–41); author of famous text on counterpoint.

Chou, Wen-chung, 1923– (China; U.S.) Composer of instrumental works combining Oriental and European idioms.

Christoff, Boris, 1918– (Bulgaria) Bass; baritone (best known for his performances of *Boris Godunov).*

Cilèa, Francesco, 1866–1950 (It.) Composer of operas *(Adriana Lecouvreur)* and chamber music.

Cimarosa, Domenico, 1749–1801 (It.) Composer of more than 60 operas *(Il matrimonio segreto)* in both comic and serious styles.

Clarke, Jeremiah, *c.* 1673–1701 (Eng.) Organist and composer of vocal works; wrote the *Trumpet Voluntary* often attributed to Purcell.

Clemens, Jacobus (called "Clemens non Papa") *c.* 1510–*c.* 56 (Netherlands) Composer of sacred and secular polyphonic vocal works.

Clementi, Muzio, 1752–1832 (It.) Pianist, teacher, and composer in the Classical style. In his more than 100 sonatas he did much to establish the pianistic idiom of the Classical period.

Cliburn, Van, 1934– (U.S.) Pianist; first American to win Tchaikovsky Prize in Moscow (1958).

Coates, Albert, 1882–1953 (Rus.; Eng.) Conductor of opera and symphony (Imperial Opera of St. Petersburg; Berlin State Opera; Vienna Philharmonic; Johannesburg Symphony).

Coates, Eric, 1886–1957 (Eng.) Viola player and composer *(Sleepy Lagoon; Knightsbridge Suite).*

Cohan, George Michael, 1878–1942 (U.S.) Composer of Broadway musicals and popular songs.

Cohen, Harriet, 1895–1967 (Eng.) Pianist; played first performances of works by many contemporary composers.

Cole, Nat "King," 1917–65 (U.S.) Pianist and singer in sensitive jazz style.

Coleman, Ornette, 1930– (U.S.) Innovative jazz saxophonist.

Coleridge-Taylor, Samuel, 1875–1912 (Eng.) Composer of choral and orchestral works *(The Song of Hiawatha).*

Coltrane, John William, 1926–67 (U.S.) Inventive saxophonist; avant-gardist in modern jazz.

Compère, Louis, *c.* 1455–1518 (Flanders) Composer of sacred and secular polyphonic vocal works.

Confrey, Edward (Zez), 1895–1971 (U.S.) Composer of piano pieces in clever, semi-jazz style *(Kitten on the Keys; Stumbling; Dizzy Fingers).*

Converse, Frederick Shepherd, 1871–1940 (U.S.) Composer of operas, symphonic works *(Flivver Ten Million; The Mystic Trumpeter),* and chamber works.

Coperario (John Cooper), c. 1575–1626 (Eng.) Lutanist; organist; composer of fantasies for viols, music for court masques, and songs.

Corelli, Franco, 1923– (It.) Operatic tenor.

Cornelius, Peter, 1824–74 (Ger.) Critic; champion of the music of Liszt and Wagner; composer of operas and songs.

Cortot, Alfred, 1877–1962 (Fr.) Pianist; member of trio with violinist Jacques Thibaud and cellist Pablo Casals; founded the École Normal de Musique.

Costeley, Guillaume, 1531–1606 (Fr.) Organist to Charles IX and composer of lyrical, expressive chansons.

Couperin, Louis, c. 1626–61 (Fr.) Composer and organist; first of long line of Couperins who were organists at St. Gervais in Paris; uncle of François Couperin.

Courboin, Charles Marie, 1886–1973 (Belg.) Organist and designer of organs.

Coward, Noel, 1899–1973 (Eng.) Author and composer of songs for musical comedy.

Cowell, Henry Dixon, 1897–1965 (U.S.) Pianist, teacher, scholar, and composer of the early avant-garde. His approach to the piano was unorthodox. He introduced new ways of playing "tone clusters" with fists, elbows, and forearms, and wrote music to be played on the strings of the piano *(Banshee).* He was one of the first to use percussion instruments as part of chamber groups. In 1927 he founded the "New Music Quarterly." In his later years he did extensive studies of folk music from all parts of the world, utilizing exotic themes in his compositions. He invented the "Rhythmicon" with Leon Theremin. His total output of works is large, and includes works in many forms (operas, 19 symphonies, and many varieties of chamber music).

Cramer, Johann Baptist, 1771–1858 (Ger.) Pianist and composer; wrote a great number of piano sonatas and concertos, but is best known for his études.

Crawford, Ruth Porter, 1901–53 (U.S.) Composer who wrote in a highly dissonant manner for unusual sound combinations *(Three Songs* for contralto, oboe, piano, and percussion with orchestral ostinato). She was also noted for sensitive settings of many American folk songs.

Creston, Paul, 1906– (U.S.) Composer of 5 symphonies and many works featuring unusual solo instruments (marimba, saxophone, trombone) in melodic, non-experimental style.

Cristofori, Bartolommeo, 1655–1731 (It.) Inventor of the piano which bears his name.

Croft, William, 1678–1727 (Eng.) Organist and composer (anthems, keyboard works) in conservative Baroque style.

Crosby, Harry ("Bing"), 1903–77 (U.S.) Outstanding singer of popular ballads.

Crotch, William, 1775–1847 (Eng.) Organist and composer of oratorios, anthems, and keyboard works; principal of the Royal Academy of Music.

Crüger, Johann, 1598–1662 (Ger.) Composer of many well-known chorales ("Nun danket alle Gott," or "Now Thank We All Our God"; "Jesu, meine Freude," or "Jesus My Joy").

Crumb, George, 1929– (U.S.) Composer of works in poetic, unorthodox style *(Night Music, I, II);* Pulitzer Prize, 1968.

Cui, César Antonovitch, 1835–1918 (Rus.) Critic and composer; member of "The Russian Five."

Curtin, Phyllis, 1922– (U.S.) Operatic soprano.

D

Dahl, Ingolf, 1912–70 (Ger.; U.S.) Teacher (U.S.C.) and composer in neo-Classical style *(Music for Brass Instruments).*

Dallapiccola, Luigi, 1904–75 (It.) Composer of operas *(Il prigioniero),* chamber and symphonic works *(Variations for Orchestra),* and choral music. His music is expressive and dramatic, making free use of twelve-tone technique.

Damrosch, Frank, 1859–1939 (Ger.; U.S.) Choral conductor and founder of the Institute of Musical Art.

Damrosch, Walter Johannes, 1862–1950 (Ger.; U.S.) Conductor and composer. As conductor (New York Symphony Society), he played works of Brahms and Tchaikovsky for the first time for American audiences. He was the first to conduct a weekly series of music appreciation programs for school children by radio. His compositions include operas *(The Scarlet Letter; The Man Without a Country)* and many songs ("Danny Deever").

Da Ponte, Lorenzo, 1747–1838 (It.; U.S.) Librettist for Mozart's *Marriage of Figaro, Don Giovanni,* and *Così fan tutte.*

Daquin, Louis-Claude, 1694–1772 (Fr.) Organist and composer of keyboard works *(Le Coucou).*

Dargomyzhsky, Alexander Sergeyevitch, 1813–69 (Rus.) Composer of operas *(Russalka; The Stone Guest).* He was one of the first to bring exotic melodic elements into music.

Darré, Jeanne-Marie, 1905– (Fr.) Virtuoso pianist.

Dart, Thurston, 1921–71 (Eng.) Musicologist and virtuoso player of early keyboard instruments.

David, Félicien, 1810–76 (Fr.) One of the first to study the music of the Near East; composer of symphonic works *(Le Désert)* and operas *(Lalla Roukh).*

David, Ferdinand, 1810–73 (Ger.) Violinist who first performed Mendelssohn's Violin Concerto.

Davidovsky, Mario, 1934– (Argentina; U.S.) Composer of expressive works for various combinations of instruments and electronic sounds *(Synchronisms).*

Davies, Sir Henry Walford, 1869–1941 (Eng.) Organist, teacher, and composer of works for chorus, orchestra, and chamber groups. One of the first to broadcast a series of educational musical programs.

Davies, Peter Maxwell, 1934– (Eng.) Composer in wide range of styles and forms.

Davis, Colin, 1927– (Eng.) Conductor (B.B.C. Symphony Orchestra; London Symphony; Royal Opera).

Dawson, William Levi, 1898– (U.S.) Composer, conductor, and teacher; scholar of Negro folk songs.

De Koven, Henry Louis Reginald, 1859–1920 (U.S.) Critic; composer of operas and operettas *(Robin Hood,* which contained the popular song "O Promise Me").

Delannoy, Marcel, 1898–1962 (Fr.) Composer of ballets, operas, symphonic works.

Delibes, (Clément-Philbert) Léo, 1836–91 (Fr.) Composer who set new styles and standards for ballet music *(La Source; Coppélia; Sylvia);* the exotic-flavored *Lakmé* and tuneful *Le Roi l'a dit (The King Said So)* were his most successful operas.

Deller, Alfred, 1912– (Eng.) Countertenor who has specialized in performances of works by Purcell and Handel.

Dello Joio, Norman, 1913– (U.S.) Composer of operas *(The Triumph of St. Joan),* ballets *(Diversion of Angels),* orchestral and chamber works, sonatas and shorter works for piano, and choral works *(A Jubilant Song).*

Del Monaco, Mario, 1915– (It.) Operatic tenor.

De Los Angeles, Victoria, 1923– (Sp.) Operatic and concert soprano.

Denisov, Edison, 1929– (Rus.) Composer of experimental and vocal works.

Densmore, Frances, 1867–1957 (U.S.) Authority on Plains and Pueblo Indian music.

Dent, Edward Joseph, 1876–1957 (Eng.) Music scholar, particularly of opera. Has translated many librettos into English.

De Reszke, Edouard, 1853–1917 (Poland) Operatic bass equally at home in Italian, French, and German operas.

De Reszke, Jean, 1850–1925 (Poland) Operatic tenor who became an outstanding vocal teacher.

Dessau, Paul, 1894– (Ger.) Composer of operas and chamber music, but best known for his revolutionary songs written for films and plays (often in collaboration with Berthold Brecht).

Dett, Robert Nathaniel, 1878–1943 (Canada; U.S.) Teacher; composer of piano works ("Juba Dance") and choral works. Collected and arranged many Negro spirituals; conductor of the Hampton Choir.

Deutsch, Otto Erich, 1883–1967 (Aus.) Musicologist; authority on Schubert.

Diabelli, Anton, 1781–1858 (Aus.) Composer and publisher. Beethoven's 33 Variations, Op. 120, are based on a simple waltz by Diabelli.

Diaghilev, Sergei Pavlovitch, 1872–1929 (Rus.; Fr.) Founded the Ballet Russe in revolt against traditional ballet; commissioned scores by Auric, Debussy, Falla, Milhaud, Poulenc, Prokofiev, and Ravel.

Diamond, David, 1915– (U.S.) Composer of a large amount of orchestral and chamber music in a dissonant, often mystical, style.

Dickinson, Peter, 1934– (Eng.) Teacher and composer, in modern eclectic style, of chamber music and vocal works.

Dieren, Bernard van, 1884–1936 (Holland; Eng.) Composer and author (*Down Among the Dead Men*).

Dittersdorf, Karl Ditters von, 1739–99 (Aus.) Violinist (string quartet companion of Haydn and Mozart) and composer of many operas (*Doktor und Apotheker*), symphonies, ballets, chamber and piano works in Classical idiom.

Dohnányi, Ernst von, 1877–1960 (H.; U.S.) Pianist, teacher, and composer in all forms in late Romantic style; best-known work: *Variations on a Nursery Song* for piano and orchestra.

Dolmetsch, Arnold, 1858–1940 (Fr.; Eng.) Violinist and instrument maker; leading revivalist of 16th- and 17th-century music.

Donizetti, Gaetano, 1797–1848 (It.) Composer of operas centering on singers rather than drama (*Linda di Chamounix; Lucia di Lammermoor; La Fille du régiment; La Favorite*).

Dorati, Antal, 1906– (H.) Conductor of ballet and symphony orchestras (Dallas Symphony; Minneapolis Symphony).

Dorian, Frederick, 1902– (Aus.; U.S.) Musicologist (*The History of Music in Performance*).

Dorsey, James ("Jimmy"), 1904–57 (U.S.) Jazz clarinetist-saxophonist.

Dorsey, Thomas ("Tommy"), 1905–56 (U.S.) Bandleader and jazz trombonist known for his controlled, sentimental style.

Dragonetti, Domenico, 1763–1846 (It.; Eng.) Double-bass virtuoso; friend of Beethoven.

Drdla, Franz, 1868–1944 (Moravia) Violinist and composer (*Souvenir*).

Drigo, Riccardo, 1846–1930 (It.) Conductor and composer of operas and ballets ("Serenade" and "Valse Bluette" are from his most successful ballet, *Harlequin's Millions*).

Dubois, (Clément-François) Théodore, 1837–1924 (Fr.) Organist; teacher; composer of comic and grand operas, orchestral, choral, and chamber works; director of Paris Conservatory (1896–1905).

Dukas, Paul, 1865–1935 (Fr.) Composer of colorful orchestral works (*L'Apprenti Sorcier*); an important opera (*Ariane et Barbe-Bleue*); a successful ballet (*La Péri*); and assorted shorter works, including a sonata for piano.

Dukelsky, Vladimir (Vernon Duke), 1903–1969 (Rus.; U.S.) Prolific composer of symphonies, concertos, ballets, chamber and vocal works. As Duke, he has written many scores for films and Broadway. Best-known song: "April in Paris."

Dunstable, John, *c.* 1370–1453 (Eng.) Composer whose polyphonic motets were important influences on the development of music in the early Renaissance period.

Duparc, (Marie-Eugéne) Henri Fouques, 1848–1933 (Fr.) Composer of a small number of hauntingly beautiful songs ("Phidylé"; "Invitation au Voyage").

Dupré, Marcel, 1886–1971 (Fr.) Organist and composer (symphonies for organ): famous for his concert improvisations.

Durand, Marie-Auguste, 1830–1909 (Fr.) Founder of publishing house that is now Durand & Cie; publisher of works by many ranking French composers.

Durante, Francesco, 1684–1755 (It.) Teacher and composer of Neapolitan school. His music, mostly for the church, is quite dramatic in its use of chromatics and unexpected harmonic progressions. Teacher of Jommeli, Paisello, Pergolesi, and Piccini.

Durey, Louis, 1888– (Fr.) Critic and composer of operas, chamber music, and songs; member of "Les Six."

Duruflé, Maurice, 1902– (Fr.) Organist; composer of organ works and a much-performed Requiem.

Dussek, Johann Ladislaus, 1760–1812 (Bohemia) Pianist and composer whose many works for piano (12 concertos, 40 sonatas) are comparable to those of Weber in their exploration of the technical and poetic resources of the instrument.

Dylan, Bob, 1941– (U.S.) Composer and singer of folk songs.

Dzerzhinsky, Ivan Ivanovitch, 1909– (Rus.) Composer of operas (*Quiet Flows the Don*).

E

Eberl, Anton Franz Josef, 1765–1807 (Aus.) Pianist and composer. Some of his piano compositions were originally credited to his friend Mozart.

Eberlin, Johann Ernst, 1702–62 (Bavaria) Organist; composer of sacred works and organ music.

Eccles, John, *c.* 1650–1735 (Eng.) Violinist; composer of songs and music for dramatic works.

Eckstine, William ("Billy"), 1914– (U.S.) Jazz singer who did much to popularize "progressive" jazz style.

Eddy, Nelson, 1901–67 (U.S.) Operatic baritone, best known for his work in musical films and radio.

Effinger, Cecil, 1914– (U.S.) Composer; first inventor of a usable musical typewriter.

Egge, Klaus, 1906– (Norway) Composer of symphonic and chamber works with some national color.

Ehrling, Sixten, 1918– (Sweden) Pianist and conductor (Detroit Symphony).

Eichheim, Henry, 1870–1942 (U.S.) Composer of works combining Oriental melodies and rhythms with early 20th-century European musical styles.

Einem, Gottfried von, 1918– (Switz.; Aus.) Composer of operas (*Dantons Tod*), some orchestral works.

Einstein, Alfred, 1880–1952 (Ger.; U.S.) Musicologist; author of books on Gluck, Mozart, and Schubert; major work: *The Italian Madrigal*, in 3 volumes.

Eisler, Hanns, 1898–1962 (Ger.) Composer of complex twelve-tone instrumental works, including several film scores and direct "peoples" songs (some for plays by Berthold Brecht).

Elman, Mischa, 1891–1967 (Rus.; U.S.) Violinist; started successful concert career at age of 13.

Eloy, Jean-Claude, 1938– (Fr.) Composer using experimental idioms.

Elwell, Herbert, 1898– (U.S.) Critic; composer of orchestral, choral, and chamber works, and a ballet (*The Happy Hypocrite*).

Emmett, Daniel Decatur, 1815–1904 (U.S.) Composer of popular songs ("Dixie"; "Old Dan Tucker"); member of Bryant's Minstrels.

Enesco, Georges, 1881–1955 (Rumania) Conductor; violinist; composer of a large body of works for symphonic and chamber groups, often based on Rumanian folk music (*Rumanian Rhapsody*).

Engel, A. Lehman, 1910– (U.S.) Composer, best known for his music for plays (*Within the Gates*) and ballets; author of *History of American Musical Theater*; conductor of Broadway musical shows.

Engel, Carl, 1884–1944 (Fr.; U.S.) Musicologist (music division of the Library of Congress); editor of *Musical Quarterly*; Author of *Alle Breve* and *Discords Mingled*; composer of songs and short works for piano.

Érard, Sébastien, 1752–1831 (Fr.) Maker of harps and pianos; inventor of the double-action harp and the double-escapement piano action, which allows for rapid repeated notes.

Erkel, Franz, 1810–93 (H.) Conductor (Budapest Philharmonic); composer of songs, including the Hungarian National Hymn, and the first Hungarian operas.

Expert, Henry, 1863–1952 (Fr.) Musicologist; editor of multi-volume collections of French music of the 15th and 16th centuries.

F

Falconieri, Andrea, 1586–1656 (It.) Lutanist and composer of instrumental and vocal works.

Fall, Leo, 1873–1925 (Aus.) Composer of light operas (*Die Dollarprinzessin*).

Farinelli (real name, **Carlo Broschi**), 1705–82 (It.) Celebrated castrato.

Farnaby, Giles, *c.* 1560–1640 (Eng.) Composer of many keyboard and vocal works.

Farrant, Richard, *c.* 1530–81 (Eng.) Composer of much enduring sacred music.

Farrar, Geraldine, 1882–1968 (U.S.) Operatic soprano.

Farrell, Eileen, 1920– (U.S.) Operatic and concert soprano.

Farwell, Arthur, 1872–1952 (U.S.) Composer of music based on folk and Indian themes; established the Wa-Wan Press in 1901 to publish works by American composers.

Fasch, Johann Friedrich, 1688–1758 (Ger.) Composer of sacred cantatas, concertos, and orchestral suites admired by J. S. Bach.

Fayrfax, Robert, 1464–1521 (Eng.) Composer of sacred and secular vocal music.

Feldman, Morton, 1926– (U.S.) Composer of experimental music that leaves much to the option of the performer.

Fellowes, Rev. Edmund Horace, 1870–1951 (Eng.) Musicologist and editor (*The English Madrigal School*, 36 vols.; *The English School of Lutenist Songwriters*, 31 vols.; *The Complete Works of William Byrd*, 20 vols.), and co-author of *Tudor Church Music*, 16 vols.

Ferrabosco, Alfonso, 1543–88 (It.) Composer of madrigals; spent time in England, where he introduced the Italian madrigal style to English composers.

Ferrabosco, Alfonso, c. 1575–1628 (Eng.) Composer of songs and works for viols; wrote music for the masques of Ben Jonson. Son of Alfonso Ferrabosco, above.

Ferrier, Kathleen, 1912–53 (Eng.) Contralto; first Lucretia in Britten's *Rape of Lucretia.*

Festa, Costanzo, c. 1490–1545 (It.) Composer; one of the early Italian madrigalists.

Fétis, François-Joseph, 1784–1871 (Belg.) Historian; theorist; critic (carried out a major revision of the music of the Roman church); author of *Biographie universelle des musiciens et bibliographie générale de la musique,* 8 vols., and *Histoire générale de la musique,* 5 vols.

Feuermann, Emanuel, 1902–42 (Aus.; U.S.) Concert cellist.

Fibich, Zdenko, 1850–1900 (Czech.) Composer of a large catalogue of operas, choruses and songs, instrumental works (*Poème,* Op. 41).

Fiedler, Arthur, 1894–1979 (U.S.) Conductor of Boston Pops concerts since 1930.

Field, John, 1782–1837 (Ireland; Rus.) Pianist and composer (mainly of piano works which influenced Chopin).

Fine, Irving, 1914–62 (U.S.) Teacher (Brandeis University) and composer (symphony; music for *Alice in Wonderland; Partita* for wind quintet; string quartet).

Finney, Ross Lee, 1906– (U.S.) Teacher (Smith College, Mt. Holyoke, University of Michigan) and composer of adventurous yet solid orchestral and chamber works.

Fischer, Johann Kaspar Ferdinand, c. 1665–1746 (Ger.) Composer of keyboard suites and a series of 20 preludes and fugues for organ, each in a different key, which undoubtedly influenced J. S. Bach's *Well-tempered Clavier.*

Fischer-Dieskau, Dietrich, 1925– (Ger.) Baritone performing both opera and lieder.

Fitelberg, Jerzy, 1903–51 (Poland; U.S.) Composer of orchestral and chamber music (5 string quartets; 2 violin concertos).

Fitzgerald, Ella, 1918– (U.S.) Popular jazz vocalist.

Fitzwilliam, Viscount Richard, 1745–1816 (Eng.) Collector of manuscripts, principally of 16th- and 17th-century English keyboard music (the collection is housed at the Fitzwilliam Museum in Cambridge). *The Fitzwilliam Virginal Book* has been published in 2 volumes, edited by J. A. Fuller-Maitland and William Barkley Squire.

Flagstad, Kirsten, 1895–1962 (Norway) Dramatic Wagnerian soprano.

Fleisher, Leon, 1928– (U.S.) Pianist; winner of 1952 prize at Brussels International competition.

Flotow, Friedrich von, 1812–83 (Ger.) Composer of operas (*Martha*).

Floyd, Carlisle, 1926– (U.S.) Composer of music for ballet, songs, and opera (*Susannah*).

Fomin, Evstigney Ipatovitch, 1761–1800 (Rus.) Early Russian composer of operas. His subject matter ranged from Russian

history to the fanciful (*The Americans*). His style was modeled on Italian opera.

Foote, Arthur, 1853–1937 (U.S.) Composer of orchestral, chamber, and choral works written in late 19th-century idiom.

Ford, Thomas, c. 1580–1648 (Eng.) Lutanist and composer of "ayres" and madrigals ("Since first I saw your face").

Forkel, Johann Nikolaus, 1749–1818 (Ger.) Music historian who wrote the first biography of J. S. Bach (1802).

Forsyth, Cecil, 1870–1941 (Eng.; U.S.) Composer of operas, instrumental works, sacred music, and songs; best known for his book *Orchestration* (1914).

Foss, Lukas, 1922– (Ger.; U.S.) Conductor (Buffalo Symphony) and avant-garde composer (*Time Cycle* for soprano and orchestra; *Echoi* for chamber group).

Fournier, Pierre, 1906– (Fr.) Cellist.

Fox-Strangways, Arthur Henry, 1859–1948 (Eng.) Writer; one of the first to study the music of India (*The Music of Hindustan*).

Françaix, Jean, 1912– (Fr.) Composer, best known for his witty concertino for piano and orchestra.

Francescatti, Zino, 1905– (Fr.) Violinist.

Franck, Melchoir, c. 1579–1639 (Ger.) Composer of sacred and secular vocal music.

Franco of Cologne: 13th-century theorist who codified the rules for notating the measurement of musical time.

Franklin, Benjamin, 1706–90 (U.S.) Statesman; invented the glass harmonica and wrote a string quartet that makes use only of open strings.

Franz, Robert, 1815–92 (Ger.) Composer of several hundred songs.

Frederick II (the Great), 1712–86 (Prussia) Patron of Quantz and C. P. E. Bach; flutist; composer (flute sonatas and concertos). J. S. Bach's *Musical Offering* is based on a theme by him.

Fricker, Peter Racine, 1920– (Eng.) Teacher and composer of highly original symphonic and chamber music.

Friedberg, Carl, 1872–1955 (Ger.; U.S.) Pianist.

Friml, Rudolf, 1879–1972 (Bohemia; U.S.) Composer of operettas (*Rose Marie; Vagabond King*).

Friskin, James, 1886–1967 (Scot.; U.S.) Teacher (Juilliard); pianist specializing in Bach; composer of chamber music.

Froberger, Johann Jakob, 1616–67 (Ger.) Organist (pupil of Frescobaldi) and composer of keyboard canzonas, ricercars, fantasias, and toccatas. His partitas established the form and order of the keyboard dance suite.

Fry, William Henry, 1813–64 (U.S.) Composer of first opera by an American (*Leonora,* 1845); also symphonic works with programmatic titles (*Santa Claus* Symphony; *Niagara*).

Furtwängler, Wilhelm, 1886–1954 (Ger.) Conductor (Berlin State Opera; Berlin Philharmonic; Bayreuth and Salzburg festivals).

Fux, Johann Joseph, 1660–1741 (Aus.) Composer of many keyboard works, operas, oratorios, masses, and other religious music, but best known for his work as a theorist (*Gradus ad Parnassum*).

G

Gabrilovitch, Ossip, 1878–1936 (Rus.; U.S.) Pianist and conductor (Detroit Symphony).

Gaburo, Kenneth, 1927– (U.S.) Composer of expressive works in experimental style (antiphonies for traditional instruments and electronic sounds).

Gade, Niels Wilhelm, 1817–90 (Denmark) Composer of 8 symphonies, cantatas, and chamber music in Romantic style with Scandinavian flavor.

Galilei, Vincenzo, c. 1520–91 (It.) Composer; member of the *Camerata di Bardi.* His songs with lute accompaniment played a large part in the development of the recitative style of early opera. Father of the famous astronomer Galileo Galilei.

Galindo, Blas, 1910– (Mex.) Composer who mixes Mexican-Indian ideas and instruments with international contemporary style (ballets; concerto for piano; orchestral works; chamber, choral, and piano works).

Galliard, Johann Ernst, 1687–1749 (Ger.; Eng.) Oboist and composer of music for masques and other theatrical forms of his time, plus cantatas, oratorios, and sonatas for various solo instruments.

Galli-Curci, Amelita, 1882–1963 (It.) Operatic coloratura soprano.

Gallus, Jacobus (real name, **Jacob Händl**), 1550–91 (Carniola) Composer of masses and motets, often for multiple choirs.

Galpin, Rev. Francis William, 1858–1945 (Eng.) Clergyman who became an authority on the history of musical instruments and ancient music (*A Textbook of European Musical Instruments; The Music of the Sumerians, Babylonians and Assyrians*).

Galuppi, Baldassare, 1706–85 (It.) Composer of more than 100 operas (one of the founders of opera-buffa style) and 12 keyboard sonatas in early Classical style.

Ganz, Rudolph, 1877–1972 (Switz.; U.S.) Pianist, teacher, and conductor (St. Louis Symphony; New York Philharmonic Young People's Concerts); director of Chicago Musical College; played many première performances of works by important contemporary composers.

Garcia, Manuel del Popolo Vicente, 1775–1832 (Sp.) Operatic tenor, voice teacher, and composer of many operas and ballets.

Garcia, Manuel Patricio Rodriguez, 1805–1906 (Sp.; Eng.) Famous vocal teacher (Jenny Lind) who, in order to make a scientific study of voice production, invented the laryngoscope. Son of Manuel del Popolo Vicente Garcia.

Garden, Mary, 1877–1967 (Scot.; U.S.) Operatic soprano; created role of Mélisande in Debussy's *Pelléas and Mélisande.*

Garner, Errol, 1921–77 (U.S.) Jazz pianist with unique improvisational style.

Gastoldi, Giovanni Giacomo, c. 1550–1622 (It.) Composer of madrigals, canzonettas, and gay balletti that strongly influenced Morley and other English composers of the Elizabethan period.

Gatti-Casazza, Giulio, 1868–1940 (It.) Director of La Scala (1898–1908) and the Metropolitan Opera (1908–35).

Gay, John, 1685–1732 (Eng.) Librettist of *The Beggar's Opera.*

Gedda, Nicolai, 1925–   (Sweden) Operatic tenor.

Geminiani, Francesco, 1687–1762 (It.; Ireland) Violinist and teacher. Composer of sonatas, concertos for strings which use shifts of position and double stops with new freedom; author of one of the first violin methods, *The Art of Playing on the Violin.*

Gerhard, Roberto, 1896–1970 (Sp.; Eng.) Composer of operas, ballets *(Pandora),* concertos, chamber music, and incidental music for several of Shakespeare's plays. His style was derived from a tightly organized serial twelve-tone technique.

German, Sir Edward, 1862–1936 (Eng.) Composer of operas, symphonic works, and chamber works; best known for incidental music for plays *(Henry VIII; Richard III).*

Gesualdo, Don Carlo, c. 1560–1613 (It.) Lutanist and experimental composer of the Renaissance. In expressing the mood of the text of his madrigals, he used dissonance, unusual harmonic progressions, and dynamic contrasts with amazing originality (6 volumes of 5-part madrigals).

Gevaert, François Auguste, 1828–1908 (Belg.) Composer of operas, cantatas, ballads, and songs; musicologist and educator (Director of Brussels Conservatory); author *(Histoire et Théorie de la musique de l'antiquité; Traité général d'instrumentation; La Mélopée antique dans l'église latine; Traité d'Harmonie théorique et partique).*

Ghislanzoni, Antonio, 1824–93 (It.) Dramatic poet; librettist of many operas *(Aida).*

Giacosa, Giuseppe, 1847–1906 (It.) Playwright; co-librettist with Luigi Illica for Puccini's *Tosca, La Bohème* and *Madame Butterfly.*

Giannini, Vittorio, 1903–66 (U.S.) Composer of opera *(The Scarlet Letter; The Taming of the Shrew),* orchestral and band music, and chamber music; first director of North Carolina School of the Arts.

Gibbons, Orlando, 1583–1625 (Eng.) Organist and composer whose style fused traditional polyphonic writing with the newer homophonic techniques (anthems; *Fantasie* for viols; keyboard works; madrigals and motets).

Gieseking, Walter, 1895–1956 (France; Ger.) Pianist noted for his performances of Debussy and Mozart.

Gigli, Beniamino, 1890–1957 (It.) Operatic tenor.

Gilbert, Henry Franklin Belknap, 1868–1928 (U.S.) Composer who used Negro, folk, and American-Indian thematic elements in his orchestral works *(Comedy Overture on Negro Themes; The Dance in Place Congo; Negro Rhapsody; Indian Sketches).*

Gillespie, John Birks ("Dizzy"), 1917– (U.S.) Jazz trumpeter; early performer in 'progressive' jazz, 'bebop' style.

Gilels, Emil, 1916–   (Rus.) Brilliant pianist.

Gillis, Don, 1912–   (U.S.) Composer of symphonies and string quartets; best

known work his good-humored Symphony No. 5½.

Gilmore, Patrick Sarsfield, 1829–92 (Ireland; U.S.) Bandleader renowned for music festivals where he conducted large choral and instrumental groups. Composer of "When Johnny Comes Marching Home."

Ginastera, Alberto, 1916–   (Argentina) Composer of ballets, orchestral and chamber music, and songs. His opera *Don Rodrigo* (1964) and opera *Bomarzo* (1967) are vividly dramatic works that utilize, expressively, many experimental techniques.

Giordano, Umberto, 1867–1948 (It.) Composer of operas *(Andrea Chénier).*

Glazunov, Alexander Konstantinovitch, 1865–1936 (Rus.) Composer (pupil of Rimsky-Korsakov) in almost all forms: 8 symphonies; ballets *(Raymonda);* orchestral suites *(The Seasons);* symphonic poem *(Stenka Razin);* concertos (for violin, for piano, and for cello).

Glière, Reinhold Moritzovitch, 1875–1956 (Rus.) Composer of songs, chamber music, symphonies, operas, ballets *(The Red Poppy),* and concertos (for violin, for harp, for cello, for coloratura soprano). His works, often based on folk tunes, are frequently given programmatic titles: Symphony No. 3, *Ilya Muromets;* overture, *25 Years of the Red Army.*

Gluck, Alma, 1884–1938 (Rumania; U.S.) Concert and operatic soprano.

Gnessin, Mikhail Fabianovitch, 1883–1957 (Rus.) Composer of operas, dramatic music, symphonic works, chamber music, piano and vocal works (many of which were inspired by and reflect Jewish folk songs and traditions).

Gobbi, Tito, 1915–   (It.) Operatic baritone.

Godard, Benjamin, 1849–95 (Fr.) Violinist; composer of operas, symphonic works, chamber works, and songs. His numerous piano works are an important part of the young pianist's repertoire; his best-known work is the *Berceuse* from his opera *Jocelyn.*

Godowsky, Leopold, 1870–1938 (Rus.; U.S.) Pianist and composer who wrote exclusively for the piano: *Triakontameron* (including *Alt Wein), Java Suite, Miniatures* for 4 hands, studies based on Chopin études and a sonata, all reflecting his prodigious piano technique, especially for the left hand.

Goeb, Roger, 1914–   (U.S.) Composer of 4 symphonies and other orchestral works, plus chamber works for various instrumental combinations *(Prairie Song* for woodwind quintet; Concertino for trombone and strings).

Gold, Ernest, 1921–   (Aus.; U.S.) Composer of many successful film scores *(Exodus; The Defiant Ones).*

Goldberg, Johann Gottlieb, 1727–56 (Ger.) Harpsichordist for whom Bach wrote his *Aria with 30 Variations.*

Goldberg, Szymon, 1909–   (Poland) Violinist and conductor.

Goldman, Edwin Franko, 1878–1956 (U.S.) Bandmaster who expanded the repertoire of bands by arranging orchestral and instrumental works for band and by com-

missioning many contemporary composers to write for band.

Goldman, Richard Franko, 1910–80 (U.S.) Musicologist, bandmaster, composer of works for a wide variety of instrumental organizations and combinations, librettist, teacher, translator, and author *(The Band's Music; The Juilliard Report; The Harmony of Western Music).* Son of Edwin Franko Goldman.

Goldmark, Karl, 1830–1915 (H.; Aus.) Composer of operas *(The Queen of Sheba),* overtures *(Sakuntala), Rustic Wedding Symphony,* 2 violin concertos, chamber and choral music works.

Goldmark, Rubin, 1872–1936 (U.S.) Composer of works for orchestra, chamber groups, and songs; teacher (Juilliard School of Music) of Abram Chasins, Aaron Copland, and George Gershwin.

Golschmann, Vladimir, 1893–1972 (Fr.; U.S.) Conductor (St. Louis and Denver symphony orchestras).

Gombert, Nicolas, c. 1495–1556 (Flanders) Composer of masses, motets, chansons. His use of canon as a predominant technique undoubtedly influenced Palestrina.

Gomes, Antonio Carlos, 1836–96 (Brazil) Composer of songs, piano pieces, and operas *(Il Guarany* was a great success on its première at La Scala in 1870).

Goodman, Benny, 1909–   (U.S.) Clarinetist and bandleader who did much to popularize the style of jazz known as "swing."

Goossens, Sir Eugene, 1893–1962 (Eng.) Conductor (Rochester, Cincinnati, and Sydney symphony orchestras); composer of operas *(Judith),* piano works *(Kaleidoscope),* chamber music, 2 symphonies, an oboe concerto, and an oratorio.

Goossens, Leon, 1897–   (Eng.) Oboist for whom many composers, including his brother Eugene, wrote solo works.

Gorin, Igor, 1908–   (Rus.; U.S.) Operatic and concert baritone; composer of songs.

Gossec, François Joseph, 1734–1829 (Belg.; Fr.) Conductor and composer of operas, oratorios, chamber music, and symphonic works. An ardent believer in the aims of the French Revolution, Gossec wrote large-scale works calling for great numbers of instrumentalists and singers. He was, in many ways, the "father" of the later music festivals utilizing hundreds—even thousands—of performers.

Gottschalk, Louis Moreau, 1829–69 (U.S.) Pianist and composer of operas, symphonic poems, piano pieces, and songs. He was among the first to use Afro-Spanish dance rhythms in concert music.

Goudimel, Claude, c. 1505–72 (Fr.) Composer (masses, motets, and chansons) and theorist; known for his settings of the hymns in the Huguenot Psalter (1564).

Gould, Glenn, 1932–   (Canada) Pianist, recording artist, and composer, known for his highly individual approach to the music of Bach and Schoenberg.

Gould, Morton, 1913–   (U.S.) Conductor and composer of orchestral works *(Spirituals for orchestra; Latin American Symphonette),* ballets *(Fall River Legend),* a Broadway musical *(Billion Dollar Baby),* symphonies, concertos, and piano sonatas. Gould has also done many brilliant orchestral arrangements of popular melodies.

Grabovsky, Leonid, 1935– (Rus.) Composer of moderately experimental music with nationalist undertones.

Graffmann, Gary, 1928– (U.S.) Pianist.

Grainger, Percy Aldridge, 1882–1961 (Australia; U.S.) Pianist and composer of many works based on folk songs or folk-like material *(Molly on the Shore; Shepherd's Hey; Handel in the Strand).* He arranged his gay, buoyant music using "elastic" scoring: allowing the works to be played by a variety of instrumental combinations.

Granados, Enrique, 1867–1916 (Sp.) Composer of Spanish Nationalist school: operas, symphonic poems, chamber music, and songs. His best-known work is the opera *Goyescas,* musically based on a 2-volume suite for piano.

Grandjany, Marcel, 1891–1975 (Fr.; U.S.) Harpist and teacher: composer of works for harp in a post-Impressionist style.

Graun, Karl Heinrich, 1704–59 (Ger.) Composer of Italian-style operas, concertos for flute and for harpsichord, and trio-sonatas, as well as church music (Te Deum; passion-cantata, *Der Tod Jesu).*

Graupner, Christoph, 1683–1760 (Ger.) Prolific composer of operas, more than 100 symphonies, 50 concertos for various instruments, 80 overtures, many solo and trio-sonatas, and more than a thousand sacred works.

Graupner, Johann Christian Gottlieb, 1767–1836 (Ger.; U.S.) Composer and teacher who organized the Boston Philharmonic Society; also was one of the founders of the choral society which later became the Handel and Haydn Society.

Greenberg, Noah, 1919–66 (U.S.) Founder of Pro Musica Antiqua, a group specializing in performances of Renaissance vocal and instrumental music. Revived the *Play of Daniel* and the *Play of Herod,* medieval sacred music dramas.

Gretchaninov, Alexander Tikhonovitch, 1864–1956 (Rus.; U.S.) Composer of operas, ballets, incidental music for plays, orchestral works, a vast output of sacred music *(Missa Oecumenica* for solos, chorus, and orchestra), chamber music, songs, and many works for children.

Grétry, André Modeste, 1741–1813 (Belg.; Fr.) Composer, best known for his dramatic and lyrical *opéras-comiques.* His masterpiece, *Richard Coeur de Lion,* is one of the earliest suspense-laden "rescue" operas.

Grey, Madeleine, 1897– (Fr.) Soprano who specialized in contemporary French songs. Well known for her recordings of Canteloube's arrangements of *Songs of the Auvergne.*

Griffes, Charles Tomlinson, 1884–1920 (U.S.) Composer of works for piano *(Roman Sketches,* which includes *The White Peacock;* Sonata in F), for orchestra *(The Pleasure Dome of Kubla Khan),* works for chamber combinations based on exotic subject matter, and songs set to both German and English texts.

Grofé, Ferde (Ferdinand Rudolph von), 1892–1972 (U.S.) Composer and arranger (he scored Gershwin's *Rhapsody in Blue* for Paul Whiteman's band). His descriptive orchestral suites mostly have geographical titles *(Grand Canyon; Mississippi; Niagara Falls; Hollywood).*

Grout, Donald Jay, 1902– (U.S.) Teacher (Cornell University) and musicologist; author of *A Short History of Opera* (1947) and *A History of Western Music* (1960).

Grove, Sir George, 1820–1900 (Eng.) Editor of Grove's *Dictionary of Music and Musicians;* first director of the Royal College of Music (1882).

Grovlez, Gabriel (Marie), 1879–1944 (Fr.) Conductor (Paris Opéra); composer of operas, symphonic poems, piano pieces, and songs.

Gruber, Franz Xaver, 1787–1863 (Aus.) Organist; composer of "Silent Night" to words by Joseph Mohr.

Gruenberg, Louis, 1884–1964 (Poland; U.S.) Composer using jazz idioms in his operas, 5 symphonies, symphonic poems, piano and violin concertos, chamber works *(Indiscretions* for string quartet; *Jazzettes* for violin and piano), piano pieces *(Jazzberries),* and vocal works *(Daniel Jazz).*

Guarneri (Guarnerius) family: Andrea (c. 1625–98); **Pietro Giovanni** (1655–1720); **Giuseppe** (1666–1740); **Pietro** (1695–1762); and **Giuseppe Bartolomeo,** or **Giuseppe del Gesù** (1687–1744) Italian violin-makers of Cremona.

Guarnieri, Camargo, 1907– (Brazil) Conductor; composer of orchestral works *(Dansa Brasiliera),* concertos for piano and for violin, songs, and piano pieces.

Guilbert, Yvette, 1867–1944 (Fr.) Noted singer of French café and folk songs.

Guilmant, Alexandre (Félix), 1837–1911 (Fr.) Organist, composer of works for organ (sonatas; symphonies), and editor *(Archives des maîtres de l'orgue).*

Guion, David, 1895– (U.S.) Composer and arranger of choral and instrumental works using American folk songs *(Sheep and Goat Walking to the Pasture; Alley Tunes).*

Gurlitt, Cornelius, 1820–1901 (Ger.) Organist and composer of operas, sonatas, songs. Best known for teaching pieces for piano.

Guthrie, Woody, 1912–67 (U.S.) Most original composer of contemporary folk songs: *Dust Bowl Blues.*

Gyrowetz, Adalbert, 1763–1850 (Bohemia) Composer of symphonies, string quartets, trios, and violin sonatas in Classical style, in addition to much church music.

H

Hába, Alois, 1893–1973 (Moravia) Composer using micro-intervals (quarter tones, sixth tones). He also composed in more conventional tonal idioms.

Hadley, Henry (Kimball), 1871–1937 (U.S.) Conductor (San Francisco and Seattle symphonies). Conducted the opening concert of the Berkshire Music Festival (1933); founder of the National Association of American Composers and Conductors; composer of operas and sym-

phonic works, many with programmatic titles (Symphony No. 5, *Connecticut;* tone poem, *The Ocean),* and choral works.

Hageman, Richard, 1882–1966 (U.S.) Composer of operas, film scores, and songs.

Hahn, Reynaldo, 1875–1947 (Venezuela; Fr.) Critic *(Le Figaro);* music director of Paris Opéra; composer of operas, symphonic works, ballets, violin concerto and sonata, piano pieces, and songs.

Haieff, Alexei, 1914– (Rus.; U.S.) Composer of ballets, symphonies, concertos, chamber music of various kinds in neo-Classical style.

Halász László, 1905– (H.; U.S.) Opera conductor (New York City Opera Company) who premièred many contemporary operas.

Halévy, Jacques-François-Fromental-Élie, 1799–1862 (Fr.) Composer of dramatic "grand" and light operas *(La Juive; L'Éclair);* professor of theory and composition at the Paris Conservatory.

Halffter, Ernesto, 1905– (Sp.; Portugal) Composer of operas, symphonic and chamber works, and a ballet *(Sonatina);* a protégé of Falla, his style is not so much Spanish as it is neo-Classical.

Halffter, Rodolfo, 1900– (Sp.; Mex.) Composer of ballets, concertos, piano works, and songs; like his brother Ernesto, he was influenced by Falla. His early works are Spanish-flavored; later he adopted a more international contemporary style.

Hallé, Sir Charles, 1819–95 (Prussia; Eng.) Pianist and conductor; founded the Hallé Orchestra in Manchester in 1857.

Hamilton, Iain, 1922– (Scotland) Teacher (Duke University); composer of a ballet *(Clerk Saunders)* and instrumental works, including several symphonies.

Hammerstein, Oscar II, 1895–1960 (U.S.) Writer of song lyrics; famous for his collaborations with Rudolf Friml *(Rose Marie),* Sigmund Romberg *(Desert Song),* Jerome Kern *(Show Boat),* and Richard Rodgers *(Oklahoma!; South Pacific).*

Hammond, Laurens, 1895– (U.S.) Inventor of the electronic Hammond organ, the Novachord, the Solovox, and a "chord organ."

Hampton, Lionel, 1913– (U.S.) Jazz pianist, drummer, and bandleader; best known for his inventive performances on the vibraphone.

Hanslick, Eduard, 1825–1904 (Aus.) Critic who championed the works of Brahms as opposed to those of Wagner, whose characterization of Hanslick lives in the character of Beckmesser in *Die Meistersinger.* Actually, Hanslick was one of the most readable and knowledgeable music critics.

Hanson, Howard, 1896–1981 (U.S.) Composer and educator; first director of the Eastman School of Music. Through his active leadership in various musical organizations, he worked diligently to further the cause of American music. His compositions—modern Romantic in style—include an opera *(Merry Mount),* 4 symphonies, choral works, symphonic poems, piano music, songs, and chamber music.

Harrison, Lou, 1917– (U.S.) Composer of opera *(Rapunzel)*, incidental music for plays, ballets, a symphony, chamber works, piano pieces, songs, and sinfonias for percussion orchestra. A student of Oriental music, Harrison's style is subtly and delicately exotic in flavor.

Harsányi, Tibor, 1898–1954 (H.) Composer of operas, ballets, and orchestral, chamber, and piano works based on folklike melodies and jazz syncopations.

Hart, Frederic Patton, 1895– (U.S.) Teacher (Sarah Lawrence College and Juilliard); composer of opera, ballet-opera *(The Romance of Robot),* chamber works, piano pieces, songs, and works for chorus.

Hartmann, Karl Amadeus, 1905–63 (Ger.) Composer of 8 symphonies, works for various instrumental combinations, piano pieces, and songs, mostly in the twelve-tone technique.

Harty, Sir Hamilton, 1879–1941 (Ireland; Eng.) Conductor of Hallé Orchestra (1920–33); composer of a symphony, works for orchestra and voices, violin concerto; best known for his arrangements of Handel's *Water Music* and *Fireworks Music* for modern orchestra.

Hasse, Johann Adolph, 1699–1783 (Ger.) Composer of many operas in Italian style; also oratorios and other sacred forms, as well as concertos, trios, and sonatas. Hasse's operas were highly popular during his lifetime, but soon dropped from the repertoire.

Hassler, Hans Leo, 1564–1612 (Ger.) One of the most important German composers. A student of the Gabrielis in Venice, he wrote many sacred works, as well as tuneful dance music and secular canzonettas and madrigals.

Hauer, Josef Matthias, 1883–1959 (Aus.) Theorist and composer who presaged Schoenberg's twelve-tone technique with his arbitrary arrangement of the twelve chromatic tones into patterns he called "tropes." In this style he wrote an opera, oratorio, orchestral pieces, string quartets, piano pieces, and songs.

Hawkins, Sir John, 1719–89 (Eng.) Historian, whose 5-volume *General History of the Science and Practice of Music* (1776) was the first history of music published in England.

Haydn, (Johann) Michael, 1737–1806 (Aus.) Brother of Franz Joseph Haydn; composer of more than 400 sacred works, as well as numerous instrumental compositions and many operas. His masses were highly regarded by the Empress Maria Theresa and Prince Esterházy.

Hebenstreit, Pantaleon, 1669–1750 (Ger.) Virtuoso performer on the dulcimer, which he improved and developed into a concert instrument.

Heckel, Wilhelm, 1856–1909 (Ger.) Instrument maker who invented the heckelphone, a baritone oboe.

Heifetz, Jascha, 1901– (Rus.; U.S.) Virtuoso violinist; one of the few outstanding performers who has commissioned works for his instrument.

Heinrich, Anthony Philip, 1781–1861 (Bo-

hemia; U.S.) Self-taught prolific composer in the 1840's and 50's whose inflated orchestral works, with titles such as *Pocahontas* and *Grand American Chivalrous Symphony,* made him a highly respected and influential musician in the United States at that time.

Heller, Stephen, 1813–88 (H.; Fr.) Pianist and composer of often poetic piano music, including his well-known études.

Helmholtz, Hermann von, 1821–94 (Ger.) Scientist whose work *On the Sensations of Tone as a Physiological Basis for the Theory of Music* is one of the basic texts in the study of acoustics.

Hendl, Walter, 1917– (U.S.) Conductor; director of the Eastman School of Music; composer of sensitive incidental music to the folk-play *Dark of the Moon.*

Henry VIII, 1491–1547 (Eng.) King of England (1509–47); competent, if not highly talented, composer of vocal works.

Henschel, Sir George, 1850–1934 (Silesia; Eng.) Singer in opera and recitals; first conductor of the Boston Symphony (1881–84).

Henselt, Adolph von, 1814–89 (Ger.) Pianist and composer, principally of works for piano: concerto, short piano pieces, and études.

Henze, Hans Werner, 1926– (Ger.) Composer of operas *(Boulevard Solitude; König Hirsch),* ballets, 5 symphonies, chamber works, cantatas, and madrigals. His style is eclectic, in that it utilizes almost every contemporary technique to achieve theatricality.

Herman, Woody (Woodrow Wilson), 1913– (U.S.) Bandleader and clarinetist for whom Stravinsky wrote his *Ebony Concerto.*

Hérold, Louis-Joseph-Ferdinand, 1791–1833 (Fr.) Operatic composer known today chiefly for his *Zampa.*

Herrmann, Bernard, 1911–76 (U.S.) Conductor active in radio and theater; composer of dramatic works (opera, *Wuthering Heights)* and film scores *(Citizen Kane),* also symphonic and other instrumental works.

Heseltine, Philip, 1894–1930 (Eng.) Critic-author *(Frederick Delius; Carlo Gesualdo)* and composer (using pen-name of **Peter Warlock**) of vocal works and orchestral settings of Renaissance dances *(Capriol Suite).*

Hess, Dame Myra, 1890–1965 (Eng.) Pianist.

Higginson, Henry Lee, 1834–1919 (U.S.) Boston banker who founded (in 1881), and subsidized, the Boston Symphony Orchestra.

Hill, Edward Burlingame, 1872–1960 (U.S.) Teacher and composer of symphonic poems *(Lilacs),* 3 symphonies, chamber and choral music.

Hiller, Ferdinand, 1811–85 (Ger.) Conductor of opera (Dresden) and concert (Leipzig). Composer of many large-scale works, but better known for his conservatively romantic songs and piano pieces.

Hiller, Johann Adam, 1728–1804 (Ger.) First conductor of the Leipzig Gewandhaus concerts. Composer of early important

Singspiels *(Die Jagd,* or *The Hunt)* which led to style of German Romantic opera.

Hiller, Lejaren A., Jr., 1924– (U.S.) Teacher (University of Illinois) and composer-engineer who has programmed a computer to invent music *(Iliac Suite for String Orchestra; Computer Cantata),* and has written works in various experimental media *(Cuthbert Bound,* a 1-act electronic fantasy).

Hoffmann, Ernest Theodor Amadeus (E.T.A.), 1776–1822 (Ger.) Writer and composer whose stories and essays did much to establish the basis of Romantic music and literature. Schumann's *Kreisleriana* is named after Kapellmeister Kreisler, a pen-name of Hoffmann.

Hoffmann, Richard, 1925– (Aus.; U.S.) Composer of large-scale works (concertos for piano, cello) in modified twelve-tone technique.

Hofhaimer, Paul, 1459–1537 (Aus.) Organist, lutanist, composer of organ works and part songs, and teacher of many outstanding organist-composers of the 16th century.

Hofmann, Josef, 1876–1957 (Rus.; U.S.) One of the greatest pianists of the 20th century (his career began at age 10); director of the Curtis Institute (1926–38).

Holbrooke, Josef, 1878–1958 (Eng.) Composer of colorfully orchestrated music in many forms: opera, ballet, symphonic poem, and a large quantity of chamber music.

Holden, Oliver, 1765–1844 (U.S.) Carpenter, minister, musician, composer of strong hymn tunes ("Coronation"—"All Hail the Power of Jesus' Name").

Holiday, Billie, 1915–59 (U.S.) One of the great "blues" singers.

Holst, Gustav Theodore, 1874–1934 (Eng.) Prolific composer whose interests and influences were English folk music and Hinduism. Experimental for his time, Holst's most-played works are his 2 Suites for Military Band (he was one of the first eminent modern composers to write for this medium), the orchestral suite *The Planets,* and *Hymns from the Rig-Veda* for voices.

Homer, Louise, 1871–1947 (U.S.) Operatic soprano; wife of Sidney Homer.

Homer, Sidney, 1864–1953 (U.S.) Composer of songs ("A Banjo Song"; "Song of the Shirt") and chamber music.

Hornbostel, Erich Moritz von, 1877–1935 (Aus.) Ethno-musicologist in fields of American Indian, Japanese, Turkish, Indonesian, and Brazilian music.

Horowitz, Vladimir, 1904– (Rus.; U.S.) Virtuoso pianist.

Hovhaness, Alan, 1911– (U.S.) Composer of works with exotic titles for variegated instrumental combinations *(Lousadzak; Arekaval; Ukiyo-Floating World).* His style is based on a fusion of Armenian, Oriental, and European techniques, with emphasis on melodic manipulation and delicate instrumentation.

Howard, John Tasker, 1890–1964 (U.S.) Writer dedicated to American music *(Our American Music; Stephen Foster, America's Troubadour).*

Hubay, Jenö, 1858–1937 (H.) Violinist, teacher (Budapest Conservatory), and composer of operas, symphonies, works for violin.

Huberman, Bronislaw, 1882–1947 (Poland) Violinist; founded, in 1936, the Palestine Symphony Orchestra, made up of dispossessed Jewish musicians.

Hucbald, c. 840–930 (Flanders) Musical theorist.

Hull, Arthur Eaglefield, 1876–1928 (Eng.) Author of *Dictionary of Modern Music and Musicians* (1924), *Modern Harmony* (1914), and *Scriabin* (1916).

Hume, Paul, 1915– Organist, teacher, and outstanding music critic.

Humfrey, Pelham, 1647–74 (Eng.) Composer of secular and sacred songs, and anthems; master of the Children of the Chapel Royal, one of whom was Henry Purcell.

Hummel, Johann Nepomuk, 1778–1837 (Ger.) Pianist and composer considered during his time to be the equal of Beethoven. In addition to operas, ballets, cantatas, and other church music he wrote many works featuring the piano: concertos, concertinos, trios, quintets, and numerous piano solos. His best-known work is his septet in D minor for flute, oboe, viola, horn, cello, double bass, and piano; it was featured at the first concert given by the New York Philharmonic in 1852.

Humperdinck, Engelbert, 1854–1921 (Ger.) Composer who achieved fame for his folk-like children's opera *Hänsel and Gretel.* He also wrote 4 other operas, incidental music for Ma Rheinhardt's production of *The Miracle,* a choral ballade, a symphony, and many songs.

Huneker, James Gibbons, 1860–1921 (U.S.) Critic and author (*Mezzotints in Modern Music; Chopin: the Man and His Music;* and the novel *Painted Veils*).

Husa, Karel, 1921– (Czech.; U.S.) Teacher (Cornell University) and composer of orchestral works, string quartets, and piano pieces.

I

Ibert, Jacques, 1890–1962 (Fr.) Composer of operas, ballets, symphonic works (*Escales,* or *Ports of Call*), *Concertino da Camera* for saxophone and chamber orchestra, piano suites (*Histoires,* which contains the popular *"Le petit âne blanc,"* or "The Little White Donkey").

Illica, Luigi, 1857–1919 (It.) Librettist (Puccini's *La Bohème, Madame Butterfly,* and *Tosca;* Giordano's *Andrea Chénier*).

Imbrie, Andrew Welsh, 1921– (U.S.) Teacher (University of California) and composer of a symphony, 2 violin concertos, an opera (*Three Against Christmas*), string quartets, and other chamber works.

d'Indy, Vincent, 1851–1931 (Fr.) Co-founder in 1896 of the Schola Cantorum; composer, in a style related to that of his teacher Franck, of stage works (*Fervaal*), 3 symphonies, the symphonic trilogy *Wallenstein,* the symphonic variations *Istar,* and the tone poem *Jour d'été à la montague,* or *Summer Day in the Mountains.* D'Indy was also a prolific composer of chamber music, including many vocal works and works for piano and for organ.

Ippolitov-Ivanov, Mikhail Mikhailovitch 1859–1935 (Rus.) Teacher (Tiflis; Moscow Conservatory) and composer of symphonic works, including his well-known *Caucasian Sketches;* conductor at Bolshoi Theater.

Ireland, John, 1879–1962 (Eng.) Teacher (Royal College of Music) and composer of orchestral, choral, and chamber works, plus many songs.

Isaac, Heinrich, c. 1450–1517 (Netherlands; Italy) Composer of polyphonic masses, motets, and secular works.

Iturbi, José, 1895– (Sp.) Pianist and conductor.

Ives, Burl, 1909– (U.S.) Folk-singer; author of *Wayfaring Stranger.*

J

Jackson, George Pullen, 1874–1953 (U.S.) Author of: *White and Negro Spirituals; White Spirituals in the Southern Uplands; Story of the Sacred Harp.*

Jackson, Mahalia, 1911–72 (U.S.) Singer of gospel songs.

Jacob, Gordon, 1895– (Eng.) Teacher (Royal College of Music) and composer of symphonies, concertos, chamber music; arrangements of music for film and ballet.

Jacopo da Bologna, 14th century (It.) Composer of madrigals and *ballate.*

James, Philip, 1890–1976 (U.S.) Composer of works for orchestra (2 symphonies, overtures, suites), chamber groups, chorus, and organ.

Janáček, Leos, 1854–1928 (Moravia; Czech.) Composer of operas (*Jenufa; The Makropulos Affair*), symphonic poems and rhapsodies (*Taras Bulba*), choral and chamber works (*Slavonic Mass;* 3 string quartets), and arrangements of folk songs. His music has made its way slowly, but Janáček has finally been recognized as one of the major composers of his time.

Janequin, Clément, c. 1485– c. 1560 (Fr.) Composer of masses, motets, and programmatic chansons (*La Bataille; Le Chant des oiseaux*).

Janigro, Antonio, 1918– (It.; Yugoslavia) Cello soloist and conductor of *I Solisti de Zagreb.*

Janssen, Werner, 1899– (U.S.) Conductor (Utah; Portland Oregon; San Diego) and composer of descriptive music (*New Year's Eve in New York*), chamber music, and film scores.

Jaques-Dalcroze, Émile, 1865–1950 (Aus.; Switz.) Composer and educator. His belief that music must be understood in the body led to his development of a system of training named Eurhythmics which has had a continuing influence on the training of both musicians and dancers.

Jarnach, Philipp, 1892– (Fr.; Ger.) Teacher and composer of chamber music; completed Busoni's opera *Doktor Faust.*

Järnefelt, Armas, 1869–1958 (Finland) Conductor (Stockholm and Helsinki) and composer of orchestral works (*Berceuse; Praeludium*), songs, piano pieces, and vocal works.

Jenkins, John, 1592–1678 (Eng.) Composer of *Fancies* for viols and light pieces he called "Rants." In addition to songs and anthems, Jenkins wrote some of the earliest English works for violin.

Jensen, Adolf, 1837–79 (Ger.) Composer of cantatas, piano pieces, an opera, and over 150 lyrical songs.

Jepson, Helen, 1905– (U.S.) Operatic soprano.

Jeritza, Maria, 1887– (Ger.; U.S.) Operatic soprano.

Joachim, Joseph, 1831–1907 (Ger.) Violinist, teacher, and composer, primarily of violin and viola solos. As a violinist, he played serious works for the instrument with few purely virtuoso works, although he composed such (*Hungarian Concerto*). The Joachim Quartet, which he founded, was the outstanding chamber music group of the 19th century. Joachim wrote cadenzas for the violin concertos of Mozart, Beethoven, and his friend Brahms.

Johanos, Donald, 1928– (U.S.) Conductor (Dallas).

Johnson, Edward, 1878–1959 (Canada) Operatic tenor; general manager of the Metropolitan Opera Company (1935–50).

Johnson, Hunter, 1906– (U.S.) Highly original composer of a symphony, ballet (*Letter to the World* for Martha Graham), piano sonata, and chamber music.

Johnson, James Weldon, 1871–1938 (U.S.) Composer of light opera and songs ("My Castle on the Nile," and, with his brother Rosamond, "Lift Every Voice and Sing"). He also published collections of spirituals.

Johnson, J. Rosamond, 1873–1954 (U.S.) Bass singer and composer of a ballet, songs, and many arrangements of Negro spirituals.

Jolivet, André, 1905– (Fr.) Composer of moderately experimental works, including a comic opera, a symphony, other works for orchestra, church music, and piano music.

Jommelli, Niccolò, 1714–74 (It.) Composer of more than 70 dramatic operas and a large amount of church music, including the *Miserere* for 2 voices.

Jones, Charles, 1910– (Canada; U.S.) Composer, in moderately dissonant idiom, of works for orchestra, chorus, piano, and chamber groups.

Jones, Robert, c. 1575–1617 (Eng.) Lutanist and composer of lyrical ayres or lute songs, and madrigals.

Joplin, Scott, 1868–1917 (U.S.) Ragtime pianist; composer of "Maple Leaf Rag" and the opera *Treemonisha.*

Jullien, Louis Antoine, 1812–60 (Fr.) Eccentric, brilliant showman-conductor of spectacular concerts as well as solid concerts of classic and contemporary works. He did much to establish high standards of orchestral playing in Great Britain.

K

Kabalevsky, Dmitri Borisovitch, 1904– (Rus.) Pianist and composer of skillful, direct music in a conservative style. He has written 4 symphonies and other orchestral works (*The Comedians,* a suite); ballets; operas; violin, cello, and piano concertos; sonatas, sonatinas, and preludes for piano.

Kadosa, Paul, 1903– (H.) Pianist and composer of an opera; 5 symphonies; other symphonic and chamber works; concertos for piano, viola, violin, and string quartet; a cantata; and a large amount of piano music in both large and small forms. His music strongly reflects his Hungarian background in its rhythms and folk melodies.

Kalinnikov, Vassili Sergeivitch, 1866–1901 (Rus.) Composer of symphonic poems, 2 symphonies of which the first, in G minor, has had some popularity, vocal works, and piano pieces.

Kalliwoda, Johann Wenzel, 1801–66 (Czech.; Ger.) Conductor, violinist, and composer of several operas; 7 symphonies and other orchestral works; concertos and chamber music for strings; masses and secular vocal works.

Kálmán, Emmerich, 1882–1953 (H.) Composer of tuneful operettas (*Countess Mariza*).

Kapell, William, 1922–53 (U.S.) Pianist.

Karajan, Herbert von, 1908– (Aus.) Virtuoso conductor.

Karg-Elert, Sigfrid, 1877–1933 (Ger.) Organist and composer of many works for the organ in a contrapuntal Impressionist style (10 *Poetic Tone Pictures;* 3 *Pastels, Cathedral Windows*), He was a master of improvisation in both free and fugal forms.

Katims, Milton, 1909– (U.S.) Violist and conductor (Seattle Symphony).

Kay, Ulysses Simpson, 1917– (U.S.) Composer of orchestral works, chamber music, short operas, vocal music, and a notable film score: *The Quiet One.*

Keats, Donald, 1929– (U.S.) Composer of expressive works for orchestra, chamber groups, and chorus.

Keiser, Reinhard, 1674–1739 (Ger.) Composer of church music (passions, oratorios, motets, cantatas), but most notable for his more than 100 operas, ranging in style from the formal Baroque to the light Rococo. His dramatic works contrast virtuoso arias with lyric songs, always with expressive accompaniments.

Kelly, Michael, 1762–1826 (Ireland) Tenor (created role of Basilio in Mozart's *Marriage of Figaro*) and composer of music for many stage works.

Kennen, Kent Wheeler, 1913– (U.S.) Composer of a symphony and various works for solo instrument and orchestra: viola and orchestra; trumpet and orchestra; oboe and orchestra; flute and orchestra (*Night Soliloquy*); piano and orchestra. Author of several textbooks on music; arranger.

Kennedy-Fraser, Marjory, 1857–1930 (Scot.) Singer, pianist, collector and arranger of folk songs (*Songs of the Hebrides* in 3 volumes).

Kenton, Stanley Newcomb (Stan), 1912–79 (U.S.) Jazz musician who encouraged his arrangers to write virtuoso works, featuring the coloristic possibilities of the big dance band.

Kerll, Johann Carpar, 1627–93 (Ger.) Organist; composer of operas, church music, and many pieces for organ and harpsichord.

Kertesz, Istvan, 1929–73 (H.) Conductor.

Ketèlby, Albert William, 1875–1959 (Eng.) Composer of many "light Classics" (*In a Persian Market; In a Monastery Garden*).

Key, Francis Scott, 1779–1843 (U.S.) Famous as the author of the words of "The Star-Spangled Banner."

Khatchaturian, Aram, 1903–1978 (Rus.) Composer of symphonies; symphonic poems; concertos for violin, for piano, and for cello; ballets (*Gayane,* which includes his most popular work: *Sabre Dance);* various chamber works; and piano pieces.

Kipnis, Alexander, 1891– (Rus.; U.S.) Operatic bass.

Kirchner, Leon, 1919– (U.S.) Teacher (Mills College; Harvard) and composer of chamber works, 2 piano concertos, 3 string quartets (No. 3 including electronic sounds) in an individual, dissonantly romantic style.

Kirkpatrick, Ralph, 1911– (U.S.) Harpsichordist and scholar; author of definitive biography of Domenico Scarlatti.

Kleiber, Erich, 1890–1956 (Aus.) Conductor of opera and symphony.

Klein, Lothar, 1932– (Ger.; U.S.) Teacher (University of Texas) and composer, in modified 12-tone idiom, of works for orchestra (*Epitaphs; Musique à Go-go*), voice, and chamber groups.

Kleinsinger, George, 1914– (U.S.) Composer best known for his good-humored works, such as *Tubby the Tuba, Brooklyn Baseball Cantata,* and the chamber opera *Archy and Mehitabel.* He has also written a symphony, concertos, and scores for film and television.

Klemperer, Otto, 1885–1973 (Ger.) Conductor of opera and symphony.

Klindworth, Karl, 1830–1916 (Ger.) Pianist, teacher; best known for his piano arrangements of *Ring of the Nibelungs.*

Knipper, Lev Konstantinovitch, 1898– (Rus.) Composer of 14 symphonies, operas, and chamber works. A student of the music of Asiatic Russia, he is an ardent nationalist in his works. The melody of the patriotic song "Meadowland" comes from his Symphony No. 4.

Kodály, Zoltán, 1882–1967 (H.) Composer whose works are based on Hungarian folk music which he and his friend Béla Bartók collected and studied. Kodály wrote 3 operas, from one of which, *Háry János,* he extracted a popular orchestral suite; large choral works, including *Psalmus Hungaricus, Missa Brevis* (the basis of an eloquent ballet choreographed by José Limon), and a Te Deum; concertos and other orchestral works; and a large number of interesting songs and piano pieces. A revered musical leader in Hungary, Kodály developed an effective system of teaching the elements of music to children.

Koechlin, Charles, 1867–1950 (Fr.) Composer, in a restrained yet eloquent style, of chamber works, piano pieces and songs, symphonic poems, suites, and ballets. A dedicated teacher (Poulenc, Sauget), he wrote several textbooks on music theory and orchestration.

Kolisch, Rudolph, 1896– (Aus.) One of the few left-handed violinists; founder of the Kolisch Quartet, which played classic standards from memory and specialized in contemporary works, and, later, the Pro Arte Quartet.

Korngold, Erich Wolfgang, 1897–1957 (Aus.; U.S.) Composer of operas; incidental music for plays; concertos for piano (left hand alone) and violin; and chamber works. Starting his career as a child prodigy, he spent much of the later part of his life in Hollywood, writing music for films.

Kósa, György, 1897– (H.) Pianist and composer of operas, ballets, 6 symphonies, chamber music, piano pieces, oratorios.

Kostelanetz, André, 1901–80 (Rus.; U.S.) Conductor and arranger of popular music emphasizing a rich, fully orchestrated sound; he commissioned many contemporary American composers, including Copland (*A Lincoln Portrait*) and Schuman (*New England Triptych*).

Koussevitzky, Serge Alexandrovitch, 1874–1951 (Rus.; U.S.) Double-bassist, conductor, and publisher who championed most of the outstanding composers of the first half of the 20th century. One of the great virtuosos of the double bass (often playing concertos originally written for the more agile cello), Koussevitzky turned to conducting in 1908. Until 1920 his activities were centered in Russia. Then he moved to various European cities until he was given the post of conductor of the Boston Symphony Orchestra in 1924—a post which he held for 25 years. In the early part of his career he operated a publishing house, specializing in such contemporary composers as Scriabin, Prokofiev, Rachmaninoff, and Stravinsky. Through his concerts and later his commissions he vigorously encouraged the works of Ravel, Honegger, Bartók, and the previously neglected Americans: Copland, Harris, Piston, Schuman, and Hill. In 1940 he organized the Berkshire Music Center, which has played an important part in developing the musical life of the United States. The Koussevitzky Foundation, established in memory of his first wife, has awarded commissions to composers writing in a wide range of styles. Although he emphasized contemporary works, Koussevitzky was at home in all styles—always infusing his performance with sincere emotional enthusiasm.

Krauss, Clemens, 1893–1954 (Aus.) Conductor of opera and symphony; wrote the libretto of *Capriccio* by Richard Strauss.

Krebs, Johann Ludwig, 1713–80 (Ger.) Organist and composer (pupil of, and assistant to, J. S. Bach). His works are mostly for keyboard instruments.

Kreisler, Fritz, 1875–1962 (Aus.; U.S.) Outstanding violinist and composer of many of the most popular violin solos (*Caprice Viennois; Schön Rosmarin; Liebesfreud; The Old Refrain*), as well as violin pieces in the Baroque style which he attributed to Baroque composers. Of his operettas, *Apple Blossoms* was the most successful.

Krenek, Ernst, 1900– · (Aus.; U.S.) Composer of operas (*Jonny spielt auf,* 1927), choral works, ballets, symphonies, concertos, chamber music, sonatas and sonatinas for piano, and song cycles. His book *Music Here and Now* is strongly supportive of the theories of Arnold Schoenberg. Highly successful at first, Krenek has since been to some extent ignored, although he has produced a wealth of important works.

Kreutzer, Rodolphe, 1766–1831 (Fr.) Composer and violinist to whom Beethoven dedicated his famous "Kreutzer" Sonata for violin and piano. He wrote operas, violin concertos, and sonatas for violin; his *40 Études ou Caprices* continue to be standard fare for the violinist.

Kuhnau, Johann, 1660–1722 (Ger.) Organist (preceding Bach at St. Thomas in Leipzig) and composer of cantatas and works for harpsichord, the best known of which are the descriptive Bible Sonatas. Kuhnau was one of the first to write true harpsichord sonatas.

Kupferman, Meyer, 1926– (U.S.) Teacher (Sarah Lawrence College) and composer, in eclectic contemporary idiom, of stage works (*In a Garden; Doctor Faustus Lights the Lights*) and symphonic and chamber music, including a *Cycle of Infinities* for various combinations of instruments.

Kurka, Robert, 1921–57 (U.S.) Composer of 2 symphonies, concertos, chamber music, and the successful opera *The Good Soldier Schweik.*

L

Lalo, Édouard, 1823–92 (Fr.) Violinist and composer whose *Symphonie espagnole* for violin and orchestra reflects his Spanish ancestry. He also wrote an opera (*Le Roi d'Ys*), a ballet (*Namouna*), and many works for violin chamber groups.

Lambert, Constant, 1905–51 (Eng.) Composer and conductor (Sadler's Wells Ballet). His most successful work is the jazz-based *Rio Grande* for piano, chorus, and orchestra. Lambert was author of the stimulating book *Music Ho!: A Study of Music in Decline.*

Lamoureux, Charles, 1834–99 (Fr.) Violinist and conductor; founder of the Concerts Lamoureux.

Landini, Francesco, 1325–97 (It.) Organ virtuoso and performer on the lute, flute, and guitar. Composer of expressive ballate, madrigals, and caccias; his use of a particular cadence caused it to become known in music theory as the "Landini cadence."

Landowska, Wanda, 1877–1959 (Poland; U.S.) Harpsichordist who renewed interest in the instrument through her performances, her teaching, and her commissioning of con-

temporary composers (Poulenc; Falla) to write works for it.

Lang, Paul Henry, 1901– (H.; U.S.) Musicologist, critic, teacher (Columbia University), editor of the *Musical Quarterly,* author of *Music in Western Civilization* (1941) and *Handel* (1965).

Lanner, Joseph (Franz Karl), 1801–43 (Aus.) Violinist and composer; he and his colleague Johann Strauss the Elder popularized the Viennese waltz.

La Rue, Pierre de, *c.* 1460–1518 (Netherlands) Composer of highly intricate polyphonic masses, motets, and chansons.

Lawes, Henry, 1596–1662 (Eng.) Composer of anthems, settings of psalms, and music for masques (Milton's *Comus*).

Lawes, William, 1602–45 (Eng.) Composer of sacred and secular vocal works ("Gather ye rosebuds while ye may"), and collections of short pieces for stringed instruments.

Lawrence, Marjorie, 1909– (Australia; U.S.) Operatic and concert soprano. Crippled by infantile paralysis in mid-career, she continued to give concerts and sing in opera (Venus in *Tannhäuser*).

Layton, Billy Jim, 1924– (U.S.) Composer, in moderately dissonant style, of works for orchestra, voices, piano, and chamber groups.

Lazarof, Henri, 1932– (Bulgaria; U.S.) Teacher (U.C.L.A.); composer of compact, non-tonal concertos, a symphony, and chamber music for various combinations, including flute and vibraphone.

Leclair, Jean Marie, 1697–1764 (Fr.) Violinist and composer of violin sonatas and concerti grossi.

Lecuona, Ernesto, 1896–1963 (Cuba) Composer of light, Caribbean-flavored music (*Malagueña; Andalucia; Siboney*).

Lees, Benjamin, 1924– (Manchuria; U.S.) Composer of much instrumental music, including symphonies and concertos (of which that for string quartet and orchestra is frequently played).

Legrenzi, Giovanni, 1626–90 (It.) Composer of operas and important early trio-sonatas.

Lehár, Franz, 1870–1948 (H.) Composer of such tuneful operettas as *The Merry Widow* and *Zigeunerliebe,* or *Gypsy Love.*

Lehmann, Lilli, 1848–1929 (Ger.) Famous operatic and concert soprano who was one of the founders of the Salzburg festivals.

Lehmann, Liza (Elizabeth Nina Mary Frederica), 1862–1918 (Eng.) Soprano and composer of light operatic works and song cycles (*In a Persian Garden*).

Lehmann, Lotte, 1888– (Ger.; U.S.) Operatic and concert soprano.

Leibowitz, René, 1913–72 (Poland; Fr.) Composer (leading French exponent of Schoenbergian 12-tone theories) of chamber music works and orchestral works (*Variations*). In addition, he was a conductor, and author of *Schoenberg and His School.*

Leinsdorff, Erich, 1912– (Aus.; U.S.) Conductor of symphony (Rochester Philharmonic; Boston Symphony) and opera (Metropolitan Opera Company).

Le Jeune, Claude, 1528–1600 (Fr.) Composer who wrote in a style known as *vers mesurez:* capturing the long and short rhythmic values of the words of a poem rather than fitting the text into an even meter. Le Jeune composed settings of the Genevan Psalter and a dozen of the psalms.

Lekeu, Guillaume, 1870–94 (Belg.) Composer who, in his brief life, wrote several enduring works, including a rhapsodic sonata for violin and piano and an elegiacal *Adagio* for strings.

Leoncavallo, Ruggiero, 1858–1919 (It.) Composer of the famous opera *I Pagliacci* and more than a dozen other operas, including a setting of *La Bohème.*

Leonin (Leoninus), *c.* 1160 (Fr.) One of the first composers to emerge from the anonymity of the Middle Ages. At Notre Dame, in Paris, he wrote sacred works using the technique of paralleling known as ORGANUM and employing set rhythmic patterns, or modes.

Leschetizky, Theodor, 1830–1915 (Poland) Pianist and teacher; a pupil of Czerny, he numbered among his own pupils such famous performers as Paderewsky, Schnabel, Vengerova, and Gabrilovitch. His "method" of piano playing continues to be the basis of much piano teaching of today.

Lesueur, Jean François, 1760–1837 (Fr.) Composer of operas (*La Caverne; Le Triomphe de Trajan*), masses, Te Deums, passions, oratorios, and other sacred works. He held many important musical posts off and on during a tempestuous career—music director at Notre Dame (1786–88), maître de chapelle to Napoleon and to Louis XVIII. He was professor of composition at the Paris Conservatory from 1818 until his death, numbering among his pupils Berlioz, Gounod, and Ambroise Thomas.

Levant, Oscar, 1906–1972 (U.S.) Pianist (particularly known for his interpretations of Gershwin's piano works). Levant was the composer of a piano concerto, a string quartet, *Nocturne* for orchestra, and film scores, and he was the author of a witty, brilliant book: *A Smattering of Ignorance* (1940).

Levy, Marvin David, 1932– (U.S.) Composer of an opera buffa (*The Tower*), an opera commissioned by the Metropolitan Opera Company (*Mourning Becomes Electra*), an oratorio, and a symphony.

Lhévinne, Josef, 1874–1944 (Rus.; U.S.) Virtuoso pianist known for his performances of Chopin.

Lhévinne, Rosina, 1880–1976 (Rus.; U.S.) Concert pianist and teacher (Juilliard School of Music); wife of Josef Lhévinne.

Liadov, Anatol Konstantinovitch, 1855–1914 (Rus.) Composer strongly influenced by Russian folk music. In addition to composing works for piano (*Tabatière*) and for orchestra (*Baba Yaga; Enchanted Lake*), He made arrangements of many Russian folk songs, including *8 Russian Folksongs* for orchestra.

Liapunov, Sergey Mikhailovitch, 1859–1924 (Rus.) Pianist and composer of brilliant works for piano (*Rhapsody* on Ukranian themes for piano and orchestra; 2 piano concertos; short piano pieces), 2 symphonies, symphonic poems, and settings of Russian folk songs.

Liberace, Walter, 1919–   (U.S.) Most successful pianist-showman.

Liebermann, Rolf, 1910–   (Switz.) Composer, in modified 12-tone technique, of operas, orchestral works *(Concerto for Jazzband and Orchestra),* cantatas, film music; director of Hamburg Opera.

Lieberson, Goddard, 1911–   (Eng.; U.S.) Writer and composer of orchestral suites, chamber works, and songs; for many years the president of Columbia Records.

Lieurance, Thurlow, 1878–1963 (U.S.) Composer and student of American Indian music. He is best known for his songs, particularly "By the Waters of Minnetonka."

Ligeti, György, 1923–   (Rumania; H.) Composer of many works in experimental vein, including a *Poème symphonique* for 100 metronomes.

Lincke, Paul, 1866–1946 (Ger.) Composer of light operettas. The well-known song "Glow-worm" comes from his operetta *Lysistrata.*

Lind, Jenny, 1820–87 (Sweden) Operatic, coloratura soprano, known as "The Swedish Nightingale."

Lipatti, Dinu, 1917–50 (Rumania) Pianist known chiefly through his recordings.

Lobkowitz, Prince Franz Joseph von, 1772–1816 (Aus.; Czech.) Patron to whom Beethoven dedicated some of his most important works (3rd, 5th, and 6th symphonies; the 6 quartets, Op. 18). The prince was one of the founders of the Prague Conservatory of Music.

Locatelli, Pietro, 1695–1764 (It.; Netherlands) Violinist, composer of concerti grossi, violin concertos, and many works featuring the violin.

Locke, Matthew, *c.* 1630–77 (Eng.) Composer of incidental music (Shadwell's *Psyche;* Shirley's masque *Cupid and Death;* Shakespeare's *Tempest* and *Macbeth*). He also composed anthems and instrumental suites, and wrote one of the earliest English textbooks on keyboard realization of figured bass.

Loeffler, Charles Martin, 1861–1935 (Alsace; U.S.) Composer in almost every medium, using an eclectic, Impressionistic style. His most often performed orchestral works are *A Pagan Poem* and *La Mort de Tintagiles.*

Loeillet, Jean-Baptiste, 1680–1730 (Belg.; Eng.) Flutist and harpsichordist; composer of suites and sonatas for harpsichord, for flute, and for violin.

Loesser, Arthur, 1894–1969 (U.S.) Pianist, critic, and teacher (Cleveland Institute of Music); author of *Men, Women and Pianos: A Social History.*

Loesser, Frank, 1910–69 (U.S.) Composer and lyricist of musical comedies *(Guys and Dolls; Where's Charley?; The Most Happy Fella)* and popular songs ("Baby, It's Cold Outside"; "Praise the Lord and Pass the Ammunition").

Loewe, Frederick, 1904–   (Aus.; U.S.) Concert pianist who composed highly successful musical shows *(Brigadoon; Paint Your Wagon; My Fair Lady).*

Loewe, Karl (Gottfried), 1796–1869 (Ger.) Composer of operas, oratorios, and chamber music, but best known for his ballades: settings of German poems ("Erlking"; "Edward").

London, George, 1920–   (Canada; U.S.) Operatic bass baritone.

Lopatnikov, Nikolai, 1903–   (Estonia; U.S.) Teacher (Carnegie Institute of Technology) and composer of symphonies, concertos for piano and for violin, chamber music, and piano works.

Lortzing, (Gustav) Albert, 1801–51 (Ger.) Actor, singer, conductor, and composer-librettist of light comic operas *(Czaar und Zimmermann,* based on Tsar Peter the Great's brief career as a carpenter) and German Romantic opera *(Undine; Hans Sachs)* which anticipated some of Richard Wagner's later works.

Lotti, Antonio, *c.* 1667–1740 (It.) Organist (St. Mark's in Venice), teacher (Galuppi; Marcello), and composer of operas and a large quantity of vocal music, including oratorios, masses, motets, and madrigals.

Lourié, Arthur (Vincent), 1892–1966 (Rus.; U.S.) Moderately experimental composer of often mystical works: operas; the cantata *La naissance de la beauté* for women's voices and piano; *Liturgical Sonata* for orchestra, piano, and chorus; several symphonies; and piano pieces.

Lowens, Irving, 1916–   (U.S.) Critic and authority on the history of early American music, and the author of *Music in America* and *Music and Musicians of Early America.*

Luca, Giuseppe de, 1876–1950 (It.; U.S.) Operatic baritone.

Luening, Otto, 1900–   (U.S.) Flutist, conductor, teacher (Bennington College; Columbia University), and composer of opera *(Evangeline),* symphonic works *(Louisville Concerto),* and much chamber music. Luening was one of the founders of the Columbia-Princeton Center for Electronic Music and has composed several works for that medium, including *Poem in Cycles and Bells* with Vladimir Ussachevsky.

Luigini, Alexandre, 1850–1906 (Fr.) Composer of comic operas and successful ballets *(Ballet égyptien).*

Luther, Martin, 1483–1546 (Ger.) Religious leader and composer who assigned music a high place in his reformation of church practices. Luther encouraged composers to write original hymn tunes or adapt melodies from folk songs and plainchants. He wrote words to many of these chorales and composed the melodies for others, notably "Ein' feste Burg" and "Mit Fried und Freud."

Lutoslawski, Witold, 1913–   (Poland) Composer who has used experimental techniques in his symphonic works *(Symphonie; Musique Funèbre)* and chamber works.

Luzzaschi, Luzzasco, 1545–1607 (It.) Organist, teacher (of Frescobaldi), and composer of dramatic madrigals.

Lvov, Alexei, 1798–1870 (Rus.) Violinist and composer of operas and works for violin, best known as the composer, in 1833, of the old Russian national anthem, "God Save the Czar."

M

Maazel, Lorin, 1930–   (France; U.S.) Conductor who started his brilliant career in New York at age 9. Most recently, Maazel has alternated conducting between Berlin and Cleveland (opera and symphony orchestras).

MacDowell, Edward Alexander, 1861–1908 (U.S.) Educator (established music department at Columbia University, 1896) and composer of symphonic poems, 2 suites for orchestra (No. 2 entitled *Indian Suite*), 2 piano concertos (A Minor; D Minor), choral works, songs, and a great number of piano pieces *(Woodland Sketches; New England Idyls; Sea Pieces; Concert Études; 4 piano sonatas).* MacDowell was the first American composer to become successful in Germany as well as at home—his "To a Wild Rose" was one of the most popular piano pieces of the early 20th century. His large-scale works are heroic and dramatic; his smaller works are poetic and intimate, and are filled with colorful, sensitive harmony that falls stylistically between Grieg and Debussy.

Macfarren, Sir George Alexander, 1813–87 (Eng.) Educator (principal of the Royal Academy of Music, 1876); author of textbooks on music theory; and composer of operas, oratorios, songs, chamber music.

Mackenzie, Sir Alexander Campbell, 1847–1935 (Scotland; Eng.) Educator (principal of the Royal Academy of Music, 1888–1924) and composer of operas, rhapsodies and suites for orchestra, works for violin and orchestra, songs, and chamber music. Many of Mackenzie's works are based on Scottish material: *Pibroch Suite; Scottish Concerto; Scottish Rhapsodies).*

Maderna, Bruno, 1920–73 (It.) Conductor and composer of works in an expressive, experimental vein, sometimes involving electronic sounds *(Sintaxis).*

Maelzel, Johannes Nepomuk, 1772–1838 (Ger.) Inventor, best known for his metronome. This friend of Beethoven's also invented an automatic chess player and various mechanical instruments.

Makeba, Miriam, 1932–   (South Africa) Outstanding singer of African folk songs.

Malipiero, Gian Francesco, 1882–   (It.) Educator; scholar; and composer of 9 symphonies, 4 piano concertos, many operas, 7 string quartets, and other chamber music—including a large quantity of piano pieces. Malipiero edited the complete works of Monteverdi, plus the works of other Italian composers of the Baroque period.

Mannes, David, 1866–1959 (U.S.) Violinist, conductor, educator; founder of the Mannes School of Music (1916), which, under his son **Leopold** (1899–1964), became the Mannes College of Music.

Marcello, Benedetto, 1686–1739 (It.) Writer and composer of settings of 50 psalms, concerti grossi, and sonatas. His book *Il teatre alla moda* is a sharp satire on the operatic world of his day.

Marchal, André, 1894– (Fr.) Blind organist famous for his improvisations.

Marchand, Louis, 1669–1732 (Fr.) Organist and composer of works for harpsichord and for organ. He and Bach were to meet in an improvisational contest in Dresden, but Marchand withdrew—supposedly because he realized Bach's superiority.

Marenzio, Luca, 1553–99 (It.) Composer of extraordinarily expressive and inventive madrigals and motets.

Markevitch, Igor, 1912– (Rus.; Fr.) Conductor and composer of ballets *(Rebus; L'Envoi d'Icare)*, works for piano and orchestra, and oratorios.

Marschner, Heinrich (August), 1795–1861 (Ger.) Composer of operas in the German Romantic style established by Weber: *Hans Heiling; Der Templer und die Jüdin.*

Martenot, Maurice, 1898– (Fr.) Inventor, in the early 20's, of the "Ondes Martenot," an electronic instrument which has been written for by Varèse, Milhaud, and Messiaen.

Martin, Frank, 1890–1974 (Switz.) Composer of delicate-hued instrumental works based on non-dogmatic use of 12-tone technique *(Petite Symphonie Concertante; concertos; chamber music).*

Martín y Soler, Vicente, 1754–1806 (Sp.; Aus.; Rus.) Composer of operas, many with librettos by Lorenzo Da Ponte *(Una Cosa rara,* quoted by Mozart in his opera *Don Giovanni).*

Martinelli, Giovanni, 1885–1969 (It.; U.S.) Operatic tenor.

Martini, Giambattista (Padre), 1706–84 (It.) Teacher (of Mozart, Gluck, Grétry); composer of chamber music and sacred music.

Martinon, Jean, 1910– (Fr.) Composer of works for orchestra, chamber groups, and chorus; conductor of Chicago Symphony (1963–68).

Martinu, Bohuslav, 1890–1959 (Czech.; U.S.) Composer, in skillful, dissonant, contrapuntal style, of operas, ballets, 6 symphonies, concertos, and much appealing chamber music.

Martirano, Salvatore, 1927– (U.S.) Teacher (University of Illinois), composer of effective non-traditional music: *O,O,O,O, that Shakespeherian Rag* for chorus and instrumental ensemble; *Cocktail Music* for piano.

Marx, Joseph, 1882– (Aus.) Teacher and composer of symphonic works, chamber music, and especially songs.

Mascagni, Pietro, 1863–1945 (It.) Composer whose early opera *Cavallieria Rusticana* (1888) is the well-known partner of Leoncavallo's *I Pagliacci.* Although he wrote many more operas, Mascagni achieved moderate success with only two of them: *L'Amico Fritz* (1891) and *Iris* (1898).

Mason, Daniel Gregory, 1873–1953 (U.S.) Teacher (Columbia University); composer (symphonies, chamber music, and a much-performed overture: *Chanticleer);* and author of many books *(From Grieg to Brahms; The Dilemma of American Music).*

Mason, Lowell, 1792–1872 (U.S.) Music educator, editor of many collections of vocal music, and composer of many hymn tunes.

Massenet, Jules, 1842–1912 (Fr.) Composer of some of the best-known French operas: *Manon* (1884), *Le Cid* (1885), *Thaïs* (1894), and *Le Jongleur de Notre-Dame* (1902). Massenet's style is based on easy-flowing melodies of great charm, as, for example, the popular "Meditation" from *Thaïs.* In addition to more than 20 operas, he wrote colorful suites for orchestra—most of them with descriptive titles: *Scènes pittoresques; Scènes dramatique.*

Mattheson, Johann, 1681–1764 (Ger.) Composer of operas, oratorios, keyboard suites, and flute sonatas; more importantly, a prolific writer on musical affairs of his day.

Matzenauer, Margarete, 1881–1963 (H.; U.S.) Concert operatic soprano, and, at times, contralto.

Maurel, Victor, 1848–1923 (Fr.; U.S.) Operatic baritone; creator of role of Iago in Verdi's *Otello* and title role in *Falstaff.*

Mayuzumi, Toshiro, 1929– (Japan) Composer, interested in sonorities, of works (often with descriptive titles) for orchestra, wind ensemble, and chamber groups. He has also written the score for the film *The Bible.*

McBride, Robert, 1911– (U.S.) Virtuoso woodwind performer, teacher (Bennington College; University of Arizona), and composer of witty instrumental works *(Fugato on a Well-Known Theme* for orchestra; *Workout* for piano and oboe; *Let-down* for English horn and piano) and a ballet for Martha Graham *(Punch and the Judy).*

McCormack, John, 1884–1945 (Ireland; U.S.) Concert and operatic tenor.

McDonald, Harl, 1899–1955 (U.S.) Composer of orchestral and chamber music, including 4 symphonies, of which No. 2, *The Rhumba Symphony,* achieved the most success.

McKay, George Frederick 1899– (U.S.) Teacher (University of Washington) and composer of orchestral and chamber music works.

McPhee, Colin, 1901– (Canada) Ethno-musicologist and composer whose works often reflect his research in the music of Mexico and Bali *(Balinese Ceremonial Music).*

Medtner, Nikolai Karlovitch, 1880–1951 (Rus.; Eng.) Pianist and composer, in Brahmsian Romantic style, of works predominantly for piano or voice: piano concertos, piano sonatas, *Fairy Tales* for piano, many songs, and a *Sonata-Vocalise.*

Mehta, Zubin, 1936– (India; U.S.) Brilliant young conductor (Metropolitan Opera; Montreal and Los Angeles symphonies); son of well-known violinist and conductor **Mehli Mehta** (1908–).

Méhul, Étienne-Nicolas, 1763–1817 (Fr.) Composer of about 30 operas, mostly with spoken dialogue (opéra comique), on subject matter in tune with the revolutionary fervor of the time. His best-known work is the biblical opera *Joseph* (1807).

Melba, Dame Nellie, 1861–1931 (Australia) Operatic coloratura soprano who was so popular that a type of toast and a peach dessert were named after her.

Melchoir, Lauritz, 1890–1973 (Denmark; U.S.) Operatic tenor famous for his singing of Wagnerian roles.

Mellers, Wilfrid Howard, 1914– (Eng.) Composer and musicologist; author of *François Couperin and the French Classical Tradition; Music and Society;* and *Music in a New Found Land,* a study of American music.

Mengelberg, Willem, 1871–1951 (Netherlands) Conductor of Concertgebouw Orchestra and New York Philharmonic.

Mennin, Peter, 1923– (U.S.) Educator (president of Juilliard School of Music) and composer of 7 symphonies, several concertos, chamber music, and choral works. Mennin's style is lean and athletic, featuring polyphonic development of long-lined melodies.

Mennini, Louis, 1920– (U.S.) Teacher (Eastman School of Music; North Carolina School of the Arts) and composer of chamber operas and works for orchestra and chamber groups.

Menotti, Gian Carlo, 1911– (It.; U.S.) Composer and librettist of some of the most popular operas in English: *The Old Maid and the Thief* (1939); *The Medium* (1946); *The Consul* (1950); *Amahl and the Night Visitors* (1951); *The Saint of Bleecker Street* (1954). He has also written a madrigal-ballet *(The Unicorn, the Gorgon and the Manticore)* and Martha Graham's *Errand into the Maze.* Menotti's style is eclectic, using any contemporary or traditional types of sounds he needs for his dramatic purpose, and always eminently singable.

Menuhin, Yehudi, 1916– (U.S.) Violinist who made a sensational debut as soloist in the Mendelssohn Violin Concerto in 1923. He has played many sonata recitals with his sister **Hepzibah** (1920–). In recent years Menuhin has become the conductor of the Bath (England) Chamber Orchestra and has also steeped himself in the study of Indian music and philosophy.

Merrill, Robert, 1917– (U.S.) Operatic baritone.

Mersenne, Marin, 1588–1648 (Fr.) Author of important books on music theory *(Harmonie universelle).*

Merulo, Claudio, 1533–1604 (It.) Virtuoso organist and composer of canzonas and toccatas for organ, as well as many madrigals and motets.

Messager, André, 1853–1929 (Fr.) Conductor of concert and opera (including the first performance of Debussy's *Pelléas et Mélisande)* and composer of many melodious operas and ballets.

Messiaen, Olivier, 1908– (Fr.) Organist, pianist, teacher (of Boulez and Stockhausen), and composer of many works noted for their wide-ranging melodic sources (Gregorian chant, bird calls, Oriental scales) and their unusual instrumental sonorities, including melodic percussion instruments and electronic sounds generated by the "Ondes Martenot." Organist at Trinity Church in Paris, Messiaen writes works that are often based on a deep religious feeling—Roman Catholic, as in the *20 Regards sur l'enfant*

Jésus and *La Vision de L'Amen* for piano; and Hindu, as in *Turangalila* for orchestra.

Metastasio, Pietro Antonio Domenico Bonaventura, 1698–1782 (It.; Aus.) Librettist for Handel, Gluck, and Mozart who established operatic form in the early and middle 18th century; in particular, emphasizing the aria as the most important ingredient of opera.

Meyer, Leonard B., 1918– (U.S.) Educator (Chicago University) and writer; author of *Emotion and Meaning in Music* and *Music, The Arts, and Ideas.*

Miaskovsky, Nikolai Yakovlevitch, 1881–1950 (Rus.) Teacher (Moscow Conservatory) and composer of 27 symphonies and a variety of church music.

Michelangeli, Arturo Benedetti, 1920– (It.) Pianist.

Mihalovici, Marcel, 1898– (Rumania; Fr.) Composer in freely dissonant idiom of operas and orchestral and chamber music works.

Milán, Luis, c. 1500–c. 1561 (Sp.) Composer of important early lute music, particularly a set of fantasias in free rhapsodic form, and a group of pavanes. He wrote largely for the vihuela, a 6-string Spanish guitar.

Miller, Glenn, 1904–44 (U.S.) Trombonist; arranger and leader for his own big dance band.

Milstein, Nathan, 1904– (Rus.; Fr.; U.S.) Concert violinist.

Mimaroglu, Ilhan Kemaleddin, 1926– (Turkey) Composer in experimental style, including electronic sounds, of works for small instrumental ensembles.

Mitropoulos, Dimitri, 1896–1960 (Greece; U.S.) Pianist and conductor (Minneapolis Symphony and New York Philharmonic).

Mompou, Federico, 1893– (Sp.) Composer of charming, refined piano pieces and songs.

Moniuszko, Stanislaw, 1819–72 (Rus.; Poland) Composer of songs and operas, including *Halka,* the first opera in a Polish nationalist vein.

Monk, Thelonius, 1918– (U.S.) Jazz pianist and composer.

Monn, Georg Matthias, 1717–50 (Aus.) Composer of symphonies, concertos, and chamber music in early Classical style.

Monsigny, Pierre-Alexandre, 1729–1817 (Fr.) Composer of early French comic operas.

Monte, Philippe de, 1521–1603 (Belg.; Aus.) Composer of sacred and secular vocal works.

Montemezzi, Italo, 1875–1952 (It.) Composer of operas, of which *L'Amore dei tre re* is best known.

Monteux, Pierre, 1875–1964 (Fr.) Conductor of ballet, opera, and symphony (Diaghilev's Russian Ballet, Boston Symphony, Orchestre Symphonique de Paris). Monteux conducted the first performances of Stravinsky's *Rite of Spring* and *Petrouchka,* Ravel's *Daphnis et Chloë,* and Debussy's *Jeux.*

Moore, Douglas, 1893–1969 (U.S.) Teacher (Columbia University) and composer of works reflecting Moore's American background: operas (*Ballad of Baby Doe; The Devil and Daniel Webster; Carry Nation*), symphonic works (*Pageant of P. T. Barnum*), and much chamber music.

Moore, Gerald, 1899– (Eng.) Outstanding accompanist for singers; author of *The Unashamed Accompanist.*

Moore, Thomas, 1779–1852 (Ireland) Poet and composer of songs, many based on Irish folk tunes.

Morel, Jean, 1903–75 (Fr.; U.S.) Conductor and outstanding teacher of conducting (Juilliard School of Music).

Morini, Erica, 1904– (Aus.; U.S.) Concert violinist.

Moross, Jerome, 1913– (U.S.) Composer of theatrical scores (*Frankie and Johnnie* ballet, 1938; *Ballet Ballads,* 1948; *The Golden Apple,* 1955).

Morton, Ferdinand ("Jelly Roll"), 1885–1941 (U.S.) Early jazz pianist.

Moscheles, Ignaz, 1794–1870 (Czech.; Ger.) Pianist and teacher (Leipzig Conservatory).

Mossolov, Alexander Vassilievitch, 1900–73 (Rus.) Composer whose early works, such as *Iron Foundry,* celebrated a mechanist society. He later composed more conventional symphonies, concertos, and cantatas.

Moszkowski, Moritz, 1854–1925 (Poland; Ger.; Fr.) Pianist and composer of many brilliant and delightful piano pieces, an opera (*Boabdil*), violin and piano concertos. His popular *Spanish Dances,* often heard in orchestral form, were originally written for piano, four hands.

Mozart, Maria Anna, 1751–1829 (Aus.) Wolfgang Amadeus Mozart's sister "Nannerl." She was an excellent pianist, often appearing in concert with her younger brother.

Mozart, Leopold, 1719–87 (Aus.) Violinist, composer, and teacher. As violinist he was a member of the Archbishop of Salzburg's orchestra. As composer he wrote symphonies, oratorios, concertos, and chamber music, and is believed to have written the well-known "Toy" Symphony, formerly ascribed to Haydn. As teacher he concentrated on the musical up-bringing of his children, "Nannerl" and Wolfgang, but he also wrote one of the most important texts on the art of playing the violin.

Muck, Karl, 1859–1940 (Ger.) Conductor of opera and symphony.

Muffat, Georg, 1653–1704 (Alsace; Ger.) Organist and composer who combined the styles of his teachers, Lully and Corelli, in writing early German instrumental music: orchestral suites, sonatas, concerti grossi, and organ toccatas.

Muffat, Gottlieb, 1690–1770 (Aus.) Organist and composer of important organ toccatas and harpsichord suites; one of the early composers in a style that became known as Classical; son of Georg Muffat.

Munch, Charles, 1891–1968 (Fr.) Conductor of the Boston Symphony Orchestra (1949–62) and the new government-subsidized Symphony Orchestra of Paris (1967).

Munsel, Patrice Beverly, 1925– (U.S.) Operatic soprano.

Muratore, Lucien, 1876–1954 (Fr.) Operatic tenor.

Mustel, Victor, 1815–90 (Fr.) Instrument maker; inventor of the celesta.

Muzio, Claudia, 1889–1936 (It.) Operatic soprano.

N

Nabokov, Nicolas, 1903– (Rus.; U.S.) Composer of orchestral and chamber music works, an opera (*The Holy Devil*), and ballets (*Union Pacific*).

Nancarrow, Conlon, 1912– (U.S.; Mex.) Composer of complex, dissonant works for player-piano, including a dance score for Merc Cunningham.

Nardini, Pietro, 1722–93 (It.) Composer of concertos, sonatas, and other works, principally for violin.

Narvaez, Luis de, early 16th century (Sp.) Composer of music for lute, including some of the first music to be written in variation form.

Neel, Boyd, 1905– (Eng.; Canada) Conductor (The Boyd Neel Orchestra) and educator (Toronto University).

Neri, Saint Filippo, 1515–95 (It.) His musical services in the oratory of the church of San Girolamo della Carità, in Rome, led to the oratorio.

Neveu, Ginette, 1919–49 (Fr.) Violinist.

Nevin, Ethelbert Woodbridge, 1862–1901 (U.S.) Composer of songs ("The Rosary"; "Mighty Lak' a Rose") and graceful piano pieces (*Water Scenes,* which includes the popular "Narcissus").

Newman, Ernest, 1868–1959 (Eng.) Music critic and author of many books, including *A Musical Critic's Holiday, Stories of the Great Operas,* and, in 4 volumes, *The Life of Richard Wagner.*

Nichols, Ernest ("Red"), 1905–65 (U.S.) Cornettist and leader of one of the first popular dance bands: Red Nichols and His Five Pennies.

Nicolai, Otto, 1810–49 (Ger.) Composer of orchestral and chamber music works and several operas, of which *The Merry Wives of Windsor* was the most successful.

Nielsen, Carl August, 1865–1931 (Denmark) Conductor and composer of several operas; 6 symphonies; concertos for violin, flute, and clarinet; 4 string quartets and other chamber music; cantatas; songs; and works for piano and for organ. Nielsen's music is Romantic yet modern. Appreciation of his works has been growing steadily and his symphonies have gradually made their way into the repertoire.

Nikisch, Arthur, 1855–1922 (H.; Ger.) Conductor (Leipzig, Berlin, Boston, London).

Nilsson, Birgit, 1918– (Sweden) Operatic soprano.

Nilsson, Bo, 1937– (Sweden) Composer of controlled "chance" music.

Nin (y Castellanos), Joaquín, 1879–1949 (Cuba) Pianist and composer of Spanish-tinted works for piano, violin, voice, and orchestra.

Nono, Luigi, 1924– (It.) Innovative composer who has written vocal works in which words are prismatically fractured so that the listener is made aware of the many sounds which make up a syllable or word.

Nordica, Lillian, 1857–1914 (U.S.) Operatic soprano.

Nordoff, Paul, 1909–77 (U.S.) Teacher and composer of orchestral and chamber music works, several concertos, piano works and transcriptions, and songs.

North, Alex, 1910– (U.S.) Composer of outstanding film scores *(Streetcar Named Desire; Viva Zapata),* modern dance ballets, a work for children *(Hither and Thither of Danny Dither),* and the song "Unchained Melody."

Nottebohm, Martin Gustav, 1817–82 (Ger.) Musical scholar who edited Beethoven's sketch-books.

Novaës, Guiomar, 1895–1979 (Brazil) Pianist.

Novello, Vincent, 1781–1861 (Eng.) Organist, editor of sacred vocal works, and founder (1811) of the music publishing firm of Novello & Co.

Noverre, Jean-Georges, 1727–1810 (Fr.) Dancer, choreographer, and writer whose book *Letters on Dancing and Ballets* (1760) exerted a strong influence on the operatic theories of Gluck.

O

Obrecht, Jacob, 1452–1505 (Netherlands) Composer of polyphonic vocal works: masses, motets, chansons.

Ockeghem, Johannes (Jean, Jan), 1430–95 (Flanders) Composer, teacher, and musician in the French court. Ockeghem's masses, motets, and chansons are notable for their flowing long-line melodies that undergo highly ingenious contrapuntal treatment. Through his pupil, Josquin Des Prés, Ockeghem's style spread to Italy, France, and Germany and became the basis of later Renaissance musical practice.

Odington, Walter (Walter of Evesham), early 14th century (Eng.) Benedictine monk who wrote *De speculatione musices,* an important treatise on music theory.

Odo, or Otto, of Cluny, 879–942 (Fr.) Composer of sacred music and author of *Dialogus de musica,* a text on music theory that was based on Odo's own teaching in the choir school of the Benedictine monastery at Beaune.

Ogdon, John, 1937– (Eng.) Pianist; winner of the Tchaikovsky Competition in Moscow in 1962.

O'Hara, Geoffrey, 1882–1967 (Canada; U.S.) Composer of many popular songs ("K-K-K-Katy"; "Give a Man a Horse He Can Ride").

Oliver, Joseph ("King"), 1885–1938 (U.S.) Cornettist; leader of the King Oliver Creole Jazz Band, which for a while included the young Louis Armstrong.

Orbón, Julián, 1925– (Sp.; Cuba) Composer of works for symphony and small instrumental ensembles *(Partita* for harpsichord, string quartet, melodic percussion instruments, and harmonium).

Orff, Carl, 1895– (Ger.) Teacher (Munich) and composer of operas *(The Moon),* chamber music, musical plays, and, most successfully, two lusty cantatas: *Carmina Burana* (1937) and *Catulli Carmina* (1943). Orff's style in these last is based on rhythmic propulsion, with melodies in chang-ing meters being chanted over the motor rhythms of instrumental ostinatos. Orff's preoccupation with rhythm led him to develop a method to train young children by means of percussion instruments.

Ormandy, Eugene, 1899– (H.; U.S.) Conductor of Minneapolis Symphony (1931–36) and Philadelphia Orchestra (1936 to the present).

Ornstein, Leo, 1895– (Rus.; U.S.) Pianist, teacher, and composer of many violent works during the World War I period: sonatas, *Poems of 1917,* and *Wild Men's Dance* for piano; symphonic and chamber music works.

Orrego Salas, Juan, 1919– (Chile; U.S.) Teacher (Indiana University) and composer of instrumental and vocal works in a style that is based on Chilean music and moderately dissonant neo-Classicism.

Ouseley, Sir Frederick Arthur Gore, 1825–89 (Eng.) Teacher (Oxford), composer (sacred music; preludes and fugues for organ), and author of texts on theory.

Overton, Hall, 1920–72 (U.S.) Teacher (Juilliard); experimental jazz pianist; composer in free dissonant style.

Ozawa, Seiji, 1935– (Japan) Conductor (Boston Symphony).

P

Pachelbel, Carl (Charles) Theodore, 1690–1750 (Ger.; U.S.) Organist and harpsichordist; one of the first well-trained European musicians to settle in the United States, where, in 1736, he gave the first concert of record in New York. Son of Johann Pachelbel.

Pachelbel, Johann, 1653–1706 (Ger.) Organist and composer of organ and harpsichord pieces that are direct and appealing to the listener, challenging to the performer. His fugues and chaconnes, written in idiomatic keyboard styles, undoubtedly influenced J. S. Bach.

Pachman, Vladimir de, 1848–1933 (Rus.) Poetic and eccentric concert pianist.

Paderewski, Ignace Jan, 1860–1941 (Poland) Statesman, composer, and one of the most popular concert pianists of all time. Always deeply patriotic, Paderewski worked for Poland's independence from Russia and served as first prime minister of the new Poland in 1919–20. After the invasion of Poland at the beginning of World War II, he became president of its government in exile in 1940. In spite of his busy political and concert life Paderewski managed to compose a great many works—mostly for piano, but including a symphony, an opera, a concerto, and a sonata for violin and piano. His *Minuet in G* is one of the most-played (or played-at) of all piano compositions.

Paine, John Knowles, 1839–1906 (U.S.) Organist, teacher (Harvard), and composer of works in large forms. Paine wrote in a conservative Romantic style which reflects his training in Germany. Most successful of his works were his *Spring Symphony* and incidental music to a production of Sophocles' *Oedipus tyrannus.*

Paisiello, Giovanni, 1740–1816 (It.) Composer who started his career writing church music, but became famous for his operas, of which he wrote 100; he also composed sonatas and concertos for piano, and symphonies.

Paladilhe, Émile, 1844–1926 (Fr.) Composer of several operas and masses, but best known for his lyrical songs.

Palmgren, Selim, 1878–1951 (Finland) Pianist and composer of operas, concertos, sonatas, and short pieces for piano, including the well-known *May Night.*

Panassié, Hugues, 1912–75 (Fr.) One of the earliest serious jazz critics and historians; author of *Le Jazz Hot* (1934) and *Dictionary of Jazz* (1954).

Panufnik, Andrzej, 1914– (Poland; Eng.) Conductor (Warsaw; Birmingham); composer of instrumental works.

Paradies, Pietro Domenico, 1707–91 (It.; Eng.) Composer of sonatas for harpsichord.

Paray, Paul, 1886– (Fr.) Conductor (Lamoureux Orchestra; Colonne; Detroit) and composer of symphonic and chamber music works, a mass in memory of Joan of Arc, and a ballet.

Parker, Charles ("Bird"), 1920–55 (U.S.) Creative jazz saxophonist.

Parker, Horatio William, 1863–1919 (U.S.) Organist, teacher (Yale), and composer of operas *(Mona),* orchestral works, many choral compositions, including his oratorio *Hora Novissima,* a great deal of chamber music, and many songs.

Parry, Sir Charles Hubert Hastings, 1848–1918 (Eng.) Educator (Royal College of Music; Oxford), music historian, and composer of operas, symphonic and chamber music works, oratorios and other choral music.

Partch, Harry, 1901–74 (U.S.) Innovative theorist, inventor, and composer of music which turned its back on almost every aspect of traditional European music. To achieve the sounds he imagined, Partch devised a scale in which the octave is divided into 43 microtones. To play this music he invented or adapted a whole series of new instruments, including "cloud chamber bowls" made of pyrex; the "chormelodeon" (a harmonium tuned to the 43-tone octave); enlarged kitharas; and modified marimbas. The effect of such instruments is mystical, exotic, and unsettling. Partch has written particularly eloquent dance and theater music *(Ring Around the Moon; King Oedipus; The Bewitched),* as well as a recorded series of brief works entitled *And on the Seventh Day Petals Fell in Petaluma.*

Pasdeloup, Jules-Étienne, 1819–87 (Fr.) Conductor who established a series of popular orchestral concerts in Paris in the middle of the 19th century.

Pasquini, Bernardo, 1637–1710 (It.) Composer of operas, sacred music, and harpsichord pieces.

Patti, Adelina, 1843–1919 (Sp.; Wales) Operatic coloratura soprano.

Paumann, Conrad, c. 1410–73 (Ger.) Organist and composer of some of the earliest organ music.

Paumgartner, Bernhard, 1887-1971 (Aus.) Conductor, director of the Salzburg Mozart um, and biographer of Mozart.

Pears, Peter, 1910- (Eng.) Tenor who has sung leading roles in the premières of Benjamin Britten's operas.

Pedrell, Felipe, 1841-1922 (Sp.) Teacher (of Granados, Falla, Gerhard), critic, and scholar whose vision led to the rise of the late 19th-century Spanish nationalist school of composition; composer of operas, orchestral works, chamber music, and vocal works.

Peerce, Jan, 1904- (U.S.) Concert and operatic tenor.

Peeters, Flor, 1903- (Belg.) Organist, director of Antwerp Conservatory, and composer of many organ works in moderately dissonant style.

Pelletier, Wilfred, 1896- (Canada) Conductor (Metropolitan Opera; Quebec Symphony) and director of Montreal Conservatory.

Penderecki, Krzyastof, 1933- (Poland) Outstanding composer, in an eloquent avant-garde style, of large-scale works for orchestra *(Threnody for the Victims of Hiroshima),* chorus *(Requiem*—one of the most performed contemporary works), and chamber groups.

Pepusch, Johann Christoph, 1667-1752 (Ger.; Eng.) Organist, composer of incidental music for masques, and adapter of the tunes used in *The Beggar's Opera.*

Pergolesi, Giovanni Battista, 1710-36 (It.) Composer of church music, trio sonatas, and sonatas and concertos for strings and for harpsichord. Best known for the comic opera *La Serva padrona,* written to be played between acts of a serious opera.

Peri, Jacopo, 1561-1633 (It.) Singer and composer of two of the earliest operas: *Dafne* (1597) and *Euridice* (1600). Only the music of *Euridice* survives.

Perotin or Perotinus, c. 1160 (Fr.) Composer of important 2-, 3-, and 4-part sacred music using the paralleling technique known as organum, which had also been used by Leonin, Perotin's predecessor at the church in Paris which later became Notre Dame.

Persichetti, Vincent, 1915- (U.S.) Pianist, teacher (Juilliard), and prolific composer in all musical forms except opera. In addition to symphonies and other large-scale works, including an effective song cycle *(Harmonium,* based on poems of Wallace Stevens), Persichetti has written many compositions to fill gaps in the contemporary repertoire. Such works include a series of serenades for small groups of instruments, a *Little Piano Book,* sonatas and sonatinas for 1 and 2 pianos, band music, and choral music. His devout and joyous *Hymns and Responses* represents one of the few attempts by contemporary composers to make their music accessible to church groups.

Peter, John Frederick, 1746-1813 (Holland; U.S.) Organist at Moravian church in Bethlehem, Pa., and composer, in a Haydnesque style, of church music and possibly the first chamber music works written in America: 6 string quartets.

Peters, Carl Friedrich, 1779-1827 (Ger.) Founder, in 1814, of C. F. Peters, music publishers.

Peters, Roberta, 1930- (U.S.) Operatic soprano.

Petrassi, Goffredo, 1904- (It.) Composer of operas, symphonic works, concertos, chamber works, and much music for chorus and solo voice.

Petri, Egon, 1881-1962, (Ger.; U.S.) Teacher (Berlin; Cornell University; Mills College; Basel) and concert pianist.

Petrucci, Ottaviano dei, 1466-1539 (It.) Publisher and printer of the first collection of part songs, *Harmonice musices odhecaton A,* in 1501.

Peuerl, Paul, c. 1570-1625 (Aus.) Organist and composer of instrumental music, including the then-new 4-movement variation dance suite.

Pezel, Johann Christoph, 1639-94 (Ger.) Composer whose hearty music for municipal wind bands has recently been revived and recorded.

Pfitzner, Hans, 1869-1949 (Rus.; Ger.) Prolific composer of works in all forms. His opera *Palestrina* and some of his songs enjoyed success in Germany, but his music has not made its way out of its homeland.

Philidor, Anne Danican-, 1681-1728 (Fr.) Composer of works for flute and founder of the Concert Spirituel in Paris.

Philidor, François André Danican-, 1726-95 (Fr.) Composer of many light and grand operas, of which *Tom Jones* was the most successful.

Philipp, Isidor, 1863-1958 (H.; Fr.) Pianist; teacher (Paris Conservatory); editor and compiler of several technical methods.

Philips, Peter, c. 1560-1628 (Eng.; Belg.) Organist and composer of madrigals, motets, and keyboard works.

Phillips, Burrill, 1907- (U.S.) Teacher (Eastman; University of Illinois) and composer of ballets, orchestral works *(Selections from McGuffey's Reader),* chamber music, and several interesting piano pieces.

Piatigorsky, Gregor, 1903-76 (Rus.; U.S.) Concert cellist.

Piccini, Niccola, 1728-1800 (It.; Fr.) Prolific composer of operas; best known as unwilling antagonist to Gluck in a political struggle between those Parisians who supported Italian opera and those who favored Gluck's new dramatic theories. Piccini wrote more than 100 operas. Many were popular when first produced, but none has become a staple of operatic fare.

Pick-Mangiagalli, Riccardo, 1882-1949 (Bohemia; It.) Composer, in moderately contemporary idiom, of stage works, orchestral pieces, chamber music, piano pieces, and songs.

Pierné, (Henri Constant) Gabriel, 1863-1937 (Fr.) Organist successor to César Franck; conductor; and prolific composer of music in a light style.

Pijper, Willem, 1894-1947 (Holland) Educator (director of Rotterdam Conservatory) and composer of symphonies, concertos, operas, and much fine chamber music.

Pilkington, Francis, c. 1560-1638 (Eng.) Composer of lyrical lute songs, several sets of madrigals and pastorales, and some sacred music.

Pinkham, Daniel, 1923- (U.S.) Organist; conductor; and composer of strong works for orchestra, small ensembles, and harpsichord, and of effective choral music *(Easter Cantata* for chorus, brass, and percussion).

Pinza, Ezio, 1892-1957 (It.; U.S.) Bass who, after a distinguished career in opera, became a Broadway star in *South Pacific.*

Pischna, Josef, 1826-96 (Bohemia) Pianist and teacher whose technical exercises have been widely used.

Pisk, Paul Amadeus, 1893- (Aus.; U.S.) Teacher and composer, in modified 12-tone technique, of much fine chamber music.

Piston, Walter, 1894-1976 (U.S.) Teacher (Harvard) and composer of 9 symphonies. concertos (including 1 for violin and 1 for 2 pianos). much distinguished chamber music. and the popular ballet score *The Incredible Flutist.* He has also authored widely-used textbooks on music theory and orchestration. Piston's music is. in fast movements. energetic and busy: in slow movements. it is lyrical in a restrained fashion—and an element of jazz is often apparent. Piston's style is based on dissonant. tonal counterpoint. He is one of the most honored of American composers and has been awarded several Pulitzer prizes.

Pizzetti, Ildebrando, 1880-1968 (It.) Teacher (Accademia di Santa Cecilia, Rome) and composer of many operas on dramatic subjects *(Fra Gherardo* has been most successful), orchestral works, chamber music, and songs.

Planquette, Jean-Robert, 1848-1903 (Fr.) Operetta composer best known for his *Chimes of Normandy.*

Playford, John, 1623-86 (Eng.) A key figure in English musical life who established a music publishing business that brought out many important collections, such as *The English Dancing Master* (1651), and books of psalms and rounds. His son **Henry** (1657-1720) continued the business, publishing works of Purcell and Blow.

Pleyel, Ignaz Joseph, 1757-1831 (Aus.; Fr.) Composer of symphonies, concertos, and string quartets in the Classical style, and founder of the piano manufacturing firm Pleyel and Company.

Poldini, Eduard, 1869-1957, (H.) Composer of operettas and light piano pieces *(Poupée valsante,* or *The Dancing Doll).*

Ponce, Manuel María, 1882-1948 (Mex.) Composer of works for orchestra and chamber groups, often using Mexican musical idioms. His best-known work is his charming song "Estrellita."

Ponchielli, Amilcare, 1834-86 (It.) Composer of operas, of which *La Gioconda,* with its *Dance of the Hours* ballet, has been most successful.

Pons, Lily, 1904-76 (Fr.; U.S.) Coloratura operatic soprano.

Ponselle, Rosa, 1897-1981 (U.S.) Operatic soprano.

Poot, Marcel, 1901– (Belg.) Educator (director of Brussels Conservatory) and composer of operas, ballets, symphonic works, and chamber music which are often inspired by people and events of the day: the films of Chaplin, Lindbergh's crossing of the Atlantic, jazz, and so forth.

Popper, David, 1843–1913 (Czech.; Aus.) Cellist and teacher (Budapest Conservatory); composer of works for cello, including concertos and a widely used series of études.

Porpora, Nicola Antonio, 1686–1768 (It.) The most famous singing teacher of his day (Haydn served him as valet/accompanist in order to learn how to write for the voice) and composer of solo cantatas, works for strings, and about 50 operas. His knowledge of the art of singing was so complete that he was able to write tremendously florid—yet singable—arias that exploit the voice to its fullest.

Porta, Costanzo, c. 1530–1601 (It.) Composer of sacred and secular vocal music.

Porter, Cole, 1892–1964 (U.S.) Composer and lyricist of some of the most skillful and sophisticated musical comedies: *The Gay Divorcee* (1932), *Anything Goes* (1934), *Dubarry Was a Lady* (1939), and *Kiss Me Kate* (1948). Porter started his song-writing career at Yale, where he wrote material for student shows as well as the Yale "Bulldog Song." His popular songs include such "standards" as "Begin the Beguine," "My Heart Belongs to Daddy," "Night and Day," and "Don't Fence Me In."

Porter, Quincy, 1897–1966 (U.S.) Teacher (New England Conservatory; Yale) and composer of several works for orchestra and a large amount of fine chamber music, including 10 string quartets and other works featuring strings—an outgrowth of Porter's early career as a violinist. His *Concerto Concertante* for 2 pianos and orchestra was awarded a Pulitzer prize.

Pousseur, Henri, 1929– (Belg.) Composer of works in experimental style, including the use of electronic sounds.

Powell, John, 1882–1963 (U.S.) Pianist and composer of works featuring the piano, including concertos, sonatas, and *Rapsodie Nègre* (1918), his most popular composition.

Powell, Mel, 1923– (U.S.) Jazz pianist (with Benny Goodman's Band), teacher (Yale), and composer of works for solo instruments and chamber groups in a style that utilizes many experimental elements, including electronic sounds.

Power, Lionel, d. 1445 (Eng.) Composer of important early polyphonic sacred vocal works.

Praetorius, Michael, 1571–1621 (Ger.) Composer of many sacred and secular works, including skillful settings of Lutheran chorales for 2 voices *(Bicinia)* and 3 voices *(Tricinia)*. His most important contribution was his *Syntagma musicum* in 3 volumes, which consists of: a history of music; a complete description, with woodcut illustrations, of known musical instruments; and a discussion of musical style and performance of the music of his time.

Presley, Elvis, 1935–1977 (U.S.) Highly successful rock 'n' roll singer.

Presser, Theodore, 1848–1925 (U.S.) Musician-publisher.

Previn, André, 1929– (Ger.; U.S.) Pianist, composer, and conductor (London and Pittsburgh symphonies).

Prey, Hermann, 1929– (Ger.) Concert and operatic baritone.

Price, Leontyne, 1927– (U.S.) Concert and operatic soprano.

Primrose, William, 1903– (Scot.) Viola soloist; commissioned Bartók's viola concerto which was completed after Bartók's death by Tibor Serly.

Prout, Ebenezer, 1835–1909 (Eng.) Teacher (Dublin) and composer of symphonic, chamber, and choral music; best known for his textbooks on music theory.

Provenzale, Francesco, 1627–1704 (It.) Composer of operas in the style that became known as "Neapolitan," preceding the great genius of that style, Alessandro Scarlatti.

Pugnani, Gaetano, 1731–98 (It.) Violinist, teacher, and composer of concertos, sonatas, and duos for violins, plus 6 string quartets.

Purcell, Daniel, c. 1663–1717 (Eng.) Organist and composer, principally of music for theatrical productions, plus some sacred vocal music. Brother of Henry Purcell.

Q

Quantz, Johann Joachim, 1697–1773 (Ger.) Flute virtuoso and composer of about 500 works, including 300 concertos for flute. For most of his life he was Frederick the Great's flute teacher and court composer.

Quilter, Roger, 1877–1953 (Eng.) Composer of many sensitive songs ("Now Sleeps the Crimson Petal") and light orchestral and choral works.

Quinault, Philippe, 1635–88 (Fr.) Playwright, best known as the librettist for most of Lully's operas. Several of his librettos were set by later composers as well: *Roland* by Piccini and *Armide* by Gluck.

R

Rabaud, Henri, 1873–1949 (Fr.) Conductor, director of Paris Conservatory, and composer of operas and works for orchestra, chorus, and chamber groups.

Raff, Joseph Joachim, 1822–82 (Switz.; Ger.) Pianist, teacher, and composer, in Romantic vein, of 11 symphonies (some with descriptive titles), concertos for violin and for piano, much chamber music, songs, and piano pieces.

Rainier, Priaulx, 1903– (South Africa; Eng.) Teacher (Royal Academy of Music) and composer of dissonant, yet tonal, works, including several string quartets; a chamber symphony for strings; songs; and pieces for violin, clarinet, and piano.

Rasoumovsky, Prince Andrei Kyrillovitch, 1752–1836 (Rus.) Patron of Beethoven, who dedicated his 3 string quartets, Op. 59, to him.

Rathgeber, Valentin, 1682–1750 (Ger.) Com-

poser of secular choral works and keyboard works of unusual charm.

Ravenscroft, Thomas, c. 1590–c. 1633 (Eng.) Composer, but best known as publisher of popular collections of rounds and catches: *Pammelia* and *Deuteromelia.*

Rawsthorne, Alan, 1905– (Eng.) Composer, in a fluent eclectic style, of symphonies, concertos, chamber music, and songs.

Rebikov, Vladimir Ivanovitch, 1866–1920 (Rus.) Composer of operas and other theatrical works (some for children), symphonic and chamber music, and much delightful piano music written in a mildly dissonant style.

Reed, Gardner, 1913– (U.S.) Teacher; author of an authoritative book, *Thesaurus of Orchestral Devices;* and composer of songs, chamber music, and much music for orchestra, often with descriptive titles *(Night Flight; Dance of the Locomotives).*

Reese, Gustave, 1899– (U.S.) Teacher (New York University) and musicologist; author of *Music in the Middle Ages* and *Music in the Renaissance.*

Reger, Max, 1873–1916 (Ger.) Teacher (Leipzig Conservatory), pianist, and prolific composer of instrumental and vocal works that combine Baroque details in massiveness with Romantic harmonic and melodic tendencies. Reger's orchestral and chamber music has been slow to make its way outside of Germany, although his unaccompanied violin sonatas and cello suites and his organ fantasias and choral preludes have gained favor with performers.

Reicha, Anton, 1770–1836 (Czech.; Fr.) Teacher (of Liszt); composer-friend of Beethoven and Haydn who wrote operas and symphonic works, but is best known for his chamber music: 24 woodwind quintets; 6 quartets for flute, violin, viola, and cello; an octet for winds and strings.

Reinagle, Alexander, 1756–1809 (Eng.; U.S.) One of the earliest European professional musicians to emigrate to the U.S. and enrich the musical life of his new country by serving as performer, conductor, impresario, and composer of harpsichord sonatas, songs, and incidental music for plays.

Reinecke, Carl Heinrich Carsten, 1824–1910 (Ger.) Conductor (Leipzig), pianist, and composer of operas, symphonies, concertos and sonatas for piano, cantatas, and much chamber music. Ironically, his most played works are the cadenzas he wrote for the piano concertos of Bach, Mozart, and Beethoven.

Reiner, Fritz, 1888–1963 (H.; U.S.) Virtuoso opera and symphony conductor (Dresden and Metropolitan operas; Rittsburg and Chicago Symphony orchestras); teacher of conducting at the Curtis Institute of Music where his pupils included Leonard Bernstein, Max Goberman, and Walter Hendl.

Reményi, Eduard, 1830–98 (H.; U.S.) Violin virtuoso for whom Brahms served as accompanist at the age of 19, and from whom Brahms learned about Hungarian folk music.

Resnik, Regina, 1922– (U.S.) Operatic soprano.

Respighi, Ottorino, 1879–1936 (It.) Composer of operas, concertos for violin and piano, chamber music, and songs, but best known for his colorfully orchestrated symphonic works *(The Fountains of Rome; The Pines of Rome; Roman Festivals),* ballet score *(La Boutique Fantasque,* after Rossini), and arrangements of Renaissance and Baroque pieces.

Rethberg, Elisabeth, 1894– (Ger.) Operatic soprano.

Réti, Rudolf, 1885–1957 (Yugoslavia; U.S.) Composer of opera, a piano concerto, and chamber music works; author of an important book on music theory: *The Thematic Process in Music.*

Reutter, Hermann, 1900– (Ger.) Composer of dissonant, yet tonal, operas, oratorios, concertos, and chamber music.

Revueltas, Silvestre, 1899–1940 (Mex.) Highly original composer of Mexican-based ballets, orchestral works, chamber music, and songs.

Reynolds, Roger, 1934– (U.S.) Composer, with a background in engineering, of sensitive and colorfully-scored works for orchestra *(Graffiti),* voices *(The Emperor of Ice Cream),* chamber groups *(A Portrait of Vanzetti* for narrator, winds, percussion, and tape), and piano.

Rezniček, Emil Nikolaus, 1860–1945 (Aus.) Conductor and composer of operas *(Donna Diana)* and symphonic works.

Rheinberger, Josef, 1839–1901 (Liechtenstein; Ger.) Highly esteemed teacher of composition and composer of works for organ.

Ricci, Ruggiero, 1918– (U.S.) Concert violinist who made his debut as a child prodigy in 1929.

Richter, Franz Xaver, 1709–89 (Moravia) Prolific composer of symphonies and chamber music works in early Classical style.

Richter, Hans, 1843–1916 (H.; Ger.) Outstanding conductor (Bayreuth; London) of the Classical repertoire, but his chief claim to fame is his conducting of *The Ring of the Nibelungs* cycle at Bayreuth in 1876.

Richter, Sviatoslav Teofilovitch, 1914– (Rus.) Concert pianist.

Ricordi, Giovanni, 1785–1853 (It.) Founder of the music publishing firm of G. Ricordi & Co. He and his son **Tito** (1811–88) discovered and backed Verdi. His grandson **Giulio** (1840–1912) did much to further the career of Puccini.

Riegger, Wallingford, 1885–1961 (U.S.) Composer in a transparent, jazz-influenced, 12-tone idiom. Riegger's early works, such as his *Study in Sonority* (1927) for 10 violins or multiples thereof and *Dichotomy* (1932), were written in an advanced style for the time. For the next decade he composed outstanding scores for such modern dancers as Martha Graham, Doris Humphrey, Anna Sokolov, and Hanya Holm and intriguing chamber works for woodwinds. Public recognition came late—on the heels of his 4 symphonies, 2 string quartets, piano concerto, and *Dance Rhythms* for orchestra.

Riemann, Hugo, 1849–1919 (Ger.) Outstanding theorist, musicologist, and editor of collections of early music.

Ries, Ferdinand, 1784–1838 (Ger.) One of Beethoven's few piano students and author of an authoritative book on Beethoven; composer of violin and piano works in an early Romantic style.

Rieti, Vittorio, 1898– (Egypt; It.; U.S.) Teacher (Queens College, N.Y.) and composer of operas, ballets, symphonies, and chamber music.

Rinuccini, Ottavio, 1562–1621 (It.) Poet whose librettos were the bases of the first operas: *Dafne* (1594), *Euridice* (1600), *Arianna* (1608).

Rivier, Jean, 1896– (Fr.) Composer of symphonies, concertos, and works for chamber groups.

Robeson, Paul, 1898–1976 (U.S.) Actor and bass singer.

Robinson, Earl, 1910– (U.S.) Composer of works based on folk idiom *(Ballad for Americans).*

Rochberg, George, 1918– (U.S.) Teacher (University of Pennsylvania) and composer of symphonic and chamber music works that are personal and highly communicative. Involved for some time with the 12-tone technique, Rochberg has recently turned to a less doctrinaire approach to composition.

Rockstro, William Smyth, 1823–95 (Eng.) Historian and music theorist.

Rode, Jacques Pierre Joseph, 1774–1830 (Fr.) Violinist and composer of concertos and étude-caprices for violin.

Rodzinski, Artur, 1894–1958 (Dalmatia; U.S.) Conductor of opera and orchestra.

Roger-Ducasse, Jean-Jules Aimable, 1873–1954 (Fr.) Teacher (Paris Conservatory) and composer of orchestral and chamber music works.

Rogers, Bernard, 1893–1968 (U.S.) Teacher (Eastman) and composer of operas and large-scale orchestral and choral works, including the colorfully scored *Passion, The Raising of Lazarus,* and *The Exodus.*

Rolland, Romain, 1866–1944 (Fr.) Musical scholar and author, best known for his *Musicians of Former Days* (1933) and the novel *Jean-Christophe* (1912).

Romberg, Sigmund, 1887–1951 (H.; U.S.) Composer of such popular operettas as *Blossom Time, The Student Prince, The Desert Song,* and *Up in Central Park.*

Rorem, Ned, 1923– (U.S.) Composer, in conservative contemporary style, of operas, piano concertos, orchestral and chamber music works, and, particularly, a large number of sensitive and effective songs; also the author of *Music From Inside Out, New York Diary,* and the *Paris Diary of Ned Rorem.*

Rosbaud, Hans, 1895– (Aus.) Conductor.

Rose, Leonard, 1918– (U.S.) Teacher (Juilliard) and concert cellist.

Rosenmüller, Johann, c. 1620–84 (Ger.) Composer of church music and chamber music for strings.

Rosenthal, Manuel, 1904– (Fr.) Conductor, composer, and arranger of Offenbach's music for the ballet *Gaîté Parisienne.*

Rosenthal, Moriz, 1862–1946 (Poland) Virtuoso concert pianist.

Ross, Hugh, 1898– (Eng.; U.S.) Choral conductor, principally of the New York Schola Cantorum.

Rossi, Salomone, c. 1575–c. 1630 (It.) Composer of madrigals of great interest, including some of the first to have an instrumental accompaniment, and several books of *Sinfonie e gagliarde,* which are examples of one of the earliest type of trio sonata. One of the few Jewish composers of his time, he referred to himself as Ebreo—that is, Hebrew.

Rostropovich, Mstislav, 1927– (Rus.) Phenomenal concert cellist who has given marathon series of concerts playing all the masterworks for cello and orchestra. As a pianist he appears as accompanist for his wife, soprano Galina Vishnevskaya. In 1977 became music director of National Symphony Orchestra.

Rouget de l'Isle, Claude-Joseph, 1760–1836 (Fr.) Composer of the "Marseillaise" (1792).

Rousseau, Jean-Jacques, 1712–78 (Fr.) Author of many books, of which *Émile* is best known; compiler of a dictionary of music; composer of the charming one-act opera *Le Devin du village (The Village Sorcerer).*

Roussel, Albert, 1869–1937 (Fr.) Composer of stage works, symphonic and chamber works, piano pieces, and songs—all skillfully composed and colorfully orchestrated. The symphonic suite from his ballet *Le Festin de l'araignée (The Spider's Feast)* is his most frequently played work.

Rowley, Alec, 1892–1958 (Eng.) Composer of charming chamber music, several concertos, vocal music, and piano pieces.

Rózsa, Miklós, 1907– (H.; U.S.) Composer of orchestral and chamber music; best known for his film scores.

Rubbra, Edmund, 1901– (Eng.) Composer of often-complex symphonies and concertos, chamber music, and vocal works.

Rubinstein, Anton, 1829–94 (Rus.) Virtuoso pianist, teacher, and composer of operas; 6 symphonies (often with descriptive titles: *Ocean Symphony* in 7 movements; *Dramatic*); concertos for piano, violin, and cello; chamber music; songs; and many piano pieces, including such favorites as *Melody in F* and *Kamennoi Ostrow.*

Rubinstein, Artur, 1886– (Poland; U.S.) Outstanding concert pianist.

Rubinstein, Nicholas, 1835–81 (Rus.) Pianist and educator; first director of the Moscow Conservatory (1866); brother of Anton.

Ruckers, Hans, c. 1550–c. 1623 (Belg.) Founder of a dynasty that made some of the finest harpsichords of the Baroque period.

Rudel, Julius, 1921– (Aus.; U.S.) Operatic conductor; music director of New York City Opera Company and music advisor for the Kennedy Center of the Arts, Washington, D.C. Rudel has commissioned and performed many new operas by Americans—Giannini, Ward, Weisgall, Moore.

Rudhyar, Dane, 1895– (Fr.; U.S.) Composer of orchestral and piano works. He attempted to translate into tone, in an idiom that had much in common with the late works of Scriabin, his Hindu-derived philosophy. After 1940, Rudhyar concentrated on writing books rather than music.

Rudolf, Max, 1902– (Ger.; U.S.) Conductor (Cincinnati) and author of an important textbook on conducting: *The Grammar of Conducting.*

Ruffo, Titta, 1877–1953 (It.) Operatic baritone.

Ruggles, Carl, 1876–1971 (U.S.) Composer of unique works, in a non-compromising, dissonant style, for orchestra *(Men and Mountains; Sun-Treader; Organum)* and unusual combinations of instruments *(Men and Angels,* for brass; *Polyphonic Composition* for 3 pianos). For most of his life Ruggles' music was almost unknown to the general musical public. Recently it has received more performances and recordings, and Ruggles is attaining a stature almost equal to that of his fellow-composer Charles Ives.

Russolo, Luigi, 1885–1947 (It.) One of the leaders of the Futurist movement in Europe during the World War I period. Some of Russolo's theories of the future of music, as outlined in a manifesto, have to some extent come true.

S

Sabata, Victor de, 1892–1967 (It.) Conductor and composer.

Sachs, Curt, 1881–1959 (Ger.; U.S.) Teacher (New York University) and musical scholar; author of *World History of the Dance; The History of Musical Instruments; Rhythm and Tempo.*

Sachs, Hans, 1494–1576 (Ger.) Poet; composer; shoemaker; one of the most inventive members of the guild of mastersingers; the philosophic leading character in Wagner's opera *Die Meistersinger von Nürnberg.*

Salieri, Antonio, 1750–1825 (It.) Teacher of Beethoven, Schubert, and Liszt; composer of once-popular operas, as well as instrumental works and much church music.

Salomon, Johann Peter, 1745–1815 (Ger.; Eng.) Violinist, and the man who induced Haydn twice to visit England and write the 12 symphonies known as the "Salomon" or "London" symphonies. Salomon also suggested to Haydn the idea of writing *The Creation.*

Salzedo, Carlos, 1885–1961 (Fr.; U.S.) Virtuoso harpist, teacher, and composer of works featuring one or more harps.

Saminsky, Lazare, 1882–1959 (Rus.; U.S.) Conductor and composer of works often based on Jewish sources.

Sammartini, Giovanni Battista, 1701–75 (It.) Organist, and one of the first composers to write in what was to become the Classical style. His works include more than 20 symphonies, sonatas, and sacred vocal music.

Sanjuán, Pedro, 1886– (Sp.; U.S.) Composer of instrumental works based on Spanish-Cuban ideas.

Sapp, Allen Dwight, 1922– (U.S.) Educator (University of Buffalo) and composer, in dissonantly contrapuntal style, of music for orchestra, chamber groups, piano, and voice.

Sarasate, Pablo Martin Melitón, 1844–1908 (Sp.) Violin virtuoso for whom Bruch wrote his *Scottish Fantasy* and Lalo his *Symphonie espagnole;* composer of many works for violin, including *Zigeunerweisen,* or *Gypsy Airs,* and several books of Spanish dances.

Sargent, Sir Harold Malcolm, 1895–1967 (Eng.) Conductor of opera, ballet, and symphony.

Sauguet, Henri, 1901– (Fr.) Composer of much sophisticatedly light music, following the lead of his idol, Satie: operas, ballets, film music, piano pieces, and many charming songs.

Sax, Adolphe, 1814–94 (Belg.; Fr.) Instrument maker who invented the saxophone family and the saxhorn family, which included the flügelhorn, baritone horn, and tuba.

Sayão, Bidú, 1902– (Brazil) Concert and operatic soprano.

Scharwenka, Franz Xaver, 1850–1924 (Poland; Ger.) Composer of concertos and many shorter works for piano.

Scheff, Fritzi, 1879–1954 (Ger.; U.S.) Operatic soprano who turned to the field of the operetta, where she starred in such works as Victor Herbert's *Mlle. Modiste.*

Scheidt, Samuel, 1587–1654 (Ger.) Composer of sacred vocal works and instrumental dances, but most importantly, Scheidt established the style of the choral prelude for organ. Scheidt is one of the three "S's" of early German music—the others being Schütz and Schein.

Schein, Johann Hermann, 1586–1630 (Ger.) Composer of many chorale tunes, madrigals, solo songs, polyphonic vocal works, and instrumental suites.

Schelling, Ernest, 1876–1939 (U.S.) Pianist, conductor (a pioneer in presenting symphonic concerts for young persons), and composer whose ironic orchestral work, *A Victory Ball,* was highly successful.

Schenker, Heinrich, 1868–1935 (Aus.) Pianist and composer, but best known for his somewhat limited, although valuable, method of structural analysis.

Scherchen, Hermann, 1891–1966 (Ger.; Switz.) Conductor with command of a wide range of styles, with special emphasis on contemporary music. His *Handbook of Conducting* is one of the outstanding works on the subject.

Schering, Arnold, 1877–1941 (Ger.) Musicologist who specialized in music of the Baroque period, particularly J. S. Bach; his *History of Music in Examples* (1931) was the forerunner of the now numerous historical anthologies of music.

Scherman, Thomas, 1917–79 (U.S.) Founder and conductor of the Little Orchestral Society in New York City which emphasizes performances of works of all periods outside the standard repertoire.

Schikaneder, Emanuel, 1751–1812 (Aus.) Actor and librettist for many Singspiels, including Mozart's *The Magic Flute;* in that work he created the role of Papageno.

Schillinger, Joseph, 1895–1943 (Rus.; U.S.) Composer and music theorist who evolved a method of composing and arranging based on mathematical formulas. At the end of his life he was concerned with applying his principles to the visual arts as well as music.

Schindler, Anton, 1795–1864 (Moravia) Violinist, conductor, and biographer of his friend Beethoven, for whom, at various times, he acted as secretary and general factotum.

Schindler, Kurt, 1882–1935 (Ger.; U.S.) Conductor and founder of the New York Schola Cantorum; arranger and editor of many volumes of folk songs *(60 Russian Folk Songs; Folk Music of Spain and Portugal).*

Schiøtz, Aksel, 1906– (Denmark; Canada) Opera and concert tenor; teacher (University of Toronto; University of Colorado).

Schipa, Tito, 1889–1965 (It.) Operatic tenor.

Schirmer, Gustav, 1829–93 (Ger.; U.S.) Founder of the music publishing house of G. Schirmer, Inc. The business grew under the management of his sons **Rudolph Edward** (1859–1919) and **Gustave** (1864–1907), who founded the Boston Music Company. **Gustave, 3rd** (1890–1965) continued the management of the firm. In addition to its vast catalogue of musical editions, G. Schirmer, Inc., made an important contribution to the field of music through its publication of the *Musical Quarterly,* founded in 1915 under the editorship of O. G. Sonneck.

Schmitt, Florent, 1870–1958 (Fr.) Prolific composer, in post-Impressionist style, of ballet, symphonic works, film and theater scores, choral music, chamber music, songs, and piano pieces.

Schnabel, Artur, 1882–1951 (Aus.; Switz.) Pianist famous for his playing of Beethoven, Schubert, and Brahms; teacher; composer of complex dissonant works for orchestra, piano, and small instrumental ensembles.

Schneider, Alexander, 1908– (Lithuania; U.S.) Concert violinist; member of the Budapest Quartet; conductor of chamber orchestras; and co-founder, with Pablo Casals, of music festivals at Prades, France, and Puerto Rico.

Scholes, Percy Alfred, 1877–1958 (Eng.) Musical scholar and author *(Oxford Companion to Music; The Puritans and Music in England and New England;* biographies of the 18th-century music historian Dr. Burney and of Sir John Hawkins).

Schorr, Friedrich, 1888–1953 (H.; U.S.) Operatic baritone.

Schott, Bernhard, 1748–1817 (Ger.) Founder of the important publishing house of B. Schott's Söhne, which first brought out works by Beethoven, Wagner, Rossini, and Hindemith.

Schrade, Leo, 1903–1964 (Ger.; U.S.) Musical scholar and teacher; author of *Monteverdi: Creator of Modern Music;* editor and transcriber of early music, such as Luis Milán's music for the vihuela.

Schröder-Devrient, Wilhelmine, 1804–60 (Ger.) Operatic soprano who created the roles of Senta in Wagner's *The Flying Dutchman* and of Venus in his *Tannhäuser.*

Schuller, Gunther, 1925– (U.S.) French horn player (Metropolitan Opera); educator (president of the New England Conservatory, 1967); composer of a successful opera (The Visitation), a symphony for brass instruments, and chamber music, often for unusual instrumental combinations (quartet for double basses). Schuller coined the term "third stream" to describe one aspect of his compositional style that combines avant-garde jazz and concert music.

Schultze, Norbert, 1911– (Ger.) Composer of music for stage and film; his "Lili Marlene" was the most popular song to come out of the World War II period.

Schumann, Clara Wieck, 1819–96 (Ger.) Concert pianist, wife of Robert Schumann, and close friend of Brahms. Her masterful performances did much to popularize the piano music of these composers.

Schumann, Elisabeth, 1885–1952 (Ger.; U.S.) Concert and operatic soprano.

Schumann-Heink, Ernestine, 1861–1936 (Czech.; U.S.) Concert and operatic contralto; created role of Klytemnestra in Strauss's opera Elektra.

Schwarzkopf, Elisabeth, 1915– (Ger.; U.S.) Concert and operatic soprano.

Schweitzer, Albert, 1875–1965 (Alsace; Africa) Philosopher; physician; organist specializing in J. S. Bach; author of a penetrating, controversial book on the music of Bach.

Scott, Cyril Meir, 1879–1970 (Eng.) Composer whose style was consistent with his philosophy of somewhat voluptuous mysticism, coupling Debussy-like harmony with fairly conventional structure and rhythm. Scott composed works for orchestra, chorus, chamber groups, solo voice, and, especially, piano. Lotus Land, his most popular piano piece, has been arranged for all sorts of combinations—from a Fritz Kreisler version for violin and piano to chamber orchestra and cocktail-lounge jazz group. Scott wrote several books about himself (My Years of Indiscretion) and music (Music, Its Secret Influence Throughout the Ages).

Scott, Tom, 1912–1961 (U.S.) Composer whose works reflect his interest in folk music: Plymouth Rock; Hornpipe and Chantey; Johnny Appleseed, for orchestra; chamber music; and many folk song arrangements.

Scribe, Eugène, 1791–1861 (Fr.) Librettist for operas by Auber, Meyerbeer, Halévy, and Boieldieu.

Searle, Humphrey, 1915– (Eng.) Composer, in a style that is basically—but not dogmatically—derived from the 12-tone technique, of stage works, symphonies, piano concertos, chamber music, songs, and piano pieces. His Twentieth Century Counterpoint is an important textbook and guide to certain aspects of contemporary music.

Seeger, Charles Louis Jr., 1886–1979 (Mex.; U.S.) Teacher, musicologist, and composer.

Seeger, Pete, 1919– (U.S.) Folk singer and author-composer of many topical folk songs reflecting Seeger's concern with contemporary social conditions.

Segovia, Andrés, 1893– (Sp.) Concert guitarist who, through his virtuoso performances, restored the guitar to its early status as a vehicle for serious music.

Seiber, Mátyás, 1905– (H.; Eng.) Teacher and composer, in an eclectic contemporary style, of works for stage, orchestra, and chamber groups.

Seidl, Anton, 1850–98 (H.; U.S.) Virtuoso conductor of opera and symphony (N.Y. Philharmonic) who conducted the first performance of Dvořák's "From the New World" Symphony.

Sembrich, Marcella, 1858–1935 (Poland; U.S.) Concert and operatic coloratura soprano and teacher.

Senesino, Francesco, c. 1680–c. 1750 (It.) Male mezzo-soprano who was one of the stars in Handel's opera company in London.

Senfl, Ludwig, c. 1490–c. 1543 (Switz.; Ger.) Court musician and composer of expressive sacred vocal works.

Serkin, Rudolf, 1903– (Bohemia; U.S.) Concert pianist; teacher (Curtis Institute); founder and director of the Marboro, Vermont, summer music festival.

Serly, Tibor, 1900– (H.; U.S.) Violinist, teacher, and composer who completed Bartók's viola concerto from the composer's sketches.

Sermisy, Claude de, c. 1490–1562 (Fr.) Composer of eloquent vocal works: chansons, masses, and motets.

Sessions, Roger, 1896– (U.S.) Distinguished educator (Princeton), author (Harmonic Practice; The Musical Experience of Composer, Performer, Listener), and composer—of operas (The Trial of Lucullus; Montezuma), 7 symphonies, concertos for piano and violin, sonatas, and other chamber music. His style is dissonant in a non-doctrinaire way. The sometimes thick texture of his music and the uncompromising demands it makes on the listener have prevented Sessions from becoming a "popular" composer—although his early orchestral suite, The Black Maskers, has appeared on many programs.

Ševčik, Otakar, 1852–1934 (Czech.) Teacher (Kiev; Prague; Vienna) of many outstanding violinists, including Zimbalist, Kubelík, and Erica Morini; author of many pedagogical works for violin.

Shankar, Ravi, 1920– (India) Outstanding performer on the sitar whose concerts have changed American and European attitudes toward the music of India; composer of musical scores for film (Pather Panchali) and dance.

Shapey, Ralph, 1921– (U.S.) Conductor specializing in performances of new music; educator (University of Chicago); and composer of works that are highly dissonant and experimental in subdividing the orchestra in unusual spatial groupings (Incantations for soprano and 10 instruments; concerto for violin).

Shaporin, Yuri Alexandrovitch, 1889–1966 (Rus.) Composer of works with programmatic or theatrical base, an opera (The Decembrists), incidental music for plays, songs, and symphonic works.

Sharp, Cecil James, 1859–1924 (Eng.) Collector and authority on English and English-American folk music. Sharp's efforts, in the early 1900's, to preserve folk songs as he found them in rural England

and the Appalachian area of the United States laid the foundation for the great contemporary interest in folk music in both countries.

Shaw, Robert, 1916– (U.S.) Choral and orchestral conductor (Cleveland; Atlanta) whose outstanding performances and recordings of choral works with the Collegiate Chorale and the Robert Shaw Chorale set professional standards for what had been, essentially, an amateur music-making movement.

Shebalin, Vissarion Yakovlevitch, 1902– (Rus.) Educator (Moscow Conservatory) and composer, in moderately dissonant style, of interesting works for piano, orchestra, and chamber groups.

Shepherd, Arthur, 1880–1958 (U.S.) Teacher (Western Reserve) and composer of works for voice, chamber groups, and orchestra (Fantasy on Down East Spirituals).

Shifrin, Seymour, 1926– (U.S.) Teacher (University of California; Brandeis) and composer of complex, delicate chamber music.

Siegmeister, Elie, 1909– (U.S.) Composer of vocal and instrumental works, often with topical titles (Strange American Funeral; Sunday in Brooklyn).

Siepi, Cesare, 1923– (It.) Operatic bass.

Silbermann, Gottfried, 1683–1753 (Ger.) Builder of keyboard instruments: organs, clavichords, harpsichords, and the first German piano.

Silcher, Friedrich, 1789–1860 (Ger.) Collector and editor of German folk songs; composer of many choral works and songs, including the popular "Lorelei."

Sills, Beverly, 1929– (U.S.) Outstanding dramatic and coloratura operatic soprano.

Sinatra, Frank (Francis Albert), 1915– (U.S.) Successful baritone singer of popular songs and film actor.

Sinding, Christian, 1856–1941 (Norway) Composer, in a style combining elements of Norwegian music and rhapsodic Romanticism, of symphonies, concertos, chamber music, and piano pieces, of which "The Rustle of Spring" (Frühlingsrauschen) is the most popular.

Singher, Martial, 1904– (Fr.) Concert and operatic baritone.

Skalkottas, Nikos, 1904–49 (Greece) Composer, in modified 12-tone idiom and showing Greek influences, of orchestral works, concertos, chamber music, songs, and piano pieces. His set of Greek Dances for orchestra is his best-known work and has been recorded.

Skilton, Charles Sanford, 1868–1941 (U.S.) Teacher (University of Kansas), and student of American Indian music, often using Indian thematic material in his compositions: Two Indian Dances and Shawnee Indian Hunting Dance for orchestra. He also wrote several operas, and vocal and chamber music works.

Skrowaczewski, Stanislaw, 1923– (Poland; U.S.) Conductor (Minneapolis Symphony) and composer of symphonies and chamber music.

Slonimsky, Nicolas, 1894– (Rus.; U.S.) Conductor; musicologist gifted with prodigious memory; author (Music Since 1900; Lexicon of Musical Invective); editor of Baker's Biographical Dictionary of Musicians, 5th edition; composer of clever piano pieces (Studies in Black and White).

Smart, Sir George, 1776–1867 (Eng.) Conductor (Philharmonic Society of London) and composer of sacred and secular vocal works.

Smith, William O. 1926– (U.S.) Teacher (University of Washington), virtuoso clarinetist, composer of works for small groups, usually featuring clarinet, using experimental techniques integrating jazz and electronic sounds.

Smyth, Dame Ethel, 1858–1944 (Eng.) Composer of opera, and orchestral and choral works.

Soler, Padre Antonio, 1729–83 (Sp.) Composer of many fine works for harpsichord in a style reminiscent of his teacher, D. Scarlatti, and a large number of religious and secular vocal works.

Sollberger, Harvey, 1938– (U.S.) Teacher (Columbia), flutist, and composer of intriguing chamber works.

Solomon, 1902– (Eng.) Concert pianist.

Solomon, Izler, 1910– (U.S.) Conductor (Indianapolis Symphony).

Solti, Georg, 1912– (H.) Conductor.

Somers, Harry Stewart, 1925– (Canada) Composer, in moderately dissonant style, of orchestral works and chamber music.

Sonneck, Oscar George Theodore, 1873–1928 (U.S.) Musicologist, specializing in early American music; first chief of music division of the Library of Congress; first editor of Musical Quarterly.

Sontag, Henriette, 1806–54 (Ger.) Soprano who sang in early performances of works by Weber, Beethoven, and Rossini.

Sowande, Fela, 1905– (Nigeria) Composer writing in a style that combines elements of Nigerian and European music.

Sowerby, Leo, 1895–1968 (U.S.) Organist and composer of works in all media, particularly for organ and chorus.

Spaeth, Sigmund, 1885–1965 (U.S.) Musicologist; author-editor (Barber Shop Ballads) famous for his role as "tune detective" on radio.

Speaks, Oley, 1874–1948 (U.S.) Composer of many well-known songs ("On the Road to Mandalay"; "Sylvia").

Spitta, Julius August Philipp, 1841–94 (Ger.) Musicologist; editor of early German music; author of authoritative biography of J. S. Bach.

Spohr, Ludwig (Louis), 1784–1859 (Ger.) Violin virtuoso; one of the first orchestral conductors; chamber music player who did much to popularize Beethoven's early string quartets; prolific composer of operas, oratorios, 9 symphonies, 15 violin concertos, 2 clarinet concertos, much chamber music, including more than 30 string quartets, violin duets, and works featuring the harp (his first wife played this instrument). Spohr was adventuresome in exploring new instrumental combinations such as double string quartet; concerto for string quartet and orchestra; a septet for piano, strings, and woodwinds. His compositional style is that of early Ro-

manticism—highly chromatic and somewhat free in form (his 8th violin concerto is titled "In the style of a dramatic vocal aria").

Spontini, Gasparo, 1774–1851 (It.) The favorite opera composer of Napoleon and the Empress Josephine. He was a master of the dramatic and spectacular, and was a founder of French "grand" opera. His La Vestale is still performed, but his Fernand Cortez and Olympie, while successful at first, have not maintained their places in operatic repertoire.

Stadler, Anton, 1753–1812 (Aus.) Clarinet player for whom Mozart wrote his clarinet quintet and concerto.

Stainer, Sir John, 1840–1901 (Eng.) Educator (Oxford), organist, and composer of often-performed anthems and other church music, including the well-known Sevenfold Amen.

Stamitz, Johann Wenzel Anton, 1717–57 (Bohemia) Conductor and developer, at Mannheim, of the first virtuoso orchestra, famous for its precision and its controlled crescendos. Stamitz is one of the founders of the Classical style of composition through his more than 50 symphonies, concertos, and sonatas. Members of Stamitz's orchestra and his sons **Karl** (1745–1801) and **Anton** (1754–1809) carried his orchestral and compositional ideas to various capitals in Europe.

Stanford, Sir Charles Villiers, 1852–1924 (Ireland; Eng.) Educator (Cambridge) and important composer of operas, symphonies, chamber music, choral works, and songs. A leader of a new English nationalist movement in music, he used English and Irish folk material in his works.

Starer, Robert, 1924– (Aus.; Israel; U.S.) Composer of dance scores, orchestral works, chamber music, and songs in a freely dissonant style.

Steber, Eleanor, 1916– (U.S.) Operatic soprano.

Steffani, Agostino, 1654–1728 (It.; Ger.) Music director, diplomat, and composer of operas, vocal duets, and chamber music, including a much-performed Stabat Mater.

Steinberg, Maximilian, 1883–1946 (Rus.) Educator (director of Leningrad Conservatory) and composer of ballet scores, symphonies, chamber music, songs, and piano works.

Steinberg, William, 1899–1978 (Ger.; U.S.) Conductor (Palestine Symphony; Pittsburgh).

Steiner, Max, 1888–1971 (Aus.; U.S.) One of the pioneers in writing scores for films (Gone With the Wind; The Informer).

Steinway & Sons: famous piano makers in America and Germany. The founder of the American firm, in 1853, was **Henry Engelhard Steinweg** (1797–1871), who changed his name to Steinway in the 1860's.

Stern, Isaac, 1920– (Rus.; U.S.) Concert violinist.

Steuermann, Eduard, 1892–1964 (Poland; U.S.) Outstanding teacher (Juilliard), composer, and pianist who played the

premières of almost all the works of Schoenberg, Berg, and Webern that use piano.

Stevens, Halsey, 1908– (U.S.) Teacher (University of Southern California) and composer of orchestral and chamber works, songs, and piano sonatas.

Stevens, Risë, 1913– (U.S.) Operatic soprano.

Still, William Grant, 1895– (U.S.) Important composer of symphonic works (Afro-American Symphony), stage works (the ballet Lenox Avenue; opera, Troubled Island), band and choral pieces, including "And They Lynched Him on a Tree" for narrator, chorus, and orchestra.

Stockhausen, Karl Heinz, 1928– (Ger.) Composer interested in every aspect of experimentation with sound—ranging from Gruppen for 3 chamber orchestras to Zeitmasse for 5 woodwinds. Some of his music is highly controlled; some depends on the element of chance.

Stokowski, Leopold, 1882–1977 (Eng.; U.S.) Conductor (Philadelphia, Houston, American symphony orchestras) who consistently championed the cause of the contemporary composer. Stokowski was the first major conductor to concern himself with the scientific placement of instruments and microphones in recording studios.

Stolz, Robert, 1880–1975 (Aus.) Composer of operettas (Two Hearts in ¾ Time), film scores, and songs.

Stradella, Alessandro, c. 1645–82 (It.) Composer whose dramatic life story has made him the hero of several operas. He wrote operas, oratorios, and some of the earliest concerti grossi.

Strang, Gerald, 1908– (Canada; U.S.) Composer whose works have always been in an experimental vein. He was one of the first composers to use a computer to create an expressive composition.

Straus, Oscar, 1870–1954 (Aus.) Composer of one of the most popular operettas: The Chocolate Soldier.

Strayhorn, William ("Billy"), 1915–67 (U.S.) Jazz pianist and arranger; collaborator with Duke Ellington on many Ellington specials; composer of "Take the 'A' Train."

Strepponi, Giuseppina, 1815–97 (It.) Singer who became the second wife of Verdi.

Striggio, Alessandro, c. 1535–c. 95 (It.) Composer of stage works and madrigals.

Stringfield, Lamar, 1897– (U.S.) Composer of works based on American themes: From the Southern Mountains, suite for orchestra; Virginia Dare Dance for 5 winds.

Stuart, Leslie, 1866–1928 (Eng.) Composer of operettas, of which the most successful was Floradora (1899).

Subotnick, Morton, 1933– (U.S.) Composer whose works reflect his interest in electronic music (Silver Apples of the Moon) and mixed media experiments.

Suk, Josef, 1874–1935 (Czech.) Violinist and composer, in a style somewhat reminiscent of his father-in-law Dvořák, of works for orchestra and chamber groups.

Sumac, Yma, 1927– (Peru) Singer known for her extraordinary compass of about 4 octaves.

Supervia, Conchita, 1899–1936 (Sp.) Operatic mezzo-soprano.

Suppé, Franz von, 1819–95 (Dalmatia) Composer of operettas, ballets, and incidental music for stage works. His overtures *Poet and Peasant; Morning, Noon, and Night in Vienna;* and *Light Cavalry* are among the most-played "light classics."

Surinach, Carlos, 1915– (Sp.; U.S.) Composer of rhythmically exciting and colorfully scored works, including scores for dance (*Ritmo Jondo* for Doris Humphrey; *Acrobats of God* and *Embattled Garden* for Martha Graham), chamber music, and songs.

Susskind, Walter, 1913–80 (Czech.; Canada; U.S.) Conductor (Toronto; St. Louis).

Süssmayer, Franz Xaver, 1766–1803 (Aus.) Composer best known for his work in completing the Requiem Mass of his teacher, Mozart.

Sutherland, Joan, 1926– (Australia) Outstanding operatic soprano who is at home in coloratura dramatic roles from Handel to Bellini.

Svanholm, Set, 1904–1964 (Sweden) Operatic tenor.

Swarowsky, Hans, 1899– (Aus.) Conductor, well known via his many recordings, and teacher of conducting.

Swarthout, Gladys, 1904–69 (U.S.) Operatic alto.

Sweelinck, Jan Pieterszoon, 1562–1621 (Holland) Organist, teacher, and composer of sacred vocal works and, particularly, organ fugues. He is one of the founders of German instrumental style and is credited with the first use of the pedals to carry a voice in a fugue.

Sydeman, William, 1928– (U.S.) Teacher (Mannes College of Music) and composer, in an expressively dissonant style, of orchestral works and much ingenious chamber music.

Szell, George, 1897–1970 (H.; Aus.; U.S.) Outstanding conductor (Metropolitan Opera; Cleveland Orchestra) and piano soloist, accompanist, and chamber music performer.

Szigeti, Joseph, 1892–1973 (H.; U.S.) Concert violinist who consistently championed works by contemporary composers.

Szymanowski, Karol, 1882–1937 (Poland) Pianist, educator (director of Warsaw Conservatory), and composer, in a style evolving from those of Chopin, Scriabin, and Debussy, of colorful and often virtuosic works for orchestra, violin, piano, and voice.

T

Tailleferre, Germaine, 1892– (Fr.) Composer of light instrumental works and songs; member of the French group of composers known as "Les Six."

Takemitsu, Toru, 1930– (Japan) Composer of works in experimental idioms for string quartet and orchestra.

Tallis, Thomas, c. 1505–85 (Eng.) Composer of some of the finest sacred vocal music of the Renaissance period; he and Byrd are considered to be the founders of English church music. Tallis' *Spem in alium*

for 40 voices is often quoted as an example of a high point of contrapuntal skill.

Taneiev, Sergei, 1856–1915 (Rus.) Pianist, teacher (Moscow Conservatory), and composer of symphonic and chamber music works, operas, and choruses.

Tansman, Alexander, 1897– (Poland; Fr.) Pianist and composer of melodically and rhythmically interesting works for stage, orchestra, chamber groups, and piano. His best-known works are his mazurkas, his children's pieces, and *Sonatine transatlantique* for piano and *Three Pieces for Guitar,* recorded by Segovia.

Tartini, Giuseppe, 1692–1770 (It.) Violinist and scientific theorist whose investigations led him to improve the violin bow; teacher, composer of many violin concertos, solo sonatas, and trio sonatas. His best-known work is his Violin Sonata in G-minor, known as "The Devil's Trill."

Tauber, Richard, 1892–1948 (Aus.) Operatic tenor also known for his work in operettas.

Taverner, John, c. 1495–1545 (Eng.) Composer of some of the greatest religious choral music of the early 16th century; his beautiful mass based on the secular tune "The Western Wynde" is available on recordings.

Taylor, (Joseph) Deems, 1885–1966 (U.S.) Composer of successful operas (*The King's Henchman; Peter Ibbetson*), works for orchestra and chamber orchestra (*Through the Looking Glass,* a suite), incidental music for stage works, and cantatas. He was the author of *The Well-Tempered Listener* and *Of Men and Music.*

Tcherepnin, Alexander, 1899– (Rus.; Fr.; U.S.) Composer, in a moderately dissonant style reflecting Russian and Oriental influences (he lived for a while in Japan), of operas, ballets, symphonic and chamber works, songs, and piano pieces.

Tcherepnin, Nicolas, 1873–1945 (Rus.; Fr.) Conductor of opera and Diaghilev's Russian Ballet, composer of stage and orchestral works; made the playing version of Mussorgsky's opera *Fair at Sorotchinsk.* Father of Alexander Tcherepnin.

Tebaldi, Renata, 1922– (It.) Operatic soprano.

Terry, Charles Sanford, 1864–1936 (Eng.) Scholar-author of many authoritative books on J. S. Bach and his music.

Tertis, Lionel, 1876–1975 (Eng.) Outstanding violinist.

Tetrazzini, Luisa, 1871–1940 (It.; U.S.) Operatic soprano.

Teyte, Maggie, 1888–1976 (Eng.) Concert and operatic soprano known for her singing of French songs, particularly those of Debussy, who coached and played accompaniments for her.

Thalberg, Sigismond, 1812–71 (Switz.; Aus.) Virtuoso pianist, rivaling Liszt, and composer of showy piano pieces.

Thayer, Alexander Wheelock, 1817–97 (U.S.) Diplomat and author of the authoritative life of Beethoven.

Thebom, Blanche, 1918– (U.S.) Operatic mezzo-soprano.

Theremin, Leon, 1896– (Rus.) Scientist; inventor of various electronic instruments including the Theremin, a metal elec-

tronic wand that produces a tone whose pitch and dynamics vary as the player's hand moves in relation to the wand, which is actually an antenna connected to an oscillator.

Thibaud, Jacques, 1880–1953 (Fr.) Concert violinist; member of trio with Cortot and Casals.

Thomas, Charles Louis Ambroise, 1811–96 (Fr.) Educator (director of Paris Conservatory) and composer of lyric operas.

Thomas, John Charles, 1891–1960 (U.S.) Concert and operatic baritone.

Thomas, Theodore, 1835–1905 (Ger.; U.S.) Conductor of one of the first touring orchestras in the United States; founder and first conductor of the Chicago Symphony Orchestra. Thomas introduced the works of many of the great European composers to American audiences.

Thompson, Randall, 1899– (U.S.) Teacher (Harvard) and composer of symphonies, chamber works, songs, and choral works, of which *The Peaceable Kingdom, The Testament of Freedom,* and *Alleluia* have had many performances.

Thomson, Virgil, 1896– (U.S.) Composer of sophisticatedly simple works, reflecting his admiration for the works of Satie: operas (*Four Saints in Three Acts; The Mother of Us All*), orchestral works (*Symphony on a Hymn Tune: Wheatfield at Noon*), important chamber music (*Sonata da chiesa* for 5 instruments; several string quartets), a series of witty portraits for various instruments, and colorful film scores (*The Plough that Broke the Plains; Louisiana Story*). Thomson was, for about 15 years, one of the most admired and most quoted American music critics. He is the author of *The State of Music* and *The Art of Judging Music.*

Tibbett, Lawrence, 1896–1968 (U.S.) Concert and operatic baritone.

Tinctoris, Johannes, c. 1446–c. 1510 (Belg.) Composer of sacred choral works; important theorist and author of the first printed dictionary of music (c. 1475).

Tiompkin, Dmitri, 1894–1979 (Rus.; U.S.) Pianist; composer of many film scores (*High Noon*).

Tippett, Michael Kemp, 1905– (Eng.) Composer of successful works for orchestra (symphonies; *Variations on a Theme by Corelli* for string orchestra), chamber groups (string quartets; sonatas for horns), songs, and the much-performed oratorio *A Child of Our Time.*

Toch, Ernst, 1887–1964 (Aus.; U.S.) Teacher (University of Southern California); author of the important theory book *The Shaping Forces in Music;* and composer, in a nondogmatic, dissonant, contrapuntal style, of operas, orchestral works, a variety of chamber works, songs, effective piano pieces, and film scores. One of his most performed works is the *Geographical Fugue,* a witty work for speaking voices.

Tomkins, Thomas, 1572–1656 (Eng.) Composer of keyboard works, fantasias for viols, many effective madrigals, a number of anthems, and other religious works.

Tommasini, Vincenzo, 1880–1950 (It.) Composer of works in all media; best known for his ballet *The Good-humored Ladies,* based on works by D. Scarlatti, written for Diaghilev's Russian Ballet.

Torelli, Giuseppe, 1658-1709 (It.) Violinist, and one of the early group of violinist-composers who developed the form of the concerto grosso and the Italian style of composing for the violin.

Torkanowsky, Werner, 1926- (Ger.; U.S.) Violinist and conductor (New Orleans Philharmonic).

Toscanini, Arturo, 1867-1957 (It.; U.S.) Outstanding conductor of opera (La Scala; Metropolitan Opera) and symphony orchestras (New York Philharmonic; National Broadcasting Co.—N.B.C.—Symphony). Toscanini was famed for his faithful adherence to the composer's score, his prodigious memory, his demand for perfection on the part of singers and instrumentalists, and his outspoken opposition to the Fascist and Nazi movements. He conducted the first performances of many important works, including the operas *Pagliacci, La Bohème,* and *The Girl of the Golden West.*

Tourel, Jennie, 1910-73 (Canada; U.S.) Concert and operatic mezzo-soprano.

Tourte, François, 1747-1835 (Fr.) Inventor of the modern form of the violin bow.

Tovey, Sir Donald Francis, 1875-1940 (Eng.) Pianist, composer, teacher (Edinburgh University), and musical scholar; author of *Essays in Musical Analysis* and *Musical Articles from the Encyclopædia Britannica.*

Traubel, Helen, 1899-1972 (U.S.) Operatic soprano.

Tucker, Richard, 1914-75 (U.S.) Operatic tenor.

Tudor, David, 1926- (U.S.) Pianist; collaborator with John Cage in concerts of avant-garde music.

Tunder, Franz, 1614-67 (Ger.) Organist and composer of organ works and cantatas based on Lutheran chorales.

Tureck, Rosalyn, 1914- (U.S.) Pianist, teacher, and scholar specializing in the works of Bach.

Turina, Joaquín, 1882-1949 (Sp.) Composer of stage works and much instrumental music, especially piano pieces, based on Spanish material.

Türk, Daniel Gottlob, 1756-1813 (Ger.) Composer of works for piano, orchestra, organ, and voice.

Tye, Christopher, *c.* 1500-73 (Eng.) Composer (sacred music; works for strings).

Tyrwhitt, Gerald. See **Berners, Lord.**

U

Ussachevsky, Vladimir, 1911- (Manchuria; U.S.) Teacher (Columbia); cofounder of Columbia-Princeton Electronic Music Center; and composer of electronic works *(Sonic Contours; Underwater Waltz; Metamorphosis;* and, with Otto Luening, *Poem of Cycles and Bels).*

V

Valen, Fartein, 1887-1952 (Norway) Composer of symphonies, a concerto and sonata for violin, string quartets, songs, and chamber music in an expressive, dissonant style.

Vecchi, Orazio, 1550-1605 (It.) Composer of sacred and secular vocal music; his *L'Amfiparnasso* (1597) is the outstanding example of the "madrigal comedy"—an attempt to fuse the madrigal style with that of the commedia dell'arte.

Vengerova, Isabelle, 1877-1956 (Rus.; U.S.) Pianist and outstanding teacher (Curtis Institute).

Venuti, Giuseppe (Joe), 1904- (U.S.) One of the few outstanding jazz violinists.

Veracini, Francesco Marie, 1690-*c.* 1750 (It.) Composer of sonatas and other works featuring the violin.

Viadana, Lodovico (da), *c.* 1564-1645 (It.) Composer of sacred and secular choral works; his *Ecclesiastical Concertos* are among the earliest choral works to be written with a non-doubling bass part for organ, with the organist expected to supply a harmonic support.

Viardot-García, Pauline, 1820-1910 (Fr.) Operatic soprano; member of the famous Garcia singing family.

Victoria (Vittoria), Tomás Luis de, *c.* 1549-1611 (Sp.) Outstanding composer, in rich polyphonic style, of motets and other religious choral works.

Vierne, Louis, 1870-1937 (Fr.) Organ virtuoso, in spite of his blindness; teacher (of Dupré and Nadia Boulanger); and composer of choral and organ works, including 5 symphonies for organ.

Viganò, Salvatore, 1769-1821 (It.) Dancer, composer, choreographer for whom Beethoven composed the ballet *The Creatures of Prometheus.*

Villa-Lobos, Heitor, 1887-1959 (Brazil) Educator (one of the few outstanding composers who concerned himself with music education in the primary and secondary schools) and a prolific composer of more than 2000 works in all media. His style is highly unique, combining Brazilian music—itself a composite of Portuguese, African, and indigenous Indian elements—with traditional as well as 20th-century European techniques, and colorfully scored for instruments, often including native Brazilian percussion instruments. Most-played and recorded are his 8 *Bachianas Brasilieras* for various combinations of instruments and voice; a series of *chôros* for a wide range of resources from solo guitar to large orchestra and chorus; piano works as direct and appealing as his 3 sets of children's pieces, *Prole do Bebé,* and as virtuosic as the *Rudepoema,* written for Artur Rubinstein. Villa-Lobos composed a dozen symphonies, ballets *(The Emperor Jones* for José Limon), 15 string quartets, symphonic poems, and a great deal of almost every kind of music composable.

Viotti, Giovanni Battista, 1755-1824 (It.; Fr.; Eng.) Violinist, teacher, and composer known chiefly for his 29 violin concertos.

Vitali, Giovanni Battista, *c.* 1640-92 (It.) Composer of early violin sonatas, trio sonatas, and dance music for strings.

Vitry, Philippe de, 1291-1361 (Fr.) Theorist whose treatises on rhythm and counterpoint do much to explain the practices of such 14th-century composers as Machaut.

Vogler, Georg Joseph (the Abbé), 1749-1814 (Ger.) Organist, master-improviser, composer, teacher of many famous musicians (Weber, Meyerbeer), theorist, and author of a textbook on music theory.

Volkonsky, Andrey, 1933- (Switz.; Rus.) Musicologist and composer using experimental techniques.

W

Wagenaar, Bernard, 1894-1971 (Holland; U.S.) Teacher (Juilliard), and composer of expertly written music for orchestra (4 symphonies; *Triple Concerto* for flute, harp, cello, and orchestra), chamber groups, piano, and voice.

Wagenseil, Georg Christoph, 1715-77 (Aus.) Court composer who wrote symphonies, sonatas, concertos, divertimentos featuring violins and harpsichord, operas, and much religious music.

Wagner, Cosima, 1837-1930 (It.; Ger.) Daughter of Franz Liszt, wife of Hans von Bülow and later Richard Wagner. After Wagner's death, Cosima managed the Bayreuth Festival until her son **Siegfried Wagner** (1869-1930) took over in 1909.

Wagner, Wieland, 1917-66 (Ger.) Stage director who boldly applied contemporary theories of non-literalness in restaging the operas of his grandfather, Richard Wagner.

Waldteufel, Emil, 1837-1915 (Fr.) Pianist (to the Empress Eugénie) and composer of much light dance music, including *The Skaters* waltz.

Wallenstein, Alfred, 1898- (U.S.) Cellist and conductor.

Waller, Thomas ("Fats"), 1904-43 (U.S.) Outstanding jazz pianist, organist, and vocalist; composer of "Honeysuckle Rose," "Ain't Misbehavin'."

Walter, Bruno, 1876-1962 (Ger.; U.S.) Pianist, composer, and conductor of opera and symphony orchestras; he was one of the supreme conductors of the works of Mozart, Beethoven, Brahms, and especially Mahler.

Walther (Walter), Johann, 1496-1570 (Ger.) Singer; composer of instrumental and vocal works; friend and collaborator of Martin Luther, for whom he arranged and published the first settings of chorale tunes (*Geystlich Gesangk-Buchleyn,* 1524).

Walther, Johann Gottfried, 1684-1748 (Ger.) Composer of skillful organ chorale preludes; author of a model dictionary of music and musicians.

Walton, Sir William (Turner), 1902- (Eng.) Composer of outstanding works in a conservative contemporary idiom: the opera *Troilus and Cressida;* concertos for violin, viola, and cello; the oratorio *Belshazzar's Feast;* the overture *Portsmouth Point;* and, at the age of 21, the brilliant, witty *Façade* to poems by Edith Sitwell. Walton has also contributed notable scores for films: *Henry V; Richard III; Escape Me Never; Hamlet.*

Ward, Robert, 1917– (U.S.) Educator (director, North Carolina School of the Arts) and composer, in conservative contemporary style, of operas (*The Crucible*); symphonic works (*Jubilation Overture; 3 symphonies*); band music; chamber and choral music; and a successful work for children, *Jonathon and the Gingery Snare.*

Warlock, Peter. See **Heseltine, Philip.**

Warren, Leonard, 1911–60 (U.S.) Operatic baritone.

Watts, Andre, 1946– (Ger.; U.S.) Concert pianist.

Waxman, Franz, 1906–1967 (Ger.; U.S.) Composer best known for his evocative film scores.

Webbe, Samuel, 1740–1816 (Eng.) Composer of much vocal music; remembered for his excellent catches and glees, as was his son **Samuel, Jr.** (1770–1843).

Weber, Ben, 1916– (U.S.) Composer of lyrically dramatic works for instruments.

Webster, Beveridge, 1908– (U.S.) Teacher (Juilliard) and concert pianist.

Wedge, George (Anson), 1890–1964 (U.S.) Educator (dean of Juilliard School of Music); eminent theorist and author of many texts on music theory.

Weelkes, Thomas, c. 1570–1623 (Eng.) Outstanding composer of madrigals.

Weinberger, Jaromir, 1896–1967 (Czech; U.S.) Composer of operas (*Schwanda, the Bagpiper*), orchestral works (*Polka and Fugue* from *Schwanda; Under the Spreading Chestnut Tree* variations), and pieces for chorus, piano, and violin.

Weiner, Leo, 1885–1960 (H.) Teacher (Budapest Academy of Music) and composer of orchestral and chamber music works, often utilizing Hungarian material.

Weingartner, Felix, 1863–1942 (Dalmatia; Switz.) Eminent scholarly conductor (Berlin; Vienna; Darmstadt), teacher of conducting, author of books on conducting and the music of Beethoven. He was also a prolific composer.

Weinstock, Herbert, 1905–71 (U.S.) Musical scholar; author of *Tchaikovsky; Men of Music* with W. Brockway; *The Opera: A History of Its Creation and Performance;* and *Rossini, A Biography.*

Weisgall, Hugo, 1912– (Czech; U.S.) Teacher (Queens College, N.Y.; Juilliard) and composer of successful operas (*The Tenor; The Stronger; Six Characters in Search of an Author; Athaliah*), songs, and choral music.

Weiss, Adolph, 1891– (U.S.) Bassoonist and composer of some of the first American works utilizing the 12-tone technique.

Wellesz, Egon, 1885–1974 (Aus.; Eng.) Composer of operas, symphonic and chamber works, and vocal works; scholar whose work in the field of Byzantine music has resulted in several authoritative books on the subject: *A History of Byzantine Music and Hymnography;* co-editor, *Monumenta Musicae Byzantinae.*

Wert, Giaches de, 1535–96 (Flanders) Composer of expressive madrigals.

Wesley, Samuel, 1766–1837 (Eng.) Organist; composer of organ and sacred choral works; popularizer of the works of J. S. Bach in England.

Westrup, Jack Allan, 1904– (Eng.) Teacher (Oxford) and musical scholar; co-author with F. L. Harrison of *The New College Encyclopedia of Music;* senior editor of the *New Oxford History of Music.*

White, Clarence Cameron, 1880–1960 (U.S.) Composer of many works based on Negro themes: *Bandanna Sketches* for violin; the opera *Ouanga;* and a string quartet.

White (Whyte), Robert, c. 1530–74 (Eng.) Composer of sacred music.

Whiteman, Paul, 1890–1967 (U.S.) Dance bandleader who was called "The King of Jazz" because of the popularity of his music. His background as a symphony musician led him to try to bridge the gap between jazz and concert music, leading to a hybrid "symphonic jazz" and the encouragement of George Gershwin (who wrote *Rhapsody in Blue* for Whiteman's first concert, in 1924) and Ferde Grofé. During the 1920's and 1930's Whiteman's band included many of the top jazz musicians of the time.

Whithorne, Emerson, 1884–1958 (U.S.) Composer whose moderately dissonant descriptive works were quite popular in the 1920's (*New York Days and Nights,* for orchestra).

Whitney, Robert, 1904– (Eng.; U.S.) Conductor of Louisville Orchestra which, under his direction, commissioned, performed, and recorded (under a grant from the Rockefeller Foundation) scores by outstanding contemporary composers.

Widor, Charles-Marie, 1844–1937 (Fr.) Organist (St. Sulpice in Paris); teacher at Paris Conservatory (Albert Schweitzer was his student); editor of Bach's organ music; and composer of works in all media, especially organ, for which he wrote 10 symphonies.

Wieniawski, Henryk, 1835–80 (Poland; Rus.) Virtuoso violinist, teacher (Leningrad; Brussels), and composer of highly idiomatic works for violin (*Légende; Souvenir de Moscou;* 2 concertos).

Wieprecht, Friedrich Wilhelm, 1802–72 (Ger.) Bandmaster, inventor of the tuba; involved in losing court battle with Adolphe Sax over invention of the saxhorns.

Wigglesworth, Frank, 1918– (U.S.) Composer, in neo-Classic vein, of symphonies, chamber music (*Telesis,* for chamber orchestra and percussion; *Quintet for Brass*), and choral works.

Wilbye, John, 1574–1638 (Eng.) Outstanding composer of madrigals.

Wilder, Alec, 1907–80 (U.S.) Composer of skillfully written stage works and chamber operas, ballets, and film scores.

Willaert, Adrian, c. 1480–1562 (Flanders; It.) Organist, teacher, and composer who first exploited the use of the 2 organs and choirs at St. Mark's in Venice. He also composed important instrumental pieces (fantasias and ricercars) and madrigals.

Willson, Meredith, 1902– (U.S.) Flutist (New York Philharmonic) and composer of works for orchestra, chorus, and band; best known for his popular musical comedy *The Music Man.*

Wilson, John, 1595–1674 (Eng.) Singer; court lutanist to Charles I and II; composer of music for stage works, including plays by Shakespeare (in one of which he sang), and many songs ("In the Merry Month of May").

Winternitz, Emanuel, 1898– (Aus.; U.S.) Curator of musical instruments at the Metropolitan Museum of Art (New York City); author of *Musical Instruments of the Western World.*

Wittgenstein, Paul, 1887–1961 (Aus.; U.S.) Concert pianist; having lost his right arm in World War I, he commissioned outstanding composers to write concertos for him: Ravel, Prokofiev, Strauss.

Wolf, Hugo, 1860–1903 (Aus.) Composer of outstanding lieder, or art songs; for 4 years an outspoken critic for the Vienna *Salonblatt,* arguing the merits of Wagner, Bruckner, and Berlioz as against Brahms and Italian opera composers. Wolf's main interest was in writing for voice—in opera (*Der Corregidor*), chorus, and art song. He wrote few instrumental works (an early symphonic poem; the *Italian Serenade*—which was originally written for string quartet). Of his almost 300 songs, the principal cycles are the *Italienisches Liederbuch; Spanisches Liederbuch;* and settings of poems by Goethe, Moricke, and Eichendorff. Most of these were written in great bursts of inspiration between 1888 and 1897. His remaining years after 1897 were mostly spent in a mental institution, as though his creative fever had burned out his sensitive mind.

Wolf-Ferrari, Ermanno, 1876–1948 (It.) Composer of light operas (*The Secret of Suzanne*) and more serious ones (*The Jewels of the Madonna*). His oratorio *La Vita nuova,* based on writings by Dante, has had a number of performances.

Wolfe, Jacques, 1896– (Rumania; U.S.) Composer of many songs in the manner of Negro spirituals ("De Glory Road"; "Short'nin' Bread").

Wolfe, Stanley, 1924– (U.S.) Teacher (Juilliard) and composer of 4 symphonies.

Wolff, Christian, 1934– (Fr.; U.S.) Composer of works based on "chance," mostly for small ensembles.

Wolpe, Stefan, 1902–72 (Ger.; U.S.) Teacher and composer, in a variety of contemporary idioms, of works (such as his Symphony No. 1) which, because of their complexities, have received infrequent performances.

Wood, Sir Henry Joseph, 1869–1944 (Eng.) Conductor who began the Promenade concerts in London, introduced many contemporary scores to England, and made orchestral transcriptions of old music such as Jeremiah Clarke's *Trumpet Voluntary.*

Woodworth, George Wallace, 1902– (U.S.) Teacher (Harvard), and for many years the eminent conductor of the Harvard-Radcliffe chorus; editor of many editions of choral music.

Wuorinen, Charles, 1938– (U.S.) Teacher (Columbia University) and composer, in an integrated variety of contemporary styles, including electronic sounds, of three impressive symphonies, concertos, and chamber music.

X

Xenakis, Yannis, 1922– (Greece) Composer, in advanced contemporary techniques, utilizing his background in architecture, of probing, brilliant works for orchestra, chamber groups, and tape (*Duel* for 54 instruments; *ST/4-2* for string quartet). In 1968 George Balanchine composed a ballet called *Xenakis* based on two of this composer's works: *Métastasis* and *Pithoprakta*.

Y

Yon, Pietro Alessandro, 1886–1943 (It.; U.S.) Organist (St. Patrick's Cathedral in N.Y.) and composer of sacred vocal and organ works. His *Gesù Bambino*, originally for organ, became quite popular.
Youmans, Vincent, 1898–1946 (U.S.) Composer of songs for musical comedies, Broadway, and Hollywood (*No, No, Nanette; Hit the Deck; Flying Down to Rio*). His many highly successful songs include "Tea for Two," "Without a Song," "Great Day," "Carioca," "Time on My Hands," and "Hallelujah."
Young, La Monte, 1935– (U.S.) Composer-theorist, in extreme avant-garde vein, of environmental works based on the drone.
Young, Victor, 1900–56 (U.S.) Composer of film scores (*Around the World in 80 Days*) and many popular songs ("Sweet Sue"; "My Romance").
Yradier, Sebastián, 1809–65 (Sp.) Composer of songs so Spanish in feeling that Bizet used one for his "Habañera" in *Carmen*, thinking it a folk song. Yradier composed the popular "La Paloma" and "Ay Chiquita!"
Ysaÿe, Eugène, 1858–1931 (Belg.) Violinist, conductor (Brussels; Cincinnati), and composer, primarily for violin (8 concertos; 6 sonatas). Franck's violin sonata is dedicated to him, as is Debussy's only string quartet—which received its première at the hands of the Ysaÿe Quartet.

Z

Zabaleta, Nicanor, 1907– (Sp.) Virtuoso harp player.
Zarlino, Gioseffo, 1517–90 (It.) Outstanding music theorist of the late Renaissance period; his viewpoint represented that of his teacher Willaert and his contemporary Palestrina—in opposition to the "radicals" of the day who were formulating ideas that led to the beginning of opera. His most famous book is the *Istituzioni armoniche*.
Zimbalist, Efrem, 1889– (Rus.; U.S.) Violinist, composer, educator (director of the Curtis Institute, 1941–68).
Zipoli, Domenico, 1688–1726 (It.; Argentina) Composer of interesting keyboard works: sonatas, toccatas, fugues.

ACKNOWLEDGMENTS

We wish to express our appreciation to the copyright owners, publishers, and agents listed below who have so kindly granted us permission to use musical examples from works by the following composers:

Albéniz, Isaac—Tango in D: Copyright 1924 by B. Schott's Soehne; reprinted by permission of the original copyright owners and their U.S. representatives, Associated Music Publishers, Inc.

Bach, C. P. E.—"Abschied von meinem Silbermannischen Claviere": Copyright 1936 by Universal Edition; reprinted by permission of the original copyright owners and their U.S. representatives, Theodore Presser Company.

Bach, J. C.—Sonata, Op. 17, No. 4: Used by permission of C. F. Peters Corporation.

Barber, Samuel—*Adagio for Strings:* Copyright 1952 by G. Schirmer, Inc. Sonata for Piano: Copyright 1950 by G. Schirmer, Inc. Used by permission.

Bartók, Béla—*Music for Strings, Percussion, and Celesta:* © Copyright 1937 by Universal Edition; renewed 1964; copyright and renewal assigned to Boosey & Hawkes, Inc., for the U.S.A. Copyright for all other countries, Universal Edition. String Quartet No. 5: © Copyright 1936 by Universal Edition; renewed 1963; copyright and renewal assigned to Boosey & Hawkes, Inc., for the U.S.A. Copyright for all other countries, Universal Edition. Reprinted by permission of Boosey & Hawkes, Inc., and Universal Edition.

Berg, Alban—*Lyric Suite:* Copyright 1927 by Universal Edition; renewed 1955 by Helene Berg; reprinted by permission of the original copyright owners and their U.S. representatives, Theodore Presser Company. Violin Concerto: Copyright 1936 by Universal Edition; reprinted by permission of the original copyright owners and their U.S. representatives, Theodore Presser Company. *Wozzeck:* Copyright 1931 by Universal Edition A. G., Vienna; renewed 1958; reprinted by permission of the original copyright owners and their U.S. representatives, Theodore Presser Company.

Binchois, Giles—Rondeau: Reprinted by permission of the publishers from *Historical Anthology of Music,* Volume 1, by Archibald Davison and Willi T. Apel; permission granted by Harvard University Press; Copyright 1946, 1949 by the President and Fellows of Harvard College.

Copland, Aaron—*Appalachian Spring:* Copyright 1945 by Aaron Copland. *Piano Fantasy:* Copyright 1957 by Aaron Copland. Piano Sonata: Copyright 1942 by Aaron Copland. *Sonata for Violin and Piano:* Copyright 1944 by Aaron Copland. All reprinted by permission of Aaron Copland, copyright owner, and Boosey & Hawkes, Inc., sole publishers.

Debussy, Claude Achille—*The Afternoon of a Faun:* Permission for reprint granted by Jean Jobert Editions, Paris, copyright owners, and Elkan-Vogel Co., Inc., Philadelphia, agents. "Feuilles mortes," "General Lavine," "La puerta del vino," and "Les Tierces alternées" from Preludes, Book II; "Golliwog's Cakewalk" from the *Children's Corner* Suite; "Des Pas sur la neige" from Preludes, Book I; *Pelléas et Mélisande;* and Prelude, *Pour le Piano:* Permission granted by Durand & Cie, Paris, copyright owners, and Elkan-Vogel Co., Inc., Philadelphia, agents.

Dowland, Robert—*Varietie of Lute Lessons:* © Copyright 1957 by Schott & Co., Ltd.; reprinted by permission of the original copyright owners and their U.S. representatives, Associated Music Publishers, Inc.

Dufay, Guillaume—Agnus Dei from the Mass *L'Homme armé:* Reprinted by permission of the publishers from *Historical Anthology of Music,* Volume 1, by Archibald Davison and Willi T. Apel; permission granted by Harvard University Press; Copyright 1946, 1949 by the President and Fellows of Harvard College.

Dukas, Paul—*The Sorcerer's Apprentice:* Permission granted by Durand & Cie, Paris, copyright owners, and Elkan-Vogel Co., Inc., Philadelphia, agents.

Falla, Manuel de—"Danza del terror" and "Pantomine" from *El amor brujo:* Copyright 1924 by J. & W. Chester, Ltd.; used by permission of G. Schirmer, Inc.

Frescobaldi, Girolamo—"Toccata quarti toni": Used by permission of Edward B. Marks Music Corporation.

Gabrieli, Andrea—"Ricercare del 12° tono": Reprinted by permission of the publishers from *Historical Anthology of Music,* Volume 1, by Archibald Davison and Willi T. Apel; permission granted by Harvard University Press; Copyright 1946, 1949 by the President and Fellows of Harvard College.

Gervaise, Claude—Galliard and Pavane: Reprinted by permission of the publishers from *Historical Anthology of Music,* Volume 1, by Archibald Davison and Willi T. Apel; permission granted by Harvard University Press; Copyright 1946, 1949 by the President and Fellows of Harvard College.

Goldman, Richard F.—Duo for Tubas: Used by permission of Mercury Music Corporation.

Gottschalk, Louis M.—"Yankee Doodle" from *L'Union:* Copyright 1956 by Theodore Presser Company; used by permission.

Harris, Roy—Symphony No. 3: Copyright 1940 by G. Schirmer, Inc.; used by permission.

Hindemith, Paul—Chanson for Chorus, "En Hiver": © Copyright 1943 by Schott & Co., Ltd. *Ludis Tonalis:* © Copyright 1943 by Schott & Co., Ltd. "Nachtstück" from

Suite 1922: © Copyright 1922 by B. Schott's Soehne. *Tanzstücke:* © Copyright 1928 by B. Schott's Soehne. Reprinted by permission of the original copyright owners and their U.S. representatives, Associated Music Publishers, Inc.

Ives, Charles—*Concord Sonata:* © Copyright 1947 by Associated Music Publishers, Inc.; used by permission.

Josquin Des Prés—Motet, "Tu pauperum refugium": Reprinted by permission of the publishers from *Historical Anthology of Music,* Volume 1, by Archibald Davison and Willi T. Apel; permission granted by Harvard University Press; Copyright 1946, 1949 by the President and Fellows of Harvard College.

Lassus, Orlando—"Beatus homo," "Expectatio Justorum," "Justi tulerunt Spolia," "Oculus non Judit," "Qui Sequiter Me," and "Servi Boni" from *Cantiones Duarum Vocum:* Copyright 1941 by Music Press Inc.; used by permission of Mercury Music Corporation.

Machaut, Guillaume de—"Ma Fin est mon commencement" from *Musikalische Werke:* Copyright 1926 by Breitkopf & Härtel; used by permission of the original copyright owners and their U.S. representatives, Associated Music Publishers, Inc.

Milhaud, Darius—*Saudades do Brasil* No. 7, 8, and 9: Copyright 1922 by Editions Max Eschig; reprinted by permission of the original copyright owners and their U.S. representatives, Associated Music Publishers, Inc.

Neusiedler, Hans—Lute Dance: Reprinted by permission of the publishers from *Historical Anthology of Music,* Volume 1, by Archibald Davison and Willi T. Apel; permission granted by Harvard University Press; Copyright 1946, 1949 by the President and Fellows of Harvard College.

Persichetti, Vincent—"Little Piano Suite No. 10" from *The Little Piano Book:* Permission for reprint granted by Elkan-Vogel Co., Inc., Philadelphia, copyright owners.

Prokofiev, Sergei—*Classical Symphony:* Copyright 1926 by Edition Russe de Musique; copyright assigned to Boosey & Hawkes, Inc. Concerto No. 3 for Piano and Orchestra: Copyright by Edition A. Gutheil; copyright assigned to Boosey & Hawkes, Inc., 1947. *Peter and the Wolf:* Copyright

by Edition A. Gutheil, English edition copyright 1942 by Hawkes & Son, Ltd., London. *Visions fugitives* No. 5: Copyright 1922 by Breitkopf & Härtel (Edition A. Gutheil); copyright assigned 1947 to Boosey & Hawkes, Inc. Reprinted by permission of Boosey & Hawkes, Inc.

Puccini, Giacomo—*La Bohème, Madame Butterfly, Tosca,* and *Turandot* (© 1926 and 1929 by G. Ricordi & C., Milan): By courtesy of the publisher, G. Ricordi & C., Milan, all rights reserved, and Franco Colombo, Inc., sole U.S. agents for G. Ricordi & C.

Rachmaninoff, Sergei—Piano Concerto No. 2: Copyright by Edition A. Gutheil; copyright assigned 1947 to Boosey & Hawkes, Inc.; reprinted by permission of Boosey & Hawkes, Inc.

Ravel, Maurice—"Laideronnette" from *Mother Goose* Suite, Forlana and Rigaudon from *Le Tombeau de Couperin,* and *Valses nobles et sentimentales* No. 3: Permission granted by Durand & Cie, Paris, copyright owners, and Elkan-Vogel Co., Inc., Philadelphia, agents.

Satie, Erik—*Gnossienne* No. 2 and Saraband No. 1: By courtesy of Editions Salabert, Paris, copyright owners, and their U.S. representatives, Franco Colombo, Inc.

Schoenberg, Arnold—Opus 19, No. 3, and Opus 19, No. 5: Copyright 1913 by Universal Edition; used by permission of Universal Edition A. G., Belmont Music Publishers, and Mrs. Arnold Schoenberg. Suite for Piano, Opus 25: Copyright 1925 by Universal Edition; used by permission of Universal Edition A.G., Belmont Music Publishers, and Mrs. Arnold Schoenberg.

Schuman, William—Symphony No. 3: Copyright 1942 by G. Schirmer, Inc. Symphony No. 6: Copyright 1952 by G. Schirmer, Inc. *Symphony for Strings:* Copyright 1943 by G. Schirmer, Inc. Used by permission.

Strauss, Richard—*Don Juan, Don Quixote,* and *Till Eulenspiegel:* Used by permission of C. F. Peters Corporation.

Stravinsky, Igor—*Firebird* Suite: Copyright 1920 by J. & W. Chester, Ltd.; used by permission of G. Schirmer, Inc. *Petrouchka:* © by Edition Russe de Musique; all rights assigned to Boosey & Hawkes, Inc.; revised version © 1947 by Boosey & Hawkes, Inc.; reprinted by permission of Boosey & Hawkes, Inc. *Rite of Spring:* © 1921 by Edition Russe

de Musique; copyright assigned 1947 to Boosey & Hawkes, Inc.; reprinted by permission of Boosey & Hawkes, Inc. *Serenade en la:* © 1926 by Edition Russe de Musique; copyright assigned 1947 to Boosey & Hawkes, Inc.; reprinted by permission of Boosey & Hawkes, Inc. *Symphony of Psalms:* © 1931 by Russe de Musique; renewed 1958; copyright and renewal assigned to Boosey & Hawkes, Inc.; revised version © 1948 by Boosey & Hawkes, Inc.; reprinted by permission of Boosey & Hawkes, Inc. Symphony in Three Movements: © 1946 by Schott & Co., Ltd.; reprinted by permission of the original copyright owners and their U.S. representatives, Associated Music Publishers, Inc.

Vaughan Williams, Ralph—Symphony No. 4: Used by permission of the publishers, Oxford University Press. *London Symphony:* Used by permission of Stainer & Bell, Ltd., London, and Galaxy Music Corporation, New York, sole agent. *Pastoral Symphony:* Copyright 1924 in U.S.A. by Vaughan Williams; permission granted by J. Curwen & Sons, Ltd., London, and G. Schirmer, Inc., sole agents for the U.S.A.

Wagner, Richard—Piano Vocal Score for *Tristan and Isolde:* Copyright renewal assigned, 1934, to G. Schirmer, Inc.; used by permission.

Webern, Anton—"Wie bin ich froh!" from *Drei Lieder,* Opus 25: Copyright 1956 by Universal Edition A.G., Vienna. Variations for Piano: Copyright 1937 by Universal Edition A.G., Vienna. Reprinted by permission of the original copyright owners and their U.S. representatives, Theodore Presser Company.

. . . Acknowledgment is also made for the following:

Edward Dent's English words, used in excerpts from *Don Giovanni* and *Fidelio,* by permission of Oxford University Press.

Cunctipotens genitor (free organum), *Cunctipotens genitor* (melismatic organum), and *Musica enchiriadis:* reprinted by permission of the publishers from *Historical Anthology of Music,* Volume 1, by Archibald Davison and Willi T. Apel; permission granted by Harvard University Press; Copyright 1946, 1949 by the President and Fellows of Harvard College.

PICTURE SOURCES

Picture Research by Natalie Siegel

We are indebted to all those who gave of their time and help in providing the hundreds of illustrations for this book. Without their patience and assistance, many of the pictures could not have been obtained.

The source of each picture used in the encyclopedia is listed below; our especial thanks go to these individuals, organizations, and institutions.

Position key: b—bottom; **l**—left; **m**—middle; **r**—right; **t**—top.

Agence France Presse (Pictorial Parade): 102t; 268t

AGIP (Pictorial Parade): 329tr

Michael Alexander (Black Star): 452b

Alinari (Art Reference Bureau): 21t; 133m; 386b

American Broadcasting Company: 502br

Ampex: 585

Anderson (Art Reference Bureau): 650

Angel Records: 10; 49b; 592

Archives Photographiques, Paris: 135; 499t; 608b

Myra Armstrong (Hurok): 492r

Art Institute of Chicago: 365b

ASCAP: 205b

Ashmolean Museum, Oxford (Hill Collection): 335

Associated Music Publishers: 329ml

Atlantic Press (Pictorial Parade): 115t; 324

Erich Auerbach: 640b

Austrian Information Service: 60; 120mr & br; 156t; 177b; 243b; 278r; 294–6; 297b; 340bl; 342; 344; 346; 375tr; 519; 548; 557–l; 559; 561; 661; 669

Ed Badeaux: 188m

Bärenreiter-Bild-Archiv, Kassel-Wilhelmshöhe: 28; 30; 33–5; 39; 121t; 177t; 530;

Book Design by
REMO COSENTINO

Diagrams

All diagrams, with the exception of those in the color section, by Charles J. Berger. The microphone diagrams on page 324 are based on drawings from *The McGraw Hill Encyclopedia of Science and Technology:* copyright 1960 by McGraw-Hill Book Company; used by permission. The organ diagrams on page 391 are based on original drawings prepared for us through the courtesy of Mr. Walter Holtkamp of The Holtkamp Organ Company, Cleveland

Color Section
(Pages I–XXIV, following page 320)

INDEX TO MUSICAL EXAMPLES

Each article title, when given as an index entry, is identified by means of a boldface page number (for instance: **3**). Such a number signifies main coverage. Lightface page numbers (3) indicate pages on which further information will be found.

Asterisks (*3) designate pages on which relevant illustrations and captions appear. Roman numerals (III) indicate color pages (the color section follows page 320).

Cross references here refer to entries in the index, not to articles within the body of the encyclopedia.

INDEX TO MUSICAL EXAMPLES: A separate index of musical examples will be found on page 702. These are listed by composer.

GLOSSARIES: Information in specialized areas will be found by consulting:

Signs and Symbols Used in Music: page 670
Foreign Terms and Phrases Used in Music: page 671
Abbreviations Used in Music: page 673
Famous Names in Music: page 674